FINANCING CATHEDRAL BUILDING IN THE MIDDLE AGES

'quod sine caritate fidelium Christi et elemosynis nunquam poterit consummari'

✳

which can never be completed without the generosity of and alms from the christian faithful

THE KING OF FRANCE COMMENDING THE CONSTRUCTION OF THE CATHEDRAL OF SENLIS (AROUND 1155)

FINANCING CATHEDRAL BUILDING IN THE MIDDLE AGES THE GENEROSITY OF THE FAITHFUL

WIM VROOM

TRANSLATION
ELIZABETH MANTON

Routledge
Taylor & Francis Group
LONDON AND NEW YORK

This book has been made possible by a grant from Stichting Charema, Fonds voor Geschiedenis en Kunst.

First published in 2010 by Amsterdam University Press Ltd.

Published 2025 by Routledge
4 Park Square, Milton Park, Abingdon, Oxon OX14 4RN
605 Third Avenue, New York, NY 10158

Routledge is an imprint of the Taylor & Francis Group, an informa business

ISBN: 9789089640352 (hbk)
ISBN: 9781041179450 (pbk)
ISBN: 9781003695691 (ebk)
NUR 684

Cover design : Suzan Beijer, Weesp, the Netherlands
Coverpicture: Detail of the retable of the high altar of the León Cathedral. See fig. 33
Endpaper: Fabric account Autun cathedral 1294-'95

Printed in the United Kingdom
by Henry Ling Limited

TO ELINE

TABLE OF CONTENTS

PART TWO THE FINANCING OF CATHEDRAL-BUILDING IN THE MIDDLE AGES

PREFACE

As a student of economics, the time came when I had to choose a topic for my Master's thesis. Already from an early age I had been fascinated by the history of architecture, and moreover, like many members of my generation, I had been captivated by a book I read just after the war, entitled *Geschiedenis eener kathedraal* (History of a Cathedral). Its author was Dr F.G.L. van der Meer (1904-1994), later a renowned professor in Nijmegen. The book's compelling opening lines resonate like a trumpet call: '*Nog altijd, in het oude Frankrijk, verschijnt de kathedraal eerder aan de horizon dan de stad. Plotseling duikt vanachter de golvende hellingen, ijl en grijs, de akropool met den bussel torens.*[...] *En ineens splijt het stadshart open en spat de gevel omhoog en het waait*' (Even today, in old France, the cathedral appears on the horizon first, before the city. From behind the rolling hills there suddenly emerges, slender and gray, the acropolis with its clustered towers. [...] And all at once the heart of the city cleaves open, and spits the edifice up, and the wind blows).

Could a study investigating the economic and historical conditions under which these wonders of human creative capacity were realized perhaps furnish a bridge between the subject I was studying and my intense interest in medieval church-building? I settled on an aspect that had until then been neglected in the literature: the financing of the building of cathedrals. My professor, Dr I.J. Brugmans, was quick to assent. A few years previous, the first volume of the Utrecht Cathedral fabric rolls had been issued, published as part of the *Rijks Geschiedkundige Publicatiën* series in 1948 - an almost ideal starting point for further research. But it seemed wise also to consult Prof. Van der Meer for advice. To my enquiry I received a letter by return post on 26 May 1952, telling me, 'I cannot help you, but only fear that you will find yourself in a chaotic field of ruins and forbidding happenstances'. This lapidary phrase from an eminent scholar had the force of a challenge, and helped lay the foundation for a lifelong fascination in cathedral-building and the ecclesiastical world that drove it, resulting first in a Master's thesis (1953), then in a doctoral thesis (in 1981, beautifully published by Gary Schwartz) and now, nearly 30 years later, in a much revised and expanded edition of that book in English. A conclusion it may be, but not, of course, the last word: a theme such as this – like the cathedrals themselves – is never finished.

A survey of this type would be unthinkable without the assistance and support of many people. In some cases this assistance related purely to matters of content, whilst in others it was personal in nature; sometimes such distinction – happily – cannot be made. There are several whom I would like to mention by name. Hans (later Prof. Joh.) de Vries was without question the centre of the small group of students who chose economic history as an elective, and continued to be a mainstay and an anchor for me later on. Dr W. Jappe Alberts (†), later my doctoral co-supervisor, manifested his confidence in the endeavour by furnishing me with transcripts of the as yet unpublished cathedral-building works rolls. Along with my supervisor Prof. J.H. van Stuijvenberg (†) – an economic historian in the truest sense – it was especially Kees (Prof. C.J.A.C.) Peeters, eminent and erudite architectural historian and author of the authoritative book on Utrecht Cathedral, who was a source of support and inspiration.

Archival research is the most exciting aspect of a study of this kind: aside from the buildings themselves, it is the old archival sources that imbue this work with that crucial historical sensation. This research entailed travel – usually brief interruptions of holiday trips – in England, France and Spain; in the last stopping at the *archivos catedralicios*, still preserved in the very place of their inception and still administered by learned *canonigos archiveros* (fig.1). Of immense value was my participation in a number of inspiring *colloques* organized by the indefatigable husband-and-wife team Jean and Odette Chapelot in Vincennes. Here we first broached the major social themes related to the medieval building lodge in the broader sense; one of these colloquia, held in June 2002, was dedicated entirely to the issue of financing. Participants included many young, recent PhD graduates of the famous *École des chartes* in Paris, with whom I enjoyed fruitful discussions and who kindly allowed me to consult their unpublished theses. Amadeo Serra Desfilis, one of the speakers at the 36th '*Settimane di*

Studi' in Prato in 2004 – entitled *L'Edilizia prima della rivoluzione industriale* – organized a wide-ranging conference in Valencia in November 2007 on the subject of architecture and building in Europe in the Middle Ages and the modern day. Financing was amongst the themes dealt with on this occasion, too, which again fostered valuable contacts with Amadeo, Joan Domenge Mesquida (Barcelona) and others.

My greatest inspiration has come from exchanges with friends and colleagues at home in the Netherlands. Here I will limit myself to mentioning *Signum*, a liaison group with a membership of keen archival researchers and activities centring on the study of ecclesiastical institutions. I would like to thank Bram Kempers and Lex Bosman for agreeing to read and critique portions of the manuscript, and especially Bram and Elian van den Hoven van Genderen for their valuable suggestions on transforming the 1981 doctoral thesis into the book now before you.

Assistance and support in the last stages have been of vital importance. Jan Kuys kindly agreed to read the manuscript in depth and provide constructive feedback. Elizabeth Manton carried out the difficult task of translating a Dutch text filled with jargon and technical terminology into English with precision and great sensitivity to the idiosyncrasies of her language. David Lepine (Exeter) was indispensable when it came to finding the right phrasing for the book title. And last but not least, my thanks to Amsterdam University Press. Director Saskia de Vries took a great interest in this project from the very outset, and put me in touch with the best editor an author could wish for: Aggie Langedijk, without whose support, dedication and specialized knowledge the manuscript could never have been realized. My thanks are also due to Paulien Retèl, Christine Waslander, Maaike Groot and Marianne de Raad. The book's design is the work of Suzan Beijer, whose professional expertise and immense insight have yielded this beautiful result.

I would like to dedicate this book to my wife Eline, who passed away in 2004. How excited she would have been to see the publication of this book, 30 years after my PhD! Together we shared the enthusiasm of countless cathedral trips. For nearly 40 years she was, in her quiet, serene, perspicacious way, the pillar of strength in my life. Our two sons, Gijs and Floriaan, gained a true understanding of what their father was engaged in as they got older, and showed their increasing appreciation for it, though I cannot say whether they will read this book from cover to cover. Finally, I would like to express my gratitude to my life partner now, Marja, who has taken an infectious pleasure in my work and shared an intense interest in the concluding phase of the book's development.

Amsterdam, June 2010

1
Room on the north side of the cathedral church of Palma de Mallorca, between the chapter cloister and one of the chapels, which until recently housed the *Archivo Capitular* of the cathedral. In 1530 one of the canons was elected as the first archivist of the chapter. The bookcase dates from 1710.

LITERATURE
Pascual 1995, p. 288.

VIII
VII

INTRODUCTION

On 18 February 1599, the young Dutch poet Pieter Cornelisz. Hooft paused in the city of Paris whilst making his Grand Tour to Italy. Crossing the bridge over the Seine that afternoon, he entered the oldest part of the city, the Île de la Cité. 'Hereupon has been built', he noted in his travel memoir (*Reis-heuchenis*), 'the church of Our Lady; which is a work that, though not beautiful, is exceptionally large & surely cost a great deal [...]'.[1] His are the very matter-of-fact and accurate observations of a Dutch merchant's son. Particularly noteworthy, however, is how his remark mingles a patently negative aesthetic judgement on what to modern eyes is a supremely impressive monument with an aside about the large sum of money spent on it. Hooft had passed through Chartres the day before but had found the cathedral there not even worth mentioning. His negative view of Gothic architecture was by no means exceptional at the time; indeed, placing medieval architecture a few rungs below that of Classical Antiquity was a definite mark of good taste.[2]

Negative appraisals of Gothic style and of medieval architecture in general have been turned on their head since Hooft's day. From the Romantic period onwards, the Gothic cathedral has been held up as the foremost expression of medieval Christian culture and the worthy counterpart of the temples of Antiquity and, at the same time, as a pinnacle of engineering skill and product of a new urban freedom.[3] It stood, quite simply, as the symbol of an era. French historian Georges Duby's volume on medieval civilization reflects this sentiment in its title, *The Age of the Cathedrals*.[4] The same swell of appreciation is evident in a stream of scholarly publications whose steady expansion continues to this day. Since the nineteenth century, the medieval cathedral has been examined through any number of lenses, from that of architectural history to iconology, to theology, liturgy and philosophy.

And yet it would seem that the lofty spiritual values that cathedrals were assumed to embody also served, in fact, to obscure certain avenues of investigation. Not until recently have the material and economic conditions surrounding the construction of these vast churches received any significant measure of attention. With a few exceptions, curiosity about such aspects of cathedral-building only started to gain steam from around the 1920s onwards. That curiosity came in the wake of a growing interest in economic and social history, on the one hand, and a gradual rise in the significance accorded the contextual study of the society in which these architectural masterpieces came into being, on the other.

For anyone embarking on this field of enquiry, there are two possible paths from which to choose. One leads to the study of organizational and technical aspects of cathedral building operations, encompassing the division of construction-related tasks, the role of the architect and significance of architectonic design methods, the acquisition of building materials and engineering apparatus and how they were used in building. These aspects have been a focus of scholarly study for many decades now[5] the *Bauhütte*, *bouwloods*, lodge or *loge*, long a source of inspiration for the high-flown ideals of the freemasons, have since been divested of myth and legend and restored to the domain of historical fact.[6]

The other path leads to the commissioning party: the ecclesiastical – or occasionally secular – administrations whose initiative it was to build a cathedral and who bore the responsibility for its erection and maintenance. Their task consisted of gathering together the funds needed to sustain building works over both the short and longer term. The question immediately arises as to how these administrative entities went about generating a public base of support that could be tapped for a varying array of income sources. To answer this question we must examine a series of factors, namely, where these resources came from and how they were gathered, the total sum available to fund the building works, and how this sum fluctuated over time.

The present study, of which the first edition was published in 1981, takes the latter path. This choice was motivated by the consideration that whereas studies on the organization and working methods applied in church-building operations were already fairly well-represented at the time, a comprehensive examination of the financing of cathedral-building was still lacking. Without a doubt, it is the near absence of relevant serial sources that is primarily to blame, in particular of sources containing financial data over an unbroken period of years of a cathedral's construction. Not only are there few such extant sources, but they have garnered hardly any attempt at systematic investigation, let alone publication.[7] The series of account rolls documenting the construction of the Dom in Utrecht is one of the few that meets the basic criteria and, as such, provides what is the almost ideal foundation for this study.

In the decades since this book's first publication, precisely the financial and economic side of cathedral-building has seen a considerable growth in scholarly interest. A number of conferences have been organized around this theme,[8] and accounts kept by the fabrics of three cathedrals – those at Exeter, Freising and Osnabrück – have since been published.[9] No self-respecting study on cathedral-building fails to at least make mention of the financial sources that determined the pace of building. In some cases, methods of financing are even the central focus of analysis, as in studies on the Spanish cathedrals in Oviedo, Toledo, Malaga, Murcia, Segovia and Mallorca, and the French cathedrals in Troyes, Rouen, Limoges, Sens and Bourges.[10]

This survey is bounded by a number of different parameters, the three most important of which are described here. First, it is limited to cathedrals in the strict sense of Episcopal churches – in other words, churches housing the bishop's cathedra. This criterion begs the question: Why only cathedrals and not other types of churches, such as abbey, monastic, collegiate or parish churches? Of paramount importance here is the elevated position that cathedrals occupied in the hierarchy of the ecclesiastical establishment, resulting in a system of financing for building works that was likewise distinct from that at other churches. This is not to say that building at these other churches was not funded by some of the same income sources used for cathedrals but, rather, that cathedrals could activate those income sources at a different level and, as such, via different organizational mechanisms. It is therefore their place at the top of the ecclesiastical hierarchy, and not mutual compatibility of scale or architectural design, that makes cathedrals eminently suitable for a comparative study. Closely related to this is the fact that underpinning all cathedrals was *l'énorme machine institutionelle de l'église*[11] that helped to access income sources and ensure a steady flow of funds. Cathedrals, more than any other type of church or ecclesiastical building – especially from the thirteenth century onwards – show a large measure of unity and continuity in both the nature and arrangement of ecclesiastical institutions involved in the building works.

Of foremost importance to the cathedral's fundamental position in the Church hierarchy were the bishopric, bishop and chapter. Even though the cathedral church ranked highest in any diocese, there were no direct ties with the faithful, whose spiritual care depended not on the cathedral, but on their own parish church. This elevated and at the same time isolated position within the ecclesiastical establishment had very far-reaching consequences where the collection of building monies was concerned, sometimes serving to favour the cathedral over a city parish church, at other times not. In principle, the present study bears upon all cathedrals that fall within the ambit of Western Christianity, with the exception of those in Italy. As shall be explained, the construction of the *duomi* in Italian cities was by and large the preserve of civic administrations, and not of bishop and chapter. Italian cathedrals will therefore only be mentioned in passing.

The second parameter for this survey relates to the time span it covers. The large measure of unity in the institutional structure of the bishopric and chapter did not develop overnight. It was not until partway into the thirteenth century that special administrative bodies – designated as *fabrica ecclesiae* – emerged as separate entities within chapter administrations everywhere, charged with specific responsibility for care of the building. And thus it is here that our investigation begins, though the preceding period will also receive some consideration. Serial sources pertaining to finances, and specifically the cathedral fabric rolls, only begin to turn up with any frequency starting in the fourteenth century, increasing in volume from the fifteenth century onwards.[12] The focus of this survey therefore lies in the later Middle Ages. Where the Utrecht Dom is concerned, the Middle Ages stretch to as late as 1580, the year in which the cathedral was prohibited from continuing to celebrate divine services.

The third parameter arises from the scarcity of primary sources. Where these do exist, they are difficult to access. This field of enquiry, by its very nature, demands the exploration of various disciplines: economic history – particularly the history of prices and wages and monetary history – Church history – most especially the history of ecclesiastical institutions, but also of theology, devotion and religiosity – and, finally, architectural and art history. However, the topic that concerns us here occupies no more than a small and sometimes hidden role within each of these domains. Consider the complex edifice of medieval canon law, for instance, in which the cathedral fabric is only a marginal player and therefore in many cases deemed hardly worth mentioning. The same is true of the extant sources, where we must dig deep within vast cathedral archives to uncover the paper trail left by a cathedral fabric. Here we are made to realize that, contrary to what might otherwise be assumed, cathedral-building and upkeep by medieval Church administrators was but one spoke amongst many in the great wheel of the church organization, and was therefore of far less administrative and managerial concern than countless other vital Church interests.

Since this book's first publication as a dissertation in 1981, each of these various disciplines has been inundated with new literature. Alongside monographs on cathedrals and publications of primary source material, we now also have studies on cathedral chapters, on episcopal cities and the topographical function of cathedrals within them, on the diocesan organization – on, in short, the entire institutional framework within which cathedral-building took place. Much has likewise been written, with some illuminating insights, about indulgences and cults of the saints and their relics, each of fundamental financial importance for building works. Architectural and art history have assigned greater influence and significance to the role of commissioners. Review of this new and at times innovative literature has led to myriad small and larger changes to the original text, and in some cases to the rewriting or addition of passages.

The book's original division into two sections remains unchanged. Part one, *The sources of income for cathedral-building in the Middle Ages*, is general in nature and organized into two chapters. The first, *The cathedral fabric*, looks at which party should properly be considered the master or commissioner of the building works. The second chapter, *Sources of income for the building works*, provides a systematic overview of the income sources that could be and were engaged to finance cathedral building works, and discusses the actual methods used to do so. Also addressed to a lesser extent is the question of how these income sources evolved over time. The income structures of specific cathedral fabrics are not discussed here, nor is the question of why certain cathedrals or groups of cathedrals experienced spikes of building activity at certain times or what made building campaigns sometimes come to an abrupt end.

Part two, *The financing of cathedral-building in the Middle Ages*, homes in on the actual financing of cathedral building works. The first chapter, on the financing of Utrecht Cathedral, comprises a case study centring on works at a single cathedral: the Utrecht Dom. This choice was prompted by the exceptional wealth and completeness of the source material preserved there, encompassing both the long period in which the building lodge was in continuous operation and the decades preceding the Reformation, when building activity had all but ceased. Continuing our systematic approach, this chapter is cast on diachronic lines, with an emphasis on analysing how the nature and size of income sources – and, with them, expenditures for construction and furnishings – evolved over a period of almost three centuries. The unusual circumstance that the city's oldest parish church, the *Buurkerk*, underwent several extensive renovations in the shadow of the neighbouring Dom during the same period, and that financial records for these renovations have also been preserved, furthermore presents an opportunity to shed light on the contrast between financing the building of a cathedral as opposed to that of a parish church.

The second chapter places the financing of building works at Utrecht's cathedral in a broader context by turning to a brief consideration, based on recent research, of such financing at eight other cathedrals. Two cases concern late medieval building campaigns: the construction of the transept at Sens and of the north tower at Bourges, both of which were fairly clear-cut building projects funded by separate financial sources. Osnabrück possesses a series of account rolls extending from the late fifteenth into the first half of the sixteenth century, which describe relatively modest expenditures for construction and furnishings in the period just preceding the Reformation. Archival data on Exeter and Troyes is early, but also very fragmentary. From the small number of published sources, it appears that the scale of building works at the cathedral of Toledo was probably amongst the most extensive in Europe. In the case of the cathedral of Milan – one of the largest in Europe – registers of accounts and other sources paint an exceptionally clear picture of spectacular building activities during the early years between 1387 and 1391. Segovia gives us the last of the Gothic cathedrals, where construction began in the sixteenth century and did not finish until the seventeenth; here the archives are preserved almost in their entirety. Finally, a brief discussion of financing for the construction of St Peter's in Rome – not a cathedral, but the mother church of all churches in the Christian world – closes this chapter.

The book's concluding section examines general questions about the scale of church building operations and, in particular, what parameters those commissioning the work set in framing their ambitions. Did the building patrons have any insight into the immensity of the task before them when they launched a building project? Did they try to estimate the financial means they would need and over how many years they would need them in order to finish all or part of the building?

The ensuing discussion of this subject may well demand a large measure of perseverance on the part of the reader, the same as might be required for technical analyses of architectural forms and structures in other studies. The history of how the network of incoming and outgoing cash flows were developed and perpetuated, and also of the drive amongst successive generations to continue the work their predecessors had begun, is as complex and diverse as the evolution of architecture and construction engineering. The story of how cathedral-building was financed is not only – or even primarily – about success versus failure, and even less about the capacity or otherwise of administrators to manage financial means. Behind the shifting fortunes that every cathedral experienced rises the edifice of Church institutions and customs, themselves tightly interwoven with medieval society. By placing a spotlight on these aspects, we can illuminate a facet of cathedral-building that, whilst perhaps less impressive or edifying, is certainly as fascinating as the built and sculpted monuments themselves – monuments that even today leave no one unaffected.

PART ONE THE SOURCES OF INCOME FOR CATHEDRAL-BUILDING IN THE MIDDLE AGES

Seat of an archbishopric
Seat of a bishopric
Boundaries of Church provinces
ATLANTIC OCEAN
NORTH SEA
MEDITERRANEAN SEA
76
62
216
98
101
213
81
58
131
65
211
105
157
68
164
212
45
49
186
192
99
13
44
9
60
160
132
90
57
27
103
29
194
67
174
181
154
205
152
21
171
144
117
47
155
48
202
94
175
197
128
10
135
18
193
89
34
130
17
150
46
162
100
73
52
110
33
209
125
168
96
66
166
107
137
28
4
42
158
210
59
54
93
72
134
14
95
5
119
7
200
15
191
92
104
19
161
31
112
11
40
167
143
124
3
129
12
116
190
217
140
43
83
146
64
163
39
184A
51
176
173
218
97
207
75
179
20
55
184
25
187
188
56
6
172
201
142
54A
23
177
84
127
78
77A
41
114
8

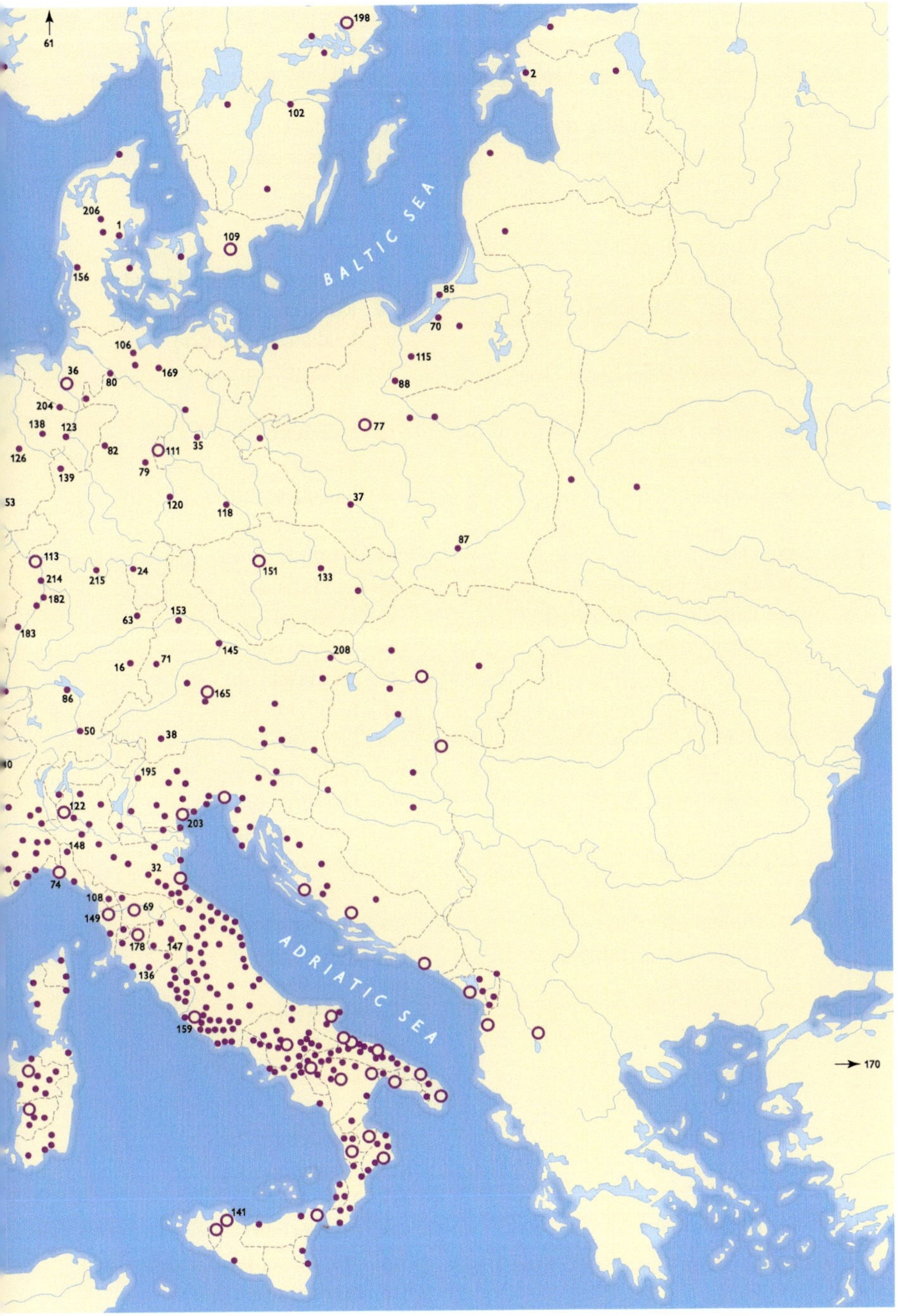

2

Ecclesiastical map of archbishoprics and bishoprics in Roman Catholic Europe around 1500, showing boundaries of the Church provinces

Archbishoprics and bishoprics mentioned in the text are indicated with a number (see p. 28-29)

LITERATURE
Atlas zur Kirchengeschichte, map 71.

1 Aarhuus (DK)
2 Abø (FI)
3 Agde (F)
4 Agen (F)
5 Aire-sur- l'Adour (F)
6 Albarracin (SP)
7 Albi (F)
8 Almería (SP)
9 Amiens (F)
10 Angers (F)
11 Apt (F)
12 Arles (F)
13 Arras (F)
14 Astorga (SP)
15 Auch (F)
16 Augsburg (G)
17 Autun (F)
18 Auxerre (F)
19 Avignon (F)
20 Avila (SP)
21 Avranches (F)

23 Baeza (SP)
24 Bamberg (G)
25 Barcelona (SP)
26 Basel (CH)
27 Bayeux (F)
28 Bazas (F)
29 Beauvais (F)
30 Besançon (F)
31 Béziers (F)
32 Bologna (IT)
33 Bordeaux (F)
34 Bourges (F)
35 Brandenburg (G)
36 Bremen (G)
37 Breslau/Wrocław (P)
38 Bressanone/Brixen (IT)
39 Burgo de Osma (SP)
40 Burgos (SP)

41 Cadix-Ceuta (SP)
42 Cahors (F)
43 Calahorra (SP)
44 Cambrai (F)
45 Canterbury (GB)
46 Chalon-sur-Saône (F)
47 Châlons-en-Champagne (F)
48 Chartres (F)
49 Chichester (GB)
50 Chur (CH)
51 Ciudad Rodrigo (SP)
52 Clermont-Ferrand (F)
53 Cologne (G)
54 Condom (F)
55 Coria (SP)
56 Cuenca (SP)
57 Coutances (F)
58 Coventry (GB)

59 Dax (F)
60 Dol-de-Bretagne (F)
61 Drontheim (Nidaros) (N)
62 Durham (GB)

63 Eichstätt (G)
64 Elne (F)
65 Ely (GB)
66 Embrun (F)
67 Evreux (F)
68 Exeter (GB)

69 Florence (IT)
70 Frauenburg/Frombork (P)
71 Freising (G)

72 Gap (F)
73 Geneva (CH)
74 Genoa (IT)
75 Gerona (IT)
76 Glasgow (GB)
77 Gnesen/Gniezno (P)
78 Guadix (SP)

79 Halberstadt (G)
80 Hamburg (G)
81 Hereford (GB)
82 Hildesheim (G)
83 Huesca (SP)

84 Jaén (SP)

85 Königsberg/Kaliningrad (R)
86 Konstanz (G)
87 Krakau/Krakow (P)
88 Kulm (Chemlza) (P)

89 Langres (F)
90 Laon (F)
91 Lausanne (CH)
92 Lavaur (F)
93 Lectoure (F)
94 Le Mans (F)
95 Léon (SP)
96 Le Puy (F)
97 Lerida (SP)
98 Lichfield (GB)
99 Liège (B)
100 Limoges (F)
101 Lincoln (GB)
102 Linköping (SE)
103 Lisieux (F)
104 Lodève (F)
105 London (GB)
106 Lübeck (G)
107 Lugo (SP)
108 Lucca (IT)
109 Lund (SE)
110 Lyon (F)

111 Magdeburg (G)
112 Maguelone (F)
113 Mainz (G)
114 Málaga (SP)
115 Marienwerder/Kwidzyn (P)
116 Marseille (F)
117 Meaux (F)

118 Meissen (G)
119 Mende (F)
120 Merseburg (G)
121 Metz (F)
122 Milan (IT)
123 Minden (G)
124 Mirepoix (F)
125 Mondoñedo (SP)
126 Münster (G)
127 Murcia (SP)

128 Nantes (F)
129 Narbonne (F)
130 Nevers (F)
131 Norwich (GB)
132 Noyon (F)

133 Olomouc /Olmütz (CZ)
134 Orense (SP)
135 Orléans (F)
136 Orvieto (IT)
137 Oviedo (SP)
138 Osnabrück (G)
139 Paderborn (G)
140 Palencia (SP)
141 Palermo (IT)
142 Palma de Mallorca (SP)
143 Pamplona (SP)
144 Paris (F)
145 Passau (G)
146 Perpignan (F)
147 Perugia (IT)
148 Piacenza (IT)
149 Pisa (IT)
150 Poitiers (F)
151 Prague (CZ)

152 Quimper (F)

153 Regensburg (G)
154 Rheims (F)
155 Rennes (F)
156 Ribe (DK)
157 Rochester (GB)
158 Rodez (F)
159 Rome (IT)
160 Rouen (F)

161 Saint-Bertrand-de-Comminges (F)
162 Saintes (F)
163 Salamanca (SP)
164 Salisbury (GB)
165 Salzburg (A)
166 Santiago de Compostela (SP)
167 Santo Domingo de la Calzada (SP)
168 Sarlat (F)
169 Schwerin (G)
170 Sebaste /Sivas (T)
171 Sées (F)
172 Segorbe (SP)
173 Segovia (SP)
174 Senlis (F)
175 Sens (F)
176 Seo de Urgell (SP)
177 Sevilla (SP)
178 Siena (IT)
179 Sigüenza (SP)
180 Sion/Sitten (CH)
181 Soissons (F)
182 Speyer (G)
183 Strasbourg (F)

184 Taragona (SP)
184a Tarazona (SP)
185 Tarentaise (F)
186 Thérouanne (F)
187 Toledo (SP)
188 Tortosa (SP)
189 Toul (F)
190 Toulon (F)
191 Toulouse (F)
192 Tournai (B)
193 Tours (F)
194 Tréguier (F)
195 Trent (IT)
196 Trier (G)
197 Troyes (F)

198 Uppsala (SE)
199 Utrecht (NL)
200 Uzès (F)

201 Valencia (SP)
202 Vannes (F)
203 Venice (IT)
204 Verden (G)
205 Verdun (F)
206 Viborg (DK)
207 Vich (SP)
208 Vienna (A)
209 Vienne (F)
210 Viviers (F)

211 Wells (GB)
212 Winchester (GB)
213 Worcester (GB)
214 Worms (G)
215 Würzburg (G)

216 York (GB)

217 Zamora (SP)
218 Zaragoza (SP)

KEY

A	Austria	IT	Italy
B	Belgium	L	Luxembourg
CH	Switzerland	N	Norway
CZ	Czech Republic	NL	Netherlands
DK	Denmark	P	Poland
F	France	R	Russia
G	Germany	SE	Sweden
GB	Great Britain	SP	Spain
IT	Italy	T	Turkey

CHAPTER ONE

MANAGING THE CATHEDRAL CHURCH: THE CATHEDRAL FABRIC

In the period between around 1200 and 1500, the ecclesiastical map of Europe was divided into some 700 bishoprics (fig. 2).[1] Though all equal in the eyes of canon law,[2] historical maps of the Church in Europe show that, in geographic terms, there was a world of difference between the various dioceses.[3] Italy counted 275 bishoprics,[4] France 130,[5] Spain 49,[6] Germany 46,[7] England no more than 21,[8] and the whole of Scandinavia 11.[9] Vast bishoprics might lie alongside very small ones, even within a single country.[10] The Breton bishopric of Dol had a scant 96 parishes,[11] whilst the neighbouring mid-sized bishopric of Amiens boasted 763.[12] Chartres, geographically the most extensive diocese of any in France, counted 963 parishes,[13] whilst Rouen had 1400.[14] The very largest bishoprics, such as Konstanz and Liège, had as many as 1700 parishes.[15]

These great disparities in geographic scale (which could in part determine a diocese's importance) can be traced back to the history of the origins of diocesan organization. From the fourth century onwards, the organizational structure of the late Roman Empire, with the *civitas* as its smallest unit, also came to define that of the Church, such that in both the densely populated regions of Rome as well as farther afield in the Empire's Romanized provinces, the constructs of *civitas* and diocese came down to the same thing. This explains the plethora of small bishoprics, some of them later subsumed by others, in the heavily urbanized and settled regions of central and southern Italy and southern France, and the far larger dioceses of northern Italy and the rest of Gaul.[16]

Later on, especially between the seventh and tenth centuries, when additional bishoprics were established in newly conquered and converted territories where there had been little to no prior contact with Rome, diocesan boundaries were expanded still farther.[17] Here it was often the German kings who took the first step. In these areas the borders of the bishopric sometimes coincided with the original territory that missionary bishops had gone to christianize.[18] The bishopric of Utrecht was amongst the major dioceses of Europe.

It took until the eleventh century – and in areas controlled by the Teutonic Knights until as late as the latter half of the thirteenth[19] – for the system of Church hierarchy to become established, constituting an archdiocese led by an archbishop and a number of suffragan bishoprics each under a bishop. Even in later periods, however, Church organization remained subject to changes and regrouping.[20] Best known is Pope John XXII's foundation of sixteen new bishoprics in southern France between 1317 and 1318, which came at the expense of exceedingly large and wealthy dioceses such as Toulouse, Clermont, Albi and Narbonne.[21] The last bishoprics to be founded in the Middle Ages were the four created in the kingdom of Granada in 1486 after the expulsion of the Moors.[22]

Each bishopric had a cathedral – that is to say, a cathedral church – the *ecclesia cathedralis*, where the bishop's throne, or *cathedra*, stood.[23] This church was also the mother church of the diocese, the *matrix ecclesia*, and accorded the canonical status of parish church of that diocese.[24] Medieval Europe thus had to build and maintain some 700 greater and lesser cathedrals, or else reclassify existing churches as cathedrals, as occurred at Benedictine abbeys in southern France. These cathedrals diverged very widely in status and prestige: whereas some were centres of learning and civilization, others lay far removed from the civilized world in vast, scarcely inhabited bishoprics in Scandinavia and eastern Europe, with parishes at a distance of two months' travel from the cathedral.[25] The bishop of Wroclaw (Breslau) lamented in 1406 that his cathedral was established '*in loco horroris et vaste solitudinis*' (in a place of dread and desolate isolation).[26] Yet in these areas, too, where parish churches were still few and far between, establishing the *matrix ecclesia* was imperative.[27]

Who bore responsibility for the cathedral as a building, and thus for its maintenance? Canon law prescribed certain rules that require consideration, separate from their application in practice. No more than cursory examination is needed here to understand how the management of Church property developed and the role accorded the church building, which was itself part of that property.

In the early Christian Church it was the bishop who exercised full authority over property and income accruing to the bishopric. He administered the diocese's ever-expanding pool of endowments, including all bequests and gifts, and spent it as he saw fit, with the important caveat that allocations stipulated by the giver (such as care of the poor or construction works) had to be honoured.[28] The fifth century saw further restrictions imposed. Abuses of spending freedoms by certain Italian bishops led Popes Simplicius (468-483) and Gelasius (492-496) to tighten the rules: thenceforth all bishops would have to divide incoming monies into four parts, with one part earmarked for the clergy, a second for the bishop's own household, a third for the poor and a fourth for the upkeep of church buildings in the diocese (the *quarta fabricis applicanda*). This quadripartition concerned both income arising from diocesan property as well as donations from pious parishioners (*redditus et oblationes*). Initially applied only to the Italian bishoprics, this rule of division gained greater currency from the eighth century onwards, and then particularly in Gaul; contemporary Spain and Sweden, amongst others, applied a division into three parts, in which care of the poor was not assigned a separate share of the revenues.[29]

The cohesion of episcopal property did not last long. As early as the fifth century, the process of pooling assets according to their source and intended use was already underway, and not only cathedral churches, but also abbeys and especially parish churches with them, increasingly gained a certain measure of independence in disposing of their own property.[30] Initially, however, bishops did keep full control over cathedral property and cathedral income (not to be confused with diocesan property). They led a communal, celibate life with the clergy attached to their cathedral, as they had done since the early Christian era. It is to this group of clerics that we can trace the origins of the later cathedral chapter. But not until after the recognition of the Benedictine-inspired rule of Bishop Chrodegang of Metz in 755-756 and the Council of Aachen's ratification of more normative *Institutiones* in 817 can we speak of chapters in the proper sense. Now, for the first time, bishops possessed legal leverage to introduce a form of common life amongst clerics attached to the cathedral, prescribing prayer at the appointed canonical hours, for example, whilst leaving them free to hold personal property. These *clerici canonici* were furthermore tasked with advising and actively supporting the bishop with the direction of his bishopric. Up through the eighth century, these two households still existed more or less as one.[31] There are indications that bishops continued to practise the old standard of quadripartition to allocate cathedral property and income up into the ninth century, and possibly even longer.[32] Later developments affecting cathedral holdings would interfere with this old rule and undercut its practical usefulness.

This general rule for a quadripartite or tripartite division of all Church incomes was included in the *Decretum* compiled by Gratian in 1140 and subsequently incorporated into general canon law;[33] it also figures as an established tenet in later canonical literature.[34] Yet in practice the rule had little real consequence as an allocation standard in the period that concerns us here, and almost nowhere do we find any mention of a share reserved for the building fund (the fabric).[35] Commenting on the custom of quadripartition in relation to the Dom tower's construction in Utrecht, Geert Groote (1340-1384) remarked that, '*quid de parte fabrice sit, nescio*' (of the fabric's share I know nothing).[36] The secularization that eroded Church holdings in general during the ninth and tenth centuries may be to blame for the fact that the fabric's share – as the least imperative of the four recipients – could even be the first to fall prey to greed amongst the laity.[37] Yet here and there the allocation standard continued to be applied for certain portions of Church income. In 1186, for example, the pope ordered that gifts offered at the grave of St Thomas Becket (1118?-1170) in Canterbury were to be divided into four parts (with one reserved for the cathedral).[38] As a general canonical regulation, quadripartition served to mark out certain duties and rights attached to property holdings, and in this sense at least, its significance persisted, albeit of secondary importance at times.[39]

Cohesion of cathedral property in the narrower sense also crumbled and, with it, the exclusive authority of the bishop. It is not unthinkable that responsibility for the cathedral had already by and large been settled on the chapter by the time a separate endowment for the canons, the *mensa capituli*, was founded. The creation between the ninth and twelfth centuries of such *Sondervermogen* in the episcopal cities of the Frankish kingdom as well as elsewhere was impelled by a multitude of factors and transpired under varying conditions and over lengthy periods where certain phases were concerned.[40] Over time, this capitular property would come to fulfil most of the functions of the former cathedral holdings, covering the costs of living for clerics (with the exception of the bishop, for whom an independent endowment, the *mensa episcopi*, was reserved from the twelfth century), hospitality, care of the poor and building maintenance for both the cathedral and the residences and auxiliary buildings.[41] Bishops used this opportunity to divest themselves of an array of financial obligations, including those relating to the cathedral. A well-known Parisian charter of 829 furnishes an example of how the burden of responsibility for church buildings was implicitly transferred onto the canons, to be borne by the chapter. Summing up the various of elements of his property to be apportioned to the chapter, the bishop concluded by adding, '*insuper et tectorum curam fratribus deputatorum, ne collapsa deperant, ad se pertinere noverint*' (wherefore the brethren must realize that the care of the roofs entrusted to them – such that these do not collapse into ruin – falls to them).[42] This passage may well have had far-reaching consequences for Paris's cathedral: of the two churches within the cathedral complex, it was not the ancient and original episcopal church of St Etienne for which a glorious future beckoned but, rather, the younger and – initially – relatively unimportant collegiate church of Notre Dame.[43]

Already there was a general tendency towards splitting Church property into distinct components, each earmarked for a specific purpose and each to a certain degree also independently managed. The

De b̄ndictōe capsarū p
reliquijs seu sāiarijs con
seruādis R xix·
De benedictōe baptiste
rij· R xx·
De b̄ndictōe cāpane
De benedictōe in R i·
īposicōe p̄mi lapidis ec
clesie noue edificande·
Sequitur rubrica.
Pontifex paratus a
micto alba et plu
uiali mitra et baculo pas
torali p̄nte lapide qui p̄
mus in fundamēto ecclie
locandus est· Incipit.
Adiutoriū nrm̄ in nōie
dn̄i Sit nomen dn̄i be
nedictum Lapidē quē
reprobauerūt edificātes
Tu es petrus et sup hāc
petram edificabo eccl'· R
Glia pr̄i et filio et sp̄ui·
Dn̄e exaudi orōem meā·
Et clamor m̄s ad te ue·
Oremus· Collecta·

Domine ihesu xp̄e fili
dei uiui qui es uerus
omp̄c deus splendor et
ymago p̄ris uita et et
na qui es lapis angu
laris et sine manibus
excisus et īmutabile
fundamentū hūc lapi
dem collocandū in tuo
nōie cōsecramus· et tu
qui es principiū et in
crementū· et cōsūmacō
istius op̄is qd̄ debet ad
laudem et ad glām tu
nōis inchoari· Qui cū
p̄re et sp̄u scō· Oratio·
Dn̄e scē p̄r omp̄s
eterne deus bene
dicere dignare hūc la

emergence of designated funds for special purposes was further encouraged by the circumstance that cathedral property, now enlarged by donations, was burdened with myriad responsibilities for, amongst other things, services for the dead and distributions to the poor, as well as '*ad luminaria sive restaurandam ipsam ecclesiam*' (for the illumination or maintenance of the cathedral itself). The practice of hiving off special funds in turn elicited new donations, the importance of which eventually superseded a fund's original capital.[44]

Almost nothing is known about the administration of funds set aside for maintenance and lighting. In an 866 inventory from the archbishopric of Cologne, the cathedral sacristan (to whom cathedral maintenance fell) received an income independent of that allocated to the clergy and the hospital (the old quadripartite division provided the standard), though it is unclear who actually managed this fund.[45] Though the bishop's transfer of capitular properties onto the canons inherently included the transfer of financial responsibility for the cathedral, this in no way implies that he lost all say in matters of cathedral management. It is quite possible that the officer directly in charge of building monies – the rural dean or archdeacon, the *camerarius* or, as at Cologne, the *custos* – was appointed by and accountable to the bishop.[46]

Sources dating from the later Middle Ages – being far more numerous than those from the preceding period – reveal that in many episcopal cities the management of the cathedral and therefore of building works lay largely in the hands of the chapter. This remarkable development – for what was the cathedral if not the church of the bishop? – can be better understood when considered within the broader context of the relationship between the bishop and chapter. From the thirteenth century onwards, cathedral chapters increasingly evolved – usually at the expense of episcopal prerogatives – into highly autonomous, legally and financially independent, wealthy associations.[47] Not until the beginning of the fourteenth century did the relationship between the bishop and chapter attain stable legal ground. The onetime ideal of the bishop and chapter as '*unum corpus*', as formulated by the thirteenth-century canonist Hostiensis, was now a definite thing of the past.[48]

3
Folio from the Pontifical of the church of St Mary, c. 1455. Parchment, 380 x 280 mm
Utrecht, University Library, ms. 400, f. 63v

This Pontifical contains the liturgy of blessing and laying of the first stone for a new church. Depicted inside the historiated initial D beginning the word *Domine* is a bishop, who is shown blessing the first stone. Behind him is a (sub)dean holding a girdle book. Three building labourers hold the stone upright, one of them using a pickaxe. At the bottom of the page two sculptors are shown at work.

LITERATURE
Exh. cat. Utrecht 1972, no. 44.

Disputes about competency remained unavoidable, however. Authority over the cathedral was only one of the issues at stake and, from the participants' point of view, not even the most important one. As such, decisions relating to the cathedral church are usually found towards the end of the records, in this case the documents settling conflicts between the two parties – the *compositiones* – and (from the fourteenth century onwards) the extensive agreements known as *Wahlkapitulationen*, used mostly to grant concessions to the chapter, which the bishop swore in the chapter's presence to uphold upon his accession to office.[49] One very good gauge of internal power relations lies in the way jurisdiction over the church building and its surrounding lands was divided. In the fourteenth and fifteenth centuries, the chapter of Chartres demanded spiritual and temporal jurisdiction over the cathedral, thus also giving it authority over building operations and all persons associated therewith.[50] In a document of 28 January 1280 describing how a dispute was settled between the chapter and the bishop of Elne, the latter refers to the college of canons as the cathedral's '*dominus principalis*' (true master).[51] In Paris, the canons of Notre Dame likewise wished to be recognized as the true masters of their cathedral; a complicated division of jurisdictional powers in 1283 defined distinct spheres of competency, whereby authority for the church and choir was allocated to the chapter and authority for the actual presbytery went to the bishop. Here too, '*operarii*' (labourers) and '*servientes*' (servants) connected with building operations came under the express jurisdiction of the chapter.[52]

In fact, the bishop was little more than a guest in his own cathedral.[53] Canon law obligated him to be present in his cathedral on Church feast days at the least, but by the later Middle Ages there were many bishops who never or only seldom officiated in their own churches.[54] In some cases they even required the chapter's permission to do so, and more than once were refused; indeed, it could happen that the bishop did not even possess a key to his church.[55] In 1496 and 1497 the canons at Poitiers refused to let the bishop use the crosier and mitre, which belonged to the chapter and were kept in the cathedral.[56] And sources show that even the English bishops who had donated large sums towards building works only rarely presided at services in their cathedrals.[57]

Another canonical prescription was that the bishop had to live in the immediate vicinity of his church.[58] As such, every episcopal city provided a – sometimes fortified – palace for the bishop's use. Situated near the cathedral, the residence was oftentimes connected to it by a gallery or chapel; never, however, was it built to adjoin the cathedral as the chapter buildings were.[59] In many instances the palace lost its residential function and came to serve solely as an administrative building.[60] It was not uncommon for political conflicts with the chapter or, even more frequently, with private citizens to force the bishop to leave the city and temporarily or permanently withdraw to some noble estate.[61] In 1296 the bishop's official at Rheims declared that, 'He who is the archbishop of Rheims has two important adversaries: the chapter of Rheims and the citizenry'.[62] In the late medieval period, bishops were rarely, if ever, present in their city; they, and incidentally many canons like them, were not 'residentiary', to use the technical term.[63]

The above already gives an indication of the chapter's importance as the foremost, if not sole, administrator of cathedral building operations – that is to say, the cathedral fabric – during the later Middle Ages. Nevertheless, let us first consider the role and position of the bishop, as it was he who was the initiator of all church building works in the diocese, according to canon law, certainly where his own cathedral was concerned (fig. 3 and 4).[64] In the words of Pope Innocent III (1198-1216), no bond between a bishop and the abbeys and churches in his diocese was as profound as that between him and his cathedral: '*cui est spirituali conjugio copulatus*' (with which he is joined in a spiritual marriage).[65] Whilst his direct influence on building operations varied from one place to another, the bishop's role as chief supervisor *ex officio* of the cathedral was the same everywhere.[66] As the bishopric's spiritual leader, he held exclusive authority to institute certain measures or spiritual benefits (such as indulgences) to support the building works. And it is rare that bishops would refuse to do so; indeed, such measures provided an easy, informal and efficient way of fulfilling the duty to lend financial support to their cathedral's con-

struction. Once extended, the chapter guarded such privileges and indulgences with care,[67] ensuring that they were confirmed and, where necessary, expanded by newly appointed bishops; in some cases such confirmation was included in the bishop's inaugural oath.[68] Post-Tridentine canon law likewise accorded the bishop primary responsibility for the welfare of the cathedral. For this he was obliged to pledge at least one-quarter of his official income as a surety (the old quadripartition), which was assumed to leave enough for him to live as befitted his station. Only when new construction projects or renovations were necessary and the customary income was insufficient could he be compelled to make good on his pledge with a cash contribution.[69] However, this by no means implied direct involvement in running the fabric; at best, it represented the fulfilment of basic canonical obligations.

Up until the twelfth century, bishops in the German empire were particularly inclined to view the erection of immense cathedrals as the ultimate expression of their office,[70] as is attested with admiration and approval in various narrative sources, chronicles and bishops' *vitae*.[71] In one case, they tell of a bishop who cherished an almost humble affection for his cathedral: in 1171 the bishop of Norwich insisted on sitting at the entrance to his cathedral so that he could personally, *in propria persona*, accept donations from the faithful.[72] Where new building projects came at the bishop's initiative, it was he who actually drove the enterprise; he might join with the chapter to generate new sources of income to fund the vast building programme, put in place administrative or, in some cases, technical measures, and prevail upon his chapter where necessary. Bishop Gerard I of Cambrai (1012–1051) set off on horseback himself to personally seek out suitable quarries, prompted by the fear that death might overtake him before his cathedral was completed.[73] Bishop Poppo of Trier (1016–1047) spent so long in fascinated observation of building activities at his cathedral that – being bareheaded in the summer sun – he suffered sunstroke.[74] Particularly striking and detailed is a report concerning the activities of Bishop Geoffroy de Montbray of Coutances (1049–1093), describing how he travelled to Apulia and Calabria with Robert de Guiscard ('*parochianus suus*') and a company of Norman barons to accumulate valuables and money to fund construction of his cathedral. Even on his deathbed, the bishop continued to fret about the building operations. Elsewhere this source tells us that '*ad aedificationem et incrementum ecclesiae suae omni nisu et voluntate per noctem erat et per diem*' (to the construction and expansion of his cathedral he dedicated himself fully both night and day).[75] Bishops cited all manner of reasons to justify new building projects: their cathedral was too small or too ramshackle to accommodate visiting pilgrims, the new building would in fact be the restoration of a former and now ruined situation, or the new building project, having already commenced, carried an obligation to finish it.[76]

During the second half of the eleventh century, sources show mounting criticism of the zeal and ostentation with which these spiritual building masters pursued their projects: their overblown ambitions could only be realized by relying on enforced labour from serfs and financial resources to which the bishop had no legal claim.[77] These sources make clear that even where bishops took the initiative, cooperation with the chapter was essential. But conflicts could not always be avoided. In Lisieux, the canons accused Bishop Arnulfus (1141-1182) of precipitous action in the cathedral building operations begun around 1170, and thus of squandering Church income.[78] In Rouen, the archbishop appealed to Pope Innocent III in 1198 when some of the canons proved unwilling to contribute a portion of their income towards cathedral works.[79] Caesarius of Heisterbach (1180-1240) relates how Cologne's Archbishop Engelbert (1216-1225) attempted – to no avail – to enlist capitular support for new building plans.[80] But on the whole it was undeniably the bishops who predominated during this period.[81] Thus, the chapter of Beauvais ceded revenues for construction in 1225, '*ordinationi [...] Milonis episcopi*' (by order of Bishop Milon [1217-1234]).[82] A more dramatic example is provided by Bishop Bernard de Castanet who, in 1277, just a day after arriving in the heretical and rebellious diocese of Albi and even 'before the meal', decided with a hastily reformed chapter to rebuild the cathedral. Intense and heated conflicts ensued with both the *boni homines* (worthy persons) of the city and members of his own chapter.[83]

From the thirteenth century onwards, however, the chapter's influ-

4
Dietrich III von Isenberg, bishop of Münster (1218-1226), with the first stone of the cathedral as an attribute, c.1230
Statue on the eastern side of the *Paradies*, the porch of the west transept
Münster, St Paul's Cathedral

The laying of the first stone was a prerogative reserved for the bishop. Bishop Dietrich was elected to his office in 1218, on 22 July, the feast of Mary Magdalene. On this same day in 1225 he laid the first stone of his cathedral and established the annual feast of the church's dedication. He died one year later, also on 22 July. The banderol refers to this coincidence:
+Eligor et morior, Opus inchoo. Festa Mariae +Dedico. Sunt anni plures, sed terminus unus

LITERATURE
Stimmen aus Maria Laach 65 (1903), p. 324; Iogna-Prat 2006, p. 574.

ence in building affairs grew apace throughout Europe, though here and there bishops long maintained full or partial control as building patrons. Thus, in 1263 the chapter at Coutances demanded a voice in major building activities, but also recognized the bishop's right to govern the fabric.[84] In Sens the archbishop agreed to definitively relinquish his authority over the fabric to the chapter in 1279;[85] in Limoges the bishop stepped down in favour of the chapter around 1300,[86] whilst the bishop of Auxerre was not to do so until the fourteenth century.[87] The cathedral at Lisieux did not even have its own fabric until 1383, towards which the chapter subsequently paid an annual fee of 30 l.t. (approximately one year's wages for an unskilled labourer), and the bishop contributed certain proceeds worth double that amount.[88] Many bishops managed to keep at least some control over how the fabric was run, as attested by the bishop's right to, for example, appoint a canon as his representative on the fabric's governing board or to be present at the fabric's yearly rendering of accounts – as was the case at Rodez in the thirteenth century,[89] Prague,[90] Lisieux[91] and Paris[92] in the fourteenth, and a century later at Troyes[93] and Augsburg,[94] amongst others. In Spier, the *Wahlkapitulationen* of 1272 and 1290 reveal that the bishop even held the right to appoint both masters of the fabric from the college of canons.[95]

Of particular interest is the situation in Cologne, where a conflict between the archbishop and chapter about the fabric's administration spilled over into the public arena. On 25 July 1365, Archbishop Engelbert III (1364-1368) and the chapter decided that each would thenceforth designate one canon from the chapter as *magister fabrice*. Amongst other things, these masters of the fabric were charged with ensuring that all monies accruing to the cathedral fabric were spent solely on building, and with rendering account of their expenditures and policy to the archbishop and chapter four times a year. Theirs was a compromise that neatly bypassed canonical complexities. Even the archbishop avoided using legal grounds, instead using history to validate his claims. Apparently, his predecessors Walram (1332-1349) and Wilhelm (1349-1362) had succeeded in thoroughly appropriating control over the fabric. Whereas the chapter had previously governed the building works in peace, or so it asserted, the unlawful intervention of these archbishops had put it out of commission. Engelbert, for his part, argued that the privilege of exclusive governance was the archbishop's by time-honoured right and that it was on this basis that some of his predecessors had exerted their full authority over the fabric in actual fact. Despite the 1365 agreement, the Cologne fabric continued to be a bone of contention between the two parties. Around 1400, the archbishop seems to have retaken the reins. The city took the chapter's side as the conflict dragged on, addressing a complaint to the archbishop of Trier in 1419 in which it accused the local archbishop of crimes such as using fabric funds for purposes other than that for which they were intended, namely, the cathedral works. In 1446 the 1365 agreement was reinstituted, thus securing the archbishop's influence in cathedral building affairs.[96]

The scarcity of sources makes it difficult to pinpoint precise reasons for this erosion of the bishop's voice in building affairs. Antinomy between the bishop and chapter and the canons' increasing power were certainly amongst them.[97] Where the bishop was concerned, another possible factor was already briefly indicated above in relation to the Paris charter of 829. It is probable that when the bishop shifted financial responsibility for the cathedral onto the chapter's shoulders, he in fact transferred his share of authority right along with it. A number of clues point in this direction. In Langres, the bishop ceded control over the cathedral to the chapter between the years 1163 and 1170, precisely during a period of construction.[98] In London, control over St Paul's old fabric lay in the hands of the bishop; the new fabric, tasked with financing construction of the new Gothic cathedral, was run by the chapter.[99] When in 1253 the bishop of Arras was acquitted of almost all duties connected with furnishing and maintaining the church buildings in return for a lump sum payment from the chapter, it follows that he also surrendered any possible entitlement to the fabric's governance.[100] The bishop of Aarhuus laid claim to the cathedral's proceeds from oblations, but between 1215 and 1224 relinquished two-thirds thereof to the cathedral church owing to its neglected state, and the remaining third to the chapter.[101] In the later Middle Ages the bishop might still initiate new works on personal grounds, even when he was not or no longer at the head of the church fabric. This is signalled by the fact that the arrival of a new bishop sometimes meant the resumption of building projects, though this by no means implies any structural financial support from his side.[102]

As a rule, it was the chapter that acted as the de facto cathedral-building works patron in later centuries. Thus, the roles had been reversed: the grand building plans once proudly promulgated by eleventh- and twelfth-century bishops were now proclaimed by canons. On 13 July 1506, the canons of Seville stated with pride that it had been the Lord who had given them the courage to begin so monumental a work without looking to any king, overlord or state for aid – '*syn ayuda de rey ni de otro pryncipe ni persona de estado*' – and that aid was furthermore unnecessary, save from the cathedral clergy.[103]

At times the episcopal contribution to cathedral upkeep declined to levels deemed unacceptably low. During his 28-month episcopacy in the late fourteenth century, Bishop Pierre d'Ailly of Le Puy had enjoyed three full years' income of his bishopric but, as his successor noted indignantly, had never once read the mass in his cathedral and had donated only 20 s. 6 d. (ten days' wages) for its maintenance.[104]

In times of financial crisis, it occasionally became necessary for the chapter to seek legal recourse to remind the bishop of his obligations to the cathedral.[105] Enforced episcopal contributions of this kind did not, however, provide legal grounds to claim a share in the fabric's governance, which usually remained firmly in the hands of the chapter. Not until the seventeenth and eighteenth centuries would some bishops succeed in wresting their former dispositional rights over the cathedral from the all-powerful and obstinate chapter.[106]

When the chapter assumed responsibility for the cathedral church, how did it go about fulfilling its task? To answer this question, we must trace a broken trail of evidence. The old cathedral patrimony was, as previously mentioned, subject to myriad forms of division. A special endowment – the *mensa capituli* – was apportioned to the chapter and, once formed, saw further fragmentation. The unity of chapter funds collapsed in part as a result of the establishment of prebends, or independent incomes for each canon.[107] Common life experienced a gradual dissolution from the tenth century on. Canons lived

5
Seal of the fabric of Metz Cathedral, thirteenth century
Wax, 52 x 32 mm
Metz, cathedral of Notre-Dame

The fact that the fabric had the authority to use its own seal to authenticate documents signals a significant measure of independence.

apart in private homes, usually situated within the immunity of the cathedral precinct, and only convened – if they were residentiary – to pray the canonical hours and for chapter meetings.[108] In time a *numerus clausus* was established, whereby a fixed number of canonries were attached to each cathedral based on its wealth and importance; the total number could vary from fourteen to as many as a hundred.[109]

But there was another approach to apportioning chapter property that is of greater interest here, namely, that of creating property endowments earmarked for specific ends, such as hospitality for guests, care of the poor and so on.[110] Such *Sondermassen* (whose formation was in many cases prompted by a donor's stipulations, thereby conferring a certain measure of legal independence) might be reserved for the works – or at least cathedral upkeep – often in combination with interior illumination and curation of the church treasury; this endowment was sometimes referred to as the *luminare*.[111] According to the Chrodegang Rule and later canon law, supervision of church buildings and responsibility for lighting and tolling of the bells were to be entrusted to the *custos*,[112] whilst the treasurer administered the treasury proper. Following the disbandment of common life, however, the two offices were almost invariably conjoined into one.[113] The position of the treasurer/*custos* position within the capitular hierarchy was not the same everywhere. His office, together with that of the dean, *scholasticus*, cantor and others, normally represented the *dignitates* of the college; he held the office for life and was granted certain jurisdictions, enjoyed precedence over the regular canons and drew a larger prebend from which he was also expected to finance the duties of his office.[114]

Should we thus conclude that, as a general rule, the treasurer/*custos*, whose responsibilities included maintaining the church building, had also assumed responsibility for everything relating to the cathedral works? And if so, did he answer first to the bishop – who, as we have seen, exercised considerable influence in building affairs until well into the twelfth century – or was he perhaps even the executor of the latter's plans? A definitive answer to these questions is impossible; if anything, the scant historical sources point up a high degree of local divergence in this regard. Whilst at many cathedrals the treasurer/*custos* was indeed the dignitary in charge of the works, this was by no means the rule.[115] A single example will suffice. Where major building campaigns were concerned, it was undoubtedly necessary to designate separate, oftentimes new, sources of income.[116] Coutances's bishop, Geoffroy de Montbray (1049-1093), entrusted the management of this income not to the *custos* but to the capitular *camerarius*, and kept decision-making authority over expenditures firmly in hand: '*redditus episcopi necessitatibus et operibus ecclesiae [...] per manum praefati camerarii expendebat*' (the income intended for the bishop's personal expenses and for the cathedral works he managed through said chamberlain).[117]

Not until the *fabrica ecclesiae* took shape within the cathedral chapter did governance of the cathedral and of funds earmarked for upkeep and building develop a large measure of uniformity.[118] The present survey is therefore limited in large part to the period in which the management of incomes and responsibility for the building, its furnishings and upkeep were entrusted to the cathedral fabric (fig. 5).

How and when various fabrics developed into administrative bodies charged with overseeing church construction, maintenance, décor and sometimes lighting, endowed with their own income and occasionally private estate for that purpose, is impossible to trace in the case of most cathedrals: our knowledge about the internal organization of chapters during this period simply falls short. Moreover, we must distinguish between the term *fabrica*, which can also refer to the physical church building,[119] and the administrative body described above, for which other terms – such as *opus* or *opus fabrice* – were also used. In northern France the term *fabrica* appears to have come into vogue for cathedrals from the beginning of the thirteenth century, but as an entity it may have existed well before then.[120]

One thing that is clear, however, is that many cathedral fabrics were created to redress a situation – now viewed with disfavour – in which authority over the building and control over property and income was vested in a single dignitary. It would appear that the cathedral fabric occasionally assumed certain tasks that had originally fallen within the domain of the *custos*. Here and there the *custos* might still have responsibilities harking back to his former role, such as in Münster

(Westphalia) in the second half of the thirteenth century, where the *custos* continued to have charge of reparations to vestments and clocks totalling under 6 d.; anything exceeding this small sum was for the fabric's account.[121] The *custos* in Liège saw his responsibilities pertaining to the church building curtailed to a minimum when his role was redefined in 1342.[122] In York, though the treasurer remained titular head of the fabric, actual responsibility went to two *custodes operis* (masters of the fabric).[123] And as late as 1485, in a capitular statute later approved by the pope, the *custos* at Augsburg was divested of his sole authority over cathedral building works; henceforth two canons – one designated by the bishop and the other by the chapter – would direct the works and fabric together with the *custos*, with the privilege of hiring and firing the architect explicitly reserved for the bishop and chapter.[124] As each of these examples show, certain vestiges of a form of governance long consigned to the past in fact persevered right up into the late Middle Ages.[125]

The conflicts inevitably caused by a cathedral fabric's creation and the ensuing restriction of the duties of the treasurer/*custos* (or those of any other dignitary) provide some insight into the considerations leading to their creation and moreover highlight key differences in the two forms of management. Responsibility for the cathedral church was taken out of the hands of a single dignitary and transferred onto an *officium* that was invariably controlled by the chapter, sometimes in coordination with the bishop, and which was designated, as previously mentioned, by the term *fabrica ecclesiae cathedralis*, or 'cathedral fabric'. It may be that this shift in power shares a common thread with developments affecting the office of the provost (*praepositus*), who was likewise divested of much of his responsibility for the chapter's properties when this was transferred onto the chapter corporate.[126]

One possible reason for divesting the treasurer of management tasks could be – as it was for the provost – a dereliction of duties. In 1218 Bishop Guillaume de Beaumont of Angers, spurred by his canons' complaint that the sacristans (who were almost certainly in the treasurer's service) were neglecting their responsibility for the ecclesiastical *utensilia*, decided that, starting with the next treasurer, the chapter would deduct a sum of 60 l.t. from that official's annual income, together with all offerings (*oblationes*) made in the church and 25 pounds of wax; these would be used to pay for church lighting and embellishment and the tolling of the bells. The bishop emphasized that this money was to be spent exclusively for these purposes: '*ne quod statutum est ad decorem domus Domini ad privatas utilitates aliqua occasione trahatur*' (in order that what is intended for the embellishment of the house of the Lord is not for any reason whatsoever wrongfully expended for private ends). Its management was entrusted to two or more *boni homines* – presumably canons or chaplains – who were delegated by the chapter but still obliged to swear loyalty and obedience to the treasurer. Quite clearly, this episcopal decision formed the first step towards an independent cathedral fabric.[127]

Another common incentive for establishing a fabric was a plan for new building or radical renovations to the cathedral. In this case it was not mismanagement that was at issue; rather, new circumstances required a new form of organization.[128] Here as elsewhere, conflict was inevitable: the treasurer was made to surrender his right to certain revenues, such as the *oblationes*,[129] which would henceforth flow into the fabric, and found himself at risk of losing all or part of his jurisdiction over the building. Not surprisingly, he resisted this course of events.

A clear example of the transition from a personal to a corporate form of administration – from treasurer to fabric – is provided by Rheims. When the cathedral burnt down in 1210, work immediately commenced on its reconstruction. Three years into the building campaign, financing became precarious when the chapter withdrew its temporary monetary support. In September of 1215 the chapter and treasurer reached an agreement, the terms of which included that all offerings collected in the cathedral, along with a number of other revenues, would in future accrue not to the treasurer but to the *ecclesia Remensis*. The treasurer was effectively discharged of his financial obligations for the cathedral, with the exception of a handful of specified duties. His *dignitas* and secular jurisdiction in the cathedral remained unchanged, however. Five years later we see the treasurer forced to sacrifice still more rights. His authority to appoint the under-treasurer – synonymous with the master of the fabric in later documents – likewise shifted to the 'church of Rheims'; that is, to the chapter.[130]

In Tournai, too, works carried out from 1218 until 1233 gave rise to a decades-long conflict between the chapter and treasurer. The latter was deprived of the oblations, which together with offerings garnered from relics – and apart from an indemnification of 18 l.par. – were redirected to the fabric. To safeguard against idleness ('*ut non sint ociosi tota die*'), the treasurer was permitted a number of honorary tasks, including supervision of trade activities in the church and cloister.[131]

The situation in Lausanne was no different. On 18 June 1226, the archbishop of Besançon and the bishop of Lausanne stepped in to settle a dispute that had the chapter pitted against the treasurer and his appointed sacristan '*super custodia operis et oblationum que offeruntur ad opus*' (concerning supervision of the building fund and the offerings presented for the building fund). They decreed that this task and income did not fall within the treasurer's or sacristan's domain and laid down terms whereby the sacristan would be permitted to continue overseeing the '*opus et oblationes operis*' (building fund and associated offerings) provided he performed his duties '*ad consilium capituli*' (following the chapter's counsel). The chapter was furthermore granted the right to appoint a *socius* to work alongside him, to which end it named the *cellerarius* some weeks later. Both officials were appointed for a term of one year, were accountable to the chapter and could not spend anything above 10 s. without its consent. As such, it was the chapter that actually held the reins.[132]

Circumstances at Soissons paint an even more revealing picture of the power relationships at play. The arrival of important relics from Constantinople in 1205 fired expectations of high revenues from offerings. It seems the treasurer claimed this income at first, but an agreement with the chapter and bishop subsequently stipulated that over the initial years from 1205 until 1208 he would receive a share equalling one-quarter, increasing after 1216 – when the income was expected to have declined – from one-third to one-half. In that year the fabric is mentioned by name. It is likely that the bishop and chapter formulated a joint plan of designating a separate building fund sometime between 1205 and 1216, in precisely the years that the choir was being erected. Here the bishop, as benefactor of his cathedral and in harmonious alliance with the chapter, provided the major stimulus for building.[133]

The large-scale new building works conceived at Cologne and, in particular, the newly founded or reorganized fabric likewise prompted power shifts within the chapter. In the cartularies we find mention of a *nova fabrica*; the modifying term 'nova' suggests that new sources of income, separately managed, were being tapped for the new construction. Comparable new funds for the fabric are also found elsewhere, including in Utrecht, London and Prague.[134] The oldest charter, dated 25 March 1247, relates to the construction of Cologne's Gothic cathedral and sets out an agreement between the chapter and the treasurer whereby the latter would cede all oblations donated at the altar of St Peter for a period of six years, excepting those brought during the mass, '*ad opus nove fabrice majoris ecclesie*' (for the cathedral's new building fund). For his recompense, he was made to settle for an annual salary of 30 marks.[135] The treasurer continued to be in charge of maintenance at the old cathedral, which remained in use for centuries.[136] Though this temporary arrangement did hold, disputes were bound to occur. A charter of 19 July 1325 lays down definitive agreements between the chapter and treasurer, the terms of which included an increase of the annual remuneration to 100 marks. For his part the treasurer would cede to the fabric his claim to all revenues received by the cathedral, including oblations, whilst expressly reserving his jurisdictional privileges.[137]

Wherever the treasurer/*custos* (or any other dignitary to whose prebend a lifetime office was attached) saw himself replaced by a fabric administrator accountable to the chapter, the chapter as a corporate body strengthened its hold on the cathedral and all matters pertaining to the works. And insofar as the bishop could name the *custos* but had no say in who was appointed master of the fabric, the establishment of the fabric also served to restrict the episcopal influence on building affairs. Governance of the fabric was characterized by a considerable degree of uniformity.[138] The chapter, possibly in consultation with the bishop, appointed or elected one or more of its member canons – sometimes a lower cleric – to administer the fabric for a cer-

6
Relief carving commemorating the commencement of the cathedral building works, 1394
Second pier on the north end of the nave
Pamplona Cathedral

Three canons kneeling before the Virgin and Child; the inscription reads: *capitulum ecclesiae Pampilonensis anno* MCCCXCXIIII; the first stone was laid on 24 May 1394. On the vaults of the chapel of St Martin above this relief is the coat of arms of Bishop Martin de Zalba (1377-1403).

LITERATURE
La catedral de Pamplona, vol. 1, pp. 246-247.

tain period of time (generally a year). The attached title was, variously, *magister, rector, provisor,* in some cases *director* (fig. 20) or *procurator fabrice*, on occasion *structuarius, yconomus* or, in Spain, *obrero* or *mayordomo.*[139] The position of fabric administrator was considered an *officium simplex* (simple office); its administrators – *officiales* or *officiati* – held neither right of priority nor jurisdiction, only serving temporarily to supervise certain ecclesiastical properties.[140] At fixed intervals, usually once a year, they were obliged to render account of their administrative activities before the chapter and, occasionally, the bishop.[141] Their authorities, which were laid down in capitular statutes and might be confirmed by oath, were remarkably limited: they were required to consult the chapter in any transaction of note[142] and were not permitted expenditures above a certain – sometimes minimal – amount without first obtaining approval from their fellow canons.[143] Officially, it was the chapter that was the building patron (fig. 6); in actual fact, the *magistri fabricae* were tasked with the supervision and financial management of building operations. It was a taxing job with considerable responsibility, and one that a single canon might fulfil for many successive decades (fig. 7).[144] Indeed, in Seville the *mayordomo de Fábrica* was referred to as the *padre de la catedral.*[145]

The specific details of how this supervision and all administration surrounding the building works and upkeep were organized is discussed below in connection with the cathedral works at Utrecht. Naturally, there were considerable differences in terms of scale and structure, which depended not only on a cathedral and chapter's prominence but even more so on the scope of the building works. For a fabric charged with maintaining a small cathedral complex or church where no further construction was planned, a limited staff and small budget could suffice, and as institutions these fabrics had a similarly low profile.[146] Fabrics at large cathedrals with building operations in full swing, by contrast, were impressive, wealthy organizations employing a large number of permanent, salaried workers. These comprised both clerics and secular staff, some garbed in the colourful robes of their office, all subordinate to the presiding *magistri fabrice* and charged with any of the countless organizational, technical or artistic facets of the project's management – from bookkeepers to *collectores*

7
Tombstone of the canon Johann von Hattstein (1455-1518), by the sculptor Peter Schro, c.1520
South wing of the ambulatory
Mainz Cathedral

The erudite, humanistically-grounded canon Johann von Hattstein served as *magister fabricae* of Mainz Cathedral for nearly 40 years. The tombstone, which was inspired by Michelangelo's *Pietà*, included quotes from the New Testament in Latin, Greek and Hebrew. A lengthy inscription praises him as an astute and erudite man.

LITERATURE
Gottron 1951, p. 56; Arens 1982, pp. 156-157.

and *petitores* from the cathedral and diocese, from the custodians of oblations to the architect, goldsmith, bell-ringers, porters and other functionaries[147] – alongside dozens or even hundreds of unskilled labourers and craftsmen of all kinds who were in the fabric's temporary employ. Various cathedral fabrics, including those at Basel, Strasbourg, Rodez, Rouen and Palma, also claimed their own private residence.[148] According to a 1425 inventory, the *Hôtel de la fabrique* in Rouen numbered seven chambers, one being designated as the bedchamber for the procurator of the fabric, and serving as the repository for the fabric's archives.[149]

One specific area deserves closer consideration: who, or which body, governed the chapter in its role as the actual administrator of the fabric? A common characteristic of cathedral fabrics is that, at least in theory, they were governed separately from the endowments and income set aside to cover the canons' costs of living.[150] Even where the management of chapter properties was wholly or partially centralized, the fabric formed a distinct fund with its own sources of income, usually its own properties and its own financial administration.[151] One consequence of this arrangement was that the fabric's financial position did not need to have any direct link with that of the chapter; well-endowed prebends by no means implied a thriving fabric, nor vice versa.

The key weakness in the organization of many cathedral fabrics was the lack of a clearly delineated sphere of activity. Its foremost duties consisted of building and maintaining the cathedral, usually in conjunction with all non-privately owned buildings within the precinctal immunity such as the cloister, chapter hall and cathedral school. It also bore a major share of the costs for furnishings and embellishments in the church building: clocks, organs, the high altar, Church vestments and the sacristy inventory were in many cases all financed by the fabric fund, sometimes together with a portion of the costs for church lighting and the liturgy and mass. Moreover, the fabric might also take on the administration of ecclesiastical foundations, which certainly provided income but also entailed costs. Added to this were all manner of administrative costs, such as salaries and legal fees.[152] On occasion, however, we find the chapter charging an

GO·SVM
ΟΥΚ·ΕΣΤΙΝ·Ο ΘΕΟΣ·ΘΕΟΣ ΝΕΚΡΩΝ·ΑΛΛΑ·ΖΩΝΤΩΝ

array of expenditures related to representation and lawsuits to the fabric fund – severely undermining its original purpose – which in no way had anything to do with construction or upkeep.[153] Drained of resources in this way, it could happen that a cathedral fabric devolved into a general fund for sundry expenditures.[154] Cathedral chapters might then withdraw funds from the fabric when it suited them in the form of loans to finance typical capitular interests.[155]

As long as the chapter fulfilled its responsibilities of providing for the building, its furnishings and divine services, there were no legal grounds for accusations of mismanagement.[156] A further obligation was that the chapter had to comply with the allocations stipulated by donors: gifts offered for the works had to be spent on the works. But beyond these simple parameters, the chapter had considerable leeway in spending, possibly reinforced by the fact that in many instances chapter funds had facilitated the fabric's very creation.[157] Only where the chapter failed to observe these parameters was there a clear case of mismanagement.

Nevertheless, mismanagement and usurpation certainly did occur, and where they did, the bishop's position usually prompted him to defend the interests and rights of the fabric. In fourteenth-century Rheims, oblations that had been expressly earmarked for cathedral building works early in the previous century were appropriated from the building fund by the chaplains for their own pocket, with the canons' knowledge; in 1325 the archbishop forcefully defended the fabric's claim thereto.[158] During his episcopal visitation in 1439, the bishop of Lincoln's third enquiry to the canons concerned the sorry architectural state of the cathedral, completed some four decades before. Responding to a question from the bishop, the dean reported that monies were being withdrawn from the fabric and other funds to finance loans and gifts. The meeting subsequently promised rapid recovery of these debts to secure the cathedral's immediate renovation.[159] One year later, in 1440, the bishop of Salisbury issued a charter likewise prohibiting reckless loans from the fabric fund to the chapter and canons.[160]

With the exception of those cases in which the bishop or, as we shall see, the city participated in the fabric's management, both the administration and governance thereof lay in the hands of a single body: the chapter. Perhaps the explanation for why neither Church law nor later canonical literature makes any or only minor mention of the cathedral fabric and provides no guidelines whatsoever for its organization is quite simply that cathedral fabrics were not faced with forces representing other, possibly opposing interests, so there was little need to formulate any general legal frameworks. Where parish church fabrics were concerned, the situation could hardly have differed more. Comparison of the two provides some interesting insights.

Parish church fabrics begin to appear from the first half of the thirteenth century, at the same time that most cathedral fabrics were brought into being.[161] One major difference between the two lay in the fact that the former were generally administered exclusively by laymen, usually churchwardens designated by members of the civic government.[162] The legal history of the parish fabric's creation is not of interest here, and in fact varies from one place to another. In every case, however, it was the parishioners' desire to exercise control over their oblations, donated for a specific purpose, and to take charge of organizing their pious foundations that formed the key constitutive element driving parish fabrics' creation. In cities, the churchwardenship generally fell to members of the civic government, who served as senior churchwardens and in turn appointed and supervised the actual churchwardens. Parish priests were generally excluded from any form of administrative participation except in rural areas. As the parishioners' representatives, churchwardens took on responsibility for at least a portion of the physical church building. It would be beyond the scope of this survey to explore Church authorities' attitudes when confronted with this new entity, from the thirteenth century or earlier, or to trace its impact on Church law; for our purposes it is enough to know that whilst diocesan canon law reluctantly recognized that the parish church fabric was run by laymen, it also attempted to secure that body's ecclesiastical character and holdings by stipulating various measures – such as granting Church authorities the right to audit the accounts and requiring the fabric to seek approval for the sale of immovable property.[163] Thanks perhaps to their double supervision (by the civic government and Church authorities), the persistent appropriation of resources for unintended uses is far less frequent here than at cathedrals.[164] Diocesan canon law imposed narrow parameters on the permissibility of certain administrative activities, such as lending and borrowing money and its use for other ends.[165] Moreover, it was ultimately the parish community that the churchwardens represented, whereas a cathedral's *magistri fabrice*, installed by the chapter, had no such official function for representing the congregation; at best, he represented the bishop, who came to see himself acquitted of responsibility for his cathedral in the late Middle Ages. From a legal perspective, therefore, the parish fabric was considerably more independent.

It is also essential to recognize the very real distance separating the ecclesiastical position of cathedrals from that of parish churches. The parish church was expected to look after spiritual welfare: the faithful came here to hear mass, make confession, wed and, finally, be buried in or near the church. A cathedral was first and foremost the seat of a bishop and, as *matrix ecclesia*, a symbol of diocesan unity, where synods brought hundreds of clerics together from throughout the diocese.[166] In practice, however, the cathedral was very much the chapter's church.[167] The countless masses said here were intended for the salvation of a single benefactor's soul, and primarily clerics attached to the cathedral were buried in or around the church.[168]

Under the provisions of canon law, each church was circumscribed by a zone of local immunity.[169] That zone was generally far more extensive at cathedral churches than at parish churches. Not only did it have to contain the cathedral itself, but also such annexes as the cloister, chapter hall and school, refectory and infirmary, the episcopal palace, residences for cathedral clergy, a churchyard and miscellaneous other church buildings all traditionally established there.[170] With all the canons and other clerics tied to the cathedral, plus servants, the number of permanent residents living within the *claustrum* confines could number in the hundreds.[171]

A prescript issued by Pope Leo I in 459 and incorporated in the *Decretals* stipulated that cathedrals could only be established in a *civitas* (even a *castellum* like Utrecht was deemed undesirable).[172] Thus, in France and the German empire, the cathedral complex comprised the oldest core of the city.[173] Spanish cathedrals were typically built in the city centre on the site of a pre-Reconquista mosque.[174] Where rebuilding plans were especially ambitious, the available space could be inadequate; then, as happened at Bourges and Narbonne,[175] the old Gallo-Roman walls would have to make way. New building could engender drastic topographical restructuring, bringing a whole host of legal, economic and architectural difficulties.[176]

Cathedral immunity created an isolated enclave that was wholly or partially sealed off in the form of a fortress with gates, walls or moats, or at the very least demarcated by boundary stones.[177] To pass through its gates was to enter a different world, one regulated by ecclesiastical jurisdiction. Neither in legal nor geographic terms would the cathedral complex ever become fully integrated in the surrounding city, not even when annual fairs or even daily commerce populated its precinctal immunity with shops and market stalls.[178]

Yet it was by no means impossible for laymen to gain a voice in the administration of a cathedral fabric. Indeed, in Italy this was even customary. North of the Alps, secular participation penetrated through to only a handful of episcopal cities in the German empire, France and England. Though it might be expected that laymen would have the best chances of securing a position of control in fabric affairs in cities where the cathedral still fulfilled its traditional parish functions, this was not necessarily the case. Various cathedrals continued to serve as parish churches up through the late Middle Ages, in addition to the key parish duties they always continued to fulfil on behalf of inhabitants of the cathedral immunity.[179] A cathedral might reserve one bay, an arm of the transept or even the nave for parishioners;[180] occasionally, the parish was provided with a separate chapel, as in Toledo and Rouen, sufficiently distant from the choir to ensure that proceedings of the parish liturgy did not disturb the canons' recitation of the Divine Office in the choir, or vice versa.[181] Elsewhere the chapter succeeded in ejecting the parish from the cathedral and finding accommodation in another church within the precinctal immunity.[182] Alternatively, a select altar in the cathedral – often one dedicated to the Holy Cross and placed under the rood loft – could serve as the parish altar.[183] In Rodez this altar was run on a par with the other parish churches by a separate, fully fledged fabric independent of the cathedral, with responsibility resting with the consuls of the *cité*.[184] Even so, we find no evidence of lay influence in building affairs in the majority of these cathedrals.

The criterion for lay participation in or even assumption of control over the cathedral fabric should instead be sought in those episcopal cities where burghers launched a conscious effort to take charge of administering their donations for the works. Such efforts not only imply that burghers shouldered a relatively large share of the financial burden for building but, even more importantly, signal a political climate in which they thought to break through the Church's exclusive authority over cathedral-building and governance of the associated funds, and were able to succeed in that endeavour. Thus, the fifteenth-century civic treasury of the Catalan city of Tortosa collected and administered all monies brought to the cathedral by individual citizens, keeping lists of names and associated sums and acting wholly independent of the cathedral fabric.[185]

Naturally, the degree to which burghers participated varied. The bishop of Amiens is recorded in a 1236 charter as applying to his clerics and laymen for their 'consent' ('*accedente consensu Ambianensis cleri et populi*'),[186] but concerning a matter chiefly civil in nature: the relocation of the collegiate-cum-parish church of St. Firmin, originally part of a *groupe episcopale*, to the premises of the city's hospital, which likewise had to move.[187] Preparations for construction of the crossing tower at Troyes cathedral – use of which was possibly, as elsewhere, shared with the city – went a step farther. Work only began in 1413 after the conclusion of various meetings: '*et tousjours les clers, bourgeois et habitans de Troyes presens, qui d'un commun consentement ont conclu de fere le dit clochier*'. A layman was appointed as the '*maistre d'œvre [...] lequel a accepté la charge de savoir depar les habitans et rapporter devers eulx [...] comment l'argent des aides et suffraiges qu'ilz ont toux promis d'y fere sera despensé [...]*'.[188] Similarly, the two canons who ran the fabric at Palma were joined by an additional two lay administrators whenever the city made sizable contributions.[189]

North of the Alps it was rare to see laymen installed as masters of

8
Counting table of the register clerk (*Schaffner*) of the *Frauenwerk*, or fabric, of Strasbourg Cathedral, made between 1585 and 1656
Walnut with bone inlay; h. 80.5 cm, top 98 x 153 cm
Strasbourg, Musée de l'Œuvre Notre-Dame

The table was used during the collection of rents and other revenues and when paying out wages and other expenses. The top is inlaid with two identical bone-encrusted rectangles each made up of 20 compartments. The vertical columns correspond with the unit of account, in this case the pound (lb.), subdivided into the solidus, denarius and half-denarius. The horizontal columns contain compartments for numbers up to 10, up to 100, up to 1000, up to 10,000 and up to 100,000. By casting counters on the table a large number of – usually – small quantities could be added up with ease.

LITERATURE
Musée de l'Œuvre Notre-Dame, notice et guide à travers les bâtiments et collations, Strasbourg 1971, p. 16; Doré 2007, p. 37.
Written communication from Marie-José Forte, Strasbourg.

the fabric. Amongst the exceptions are Palma and Huesca,[190] Lincoln,[191] Lübeck,[192] Hamburg,[193] Bremen,[194] Meissen,[195] Strasbourg[196] and, for a time, Regensburg.[197] The grounds for lay participation in running cathedral fabrics are not always clear. In the case of both Spanish cathedrals, it was prompted by major short-term financial contributions from the city. The burghers' wish to share in planning and controlling how their offerings[198] were spent was manifest in Hamburg. Since 1269(?) Hamburg's cathedral fabric had been led by two *structuarii*: one canon and one city councillor, though both were chosen by the chapter. Moreover, the lay *structuarius* was tasked only with monitoring that the cathedral building works did not damage the city and that the fabric spent its money as intended.[199] In Lübeck the canons remained lord and master of the cathedral fabric until around 1220. Between 1227 and 1234 the city and chapter became entangled in disagreements: the city was withholding oblations intended for the cathedral, thus acting in violation of canon law.[200] An amicable settlement reached in 1256 provided that of the four *structuarii*, two would be chosen from the chapter by the bishop and two would be chosen by the council from amongst its members. Thus, it seems a balance of power between the two parties was achieved, at least until the sixteenth century. In 1529 the bishop ordered that only a vicar, and not a layperson, could serve as *operarius*.[201] In Bremen we first find mention of a lay *procurator fabrice* in 1310. It is indicative that as soon as the populace slid into a period of political upheaval and economic hardship a half century later, the archbishop temporarily succeeded in driving lay administrators from the fabric.[202] Nevertheless, the '*buw sunte Peters*' continued under the supervision of both a lay and a clerical '*buwmeister*' until 1547.[203]

In Regensburg the situation was exceptional. From the account rolls for 1459 we know that here, as everywhere, the fabric's administration was vested with a canon. The fabric is first mentioned in 1266. By 1281, if not earlier (the start of the building campaign can be dated to around 1275), its management was in the hands of laymen – *procuratores fabricae* – who maintained close ties with the bishop. The latter gave them express authority to collect money for the cathedral in all parishes in the bishopric. It is not until 1377 that the records mention a *magister fabricae*, here a canon who initially worked together with the lay procurator. After 1400 this procurator disappears from the records: evidently the chapter had succeeded in ousting the bishop and burghers from positions of authority over the fabric.[204]

Only in Strasbourg did the civic council manage to acquire almost full authority over the cathedral fabric. One factor that certainly served in its favour was that the city had no other competing parish churches.[205] The so-called second chronicle of Jakob van Königshofen (c. 1385) relates how after the burghers had defeated Bishop Walter von Geroltzeck in Hausbergen in 1262, the chapter took full control of the cathedral fabric. But some 30 years later, in 1290, the older canons, perceiving the extent of their younger colleagues' mismanagement, prudently transferred its administration to the local city government. These episodes would have coincided with work on the nave, completed at a rapid pace between around 1240 and 1275, and the construction of the enormous façade that began two years later.

In reality, things did not occur in exactly the way the chronicle describes. There is no direct link with the political events of 1262, since the appointment of a lay fabric administrator was in fact already recorded in the previous year. The sources continue to list the names of canons who served as bishop-appointed *rectores fabrice*. Four years later, in 1286, the cardinal legate confirmed all indulgences granted to the fabric in a declaration directed not to the chapter but – very unusually – to the city magistrate. Even so, after 1290 we only know the names of lay *Münsterpfleger*. Clearly, at some point between around 1282 and 1286, the city succeeded in gaining not merely participation, but a virtual monopoly over the fabric (figs. 8, 9). It was to mark the dawning of the era of the *Ratspflegschaft* over the *Frauenwerk*, as the cathedral fabric was called. The city magistrate appointed the *Pfleger* and bore responsibility for the cathedral; the bishop's and chapter's joint role as building patron was no more than a formality.[206] The initial impulse for this development can be traced back to the city patriciates' foundation of the *Fruhealtar* or *Fruegealtar*, recorded as early as 1252,[207] which had been dedicated to the Virgin and set in a niche of the rood loft and was, significantly, withdrawn from the bishop's canonical authority. In 1264 the city patrician Heinrich Wehelin, who would

9
Seated man, presumed to be *Pfleger* of the *Oeuvre Notre-Dame* in Strasbourg, c.1420
Stone
Strasbourg, Musée de l'Oeuvre Notre-Dame

The statue was unearthed near the house of the *Oeuvre Notre-Dame* in 1864.

LITERATURE
Exh. cat. *Strasbourg 1400, un foyer d'art dans l'Europe gothique*, Strasbourg (Musée de la ville de Strasbourg) 2008, p. 129.

later serve as churchwarden, established another altar in a central position in front of the rood loft. Beginning in 1291 this altar also took the designation *altare fabrice*, and would ultimately supersede the *Fruegealtar*.[208] This second altar had its own priest, who not only received offerings for the works but also presided at the presentation of the fabric accounts.[209] Masses were furthermore said here for living and deceased benefactors of the building works – a practice that was also customary at cathedrals, where the laity had no influence on the affairs of the fabric at all.

In fact, the city had such a degree of mastery over what it considered its own 'house' that it could exploit its position of sole control. The fabric's monetary resources were diverted from the purpose for which they had been consigned and put to purely profane use.[210] As the cathedral preacher Johann Geiler (1445-1510) bluntly framed it: whomsoever gives money to the *Frauenwerk* wishes to see it spent on the building or the divine office, and not on the horse market at a tournament.[211] By the fourteenth century the *Frauenwerk* had become thoroughly interwoven with the civic government, prompting Geiler to lament: '*es ist etlicher meynung unser frouwen werck und die stat sy ein ding*' (many are of the opinion that the Frauenwerk and the city are one and the same thing). This laicization drew protest from the chapter and especially the bishop, who felt it his duty to resist the pervasive corrosion of the fabric's ecclesiastical nature.[212] In 1442 the chapter prevailed in sending one of its members to deputize at the rendering of accounts, though this right may not have been effectuated until later.[213] Here we encounter a situation opposite to that at Cologne and Bremen, where city and chapter had to rally to protect the fabric's interests when these were compromised by myriad forms of episcopal mismanagement.[214] It was on this ground that, in 1419, Cologne's city magistrate recommended himself as a candidate co-administrator of the cathedral fabric to the archbishop of Trier (who was acting as intermediary).[215] In Strasbourg, by contrast, the bishop and chapter formed a united front to defend those very same fabric interests.

The very state of affairs that was atypical north of the Alps was the rule in such Italian episcopal cities as Pisa, Genua, Lucca, Milan, Florence,

Perugia, Siena and Orvieto, where from early on the civic commune was closely involved in the cathedral's management.[216] The roots of this development can be traced back to the strong ties that had bound city and church/diocese ever since late Antiquity. Thus, around 1100 the bishop's church still served to represent and personify communes that did not yet have their own legal capacity for action, which also meant that the bishop accepted donations for the city coffers. At the same time, we see cases where the commune received donations on behalf of a church.[217] Lay participation in the management of cathedral property had a long tradition here, dating back to as early as late Antiquity. But from the end of the eleventh century, we see the bishop withdrawing from his one-time role as lord of the city. Compared with his more powerful colleagues north of the Alps, the Italian bishop occupied a role of little consequence in social, economic or even ecclesiastical terms.[218] The eleventh century saw the first removal of cathedrals to the old urban centres, near – and sometimes sharing a square with – an existing or planned *palazzo di comune*. In Florence, Siena and elsewhere, the *duomo* functioned as the political and spiritual hub of the city and remained so even after town halls – with their bells tolling the meetings – began appearing from the beginning of the fourteenth century; the cathedral was at once the *matrix ecclesia* of the diocese and the *conventus civium* of the city.[219] Lay participation in fabric affairs took on an organized and institutionalized character. Throughout the Middle Ages, these cities regarded their cathedrals as symbols of urban liberty and independence: '*nostrae religionis, verum etiam hujus civitatis decus et ornamentum*'.

Italian cities assumed responsibility for the construction of their cathedrals, but this does not mean the Church authorities were excluded from all aspects of governance. During a meeting of the guilds and citizens of Perugia on 22 March 1300, the commune affirmed that it was responsible not only for the dignity of the Palazzo Publico and city square, but also for the construction of the new cathedral. Whereas the city council could not impose laws ('*non possumus imponere legem*') for the bishop and chapter, it enjoined their cooperation in the matter of the building plans – which concerned especially the securing of indulgences from Rome.[220] Late thirteenth-century Siena, Perugia and Orvieto each installed a monk as the *operarius* – head of the *Opera*, or cathedral fabric – over several successive decades. Whilst these monks enjoyed a special relationship with the bishop and chapter, the chief reason for their appointment must have been their excellent administrative abilities and knowledge of art.[221] Occasionally, a city managed to deprive the clergy of any involvement in the *Opera* whatsoever. Pope Martin V proved receptive to the Orvieto city council's argument in 1220 that participation by the chapter in the *Opera's* administration would effectively alienate the devotion of citizens ('*esset remotio devotionis civium*').[222]

The precise manner in which Italian civic authorities ran the cathedral *Opera* differed from one city to another. Two examples shall suffice here.[223] In Milan, the city did not merely deputize a few council members and masters of the fabric, but had a hand in directing the fabric of the cathedral of Santa Maria Maggiore at every level.[224] What is striking is the sheer number of people involved – sometimes several hundred.[225] When building began in May 1386, it was with a 29-member committee: 20 lay members and nine clerics attached to the old cathedral. A new arrangement was put in place[226] on 16 October 1387, when a meeting of Duke Gian Galeazzo Visconti of Milan, the chapter, city administration and citizens elected a committee of 100, comprising 80 laymen and 20 clerics. This did not include a number of salaried fabric officers. This committee was split into 25 *squadri* of four persons each, always including one canon. Daily supervision of the cathedral and building works rotated amongst the *squadro* each week. This arrangement, approved by the duke of Milan only the previous day and – after the fact – by the archbishop, saw numerous revisions. In 1388 the committee was extended to include, amongst others, the archiepiscopal vicar-general and 118 citizens representing the gates of the city. In 1394 and 1395, representation for each district – to which the city gates lent their names – again saw significant upwards adjustment. Not until the fifteenth century did the building committee begin to shrink in number, ultimately leaving a kind of governing council of 20 delegates for the archbishop, chapter, duke and city.[227]

Sources pertaining to the cathedral fabric administration in Florence are plentiful.[228] Here (as elsewhere in Italy) the city's intense engagement in the building works encompassed not only the cathedral, but equally the major abbey churches; curiously, parish churches were fully dependent on their parishioners for financing.[229] According to a document of 1226, the construction of the new cathedral ('*Opus Sancte Reparate*') was initially still guided by two episcopal representatives (a canon and a chaplain) and another two for the commune.[230] In 1321 the city ceded its administrative rights to the five largest guilds, which took charge of the administration in turns. On 2 October 1331, the powerful *Arte della Lana*, or wool guild, gained exclusive authority over the *Opera*, creating a situation that was unique in Italy and would last for over a century.[231] A document dated 24 December 1331 records only four *operarii* as administrators, all members of the wool guild, whose activities were supervised by the guild consuls. Clearly, the chapter and bishop no longer played any role in the administration.[232] Of particular importance and very characteristic of this arrangement was the interconnectedness of civic subsidization for building (as the commune's agents, the guilds did not themselves supply funds) and civic influence on the fabric's governance. Whereas the city initially furnished its subsidies directly to the chapter, by 1293 – several years before construction commenced – the four *operarii* already had the authority to control revenues assigned by the city.[233] When these subsidies ceased for various reasons in later years, it meant not merely a significant reduction in the scale of building operations, but also the termination of the city's role in their management.[234] In the period between 1303 and 1318, and again between 1323 and 1330, the chapter shouldered the *Opera's* administration, though it was to be for the last time.[235] In fact, building activity had all but stopped during these years. As a document of 1331 unequivocally declares, '*nulla fuit assignata pecunia per Comune Florentie, ita quod remansit iam est longum tempus et est absque hedificatione aliqua*' (no money having been allocated by the civic commune of Florence, the work halted for a long time and construction has ceased).[236]

CHAPTER TWO

SOURCES OF INCOME FOR THE BUILDING WORKS

INTRODUCTION

Before turning to investigate the various income sources that could be used to finance cathedral construction, we must first answer the question: What role did the Church accord to church buildings; what were their theological and moral foundations?

Posited in this way, the answer seems straightforward: a church building embodied the spiritual community of the Church and was necessary for performing divine services. However, this idea did not begin to take shape until the Carolingian era. Church fathers placed no great importance on the church building itself as a site for divine services; God was *illocalis*, 'without place'. But as the Church evolved into an institution with a cherished ideal of embracing the whole of society, theologians developed the notion that the church of stone (and the sacred area surrounding it) was the single most effective vehicle for representing the religious idea of the Church, in the same way that Christ was the incarnation on earth of the Son of God. For the faithful to gain admission to the spiritual temple, and thus to the gates of heaven, they had first to pass through the physical church of stone.[1] Describing his cathedral church in 1025, the bishop of Cambrai writes, 'We call this House "church" because it contains the "Church", which is to say the people whom He has called together to live in harmonious accord in that House'.[2] Tournai's fifteenth-century *liber fabricae* describes the cathedral as a haven for the faithful who, crossing its threshold *singuli*, one by one, were roused *universi*, as a community.[3] The erection of a church was deemed an *opus pietatis* (pious work)[4] that, beyond these theological aspects, was also marked by moral complexities. Such complexities only became problematic when religious building patrons sought to construct on a greater, more costly and more elaborate scale than was strictly necessary for divine services and the cure of souls. To justify, and even encourage, such excessive building pursuits, they deployed the familiar psalm verse about the splendour of the Lord's house[5] and cited familiar clichés: that the church building was the earthly reflection of the heavenly Jerusalem,[6] or that in the era *sub gratia*, which began with Christ's birth, the Church had become the successor to the temple of Solomon;[7] if neither expense nor effort had been spared for the latter, did it not follow that even more be invested in Christ's residence on earth? The contrast between the sumptuous stone edifice of the church and the small wooden houses surrounding it only served to strengthen people's yearning for the heavenly Jerusalem.[8] Moreover, the scholastic system of virtues expressly provided for large expenditures towards works conceived on a large scale; *liberalitas* (magnanimity) and especially *magnificentia* ('*grandezza*') were viewed as virtues, inspiring '*uti divitiis* [...] *in alicuius magni operis expletionem*' (the use of wealth to realize a great work).[9] As a young prelate, one of the foremost builder-bishops in France, Arnulfus of Lisieux (1105-1182), dreamed of conjoining the ideal of *sanctitas* (saintliness) with that of *magnificentia*, but in advanced years was forced to concede that he had fallen short of his goal.[10]

Countervailing this dominant viewpoint was a current of morally and theologically based opposition to any form of luxury or excess in ecclesiastical structures and their décor, which continued from the early Christian era onwards.[11] The full battery of arguments and motivations mobilized in this context need not concern us here;[12] the relevant aspect for our purposes is the criticism directed specifically at the use of money for building churches instead of for causes more in tune with the Gospel. Additional, albeit later, criticism also targeted the use of certain individual income sources and money-collecting methods.[13]

10
Bound parchment volume with a miniature of the Virgin and Child from the *libro de fabrica* of the cathedral of Palma de Mallorca, 1406
Palma, Archivo capitular de la catedral de Mallorca

LITERATURE
Pascual 1995, fig. 158.

These moralists focused on the idea that money or goods expended on non-essential or excessive building activities was money diverted away from the poor. St Bernard of Clairvaux (1090-1153) was without question their most eloquent and fervent advocate. In his *Apologia*, directed primarily against the Benedictines at Cluny, he declaimed, 'The Church is radiant in its walls and destitute in its poor [...]; it serves the eyes of the rich at the expense of the poor'.[14] This was to become a celebrated passage, cited in innumerable theological and canonical treatises and handbooks.[15] Similar declarations come down to us from later centuries from not only the statutes of such strict monastic orders as the Cistercians, Carthusians and mendicants,[16] but also from the likes of St Anthony of Florence, archbishop of that city from 1446 until 1459.[17] Writing in his *Contra turrim Trajectensem* ('Against the tower of Utrecht'), Geert Groote (1340-1384) commented that the Dom tower in Utrecht 'was erected using the wealth of Christ's poor at such immense and almost endless cost'.[18] Citing a host of references and arguments, a canonist like Thomassinus (1619-1695) could make the case that all Church income and goods should properly be designated as the *patrimonium pauperum* (patrimony of the poor).[19]

Viewed from a positive canonical perspective, the notion prescribing that the full *superfluum* (superfluous monies) be spent on the poor was untenable. The early Christian four-part (or three-part) division, as described in the *Decretum Gratiani*,[20] guaranteed a full share of Church revenues for the building works. Thomas Aquinas referred to this practice when addressing the question (which he answers in the negative) of whether a bishop commits a mortal sin if he does not distribute the entirety of Church properties entrusted to him amongst the poor.[21] This was not to say that, from a moral standpoint, supporting the poor was not preferable to church-building,[22] yet neither was it a moral imperative, and even less a canonical rule. Honorius of Autun (first half of the twelfth century) states unequivocally that: '[...] *bonum est ecclesias aedificare* [...] *sed multo melius est eiusdem sumptus in usus indigentium expendere*' (it is good to build churches, but it is far better still to spend those sums for the needy).[23]

It is impossible to judge to what extent, if any, these critical voices, which formed a constant counterpoint to medieval church-building, negatively impacted the inflow of revenues for the fabric. Where criticism targeted specific methods of money-collecting or the use of certain income sources for cathedral construction, however, this is easier to assess. All the same, it is important to realize that cathedral building campaigns – certainly on the monumental scale in which these took place – were exposed to constant moral opposition from parties that, in many cases, spoke from positions of authority.

This chapter discusses the primary revenue sources to which a cathedral could have access and, in particular, the nature and origins of these revenues. Whilst some indication will be given of the scale and relative significance of the total amounts these various income sources generated, such quantitative aspects are dealt with chiefly in Part II, in the chapter on funding for the works at the cathedral of Utrecht.

Our best historical source of information about the origins of construction monies is, as already noted, the fabric account rolls: records of a fabric's receipts and expenditures that were presented and audited, usually once each year, to an authorized body (typically the chapter, occasionally joined by the bishop).[24] Fabric rolls for the period stretching from the Middle Ages through the first half of the sixteenth century are preserved at some 80 cathedrals (figs 10, 11, 12, 13, 65, 75, 84, 90). The oldest – a small handful – date from the latter half of the thirteenth century;[25] the fourteenth century is somewhat better represented, whilst the majority date from the fifteenth century and later. Though this may seem a fair amount, most are of little practical value in the investigation that concerns us here, as they contain substantial lacunae or else represent only a brief span of years. Many account rolls furthermore document periods in which the church and its interior changed but little; they are maintenance records only, with identical categories of minor expenditures year in and year out. The series of fabric rolls from Utrecht Cathedral form an exception, recording an important period of building works virtually without gaps.

Whereas serial accounts shed light on the quantitative side of receipts and expenditures especially,[26] we learn more about their qualitative aspects from historical sources of an institutional or legal and administrative nature: synodal statutes, episcopal mandates, the

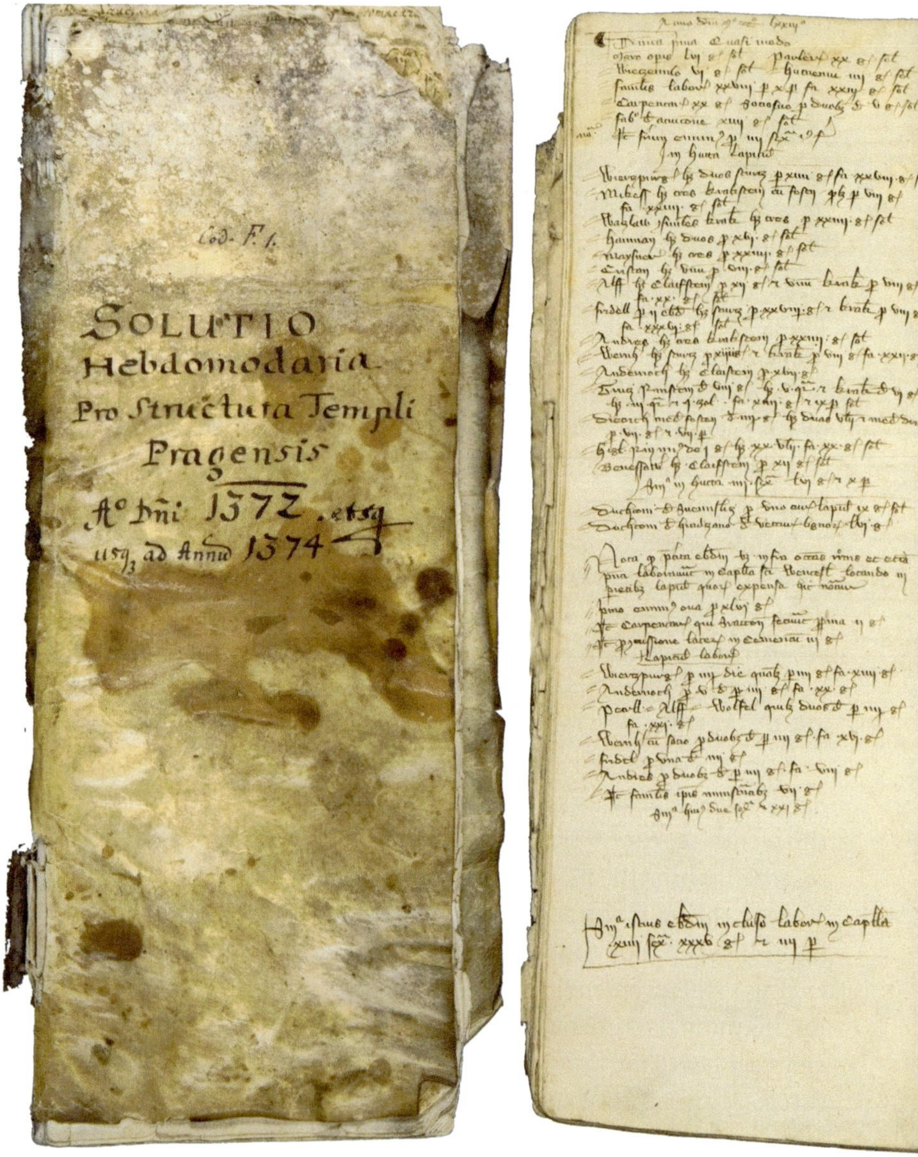

11
Left. Bound parchment volume of the fabric rolls of Prague Cathedral, 1372-1374, with the title *solutio hebdomodaria pro structura templi Pragensis* (weekly payment for the construction of the cathedral of Prague)
Prague, Prager Burgarchiv

Right. Pages from the fabric rolls of Prague Cathedral; expenditures for wages in the week of 24 April 1373
Prague, Prager Burgarchiv

LITERATURE
Die Kathedrale von St. Veit, pp. 50-51.

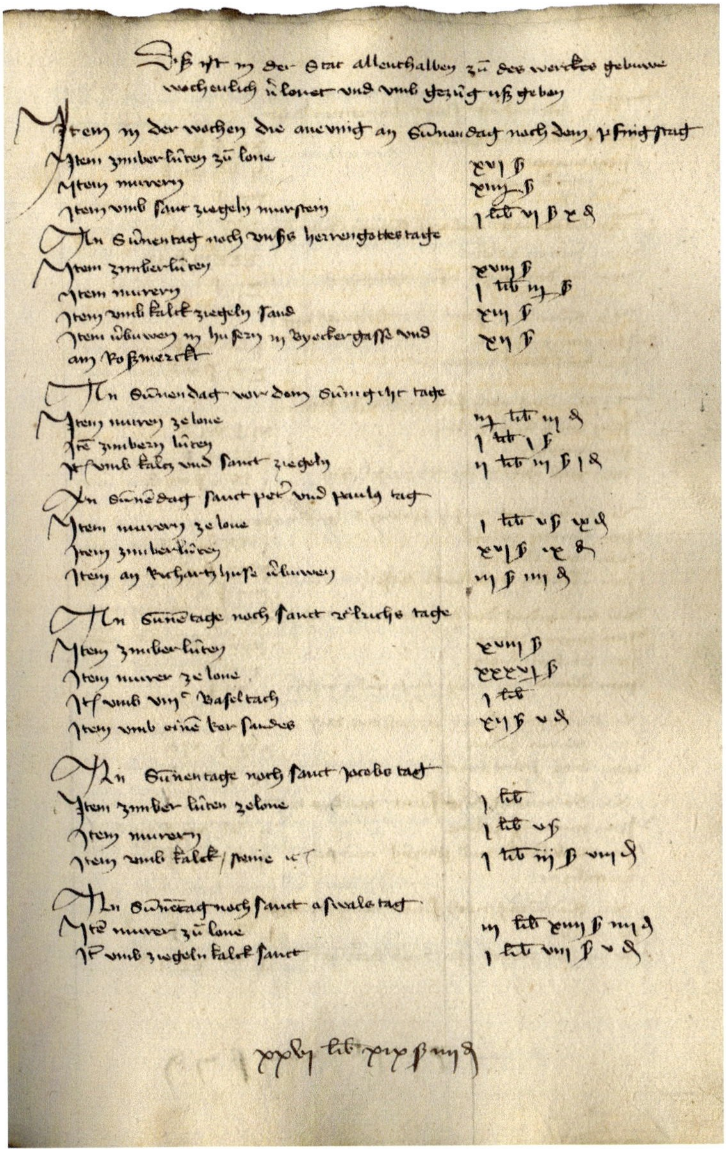

12
Page from the fabric rolls for 1438/39 from Strasbourg Cathedral
Strasbourg, Archives de la ville

LITERATURE
Doré 2007, p. 36.

rights and customs of cathedral chapters and the minutes of chapter meetings. This category of documentation reveals facets of the plans and intentions of the ecclesiastical patrons of the building works, and additionally provides insight into the ecclesiastical and institutional frameworks within which cathedral-building took place. In contrast, fabric records primarily show whether, and then mainly to what extent, official measures and precepts had any effect.

Cathedral construction was never funded by any one single, or even only a mere handful, of income sources: bishop and chapter had to traverse various paths to secure the necessary resources. Since cathedrals and chapters were characterized by a relatively high degree of organizational uniformity, and bishops everywhere exercised the same ecclesiastical authority, the resources they utilized were in many cases similar, if not identical, as were the measures they put in place to generate money for building. The precise constellation of income sources and, more specifically, the extent to which they were successful in tapping these sources were what endowed each cathedral fabric with its own unique financial organization. Where one fabric might concentrate on income from property revenues,[27] another relied on contributions gathered from the diocese's faithful through church collections or tithes, or on offerings from pilgrims or a large donation from the bishop. Naturally, the size of the resulting individual budgets could differ considerably.

A discussion of the various income sources employed by cathedral fabrics can be framed by any number of classification criteria. The criterion applied here derives from and links up with the dictates of ancient canon law. In the period at issue, legislation assigning individual responsibility for the cathedral church was all but non-existent, with the sole exception of the previously cited four- or three-part division of church revenues. Such responsibility was determined by local custom *(consuetudo)*, though never codified to my knowledge. Canonists' handbooks and treatises from the period after the Council of Trent, however, attest to their efforts to delineate responsibility for the church building (in German: *Baulast*) in clearer terms and to formalize them in the canonical system. There is no question that legislation formulated at this time fixed a pattern of responsibilities that had already been in use in the Middle Ages, albeit in a less binding form.[28]

Post-Tridentine canonists now applied a differentiation amongst building activities that were necessary and those that were not (and not between construction and upkeep, which they deemed irrelevant).[29] No one could be impelled to carry out non-essential building activities; these were undertaken voluntarily. This meant that where a bishop launched a monumental, extravagant new building campaign, his successor was not financially bound to continue the work.[30] Canon law concerned itself solely with essential building works and the associated expenses. It also assumed the existence of a cathedral fabric. The canonists were not interested in revenues or their arrangement; rather, they furnished rules for churches that had no fabric or whose quarter of the revenues proved insufficient for the fabric's needs.[31] Naturally, this latter problem was quick to arise for construction on anything more than a modest scale.[32] In such cases they stipulated – with due observance for local custom[33] – that the bishop had principal accountability to contribute a quarter of his income (Pope Gelasius's quarter again), together with any superfluous episcopal income – depending on the shortage – this being what remained after deducting his costs of living as appropriate to his station (*congrua sustentatio*). If funding still proved inadequate, the bishop could require the chapter to shoulder a portion of the building expenses from its own revenues, again insofar as these exceeded what was needed to sustain its members as befitted their status. Where financial liability for essential cathedral works was concerned, the bishop and chapter were thus first in line, and it was only after they had contributed their shares that one could also be demanded from the lower cathedral clergy.[34] If the sum total still fell short, it became the diocesan clergy's turn to lend financial support, in the form of the fruits of vacant ecclesiastical benefices. Finally, the faithful could be solicited for donations, the local lord, if there was one, first amongst them.[35] In cases of dire necessity, the populace could additionally be compelled to perform the necessary corvee services.[36]

As already indicated, the precepts described above were of limited consequence because they related to building maintenance only. Cathedral expansions fell outside their scope, except in cases where swelling church attendance meant the available space no longer sufficed.[37] Superficial changes in form, elevation or layout unconnected with critical expansion or repairs of any sort were therefore voluntary undertakings.[38] In the eyes of canon law, the financing of cathedral-building was almost invariably at the discretion of those who wished it.

This canonical sequence of responsibility and accountability for the cathedral can serve as the basic starting point for a discussion of the origins of cash resources used towards its construction. Leading on from the rules discussed above, we shall now turn our attention to the contributions of, respectively, the bishop, the chapter and its members, the bishop and chapter jointly, the pope, the king and the overlord (if not the bishop himself), the city and, finally, the clergy of the bishopric and the faithful both within the diocese and beyond. This hierarchy is also useful in illuminating socio-economic facets, providing insight into the social provenance of resources and addressing the question of which individuals and official bodies or groups shouldered the financial burden of cathedral-building. As with any major work of art, one of the exciting aspects of studying cathedrals lies in learning 'the material conditions under which they were commissioned and created'.[39]

We do well to keep in mind that income sources may be classified according to countless other criteria than those selected here, criteria that can only be given secondary consideration in our present line of enquiry. For instance, there is an important distinction to be made between sources of revenue that were available exclusively for cathedral works and those that could also be used for works at other churches, such as parish, chapter and monastery churches.[40] In the latter case, the competition between cathedral and other church fabrics was one the cathedral fabric often lost: certainly in the late Middle Ages, there was many a bishopric in which the magnitude and prestige of parish churches or monastery and abbey churches won out over those of the cathedral. Another key dividing line – one that cuts straight

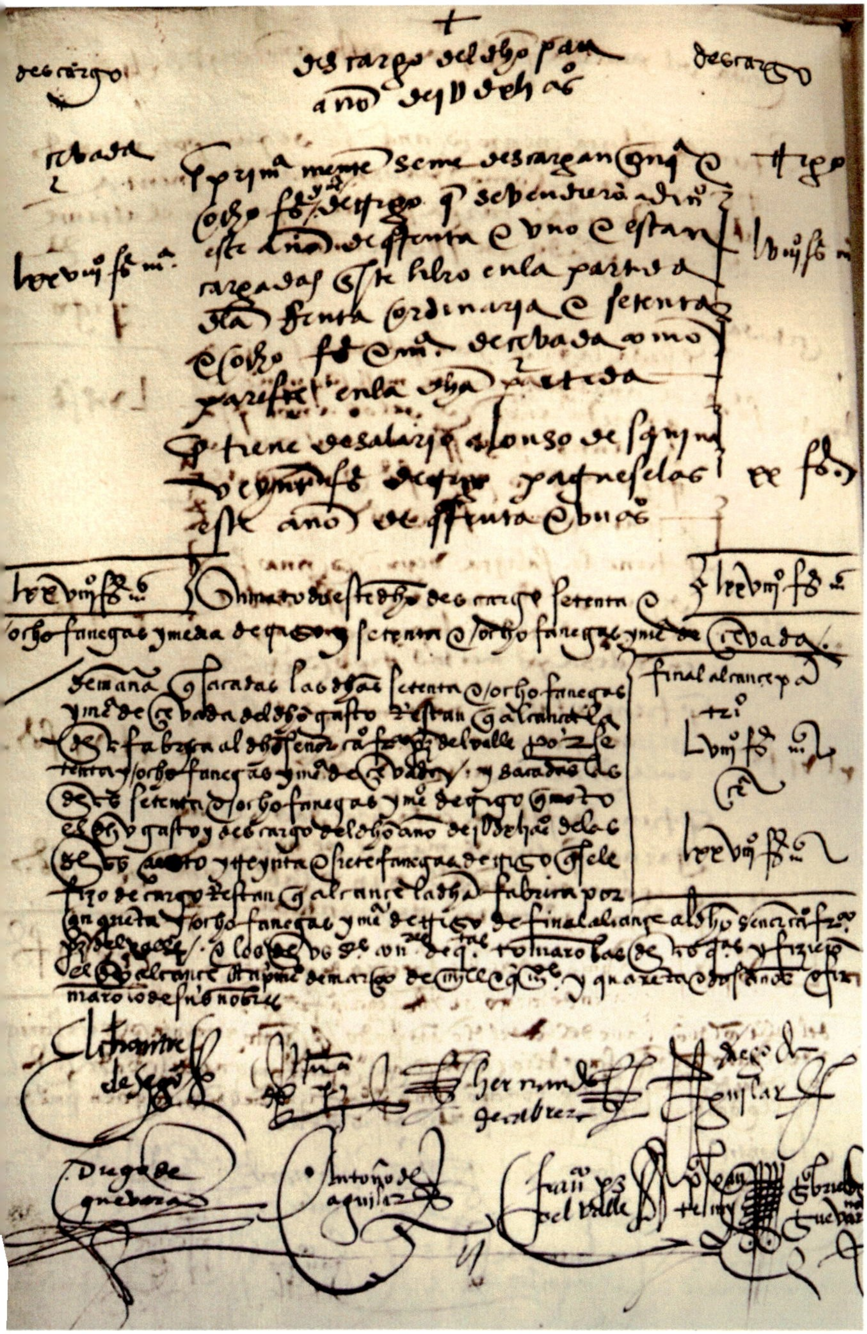

13
Page from the fabric rolls of Segovia Cathedral for the year 1541
Segovia, Archivo de la Catedral de Segovia, inv. C 229 bis

The last page of the fabric rolls contains the settlement of all receipts and expenditures in kind, listed under the heading *pan*. The account rolls were audited on 1 March 1542 and signed by the *canonigo fabiquero*, the chantre (standing in for the bishop) and five other canons.

LITERATURE
Cillanueva de Santos 2009, p. 342 ;
M.A. Cillanueva de Santos, *Análisis de los libros de fábrica de la catedral de Segovia (1524-1699)*, (diss.) Complutense University of Madrid 2008, E-prints complutense, pp. 580-581 and 388, 390, 393 n. 200, 411, 590, 602.

across the categories applied here – is that between ordinary and extraordinary income sources. Amongst the first are sources tapped to fund necessary, basic fabric activities, such as maintenance costs, outlays for divine services, and an array of fixed expenses; new building was excepted, as were expenditures for precious works of art.[41]

Occasionally, the *Novum Opus* controlled special income sources created expressly for the works, which could be administered together with or separate from its regular income.[42] Running alongside and to a certain extent parallel to this distinction is the one between perpetual and temporary income sources. Certain revenues, sometimes of great value, might accrue to the fabric for only a limited number of years, or even as a lump sum, whilst others were sustained for centuries.

Another key difference is that between the regular income for the works and the monetary resources secured using a range of financing methods to fund phases of heightened building activity, amongst other things. The latter category includes money acquired via loans, capitalization on assets, the sale of life and hereditary annuities or by saving credit balances over successive years.[43] The fabric could also put surplus resources to productive use. Thus, the chapter might allow the fabric to invest in putting up houses and shops flanking the buttresses and gates or on as yet unexploited building plots surrounding the cathedral, and to lease them to tradesmen and craftsmen. Income garnered from these rents could be considerable.[44] These financing and investment methods, occasioning receipts and expenditures of a potentially complex nature, must be seen as separate from the fabric's acquisition of non-recoverable resources. Though they are not discussed in this section, such business and economic aspects of the fabric's activities will be investigated further in the section on the Utrecht Dom.

The notion of 'the provenance of contributions', which informs any discussion of income sources for cathedral-building, must be specifed at every turn. A single person or institution could be invested with multiple capacities and functions, and then we must ask, for example, whether a bishop's contribution was made from his position as religious head of the bishopric, as overlord or as private benefactor?[45] Was a contribution made by a canon a private donation, a penalty imposed by the chapter, a fixed sum agreed in consultation with his fellow canons or a bequest for an anniversary obit? Many revenues also had an indirect, derivative aspect: gifts and contributions for the building works could come to the fabric by way of an intermediary, or the cathedral might simply acquire control of long-existing revenues. Revenues of the latter type immediately beg the questions of which party had originally been entitled to them, as well as from which alternative allocations they had been diverted and who had the authority to modify such allocations. The fabric received much of its income indirectly, by circuitous means; why this was typical of cathedral fabrics, as opposed to parish church fabrics, will be discussed in considerable detail further on. These same circuitous derivations sometimes make it difficult to trace the exact source of certain contributions, whether this was the person legally entitled to the revenues – thus, he who assigned them to the fabric – or the one who had actually generated them. Moreover, the very term 'contribution' obscures its compulsory or nearly compulsory character. It is unavoidable, therefore, that different sources of income must be treated from different vantage points, whilst some must be discussed in multiple contexts.

In the next section we will turn to a discussion of the cathedral fabric's income. But before doing so, we must first consider the fabric's level of involvement in all the aspects entailed in church construction and furnishing. Cathedrals fulfilled a number of ancillary functions, serving as the final resting place of the bishop, chapter members and lower cathedral clergy, of kings and lords and, sometimes, lay magnates,[46] as well as accommodating obit celebrations at various altars. From the beginning of the thirteenth century, these functions came to demand architectural interpositions and provisions that could have a defining impact on a cathedral's appearance, even overshadowing it; this is especially true where the addition of private chapels is concerned. Chapels, their altars, and other features such as stained glass windows and partitions were always included in obit foundations. Masses were read there, along with other services intended for the salvation of the founders. Whereas a chapel's construction and furnishings were a one-off expense, the obits held there had to be paid year in, year out from the bequest. In a certain sense chapels were private domains within the cathedral, intended for the clerics or families to which they owed their foundation and endowment. In many cases they formed an integrated whole with the cathedral, as side chapels projecting around the apse, choir and nave.[47] During the later Middle Ages, however, these funerary and other chapels evolved into separate units, fully independent of the cathedral in their construction, design and scale. In Spain such chapels sometimes all but smothered the physical fabric of the church.[48] Yet for our present purposes we must leave aside the fascinating question of how this late medieval 'individualization of cathedral space'[49] progressed throughout Europe.

Another question – this time one that must be addressed – concerns which funding mechanisms were used for the construction and maintenance of these chapels. And, related to this, the issue of how responsibility for obit foundations, and thus for chapels, was arranged. There is no uniformity here. Furthermore, though there is no lack of legal documents, such as foundation deeds and testaments, they usually fail to provide any details about precisely how the financial aspects were actually managed.[50] The wealth of possible approaches can be illustrated by a handful of examples.

Around 1300 the chapter at Huesca sold eight side chapels, the construction of which was already provided for in the plan of the cathedral, to families who would be entitled to bury their dead there; the receipts of 3000 and 4000 *sueldos* per chapel counted as a contribution towards the building costs.[51] In Tortosa, the bishop and chapter arranged for the erection and foundation of a chapel around 1350, shortly after the first stone of the new cathedral was laid. Here any founder of a chapel was obliged to pay the masters of the fabric at least 4000 sol.barc. (approximately ten annual wages of a *manobre*) for the building, plus an annual remuneration of 18 l.barc. (less than a year's wages) for the chantry.[52] The contract was concluded directly between the founder and the stone mason, but witnessed by chapter representatives; the canons additionally dictated the iconographic programme, though they did offer it for the patron's approval.[53] In Barcelona, too, founders of a benefice or an annual service for the salvation of their souls paid a fixed donation to the masters of the fabric, usually amounting to 2000 sol.barc. (estimated at five annual wages of a *manobre*[54]), '*in adjutorium confeccionis seu construccionis vestre capelle*' (in aid of the creation or construction of your chapel).[55] In Rodez founders paid a sum to the fabric to help finance the construction of their chapels.[56] In the majority of cases, chapels were built at the founder's expense ('*suis expensis*'). The chapter's master of the fabric still reserved the right to supervise construction, though this did not necessarily enhance the architectural homogeneity of the result.[57] On one single occasion we see a founder granted exceptional leeway, when a canon of Santo Domingo de la Calzada was permitted in 1447 to build a chapel '*a su costa y a su voluntad*', provided it augmented the '*nobleça*' of the cathedral.[58] In some instances founders managed the construction of their chapels themselves,[59] in others control lay in the hands of the fabric to which the performance of the obits was also entrusted. In 1352 the cathedral fabric in York granted Archbishop Zouche permission to commission a chapel to be built at his personal expense, for which he was allowed to employ the cathedral's master of the works.[60] This shifting spectrum of approaches reflects the evolving power relations between the various parties involved: the chapter and fabric on the one hand, and the bishop, individual members of the cathedral clergy, aristocratic and urban families, and guilds and confraternities on the other.

Another major category of expenses is one that in many cases was paid for with no or only partial recourse to fabric funds, and administered wholly outside its jurisdiction: the large items of church furniture that, unlike chapels, usually did not require major structural modification of the cathedral. It is important to differentiate between furnishings connected with a chapel or obit foundation and those that composed part of the cathedral proper. Included in the first group are not only tombstones and monuments, but also altars with their retables, paraments and so on. As a rule, their fabrication and upkeep were funded and managed as part of the obit foundation to which they belonged, though, again, with the full gamut of local variation.

Other church furniture belonged to the cathedral itself, including the retable for the high altar, glass windows, choir hangings, organ, church bells, reliquary shrines, liturgical books and vessels, and paraments.[61] Many of these objects were supplied as gifts (figs 18, 19, 40, 41). The associated expenditures were then usually simply recorded in the fabric rolls, though occasionally a separate budget and separate administration of receipts and expenditures were maintained for specific donors such as the bishop or a canon. Late medieval donors much preferred to present ready-made artworks as expressions of their personal piety, and private artistic patronage sometimes dominated the aspect of the cathedral. The *Liber confraternitatis fabricae* from the cathedral of Tournai accuses the devout of furnishing the cathedral with nothing but pompous trimmings whilst neglecting building works and repairs.[62] Chapters adopted a similar approach to such artworks as they did to chapels, making an obvious effort in their roles as protectors, custodians and, in a certain sense, owners of the cathedral church to preserve authority over the nature, scale, design and iconography of donated pieces.[63] But they were not always successful. In 1493, for example, Archbishop and Cardinal Mendoza of Toledo made plans for a sepulchral monument in the form of an open triumphal arch, to be placed in a prominent spot to the left of the main altar. He held that its design evinced great beauty; the chapter rebutted that it was '*diformidad*'. Disagreement over the tomb's construction dragged on, with the chapter still adamant in its resistance upon the archbishop's death in 1495. Intervening in a secret night-time raid, Queen Isabella and Mendoza's successor, Cardinal Cisneros, had part of the choir screen dismantled so that the cardinal could ultimately be interred in his preferred spot after all.[64]

The activities of these various stakeholders in the expansive cathedral domain notwithstanding, the fact remains that construction and also a significant share of the outfitting lay in the hands of the chapter and was charged to the fabric; therefore, we shall primarily focus on the latter's activities.

Any investigation into how cathedral-building was financed must be founded on an analysis of the monetary value of receipts for and expenditures on construction and upkeep. As has already been noted, it is only from the period in which fabric rolls have survived – from the end of the thirteenth century at the earliest – that we can gain any real degree of quantitative insight into such financing. But here we encounter a difficulty: how are the sums to be compared and, furthermore, presented in a meaningful way, as they are expressed in diverse coinage and varying monetary systems over a period exceeding two centuries and an area covering the whole of Europe? Conversion into a metal unit, such as grams of gold or silver, is no solution: not only do values of coinage in precious metals diverge widely, but as a metric they hold little tangible appeal.

One useful approach is to convert the overall or annual total building investment into the annual wages of an unskilled building labourer. This implicitly assumes that there was no significant variation in the labour productivity of basic building tasks over the centuries and large territory concerned, as is justified by the absence of major technical or organizational innovations.[65] Fluctuations in income purchasing power are not relevant here. This approach further assumes that outlays for all the requisite construction materials on the one hand, and all wages on the other, evolved in a parallel fashion both over time and across the entire territory. In fact, this is only partly true.[66]

Several criteria must be met in order to define a good and valid measure. First, the daily wage of a building labourer engaged in unskilled labour at the construction site (referred to as a labourer, *opperknecht, manovale, peón, manoeuvre, manobre, Tagwerker*, etc.) must form the basis; the nature of their work was the same everywhere, and therefore comparable. The next step is calculating a reliable annual wage. This means we have to know how many days a labourer actually worked each year. That number turns out to be fairly constant, ranging from around 250 to around 280 days a year.[67]

We will therefore take a 250-day working year as our standard, with 180 days paid at the summer rate and 70 at the winter rate. This number of working days reflects that averaged by the fabric attendant, the *famulus loedzae* (elsewhere known as *valet de fabrique* or *Hütteknecht*), who was appointed as the supervisor of the lodge at the Utrecht Dom. The calculated wage is therefore a wage type, representing the upper limit of what an unskilled building labourer could earn when sustainably employed in the cathedral building works. The resulting index for the scale of building operations in any given year or over a certain period therefore has no bearing on the actual number of workers involved in construction, but instead indicates how many unskilled labourers could have been employed for that sum, thus providing an indication of the size of the works, of the costs of church furniture or of cash resources available for building, upkeep and furnishings. From this point onwards, we shall apply this measure wherever possible.[68]

ONE THE BISHOP'S CONTRIBUTIONS

A bishop could contribute to his cathedral on either the basis of his canonically founded responsibility for the church building or personal initiative – *'ultra quam iustitia exegerit'* (above what propriety demands), in the words of the bishop of Salisbury in 1219.[69] It is with his core obligation that we will begin.

Canonists working after the Council of Trent laid down the following rule of thumb: in the absence of a cathedral fabric, or when that fabric did not have sufficient income, the bishop was to be held accountable with a quarter of his income. If after the deduction of this sum he was still left with more ecclesiastical income than needed to maintain an appropriate style and standard of living, the *superfluum* was also to be invested in the building works. Only where these contributions failed to raise what was needed for essential building activities would other parties be expected to step in, beginning with members of the chapter.[70]

As far as can be deduced from the scarce – predominantly French – sources, local rules were different, and varied widely.[71] Only occasionally is the bishop's obligation expressed in general terms: in 1422 the archbishop of Sens had to pledge to the chapter that '[...] *in reparationibus ecclesie a modo fiendis, contribuet cum capitulo, quantum ius et iusticia suadebunt*' (for the imminent repair of the church he, together with the chapter, will contribute as much as duty and sound judgement may dictate).[72] The chapter at Toul was hardly more precise in its formulation: '*item tenetur pro posse sponsae suae matrici ecclesiae ipsam adornare et adiuvare in sua aedificatione et manus adjutrices porrigere modis omnibus er curam indefessam habere*' (equally he is bound to provide for the adornment and support of the building, his bride the mother church, according to his means, and to lend a helping hand in every possible way and to take constant pains to do so).[73]

There were also arrangements of an entirely different order. The bishop could be charged with the care of a specific part of the building, for example. According to a deed of 1124, the bishop of Paris was responsible for the preservation of certain components of the vaulting in the old cathedral.[74] A good century and a half later we read that he, like the archbishop of Bourges, was responsible for the maintenance of the bells.[75] The legal grounds for such obligations elude us. Even more intricate were the differentiations made at Ely Cathedral. After the collapse of the crossing tower in 1322, the bishop rebuilt the choir at his own cost – and doubtless in a grander style than necessary – whilst the sacristan took charge of rebuilding the octagon on behalf of the monastery; the two building campaigns each had their own separate administration and were even entrusted to different architects.[76]

At the opposite extreme are the remarkable terms drawn up by the bishop and chapter of Arras in July 1253. Their solution, perhaps made to their mutual benefit, allowed that in exchange for a one-time payment of 400 l.par. the bishop and his successors thenceforth '*sunt et erunt liberi et immunes ab omnimoda refectione et retentione*' (be and remain free from and not accountable for tributes for repairs or maintenance of any kind whatsoever) for the cathedral, with a few specified exceptions. The fact that an erudite canonist like Pope Innocent IV confirmed their agreement indicates that settlements of this kind did not contravene canon law.[77]

Cooperation between the bishop and chapter was not always harmonious. In Prague the archbishop accused his chapter of appropriating gifts made to the cathedral that were his by right; the chapter rejoined by charging him with running his church into the ground, '*ecclesiam destruere tam solempnem*'.[78] Occasionally, it became necessary to seek legal recourse to compel a bishop to meet his financial commitment to his cathedral. The fifteenth and sixteenth centuries furnish diverse examples of French cathedrals where the bishop was ordered by the highest courts – the *parlements* – to pay a lump sum or annual contribution towards the costs of repair.[79] In these cathedrals, the structural conditions were so poor or the fabric revenues had declined to such an extent that patently critical new building works could not be brought to any reasonable form of completion. Rulings of this type arose from court decisions or settlements at Beauvais,[80] Sens,[81] Bordeaux,[82] Paris,[83] Sarlat,[84] Auch,[85] Vannes,[86] Limoges,[87] Gap,[88] Lavaur,[89] Agen,[90] Narbonne[91] and others. In the last-named instance, the *parlement* of Toulouse determined in 1521 that the archbishop would contribute '*ad causam reparationis et continuationis edificii ecclesie*' (for the repair and continuance of the church building) '*terciam partem fructuum dicte dignitatis archiepiscopalis Narbonensis*' (one-third of the profits of the aforenamed archiepiscopal office); clearly the old tripartite division still found application in this southern French diocese. Such coerced contributions were sometimes impelled by dire necessity, as in Bordeaux, where the archbishop assumed nearly half the total annual construction costs after 1510, equalling 50 annual wages of an unskilled labourer between that year and 1518.[92] In Bourges the archbishop's annual contribution for construction of the tower was reckoned by the king in 1508, and subsequently authorized in a 1510 suit in the *parlement*, at 3000 l.t. a year, this being the difference between the income from his *mensa* and his costs of living.[93] A different means of forcing the bishop to contribute was that applied by the chapter at Ribe (Denmark). There, Bishop Peter (1345-1364) committed himself and his successors to a yearly payment of 1 mark's worth of grain, for which he had to offer his mitre and crosier as sureties.[94]

More interesting than the contributions imposed on bishops for cathedral repairs or to revive flagging new building campaigns are those they gave for cathedral construction voluntarily. There is a vital distinction to make between indirect contributions, in the form of special episcopal measures, and actual monetary assistance. In most cases, a bishop enacted such measures – sometimes in coordination with the chapter – in his capacity as head of the diocese, and possibly also as local lord.[95] He granted indulgences to benefactors of the works and incorporated special provisions for the fabric in synodal statutes.[96] He could also issue a special mandate, the so-called *mendicatoria*, to activate the cathedral's intricate system for gathering money for the building works from various sources throughout the diocese; he was empowered to do so by either the authorities of the episcopal office or those specially delegated by the pope, such as the authority to grant dispensations and commutations.[97] As already noted, there was usually little reason for the bishop to refuse to mobilize these sources of income,[98] except where prestige or jurisdiction were at stake.[99]

Alternatively, the bishop could present the cathedral fabric with ecclesiastical revenues that had a variety of possible allocations, including those that he could otherwise have used to enlarge his own *mensa*. Amongst such revenues were the fruits of recently vacated benefices; instead of immediately being settled on the new benefice holders, they might come under a papal reservation, such that the pope could allow their use for general ecclesiastical, or even non-ecclesiastical, designations. Such designations could include the building works, but equally the *mensa* of an impoverished or debt-ridden episcopate. Where the bishop agreed to assign such revenues to the fabric, it sometimes meant the sacrifice of considerable financial gains on his part. However, the bishop's obvious stake in these revenues notwithstanding, we will consider them as contributions from the diocese.

There is no doubt that, at least in the official Church order, the bishop stood at the head of the cathedral, the mother church of his diocese. Church portal and glazing iconography abounds with representations centring on the historical succession of bishops from the time of a particular episcopate's foundation, sometimes also introducing references to the bishop's financial contribution to the works.[100] And yet the bishop's role in amassing construction monies is difficult to define or predict. Sometimes he gave little or nothing, even in cases where the cathedral building campaign came at his initiative;[101] or he might confine himself to the bequest of a single artwork. Elsewhere he was not only the initiator and hence driving force, but also the financial mainstay of the enterprise. This was particularly common in the period before the chapter got control of the cathedral fabric.[102] It would be going too far to cite the many examples of just how varied episcopal engagement in the cathedral works was. Nevertheless, certain kinds and forms of contributions should be expected from the bishop more than from anyone else. He could contribute from his position as the religious head of the diocese, drawing on his official income for example, or as the lord of a demense or city.[103] If he came from a wealthy family, he could donate private funds. Lastly, he could contribute as a member of the chapter (such as by providing paraments upon ascending to office).[104] In practice, however, it is difficult to distinguish one category from another.[105]

Of greater relevance here is the difference between contributions given in a lump sum and those repeated over the course of several years. Contemporaries made clear distinctions in the various ways in which bishops could support the building works. Concerning the enthusiastic builder-bishop Guillaume de Seignelay (1207-1220) of Auxerre, who took personal charge of financing the rebuilding campaign begun at his initiative in 1215, records relate that he relinquished his jurisdictional dues – in other words, his salary – and donated a further 700 l.t. '*de proprio*' (from personal means) in the first year, and upwards of 5 l.t. to 10 l.t. a week in the years thereafter. In addition, he allocated pious offerings to the building fund and organized collections in his bishopric and the surrounding dioceses. All together, he thus granted certain official revenues to the works, subsidized it with sporadic and periodic contributions – presumably deriving from his private estate – and established special measures to benefit the cathedral.[106]

Periodic contributions like these formed the most important source of funding because they provided a degree of surety for the continuity of a building campaign (always so essential). Sources from the eleventh and twelfth centuries say much on this topic, but in fact tell us little. Chronicles and other narrative sources relate that bishops of the time often shouldered the financial burden of building projects, which in many cases were also begun by them. One tells of Bishop Meinwerk of Paderborn (1009-1036) who, having inherited a neglected cathedral from his predecessor, invested his private means '*sumptu ingenti et munificentia singulari construxit*' (to continue the building with vast sums and exceptional munificence).[107] An account of the life of Bishop Otto von Bamberg (1102-1139) recounts that the generosity he displayed in order to speed up reconstruction after the fire of 1117 was such '*ut cunctis stuporem, multis quoque invidiam tanta pecuniae profusio pareret*' (that all were amazed, and many even jealous of the great amount of money he so lavishly spent on the building).[108] Many texts speak of bishops who rebuilt their cathedrals '*propriis*' or '*suis sumptibus*' (at personal expense), suggesting the use of revenues intended for their own sustenance (the *mensa episcopalis*) or private funds.[109] We have no way of knowing what the actual circumstances were, however.

After the second half of the twelfth century, our sources become more precise. Some bishops showed themselves willing, even without the chapter's support, to grant an annual sum or a portion of the revenues due them to support the building works for an agreed number of years. The martyrology of Gaultier de Mortagne, bishop of Laon from 1155 until 1174, tells us that apart from two valuable tapestries, he also '*dedit novissimo operi Laudunensi centum libras preter viginti libras bone monete, quas eidem operi ab initio contulerat annuatim*' (gave to the very recent lodge of the cathedral of Laon one hundred pounds of good coin in addition to the twenty pounds of good coin that he had contributed annually for the construction of the cathedral from the beginning); thus a combination of a one-time and an annual donation.[110] From fabric rolls preserved at Exeter we learn that the bishops Thomas Bitton (1292-1307) and Walter Stapeldon (1308-1326) each donated £124 18 s. 4 d. (80 annual wages of an unskilled building labourer) annually over the course of a quarter-century for the cathedral rebuilding campaign begun around 1270; of the fabric's total yearly income during this period – which was then the highest it would ever be – one-half came from the bishops. In 1361 John Thoresby, archbishop of York (1352-1373), laid the first stone of the new choir and marked the occasion by donating £100 to the fabric and pledging a further £200 (equal to 50 annual wages) each year until the choir was complete; by the time of his death this amount had swelled to over £2300.[111] It is likely that the archbishops of Canterbury provided financial backing for the construction of the nave, begun in 1317, in the same way.[112] In Germany, too, late medieval bishops occasionally supported the building works. Thilo, bishop of Merseburg from 1466 until 1514, made a gift of 3000 gulden, to which he added another 200 gulden yearly – the same as the chapter – to rebuild the nave, in order that 'his palace would not appear more precious than his church'.[113]

After the Hundred Years' War (1337-1453), French bishops who wished to support their afflicted or neglected cathedrals likewise provided major subsidies, drawing them out over several years.[114] Two examples will suffice here.[115] In Troyes, the bishops Louis and Jacques de Raguier, an uncle and nephew, are recorded in the fabric rolls as donating 167 l.t. in 1479/80 and 250 l.t. in 1482/83, *'pour faire la nef neufve'*, with additional subsidies for a period of four years after 1486-87 towards expenditures for building materials and the wages of initially six, and later twelve, building labourers. The total came to around 2000 l.t., or some 80 annual wages.[116] Similarly, construction of the transept arms and portals at the cathedral of Sens between 1490 and 1520 profited from the archbishop's financial support: starting in 1492 and over a 25-year period, Archbishop Tristand de Salazar (1474-1519) carried five percent of the building budget, donating some 22,000 l.t. in all. He furthermore contributed to the interior furnishings, with sums ultimately totalling over 3000 l.t. for an altar founded in his name, and 300 l.t. for a choir hanging. In his will he bequeathed another 1200 l.t. for the completion of the tower.[117]

Sporadic contributions from bishops are even more difficult to sum up in global terms; naturally, there are countless references to episcopal bequests and donations from far and wide. They are mentioned in obituaries, wills, chronicles, vitae and also fabric rolls.[118] We are immediately struck by their enormous variation in value: the gifts ranged from incredibly large to downright negligible. Yet even gifts in the first category indisputably signal a lesser degree of episcopal involvement in the building works. Bishop Milon de Nanteuil of Beauvais, who initiated building at his cathedral, supported the campaign's initial phase from 1225 for ten years, whereas his successors Robert de Cressonsac (1237-1248) and Guillaume de Gretz (1249-1267) contented themselves with granting large lump sums.[119] Similar variances are seen at Soissons in the same period.[120]

Sporadic gifts typically fit within the existing financial plan, and usually came with a specific designation attached. A donation of 100 l.t. made in 1405 by the bishop of Le Mans was earmarked for the recently begun northern transept.[121] The archbishops of York subsidized construction of the nave with sporadic gifts after 1291, and one gave a further sum of 50 marks '*pro celeriori promocione operis in instante estate*' (to accelerate building work in the summer to come).[122] In 1413 the bishop of Lodève donated 1000 l.t. for his cathedral, left unfinished and in disrepair in the wake of war and impoverishment, '*non completa, imo ventis et pluviis aperta et indecenter patefacta*' (incomplete, and indeed even open to rain and wind, and indecorously exposed thereto), though in fact this sum would scarcely have covered the costs of paying seven stonemasons for a single year.[123]

A distinct category of sporadic contributions are bishops' testamentary dispositions. A bishop's last will and testament provided an unparalleled opportunity to honour his cathedral. And yet it is remarkable that in many wills we find no, or only vague, gifts to the fabric, or donations of precious items that were useless in advancing construction.[124] Frequently, the cathedral fabric figures as one party in a long list of persons and institutions remembered with sums large or small.[125] This is even true of certain bishops who are documented as benefactors of their cathedrals. To his Notre Dame in Paris, Maurice de Sully (1160-1196) left 100 l. '*ad tectum nove fabrice ecclesie faciendum plumbeum*' (to lay lead cladding on the new cathedral), and 20 marks of gold for an antependium to grace the high altar, together with a chalice and censer; a gift of modest proportions within the entirety of his testamentary disposition, and yet he is seen as the force that propelled the building campaign all the same.[126] The bequest of 1000 marks (160 annual wages of an unskilled labourer) left by the bishop of Wells, Nicholas Bubwith (1407-1424), for completion of the library and construction of the north tower on the west façade is by far the largest gift left a church fabric in any of the many English wills we have from this period. Yet it represents less than a one-third share of all the legacies making up Bubwith's will, and the same as the sum he bequeathed for improvements to the Somerset roads.[127]

When viewed from the fabric's position, too, the majority of episcopal bequests were modest in size. The 1253 bequest of 150 marks (£100) left by Hugh of Wells, bishop of Lincoln, is paltry in comparison with the total annual income of the diocesan fabric confraternity, constituting some 1000 marks a year.[128] The same is true of sporadic donations. The fairly sizable gift of 480 lire imp. (around thirteen annual wages of an unskilled labourer) made by the archbishop of Milan in 1390 is nothing when compared with the vast revenues – 50 times this sum – that the fabric was receiving each year.[129] Conversely, bequests could also play an important role for the fabric. Amongst the legacies left by Archbishop Etienne de Bécart of Sens (1292-1309) was 1200 l.t. for the works, a sum higher than the fabric's income, which amounted to 437 l.t. in 1295 and 623 l.t. in 1319.[130]

Only in exceptional cases did the cathedral building works assume a central place in a bishop's last will and testament.[131] Two well-known examples follow, which additionally show that the boundaries between a lump sum gift and one repeated each year were vague, in that a bequest could be so large that it might fund building operations over the course of several successive years.

The first example concerns William of Wykeham, bishop of Winchester (1366-1404), whose will is dated 24 July 1403. On a previous occasion, having failed in an attempt to squeeze an annual contribution from the cathedral prior and monastery, he simply took control of reconstructing the church nave himself. Contributions from the monastic community remained limited to the supply of scaffolding and of sand and lime from its own estates, and permission to reuse material from the demolished old nave.[132] At his death, Wykeham left 2500 marks to complete a carefully delineated section of the nave, as well as an additional gift meant for glazing certain windows, comprising 3000 marks (£2000) and equalling the annual wages of 500 unskilled building labourers. The bishop furthermore gave instructions for both the supervision of finances and artistic guidance for the building. Yet even acknowledging the core emphasis his will put on the cathedral's completion, Wykeham's bequests to other institutions and parties nevertheless exceed those for the cathedral, which amounted to £2875, to which we may add a series of £900 payments already distributed during his lifetime. We might even question whether the cathedral nave really had the highest priority amongst his building activities at all after 1394, given that we know he also incurred 20,000 marks for the building and repair of his residences from 1366 onwards.[133]

The second example concerns the detailed testament drawn up for Louis I d'Amboise, bishop of Albi (1474-1502), on 28 January 1485, in which bequests for the cathedral were again central. In as early as 1479 he had obtained papal permission to dispense freely over not only goods obtained *ex industria* (through careful management) or by inheritance and donation, but also those due him from both the 'church of Albi' (the *mensa episcopalis*) and other secular and regular benefices (which he possessed in ample measure). Expenses for his comparatively modest burial, the memorial service and some ten monetary bequests can be estimated at no more than 6000 l.t. To the cathedral he not only bequeathed his library, his breviary, his large missal and several paraments, but also 200 marks of silver from which to fashion a gilded silver retable for the high altar. Most notable, however, were his financial stipulations for the completion of the tower – the visibility of which was assured by raising it to 25 *cannae*, or approximately 44 metres, above the nave – and for the creation of a south portal. These pledges he actually fulfilled during his lifetime, providing 282 ½ l.t. in the first year, and 2000 l.t. each year thereafter. If the tower and portal were incomplete at his death, his will provided that additional monies would be allocated to those projects.[134]

When late medieval bishops provided extensive financial support for cathedral construction, it was very often with a view to deriving personal honour from the erection or completion of a circumscribed portion of the building.[135] In some cases they wished their names to be connected with the structure in a very literal sense. To the gift in his abovementioned testament of 1424, Bishop Bubwith of Wells attached the proviso that the prospective north tower bear his name, just as the south tower had been named for his predecessor: '*vocetur et nuncupetur Bubbewithtoure*' (to be named and called Bubbewithtoure).[136] Other bishops were content with no more than the addition of their coat of arms.[137] Towers enjoyed a definite preference amongst episcopal donors, perhaps because they could simultaneously serve as symbols of their secular power. The bishop of Burgos, one chronicle tells us, funded the completion of the west towers with his private means from 1442.[138] The addition of the large crossing tower at Bayeux Cathedral, planned as far back as 1425, had to wait until Bishop Louis de Harcourt – who, like most French bishops of the time, was not residentiary – proved willing to finance construction of the masonry substructure. Having been despatched to the bishop to petition for funds, the master of the fabric returned on 26 September 1477 to share the happy news with his fellow canons. From October 1477 until August 1479, a sum of 4092 l.t. 12 s. 6 d. flowed into the campaign, equal to 108 stonemason's wages. Only the lead-clad *bonnet* had to be funded from the fabric's regular income between May 1483 and October 1486.[139] In Rodez, Bishop François d'Estaing likewise financed the construction of an imposing tower from 1510 onwards; in subsequent legal proceedings he cited the great costs entailed as the most important reason why he had been unable to meet his obligations for the repair and maintenance of the priory at Villeneuve, which it seems was attached to his *mensa*: all its revenues, he said, had been used up for the tower. Testifying as witnesses, the bishop's master builder and treasurer both affirmed that 100 to 120 labourers were employed on a daily basis and that the total annual expenses ran up to 5000 l.t. This sum is five times what the fabric spent on the works in 1507/08 and 1509/10. Without their episcopal patrons, neither the tower at Rodez nor that at Albi would ever have been realized.[140] Similarly, the final phase of construction on Rouen's south façade tower ('*tour de beurre*') and its crossing tower could only be completed in the sixteenth century thanks to large gifts and sureties from its archbishops.[141] Hampered by exceptionally poor finances, the tower of the cathedral at Oviedo was saved in 1524 by a one-time gift of 600 gold ducats from the bishop, who was '*movido de caridad*' (moved by charity); the canons kissed his hand in gratitude.[142]

Even in instances where a tower was named for the bishop, as at Wells, this need not necessarily signal episcopal support. The construction of the large free-standing cathedral tower in Bordeaux, for which Archbishop Pey de Berland laid the first stone in 1440 and which to this day still bears his name, received no or little financial support from him; we do not find any contributions of significance either during his lifetime or in his will. Even after a cult of worship developed around his grave for 30 years or more after his death in 1456, the gifts received there did not enrich the cathedral fabric.[143]

Another typical feature of late medieval episcopal artistic patronage was the bishops' tendency to bypass the fabric and pay tribute to the cathedral church with an artwork of their own – a stained glass window, a retable for the high altar, a bell, a rood loft, a reliquary shrine or a set of paraments (*capella integra*). Such artworks, displaying the bishop's coat of arms, portrait or an inscription, proclaimed his importance as patron and promoter of the arts and cathedral benefactor as no gift to the general building fund could ever have done.[144]

It has already been noted that, apart from such financial support as canon law prescribed in cases of neglect, there is no clear trend to be discerned in the nature, size and duration of bishops' contributions towards the splendour of their cathedrals. The fact that they themselves initiated campaigns and established the necessary sources of income in various instances, or that they retained a considerable voice in the fabric's affairs, in no way guaranteed large contributions *de proprio* (from personal funds) for the works. But neither did a bishop's nearly permanent physical absence necessarily translate into a lack of interest in his cathedral. Bishop Stillington of Wells, who occupied the episcopal see for a quarter-century from 1466 until 1491, was in residence for a mere four weeks; nevertheless, it was he who sponsored the campaign for a Lady Chapel alongside the cloister.[145]

Differences in the size of bishops' financial contributions will have had less to do with their personal preferences and inclinations, their social background or the extent of their personal wealth, and more with the historical evolution of the episcopal office. To begin with, the bishop found himself up against the chapter, which often acted peremptorily. In some cases he fulfilled a dual role in his episcopate: not only was he the religious head of the diocese, he also exercised temporal sovereignty within all or part of its borders. It is possible that local research, whilst beyond the scope of this study, could shed considerable light on these aspects.[146] One recent study, for example, has linked episcopal patronage of presumed fundamental importance for the construction of the cathedrals at Albi, Narbonne, Limoges and Rodez in southern France from the latter half of the thirteenth century with their bishops' expanding secular power in the region and the increasing revenues generated by growing and better-managed Church property.[147] The bishops of Utrecht, by contrast, never made any substantial contributions to the construction of their Gothic cathedral that we know of. Possibly this can be explained by the fact that Utrecht's bishops regarded themselves as lords first and foremost – their chief concern the defence of an ever-imperilled and eroding secular power – to which their role as religious leader of a large diocese was secondary.[148]

TWO THE CHAPTER'S CONTRIBUTIONS

As already indicated, canonists prescribed that the college of canons came second, after the bishop, in the chain of accountability for the cathedral church.[149] The situation was different in practice. More often than not, the bishop had relinquished his authority over the cathedral, whether willingly or unwillingly, without having also been released from all financial responsibility. Jurisdiction over the building and the precinctal immunity tended to rest with the cathedral chapter, as did control over the fabric.[150] Certain financial rights and duties attended this situation. Amongst these rights was the chapter's authority to collect various revenues associated with its jurisdiction over the cathedral and precinctal immunity and to allocate them as it saw fit, albeit with the bishop's approval – for example, to increase prebendary stipends or to cover general capitular expenses. Included in these revenues were alms given in the cathedral, burial fees and rents from buildings leased within the cathedral precinct. Naturally, the chapter could also assign these cathedral revenues to the fabric. Canon law even furnished legal grounds for doing so, with a provision stating that responsibility for cathedral maintenance lay with those who enjoyed its ecclesiastical income. Generally speaking, local *consuetudo* determined to what purposes these sometimes very valuable revenues were put.[151]

Practices surrounding the allocation and division of the oblations illustrate this most clearly. Offerings of varying nature and sometimes immense value could be brought to the cathedral on any number of occasions, at various sites and for all sorts of causes. Though it was usually the chapter that had overall charge of these gifts,[152] their division amongst entitled parties gave rise to countless problems and conflicts.[153]

To begin with, the express wishes of the donor – provided they were known – had to be honoured: receipts from a collection box for the poor, for instance, had to benefit the poor. Yet what if the donor's intentions were unclear? Some canonists and theologians, and even ecclesiastical councils, held that the old four-part rule of division applied in such cases.[154] But were their prescriptions borne out in practice? In 1186 Pope Urban II ordered the archbishop of Canterbury to split offerings brought to the grave of St Thomas Becket (1118?-1170) into four shares, with one going to the church.[155] Properly speaking, the cult of St Thomas did not really start until after the translation of his relics on 7 July 1220. Detailed records tell of the impressive revenues garnered from donations left at his shrine between 1213 and 1383,

14
Santiago Alfeo, late fourteenth century
On the banderol: *Eice arca hoperis beati Iacobi apostl.* (This is the offertory chest of the *Opus* [fabric] of the sainted Apostle James) Polychromed stone
Installed on an offertory box in the shape of a capital which was placed against the north crossing pier, dated 1497
Cathedral of Santiago de Compostela

Santiago Alfeo is not the apostle St James the Greater to whom the cathedral is dedicated, but the apostle St James the Less, son of Alphaeus. The statue may have been produced following the archbishop's legal ruling in 1393 ordering the chapter to replace the sign which he had removed from where it stood at the fabric offertory chest, bearing an inscription that corresponds with that on the banderol.

LITERATURE
M. Chamoso Lama, *La catedral de Santiago de Compostela*, León 1976, pp. 71 and 76 (fig.); López Ferreiro 1898-1911, vol. 6, p. 258.

furnishing 20 to 25 percent of the monastery's centrally administered income (the monastery fulfilled the function of a chapter at Canterbury). However, there are no indications that any part of that revenue was officially designated for the works: clearly, the pope's orders were not followed.[156] Indeed, in English cathedrals it was rare for receipts from saints' shrines to go to the building.[157] Another illustrious illustration concerns the offerings brought to the shrine of the Three Kings in Cologne Cathedral. These relics, acquired from Constantinople, had been presented to Archbishop Rainald von Dassel by Frederick Barbarossa in 1164. The prelate in turn granted not only the holy remains, but also the right to dispose over the prospective oblations to the chapter.[158] In 1189 Archbishop Philipp von Heinsberg confirmed his predecessor's pledge and furthermore allowed the canons '[...] *liberam potestatem ordinandi de ipsis elemosinis ad supplementum prebendarum suarum prout poterunt diligentius et melius*' (complete freedom to make arrangements for the gifts to supplement their prebends, as well and as scrupulously as they are able). Though the new building campaign was not yet underway at the time, receipts from the shrine certainly did not go to fund construction even after it was launched in 1248.[159] Similarly, offerings made at the grave of Bishop Symon (1297-1315) at Salisbury Cathedral[160] and of St Hugh and other bishops at Lincoln Cathedral (where profits actually suffered a sharp decline after the first quarter of the fourteenth century)[161] accrued to the chapter, not the fabric.[162] Devotional gifts for the grave of St Thomas Cantilupe in fifteenth-century Hereford were set aside for the fabric only when and as required for the construction programme.[163]

It goes without saying that decisions about the allocation of offerings could also go in the fabric's favour. Pope Leo IX (1049-1054) possibly set an example by dedicating a tenth of the offerings made in St Peter's in Rome, reserved by his predecessors for their own ends, to the '*decor*' (ornamentation) of the basilica.[164] Cathedral fabrics could always count on revenues from certain collection boxes in the church, but their assignment required an explicit decision by the chapter, or bishop and chapter together. This is described in the so-called *liber niger* (black book) kept by the chapter at Coutances, where cathedral construction began early in the eleventh century: '*auxiliantibus etiam canonicis, redditibus medietatis altaris ad tempus operi concessis*' (to which the canons now too made their contribution by temporarily making half the receipts from the altar available for the works).[165] In 1205 the bishop of Soissons determined that future offerings made for the relic of St Stephan, lately acquired in Constantinople, would be divided into equal halves, with one half '*ad opus ecclesie*' (for the cathedral building works) and the other for the city bridge.[166] In Vannes, the bishop and chapter decided on 30 October 1419 that one-third of all donations from the faithful at the grave of St Vincent Ferrer (a famous preacher and miracle-worker who had met his unexpected end there half a year before) would be deposited in the fabric fund.[167] Some chapters established a collection box expressly for donations to the works[168] or designated an existing box for this purpose.[169] In a great many cathedrals, nearly all the alms, excepting the so-called mass oblations, accrued to the fabric; indeed, some canonists even viewed this as the normal state of affairs.[170] A case in point are the arrangements made by the bishop and chapter of Arras in July 1257.[171] Of especial interest are the circumstances that surrounded the division and use of offerings collected at the cathedral of Santiago de Compostela, where the constant influx of pilgrims to the grave of St James yielded revenues on a scale that guaranteed considerable financial support for the chapter and cathedral alike.[172] Here, as at cathedrals elsewhere, certain strict rituals had to be observed.[173] Twelfth-century pilgrims brought their gifts in coin and kind to the main altar, which was dedicated to St James. Initially, a portion of the gifts (specifically: two-ninths) was earmarked for the *obra*, as the cathedral fabric was called.[174] By the time the renowned Bishop/Archbishop Diego Gelmirex (1100-1140) held the episcopate, the cathedral even had a separate donations box designated only for the works.[175] A change came in the first half of the thirteenth century, when it was determined that gifts at the high altar would be shared between the archbishop and chapter; henceforth the *obra* would have to be satisfied with proceeds from the '*arca operis beati Jacobi*' (the blessed James's collection box for the *obra*).[176] This decision marked the start of frequent conflict between the chapter and *obra*, as each vied to gain pilgrims' favour. Santiago's archbishops had to fix rules setting out precisely how the church's various officers were to welcome the pilgrims who, arriving at the cathedral wholly disposed to give but equally unsuspecting, sometimes knew how they wanted their offerings to be spent and sometimes did not.[177] A decree dating to around 1250 includes in its stipulations that in the morning pilgrims are to be brought to the high altar first, and only then to the *arca operis*; in the afternoon, the sequence is reversed (fig. 15). Pilgrims were also to be asked outright about the desired purpose of their gifts. Attendants at the *obra* collection box were not allowed to solicit pilgrims but could, where appropriate, direct their attention to it and show it to them. Supervision was put in place to ensure that every point where offerings could be made was accessible for the same number of hours.[178] A century later, around 1350, the *arca operis* had acquired a statue of Santiago Alfeo[179] (St James the Less) and a sign reading: '*Eice arca hoperis beati Iacobi apostl*' (This is the collection box of the blessed Apostle James for the *obra*) (fig. 14). Around 1390 the chapter had the sign removed, much to the *obra*'s dismay, together with the candleholders and candles that had burnt before the statue of St James the Less. A suit followed, in which the chapter was found in the wrong. The archbishop ordered that the contested inscription be reapplied in bold letters ('*en letteras gruesas*'), so that it could be read from a long distance.[180] After this episode the chapter seems to have ceased challenging the *obra*'s rights. A wholly different solution was devised at Vannes: here the chapter was entitled to the oblations, but leased the profits to the fabric at a fixed annual sum.[181]

Monies offered in the cathedral could make or break a construction campaign, and it is to this aspect that we shall turn next. The above examples of how receipts from the cathedral's ecclesiastical revenues were divided have widespread application and offer clear illustrations of the large measure of freedom the chapter (and bishop) had in apportioning alms. Donor stipulations and the chapter's ultimate responsibility for the church building imposed certain parameters. Whenever building operations were up and running, it was in the chapter's interest to maximize the flow of alms into the fabric; on these occasions it used every means at its disposal to swell the tide of pilgrims and the faithful.

15
Welcoming pilgrims at the grave of St James in the choir of the cathedral of Santiago
Frontispiece of the *Cartularium* of the hospital of St James in Tournai, by the Master of the Dresden Hours, c. 1489
Tournai, Bibliothèque de la ville

This is a realistic representation of the ritual manner in which pilgrims venerated St James in the choir of the cathedral, where a thirteenth century statue of him was installed behind the shrine. In the centre a pilgrim is shown giving a devotional accolade backwards over the shoulder of St James. In front of the shrine is the high altar, to the left of which the *custos arche operis beati Jacobi* guards the sickles with which St James was reputed to have been beheaded. Pilgrims are standing and kneeling around the altar.

LITERATURE
Vanwijnsberghe 2002, pp. 1509-1546.pp. 71 and 76 (fig.); López Ferreiro 1898-1911, vol. 6, p. 258.

ihs

This section first addresses contributions for building and upkeep that the chapter or individual canons provided on the basis of either formal decrees or time-honoured customs. The route by which these contributions entered the fabric fund was determined in part by how the chapter's holdings were managed. Where such management was largely or fully centralized, the endowment's administrators were responsible for making disbursements on the chapter's behalf.[182] Where the canons' salaries consisted in large part of profits from their own personally controlled prebendary endowments (the values of which could come to diverge widely over time),[183] the canons were required to make their contributions to the fabric individually. In instances where the former applied, the chapter could apply measures such as ceding certain surplus profits to the fabric each year.

When it comes to financing the building works, however, the key issue – apart from the size of the contributions – is not so much whether the monies were collected on an individual or a collective basis but rather whether the contributions benefited the fabric fund in perpetuity or for a specified number of years or only sporadically.

1 • PERPETUAL CONTRIBUTIONS

Perpetual contributions comprise the subsidies and payments established and pledged by capitular statute for an unlimited or very lengthy period of time, though this is not to say that these sums were actually available to the fabric every single year. There is a significant degree of uniformity in the nature of the measures that different cathedral chapters – and indeed other collegiate church chapters as well – adopted on behalf of their fabrics.

THE FRUCTUS PREBENDAE DEFUNCTORUM

Chief amongst such measures was the chapter's allocation of the *fructus prebendae defunctorum* – revenues attached to a canon's prebend which, having been released upon his death or for some other reason, were withheld from his successor for a certain period (one, two or several years).[184] An old custom – our first examples go back to the eleventh century – dictated that upon a canon's death his heirs be granted a sum equal to the prebendary income he would have received over a single year (the so-called *annus gratiae*), which they should use to settle his debts and found an obit celebration in his name.[185] In later years it became customary whenever a prebend fell vacant to withhold some share of the fruits from the new beneficiary for a second, third or even fourth year, and to put the sum towards a general expense, such as enlarging the chapter's endowment,[186] enriching prebendary benefices[187] or repaying debts.[188] The chapter could also choose – as it very often did – to designate the fabric as the beneficiary. In most cases we have no way to trace when such decisions were made; dated capitular statutes usually only renewed arrangements that had long been in place. Plans for a building campaign could occasion such an allocation, but this was by no means always the case. The earliest extant decision we know of relating to an allocation to the cathedral works dates to the period between 1165 and 1181. The bishop and chapter of Bayeux at the time were determined to divert all profits arising from the prebends of canons who had died or taken their vows, with the exception of a few entitlements for new prebendaries, to the fabric for a term of one year. At their request, Pope Alexander III, the famed canonist, confirmed the decree,[189] but not without reservations. In fact, the pope remarked, deceased canons were best served, where the salvation of their souls was concerned, when such profits were distributed amongst the poor, as other churches did; however, he continued, given that what you intend is not strange to an *opus pietatis* (pious work), we confirm your decree, under the understanding that it will be valid for a term not exceeding the duration of building.[190] This papal limitation indicates a moral preference for designations that would aid the poor, and furthermore signals that the designation of these revenues for building projects was still relatively unheard of in Rome.[191]

Most of the statutes that have come down to us date from the thirteenth century[192] or later, the majority of them from German cathedrals.[193] However, this should not be taken to mean that it was common German practice to divert some or all of the first year's profits of vacant benefices (the *annus carentiae*); of the 31 cathedrals that did so, only ten allotted these profits to the fabric.[194]

Where the fabric was allowed to enjoy these revenues, the financial gain could vary considerably. Amongst other things, it depended on the number of canonries at a cathedral and how many of them fell vacant each year, as well as on the value of the prebends and the number of years they were allotted to the fabric. Equally important was whether any portion of the prebend accrued to the new beneficiary during that year (or years). The 1317 papal decretal *Suscepti regiminis* – the only mention of this problem in the *Corpus Iuris Canonici* – sought to redress lengthy absenteeism amongst expectant canons by explicitly reserving for them at least a portion of their benefice during the first year.[195] In Speyer the fabric enjoyed the full fruits over three years, in Paderborn only one year, which the successor could moreover buy off for a relatively minimal sum, whilst elsewhere the term might comprise no more than six months.[196] Occasionally, new chantry priests were also compelled to observe a certain waiting period.[197] Prebendaries vacated due to the death of the holder were subject to different rules than those freed up through exchange or retirement. Finally, the share deducted from the benefices of residentiary canons was smaller than that withheld from those who were not resident.[198] The sum of these variables resulted in an exceptionally complex constellation of rules that differed from one place to another and which was furthermore liable to constant modification and supplementation.

ADMISSION DUES

A second, albeit less important, contribution that capitular statutes assign to the fabric is the portion of the sum that every new canon had to pay upon joining the chapter. A custom perhaps even more common than the *annus gratiae* was one under which new residentiary canons hosted a feast for their fellow brethren upon taking possession of the office.[199] In some instances they were further required to provide a new, often silken, cope for the chapter's vestry.[200] Starting from the fourteenth century, such dues in kind were typically converted into a fixed, sometimes considerable, sum of money. In that case the chapter could determine how it was to be apportioned. One share usually went to the fabric, possibly with a proviso such as that it was to be spent on bettering the paraments. In Salisbury, members of the chapter were offered a choice between a feast in their home or a fine of £40 payable to the fabric; chapter minutes from the early fourteenth century show that most opted for the latter.[201] Elsewhere, the admission dues and celebratory reception continued side by side. New canons at Chichester spent an obligatory 150 marks on the admission feast plus, according to a 1251 statute, donated a further 25 marks to the chapter and the same to the fabric fund.[202] For the newly admitted, a contribution to the cathedral was thus only one amount due amongst many.[203] Dates are usually impossible to trace where such regulations are concerned,[204] though they do not seem to be exceptionally old. On rare occasions it was a new building project that actually prompted a statute designating admission dues to the fabric, as at Prague in 1350 and Troyes in 1363.[205] As far as other cathedrals were concerned, particular arrangements continued to vary according to the place and time, occasionally also being applied to new chantry priests and other benefices attached to the cathedral.[206] The resulting revenues were never of any great value: in Sens the profits ranged between 5 l.t. and 70 l.t. over the fifteenth and first half of the sixteenth century, thus no more than two years' wages of an unskilled labourer.[207]

FINES

Included amongst the chapter's entitlements was the authority to levy fines on negligent members of the cathedral clergy. All or some of these receipts could likewise be designated to the fabric by capitular statute. Negligence usually related to absence from daily choral services, for which the absent cleric either paid a fine or surrendered his attendance stipend.[208] Vicars and chantry priests were subject to a similar rule on occasion. Other lapses, including unseemly dress, indecorous behaviour in the choir, name-calling[209] and unchaste conduct, were also fined. The canon Robert Gifford of Wells, guilty of this last transgression, was fined a sum of 1265 s., to be paid to the cathedral's master workman. Another canon accused of adultery near the end of the fifteenth century was banished from the church and city for two years, during which time all his daily distributions and other emoluments would accrue to the fabric; he was furthermore made to pledge payment of £10 to the fabric if he were to be caught in the same offence again.[210] After the cathedral had been repaired and no longer needed the funds, such as in Aarhus in 1388, fines were once again paid into the chapter.[211]

ABSENCE DUES

Closely related to these fines were the fees that non-residentiary canons were made to pay.[212] Deducted from their prebends in most cases, these monies could also be assigned to the fabric by capitular statute, and indeed later canon law assumes this to be the normal state of affairs. In the Middle Ages, however, the practice was not as widespread. In Angers, the chapter held back 5 l.t. from the prebend of every non-residentiary canon after 1209, which it allocated to the building works.[213] In Verden[214] and Paderborn[215] a similar regulation applied, but only to the prebends of canons who were absent without leave (*portiones absentium*). These may be understood as fines, but equally as charges for dispensation. The canons of Speyer Cathedral were able, following the fire of 1289, to acquire a *licentia deessendi de ecclesia* (permission for non-presence in the cathedral) for one or two years if they ceded half of their prebend, appraised at a certain value, for cathedral repairs; they also had to delegate a vicar at their own expense.[216] It goes without saying that these revenues tended to be of lesser consequence.[217]

MORTUARY GIFTS

The same is true of receipts in the form of mortuary gifts or *mortuaria*,[218] comprising valuable objects from the estates of the deceased given to the parish church[219] or to the cathedral in the case of canons. Listed in fabric rolls from the cathedral of York, for example, under the heading '*mortuaria canonicorum*' (mortuary gifts from the canons), are profits from horses, or else a corresponding commutation payment, bequeathed by deceased canons.[220] Elsewhere, such as at Troyes and Utrecht, canons left a *pallium* to the fabric upon their deaths, or a fixed amount in its stead.[221] It is not clear whether such bequests were motivated by long-held custom or an actual obligation.[222]

PREBENDAL INCORPORATION

A sixth perpetual or sustainable form of contribution to the building fund was one that, though effective, was rarely applied. This was the option, conditional upon Church approval, of incorporating a prebendary benefice into the fabric,[223] whereby the occupation of a single seat in the chapter simply devolved, as it were, from a natural person to the fabric, either permanently or for a fixed term. The associated revenues thus flowed into the fabric fund.[224] It was not often that chapters sought recourse to this rigorous measure, even though it entailed no real sacrifice for either the chapter as a whole or its members.[225] But the incorporation of a prebend hinged on a canonical procedure, the formalities of which posed a considerable obstacle. Not only the bishop's consent was needed, but also, it seems, the pope's, and their approval was only forthcoming if there was a demonstrable *necessitas* (necessity) and *evidens utilitas* (apparent usefulness) for the fabric. It is easy to understand why Church authorities only resorted to this measure under very exceptional circumstances, for what it meant, after all, was the formal redesignation of Church revenues.[226] We find a handful of cases in which this step was taken. In 1220 the pope authorized the bishop and chapter of Metz to assign the fruits of all newly released prebends to the fabric for a period of ten years, on the grounds that the cathedral had so many canons that the measure would not disadvantage the choral services.[227] Some centuries later, in 1453, the canons decided to apply for the suspension of the next vacant prebend in order that the organ could be completed.[228] At Bremen in the beginning of the fourteenth century, the *prebenda defunctorum* was replaced with the incorporation of one prebend, to accrue to the fabric.[229] In 1397, the pope granted his permission for the cathedral of Bordeaux to incorporate one prebend, amongst other things to fund cathedral upkeep and liturgical books.[230] The fabric of the cathedral of Meaux shared in the '*grossus fructus unius prebende integre*' (total profits of one full prebend) during the sixteenth century, and possibly longer,[231] as did the cathedral fabric at Soissons.[232] During his sojourn in Regensburg in 1541, Cardinal Gaspar Contarini (1483-1542) is recorded as having '*extinxit unam prebendam*' (extinguished a prebend) to benefit the cathedral fabric there,[233] whilst as late as 1568 the cathedral fabric in Utrecht incorporated a prebend known, quite aptly, as the '*prebenda sancti Martini*' (prebend of St Martin),[234] though with certain restrictions attached. Both these latter instances of incorporation concern penniless and impoverished fabrics, deprived in times of difficulty of the income they had relied upon for centuries.[235] In rare cases a chapter decided to annex to the fabric the fixed annual salaries of certain lower chapter officers, including the architect, in perpetuity.[236]

The contributions summarized above[237] usually played only a limited part in funding building operations, furnishing just enough to defray the costs of day-to-day construction and maintenance. Their value varied from one place to another: some chapters made do with a grace year or admission dues, whilst cathedral fabrics elsewhere enjoyed a plenitude of financial pledges.[238] Moreover, chapters modified their statutes on a regular basis, allowing them to adjust contributions according to their needs. There was not a single canonical rule requiring the chapter to transfer any of the revenues described above to the fabric. Thus, from 1420, the chapter at Augsburg chose rather to amass a reserve fund for general expenses that tapped these very same sources (the *annus carentiae* ('*Karenzjahre*'), admission dues, fines and absence dues).[239]

2 • CONTRIBUTIONS FOR A LIMITED TERM

Chapter contributions made over a short, set period of time served to support a specific building campaign. Whilst the chapter could act in cooperation with the bishop, as we shall see, it could also decide independently, as a collective of prebendal beneficiaries, to grant significant sums of its own income for building activities – though with certain conditions attached. These types of binding settlements were made by the canons at Chichester in 1232,[240] at Hereford in 1246[241] and at York in 1296,[242] amongst others. Later examples of such self-imposed levies – referred to as *imposicio* or *tallia* in the sources – are rarer, with fourteenth-century statutes preserved at Exeter,[243] York,[244] Salisbury[245] and Cambrai.[246] On 27 November 1406, the canons at Le Mans

16
Pierrre de Fayel (c. 1344), canon of the Notre-Dame in Paris, shown as the donor of the choir screen of the Notre-Dame Inscription: *Maistre Piere de Fayel chanoine de Paris a donne CC lb par a faire ces hystoires et pour les novelles voirieres q. snt sus le cuer deceans* Relief carving by Jean Ravy Paris, Musée du Louvre

The inscription records – quite exceptionally – his contribution of 200 l.par., worth fourteen annual wages. The '*hystoires*' concerned the history of Joseph. The choir screen no longer survives.

LITERATURE
Exh. cat. *Les fastes du gothique, le siècle de Charles v*, Paris 1981, no. 40; Baron 1999, pp. 329-330; Fr. Baron, 'La partie orientale détruite du tour de choeur de Notre-Dame de Paris', *Revue de l'Art* 128 (2002), p. 17.

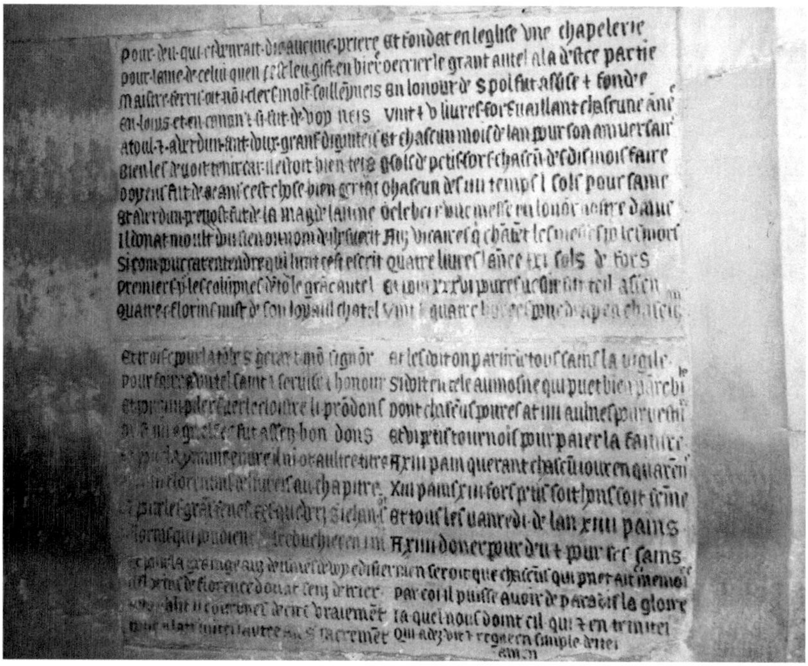

17
Inscription on the tombstone of Ferry de Void, dean of the chapter of Toul and provost and canon of the church of Ste. Marie-Madeleine in Verdun, late fourteenth century
Toul Cathedral, north wall of the north transept

French summary in verse form of all donations made by Ferry de Void during his lifetime and all foundations established by him: for the columns of the high altar, 400 florins; for the grave of St Gérard, 300 florins; for four piers in the nave, 400 agnels d'or; for the general use of the *Oeuvre*, 400 florins; for the large window near St John, 100 florins; additionally endowments for a chaplaincy and for a series of masses and for alms in kind to be given to the poor. A summary of this kind is unusual. The inscription closes with an entreaty to pray for the repose of his soul.

LITERATURE *Congrès Archéologique de France* 164 (2006), pp. 231-232.

decided to invest ten percent of all prebendal profits in the cathedral's north transept, which was finished around 1430.[247] An entry in a 1522 deed from Auxerre reveals that the canons there had decided around 1500 to relinquish two month's profits from their prebendal estates. These contributions were mandatory for all concerned.[248] In Vienne, the canons and clerics of the cathedral joined with the bishop in 1228 in promising *'certum quid de bonis suis'* (a certain portion of [the revenues from] their estate) each year for the building works. Four years on they decided to withhold certain revenues from clerics who had failed to keep their vow, and from 1250 they were even denied admission to the choral service, and thus of their stipend for attendance.[249]

That these monies were of paramount importance is borne out by the numbers. In Autun, the *'impositio* [...] *pro opere ecclesie'* ([self-]imposed levy for the cathedral building works) raised 160 l.vien. towards a total income of 400 l.vien. in 1294, when there were barely any building activities to speak of.[250] After 1412 the chapter at Sens voted to dedicate a sum of 100 l.t. to the construction of the tower over the course of several years; here the total income ranged between 300 l.t. and 400 l.t.[251] In 1490 the canons promised to raise a collective annual sum of 80 l.t. for five years to fund the construction of both portals, this being equal to around two and a half year's wages of an unskilled labourer, or ten percent of the annual building costs.[252] Such temporary contributions secured at least some measure of stability in funding and thus in the progress of operations over a certain period; as to what happened thereafter, chapters deferred that concern to the future.

3 • ONE-OFF CONTRIBUTIONS

When the chapter wished to put money towards some very specific goal, such as acquiring a costly item of church furniture, it could do so via a lump sum disbursement. The cost of new choir stalls for the cathedral of Wells were translated into a per capita sum of 30 s., payable by all residentiary canons; those who were not in residence paid a collective £200.[253] In 1397 the chapter at Sens decided to impose a one-time tax of 10 l.t. or 5 l.t. on each of its members, depending on the nature of their endowment, to enable construction of the tower; the '*recepte de messeigneurs pour le taux qui fut fait et ordonne en chapitre*' amounted to 283 l.t., or 33 annual wages of a stonemason's assistant and about as much as the fabric's income over the whole of the campaign up until then.[254] A crisis in the fabric's finances could also prompt the chapter to inject a lump sum,[255] and at times it even proved necessary to liquidate a portion of the chapter's estate to support the fabric.[256] When times were hard, the chapter's responsibility for the cathedral church could become a heavy burden to bear.[257]

The chapter's dominant role in cathedral-building and maintenance affairs has already been noted. Even where the bishop was the initiator of building activities, it nearly always fell to the chapter to see the enterprise to a satisfactory conclusion.[258] This was a difficult administrative and organizational undertaking, demanding technical and artistic insight into complex architectural issues. The chapter's own contributions served, from a purely financial standpoint, as a stabilizing element. The institutional, impersonal character of the policies and decisions described above also had its strengths, generating grants of money that laid a solid financial foundation for the fabric.

It is good to note that the various capitular contributions discussed here were not exclusive to cathedral fabrics and in theory were available to the fabric of any church with its own chapter (collegiate churches). Unlike a cathedral fabric, however, which had so many alternatives it could bank on, collegiate fabrics usually had to operate on these receipts alone.[259]

Voluntary donations in money and kind from individual canons form a category wholly separate from the official, mandatory contributions made by the chapter corporate in discharging its duty for the church building (fig. 16). Yet if the bishop's role as artistic patron of his church is difficult to define, this is even more true where the chapter is concerned. Nevertheless, there are two forms of patronage that can be distinguished as especially characteristic. The first was a pledge drive held amongst the canons, sometimes in coordination with the lower cathedral clergy, to subsidize a gift made over a succession of years. The line between this and a mandatory contribution is not entirely clear: though the canons signed up to pledge an amount out of their own free will, their ties with the group would have made it difficult for them to refuse any invitation to do so. In Beauvais, the accounts for 1499-1500 show the chapter launching a pledge drive whereby canons could donate a given sum over several years to fund construction of the transept.[260] In most cases these initiatives were connected with the commission of a precious and intricate artwork, such as a reliquary shrine, rood loft, organ or portal. A decision taken on 2 August 1503 by the chapter of Metz pronounced that '[...] *chacun promit de faire son offrance selon ses facultéz pour la structure de ce sacré tabernacle; le primicier promit de donner cent florins* [...] *en six ans, le chantre soixante francs dans le mesme terme* [...]', and so the list goes on.[261] In some cases the fabric commissioned an item of church furniture and supplied the principal funding for it, and then invited members of the canonry to donate further components. In drawing up the commission for a rood loft at the cathedral of Troyes in 1382, pictorial elements were explicitly not included: '[...] *senz les ymaiges, lesquelles les messeigneurs feront faire à leur plaisir et à leur propres couz et despens*'.[262]

In the second place, sources show that canons and other cathedral clergy were particularly inclined to commemorate the fabric in their wills (fig. 17). Of course, residentiary clerics had typically spent many decades living in the cathedral precinct, had prayed there every day, had led the fabric in some cases and usually were also buried there.[263] Their bequests were seldom large though, and the practice was by no means customary, let alone required.[264]

THREE JOINT CONTRIBUTIONS FROM THE BISHOP AND CHAPTER

The bishop and chapter sometimes made joint agreements wherein they committed themselves to large financial pledges for the building works. Instances of such agreements are infrequent; most examples date from the late twelfth and the thirteenth centuries, when cathedrals were still inherently the products of solidary cooperation between the bishop and chapter, and were made at the start of a building campaign. Though the sums pledged on both sides tended to be quite large, they were explicitly restricted in years, usually serving to cover most of the expensive early phase of building.

In many cases we can only speculate as to the actual size and nature of these contributions. Following the disastrous fire of 1194, and prompted by a visit from the papal legate Cardinal Melior of Pisa, the bishop and chapter of Chartres agreed to provide a '*pars non modica*' (not insignificant portion) of their revenues for the rebuilding campaign for a term of three years. The sums, which must have been considerable, can be linked with a reorganization of the chapter's estate in the preceding year, when the provosts had been divested of their administrative duty.[265] When the three-year term came up for renewal, however, neither the bishop nor chapter proved willing, and the ensuing lack of funds was so great that the building labourers could not be paid their wages. Fortunately, miracles effected by the Virgin soon brought financial relief.[266] The rapid progress made early on in construction of the new cathedral at Rheims may likewise have been borne by short-term, large subsidies from the archbishop and chapter; in 1213 the campaign threatened to stagnate – just as at Chartres – exactly three years after it had begun.[267]

Usually it was the bishop who initiated joint contributions of this kind. But securing the chapter's agreement was not always an easy matter. Attempts by Archbishop Engelbert I of Cologne (1216-1225) to convince the chapter to support new building activities with a pledge of 300 marks each year until the work was complete were unsuccessful.[268] The archbishop of Rouen's financing plans encountered similar resistance from some members of the chapter, so, changing tactics, he induced Innocent III to issue a decree in 1198, in which the latter unhesitatingly declared that in so laudable an effort as dedicating a share of the chapter's income for cathedral construction, the decision of the archbishop and of the '*major et sanior pars*' (greater and wiser part) of the chapter was binding.[269]

Arrangements made by Bishop Milon de Nanteuil and his chapter when cathedral construction began at Beauvais in 1225 had also proceeded '*ordinationi* [...] *Milonis episcopi*' (by order of Bishop Milon). From the episcopal charter that has come down to us in fragmentary form, it moreover becomes clear what a *pars non modica* as referred to in the Chartrian *liber miraculorum* (book of miracles) could actually entail.[270] The bishop pledged not only the considerable yield from the *annualia* (see below), but also granted a one-tenth share of various revenues to the building works for the duration of ten years, including the annual income from almost all of his religious and temporal holdings both within and outside the diocese. The canons pledged one-tenth of their prebends for the same term (with the exception of their distributions for attending choral services each day). Immediately after taking up his office, Bishop Bernard de Castanet and the chapter of Albi allocated similar income sources to the cathedral building works there: a share of one-twentieth of the profits of the episcopal *mensa* and of the canon's prebends, which, though not in themselves large, bore a term of 20 years.[271] Thus, both the bishops and chapters at Beauvais and Albi alike were willing to donate a full year's profits from their *mensa* and prebends, respectively, alongside other contributions. Voluntary levies like this must have entailed a considerable sacrifice on the part of those making them. In Salisbury, where from 1219 the bishop and chapter had supported construction of the new cathedral with annual contributions for successive periods of seven years, the renewal of the contribution in 1233 for another seven years was hardly welcomed by the canons, and the bishop's averal that '*parati sumus deo dante onus fabrice una vobiscum ultra quam iustitia exegerit supportare*' (we are prepared to, God willing, share the burden of the fabric together with you, even beyond the dictates of propriety) is perfectly understandable. At the capitular meeting organized to decide the matter, all member canons, both residentiary and non-residentiary, were required to be present, or at least represented; their subsequent decision explicitly stated that a renewal of the statute on this occasion in no way implied any obligations in respect of the future.[272]

At other times, the bishop's and chapter's contribution was more modest. In 1209 the bishop of Angers committed himself and, if needed, his successors to a grant of 30 l.t. '*de redditu suo*' (from his own income) for at least ten years for the completion of the south transept, together with 50 l.t. as compensation for five meals that he owed the canons on Christian feast days; in other words, the canons sacrificed their future banquets for the cathedral's construction.[273]

The bishop's share did not necessarily have to equal that of the chapter. In an agreement concluded between the bishop and chapter of Narbonne on 4 July 1267, the former committed himself to an annual contribution of 250 l.t. from his own *mensa*, whereas the chapter pledged only 50 l.t. – a clear indication that the bishop's financial resources surpassed those of the chapter.[274] In Exeter, the contribution made by the chapter in the first quarter of the fourteenth century amounted to exactly one-half of the considerable sums pledged by the bishop.[275]

Such arrangements continued to be applied in later centuries. In 1378 the bishop and chapter of Tortosa decided that since the offerings of the faithful yielded too little *'ad continuacionem et perfeccionem ecclesie'* (for the continuation and completion of the church), they themselves would pledge one-tenth of their incomes for 50 years.[276] The cathedral of Condom, begun in 1505, could be consecrated in 1531 thanks to shares relinquished by the bishop (as much as one-third of the episcopal *mensa*) and chapter in 1507.[277] We also find instances of cooperation of a different kind. In 1546, during a large-scale campaign to expand the cathedral into a hall church, the archbishop and chapter of Zaragoza achieved a harmonious accord in which the former – also the campaign's initiator – paid for the building materials and costs of labour whilst the latter took responsibility for preparing the still fully occupied building site, scaffolding, equipment and apparatus, and water transport. A condition stipulated by the bishop here was the inclusion of his coat of arms.[278]

FOUR **PAPAL CONTRIBUTIONS**

Papal involvement in the affairs of the cathedral fabric was usually indirect: the pope's consent and cooperation was quite simply necessary, or at least desirable, for certain building-related measures. Only under highly exceptional circumstances would the pope take a personal concern in how building was financed at any specific cathedral.[279] For example, Clement V (1305-1314; Bertrand de Got) had served as bishop of Saint-Bertrand-de-Comminges (1295-1299) and archbishop of Bordeaux (1299-1305) before ascending to the papacy and was a driving force behind the building works at both cathedrals. In a mandate of 30 January 1313, he affirmed that the first of these cathedrals had been constructed *'de bonis nostris'* (from [the income from] our estate). To ensure the cathedral's completion, he charged two canons with levying a sum of 1000 l.t. on the revenues issuing from a number of archdioceses attached to the bishop's *mensa*, which the latter was obligated to pay.[280] In 1308 he granted the cathedral of Bordeaux an indulgence of fourteen years and fourteen quarantines[281] – extremely high for the time – to be extended to anyone who visited the church on the day marking the translation of the relics of its patron saint, St André.[282] In 1307 he had furthermore already demonstrated his dedication to his one-time cathedral by designating the first-year's fruits of all newly vacated diocesan benefices, exempt and non-exempt alike (to which he was entitled), to the fabric for an exceptionally lengthy term of 20 years. The resulting profits, combined with his own 1314 testamentary bequest of 10,000 fl. (around 35,000 l.t. or 3500 annual wages), formed by far the most important contribution to the building fund.[283]

Urban v (1362-1370), having been born in the region of Mende, had developed a fondness for the cathedral there.[284] In 1369 he himself took the initiative for the cathedral's reconstruction, allocating income intended for the see, which had been vacant since the end of 1368, for that purpose.[285] In the same year, the treasury of the Camera Apostolica furnished the fabric with 6000 fl., this apparently representing the profits of the episcopal seat, which would remain unoccupied for over two years.[286] The pope's early death cut building activities short for a time, though the nave could still be finished. He furthermore donated a range of precious objects, including a reliquary shrine for a thorn from Christ's crown of thorns, a shrine for the head of St Blasius, the church's patron saint, and, just before his death, a series of tapestries previously given to him by the king.[287] On this gift the pope placed the unusual condition that the relics and precious objects were under no circumstances to be alienated – a stipulation that was all but overstepped several decades later.[288]

At the cathedral of Lyon we see papal intervention of an entirely different order. Having once been a canon of that cathedral and returning with the ecumenical council to reside there from 1244 until 1251, Innocent iv (1243-1254) stimulated the works by addressing a long string of unusually elaborate letters to archbishops and bishops of dioceses both in and outside of France, instructing them to welcome the messengers despatched by the chapter of Lyon to collect gifts from '*per diversas mundi partes*' (every part of the world) for the building works, and to grant them permission to traverse their dioceses. His successor Alexander IV (1254-1261) confirmed these measures and also issued a series of indulgences. Here, however, there was never any question of direct financial support.[289]

Most of the time papal measures were limited to granting spiritual favours or special privileges and issuing confirmations for local arrangements – by and large routine tasks that could be dealt with, for a fee, by the papal chancellery. Foremost amongst these spiritual favours were indulgences. From the time of the Fourth Lateran Council (1215), the pope reserved sole authority to grant partial indulgences above 40 days and, more importantly, plenary indulgences.[290] Indeed, in the later Middle Ages there was not a single cathedral that did not have one or more papal writs of indulgence at its disposal. The Camera Apostolica reaped the benefits: officials of the papal curia demanded stiff fees for preparing documents and administration at the very least. Financial proceeds from indulgences will be discussed later, in connection with contributions from the faithful.

The pope was always approached for permission or confirmation of measures that hinged on canon law. Where matters such as the incorporation of a canon's prebend or parish church in a cathedral fabric were concerned, only episcopal and capitular permission were absolutely requisite, whilst papal approval was, if not necessary, certainly highly desirable.[291]

The legal relationships involved in allocating benefice profits to the cathedral building works during the first year after the benefice was vacated – the *fructus primi anni* (fruits of the first year) or *annualia* – were rather more complex.[292] Starting from the eleventh century, it had become customary, whenever revenues attached to a Church office were released on the death or resignation of the holder, to deduct some portion from the newcomer's salary over an initial period; usually the collator enjoyed all or some of this income for a period of one or more years. It was on this basis that the bishop and chapter could, under certain circumstances, avail themselves of these funds to serve their own ends – to bolster the chapter's estate, to found an obit for a deceased prebendary or to support the cathedral fabric. This is yet another example of an indirect source of income that could support any number of causes, the building works included, and which shall be considered in greater detail in the section on contributions collected in the diocese. In fact, many bishops acquired authorization from the pope – who seems, with some exceptions, to have exercised supervisory control over the *annualia* – to use the *annualia* from all vacated benefices for a set period, though there were certain conditions. It is mainly in the thirteenth century that we see popes granting this right, where its purpose was to allow the bishop to relieve his bishopric from heavy debts.[293] Occasionally, even secular rulers enjoyed these profits.[294] At a very wide range of cathedrals, popes furthermore gave their approval for the *annualia* from all benefices to be spent on construction.[295] By the early fourteenth century, however, popes carried their entitlement to grant such general privileges to its logical consequence, and thenceforth exercised authority over not only the *annualia* or the annates but also, and equally, over the annual profits of all benefices vacated within a given area and period of time.[296] In 1306 the pope first claimed the *annualia* from all vacant benefices in England, Scotland and Ireland for the Camera Apostolica, followed ten years later by a papal reservation across the whole of Europe (with the exception of France and a few other areas, which first conveyed the annates to Rome in 1326). In 1326 the papal entitlements were pared back down to only those benefices in the collation of the Holy See. Nevertheless, so broadly did the very notion of collation come to be defined that the levy of the annates developed into a fairly standard papal tax. Though later limited to a portion of the annual profits, the annates comprised a key source of income for the Camera Apostolica until at least the mid-fifteenth century, when their financial importance waned with concordats, custom and the institution of fixed contributions.[297]

These developments came with certain consequences. It goes without saying that any appropriation of the annates almost always depended on papal approval. That the annates lost some of their significance for cathedral building works during this period is fairly logical. In some cases there is an indication that annates which did accrue to the fabric fund came at the direct expense of the Camera Apostolica, and as such they represent a papal donation. An entry concerning the annates of the bishopric of Thérouanne in accounts kept by papal *collectores* (tax collectors) for the periods 1388-1390 and 1390-1393 relates that: '*dom. noster Papa in reparationem dicte ecclesie Morinensis remisit et donavit*' (the pope, our lord, has transmitted and bestowed [these] for the repair of said cathedral of Thérouanne).[298] Yet incidental gifts of this kind do nothing to change the fact that the pope was only very seldom directly involved in financing cathedral construction. Our discussion of the *annualia* here has been limited to the pope's prerogative to grant permission for their designation for the works. Their significance in financial terms will be considered later, when we explore contributions from religious holdings in the diocese.

FIVE CONTRIBUTIONS FROM THE RULER: EMPEROR, KING AND LORD

Liberalitas was generally held to be the definitive virtue of a sovereign, and his munificence was certainly also expected where church-building was concerned.[299] However, there was no canonical imperative upon the emperor, king or lord to take on any specific responsibility for cathedral churches. And yet at the same time it would be wrong to see their gifts and bequests as ordinary contributions from the faithful. In fact, there were many instances in which special relationships did exist, though their nature varied from one region to another.

In many bishoprics the bishop was also the local lord and might support the building works in this latter capacity by allocating some of his temporal income to the fabric. Identifying and isolating these contributions proves impracticable, however, as extant sources do not explicitly distinguish when bishops donated money from their positions as lords.

Where a ruler was the founder of a bishopric and its cathedral, he might also assume the role of building patron.[300] Prime examples are the imposing *Kaiserdome* in such cities as Bamberg, Speyer, Worms and Mainz, which rose at an incredible pace during the tenth and eleventh centuries thanks to imperial patronage.[301] Various texts have come down to us containing striking references to the emperor's role not only in providing resources, but in personally commissioning the work as well. Emperor Henry II (973-1024) had already begun building the Bamberger Dom before actually establishing the bishopric in 1007 as a missionary base for converting the Slavs; the cathedral consecration ceremony would follow on 6 May 1012.[302]

The cathedral of Speyer, in the last of the bishoprics to be founded along the Rhine, was long the largest church in Christendom and dominated the city entirely.[303] The Salic emperors chose the cathedral as their dynastic final resting place and locus of their dynastic obits.[304] Concerning Emperor Henry III (1017-1056), sources recount that '*Spira fit insignis Henrici munere regis*',[305] and a vita of Emperor Henry IV (1056-1106) reports that '*imperator vero famosum illud ac laboriosum opus Spirensis monasterii habebat in manibus*' (the emperor was at the head of the famous, intensive operations for the construction of Speyer Cathedral).[306] There is no doubt whatsoever that imperial donations and allocation of income to the bishop and chapter provided the financial means to make building possible.[307] It is revealing, moreover, that in the late Middle Ages, when imperial power suffered a sharp decline, we come to find the same organization and income sources operating in the cathedral fabric at Speyer as everywhere else.[308]

In France the king was entitled and obliged to provide a special type of protection to many of the churches in his realm. This *gardia specialis*, or *garde royale*, extended not only to all churches situated within the royal domain and supposedly founded by the king, but also, from the thirteenth century onwards, to nearly all cathedrals in France.[309] Though this in no way put the king (or whomever held the *garde*) under obligation to support church-building campaigns, there was certainly an assumption that his assistance would be forthcoming.[310] The roles could also be reversed, with the king profiting from the cathedral fabric, as occurred in 1230, when he laid claim to 1500 l.t. in building materials to use for the city wall at Angers.[311]

After the Hundred Years' War (1337-1453), French kings were fairly systematic in financing the construction of cathedrals (and of churches generally).[312] The country's recovery on all fronts was a process in which the king played a leading role. It appears that he reserved part of the proceeds from the *gabelle du sel*, an indirect tax on salt levied everywhere from 1347 onwards, for church building works.[313] This is suggested by the many charters in which the king granted tax receipts from a given region to cathedrals and parish churches for a specified period. The cathedrals of Evreux,[314] Sens,[315] Senlis,[316] Rouen,[317] Bourges,[318] Beauvais,[319] Rheims,[320] Troyes[321] and, in the seventeenth century, Orléans and again Evreux[322] all profited from this income source on a fairly large scale. The actual benefits varied depending on the extent of the entitlements granted, but could be considerable, even dominating the fabric's budget.

One example of royal support will suffice here.[323] The cathedral of Troyes enjoyed the king's assistance in various ways and at various times. In 1366 and over the following four years, the fabric received an annual sum of 200 l.t. from the king, representing around 30 percent of its income in the first year.[324] From the end of the fifteenth century, the chapter spared no expense or effort in attempts to secure a share of the salt tax for the fabric. A trip to Paris in 1486 yielded naught,[325] so a repeat attempt was made after 1495. In 1503/04 the master of the fabric spent over 140 l.t. on a trip to court, hoping to obtain privileges similar to those that the cathedral of Rheims had enjoyed since 1484.[326] His mission met with success: for at least three decades the fabric drew a very significant portion of its income from the salt tax. From 1 September 1506 the fabric received 1 d.t. of every minot of salt sold in salt storehouses throughout the kingdom, with the exception of Normandy and Languedoc, for a term of six years.[327] During the first term this yielded a revenue of 5114 l.t., which came to around half the fabric's net income in the last year. Renewal of the privilege proved no simple matter, however. In 1514/15 the master of the fabric paid out 741 l.t. in expenses, rights and gifts for officials in the diocesan chancery;[328] two years later the influx of tax monies resumed, totalling over 10,500 l.t. in eight successive years between 1516/17 and 1526/27, and in some years as much as 40 percent of the net income.[329] But in

1522/23 the fabric was again spending 365 l.t. on costly gifts (32 dozen napkins and an 87 ell of tablecloth) to effect another eight-year renewal of the charter after its expiry on 1 October 1523.[330] In 1532/33 we read mention of legal proceedings, but the charter was renewed once more; the income in 1536/37 was 2300 l.t., or 57 annual wages of a *manoeuvre*.[331]

A different indirect form of royal support is seen in Spain, where a predetermined number of building labourers employed in the cathedral (or another church) works could be granted exemption from royal taxes and other obligations: '*el privilegio de los excusados*'. We know of countless examples of this practice dating from the latter half of the twelfth century through the fifteenth. It is quite possible that the privilege, attesting a monarch's overall engagement in the cathedral's construction, was altogether common.[332]

Donations from kings, lords and local nobility in the form of artworks for the cathedral comprise a study unto itself.[333] The windows of large cathedrals enjoyed an especial preference amongst royal and aristocratic artistic patrons (fig. 25), and in a few instances we can identify the donors pane for pane.[334] It would be beyond the scope of the present survey to gauge the scope of this type of patronage and the sums involved. Interestingly, it has been noted that French kings often elected to subsidize windows during periods in which the episcopal see was vacant, and thus when they had control over the revenues.[335] However, it would be wrong to assume a priori that those who donated large glazed windows should also be reckoned amongst the cathedral's benefactors; in fact, the opposite was more likely to be true.[336]

On the whole, it is important not to overestimate the share that kings and other lords contributed towards the financing of cathedral works, and certainly not during the period in which the chapter governed the cathedral fabric. To gain a clear picture of royal architectural patronage, we may turn to the kings of England.[337] Not one of the main three building patrons amongst them – Henry III (1216-1272), Edward I (1272-1307) and Edward III (1327-1377) – supported cathedral works to any significant degree. Henry III stands out only for his gift to Wells Cathedral in 1220 of 60 large oaks from one of his forests and, four years

18
Stained glass windows: the donor with a model of the window as an attribute

Arnould de Collongues, dean of the chapter of Lyon from 1241 until 1250, donor of the north rose window
Outermost band on the left: the donor with a model of the rose window, with the inscription *Li doien ernous me fecis facere* (the dean Arnould had me made)
Lyon Cathedral

19
Stained glass windows: the donor with a model of the window as an attribute

Renaud de Forez, archbishop of Lyon (1193-1226), donor of a lancet window in the apse
Bottommost scene: the archbishop kneeling with a model of the window
Lyon Cathedral

later, of a trivial sum of 5 marks for twelve years.[338] From 1227 the new cathedral at Salisbury profited from the proceeds of certain fines assigned to it by the king,[339] who had also given a sum of money to the fabric to mark the laying of the first stone in 1220.[340]

It is a fact well established that temporal rulers' engagement in ecclesiastical building activities nearly always centred on monasteries. Louis VIII of France (1223-1226) founded the Cistercian abbey of Royaumont, for example, and bequeathed all his valuables to its construction upon his death.[341] Edward I, having returned from a dangerous sea voyage, gave thanks by founding the Cistercian abbey of Vale Royal in 1274.[342] The notion that the welfare of their souls was better tended by the eternal prayers of the monks than by the secular canons will have played some part.[343] This belief took tangible shape in the designation of those same monasteries as royal resting places. The dukes of Burgundy drove the rapid pace of construction of the Carthusian monastery of Champmol near Dijon from 1377, which they intended as their final resting place; the sums they put towards its realization were on a level rarely equalled at any cathedral, with expenditures in 1386 coming to the equivalent of 520 annual wages of an unskilled labourer.[344] Gian Galeazzo, lord and later duke of Milan (1378-1402), lost interest in the construction of his city's cathedral soon after the campaign commenced in 1386, and instead channelled his chief energies and financial support into building the Certosa near Pavia, also choosing it as his mausoleum.[345] The fairly substantial sums of money he had pledged to the cathedral works were honoured only in very small part, and his testament makes no mention of the cathedral. When he became indirectly involved in a dispute between the cathedral fabric and an architect in 1401, his irritated reaction was that he wanted nothing more to do with the cathedral's construction: '*fiat, hedificatur et construatur in omnibus et per omnia secundum libitum et dispositionem suorum civium et hominum Mediolanensium ac deputatorum fabricae*' (the cathedral's creation and construction in every detail and in every part should be left to the plans and fancies of its citizens, the residents of Milan, and of the representatives of the fabric).[346] It is equally to be expected that the personal interest of Henry III (1216-1272) was drawn first and foremost to the construction of

Westminster Abbey. The abbey preserved the remains of its sainted founder and the last Anglo-Saxon king, St Edward the Confessor (1042-1066); it had long served as the coronation church and was soon to become the royal burial place as well. Between 1245 and 1272 the king funded its construction with the fabulous sum of £50,000, around double the king's annual total income and equal to 24,000 annual wages of an unskilled building labourer.[347] Paternal encouragements notwithstanding, his son and successor, Edward I, declined to perpetuate his father's patronage of the works.[348]

Where a cathedral also served as the royal mausoleum and coronation church, it was more reasonable to expect financial support from the secular ruler.[349] Such was the case at the cathedral of Pamplona, retained by the Evreux dynasty as the royal resting place.[350] Here King Charles II of Navarre (1349-1387) commissioned and personally funded the construction of a '*capilla real*' between 1351 and 1353, the administration of which he entrusted to the canon appointed as the cathedral's master of the fabric; thus he founded his palace chapel within the cathedral.[351] Wedding and baptismal ceremonies for the House of Evreux also took place in the cathedral.[352] Moreover, the monarchy made efforts to achieve alignment between the Kingdom of Navarre and the borders of a new Church province with its archiepiscopal seat in Pamplona.[353] On 1 July 1390 the cathedral's east end collapsed. On 27 May 1394 King Charles III (1387-1425) laid the first stone of a new cathedral. Initially, the usual sources of income – presumably monies allocated by the bishop and chapter – provided sufficient means, but after three years there was no longer enough to pay the labourers. The king intervened, forcing the chapter to make good on former pledges and to take on new commitments. He himself furnished key support for the building from 24 May 1397 until 1425, with a series of financial grants that included percentages of certain royal revenues and large sums of money from tax receipts for periods of ten to twelve years or over his entire lifetime.[354] Though there is no question that the cathedral was the work of the bishop and chapter, the king supplied far and away the most important financial backing during the first phase of the campaign: from 1387, and especially after 1401, until 1425, he donated a sum total exceeding 32,000 l., represent-

20
The first five *directores fabrice* of the Prague Cathedral, the canons Busek (d. 1350), Nichols Holubec (d. 1355), Benes Krabice (d. 1375), Andre Kotlik (d. 1380) and Wenceslas of Radec (d. 1417)
Busts along the interior of the triforium
Prague, St Vitus's Cathedral

These statues belong to a cycle of 21 life size busts of individuals who took an initiative in building the cathedral of Prague and led building activities there, starting with Emperor Charles IV and his family, next the three first archbishops, and last the five first masters of the fabric and two first architects, Mathieu van Arras and Peter Parler.

LITERATURE
Beneškovská & Hlobil 1999, pp. 94-101, 152-155.

ing some 14 percent of his overall building expenditures and around 20 percent of what he spent on his palace.[355] The heraldic decorations that embellish the vaults in honour of the House of Evreux are a testament to this royal patronage.[356]

The early phase of construction at the cathedral of Palma was initiated by a large gift from the first king of the independent kingdom of Mallorca, James II (1276-1311), in 1306.[357] Renovated to enable the celebration of the Christian divine service, the mesquita where '*nomen execrabilis Machometi*' (the name of the accursed Mohammed) had once been venerated assumed a new guise as the city's cathedral in the years following the Reconquista in 1229 and appointment of the first bishop in 1238 – a course of events mirrored in many Spanish cities.[358] A gift from the king facilitated the addition of a royal sepulchral chapel dedicated to the Holy Trinity and of the Capilla Real encircling the existing apse between 1306 and 1330, thus making an unmistakable statement about the cathedral's political significance. Moreover, the royal clerks administered the finances during this period. In 1309 the king also launched a collection for the cathedral on the island of Menorca.[359] The royal contribution comprised 2000 l., or around 320 annual wages of a *manobra*,[360] which may be compared with the largest episcopal donation of only 250 l. Successive building campaigns in the second half of the fourteenth century could no longer count on much royal support, however.[361]

In other Spanish kingdoms, royal sponsorship of cathedral building works was likewise expected. The imperative of expelling the Muslims and restoring the political and religious unity of Spain engendered a system of political and economic relations between the monarchy and episcopate in which the authority of the former grew increasingly dominant.[362] The king's right to dispose of various Church revenues and, if he wished, to assign them to the cathedral building works will be addressed in the next section.

Direct financial support by monarchs is a different story; whilst there is no doubt that many cathedrals received such support, it can only rarely be quantified and almost never assimilated into a comprehensive picture.[363] As a source of income, this support was neither certain nor structural. Without exception, it continued to be the chapter that commissioned cathedral works. Such was the case in Seville, where the canons declared in 1506 that it had been the Lord who had given them the courage in 1401 to begin so lofty a temple, unaided by king or monarch. Nevertheless, following the collapse of its central dome, Ferdinand the Catholic promised 10,000 gold ducats, to be paid over ten years from 1515, under the condition that construction of the Capilla Real be completed.[364]

Another motive that might prompt a royal house to support cathedral construction was the prospect of raising the cathedral to the status of a national shrine – as a coronation church,[365] as a dynastic mausoleum and sometimes as the final resting place of a sainted monarch or depository for his relics. In almost every case, the absence of data makes it impossible to reconstruct the consequences this had for construction financing.[366]

An exception to this is the cathedral of Prague. Here the cathedral was not only the main church of its diocese, but also a dynastic mausoleum, a coronation church and the final resting place of the national patron saint, Duke Wenceslas (907-929). On 23 October 1341, Jan de Luxembourg, king of Bohemia (1310-1346), permanently allocated the tithes on the profits of certain Bohemian silver mines to the building works at the new cathedral, the first stone of which was not actually laid until November 1344 (fig. 21). The donor's motives and intentions are meticulously recorded in the deed. The king proclaims himself patron of the cathedral (in itself a legal ground for financial support)[367] and recalls a vow made to his saintly predecessor Duke Wenceslas, in whose name he had claimed many victories. He instructs that the sums, which were doubtless large, be put firstly to new graves for St Wenceslaus and St Adalbert (second bishop of Prague, 956-997), whose remains would be elevated,[368] and secondly to obits for members of the royal household.[369] The donation thus intermingles political with religious motives: King Jan sought to promote the St Vitus Cathedral to the status of national shrine and head church of a Church province, the borders of which would coincide with those of the kingdom. It was on these grounds that he was able to convince the pope to elevate the bishopric of Prague to an archbishopric on 30 April 1344; the latter also conferred on the archbishop the right to anoint and

21
Plaque commemorating the building of Prague Cathedral (1344-1396)
Stone, 114 x 120 cm
Installed at the *Porta Aurea*, the south entrance to the cathedral
Prague, St Vitus's Cathedral

The Latin inscription records the elevation of the bishopric of Prague to an archbishopric on 3 March 1344, the laying of the first stone of the choir on the same day, the dedication of the choir in 1385, the laying of the first stone of the west end in 1395 and the translation of the relics of St Adalbert in 1396. It concludes with a reference to the *director fabrice*, the canon Wenceslas of Radec, and the *magister fabrice*, the architect Peter of Gmünd.

LITERATURE
Beneškovská & Hlobil 1999, pp. 149-151; *Die Kathedrale von St. Veit*, p. 80.

crown the king of Bohemia.[370] Several months later, on 21 November, the time was ripe to lay the first stone of the new cathedral. Jan's son, King (later Emperor) Charles IV (1347-1378), was possibly even more assiduous in his support for the building works and furnishings.[371] In later centuries, too, building campaigns continued to hinge on royal initiatives.[372]

It is interesting to trace how the dukes and archdukes of Austria strove to achieve similar objectives for the cathedral of St Stephen in Vienna, which they hoped to see as the coronation church and mausoleum of Austria.[373] However, their efforts were too late in bearing fruit to have any impact on construction financing. It was not until 1469 that St Stephen's became a cathedral, when the small bishopric of Vienna was split off from Passau,[374] and not until 1486 that Margrave Leopold III (1073-1136), the prospective national and dynastic saint, was canonized. By that time the construction of St Stephen's, intended as a cathedral but in the event serving as a parish church, and as collegiate church from 1365, was all but finished.[375]

The cathedrals of Prague and, later, Vienna combined functions that in France and England were distributed amongst different churches; as cathedral, coronation church, royal mausoleum and final resting place of a canonized monarch, they were each political instruments designed to strengthen the dynastic position of the royal house, as well as symbols of the unity of the ecclesiastical and temporal domains. The same was true of the cathedral of Krakow. It was dedicated in the first place to the national patron saint, Bishop Stanislaus (1071-1079), who had been canonized in 1254 and whose relics were immured within the cathedral itself. Coronations were conducted at his grave beginning in 1320, and from 1370 the cathedral also became the dynastic mausoleum. The royal castle was even built in close proximity to the cathedral, as in fact it also was in Prague.[376] Under circumstances like these, a monarch might be expected to take the first steps towards building a cathedral and supporting the early construction phase. In Prague, it is indicative of the king's later lack of involvement in building activities that he refused to attend a feast hosted by the archbishop at the choir's consecration in 1385; the meal intended for the king went to feed several hundred of the poor instead.

Yet the king and queen were both present to celebrate the laying of the first stone of the nave on 2 June 1392.[377]

SIX CONTRIBUTIONS FROM THE CIVIC ADMINISTRATION AND URBAN INSTITUTIONS

A city's willingness to provide financial support for building projects to a certain extent ran parallel to its share of power in the cathedral fabric – much as it did for the bishop and chapter. Given what has already been said about the relationship between cities and cathedrals, it is wholly understandable, albeit surprising, that cities took little to no interest in cathedral building affairs. Of course, in principle, the city had no stake in the cathedral church; it served the chapter, whereas the city identified primarily with the interests of its parish churches. In fact, the glaring conflicts of political interest that not infrequently marked the relationship between city, bishop and chapter could even have a direct negative impact on cathedral works. The 'book of miracles' of Chartres lamented around 1210 that burgers refused to lend their support for the cathedral's construction.[378] Occasionally, cathedrals were even involved in violent incidents. In Laon, rebelling local worthies killed the bishop on 25 April 1112 and set fire to his palace, the canons' residences and even the cathedral itself.[379] In 1116 or 1117 a raging mob pursued the bishop (later archbishop) of Santiago de Compostela, Diego de Gelmirez, up to the very altar and there proceeded to pelt him with a shower of stones. The church, still under construction at the time and covered with only wood and hay, caught fire in the process, and the episcopal palace suffered damage as well. Renewed rebellion in 1136 left the high altar damaged.[380] In Rheims, the citizenry's revolt against their archbishop and chapter led the canons to withdraw from the city for 26 months between 1234 and 1237; in the summer of 1235 the burgers built their barricades using not only paving stones, but also the '*tumbas coementariorum et lapides adfabricam majoris ecclesie deputatos*' (the tombstones and stones intended for building the cathedral).[381] In 1272, conflicts between the Benedictine priory of Norwich Cathedral and the city involving the priory's exempt rights in the area around the cathedral led burgers to launch a heavy three-day attack on the religious complex, in which they set fires and caused immense damage to ecclesiastical buildings and their contents.[382]

A cathedral's topographical position in a city, sometimes within the ancient Gallo-Roman walls of the *civitas*, combined with its bishop and chapter's rights of immunity within the cathedral precinct, could likewise lead to lengthy legal and economic conflicts with the city,[383] in which the cathedral was sometimes the clear loser. In Narbonne, the consuls' refusal between 1349 and 1354 to tear through the town wall in order to make room for the cathedral nave led to legal proceedings and the result that the nave was never built at all.[384]

Even where the city or civic administration showed obvious concern for the cathedral's interests, it did not necessarily follow that the city also provided financial support. In 1521 the city administrators of Burgos backed the bishop's wish, against the interests of the chapter, to move the choir stalls in order that the faithful, '*los legos*', could have a better view of the altar – without, however, offering to alleviate the costs.[385] A famous case concerns events ensuing from a 1521 plan to erect a transept for the daily choir offices and *capilla real* in the middle of Córdoba's old mosque, which had served as the cathedral since 1239. The bishop insisted on a central location rather than a hidden corner in the mosque's vast forest of columns, to which the chapter assented in half-hearted support. But the city council was adamantly against wrecking the old mosque: it was '*unico en el mundo*', and moreover the plan would damage old graves and chapels of eminent city residents. On 4 May 1523 the council issued an ordinance – proclaimed throughout the city – prohibiting building labourers from signing contracts to demolish any part of the old edifice, on pain of death. The bishop countered on 8 May with a threat to excommunicate any party – read: the civic administrators – who resisted the building plans. The case was submitted to Emperor Charles V, who declared himself unable to block the construction, though he later expressed his deep regret over the entire affair.[386]

It could also happen that a city claimed a share of the alms that the faithful brought to the relics. The consuls who led civic administrations in southern France viewed themselves as the owners of such holy relics – the true guardians of the city after all – a view that led to a clash with the chapter of the cathedral of Lavaur in 1491.[387] In Trier the city laid and held claim to the key to the most important relics from the fifteenth century, and in 1512 demanded one-third of the alms collected on days that the Holy Robe of Christ was displayed, as well as reimbursement for two-thirds of the city's expenditures towards security and supervision during that time.[388]

In regions north of the Alps, where cathedral administration was in the hands of the chapter, any kind of consistent civic monetary support for the cathedral fabric was an exception to the rule. Typical here was the attitude taken by the consuls of the *cité* of Rodez. Having been invited by the chapter to join other benefactors in donating a sum of money for a new nave pillar, they first deliberated at great length before finally assenting, with the caveat that their – small – gift of 50 l.rod. implied no promise for the future. And when the first stone of that pillar was laid on 20 September 1466, in a ceremony adorned with a procession and music, some consuls did not even bother to attend.[389]

Now and again we do find instances of cooperation between chapter and city. In 1457 the chapter of Sens was able to elicit the civic administration's interest in the preservation of its neglected cathedral; in a joint letter they appealed – unsuccessfully – to the king for financial support.[390] In Troyes, the rolls contain various entries for contributions of 30 l.t. or 40 l.t. from '*les habitants de la ville de Troyes*',[391] and on a handful of occasions the civic administration itself subsidized the building: in 1496 with 120 l.t. and in 1298 with 80 l.t. for the nave.[392] In Tortosa, the chapter and city agreed to join forces in 1439 in order to facilitate rapid completion of the chevet, sharing in both the costs and financial management.[393] The cities of Meaux and Châlons-en-Champagne likewise donated sums for the works from time to time.[394] In 1511 the civic authorities in Huesca decided to assist the '*Obra de la*

Seu', on the condition that the bishop would also contribute towards the nave vault.[395]

Far more common was for cities to fund the construction of towers and belfries, which were generally used for purely profane, civic purposes. Such was the case in Troyes in 1412/13 and subsequent years. In Sens the city donated bell metal in 1377/78,[396] and during the reconstruction of the large south tower in 1533 made a grant of 300 l.t.; this latter project seems to have been a joint endeavour of the chapter and city.[397] Construction of the tower at Rouen likewise prompted a small gift of 30 l.t. from the civic administration.[398] In Lausanne, the prince-bishop led the way for the installation of a time clock in the cathedral tower '*pro bono statu*' of the Church and city, levying a tax on both quarters of the city to contribute to the cost of its purchase.[399]

Even where the city had a vested interest in the construction of a tower, this by no means implied a willingness to provide funds. When in 1524 the chapter of Konstanz proved unable to complete the tower planned and formally agreed to house the civic alarm-bell and guard-house, the city reminded the chapter of its obligation and even demanded that the project be accelerated, though without granting any financial assistance.[400]

As might be expected, the situation was entirely different in Italian cities. For our purposes it is enough to consider the single example of Florence, which provides a good illustration of the state of affairs in general. The city of Florence and its citizens saw the construction of the *duomo* as a matter that concerned the entire *Comune*, a '[...] *concetto* [...] *composto dell'animo di piu cittadini uniti insieme in un sol volere*'.[401] We have already seen that civic subsidies determined the actual pace of building here,[402] evident in periods when civic funding dried up in the wake of political shifts (1303-1318 and 1323-1330): '*opus* [...] *ecclesie Florentine* [...] *lente processit, immo quasi derelictum est propter deffectum pecuniae*' (work on the cathedral of Florence progressed slowly; it even appeared to have ceased due to lack of money).[403] From the civic vantage point, the cathedral was but one of a multitude of building projects and so, in typical fashion, funds for erecting both the city walls and the *duomo* came in part from the same civic revenues.[404] The city subsidized the *Opera del Duomo*, as the fabric was called, in myriad ways – initially through the sporadic allocation of monies,[405] but progressing towards a system of more routine contributions as time went on. As a speedy measure for gathering necessary funds, the city levied a two-year tax of a small percentage (between one-quarter and one percent) on citizens' property holdings, calculated according to set rules.[406] Shortly before, in August 1418, the civic authorities had already decided to tax all payments made from the city treasury by 1.66 percent (4 d. per lire) to support the cathedral works.[407] Starting in 1318 and extending over the next ten years, the cathedral benefitted from the proceeds of inquisition monies, of which the *Comune* could collect a one-third share.[408] After the administration of the *Opera* devolved onto the *Arte della Lana* in 1331, and as the century progressed, contributions from the *Comune* gradually came to follow a pattern. Funds entered the *Opera* via three avenues: from the direct allocation of certain revenues of the *Comune*, such as a percentage of the rent on all taxes, known as the *gabella di Santa Maria del Fiore*; from statutory contributions, such as the tax on wills or on certain penalties; and finally from the allocation of one particular endowment, comprising the usufruct of the forests of the Cornuolo mountains, in perpetuity.[409] Contributions were subject to constant change as funds dispensed by the city were adjusted to meet the requirements of the building campaign. For example, the costs of vault construction in 1364 prompted the city to temporarily double all percentages.[410]

Yet civic management and strong civic financial support was a double-edged sword. Not only was there constant haggling over the subsidies during hard times but, as happened in Strasbourg, the city drew from the *Opera* during such periods in its turn: unexpended cash and credit balances disappeared '*in capsam* [...] *Comunis*' (into the city treasury) or were spent on other construction projects, such as the Loggia degli Lanzi.[411]

Though the Florentine *Opera* tapped sources also favoured by cathedral churches elsewhere (diocesan collections, alms for the relics of the patron saint),[412] the receipts over the long term amount to little when weighed against the financial support given by the city.[413] In its conspicuously one-sided dependence on the civic administration and civic financing for its construction, the *duomo* of Florence much resembles cathedrals in other Italian cities, albeit with considerable differences in organization and efficiency.[414]

SEVEN CONTRIBUTIONS FROM ECCLESIASTICAL PROPERTY AND FISCAL SOURCES IN THE BISHOPRIC

The cathedral was the '*primitiva mater et domina omnium ecclesiarum*' (first mother and mistress of all churches) in the diocese.[415] We do well to remember that this appellation was not merely a mystical turn of phrase but also and especially a designation bearing canonical significance and consequences: the cathedral had privileges over other churches in the bishopric, of which it could furthermore make systematic use to raise funds for the building works.

Contributions generated from within, and sometimes even far beyond, the bishopric can be divided into two groups: those deriving from religious property and those made by the faithful. It is to the first type that we shall turn in the section below.

Where the religious property of the bishopric is concerned, there were three categories of income to which the cathedral fabric might have access for longer or short periods: first are the fruits of benefices incorporated into the fabric, second the *annualia*, and third the tithes (*decimae*) and first fruits of the harvest (*primitiae*) to which parish church fabrics had claim. All are indirect revenues, existing independent of and bearing no relation whatsoever to the cathedral works. Of primary interest here are the basis and conditions on which these revenues were permitted to bypass a host of other possible beneficiaries and, for a brief or extended period of time, were allocated to the cathedral. Usually this required a decree from the bishop and chapter, and sometimes also confirmation from the pope. In accruing to the works of the first church of the diocese, these revenues were by definition being diverted from their true designation. In areas where the king had acquired rights to such ecclesiastical income, as in Spain and Sweden, his cooperation was also a requisite.

As the continuity of the cathedral fabric was anchored in income from Church property, its prosperity depended on the scale and wealth of those holdings. And since these profits came by and large from agrarian activity, it is sometimes said that '*les cathédrales naquirent* [...] *de la prospérité des campagnes*' or '*sont le fruit des moissons*'.[416] As the discussion that follows will show, such axiomatic sayings have little absolute value.

1 • BENEFICES INCORPORATED INTO THE CATHEDRAL FABRIC

Incorporation has already been discussed as a legal measure available to the chapter: in exceptional circumstances, and only provided papal permission was forthcoming, a canon's prebend could be incorporated into the cathedral fabric. In general, incorporation comprised the sustained (or sometimes temporary) ecclesiastically sanctioned integration of a benefice – almost invariably a priesthood – within a Church institution.[417] There were two different contexts in which incorporation could take place.[418] The first was the mass movement in certain regions towards seeking restitution of ecclesiastical properties still held in lay possession, in direct contravention of canonical prohibitions, particularly as formulated in the second and third Lateran Councils of 1139 and 1179, respectively.[419] Monasteries reaped the greatest benefit from this reformist movement. In one exceptional case we find a layman granting his church to the bishop and chapter with express instructions to use the profits for cathedral construction and furnishings: in York at some point before 1173, the Baron William Percy II donated the church of Topcliffe, which was his by right, to the archbishop and chapter for this specific purpose. The receipts were considerable, amounting to around £90 (some 25 annual wages) in the fifteenth century, and representing a quarter of the fabric's total income.[420]

Alternatively, a Church authority could intervene to incorporate a benefice[421] – in most cases the property and other income entitlements attached to a priesthood – whereby these goods and their administration were permanently subsumed within a given Church body. Here the motive was purely financial. Stringent canonical rules and conditions guarded the implementation of this drastic measure.[422] Naturally, the institution that benefitted had to fund the priest's living, and sometimes other ecclesiastical expenses as well, including those of the church building itself. Church authorities required sufficient grounds to justify such incorporations; the institution's *insupportatio onerum* (incapacity to fulfil obligations) was one such.[423] Understandably (since the benefice might still draw income from pastoral goods), the right of patronage had to rest with the institution or persons that had effected the incorporation.[424]

The right of incorporation fell within the bishop's jurisdiction; as an eternal right, however, it was conditional on the chapter's consent.[425] Permission from the pope was initially only needed for the incorporation in an episcopal or capitular *mensae*,[426] but explicitly not when it concerned the cathedral fabric.[427] But in fact, the late medieval popes managed quite successfully to pre-empt this episcopal authority. Parish churches were incorporated on a huge scale to benefit monasteries and bishops' and chapters' *mensae*. Whilst incorporation in a cathedral fabric with an express designation of the profits for the building works was by no means rare – some 20 cases are known – their share in the overall number of actual incorporations is trivial. A glance through the papal registers shows that Clement V (1305-1314), for example, admitted 82 incorporations, but not one for a cathedral fabric,[428] whilst of the 281 instances in which John XXII (1316-1334) gave his consent for incorporation, 145 concerned monasteries and another 81 episcopal *mensae*,[429] but again not one the construction or upkeep of a cathedral.[430]

We find scattered examples of parishes being incorporated into cathedral fabrics from the thirteenth century onwards:[431] in Exeter, Canterbury, Agde, Rodez, Narbonne, Quimper, Béziers and Limoges in the thirteenth century,[432] in Hereford, Würzburg, Wells, Salisbury, Münster, Cambrai, Speyer and Angers in the fourteenth century,[433] in Canterbury, Magdeburg, Rodez, Uzès, Vannes and Nevers in the fifteenth century,[434] and in Metz in the sixteenth century.[435] Such annexed churches were usually collated by the bishop or chapter. Deeds issued by the pope or bishop sometimes disclose their motivation in enacting the incorporation. For example, in Magdeburg the fabric's regular income was so little that not only could new building not continue, the existing structure likewise stood in a state of disrepair. The incorporation of two churches in the fabric of Rodez was justified '*propter fructuum et reddituum* [...] *fabrice* [...] *diminutionem eorumque carentiam, necnon raram Christi fidelium elargationem*' (on account of the diminution of the profits and revenues of the fabric, on account of the cessation thereof and also on account of the scant increase in the number of the faithful). Moreover, here, as in Nevers, the Hundred Years' War had made completing the cathedral impossible. We know that the bishop of Würzburg broached the matter of the fabric's lack of a permanent income, but we do not know the outcome. Unlike some hospitals and universities, church fabrics were never simply given the profits of incorporated churches. The gains could be very limited, as in Uzès where, at no more than 10 l.t., they represented just four month's wages. In Hereford the cathedral parish yielded £20 for the fabric in 1290, amounting to almost nine annual salaries, whilst in 1415 a church subsumed within the fabric of York Minster in 1377 '*propter maliciam temporum*' (owing to the ill times) provided £27, or five percent of its income and over six years' wages. By contrast, the incorporation of two churches by the fabric of Rodez Cathedral in 1427, described in the associated petition (*supplicatorium*) to the pope as '*quasi ad medium constructa*' (almost half built), was very much intended to stimulate building operations, generating an estimated 278 l.t. Two fabric rolls over the years 1507/08 and 1509/10 reveal that the three incorporated priories yielded net profits of 622 l.t. and 570 l.t., respectively, or 57 and 54 percent of the net income.[436]

Nevertheless, this notable source of income, requiring no major sacrifices for anyone connected with the cathedral works – except in instances where the bishop or chapter donated a church previously incorporated into their own *mensae* – was clearly of secondary significance. Like the incorporation of canons' prebends discussed above, the incorporation of a church was typically prompted by the imperative of supplementing the fixed income of a cathedral fabric in dire straits.

2 • THE ANNUALIA: PROFITS FROM VACANT BENEFICES

In contrast to the proceeds from incorporated benefices, those obtained from diocesan benefices over the first year after being vacated can more properly be classified as income for the works. Several aspects of this income source, too, have already been noted above.[437] In Beauvais (1225), Narbonne (1267) and Albi (1277), the allocation of the *annualia* formed part of a constellation of temporary financial measures that the bishop and chapter established jointly when launching their building campaign. From the early fourteenth century, as we have seen, the pope began to claim exclusive rights to this key income source.[438] There was also a further special type of *annualia*, the *prebende defunctorum* (prebends of the deceased), which chapters regularly began assigning to the cathedral fabric in the late twelfth century.

A distinction must be made between profits from the period in which a benefice was actually vacant and that in which the new beneficiary had taken up the duties of his office but still had to forgo his salary. The terminological distinctions can be slippery here: the first category of income was called the *fructus intercalares* or *fructus medii temporis* (intermediary profits), whilst the second, when they were annual profits, were known as the *fructus primi anni* (profits over the first year)[439] or *annualia*, and when semi-annual as the *medii fructus* (profits over the first half-year), or annates in the proper sense.[440]

Only in exceptional cases were the *fructus intercalares* of episcopal benefices invested in the cathedral works. The only example we know of concerns Bishop Reginald of Wells (1187-1191), who temporarily granted such revenues to the cathedral '*in usus operationis* [...] *donec per dei miserantis auxilium consummetur*' (for the construction of the cathedral until, with God's compassionate aid, it is finished).[441] These monies, like the annates, were to devolve to the pope from the beginning of the fourteenth century until at least the Council of Konstanz (1416).[442]

The *annualia* represented a more common income source for the cathedral works: we know of at least 50 cathedrals that enjoyed these revenues between the thirteenth and sixteenth centuries, albeit usually over a short period only.[443] Later canonists even considered this to be the normal state of things,[444] though in reality it was not. Allocations of diocesan *annualia* to the works were as infrequent as the incorporation of parish churches in the cathedral fabric; the number of papal allocations for other purposes far exceeded those for cathedral building works, also in the period in which the pope enjoyed exclusive rights.[445] In some instances, the cathedral's dismal financial situation was advanced as a legitimate justification. In Tournai, for example, revenues held by the fabric were so meagre in 1360 that even a hundred times the amount would have been insufficient to repair the building.[446]

Highly diverse stipulations could be attached to the *annualia* assigned to cathedral fabrics. The most common restrictions concerned, first, the number of years for which the right to raise the *annualia* was granted; second, the nature of the benefice at issue; and third, the share of the profit to be taken for one or more years after the vacancy arose. We can trace the widely diverging financial significance of the *annualia* to precisely these restrictions.

The very comprehensive and extended privilege that Pope Clement (1305-1314) conferred on the cathedral of Bordeaux in 1307, namely, the profits of all diocesan benefices for a year after their vacancy for a term of 20 years, has already been cited as a unique example of personal papal interest in a cathedral.[447] On the whole, where such documents state a term, it tends to be shorter – ranging from two to ten years – though a great many bishops and chapters contrived to get the terms renewed. Some cathedrals even enjoyed the *annualia* over several centuries. From 1277 until well into the sixteenth century, the cathedral fabric of Rodez collected the half-year's profits of all benefices in the collation of the bishop and chapter.[448] In Narbonne, the fabric's right to draw the half-year's profits of all vacant benefices (with the exception of those collated by exempt Church institutions) was continuously renewed from 1267 onwards and fixed '*in perpetuum*' by official papal privilege in 1498. Over time these receipts could come to be regarded as part of a fabric's regular fixed income, and not directly connected with a particular building campaign.[449] The volume of the *annualia* grew considerably in the period around 1350 as the result of a surge in vacancies after the Black Death.[450]

Questions regarding which benefices the *annualia* could be raised over were closely linked with that concerning which Church body was authorized to extend this right. The bishop and chapter required papal permission for any allocation beyond that of the *annualia* of benefices in their collation. One of the first cases (earning it a place in the *Corpus Iuris Canonici*) in which a pope permitted a bishop – presumably at the latter's request – to take the profits of all diocesan benefices was in Toul; in 1223 the bishop was granted this right for a three-year term in order to pay off the bishopric's debts.[451] On 11 November 1225 Bishop Milon of Beauvais likewise requested the requisite papal confirmation (which he received) after having decided with the chapter several days previously to assign all diocesan *annualia* to the building works for a period of ten years.[452] Such precedents failed to set a common standard, however, and questions of competence remained. The bishop of Quimper stated explicitly in 1239 that he would restrict himself to benefices in his collation and therefore did not seek confirmation from the pope, whilst the bishop and chapter of Geneva did the same in 1245 yet felt compelled to secure papal approbation. Generally speaking, however, the thirteenth century saw the pope successfully expand his authority over the *annualia*. In Narbonne we find a clear illustration of this, where the archbishop and chapter resolved to supplement gifts from their own *mensae* with the full annual profits of the *annualia* in order to fund construction; the pope subsequently ordered the supplement reduced to a half-year's share. This brings us to the third restriction: the share of the profits allowed to be drawn from the benefice over – usually – the first year after its release. Here, an important factor in the pope's final decision was the notion that a new beneficiary should be allowed at least some part of his salary to prevent absenteeism and neglect of duties, as well as the tacit knowledge that this would enhance a benefice's appeal for new candidates, who were often nominated and appointed by the pope himself. Accordingly, the 1317 papal decree *Suscepti Regiminis* (included in the *Corpus Iuris Canonici*) set down rules to this effect;[453] from that moment onwards the levy nearly always represented one-half of the annual profits.

By the early fourteenth century, increasing papal reservations were beginning to detract from the real value of the *annualia* for the building works. Occasionally, popes granted the privilege, but then with an emphatic reiteration of their papal rights, such as in Sarlat in 1365. Here the customary phrasing read – to cite a random example (from Châlons-en-Champagne in 1285) – 'that we, the pope, by virtue of our apostolic authority grant to you permission to collect the first year's profits, revenues and gains from all prebends and other ecclesiastical benefices at your [= the dean and chapter] disposal, such as shall be vacated during a period lasting from one to five years in the city and diocese of Châlons-en-Champagne, and we allow that you should use these to build the choir'.[454] As we have already seen, however, once this privilege had been granted by the bishop, and possibly confirmed by the pope, various chapters in Spain and southern France managed to secure its renewal year after year.

The dearth of extant account rolls from this period make it difficult to provide an indication of the scale of these profits. We know that in Rodez the receipts for the 1293/94 financial year included '*medietas redditum ecclesiarum vacantium*' (half of the revenues of vacant churches), comprising approximately 20 percent of its income.[455] By the sixteenth century the fabric's share had dwindled to one-quarter, which nonetheless yielded 232 l.t. in 1507/08 and 186 l.t. in 1509/10, or 20 and 17.5 percent of its respective incomes in those years.[456] In Gerona, receipts from the annates '*quod est medium beneficii*' (this being half of the benefice) were variable, generating a mere 655 s., or four percent of its net income, in 1369/70; 2524 s., or 15 percent, in 1370/71; and 2226 s., or 16 percent, in 1375/76.[457] The annates dominated the small budget of Elne Cathedral during periods in which the works were inactive, making up over 45 percent of its income in 1415, 75 percent in 1416 and as much as 90 percent 1441 and 1448.[458] In Autun, by contrast, the account for 1294 relates that '*recepta beneficiorum vacancium in civitate et dyocesi Eduensi, auctoritate apostolica fabrice [...] convertenda*' (the revenues from benefices that are vacant in the city and the diocese of Autun and which the Holy See has confirmed may be spent for the cathedral fabric) contributed only 12.5 l.t., or just over three percent of the income.[459] The annates raised in Palma de Mallorca in 1393/94 and 1397/98 represented one-third and one-sixth of the total income for those years, respectively, though in fact this amounted to 1260 llivres (around 35 annual wages) in the first year, dropping to 957 llivres (around 25 annual wages) in the second.[460] A 1387 account for the Halberstadt fabric reveals that a mere eleven parishes rendered their *annualia*.[461]

The task of collecting these monies was hardly a sinecure. In order to stem fraud and evasion, the diocesan synod of Barcelona determined in 1354 that episcopal notaries and anyone charged with collating benefices were obligated to notify the cathedral *operarii* of each and every new vacancy within two weeks, on penalty of excommunication and a monetary fine.[462] In 1338 Huesca's fabric administrators set out for two months in summer to collect the proceeds of vacant clerical benefices, armed with official documents and powers of excommunication; they found themselves confronted with parish priests who were absent and priests who had gone into hiding or, in some cases, who refused outright on principle.[463]

There is one question that has yet to be answered: from whom had these revenues ultimately devolved? Cases where a fabric's *annualia* came at the direct expense of papal reservations may appropriately be deemed donations from the pope. Yet in doing so we must remember that it was ultimately the new benefice-holder who was forced to forgo the fruits attached to his ecclesiastical office in favour of some recipient or other, even if we can safely assume that he would have cared little whether that money ended up with the papal court, the bishop and chapter, or the cathedral fabric. After the Council of Trent, canonists rightly held that the *annualia* were in fact contributions from the diocesan clergy for the building works; after all they, second only to the bishop and chapter, bore the '*onus fabrice*' (burden of the fabric) of the cathedral. A handful of medieval deeds express similar ideas, calling it the duty of the diocesan church to support the mother church.[464] Defending the designation of the *annualia* for the reconstruction of his cathedral in 1268, the bishop of Meaux argued 'that the daughters, moved by compassion, must salve with wine and oil the wounds of the much distressed mother'.

3 • INCOME FROM THE CHURCH'S FISCAL SOURCES: THE TITHES

Spain and Scandinavia were the only countries in which the cathedral works occasionally shared in the receipts of the Church's fiscal levies – the tithe (in all its shapes and sizes) – and other Church taxes,[465] which in some cases formed far and away the most important source of income for the cathedral fabric in these countries.

In Spain, as previously mentioned, provisions adopted in the early sixth- to late seventh-century provincial councils (Toledo 693) had put in place specific legislation under which the diocesan estate, once controlled as a single entity, was split into three shares. Later this division would also be applied to the tithes, which were slowly but steadily introduced into the Christian part of Spain and territories captured from the Moors from the end of the eleventh century and established as a compulsory ecclesiastical levy of one-tenth of the harvest.[466] One share was destined for the bishop's and chapter's *mensae*, another for the episcopal parish clergy, and the last for the diocesan church fabrics, the '*tercias fabricae*'. In exchange for partaking of this income, the bishop accepted responsibility for keeping all parish churches in his diocese in good repair; with this condition met, he could use what balance remained as he saw fit.

In nowhere less than Castile we find that for decades, and even centuries, a portion – admittedly small – of this vast income source, by far the most important in the Church's arsenal, was allocated to cathedrals. To understand how this came to be, we must look to the recapture of Spain from the Moors. The Reconquista represented the single most important mandate to be issued jointly by the pope, bishops and kings of Spain.[467] For centuries the Reconquista legitimized ecclesiastical measures of every kind,[468] including the construction of cathedrals, often on the site of a demolished mosque. In the thirteenth-century law book *Las Partidas*, we read that, 'The kings of Spain deserve glory; they turn mezquitas into churches, cast out the name of Mohammed and replace it with the name of Jesus Christ'.[469]

It was against this background that efforts were made to achieve a substantial measure of centralization in administering the vast tithal revenues. Pope, bishops and king jockeyed for control of the income sources in an ever-shifting balance of power, with kings lending support for the enforcement of the church levy, whilst at the same time demanding certain revenues from the bishops.

In some cases the tithes accrued to the cathedral building works. In 1194 the king and the archbishop of Toledo gave the bishop of Cuenca – an area taken from the Moors in 1177 – permission to lay claim to a portion of the tithes and spend this on building the cathedral.[470] In 1222, five years before the first stone of the cathedral at Toledo was laid, the archbishop obtained the pope's approval to take the third share of all tithes intended for the parish churches for a term of five years and invest them in the cathedral fabric, thus depriving the maintenance funds of other archdiocesan churches. Plans to make the future cathedral of Toledo the first church of Spain seem to have lent it a unique status as the visible symbol of the Spanish victory over the Moors, for which even the interests of all the countless parish churches were no match.[471]

The Reconquista legitimated diverting Church revenues from the ends for which they had originally been conceived. In 1219 the Spanish bishops first gained permission from Rome to spend a portion of the fabric tithes due them over a certain period on a crusade against the Moors, though they could also use this money to relieve their bishoprics of debt.[472] Shortly thereafter, in a deed of 15 April 1247, Pope Innocent IV first ceded the illustrious *tercias reales* ('the third portion for the Crown') to the king of Castile, albeit for a limited period, in order to fund the imminent recapture of Seville; this consisted of a one-third portion of two of the three tithe designations, namely, that for the clergy and that for the fabrics, and thus a two-ninths' share, '*dos novenos*', or more than 22 percent of all the tithe monies.[473] From that point, the Crown possessed the privilege, unique in Europe, of almost uninterrupted control over this key Church revenue source. As a gesture of thanks for the conquest of Granada in 1492 – the final act of the Reconquista – Pope Alexander VI established this concession in perpetuity, though in fact the *tercias reales* had long since shed any relation with the struggle against the Moors.[474]

Initially, this concentration of Church income in the hands of the king had a negative impact on ecclesiastical building activities in various bishoprics, since the *tercias* ostensibly intended for parish church fabrics now partially accrued to the Crown instead. By the second half of the thirteenth century, ecclesiastical building, including cathedral-building, had stagnated as a result.[475] Yet the king could also join hands with the pope to confer this source of income on a cathedral fabric in turn. In 1255, for example, the fabric at León acquired the fabric tithes from a number of parishes through allocation by the pope, who was friends with the king.[476] However, in 1303 the bishop restored control of certain of the cathedral fabric's tithes back to the chapter as '*la obra está en bon estado, merced a Dios*'.[477]

It is no longer always possible to trace the avenues by which individual cathedral fabrics gained access to income from various tithes. Nor is it clear whether tithes assigned to the cathedral had their origins in the traditional one-third share of the tithes designated for the upkeep of diocesan churches. In a few dioceses, such as Santiago de Compostela,[478] Huesca[479] and Pamplona,[480] the cathedral works benefitted from a different tithe – the *primitiae*[481] – drawn from the parish churches. In Huesca this assignment was complicated by the fact that both the bishop and the pope had jurisdiction over a portion of the *primitiae* and both, on 28 and 29 November 1273, respectively, ceded the *primitiae* due them to the building works for a term of five years. In 1399 the bishop once again allotted the *primitiae* to the fabric, this time for the roof and construction of a new cloister. At the beginning of the fifteenth century, Huesca's fabric administrators took to the roads with a donkey, stopping to collect the annual tithe in every village with more than ten hearths. According to the fabric rolls for the first half of that century, the *primitiae* comprised the largest share of the fabric's income there, around 60 percent, yet amounting to no more than five or six annual wages of one *peón* (day labourer).[482]

The collection of the tithes could pose major problems for the fabric. Sometimes tithes were portioned off and farmed out to the highest bidder – often a canon, as in León.[483] In 1409 the cathedral of Zaragoza received the '*gratia quinti decimarii*', the fourth most valuable tithes from villages with more than nineteen hearths, for the duration of the building campaign. Yet in the first collection year, the costs of visiting 355 parishes in four archpresbyterys exceeded the gains, in part because many parishes refused to pay on legal grounds.[484] In the bishopric of Murcia, the pope's and bishop's designation of tithes to pay for the cathedral's construction triggered protests in a neighbouring city, whose own walls and towers were in a state of deterioration.[485] Where parishes remained stubborn and unwilling to cooperate, they could expect to face lawsuits.[486] In the small and secluded bishopric of Mondoñedo, local clergy were actually prohibited from speaking, drinking, eating or even greeting (*salve*) parishioners who took or concealed property belonging to the fabric. Repeat recalcitrants were made to stand with candle in hand as the parish priest uttered a ritual curse over each of the 366 bones in his body; like the burning candle submersed in holy water, so too would the soul of any person who was publically excommunicated perish in the flames of hell.[487]

A special type of tithe that proved exceptionally important for the cathedral fabric's income in the late Middle Ages was that collected from the richest household in the parish, the *casa excusada*.[488] This tithe was expressly designated for the cathedral fabric, first in the fourteenth century in the bishopric of Baez-Jaeca (a diocese with two cathedrals), followed in the fifteenth by those of Toledo, León, Malaga, Granada and Seville.[489] It is during the latter period that we can begin to gain some insight into the significance of this source of income. Between 1418 and 1448 the *excusados* was the second most profitable tithe in the whole of the bishopric of Toledo, supplying 90 percent of the fabric's income at a yearly average of 170 annual wages of a *peón*.[490] Around 1500 the receipts from Seville Cathedral's ecclesiastical rents reached a staggering sum of between 1.6 and 1.85 million *maravedís*, worth 350-410 annual wages of a *peón*; in 1511 and 1515 the *excusados* contributed 39 percent of its income.[491] In Murcia the *diezmos* (tithes) collected in 1522 provided nearly 40 percent and in 1545 nearly 90 percent of the fabric's income.[492] For many cathedral fabrics, tithal receipts formed far and away the most important source of revenue. We have no explanation for why a large number of cathedrals was able to access this income flow whilst others were not; it may be that those situated in regions which had been caught up in lengthy struggles against the Moors had an advantage.[493] In certain bishoprics all the constituent parishes were furthermore made subject to a tax, first in kind and later also in coin, to fund the construction of the cathedral, their mother church.[494]

The so-called *Voto de Santiago* occupies a category of its own.[495] A tax in grain, it was imposed on all farmers throughout Spain – again, in principle. As a rule, the receipts were apportioned in one-third shares to the chapter, the archbishop of Santiago and the cathedral fabric (and later also the hospital). The history of this tax similarly typifies the Reconquista ideology, as well as the attempts to promote St James as the patron saint of Spain and Santiago as the principal seat of the Church in Spain. The basis for these efforts lay in a mid-twelfth century capitular charter (later proven a forgery) purporting that during the Battle of Clavijo against the Moors in 834, St James, the '*hispanorum protector*', had appeared to the king and promised him victory in exchange for the latter's pledge to impose an eternal tax on all remaining Moors in the conquered territories, with the proceeds going to St James. The levy thus comprised an ecclesiastical tax under royal protection and was in fact a gift from the king to the church of St James. From 1492 the pope allowed the king to levy the tax in the newly captured territory of Granada as well. However, in practice the tax proved difficult to enforce: in many bishoprics the collections were boycotted, so that at one point only 65 percent of Spanish territories actually paid it.[496] Even so, the *Voto de Santiago* was amongst the most important of the ecclesiastical taxes. Though we know next to nothing about the extent of the receipts at any time from the end of the twelfth century onwards, nor about the share that was actually reserved for the cathedral building works,[497] it was a privilege that was indisputably of immense financial value over the centuries – until 1834, when the tax was finally retired – for the clergy, cathedral and hospital of Santiago, the wealthiest of all bishoprics in Spain.[498]

In Scandinavian lands the tithes could also be used to benefit cathedral building works. And here, too, they formed the most important ecclesiastical income source by far. From the twelfth century their division was guided by a rule of four shares, with one each for the bishop, parish priest, parish church and poor, though in Sweden parish priests drew a third and the other parties two-ninths each.[499] Within a system of administration that, as in Spain, was more highly centralized than elsewhere in Europe, kings and bishops competed with each other to gain the greatest possible authority. In Sweden, Norway and Finland, a portion of the shares for the provincial churches and, less often, for the poor, occasionally went to fund cathedral construction.[500]

The cathedral of Linköping presents a typical case in point and says a great deal about mutual balances of secular and religious power in Sweden.[501] Responding to an entreaty from the bishop in 1245, the pope enjoined clerics (confirmed by the papal legate two years later) to give a tenth part of their parish fabric *decimae* to the cathedral building works and also to stimulate their flock to contribute: since all churches in the diocese '*sunt edificate ad plenum*' (are completely finished), it fell to the sons to come to their father's aid.[502] In 1280, again moved by an episcopal petition, it was this time the king who laid a claim – far heavier – on the parish church tithes; not one-tenth, but fully half, or five times the former amount, was to be rendered for the cathedral works. Realizing that a unilateral decree would fail to garner support, the king found himself compelled to consult a council of prominent men, possibly including parochial representatives, to justify the unpopular order. The special levy was renewed once, and thus applied for a total of sixteen years.[503]

In 1321 the king confirmed the mandates issued by the pope and his 1247 legate for the full term of the building campaign, namely, for six years. His one-sided decision appears to have met with resistance. In 1328 the bishop had to assemble a council of spiritual and secular leaders (including pre-eminent canons) whose task it was to establish when the cathedral would actually be '*perfectam et omnino completam*' (finished and wholly complete).[504] Ultimately, it was the bishop who prevailed: in 1337 the tithes were assigned to the cathedral fabric – with the king's approval – in perpetuity.[505]

Bit by bit, the cathedral fabric in Linköping (and elsewhere[506]) gained access not only to the tithes intended for the parish churches but also to those reserved for the poor; from 1410 onwards one-third of the entire bishopric's portion for the poor was allocated to the construction of the chapel in which obits for benefactors were read, amounting to around 7.5 percent of the total receipts from all tithes.[507]

It has rightly been noted that the faithful saw the cathedral of Linköping as an eternal devourer of tithes that by rights belonged to the poor and the parish churches.[508]

The last ecclesiastical tax that deserves mention here is the *Votum Olavi* or *Olafsskat*, which began as a votive offering at the grave of King Olav (1015-1030), the national saint of Norway, in the cathedral of Nidaros/Drontheim, but evolved into a tax in kind levied by the Norse archbishop. Since the pilgrimage route to this saint's resting place also took in Sweden, the bishop of Uppsala was able to impose the same tax in the northern provinces of his diocese. In Norway, two-thirds of the receipts accrued to the fund of the Drontheim fabric, whilst in Sweden the same share paid for the maintenance of a chapel dedicated to Sts Olav and Erik (the latter being the Swedish national saint; d. 1160) in Uppsala Cathedral.[509]

It is hardly a coincidence that only Spain and Scandinavia had the custom of allocating – or, one might say, annexing or usurping – a portion of the tithe proceeds for the construction of cathedrals. The two regions share clear parallels in that both had to be conquered or reconquered for Christianity from non-believers and pagans. It is telling that in 1245 and 1247 Pope Innocent IV granted the kings of Sweden and Spain, respectively, the right to spend one-third of the fabric tithes on campaigns against the heathens, '*contra paganos et barbaros*';[510] clearly, the pope regarded both countries as frontlines in the battle against paganism. Equally remarkable is that both Spain and Norway created an ecclesiastical tax focused around the cults of their national saints. The centralized control exercised by the pope, episcopates and rulers will certainly have been a key factor in this development.

Given the fragmentary quantitative data available, it is difficult to gauge how much real financial significance the tithes had for cathedral fabrics. However, considering their permanent character, the significance of these revenues must have been considerable; certainly this was true for the cathedrals of Toledo and Seville, and probably also for that of Linköping.

In principle, the tithes were an ecclesiastical tax levied by the clergy on parishioners, and as such they represent a form of revenue ultimately stemming from the faithful. Compulsory in nature, these funds were furthermore used for other purposes than those for which they had originally been raised – a practice that occasionally met with resistance, as in Sweden. In the next chapter we will turn to consider contributions from the faithful. Ostensibly, they were freely given, though bishops and chapters sometimes brought moral pressure to bear to stimulate giving.

EIGHT VOLUNTARY CONTRIBUTIONS FROM THE FAITHFUL

In 1325, over three-quarters of a century after launching the cathedral construction campaign in Cologne, the chapter remarked that, given the high cost of building, it absolutely could not go on without the *oblationes* from the high altar, '*quia ipsius sumptus fabrice pro magna sui parte ex Christi fidelium elemosinis et oblationibus proveniunt*' (because expenses for the works are for the main part paid for from the alms and offerings of the faithful).[511] Around 1155 the king of France used similar words in commending the *opus insigne* (distinguished work) of the cathedral of Senlis: '*quod sine caritate fidelium Christi et elemosynis nunquam poterit consummari*' (which can never be completed without the generosity of and alms from the faithful).[512] Even more to the point is the chronicler of Durham's assertion that the pace of construction rose and fell with the magnitude of offerings made, '*circa opus ecclesiae modo intentius modo remissius agebatur, sicut illi ex oblatione altaris et coemeterii vel suppetebat pecunia vel deficiebat*' (as regards the construction of the cathedral, work was carried out with greater or lesser diligence by turns, depending on whether money made in offering at the altar and cemetery were at his [Bishop Ranulphus (1109-1128)] disposal or absent).[513] We may well be given pause to wonder if cathedrals were in fact built by the generosity of the faithful.[514]

If we consider the situation in Chartres after the 1194 fire, the *Liber miraculorum* compiled around 1210 tells us that for three years afterwards the building works depended primarily on contributions from the bishop and chapter, '*verum ad tanti structuram operis laicorum munera vel auxilia nequaquam sufficerent nisi (ut) episcopus et canonici tantam* [...] *ex propriis redditibus tribus annis pecuniam contulissent*' (but gifts and aid from the laity would never have been sufficient to create so large a structure if the bishop and canons had not for three years contributed so much money from their own incomes). When that three-year term ended there was not even enough money left to pay the workers.[515] It was not until the mother of God, whose tunic – a highly venerated relic – was kept behind the high altar, performed a great miracle, followed by many more, that the tide changed.[516] Soon droves of pilgrims came flooding in from far and wide, leaving behind donations for the works.[517] From that moment on, contributions from the faithful outweighed all others. But what really interests us in this example is the fact that an event with no direct bearing on the building works provided the impetus for countless pilgrims to offer their savings for that very purpose. Clearly, it will be necessary for us to explore in greater depth the motives prompting people to give over their earthly belongings to support the creation of cathedrals, particularly in view of the Church authorities' conscious efforts to appeal to precisely these underlying motivators.

To begin with, there was of course the allure of the physical building, or the building plan, which might stimulate contributions. Moralists were fully cognizant of this fact. St Bernard of Clairvaux (1090-1153) described the fascination that the grandeur of a richly appointed church could arouse: '[...] the very sight of these costly but wonderful illusions inflames men more to give than to pray. In this way wealth is derived from wealth, in this way money attracts money [...] Eyes are fixed on relics covered with gold and purses are opened'.[518] In his treatise *Contra turrim Trajectensem* ('Against the tower of Utrecht'), Geert Groote (1340-1384) conjures for us a traveller whose awestruck gaze encounters the cathedral's magnificent tower, spurring him to approach a few of the city's proud citizens to learn the true dimensions of this collosus.[519] Some fabrics endeavoured to stimulate giving by

22
Procession on the occasion of the display of relics in Bamberg, 1509
Pen drawing with colour wash, 440 x 290 mm
Folio from manuscript.
London, British Library
Add. ms. 15689, f. 36r

The *ostensio reliquiarum* was held in Bamberg once every seven years on the anniversary of the cathedral's dedication (6 June). The earliest display is presumed to have taken place in the late fourteenth century; the last was in 1515. In eleven displays 135 relics were presented from a specially constructed platform outside the cathedral church, loudly elucidated by a *vocalissimus* or *Ausschreier*. This was followed by a procession with the reliquary shrine of the emperor-saint Henry II. The manuscript was charged to the care of the cathedral *custos*, who also collected offerings for the fabric.

LITERATURE

Facsimile: Das Bamberger Heiltum von 1508/1509 der British Library London (Add. ms. 15689), ed. Historischer Verein Bamberg 1998; Kühne 2000, pp. 275-292.

setting up a model of the completed church or a drawn or painted representation (*Schaubildriss*) next to the collection box.[520] Bishops never failed to describe the deplorable state to which the cathedral, the mother church of the diocese, had deteriorated after a fire, nor to portray in words the future splendour of the new building. In 1445 the bishop of Lübeck spoke of the enormous scale of the great building campaign there and of the church's soaring towers, battered by blasts of wind and torrents of rain; should support fail to be given, then '*verisimiliter tocius machine celsitudo tenderet in ruinam*' (verily these monumental heights shall fall into complete ruin).[521] In a letter of indulgence dated 1275, the bishop of Strasbourg compares the rising cathedral nave with flowers in the month of May, '[...] *quia opus ecclesie Argentinensis sicut flores maji variis ornatibus consurgens in altum, oculos aspiciensium magis et magis allicit et eisdem dulcibus oblectaminibus alludit*' (because the edifice of the cathedral of Strasbourg, like May flowers that shoot forth in colourful array, increasingly draws the gaze of observers, caressing their eyes with sweet grace) (fig. 24).[522] Certain bishops even entertained the idea that, aside from being marvellous to behold, the sight of a cathedral might actually elicit feelings of devotion.[523]

And yet church-building, to say nothing of cathedral-building, could never in itself fire imaginations and open purses in sufficient measure. It was not without a note of irony that Geert Groote declared never to have met anyone who had donated a large sum to the building works out of the pure fullness of his heart; and what is more, he says, hardly anyone could be brought to do so.[524]

One factor of key significance here is the notion, advanced by most theologians and moralists, that church-building qualified as an *opus pietatis* (a pious work). This presented a different motive for relinquishing money and possessions: after all, if a gift for the building campaign was a good work, then it would yield benefits both in this life and in the afterlife to come.[525] In fact, the early Church fathers, drawing in part on Old Testament texts, had also already maintained that voluntary gifts could wipe out sins and the need for penance. As water extinguishes fire, they said, so alms extinguish sin.[526] Concerns of spiritual salvation were part and parcel of medieval alms-giving, for

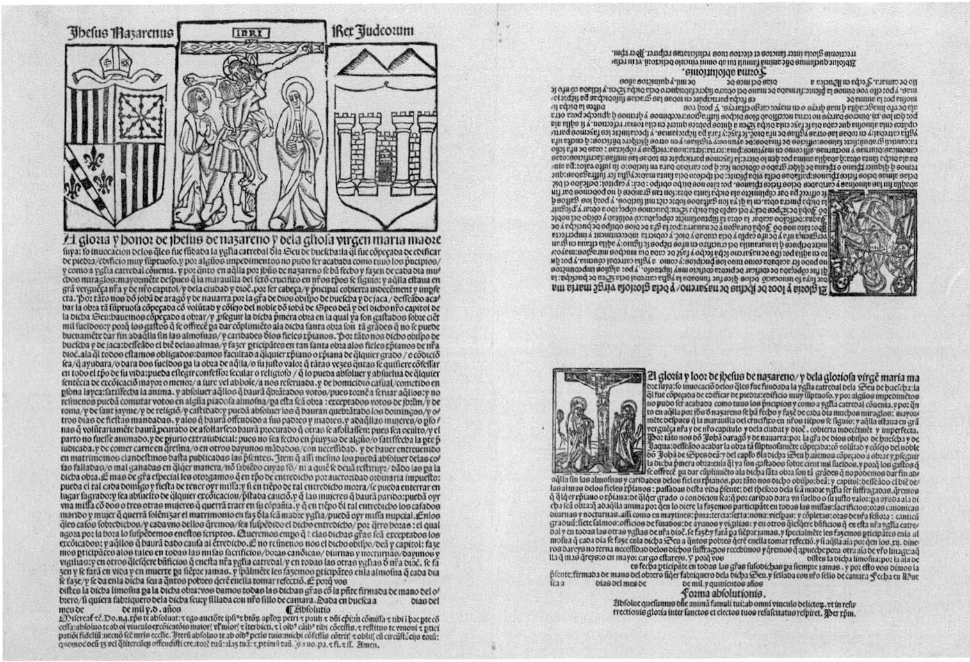

23

Confessional letter, or *confessionale*, and two confraternity letters printed on a single broadside
Broadside incunables, 277 x 167 mm, 108 x 162 mm and 108 x 162 mm, respectively, printed by Georg Coci in Zaragossa, c.1500
Huesca, Archivo de la Catedral

The large leaf records how Bishop Juan de Aragón y Navarra (1484-1526) granted a series of spiritual privileges to all who would give 2 sueldos to the fabric (less than a day's wage for an unskilled building labourer), motivated thereto by the great expense of building the cathedral of Huesca, which had already consumed more than 100,000 sueldos (construction of the vaults began in 1497). Whomever held such a letter would be permitted to choose his or her own confessor, who could then at any time lift certain types of excommunication and release the holder from sins the remission of which was reserved for the bishop. The holder would moreover share in the fruits of the prayers and other good works performed in the cathedral and other churches in the diocese. Blank spaces were provided in which to fill in the name of the donor and the date. The document had to be signed by the master of the fabric. Affixed to the Spanish text is an absolution form in Latin for the confessor's use. The small-format forms grant the holder the right to apply the fruits of the aforementioned good works and prayers to the soul of someone who had died. These forms likewise contain blanks for the names of the donor and the deceased and for the date.

LITERATURE Durán Gudiol 1991, pp. 130-131; F.J. Norton, *A descriptive catalogue of printing in Spain and Portugal 1501-1520*, Cambridge 1978, no. 1296 (confessional letter for the cathedral of Coria, c.1505).

24
Indulgence letter from Bishop Konrad von Lichtenberg of Strasbourg on behalf of cathedral benefactors, 1275
Cartularium Oeuvre Notre-Dame
Strasbourg, Archives de la ville

'Because the edifice of the cathedral of Strasbourg, like May flowers that shoot forth in colourful array, increasingly draws the gaze of observers, caressing their eyes with sweet grace', the bishop grants a 40-day indulgence to all those who caused the large bell to toll in support of the church building works, and a 20-day indulgence to all those who pray for the deceased when they hear the bell toll.

LITERATURE
Doré 2007, p. 157.

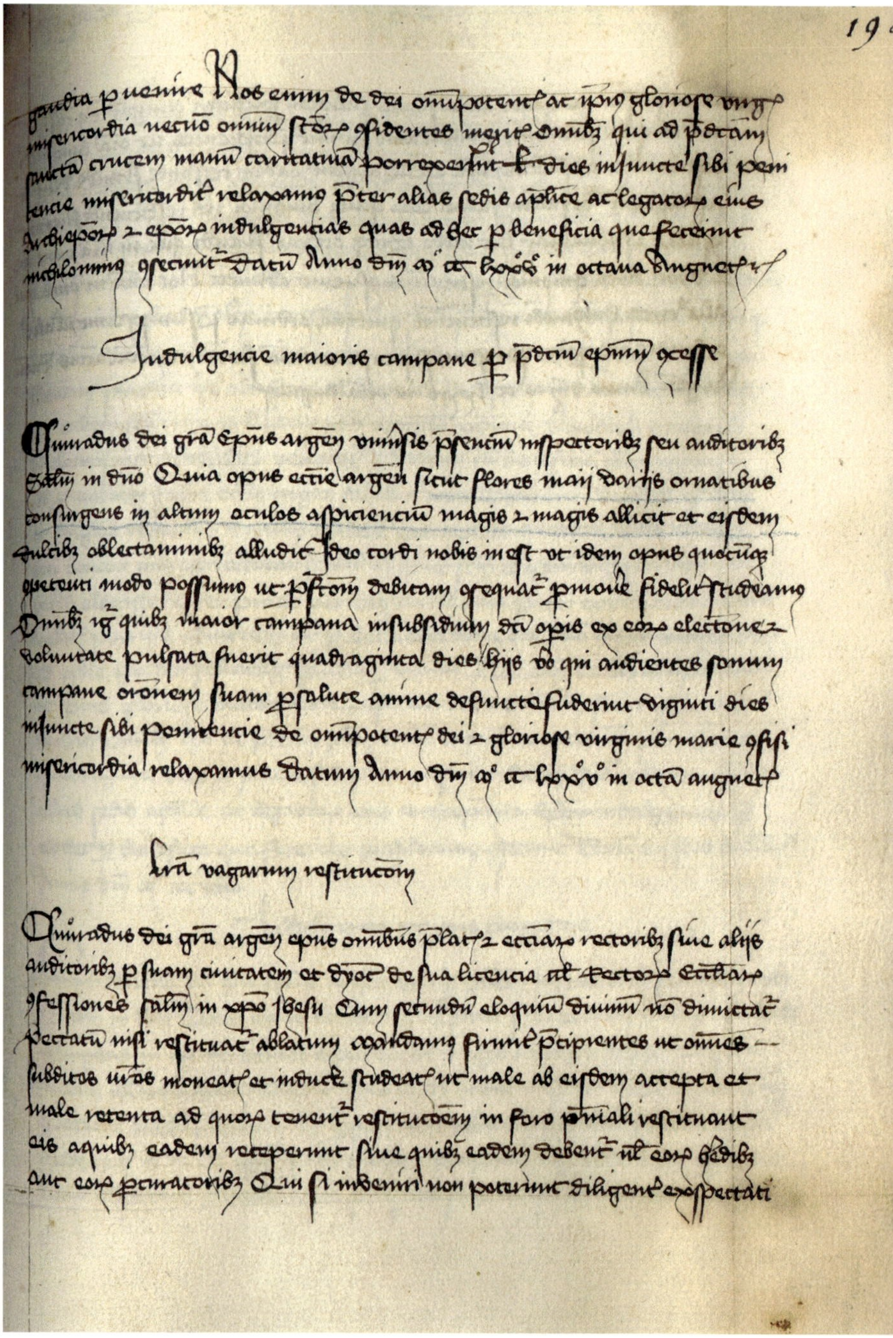

unconditional donations, too, though they were never of any great consequence. The wish to be relieved of some ailment or illness in the here and now could also motivate the faithful to offer money for a range of charitable or religious efforts, including the construction and furnishing of churches. Status and prestige could likewise play a role. Non-worldly motives such as securing one's spiritual welfare might go hand in hand with patently temporal political, social and economic aspirations. We have already briefly seen some of these same factors at play in contributions from bishops and rulers.

These intertwined religious and worldly expectations, which gave rise to a collection of observances, customs and institutions that in turn laid the foundation for medieval donating practices in general, were of fundamental importance in funding the construction and upkeep of all churches, including cathedrals.[527]

1 • VENERATION OF RELICS

Chief amongst the incentives for the faithful to open their purses may have been the fact that a church could bring them into direct contact with saints' relics. The practice of venerating the physical remains of martyrs dates back to the very beginnings of Christianity. There are a number of features that typify the history of this form of devotion.[528] From early on, the presence of saints' relics, often occasioning the erection of a church on or near the site, became a draw for pilgrims. Initially, their gravesites were left intact but, from as early as the fourth century, people began opening the graves and removing the bodily remains, and later felt no qualms about taking those remains apart (*dismembratio*), with Church consent. The eighth and ninth centuries saw the distribution of the dismembered bodies of saints across the length and breadth of Europe. Objects belonging to the saint or things that he or she had touched, even objects that had touched only the bones, were also traditionally classified as relics. Every church of any consequence had an opportunity to acquire its own assemblage of relics in this way.[529] Following the installation of the Latin empire in Constantinople in 1204, much of the Byzantine store of relics was

25
Historiated initial of the charter, documenting the acquisition of relics by bishop Johann Senn von Ensingen
Basel 1360, pen and ink and watercolour on vellum, 40 x 52 cm
Staatsarchiv des Kanton Basel-Stadt

The bishop applied to the pope for relics after a 1356 earthquake resulted in damage to the cathedral. He received thirteen, including a tooth of St Paul's. The illumination shows St Paul – with his attribute of a sword – presenting this relic to the bishop, who in turn offers it, now in a reliquary, to the Virgin, to whom the cathedral is dedicated. An indulgence was issued for veneration of the relics, which attracted countless pilgrims and many offerings. In 1363 the bishop was able to consecrate the new high altar.

LITERATURE
Exh. cat. Basel 2001, pp. 10, 152.

channelled into the West as well, including some of great religious value. Cathedrals got their share of this treasure.[530] Later centuries continued to see relics donated as gifts (fig. 25), exchanged, bought and sold, and even plundered and stolen.

As early as the seventh century, and continuing on into the eleventh and twelfth, relics might be 'elevated' (*elevatio*), meaning that the physical remains were removed from their original resting place and installed in a visible spot under the altar or, as was preferred in the later Middle Ages, in a shrine behind or on the high altar. The masses of pilgrims were thus granted direct, sometimes even physical, access to the venerated remains.[531] Up until the end of the twelfth century, the solemn elevation that formed part of a saint's canonization and heralded the official beginning of his veneration was performed under the bishop's authority, and indeed often by the bishop himself. Eyewitness accounts from this period paint an arresting picture of the emotion and ecstasy charging the crowds that converged on such occasions.[532] It is difficult to overstate the emotive role that relics played in medieval spirituality; they were 'the strongest links with the invisible world',[533] and indeed, confidence in saints' powers knew no bounds. From the thirteenth century on, canonization and *elevatio* grew increasingly subject to papal jurisdiction, as did the solemn *translatio*, whereby the relics were conveyed to a new, more dignified accommodation, such as a shrine (fig. 33).[534] Accordingly, it was not unusual for the pope to have sole authority to grant important indulgences specifically intended to attract a great influx of pilgrims.[535] Papal control over all matters relating to the veneration of relics also finds expression in the *canones* of the Fourth Lateran Council (1215), which stipulate that no new relics were to be venerated without permission from the Apostolic See and that relics were not to be bought or sold nor taken out of their *capsa* (receptacle) for display. During the late Middle Ages, images of saints fulfilled a function comparable to that of their relics, and could likewise become a focus of worship and pilgrimage. Inherent in the devotion paid to relics was the expectation of a miracle, which of course depended on the saint's intercession. Miracles, moreover, provided an incontrovertible proof of the authenticity of relics.[536] Anyone who came to visit the grave of a saint did so either

potuint de premissis demonstrauit
est romanus corporale prestitit iuramentum sic
Quinquagesimo nono Pontificatus dni Innocenti
Petrus olim de

to thank him or her for an act performed or prayer answered on the suppliant's behalf, or in hopes of being freed from some ailment or illness.[537] Alternatively, a journey ending at the saint's gravesite could represent the culmination of a penance, as pilgrimage was also at times imposed as a penalty by temporal judges.[538]

The possession of illustrious relics lent a cathedral prestige and marked and signalled its status,[539] and competition was rife amongst cathedrals and between them and abbeys and other churches.[540] The financial side of such ownership was of the utmost importance, for pilgrims never visited the shrines of saints whose solace and blessings they sought with empty hands. The possession of an illustrious relic assured the church that owned it of a continuous source of revenue.[541] In the pages that follow, we will explore the ways in which bishops and chapters used their cathedrals' relics to benefit building works.

Every church owned one or more relics, but these differed in terms of their significance, and churches themselves differed in the ways in and degrees to which they were able to exploit them.[542] In the eleventh and twelfth centuries – a period characterized by a contemporary witness as the *saeculum reliquiarum*[543] – monasteries and abbeys in particular led the mass movement towards venerating relics.[544] One miracle-working saint attracted so many worshippers to his English abbey in the twelfth century that the abbot urgently petitioned him to stop performing miracles so that the cloister might enjoy a return to its former peace and insignificance.[545] After the twelfth century, bishops and popes came to assume a growing role in stimulating the veneration of relics, which was no doubt due in part to their authority to grant indulgences.[546] A few cathedrals acquired relics that drew the devout from far and wide, but in fact the contemporary, usually monastic, saints whose remains enjoyed the greatest popularity in the late Middle Ages were typically found in monastery churches, whilst images of wonder-working saints and miraculous hosts, which often brought throngs of people flocking to a church – albeit only for brief periods – were more likely to be found in parish churches, cloisters and chapels than in cathedrals.

It would be beyond the bounds of this study to determine whether or to what extent the veneration of saints and saints' relics and belief in their miracle-working powers were but a panacea for the masses, the elaborate orchestration – and all resulting profits – of which were actually controlled by the upper echelons of a clerical hierarchy whose members felt little spiritual affinity with such enterprises. One modest example argues against this notion. On 5 June 1476, Johannes van Drakenborch, a canon of Utrecht and for many years master of the cathedral fabric, travelled to Lier in Brabant to give thanks to St Gummarus for interceding to effect an unexpected recovery after he had lain in sickbed for 23 weeks; this miraculous cure was the 73rd such in the book of miracles of this saint. This very same Van Drakenborch shared in directing the immensely successful, tightly regulated reliquary circuits through the bishopric in support of the cathedral buildings works, which will be discussed in detail below.[547]

2 • INDULGENCES

Second in significance were indulgences. An indulgence (*indulgentia*) can be described as an extra-sacramental remission granted on reasonable grounds from such punishments as might remain after the forgiveness of sins (confession), and for which penance was required in either this world or the next. Indulgences were granted from the accumulated merits of Christ and his saints (the *thesaurus ecclesiae*, or treasury of the Church) by designated Church authorities and by virtue of the Church's jurisdiction.[548] The first real indulgences date from the beginning of the eleventh century, though the concept would not attain its full theological complexity until 1350. There were two main categories of indulgences: plenary indulgences, providing full remission from all sins for which penance was due, and partial indulgences, providing only limited remission. The latter type soon developed to encompass temporal units of specific numbers of days and years, sometimes together with a number of quarantines (*quarantena*, a reduction of Church penances such as fasting).[549] An indulgence for a certain number of days or years represented the remission of punishments for sins that would be meted out in Purgatory, and corresponded to the numbers of days or years of real penance prescribed by the early Christian church.

An indulgence was only granted where there were reasonable grounds to do so (*causa justa et rationabilis*);[550] specifically, it had to serve some pious purpose pleasing to God. According to Thomas Aquinas (1225-1274), this encompassed the *honor Dei* (honour of God), *utilitas ecclesie* (interest of the Church) and *utilitas proximi* (interest of your fellow man).[551] Recitation of prayers, churchgoing, venerating relics, listening attentively to a sermon and even attending devoutly to a cathedral bell[552] could all be tied to an indulgence.[553] Where the interests of the Church or fellow man were at issue, it was an obvious step to link indulgences with alms. The possibility of substituting alms for penances was nothing new. Indeed, a gift of alms by its very nature possessed the power to blot out the need for penance, thus laying a further link between indulgences and monetary offerings. Despite occasional criticism from the twelfth century on,[554] this link held firm until the Council of Trent.[555]

Church authorities issued indulgences in recognition of monetary and other forms of support given to any of a myriad of religious and temporal causes: for participation in or financial support for the Crusades, for acts of charity, even for subsidizing bridge-building. But the largest number of indulgences was distributed for physical or financial aid for the construction and furnishing of churches.[556] Historically, they are also amongst the first indulgences, with the very earliest being issued by bishops in northern Spain and southern France in the first half of the eleventh century.[557] From the twelfth century, and even more so the thirteenth, granting indulgences on this basis became a widespread custom. In time, preferences developed for certain phrasings that we find repeated in countless writs of indulgence. One recurring passage declares that the indulgence is granted to those '*qui manus adiutrices porrexerunt*' (who have offered a helping hand):[558] anyone who either literally lent an unpaid hand in building activities or made a donation acquired the indulgence. Apart from a gift of alms for the building works, indulgences usually also required the recipient to visit the relevant church on certain specified feast days. The financial gains on granting indulgences in return for churchgoing and almsgiving could be considerable; as we shall see there were various means by which bishops and chapters engaged these indulgences for the building fund.

It goes without saying that any bishop would be more inclined to supply his own cathedral church with indulgences and other spiritual privileges than he would other churches in his bishopric. Given that a bishop exercised spiritual authority in his own diocese, he was entitled, if he chose, to grant exclusive rights for the fabric to, for example, organize diocesan fundraising campaigns in aid of the construction of its first church. From the fourteenth century onwards, bishops increasingly sought to acquire indulgences from the pope – an endeavour that generally came down to developing and maintaining good relations with the papal curia. Though it seems reasonable to expect that bishops and chapters had easier access to this network than someone like a parish churchwarden, sources indicate that in fact cathedral fabrics did not receive the greater share of such indulgences. Of the 335 or more indulgences issued by the metropolitan and pope for churches and monasteries in the archbishopric of Cologne between 1225 and 1590, only sixteen were earmarked for the cathedral. Similar ratios may be expected elsewhere.[559] It is worth remembering that neither relics nor indulgences were exclusively, or even primarily, reserved to support cathedral-building.

Cathedral fabrics had two roads by which they could stimulate the faithful to contribute to the building fund. The first was by and large passive: the faithful were encouraged to visit the cathedral *en masse*. The second was active: the cathedral fabric despatched its collectors on a circuit of the entire diocese to solicit gifts from the faithful. In terms of generating funds, there is no real fundamental difference between these two approaches; in both cases the stimulus for giving centred on the cult of relics and veneration of saints, paired with the prospect of earning an indulgence. Yet in practice, the difference was immense. Churches where visitors were to be welcomed required various special adaptations: the relics had to be accessible, the large crowds of pilgrims had to be received in proper fashion, if major indulgences were being issued there had to be provisions for those wishing to make confession, and of course facilities had to be put in place so that the faithful could make offerings. A campaign that travelled out into the diocese, by contrast, required the fabric to set up an intricate substructure, often involving cumbersome collection procedures, in order to funnel donations from the entire bishopric into the fabric fund. These organizational distinctions justify our separate treatment of gifts from the faithful brought to the cathedral versus those collected in the diocese.

NINE DONATIONS MADE FOR THE FABRIC IN THE CATHEDRAL

Donations that were brought to the cathedral did not automatically accrue to the works; this conclusion was already drawn in the preceding discussion on contributions from the chapter.[560] There were collection boxes that had other designations and for that reason did not benefit the fabric. Or the proceeds from a collection box might be shared between the fabric and the chapter or bishop, though agreement on such division was generally subject to its share of strife.

Of what consequence, then, were the alms brought to the cathedral specifically to fund the building works? There is a clear line dividing ordinary and extraordinary years. In ordinary years a fabric's need for resources was comparatively limited, albeit constant. Its outlays comprised a range of fixed annual expenses, costs for maintaining and furnishing the building and costs arising from day-to-day building activities. Year in, year out, donations flowed into the fabric fund in a pattern of unchanging and almost monotonous regularity, and there were always opportunities to earn ordinary indulgences and to venerate relics. In extraordinary years, by contrast, the building works were operating at full steam. Sometimes a new devotional movement developed spontaneously and supplied the incentive for a building campaign; at other times, it was the plan for a new building or restoration that came first. Where a cathedral stood in disrepair following a disaster such as a fire, the bishop and chapter might be spurred to set up devotional frameworks to propel large-scale almsgiving. Indulgences and the veneration of relics served as primary stimuli, and in this sense there was no essential difference between ordinary and extraordinary years. The distinction lies, rather, in the special status of the indulgences and the topical interest of a relic or miraculous image, which invested devotions with a greater intensity. In these cases the alms collected over a few years might be several times the amount otherwise gleaned over an entire decade. In view of these differences, ordinary and extraordinary years must be dealt with independently.

1 • ORDINARY YEARS

Every cathedral always had one or more collecting boxes and chests into which the faithful could drop their gifts in money and kind throughout the year (fig. 37).[561] Several times a year the *magistri fabrice* emptied these containers, sometimes in the presence of witnesses, at which time the contents were counted and entered in the account rolls under such headings as '*de pecuniis repertis in tronco fabrice*' (from the monies found in the collection box of the fabric)[562] or '*inventum est in archa ferrata*' (is found in the ironwork chest)[563] or '*dou tronc, qui est au cuer de lad. eglise*'.[564]

The fabric collection box or chest, like all the other almsboxes, occupied a permanent spot in the church, recognized by and familiar to the faithful.[565] The chapter of Narbonne turned this power of habit to the advantage of the cathedral building works in a way that cannot help but amuse us now: when a special papal collection box for the Crusade was set up in the cathedral in 1309, the chapter hurried to place the fabric box alongside it, which had the intended effect that gifts meant for the Holy Land ended up in the fabric fund. The pope, upon hearing of the ploy, flew into a rage and commanded the chapter to put the fabric box back in its usual spot.[566] At large cathedrals, the viewing of relics was sometimes accompanied by specific, daily recurring rituals.[567] Around 1250 the cathedral of Santiago de Compostela

26
Interior view of Basel Cathedral, c. 1850
Watercolour, 259 x 199 mm
Basel, Staatsachiv

View of the nave and the rood loft separating the nave from the crossing as they were in the period after the Reformation (1529) and before the major restoration campaign of 1852, when the rood loft was moved. The spot occupied by the communion table, at the foot of the stairs to the crossing and choir, was where the fabric had its primary offertory box up until 1529. This spot was variously referred to as the *locus petitionis fabricae*, *der Bitt* or *der Heischeplatz*. On feast days the cathedral's precious reliquaries were displayed here, most importantly the famed cross donated by Emperor Henry II in 1019. The cathedral's parish altar of the Holy Cross, which was also used by the *confraternia fabricae* (fabric confraternity), was situated in the crypt beneath the crossing.

LITERATURE
Exh. cat. Basel 2001, pp. 8, 40-41, 168.

held a brief ceremony each morning, after sounding the bells for morning mass, to signal that pilgrims could start visiting the relics of St James, earn their indulgence and make their offerings. In this ceremony, the priest jointly responsible with the lay *custos* for guarding the *archa operis* was supposed to don his surplice and mount a dais above the *archa* when the cleric whose duty it was began to proclaim the indulgence. As soon as the cleric had loudly announced the *archa operis* as the first collection point, the lay *custos* was to address the pilgrims in their diverse languages and draw their attention to the *archa*, saying to the French, *'zee larcha de lobra mon señor Samanin; zee lobra de lagresa* [...]' and to those from Lombardy and Tuscany, *'O miçer lombardo, queste larcha de la lavoree de micer Saiacome. Questo vay a la gage fayr'*. The *custos* and priest each held a long wand with which they tapped pilgrims on the shoulders and arms to indicate that the indulgence had been granted.[568]

Many cathedrals also had almsboxes, collection chests and alms dishes that were deployed only on certain days of the year, namely, on Christian feast days and especially during Easter and Holy Week, the anniversary of the church's consecration or the patron saint's feast day. On these days, a servant of the fabric or one of the lower cathedral clergy would take his place behind the open container or chest, which was placed in proximity to the shrine, an altar or a miraculous image, in order to monitor the faithful as they gave alms, to show or point out the relics or to present them to be kissed,[569] and to receive any offerings.[570] The sums garnered on these special occasions were recorded in the fabric rolls under headings such as *'recepi a custodibus altarium de venia ecclesie'* (I have received from the *custodes* at the altars [as revenues from] the cathedral indulgences),[571] *'de l'escrin desd. reliques'*[572] or *'rec. des troncs des reliques et de la nef ouverts le 10 juillet* [...]'.[573] The *Münster* of Basel had a collection box – referred to as *die Bitt* or *truncus magnus* – set up before the centre of the rood loft, decorated on feast days with reliquaries and attended by not only a chantry priest but a layman as well, known as the *bytter am buw* or *petitor* (fig. 26).[574] Some cathedrals also organized plate collections, but this practice was not widespread.[575]

27
List of relics and indulgences of the cathedral of Santiago de Compostela
Broadside incunable, 313 x 207 mm, printed by Gonzalo de la Passera, c.1495
Simancas, General Archive of Simancas

The left-hand column provides a summary of all relics in the possession of the cathedral of Santiago, beginning with the body of the Apostle St James the Greater, which was preserved in its entirely under the high altar. The right-hand column documents the indulgences available to earn in the cathedral on a daily basis, on exceptional days, on special occasions and, lastly, during the Jubilee year, which was celebrated each year that the feast day of St James (25 July) fell on a Sunday.

LITERATURE
Einblattdrucke des xv. Jahrhunderts, no. 352; A. Rey Soto, *La imprenta en Galicia, el libro gótico*, Madrid 1934, pp. 157-161 and facsimile t.o. p. 34; Vázquez de Parga *et al.* 1993, vol.1, p. 152, vol. 3, fig. XVII.

Over the course of a year, a cathedral could thus anticipate a concentration of gifts in money and kind on those days when an indulgence could be earned or special devotions paid to a saint. As a rule, the faithful were required to give alms in order to earn the indulgence, as well as visit the church on several specific feast days and, usually, their octaves.[576] The majority of such – partial – indulgences were provided at the bishop's initiative. Whenever building plans were in the works or the fabric was short of funds for any other reason, it was standard practice for the diocesan bishop to issue an indulgence. Yet there were limits to the bishops' powers. Not only did their religious jurisdiction to grant indulgences extend only to territories within their dioceses, but there were also certain restrictions on the nature and scope of these indulgences. The most important restrictions were laid down by the Fourth Lateran Council of 1215, warning bishops not to get carried away and issue more than one 40-day indulgence, except in rare exceptions.[577] Episcopal indulgences were unlimited in their validity, however (*indulgentiae perpetuae*). In the later Middle Ages, when an indulgence of 40 days no longer had the power to impress anyone, cathedral fabrics endeavoured to secure more, and especially larger, indulgences for churchgoing and donations to their cathedrals. There were various ways in which they could do this.

Firstly, the bishop and chapter could attempt to get a partial papal indulgence from Rome. Indeed, the registers of petitions to the pope teem with such requests.[578] There were no restrictions on papal jurisdiction in this regard. Popes in the thirteenth century, and even into the fourteenth, continued to be relatively reticent in exercising their rights: the indulgence for one year and 40 days that Pope Innocent IV issued for building works at the cathedral of Cologne in 1248 was exceptionally high for the time.[579] From the second half of the fourteenth century, the number and size of papal indulgences saw an exponential rise; episcopal indulgences seemed downright shabby in comparison. Clement V's large 1308 indulgence of fourteen years and fourteen quarantines to support the works at his beloved former archiepiscopal cathedral of Bordeaux, granted to anyone who visited the church on the day of the translation of its patron saint, St Andrew, has already been mentioned.[580] Sometimes the terms swelled to grotesque pro-

¶ He sunt reliquie que habentur in hac sanctissima eccle-
sia compostellana: in qua corpus beati iacobi zebedei in
integrum.

Primo ⁊ principaliter Corpus ipsius beati ia-
cobi zebedei nepotis virginis marie: ⁊ fratris
beati iohannis apostoli ⁊ euangeliste: totum
integrum sub altari maiori.
Item corpus beati athanasij ⁊ beati theodori
discipulorum ipsius apostoli. Corpus beati siluestri marty-
ris. corpus beati cucufati martyris: ⁊ corpus beati fructuo-
si episcopi.
Item in thesauro predicte ecclesie caput beati iacobi al-
phei: quod cunctis magnifeste monstratur.
Item sunt in sacrario predicte ecclesie ⁊ in capella sancti sal-
uatoris ꝙ plurime reliquie quarum nomina vix nominari
possunt.
Item in predicto sacrario est quedam ymago in qua est de-
ns beati iacobi alphei apostoli.
Item quattuor cruces: in quibus sunt inserte ptes de ligno
crucis domini nostri iesu christi.
Item vna spinarum corone eiusdem domini nostri.
Reliquie sequentes sunt in quadam custodia argentea re-
condite que in thesauro eiusdem sanctissime compostellane
ecclesie reseruatur. Necnon ⁊ alie ꝙ plurime quarum nomi
na prolixum esset scribere.
Primo ⁊ principaliter de ligno sancte crucis. De baculo p-
prius domini nostri ihesu christi.
Item de sepulchro in quo reconditū fuit suum sanctissimū
corpus. Item de mensa in qua idē dominus noster ihesus
christus cum discipulis suis vltimum porrexit cenam.
Item de sepulchro virginis marie ⁊ de baculo eiusdem.
De tumba beati iacobi apostoli.
Item de reliquiis beati thome apostoli.
Item de sindone beati thome.
Item de veste virginis marie.
Item de ossibus sancti pauli apostoli.
Item de ossibus sancte thadee.
Item de ossibus sancti barnabe apostoli.
Item de ossibus sancte luce euangeliste.
Item de ossibus ⁊ carne sancte agnine.
Item de abacuc propheta.
Item de veste sancti Nicholai.
Item de ossibus sancti gregorij pape.
Item de ossibus sanctorum cosme ⁊ damiani.
Item de ossibus sanctorum thimothei Sixti ⁊ marcellini.
Item reliquie beati vincentij martyris.
Item de capillis beati marie magdalene.
Item de veste beate martini episcopi.
Item de sanguine beati sebastiani.
De cilitio sancti thome cantuariensis episcopi.
Item dens beati siluestri ⁊ de eius corpore.
Pars cuiusdam dentis beati petri alexandrini.
¶ Has venerabiles reliquias infra scriptas inclusas in qua
dam ymagine aurea beati iacobi misit huic sancte ecclesie
eiusdem apostoli illustrissima ducessa Helionor et prosapia
regis progenita de scotia. Uxor domini ducis Austrie.
Primo de sancto cassiano episcopo ⁊ martyre.
De sanctis christophoro ⁊ gregorio martyribus.
De sancto accasio ⁊ sancto magno confessoribus.
De sanctis eugenio ⁊ albino episcopis ⁊ confessoribus.
De sanctis gallo ⁊ vdrainico confessoribus.
De sanctis dauid ⁊ [illegible] confessoribus.
De sancta vrsula virgine ⁊ martyre.

¶ DEO GRATIAS.

¶ Extra muros vrbis ad partem occidentalem requiescit
venerandum corpus beate Susanne virginis ⁊ martyris.

¶ He sunt indulgentie concesse a sanctis patribus ⁊
summis pōtificibus dicte sancte ecclesie cōpostellane.

Primo ꝙ quicunqꝫ venit in peregrinatione ad
ecclesiam beati iacobi zebedei que est in prouin-
cia galecie quocunqꝫ tempore est ei remissa ter-
tia pars omnium peccatorū suorū. Et si veniēdo
stando vel redeundo decesserit habita penitentia
de cōmissis omnia peccata sunt ei remissa.
Item omnes qui incedunt omnibus diebus dominicis ad
processionem dicte sancte ecclesie beati iacobi habent ꝑ qua
libet processione ⁊ sacratione quadraginta dies indulgētie
⁊ sic per totam septimanam. ⁊ si est festum habent trecētos
dies. Preter predictam indulgentiam. s. tertiā partem omni
um peccatorum suorum.
Item in vigilia sancti iacobi. ⁊ in die ⁊ in festo dedicatiōis
eiusdem ecclesie sic habent sexcentos dies indulgentie tam
in vigilia ꝙ in die oēs pegrinatōes ibi ꝯcurrētes vltra ꝑdi
ctā indulgentia tertie ptis omniū peccatorū suorū.
Itē omnes audientes missam ab archiepiscopo aut cardi-
nali in altari beati iacobi habent ducentos dies indulgētie
ꝑ qualibet missa vltra predictas indulgētias q̄ omnia ꝑdic-
ta peregrinis sancti iacobi ꝯfessis ⁊ vere penitentibus sunt
concessa modo predicto per bullas sanctorum patrum se-
dis apostolice ⁊ confirmata.
Item calixtus papa ꝯcessit ꝙ quando acciderit festū beati
iacobi zebedei die dominica ꝙ in toto illo anno omnes ibi
cōcurrētes in pegrinatione vere penitentes ⁊ ꝯfessi. Sunt
absoluti a pena ⁊ culpa. Item per bullam sancti calixti pap
Qui valde fuit deuotus beato iacobo. Cōcessit omnibus
pegrinis huius sancte ecclesie cōpostelle metropolitane in
galecia pegrinatōis causa venientibus ꝙ qn festum beati ia
cobi acciderit die dominica. In vigilia ⁊ in die habeāt ple-
nā indulgentiā oium peccatorū. A pena ⁊ culpa. Et sic ꝑ to-
tum annum: incipiendo prima die mensis ianuarij vsqꝫ ad
vltimam diem mensis decēbris proxime future ⁊ inclusiue.
Item per bullā predicti pape calixti q̄ per successores est cō
firmata cōceditur ⁊ mādatur ꝙ quicunqꝫ illas remissiones
siue preuilegia seu indulgentias ꝑdicte ecclesie cōpostella-
ne dubitauerint ⁊ firmiter nō crediderint: maiorem excōica
tionis sententiam auctoritate apostolica sunt incursuri.

Confirmationes indulgentiarum predictarū per dominū
papam innocentiū secundum ⁊ Leonem sancte memorie. ⁊
alios summos pontifices sunt confirmate ⁊ concesse.

¶ Itē gratiose est concessum eidem ecclesie cōpostellane
per summos pontifices predictos ꝙ in festo eiusdem apo-
stoli: ⁊ in trāslatione ac in omni tempore: quicunqꝫ peregri-
nandi causa ad predictam ecclesiam accedere proposuerint
a die quo de domo sua viam arripuerint: valeant eligere cō
fessorem idoneum qui auctoritate apostolica ⁊ ab omnibus
casibus sedi apostolice pertinentibus. Ueniendo. Stando.
Uel redeundo. Absoluere valeat.
Item continetur in dicta bulla ꝙ si quis peregrinus veniēd
ad ecclesiam compostellanam confessus ⁊ contritus. Et in
via stādo vel redeundo decedat. ab omnibus suis peccatis
sit penitus absolutus.

¶ Deo gratias.

¶ Presens ecclesia in qua vt predictū est indubitanter re-
quiescit integrum. nec aliqua particula minutum. Uenerā-
dū corpus beatissimum iacobi zebedei apostoli. incepta fuit
era millesima centesima decima sexta. Completa autem
miro vt patet opere in annis quadraginta quattuor.

¶ Gundisaluus de la passera natione astur.

portions, with Pope Leo x (1513-1521) issuing indulgences of thousands of years for churchgoing and almsgiving.[581] The financial interests of the Camera Apostolica played a large part in this development. Officials in the papal court demanded, at the very least, considerable sums in document sealing duties and administrative fees.[582] And yet there was not a single cathedral that was able do without one or several such papal bulls of indulgence.

Another way cathedral fabrics could mitigate the provisions of the Fourth Lateran Council was to procure a collective letter of indulgence. Specifically, cardinals and bishops could issue a collective letter wherein each one granted an indulgence of 100[583] or 40 days for the benefit of the cathedral building works; together, these small indulgences could mount to an impressive number of years. Collective indulgences presupposed a gathering of many prelates together in one place.[584] Most such letters were therefore published in Rome and Avignon, and others in cities where councils convened. It was in this way that, after his cathedral burned down in 1273, the bishop of Regensburg was able to secure an indulgence from 22 of the bishops and archbishops in attendance at the Council of Lyon in 1274;[585] the bishop of León achieved a similar success for his cathedral, begun in 1255.[586]

In the third place, a cathedral fabric could capitalize on all the various indulgences it had acquired over the course of time. As mentioned

28
Chest, early thirteenth century
Oak, (124 x 66 x 78 cm)
Chichester Cathedral, on loan from the parish of Climping (Sussex)

In 1199, Pope Innocent III issued a decree aimed at expanding the financial base for the Crusades, in which he ordered that all churches throughout Western Christendom install offertory boxes into which the faithful could deposit alms to help recapture the Holy Land. This chest is one of the surviving examples and comes from the parish church of St Mary in Climping, Sussex. It includes two features known to be common amongst chests used to collect funds for the Crusades: three locks for three different key holders and a slot in the lid for coins, which feeds into a locked box on the inside left. The Chichester Cathedral treasury has two more such 'Crusader' chests.

LITERATURE
Riley Smith 1995, p. 58. Kindly communicated by Michael Moriarty, Sub-treasurer of Chichester Cathedral.

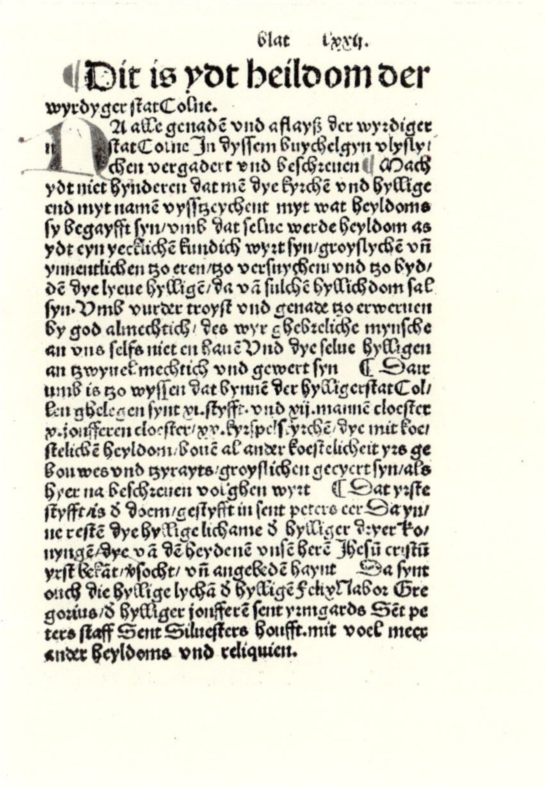

Blat lxxii.

Dit is ydt heildom der wyrdyger stat Colne.

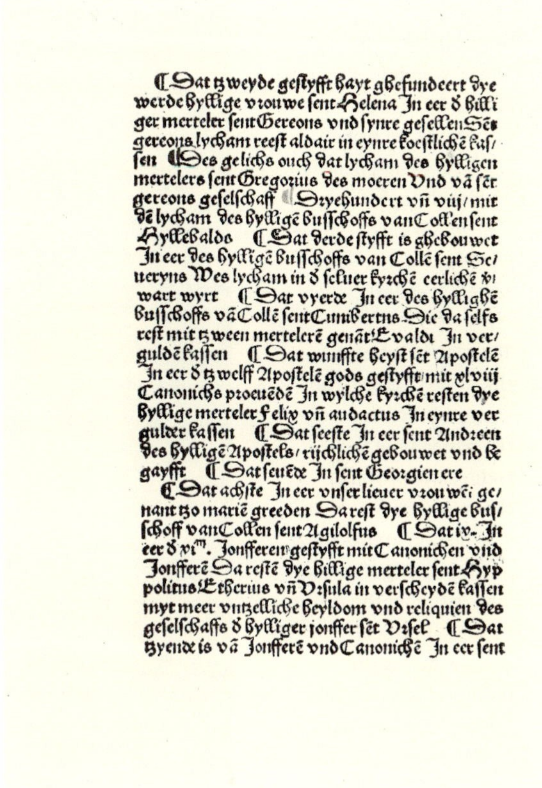

29

Pilgrim guidebook *Beschryvonghe des aflayss und heyldoms der Stat Colne*, folios 3v and 72r.
Incunable, printed by Johannes Koelhoff von Lübeck in Cologne, 18 February 1492, 4°
Göttingen, State and University Library, ms. 327

The first 71 folios of this guide for pilgrims visiting the city of Cologne provide a summary of indulgences, grouped according to the calendar days on which they were available to earn in the various churches of Cologne, starting with the cathedral. The text for new year's day reads: '*Im doem der syn almyssen gyfft tzo dem bouw off tzyrait der kyrchen, der verdyent 22 iair, 6230 dagen* [in the margin: 22 *karenen* (fasting periods)]. *Dair tzo werden sy deylhafftich alle der gueder wercken, dye gesehyen in 7000 myssen* [...]'.
Folios 72-78 contain an overview of the all the relics to be found in Cologne: '*Dit is ydt heildom der wyrdyger stat Colne*'. It starts with a list of all the churches and monasteries, followed by an inventory of the cathedral relics, beginning with the bodies of the Three Magi.

LITERATURE

Falk 1879, pp. 67-69; *Gesamtkatalog der Wiegendrucke*, Stuttgart/ New York 1968 (2nd ed.), no. 8.

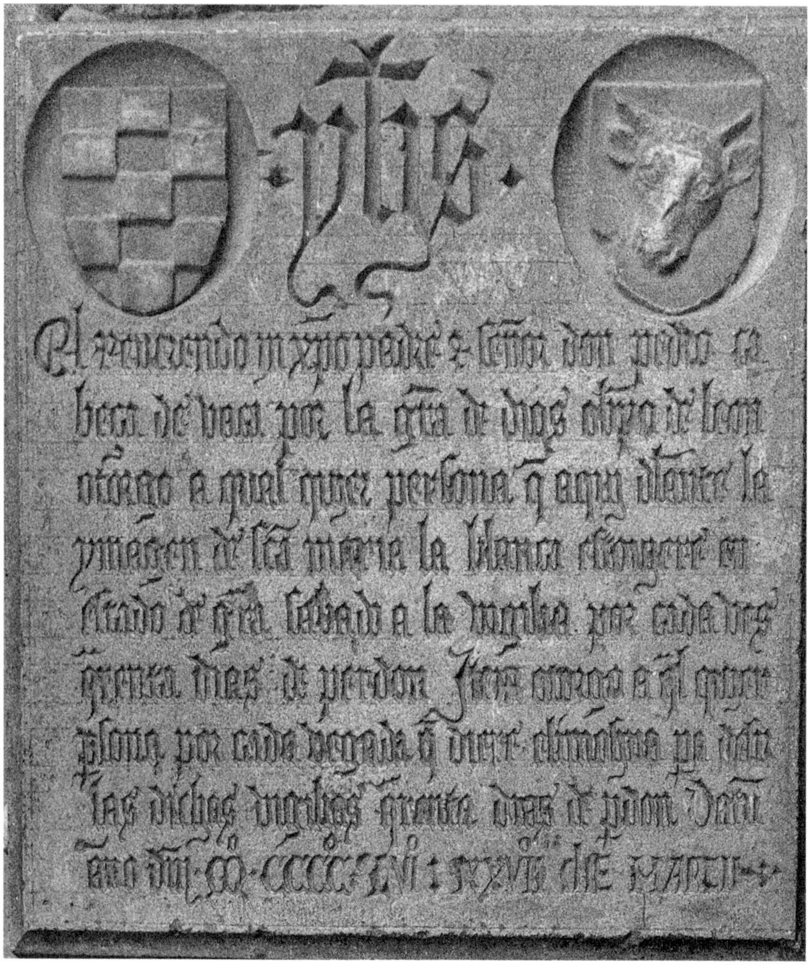

30
Stone slab incised with the indulgence issued by Bishop Cabeza de Vaca of León (1440-1459) on 27 March 1456
Central portal of the west façade
León Cathedral

The slab is set next to the *Virgen Blanca*, the statue of the Virgin on the trumeau of the right-hand portal of the west façade.
The bishop grants the 40-day indulgence to all who gather at the statue of Santa Maria la Blanca during the memorial service held for the deceased (*vigilia*) on Saturdays, provided they are in a state of grace, and to all who give such alms as they see fit on these days, and on each occasion they do this.

LITERATURE
La Catedral de León, p. 313; *Reallexikon zur deutschen Kunstgeschichte*, in voce *'Ablass (-Tafel)'*, concerning other similar sculpted indulgence letters.

above, a great many letters of indulgence – both episcopal and papal – retained their validity even after the building campaign for which they had been conceived was no more than a distant memory.[587] At the chapter's request, new bishops generally confirmed indulgences issued by their predecessors, and often added another of their own.[588] In some instances, indulgences were issued for a period described as ending when the building campaign was finished – a vague time limit that in fact came down to no limit at all.[589] In a typical expression of late medieval 'arithmetic piety', or *Heilsarithmetik*, a cathedral's stock

31
Stone relief carving depicting a pope presenting a bull of indulgence to a bishop kneeling before him, late thirteenth century
Salamanca, *Catedral Vieja* (old cathedral)

The inscription documents indulgences issued to the cathedral of Salamanca by popes Clement IV (1265-1268) and Nicholas IV (1288-1292), four archbishops and 29 bishops, designated for church-going on feast days and for supporting the *Obra* and *luminaria*.

LITERATURE
M. Villar y Macias, *Historia de Salamanca*, vol. 1, Salamanca 1887, pp. 134-135.

of indulgences could thus, bit by bit, tally to an impressive and sometimes absurdly high total.[590]

Fabrics would publish the text (or a summary) of their indulgence to distribute throughout the bishopric in manuscript or, later, in printed form, in Latin and/or the local vernacular. They also compiled inventories listing all their indulgences in hierarchical and chronological order, together with the days on which they could be obtained.[591] Some lists were accompanied by precise reckonings of the total number of years' and days' worth of indulgences the faithful could earn on cer-

32
Indulgence plaquette with an image of the Virgin and Child, Lower Saxony, c.1290
Engraved copper, approx. 40.5 cm
Halberstadt, Domschatz

The plaquette, which was nailed to the south door of the church of Our Lady in Halberstadt, summarizes all indulgences issued by cardinals, archbishops and bishops, as well as by popes Nicholas IV and Innocent IV, for those who visited the collegiate church on specific feast days, totalling eight years, 85 days and ten quarantines. The church was situated inside the cathedral immunity.

LITERATURE
Reallexikon der deutschen Kunstgeschichte, in voce *'Ablass'*; J. Flemming & E. Lehmann, *Dom und Domschatz zu Halberstadt*, Vienna 1974, ill. 167, pp. 225-226.

tain feast days, or by a list of feast days specifying numbers and types of indulgences (fig. 27, 29). The fact is that on every feast day of any import, cathedral visitors could always expect to earn some sort of indulgence.[592] Literally hundreds of such lists must have circulated within any given bishopric.[593] The advent of printing from the second half of the fifteenth century provided an enormous impetus for the dissemination of indulgences in general, though cathedrals did not benefit as greatly.[594]

Inside, cathedrals would post lists of the indulgences on offer for all to see, sometimes engraved in brass or carved in stone, thus enhancing their status and prestige (figs 30, 31, 32).[595] The fabric of the *Münster* in Basel employed a special lay functionary – the aforementioned *petitor* – to announce indulgences in the cathedral; one of his duties was to stand in the cathedral on Sundays and feast days, and Monday and Friday during the week, and from the early morning hours on to call out in a loud voice, '*Stürend an den buw unser lieben frowen und lösend den grossen aplos und gros gnod, so do geven ist von heiligen bäpsten, concilien, cardinälen, ertzbischofen und bischofen, des von gottes gnoden vil est* [...]'.[596]

Lastly, popes had the power to grant full, or plenary, indulgences. Unlike partial indulgences, these were – initially – unconnected with pilgrimage or church-building, and available only to those who joined the Crusades. But starting from the first Jubilee year in 1300, plenary indulgences also came within reach for pilgrims visiting the Roman basilicas, and from about 1350 churches outside Rome also began to profit from these indulgences on a large scale.[597] But it was not until the papacy of Boniface IX (1389-1404), sometimes rightly referred to as the father of the plenary indulgence for churchgoing, that the floodgates were truly opened.[598] Plenary indulgences could be earned on only a handful of days each year (designated the 'time of grace'), and most were restricted to one or a few years; this aspect will be treated in our discussion of revenues in exceptional years. However, cathedrals, like other churches, also managed to obtain papal plenary indulgences that were renewed each year. Such was the case at the cathedral of Oviedo from 1438 until after 1480.[599] Another example is the *pardon annuel* granted to the cathedral of St John the Baptist in Lyon. In 1392 the duke of Berry gave this church a relic of the jawbone of St John; to commemorate the gift, he procured an annual plenary indulgence from the pope, to be offered to the faithful on the vigils and feasts of St John (23 and 24 June) and Sts Peter and Paul (28 and 29 June), with which to fund the completion of the nave and façade.[600] Observance of this indulgence continued for several centuries, with an altar placed before the rood loft where the venerated relics could be displayed and a collection box set alongside.[601] The resulting receipts were administered strictly separate from those on older indulgences – the *venia antiqua* – which were granted to the faithful year-round.[602] As the profit figures that are preserved to us in fragmentary form after 1397 show, the alms presented on those four days equalled or exceeded those left over the whole of the remaining year, though the totals never rose above two to six annual wages of an unskilled workman, and never contributed more than fifteen percent of the revenues.[603]

Throughout the year the faithful could also leave their offerings at the shrine of the patron saint or before relics or miraculous images. In Ely, for example, receipts from devotion to St Etheldreda, the seventh-century patroness of the later cathedral, were entered in the fabric rolls under three different headings.[604] Pilgrims made their offerings first at her shrine, placed, as was the English custom, behind the high altar (*de feretro*),[605] next at the place inside the church where a fountain had gushed forth at the saint's exhumation (*de cruce ad fontem*), and finally at a pillar alongside the high altar, where amongst the many later ex votos hung a pair of handcuffs from which a man had miraculously been freed thanks to the saint's intercession (*de bogis*).

Devotion was usually concentrated around certain days of the year. On the commemorative anniversary of the saint's death or translation of his relics, as well as on other occasions, the shrine that was otherwise fully or partially shielded from view was revealed for pilgrims to admire in its full glory.[606] Some cathedrals brought out their entire inventory of relics, kept in precious reliquary holders, and presented them to the public in ceremonies held each or every so many years – following a strict protocol – often carrying them outside[607] in procession, or else displaying them on altars inside the church. Almsgiving invariably formed a fixed part of such festivities.[608]

Church authorities made conscious efforts to stimulate and propagate pilgrimage. In Ely, Canterbury, Chartres and elsewhere, saints' days were planned to coincide with annual fairs.[609] If rewards of indulgences were common for the ordinary veneration of relics, this was especially true during a feast of the holy relics.[610] Such occasions provided yet another opportunity for a fabric to boost the number of indulgences its cathedral had to offer; for example, it might offer an indulgence of 40 days for veneration of each composite part of a relic, whereby the sum total of indulgence days for all these innumerable parts could rise to astronomical heights. The late medieval inclination to extravagance and immoderation is much in evidence here. As they did for their indulgences, cathedrals also published inventories of their relics (figs. 27, 29). One such from the cathedral of Magdeburg reads: '*de Summe der stucke des hilghedoms die ist 7118 stucke; de summe des aflates ist 49826 jahre*'.[611] German churches more than any others used printing to propagate their collections of relics. *Heiltumsbüchlein*, printed manuals and guidebooks which contained descriptions and sometimes pictures of the relics together with explanations of what to do during a visit and tallies of indulgences to be earned down to the day, have also been preserved at various cathedrals (fig. 34).[612]

Another strategy for enhancing or maintaining the appeal of a pilgrimage site and stimulating a steady flow of pilgrims was to record the miracles that had taken place there. There was a long-standing tradition of drawing up official written statements of the miracles effected through individual saints' intercessions.[613] Those who had benefited from a miracle showed their thanks by going to the church where the miracle-working saint was honoured in order to relate, sometimes before witnesses, the facts of the case. A cleric would note down the miracle and then record it for posterity in a book kept or made for that purpose. In 1330, many centuries after the first miracles had taken place at Coutances, the bishop commissioned such a book: '*item ordinamus quod omnia miracula que de cetero evenient in ecclesia per custodem luminaris in uno libro ad hoc deputato perpetuo erunt scripta*' (we further order that all miracles which may occur in the church be recorded by the *custos* of the candles in a book that will

33
Panel from the retable of the high altar of the Capilla Major, 1427-1434
By the painter Nicolás Francés, active between 1427 and 1467/68
León Cathedral

According to a recent reconstruction, the centre of this enormous retable (13 x 6 metres) contained scenes from the life of the Virgin, with to the left scenes from the life of San Alvito, bishop of León, and to the right from the life of San Froilán, bishop and patron saint of León. To the far right were scenes from the life of St James. The scene reproduced here shows the translation of the saint's relics on a wagon drawn by two oxen, to be borne to the cathedral of Santiago de Compostela. The detail of a pilgrim making his offering is the cover illustration of this book.

LITERATURE
La Catedral de León, pp. 150-167.

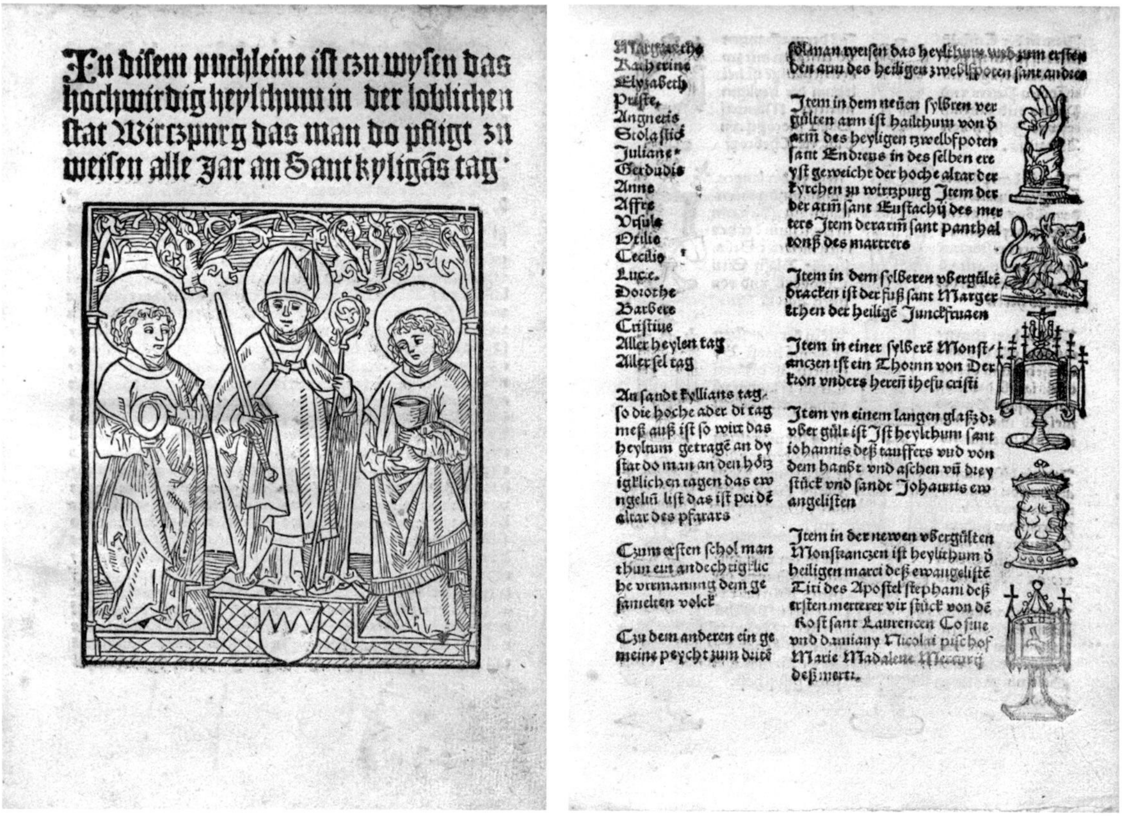
In disem puchleine ist czu wyssn das hochwirdig heylthum in der loblichen stat Wirczpurg das man do pfligt zu weisen alle Jar an Sant kyligās tag

Katherine
Elyzabeth
Puscie
Angnetis
Scolastice
Juliane
Gerdrudis
Anne
Affre
Ursule
Otilie
Cecilie
Lucie
Dorothe
Barbere
Cristine
Aller heylen tag
Aller sel tag

34

Heiltumsbuch (book of shrines) of Würzburg, title page and folio 3a Incunable, printed by Hans Mayr in Nuremberg, 1 June 1493. Vienna, Austrian National Library

Books of shrines contain a list of relics put on display, often together with a summary of the associated indulgences on offer. Of the books that have been preserved, only a few concern displays in or in behalf of cathedrals; those that do are for Bamberg, Cologne, Le Puy, Trier, Vienna and Würzburg. The exhibition of relics conducted by the cathedral of Würzburg took place each year on the feast day of St Kilian (8 July), the patron saint of the diocese. Attended by the full ranks of the city's clergy, the *exclamator reliquiarum* stood inside or in front of the cathedral church and in a loud voice recited the names of the relics on show, pointing to each reliquary with a staff as he did so. From 1401 onwards there was a papal plenary indulgence available to earn by anyone who supported the building works or *Stift*.

The title page contains an illustration of the three Frankish patron saints: Bishop Kilian with his companions Sts Colman and Totnan.

LITERATURE

Falk 1879, p. 79; Boeren 1962, pp. 87-89; W. Engel, 'Das Würzburger Heiltum des späten Mittelalters', *Würzburger Diözesangeschichtsblätter* 11/12 (1949/1950), pp. 127-158.

henceforth be kept for this purpose).[614] From these books cathedrals then made up extracts of the most memorable miracles.[615] Aside from those known to us from abbeys,[616] the miracle compilations that have come down to us from before 1300 alone include those of the cathedrals of Durham (early twelfth century), Coutances (twelfth century), Laon (1146), Canterbury (after 1170), Norwich (twelfth century), Worcester (early thirteenth century), Chartres (around 1210), Paris (twelfth century), Tournai (twelfth century), Lausanne (after 1232) and Strasbourg (1280).[617] The early twelfth-century book of miracles from Notre-Dame de Coutances, like that from Chartres,[618] had unmistakable roots in propagandistic aims: '*ad laudem suae majestatis et incrementum ipsius ecclesie*' (to praise its dignity and promote the cathedral). Rivalry with the neighbouring diocese of Bayeux composes one of its themes. In the sixth miracle, for example, we learn how Vitalis, a man whose village in the bishopric of Bayeux lay about equidistant from Coutances, refused to take part in the parishioners' procession to Coutances, for which solemn vows had been made, arguing that the mother of God of Bayeux and that of Coutances were one and the same. For this he was punished with a broken leg and paralysis. It was only after making a remorseful confession at the altar in the cathedral of Coutances that he was cured. Following these events, Vitalis served the building works at Coutances for one week as a carpenter, for which he accepted no pay. He furthermore pledged himself a serf of the Virgin Mary and promised an annual tribute for the remainder of his life.[619] Particularly this last passage, quite obviously served up for emulation, makes it clear that the fabric also expressly intended these stories of miracles to boost its long-term interests. Typically, such stories, or rather, series of them, looked back to a period of intense but brief devotion in the recent or distant past. Their compilation formed part of a cathedral's attempts to uphold its renown as a pilgrimage site by any means possible: once the flow of pilgrims got underway, it was essential to keep it going.

It is difficult to make generalizations about profits garnered from regular donations in years in which there were no special religious incentives (extraordinary indulgences, special displays of relics, a concen-

35
Procession with the reliquary shrine of St Honoratus
Detail of the tympanum of the portal dedicated to St Honoratus, c. 1260 (heavily restored)
Amiens Cathedral, south transept

In 1240 the bishop and chapter decided to conduct the reliquary shrine containing the *gloriosissimum corpus* of St Honoratus past all the diocesan parishes to collect money for the building works. St Honoratus was a sixth-century bishop of Amiens who venerated as a miracle-worker. The portal illustrates the miracle of the statue of Christ, which bowed down before the saint during the shrine's visit to a church.

LITERATURE
Murray 1996, pp. 119, 138-139; Cecilia Gaposchkin in Blick & Tekippe 2005, pp. 217-242.

36
Copper collection box, engraved with representations of St Peter, St Paul and a bishop-saint, possibly Martin, sixteenth century
Strasbourg Cathedral

The collection box may have been used by pardoners when they circuited the diocese.

LITERATURE
Doré 2007, pp. 57, 325.

37
Alms chest made by the blacksmith Juan Barba, 1572
Seville Cathedral

Alms collected in this chest may have been intended for the *Obra*.

LITERATURE
La Catedral de Sevilla, fig. 551.

tration of miraculous events). Receipts varied according to time and place but seem, judging from the extremely scarce, mostly chance, available data, to rarely have contributed any significant share of the fabric's income. To a lesser extent, the same is true of relics displayed in lengthy rotations (*turnus*), for example of seven years (fig. 22). In Bamberg, alms given during these years amounted to double that of 'normal' years.[620] But these receipts did not necessarily even play a role in the building works, and in cathedrals in England, as wells as in Cologne and Santiago, receipts from the saint's relics only accrued to the fabric in part, if at all.[621]

Receipts *'des troncs'* and *'du coffre'* at the cathedral of Rouen, by contrast, were exceptionally large. In the fifteenth century the fabric's total share of income from offerings varied from 10 to 49 percent – far more than from monies collected in the diocese.[622] Usually, however, alms offered in the cathedral were of less consequence. Annual revenues for the building works from devotional offerings made to St Etheldreda at Ely fluctuated between £25 (twelve annual wages) and £50 (24 annual wages) in the years from 1302 until 1360 – the same period that saw the famous octagon raised above crossing – which represented 8 to 25 percent of the sacristan's salary.[623] Account rolls from the cathedral fabric at Troyes over the years 1294–1300, when the transept was under construction, reveal low profits from the collection box in the choir and from alms offered for the relics, ranging between 18 l.t. and 36 l.t., compared with the fabric's total income of around 250 l.t.[624] In the last quarter of the fourteenth and first decade of the fifteenth centuries, various rolls show that *oblationes* given for the relics and at the mass of the Holy Spirit equalled about three years' wages of an unskilled labourer and comprised around 15 percent of the total net income.[625] In 1516, when work on the façade was underway, gifts brought to the cathedral for the collection box and relics totalled 583 l.t., or 19 percent of the net income and – in a departure from the norm – slightly more than profits from the diocesan collection.[626] In the cathedral of Sens, proceeds from the collecting box yielded 10 to 20 percent of its total revenues in the fourteenth century,[627] which saw no significant building activity, and similar percentages when the transept was being built from 1490 on, even though overall receipts were higher.[628] Proceeds from the *cippi* (wooden collection chests) in Freising were higher percentage-wise – sometimes reaching 50 percent, but usually averaging 20 percent of the total income – in the years between 1447 and 1500, when there was moderate building activity on the tower and vaults, but when translated into absolute terms, this comes to no more than ten years' wages.[629] Details of collection box receipts culled from scattered publications on the cathedrals of Clermont-Ferrand (1334/35),[630] Limoges (1388-1391),[631] Amiens (1358),[632] York (1415),[633] Strasbourg (1382 and 1419),[634] Regensburg (1459)[635] and Rodez (1507/08 and 1509/10)[636] point in the same direction, with gains from this source yielding between 4 and 15 percent of fabrics' net income.

In addition to these devotional alms, cathedral fabrics could also expect to receive large and small individual donations throughout the year, whether in money or in kind, to which no devotional motivations were attached. Donations in kind typically consisted of trinkets of all sorts and garments. Usually the fabric rolls distinguish these types of gifts from offerings left in the collection boxes and plates by listing the donor's name. In ordinary years such lay gifts were infrequent and inconsequential.[637] In York[638] and Regensburg[639] this income from the living was entered under the same heading as bequests from the deceased, and yielded little, as it did in Basel[640] Troyes,[641] Rodez[642] and Limoges.[643]

Where cathedral churches are concerned, we should in general only expect larger voluntary gifts from bishops, members of the chapter, other cathedral clergy and lords.[644]

2 • EXTRAORDINARY YEARS

There were also periods in which the inclination of the faithful to give was intensified. Very occasionally, a cathedral building campaign or a structure's lamentable state in the aftermath of some disaster was sufficient to stir emotions that elicited a spontaneous flood of donations.[645] Whilst bishops and chapters did seek to guide these impulsive swells of gift-giving sentiment and to lay sustainable devotional parameters for them, they usually met with no more than marginal success at best.[646]

38
Pilgrim badge depicting the enthroned Virgin and Child, the *Tunica* and kneeling worshippers, c.1350-1400
Inscription: *SANTA BEATE MERIE CARTOSESIS* (the blessed Mary of Chartres)
Lead-tin alloy, 67 x 44 mm
Found in Nieuwlande (Zeeland, NL)
Cothen, Collectie familie van Beuningen, inv. 2130

The pilgrimage to Chartres Cathedral reached its apex in the twelfth and thirteenth centuries, when the cathedral was under construction; the chief objective of the pilgrimage was the relic of the *Sancta Tunica*.

LITERATURE
Van Beuningen & Koldeweij 1993, fig. 445 and p. 325.

A practice that is particularly interesting to note in this context is actual lay participation in building monasteries and churches. Manpower from unskilled laymen could take various forms, and we find instances from the early Middle Ages[647] until well into the early modern period.[648] These forms of participation are relevant to our discussion here, despite the fact that they were not always connected with extraordinary devotions. Such participatory labour could also be involuntary, with its roots in feudal obligations. The corvee duties required of early medieval serfs made a definite and vital contribution to the maintenance and construction of many a church and chapel.[649] And though it could be bought off from the twelfth century onwards,[650] enforcement of this feudal service persevered in some places on into the eighteenth century. On certain days, then, farmers would be required to report with their carts and their draught animals to carry materials to the building site. In a few cases certain *villae* (villages) were under obligation to not only provide labour and transport but also to purchase building materials for regular maintenance of the church.[651] Equally non-voluntary was participation imposed as a penance, such as when inquisitors sentenced penitent heretics to contribute to a rebuilding campaign for a certain period of time.[652]

Voluntary participation was altogether different and almost always had a ritual character. Personal atonement or redemption were the main motivations for individuals and groups to put their skills at the disposal of a church building campaign. This was the case for the carpenter Vitalis at Notre Dame in Coutances, as we have already seen, and also, as tradition has it, for one of the 'four sons of Aymon', Renaud de Montauban, at the cathedral of Cologne.[653] Bishops,[654] kings[655] and rulers sometimes set the example by performing an *opus humilitatis* (work of humility) themselves. Often the faithful were spurred to participate by the promise of an indulgence; here the clause *manus adiutrices porrigere* (offer a helping hand) was taken quite literally.[656] Thus when, in 1443, the then dying pope granted a plenary indulgence to anyone who would, amongst other things, provide at least fifteen days labour at the cathedral of Liège or, alternatively, a sum equal to fifteen days' wages, many of the poor opted for manual labour.[657] In 1330, parish priests in the bishopric of Strasbourg, instructed by the bishop,

39

Stained glass window depicting the miracles of Notre Dame, detail, c.1200
East bay of the south nave aisle
Chartres Cathedral

The window is situated above the spot where the statue of the Virgin stood, with next to it the fabric offertory box. The representations of almsgiving in money and in kind served as a direct invitation for pilgrims to make their offerings here. Uppermost medallion: the miraculous statue of the Virgin with two angels. Centre medallion: pilgrims kneeling before the statue of the Virgin and placing an offering in the offertory box. Left and right-hand medallions: men drag heavily laden carts to the statue of the Virgin. Bottommost medallions and two quarter-medallions: butchers – the donors? – at work. Half-medallions above to either side: left, a man and a child holding a stone; right, a man carrying two animals to the altar.

LITERATURE
Manhes-Deremble 1993, pp. 208-209 and no. 38; Kurmann-Schwarz & Kurman 2001, pp. 153-154; Blick & Tekippe 2005, p. 158.

called upon all diocesan residents who owned their own conveyance to aid in transporting stones from the quarry near the cathedral, with an episcopal indulgence for their reward. The fabric also distributed wine amongst the farmers, donated for this purpose by a pious patron.[658] Around 1260 the *Comune* of Siena asked everyone who owned a pack animal to help carry building materials to the cathedral twice a year, again in return for an episcopal indulgence.[659]

A third form of active participation is distinguished from the foregoing by its mass, albeit brief, character. The eleventh and twelfth centuries, and later in a few instances, saw the emergence of religious building movements that spread so quickly as to arouse amazement in contemporary observers.[660] Abbeys had an especially large hand in this development.[661] We find instances of large-scale voluntary participation at cathedrals, such as Chartres in 1145, from thence to Normandy and elsewhere,[662] in Chartres once again three years after the fire of 1197,[663] in Auxerre in 1215[664] and in Le Mans in 1234.[665] Labouring in the building works was considered an act of humility, and many accounts are careful to point out that even the mighty of this earth allowed themselves to be harnessed to the carts.[666] From quite early on we find indications that this ritualized building movement was actually being orchestrated. Sometimes the carts were blessed, sometimes the participants sang during their journey, at others they kept utter silence.[667] A letter dating to around 1145 addressed by the archbishop of Rouen to his colleague in Amiens reveals that the former exercised some measure of supervision over the movement, which had spread to his bishopric from Chartres. From members of the religious confraternities that had formed there he extracted certain promises, namely, that they would confess with contrition, keep unity of purpose and observe humility and obedience. Having received their bishop's blessing, these groups would pick up their carts and set out, led by one of their own number, for the cathedral or for other churches in the diocese, or even beyond.[668] A half-century later these pilgrims, now under clerical leadership, made their way parish by parish back to the Notre Dame in Chartres, there sleeping – as was the ritual custom – in the cloister and church, passing part of the night singing psalms and lauds to Mary.[669] So many were these guests in number that the priests, rising in the early hours for Matins, were unable to cross the cloister.[670] It is difficult to judge the exact impact a movement of this kind could have had on the building works. In practice, its significance was primarily symbolic, serving to enhance the prestige of the church concerned. It is for precisely this reason that local chroniclers typically revert to stereotyped phrasing when describing these events in their histories. Moreover, the scale of the movement will have varied greatly from place to place. In Le Mans, for example, its activities consisted of no more than a long week's worth of hauling debris and sand from the newly completed choir.[671]

There can be no question that donations from the faithful in money and kind were of fundamental importance to the economy of the fabric. A gift of free manpower counted every bit as much as an offering. Chartres's *liber miraculorum* relates that after 1197 the carts in which pilgrims arrived were filled with grain, wine, iron and all manner of provisions needful for building, as well as with silver and other precious objects.[672] In the same letter of around 1145 cited above, the metropolitan of Rouen describes how in his cathedral, too, the faithful '*praesentant oblationem suam non sine disciplina et lacrimis*' (offered their gifts not without self-mortification and tears).[673]

Elsewhere, bishops and chapters adeptly yet subtly fanned the flames of rivalry between different groups and individuals. We see this in the matter of church glazing, for example.[674] A passage in the *Actus pontificum Cenomannis* recounts how the various trades of the city of Le Mans had engaged themselves to supply the church lights for the consecration of the cathedral's new choir in 1254. The vintners, however, had failed to join in, and now deliberated on what might yet be done: '*alii fecerunt momentaneum luminare, faciamus vitreas, que illuminent ecclesiam in futurum*' (others furnished lights for a brief time, let us put up glass that will continue to illuminate the cathedral on into the future). They agreed to install a stained glass window picturing their trade, and others quickly followed their example.[675] The fabric also invited illustrious laymen, guilds and confraternities to donate certain components of the structure, such that one might pledge a contribution towards a vault, another a pillar or portal.[676] With the addition of an inscription, a coat of arms or even the donor's

40
Stained glass windows: the donor with a model of the window as an attribute

Three cloth merchants as the donors of a lancet window in the northeast radiating chapel, c. 1270-1280
Inscription: *La verrière des drapiers*
Sées Cathedral

LITERATURE
M. Callia Bey & V. David, *Les vitraux de Basse-Normandie*, Rennes 2006, pp. 222-224.

41
Member of the aristocratic Mowbray and Clare family as the donor of a window in the north wall of the nave, fourteenth century
York Minster

portrait on the structural element, the benefactor could be assured of praise for his generous gift.[677] The chapter, knowing that the fabric required a regular income to stay afloat during the initial phase of the building campaign, did what it could to spur the faithful to donate over multiple successive years, and to this end sometimes launched a pledge drive for voluntary gifts. Chartres's *liber miraculorum* notes that some laypersons made solemn promises to undertake a pilgrimage to Notre Dame each year and give alms for the building works. In one case, it tells of a rich but God-fearing man who witnessed a miracle on the way to Chartres; arriving there, he urged bystanders to '*ut annis singulis ad ejusdem ecclesie fabricam sua transmittant vel deferunt munera*' (send or bring their donations for the construction of that cathedral year after year).[678] Vitalis the carpenter likewise committed himself to an annual tribute for the construction of Notre Dame in Coutances, thereby providing a model, as we have seen.[679] The monastery at Canterbury opened a pledge register in 1369, eight years before breaking ground for the nave, which lists 24 individuals who promised gifts of between £2 and £20 each year.[680] Such gifts were freely given and in this respect differ from the compulsory contributions from the bishop and chapter discussed above. Following the 1207 fire that reduced the Ottonian cathedral of Magdeburg to ashes, various rulers and liege lords pledged annual contributions; however, a later chronicle adds that '*se heildent doch kume ein jar*'.[681] It was quite common for such pledge drives to encompass an entire diocese, making them fundamentally different from parish lists, which remained strictly local.[682] And it was the former that evolved into diocesan fabric confraternities, to which our discussion shall turn when we examine contributions from throughout the bishopric.

Unique in their power to stimulate donations for the building works were plenary indulgences, offered during a brief period – the time of grace, ranging from several weeks to select months – over no more than a single year or several years.[683] As we have seen, in the period before the fifteenth century, plenary indulgences were generally not or only rarely issued outside Rome. Typically, they came with additional exclusive privileges and special conditions attached, forming part of

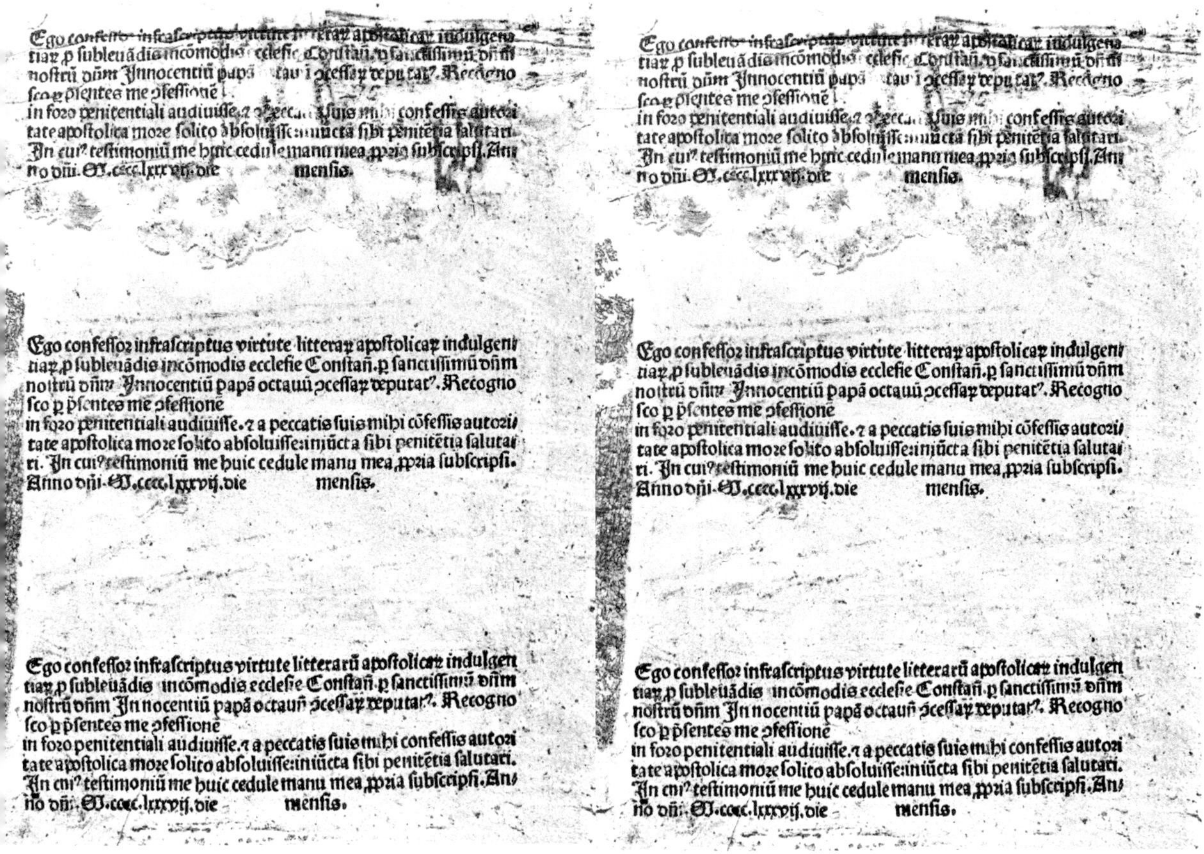

42

Proof of confession for the acquisition of the plenary Jubilee indulgence to benefit the cathedral Konstanz
Six identical forms on a single uncut leaf, 300 x 220 mm, printed by Michael Wenssler in Basel, 1487
Mainz, Gutenberg Museum

The undersigned declares that he has, in his position as confessor and by virtue of the indulgence bull issued by Pope Innocent VIII in behalf of the cathedral of Konstanz, heard the confession made by NN, has released him from the sins which he committed and has imposed a penance. In witness whereof the confessor signs and dates the form. Upon presenting this statement from his confessor the holder could earn the Jubilee indulgence of 13 January 1487, granted by the pope in return for visiting Konstanz Cathedral and ten parish churches. By this time the campaign to build the side chapels of the *Münster* of Konstanz was fully underway.

LITERATURE
Einblattdrucke des XV. Jahrhunderts, nos 430-435; Eisermann 2004, vol. 2, pp. 294-295; 599-600 (bull issued by Innocent VIII).

43
Indulgence chest, c.1500
Oak with iron fittings, 40.7 x 82.5 x 47.5 cm
Braunschweig, Städtisches Museum

The chest can be lifted from the sides; the front is fitted with three locks, possibly one for each of three competent parties. It was probably used to store the indulgence receipts – typically in the form of thousands of small coins. A link has been proposed with the activities of the preacher of indulgences Johann Tetzel (c. 1465-1519), but this remains unverified.

LITERATURE
F.J. Christiani, 'Tetzels Ablasskiste', *Miszellen Städtisches Museum Braunschweig*, no. 37 (1983).

their appeal. To get a plenary indulgence, it was usually necessary to make a repentant confession,[684] to which end confessors were specially authorized on such occasions to release penitents from the *casus reservati*, allowing them to remit sins otherwise under papal or episcopal reserve.[685] The pope could further issue a plenary indulgence that applied *per modum suffragii* (by means of intercession) to souls residing in Purgatory.[686] In addition to the plenary indulgences that were applied from the moment of acquisition, it was also possible to postpone a plenary indulgence for the hour of death (*semel in mortis articulo*).[687] These future indulgences represented a privilege bestowed in ever-growing numbers during the fifteenth century, taking the form of a confessional letter (usually printed), or *confessionale*,[688] that entitled the holder to choose any priest to be his confessor when he came to that most critical hour of his life; this priest could release him from all sins – including those reserved for popes and bishops – and, more importantly, grant him the plenary indulgence (fig. 23).[689] There is a fundamental difference between these indulgences and ordinary papal and episcopal indulgences in terms of the former's unrestricted scope, associated privileges and limited time of grace. Moreover, the particular type of indulgence at issue here hinged on visiting the cathedral during that time of grace, occasionally in combination with other churches in the city. They are distinct from the papal indulgences available in any of various churches in a bishopric, the proceeds of which also accrued – at least in part – to the cathedral fabric. We will return to treat this latter type in our discussion of contributions from the diocese. Naturally, such large papal pardons, issued to a cathedral alone, implied a great flood of pilgrims into the episcopal city. Indeed, from the moment of their ceremonial promulgation up through their official termination, such indulgences dominated the religious life of a city, and its secular life too. The time of grace was a period of penitence and introversion, in which processions alternated with preaching, in which dozens of confessors, many commandeered from nearby cloisters, stood in attendance all through the day to assist the throngs of pilgrims who arrived from far and wide to confess their sins and earn the indulgence within the allotted time.[690] Inside the church were special collecting boxes into which the faithful could deposit their gifts, which, though not a prerequisite for earning the indulgence, were nevertheless customary. Expectations for yields on these occasions were high: in 1467 the cathedral of Cologne installed an indulgence alms-chest that required six men to lift it (fig. 43).[691]

It is important to distinguish between plenary indulgences, which were issued by the pope for a specific purpose and were just guests in the cathedral, as it were, and indulgences that the pope granted expressly for a single cathedral (or church). The difference lies more in the principle than in the practical consequences; in the case of the former, the profits were the pope's but the cathedral fabric received a share, whilst in the latter the situation tended to be the opposite. A famous example concerns the cathedral of Saintes. At the king's instigation, the chapter dean, Raimundus Peraudi (1435-1505), was able to secure an indulgence for the cathedral on 3 August 1476, half the proceeds of which would support the cathedral building works for ten years, the other half the battle against the Turks. In an important theological innovation, this indulgence was the first that could be applied to souls in Purgatory. Yet upon its renewal in 1487, we find that we are in fact dealing with a papal indulgence for the crusade against the Turks: whilst the indulgence was renewed, the cathedral's portion of the profits was not.[692] For the youthful Peraudi, who would rise to become a bishop and cardinal, an illustrious future awaited as a commissary of indulgences and adroit propagandist for major papal indulgences throughout all of northwestern Europe.

Amongst these large general papal indulgences were the crusade indulgences and the closely related Jubilee indulgence.[693] The first true Jubilee year, being a year of full forgiveness of sins and remission of associated punishments,[694] was proclaimed by Pope Boniface VIII in 1300. Subsequent popes in turn continued to declare certain years an *annus jubilaeus*, in intervals varying between 100, 50, 33 and 25 years.[695] Whereas the faithful initially had to make a pilgrimage to Rome to share in the plenary pardon, by the time of the second and especially third Jubilee, popes had devised a way for those incapable of undertaking the long Roman journey to enjoy the spiritual benefits of the indulgence as well.[696] At the close of the third Jubilee year in 1390, the plenary indulgence was made available for the first time in large parts of Europe,[697] with one-half of the resulting revenues going to Rome and the other half to meet local religious needs. The pope selected several churches in each diocese, usually including the cathedral, where for a certain space of time the faithful would be able to earn the indulgence under the same conditions as applied in Rome and *ad instar jubilei* (as for a Jubilee).[698] To describe the process by which indulgences were propagated in various Church provinces by the indulgence commissaries, who were further charged with collecting the resulting income, would require a chapter unto itself and need not concern us here. The division of such funds, however, is relevant for our purposes.[699] There were countless interested parties in the late Middle Ages, running the gamut through to the overlord.[700] One share, as stated, always went to the fabric of the church that hosted the Jubilee indulgence; usually this was half or a third of the local receipts.[701]

Plenary indulgences issued by the pope specifically to benefit building works at cathedrals and other churches varied according to the privileges and ceremony with which they were promulgated and celebrated. Of particular relevance is the actual length of an indulgence's validity. The simplest types were obtainable on certain days every year; they have already been discussed above. There were also jubilees (occasions on which extraordinary, usually plenary indulgences were offered in connection with a public display of the relics), which were celebrated with certain regularity (*turnus*) (fig. 44).[702]

Where a *turnus* spanned a few years – perhaps five or seven – the devotional event cannot be expected to have yielded significantly more than in ordinary years. Whether this was very much different for a *turnus* lasting 25, 50 or 100 years is doubtful. In 1220, the year of the translation of St Thomas's remains 50 years after his martyrdom, proceeds from the collection boxes in Canterbury (of which only a very small part went to the building works, as we have seen) totalled around three times the average yield between 1213 and 1222. By the second Jubilee in 1270, however, receipts were less than double the 1263-1273 average, and proceeds from the third Jubilee in 1320 and fourth in 1370 provided even less than the most profitable years between 1314-1323 and 1370-1383, respectively.[703] In Lyon the cathedral had not only the annual aforementioned plenary indulgence, but also celebrated a Jubilee whenever Corpus Christi coincided with the feast of its patron saint, St John (24 June) – an overlap that occurred every 50 to 90 years. Concerning the first celebration in 1546, we know that collection box profits, though at 186 l.t. totalling seven times the gains on the annual pardon, were too small to even cover the purchase of decorations for the cathedral.[704]

As this handful of figures shows, these oftentimes expensive devotional ceremonies were not exclusively, or even primarily, organized as a means of amassing alms, but just as much to advance the prestige of a church, its venerable treasury of relics and its exalted privileges. The same is not true of plenary papal indulgences, issued for a certain number of years and a brief time of grace, with or without special privileges attached: these were intended first and foremost to help fund the construction of a church. The fifteenth and sixteenth centuries saw the papal chancery issue a fairly large number of such indulgences, with a share of the profits – usually a third[705] – almost always claimed by the pope. A few examples will shed light on certain facets of this form of indulgence.

On 1 October 1390, even as Pope Boniface IX's Jubilee year drew to a close, the cathedral fabric of Milan managed to get possession of the *ad instar jubilei* indulgence for its building works. Anyone who wished to earn the indulgence had to visit the cathedral and four other churches in Milan and donate a sum equal to one-third of the costs of a trip to

44
Le grant pardon de Nostre Dame de Rains
Broadside incunable, 315 x 197 mm, attributed to the Parisian printer Guy Marchant, 1482
Rheims, Bibliothèque Municipale

French summary of the indulgence bull issued by Pope Pius II (1458-1564) on 1 April 1460.
The pope grants a plenary indulgence once every seven years in perpetuity to all who will go to the cathedral after Vespers and there make a gift of their temporal goods to the fabric on the feast day of St Luke (18 October, the anniversary of the church's dedication), the day thereafter and on the vigil day (day before the feast day). For the feeble and the elderly, an offering to the fabric suffices. The archbishop and chapter are empowered to appoint confessors who can release the faithful from all their sins, including those the remittance of which is reserved for the Holy See, and can commute

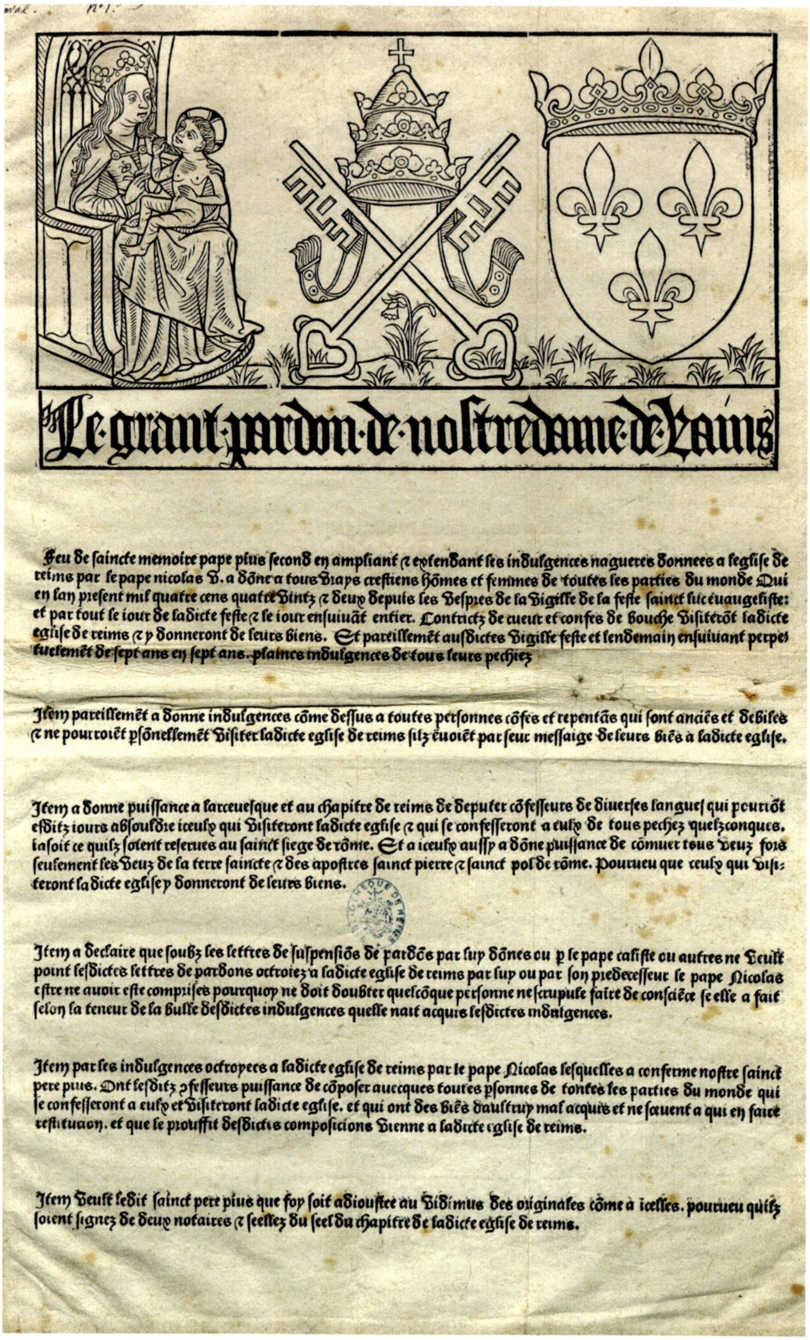

Le grant pardon de nostre dame de Rains

Feu de saincte memoire pape pius second en ampliant ⁊ extendant les indulgences nagueres donnees a leglise de reims par le pape nicolas V. a dōne a tous vrays crestiens hōmes et femmes de toutes les parties du monde Qui en lan present mil quatre cens quatre vintz ⁊ deux depuis les vespres de la vigille de la feste sainct luc euangeliste: et par tout le iour de ladicte feste ⁊ le iour ensuiuāt entier. Contrictz de cueur et confes de bouche visiterōt ladicte eglise de reims ⁊ y donneront de leurs biens. Et pareillemēt ausdictes vigille feste et lendemain ensuiuant perpetuelemēt de sept ans en sept ans. plaines indulgences de tous leurs pechiez

Item pareillemēt a donne indulgences cōme dessus a toutes personnes cōfes et repentās qui sont anciēs et debiles ⁊ ne pourroiēt psōnellemēt visiter ladicte eglise de reims silz enuoiēt par leur messaige de leurs biēs a ladicte eglise.

Item a donne puissance a larceuesque et au chapitre de reims de deputer cōfesseurs de diuerses langues qui pourrōt esditz iours absouldre iceulx qui visiteront ladicte eglise ⁊ qui se confesseront a eulx de tous pechez quelzconques. iasoit ce quilz soient reserues au sainct siege de rōme. Et a iceulx aussy a dōne puissance de cōmuer tous veuz fors seulement les veuz de la terre saincte ⁊ des apostres sainct pierre ⁊ sainct pol de rōme. Pourueu que ceulx qui visiteront la dicte eglise y donneront de leurs biens.

Item a declaire que soubz les lettres de suspensiōs de pardōs par luy dōnes ou p le pape caliste ou autres ne veult point lesdictes lettres de pardons octroiez a ladicte eglise de reims par luy ou par son predecesseur le pape Nicolas estre ne auoir este comprises pourquoy ne doit doubter quelcōque personne ne scrupule faire de consciēce se elle a fait selon la teneur de la bulle desdictes indulgences quelle nait acquis lesdictes indulgences.

Item par les indulgences octroyees a ladicte eglise de reims par le pape Nicolas lesquelles a conferme nostre sainct pere pius. Ont lesditz cōfesseurs puissance de cōposer auecques toutes psonnes de toutes les parties du monde qui se confesseront a eulx et visiteront ladicte eglise. et qui ont des biēs daultruy mal acquis et ne sceuent a qui en faire restitucion. et que le prouffit desdictes composicions vienne a ladicte eglise de reims.

Item veult ledit sainct pere pius que foy soit adioustee au vidimus des originales cōme a icelles. pourueu quilz soient signez de deux notaires ⁊ seellez du seel du chapitre de ladicte eglise de reims.

Rome. The validity of the indulgence was exceptionally long; whereas the time of grace was generally not above fifteen days, here it ran from 15 February until 8 September 1391, with a subsequent extension until Easter (14 April) 1392. Receipts exceeded all expectations, with at least 34,700 lire imp. (910 yearly wages of a *manovale*) in 1391 alone, representing 60 percent of the fabric's already exceptionally high income.[706]

In the case of Troyes, where the cathedral enjoyed these papal indulgences several times in succession, the fabric's profits are also documented. On 21 October 1451 Pope Nicholas V issued a plenary indulgence for a term of seven years, having been petitioned by the king to do so in connection with the resumption of works in the nave. The indulgence was available to all who visited the cathedral on Low Sunday (and from 1452 also on Easter) and gave alms for the nave's completion. A quarter of the profits were to be reserved for Rome.[707] In 1451/52 the gross receipts came to 1155 l.t., from which the papal quarter and over 200 l.t. in expenses were deducted, leaving the fabric with 876 l.t., or over 41 yearly wages of an unskilled labourer. Several years later, in 1461, Pope Pious II renewed the indulgence for an undocumented number of years; now the time of grace spanned one week, from Easter until Low Easter, and the papal share comprised one-third. Preachers promoted the pardon in all the surrounding dioceses. Net proceeds (after deduction of the Roman portion) over five years between 1461 and 1470 were recorded at between 546 l.t. and 245 l.t. a year.[708] At just under half of the fabric's income, these were considerable sums.[709]

The papal indulgence for the cathedral of Vannes brings another aspect to light, namely, that the pope could repeal or postpone indulgences granted by his predecessor or reissue them under new conditions. In this case, Pope Nicholas v (1447-24 March 1455) issued a plenary indulgence when construction of the nave began on 20 September 1451, available to anyone who visited the cathedral on the feast day of Sts Peter and Paul (29 June) and made an offering for the building works. There is no mention of a papal share. Three years later, on 15 May 1455, the new pope, Calixtus III (8 April 1455-1458), suspended this indulgence in order to give precedence to another for a crusade against the Turks.[710] For Vannes, the timing was terrible; the 1455 feast

vows (except pilgrimages to Jerusalem or Rome). The confessors may furthermore make a *compositio* (settlement) on behalf of the cathedral fabric with anyone who holds unlawfully acquired goods with no known owner.
The indulgence was probably prompted by the fire that destroyed the roof on 23 July 1481

LITERATURE
A. Claudin, *Histoire de l'imprimerie en France au xve et au* XVIe *siècle*, Paris 1900, vol. 1, pp. 220-222 (with facsimile); *Einblattdrucke des XV. Jahrhunderts*, no. 1076 and index in voce '*summa(rium)*'; Fournier 1923, p. 120 n. 1; *Gesamtkatalog der Wiegendrucke*, Stuttgart/New York 19682, no. 107; Eisermann 2004, vol. 1, p. 42 no. 68.

of Sts Peter and Paul had been earmarked as the day on which Vincent Ferrer, who had died in Vannes in 1419 and was buried there, was to be canonized. To make up for the loss, the pope extended the indulgence for another ten years after the suspension expired on 6 March 1460, at which time the cathedral was still due seventeen years. However, new papal conditions now stipulated that one-third of the profits from the remaining years be ceded for the war against the Turks. The plenary indulgence remained in effect until 29 June 1476. Two years later the cathedral had secured another one, this time for four years – a generous term if we consider that the new nave had already been consecrated on 17 March 1476.[711]

While the possibility of acquiring indulgences allowed a cathedral fabric to exert some measure of control over a short-lived, though at times exponential increase in its income, this was much less so in the case of receipts resulting from a surge in veneration – and donations – for a saint. The sudden emergence, and often equally rapid decline, of certain devotions was bound up with an array of unpredictable factors, including the occurrence – or absence – of miracles. We must take care to distinguish between such swells of devotion and the annual cycle of ordinary devotions, discussed above. An example of the former is related in the Chartrian *liber miraculorum*: at a critical turning point, when financial support from the bishop and chapter had ceased, the Virgin Mary interceded on the cathedral's behalf with a great and astounding miracle at the Marian altar, restoring to a mute child his power of speech.[712] As news of this marvel spread, the crowds streaming to the church waxed so large that – in a superbly orchestrated scene – the boy had to climb atop a wooden dais raised over the fabric's collection box so that all could hear as he roused the faithful to give alms for the building works.[713] This first miracle unleashed a series of others, which together in large part propelled the great building movement described above. Numerous miracles befell pilgrims as they transported building materials to the cathedral, saving them from various misfortunes. There can be no doubt that the exceptional pace of building – the cathedral was largely finished by around 1220[714] – owed primarily to contributions made by pilgrims in the years after

1197 (figs 38, 39). One century later, Our Lady of Chartres and her *sancta Tunica* (blessed tunic) had, it seems, been forgotten. In her place was St Piat, and at the beginning of the fourteenth century '*le corps de saint Piat florissait en miracles*' (the body of St Piat flourished in miracles). Veneration for this sainted bishop, whose remains were discovered in a dismembered, though unharmed, state upon the opening of his shrine in 1310, paved the way for, amongst other things, a chapel in his name and the commission of a new shrine.[715]

One strategy used to promote devotions was the ceremonial transfer of a relic to a new resting place (translation).[716] It has rightly been noted that the ceremonial rehousing of the skull of St Nicasius, a fifth-century bishop of Rheims, in a new reliquary in 1213 was in fact a strategy conceived by the chapter to attract outside funds after the three-year term of archiepiscopal and capitular financial support for the cathedral, begun in 1210, expired.[717] The ceremonial opening of a shrine (*visitatio*), as with the aforementioned '*capsa sancti Piati*', had a similar objective.

England was particularly rich with shrines where veneration sparked and sustained building activities.[718] More than half of its nineteen cathedrals could boast such a shrine, usually dedicated to a local saint (figs 45, 46).[719] Amongst them, the cult of Thomas Becket occupies a special position. Having been assassinated at the king's behest in 1170, the bishop was canonized after just three years. The translation of his body 50 years later, on 7 July 1220, and the celebration of the first Jubilee marked the actual beginning of the great pilgrimage to Canterbury in the thirteenth, fourteenth and fifteenth centuries.[720] As one maxim went, '*translato Thoma, succedunt prospera cuncta*' (all prospers since the translation of Thomas).[721] English bishops therefore set about translating the relics of their own local saints in similar fashion. But in the event, as we have already seen, it by no means followed that the alms of the faithful all flowed into the building works.

Another option was to acquire new relics (fig. 25). The cathedral chapter of Troyes enjoyed a uniquely advantageous position in this respect: after the capture of Constantinople in 1204, it was the bishop of Troyes, Garnier de Tramel, who was appointed to manage the full

45
Shrine of Thomas Cantilupe, bishop of Hereford (1274-1282), used from 1287 until 1349
Hereford Cathedral, north transept

This shrine was the locus of miracles in the years after 1287, contributing to the canonization of Thomas Cantilupe in 1320. The shrine was used from 1287 until 1349 and the offerings made during this period were enormously important in financing the cathedral's construction. The base of the monument, which is carved with reliefs of mourning knights (the plinth is modern), is the original sepulchre, which consisted of a tomb covered with a marble slab and on top of it a copper sheet bearing the figure of the bishop. Presumably it was Cantilupe's successor who decided fairly early on to transform the tomb into a shrine in which the relics could be venerated. The first miracle was recorded in 1286, indicating that the shrine was already drawing worshippers. The base was adapted and made slightly broader, and a second level of open arches was added store of Byzantine relics. Before his death in 1205, he had ensured that a number of illustrious remains, including the body of the holy virgin St Helena of Athyra, were reserved for his cathedral. They reached their destination sometime before 1215, and in fact it was not until then that the chapter was able to make real progress in its campaign to rebuild the cathedral that had burnt down in 1188. Then, and even more so after the devastating 1228 storm that destroyed freshly rebuilt sections of the cathedral church, various measures were put in place by the chapter to propagate St Helena's fame as a miracle-working saint.[722]

Concerted attempts were also made to find forgotten remains of saints buried under church floors, with solemn elevations resulting from such happy discoveries, of which eleventh- and twelfth-century sources leave us with some striking descriptions.[723] In 1330 an antique sarcophagus with the presumed remains of the fifth-century bishop St Zenobius was unearthed in the cathedral of Florence, serving to kick-start the building campaign that had been stagnating since 1323. His translation was performed in the presence of a large host of bishops, who granted their indulgences for the thronging faithful. '*Per qual tralazione*', Villani writes, '*quasi tutto il populo e persone di Firenze devote, uomini e donne, piccoli e grandi, v'andarono con grande devozione e offerta*'.[724]

Last but not least, the first years following the canonization of a saint could spell large revenues for the church in which his remains were preserved. In 1457 the canons of Salisbury were granted a request for the sanctification of their first Norman bishop, Osmund (d. 1099), by which they intended to attract pilgrims and thus accumulate the financial resources needed to make necessary repairs to the tower.[725]

There is little quantitative data tracing the financial impact these brief yet intense devotions had on the building works. We do, however, have some figures from York Cathedral relating to devotional offerings for the fabric made at the grave of the Archbishop Richard Scrope, who had been revered as a saint since his execution following an armed action against Henry IV in 1405, in spite of protest from the king and the archbishop of Canterbury. In 1415 the '*recepta oblacionum ad sepulturam Magistri Ricardi Lescrope*' (offers received for the grave of

through which the bishop's portrait remained visible. During the ceremonial translation of the relics on 3 April 1387 the bones were placed inside a wooden *feretrum* (litter), possibly in the shape of a catafalque, which was placed on the top of the tomb and covered with a canopy that could be raised and lowered by means of a pulleys; remnants of this mechanism have been preserved, but the *feretrum* and canopy are lost. In 2008 the medieval shrine base was fitted with a new canopy, donated by Sir Roy Strong, designed by the architect Robert Kilgour and painted by Peter Murphy; a single extant relic was placed back inside at that time.

LITERATURE

Jancey 1982; G. Marshall, 'The shrine of St Thomas de Cantilupe in Hereford Cathedral', *Transactions of the Woolhope Naturalists' Field Club* 1930-1932, pp. 34-50; Nilson 1998, pp. 47-49; *A Guide to the fabric of the newly restored shrine of Saint Thomas of Hereford, celebrating the saints a Hereford Cathedral*, Hereford 2008.

master Richard Scrope) totalled over £73, representing almost twelve percent of the fabric's income, and in 1418 as much as £150, or over 20 percent of its income, which reached a record height of £696 in that year, this being equivalent to around 170 annual wages of an unskilled labourer.[726]

A second example concerns gifts brought to the tomb of St Thomas Cantilupe in the cathedral of Hereford, and perhaps paints a more typical picture of the nature of temporary devotional cults. Fabric rolls are preserved from 1290/91, a year in which veneration for this saint was probably at its peak, and from 1386/87.[727] On 3 April 1287 the body of Thomas Cantilupe, who had died in 1282 and was venerated as though sainted, was transferred to a new grave in the cathedral (fig. 45). A first miracle took place a week before this rite, and from that moment on the chapter had all the miracles that occurred or were reported there put in writing. In 1305 the king and an assortment of bishops and high clerics and nobles petitioned the pope to confer sainthood on Thomas Cantilupe. The canonization procedure was launched on 13 July 1307, with the papal commission spending eleven weeks at the cathedral of Hereford to inspect the tomb, draw up an inventory of the offerings made in coin and especially in kind, and to interview the '*custodes tumuli*' (gravesite supervisors) about the nature of the miracles. From the list of 470 miracles recorded from 1287 on, they selected 207 for the canonization dossier, from which a final selection of seventeen was tendered as incontrovertible evidence in the canonization bull. But by 1307, crowds at the tomb and almsgiving there were already on the wane. Neither Cantilupe's canonization in 1320, nor the translation of his remains to a new shrine in 1349 was able to revive the cult to any extent. Records of the offerings there provide striking confirmation of the characteristically short-lived popularity of such cults. The proceeds from offerings at the tomb alone comprised £179 in 1290, or more than 92 annual wages of an unskilled labourer and over 60 percent of the total income of £286. Clearly, it was no exaggeration when the papal commissaries declared in 1307 that the financial proceeds from the gravesite '*fuerent (!) cathedralis ecclesia de duabus navibus amplicata et fabricatum in parte maximum campanile*' (have enlarged the cathedral with two aisles and in part erected the high bell tower).[728] Barely a century later, in 1386, offerings at the shrine only raised £1½ of the fabric's total income of £79. The miraculous cures had already long been consigned to a distant past; indeed, by far the greatest number of miracles had taken place in the first year (1287), whilst by 1300 only no more than nine were recorded, and in 1312 only one.

TEN MONEY COLLECTED IN AND OUTSIDE THE DIOCESE

No matter how wealthy a cathedral was in its indulgences, or how impressive its collection of relics, the bishop and chapter could do no more than wait and see if the faithful would actually be willing to undertake the often difficult and expensive journey to a cathedral.[729] Given this fact, churches and monasteries began quite early on to seek out opportunities for turning the wait-and-see approach into an active one, bringing the rich blessings proffered by indulgences and the veneration of relics to the faithful to reap a similarly rich harvest of gifts and offerings for the church. Here, too, we must distinguish between collection campaigns launched for a delimited, temporary period and those that continued over many decades or even centuries. We shall first briefly consider the former category.

1 • SHORT-TERM DIOCESAN COLLECTIONS

Short-term diocesan collections had their basis in the same papal indulgences discussed above. Those indulgences and spiritual benefits could only obtained by visiting the cathedral itself, sometimes in combination with a number of other churches in the same city. But it was equally possible for papal indulgences to be made available in

designated churches throughout an entire bishopric or Church province, or to omit the stipulation of a church visit. In such cases it became necessary not only to propagate the indulgence over a large territory, but also to collect the monies from near and far; two examples follow below.

Records concerning the financial results of an indulgence that Pope Eugene IV bestowed on the cathedral of St Lambert in Liège for a term of three years on 24 April 1443 present us with a fairly complete picture. Anyone who laboured in the building works for 30 days, or fifteen for those less well-off, or alternatively donated a sum equivalent to as many days' wages, and who furthermore fasted every Friday for a full year, would receive the right to choose *in articulo mortis* (at the hour of death) any confessor he wished to release him from all sins, including the *casus reservati* (reserved cases), and confer on him a plenary indulgence. Those who earned this indulgence received a confessional letter, or *confessionale* (fig. 23), the granting of which the masters of the fabric recorded in a registry. The funds raised over three years, from mid-August 1443 until 7 April 1446, came to more than 17,221 l.lod., or 25 to 30 times the annual wage of an Utrecht labourer. This amount still included expenses, the quarter reserved for the Dominicans in exchange for their aid in propagating the indulgence, and the salary of the chaplain charged with its complex administration. Over two-thirds of the earnings on this indulgence came from outside the city of Liège.[730]

The second example relates to the *ad instar jubilei* indulgence – an indulgence that was exceptionally broad in scope – which the chapter at Konstanz managed to obtain from Rome to rebuild its two towers after fire damaged the cathedral in 1511.[731] The indulgence was granted by Pope Julius II on 18 September 1512 for a term of three years from the first day of Lent of the following year (9 February 1513).[732] A unique feature of this indulgence was that it could be promulgated in not only the bishopric of Konstanz, but also in the dioceses of Chur, Augsburg and Strasbourg. It could be obtained in the cathedrals of any of these four bishoprics, as well as in their collegiate churches and in populous parishes where there were enough priests on hand to preach and hear confessions.[733] In order to earn the plenary indulgence[734] the suppliant had to visit a church and donate a sum of money equivalent to the amount needed to sustain his family for one week (with a possible reduction for especially prolific families); those who lived alone had to surrender one or half a month's salary, as determined by the confessor. Also eligible for the indulgence were those who donated or transported construction materials or who laboured unpaid or provided free labour for six days. Those favoured with wealth and power were expected to give more, whilst the poor might receive dispensation. Even before the cathedral's first indulgence campaign could be rounded off, however, it encountered a hitch, in the form of Pope Julius II's

46
Crippled pilgrims, drawing oil at the grave of St William, archbishop of York
Stained glass window in the north choir aisle, by the workshop of John Thornton, c.1414
York Minster

St William Fitzherbert, archbishop of York (1142-1154), was venerated as a martyr in York and canonized in 1227. Countless miracles took place at his grave. The large stained glass window dedicated to him, privately endowed by a baronial family, contains 105 panels with scenes from the saint's life, posthumous miracles and veneration at his shrine. Oil that had been brought into physical contact with the grave was collected for its healing effect.

LITERATURE French 1999, p.80, plate 12; Nilson 1998, pp.104-105, 164.

death on 21 February 1513. Following custom, the indulgence had to be requested anew from the incoming pope. The chapter decided to make a virtue of necessity and solicited Rome for greater benefits and compensation, including a reduction of the pope's one-third share in the proceeds as negotiated in 1512[735] and the right to tender the indulgence in additional dioceses, namely, the bishoprics of Mainz, Bamberg, Salzburg, Passau, Würzburg and Magdeburg.[736] Wary of provoking needless irritation from Rome, the chapter elected to hold off on pushing the latter request. Yet to its bewilderment the new pope, Leo x, immediately responded by demanding not a third, but half the gross profits. The indulgence continued under this condition for only one further year, and plans for a third campaign were abandoned.

Meanwhile, the receipts proved considerable. They are known to us only from Roman sources and document the gross amounts, thus before deduction of the very high costs.[737] In fact, one of these costs was the one-third, later possibly one-quarter,[738] share of receipts from the diocese of Konstanz that was designated for the bishop – a glaring indication of how little concern this prelate actually spared his spiritual bride. The gross profits less the portion for Rome came to 7108 rhinegulden in 1513, and 4474 rhinegulden in 1514, equalling 197 and 124 annual wages of a stonemason, respectively.[739] A large part of the profits was also needed to pay outlays for propaganda and collection of the monies. The latter was the chapter's responsibility, delegated to individual canons, with the Augsburg Fugger banking firm charged with securing the pope's share. Great risks attended the transportation of the collected profits. On 23 August 1513 one of the cathedral canons solicited his brethrens' advice on how best to get the indulgence monies from Strasbourg to Konstanz; the quantity of coins was '*da wa es muntz sin* [...] *ze schwär zu ross ze füren*', inspiring his request to stash the coins in small vessels disguised as merchandise and have them transported by a wagoner.[740]

2 • LONG-TERM DIOCESAN COLLECTIONS: THE MENDICATORIA

Collections of a more permanent duration both within and occasionally also outside the diocese had a far greater impact on funding cathedral construction. Unlike collections linked with a papal plenary indulgence and restricted to a few years, which only made their appearance in the fifteenth century, collections initiated by the bishop and chapter are documented from the beginning of the twelfth century. These early instances were hardly organized, and it is only towards the end of the twelfth century that we find episcopal missives, addressed to all the clergy of a bishopric, giving such collections a more definite structure. Around 1200, and possibly even slightly earlier, convention turned to the use of a certain type of elaborate document that, minor differences aside, gained acceptance in countless dioceses. As complex episcopal mandates welding elements of unmistakably varied provenance into a single end product, these documents should not be classified as letters of indulgence on the basis of one or another of those elements, as has been done in the past; rather, they can more properly be designated as *mendicatoria*, or 'begging-letters'.[741]

Mendicatoria serve as a good starting point from which to explore the complicated diocesan collection campaigns. We have analysed various such documents, dating from the end of the twelfth to the sixteenth centuries and originating from bishoprics throughout Europe. Given the broad similarity in content and formulations used in these letters, our selection is deemed to provide an accurate representation.[742] Such differences as do exist concern not only variations between *mendicatoria* from different bishoprics, but also between versions issued by successive bishops in a single diocese; though earlier *mendicatoria* were generally confirmed by a new bishop, he might also add or amend key points. This aspect will be addressed in greater depth in our discussion on the series of such letters from Utrecht. For now we shall take a cursory look at the content of these documents and go on from there to identify their component parts, the varying nature and provenance of the resulting revenues, and the factors that determined their value.

As stated, these episcopal mandates were addressed to the community of diocesan clergy. In them, the bishop usually began by listing the cathedral fabric's needs. He appealed to the love the faithful bore the cathedral – mother church of the diocese – and called on their generosity. In flowery language he would describe the lamentable state to which the cathedral had been reduced following fire or storm and rain, and also, conversely, the beauty of the cathedral and its high rank in the hierarchy of diocesan church buildings.[743]

In consideration of this financial need, or alternatively to ensure that the great work could be completed at a reasonable pace,[744] the bishop announced his decision to despatch one or more *nuntii* (messengers) to visit all churches in the bishopric on behalf of himself and the chapter. Clerics were obligated to allow the messengers into their churches; sometimes they were even required to offer them fitting hospitality in the rectory to prevent their being forced to seek shelter in taverns or other such unworthy places and thus discredit the whole enterprise.[745] Wishing to reassure the clergy concerning the hospitality demands being imposed on them, the archbishop of Besançon announced that the messengers would arrive '*in paucis equitaturis et modica familia*' (with only a few horses and a modest retinue).[746] Who exactly these messengers were is not always stated in so many words. Generally, they are described as '*nuntii eiusdem ecclesie, latores presencium*' (messengers of the cathedral, bringers of this letter),[747] arriving with or without relics from the cathedral.[748] *Mendicatoria* can be equally vague when it comes to the purpose of their visit. They are referred to as '*nuntii* [...] *fidelium suffragia ad hujus fabricam petituri*' (messengers to petition the faithful to aid the fabric of this cathedral),[749] '*nuntii, super premisso negotio promovendi deputati*' (messengers sent to advance the progress of the aforementioned matter)[750] or, more straightforwardly, '*nuntii* [...] *ad proponendum verbum Dei in ecclesiis vestris et pro colligendis fidelium elemosunis pro dicta structura*' (messengers to preach the word of God in your churches and collect contributions from the faithful for the said construction).[751] Simply stated, these messengers were the campaign's propagandists and the procurers of all that was given to the cathedral by parishioners, whether in obligatory collections or otherwise.[752] In most cases the bishop included a provision requiring parish priests to recommend the cathedral fabric to their congregations, sometimes with instructions for how and when this was to be done – for example on certain Sundays and feast days, or on all the days on which mass was read over the course of a full month following receipt of the letter, or on all Sundays and feast days up until the *dies reportationis*, this being the day on which the donations were to be handed over.[753] The collections themselves were also held on specific days, sometimes during a period designated by the *nuntii* or stated in the letter. To assure admittance for the cathedral's collection campaign, the bishop would usually order any interdict laid on the church to be raised for its duration,[754] and moreover prohibited other churches and ecclesiastical institutions from carrying out competing collections in the same period.[755] A common provision prescribed that the actual gathering of the monies be entrusted to one or more reliable parishioners, whom the parish priest appointed as *collectores*.[756] In some cases the *collectores* went door to door to receive donations from their fellow parishioners.[757] They were to keep all gifts intended for the cathedral in their possession and transfer them either to their parish priest or dean, or directly to the episcopal emissary on a specified day, the *dies reportationis*, and location, the *locus reportationes*.[758]

At the very least, therefore, the *nuntii* delivered the letters and collected the donations. But often their task was broader. When they brought relics with them or had explicit permission to ascend the pulpit or even to read the mass, their role was a more active one; then they were charged with conducting the collection and also, in many instances, with taking the donations then and there before continuing their journey. To invest the collection with a dignity befitting the occasion – thus assuring its chances of success – parish clergy and the faithful were expected to greet the cathedral's relic-bearing *nuntii* at the outer parish limits in ceremonial array, with parish pennants waving, candles alight and church bells tolling. They were also to observe the day of the collection as a Sunday: all parishioners who were of age were prohibited from performing heavy labour and were required to attend the church and remain there '*donec ipsum negotium sit finitum*' (until the task [the collection] is finished).[759]

The two methods of collecting – carried out by the parish priest and parishioners or by the episcopal messengers – could also coincide. In Prague, parish priests were to report on the *dies reportationis* to deliver alms from the faithful '*tam per socios dicti negotii, tam per vos acquisitas*' (collected both by the brethren with the stated task and by you [the parish priests]).[760] The archbishop of Mainz ordered that lists, *cartulae*, be drawn up rendering separate accounts of the gifts and providing an overview of the size of receipts from each source.[761] In Milan, messengers conducted the mass and also preached, but it was up to the local clergy, accompanied by two consuls and two further laymen, to go door to door for the money.[762]

The fabric was also assigned other monies in addition to these collection receipts. For example, parish priests usually had a duty to urge parishioners who were *in extremis* (in their last hour) to remember the cathedral in their wills.[763] Confessors, or even the *nuntii* themselves, could have an episcopal privilege permitting them to convert (*commutare*) certain pledges or imposed penances such as a pilgrimage or a fourteen-day fast into the payment of a certain sum of money to support cathedral construction.[764] Such a provision was almost always included for those individuals who wished to atone for the possession of goods acquired by plunder, theft, usury or other unlawful means and whose rightful owner could no longer be traced. In return for surrendering these *bona injusta* and *bona incerta* (goods of uncertain origin) to the building works, they received absolution.[765] Sometimes the bishop further stipulated that the cathedral building works was the sole party eligible for the restitution of such ill-gotten gains. Finally, there were the contributions from the confraters and consorors of the fabric confraternity, the foundation of which was sometimes also announced in the letter.[766] Generally speaking, anyone who registered as a member of a *fraternitas* accepted the moral obligation to pay admission dues and a yearly contribution,[767] for which not only the precise sum might be stipulated, but also the minimum term over which it was to be paid.[768]

Most *mendicatoria* are not clear as regards the collection of gifts intended for the fabric. If the *nuntii* did not actually take along the assembled offerings themselves, then the parish priest had to deliver them on a pre-agreed day – sometimes known as the *dies reportationis*[769] – directly into the hands of the *nuntii* or representatives of the cathedral fabric. A *dies reportationis* usually applied to an entire diocese, on which the parish priests were required to transfer the offerings in the presence of the dean.[770] In Prague the deans were then charged with recording which of the priests had failed to show up and to make an immediate report of their names to the bishop. These regulations were attended by religious penalties of various kinds to be imposed on both recalcitrant clergy and on laypeople who refused to cooperate or committed fraud, the implementation of which sometimes rested in part with the *nuntii*.[771]

Naturally, the bishop's letter was not confined to publicizing stipulations and penalties against various forms of obstinacy. Based on the powers vested in him as bishop, he bestowed countless spiritual benefits and privileges beginning, of course, with an indulgence for all benefactors of the cathedral fabric. Whilst these generally did not exceed the set limit of 40 days, the bishop could annex indulgences granted by popes, cardinals and other bishops to his own and declare these valid.[772] This practice could turn a *mendicatorium* into something of a collective bull of indulgence. One such *mendicatorium*, issued by the bishop of Würzburg, summarizes seven indulgences of 40 days to be granted to benefactors of the fabric, and more especially to those who combined a gift of alms with a visit to the cathedral on stated days.[773] In such cases as this, the episcopal letter would also encourage pilgrimages to the cathedral.

Linking up with the indulgence itself was a series of additional privileges, listed in the same sequence and in nearly identical phrasing in most *mendicatoria*.[774] One special privilege allowed cathedral benefactors to have their usual confessor absolve them of sins that normally fell under the episcopal reserve – the *casus reservati*[775] – such as breaking faith (provided such faith was later restored),[776] abusing one's parents (except bodily),[777] and perjury and breaking an oath (but only when frivolously sworn).[778] Occasionally, the bishop stipulated that parishes should announce the indulgences and spiritual benefits on offer in the local language from the pulpit.[779] For the priests who invested their energies in implementing the bishop's instructions, there was a special benefit consisting of an indulgence that lifted all sins of negligence they might have unwittingly committed whilst saying mass or praying the canonical hours, whether through forgetfulness, carelessness or mindlessness.[780]

Frequently, the bishop granted all benefactors a share in the common spiritual fruits of the prayers and good works carried out in and by diocesan churches and cloisters.[781] Sometimes he added some further specification entailing special obligations on the diocesan clergy.[782] In the diocese of Strasbourg, as we learn from the 1275 letter, all priests, both regular and secular, were required to read no less than three weekly masses for cathedral benefactors: one for the deceased, one for the remission of sins and one in honour of the Virgin Mary; the chapter calculated the cumulative total at 80,000 masses each year.[783] In 1326 the bishop of Vich worked out that four compulsory masses from 1500 priests in the city and diocese would come to 6000 masses to be said for the souls of brothers and sisters both deceased and living.[784] A 1525 *mendicatorium* from Regensburg reckons the number of masses celebrated in the cathedral at 7254.[785] In Cologne, the archbishop ordered every priest to read two masses each month for living and dead benefactors, and all lower clergy to recite two Psalters each year for the same; furthermore, after reading from the gospels on Sundays and feast days, parish priests had to invite their congregation to kneel together to recite the Our Father and Ave Maria. In the episcopacy of Würzburg, the recitation of the Credo was followed by a number of psalms, these to be accompanied by a collection and the tolling of the church bells. The bishop of Toul made it mandatory for the faithful to attend the thrice-yearly choral masses for cathedral benefactors, and the bishop of Gerona announced his appointment of four priests to read masses for them in the cathedral.

As a rule, such benefits and privileges applied to everyone who supported the cathedral building works, though in the case of members of the fabric confraternity, the beneficiaries were listed by name and might enjoy additional special privileges. For example, it was very common to give them the right to a church burial, even where the parish concerned had been placed under an interdict.[786] In the bishopric of Toul, these confraters and consorors were also granted complete and exclusive freedom in selecting their own confessors each year, which they could do within a month after making their donation; this confessor would also be able to absolve them of reserved sins.[787]

To offer a simple paraphrase of an episcopal *mendicatorium* or cathedral-buildings mandate would fall short of our purpose here. In its most intricate form a *mendicatorium* encompassed a constellation of myriad heterogeneous constituents. The section that follows shall first set out their historical components, insofar as possible, and proceed from there to examine various types of contributions. Bishops' *mendicatoria* employ various approaches to summon the faithful to donate to the building works. Though many bishoprics did not take every single path mapped out in the *mendicatoria* and also acquired lay contributions outside the framework of such mandates, they will nevertheless all be dealt with here. To conclude our discussion, we will explore the financial impact that all these revenues from the diocesan faithful had on the cathedral building works.

HISTORICAL COMPONENTS OF *THE MENDICATORIA*

THE FABRIC CONFRATERNITY

Of all the variegated historical roots from which *mendicatoria* derive, the notion of the fraternal community can be traced back the farthest. During early Christian times the idea took shape that the fruits of one's prayers and good works could be extended to others, manifesting itself as early as the sixth and seventh centuries in the establishment of confraternities of prayer amongst countless monastic communities,[788] later also coming to include the lay benefactors of that monastery. Men and women who were affiliated with a confraternity would partake, both in life and after death, of the spiritual merits that the members of the monastic community had amassed during a lifetime of prayer and penance.[789] From the eighth century onwards, synods also gave rise to such religious associations, formed between the participants and their followers, sometimes involving precise prescriptions for the number of masses to be read and Psalters to be recited for the souls of the deceased.[790] The spirit driving these confraternities evolved in various directions, though always circumscribed by the notion of the religious brotherhood, and resulted in a diverse range of organizational forms. One was the *fraternitas*, which as a strictly local socio-religious association was tied to a particular church, where it typically maintained its own chapel or altar.[791] The group's activities were both internal and external in focus. The confraters, and later also consorors, socialized with each other (holding an annual banquet) and organized anniversary obits for deceased members; they also carried out good works or exercised some special form of devotion. Some confraternities were established with the express aim of supporting a parish church building works.[792] At the same time, the original idea for interlocal religious brotherhoods was also sustained, both in the international confraternities attached to major abbeys and monastic orders such as the Antonines,[793] and in the cathedral fabric confraternities named in *mendicatoria*.[794]

Those who felt prompted to make an annual contribution to the building works were welcomed into the confraternity of the cathedral. In Spain the oldest cathedral confraternities date to around 1100. In Pamplona we find Pope Urban II approving the foundation of a confraternity in support of the cathedral in 1091.[795] At the cathedral of Seo de Urgel, Bishop Odón (1095-1122) fixed an especially comprehensive set of rules for the fabric confraternity – rules that already contain many of the ingredients that would later come to characterize most *fraternitates*: the opportunity to earn an indulgence, annual contributions from members and masses to be read for the souls of dead and living brethren.[796] Within the span of less than a century, cathedral fabric confraternities had proliferated far and wide, arriving in Lisieux about 1166,[797] in Noyon around the same time,[798] in London before 1175,[799] in Bayeux between 1184 and 1205[800] and in Strasbourg between 1190 and 1202.[801] It is to this period as well that we must trace the development of the organizational model that would remain current throughout the Middle Ages.[802] The process of founding a diocesan confraternity was not always a smooth one. In 1166 Bishop Arnulf of Lisieux complained to the pope about the fate of two priests he had sent out '*ob constituendas fraternitates ad reedificationem ecclesie nostre*' (to establish brotherhoods for the rebuilding of our cathedral): having reported to the monastery of Grestain, they were beaten up by two of the local monks who proceeded to kick them around in the mud.[803] But this was not to be the end of his woes. A few years later we find him appealing to his colleague in Noyon to inflict severe punishments on a group of priests who had been passing through the bishopric to collect donations for the cathedral, but had absconded with the money instead.[804]

A letter from the bishop of Bayeux (between 1184 and 1205) provides clues to a complicated substructure. In the letter he announces the reestablishment of an existing but 'dozing' brotherhood. The members paid 6 d.and. a year for a period of at least five years. In return, they were guaranteed a church burial – possible interdicts notwithstanding – and an indulgence, as well as the assurance that masses with canonical hours for deceased brethren would be read in all diocesan parishes and abbeys. Two parishioners and a parish priest would be tasked with taking in and guarding the donations until such time as the *nuntii* came to pick them up, and they were to be given a hospitable welcome (an apparently not unnecessary instruction, given the experiences of the Lisieux *nuntii*). Around the same time a London diocesan fabric confraternity was founded to bolster the fire-damaged cathedral of St Paul's. From a 1175 episcopal letter addressed to the clergy and faithful of that diocese, we learn that its creation had already been proposed at the diocesan synod, where all the assembled priests had agreed to read 30 masses for the fraternity's members each year – fifteen for the living and fifteen for the dead – to which the chapter had added another two masses per week. Confraternity members would moreover be entitled to a church burial, regardless of any interdict. They would in turn be expected to pay an annual contribution, though poor brethren were exempted. The bishop's writ was to be circulated amongst the archdeacons and deans and, through them, to all the parish churches; the parish priests were ordered to make the letter's contents known to their congregations during the celebration of the mass on Sundays and feast days. The bishop of London also hoped to make membership attractive to faithful from outside the bishopric and to this end applied to Pope Alexander III (1159-1181) for a papal recommendation for his cathedral fabric confraternity. Armed with this recommendation, the bishop could make his appeal to prelates in surrounding dioceses that much more convincing. One such, the bishop

47
Stone partition of the Works Chantry, the northernmost chapel in the south transept, c.1350
Lincoln Cathedral

Inscribed in the arch framing the door are the words: *'Oremus pro benefactoribus istius ecclesie'* (let us pray for the benefactors of this church). Beneath it on either side are two clerics, the chaplains of the Works Chantry, kneeling in prayer; at the top is the seated figure of a bishop, with above him the royal arms. The uppermost section of the partition has been heavily restored, and the statues crowning the entryway are modern. Masses founded by the fabric for living and deceased cathedral benefactors were read in this chapel. The Works Chantry is the oldest of the three major chantries in Lincoln Cathedral, and was probably founded as early as c.1200.

LITERATURE Hill 1965, p. 113.

of Winchester, agreed on 18 May 1175 to allow *nuntii* from London to traverse his bishopric to promote the confraternity.[805]

Nearly all *mendicatoria* include provisions on a confraternity as one ingredient - sometimes the principal one - in a wider assemblage of measures.[806] The role of a fabric confraternity differed from one bishopric to another. In Utrecht its significance was secondary, whilst in Cologne the collection campaign organized from the fourteenth century onwards was carried out entirely under the auspices of the brotherhood of St Peter's.[807] One factor determining such differences was the term for which a brotherhood was established. Some seem to have been intended to generate financial support for a single building campaign, and thus were set up for five, seven or ten years, though very often with extensions thereafter.[808] Many others, however, appear to have been founded in perpetuity and managed to continue their meagre existence for several hundreds of years.

A second factor in such differences was the degree of formality and ceremony attending the masses and divine offices said for benefactors chiefly in the cathedral church. For example, in a decision dated 20 December 1362, the chapter of Metz agreed to establish an annual '*anniversaire solenneil, vigile et messe a grant aulteil pour tous les bienfaicteurs de l'euvre et soneront les grosses cloches*', to be funded by the fabric. Many cathedrals housed an altar designated for the confraternity, at which masses for the confraters and consorors were read.[809] As early as 1217, we find an altar dedicated to St Thomas Becket in the cathedral of Auxerre, '*quod et de confratria dicebatur, eo quod pro confratribus ecclesie missa ibi cotidie celebretur*' (this also having been called the altar of the confraternity, since masses for the members of the cathedral confraternity were daily read there).[810] A similar altar could be found in the cathedral of Basel.[811] In the cathedral of Strasbourg, confraternity masses were said at the previously cited altar of the city council, situated in front of the rood loft.[812] At Lincoln, the fabric had charge of the 'works chantry' from the end of the twelfth or beginning of the thirteenth century, which was accommodated in one of the chapels of the transept; as in Strasbourg, the cost of the three or four chaplains attached to it was borne by the fabric fund. Unto this day an inscription above the chapel entrance reads '*Oremus pro bene-*

48
Detail. Stone partition of the Works Chantry, the northernmost chapel in the south transept, c. 1350 Lincoln Cathedral

Two chaplains of the Works Chantry, kneeling in prayer

factoribus istius ecclesiae' (let us pray for the benefactors of this church), to either side of which are relief carvings of two chantry priests in prayer (fig. 47, 48).[813] In Troyes a special votive office in honour of the Holy Spirit was read for cathedral benefactors every Monday.[814] Such confraternity altars formed a tangible expression of the *fraternitas* spirit and formed the focus of devotions and services organized by the cathedral fabric. In the Utrecht Dom it was the altar of St Martin in the north transept arm – also known as the *oflaet-altaar* – that served this purpose,[815] and in Lund sources mention an *altare fabrice* in 1384.[816] In many instances, such as in Strasbourg and Utrecht, this altar was also where gifts in currency and kind for the building works were collected. On occasion we encounter references to a local nucleus of members, such as in Troyes, where brothers of the confraternity of St Peter came together on the saint's feast day for a civic procession and annual sermon by the bishop thereafter.[817] In Basel it was the cathedral clergy that assembled once a year during the Ember Days of December for a confraternal procession through the cloister, carrying relics, a cross and pennants. On this occasion they invested extra effort in soliciting new members from the crowds that came to witness the spectacle.[818]

Another widespread and age-old custom was the compilation of a register in which to record the names of all benefactors, and of confraternity members in particular (fig. 49).[819] In the *liber confraternitatis fabricae ecclesiae Tornacensis*, belonging to the Tournai brotherhood founded in 1361, we find not only an overview of indulgences and a description of the miracles attributed to intercession by the Virgin and various saints, but also a wonderful paean to the cathedral: with its ceaseless singing of the choral offices, the glorious interior and the erudition of its clerics, it forms the '*lux suprema ac laus magnifica*' of the city. The cathedral is a source of solace for all who enter there, 'because they come one by one, but are as roused as a community'.[820]

The masters of the *Frauenwerk* in Strasbourg recorded the names of benefactors and their gifts in the *liber donationum* (book of donations);[821] deeds relating to important donations in money and kind[822] and bequests of property components such as rents, estates and houses were copied in this codex, amounting to some 6000 entries in all.[823]

Each donor of a bequest was assured commemoration in the form of at least the mention of his name around the anniversary of his death as well as the common prayers of all the faithful then present. From the beginning of the fourteenth century, the *capellanus fabrice* (fabric chaplain) would call upon the faithful during the mass, urging them, '*Lieben Kinder, helffent mir got getruwentlichen bitten vor alle die menschen, lebenden und totten, die ir almosen und stür habent geben an das werck unser lieben frouw und deilsam hant gemacht alles gutz, daz hie geschit, mit singen und mit lesen, der namen harnoch geschriben stont und fallent in diser wuchen; zu dem ersten gedenckent durch gotz willen des erbern manns* [...]'.[824] This was followed by reading out the names of those who had died in that week, for instance: '*item obiit her Johans Schultheis Zorn seliger, ein fromer türer Ritter, ein sunderbarer liebhaber unser lieben frowen und ires werks, der bij sinem leben das werk mit vil sinen hengesten und pferden und nach sinem tode ietzund mit sinem harnasch und einem pferde aber begobet hat; orate pro eo*'.[825] Finally, those assembled recited the Our Father and Ave Maria to bring peace to the souls of the deceased. Codices like the *liber donationum*, begun in 1263 and maintained until around 1520, were arranged around the liturgical calendar, much like the *obituaria* and *necrologia* of the many monasteries and chapters that had been forming internal and external confraternal alliances since the early Middle Ages.[826]

In their structure and set-up, cathedral fabric confraternities were no different from the other religious confraternities active within any given bishopric; their members enjoyed comparable privileges under the same conditions. Similarly, the practice of issuing confraters and consorors with written, and later printed, confraternity letters bearing the holder's name as proof of membership was common to all confraternities (figs. 50, 51). Whereas some of these other associations were also set up to support church works, yet others looked after the interests of hospitals, large abbeys or monastic orders. As we shall see, these brotherhoods, which likewise depended on collections to secure their funds, might coordinate their diocesan efforts with the confraternity attached to the cathedral.

THE RELIC TOUR

Rarely absent from *mendicatoria* are provisions for taking the cathedral relics around the diocese, and indeed this forms the second cornerstone of the intricate system of begging for funds.[827] In a general way the presence of relics lent the clerics who carried them authority and prestige. When the time came to collect Church taxes in eighth-century Ireland, for example, the relics came along for good measure.[828] Shortly after the mid-eleventh century we find a first mention of monks and other clerics from monasteries and churches between the Loire and Scheldt taking their relics into the countryside to collect alms for their churches.[829] It may be that the practice had its origins in this region; in any case, it is not long thereafter, around 1100, that we find an English abbot despatching his monks with the monastery relics and a freshly acquired episcopal indulgence to garner funds for the church that had burnt down a short time before.[830] Even at this early date the collectors carried letters of recommendation from the king.[831] Several decades later, clerics were also collecting in Spain[832] and southern Germany.[833] The first such travelling campaign for a cathedral that we know of concerns Laon.[834] In 1112 a party of seven canons and laymen set out for a three-and-a-half-month journey through northern France to beg alms after the cathedral church was burned down by burghers of the commune.[835] A second trip a year later, this time lasting over five months, brought them all the way to England,[836] with many miracles occurring along the way that were later recorded by the monk Herman.[837] As was also done elsewhere, the relics were borne along in a precious shrine.[838] Amongst the recorded miracles of the trip there is one that is interesting to note, concerning the cure of an old blind goldsmith from Artois who had himself made that very shrine for the Virgin Mary in his younger years and whose only wish was to be allowed to see the work of his youth once more. His prayer was answered with alacrity.[839]

In their very earliest phase these begging expeditions, in which 'the saints themselves earned money for their church',[840] were enterprises almost devoid of organization, let alone authorization.[841] The *Book of Miracles* from Laon exudes the spirit of enthusiasm and adventure, and a comparable aspect of improvisation continues to dominate during the construction of the cathedral at Salisbury more than a century later. Here the bishop initially requested the lower clergy to go out and collect donations for the new building project. A few agreed, but the following day, whether spurred by the devil or ill counsel, they reneged with an unanimous refusal. Not knowing what else to do, the bishop turned to his canons, '*cum lacrimis et suspiriis*' (with tears and sighs). They proved amenable, and even before Christmas seven of their number set off for the surrounding dioceses.[842]

Already at a fairly early stage, however, these fundraising campaigns came into the hands of professional *questores* (pardoners), and what had begun so spontaneously petrified into an institution. The need for rules and regulations from higher up now proved unavoidable, and the growing number of such initiatives furthermore compelled Church authorities to lay down restrictive measures to end their unchecked proliferation.[843] Provincial ecclesiastical councils and synods began to issue prohibitions around the same time that moralists took to launching pointed criticisms. It hardly takes any great power of the imagination to see how easily this form of collection might engender skimming and abuses.[844] Guibert, abbot of Nogent (1053-1121/5), censured the brutish way in which the pardoners of a well-known church - perhaps the cathedral of Laon - fulfilled their mission.[845] The oldest canonical provisions relating to collections are even slightly earlier than this; around 1109 the ecclesiastical council of Poitiers decided to forbid preaching by '*sanctorum reliquias causa pecuniae et quaestus circumferentes*' (those who travel around with the relics of saints in order to collect money).[846] A century later, in 1210, similar prohibitions were issued at the local level by several synods in northern France, with that issued under Bishop Eudes de Sully in Paris being the most important.[847] These decisions in turn laid the basis for Canon 62 as formulated during the Fourth Lateran Council in 1215 and subsequently incorporated in the collection of Decretals.[848] As regards the limitations imposed on pardoners' activities,[849] there is one in particular that is relevant here: in order to provide a modicum of assurance that pardoners would not operate under false names and propagate heretical beliefs in their preachings, and moreover to prevent them from 'reaping another man's harvest', their activities now had to be authorized by a bishop.[850] Later councils and synods simplified enforcement by requiring local clergy to obtain an admittance letter from the bishop or his official for any form of collection campaign whatsoever, including those that had papal approval.[851] An indirect outgrowth of these various provisions was that jurisdiction to decide whether or not to admit organized collections, with or without relics, devolved to the highest power in the diocese – the bishop.

This development had two consequences. Firstly, the bishop (or in fact, as we shall see, the chapter) could now not only organize collections to benefit the cathedral but could also give them precedence over other collections, '*negotium fabrice nostre matricis ecclesie [...] in omnibus speciali prerogativa gaudere*'.[852] Secondly, decision-making authority about whether or not to admit individual 'quests' (collection campaigns) from other churches, monasteries and institutions fell to the bishop (and chapter). We will explore this admission policy in depth below.

THE INDULGENCE

A third element nearly always found in *mendicatoria* is an indulgence. The bishop granted this indulgence to all benefactors, or to the brothers and sisters of the *fraternitas* in particular, together with any indulgences previously acquired by the cathedral. Understandably, he attempted to boost the total tally of indulgences as high as possible. In Würzburg the bishop and chapter invested three years of effort prior to 1240 into gleaning indulgences wherever they could;[853] a similar initiative was launched by the bishop of Osnabrück for his cathedral church between 1254 and 1255.[854] No one felt any hesitation about counting up indulgences and categorizing spiritual benefits for easy reference. Under the heading '*de indulgenciis s. Martini episcopi*' (indulgences of the bishop St Martin), the chronicle of the 'New Church' (*Nieuwe Kerk*) of Delft lists all the indulgences and spiritual benefits the faithful would be able to earn in Delft in return for donations for the cathedral of Utrecht: '*somma indulgenciarum: novem anni, 1550 dies, 12 karene et missarum innumerabilium multitudo*' (total of indulgences: nine years, 1550 days, twelve fasting periods of 40 days and countless masses).[855] The parish priests were required to proclaim these indulgences from the pulpit, sometimes according to detailed instructions.[856] Even as late as 1530 the printed synodal statutes of the bishopric of Troyes contained – presumably following older custom – the provision that '*Chascun dimenche doivent recommander les curez à leurs parrochiens l'œuvre de l'église Sainct Pierre de Troyes en la manière qui s'en suyt: "J'ay commendement de par Mgr l'évesque de vous recommander chacun dimenche l'œuvre de l'église Monseigneur S. Pierre de Troyes, qui est la cathédrale église de ceste éveschié et la mère de toutes les autres églises là ou on a prins la sainct cresme de quoi vous estes oings au saint sacrement de baptesme. Et pour ce chascun y doit avoir singulière dévotion et y faire du bien selon sa puissance* [...]"', upon which followed a summary in the vernacular comprehensible for all concerning the full range of indulgences and spiritual benefits that the bishop extended to benefactors.[857]

THE WHITSUNTIDE PROCESSION

Aside from these three immediately recognizable constituents, the *mendicatoria* also contain other, more obscure elements borrowed from other ecclesiastical customs and institutions. More difficult to prove but of potentially vital relevance for the history of the origins of cathedral-building collections are the links between these fundraising campaigns and Whitsuntide processions, known as *cruces banales* or *sinodali banno.*[858] Most *mendicatoria* open by noting that the cathedral is the mother church of the diocese, on which ground the bishop justifies his mandate to the clerics. This same priority entitlement of the cathedral served as a basis for the age-old obligation on the faithful, possibly tracing back to the sixth century and at any rate customary in tenth-century French, English and German bishoprics, to assemble with their parish, usually around Whitsuntide, and process to the cathedral bearing their boundary crosses, the parish pennant and the relics, and there present their donations, the *pentecostalia.*[859] In the more distant past such Whitsuntide processions may have been held to coincide with synods, as initially the faithful, too, were expected to attend episcopal synods, or to at least send delegates.[860]

These processions were compulsory and probably far from popular. One of the twelfth-century *miracula* of the cathedral of Coutances draws a line between, on the one hand, the '*debita processio et oblatio* [...] *sicut debitur et solitum est in eisdem diebus reddere matribus ecclesiis*' (procession with offerings due, such as people are accustomed to hold in those days to benefit the mother churches, in accordance with the requirement), which the residents of a village had to make to their cathedral in Bayeux and, on the other, their pilgrimage to Notre Dame in Coutances '*communi et spontaneo voto*' (based on a communal and spontaneous vow).[861] Amongst the fixed elements of the Whitsuntide procession was the obligatory *oblatio* to be rendered by each hearth or each parishioner, originally consisting of a specified amount of wax and later a sum of money, usually some small coin; this contribution was known variously as the *nummi pentecostales* or *pentecostales oblationes* (Pentecostal contribution) or *pentecostales* (Pentecostal offering).[862] In some bishoprics the custom of this pilgrimage continued for many years,[863] though it shed its compulsory character along the way. Synodal statutes continue to recommend an annual procession to the cathedral up through the late Middle Ages.[864] In addition, we find that certain groups of parish churches – so-called regional processional groups[865] – were required to visit a nearer abbey or collegiate church, possibly designated as a daughter church of their mutual mother church, with a procession there perhaps replacing the original journey to the cathedral and authorized by the bishop in order to help generate funds for selected abbeys or churches.[866] Around 1200, however, the processional element seems to have fallen into disuse,[867] leaving only the obligatory small fixed sum payable by every person, hearth or parish; the mandatory pilgrimage to the cathedral was thus commuted to the payment of a stipulated amount.[868]

What, then, are the points of overlap between collections for the cathedral works and the *pentecostalia*? To begin with: the nature of the benefits. Pilgrims to the cathedral, too, could earn an indulgence and become members of the cathedral confraternity.[869] The episcopal mandates by which clerics urged the faithful to undertake pilgrimages are framed in phrasings analogous to those of *mendicatoria*.[870] Where the procession disappeared but the payment rule remained, the methods employed to collect the *pentecostalia* could be similar to those used to collect monies for the cathedral works. An early example from the late twelfth century concerns a Benedictine monastery near Brussels that, being entitled to certain *pentecostalia*, arranged with parish priests to despatch its monks around Whitsuntide to collect the proceeds from their parishes.[871] Cathedrals steered the same course. Where processions fell into disuse, the Pentecostal alms had to be gathered by the parish clergy and conveyed in full to the episcopal or capitular *nuntii*;[872] both types of collections (as we shall see) relied on local Church functionaries. In the second half of the twelfth century, the bishopric of Lincoln had already put its collection in the hands of the archdeacons, and it was they who determined where and when the faithful were to assemble for the ritual transfer of the *pentecostalia* to the capitular *nuntii*.[873] In other English dioceses, and elsewhere such as in Amiens, these monies were collected by deans, who then delivered them during synods.[874] And, like cathedral collections, the Pentecostal levy could be designated to the fabric, whether in full or in part.

Yet none of this provides much insight into the actual relationship between the *pentecostalia* and diocesan collections for the building works. It is quite possible that certain aspects of Whitsuntide processions served as a model for cathedral works collections.[875] But it is unlikely that the diocesan cathedral campaigns were simply a replacement for the old obligatory processions: both revenue flows continued side by side until far into the Middle Ages, sometimes even enriching the fabric simultaneously, yet wholly independent of each other. Overall, information about the designation of the *pentecostalia* is scarce. Often the bishop received a portion,[876] as did, sometimes, the chapter[877] or some dignitary;[878] usually the *luminare* (church lights) or the church fabric was also assigned a share.[879] In 1136 the bishop of London allocated half the Pentecostals due him to the repair of the fire-damaged cathedral,[880] whilst in 1204 the bishop of Winchester ceded all Pentecostals to the sacrist charged with providing the cathedral lights.[881] As mentioned, some fabrics tapped both these sources. In the bishopric of Exeter, the *oblaciones pentecostales* accrued to the cathedral fabric from at least the beginning of the thirteenth century, to which a number of fourteenth-century account rolls add the *venia sancti Petri* (the indulgence of St Peter) collected in each archdeaconry.[882] Might these once separate revenues have been merged through King Henry VIII's charter of 9 November 1539 confirming the old law under which all households had to pay 1 farthing for the cathedral works and announcing that these offerings would be gathered by cathedral messengers?[883]

In Rouen the cathedral fabric had to share the proceeds from the *pentecostalia*, there known as the *débite*[884] and levied until 1789, with the chapter.[885] The fabric rolls record these tax receipts – which apparently were rendered by clerics at the winter and summer synods – as distinct from those of the quest, gathered both in that and a handful of neighbouring episcopal dioceses. The *débite* were never all that profitable, providing only between 183 l.t. and 100 l.t. at the end of the fifteenth and in the sixteenth centuries, as opposed to the quests, which yielded between 600 l.t. and 1400 l.t. over the same period.[886]

THE COLLECTION FOR THE CRUSADES

Another possible source of inspiration for the organizational structure of episcopal collections for the cathedral works were the crusade collections, which were fundraising campaigns conducted throughout western Christendom, instituted by the pope or under his auspices, to collect funds for or in connection with the Crusades. More probable, however, is that these enterprises represent a parallel development.[887]

The use of collection boxes to gather parish contributions for the cathedral building works (see below) may well have stemmed from crusade indulgence usages. In England this method of collecting alms for the Crusades was already in use in 1166, albeit initially under the auspices of the king.[888] In 1199 Pope Innocent III issued an ordinance stipulating that each parish church set up a collecting box where offerings for the Crusades could be deposited in return for absolution from sins (fig. 28); later on parishes were required to hold weekly services.[889]

Similarly, the mendicatorial clause stipulating that the faithful were to attend their parish church on the day of the *nuntii*'s arrival and to observe that day as a Sunday may have been inspired by papal crusade bulls.[890] Indeed, this would hardly be surprising,[891] considering that both types of collections were intended to cover a large territory to glean funds for a cause in which potential donors felt no personal involvement. The need for a degree of coercion – by requiring church attendance and the observance of a day of rest – was unavoidable. It is easy to understand why precisely these clauses met with sharp protest from some moralists. Around 1300 Hugh of Newcastle decried the fact that 'the common folk and the poor, who must live from their labours, are also compelled by these letters to assemble in the church on days on which no feast is celebrated to surrender their wages and hear a sermon'.[892] By the late Middle Ages we find the 'Sunday clause' gone from most *mendicatoria*.[893] A 1396 synodal statute from Tours even prescribes that pardoners are only permitted to come on Sundays and feast days, '*afin que les bonnes gens par telle occasion ne soyent retrais de faire leur besoigne*'.[894] Even so, around 1450 we hear an auxiliary bishop from one of the suffragan dioceses of the archbishopric of Mainz complain that cathedral messengers were ignoring the rule that collections be conducted only on Sundays and feast days; with a disgraceful disregard for the limits of their authority, they forced the poor common folk to lay down their labours in the field on working days in order to go to the parish church. Moreover, if any were absent during the sermon or failed in the messengers' eyes to render an adequate sum for the cathedral, these men were not above raining down excommunications from the pulpit.[895]

The direct model for bishops' campaigns for the cathedral works were the papal privileges attached to collections run by the oldest military orders – the Knights Hospitaller (founded around 1108) and the Knights Templar (founded 1119; confirmed by the pope in 1128). The Hospitallers first gained these privileges between 7 May 1139 and 1142,[896] and the Templars perhaps earlier, between 12 February 1133 and 1137,[897] but certainly by 9 January 1144.[898] In this case, the pope addressed a letter to all the archbishops, bishops, abbots and prelates of his Church, urging them to exhort their flocks to organize collections. Those who donated property and joined the fraternity of a military order would see a one-seventh portion of the punishment for their sins remitted and would be entitled to a church burial, even if their parish church should fall under an interdict. In addition, the annual festive arrival of the Templars and Hospitallers ('*in iocando eorum adventu*') at the church was required to be honoured with the celebration of the divine office.

Several decades after issuing these privileges, between 15 May 1166 and 1179,[899] the pope received a serious complaint ('*querelam gravem*') from the Hospitallers concerning sabotage of papal instructions: local clergy were claiming a portion of the proceeds, even refusing the brethren entry into their churches, and were failing to render bequests due them. The pope responded by ordering bishops to clamp down on these abuses. Texts of these papal privileges for Hospitallers and Templars were compiled in official form books kept by the papal chancery, where they served as templates when the occasion arose to extend similar privileges to such institutions as the orders of Saint James of Altopascio, the Santo Spirito in Rome and Saint Lazarus in Jerusalem.[900]

The link between these papal privileges and the *mendicatoria* is unmistakable, with striking correlations not merely in terms of content, but also in word choice and formulation. The oldest episcopal *mendicatorium* known to this author, one issued not for a cathedral but on behalf of the Cistercian monastery of Fontguillem, dates from the same period as the papal privileges: between 1126 and 1138 the bishop of Bazas (*dép.* Gironde) instructed his clerics to give a fitting welcome to *nuntii* from this monastery and to encourage the faithful to give alms and join the monastic confraternity, for which he granted an indulgence of 40 days.[901] Still absent from this deed are the familiar provisions for the suspension of any interdicts upon the arrival of the *nuntii*[902] and burial of confraternity members. Another, somewhat later *mendicatorium*, issued by the bishop of Bayeux between 1165 and 1205, does include the clause on lifting interdicts for confraternity members.

It is likely that bishops formulated their *mendicatoria* in such uniform terms not so much in emulation of the Hospitallers, Templars and other religious organizations issued with papal bulls, but in order to be able to compete with these powerful begging campaigns, which enjoyed an exemption that put them beyond the bishop's jurisdiction.[903] As we shall see, those campaigns could form a considerable

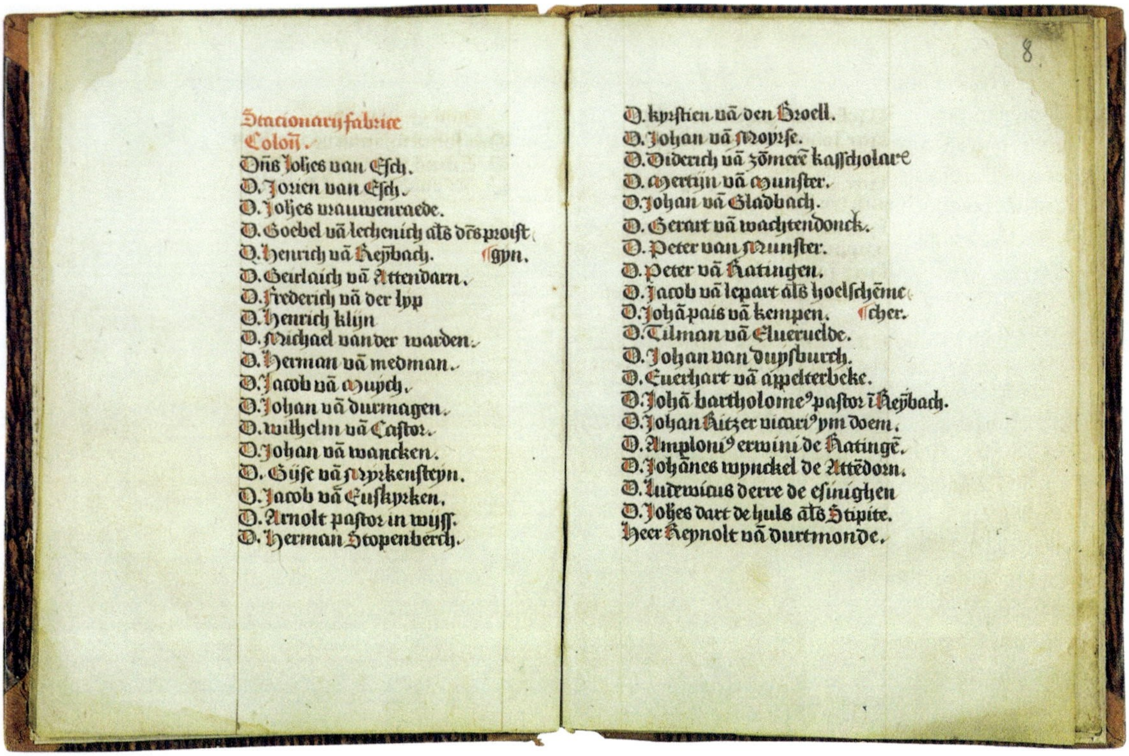
Stacionarij fabrice
Colon̄.
Dn̄s Johes van Esch.
D. Jorien van Esch.
D. Johes wrauwenraede.
D. Goebel vā lechenich als dēs proist
D. Henrich vā Keysbach. gyn.
D. Gerlaich vā Attendarn.
D. Frederich vā der lyp
D. Henrich klyn
D. Michael vander warden.
D. Herman vā medman.
D. Jacob vā Murch.
D. Johan vā durmagen.
D. wilhelm vā Castor.
D. Johan vā wancken.
D. Gijse vā Nyrkensteyn.
D. Jacob vā Euskyrken.
D. Arnolt pastor in wyss.
D. Herman Stopenberch.

8
D. kyrstien vā den Broell.
D. Johan vā Moyrse.
D. Diderich vā zōmerē kasscholare
D. Mertyn vā Munster.
D. Johan vā Gladbach.
D. Gerart vā wachtendonck.
D. Peter van Munster.
D. Peter vā Ratingen.
D. Jacob vā lepart als hoelschēme
D. Johā pais vā kempen. cher.
D. Tilman vā Elueruelde.
D. Johan van Duysburch.
D. Euerhart vā appelterbeke.
D. Johā bartholome[9] pastor ī Keysbach.
D. Johan Ritzer vicari[9] ym Doem.
D. Amploni[9] erwini de Ratinge.
D. Johānes wynckel de Attēdorn.
D. ludewicus derre de esinighen
D. Johes dart de huls als Stipite.
Heer Reynolt vā durtmonde.

49

Confraternity book of the confraternity of St Peter, after 1508
Cologne, Historisches Archiv der Stadt Köln, Geistliche Abteilung 177/1

This fabric confraternity for Cologne Cathedral was attached to the church of St Maria im Pesch, which was situated behind the cathedral and served as the parish church for residents of the immunity. The book lists names of 180 deceased confraters and consorors, whose number included archbishops, *provisores* of the cathedral fabric, canons and architects of the cathedral church. Also listed are the *stacionarij fabrice Coloniensis* (fol. 7v); these were chantry priests who perhaps collected money for the fabric after the celebration of masses and acted as pardoners in the diocese. The confraternity functioned to support the cathedral building works. Members were assured prayers for the repose of their souls.

LITERATURE
Ad Summum 1248, p. 81 and fig. 14; Militzer 1997-2000, vol. 2, pp. 1007-1015.
Kindly communicated by Prof. Klaus Militzer.

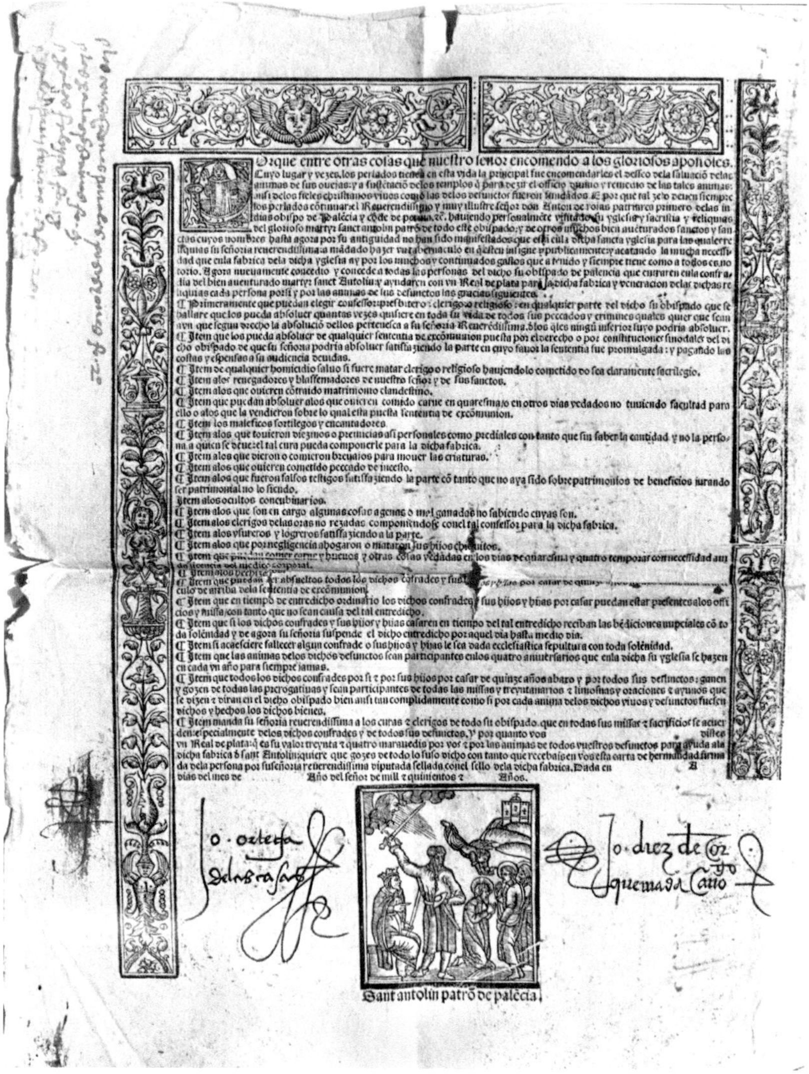

50
Carta de hermandad, for the fabric confraternity dedicated to San Antolin, patron saint of the cathedral of Palencia
Broadside post-incunable, 310 x 222 mm, c.1525
Palencia, Archivo Catedralicio

The confraternity letter was for the fabric confraternity of Palencia Cathedral, established by Bishop Antonio de Rojas (1524-1525) to rescue the fabric from its dire financial position. Prospective members had to contribute 1 silver real (worth 24 maravedís), in return for which they received a series of spiritual privileges, including the right to choose a confessor who could at any time release them from sins whose remission was reserved for the bishop. As such, the confraternity letter also served as a confessional letter (*confessionale*). Under certain conditions this confessor could also release the holder from an excommunication. Confraters and consorors further acquired the right to attend mass, marry and receive a church burial even during times of interdict. Finally, each received a share in the spiritual fruits of certain specified prayers and good works performed in the bishopric.

LITERATURE

Einblattdrucke des XV. Jahrhunderts, in voce *'Bruderschaftsbriefe'*; *Publicaciones de la Institución Tello Téllez de Meneses* 11 (1954), p. 162, no. 10.

obstruction to the interests of the episcopal collection, but bishops always dutifully gave primacy to the cathedral works campaign.

The complicated history of the origins of the episcopal *mendicatorium* cannot be explained on the basis of papal bulls for the Hospitallers and Templars alone. The constituents from which *mendicatoria* are made up are more varied and stem from older traditions than the very oldest papal privileges for any military order. They have been described above and comprise the religious confraternity, the indulgence, the custom of processing with relics, and the old prescription directing all the faithful to visit the diocesan mother church during Whitsuntide *in signum debite subjectionis* (as a sign of the requisite submission) and then 'not appear before the Lord empty-handed' (Deut. 16:16).[904]

DIFFERENT FORMS OF CONTRIBUTIONS

What are the different types of contributions specified in *mendicatoria*? The answer to this question has already in part been given above; since the episcopal mandate was made up of varying components, monies flowed into the cathedral fabric fund from a number of different sources.[905] That fabric rolls usually do not list them as distinct quantities is chiefly a consequence of the method of collection (to be discussed subsequently), but does nothing to detract from their important fundamental differences in provenance.

INCOME FROM INDULGENCES

Little need be said concerning income from indulgences. Usually every benefactor could earn the indulgence, such that each gift was simultaneously indulgence income.

CONFRATERNITY CONTRIBUTIONS

Contributions made to confraternities require more detailed explication (figs. 50, 51). Annual contributions were due from each member, the amount of which was sometimes specified in the *mendicatorium*. Typically, we distinguish between admission dues and the slightly lower annual contributions, which could be mandatory for a minimum number of years. In late twelfth-century Bayeux, the annual

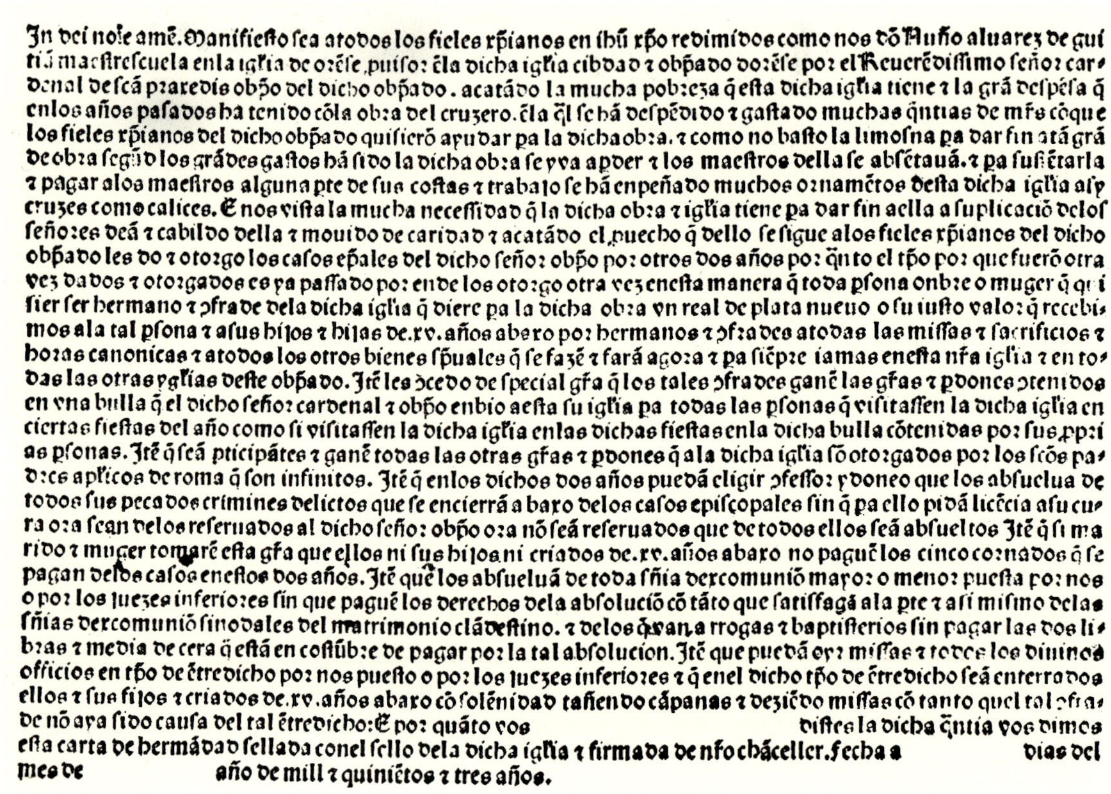

In dei noīe amē. Manifiesto sea atodos los fieles xp̄ianos en ihū xp̄o redimidos como nos dō Nuño aluarez de guítiā maestrescuela enla igl'ia de orēse, puisor ēla dicha igl'ia cibdad z obp̄ado dorēse por el Reuerēdissimo señor cardenal de sācta prarediss obp̄o del dicho obp̄ado. acatādo la mucha pobreza q̄ esta dicha igl'ia tiene z la grā despēsa q̄ enlos años pasados ha tenido cōla obra del cruzero. ēla q̄l se hā despēdido z gastado muchas q̄ntias de mrs cōque los fieles xp̄ianos del dicho obp̄ado quisierō ayudar pa la dicha obra. z como no basto la limosna pa dar fin atā grā de obra segūd los grādes gastos hā sido la dicha obra se yva aporder z los maestros della se absētauā. z pa sufrētarla z pagar alos maestros alguna pte de sus costas z trabajo se hā enpeñado muchos ornamētos desta dicha igl'ia asy cruzes como calices. E nos vista la mucha necessidad q̄ la dicha obra z igl'ia tiene pa dar fin aella a suplicaciō delos señores deā z cabildo della z mouido de caridad z acatādo el prouecho q̄ dello se sigue alos fieles xp̄ianos del dicho obp̄ado les do z otorgo los casos ep̄ales del dicho señor obp̄o por otros dos años por q̄nto el tp̄o por que fuerō otra vez dados z otorgados es ya passado por ende los otorgo otra vez enesta manera q̄ toda psona onbre o muger q̄ quisier ser hermano z cofrade dela dicha igl'ia q̄ diere pa la dicha obra vn real de plata nueuo o su iusto valor q̄ recebimos ala tal psona z asus hijos z hijas de.xv. años abaxo por hermanos z cofrades atodas las missas z sacrificios z horas canonicas z atodos los otros bienes spūales q̄ se fazē z farā agora z pa siēpre iamas enesta nr̄a igl'ia z en todas las otras yglias deste obp̄ado. Itē les cōcedo de special gr̄a q̄ los tales cofrades ganē las gr̄as z pdones cōtenidos en vna bulla q̄ el dicho señor cardenal z obp̄o enbio aesta su igl'ia pa todas las psonas q̄ visitassen la dicha igl'ia en ciertas fiestas del año como si visitassen la dicha igl'ia enlas dichas fiestas enla dicha bulla cōtenidas por sus p̄prias psonas. Itē q̄ seā pticipātes z ganē todas las otras gr̄as z pdones q̄ ala dicha igl'ia sō otorgados por los scōs padres ap̄licos de roma q̄ son infinitos. Itē q̄ enlos dichos dos años puedā elegir cōfessor ydoneo que los absuelua de todos sus pecados crimines delictos que se encierrā abaxo delos casos episcopales sin q̄ pa ello pidā licēcia asu cura ora seā delos reseruados al dicho señor obp̄o ora nō seā reseruados que de todos ellos seā absueltos. Itē q̄ si marido z muger tomarē esta gr̄a que ellos ni sus hijos ni criados de.xv. años abaxo no paguē los cinco cornados q̄ se pagan delos casos enestos dos años. Itē que los absueluā de toda sētēcia dexcomuniō mayor o menor puesta por nos o por los juezes inferiores sin que paguē los derechos dela absoluciō cō tāto que satisfagā ala pte z asi mismo delas sēnias dexcomuniō sinodales del matrimonio clādestino. z delos q̄ van a rrogas z baptisterios sin pagar las dos libras z media de cera q̄ estā en costūbre de pagar por la tal absolucion. Itē que puedā oyr missas z todos los diuinos officios en tp̄o de ētredicho por nos puesto o por los juezes inferiores z q̄ enel dicho tp̄o de ētredicho seā enterrados ellos z sus fijos z criados de.xv. años abaxo cō solēnidad tañiendo cāpanas z deziēdo missas cō tanto que el tal cofrade nō aya sido causa del tal ētredicho. E por quāto vos distes la dicha q̄ntia vos dimos esta carta de hermādad sellada conel sello dela dicha igl'ia z firmada de nr̄o chāceller. fecha a dias del mes de año de mill z quiniētos z tres años.

51

Carta de hermandad of the fabric confraternity of Orense Cathedral
Broadside post-incunable, 123 x 169 mm, printed by Joannes Gherlinck, 1503
Orense, Archivo Catedralicio

At the dean and chapter's request the bishop issued a two-year extension of the possibility to earn certain spiritual privileges. This request was prompted by financial problems in the building works. Anyone who gave 1 silver reaal or its equivalent would be allowed, together with his or her children under the age of fifteen, to share in the spiritual fruits of all masses and prayers said in the cathedral church and all other churches in the diocese. Confraters and consorors were additionally granted the same spiritual privileges as those who visited the cathedral on certain feast days (specified in an indulgence bull). They were further free to choose a confessor within the subsequent two years, who would be authorized to remit such sins as were reserved for the bishop, and were discharged from paying certain types of ecclesiastical fines. Finally, they were permitted to hear the mass and receive a church burial in times of interdict.

LITERATURE

F.J. Norton, *A descriptive catalogue of printing in Spain and Portugal 1501-1520*, Cambridge 1978, no. 562 A.

contribution of 6 d.and. was obligatory for at least the first five years.[906] The Confraternity of the Holy Cross attached to the cathedral fabric at Orléans and established around 1478 demanded from its members 2 s.par. *ingressus* (admission dues), and 4 d.par. twice each year thereafter.[907] In Limoges, the confraternity re-established in 1501 required 2 s. upon joining and then 10 d. each year,[908] compared with the 12 d.par. admission fee and 3 blancs annually stipulated by the *confrérie de la Vierge* in Senlis from 1507.[909] All who joined accepted the moral obligation to pay, sometimes on pain of excommunication.[910] This commitment by a large group of people to pay fixed annual contributions played an important role in fabric finances, despite the fact that such contributions rarely amounted to more than one or two days' wages of an unskilled labourer. But tampering with the annual nature of contributions only served to invite improper use of the religious privileges of membership. Thus, in Cologne, where the archbishop declared that all who made a one-time donation to the cathedral building works would enjoy the religious benefits and privileges of the Confraternity of St Peter during that year, found himself forced to repeal this decision in 1339: many who were ill and had never before in their lives given anything for the cathedral works could now – as they lay at death's door – reap the profits of the full range of confraternal indulgences with a single payment of 1 or 2 d. Interdicts lost their force when temporary members of the brotherhood could enjoy its privileges too.[911] Accordingly, parish priests were sometimes made to compile a register of all members to supply to the fabric *nuntii*.[912] On rare occasions we have information about the number of members considered to be desirable: on 20 December 1529 the pope established a cathedral confraternity in the diocese of Jaén, fixing the number of members at 2000 men and as many women.[913]

It is not always possible to discover the total proceeds from contributions, given that they are included under receipts from the diocesan campaign as a whole.[914] And even where the confraternity share is recorded separately, it is usually an aggregate, and not specified by contributor. In rare exceptions, however, we do find such specification, as in Halberstadt (1387 roll) and Osnabrück (1477-1528 rolls); presumably these members were residents of the episcopal city.[915] How great a share confraternity monies contributed to the fabric's overall income depended not only on the number of confraters and consorors and the amount that each paid, but especially on the time span for which the *fraternitas* had been instituted, or more specifically when it had an active membership. Over the long term, no cathedral anywhere could be sure of constant, large receipts from this source.[916] The bishop and chapter had to make continuous efforts to revive confraternities that had 'dozed off', as the bishop of Bayeux expressed it around 1200,[917] when new building campaigns demanded it. We see this in Toul, where in 1525 the bishop attempted to breathe new life into the fabric confraternity founded there in 1336.[918] We know of a few fabric confraternities that furnished significant support for the building budget for only a handful of years. For example, in 1506, the year that the north tower of Bourges Cathedral collapsed, the cathedral chapter immediately acted to found a confraternity, but it was not until after 1515 that contributions began flowing in, and after 1552 enthusiasm had already begun to ebb. Even during peak years around 1520 the *confraternitas* of the tower never supplied more than ten to fifteen percent of the fabric's total income,[919] and the sum total of all contributions made over its entire lifetime come to no more than just above half the fabric's highest annual incomes of 6000 l.t., or around 75 annual wages of a skilled labourer.[920] In Hereford, fabric rolls for the year 1290/91 show an even smaller share, with contributions '*de fraternitate totius episcopatus*' (from the brotherhood of the entire diocese) amounting to just 6½ percent of its income.[921] Curiously, these confraternal revenues could vacillate substantially. In the bishopric of Troyes, monies generated over a period of 20 years by the confraternity '*de tous les confrères et conseurs de tous les villages de ce dyocèse*', founded in 1488 to support construction work on the nave, and coexistent with the older diocesan collection, yielded sums of 812 l.t. in 1488/89, 172 l.t. in 1491/92, 203 l.t. in 1492/93, 61 l.t. in 1493/94, around 175 l.t. between 1495/96 and 1498/99, 200 l.t. between 1499 and 1501, and as much as 288 l.t. in 1507/08 – thus between one and 13 mason's wages a year.[922] Receipts in Basel reveal a similar tendency, generating between 518 lb. (16 annual wages) and 1512 l. (48 annual wages) in the period from 1399 to 1471.[923] In the case of Notre Dame in Chartres, sources documenting the cathedral confraternity furnish an exceptional wealth of detail. Established in 1516, ten years after the fire in the north tower, it provided an income of 540 l.t. (over 17 annual wages) in 1519, of which only 20 l.t. derived from the city. Given the confraternity's very modest annual fee of 6 d., we can conclude that the brotherhood counted 21,600 members, 800 of them dwelling in the city.[924] We will return to consider receipts from this brotherhood in the discussion on total revenues from diocesan collections.

TESTAMENTARY BEQUESTS

Testamentary bequests for the cathedral fabric also warrant separate consideration. We find provisions relating to bequests not only in *mendicatoria*, but in synodal statutes, too. Diocesan legislation shows an especial concern with wills and legacies in general, stipulating that parish priests attend parishioners when they made up their wills before receiving the final sacrament. Often priests were also asked to keep a register of all the wills drawn up in their presence and to present this at the synod to the bishop's official, who was charged with verifying wills.[925] Some statutes added a provision stating that when a parishioner lay on his deathbed, the priest should rouse him to expressly remember the cathedral fabric in his last will and testament. We already find a provision of this type for Notre Dame in early thirteenth-century synodal statutes from the bishopric of Paris; here, parish priests had to record the names of testators and give the complete list to their bishop during the synod.[926] The synodal statutes of Bishop Richard Poore of Salisbury (from between 1217 and 1219) lay down the same requirement: priests must get the sick to bequeath some portion of their goods, as much as God inspired them to, to the fabric of the mother church of Salisbury.[927] Similar regulations occur in synodal statutes from the bishoprics of Liège,[928] Cambrai,[929] Cologne[930] and Utrecht,[931] amongst others. In the case of cathedral fabrics managed in large part by the city, such as in Siena, these tasks were assigned not to the clergy but to city notaries, who were required to record '*utrum talis testator aliquid reliquerit dicte opere vel non reliquerit*' (whether such testator has or has not named the said fabric in his will), or risk a fine of 10 lire.[932] Sources indicate

52

Les grans pardons de nouveau donnez a leglise nostre Dame de Rouen
Broadside post-incunable, 330 x 210 mm, 1510-1513
Paris, Bibliothèque Nationale

French summary of the customary indulgences and privileges available to benefactors of the cathedral of Rouen. The vicar of the cardinal legate (Archbishop Georges d'Amboise, d. 1510) grants an indulgence of three years and three quarantines (fasting periods) for churchgoing and almsgiving in the period between the first Vespers on Passion Sunday and the last Vespers on Easter day. Benefactors of the cathedral fabric further receive the privilege of freely choosing a confessor, who can also release him or her from the *casus reservati* and commute vows (with certain exceptions), and of participating in the spiritual fruits of all masses and prayers said in the cathedral. The text concludes by listing the many papal and episcopal indulgences issued for the cathedral, *'car cest la mere*

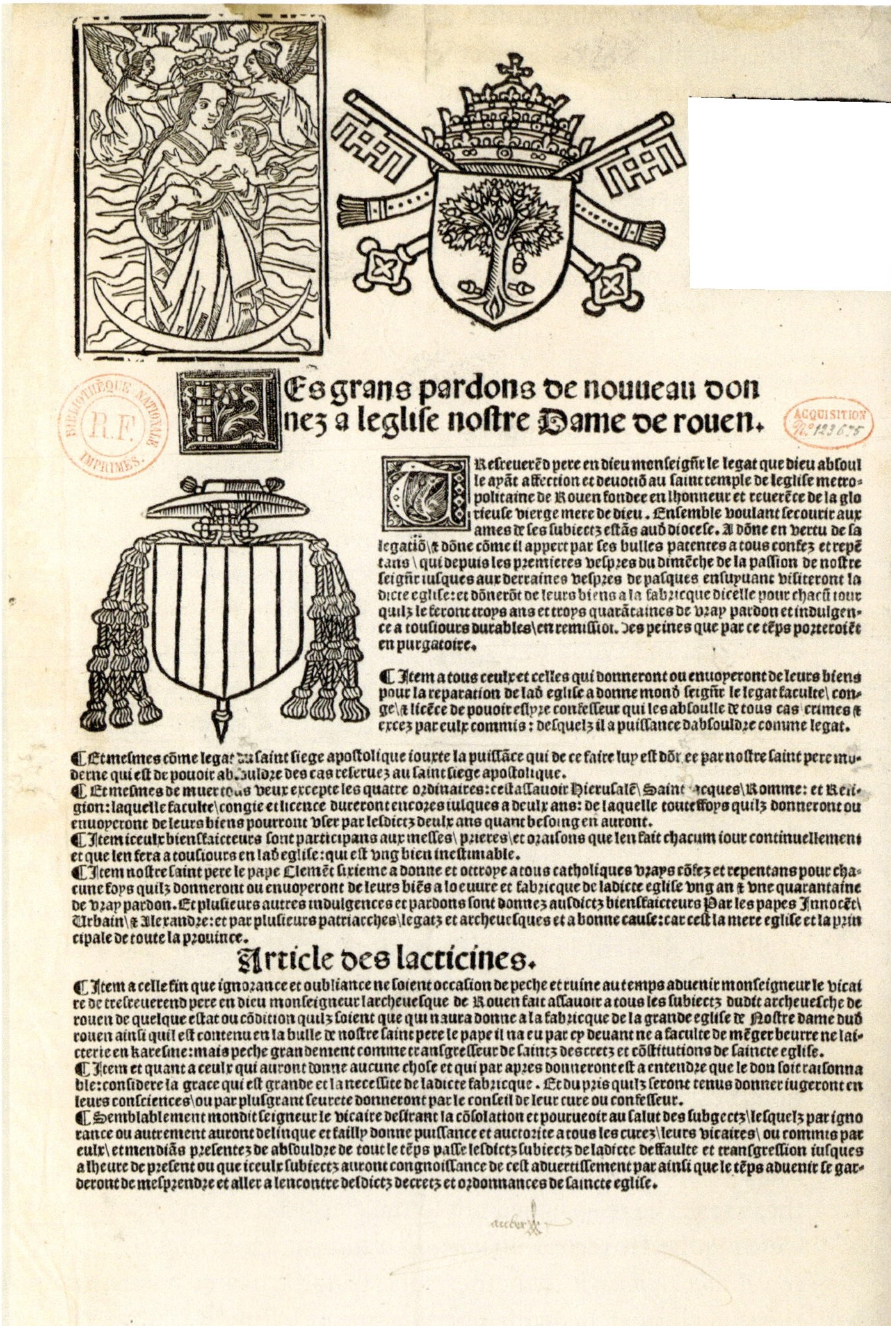

Les grans pardons de nouveau donnez a leglise nostre Dame de rouen.

Tresreuerēd pere en dieu monseignr le legat que dieu absoul le ayāt affection et deuotiō au saint temple de leglise metropolitaine de Rouen fondee en lhonneur et reuerēce de la glorieuse vierge mere de dieu. Ensemble voulant secourir aux ames de ses subiectz estās aud diocese. A dōne en vertu de sa legatiō\ & dōne cōme il appert par ses bulles patentes a tous confez et repētans\ qui depuis les premieres vespres du dimēche de la passion de nostre seignr iusques aux derraines vespres de pasques ensuyuant visiteront la dicte eglise: et dōnerōt de leurs biens a la fabricque dicelle pour chacū iour quilz le feront troys ans et troys quarātaines de vray pardon et indulgence a tousiours durables\ en remissiō. des peines que par ce tēps porteroiēt en purgatoire.

¶ Item a tous ceulx et celles qui donneront ou enuoyeront de leurs biens pour la reparation de lad eglise a donne mond seignr le legat faculte\ conge\ & licēce de pouoir eslyre confesseur qui les absoulle de tous cas crimes & excez par eulx commis: desquelz il a puissance dabsouldre comme legat.

¶ Et mesmes cōme legat du saint siege apostolique iouxte la puissāce qui de ce faire luy est dōnee par nostre saint pere moderne qui est de pouoir absouldre des cas reseruez au saint siege apostolique.

¶ Et mesmes de muer tous veux excepte les quatre ordinaires: cest assauoir Hierusalē\ Saint Jacques\ Romme: et Religion: laquelle faculte\ congie et licence dureront encores iusques a deulx ans: de laquelle toutesfoys quilz donneront ou enuoyeront de leurs biens pourront vser par lesdictz deulx ans quant besoing en auront.

¶ Item iceulx bienfaicteurs sont participans aux messes\ prieres\ et oraisons que len fait chacun iour continuellement et que len fera a tousiours en lad eglise: qui est vng bien inestimable.

¶ Item nostre saint pere le pape Clemēt sixieme a donne et ottroye a tous catholiques vrays cōfez et repentans pour chacune foys quilz donneront ou enuoyeront de leurs biēs a loeuure et fabricque de ladicte eglise vng an & vne quarantaine de vray pardon. Et plusieurs autres indulgences et pardons sont donnez ausdictz bienfaicteurs Par les papes Innocēt\ Urbain\ & Alexandre: et par plusieurs patriarches\ legatz et archeuesques et a bonne cause: car cest la mere eglise et la principale de toute la prouince.

Article des lacticines.

¶ Item a celle fin que ignorance et oubliance ne soient occasion de peche et ruine au temps aduenir monseigneur le vicaire de tresreuerend pere en dieu monseigneur larcheuesque de Rouen fait assauoir a tous les subiectz dudit archeuesche de rouen de quelque estat ou cōdition quilz soient que qui naura donne a la fabricque de la grande eglise de Nostre dame dud rouen ainsi quil est contenu en la bulle de nostre saint pere le pape il na eu par cy deuant ne a faculte de mēger beurre ne laicterie en karesme: mais peche grandement comme transgresseur de saintz descretz et cōstitutions de saincte eglise.

¶ Item et quant a ceulx qui auront donne aucune chose et qui par apres donneront est a entendre que le don soit raisonnable: considere la grace qui est grande et la necessite de ladicte fabricque. Et du pris quilz seront tenus donner iugeront en leurs consciences\ ou par plusgrant seurete donneront par le conseil de leur cure ou confesseur.

¶ Semblablement mondit seigneur le vicaire desirant la cōsolation et pourueoir au salut des subgectz\ lesquelz par ignorance ou autrement auront delinque et failly donne puissance et auctorite a tous les curez\ leurs vicaires\ ou commis par eulx\ et mendiās presentez de absouldre de tout le tēps passe lesdictz subiectz de ladicte deffaulte et transgression iusques a lheure de present ou que iceulx subiectz auront congnoissance de cest aduertissement par ainsi que le tēps aduenir se garderont de mesprendre et aller a lencontre desdictz decretz et ordonnances de saincte eglise.

that these episcopal exhortations were not disregarded.

Yet these legacies yielded the cathedral fabric little. This was primarily due to the fact that testamentary bequests eventually lapsed into no more than a simple formality. In the dioceses of Regensburg[933] and Basel[934] it became customary for wills to include a gift of small coin for the cathedral building works – a practice that continued in some areas into the nineteenth century. Practices differed from one place to another, however. Of the 356 testaments drawn up in the city of York between 1321 and 1400, only 90 incorporate a small legacy for the cathedral.[935] Conversely, the Lincoln chapter was successful in its efforts to secure bequests from the faithful precisely as a means to strengthen their ties with the mother church. Between 1480 and 1535 the annual income from these bequests ranged from £20 to £35 (around five and eight and a half annual wages, respectively), consisting of hundreds of small testamentary gifts, recorded one by one, each worth a single or a few days' wages.[936] Most late medieval donors furthermore had a habit of spreading their gifts out over a multitude of pious causes, of which the cathedral was but one, and by no means the favourite.[937] Only one-third of all wills from the diocese of Norwich contained a gift for the cathedral, whilst almost all of them (95 percent) included a bequest for a parish church, and half a donation for the mendicant orders.[938] In Cologne, half of the testaments made up in the fourteenth century include a small gift for the cathedral works, increasing in the fifteenth century to 90 percent, but then in lesser sums.[939]

Another explanation for the relatively minor role that bequests played in the cathedral fabric budget relates to how they were procured, and specifically to the fact that they usually accrued to the cathedral fabric not directly, but in a roundabout manner. In account rolls kept by the fabric of the parish church of St James in Antwerp, which belonged to the diocese of Cambrai, we can look up the year 1535/36, for example, and find under the heading '*ontfanck van de testamente, die onse vrouwe van Camerijck gemaect sijn*' (received from the bequests left for Our Lady of Cambrai) a total of eight entries, together yielding 18 ob. 10 s. 6 d.brab, or two years' wages of an unskilled workman. In fact, this parish fabric – and it is not the only one – leased the

eglise et la principale de toute la province'.
The text under the heading *Article des lacticines* points out a number of abuses connected with remittance of the obligatory abstinence from dairy products during Lent. The vicar warns that those who have contributed nothing to the building works will be committing a sin if they fail to comply with the fasting restrictions.
In addition, anyone wishing to enjoy remittance from fasting must contribute a reasonable sum to the building works; those in doubt as to the proper amount should consult their parish priest or confessor. Represented in the four woodcuts are: the Madonna in a crescent moon and the coats of arms of Pope Julius II (1503-1513), Rouen's patron St Romain (d. 683) and the cardinal legate (d. 1510). The fabric rolls show that thousands of *brevets de pardon* were commissioned by the fabric and distributed throughout the diocese.

LITERATURE
Fournier 1923, pp. 151-152.

right to collect these legacies from the cathedral fabric for the price of 1 lb.brab. (30 days' wages) each year. Thus, from a sum of almost 19 lb.brab., a mere 1 lb.brab. ended up in the coffers of the cathedral fabric.[940] In Burgos such collection of testamentary bequests for the cathedral was leased to two laymen.[941]

Large bequests from laypeople – those from lords aside – were a rarity, to which Italian cathedrals perhaps provide the exception.[942] The legacy left by the Milanese merchant Marco Carelli (c. 1325-1394) is a complete departure from the norm: in his testament, drawn up on 4 July 1393, he bequeathed nearly his entire estate '*pro fabrica ecclesiae majoris et pauperibus Christi*' (to the cathedral fabric and Christ's poor). At his death, that estate was estimated at 35,000 ducats, or a full year's wage for 1275 unskilled workmen.[943] In return, the cathedral fabric executed the will, arranged his expensive funeral and commissioned a tomb monument (fig. 83).[944]

The fabric could also receive bequests in kind. In Basel the fabric sold all goods acquired by inheritance to its regular '*unser lieber Frauen Fürkauferin*' (the regrater of Our Lady), [945] whilst the cathedral fabric in Milan ran its own shop for the purpose.[946]

THE COMMUTATION MONIES

Many *mendicatoria* created opportunities for substituting imposed penitential fasts and pilgrimages (usually excepting any requiring a voyage to Jerusalem, to Sts Peter and Paul in Rome or to Santiago de Compostela) as well as simple vows made in silence[947] with a sum of money for the building works, '*propter urgentem ipsius fabrice necessitatem*' (due to the fabric's urgent need).[948]

The moralist Hugh of Newcastle makes mention of this practice around 1300, but refuses to recognize pardoners' authority to commute penances, calling it cheating the Christian populace.[949] Yet bishops were entirely within their rights when it came to substituting certain simple vows.[950] It is possible that the preaching of the Crusades – as early as the late eleventh century it was already common for the crusader's vow to be commuted to the payment of a sum of money – provided the model for this aspect of *mendicatoria*.[951] Special laws dictated the size of the commutation sum, which in theory was to be proportionate to the lapsed vow.[952] In the case of a pilgrimage, this was the cost of the journey there and back, along with the cost of lodging at the pilgrimage destination; indeed, this is precisely the calculation basis applied by the Utrecht *mendicatorium* issued by Bishop Jan van Diest in 1327.[953] But any guess as to the actual size of receipts is no more than a shot in the dark. The Utrecht rolls record only a single entry concerning a commutation.[954] Thus, here, too, the methods of procurement serve to obscure the true value of these contributions.

A further option for commutation, which had already existed in the thirteenth century but found particular favour after the second half of the fourteenth, revolved around the pope's and, as his delegate, the bishop's use of their authorities to release the faithful both individually and generally from certain obligatory abstinences, especially the use of milk, butter and eggs during Lent, in return for the contribution of a specific sum of money for a specific ecclesiastical cause – hence the name *Butterbriefe* given to such dispensations. A case in point is the papal exemption granted on the occasion of the issue of the crusade bull of 1343,[955] from which cathedral fabrics were also eligible to profit. In Bremen, the archbishop declared on 18 January 1395 that the faithful in his bishopric would be allowed to eat meat on a certain fast day, provided they donated 1 groot (*gravis*) to the cathedral works via their parish priest.[956] There are further examples. Fabric rolls from the cathedral of Regensburg for the years 1487 and 1488 record small amounts (which furthermore had to be shared with Rome) '*occasione lacticiniorum*' (for dispensation of abstinence from dairy);[957] according to the fabric rolls for 1516, the cathedral of Bordeaux enjoyed minor proceeds '*à cause du pardon du beurre*';[958] the bishopric of Cambrai held a dispensation option since 1493;[959] and in 1526 the chapter of Châlons-en-Champagne filed a suit against Rome concerning this same dispensation.[960] Lastly, the cathedral of Rouen was able to achieve an agreeable financial result using effective propaganda. Here the first papal dispensation dates from 1479, with a renewal in 1484. One year later saw the first meeting to discuss rebuilding the new south tower, for which the first stone was laid on 10 November 1487. The rolls for that year (1487/88) mention the completion of '2 *milliers et demy de brevez fais pour le burre envoyez aux doyens et curez pour recommander la fabrique*' for 12½ l.t. The receipts '*des deniers venus de burres et letaiges*' amounted to 1378 l.t. 19 s., equivalent to 44 labourers' annual wages, and over 45 percent of the total income for that year. In later years the receipts from this source became utterly insignificant. The share that these dispensation monies contributed to the overall building costs of an estimated 24,750 l.t. hardly justifies the structure's evocative appellation of the 'Tour de Beurre' (fig. 52).[961]

UNLAWFULLY ACQUIRED GOODS

Lastly, the bishop could designate the *res male acquisite*, or unlawfully acquired goods (sometimes specifying those which had been acquired by plunder, usury or theft) for cathedral construction, at least in cases where the original owner or his heirs could not be found. As such, these goods had to meet two criteria: first, they had to be *bona restituenda*, or property that ought to be given back to the owner, and, second, the owner had to be untraceable. Where these criteria applied, he who held unlawfully acquired goods faced a moral dilemma, since he could not gain absolution through confession if he kept possession of the tainted property, '*non dimittitur peccatum, nisi restituatur ablatum*'.[962] The episcopal directive extended in *mendicatoria* provided a way out: by giving these goods to the cathedral he could be released from his sin. In actual practice, however, Church advisers did not always stick to the rule that the original rightful claimant had to be satisfied first. Towards the end of the twelfth century, the cantor of Notre Dame in Paris, the strict moralist Peter Cantor, found his Bishop Maurice de Sully culpable of advising an usurer to simply give over all his ill-gotten gains to the cathedral. Cantor counselled the man to first allow all his disadvantaged clients to be summoned and only then give the remainder to Notre Dame.[963] Indeed, late medieval literature abounds with tales of clerics who were more concerned with cashing in tainted money for the church works than with facilitating fair restitution to those who had been duped.[964]

But goods could also be obtained by questionable methods that met neither of these conditions. For instance, there was money that, though acquired by immoral means, required no restitution. A classic example cited in canonical literature is the wages of prostitution,

53
Scene from the story of the penitent cloth merchant, c.1220
Portal of the Last Judgment on the north transept
Rheims Cathedral

The scene is carved around the socle supporting the figure of Christ on the trumeau. According to tradition the image depicts the dishonest cloth merchant who begged forgiveness form the Virgin and Child as a canon looked on and – possibly – made restitution of unfairly acquired goods, the *bona injusta*.

LITERATURE
Abou-el-Haj 1988, p. 26.

which no one in their right mind would claim should be refunded to clients.[965] Though expressly prohibited in the Bible (Deut 23:28-19), scholastics maintained that this category of *bona injusta* (unlawfully acquired property) could be spent on *pia causae* (pious causes) (fig. 53). Yet moral complexities might arise to confound the recipient nevertheless. Thomas of Chobham (1156/58-1233/36) relates how Paris's loose women presented themselves before Bishop Maurice de Sully to offer a splendid stained glass window for the Notre-Dame, paid for with their earnings. The bishop reportedly turned to Peter Cantor and Stephen Langton for advice, both of whom recommended turning the gift down as public acceptance might suggest approval for the prostitutes' lifestyle.[966] A gift that was more discretely given, however, could be accepted without objections.[967]

Another category of such goods was the *bona vaga et incerta* (unattended goods of uncertain origin); in theory they had to be restored to their owners (if possible), but possession was not considered morally reprehensible. This category included discovered goods, such as found treasure and items scavenged on the shore. Goods of this last variety were typically governed by a distinct set of rules; often for example, the lord could claim entitlement.[968] But even this property of 'vague and uncertain' origin could not be allocated to the cathedral fabric without an episcopal order.[969] Basel's cathedral welcomed all categories of goods of uncertain origin and unlawful acquisition; on Sundays and feast days, the petitor charged with collection would call on the assembled, '*hat ouch yeman unfertig, unrecht gut, es sig funden gut, gestolen gut, geraubt gut, wuchergut und der rechten erben nit weisst, der gebs an der buw unser lieben frowen, so wirt er ledig gezalt der schulden*'.[970] Both *bona injusta* and *bona vaga et incerta* were more common in the Middle Ages than they are today. As an example of the first category, its suffices to cite the prohibition on charging interest. Uncertain goods are the product of an uncertain society, and occasionally we get a fascinating glimpse of this fact in account rolls from parish fabrics, where such goods and money were first deposited. In 1502, for example, the wardens of the church of St Bavo in Haarlem concluded an agreement with a buyer stating that it would dispose of '*alle dat goet dat verloren waert ende wort onder sinte Baef gebracht*' after a term of six weeks, with the proceeds to benefit the church fabric.[971] So when an innkeeper came to the church with a bible that a '*man of ghesel*' had used to pay his bill of 8 stuivers without ever returning to claim it, the church gave the innkeeper his 8 stuivers, but kept the excess profit.[972]

Were church building works the obvious beneficiary for money and goods of these types? That they ought to go *ad pios usus* (towards pious purposes) was clear. Strict moralists judged there to be only one option: distribution amongst the poor;[973] to this, Hugh of Newcastle (c. 1300) added the Crusades.[974] Geert Groote even dedicated his short treatise *Contra turrim Trajectensem*, written around 1371, primarily to this problem, since Utrecht's cathedral tower, in itself a superfluous, excessively expensive and vainglorious hulk, was built in part from the profits of the *bona injusta* and thus paid for by alms meant for the poor.[975] Though we cannot pursue his argumentation here, it is important to note that many Church authorities felt no compunction in permitting, and even promoting, the donation of tainted money to the church building works as a way to wipe the conscience clean. Sources do not always make clear who held the authority to allocate these goods. Many *mendicatoria* and synodal statutes show us bishops assigning them to the cathedral works without requesting papal consent.[976] In some cases papal privileges were honoured, such as in the 1288 synodal statutes from Liège, which made a point of recognizing any papal claims to the revenues from certain religious institutions.[977] From the thirteenth century onwards the papal registers show popes apportioning proceeds from these goods and monies to a range of causes, including cathedral-building, though often limited to a certain value and term.[978] The fabric of Haarlem's parish church of St Bavo enjoyed the fruits of one of these papal privileges, extended in 1309,[979] as did the church of Our Lady in Antwerp.[980] Around 1300 the pope also brought a new element into play: the *compositio*. Anyone who held property unlawfully could be released from the obligation to restore it, and as such be absolved of his sin, if he donated part of it to a good cause; the remainder was his to keep in good conscience.[981] With the Council of Vienne (1311/12) came a final important change. Revoking all former privileges, the pope delegated the authority to allocate these goods to the bishops.[982] Various considerations may have motivated this move. To begin with, the many and diverse privileges granted over time rendered any overview or control over ill-gotten gains entirely illusory. Added to this was the fact that Italian merchants in particular found roundabout ways to use this money, mostly acquired through usury, for their own benefit, albeit for their own or their families' spiritual welfare; many of their wills include a fixed clause stipulating that profits from usury be put towards a family chapel (and foundation of a mass) or private altar.[983] One fifteenth-century moralist, wishing to prevent such promotion of personal interests and self-glorification, recommended that usurious gains be spent on repairing existing churches rather than on new building works, as these served too much to honour the patron.[984]

From this point on, bishops almost always designated the cathedral fabric as the bishopric's only legal claimant to the *bona restituenda*,[985] and provisions to this end thus become a fixed element in *mendicatoria*. Though bishops were of course entirely free to allow other churches or Church institutions to share in these profits,[986] doing so could oblige them to indemnify the cathedral fabric in return, as we shall see.

How effective were episcopal efforts at funnelling the influx of *bona injusta, vaga et incerta* from throughout the entire diocese into the cathedral fabric fund? Were parish churches willing to relinquish all unlawfully acquired goods that parish priests and church fabrics received on a regular basis to the *collectores* from the cathedral?

Some parish churches were able to obtain their own papal privileges trumping those of the bishop. We have already seen this at St Bavo in Haarlem (15 May 1309), winning out over the Utrecht Dom, and at the church of Our Lady in Antwerp (after 1434), to the disadvantage of the cathedral at Cambrai. There were also churches that kept these goods without ever getting a papal privilege. One example is the church of St Victor in Xanten, which behaved as though the Cologne episcopate's synodal statutes simply did not exist.[987] As shall become clear in the chapter on the Utrecht Dom, cathedral fabrics might sometimes settle instead for the payment of a small redemption sum from their parishes. And yet episcopal prescripts are very much in evidence at the local level, as attested by a random will from Antwerp dated 1500 which, despite the papal privilege accorded to the church of Our Lady, lists *'item de voerg. testatoer gheeft ende maect der fabrijken van onser vrouw van Camerijck voer sijn onrechtverdich goed, dwelc hij niet en weet 13 s.'*,[988] a sum equal to 25 days' pay of an unskilled labourer.

54
Reliquary of St Stephan, fifteenth century
Sens, trésor de la cathédrale

The 1457/58 fabric rolls record that this reliquary was borne around the diocese by the cathedral pardoners.

LITERATURE
Exh. cat. Rheims 2001, p. 178.

THE FINANCIAL RESULTS

What were the factors that went into determining the financial success of these complex campaigns for the cathedral building works? On the one hand, the size of the receipts depended on countless incidental religious, political and economic circumstances rooted in time and place, such as the inclination to give alms and the prosperity of the bishopric. These factors will not be discussed here, but will be treated in Chapter three, in relation to the specific situation in the bishopric of Utrecht. On the other hand, there were a number of factors of a more general nature that, the actual and ever-changing historical situation aside, also exerted an influence on the financial results. In considering any diocesan collection for the cathedral works, we should always ask: Over what time span was the collection organized? What geographical area was covered? How did the donations reach the cathedral? Were there other collections competing with that of the cathedral, and if so to what extent? Each of these four aspects will be addressed in turn below.

THE DURATION OF THE COLLECTION CAMPAIGN

Generally speaking, there was no rule for how long collection campaigns should last. Certainly, the organizational structure called forth by a *mendicatorium* was not intended to last a few years only. Though it is true that the oldest expeditions with relics, such as those in Laon in 1112 and 1113, were one-time affairs,[989] this changed as soon as bishops began laying down official procedures. Most *mendicatoria* do not specify a campaign duration; some do state a term, however, such as a 1525 *mendicatorium* from Toul stating a period of 20 years. But in reality this term means nothing, since we know that quests were already being conducted in Toul from the first quarter of the fourteenth century.[990] Most bishops' mandates are in fact no more than a renewal and confirmation of letters issued by their predecessors; in most cases, the earliest document – the source on which all later writs were based – has not been preserved. Diocesan cathedral-building collections could go on for decades, even centuries. One study has calculated the minimum number of years that pardoners operated in each of various dioceses in France: in Amiens this was 60 years, in Clermont-Ferrand 100 years, in Arras 238 years and in Troyes no less than 277 years.[991] According to fabric rolls from the archiepiscopacy of Sens, the campaign there was already up and running at end of the thirteenth century and continued until far into the sixteenth century (fig. 54),[992] and diocesan revenues in the archbishopric of Rouen did not dry up completely until 1640/41.[993] Sources from dioceses outside France reveal similar trends. In the archbishopric of York, the pardoners of the cathedral works toured the diocese from 1227 until after 1408,[994] in the bishopric of Regensburg they were active from around 1250 until after 1525,[995] in Cologne from the beginning of construction of the Gothic cathedral in 1248 until into the sixteenth century,[996] in the bishopric of Utrecht from 1288 until 1563,[997] and in that of Pamplona from 1291 at the latest until well into the fifteenth century.[998] Implicitly, these campaigns continued even when there was no cathedral-building activity to speak of. Once established, the institution was never formally abolished, but simply spun out its idle existence – in the bishopric of Utrecht even holding on until the bitter end, when the council fathers of Trent issued an official Church prohibition on pardoners.

THE GEOGRAPHICAL AREA

The territorial expanse that a cathedral fabric's collectors were entitled to cover was usually contiguous with the boundaries of the bishopric. We have already pointed out the potentially vast differences in scale between bishoprics, ranging from several dozen parishes (as in Senlis) to a thousand (as in Chartres).[999] Accordingly, it was essential for fabrics to keep methodical records on all the episcopate's parishes. In 1414/15 the master of the fabric of the cathedral of Rouen paid 30 s. '*pour faire renouveler les 3 papiers où sont enregistrées toutes les cures de archevesquié de Rouen pour la fabrique*'.[1000] Some of these records list contributions by parish: at Freising listing more than 200 parishes,[1001] at Regensburg 486[1002] and at Utrecht over 800.[1003]

It was an obvious move for bishops and chapters to attempt to extend their radius of action as far as possible. The very earliest cathedral expeditions do not seem to have paid particular heed to boundaries or territorial jurisdictions; we can assume that the canons who set off for England from Laon in 1113 left without bothering about obtaining official Church permission.[1004] As soon as bishops acquired the right to determine which collections to admit in their dioceses – from the first half of the thirteenth century – that situation changed, and from then on all aspirants needed the bishop's authorization.

What could a bishop and chapter do if they wished to take their campaign outside diocesan boundaries? Firstly, they could try to convince the pope to issue orders to admit the collection in a territory extending beyond their diocese. We see this in a letter issued by Pope Urban IV to all clerics in the kingdom of France on 8 September 1262, in which he confirms bulls issued by his predecessors, Popes Innocent IV (1243-1254) and Alexander IV (1254-1261), ordering that messengers from the cathedral of Clermont-Ferrand, where rebuilding works had begun in 1248, be given a warm welcome and their indulgences proclaimed.[1005] A letter from Pope Innocent IV dated 27 April 1247 directs all English bishops to admit *nuntii* from the cathedral of Lyon in their churches and to allow them to speak to the faithful to encourage them '*pro subsidio fabrice*' (to support the fabric).[1006]

A sense of fellowship and of empathy for the fate of a neighbouring cathedral could also prompt a bishop to admit messengers from another episcopate's church into his own diocese – all the more so if he was not engaged in building himself. Thus, in 1243 the archbishop of Cologne felt at liberty to command his archiepiscopal clergy to prepare to receive emissaries from the church of Our Lady in Trier – not even a cathedral – and moreover to meet them in ceremonial array in each parish on the day of their arrival, which was to be treated as a Sunday.[1007] Whether this same archbishop would have been as willing to welcome a foreign collection five years later is doubtful; the first year of work on the Gothic cathedral church, 1248, already saw the appointment of a *petitor structurae majoris ecclesiae* (collector of funds for the cathedral building works),[1008] and in 1254 he refused to admit a campaign from an Augustinian monastery near Liège so as not to undercut the home campaign.[1009] A similar situation developed in the archbishopric of Rouen. In 1485 the bishop of Paris obtained permission from his *confrater* in Rouen to publish Parisian indulgences in the latter's archdiocese. But the chapter of Rouen was vehemently opposed as a fundraising campaign from outside would disadvantage progress on the Tour de Beurre. Ultimately, the king ruled in favour of the bishop of Paris, citing the fact that consent from his fellow prelate would always be the decisive factor. This incident also serves to point up the characteristic lack of cooperation between an archbishop and chapter where the interests of the cathedral works were concerned.[1010] Nevertheless, the admittance of pardoners from other cathedrals was by no means uncommon. In 1224 the bishop of Lincoln granted the bishop and chapter of Salisbury permission '*quod mittant nuntios suos predicatores per totum archidiaconatum Norhamtonie ad querendum elemosinas* [...] *ad fabricam nove ecclesie Saresbiriensis*' (to send their messengers and preachers throughout the archdeaconry of Northampton in order to amass alms for the construction of the new cathedral at Salisbury).[1011] In 1233 the archbishop of Tours applied to his colleague in Rouen to admit collections for his cathedral.[1012] Similarly, in 1291 the archbishop of Cologne informed his *confrater* in Mainz that he had appointed two clerics from that city to serve as *procuratores* for his cathedral, but this was for a period of less than one year.[1013] The bishop of Speyer recommended messengers from Strasbourg to his clerics in 1264, and granted an indulgence worth 40 days for benefactors of that cathedral.[1014] We have already seen that bishops might issue indulgences for cathedrals other than their own, just as they did, incidentally, for non-cathedral churches and religious institutions in and outside their dioceses; examples include the bishop of Metz for the cathedral of Halberstadt in 1258 and the bishop of Durham for the cathedral of York in 1312.[1015] Here it is worth noting that consent or cooperation from temporal ruling bodies seems to have been, if not requisite, at least highly desirable.[1016] Following the 1194 fire at Chartres, the occurrence of a miracle inspired King Richard to allow collectors from the cathedral to journey through his kingdom; he is even reported to have humbly borne the reliquary shrine on his own shoulders.[1017] And during a 1257 visit to King Henry III of England, the archbishop of Cologne – who supported the king's brother Richard's aspirations to the Holy Roman imperial throne – managed to draw on his political clout to promote recently begun works at his cathedral, moving the king to send requests to the archbishop of Canterbury and other English bishops to welcome messengers from Cologne.[1018] In neither France nor, as the subsequent discussion will show, in the Netherlands, were such expeditions organized without approval from the sovereign ruler or overlord. In the fifteenth century the king of France authorized diocesan campaigns for the cathedrals of Châlons-en-Champagne,[1019] Noyon,[1020] Sens[1021] and Perpignan[1022], amongst others.

Archdioceses presented a difficult case where borders were concerned: could the archbishop and metropolitan chapter compel suffragan bishops to admit and welcome messengers from the archiepiscopal cathedral, and could they impose ecclesiastical sanctions for refusal? Archbishops may initially have appropriated the powers to do so; for example, on 16 June 1191 the archbishop of Rheims called on clerics throughout the Church province to welcome messengers from the cathedral of the suffragan Senlis – thus not even from his own cathedral – and to encourage generosity from their flocks.[1023] A conflict that arose in this same Church province in the 1320s engendered a *cause célèbre* that would see the contested issue of whether or not it was compulsory for suffragan dioceses to admit metropolitan pardoners settled once and for all. The conflict started in 1223, when the bishop of Laon complained to Pope Honorius III about operations being conducted in his bishopric by pardoners from the cathedral of Rheims, where rebuilding works had been underway since 1210. The archbishop had ordered that his parish churches open their doors to these messengers, that the day of their arrival be celebrated as a Sunday and so on, all this on pain of ecclesiastical penalties for defiance.[1024] It was not until many years later, on 17 March 1246, that Pope Innocent IV finally issued a definitive ruling in the affair,[1025] and moreover one that dealt with only one item on a long list of points of contention, all of them related to the jurisdiction that the archbishop exercised over his suffragans. In this particular case the pope found against the archbishop: he had no right to grant his messengers any authority whatsoever to summon recalcitrant parish priests within his Church province to appear before the ecclesiastical court. In other words, it was up to the diocesan authorities to decide when to admit messengers from any given church into their bishopric. The verdict was deemed to merit incorporation in the collection of Decretals and thus found its way into general canon law and canonical literature,[1026] serving as a reference for provincial councils and diocesan synods.[1027]

However, the pope's ruling also went on to say that the archbishop would always be free to approach his suffragans with affectionate exhortations to welcome his *nuntii* and provide assistance. This was no formality. On 6 March 1251 the pope addressed an urgent entreaty to bishops of the Church province of Rheims – apparently at the archbishop's request – to lend the heavily debt-ridden metropolitan church as much financial support as possible, '*ut membra capiti debeant subvenire*' (just as the limbs ought to assist the head).[1028] Together these various episodes provide a clear illustration of the avidity with which archbishops (and bishops) endeavoured to stretch the boundaries of their collection campaigns, particularly during early phases of construction. Though archbishops may have brought pressure to bear to get their campaigns admitted to other bishoprics within their Church province, they could not go so far as to impose their will. Thus, whilst the '*fermes des questes faictes* [...] *es six eveschies de la province de Rouen*'[1029] generated a small, albeit sporadic, income for the fabric of that cathedral, after a number of bishops lodged their objection in 1487, the fabric only received proceeds from the *quêtes* it had leased out in Sées and Coutances.[1030]

METHODS OF COLLECTING THE CONTRIBUTIONS

It does not take any great imaginative power to envisage the array of problems that the masters of the fabric had to overcome to ensure that all the alms donated by the faithful in hundreds of parishes scattered throughout a large diocese made it safely and undivided into the fabric's treasury, year in, year out. Complaints about designated revenues being withheld from the fabric are legion.[1031] Effective control over compliance with episcopal regulations was made all but impossible by poor and sluggish communication. Bishops and chapters sought remedies to stem myriad forms of passive and open resistance to collections and of embezzlement and theft of the collected alms. Threats of ecclesiastical punishments had little effect; clearly, cooperation would have to be achieved by some other means. Specifically, the cathedral fabric would have to find some way of ensuring that all involved had an interest in the profits – both the parish priests or churchwardens who had to hand over donations for the cathedral works and the *nuntii* charged with receiving this money on behalf of the cathedral fabric and conveying it there. It was unavoidable that the cathedral fabric would quite literally have to pay a price to secure this series of transactions, with cooperation coming at the direct cost of the final profits. Over the centuries various means were developed for rewarding cooperation with collection campaigns, all of which had an impact on the methods used for collecting the alms and transferring them to the cathedral fabric. Use of these methods was in itself enough to make the otherwise simple matter of campaigning for the cathedral building works inordinately complicated. Given that the problems associated with collection are so integral to the essential nature of this source of income, it is worthwhile to examine them in greater depth.

Regulations on how donations were to be collected were far from clear cut, it may be recalled. Where actual practice is concerned, however, we can be more specific. On the payment day, or *dies reportationis*, parish priests had to personally settle payment of all gifts and alms donated to the cathedral works. Clerics were already required to convene at certain times throughout the year for the annual or biannual synod at the diocesan level, at the level of the rural deanery and, occasionally, archdeaconry, as well as for the parish synods variously known as *capitula ruralia*, *ruralia concilia*, *synodi christianitatis*, *senne*, *seend* or *kalendae*, the last harking back to the fact that they were originally held on a monthly basis. It seems that nearly every bishopric used these gatherings as an occasion to hold the *dies reportationis*.

As conventions of clerics – or their delegates – from throughout the bishopric in the episcopal city, diocesan synods had as their chief aim the promulgation of the administrative, judicial, statutory and pastoral regulations and measures framed to support religious life in the bishopric. Particularly after the Fourth Lateran Council (1215), the synod developed into an important legislative institution, issuing statutes that represent the codification of diocesan legislation.[1032] As mentioned, such statutes very often contained provisions designed to aid the cathedral fabric.[1033] Clerics were counselled on which pardoners they were and were not to receive and the conditions under which they were to do so; further, they were sometimes required to spur the faithful, both during confession and *in extremis*, to make a donation to the cathedral. Of course synods also furnished an excellent occasion for the masters of the fabric to receive donations for the works. Clerics also had other financial obligations to fulfil at the synods, such as payment of the *cathedraticum* – a special tax benefitting the bishop.[1034]

Fabric rolls for the year 1294/95 from the cathedral of Autun record receipts from 24 rural deaneries under the heading '*anno quo supra recepta queste et confratrie beati Nazarii in synodo Pentecoste*' (in the above-named year: receipts from the collection and from the confraternity of St Nazarius during the Whitsun synod).[1035] The fourteenth- and fifteenth-century fabric rolls from the cathedral of Sens include a similar category: '*recepta pro generali questa* [...] *recollecta Senonensis die synodi*' (received by way of the general collection on the day of the synod in Sens).[1036] In the bishoprics of Troyes,[1037] Utrecht,[1038] Clermont-Ferrand[1039] and Lyon,[1040] synods likewise presented the most convenient collection point. So too in Halberstadt, where in 1509 the bishop prescribed that the collected donations were no longer to be gathered by *nuntii* on horseback; rather '*ad parcendum talibis superfluis et inutilibus expensis*' – in other words, for reasons of efficiency – the money, counted and parcelled out in pouches, and each accounted for in writing, was thenceforth to be conveyed personally by the parish priests to the rural deans and brought by them to the synod.[1041]

And yet it is far from certain that later medieval bishops actually observed the Fourth Lateran Council prescription that synods be summoned at least once each year. It would appear that the frequency of synodal gatherings varied considerably according to time and place, to the extent that clerics in some dioceses might not meet for decades.[1042] Yet the regular transfer of monies was unquestionably in the cathedral fabric's interest. Fabrics therefore always also relied – sometimes exclusively – on the regular rural deanery meetings that parish priests were required to attend. As the lowest organizational unit within the Church's complex hierarchical structure, these *capitula ruralia* were led by a rural dean, known as the *oculus episcopi* (or eye of the bishop), who served as the intermediary between the highest ecclesiastical powers and the clergy at the base.[1043] As such, he also provided a link between the cathedral fabric in the distant episcopal city and priests in his own deanery.

Parish synods could function in two ways within the cathedral works collection system: as an interim phase or as the final stage. In the former, parish priests gave the monies to the deans, who in turn delivered them in person to the masters of the fabric during a diocesan synod. This may have been the arrangement in the episcopates of Autun and Sens. As early as 1240 a Scottish provincial council decreed that parish priests had to gather all alms donated for the cathedral of Glasgow in their parishes and transfer these unreduced to the deans during the first scheduled parish synod (*capitulum*), though without leaving us any clue as to how the monies got to their destination from there.[1044] In instances where the parish synod was the organizational endpoint of the collection (the latter form above), the cathedral fabric *nuntii* or *procuratores* (delegates) had to journey there to pick the funds up. This was the method applied in the archbishopric of Rouen, though more outlying parishes may also have delivered their monies for the cathedral works directly at the provincial summer and winter synods.[1045] Each year after the Octave of Easter, the *procurator* of the cathedral fabric rode out on horseback, accompanied by two servants, to spend four weeks visiting the *calendes* (priests' assemblies) of one of the archdeaconries and picking up the alms collected there; the daily routes and resting points are all minutely described.[1046] When pitched warfare discouraged the *procuratores* from making their rounds in 1431 and 1432, the rural deans nevertheless discharged their duty; as a reward for their effort, they were given extra wine and bags of spices.[1047]

An Utrecht *mendicatorium* of 18 December 1322 is also clear on this point, stating simply, '*in die reportationes, hoc est in generali eorum capitulo*' (on the day of conveyance, that is at their general meeting).[1048]

In the bishopric of Basel the cathedral fabric *nuntius* likewise attended the priests' meetings; here the rolls also record the receipts per rural deanery.[1049] Deans were actively drawn into the organization and propagation of cathedral works campaigns in other ways, too. They distributed the offertory boxes amongst parish church priests – to be discussed below – either by handing them out during the meeting or having their special paid messengers deliver them.[1050] In 1495 the cathedral of Sens sent a letter to the rural deans announcing the beginning of transept construction and asking them to commend the enterprise to their parish priests.[1051] The *litterae recommendativae* (letters of recommendation) used in some dioceses were also passed on to parish priests via the rural deans.[1052] In Rouen these *breves*, summarizing indulgences on offer, were conveyed to the priests of its 1400 parishes by the rural deans; priests had to sew the *breviculi*, possibly written on parchment, into their missals (*cousu en son missel*) and read out the text on Sundays and feast days.[1053] Deans were furthermore tasked with supervising compliance with episcopal regulations.[1054] In the episcopacy of Prague they had to report the names of priests who failed to show up at meetings to the bishop.[1055]

In certain instances we find parish priests coming together for the sole purpose of handing over donations for the cathedral works. In a *mendicatorium* of 1327, the bishop of Utrecht addresses clerics as '*vos* [...] *in capitulis vestris generalibus aut in diebus et in locis reportationum vestrarum solitis et ad hoc deputatis specialiter congregati*' (you who convene at the general rural synod or at the regular times and places designated especially for that purpose, in order to deliver the contributions).[1056] It was precisely such assemblies, convened for this purpose alone, that prompted the moralist Hugh of Newcastle to inveigh against bishops around 1300 for improperly authorizing their pardoners to round up simple ministers of the soul and take them from their work to receive episcopal instructions.[1057]

Most *mendicatoria* expressly stipulated that contributions were to be handed over without delay, deduction or reduction.[1058] Synodal statutes dating to the last quarter of the thirteenth century from the diocese of Albi prohibited both parish priests and *predicatores fabrice* of the cathedral from selling or commissioning third parties to sell any donations in kind that they received.[1059] Other statutes prohibited parish priests from demanding gifts from the pardoners or extorting money from them.[1060] Far more effective at guaranteeing that the results of the collection actually made it into the hands of the masters of the fabric intact was the practice of gathering parish contributions in a sealed coin box. We previously noted that the custom of distributing sealed collection boxes to churches may have derived from crusade collection campaigns; in England money for the Crusades was already being collected in this way in 1166.[1061] Pope Innocent III's 1199 crusade bull includes the provision that '*in singulis ecclesiis truncum concavum poni praecipimus, tribus clavibus consignatum*' (we command that a collection box locked with three keys be placed in every church) (fig. 28).[1062] According to the synodal statutes of 1372 from the Breton bishopric of Tréguier, every parish church had to install a collection box (*bixida*) for the cathedral; moreover, parish priests were required to encourage the faithful to contribute to this cause before proceeding to any other collection whatsoever, with the prospect of a 40-day indulgence for munificent donors.[1063] The fifteenth-century oath of allegiance to be sworn by the *petitor fabrice* of Speyer Cathedral charged him '*ordinando pyxides ubi prius non fuerunt, quantum ei utile et ubi expedire videbitur*' (to have collecting boxes placed where formerly there had been none, as many as he shall deem useful and there where he deems it expedient).[1064] Other dioceses, too, employed this method to garner alms for cathedral-building, including Basel,[1065] Sens,[1066] Troyes,[1067] Strasbourg,[1068] Milan,[1069] Amiens,[1070] Tours,[1071] Le Mans[1072] and Châlons-en-Champagne.[1073] What this meant in practice becomes clear from the fabric rolls of Troyes. They make an administrative distinction between receipts from the almsboxes in the city's nine parish churches ('*rec. des boistes parochiaux*') and the far more important gains from collection boxes across the entire diocese, which the clergy brought to the diocesan synod ('*rec. des boistes du Senne* [= the synod]');[1074] the latter entry was sometimes described in greater detail, such as '*rec. des boistes qui sont en toutes les paroches de l'éveschie de Troyes, esquelles sont les questes faictes pour lad. euvre esd. parroches et sont ouvertes par led. proviseurs*'.[1075] The clergy were given new collection boxes or used boxes fitted with new locks to take back with them, with the related expenses recorded each year: '*pro 400 bustiis tam novis quam veteribus ferrandis 25 s.; pro centum bustiis novis emptis 7 s.*' (for arranging for locks on 400 offertory boxes, both new and old: 25 s.; for the purchase of 100 new offertory boxes: 7 s.) (1296/97).[1076] In many Spanish bishoprics, parishes were under episcopal orders to make rounds with *bacins* (collection plates) on certain days, the proceeds of which reached the cathedral fabric by various routes.[1077]

Cooperation from both the parish church priest and fabric could make or break efforts to collect the donations for the cathedral works. Their cooperation could never simply be assumed, however, since campaigns for the cathedral works represented competition for a parish's own collection. Whilst the efficaciously locked collecting boxes could of course no longer form a temptation for sticky fingers, cooperating *con amore* was an entirely different matter. Sometimes the cathedral fabric confined itself to distributing gifts in thanks for services rendered. In the archbishopric of Rouen it was common custom, certainly in the sixteenth century, to present parish priests with gloves and a pouch of spices after the synod and (from 1540) to offer them a meal each Wednesday during the summer synod.[1078] Certain other usages that emerged, however, came at the direct cost of the fabric's net receipts.

The consequence of these usages was that actual practice diverged from the rules typically laid down in *mendicatoria* and synodal statutes. Shortly before 1300 Hugh of Newcastle was already complaining that cunning pardoners were promising parish priests a third to half of the proceeds in exchange for their ready cooperation in campaigns.[1079] English priests' rolls from the fifteenth century show parish clergy receiving a portion of all collections in this way, totalling some six or seven a year, including those not organized for the cathedral.[1080] Geert Groote describes what might be called standard procedure: the masters of the fabric of Utrecht Cathedral started out by making orders and threats, but when this failed to secure cooperation, gradually conceded a part of the proceeds to the parish priests.[1081] In some cases the bishop sanctioned the way affairs were conducted in practice. In the bishopric of Basel it was formally agreed that parish priests could keep one-third of the contents of the collection boxes when they were emptied.[1082] A synodal statute from Utrecht dating to around 1350 permits priests to take a quarter of the monies collected in their own parishes, provided the masters of the fabric were satisfied that the parish's share was being delivered at the appointed place with due frequency.[1083] Elsewhere, the local church fabric was allowed a portion of the collection revenues.[1084]

The parish fabric's or priest's participation in the cathedral collection campaign had no impact on the essential nature of this income source. Matters were different when a cathedral fabric and parish agreed to a *compositio* (settlement) wherein the chapter granted the parish church (usually the church fabric) the right to execute all the mendicatorial directives on its behalf; however, rather than relinquish the full or greater part of the proceeds, the parish was now allowed to keep them in return for annual payment of some previously agreed sum. We will have occasion to discuss this practice in detail where the bishopric of Utrecht is concerned.[1085] In the bishopric of Konstanz, too, receipts from the cathedral works collection, characteristically called the *peticio matricis [ecclesie]* (supplication for relief of the mother church) were sometimes left to the parish church in exchange for a specified payment,[1086] but only sporadically. Apparently, this was meant as a favour to parish churches that were themselves under construction, but in general the Konstanz chapter preferred – perhaps with an eye to realizing the best possible result – that the bishopric's 1400 parishes or, rather, its countless rural deaneries simply rendered their *säcklein der peticion*, whose contents of tens of thousands of sometimes bad and inferior coin of varying provenance had to be painstakingly counted, sorted and exchanged.[1087]

Clearly, profits from the diocesan campaigns for the cathedral works did not reach their destinations fully intact. One way or another, either the parish priest or the church fabric received the right to share in these revenues. But they were not the only ones. The *nuntii* did not provide their services for free either. Whereas originally clerics attached to the actual abbey, church or cathedral organizing the campaign did the collecting,[1088] by the end of the eleventh century some churches were already entrusting this task to professionals – both clerics and laypersons – who made careers out of conducting such fundraising expeditions. Yet even near the end of the twelfth century its appears that this practice had not yet taken hold everywhere: around 1170 Bishop Arnulf of Lisieux wrote that he was keeping with him several priests from the diocese of Noyon in order to set up confraternities and conduct collections for his cathedral, precisely '*quia periti et instructi super huiusmodi officio dicebantur*' (because they – it was said – were experienced and proficient in that task).[1089] The innumerable limitations established by Church authorities at ecclesiastical councils and synods were directed chiefly against these *predicatores*, *questionarii*, *mercenarii* and *questores*, whom official documents place apart from and in direct opposition to the *simplices nuntii* (ordinary messengers).[1090]

For now, we will leave it up to the reader's imagination to picture these smooth-tongued agents, bent on profit and never quick to reject as too base any means of intimidating the faithful and wheedling away their money. In the next chapter, however, we will follow closely on the heels of the Utrecht pardoners as they make their journey. From the fifteenth century on, we have a few fairly brief model sermons written in the vernacular and approved by the Church that allow a global – and therefore only minimal – impression of the way in which pardoners were supposed to publicize the merits of the saints and spiritual benefits on offer and to encourage magnanimity.[1091] By far the earliest as well as most informative and, moreover, remarkably lengthy sermon for a cathedral made by any pardoner is the *Sermon d'Amiens*, which can be dated to shortly after 1276, when construction work on the cathedral had almost finished.[1092] The sermon is in French, presumably transcribed from the words of a Dominican sent out to visit a parish on the bishop's and chapter's behalf, bearing with him relics from the cathedral of Amiens. There, on a certain morning, he ascends the pulpit to address the small assembled congregation and to describe and propagate the essence of a *mendicatorium* of which no other trace now remains. Girding himself with threats of ecclesiastical penalties, he summons the clerics to cooperate; he announces the rule that the day of his arrival be observed as a feast day, and thus as a day on which no work may be done. He describes at length the bishop's exclusive power to forgive the *casus reservati*, citing such examples as failing to keep promises and swearing false oaths; next he mentions the option to surrender unlawfully acquired goods to the cathedral; and, finally, he closes by announcing the indulgences; the whole is primed with exempla and quotes in Latin from the Bible and other texts. He enumerates the exact number of masses that the bishopric's 777 priests will read for the cure of the souls of benefactors – namely, three each – with in addition the prayers said in its 26 abbeys and 30 priories.[1093] The martyrs, so the pardoner preaches, had to suffer hellish tortures '*por avoir pardon*' and monks must lead a life of ascetism; but you, '*bele douce gens*' need do no more than give alms to the cathedral, which will in itself suffice for '*pardon et asolucion à tous ciaus et à tous celes qui leur aumosnes envoieront à l'église me Dame S. Marie d'Amiens, [.. .] qui est vostre mere eglise*'.[1094]

We find traces of the pardoner in medieval literature, too. Only take his caricatured portrayal just after 1390 in the figure of Chaucer's pardoner, making his way to Charing Cross on the outskirts of London on behalf of the hospital and chapel of Our Lady of Roncesvalles (fig. 55). He sermonizes on the theme '*radix malorum est cupiditas*' (greed is the root of all evil) (Paul, 1 Timothy 6:10) and announces his business thus:

> First I pronounce whennes that I come,
> And thanne my bulles shewe I, alle and some.
> Oure lige lordes seel on my patente,
> That shewe I first, my body to warente,
> That no man be so boold, ne preest ne clerk,
> Me to destourbe of Cristes hooly werk.
> And after that thanne telle I forth my tales.
> Bullles of popes and of cardinales,
> Of patriarkes and bishopes I shewe,
> And in Latin I speke a wordes fewe,
> To saffron with my predicacioun,
> And for to stire hem to devocioun.
> Than shewe I forth my longe crital stones,
> Ycrammed ful of cloutes and of bones, –
> Relikes been they, as wenen they echoon.[1095]

55
The Pardoner
Illustration for 'The Pardoner's Tale' from *The Canterbury Tales* by Geoffrey Chaucer (1343?-1400), c.1420-1440
Parchment, 135 x 122 mm
Cambridge, University Library, Ms. Gg IV 27, f. 306r

The illuminator's portrait of the Pardoner is not so much based on Chaucer's text (General prologue, lines 671-716) as it is, it would seem, a faithful rendering of the real thing. The Pardoner is seated on a brown horse; the saddle, harness and reins are fashioned of black leather with metal fittings. He is garbed in a purple mantle, red head cloth, a black embellished belt, green hose and black shoes. The jawbone that he holds in his left hand may be intended as an satirical representation of a relic, which Church regulations forbade from ever being displayed outside their cases.
The spelling of the text and style of the

Naturally, Church authorities sought to check the liberties taken by pardoners. A decree issued by Pope John XXII in 1317 ordered these collectors to confine their preaching – or better yet, elucidations – to the indulgences and spiritual benefits connected with the institution they represented, whether cathedral, cloister or hospital.[1096] Countless provisions state in no uncertain terms that letters for the collection campaign are never to be discussed by the *predicatores questionarii*, but only ever by the *nuntii*.[1097]

But our interest here is confined to the relationship between the cathedral fabric and the pardoners. There were two possible forms in which this relationship could be organized, depending on whether the pardoner himself took a direct interest in the size of the financial results or not. If not, then he was simply in the employ of the chapter, monastery or institution for which he made his rounds. The earliest known contract of this latter type concerns the abbey church of St Faron in Meaux. In 1094 a priest agreed to journey through the Church province of Rheims for nine years to show the saint's relics and collect alms, returning at the end of this period to hand over both relics and revenues to the abbey in return for an annual wage of 120 l.[1098] We encounter agreements of this kind up through the late Middle Ages. In fifteenth-century Speyer[1099] and Strasbourg,[1100] for example, pardoners were hired by the cathedral on an equivalent basis.

The other method, giving the pardoner a real interest in the size of the proceeds, was more common and, apparently, more attractive for both parties. In this case there were a number of possible options. The chapter could agree on a certain division of the proceeds with the pardoner, such as a ratio of two-thirds for the cathedral fabric and one-third for the pardoner.[1101] One disadvantage of this option was that the chapter had to keep full records of pardoners' journeys, or else run the risk that all or some of the cathedral's share would disappear in their agent's pocket.[1102] It was for this very reason that in fourteenth-century Toul the diocesan chapter charged a chaplain with accompanying and monitoring the pardoners on their journeys.[1103] Thus, another method was also used, one particularly prevalent in many sectors of medieval commerce and favoured by countless chapters, in which the

miniatures in this manuscript reveal Netherlandish features. This has led to the assumption that the manuscript may have been commissioned from a scribe and miniaturist with Dutch roots by Humphrey, duke of Gloucester (1390-1447), who then presented it to Jacqueline, Countess of Hainaut, to whom he was married between 1422 and 1428.

LITERATURE

J.M. Manly & E. Rieken, with a chapter on illumination by Margareth Rickert, *The text of the Canterbury Tales, studied on the basis of all known manuscripts*, vol. 1, Chicago 1940, pp. 170-182, 590-605; Hodges 2005, pl. VII; pp. 227-28, 241.

masters of the fabric farmed out the entire cathedral works collection to a pardoner for a specified period (perhaps three years, with an option for renewal) in exchange for a fixed yearly fee. The pardoner then organized the journey and paid the associated costs, along with the agreed rent for the cathedral fabric; the difference between these costs and the ultimate receipts from the collection thus represented the remuneration for his labour and efforts.[1104] Since we will subsequently be examining the full workings of this system in the bishopric of Utrecht, it is only necessary to point out a few fundamental aspects here. The practice of *committere ad firmam* (contracting out) gained currency at an early stage: already in 1213 the synod of Paris was issuing a prohibition against it, incidentally without effect.[1105] Cathedral quests were farmed out in the dioceses of Sens,[1106] Clermont-Ferrand,[1107] Troyes,[1108] Utrecht[1109] and Rouen,[1110] to name a few. There even seems to have been a practice in a scattering of places whereby pardoners themselves subleased the anticipated local proceeds from a given parish or rural deanery to the priest or rural dean, not surprisingly to the chagrin of Church authorities.[1111]

One reason why the lease of cathedral works collections continued in spite of all abuses must lie in the fact that it gave the already overburdened cathedral fabric a means to avoid the administrative hassle entailed in organizing a diocesan fundraising campaign. It made bookkeeping exceedingly simple, as the fabric collected and recorded only the lease due from the pardoner. As an example, the 1383 fabric rolls from the cathedral of Troyes give us the following entry: '*de Nicolas Bouclier, demorant à Plancy, questain pour la fabrice, a luy admoissonne pour ung an seulement, venant au senne* [synod] *1383: 16 l.t., paient à Noël et Pasques par moitié, pour ce icy 16 livres*'.[1112] Another advantageous aspect of the leasing system was that because the fabric had effectively deflected any and all financial risks of the enterprise onto its pardoners, it now had an important and relatively stable source of income to rely on and could plan its building programme accordingly. Fabrics tended to be generous in their lease contracts, such that in cases of obvious force majeur, including war, it reduced the lease fee or even remitted it entirely.

In fact, it was not only – and not even primarily – cathedrals that farmed out their quests; large monasteries, abbeys and other religious institutions, such as hospitals, did the same, and it was against this latter group that the provisions drawn up at ecclesiastical councils and synods were chiefly directed.[1113]

To sum up, we can say that depending on the method by which receipts were gathered, the financial yield on a collection campaign for the cathedral building works could be trimmed on two ends and in two different ways. On the one hand, the parish priests or church fabrics could be given either part of the profits in return for services rendered or could take over the collection themselves in exchange for a fixed payment to the cathedral. The *nuntii* we find named in *mendicatoria*, on the other hand, who were usually pardoners serving as professional collectors of alms, could also participate in the proceeds – unless they were in the chapter's employ – such that they either received a share in the collection profits or leased the entire enterprise from the chapter. Some combination of the two systems was also possible to a certain extent. The cathedral fabric might then delegate pardoners to whom it had farmed out the collection, under the condition that they leave a certain share for the parish priests; the pardoners could also come to their own arrangements with the priests about this amount. But a cathedral fabric would never go so far as to make settlements for annual payments to parish priests when it had already contracted the entire affair to professional pardoners for an agreed sum.

It need hardly be said that these *compositiones* and leases not only caused a sizable portion of the proceeds to end up lining pockets, but also altered the nature of the income source itself. Quite simply, the rent paid by a professional pardoner can no longer be considered the direct derivative of a mendicatorial prescription. At the same time, it was entirely feasible for a single diocese to host two or more cathedral collection campaigns, both tracing back to a *mendicatorium*. Where this occurred, a possible explanation is that as an earlier campaign gradually withered owing to poor or antiquated collection methods, it became necessary at a certain point – at the launch of new building operations, for example – to set up a new campaign with its own organization, perhaps arranged by professional pardoners. Rather than dispensing with the old collection, it was more or less left to continue its sorry existence ad infinitum. In the bishopric of Utrecht, it was the *reportatio sancti Martini* (conveyance for St Martin) that was the oldest, probably stemming from 1288 and received at rural synods – in principle at least. When the time came to erect the tower (around 1322), it was supplemented with the quest for St Martin, which was farmed out to pardoners not long thereafter.[1114] We find similar duplication[1115] in the dioceses of Troyes and Amiens. The oldest fabric rolls of the cathedral of Troyes (1294 and subsequent years) distinguish between receipts *'de bustiis receptis die synodi'* (from the offertory boxes, received on the day of the synod)[1116] and those categorized by rural deanery *'recepta questarum Trecensis dyocesis solutis questoribus et eorum servientibus'* (receipts from the collections in the diocese of Troyes; the collectors and their servants have been paid).[1117] Contributions from the confraternity established in the 1490s were also administered separately, at least initially, and perhaps were a replacement for the *bustii*, as the contributions were delivered at the synod: *'de tous les confrères et conseurs de tous les villages de ce dyocèse apportez par les curez et recteurs tant du senne que par tout l'an* [...]'.[1118] Collections in the archdiocese were organized along similar lines. Proceeds from the originally leased quest for the year 1341/42 appear to have been handed over by each rural deanery in a sealed box during the Whitsun synod.[1119] In 1441/42 this *queste generalle* was supplemented with a new leased quest, described in the account as *'la queste generalle de la confrarie Mons. St. Estienne qui se recoit per tout le dyocese de, apellee la petite queste'*.[1120] This brotherhood seems to have been intended to boost income generated by the large quest, which had experienced a sharp decline particularly during the Hundred Years' War (1339-1453). In terms of financial value, the confraternity contributions only began to make a real difference in the period when the transept was built, after 1489.[1121] The bishopric of Amiens also had two collection campaigns, possibly stemming from a single episcopal mandate but cut from a different cloth. According to the account for 1358, there were receipts *'pro questa'* and *'de pixidibus episcopatu'*.[1122] It may be that this *'questa'* is identical with the processional circuit of episcopal parishes made with the reliquary shrine of Bishop St Honoré from 1240 onwards, also pictured in the portal dedicated to this saint (fig. 35).[1123]

COMPETITION FROM COLLECTION CAMPAIGNS FOR OTHER CHURCHES AND ECCLESIASTICAL INSTITUTIONS

In the preceding discussion we considered three factors that could have a positive or negative impact on the total yield of a diocesan collection campaign for the cathedral works, namely, the geographic extent of the campaign, its duration and the way in which receipts were collected. There is another, fourth, factor that could have both a negative and, paradoxically, positive influence on the cathedral works campaign: competition from collection campaigns for other churches and ecclesiastical institutions.

Mendicatoria often contain a clause relating to foreign pardoners, meaning those not delegated by the home cathedral. Such clauses stipulate that the cathedral collection campaign must at all times take precedence over any other collection whatsoever. This provision was intended not only to avoid ill-fated collisions between multiple fundraising efforts, but also, and especially, to ensure that no other church or agency got to the source of profits first. At any given time there might be countless other pardoners roaming criss-cross through the bishopric for myriad religious or charitable causes. The roots of those fundraising campaigns were older than those of the cathedral works campaign, and the documents on which they were based evinced a weightier authority. We have already seen that collectors delegated by the Hospitallers and Templars had been traversing the whole of Europe since the beginning of the twelfth century.

It was by no means a foregone conclusion that the cathedral collection should enjoy priority rights. This becomes clear from events following the huge fire that struck the episcopal city of Lausanne on 15 August 1235. Collectors from both the cathedral and from the collegiate church of Saint-Maire each set off into the bishopric bearing their images of Mary to assemble money for their respective rebuilding campaigns, resulting in a conflict that was not settled until November 1236, when the canons of Saint-Maire conceded and promised to never again appeal for funds without permission from the cathedral chapter. They furthermore had to relinquish one-quarter of their earnings to the cathedral.[1124] Starting in the second half of the thirteenth century, however, it was no longer possible for anyone to make rounds without having first obtained official consent from the bishop in the form of a letter of admission. Such changes paved the way to exceptionally lucrative financial opportunities. Naturally, the bishop could demonstrate his paternal benevolence by admitting foreign collections into the diocese without attaching conditions; we have just seen that he might agree to this when approached for collections from nearby cathedrals or parish and other churches in his bishopric,[1125] but there was never any obligation on him to do so. He could also expressly forbid a campaign from entering his bishopric.[1126] But beyond this, who was there to stop him from accepting commensurate payments for the right to carry out a collection? In some instances such collections were relatively local in scope, organized, with the bishop's permission, by a diocesan monastery or hospital or, less often, a parish,[1127] in aid of some charitable cause. At the other end of the spectrum were institutions that could claim papal privileges enabling them to appeal to the liberality of the faithful year in, year out, for centuries. Aside from the military orders, these included the Antonine Order – or confraternity of the Antonines – who had been involved in running hospitals for pilgrims since the end of the eleventh century and in the thirteenth set up a network of collections spanning all of Europe in order to cover the costs. The Antonines' base of operations was their head monastery in the Dauphiné or one of their many commandries.[1128] Their patron was St Anthony Abbot, protector against deadly ergotism (*ignis sacer*); in representations he is shown with his attributes of a bell (announcing the collection) and a pig, the meat of which was thought to be an effective remedy against the dreaded disease. Similarly, the thirteenth-century Santa Spirito – or hospital of the Holy Spirit – in Rome also collected throughout all of Christendom. Other institutions covered many dioceses. The abbey of St Hubert in the Ardennes operated in at least sixteen dioceses across France, Germany and the Low Countries.[1129] The Hotel Dieu in Paris despatched its pardoners to cover large expanses of France, as well as to the southern Netherlands.[1130] Finally, of the approximately 35 church, hospital and monastery collections admitted by the archbishop of Zaragoza between 1346 and 1387, four originated in France and one in Rome.[1131]

Since it was the bishop who granted foreign pardoners entry to his diocese, it followed that, in principle at least, the resulting admission revenues accrued to him.[1132] Occasionally, this formula persisted into the late Middle Ages. A fifteenth-century *pouillé* (list of benefices) from the bishop of Tournai inventories no fewer than 44 foreign quests that he had admitted and authorized, yielding him total profits of more than 375 l.par. a year.[1133] In most cases, however, the bishop ceded his income from admission fees, whether temporarily or permanently, mostly in conjunction with supervision over the entire quest organization, to the cathedral fabric and cathedral chapter.[1134] This approach, too, was grounded in a certain logic. When outside pardoners were admitted, this constituted a direct or indirect encroachment on the campaign for the cathedral, which after all held primacy and priority; diocesan collections were, quite simply, treated as a monopoly held by the cathedral fabric, and anyone wishing to infringe on that monopoly would have to pay for the privilege. Nevertheless, sources do show the bishop as the original rightful claimant, one who was at times reluctant to relinquish his right. Thus, when the archbishop of Cologne fixed the cathedral's yearly admission charge on the Antonines at 30 marks of silver in 1301, he noted that he himself had actual claim to the payment and furthermore reserved the right to change its designation if he chose.[1135] In 1321 the bishop of Liège surrendered his right to the admission monies in perpetuity in favour of the cathedral building works, '*dedimus et ad tempus assignavimus omnes obventiones et emolumenta questuum omnium infra limites nostre civitatis et diocesis provenientes et etiam proventuras* [...], *mandantes* [...] *questuariis* [...], *ut de universis dictorum questuum emolumentis et fructibus, de quibus nobis hactenus respondere consueverunt, provisoribus dicte fabrice* [...] *de cetero respondeant* [...]' (we have donated and transferred for all time all gains and revenues that were and shall be generated by all collection campaigns held within the borders of our city and our diocese, and in respect of these have instructed the collectors, who until now were accustomed to make settlement with us, to henceforth make settlement with those charged with conducting the affairs of the said fabric).[1136]

In many cases the cathedral chapter also assumed responsibility for establishing policy on the admission of foreign quests. We see this happen in the bishopric of Utrecht after the first quarter of the fourteenth century. In a sixteenth-century written vernacular overview of all the benefits accorded to the cathedral fabric over time, we read '*dat men geen aflaten ofte eenige andere gratien in den bisdom van Utrecht vercundichen en moet, sij en sullen eerst deursien ende toegelaten worden van de heeren Decken ende Capittel ten Dom voorscr.*'.[1137] While officially the bishop was still in charge of issuing these admittance letters, he was under obligation to confirm them at pre-agreed times. In the bishopric of Halberstadt a clause to this effect was even taken up in the *Wahlkapitulation* starting in 1390: '[...] *ok zo schullen we unde willen alle iar gheven to unser fabriken to wontliken tiden unse wontlike beseghelde breve over de negotia unses heren S. Stephani unde S. Anthonii in oren plechliken formen. Unde wat darvan vallen mach, unde alle andere gulde unde toval, dat de selve fabrika heft unde hebbende wert, willen to deme buwe des domes ghenstliken volghen laten ane hinder* [...]'.[1138] In 1314 the bishop of Münster promised his chapter that he would admit no more collections until a fitting share for the cathedral fabric was agreed.[1139] The cathedral statutes of Salisbury show the bishop announcing in 1319 that foreign pardoners could not make their rounds '*absque nostri capituli consensu expresso*' (without the express consent of our chapter).[1140]

We may therefore conclude that the majority of bishoprics put their admission policy in the hands of the cathedral fabric, or the masters of that fabric.[1141] Their task was anything but easy. Indeed, they were facing a difficult dilemma: on the one hand, the priority interests of the cathedral collection and their moral duty to oppose excesses demanded a restrictive approach to granting admission; on the other, a generous admission policy created the opportunity to levy fees on a large number of quests and so enrich the cathedral fabric. The trouble with the latter strategy, however, was that a foreign pardoner would not be willing to pay high fees if he knew himself to be only one of many trying their luck in the bishopric. It is owing to precisely such difficulties that we see ecclesiastical administrations in various dioceses taking both shifting and diverging stances on this issue. The bishop of Tournai, as mentioned above, accepted payments for 44 quests. We suspect that every church or institution that applied to the bishopric was in fact also admitted – for a fee, of course – such that the Tournai *pouillé* lists not only such famous cross-diocesan border collections as those for the hospital of Santo Spirito in Rome, the Order of St Lazarus in Jerusalem, the abbey of St Cornelis in Cornelimünster near Aachen and the brethren of the hospice of St Bernard,[1142] but also comparatively insignificant collections such as that for the Church of St Willibrord in Hulst and for the parish of Ligne. The cathedral fabric at Troyes had a similar open-door policy. According to the fabric rolls there were two foreign collection campaigns operating in the diocese in 1294/95, four in 1298/99, nine in 1373 and eleven in 1409/10,[1143] whilst later fifteenth-century rolls record no less than 39 simultaneous foreign quests.[1144]

The very nature of the enterprise made exercising effective control over the comings and goings of all the pardoners associated with these various collections all but impossible, as each of them had his own sub-pardoners and helpers. Restriction of the number of petitioners was essential, even if only for that reason. In 1412 the bishop of Strasbourg limited the number of admitted quests to seven – the cathedral's campaign amongst them – mainly for this very reason.[1145] The diocese of Pamplona allowed nine foreign quests to operate in the bishopric in 1487.[1146] The synod of Speyer admitted only five in 1410.[1147] Synodal statutes issued in the bishopric of Cambrai in 1260 recognized only their own quest and three others, those for the cathedral of Rheims, for St Nicaise in the same diocese and for the Antonines.[1148] Statutes from the Basel synod of 1400 revoked all former concessions and granted admission only to the cathedral's campaign and that of the Antonines.[1149] In Utrecht the cathedral chapter was fairly precise in sticking to the admission of seven alien quests; there can be no question that the fabric's financial interests were responsible for shaping admission strategy there, and with great success, as we shall see.[1150]

What options, then, did a cathedral chapter (or fabric) have when it came to structuring its financial relationship with, for example, an individual abbey whose quest had been admitted to the diocese? Usually the canons negotiated terms with the monastery's delegate. The monastery, like the cathedral fabric, could opt to keep the collection in hand or to appoint a pardoner and either give him a share of the profits or lease them to him. This 'alien' pardoner, in turn, had to agree to terms with the bishop and members of the cathedral chapter. The masters of the fabric might claim a portion of the collection proceeds as their admission fee, but this meant that the chapter would have to delegate one of its members to monitor the pardoner on every step of his journey. In the fourteenth-century archbishopric of Bremen it was customary for messengers of the quest for St Anthony to give one-third of their receipts to the cathedral fabric *structuarius* (master of the fabric); a chapter-appointed vicar accompanied them on their journey.[1151] Many Spanish dioceses applied a rule under which one-quarter of the proceeds from non-cathedral quests were surrendered to the cathedral building works.[1152] Around 1506 the archbishop of Bourges claimed half the receipts from the collection of the Hotel Dieu in Paris to put towards construction of the tower.[1153] A chapter could also charge a local priest with securing the fabric's share of a foreign quest, as was done in the bishopric of Nevers; however, this did not solve the problem of getting the money into the fabric treasury.[1154] A simpler and more practical solution was therefore to fix the admission fee at a certain annual sum for a term of, for instance, five or ten years, after which the two parties could make new arrangements.[1155] *Cuestores* in Pamplona could choose between ceding a quarter of the monies they had collected and paying a predetermined sum to the master of the fabric by way of a 'composition'.[1156] But there was yet another option. If the monastery, which was usually several days' journey from the cathedral, was unable to find a suitable delegate or if communication with him proved too taxing, it could opt to lease the quest to the cathedral fabric.[1157] Rather than pay an admission fee, it now received an annual rent from the masters of the cathedral fabric, whilst the fabric collected the full proceeds. In many cases, however, the fabric in turn farmed out this foreign quest to a professional pardoner for an agreed annual fee. It goes without saying that a cathedral fabric could shape its relations with various monasteries and institutions in different ways; we will see that this was also true in Utrecht.

The admission of collections from cloisters, churches and other institutions had a number of implications for the cathedral chapter. Most important was that the bishop and chapter effectively put the 'alien' quest on equal footing with their own diocesan campaign for the cathedral building works. As already indicated above, the entitlements enjoyed by a group like the Antonines were no different from those laid down in cathedral works *mendicatoria*, consisting of prescribed observance as a Sunday, the obligatory welcome of messengers, temporary suspension of any interdict, penalties for obstinacy, and so forth.[1158] Such foreign quests typically hailed from abbeys, cloisters and hospitals of wide renown, whose specific spiritual benefits and blessings were thus offered to the faithful. In the first place they offered, of course, the relics of their saints, whose power to effect miracles or heal any of a diverse range of ailments exercised an immense power of attraction; they also offered papal and episcopal indulgences and such spiritual benefits as are found in nearly every *mendicatorium*, including forgiveness for certain *casus reservati*, commutations and so on.[1159] Donors could furthermore gain membership in a confraternity organized in much the same way as a cathedral fabric confraternity, with participants sharing in the spiritual fruits of the good works and prayers of the founding religious community.[1160] Even collections run by less eminent institutions to support a collegiate church or even a humble parish church were established along the same lines. Thus, a village church such as that in Assche near Brussels could gain permission from the bishop of Cambrai to send out its '*procuratores et nuntii*' after a fire in 1490 (extended for another four years in 1495), who were to be welcomed once a year and the day of their arrival marked as a Sunday; only the cathedral collection enjoyed primacy before it.[1161]

We have come back full circle to our initial premise. Amongst the general factors that had a definitive impact on the overall profits garnered by a diocesan collection we must include the possible presence of campaigns for causes other than cathedral-building. Whilst these competing campaigns might have come at the expense of the cathedral collection, they did not necessarily detract from the cathedral fabric's overall income – quite the contrary. It is true that the bishop's right – later often transferred to the chapter – to determine admission tended to downgrade the cathedral works collection to just one of many authorized fundraisers, but at the same time his associated entitlement to levy a fee for admittance meant that the cathedral fabric could enjoy a share of the receipts of all collections admitted to the bishopric, even those which had nothing to do with the cathedral building works. This fact is of major socio-historical significance for our topic. The faithful who gave alms in these 'alien' collections did so not with the intention of aiding the cathedral works but, rather, to offer financial support to the poor, the blind, the sick or for some other cause or, perhaps more to the point, to obtain a monastery or hospital's special spiritual benefits and to experience for themselves the miraculous powers of the relics to which they gave access. And yet indirectly they were also contributing to the edifice of the cathedral.

Admission fees from 'alien' collections made up an integral part of the total receipts of the diocesan cathedral works collection, representing as they did an indemnity for infringement on the cathedral campaign's exclusive right. How, then, did receipts from the cathedral quest and the foreign quest compare? Cathedral fabrics did not always make conscious and targeted use of their ability to shape an admission policy to serve the financial interests of the cathedral fabric, and from what we can tell from the scant published data, the balance usually tipped in favour of the cathedral campaign. In the bishopric of Troyes, the number of foreign quests increased in the years between 1294/95 and 1409/10 from two to eleven, but the proceeds actually decreased from 43 l.t. to 27 l.t., and the admission rights never amounted to more than a quarter of the gains on the cathedral's own collection.[1162] Fabric rolls for 1294 from the bishopric of Autun show that the two outside quests held there yielded 16 l.vien., not even ten percent of the diocesan collection, which brought in 181 l.vien.[1163] Rolls from the cathedral fabric of Sens over the years 1295/96, 1319/20 and 1341/42 reveal similar percentages, with the admitted quests paying 27 l.t., 20 l.t. and 10 l.t., respectively, or seventeen, seven and two percent of the profits from its own campaign.[1164] In the bishopric of Pamplona, 1487 admission income represented a mere three percent of receipts from the cathedral's diocesan collection.[1165] These proportions were entirely different in the bishopric of Utrecht, where the seven admitted quests contributed a far greater share of the receipts than did the cathedral's own quest. The next chapter will explore the role that quest monies played in cathedral construction there.

Generally speaking, total receipts from all diocesan collections, including the admission fees, were considerable, and usually furnished the lion's share of a fabric's income. According to the Laon *Book of Miracles*, the two journeys made by its canons to France and to England in 1112 and 1113, respectively, yielded sufficient means to finance reconstruction of the damaged cathedral.[1166] In Cologne the archbishop cited the diocesan revenues as representing the largest contribution to the building fund in 1278, 30 years after the launch of the new cathedral's construction; though he lamented that money was still very short.[1167] Fabric rolls provide us with more solid data. For example, we know the value of receipts in the archbishopric of Sens over 84 years between 1295 and 1520, which reveal that the percentage share contributed by the totality of diocesan collections remained relatively constant, unaffected by changes in the intensity of building or maintenance works. In only 20 of these years did receipts fail to rise above 20 percent of the fabric's net income; in the years around 1430 for example, it was the war – preventing synodal meetings – that was responsible.[1168] In a further 40 years the receipts yielded between 30 and 60 percent, in twelve between 60 and 70 percent and in four even above 70 percent of the fabric's income.[1169] Gains *de collecturis ecclesiarum* (from collections in the churches) in the diocese of Regensburg furnished 37, 65, 70 and 76 percent of respective revenues in 1459, 1487, 1488 and 1489.[1170] Clermont-Ferrand drew 52 percent of its resources from the diocesan collections in 1334/35.[1171] In the bishopric of Wells the *legata et collecta fraternitatis S. Andree* (gifts and collections of the confraternity of St Andrew) supplied 73 percent of the fabric's income in 1390/91, later fluctuating between 54 and 38 percent in the years from 1457 until 1505 (only five extant account rolls).[1172] Proceeds from the 882 parishes of the archbishopric of Lyon generated between 13 and 40 percent of the fabric's income between 1416 and 1499. Other cathedrals saw even greater variability in the value of their diocesan fundraising campaigns.[1173] The cathedral fabric of Troyes drew around 80 percent of its income from its own and foreign quests in the period between 1294 and 1301, but in the first decade of the fifteenth century we find this figure has dropped to 27 percent.[1174] A similar decline is evident at Rodez, where the quest conducted in the diocese, city and *burgus* furnished 29 percent of the revenues in 1293/94, but only 11 and 8 percent in 1507/08 and 1509/10, respectively.[1175] Proportionately much smaller receipts are recorded for the bishoprics of Amiens (1357/58),[1176] Gerona (10 to 11 percent between 1367 and 1377, with over a third collected by the cathedral itself)[1177] and in Strasbourg (in 1382 and 1419 a mere 8 percent).[1178]

By expressing these profit figures in the annual wages of skilled or unskilled building labourers, we can calculate real quantities that justify mutual comparison.[1179] Well-organized collection campaigns in the archbishopric of Rouen and its surrounding dioceses generated high and relatively stable revenues, especially in the sixteenth century, where the thousands of printed *brevetz des pardons* sent out to parish priests each year clearly achieved the intended effect (fig. 52). Receipts actually peaked in the years between 1531 and 1542, after the real period of building, averaging around 1100 l.t. and equal to 28 annual wages of a labourer. A hundred years earlier, in 1432, that amount had been no more than 162 l.t., or five years' wages of an *homme de bras*.[1180] In Regensburg, yields in 1459 and 1487-1489 came to respective equivalents of 22, 34, 28 and 29 annual wages of an unskilled labourer, and it was thanks to this diocesan income that building operations could continue at a fairly reasonable level. Diocesan revenues elsewhere were much lower.[1181] The *collectura per diocesim* in Freiberg yielded an amount equalling around three annual wages in the years from 1447 to 1452, and not much more in later decades; alms offered in the cathedral proved more profitable.[1182] Six extant account rolls dating to between 1390 and 1505 from the cathedral fabric at Wells report amounts totalling between 17 and 6 years' pay of an unskilled labourer.[1183] In Basel, returns from the *unser Frowen Bitte*, held four times a year on six successive Sundays and all feast days in between in every parish of the bishopric furnished little more than alms collected in the cathedral itself, with 129 lb. in 1436 and 156 lb., 157 lb. and 158 lb. in 1467, 1470 and 1476, respectively – incidentally a period that saw no construction of any consequence; all small sums when we consider that at the end of the fifteenth century the annual salary of an unskilled assistant was approximately 30 lb.[1184] Fabric rolls from the latter half of the fourteenth and beginning of the fifteenth centuries from the cathedrals of Troyes,[1185] Gerona[1186] and Amiens[1187] record diocesan collection receipts ranging from almost four to just over two years' wages of an unskilled workman.

These last figures once again serve to underscore the conclusion reached earlier, namely, that diocesan collections carried on regardless of whether an important building campaign was underway, and likewise independent of the value of the profits. The intricate diocesan organization was simply never dismantled. Once in place, that organization could easily be activated whenever the need arose. Sens Cathedral is one example, where the chapter re-established its campaign in order to build the transept; in the space of a single year revenues from diocesan monies climbed from 73 l.t. in 1488/89 to 473 l.t. in 1489/90 - a sufficient sum to pay fifteen hodsmen for a year.[1188]

Diocesan contributions collected for the construction of the cathedral of Utrecht have largely been left out of the preceding discussion. Whilst they were of the same nature as those described here, the yield was actually far higher than at other cathedrals. A key difference distinguishing the diocese of Utrecht from most other bishoprics is the ratio between its relatively high receipts from admission fees and relatively low income from the cathedral collection campaign.

The next chapter is dedicated to the financing of the Utrecht Dom, where an exceptional wealth of archival documentation justifies its use as a case study. Most, if not all, of the sources of income discussed in this section shall return again in the next. Now, however, their constellation will be specific to the makeup and size of the revenues of the cathedral fabric at Utrecht, which were definitive for the comparatively fast pace of construction of its cathedral church. To conclude our survey, Chapter four will briefly explore fabric financing at a number of other cathedrals, thus setting the situation in Utrecht in its broader perspective.

PART TWO THE FINANCING OF CATHEDRAL-BUILDING IN THE MIDDLE AGES

CHAPTER THREE

THE FINANCING OF THE BUILDING WORKS AT UTRECHT CATHEDRAL: A CASE STUDY

INTRODUCTION

Part I of this book explored how cathedral fabrics were administered. We saw that cathedral chapters in nearly every episcopal city, with the exception of those in Italy, appropriated control over the cathedral church and cathedral fabric. Bishops did in general retain some measure of influence and authority, but usually no more than what was required under canon law. We then turned to consider the sources of income that cathedral fabrics used to finance cathedral construction and furnishings. If, however, we mean to gain insight into cathedral fabric financing systems, a mere description of their income, informed by a diverse range of historical sources, will not in itself be enough. What is important, after all, is how various income sources were combined and, of course, the relative financial value of each one. Equally, we must look at financial transactions that were not actual sources of income, such as the acquisition of capital through loans and issue of hereditary and life annuities, or the liquidation of assets, even down to items from the church treasury. Such transactions could have a definitive impact on how large a pool of funds was available and thus on the plans made for building.

The only way to gain insight into these financing activities is on the basis of the account rolls kept by the cathedral fabric or other body charged with the building works. Sources of this type are hardly

56
Archive cabinet of the chapter of Utrecht Cathedral, first half of the sixteenth century
Oak, 221 x 354 x 96 cm
Amsterdam, Rijksmuseum Amsterdam, inv. BK NM 125

This cabinet was used to store archival records belonging to the cathedral chapter. Forty of the original drawers are preserved; which documents they held is unknown.

LITERATURE
Th.H. Lunsingh Scheurleer, *Catalogus van meubelen en betimmeringen*, Amsterdam (Rijksmuseum Amsterdam) 1952 (3rd edition), no. 89.

scarce. Financial records have been preserved at over 80 cathedrals, the oldest dating from the second half of the thirteenth century, the majority from the fifteenth century and later.[1] French and Spanish cathedrals offer a particularly rich source of financial documentation, whereas in other areas such as Scandinavia, Eastern Europe and the Balkans, nothing has been preserved at all. However accounts are by definition a serial source, and it is only from a complete, or nearly complete, sequence of records spanning an extended period that we can gain any real insight. For the purposes of this survey, such records must furthermore cover a period in which cathedral-building and furnishing were major concerns. Frequently, this is not the case. The impressive cycles preserved at Cambrai and Liège, for example, however valuable in other ways, shed barely any light on how building works were financed. In both cities, moreover, the cathedrals fell victim to the devastation of the French Revolution. Finally, the colourful, sometimes cryptic phrasings and indeed varying systems for classifying and entering receipts and expenditures demand additional, supplementary, historical sources to explain them. And these we find in only a handful of cathedral archives.

The long and comprehensive set of account rolls from the fabric of Utrecht Cathedral, covering a key period in its building history, furnishes an unparalleled example of how one cathedral chapter went about gleaning the monetary resources it needed for building a great cathedral. The Utrecht rolls begin in 1395/96, continuing with some lacunae until the year 1460 and without any gaps thereafter.[2] The value of the rolls is enhanced by further archival documentation relating to the cathedral, such as the chapter resolutions, extant from 1402 on, which provide additional details about certain income sources.[3] We are particularly lucky in that a large number of sources that define the fabric's rights and obligations, lay down rules and establish agreements have also been preserved. In the cathedral's various statute books we can discover which obligations the chapter shouldered to support the cathedral fabric,[4] whilst the fabric's cartulary in turn contains copies of the most important episcopal *mendicatoria*, papal privileges, writs of indulgence, judicial rulings and such like, which outline the powers, rights and duties of the fabric.[5] Similar provisions

were also set down in countless individual charters and documents (fig. 56).[6] In the fabric rolls we see how all these rules and measures were translated into real income.

The availability of so great a quantity and so varied a range of documentation presents an opportunity to investigate not only specific income sources engaged by the fabric, but also its financing in the broader sense, extending to financing transactions. Where the fabric's expenditures are concerned, we can distinguish between outlays for building, upkeep and furnishings and overhead costs on the one hand, and those that were strictly for the chapter on the other, and thus had no bearing on the fabric. In the sections that follow, we will therefore keep an eye to the full spectrum of financial activities described in the account rolls.

Here we find ourselves in the particularly fortunate circumstance that we also have the building accounts – together with other documentation pertaining to the church fabric, administered by lay churchwardens – of Utrecht's oldest parish church. This is the so-called Buurkerk, situated a stone's throw from the Dom, which underwent several large-scale renovations from 1430 onwards. With these two sets of records at our disposal, we can compare financing for cathedral-building with financing for a parish church.

THE CATHEDRAL CHURCH

With Willibrord consecrated as a bishop by the pope in 695, Utrecht became an outpost of Christianity in the region, operating under the auspices of the Frankish rulers, but at the same time in close contact with Rome (fig. 57). As a diocese, Utrecht had no precise borders as yet, and it would not be until the reign of Charlemagne that Utrecht took its position as a suffragan bishopric within the Church province of Cologne, together with the dioceses of Münster, Osnabrück, Minden and Liège (fig. 58).[7] The resulting diocese encompassed a fairly large territory, with boundaries shaped over the course of the Middle Ages that it retained until the new episcopal division of the Netherlands in 1559. Over time, Utrecht saw a considerable number of parishes established within its episcopal borders, numbering some 1200 just before 1559.[8]

The broad outlines of the earliest history of the cathedral, or rather the cathedral complex, have been well documented.[9] It lay within the Merovingian citadel, the boundaries of which more or less coincided with those of the *castellum*, or Roman fortifications, measuring a very modest 160 by 25 metres. The oldest church had been built before Willibrord's time and was probably dedicated to St Martin. A second

57
St Willibrord (658-739), the first bishop of Utrecht and traditionally regarded as founder of the Dom
Oak, h. 87 cm
Early sixteenth century, hands and model of the Dom tower may date to the seventeenth century; the crosier is missing, the polychrome has been restored
Beesd, Roman Catholic parish of H. Kruisverheffing

LITERATURE Exh. cat. *Monniken en monialen in de Nederlanden*, Ghent (St.-Pietersabdij) 1980-1981, no. 131.

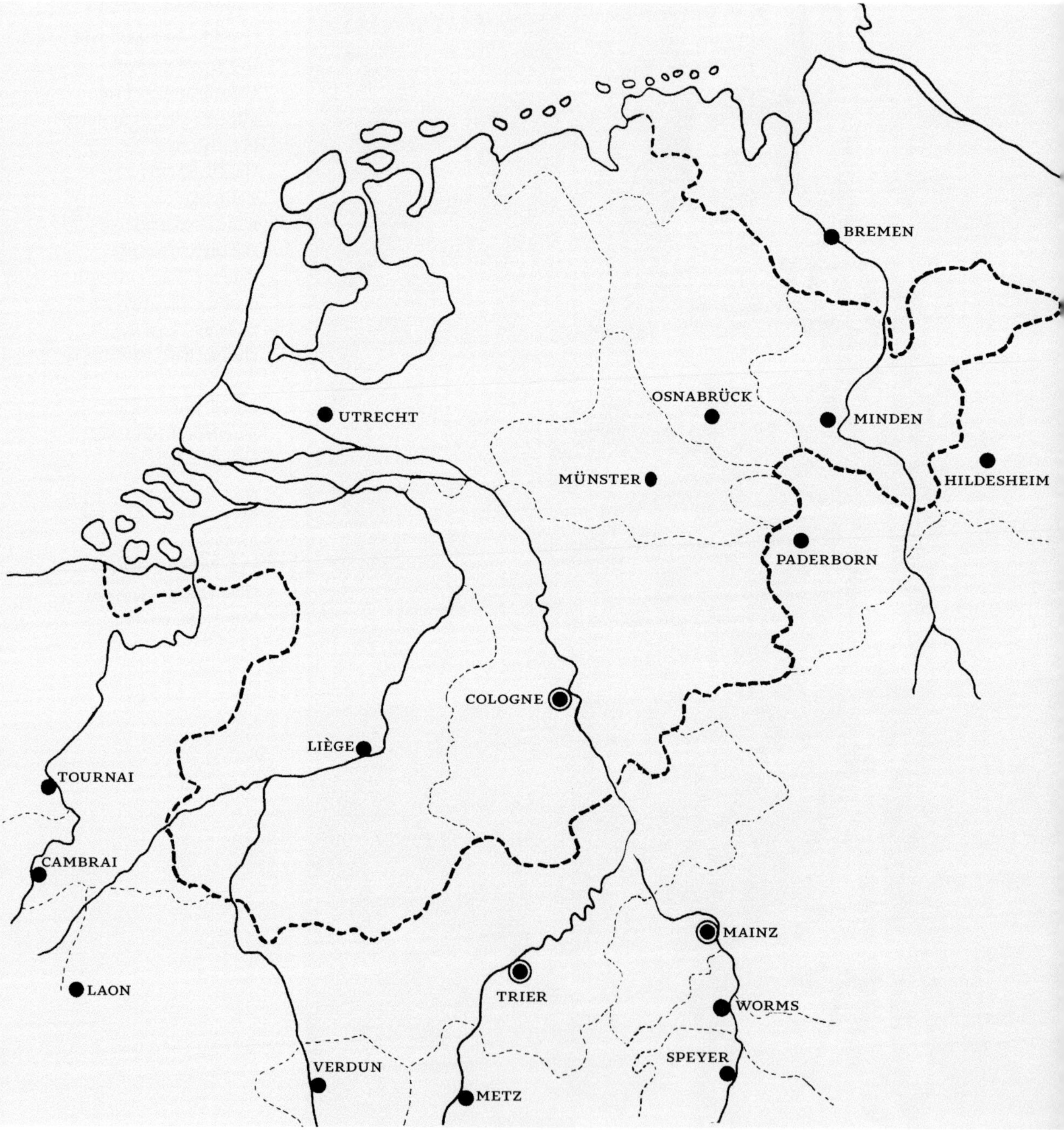
BREMEN
OSNABRÜCK
UTRECHT
MINDEN
MÜNSTER
HILDESHEIM
PADERBORN
COLOGNE
LIÈGE
TOURNAI
CAMBRAI
MAINZ
TRIER
LAON
WORMS
SPEYER
VERDUN
METZ

church, commissioned by Willibrord and dedicated by him to St Salvator, was the original cathedral, but as early as the mid-eighth century it surrendered this privileged status to the church of St Martin, which would remain the episcopal seat from that point on. Nevertheless, the church of St Salvator, characteristically also known as the Oldminster (*Oudmunster*), retained some of the privileges typically accorded a cathedral, such as the right to serve as the last resting place of the bishops. Utrecht was thus home to a cathedral complex with two churches, but was served by a single body of clerics, or *familia*, bound to the bishop. Bishop Balderic (918-975), who was the first to re-establish the see in Utrecht after the devastating Viking invasions, honoured tradition by rebuilding both buildings. Within this small enclosure the two churches stood cheek by jowl, separated only by the Chapel of the Holy Cross, which was founded perhaps sometime in the tenth century and fell under the charge of St Salvator's.[10] When fire destroyed the cathedral church of St Martin in 1017, it was restored in full glory and reconsecrated by Bishop Adelbold (1010-1026) in the company of the emperor and twelve fellow bishops.

The city of Utrecht would have to wait until the eleventh century, however, to earn its full-fledged imperial episcopal status, which came with the construction of three collegiate churches dedicated to Sts Peter, John the Baptist and Mary, respectively, under the auspices of the emperor; these churches, in conjunction with the abbey of St Paul, which had been transferred to Utrecht, traced a cross of churches around the cathedral complex (fig. 60). Eighty canons were joined under the three new collegiate churches, whilst the cathedral itself and the Oldminster had a total of 40 and 20 canons' prebends, respectively.[11] The city of Utrecht thus numbered 140 canonries in total.

Each of the five collegiate churches (the cathedral, Oldminster, St Peter's, St John's and St Mary's) and the abbey of St Paul occupied a zone in which they exercised independent ecclesiastical rights, topographically set apart from the city by canals, houses and walls (fig. 59).[12] The immunities of the cathedral and Oldminster were woven together within the narrow confines of the small Merovingian citadel.[13] As time progressed, these two churches and the Chapel of the Holy Cross would come to share this space with episcopal buildings, the old im-

58
Map of the Church province of Cologne and the surrounding dioceses before 1559

Literature
Exh. cat. *Rhein und Maas, Kunst und Kultur 800-1400*, Cologne 1972, t.o. p. 16.

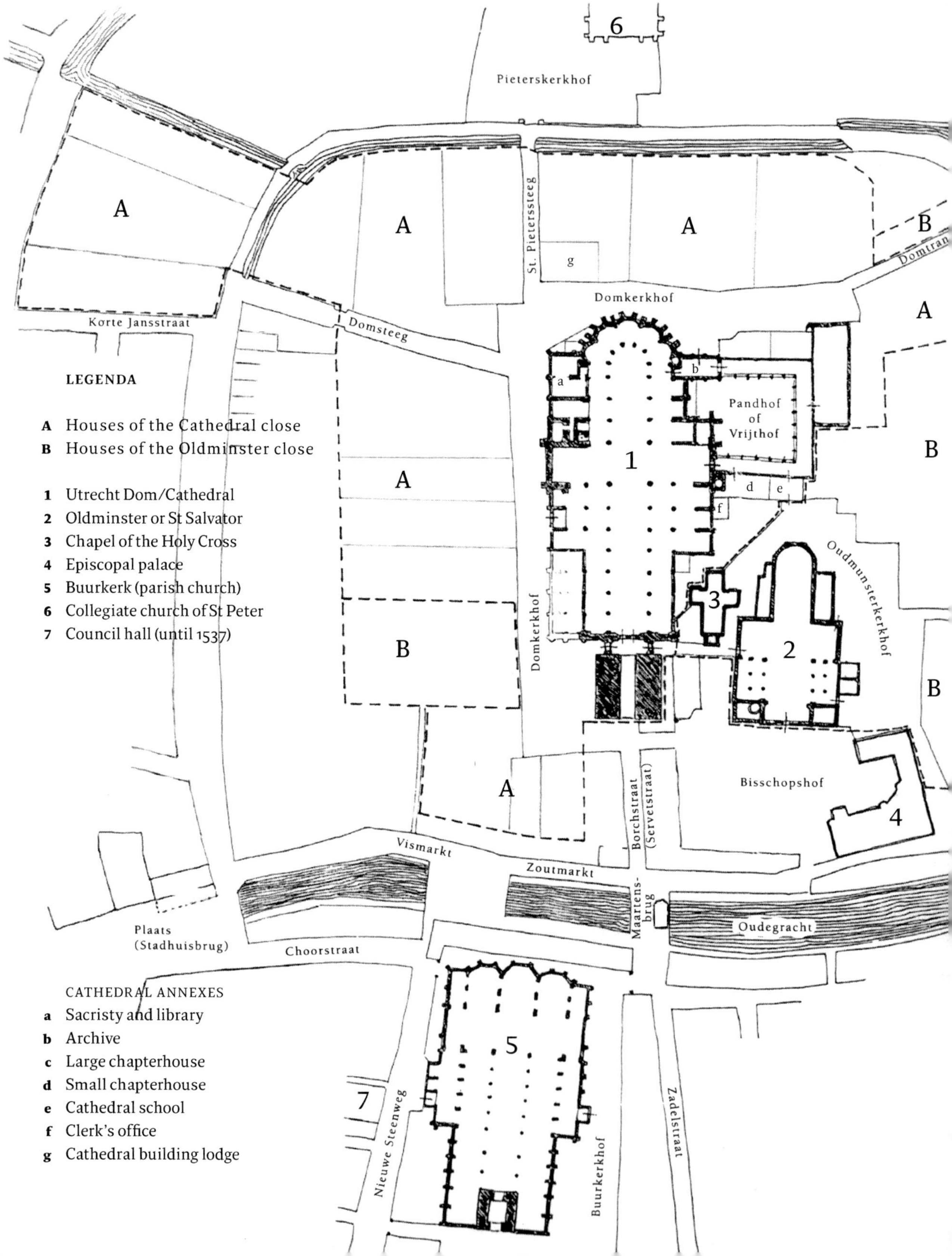

LEGENDA
A Houses of the Cathedral close
B Houses of the Oldminster close
1 Utrecht Dom/Cathedral
2 Oldminster or St Salvator
3 Chapel of the Holy Cross
4 Episcopal palace
5 Buurkerk (parish church)
6 Collegiate church of St Peter
7 Council hall (until 1537)
CATHEDRAL ANNEXES
a Sacristy and library
b Archive
c Large chapterhouse
d Small chapterhouse
e Cathedral school
f Clerk's office
g Cathedral building lodge
Pieterskerkhof
St. Pieterssteeg
Domkerkhof
Domtran
Korte Jansstraat
Domsteeg
Pandhof of Vrijthof
Oudmunsterkerkhof
Domkerkhof
Bisschopshof
Borchstraat (Servetstraat)
Vismarkt
Zoutmarkt
Maartensbrug
Oudegracht
Plaats (Stadhuisbrug)
Choorstraat
Nieuwe Steenweg
Buurkerkhof
Zadelstraat

perial palace and countless annexes such as the cloister, churchyard, the large and small chapterhouses, the cathedral school, choir house, sacristy and church library, as well as the claustral residences built for the canons, numbering some fifteen under the cathedral and ten under the Oldminster, which stood in an arch around the two churches (fig. 59, 60).[14] There is no question that the presence of the Oldminster (demolished in 1587) and Chapel of the Holy Cross (demolished in 1826) severely limited how far the Gothic cathedral could be extended in either length or breadth.

59
The precinctal immunity of Utrecht Cathedral and its immediate surroundings, mid sixteenth century

LITERATURE
De Groot 2006, pp. 344-345.

When fire swept through the city on 29 April 1253 - the largest ever to afflict Utrecht[15] - the cathedral must have been damaged as well, and it was probably not long thereafter that Bishop Henry I van Vianden (1249-1267) laid the first stone of the new Gothic church that we still see today.[16] The issue of a papal indulgence in 1265 and an episcopal indulgence in 1267 indicate the continuance of building works. But probably the works did not gain full steam until Bishop-elect John I (1268-1290), the new cathedral's *fundator*, published a *mendicatorium*

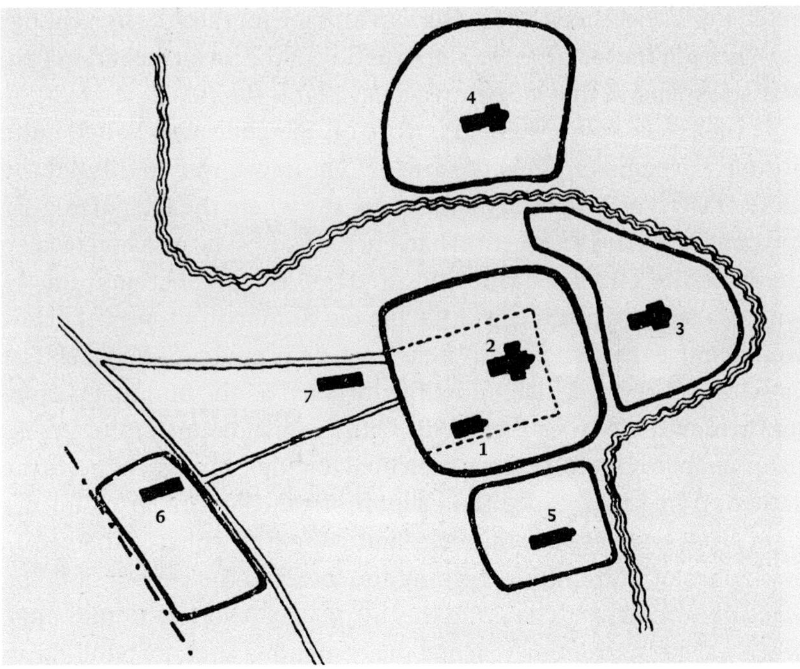

60
Schematic map of the cross of churches in Utrecht

1 Collegiate church of St Salvator
2 Utrecht Dom/Cathedral
3 Collegiate church of St Peter
4 Collegiate church of St John the Baptist
5 Abbey of St Paul
6 Collegiate church of St Mary
7 Buurkerk (parish church)

LITERATURE
Utrecht kruispunt van de middeleeuwse kerk, Utrecht 1988, p. 40.

61
The Utrecht Dom within the boundaries of the Roman *castellum*

Axonometric perspective reconstruction. The positions of the chapel of the Holy Cross, east end of St Salvator and perimeter of the Roman *castellum* are indicated by the dotted line.

LITERATURE
Haslinghuis & Peeters 1965, fig. 22.

on 8 September 1288, thereby securing sources of income on which the building works would continue to draw for centuries.[17]

The choir as we see it today bears distinct traces of a change in plans during mid-construction. An ambulatory with radiating chapels was erected before the end of the thirteenth century,[18] and shortly after 1300 three bays in the southern transept were built with abutting burial chapels for the bishops Guy van Avesnes (1301-1317) and John of Arkel (1342-1364). In the south transept, the eastern wall was raised to half height.

In Utrecht one might have expected a plan emulating the cathedral of Cologne, built with an extended four-bay choir, paired with a transept with two side aisles. Indeed, a plan of this type probably was intended, but ultimately discarded; Utrecht's extended choir numbers only three bays (as a result of which St Luke, fourth of the evangelists, has been missed out in the set of keystones in the lantern over the choir) and the aisled transept was never realized. The costly compound piers were likewise scrapped, though replaced on the north side of the choir with roughly-hewn shafts. The building also makes extensive use of cheap brick. The explanation for these design changes may lie in the fact that the construction of the tower, begun in 1321, was so expensive that it devoured all available funds.

For reasons unknown to us, work on the choir was halted quite abruptly to begin building the tower.[19] The new tower, to this day the glory of Utrecht, was built on the same site where the dilapidated old tower of St Martin's Cathedral had once stood.[20] The decision to keep the structure's traditional position and traditional functions brought with it a series of problems. Like the old St Martin's tower, the new would house the bishop's private chapel, dedicated to St Michael. The cathedral chapter, which undoubtedly acted as the building patron, had to make certain arrangements with the bishop concerning access to his chapel, both from the bishop's palace and from the chapel to the cathedral building. Since the chapter of the Oldminster claimed a right of passage between the tower and cathedral, which connected its two zones of immunity, attaching the tower to the church building was not an option.[21] The issue was ultimately resolved around 1490, when nave construction reached the contended spot, by building an

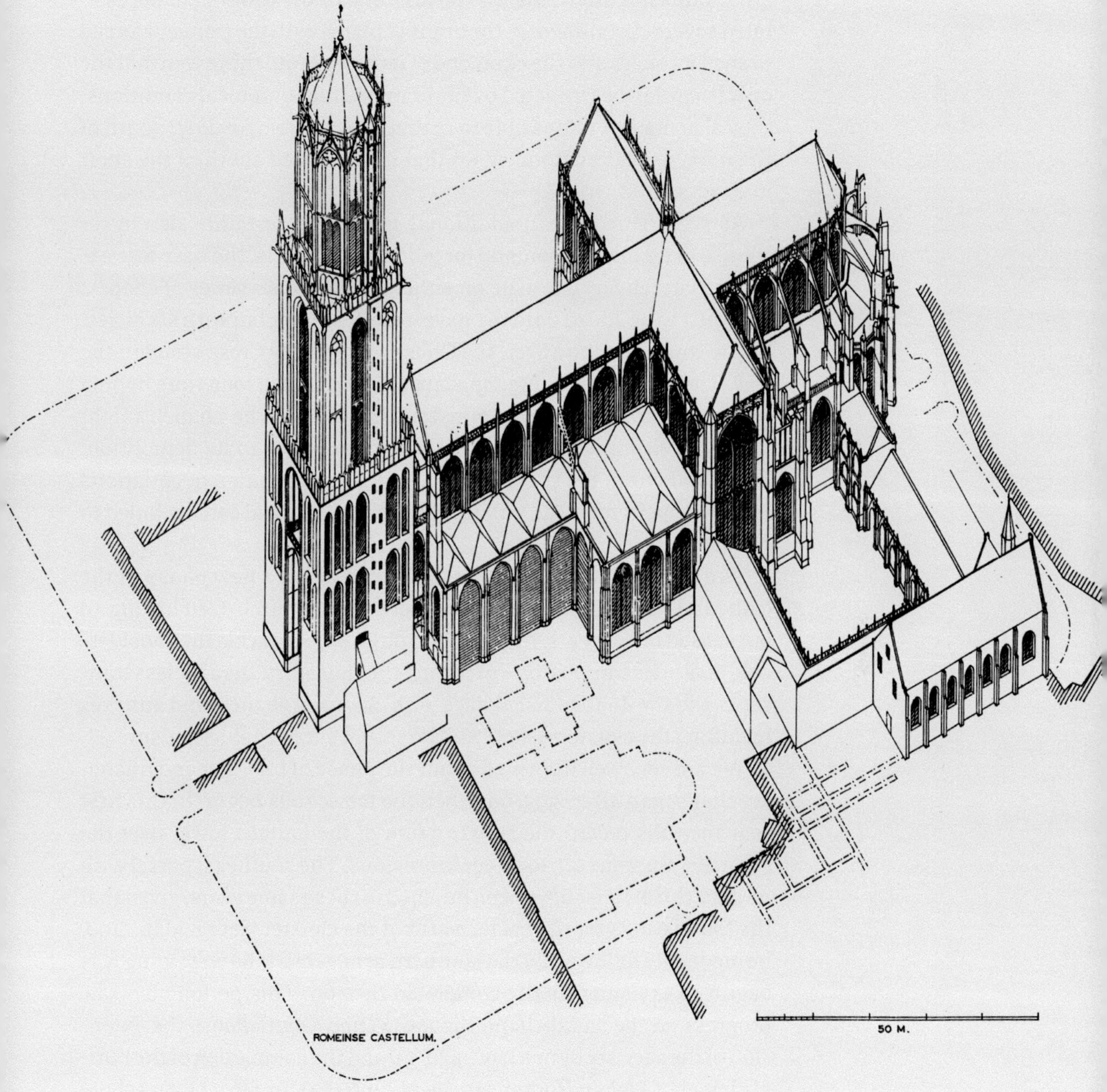
ROMEINSE CASTELLUM.
50 M.

high-level bridge – the so-called bishop's loge – connecting tower and nave. But aside from this, the positioning of the tower also necessitated severe curtailment of the original plans, with the transept forced to shed its aisles and the choir one of its bays.[22] And these were not the only irregularities inflicted by the cramped topographical conditions; they also made it impossible to realize the cloister (*pandhof*) south of the nave, as was customary, so that it was raised south of the choir instead.

As a measure to gain additional space, and certainly also in response to increasing demand for individual chapels, the nave was extended laterally by one aisle on either side. Another series of chapels was then to be added onto the nave, resulting in a plan with six aisles. At the south end, however, the Chapel of the Holy Cross stood in the way. The cathedral chapter appears to have spent a long time hoping that the canons of the Oldminster, who owned the chapel, might change their minds at the crucial hour and agree to its demolition. Fabric rolls from the years 1484, 1487 and 1491 mention negotiations on the chapel's removal, but ultimately the cathedral canons failed to get their way.[23]

The completion of the tower in 1382 heralded a new phase in the cathedral's building history. With work on the church itself having all but ceased for 60 years, the time had now come to tackle the considerable task of its completion – of raising the clerestory, the aisleless transepts and the double-aisled nave with chains of chapels and annexes including the cloister, school and large and small chapterhouses.

We are very well informed about the phase of building and financing that began after 1395/96, when the fabric rolls begin. In this first year the rolls record the construction of the lantern tower over the choir, begun some ten to 20 years previous. The southeast portal with its stair turret must have been finished in these same years, given that the foundations for the eastern arm of the cloister were laid in 1400, immediately followed by the southern arm, whilst the west wing was begun in 1436 and finally completed in 1460. This period also saw progress on the small chapterhouse (*Kleine Kapittelhuis*), the extension of the sacristy by one bay (1450/51) and the completion of the burial chapel of Bishop Rudolf van Diepholt (1464). In 1461 a new school was erected abutting the western arm of the cloister, alongside the small chapterhouse.

Lacunae in the cycle of accounts make it impossible to say precisely when work on the transepts began; it may be that the north and south arms were both raised to the level of the triforium first (around 1450?), after which the north arm was completed, followed by the south. The transepts were virtually finished by 1479, but the vaults, for which springers had been laid, were never actually raised. The glazing was not installed until the following decade, with Bishop David donating the immense north window in 1485.[24]

Meanwhile, the final phase of construction – the erection of the nave, now almost entirely lost – had also begun: 1471 saw demolition works begin on the last remaining sections of the Romanesque church of Balderic and Adelbold's time, as well as the laying of the foundation for the new nave. Entries pertaining to the demolition, which also include receipts for old building material that was sold off, continue until 1485/86. In 1484 they record the laying of the first stone *ante turrim* (in front of the tower), therefore on the west end, and in the following year the embedding of eight piers for four bays. Two years later, temporary cladding was laid across seven bays of the lateral aisles. In 1489/90 workers were laying bricks for the two spiral stairways in the westwork. It is in these years, too, that the bishop's loge must have been built.

Building progressed at a rapid pace.[25] Between 1485 and 1504 work focused on the outermost south lateral aisle and three adjoining chapels, dedicated to the canons Montfoort, Van den Veen and Zoudenbalch, respectively; the corresponding north section was built between 1505 and 1515. Each of these chapels and aisle bays were covered with stellar or net vaults. Once the side aisles had been covered with permanent cladding in 1499, work also progressed on the nave clerestory. Preparations began in 1512 for raising stone vaults, but never came to fruition. Instead, a timber ceiling was constructed between 1512 and 1515 as a substitute for the vault (fig. 64). Last came the installation of the large west window in 1517. Though foundations were laid and some slight progress made on the four northern chapels, they were never finished. Plans for the auxiliary buildings also underwent revisions during the concluding phase of building.[26] In 1495 the sacristy was enlarged with an additional bay, intended to serve as the library, with a further bay put up between 1496 and 1498. As regards the two chapterhouses, one large and one small (the latter positioned along the western arm of the cloister), the building records are not clear on all points. The small chapterhouse, with above it the *schrijfkamer* or 'clerk's office', was probably erected between 1462 and 1464. It was here that the daily meetings were held. The large chapterhouse, which hosted the general chapter meetings as well as those of the States of Utrecht, may date to around 1400, with vaults that were raised higher and repainted between 1495 and 1497.[27]

After 1517, activities focused on refurbishing and embellishing the cathedral. The tower octagon was in urgent need of repairs in 1516, and from 1520 attention turned to mitigating the contrast between its sober fourteenth-century aesthetic and the late Gothic forms of the recently completed nave[28] with the addition of decorative elements such as a costly openwork balustrade along the first stage. Building activities saw a drastic decline after 1524. Purchases of stone ceased in 1527. In fact, the cathedral was never actually entirely completed to plan; the outermost side aisles to the north and south remained unfinished, the vaults above the transept and nave were never raised, and plans for a system of abutments likewise came to naught (fig. 63). We might even speculate that the barely finished building presented an all too easy prey for the tornado that obliterated virtually the whole of the nave in 1674.

THE CATHEDRAL FABRIC AND IT'S SOURCES OF INCOME

The construction of the Gothic cathedral church was financed by the *fabrica ecclesie Trajectensis*, sometimes also known as the *nova fabri-*

ca.[29] The epithet *nova* signals the fact that when new building works began after 1253, new and separately managed sources of income were also called into being. It is possible that this initiative traces back to the first *mendicatorium* of 8 September 1288 which Bishop-elect John I of Nassau circulated amongst all the clergy of his diocese. Implicit in the appellation of a *nova fabrica* is the prior existence of an 'old' fabric fund. This we find in the *prebenda defunctorum* fund, in which the proceeds of the canons' prebends accrued over one or more years following the death of the previous occupant.

The cathedral chapter's oldest known statute concerning these prebends of the deceased dates to 1247, several years before new building works commenced, and makes it clear that it is reinstating an old custom that had fallen into disuse.[30] Similar charters have been preserved from Utrecht's other collegiate churches, but bear slightly earlier dates: St Mary's of 1202, St John's of 1231 and St Salvator's of between 1223 and 1257.[31] The last of these relates that the measure was being introduced in emulation of the metropolitan cathedral of Cologne and fellow collegiate churches in Utrecht on the grounds that the fabric had until then had no income of its own. Thus, it was the example set by Cologne that inspired the thirteenth-century chapters of Utrecht to establish separate administrative 'chambers' with their own revenue sources to defray the costs of the churches' maintenance, furnishings and religious services, and not any need for new building projects. The old *prebenda defunctorum* fund, with its earliest extant rolls running from 1 October 1402 until 1 October 1403, drew out its independent existence until 1463/64, after which, barring a brief interlude from 1487 until 1492, the chapter drew its administration into that of the new fabric.[32]

Yet even before 1463, the administration of the two fabric funds was already closely linked. Up until then the chapter had after all appointed one of its own members to serve as *collector* and manage the *prebenda defunctorum* fund; it also appointed a *procurator* or *magister (nove) fabrice* (master of the fabric) to take charge of affairs in the new fabric.[33] The *magister (nove) fabrice* administered the new fabric until 1 March, thereafter switching to the post of *collector* of the *prebenda defunctorum* fund until 1 October. This arrangement allowed him to use the overlapping months to acquaint his successor with the relevant tasks.[34] Though the master of the fabric was only appointed for a single year, he might in fact fulfil the *officium* for multiple, sometimes successive, years, and in some cases for as many as seven or eight years (fig. 62). The authorities of the office were limited. Hugo Wstinc's *Rechtsboek van de dom* (c. 1345) allows the *procuratores* a measure of freedom: on the one hand they needed the chapter's permission to begin new building works or demolish old structures and to appoint or fire architects; but on the other they were free to decide whether or not to admit foreign pardoners, contract debts and hire and fire workers, amongst other things.[35] A chapter ordinance of 1415 appears to have abridged these authorities. To begin with, the incumbent master of the fabric was now to work in much closer coordination with his *socius*, an office identical to the *prebenda-collector*; both officers now held a key to the strongbox, for example. The ordinance also placed a more definitive limit on expenditures for building materials, with anything above the nominal sum of 4 oude schilden requiring special permission from the chapter.[36] It is possible that an incident like that involving a canon named Johannes Wite had made the chapter cautious. According to a complaint that Wite – who had served as master of the fabric during the tower's construction – submitted to the pope in 1359, the fabric still owed him a large sum of money from that period, which the bishop and chapter refused to pay on grounds of mismanagement. The 1415 ordinance seems to have prevented any further conflicts on this scale.[37]

The master of the fabric was obliged to render account to the bishop and chapter. He did this before the assembled canons, one of whom might be appointed as the bishop's representative, and in the presence of the messenger, the notary and the building lodge assistant, each of whom received a remuneration.[38] From 1505/06 onwards, two prebendary canons, the *domini examinatores*, performed an initial audit of the account rolls, which was followed by formal approval in the chapter meeting a year or more later.[39]

Though the chapter kept control over the cathedral church and fabric firmly in hand, the bishop did retain certain rights.[40] A papal mandate of 1359 ordering renewed investigation into the Johannes Wite affair explicitly states that the fabric is to render account in the presence of the bishop, dean and chapter;[41] if we consult the rolls themselves, however, it turns out that the bishop's presence signified little beyond the right to an allowance for showing up.[42] The bishop also had the – possibly traditional – right, shared jointly with the chapter, to appoint the master of the fabric, though there is no actual evidence of this in practice until the incumbency of Bishop David of Burgundy (1456-1496).[43] It is likely that the bishop and chapter had an arrangement to each appoint a canon as *magister fabrice* for a two-year term, whereby the joint appointees took turns managing the accounts as de facto master of the fabric for one year and supervising their colleague in the position of *socius* in the second.[44]

From time to time the bishop might also play an informal role in cathedral building operations. For example, it was at the bishop's explicit request that the collector for the papal indulgence for the anti-Hussite Crusade released a small sum to the fabric in 1472.[45] In 1487 the chapter consulted Bishop David on the cathedral's construction – presumably owing to difficulties connected with the Chapel of the Holy Cross[46] – and Bishop Frederick of Baden wrote a letter to the chapter recommending the sculptor Gerrit Splintersz. – *unses kokenschrijvers dochter man* – when the death of Cornelis de Wael created an opening for a new architect, though to no effect, as it turned out.[47] Bishop Philip of Burgundy was more successful in his suit, managing to gain the chapter's approval for his choice of painter – Jan Gossaert – in 1518, and thus also helping to introduce Renaissance style into the Northern Netherlands.[48]

While the cathedral fabric in Utrecht had its own distinct administration – like everywhere else – there was at the same time such a complicated web of financial and administrative links between the fabric and the chambers responsible for managing chapter property that it will aid our understanding to first provide a brief overview of the system by which the chapter's property and income were managed.

The endowment of the chapter of St Martin's Cathedral, separated from that of St Salvator perhaps as early as the mid-eleventh century,[49] was subject to a gradual process typical of nearly every collegiate church: the division of the principal and apportionment of the fruits amongst individual prebends – a circumstance that can be attributed to the decline in communal living as prescribed by the Council of Aachen in favour of an independent lifestyle. Ever since the first quarter of the eleventh century, it had been the provost's responsibility to administer this endowment in its entirety and to use the proceeds to issue payments in kind to the canons. A century later, in 1122, the provost and chapter seem to have clashed, resulting in a separation of the provostal properties from the capitular endowment, which was given to the dean to administer.[50] However, the provost continued to have charge of paying prebendal emoluments from the provostal goods. In addition to this, all canons received a share in the newly organized chapter endowment, which was paid out by the dean. These various payments were made mainly in kind – in foodstuffs in particular – with only small sums in coin. After all, it was the custom for canons to dine together and sleep in the communal dormitory. In the *Liber Camerae* (c. 1215) we can still read in minute detail how revenues in kind were to be apportioned amongst the various stipendaries – at a time when the prebends were already established.[51] But as time progressed, communal life underwent a gradual decline.[52] Already in the twelfth century some of the canons were living in houses of their own within

62
Evert Zoudenbalch (1423/24-1503), canon of the Dom and master of the fabric
Panel, 54 x 34.4 cm
By a painter working in Utrecht, c.1491
Utrecht, Centraal Museum, on loan from Het Evert Zoudenbalch Huis

Evert Zoudenbalch was descended from an old and wealthy Utrecht family. In 1445 he became a canon in the Dom chapter, and served as, amongst other things, treasurer, provost of West-Friesland and vice-dean.
His chief talents were administrative, and from 1454 on he was repeatedly appointed to supervise various of the cathedral's capitular chambers. He was partial to the cathedral building works, serving seven terms as master of the fabric between 1460 and 1495, and continuing in an advisory role thereafter. In 1461 he was the chapter's representative in negotiations with the abbey of St Hubert concerning the renewal of their quest. From 1482/83 until 1490/91 he furthermore leased the lucrative quest for St Cornelius from the cathedral chapter, thus working as a pardoner.
Zoudenbalch wears a surplice and has an almuce (*almucium*) draped over his left arm.

LITERATURE
J.A.L. de Meyere, 'Portretten van Evert Zoudenbalch', *Jaarboek Oud-Utrecht* 1977, pp. 56-71; Suir 1977, pp. 7-56.

HEER. EVERT. ZOUDENBALCH. PROEST
VAN MAESTRICHT. CANONICK. ENDE
TRESAVRIER. IN. DEN DOM TVTRECHT
HEER. VAN. ORCK. ENDE. EMELOERT

the cathedral precinct, and within another century these so-called claustral homes had become the rule.[53] Payments in coin began to replace those in kind, though the latter never disappeared entirely.[54]

In 1243, shortly before construction of the Gothic cathedral began, the *vita communis* (communal life) underwent further administrative and organizational decentralization. Salaries for jobs such as baker, cook and cupbearer were reallocated for other purposes.[55] Over the century or so that followed, this fragmentation continued. Since certain goods were controlled by the prebendaries themselves, a situation developed in which individual prebendaries could assume highly divergent values; indeed, this became the rule in many places in Europe.[56] By 1341 these unequal values were giving rise to conflict, prompting a complete overhaul of the former administrative structure. The cathedral canons now agreed to once again combine the independently administered *Bona Divisa* (divided goods) under centralized control and to apportion the profits equally amongst the prebends.[57] The other administrative units, or *camere*, were likewise restructured. The new conditions, which in fact marked a return to old customs, were minutely set down by Wstinc in his *Rechtsboek van de dom*.[58] Later law books, including Gerlacus van der Donck's so-called *Talmud* (c. 1460) and another by Wouter Brock (c. 1575) provide additional details about the rights and duties attached to various types of prebends and furthermore show that, until 1586, very little changed in the way property was administered.[59]

Wstinc's *Rechtsboek* is also our first exhaustive record on the different *camere*.[60] Of these, the most important was the *Camera Major*, or 'Large Chamber', which administered the chapter's oldest properties.[61] The *Camera Minor*, or 'Small Chamber', managed goods that had been brought together to fund the requisite obit foundations for canons and chanty priests.[62] The *Bona Divisa* have already been mentioned above. Of especial importance to the chapter were the provostal goods, which did not officially belong to the chapter, but were nevertheless counted as such, and controlled by the *socius prepositi*, or provost's adjunct.[63] Finally, there was also a number of lesser chambers, including the *Bona Cervisie*, or beer goods – a specially designated fund with possible origins in a fourteenth-century foundation[64] – and the choral goods, intended for the singers or choristers.[65] Income from these various goods was distributed amongst 36 prebendary canons and the dean's double prebend. There were a number of different categories of prebends: 27 were intended for adult canons and two for the dean,[66] with another nine at one time reserved for *pueri* or *scholaren*, these being underage canons whose prebends did not yet fully share in the proceeds from certain chambers. Distributions further had to take account of the years that expectant canons had to wait for admission to their prebends, and of certain revenues reserved exclusively for resident canons; all this made the *similis collacio*, or proportional allotment, an exceptionally complicated matter,[67] as well as a not infrequent source of contention.

To sum up, the cathedral fabric was a distinct administrative and organizational unit with its own sources of income. At the same time, however, it maintained an extensive network of financial relationships with the various chambers charged with administering the chapter's endowment. This is clear not only from the fact that revenues arising from prebends of the recently deceased accrued to the fabric fund for one or a succession of years, but also from the objectives set forth for the *prebenda defunctorum* fund and for the new fabric. When discussing the duties of the *procuratores* of the new fabric, Wstinc's *Rechtsboek* tells us that '*ad officium istorum pertinet providere fabrice ecclesie, tam veteris quam nove, ad conservandam et reparandam eam de bonis elemosinarum*' (their charge includes the care of the fabric of the cathedral, both the old and the new, and to maintain and repair them using the offerings).[68] The income of the new fabric was therefore earmarked for maintenance and repairs to the old Romanesque cathedral and the new one alike; remarkably, there is not a word about new building works. Apart from being burdened with a number of emoluments, the *prebenda defunctorum* fund, which predated the Gothic building and was fully subsumed in the new fabric after 1464, was used for – as Wstinc tells us – the paraments, both the old collection of books and new books, and moreover for '*expensas, quas capitulum sibi injunxerat*' (such expenditures as the chapter imposes).[69] Yet herein lay the rub. The chapter could, if it wished, draw on the *preben-*

da defunctorum fund for a wide range of expenditures entirely unconnected with construction or furnishings, which it did – liberally.[70] Particularly after the first quarter of the sixteenth century we find the fabric assuming an ever more dependent position relative to the other chambers, though these were in turn becoming ever more lax in delimiting their competencies. The Utrecht Cathedral fabric was certainly no exception in this regard. As has already been demonstrated in Part I, many cathedrals ultimately saw their fabrics degenerate into funds for general expenses.[71]

Two questions regarding the scope of the cathedral fabric's tasks still remain to be addressed. The first is largely of technical and architectural interest: Were the resources that the chapter received and spent on building, upkeep and furnishings administered solely and exclusively within the *prebenda defunctorum* and fabric funds? Though we can answer in the affirmative, some slight elucidation is called for here. The treasurer/*custos*, who at other cathedrals might be tasked with a restricted set of duties relating to the building works, was never in any way involved in the cathedral building works in Utrecht. A few rolls from this *officium* preserved in later years only record outlays for wax and oil.[72] However, it is likely that at one time he would occasionally have borne the costs of maintenance and of purchasing paraments for the cathedral treasury.[73]

On the whole, there was an unmistakable trend towards unity of administration. We need only cite the incorporation of the *prebenda defunctorum* rolls into those of the new fabric from 1464 onwards as an example. In most cases, details about individual elements of construction or furnishings recorded in such substantiating documents as happen to have been preserved concur with figures listed in the fabric rolls.[74] In the period covered by the earliest of these, however, we find occasional reference to the creation of distinct funds with independent receipts and expenditures administered for some specific cause, the sum totals of which never made it into the fabric rolls. An example from between 1406 and 1409 concerns the *capsa S. Agnetis* (reliquary shrine of St Agnes) and another, related account set up for the manufacture of paraments, which was administered by canons who, in those years at least, had no involvement in the fabric's management. They received various revenues that strictly speaking should have gone into either the *prebenda defunctorum* or the fabric fund, including proceeds from the collection dedicated to Our Lady (*Onze-Lieve-Vrouwequest*), they borrowed money from private parties and from the chapter (the *Camera Minor*), collected outstanding debts owed to the fabric and accepted gifts in kind (gold statuettes) from the canons. All this they put towards the commission of a gold reliquary shrine for St Agnes and the purchase of a set of paraments (for which, incidentally, we also find expenditures in the *prebenda defunctorum* rolls). Perhaps it was the complicated system of financing, one that moreover extended over a number of years, that led to the creation of separate dedicated funds.[75] In general, however, there was no imperative to create distinct budgets for special causes.

The second question is broader in scope: To what extent and in what ways did private individuals and institutions contribute to the cathedral's actual construction, furnishing and embellishment independently of the fabric fund, albeit of course with the chapter's consent? We might note here that the sixteenth-century interior of Utrecht Cathedral has rightly been characterized as one that was not exceptionally rich.[76] That private individuals did actually commission sections of the cathedral works of their own accord is hardly surprising if we recall the fact that the church and its cloister also served as a graveyard; it was also home to chantries and mass foundations, mostly for the canons and lower clerics.[77] Naturally, these activities entailed the presence of burial chapels, burial tombs and tombstones, epitaphs and altars. Interment in the Dom was a privilege reserved for the few. According to Wstinc, only prelates and knights could be buried in the nave, whilst lay attendants and *scholaren* had to content themselves with the churchyard outside.[78] Gravestones that have been preserved also attest to the fact that bishops and members of the cathedral chapter, in particular, had their final resting places inside the church;[79] chanty priests and lay attendants, such as the '*blynde Joannes, organiste deser kercken*', were more likely to be laid to rest in the cloister or churchyard.[80] The placement of a tombstone required the chapter's permission; 'no one is permitted to make a grave in the cathedral or in the Pandhof without the chapter's consent' asserts Wstinc's *Rechtsboek*.[81] Naturally, the costs of a tomb or grave slab were paid for by the deceased; memorial tablets such as the preserved relief carving installed by the canon Anthonis Pot around 1500[82] were likewise put there by the founders, as the chapter minutes tell us, *suis expensis* (at their own cost).

A different procedure applied where altars were concerned. In the sixteenth century the cathedral church and tower contained 40 altars, 35 of which were connected with a chantry or mass foundation.[83] The altar block itself was paid for by the fabric.[84] Its material accoutrements, requisite attributes and decoration were the responsibility of the founder. A fifteenth-century inventory listing the possessions of the Dom chantries only takes note of the bare necessaries: paraments, a chalice, a missal and an altar cloth;[85] these items were kept in a special repository near the altar and tended by the chantry priests themselves. Some altars were furnished with curtains, a lectern, altarpiece or memorial tablet.[86] The all but total loss of this original décor makes it impossible to form any real idea of the richness of these altars.

Procedures for dividing the costs of building and furnishing grave chapels are less clear. Various such chapels were linked with the name of a bishop,[87] provost,[88] member of the chapter[89] or, in two instances, laymen.[90] Usually this was because the person concerned was entombed there or had founded a chantry at that altar, often paired with the donation of a stained glass window for the chapel. And yet in many cases such appellations were actually somewhat arbitrary. A single chapel typically contained several graves, and more than one chantry could be established at its altar. In some cases they were named for a cleric buried there long after the chapel's completion.[91] Who, then, financed the building of these chapels – of which an additional row was added along either side of the nave, in a departure from the original plans? Though the extant fabric rolls never make any mention of donations for chapel construction, they do list a few related expenditures.[92] From them we can deduce that there was no uniform method for financing the erection of private chapels. In Utrecht, unlike other places, founders probably did not oversee the construction of their chapels personally.[93] The fabric appears to have had some say in the matter, even if only indirectly. As an example, we can take the burial chapel of Bishop Rudolf van Diepholt (d. 1455), for which the relevant documentation remains.[94]

The bishop's testament, drawn up on Laetare Sunday in 1455, tells us that his chapel was '*noch niet voltimmert*' (not yet fully built) at that date. His testamentary executors, appointed on the same day, promised '*dat de capelle ende sepultuere*' would be '*voltimmert*', indicating that construction had in any case already begun. In 1456 the cathedral architect, Jacob van der Borch, who had been charged by the executors with building the chapel, signed a receipt acknowledging payment of 120 gold Rudolf van Diepholt gulden, equalling over three years' wages of an unskilled labourer, by the masters of the fabric for '*die capelle mede te maken te goeder rekeninghen*'.[95] A deed of 13 January 1469 reports that the bishop supplied a large sum of money '*om sijn memorie, capelle ende sepultuere mede te maken*', with a small portion – a debt of 300 rhinegulden attached to a claustral house – reserved in full '*totter makinge ende sieringen der capelle ende sepultuere bischop Roelofs*'.[96] Though the chapel had probably already been completed in 1469, its furnishing and the installation of the tomb and altar had to be delayed when disagreement arose between the lord of Brederode and the chapter regarding the collection of the aforementioned debt. A last chapter resolution dated 7 July 1473 concerning the '*ornatus et pictura cappelle Domini.Rodolphi*' provides proof that chapel decorations were being funded using the resources designated by the bishop.[97] Thus, whilst the masters of the fabric clearly received money to build the chapel, it seems they may have bypassed the fabric fund (there is a gap in the rolls between 1448 and 1460) when transferring it to the architect. According to the aforementioned bill of receipt, it was also the architect who assumed administrative responsibility for the building work. Whatever the case may have been, it is certain that furnishings for the chapel were financed entirely by the bishop and without the fabric's involvement.[98]

On the whole, it is difficult to form a clear picture of the fabric's financial relationships with third-party founders and benefactors.[99] This is particularly true for the many pieces of furniture and artwork not directly related to the cathedral's function as a place of burial and

63
View of the Dom of Utrecht as seen from the northwest
Preliminary drawing for a print, red chalk and pen, 403 x 347 mm
By Steven van Lamsweerde (1621-1686), 1660
London, British Museum

View of the tower, the seven nave bays, three transept bays and the northwest chapels. This was all that was visible of the Dom from this perspective; presumably the artist made a separate drawing of the choir that has since been lost.
This is the only illustration of the nave recorded from life before it was destroyed in 1674. The nave and transept bays are not supported by a system of buttresses the chapels to the north were never completed.
The tower and nave were connected via the so-called bishop's loge, through which the bishop could walk from the nave to his chapel inside the Dom tower.
On the ground floor was a passageway connecting the immunities of the Dom and Old-Minster.

LITERATURE
Wilmer 2005, p. 224.

centre of memorial services. Repeatedly, the masters of the fabric invested large sums in a wide range of interior items, including bells, paraments, organs, the high altar, the rood loft, reliquary shrines, choir stalls, books and sculpture,[100] and yet all this represents but a fraction of the cathedral's rich inventory. Many of these items were donated directly by third parties, and thus made their way into the church treasury or were placed in the cathedral without the fabric's involvement. This applies to the sacristy inventory[101] but also, more importantly, to the church's 75 windows, most of which were stained glass.[102] Anyone wishing to install sculptural work on a nave or transept pier in connection with a grave or epitaph[103] had a simple procedure to follow: the donor needed only to inform the master of the fabric of his intentions and was then free to see to the commission himself.[104]

By steering this course, the chapter furnished options for artistic patronage by individuals, bearing in mind that a donor was almost always memorialized with his coat of arms in the tapestry painting on the pier against which his sculpture was placed.[105] The personal prestige of the founder was key here; indeed, as we shall see, those who honoured the Dom with an artwork never left gifts of any consequence for the cathedral fabric fund, where the donor would be but one amongst many. The commemorative function of these items of church furniture also carried real significance.[106]

A final, intermediate form of patronage was already discussed in Part I, in which the cathedral fabric commissioned the manufacture of a precious piece of furniture at its own expense and then invited individual benefactors, members of the cathedral clergy especially, to participate in its realization by paying for some part of it. This approach offered an obvious solution particularly where artworks of intricate configuration where concerned. The separate account rolls for the *capsa S. Agnetis* lists ten small gold or gilt sculptures with the names of the canons who donated them; the bishop himself donated a further two.[107] The chapter opted for this same approach for the shrine of St Pontian, begun in 1459.[108] For the sacrament house, which the fabric commissioned, the canon Uten Enge gave thirteen statuettes and the wrought iron latticework in 1442.[109]

Each one of the revenue sources that made up the total income at the cathedral fabric's disposal is marked by its own history. In discussing them, there are two questions to keep in mind. First, which measures did the bishop of Utrecht and/or the cathedral chapter put in place in order to create or allocate revenues for the building works? It goes without saying that these measures could be amended, supplemented or withdrawn. This then prompts the question of whether and to what extent the measures applied could actually be put into practice. Could the bishop and chapter count on compliance with the rules, and were these rules effective?

We know next to nothing about measures taken to finance the Romanesque cathedral. At most, we might cite the acquisition by Bishop Balderic of the relics of Sts Benignus and Agnes from the Loire region in 964 and of St Pontian from Spoleto in 966.[110] But when it comes to the endowment of the fabric of the new cathedral, we have data stretching back to nearly the beginning of the Gothic building campaign (1253). The year 1265 marks the earliest papal indulgence for the building works, and 1288 the oldest known episcopal *mendicatorium*. The very last capitular measures to inject funds into the increasingly impoverished fabric date to just before 15 June 1580, the year of the definitive ban on reading Catholic masses in the cathedral. The implementation of all these various measures was logged in the account rolls of the *nova fabrica* and, after their merger in 1464, the *prebenda defunctorum* fund, with the earliest extant accounts dating back to 1395 and 1402, respectively. It is only from this point on that we can discover the quantitative value of different income sources and scale of the building lodge.

Though the account rolls covering the period from 1395 until 1580 present a continuous record, comprising 129 annual accounts from the *nova fabrica* and 30 from the *prebenda defunctorum* fund, one break does occur around 1525. An abrupt decline in revenues forced such a drastic reduction in building activities that the building lodge effectively ceased to exist. The chapter attempted to make ends meet by whatever means it could and thus at least keep the cathedral in good repair. Renewed funding on the eve of the Reformation extended only far enough to meet some expenses for the church interior.

As we turn now to consider specific sources of income utilized during the lengthy span of time between 1253 and 1580, it is important to note that there are three distinct periods that will continue to guide our discussion. In the first, which ends in 1395, our information is limited almost exclusively to measures aimed at financing the building works. The second, from 1395 until 1525, is of the greatest interest as our data includes figures relating to the budget and building operations. Here we are dealing with not merely a single or series of building campaigns, but with a permanent building lodge active for more than a century. In the third period, from 1525 until 1580, building had all but ceased; financing was aimed primarily at patching up the depleted income and thereby, as already noted, keeping the building in a reasonable state of repair.

ONE CONTRIBUTIONS FROM THE CHAPTER

1 • CONTRIBUTIONS BEFORE CIRCA 1525

The contributions from the chapter present a clear picture of the extent to which the cathedral canons in Utrecht conformed to the methods employed by cathedral and collegiate chapters generally for funding building and upkeep.

THE *PREBENDAE DEFUNCTORUM*

The oldest and also most important contributions were the *prebenda defunctorum*. For the cathedral church, as for the other collegiate churches, these formed the financial basis for the separate administrative unit created to meet the costs of maintaining the church building: the fabric.[111] By examining the history of this source of income in detail we can gain an excellent understanding of the degree to which it was enmeshed in the complicated division of proceeds from chapter possessions. We will recall that in his *Rechtsboek* (c. 1345), Hugo Wstinc cites the earliest known statute of 1247, enacted to reinstate an old but long-forgotten custom.[112] Under this custom, each newly admitted canon had to wait three years before he was allowed to enjoy the fruits of his prebend (granted as an expectative grace). Proceeds from the first year were designated for his deceased predecessor; the fruits of this 'year of grace' (*annus gratiae*) were needed to establish his obit and pay off his debts, with the remainder divided amongst his heirs. The fruits of the two years that followed accrued '*ad fabricam et usum ecclesie nostre*', which can only mean the upkeep and furnishing of the old, Romanesque cathedral.[113]

These proceeds – as we have seen – were administered via a separate fund until 1464. In 1257, ten years after the first statute and four years after the major city fire that supplied the incentive for rebuilding, the chapter set up a new scheme.[114] The number of years for which a canon was in expectation of his prebend remained unchanged at three, but because proceeds from the prebends were so small, in many cases not even enough to pay off the debts of the deceased, the years of grace were increased to two. This left the *prebenda defunctorum* fund, used to pay for paraments and the church treasure, with only one year, making it eminently clear that the prebendal fruits were in no way intended to fund the recently launched cathedral building works. On this same occasion the chapter determined that any canon who was non-residentiary without leave forfeited his entitlement to the years of grace, in which case the proceeds from all three years went to support the cathedral.

In 1344 the chapter decided to raise the number of years that an expectant canon had to wait to receive his prebend from three to four, with two to benefit the heirs and two the *prebenda defunctorum* fund.[115] In the event that the heirs of the deceased canon were for any reason ineligible to claim monies arising from the years of grace, such as in cases where the canon had not yet fully come into his prebend, then the proceeds of all four years accrued to the fund. Here the chapter added the important caveat that its aim was to enforce the papal bull *Suscepti Regiminis* of 1 November 1317, intended to stem absenteeism amongst newly appointed canons.[116] In the cathedral canons' interpretation of this bull, new canons who wished to take up immediate residence, in other words whilst they were still in expectation of a prebend, were entitled to half of the fruits of the years of grace – at the expense, obviously, of the heirs and the *prebenda defunctorum* fund.[117]

This was the scheme in place when the cycle of *prebenda defunctorum* accounts begins in 1402, which would remain essentially unchanged. Only in the matter of whether expectant prebendaries were to be made to wait three or four years do the canons seem to have experienced some hesitation. Gerlacus van der Donck's *Talmud* (c. 1460) mentions three years, but amended this to four in the wake of a capitular statute of 7 March 1475.[118]

We have already seen that the *prebenda defunctorum* fund, later the fabric fund, did not receive equal sums from all vacated prebends. One basic and obvious factor impacting prebendal incomes was the size of the annual harvest and the level of prices. The share of the prebend designated for the fabric was further dependent on the relative status in the chapter of both the former and the incoming canon. For both, their legal status was defined in terms that we find explained in the *Talmud* of 1460 and indeed also used in the account rolls. Where a new canon elected to take up immediate residence, the *Suscepti Regiminis* bull entitled him to half the prebendal fruits enjoyed by his predecessor. Their actual value depended on whether his predecessor disposed solely over one of the nine prebends originally intended for minors (a *plenus non supplementatus*) or also held one of the 27 supplements initially allocated only to adult canons, later by seniority (a *plenus supplementatus*). Provided he was residentiary from the start, a new canon appointed to a prebend of the latter type was known as a *medius simpliciter*, in reference to his one-half entitlement. Successors to a *plenus* with no supplement were known as a *medius non supplementatus* or a *quartarius*.[119] For the *prebenda defunctorum* fund, these complicated rules of partition presented a range of prospects. The fabric profited most in situations where a prebend with a supplement was released due to resignation (*resignatio*) or exchange (*permutacio*) – in which case there were no years of grace – and the successor elected not to reside in Utrecht straight away; here the fabric could dispose over the prebendal fruits plus the supplement for four years. Least profitable were situations in which a prebend with no supplement was released on a canon's death and the successor chose to take up immediate residence, in which case the fabric received only half the fruits of the unsupplemented prebend for two years. Between these two poles were various other possibilities.[120] The total value of revenues from the *prebenda defunctorum* fund also depended on the number of annual mutations. During the Schism of Utrecht (1423-1449), for example, this number was extremely high, since the battle for the bishop's see compelled many canons to flee the city and give up their canonries.[121] Yet these fluctuating revenues had to offset the fabric's fixed expenditures, including emoluments for individual Church officials, payments to the *Camera Minor* for certain memorial services, and the general capitular costs already discussed above, which the canons expressly charged to this account.[122]

OTHER CONTRIBUTIONS: THE *OFFICIUM TECTORIS*, *VINALIA* AND *SIGILLUM*

Capitular contributions mentioned by Wstinc, consisting of nine measures of rye and twelve *ame* of beer drawn from the provostal goods, originally accrued to the *officium* of the *tector monasterii*, or lay roofer – an office that stemmed from the period of the communal life. When this office was abolished, these contributions were reallocated to the fabric, apparently in order to pay the architect.[123] The volumes of grain and beer, valued at market price, generated sums that fluctuated considerably but were never of any consequence.

Another contribution, one of far greater significance, issued from the cathedral chapter's custom of requiring new canons to provide wine for their fellow brethren when they came into a prebend or supplement. Wstinc cites a statute dating to 1327 in this connection.[124] In time this obligation evolved into a series of payments collectively referred to as *vinalia*, or wine fees. It was not until fairly late that the fabric gained a share in these admission monies. Starting from 1424, all canons admitted to a supplement had to make certain payments, including 3 marks of silver to the fabric – a stipulation that survived up until the Reformation.[125] From 1473 on, each canon was moreover obliged to pay a small admission fee of 6 oude schilden (= ½ silver mark) into the fabric fund when he was endowed with his prebend. Initially, this sum was intended to cover the costs of a lawsuit in Rome, which were charged to the fabric.[126] In 1502 the admission dues were increased to 6 oude schilden (the *denarii vini*),[127] with another 3 marks of silver *ex officio regis Herodis* – a category left over from the Dom's annual Herod plays that were discontinued in 1499.[128] Both the dean and provost had to pay double these amounts.

Naturally, the yield on admission dues varied depending on the number of mutations. Paid in marks of silver, the value of which was based on that of the gold rhinegulden, this not insignificant source of income remained unaffected by the devaluation of the stuiver, the coin (sometimes silver) that served as the basic monetary unit. The same applied to income from other sources. The influence of currency factors on the size of receipts and expenditures will be discussed below.[129]

Lastly, it was customary for prebendary canons to leave their silver signets to the fabric when they died.[130] Those buried in the church were also expected to donate a *pannus aurifrigiatus*, or gold-embroidered tapestry.[131] In later periods the canons could buy off this requirement for a fixed sum, initially 30 gold rhinegulden, or 42 karolusgulden after 1546.[132] Invariably, the monies that accrued to the fabric from this source were small, not least because the ostensible requirements were not always honoured.

Summing up, we can say that where the period of building is concerned, the chapter never contributed revenues of any great value. Strictly conventional in nature, these were contributions of a type common throughout Europe. Nor is there any direct link between them and the new building campaign for the Gothic cathedral; in fact, the most important of these receipts – the *prebenda defunctorum* – predates the launch of the campaign.[133] At best, the chapter increased certain contributions, the admission fees in particular, to help cover construction costs. With a maximum share in the fabric's income of 20 percent, and usually much less, chapter contributions did not keep the economy of the fabric afloat during the building campaign. More important were contributions made by the diocesan faithful, to which we shall turn in a subsequent chapter.

2 • CONTRIBUTIONS AFTER CIRCA 1525

Matters changed drastically when gifts from the faithful declined to almost nothing after around 1525. Even though works at the Gothic cathedral had ceased, the high costs of maintenance and repairs remained. The chapter had no choice, beyond renouncing its responsibility vis-à-vis the building, but to allocate larger sums to the fabric or else unburden it of certain large expenses not connected with its tasks. Efforts in this direction met with only slight success during the first decade after 1525, when the chapter's own financial administration was itself in upheaval. Not until the last ten to fifteen years before the ban on reading Catholic masses in the cathedral did the chapter succeed in generating contributions that could again support spending of any note.

Capitular contributions and allocations in the period after 1525 were diverse in nature. It is vital that we keep such differences in mind. The first option at the chapter's disposal was to increase existing contributions. This it did continuously with the admission fees. In 1534 the chapter decided to raise the prebendal admission fee to 55 gold rhinegulden, thus almost doubling it, despite difficulties with the provost and dean who now had to pay this sum twice over.[134] In 1561 the fee was raised substantially yet again, prompted by a resolution taken by the Council of Trent.[135] Beginning in 1562 the treasurer, *scholasticus* and provost of Elst were also required to pay this fee upon taking up their offices.[136] The chapter minutes justify these measures by citing the fabric's dire situation: '*ob antique pietatis calorem* [...] *hac infelici tempestate infrigeratum et pene extinctum*' (because the blaze of time-honoured piety has, in this unhappy season, been cooled and almost extinguished).[137] It is also curious to note that the number of signets left to the fabric by the prebendal canons is higher after 1530.

Another means of supporting the fabric fund was to establish a charge that was actually raised from the canons. In a charter of 14 July 1562, the chapter published a statute assigning the charge levied for tolling the bells to the fabric, on the grounds that frequent use made them subject to wear and tear, and it was the fabric that bore the cost of having them cast.[138] Though a tolling fee had also been charged previously, it is not clear who the beneficiary was.[139] Far from being sounded at every death, however, the tolling of the bells remained a privilege reserved for sovereigns, canons of the city and their kin, and chanty priests. The fee itself varied according to the size of the bell and the number of times it was tolled; moreover, the charge to toll the bells for a canon from one of the other collegiate churches was higher than for a cathedral canon, and higher for laypeople than for clergymen.[140] The returns *de campanis* (from the bells) were comparatively large, sometimes as much as ten percent of the annual income. One of the first names to be listed in the fabric rolls under receipts for the death knell is the famous painter '*magister* Johannes Schorelius', canon of St Mary's, on 11 December 1562.[141]

On three occasions the chapter sought to revive the impoverished fabric fund by means of the additional extreme measure of incorporation. On 6 May 1566 it decided, in view of the fabric's meagre income and the high costs of repairing the cathedral church, and naturally with the archbishop's consent, to incorporate the chantry of Sts John the Baptist and John the Evangelist into the fabric. We know nothing of the resulting receipts as these monies made their way into the fabric treasury via the fund for absent chantry priests (see below).[142] In 1570 the fabric received, for the first time, proceeds from a prebend (without supplement), designated as the *prebenda fabrice* (prebend of the fabric) or also, very characteristically, as the *prebenda sancti Martini* (prebend of St Martin). Against these not insubstantial revenues, however, stood a fixed annual payment of 445 karolusgulden made in quarterly instalments to the archbishop. This comprised one prebend from each of the five chapters, assigned to the archbishop by the papal bull of 11 March 1561 that established new geographical boundaries and dotations for bishoprics in the Low Countries.[143] The Utrecht chapters were vehemently opposed to this measure, apprehensive of seeing a portion of their income disappear. The dispiriting conflict that ensued dragged on until July of 1568, when a compromise could be reached thanks largely to the intervention of the president of the State Council, Viglius. Under the comprise the archiepiscopal *mensa* was permitted to incorporate one canon's prebend from each of the five collegiate churches in perpetuity, but the distribution of the as-

64
Interior of the nave and choir of the Dom of Utrecht, as seen from the west
Pen, red chalk and watercolour, 544 x 422 mm
By Pieter Jansz. Saenredam (1597-1665), signed and dated 3 September 1636
The Utrecht Archives

Four of the seven bays of the nave before its collapse in 1674, together with the crossing and the choir. The choir, transept and nave were covered with a provisional simple flat timber ceiling; the springers of the stone vaults that were never built are clearly visible in the drawing.

LITERATURE
Wilmer 2005, p. 247.

sociated fruits would be substituted by a fixed sum of in total 1800 karolusgulden a year.[144] The archbishop further committed his successors to payment of both the *vinalia* and the years canons held their benefices as expectatives, which sums, as the canons rightly pointed out, formed the mainstays of the fabric's chambers.[145] The cathedral chapter would cede to the fabric whatever prebendal profit remained in excess of the stipend; between 1570 and 1579 the amount came to a mere 641 karolusgulden in total, this being no more than one-forth to one-fifth of the fabric's annual expenditures.[146] On only one other occasion did the chapter attempt to save the fabric's finances by means of incorporation. On 8 November 1577 the archbishop consented to the incorporation into the fabric of no less than four prebends in consideration of, amongst other things, necessary repairs to the tower, '*wesende een ciraet ende ornement van de gehele stadt*'; ultimately, however, a variety of factors prevented this measure from ever being carried out.[147]

Another separate category of receipts concerns profits that can best be typified as internal payments. Specifically, these were payments based on standing agreements and on an incidental basis between the different chambers and treasuries gathered under the umbrella of the capitular administration. Together, these transactions show a clear trend of increasing internal alignment amongst the chapter's various administrative chambers. In some cases payments were to the fabric's disadvantage, in others to its benefit. Before 1525 the fabric was generally the supplying party, injecting other chambers suffering financial shortfalls with a one-time or sometimes even multi-year loan or non-recoverable sum. Rather than being carried forward to the next accounting year, credit balances sometimes disappeared in a common fund *ad manus capituli* (for the chapter's disposal). After 1525, however, the fabric in its turn profited from monetary assignments of various kinds.

In 1506 the canons had already put a procedure in place under which annual surpluses on the *fructus vicariorum absencium* account (funds from chantries from which the chantry priest was absent without permission or need) were no longer divided amongst the prebends but instead assigned to the fabric;[148] additionally, the vacant chantry fund

itself would be enriched by the institution of an *annus carentiae* for each vacant chantry.[149] In actual practice the situation was more complicated and considerably less advantageous for the fabric than the capitular statute would lead us to expect. As from 1483 there was one single chamberlain who administered both the *fructus vicariorum absencium* and two other funds, that for beer (*Bona Cervisie*) and that for maintaining the vocal choir (*Bona Choralia*).[150] This conjunction opened the way for offsetting negative balances on any one of these three still independent funds using money from one of the others. Initially, it was always the fabric that compensated shortages in this fund group,[151] and not until 1519 did it too begin to profit from an occasional credit balance. After 1555, amounts received by the fabric spiked, and payments also became more regular.[152] On 11 June 1574 the chapter decided thenceforth to appoint only one person to serve as both *magister choralium* (choir master) and master of the fabric. This further streamlining of tasks would ensure that surpluses from the choir, beer and vacant chantry funds '*inopiam et tenuitatem redituum fabrice in tempore iuvare et sublevare possint*' (would, for the time being, redress and relieve the fabric's destitution and meagre income).[153]

Not only did the fabric profit from surpluses on these combined accounts on a regular basis, but from time to time its negative credit balances were also picked up by the other chambers.[154] How this was arranged initially is unclear.[155] After 1548 we find the *Bona Divisa* fund covering these shortages (which also paid the chapter's costs of representation in these years, previously charged to the fabric),[156] with the fund's chamberlain occasionally even finding it necessary to take out a redeemable annuity.[157] Between 1548 and 1580 a total of over 3000 karolusgulden was settled in this or a comparable manner.

Lastly, in various years from 1570 onwards, this same *Bona Divisa* fund also provided the fabric with considerable subsidies, '*iuxta ordinationem capituli*' (as per the chapter's orders), amounting to 2950 karolusgulden in all.[158] Rather than an emergency stopgap, however, these additional contributions were meant to finally enable the fabric to make large expenditures for upkeep and furnishing once more. Accordingly, this period saw the cathedral fabric finance the construction of, for example, a large organ costing approximately 2400 karolusgulden.[159]

The history of fabric between 1525 and 1580 warrants a number of observations. Firstly, the fabric's financial position grew ever more closely interwoven with that of the other chambers, each of which in turn lost their independent status. The entire economy of the chapter dissolved into a state of chaos. Indeed, the chapter itself characterized its entire administration over the decades leading up to 1580 as *'een laboryntes, eenen doelhoff, daer men noch eynt noch begin weet te vinden* [...] *ende zal op tlest by een hoyberch geleken moeten worden*'. Not until the cathedral church closed its doors in 1580 did the chapter attempt a rehabilitation through comprehensive fusion of the various chambers. From then on, the cathedral canons wanted to be able to see at a glance, *'bij één reeckeninge, één sommatie, één slot alle onze armoede ende rijckdom, alle onze lasten, schulden ende onschulden, incomen ende restanten op éénen dach'*.[160]

Secondly, having entered a phase of its existence in which building was out of the question, the fabric economy now found itself increasingly reliant on funding allocated by the chapter. In some years these monies comprised more than 90 percent of its by then much-diminished income. The fabric's financing and, with it, the upkeep and furnishing of the cathedral had thus become a strictly internal affair for the chapter, with almost no funds coming in from beyond the cathedral canonry. It could be posited that in losing the diocesan revenues that so defined a cathedral fabric, the very thing that marked its income as *cathedral* income had faded steadily deeper into the background. In terms of the configuration of its revenues, Utrecht's cathedral fabric had little that distinguished it from the city's four collegiate churches of the Oldminster, St Peter, St John and St Mary, which had been incapable of undertaking building works of any consequence during the building campaign for the cathedral.[161]

TWO GIFTS AND BEQUESTS

It is interesting to note that almost all of the few truly valuable monetary gifts and testamentary bequests left to the fabric came from members of the cathedral chapter. The two most important exceptions concern bequests made by two architects, who naturally were very closely involved in the building lodge and cathedral fabric. Cornelis de Wael, *archilatomus* (master mason, 'architect') from 1476 until 1505, left the fabric 156 ½ rhinegulden current, or enough to pay five unskilled workmen for a year.[162] Jacob van der Borch, who spent 31 years working as the Dom's architect, bequeathed 50 rhinegulden current at his death in 1475, equivalent to an annual wage for two unskilled workmen.[163]

All other legacies and gifts of note derived from canons attached to the cathedral, and especially from those who had served as masters of the fabric.[164] Such contributions came in the form of lump sums or the full or partial fruits of the sale of real property. Donations of real property – such as a house or parcel of land – not encumbered by heavy financial obligations were few and far between. As an example, it will suffice to cite the bequest in 1486/87 of a house situated along the St Jansveld near the meat hall (Vleeshuis), which was further exceptional in that the testatrix was a layperson, documented as a certain Agatha, most likely from Leiden. Initially, the house was let by the fabric, but in 1499 it was sold for 187 ½ rhinegulden current, or nearly seven years' wages of an unskilled labourer.[165] It would seem that the chapter had no interest in amassing a pool of capital for the fabric; this is an issue to which we shall return.

Thus far, we have been able to establish the following. Individual bequests and gifts never made any vital contribution to the cathedral fabric's income. In almost every case they came from members of the cathedral chapter, but even within this limited circle only a few were prepared to manifest their concern for the fabric's welfare by leaving a bequest. Moreover, the period in which the fabric did receive legacies of any note is limited to that when cathedral building and furnishing activities were at their height, thus between 1485 and around 1525. It was the vigorous operation of the building lodge that served as the lure, as it were, for bequests over these 40 years, and not the other way around. In this respect, the tendency in contributions from the chapter corporate was entirely opposite, with the chapter shouldering responsibility for the state of the building in difficult periods and choosing precisely those years to allocate large sums to the fabric.

If gifts of money from individual canons manifested a clear desire to make recognizable contributions to the cathedral church, especially where they were given a specific designation, this was all the more true of gifts in kind. The commission of altars, burial chapels and burial tombs, which were so integrally linked with the cathedral's functions as a centre of obits and final resting place of bishops and cathedral clergy, have already been discussed in a different context.[166] Artistic patronage in the Dom was by and large concentrated within three categories of objects: precious items and paraments kept in the sacristy, stained glass windows, and stone sculptures set against the piers. Drawing on the sources available to us, it is possible to make a fair reconstruction of how such patronage was arranged.[167]

Each year, the *thesaurier* was required to draw up an inventory of the sacristy contents. Only five of these inventories have been preserved: one from 1498 and four from the period between 1504 and 1571.[168] The most important categories in these documents are paraments and other textiles, items of gold and silver, and books. Amongst the recorded names of donors (only 49 of the 226 items listed in 1504), canons form the definite majority. The 1571 collection of 60 *pallia* – coats of arms sewn on gold cloth and velvet that the canons were obliged to bequeath – represented an impressive element of the decoration in the church choir.[169] The most prestigious contributions listed in the cathedral inventory were those made by the bishops. Of these, David of Burgundy takes pride of place with his gifts of paraments and, more importantly, a gilded silver nativity scene given in 1489.[170]

Those who donated the statues of St Martin and the apostles in the choir belonged to the aristocratic circle around Bishop John of Arkel (1342-1364).[171] The statues along the piers of the nave, aisles and transept, numbering some 20 in all, were donated by canons and placed in proximity to their graves, and as such may be considered part of their funerary memorials. There were few formalities surrounding such donations: the canon needed only inform the master of the fabric of his intention and could proceed to order the statue himself.[172] To learn the names of those who donated windows, we must turn to old descriptions of the building, capitular resolutions, the fabric rolls and other archival sources.[173] The honour of furnishing the glazing in the transept – the most prestigious windows in the building – went to Bishop David of Burgundy and the cathedral provost Simon van der Sluis. As far as we know, the remaining windows were likewise supplied by high clerics of the cathedral, the dean and *thesaurier* and, on a few occasions, by a cleric not attached to the cathedral chapter, such as the provost of the Oldminster or the great commendator of the House of the Teutonic Order. For the glazing of the ambulatory and radiating chapels, the chapter would seem to have approached Bishop Rudolf van Diepholt and a collection of nobles and rulers, most of them his liegemen, around 1450 – possibly after he emerged the victor in Utrecht's factional conflict.[174] The bishop reserved for himself the three best-positioned windows in the heart of the church.[175]

The group of donors who gave precious objects and artworks turns out to have differed in many ways from those who preferred to give the fabric a sum of money. Though our data are incomplete, it is nevertheless possible to formulate a number of conclusions. As far as we can tell, the bishops of Utrecht never provided sums of money for the building works, but were prepared to donate reliquaries, paraments and stained glass windows. Of the 73 donor names listed in the sacristy inventory, 20 were laymen. But it is the names of canons, numbering 41, that form by far the majority in this category.[176]

The fragmentary record further reveals a marked preference amongst bishops and high clergy in particular for donating objects to which their coat of arms or an inscription could be added, thus creating a permanent link with their own or their family name, over and above donating gifts of money, which disappeared into the anonymity of the fabric fund. Similarly, gifts of church furniture for chantry foundations and other memorial services were favoured amongst canons who never demonstrated any modicum of real interest in the church building.

THREE DEVOTIONAL AND INDULGENCE MONIES OFFERED IN UTRECHT CATHEDRAL

Wstinc's *Rechtsboek* (c. 1345) states that building maintenance and repairs, whether relating to the old or to the new Gothic cathedral, were to be funded *de bonis elemosinarum.*[177] Thus, he identifies offerings from the faithful as the primary and most desirable source of income for the *nova fabrica*. We find this precept borne out in the accounts. Gifts from the faithful, made in all manner of forms, were the financial mainstay of the fabric during the building period.

The Dom had all the usual facilities for receiving offerings. There were several collection boxes into which churchgoers could deposit gifts. These boxes were emptied in the presence of witnesses who were paid for this service with a *take* of wine.[178] There was also a chantry priest who was charged with collecting the *immolaciones* (offerings) brought to the church on special days, which he handed over to the master of the fabric at predetermined times after deduction of his salary and money for wax and candles. On Good Friday, Easter and other feast days, the same chantry priest took his place *in choro ante crucem* (in the choir before the cross) and *ante ymaginem beate Marie* (before the image of St Mary); the *Rechtsboek* already determined that offerings made at the Holy Cross on these days accrued to the *nova fabrica.*[179] On ordinary days the chantry priest was *sedens ante indulgentias beati Martin,*[180] that is to say, seated before the aforementioned altar of the indulgence dedicated to St Martin, which was stationed against the eastern wall of the north transept. This particular altar in fact represented the devotional nexus of the fabric.[181]

The chapter deemed partial papal indulgences to be the most prestigious privileges allotted the cathedral building works, and accordingly, these writs fill the first folios of the cathedral fabric cartulary.[182] Likewise, the list of all spiritual benefits drawn up in the Dutch language and hung in the choir for all to see, of which further copies were

65

Interior of the north transept and portion of the north side aisles and chapels of the Dom of Utrecht
Pen and chalk,
385 x 525 mm
By Pieter Jansz. Saenredam (1597-1665), signed and dated
15 September 1636
The Utrecht Archives

View of the Dom from the point separating the part of the church that still stands from that destroyed during the storm of 1674. Three bays of the lost nave are visible (one partially) on the left-hand side, with beyond them the side aisle and chapels. In the centre this leads into a view of the surviving north transept; on the right-hand side we can just distinguish one bay of the choir together with its side aisle and chapels.
Some inventory from the pre-Reformation period is still visible, including the choir stalls and the 1568 organ.

LITERATURE
Wilmer 2005, p. 248.

sent to the parish churches, began with a summary of the papal pardons.[183] The oldest and first to be listed was the hundred-day indulgence issued by Pope Clement IV on 2 May 1265, available to everyone who visited Utrecht Cathedral on the anniversary of its consecration (22 July) and on the feast day and octave of St Martin.[184] Next followed the indulgences of one year and 40 days each, issued by popes Nicholas IV (23 August 1293)[185] and Boniface VIII (9 April 1296),[186] that of three years and three quarantines issued by Boniface IX (28 September 1391)[187] and of four years and four quarantines issued by Eugene IV (3 October 1432), mostly applied for churchgoing and offerings made on certain feast days and their octaves.[188]

This list also includes a letter of indulgence for one year and 40 days proclaimed by Bishop Gerard van Munster on 15 July 1267 for all those who supported the church building works,[189] together with a collective letter of indulgence issued by 22 bishops on 5 July 1288.[190] Surprisingly, not a single indulgence was issued by one of Utrecht's own bishops until the *mendicatorium* of 1288. An inventory of indulgences compiled at the beginning of the sixteenth centuries summates: '*item van cardinalen, legaten, eertsbisschoppen ende bisschoppen 7 jaer, 1380 dagen aflaets ende 12 karenen*'.[191]

Utrecht Cathedral's collection of relics – that other magnet for the faithful – was not without distinction, although the chapter could not boast any one single famous item to lure multitudes of pilgrims.[192] Amongst the earliest documented relics are those of Sts Agnes and Benignus, conveyed from a monastery in the Loire region to Utrecht by Bishop Balderic in 964, of St Pontian, acquired in Spoleto in 966, and of St Wiro from Odiliënberg.[193] In 1421 the chapter obtained the head of St Adrian thanks to the mediation of Bishop Zweder van Culemborg.[194] A century later the chapter invested tremendous efforts to get hold of certain relics of historical value for the cathedral. Its attempts met with success at the monastery of Cognac in 1519, albeit at a high price, in the form of a relic of St Martin.[195] The cathedral already possessed other relics of this saint, including the famous hammer – preserved to this day – that he was supposed to have wielded against pagan idols.[196] We do not know whether the cathedral canons were similarly successful in their endeavour – which apparently pitted them directly against the canons of the Oldminster[197] – to obtain relics of St Willibrord from the monks of Echternach, of whom they already possessed pieces '*de carne, de ossibus, de casula et calciamentis*' (of his flesh, of his bones, of his chasuble and shoes).[198]

The cathedral observed a seven-year *turnus* (cycle) for the display of all its relics, which it did on the feast day of St Mary Magdalene (the anniversary of the church's consecration, 22 July), presenting them from the rood loft. From the protocol used for this display of saints, we learn that the bishop granted indulgences and blessed the people who streamed to the cathedral from far and wide.[199] The list of relics, arranged according to the order in which they were shown, leads us through the entire collection as preserved in *cistae, capsae, pixides, monstrancie* and *cruces* or *feretra* (boxes, reliquaries, cases, monstrances, crosses and shrines).[200] The chapter was assiduous in tending its store of relics, as is evident from the large sums paid for precious reliquaries and shrines of all kinds. In the first quarter of the fifteenth century, the chapter commissioned a valuable *capsa* to house the relics of St Agnes, which was set all around with small gilded statuettes.[201] In 1425 the skull of St Eligius was placed inside a painted reliquary case. In the second half of the fifteenth century, a costly shrine was fashioned in gilded silver for the relics of St Pontian, which was itself railed off inside a little stone structure. St Adrian's head was placed in a silver mount in 1507, and a head and arm monstrance were made for the relics of St Blaise in 1521 and 1524, respectively.[202] The precious items that some bishops donated to the cathedral treasury also contained relics: Bishop John of Arkel's (1342-1364) cross housed various remains, including several of St Thomas Becket, that could each be displayed individually,[203] whilst the famous gilded silver nativity scene given by Bishop David of Burgundy (1457-1496) contained particles '*de vestimentis et de crinibus gloriose Virginis Marie*' (of the vestments and hair of the glorious Virgin Mary).[204] And yet in spite of all these provisions, the pilgrims never came. The cathedral of Utrecht was never to become a centre of pilgrimage. It was also only in rare instances that any judge ever imposed a pilgrimage to Utrecht as penance.[205] Even as late as 1520 the cathedral chapter was still pursuing various strategies for stimulating the devotional life of its church, such as by obtaining new relics, transferring the remains of St Benignus to the cathedral[206] and preparing to set off the indulgence altar with a costly copper balustrade.[207] Clearly, pilgrims were anticipated, but they never materialized.

Proceeds from offerings and from the collection boxes, the '*recepta de immolacionibus et ex truncis*', had always yielded remarkably little – no more than a few percent of the total income. Rather, the chapter's chief financial strategy for the fabric was centred on the diocesan collections. In the years after 1525 all enthusiasm cooled, to the extent that on some occasions the costs even surpassed the profits. After the seven-year display of relics in 1557, the master of the fabric bewailed the fact that the '*cessante devotione*' (abating devotion) had compelled him to foot the bill for candles, which the offerings had always covered in previous years.[208]

Large sums of money were only ever offered in the Dom during the brief periods when one of the major papal indulgences could be earned. The cathedral fabric was able to profit from the resulting indulgence monies by two routes. In many instances the chapter managed to demand an admission fee from the organizers, usually in the form of a round sum, based on the fact that even these indulgences could not be promulgated without the consent of the bishop and chapter.[209] Revenues acquired in this manner will be considered later, in our discussion of income from the diocese. Aside from these receipts, the fabric could also claim a third, or sometimes half of the fruits of the indulgences from the cathedral itself;[210] in this respect, it was no different from church fabrics in every other city and diocese with papal pardons on temporary offer. At such times the Dom became a centre of devotion, drawing floods of the faithful from far and wide during the brief time of grace to make their confessions, visit the featured altars and deposit alms in the collection boxes furnished especially for the occasion.[211] In 1489 the city granted a safe-conduct to all who came to earn the pardon: '*verdienen sel moghen in den doem te Sinte Mertijn en vrijdaghe, saterdaghe ende sonendaghe naestcomende, daer men drie daghen voer ende drie daghen na biechtvaders toe setten sel*'.[212] Where the indulgence was connected with the crusades or the war against the Turks, the opening ceremony always centred on the veneration of the Holy Cross. On 9 October 1502, following their processional entry into the cathedral, the auxiliary bishop and both indulgence commissaries raised a large cross in the centre of the church, accompanied by the choir singing the lines '*quos preciosa sanguine redemisti*' (whom Thou hast redeemed with Thy Precious Blood) from the antiphon *O Crux gloriosa*; this indulgence remained on offer until a few days before Christmas.[213] The fabric's earnings from papal indulgences granted in the cathedral itself were modest, usually amounting to no more than a few percent of the total net annual income, or the value of a few years' wages.[214]

FOUR EPISCOPAL MENDICATORIA AND SYNODAL STATUTES

The mandates in which the bishop announced he was sending messengers to all parishes in the diocese and promised pardons and other spiritual benefits to all those who supported the cathedral building works were duly compiled by the chapter and copied into the cartulary of the cathedral fabric. And it had every reason to do so as the *mendicatoria* formed the cornerstone of all collection activities in the bishopric.

We find two diocesan sources of income recorded in the account rolls: the *reportationes sancti Martini*, or 'conveyance' for St Martin, paid by individual parishes, and the monies gathered throughout the bishopric by travelling pardoners. Each collection had its own origins, with the *reportationes* the older of the two, as the other collection was not introduced until the fourteen century. These origins and the development of both diocesan collections are known to us from the *mendicatoria* and synodal statutes.

Nineteen *mendicatoria* have been preserved from the bishopric of Utrecht - more than from any other.[215] This opens the possibility of tracing precisely how the provisions in them developed over time. The earliest of these mandates dates from the thirteenth century (1288), with another seventeen from the fourteenth (between 1308 and 1394), one from the fifteenth (1463) and one from the sixteenth (1518). This uneven distribution in no way signals any decreased collecting activity – quite the contrary. Rather, the primary cause for this seeming decline probably lies in the fact that in the years 1396, 1399 and 1440 the chapter had succeeded in getting the pope to confirm certain privileges and powers granted by the bishop, such that renewed confirmations by the bishop no longer needed to be noted down with as much precision. This is a point to which we shall return.

The oldest known *mendicatorium* was published by Bishop-elect John I of Nassau on 8 September 1288 (see Appendix four). But is it also the earliest? Certainly it is in terms of the broad nature of the document. Indeed, the bishop-elect asserts that he considers himself the cathedral's *fundator* (founder), a title not effected by any of his successors or predecessors. Moreover, nowhere in the letter does he make reference to an existing infrastructure. And yet some form of fundraising for the cathedral works, however simple, must have taken place before 1288. In fact, if we go back three years, to 27 October 1285, we see this same bishop-elect promulgating a mandate ordering the diocesan clergy to bring their collected gifts to the emissaries of the collegiate church of St John in Utrecht, which had been devastated by fire in 1279. No other fundraising campaigns (such as that for St Rumbold) were to be admitted whilst this collection was underway, excepting that for St Martin, which would seem to have enjoyed priority.[216] This supposition is supported by an indulgence issued by the bishop of Münster in 1267.[217] But we have no clues as to when the collection for St Martin was first organized, nor who established it.

Did the issue of the 1288 *mendicatorium* spell the end for all other campaigns conducted in the diocese, such as that for St John? It is impossible to say with any certainty. We only know that statutes from the synods held in Utrecht in 1292, 1293 and 1294, unlike the Liège statutes of 1288, contain no references to the travelling collectors – the *questores* – who made rounds of the diocese.[218] The 1288 *mendicatorium*, which alone of the Utrecht series opens with the words '*cum venerabilem matricem ecclesiam*' (whereas concerning the venerable mother church), does not differ in terms of either substance or form from *mendicatoria* issued in other dioceses. The epistle is addressed to the whole of the diocesan clergy and sets out the usual measures. It cites the *nuntii* who will visit the churches and for whom a fitting welcome must be prepared. Interdicts would be temporarily lifted upon their arrival, where applicable. Each parish had to send two reliable laymen to procure the monies and to deliver them, accompanied by parish clergymen, to the cathedral fabric's special messenger at the place and time that he appointed. When parishioners were *in extremis* (on their deathbeds), clerics were to advance the cause of the cathedral works. Benefactors and those who joined the fabric confraternity of St Martin were granted indulgences and had certain sins remitted. Indulgences granted in the past were confirmed. Goods acquired through plunder, theft, usury or other unlawful means and for which no owner was identified could be handed over to the cathedral fabric without reprisal, thus satisfying the need for indemnity. Imposed pilgrimages (excepting those to Jerusalem) and certain vows could be commuted to a donation to the fabric. Members of the confraternity received the special privilege of a church burial, even if their parish church had been placed under interdict; additionally, every priest in the diocese would read two monthly masses in their honour. Finally, anyone who sought to thwart or impede the collection was threatened with appropriate ecclesiastical punishments, whilst those clerics who demonstrated loyal participation were promised a share in special spiritual benefits. Enforcement of all these provisions was settled on the rural deans.[219]

There is no question that John I of Nassau's *mendicatorium* laid the foundation and springboard for all subsequent episcopal letters for the Utrecht Cathedral building works. But that is not to say that these simply repeated the text of 1288. On the contrary, numerous provisions and prescriptions were added, amended, taken out or elaborated. By examining these changes we can develop a picture of how the cathedral works collection evolved over time.

The next two *mendicatoria* of the bishops Guy of Avesnes and Frederik II van Sierck date to 2 March 1308 and 30 March 1318, respectively, and stick to the same formula. In the case of the latter – as with many such letters – it is important to note the date as it highlights the integral link between *mendicatoria* and the synodal statutes, which were publicized at the semi-annual synod.[220] Certainly, there could be no place more efficient or better suited to promulgating provisions for the cathedral works throughout the diocese than a meeting attended by a large share of the diocesan clergy, whether in person or by deputation. Both documents begin with the words '*querelam gravem*' (serious complaint), a loan phrase that we have already encountered in papal permissions for the Hospitallers' collections in the second half of the twelfth century, which made their way thence into the papal form books.[221] This serious complaint concerned the refusal of parish clerics, and indeed also of laymen, to cooperate with the collection campaign and hand over all of the collected offerings; some were even so bold as to prevent the transfer of the monies unless they could keep a portion for themselves. Now, moved by an appeal from the masters of the fabric, the bishop of Utrecht sought recourse in threats: suspension, followed by expulsion from office. Of particular interest in these *mendicatoria* are the handful of additions pertaining to how money for the cathedral works was to be gathered. Deans were to exhort delinquents to deliver all '*oblaciones, elemosinae, legata, relicta et donata*' (offerings, alms, gifts, bequests and donations) within fifteen days; obstructers would be excommunicated. The special benefits available to clerics were now awarded particularly to those who rendered their collected offerings on the day of payment (designated by the new term *dies reportationis*), whilst those found to be in defiance due to their failure to hand over the receipts in person or by delegation were suspended based on that fact alone. Additionally, the passage concerning the *bona injusta* was modified from recommendation to rule, so that anyone who kept goods acquired through plunder, theft, usury or other unlawful means without knowing who the owner was had no choice but to surrender them to the cathedral fabric. Priests, for their part, now had to encourage generosity from the faithful not only when it came time to draw up their testaments, but also during sermons and at confession. Finally, the letters provide a more precise gauge for the size of the commutation sum attached to abandoned pilgrimages and vows: '*secundum taxacionem expensarum et laborum*' (according to the estimated expenditures and effort).

The *mendicatorium* of Bishop-elect Jan van Bronkhorst (October

1322 - April 1323),[222] dated 18 December 1322 and once more opening with the words '*querelam gravem*', contains two important additions. Firstly, it sets the day of payment as the day of the priests' meeting, which was organized by the rural deans ('*in die reportationes hoc est in generali eorum capitulo*').[223] This ensured that the collection was conducted via existing organizational channels as far as possible. Secondly, and far more importantly, it marks the introduction of the *questores* into our narrative, that is to say, of the 'pardoners' or collectors who sought to take their own collection (and not the cathedral's) into the various churches of the diocese. Parish priests were only to admit pardoners who could present letters of admission from both the bishop and chapter. Doubtless this condition was based on a provision in the synodal statutes of 9 May 1310, although this refers only to letters from the bishop and his official.[224] It has rightly been noted that the chapter did not become involved in policies surrounding the admission of foreign pardoners until between 1310 and 1322, no doubt because the admission monies were being used to fund the first phase of tower construction in those years.[225] But, as another passage tells us, the cathedral reserved the most profitable period of almsgiving for its own collection. Churches that had been placed under interdict could open their doors to approved 'alien' pardoners only once a year. Pardoners for the cathedral fabric's campaign for St Martin, by contrast, were allowed to visit these churches on all Sundays and feast days during Lent, as well as over a series of other holy days on which parish priests were wont to advance the cause of the cathedral building works in their sermons to parishioners. The rules governing this appeal (*precaria*) expressly dictated that it be carried out by the parish priests, and not by the travelling *nuntii* of the cathedral fabric. It is here that we begin to see the first signs of a distinction between what would come to be known as the *reportationes* (*sancti Martini*) and the admission monies.

The *mendicatorium* issued by Jan III van Diest on 11 May 1340 copies that of 1322 word for word; however, there is also an intervening *mendicatorium* of 11 October 1327 that gives an interesting explanation of campaigning and collecting procedures.[226] Alms for the cathedral building works, it tells us, could be handed over either at the priests' meeting or on days designated for that purpose.[227] Priests were not allowed to return home from this meeting before having given an attentive ear to the fabric's letters of privilege, in order that none could subsequently claim ignorance. In rural deaneries where priests' meetings were not as frequent, the deans were now charged with designating a delivery day, as per the instructions of the cathedral fabric messengers. The letter's other additions are less relevant. They fix the sum for commuting a pilgrimage at exactly that needed to pay for the trip to the pilgrimage site and back and of lodgings befitting the pilgrim's station. Members of the confraternity of St Martin are further granted their own badge and letters affixed with the fabric's seal.[228]

Bishop John of Arkel (1342-1364) is known to have issued three *mendicatoria*. The two earliest date from 12 May 1343 and 3 May 1344, and thus from the days just before the respective first and second synods that he as bishop convened.[229] In the several days separating his arrival in Utrecht from Avignon on 8 May 1343 and the synod on 13 May, the energetic bishop ordered a *mendicatorium* to be drawn up, one that began not with the usual complaint about clerics who unlawfully withheld offerings for the cathedral building works (*querelam gravem*), but with a forceful appeal to all the Christian faithful to pool their gifts with his own ('*cum ad fabricam*'). Where the first-mentioned *mendicatorium* is concerned, this was certainly no empty phrase. In fact, this is the one key point in which the two letters, so consonant in all other respects, differ. In the 1343 letter the bishop allocates one-quarter of all the tithes that were due him to the cathedral works.[230] In the *mendicatorium* of the following year, this provision has disappeared. For the space of exactly one year, therefore, the fabric could profit from this no doubt valuable episcopal contribution. As far as we know, this is the first and indeed only financial gift that any bishop of Utrecht gave to his cathedral. We can quite easily deduce why he might have done so: as the newly appointed bishop he doubtless wished to win favour with the chapter, which had developed an exceptionally autonomous attitude during the vacancy of the see.[231]

Immediately following this is the now familiar passage in which the bishop assigns the *bona injusta* to the cathedral works. However, to this he adds – in both letters – the *bona naufragorum*, or shipwreck goods. Where the allocation of the *bona injusta* was concerned, the bishop could invoke (as he did in the synodal statutes of 1345 and 1347) a decree issued by the Council of Vienne (1311) in which the pope granted bishops, the *ordinarii*, the right to dispose over these goods.[232] Apparently, the new bishop had put his visit to Avignon (where he received the episcopal appointment) to good use by learning everything he could about the Church's official position in the controversial matter of the *bona injusta ac incerta* (unlawfully acquired and abandoned goods).[233] The measure would still elicit criticism 30 years later from Geert Groote, who provides an almost verbatim citation in his treatise, the *Contra turrim Trajectensem*.[234] Certainly the bishop was pushing the limit in laying these legal claims. Under secular law, salvage found alongshore was the local overlord's by right, who could claim all or some of the proceeds.[235] Viewed from this perspective, the bishop was well within his rights to assign any salvage that washed ashore along the small stretch of Zuiderzee coastline and the rivers within his secular territorial domain to the cathedral building works. Yet in fact the issue of *bona injusta ac incerta* was of no more than theoretical interest; as Geert Groote himself pointed out, no one – or very few – actually rendered these goods to the cathedral works.[236] Another important new element in John of Arkel's *mendicatoria* has to do with the admission policy for foreign pardoners applying for entry into the diocese, with the masters of the cathedral fabric gaining broad powers to prosecute 'false' pardoners. In his synodal statutes, too, we find John of Arkel showing a remarkable degree of interest in the cathedral fabric. Most of these synodal provisions simply repeat in brief what had already been formulated in greater detail in the *mendicatoria*, but occasionally they do elaborate.[237] The most important amendment occurs in an annotation relating to a synodal statute with a possible promulgation date of 1354:[238] clerics who fulfilled their duties in connection with the cathedral-building collection would be allowed to keep a quarter of the profits for themselves.[239] This concession – an acknowledgement of the realities of the situation – was intended to motivate clergy to cooperate with the cathedral works campaign. Whether and to what extent the bishop succeeded in this aim is unknown. John of Arkel's last *mendicatorium*, dated 25 March 1358, con-

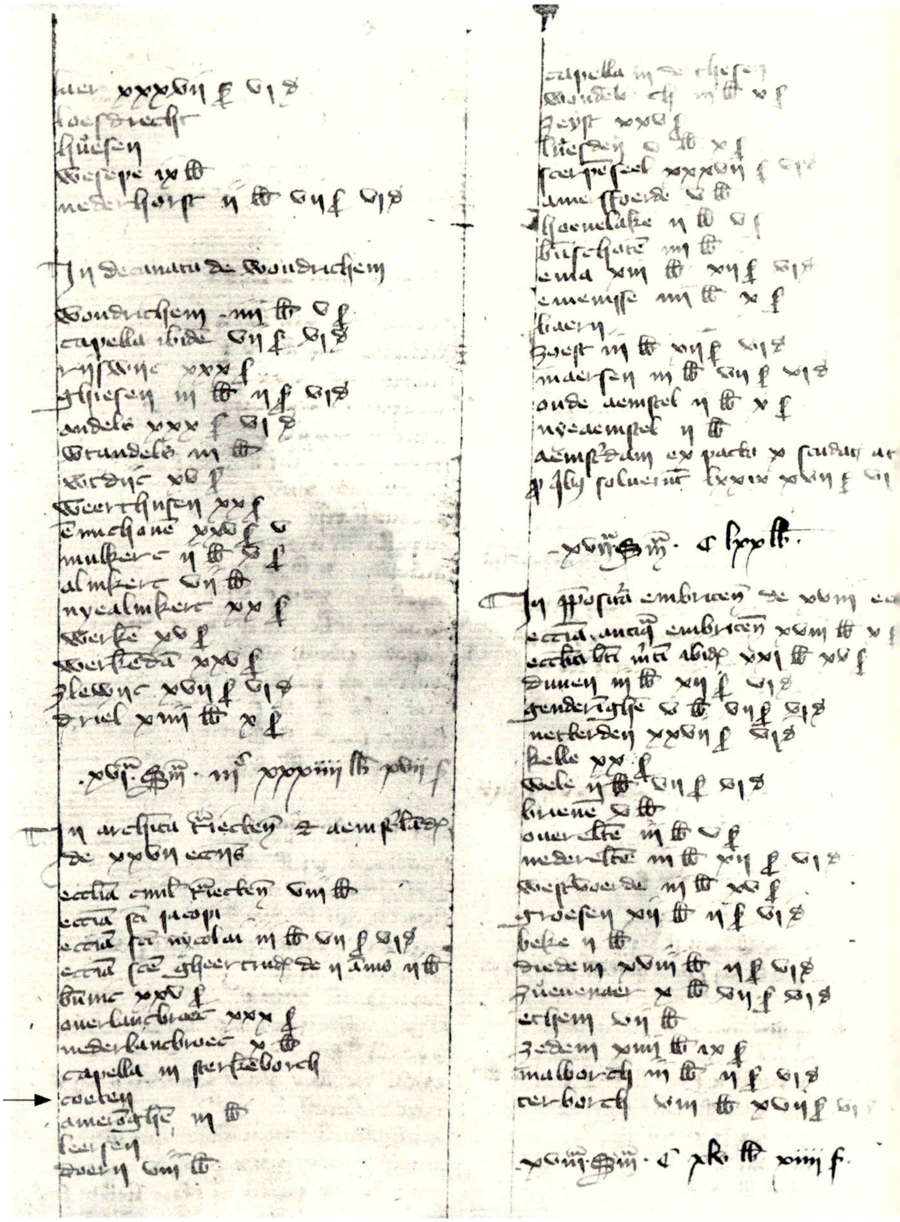

66
Receipts from the *reportationes* for St Martin in the accounting years 1400/01 and 1567/68
Pages from the Utrecht Cathedral fabric rolls
The Utrecht Archives

Receipts from the *reportationes sancti Martini* reached a peak in 1400/01. The amounts paid by each of 61 of the total 69 parish churches and chapels are listed on this page.
By 1567/68 this source of income had all but dried up. In this year the parish church of Cothen was the only one that paid the requisite sum of a mere 5 stuivers. Coincidentally, this was one of the parishes that defaulted in 1400/01.

LITERATURE
Bronnen bouwgeschiedenis, vol. 2 (1), p. 67; *Inventaris Archief kapittel ten Dom*, no. 651, vols 1 and 11.

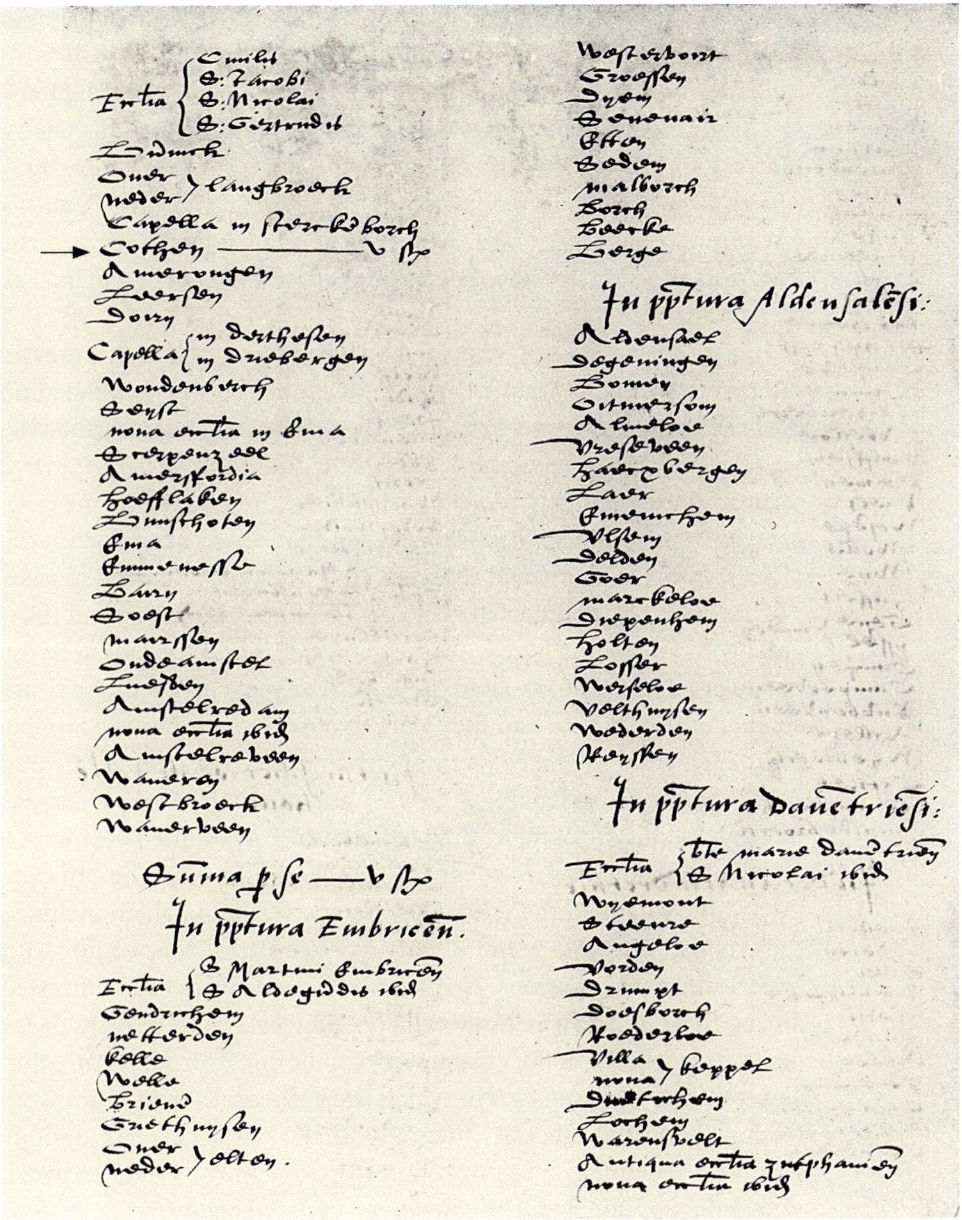

Ecclesia { [illegible] / S. Jacobi / S. Nicolai / S. Gertrudis

Lodmerck

Over / neder } Langbroeck

Capella in Sterkenborch

Cothen — v sh

Amerongen

Leersen

Doirn

Capella { in Dorthosen / in Driebergen

Woudenberch

Zeyst

nova ecclesia in Ema

Scherpenzeel

Amersfordia

Hooglanden

Leusthoven

Ema

Emmenesse

Barn

Soest

Maersen

Oudeamstel

Loesden

Amstelredam

nova ecclesia ibid

Amstelreveen

Waveren

Westbroeck

Wamelveen

Summa p se — v sh

In pptura Embricen.

Ecclesia { S. Martini Embricen / S. Aldegundis ibid

Gendringhen

Wetteringen

Kelle

Wolle

Brienen

Grethuysen

Over / neder } Velten.

Westervoort

Groessen

Dyem

Zevenaer

Etten

Zeddem

Malburch

Borch

Herbe

Berge

In pptura Aldensalensi:

Aldensael

Degeningen

Bornen

Ootmersom

Almeloe

Vriesveen

Haexbergen

Laer

Enschede

Velsen

Delden

Goor

Markeloe

Diepenhem

Holten

Losser

Wersloe

Volthuysen

Woerden

Hersten

In pptura Davantriensi:

Ecclesia { bte Marie Davantrien / S. Nicolai ibid

Nyemont

Olderre

Angeloe

Vorden

Drimpt

Doesborch

Hoederloe

Villa / nova } Keppel

Dutinchem

Lochem

Warensvelt

Antiqua ecclesia Zutphanien

nova ecclesia ibid

firms the mandate issued by Bishop Jan III van Diest on 11 October 1327 and reintroduces the '*querelam gravem*'.

Bishop Jan van Virneburg (1364-1371) quite clearly never had any intensive involvement in the cathedral-building collection. On 22 March 1364 he confirmed both the *mendicatorium* of 11 October 1327 ('*querelam gravem*') and that of 3 May 1344 ('*cum ad fabricam*'), with a few minor amendments. In the latter the provisions relating to the fraternity of St Martin have been scrapped, possibly owing to its lack of popularity.

His successor, Bishop Arnold van Horn (1371-1379), took a greater interest in the cathedral works. On 12 October 1371 he published no fewer than three *mendicatoria*. Like his predecessor, he confirmed the *mendicatoria* of 1327 and 1344. The third, additional *mendicatorium*, opening with the words '*nuncium seu nuncios*' (messenger or messengers), introduces an additional provision that seems at odds with the other mandates confirmed that day. In it, the *nuntii* make a reprise. They would pay their parish visits on a self-appointed day and time, and on that day – and here we come to the addition – the parish clergy had to order all those who had come into the years of discretion to assemble in the church, and they were to observe this day as a Sunday until such time as the collection was completed. Carrying burning candles and the parish relics, crosses and standards, and accompanied by the ringing of the church bells, the clergy (in their vestments) and common folk were to advance in procession to meet the emissaries as an homage to the relics they bore with them (which included those of the Virgin Mary and St Martin). Failure to do this would result in ecclesiastical sanctions. No other collections were to be admitted during this period. In fact, the evidence suggests that the bishop was here setting the regulatory framework for the quest for St Martin – that as yet nameless campaign in which the cathedral's own relics were taken around the diocese. Integrally linked with these regulations was a far-reaching reorganization of the questing system between 1371 and 1380, which will be considered in detail below.

To summarize, it is not until Bishop Arnold van Horn's *mendicatorium* of 1371 that the various forms of collecting documented in the fabric rolls were all established in actual fact, albeit in a different guise in some cases. The sequence of events can be reconstructed as follows.

In 1288 Bishop-elect John I of Nassau established the *reportationes sancti Martini*, or 'conveyance' for St Martin. Beginning in the early fourteenth century, we find pardoners from outside Utrecht plying their trade in the diocese, initially with only the bishop's consent. Not long thereafter, between 1310 and 1322, this authority to admit 'alien' quests devolved to the chapter. Compared to these extra-diocesan collection campaigns, the *Reportatio* for St Martin held a position of privilege.

Between 1371 and 1380 the admission policy for quests gained a cohesive character. The former year saw the bishop establish the quest for St Martin – alongside the *reportationes* – which was conducted using the relics of St Martin preserved in the Dom. This quest operated on the basis of the same conditions as the limited number of foreign quests to which, as we shall see, definitive admission was granted between 1373 and 1380.

From this point on, the diocesan campaigning infrastructure would not see any further significant modification until the end of the Middle Ages. Accordingly, later *mendicatoria* introduce few new elements. On 23 October 1370 Bishop Floris van Wevelinchoven (1379-1393) confirmed the *mendicatoria* of 11 October 1327 and 22 November 1322 (*cum ad fabricam*).[240] A new *mendicatorium* promulgated by Bishop David of Burgundy (1457-1496) on 10 May 1463 also largely duplicates that of 11 October 1327, but leaves out all provisions relating to the confraternity of St Martin and to powers of commutation, whilst adding a fine of 25 French écus, earmarked for the poor, on any cleric who opened his church doors to pardoners without valid letters of admission. The last *mendicatorium*, published by Bishop Philip of Burgundy (1517-1524) and dated 31 March 1517, once again confirms the mandate of 1327, with only a few very minor changes.[241]

In the two sections that follow we will consider both of these diocesan collection campaigns in turn, beginning with the *reportationes sancti Martini*, followed by the quests, both for St Martin and those admitted into the diocese from outside.

Each year, the clerk responsible for recording entries in the fixed categories of the fabric accounts copied the seemingly endless list of over 800 parishes established within the diocesan boundaries.[242] This list conforms to the official Church division into archdeaconries, and deaneries within them.[243] Not all parishes (and chapels) inside the diocesan borders are included, however: the 310 parishes of independent Friesland are absent.[244] Nevertheless, there are indications that these Frisian parishes did originally contribute to the *reportationes*, and continued to do so far into the fourteenth century. Around 1371 Bishop Arnold van Horn addressed a letter to the Frisian deans announcing the impending arrival of the chanty priests Theodericus van Heusden and his party on behalf of the cathedral fabric. Their task was to give the parish priests, specially convened for the occasion, an explanation and the text of the letters of indulgence and other spiritual benefits being offered in return for supporting the cathedral building works. The parish priests in turn were charged with announcing them to the faithful on the three Sundays and feast days of Lent, as well as gathering the resulting offerings, bequests and *bona injusta* and handing these over on a specified day. If the emissaries were afraid to travel with this cash on their persons, the rural deans would have to arrange for the money to be transported to Utrecht under reliable supervision.[245] Such special precautions are unusual and were never included in *mendicatoria* for the diocese as a whole. Here, however, the bishop cites the '*malefacta in aliquibus terrarum partibus dicte diocesis*' (evil deeds in certain territories of said diocese). Friesland was deemed to be distant and dangerous, which is perhaps the reason why its parishes eventually disappear from the account rolls.[246]

With the exception of these 310 Frisian parishes, then, all diocesan parishes contributed to the *reportationes* – at least in theory. The fabric rolls record receipts for the cathedral building works from each of the approximately 800 parishes, a few deaneries (Drenthe, the Vier-Ambachten) and the provostry of West Friesland aside, which all sooner or later agreed to a communal payment scheme. Yet even in the very oldest accounts we already see dozens of parishes defaulting on payments.[247] The problem of non-payment only grew worse as time passed. Whereas in 1395 and 1406 a respective 620 and 600-plus parishes were still meeting their obligations, this number had dropped to 410 by 1480, to 390 in 1506, recovering to 415 in 1520 and then sliding back to 283 only five years later, and continuing to fall steadily thereafter (fig. 66).[248] Instances of non-payment were not evenly distributed throughout the diocese: relatively speaking, parishes in the west proved best at fulfilling their obligations, those in Guelders worst.[249] An obvious question is whether this trend was in any way linked to such factors as urbanization, in the first place, and poor economic conditions in rural areas, in the second. It hardly seems likely, given the small sums involved. Naturally, large cities did contribute more than small villages did. Thus, in 1474, thirteen cities, nine in the western part of the diocese and four in the east, contributed 20 percent of the *reportationes*.[250]

The gradual decline in the relative importance of this source of income is not entirely surprising. In the oldest account roll the *reportationes* still account for 37 percent of the total income (the highest percentage known to us), whilst between 1436 and around 1470 they generated approximately 15 percent of revenues, from then until 1500 no more than 10 percent, and in successive years less and less; after 1528 this share never again rose above 5 percent. Profits from the *reportationes* also continued to deteriorate in terms of their monetary value. This paired relative and absolute decline had its roots in various factors, both particular and general. Amongst the former were political crises that had a lasting negative impact on the infrastructure of the *reportationes*, with sharp downturns being followed by partial, but never complete, recoveries. Here we can cite the Schism of Utrecht (1423-1449)[251] and the turbulent years leading up to the imposition of temporal power by Charles v (1528).[252] Parallel to these events, the advent of Luther's views in this region engendered passive resistance to the fundraising appeal, as we shall see.

The primary general cause for the steady deterioration of the *reportationes* must be sought in the gradual accretion of difficulties associated with the procurement and delivery of all those hundreds of collection sums. Repeatedly, the chapter tried to secure loyal cooperation from those involved in collecting and transmitting the monies and to simplify the entire process, but these new ways and means ate into the fabric's profits and additionally created a divide between donor and designee, thus undercutting whatever sense of engagement parishes might still have felt and dousing any impetus to pay of their own accord.[253]

In 1354 John of Arkel had already agreed to allow local clergy to keep a quarter of the proceeds as a reward for services rendered.[254] Not long thereafter his initiative was taken a step further. The chapter minutes of 1404 record – for the first time – various agreements between the masters of the cathedral fabric and the parish church priests or fabric administrators. Here we see the cathedral chapter farming out the *reportationes* for St Martin for a certain term (ranging from six to ten years); in other words, assigning the right '*om van onsser* [i.e. the cathedral] *fabrijcken wegen te eysschen ende te ontvangen sunte Martensbede, die men hiet reportationes b.Martini*' to the masters of the local fabric or priest in return for the payment of a fixed annual sum.[255] There was a huge advantage to be gained from this arrangement as the lines were clearly drawn for both parties, thus rendering much of the tiresome task of supervision unnecessary. Yet there were also drawbacks for the cathedral fabric. Some parishes found themselves unable to continue meeting the settlement rate. When their term came up for renewal, many parishes, and especially those that had been in default, were therefore allowed to negotiate a new rent at a lower rate. Monetary factors could also have an impact. Sometimes receipts from the *reportationes* were registered in a money of account, the denomination of which was initially based on a fixed-value gold coin (such as the gold rhinegulden); however, at a given point it lost this basis and ended up tied to the value of the devaluating money of account used in the rolls (such as the rhinegulden current).[256] Our discussion will return to monetary factors of this kind when considering other income sources. Here we can establish that, on balance, the *reportationes* from individual parishes oftentimes failed to make sufficient adjustment for the rising level of prices. An illustration of this is the fact that the 1525 receipts, as expressed in the money of account, amounted in Kampen to one and a half, and in Gouda to two times their share in around 1400, whereas during that same period wages increased sixfold.[257]

No doubt these agreements with the chapter were profitable for the parish churches. The sums agreed between the cathedral fabric and a parish (*compositio*) were never large, and even high-paying churches (Kampen, Haarlem) never contributed above at most 20 or 30 days' wages of an unskilled labourer each year. The churchwardens (or parish priest) in turn were entitled to the fruits of the annual cathedral-building collection. We have countless indications that parishes did indeed hold the collection; the indulgences and other spiritual benefits were too attractive not to. A list of these benefits would be circulated throughout the diocese via the synodal channels and sometimes also incorporated in the parish registers.[258] In 1508 the chapter had printed copies of the papal privileges made up in Antwerp to distribute amongst parish priests.[259] The collection itself was held on the prescribed holy days, when the impetus to give was greatest – thus during Holy Week, on Whitsunday and on other feast days.[260] A register from the church of St Lawrence in Alkmaar (second half of the fifteenth century) notes, in connection with its annual fee of 1 gold Wilhelmus schild to the cathedral fabric, '*ende daer voer so heeft die kerck sunte Martijnsbede op grote hoechtiden daer seer vele aflaten toe staan*'.[261]

Most parishes have left no data on the level of local proceeds for the cathedral-building collection.[262] Only the church of St Peter in Leiden and the so-called Oude Kerk (Old Church) and Nieuwe Kerk (New Church) in Delft have preserved details on the size of both the settlement sum and local proceeds from the *reportationes* for St Martin. These sources also tell us how such settlement sums were determined. In Leiden in 1414, the churchwardens of St Peter took the first step towards *virpachten* of the *reportationes* for St Martin, approaching the commander of the Teutonic Order in Utrecht, who held the church pastorate, to initiate negotiations with the *heren van den Doem* on their behalf. The cathedral canons responded by indicating their preference to deal with the Leiden churchwardens directly. Having thus travelled to Utrecht, the negotiations foundered on the chapter's financial terms, which were so excessive that '*die commelduyr ons niet en riet ant te gaen*'.[263] Ultimately, an agreement deemed acceptable by both parties was reached in 1418, for a sum of 8 gold Wilhelmus schilden, which was renewed for another ten years in 1428.[264] Proceeds from the '*Sinte Martinsbede des daer uutgecomen boven de 8 scilden die daer tot deze jaer of gegeven sin*' yielded 10 lb. in 1426, 32 lb. in 1427 and 40 lb. in 1428, with 8 gold Wilhelmus schilden equal to 18 2/3 lb.[265] In this last year the church of St Peter thus rendered a share of slightly less than one-half of the cathedral-building collection proceeds to the cathedral and could keep the remaining greater share for itself.

In Delft the financial arrangements were completely different. In 1434, or perhaps even earlier, the cathedral fabric began leasing proceeds from the *reportationes* for St Martin to the churchwardens of the Oude Kerk for successive ten-year periods for a fee of 4 Bavarian gulden. This arrangement was still in place in 1528, the last year that clerics went around the church '*mit sinte Martijnsborden*' (with collection dishes for St Martin); after this, the collection was no longer held in this guise. Collections were conducted on all Sundays and feast days. Proceeds from the *reportationes* for St Martin are documented from 1495/96 onwards, and show that Church feast days (Christmas, Easter and Whitsuntide) accounted for around a third of the total. The Oude Kerk benefited considerably, though profits fluctuated with the total yield from the *reportationes*. In 1510, the year with by far the highest yield, the *reportationes* generated 64 lb.vls., or over 80 times the agreed rent. From the large amount of data available from the Nieuwe Kerk, we know that the situation was similar there.[266]

For our purposes it is important to learn whether these settlement sums entitled a parish to the proceeds of the collection only, or also to the other revenues referred to in the *mendicatoria*, including bequests, commutation and conscience monies and confraternity contributions. In some cases the conditions are clear: '*mit voirwaerden off den kerckemeesters voirscr. enige testamenten die onsser kerken ten doem beset waren ofte enige onrechte off aesper guede te handen quamen, die sullen si ons nochtans bijsonder dair mede brengen ende leveren*'.[267] The fabric rolls do in fact include the annual heading '*de testamentis, vagis et injustis*', comprising not only bequests from canons and other clerics and laypersons affiliated with the cathedral (as discussed above), but also testamentary donations and occasional monetary gifts from throughout the entire diocese, '*ad purgandam conscientiam suam*' (to cleanse their consciences).[268] The number of items listed in this category saw a steady decline from some 30 a year in the beginning of the fifteenth century to rarely more than 10 during and after the Schism of Utrecht.[269] These receipts are without exception small, and certainly never enough to tip the balance. Revenue from commutations is listed in the rolls only once.[270] Contributions from the confraternity of St Martin are likewise recorded on only one occasion, in 1492.[271] However, there are hints that in various cases these revenues did all fall within the settlement sum. Many parishes, that of the nearby Buurkerk amongst them, collected the *bona injusta* without any apparent concern for the episcopal rule assigning these goods to the cathedral fabric.[272] One document, now lost, from the church archives at Veere gave the parish church outright permission to keep all monies that the faithful made in offering to St Martin behind the high altar on holy days, as well as all unclaimed unlawfully acquired goods.[273] This could explain why so few *bona injusta* ever made it into the treasury of the cathedral fabric.[274]

Synods long continued to be the preferred place for each parish to deliver the sums due, as also prescribed in the *mendicatoria*. The Alkmaar register already cited above records that its 1 gold Wilhelmus schild '*tUtrecht wart ghesent te Cantaet, dat is die darde sonendach voer Pinxteren*',[275] this being the date on which the synod was always held. An 1415 *ordinacio* relating to the respective tasks of the two masters of the Utrecht Cathedral fabric gives a very visual description of how the affair was arranged. Both administrators had to remain in attendance for the duration of the synod in order to accept the contributions, with one responsible for counting and the other for keeping the records in '*certo manuali*' (the designated manual). All receipts had to be placed in a sealed chest, to which they each held a key. Once the synod was over they had to count everything up once more.[276]

As time passed, however, synods seem to have slowly lost their role as point of payment. Indeed, the *ordinacio* of 1415 already provided for the possibility of paying the *reportationes* outside the synodal context. Occasionally, entries in the manuals or even in the official account rolls specify who actually made these payments,[277] revealing that the task was increasingly being delegated to people who were compensated for their services with a portion of the proceeds, but who had no actual interest in the fundraising appeal in and of itself. A few examples will serve to illustrate this point. Even in the very earliest accounts, we already encounter the *collectores reportationum*, charged with procuring monies in certain deaneries.[278] Pardoners took the money with them on their journey, or even farmed out the proceeds in a given area.[279] Some rural deaneries charged the provisor – the local assistant to the bishop's official – with procurement.[280] We even find a stonemason offering to convey the monies due from his parish.[281] In one account after another we find tips and gratuities for the *nuntii* who delivered the *reportationes* and for others who had helped to gather them. This system was streamlined at the end of the fifteenth century and during the sixteenth, though incidentally without achieving any change whatsoever. In 1504, *magister* Jacob Lengel, secretary of the city of Deventer, received a payment in connection with his '*commissionem recipiendi reportationes in prepositura Daventriensi*' (authority to gather the *reportationes* in the archdeaconry of the provost of Deventer).[282] Such commissioners sometimes partook in a third of the sum they delivered.[283] In most cases their task constituted not only gathering the *reportationes* due year by year, but more especially collecting the arrears. Figures from the accounts show that there was almost no church that managed to fulfil its obligations in a timely and consistent manner. Moreover, these debts mounted. Special measures were put in place to redress the situation and allow collection of the *restancie* (back payments).[284] Because the *reportationes* were in fact a redemption fee on profits from a fundraising campaign mandated by the bishop, the cathedral fabric could dispose over the full battery of ecclesiastical penalties in order to compel refractory parishes to pay. During the synod of 1508 it addressed a *monitorium* (summons) to all who refused to pay the *reportationes sancti Martini*, which was recited '*alta et intelligibili voce*' (in a loud and audible voice).[285] At what point the fabric actually sought recourse in sanctions is not clear. In the fifteenth century we find the bishop's official unhesitatingly wielding the sword of excommunication on several occasions.[286] On another, the provisors and deans were instructed '*ad extorquendum restancias reportationum b.Martini*' (to procure the *reportationes* for St Martin in arrears by force),[287] with a messenger receiving payment '*ad faciendum diversas execuciones numero 48 contra pastores*' (for launching legal proceedings in 48 cases against parish priests) in Drenthe.[288]

The problem of deficient and irregular payment of the *reportationes* assumed dangerous proportions when open refusal was to blame rather than laxity and perhaps some passive resistance.[289] In 1526 the parishes of Amsterdam refused to pay their annual fees,[290] whilst in Delft the *reportationes* for St Martin was simply held under a different name after 1528, with all the income claimed by the churchwardens.[291] Particularly revealing is an entry from 1529, which blames the Lutheran movement for parishes' unwillingness to pay the contracted sums.[292] In many cases the fabric opted for the high road and refrained from pressing its demands, sometimes reaching a compromise on the amount still due.[293] In 1554 the masters of the cathedral fabric pledged to donate a window to the church of Gouda on the condition that it first settle the balance over a long succession of years.[294] Efforts also continued to regain lost territory. As late as 1535 the bishop's official summoned several parish priests and fabric administrators who had failed to despatch the *reportationes* to the provisor of the cathedral fabric on time.[295] In 1552 the chapter managed with difficulty to secure letters from the emperor '*ad prosequendam et exigendam solucionem ende restancias reportationum b.Martini* [...]' (to collect and demand payments and also back payments of the *reportationes* for St Martin).[296] One year later the chapter issued orders to two clerical *nuntii* to gather bequests and *bona injusta* as if nothing had ever changed.[297] Even in 1570 the parish lists still brimmed with memoranda and notes. But in fact the foregoing year, 1569, would turn out to have been the last in which receipts from the *reportationes* – a sum of 17 stuivers – were ever recorded.[298]

For nearly three centuries, from 1288 until 1569, contributions from parishes throughout the diocese generated income for the fabric. In the thirteenth and fourteenth centuries the *reportationes* may well have supplied the largest share of the fabric's income. But starting from the end of the fourteenth century these profits underwent a steady decline. By that time, however, the *reportationes* were no longer the primary source of funds for the cathedral works in Utrecht, unlike similar forms of parish cathedral-building contributions in other dioceses, such as Regensburg.[299] One cannot escape the impression that the chapter let the *reportationes* slide in favour of that other diocesan income source: the quest monies, which by the second quarter of the fifteenth century had already entirely overshadowed profits from the *reportationes*. And this is hardly surprising, considering that the quests brought people in even the most remote reaches of the diocese into direct physical contact with the relics of the saints, whose miraculous powers the pardoners amplified with professional finesse.

SIX THE QUEST MONIES

Without the income generated by quests, the chapter would never have been able to finish building the cathedral. Even in the earliest preserved account from the end of the fourteenth century, it is these revenues that were the most important, supplying just under half its total available means. From what we can learn from the extant rolls, this share climbed to between 50 and 60 percent in the first half of the fifteenth century, then to between 60 and 70 percent in the second half, and even to between 70 and 80 percent in the years around 1500. Its relative contribution to the fabric's income dipped slightly thereafter, to vacillate between 45 and 70 percent, but in fact this had to do with budgetary increases resulting from major capital transactions during these years. After 1525, too, when revenues suffered a harsh decline, quest monies continued to account for a large share, around 40 percent. Not until after 1554 did this figure drop to under 20 percent. The last quest monies, recorded in 1563, amounted to not more than 2.5 percent of the fabric's income (fig. 76).

When expressed in the money of account, however, we get a different view of how the absolute values developed over time. There was an almost continual rise until 1520/21, when proceeds totalled over 4200 rhinegulden current, equalling the annual wages of 137 unskilled workmen (fig. 31). Ten years later proceeds had fallen to under 10 percent of that peak year. Though a degree of recovery followed, the quest monies would never again bring in more than a quarter of the total earned in 1520/21, and usually far less. It is no coincidence that as these revenues from the quest dried up, activities in the cathedral building lodge were called to an almost complete halt.

There are indications (to which we shall return) that the profit share these foreign quests contributed to the cathedral fabric were exceptionally high in the diocese of Utrecht, higher than in other dioceses. A strict application of its powers allowed the cathedral chapter to restrict the number of foreign quests admitted into the bishopric on the one hand, whilst claiming an extremely high share of the collection results for the cathedral buildings works from those lucky few that were admitted on the other.[300]

We have already discussed the specific powers held by the cathedral chapter in Utrecht and how it acquired them. In 1322 the admission of foreign quests was made contingent on the consent of the bishop and cathedral chapter, and thus no longer only on placet letters from the bishop.[301] John of Arkel (1342-1364), moreover, gave the cathedral chapter a series of penal authorities: the masters of the fabric were granted to '*examinare, investigare, approbare et reprobare*' (test, investigate, approve and reject) pardoners, to '*admittere et refutare*' (admit and refuse) individual pardoners and to '*arrestare, capere et punire*' (arrest, seize and punish) false pardoners.[302] This effectively placed control over the entire questing establishment in the hands of the cathedral canons. The bishop received no more than 1 ½ oude schilden in dues for sealing the admission letter for each quest allowed into the diocese; this small sum can be traced in the accounts kept by his vicar-general.[303] The need for the bishop's seal on these letters never gave rise to any difficulties. On a very few occasions the bishop deemed it advisable to in effect renew his pledge of full cooperation in granting admission to pardoners. In 1418, upon receiving a sum of money from the chapter to use in erecting his palace, Bishop Frederick of Blankenheim (1393-1423) declared that he would always make due haste in sealing pardoners' letters.[304] At the same time the chapter sought to strengthen its position in relation to the bishop even further by requesting papal confirmation of its exclusive rights.[305] Of considerable significance in this respect was a bull issued by Pope Eugene IV, dated 13 April 1440 and succinctly documented by the chapter as the '*bulla* [...] *ubi examen, admissio et correctio quorumcumque questorum committitur decano et capitulo ecclesie Trajectensis*' (bull [...] in which testing, admission and punishment of pardoners, whomsoever they be, is entrusted to the dean and chapter of the cathedral of Utrecht).[306] Though in formal terms no more than a verification of the decisions handed down by Bishop Frederick of Blankenheim,[307] in truth the bull was directed against the bishop, as is attested by the fact that the chapter addressed separate letters describing the purpose of the papal bull to the bishop, his vicar-general and the diocesan clergy. Accordingly, the fine on offenders of 1000 gold gulden fell due not to the bishop but to the Camera Apostolica and the cathedral fabric.[308] The chapter had good reason for endeavouring to secure papal confirmation of its full range of quest-related privileges once and for all. During the Schism of Utrecht, a period lasting from 1423 until 1449 in which rival candidates fought for occupancy of the see,[309] proceeds from not only the *reportationes* but also from quest admission fees had come into the hands of canons and other clerics who backed the losing candidate.[310] The chapter did not hesitate to launch legal proceedings, ending in a judgement issued by the Council of Florence on 20 August 1434. On 18 September three council-appointed clerics summoned three canons and seven other clergymen and laypeople to make satisfaction to the master of the fabric within a term of 15 days or be fined 1000 marks of silver if they continued to collect admission monies without the chapter's consent.[311] It is in this context that this seemingly unique papal confirmation should be regarded. Incidentally, it would prove to serve the chapter in good stead in other situations as well, particularly when it came to negotiating with extra-diocesan pardoners who could claim papal privileges of their own.

The admission of the quests listed in the account rolls dates from the episcopacy of Bishop Arnold van Horn (1371-1379). Prior to this period we only know that quests were indeed conducted, but not which ones or under what conditions.[312] It is possible that the admission policy was less selective during the period of tower-building after

1321 than it was subsequent to Arnold van Horn's episcopacy. Whatever the case may have been, six of the seven foreign quests that would continue to tour the diocese until far into the sixteenth century make their first appearance in the Utrecht sources between 1371 and 1380 (figs 67-73). Given the availability of extensive studies on the history of the monasteries and institutions that organized these quests, it will suffice to provide just a summary here.[313] We have sufficient grounds to presume that the first quest arranged by the bishop on 11 October 1371 was that which journeyed with the cathedral's own relics of St Martin.[314] On 31 March 1373 the bishop gave leave for the quest for the Blessed Sacrament to gather funds in the diocese for the reconstruction of the church of St Bartholomew in Meerssen, Limburg, recently devastated by fire.[315] One day later pardoners from the abbey of Kornelimünster near Aachen gained similar permission;[316] its patron, St Cornelius, was venerated chiefly as a protector against epilepsy.[317] One week later, pardoners from the renowned abbey of St Hubert in the Ardennes received their letter.[318] People applied to St Hubert to intercede against an array of illnesses and ailments, the dread rabies infection foremost amongst them.[319] Both these latter campaigns were international in the sense that they were conducted in a range of dioceses and Church provinces. On 1 March 1378 the quest for St Theobald gained the requisite permission. It is possible that this campaign can be identified with that held for St Ewoud and linked with the collegiate church of Thann (Vosges).[320] On 8 April 1378 admission followed for the quest for Mary and the Twelve Apostles, organized by the monastery of canons regular on the Oude Gracht in Utrecht.[321] Another two collection campaigns were added to the list a year later, that of the Order of the Holy Sepulchre[322] and that of the Blessed Sacrament in Amersfoort,[323] both of which led but a brief existence and never recur in the accounts. Concerning the most famous collection of them all, the quest for the Order of St Anthony that was active throughout Europe, we only know that by 1420 it was in approximately its fortieth year in the diocese of Utrecht, thus putting the date of admission at around 1380.[324] St Anthony was a popular miracle-working saint, petitioned by those suffering from so-called St Anthony's Fire and other skin afflictions. The Antonines themselves ran hospitals. The order

67
Pilgrim badge of St Martin, c.1400-1450
Lead-tin alloy, 45 x 41 mm
Found in Leiden
Cothen, Collectie familie van Beuningen, inv. 0895

This badge and others like it may have been distributed by pardoners of the quest for St Martin.

LITERATURE
Van Beuningen & Koldeweij 1993, fig. 283.

68
Pilgrim badge of St Martin, c.1450-1500
Lead-tin alloy, 40 x 40 mm
Found in Utrecht
Utrecht, Archeologisch Bouwhistorisch Centrum, inv. 0G94-80

This badge was probably cast from the mould that the Utrecht Cathedral fabric commissioned from the goldsmith Cornelius van Noert in 1487/88.

LITERATURE
Van Beuningen, Koldeweij & Kicken 2001, fig. 1198; *Bronnen Bouwgeschiedenis*, vol. 2 (2), p. 224.

69
Pilgrim badge with a Tau Cross, the attribute of St Anthony Abbot, c.1400-1500
Inscription: *S.ANTON US*
Lead-tin alloy, 42 x 43 mm
Found in Dordrecht
Cothen, Collectie familie van Beuningen, inv. 2054

Possibly distributed or sold by the pardoners of the quest for St Anthony conducted by Utrecht Cathedral.

LITERATURE
Van Beuningen & Koldeweij 1993, fig. 34.

70
Pilgrim badge of St Theobald of Thann (Alsace), c.1375-1425
Lead-tin alloy, 100 x 56 mm
Found in Amsterdam
Amsterdam, Amsterdam Historical Museum, inv. ROKI-6

Possibly distributed or sold by the pardoners of the quest for St Theobald conducted by Utrecht Cathedral.

LITERATURE
Van Beuningen, Koldeweij & Kicken 2001, fig. 1274.

71
Pilgrim badge of St Cornelius, venerated in Kornelimünster near Aachen, c.1400-1450
Lead-tin alloy, 94 x 70 mm
Found in Zwolle
Zwolle, Archeologische Dienst

Possibly distributed or sold by the pardoners of the quest for St Cornelius conducted by Utrecht Cathedral.

LITERATURE
Van Beuningen, Koldeweij & Kicken 2001, fig. 1080.

72
Pilgrim badge of St Quirinus, venerated in Neuss, c.1450-1500
Inscription: *S'QUIRINUS*
Lead-tin alloy, 72 x 42 mm
Found in Dordrecht
Cothen, Collectie familie van Beuningen, inv. 2284

Possibly distributed or sold by the pardoners of the quest for St Quirinus conducted by Utrecht Cathedral.

LITERATURE
Van Beuningen & Koldeweij 1993, fig. 317.

73
Pilgrim badge of St Hubert, c.1450-1500
Inscription: *S:HUBERT: DARDENNE*
Lead-tin alloy, 56 x 54 mm
Found in Nieuwlande (Zeeland, NL)
Cothen, Collectie familie van Beuningen, inv. 1693

Possibly distributed or sold by the pardoners of the quest for St Hubert conducted by Utrecht Cathedral.

LITERATURE
Van Beuningen & Koldeweij 1993, f ig. 200.

enjoyed a plethora of spiritual privileges from various popes, the effect of which was to give it the power to grant its benefactors benefits analogous to those typically found in episcopal cathedral-building *mendicatoria*.[325] The last quest, that of St Quirinus – patron saint of eye and ear ailments – first appears in the account for 1443, and probably originated in the Benedictine abbey of Neuss where this saint's relics were preserved.[326]

We can only guess at what motivated the cathedral chapter to admit precisely these seven quests into the diocese and refuse virtually all others. It is not unthinkable that the chapter admitted the St Quirinus quest in 1443 because it formed a group with the quests of Sts Anthony, Cornelius and Hubert, who were jointly venerated in the Church province of Cologne as the Four Holy Marshals.[327] It is remarkable that only one of the seven admitted quests hailed from an institution within the bishopric, namely, the monastery of the canons regular in Utrecht. All the rest came from beyond the diocesan boundaries. In fact, it would appear that, as a rule, the cathedral canons did not admit quests from churches, monasteries and ecclesiastical institutions within the diocese of Utrecht. Thus, the parish church of Hulst, for example, campaigned in the bishopric of Tournai, but not in its own diocese.[328] Occasionally, exceptions were made. In 1520 and 1521 the cathedral chapter forbore to demand a share in the fruits of the large-scale collection organized for the burnt-down church in Medemblik, provided its pardoners did not collect at the same time as the cathedral campaign. This particular instance of clemency may have arisen from the close ties between the archdeaconry of West Friesland and the Utrecht Cathedral chapter.[329]

It is possible that the chapter turned a blind eye to the odd collection for the simple reason that effective enforcement would have been impracticable. Certainly, the immensely successful 1487 collection organized in Holland and Friesland by the chapter of Xanten for its church of St Victor left no traces in the cathedral chapter archives.[330] And there were countless other temporary fundraising appeals held by hospitals and almshouses for perhaps a single year that seem likewise to have been left to operate unhindered.[331] At times the bishop also approved diocesan collections of which the cathedral fabric received neither notice nor profit.[332] Clearly, the system was not entirely closed.

Determining which of the prominent, annually recurring quests the cathedral chapter would admit or exclude was no easy task. The cathedral canons were barraged from all sides with lobbies for admission. In this sense, the chapter functioned like a sluice gate, channelling and regulating the great flood of collectors of varying descriptions. A leading consideration was doubtless to secure the highest possible admission revenues for the cathedral building works. It is also conceivable that the chapter's selectivity in granting admission lent the quests a certain measure of religious prestige that helped to boost overall returns.[333] Studying the account rolls and other sources, we cannot help but be impressed by the tenacity with which the chapter resisted the temptation to grant unchecked admittance and by the vehemence with which it defended its rights.

Jurisdiction in the matter of quest admissions was reserved solely and exclusively for the cathedral chapter. When the bishop's vicar-general Herman van Lochorst, dean of the Oldminster and canon of the Dom, took the initiative to admit various indulgences and quests, including that of the diocese of Tournai, the chapter responded by launching proceedings against him in 1508. Citing the losses incurred by the cathedral fabric, which were estimated at 300 rhinegulden from the Tournai indulgence alone, the chapter refused to pay Van Lochorst his attendance stipend.[334]

New candidates were granted admission in some cases and barred in others. One group that was successful in gaining admission was the Trinitarians, an order founded in 1198 and dedicated to purchasing the freedom of enslaved Christians. In 1458 they submitted an impressive series of papal bulls, issued between 1251 and 1456 (two of them forgeries), ordering clerics to permit the brethren to collect alms.[335] The cathedral chapter admitted the order for a single year, perhaps as a probationary period.[336] But a chilly welcome awaited them in the cities of Holland, which probably explains why no renewal followed.[337] Some 30 years later, in 1486, the Trinitarians came knocking again, bringing with them fresh bulls from Pope Innocent VIII in which old privileges were confirmed and a new one was granted (namely, that benefactors could appoint a confessor to grant them a full pardon at the hour of death).[338] It seems the brethren chose to approach the bishop first, because the chapter deemed it wise to send a messenger to the bishop's palace '*ad informandum dominum quod non admitteret aliquas indulgentias preter consensum capituli*' (to advise our lord not to admit any indulgences without the chapter's consent).[339] Negotiations would not start until three years later, in 1490, and it was another four before a contract was settled for a term of three years.[340] The long delay in the deliberations was due to the brethren's insistence on terms that the chapter had no wish to honour. Specifically, the Trinitarians wanted to set out with pennants bearing the papal arms and to be welcomed in corresponding state, as they were accustomed to doing in other dioceses. The chapter, mindful of the basic equality of all quests – a cornerstone of its admission policy – felt such displays would '*ducere in vilipendium*' (devalue) other quests.[341] As it happened, the quest disappeared from the diocese after the three years, never to return.[342]

Now and then other quests were also admitted for brief periods, such as those of the hospital of Santo Spirito in Rome[343] and the Teutonic Order.[344] The major Roman indulgences offered in different cities of the diocese in different years can also be counted in this category; in some cases the cathedral fabric got not only a share of the profits collected in the cathedral itself, but also a percentage of what was gathered in the diocese.[345] It further received a quarter of the proceeds from the Saintes Cathedral collection, which was dedicated in part to the war against the Turks and boasted a plenary indulgence.[346] Even the illustrious indulgence issued to support the construction of St Peter's in Rome generated funds for the fabric of Utrecht Cathedral.[347]

At the same time there were quests that not even the recommendations of persons of influence could sway the chapter into admitting. On 28 June 1495 Philip the Handsome of Burgundy applied on behalf of the Chapel of Our Lady in Halle (near Antwerp) to have its quest admitted to the provinces of Holland, Zeeland and West Friesland, which the bishop approved but the chapter refused. Philip renewed his request on 6 August, this time threatening to retract his seigneurial authorization for the chapter's quests (such authorization being requisite) if it were to impede that of Halle. On 21 August the duke announced the arrival of negotiators. The cathedral canons gave them a friendly reception with *prandium et vinum*, but still refused to give them placet letters.[348] They likewise declined to admit the quest for St Adrian, operated by the Benedictine abbey in Geraardsbergen,[349] and possibly also the quest for the Friars Minor in Paris, intended to assist poor students.[350]

Aside from the problems attending official decision-making on whether or not to grant admission, the cathedral canons were also forced to deal with quests conducted in the diocese without the chapter's permission or for periods exceeding what was agreed. Even worse were the pseudo-pardoners who fooled parish priests with forged letters and then absconded with the loot.[351] Of course, there was no fail-safe way to keep unauthorized pardoners out entirely, but certain steps were taken, such as sending messengers out to investigate individual cases, questioning parish priests as to whether they had verified the letters properly and attempting to apprehend all goods and persons involved in a false quest: '*bona, res, pecunias, litteras et personas*' (possessions, goods, monies, letters and persons).[352] On receiving a report that a false pardoner from Mount Sinai was operating in Abcoude, the chapter responded by promptly despatching its messenger, the cathedral box-maker, two labourers and three others on a hired ship with orders to seize the man. Having arrived at the site, however, they found the bird had flown the coop.[353] In 1495 an assistant in the building lodge – the *famulus in loedsa* – was rewarded with a gratuity because he had ripped bulls declaring an indulgence offered by the convent of St Bridget from the doors of Utrecht's churches since it had no permission to be promulgated there.[354]

Strangely enough, the overlord might also interfere with Dom quests in areas where the bishop exercised only spiritual jurisdiction, particularly in Holland, Zeeland and West Friesland. In 1427 the count agreed to Bishop Zweder van Culemborg's request to grant pardoners from Utrecht Cathedral safe-conduct in Holland, amounting to permission to collect, and setting a precedent from which a formal seigneurial right of authorization would subsequently develop.[355] This arrangement was also common elsewhere: in France as early as the twelfth century[356] and later also in Spain[357] and Germany.[358] Church authorities respected this right; witness Pope Adrian VI's willingness in 1522 to acknowledge admission letters issued by Philip the Good and his successors.[359]

Though permission from secular authorities signified formal approval and protection, it also entailed dependency on the overlord's judgement. The slightest sign that this approval was in jeopardy sent the cathedral canons into a panic. A case in point was when Philip the Good acquiesced to an appeal from the civic administrations to order a universal ban on pardoners in 1462. The cities felt – understandably – that the multiplicity of unstructured external collections were siphoning off their populations' wealth, sometimes at the expense of the cities' own local churches. Here, as elsewhere in Europe, lords had gradually come to lay claim to certain competencies in the domain of Church politics, including to activities relating to indulgences. The chapter assumed that the duke's universal ban applied to quests for the cathedral as well, but he was quick to send assurances that this was not the case. Even so, various cities were only too happy to use the general ban as an excuse to refuse the cathedral pardoners entry. The sluggish workings of the ecclesiastical justice machine thus had to be set in motion, with all its attendant costs and vexations.[360] Difficulties recurred in 1510, 1515 and 1518, because authorization for the cathedral's collection campaigns was deemed potentially detrimental to the papal indulgences to which the lord had promised his protection.[361] Understandably, the fabric objected to the '*insupportabiles expensas*' (unendurable expenses) now needed to obtain the authorization.[362] When a ruling was issued in favour of the fabric in 1515, the chapter immediately made certain that the news was spread far and wide so that cities could not seek recourse in sham excuses to keep cathedral pardoners outside the gates.[363]

The lord, for his part, took advantage of his own position as benevolent conferrer of permits whenever he stood to gain financially or politically from approving new indulgences from outside the bishopric to which the chapter was opposed. Papal and other collecting campaigns were submitted for the chapter's consideration under cover of forceful letters of recommendation from the lord which could not always be ignored, as seen in the case of Halle.[364]

We can now turn to consider the various financial conditions under which quests were admitted. The quest for St Martin was never an issue, given that the relics belonged to the cathedral itself and the confraternity of St Martin owed its inception and organization to the cathedral fabric. Where foreign quests were concerned, there were two options. Either the chapter could admit the quest and charge an admission fee on behalf of the fabric, leaving the organization up to the abbey, monastery or Church institution concerned, or it could obtain the rights to campaign with the abbey's relics and letters of indulgence in return for paying that abbey a certain agreed fee each year. Not surprisingly, the chapter preferred the latter type of arrangement. The first type had been contracted with the Antonines, and indeed theirs was the only campaign that managed to elude the chapter's grasp to the very end, remaining firmly in the hands of the Antonines of the Commandry in Belle in Flanders,[365] where the local preceptor appointed a pardoner. In fact, the Antonines actually denied the chapter the right to ask anything more than a nominal admission fee, demanding unconditional admittance on the basis of their papal privileges. The order had ample justification for its rather supercilious attitude. It held a papal privilege dating from 17 April 1265 that authorized it to organize collections throughout the whole of Christendom (fig. 75).[366] At the time, Europe was split into collection zones, called *balivia* or bailiwicks, the boundaries of which extended over one or more dioceses. In many, if not all, dioceses, the bishop or cathedral chapter demanded no more than a modest reimbursement for their admission letter,[367] but not so in Utrecht, making a clash with the cathedral canons there inevitable. In 1420 the Antonines suddenly refused to pay the annual fee, despite having paid it without objection for 40 years. Thenceforth they would only agree to pay one gulden to have their letter sealed.[368] This being a matter of principle, the chapter had to respond swiftly. The fabric masters had the pardoners arrested and laid the case before the court in Rome. Not until 19 November 1425 did the court finally find in their favour,[369] after which the Antonine collection was repulsed for a number of years. John III, duke of Bavaria and count of Holland, wishing to remain neutral in the affair, prohibited his subjects from giving money to either the Dom or the Antonines until the matter was settled.[370] The papal judge, later Pope Eugene IV, adopted the chapter's general line of argumentation, which is known to us from an undated manuscript containing an exceptionally lucid description of the chapter's demands. According to the canons' reasoning, the diocese of Utrecht had within it a cathedral under construction, which could not be completed '*sine communi subsidio subditorum episcopatus*' (without the combined assistance of the subjects of the diocese). It was for this very reason that the chapter had been granted, by virtue of the bishop's authority, the '*facultas exigendi et obtinendi a subditis tocius episcopatus predicti elemosinas necnon usuras, rapinas, incerta, vaga et alia bona predicta*' (right to demand and receive offerings from the subjects of the entire diocese, as well as gains from usury, goods acquired through theft, goods without an obvious owner, vagrant goods and other goods as aforementioned). As such, the admission fee was to be regarded as an indemnity for Utrecht's cathedral fabric, whose collection would yield at least 300 ducats more if the Antonines were not to conduct their campaign.[371] The papal judge's ruling fixed the admission fee at the hefty sum of 213 French francs, which remained the benchmark for admission negotiations until far into the sixteenth century.[372] Many years later, perhaps around 1517, the chapter essayed another attempt to make the Antonines conduct their quest in the same way as the others, and to expropriate its exploitation from the Antonines, whose moral misdemeanours were bringing discredit on all the quests.[373] But the Antonines refused to budge, wishing to continue running their campaign themselves. The chapter never forgave the order this obstinacy. The temporary fee reductions always promptly granted *ex gratia capituli* (as a favour conceded by the chapter) to all the other quests in periods of war and unrest were denied the Antonines alone.[374] As conditions grew steadily worse after 1527, theirs was also the last admission fee to be adjusted downwards, in 1548.[375]

All other quests in the diocese eventually ceded their exploitation rights to the cathedral fabric in exchange for an annual monetary fee

74
Reliquary of St Hubert, manufactured in the Rhineland
Gilded silver, rock crystal, 37 cm
Cologne, cathedral treasury

Cologne Cathedral, unlike that of Utrecht, owned a large number of relics of St Hubert. This collection was without doubt connected with the quest run by the abbey of St Hubert, which also operated in the archbishopric of Cologne. These relics were kept in the chapel of St Hubert, presumed to have been situated near the Huprechtshof, which was the administrative centre of the Cologne Cathedral fabric's quest operations. After the quest was discontinued the entire collection of relics was transferred to the cathedral treasury on 16 June 1557. This reliquary is the only piece that remains.

LITERATURE
Ad Summum 1248, pp. 49, 52, 63-66.

payable to the institution or monastery that owned the relics. This is the second option referred to above. This arrangement was no less susceptible to conflict, albeit for entirely opposite reasons. A clear case in point concerns the quest for St Hubert. Initially, all contact with the abbey of St Hubert was channelled via the fabric of Cologne Cathedral, which coordinated the exploitation of the quest in all its suffragan dioceses, Liège excepted. The fabric master at Utrecht paid a pension to his colleague in Cologne each year, up until 1444, when Cologne seems to have decided to give up running the quest in the diocese of Utrecht. On 7 October the abbot signed a contract with the Utrecht Cathedral fabric directly, thus without Cologne's mediation, under which he transferred the rights to exploit the quest to the chapter for a period of nine years in return for an indemnity of 32 gold rhinegulden.[376] His reasoning was that the abbey was too distant from the diocese of Utrecht to permit it to conduct the operation itself (though it never had done so anyway). The abbey already had plenty of experience working with different bishoprics, given that it ran the quest in (or had it run by) more than ten dioceses.[377] The relationship started off smoothly, and the contract was extended for the considerably longer term of 25 years.[378] A high point came in the year 1461, when the abbey sent several relics to Utrecht and further authorized the chapter to register confraters and consorors in the aristocratic confraternity of St Hubert and to confer the insignia of the order[379]. But then relations cooled. The cause was the extremely uneven distribution of quest profits between the abbey and cathedral fabric. Whilst the abbey's fee saw a small increase from 32 to 50 gold rhinegulden between 1444 and 1512, the cathedral fabric's net proceeds[380] rose from 100 to 350 gold rhinegulden; in other words, the abbey's portion shrank from 25 to 12.5 percent.[381] In 1510 the abbey laid its dispute with the chapter before the Court of Brabant and subsequently refused to renew the agreement, which was due to lapse in 1511.[382]

The case never came to trial however, as the two sides were able to reach an amicable settlement on 7 January 1513, retaining all the old provisions except that the chapter would pay the abbey 75 gold rhinegulden instead of 50 for the subsequent 20 years. It was a downright shabby result for the abbot, who had submitted such strong and – in our eyes – legitimate arguments. He posited the fundamental principle that offerings given as an act of devotion to a particular saint should be brought to the place where that saint was venerated, where his body was laid to rest and where he had caused miracles to occur. The abbey was willing to divide the devotional monies collected in the diocese of Utrecht into two equal shares, but not to accept a share of a mere 20 percent, as it had done until then.[383] Archduke Maximillian accepted the validity of this reasoning and on 9 September 1512 prohibited the chapter from performing the collection without asking the abbey's permission.[384] Meanwhile, the cathedral canons had sought out the aid of two of their most prominent confraters, both residing in the Southern Netherlands, to defend their interests. One of them, Adriaan Florensz., later Pope Adrian VI but at that time still a professor in Louvain, shrewdly raised the point that quests such as the one for St Hubert actually had two components – an indulgence element and a devotional element – that were not equal in importance. Deftly arguing the chapter's case, he asserted that the faithful gave alms not so much because of the relics brought along on the campaign (which were the abbey's), but for the indulgences and dispensations they could earn (which were granted at the bishop's behest).[385] The arguments that ultimately won the suit for the chapter were a good deal less elevated. The chapter claimed that the cathedral fabric had already been conducting the St Hubert quest for over a hundred years using the relics of St Hubert, and that these actually belonged to the cathedral. The only thing that had been agreed in 1444 was that the quest would thenceforth be conducted in the abbey's name, by virtue of additional relics that it sent for the purpose. If the abbey did not wish to accept the chapter's conditions, then the cathedral fabric would simply go back to carrying out its own St Hubert quest as it had done before 1444, without suffering any ill effect.[386] Certainly, there are no indications that the Dom itself ever possessed any relics of St Hubert whatsoever, though possibly its assertion rested on the fact that the chapter of Cologne Cathedral claimed to have relics of this saint[387] (fig. 74). The entire line of argumentation smacks of usurpation, which the abbey's apparent lack of relevant documentation rendered it powerless to expose, even in spite of the fact that it could claim ownership of the entire body of the saint, which had been interred at the abbey since 825 – thus going back for centuries. In 1515 Pope Leo x quite superfluously declared that the whole of St Hubert's body was preserved at the abbey.[388]

Around the same time a similar conflict arose between the cathedral fabric and the abbey of St Cornelius.[389] A few years on, in 1521, the abbot renewed his initial complaints about the way in which the chapter had usurped the quest, making a mockery of the fair division of proceeds.[390] Why, the abbot wondered, have we not been admitted under the same terms as in the dioceses of Trier, Cambrai and Liège, when we are equally prepared to pay fees for sealing documents and administration to the fabrics there? Here the abbot of Kornelimünster hits on the crux of the matter. For one reason or another,[391] the cathedral chapter at Utrecht had managed, unlike neighbouring dioceses, to turn the few foreign quests that it did admit into all but proprietary quests, the high profits of which accrued chiefly to the cathedral building works and not to the monasteries or institutions where the collections originated.[392]

Alongside the matter of who exploited the quests in the diocese of Utrecht is the question of how this was done. We have seen that the quest for St Antonius formed an exception, run by the commandery of Antonines in Belle and carried out by an Antonine or other cleric who leased the quest from the commandery.[393] The sum recorded in the fabric rolls each year is the admission fee, which was paid by the lessee to the cathedral fabric. Operation of all the remaining quests was, sooner or later, taken over by the cathedral fabric, though this does not mean that the canons took charge of the exploitation themselves. They in turn farmed out the right to take the relics around the diocese to a pardoner, who then assumed responsibility for organizing the collection and procuring donations. Their annual rents are entered in the fabric rolls under the heading '*recepta de questoribus*' (receipts from pardoners), as is the admission fee paid by the St Anthony quest.[394] Quest lease contracts were drawn up on set dates as part of capitular meetings.[395] Judging from those that have been preserved, the conditions were almost always identical.[396] They included the lease term (four, six, eight or more years), rent and method of payment to be determined, the surety to be arranged and the provisions for arbitration in the event of disputes. Invariably there is a clause requiring the pardoner to carry out the quest in a manner that is '*eerbaerlick ende statelick*' (honourable and dignified). The pardoner himself had to arrange to obtain a 'proxy' or authorization to collect on the relevant abbey's behalf, as well as to pay all the necessary costs – thus including the sum to which the abbey was entitled. Further provisions stated that where pardoners found themselves unable to access a certain area due to war or other unforeseen circumstances, they would be given a discount in consultation with the masters of the fabric. The appurtenances of the pardoner's office – vessels enclosing relics, portables with account books, registers, letters and bulls, a book containing the route description and other official papers – were supplied by the masters of the fabric and had to be returned to them in good condition at the close of the contract term.[397] The relics in their reliquaries and all other paraphernalia needed for the quest were most likely furnished to the cathedral fabric by each individual abbey.[398]

On the whole, the fabric was fortunate in its choice of pardoners, most of them clergymen from Utrecht – often a canon from one of the collegiate churches (fig. 62) or a chantry priest, occasionally a layman – who under ordinary conditions paid their rents on time.[399] For its part the fabric provided all possible assurances to pardoners. For example, when an assistant pardoner refused to hand over the monies he had collected to his principal, the fabric gave the latter leave to arrest the debtor and put him behind bars.[400] On a few occasions the chapter had to intervene to secure the release of imprisoned pardoners.[401]

Only the pardoners and their aides had direct contact with the faithful.[402] The cathedral fabric vouchsafed that they would be welcomed in parish churches, as indeed was required of the parish priests. Pardoners could sweeten the deal by assenting to pay the parish church priest or fabric a small sum if they were received with torches and candles and the ringing of church bells. Whether such gestures of welcome were always sincere is highly doubtful; after all, what parish interest was served in a collection that only came to reap what was properly its own harvest?[403] One known point of contention was the

75

Remains of a printed list of indulgences and spiritual benefits offered by the Antonines (?), c.1500
Broadside incunable, approx. 220 x 180 mm
Affixed to a pier in the northeastern end of the ambulatory
Groningen, church of St Martin

Rare example of a list of indulgences in Latin, preserved in the place where it originally hung. This document is presumed to list the indulgences and spiritual benefits that were conferred on the Antonines by popes Sixtus IV (1471-1484) and Innocent VIII (1484-1492) and various bishops. Some phrases are still legible: '*indulgentias ple*[*narias*]' and '[*ne*]*gotium pauperum sancti Anthonii* [...] *de suis bonis aliq*[*uid*] [...]'. This also signals an inherent link with the cathedral works in Utrecht, given that in Groningen, as elsewhere, the Antonine collection depended on permission from the cathedral chapter in Utrecht, paying an admission fee to the cathedral works fund for this right. It is not clear why this document, which seems to have been intended for the clergy, was affixed to a pier in the ambulatory.

LITERATURE
Bulletin van de Koninklijke Nederlandse Oudheidkundige Bond, vol. 65, 1966, pl. XLIV and p. 96 n. 12.
Dr C.L. Heesakkers assisted in deciphering the text.

issue of whether parish priests were to allow pardoners to ascend their pulpits to preach,[404] giving rise to the logical demand that the chapter at least delegate ecclesiastics as pardoners.[405] The fact that these quests and indulgences ran counter to local interests prompted opposition from city governments, too, unless the city or its churches also shared in the proceeds (as was the case with various papal indulgences).[406] Eventually, however, the very practice itself came to elicit resistance and protest, though incidentally without making an immediate dent in overall returns.[407] We hear criticism against the quests from, amongst others, Oldenzaal (1460), Kampen (1461), Gorkum (1469), Gouda (1510), Ouderkerk aan de IJssel (1521), Zutphen (1522), the provostry of Emmerich (1522), Deventer and Rotterdam (1524).[408] In 1488 the Saintes indulgence, the proceeds of which accrued in part to the cathedral fabric, aroused the wrath of the priest in Wageningen, who had the temerity to declaim the whole indulgence as nothing more than '*mera trufa et deceptio quedam ad extorquendum a communi populo pecunias*' (pure deceit and deception to extort money from the common people),[409] to which we might add the interesting note that promulgation of the indulgence in the Wageningen region bore no fruit thanks to the priest's pronouncements. Moreover, Luther's influence became manifest fairly early on. His name is mentioned twice in 1522 in connection with quests: first when the pardoners were instructed to distribute 500 printed leaflets setting out '*zekere wondertekenen tegen Luthers leer*'[410] and, second – and particularly revealing – when the '*doctrina magistri Martini Lutheri*' (teachings of master Martin Luther) are cited in so many words as being one of the factors responsible for the already noticeable decline in quest profits.[411]

We have already considered the financial significance of the total quest revenues. Those overall receipts were composed of sums rendered by a collection of distinct quests, not every one of which contributed as large a share nor, indeed, one that remained constant over time.

Up until 1450 the quests for St Cornelius and St Antonius were the most important collections after that for St Martin. Together these three generated upwards of 65 percent of the quest income. In that year the rent for the St Hubert quest was raised to almost double what it had been, as was that for the smaller-scale quest for Our Lady. After 1463, proceeds from the latter quest and that for St Martin experienced such sharp declines that both ended up taking a permanent backseat to the other quests.[412] Even more remarkable is the sudden surge to prominence of a quest that had previously been one of the smaller campaigns. In 1477 the rent on the St Theobald quest increased three- or fourfold,[413] after which it was this campaign and that for St Cornelius that ranked first. From that point on until around 1525, the proportionality of rents remained constant, with the quests for St Cornelius and St Theobald together furnishing a little under half, the three medium-sized quests for St Hubert, St Anthony and St Quirinus slightly over a third, and the other three, for St Martin, Our Lady and the minor collection for the Blessed Sacrament, the remaining one-sixth portion.[414] Particularly striking and, it would seem, unusual is the fact that the cathedral's own quest – that for St Martin – should have accounted for such a small part of the total quest income.[415]

It is worth noting once again that receipts from each quest were net sums. The pardoner leasing the quest from the cathedral chapter still had his expenses to pay, including the fee to the abbey (the amount of which is only recorded for the St Hubert quest), fees for having documents sealed by the bishop's vicar-general and the costs incurred by himself and his aides (of which we have no records).[416]

Before 1526, rents for all quests were contracted in gold coin; specifically, from 1442 on, in the gold rhinegulden. Usually the masters of the fabric calculated a standard exchange rate based on the money of account, though under exceptional circumstances, such as during war or upheaval, they could be accommodating and apply a lower rate *ex speciali gratia capituli* (as a special favour from the chapter).[417] By drawing up accounts in gold rhinegulden, this fundamental source of income could be shielded from the constant depreciation of the silver wit, later stuiver, that formed the basis of the monetary system in the 'Sticht', the bishop's temporal territory. The consequences this had for the financial position of the cathedral fabric shall be explored presently; for now it will suffice to note that the rise in quest revenues, as expressed in the money of account, was due in part to purely monetary factors. Yet even when expressed in gold rhinegulden and not in the money of account, which depreciated in tandem with the base silver monetary unit (the rhinegulden current), rents prior to 1526 show a clear, if not steady, upward trend. Table 1 illustrates this trend in relation to the rents in gold rhinegulden from the quests for Sts Cornelius and Hubert.

From around 1526 onwards, quest rents were no longer contracted in gold rhinegulden, but instead in the prevailing money of account, the karolusgulden.[418] This had the effect of forcing quest proceeds to depreciate in parallel with the coin on which the monetary system was based, that is to say the stuiver. Even rents entered in the money of account show a sharp downward trend, as represented in Table 1.[419]

Initially, the deterioration of the quests revealed itself not only in a decline of rents, but even more so in chronic defaulting on payments. The administrative organization of the fabric rolls makes it easy for us to trace this progression. In them, amounts due were always entered under the receipts as if they had actually been paid in full; rents that remained in arrears were then tallied under the heading '*restancie in receptis computate*' (back items, registered under receipts) and so deducted from the income.[420] Before around 1524 it was rare for pardoners to be unable to meet their payment obligations.[421] For reasons unknown to us, they defaulted on comparatively large sums between the years 1396 and 1413, but almost all paid these debts off in the subsequent years.[422] Another collapse between 1464 and 1469 did have a lasting impact, however, and although the debts concerned on this occasion were all in themselves insignificant, they did at least in part have to be forgiven. Plague, famine and opposition from Holland's urban centres were presumably to blame for this brief setback.[423] The war of 1481-83, which paralysed all economic activity in the diocesan region for years, also ate into quest proceeds for a time, but most of these debts were ultimately settled.[424]

Payment defaults after around 1524 present an altogether different picture.[425] Back payments were not only larger, but also took on a

TABLE 1 Rents from the St Cornelius and St Hubert quests as expressed in gold rhine-gulden, 1396-1526.

ST.-CORNELIUSQUEST		ST.-HUBERTUSQUEST	
		1396	**90 gold rhinegulden**
		1400	**25**
		1401-1414	**58**
		1424	**150**
		1436	**58**
		1442	**92**
1436	**80 gold rhinegulden**	1443	**100**
1442	**138**	1445	**110**
1445-1459?	**251 1/2**	1450-1475	**200**
1460	**261 1/2**		
1461	**281 1/2**		
1462	**291 1/2**		
1463-1474	**300**		
1475-1481	**325**	1475-1488	**240**
1482-1498	**500**	1488-1493	**270**
1499-1518	**400**	1494-1498	**350**
1519-1523	**470**	1499-1514	**300**
		1515-1523	**310**
1524-1526	**400**	1524-1526	**380**
Expressed in karolus-gulden, 1526-1558			
1526	**400 gold rhinegulden = 560 karolusgulden** [418]	1526	**380 gold rhinegulden = 532 karolusgulden** [418]
1527	**300**	1527	**470**
1530	**200**	1528-1529	**200**
1531	**170**	1530	**300**
1532-1535	**160**	1531	**320**
1536-1540	**200**	1532	**225**
1541-1542	**160**	1533-1542	**260**
1544-1545	**100**	1544	**150**
1548-1554	**90**	1445-1550	**145**
1555-1557	**70**	1551-1555	**125**
1558	**50**	1556-1558	**85**

chronic aspect: between 1522 and 1563 virtually not a year went by in which the fabric did not have one or more pardoners in the red. Old debts were not being settled as they once had been, and only 12 percent of all arrears arising between 1522 and 1532 were paid back within that same period. It is curious that the cathedral fabric waited until fairly late to make a severe downward adjustment in the rents, and thus to recognize that quest proceeds were not likely to recover. At first, the decline was considered merely the backwash of a temporary crisis. On 31 March 1522 the cathedral fabric granted all pardoners (with the exception of the Antonines) a reduction in their rent '*propter magnam caristiam, propter doctrinam magistri Martini Lutheri, propter guerras transysulanas, ubi non potuerunt habere cursum*' (due to the expense of provisions, due to the spread of the teachings of Martin Luther, due to the wars in the Oversticht, where the quests could not be conducted).[426] The canons appear not to have realized that they were juxtaposing incommensurate factors to explain this early decline in quest revenues. As the quests continued to lose ground, it became clear that the trend was not to be reversed. The quest for the Blessed Sacrament was not leased again after 1536, and 1543 saw the end of the quests for St Martin and Our Lady.[427] In the chapter minutes, amendments made to the lease terms were substantiated with the formulaic entry '*propter mala tempora et sectas lutheranas*' (due to the evil times and the followers of Luther). A little later the chapter opted to farm out different quests in combination, given that exploiting each one separately was no longer profitable.[428] The last receipt from quest monies to be entered in the rolls dates to 1563 (fig. 76). It is possible that the official Church ban on granting indulgences in exchange for money, issued by the Council of Trent on 16 July 1562, arrived as the final blow to Utrecht's questing establishment.[429] Whatever the case may be, in 1567 we find the chapter substantiating the foundation of new revenue sources for the fabric with the loss of quest income: '*amissio fructuum quondam ex questibus provenientium, etiam per Concilium Tridentinum sublatorum ac condemnatorum*' (the loss of revenues that previously issued from the quests, these also being abolished and condemned by the Council of Trent).[430]

Comparison of the linear progression of profits from the *reporta-*

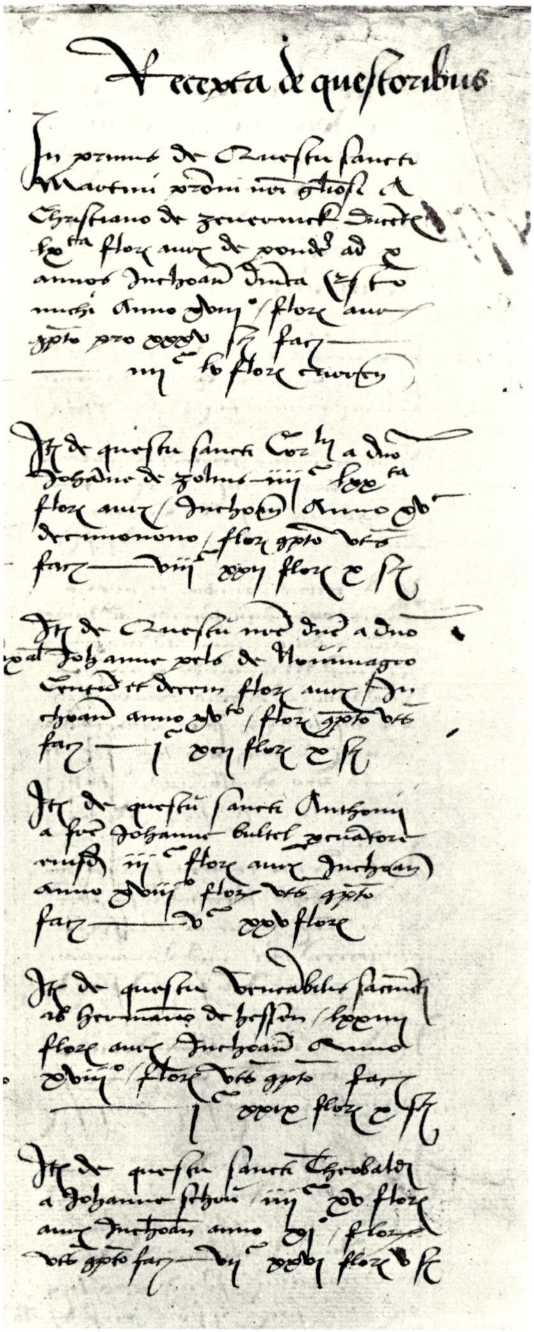

Recepta de questoribus

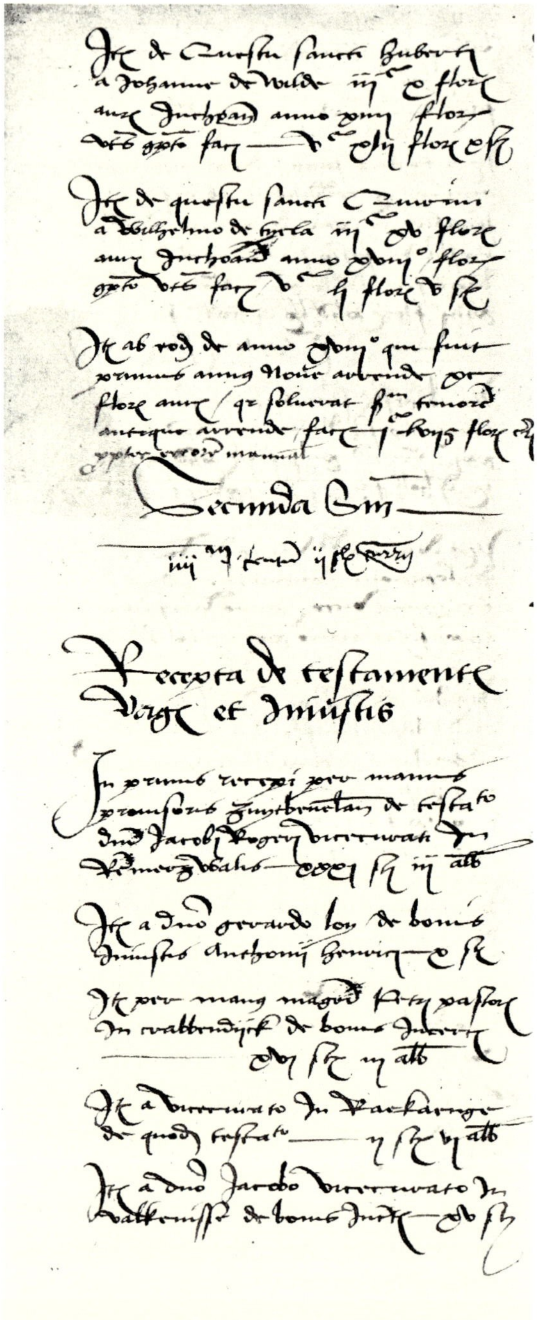

Secunda Sum[ma]

Recepta de testamentis legatis et dimissis

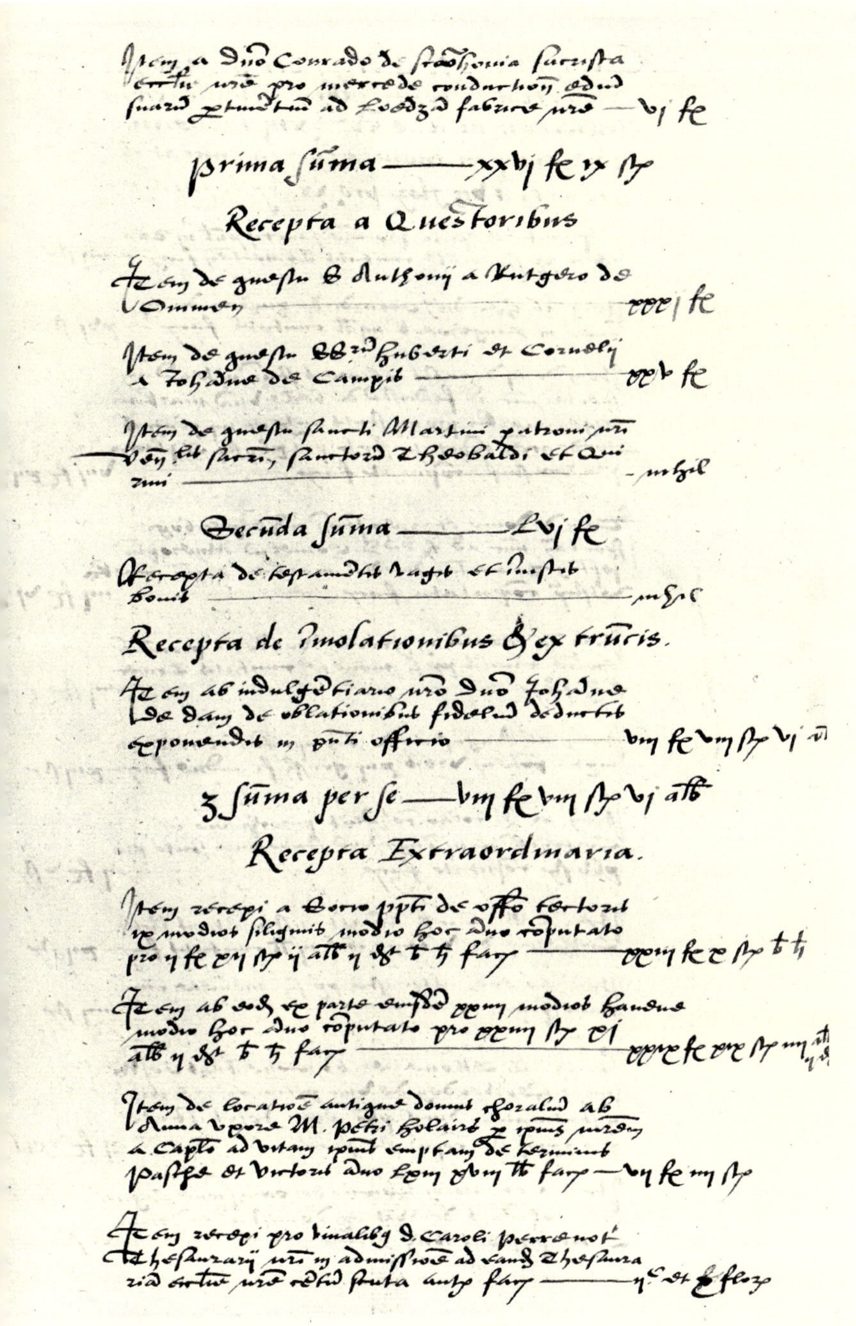
prima suma
Recepta a Questoribus
Secunda suma
Recepta de Imolationibus & ex truncis.
Recepta Extraordinaria.

76
Quest receipts in the fabric accounting years 1520/21 and 1563/64
Pages from the Utrecht Cathedral fabric rolls
The Utrecht Archives

In 1520 quest receipts peaked at 4102 rhinegulden current. This sum is comprised of the rents and admission fees for the quests for St Martin (455 rhinegulden-current), St Cornelius (822½ rhinegulden-current), Nostra Domina (192½ rhinegulden-current), St Anthony (525 rhinegulden current), Venerabile Sacramentum (129½ rhinegulden-current), St Theobald (726½ rhinegulden-current), St Hubert (542½ rhine-gulden-current) and St Quirinus (551½ and 157½ rhinegulden-current). The year 1563/64 was the last in which quest receipts were registered, with a profit of only 56 karolusgulden: 31 from the quest for St Anthony and 25 from those for St Hubert and St Cornelius combined.

LITERATURE
Bronnen bouwgeschiedenis, vol. 2 (3), pp. 474, 827; *Inventaris Archief kapittel ten Dom*, no. 651, vols 7 and 11.

tiones versus those from the quests reveals a striking difference. Contributions from the *reportationes* show a slow, gradual decline that in any case had already set in by the first year of the extant records (1395-96). Revenues from the quests, by contrast, continued to rise throughout the fifteenth century, peaking around 1525 – and then all but collapsed before the next ten years were out.[431] In Utrecht, as in many other dioceses, confidence in the age-old, seemingly popular devotions suffered a swift and lasting blow. '*Vehementer ubique frigere coepit res indulgentiarum*' (the system of indulgences is coming to a ubiquitous standstill), Erasmus wrote in 1529.[432] The teachings of Martin Luther made a huge impact also in these parts. Devotions and indulgences, with their blatant links to all manner of financial interests, came to be completely discredited.[433] So thoroughly had the image of the pardoner and trader in indulgences engraved itself in the collective memory that even long after their disappearance they continued to form a subject of ridicule and satire (fig. 77).

SEVEN INCOME FROM PROPERTY: RENTS AND ANNUITIES

Profits on estates and houses owned by the cathedral fabric, or the rights thereto, were never of any significance during the period covered by the extant rolls, though it is possible that they were somewhat higher in the fourteenth century. The extent of its holdings is known to us from a 93-item list prefacing each of the accounts, representing a kind of register or memorandum of income from immoveable property. The list was first compiled around 1365 and updated in chronological fashion until 1407. Up through 1508 it was copied over unchanged each year under the heading '*hii sunt certi redditus, spectantes ad fabricam ecclesie Trajectensis*' (these are the fixed revenues, intended for the fabric of the cathedral).[434] In examining the rolls, we learn that only 13 of those 93 items ever yielded the fabric fund any income – at least after 1395/96, this being the year of the oldest preserved roll – and that even these 13 items were not paid on a regular basis or, eventually, at all.[435] The meagre return on these old possessions, supplemented with a few immoveable properties and rights acquired after

1407, were entered jointly under the receipts heading '*recepta de certis redditibus*' (receipts from fixed revenues). This was the category used to record outstanding amounts, not those actually received. Revenues that proved uncollectible were subsequently recorded as outstanding debts under the expenses heading '*hec sunt restancie, superius per me in receptis computate*' (these are items in arrears, which I counted with the revenues above) to correct the overvalued income. Were any of these *restancie* paid in later years, they would be entered as receipts under the heading '*recepta de restanciis*' (receipts from items in arrears).[436] Thanks to this bookkeeping system, we have a clear view of the degree to which the fabric's fixed income suffered from chronic non-payment.

The root of this problem might plausibly be sought in the physical impossibility of devising an even moderately effective system for managing a body of geographically dispersed holdings, each meant to supply a small amount of income.[437] In this respect the handful of city houses that the fabric owned, like its few estates of any note, generated few difficulties.[438] A second factor contributing to payment defaults were the crisis situations that ensued after war or flooding, though these were as short-lived as they were sudden.[439] During and immediately following the years of Utrecht's civil war (1481-83), for example, not a single debtor possessed the wherewithal to pay.

Compounding the problem were monetary factors. Various of the fixed revenues were affected by inflation in the money of account. Of the eleven lease and tenancy agreements that have been examined, seven were secured against currency depreciation by being registered in gold coin or a money of account anchored in the gold coin; in the latter case, however, the value of the money of account nevertheless sometimes lost that basis.[440]

Finally, there was one other, entirely different reason why net revenues from property holdings yielded less than the already modest gross revenues would lead us to suppose. Many of these immoveable properties and valuable rights had been gifted or assigned to the fabric under onerous contracts, meaning that a portion of the profit had to be used to pay for a memorial service, an eternal light or the like. Payments for these obligations are listed as expenditures under the head-

77
Print satirizing the decadence of the Roman Catholic church Three leaves, 440 x 1410 mm. By Robert de Baudous (1574/75-after 1659); published by Jacob de Gheyn (1565-1625), dated 1605 Accompanied by a Dutch poem in 36 stanzas by Pauwels de Kempenaer (1552 or 1555-after 1620), four leaves, 230 x 11410 mm Fragments from the left-hand, the right-hand and centre leaves of the print Amsterdam, Rijksprentenkabinet; Rotterdam, Museum Boijmans Van Beuningen (version with text)

As late as 1605 - many years after the Reformation had taken root in the Northern Netherlands - three refugees from the Southern Netherlands now working in Holland produced this fiercely anti-Catholic engraving satirizing the medieval Church, elucidated by a long verse with which it was published. The print shows a church building peopled with misshapen figures who are engaged in Catholic ceremonies and all manner of devotions. The main point of criticism was the corruption of the Catholic

Church in both holy and profane matters: *'omnia sunt nummis venalia, sacra, profana'* - incense, prayers, the mass, baptism, rosaries, bulls, churches, priests, altars, wax, crosses, holy oil, saliva, ashes, mitres, relics, merits, indulgences, the Lamb of God, the keys to Heaven, Heaven, Christ and God himself.
The fragment from the left-hand leaf depicts a procession in which the statue of St Martin is borne aloft, perhaps in parody of the quest for St Martin.
The fragment from the right-hand leaf depicts a shrine with relics of St Anthony (identifiable by the tau cross) carried by clerics, intended as a satirical representation of the Antonine pardoners.
The fragment from the centre leaf shows a large offertory chest on the right, with behind it the cross and instruments of the Passion, accompanied by the text *'Aflaten der sonden'* (indulgences for sin), such as were typically erected during the major papal crusade indulgence campaigns.
To the left of this are two tables on which various items are exhibited, including Church letters and bulls in which spiritual benefits are offered in return for

hard cash: '*oorlofft*[*ot*] *trouwen*' (permission to marry; this may refer to lifting interdicts for Church marriages) and '*bulle om vleesch te eten*' (bull to eat meat). On the left, on the table with the text '*'t groot craem*' (the great booth) are bulls and letters with '*verdienste*' (merits), '*dispensa*[*tio*]' (dispensations), '*perdo*[*n*]' (pardons), '*oorloff om te sondigen*' (permission to sin), '*indulgentie*' (indulgences), '*vergevinge der sonden*' (forgiveness of sins), '*overschietende wercken*' (surplus works) and '*taxatie der sonden*' (appraisal of sins) (perhaps the *casus reservati*: '[...] *soo dat gheen quaet bedreven noyt en was soo groot of 't wert hier om ghelt vergheven*' (such that no evil act was ever so great that it could not here be forgiven for money).

LITERATURE

F. Muller, *Nederlandsche Historieplaten*, vol. 1, Amsterdam 1863, no. 432; Eekhof 1909, p. CXVI and illustration.

ing '*in pensionibus fabrice*' (annual payments by the fabric), '*in pensionibus prebende defunctorum*' (annual payments charged to prebends of the deceased), '*pro candelis*' (for candles) or payments to the *Camera Minor*.[441]

Relationships between a given revenue and the obligation entailed upon it are only clearly manifested in the new revenues that continued to augment the fabric's modest holdings – at least until 1520.[442] Items in this category were less donations to the fabric than capitular allocations of specific revenues and connected financial payouts. Between 1490 and 1520 the fabric was assigned an especially large number of revenues (tithes from Jutfaas,[443] an annual *pensio* from the parish of Sassenheim for the singing choir,[444] annuities purchased by the States of the Nedersticht)[445] in connection with certain complex, large-scale financial transactions undertaken in these years by the cathedral chapter, which will be discussed further below.

Over the course of time, the fabric's rights and obligations became so murky that in 1526 the chapter decided to step in and simplify matters by transferring equal shares of income and obligations to the accounts of the *Camera Minor*.[446]

In 1556 the fabric registered a small rise in revenues when the old building lodge, now no longer needed, was leased for 6 karolusgulden.[447]

EIGHT FINANCING TRANSACTIONS: THE CATHEDRAL FABRIC AS LENDER AND BORROWER

Up until this point, we have focused mainly on sources of income in the narrow sense. But the cathedral fabric was also regularly involved in financial transactions directly or indirectly related to acquiring or providing long- or short-term credit, which carried the potential for considerable receipts and expenditures. Such credit transactions were typically cast in complex legal moulds. The Church ban on charging interest (regarded as usury) led to the development of arrangements that in economic terms came down to the provision of credit, but nevertheless managed to uphold canonical precepts. Where the cathedral fabric was concerned, matters tended to be further complicated by the fact that the other administrative chambers were also involved in these credit transactions. This makes it particularly difficult to distinguish the boundaries setting off strictly internal payments, identified as separate revenues in the section on capitular contributions above.

Generally speaking, we have a clear view of the economic impact these transactions had on the financial position of the cathedral fabric. Stated very simply, the method used to provide credit in return for remuneration without running afoul of canon law was based on an arrangement in which the lender secured a fixed periodic remuneration by giving a principal to the borrower, who then pledged to make payments to the lender.[448] This annual or semi-annual remuneration could be based on any of various kinds of underlying agreements. It could be tied to the life of one or more individuals, in which case it was called a life annuity. A lender could purchase a life annuity by laying out a certain sum of money, ranging from eight to around sixteen times an agreed annual distribution, depending on whether it was vested in the life of an older or younger person or in one or more people. In the case of a hereditary annuity, which did not expire with the owner, the purchase price could climb to 24 or more times the periodic remuneration. Annuities from land and houses were usually secured in the same way, except that here the immoveable property or value-bearing entitlement served as security, thus resembling our modern system of mortgage lending. Life annuities were usually redeemable, and hereditary annuities always were, meaning that the party making the periodic payout was entitled to redeem the annuity contract by paying off the principal. The person receiving the payments, by contrast, could not cancel the contract.[449] These kinds of arrangements made it possible for public bodies such as cities but also church fabrics, hospitals and other institutions to lend large sums of money, variously with or without providing private property and rights as collateral.

What concerns us here, however, is not the legal form of these credit transactions, but their financial consequences for the economy of the cathedral fabric. It is important to note in this context that particularly in the sixteenth century, the chapter wielded the fabric fund as a welcome means for facilitating a much wider spectrum of financial activities.

We can distinguish two main categories of transactions, based on whether the fabric had a surplus of funds or a shortage, and within each of these categories a further two subcategories.[450] In cases of a surplus of funds, the cathedral fabric could acquire profitable real estate or a value-bearing entitlement to enlarge its income from capital (investment), or it could redeem one of its own financial obligations by refunding the principal to the creditor (debt redemption). If, on the other hand, the fabric needed funds, it could or had to contract money by selling life or redeemable annuities, possibly providing immoveable property as collateral (loan), or alternatively it could either alienate property components, resulting in the loss of future years' revenues, or redeem annuities by collecting principal sums. In the section that follows, we will examine one or more examples of each type of financial transaction, keeping in mind that there was usually some variation in the way affairs were actually conducted in practice.

1 • FUND SURPLUSES

When the fabric accounts closed with a credit balance, this surplus was usually booked as income in the next year's account. However, in the years shortly before and after 1500, the cathedral canons used a large share of the fabric's credit balances to make liquid funds available to the chapter and, more especially, to the States of the Nedersticht, in the activities of which the cathedral chapter was closely involved.[451] In 1492, for example, the cathedral fabric paid 312 gold rhinegulden current to help redeem a debt that the States of the Nedersticht had contracted from Jurgen Rotteler, adviser and chamberlain to Archduke Maximilian. The debt had been contracted when he lent 1500 rhinegulden to the States in order to settle the debt owed to Frederik van IJsselstein, who had supported Bishop David of Burgundy during the civil war (1481-83).[452] In return for its contribution, the cathedral fabric was paid an annuity of 24 gold rhinegulden from the States treasury,[453] which it continued to collect for twelve years. When the annuity was redeemed in 1504, however, the fabric received nothing of the principal, as might have been expected.[454] Insofar as we can tell, it seems the cathedral fabric did not merely provide financing, but actually helped sponsor the States. The fabric's role in financing the war that the States of the Nedersticht waged against Floris van IJsselstein was similarly imposed from outside.[455] Here the States sold redeemable annuity certificates at 'the sixteenth penny' (*de penning 16*, or at 6.25% interest) for a sum of up to 34,000 rhinegulden current, offering as collateral the revenues from the Hinderdam, a system of sluices in the river Vecht, and the city of Utrecht's excise tax on wine and flour.[456] The cathedral chapter used the fabric treasury to purchase a credit share of 3212 ½ rhinegulden current, or nearly ten percent of the entire loan.[457] From 1513/14 the fabric treasury was further burdened with payouts on a series of redeemable annuities worth around 180 rhinegulden held by several canons, which were likewise funded '*ex redditibus emptis a tribus statibus*' (from receipts purchased from the Three States);[458] presumably these canons had deposited their principals in the war fund as well. In return for purchasing the redeemable annuity certificates and making the annual associated remuneration to the canons, the fabric received a '*pensio annua ex redditibus a tribus statibus emptis*' (annual payment from the receipts purchased from the Three States) from 1515/16 onwards of almost 358 rhinegulden current, representing an ordinary return of altogether almost six percent.[459] After 1548/49 this *pensio* disappears from the rolls, however. It is unlikely that the cathedral fabric ever got back the principal paid to redeem these annuities.[460] It would thus appear that these profit-bearing investments of cathedral fabric monies conceal what was actually a drain on fabric resources to fund causes of an entirely different order – and although the fabric got to collect distributions for a certain period, it rarely got back the principal. In general, though, these types of transactions were rare.

On more than one occasion, we see the fabric spending money to redeem certain financial burdens. In 1505 the fabric had acquired several tithes in Jutfaas that generated between 50 and 170 rhinegulden a year, whilst being encumbered with a yearly remuneration of 145 gold rhinegulden current. In 1514 and 1518 the masters of the cathedral fabric bought off the annual fee with a combined sum 20 times that of the remuneration ('the twentieth penny'), amounting to over 2900 gold rhinegulden current, or the average needed to fund building for about a year.[461] From time to time the fabric paid off redeemable annuities against the 'sixteenth penny' in the same manner.[462]

2 • A NEED FOR FUNDS

The customary method by which ecclesiastical and secular institutions borrowed money was through the sale of hereditary and life annuities.[463] Yet it was but seldom that the masters of the fabric opted for this simple approach.[464] The reason why has to do with the fact that the chapter disposed over a steady inflow of endowments, the fruits of which were designated to pay for memorial services for deceased brethren. The cathedral statute books prescribed that any canon, and later also chantry priest, who wished to be buried in the cathedral church had to establish an obit. The minimum payout on such obits was set at 1 oude schild, and custom dictated that each canon had to deposit a principal sum worth at least 20 to 25 times this amount from the proceeds of his *annus gratiae* (annual fruits from a prebend after the canon's death) in the *Camera Minor* treasury, which was charged with administering obit endowments.[465] With these cash resources at its disposal, the *Camera Minor* was on various occasions able to supply credit to the fabric. Purchases of paraments were financed with the obit endowments in 1407 – doubtless with the cognizance and consent of the chamberlain of the *Camera Minor* – when three canons deposited the principal sums for their respective obits – twentyfold the aggregate of 5 oude schilden – in the fabric treasury.[466] In return, the cathedral fabric paid 5 oude schilden to the *Camera Minor* each year thereafter.[467]

Endowments of this kind were given not only for obits but also for other types of foundations: a meal for the canons each year on Laetare Sunday (mid-Lent),[468] three lamps to be kept burning through the night[469] or sermons on each of four feast days framed by church bells ringing and choral song.[470] In these instances it was not the chamberlain of the *Camera Minor*, but perhaps the treasurer or choral master who was charged with the arrangements and, as such, received the associated annual dues paid by the cathedral fabric.

Last but not least, the masters of the cathedral fabric could generate necessary cash resources by liquidating a profitable component of its property. In many cases this was not an option for the simple reason that the fabric did not own sufficient property. We need only recall the sale of the house on the St Jansveld in Utrecht for 125 gold rhinegulden in 1500; the annual profit on the lease was 5 gold rhinegulden, representing a return of four percent.[471] Sometimes the masters of the fabric had to stand by as debtors redeemed their annuities. Thus, in 1502/03 an annuity of 35 rhinegulden current paid to the fabric from the common treasury of the States of Utrecht on the four Ember days each year since 1490 was redeemed by the debtors, the *deputati ciste* (deputies of the chest), at thirteen times the annuity – 'the thirteenth penny' – for a sum of 455 rhinegulden current.[472] On rare occasions such transactions concerned a claustral house. Given their unique legal status, the sale of these types of residences could become a complex affair. The cathedral chapter's sixteen claustral houses were residences that belonged to, or were at any rate intended for, the canons. Surrounding the immunity of the Dom (as at the other collegiate churches), they were what lent the cathedral close its secluded character.[473] Each canon held a restricted property right to his house: he could dispose over the dwelling as he wished, under the understanding that it could only be sold to a fellow canon or the chapter.[474] The selling canon was then entitled to the amelioration, that is to say the profit on the sale of the house after deduction of the capitalized value of all charges on it, with the latter almost always established on the residence to pay for a memorial service.[475] The new owner accepted the liability to pay the entitled parties the *pensio* (the sum of all charges) attached to the house. Occasionally, the cathedral fabric received the amelioration on a house, in other words the net profit, variously with or without onerous conditions.[476] It also happened that the fabric gained possession of a claustral residence itself. A single example will suffice to show the intricate financial transactions this could entail. In 1507 the chapter acquired ownership of a large claustral house, apparently for the fabric's benefit. The cathedral canons sold this house to Margaretha van Broeckhuysen '*haer leven lanck duerende ende nyet langer*' (for her lifetime, but not longer) for 100 oude schilden (or 262 gold rhinegulden); she further committed to payment of a total of 17 oude schilden from the house in annual fees to the *Camera Minor* and the treasurer. The fabric collected the purchase price of 100 oude schilden, but at the same time took on the responsibility of funding Margaretha's memorial service for 4 oude schilden after her death. In fact, the widow was effectively providing credit to the fabric in a manner as sketched above.[477] Following her death, the chapter sold the house to the canon Dirk van Drakenburch. Though he did not actually pay a purchase price, he did bind himself to pay the annual fees and additionally to have certain structural renovations carried out. Moreover, upon his death the property amelioration would not fall to his estate, but to the cathedral fabric.[478] Not until that time then – in 1522/23 – did the fabric collect the purchase price of 300 rhinegulden current.[479]

What impact did these financial transactions have on the financing for cathedral-building, whether positive or negative? To begin with, it is clear from the data that it was only during the most prosperous phase of its existence, thus in the quarter-century between 1499 and 1525, that the cathedral fabric had a major hand in financial transactions.[480] Where it lent funds, it was usually *mandato capituli* (at the chapter's behest).[481] Its borrowing activity, for instance in the form of large capital sums for obits, was similarly restricted solely to these years.[482] Secondly, it is interesting to note that within this 25-year time span, the aggregate of capital receipts did not much exceed the sum of all money spent on redemptions and investments. Nevertheless, the balance did tip towards the positive. The fabric acquired credit and sold immoveable property to a total worth of around 11,300 rhinegulden current[483] and invested and redeemed annuities for a sum of around 7800 rhinegulden current.[484] Overall, therefore, the extent to which the fabric borrowed money and liquidated assets was of relatively little significance even during the period in which building activity was greatest. At times that the fabric had an acute need of cash, however, these were its only options. The enormous expenditures for bells in 1505, for instance, had to be financed with the sale of a life annuity and the receipt of endowments for several obits. Nearly 20 percent of the funds needed in that year were obtained in this way.[485]

At this point in time, the payment of costs tied to these principal sums did not yet present any difficulties since the regular income, mainly quest monies, generated more than enough to cover them. But after around 1526, the fabric's and chapter's financial circumstances degenerated into a state of upheaval and malaise. The fabric was unable to complete its periodic payouts in 1528/29,[486] and from 1532 on it had to cease its payouts to the *Camera Minor* due to its abominable financial position.[487] Not until 1570, when the St Martin prebend was designated to the fabric treasury, could these distributions be resumed.[488]

NINE THE SALE OF BUILDING MATERIALS AND CHURCH TREASURE

A final category, though not a source of income in the proper sense, was the return on sales of surplus or old building material. Many rolls include financial statements submitted by the architects (*'des loedzmeysters ceedel'*)[489] listing the sale of small stocks of building materials such as timber, lead, slates, blocks of stone suitable for tombstones and so on. Every once in a while the cathedral fabric donned the guise of trader in building materials as a service to individuals and bodies that needed exact quantities of certain hard-to-get materials. The resulting profits could be fairly substantial. It goes without saying that when building operations began to ebb in 1526, the value of this income category witnessed a swift decline.[490]

The dramatic melting down of the cathedral's ecclesiastical silver in 1577 and 1578 may be on a par with the sale of building materials from an economic standpoint – given that both concern the alienation of moveable assets – but is vastly different in terms of the underlying motives and ensuing consequences. The sale of some precious item from the treasury in order to pay off debt or even finance a building campaign was not an unusual occurrence in and of itself;[491] indeed, in the early medieval period, sales from the *thesaurus* (treasure) were even the method of choice for generating fast cash for building.[492]

The decision to melt down all of the cathedral treasure (or at least the items that were not consecrated) came as a result of political events. As early as 18 June 1577, the cathedral canons agreed to melt silver objects worth 1000 karolusgulden into coin, '*anmerckende den hogen noot van gelde ende die grote necessiteyt die de fabrijck* [...] *eijsschende is*', especially in connection with the damage that had been sustained by the tower during shelling from the castle of Vredenburg.[493] On 30 June, following an unsuccessful attempt to sell certain estates, they added a further sum of 1400 to 1500 karolusgulden. We do not know whether they ever followed through on these decisions; whatever the case may be, the sums were not settled via the fabric fund.[494]

On 17 and 18 February 1578, the chapter decided to liquidate silverwork once more in order to coin up to 8000 karolusgulden for the redemption of annuities. A committee was appointed to make the arrangements a day later,[495] and work set off apace. Complaining of the overtime he had had to put in, the secretary enumerated: '*op diversche dagen ende stonden ende meestendeel bij nacht, jae geheele nachte over heeft geassisteert*'.[496] There was ample cause for this haste. It seems the chapter had gotten wind – just in time – of plans conceived by the governor-general, Archduke Matthias, to claim all unconsecrated silver in every church and cloister in Utrecht, melt it down and mortgage the proceeds to the States-General, primarily '*tot betalinge van de ruyteren en knechten*'.[497] The governor-general announced these plans by a letter from Antwerp dated 19 February 1578; on 25 February commissioners were appointed in Utrecht to draw up inventories of its churches and cloisters.[498] When they arrived at the sacristy of the cathedral on 8 March, they found that four-fifths of the treasure had already been melted down... in behalf of the chapter.[499] They made up an inventory of the remainder, which included the famous Nativity scene bequeathed by Bishop David of Burgundy; everything on this list was melted down on 16 May, with the States-General receiving its share of the proceeds.[500]

For all that the cathedral fabric '*zoe zeer ten achteren was, zelfs geen raet en wisten, om heur kerk dicht ende in notelyke reparatien te onderhouden'*,[501] it saw scarcely anything of the wealth generated by the chapter's liquidation of the cathedral treasure. Of a yield of 16,187 karolusgulden (which was five times the fabric's annual budget in these years), more than 40 percent was used to redeem annuities. In the 1577/78, 1578/79 and 1579/80 accounting years, the fabric received no more than slightly above 2700 karolusgulden. Despite its comparatively small worth, this money did provide an important boost, contributing around 30 percent of the fabric's income in these years.[502]

Today almost nothing is left of Utrecht Cathedral's once rich treasury. All the famed works that the fabric funded at great expense over many decades in bygone centuries were sacrificed to the melting pot: the reliquary shrine of St Agnes, the shrine of St Pontian, the silver *capsae* for the head of St Adrian, the head and arm of St Blaise and the silver candelabra from the high altar. The same fate befell the precious items donated by private parties.[503] The Dom lost more inventory than any of the other collegiate churches. There is no doubt that the haste with which the cathedral chapter set to work supplying finances – for its own ends especially – carries some of the blame.[504]

THE FINANCING OF BUILDING AND FURNISHING UTRECHT CATHEDRAL

There are a variety of graphical ways of representing the cathedral fabric's receipts and expenditures in the period between 1395 and 1580.[505] Here, receipts are expressed in – or converted into – the money of account used longest in the cathedral fabric rolls, that is, the rhinegulden current (graph 1). However, as these amounts are not adjusted for inflation in the money of account, we must be cautious when drawing conclusions; the value of these graphs lies chiefly in providing a clear overview of the relative significance of difference income sources. The graph representation of the fabric's total expenditures – including those incurred by the building lodge and general, unrelated expenses – is likewise shown in the money of account, that is, the rhinegulden current (graph 2). When the various expense categories for building and furnishings are translated into the annual wages of the *famulus in loedsa*, or building lodge assistant,[506] the resulting graph allows us to track real ups and downs (graph 5), without the effects of the substantial inflation in the money of account in some decades.

We can distinguish four periods in the financial history of the cathedral fabric. In the first, running until around 1500,[507] its constellation of revenues contain comparatively few components. The relative value of the *reportationes* diminishes, whilst that of the quest monies sees strong growth. Credit transactions and internal settlements play no major part as yet. A period of prosperity follows and holds for a quarter century. Income patterns become complex in character. It is only during this period that we encounter bequests of any magnitude. The chapter takes on greater financial obligations for the building works. Its cautious spending policy further yields credit balances – sometimes large ones – and thus a substantial augmentation of available resources in the next accounting year (graph 4). More than anything, however, the internal payments and credit transactions determine the value of gross income in these years. Having assembled the most varied constellation of revenues possible, the chapter achieves its aim of generating monetary resources for the cathedral fabric. And then, rather abruptly, this period of prosperity comes to an end. Accounts kept in the years after 1525 show signs of severe budgetary crisis. The sharp decline in quest monies is the most important cause, but by no means the only one. This crisis, initially treated as a temporary setback, would in fact prove to be chronic. The chapter's miscalculation of its nature finds clear expression in the large debit balances and many and high *restancie* figures.

In general, deficits occurred where unforeseen circumstances disturbed the balance between expenditures and receipts; here, *restancie* were used to compensate for income booked under receipts but never actually collected.[508] As we might expect, large *restancie* typically went hand in hand with high debit balances. As graphs 3 and 4 show, it was not until after 1525/26 that *restancie* and debit balances took on a chronic aspect; they had occurred only sporadically before then, such as during the war years of 1480-82 and at the insolvency of a pardoner in 1498. The *restancie* were made up of unpaid quest monies, first and foremost, and also of outstanding contributions from the chapter and distributions issuing from credit transactions. Up until 1536, debtors, and pardoners in particular, did still repay small portions of their debts, around thirteen percent, and any amounts that remained outstanding were subsequently written off.

Not until the 1550s did the cathedral fabric regain a certain equilibrium, albeit at a considerably lower level than before. In this fourth period, proceeds from the quests and *reportationes* shrank to almost nothing, to be replaced by chapter-allocated revenues that would even come to dominate the budget in the decades leading up to the Reformation. The canons showed themselves willing to go beyond the call of duty to supply funds for outfitting the cathedral, and the fabric's last large expenditures, for the choir stalls and the large organ, were financed with capitular contributions.

In the discussion concerning different income sources above we already touched on how the monetary system impacted the value of revenues.[509] We will now turn to examine in greater depth the nature and mechanisms of that monetary system and how it affected cathedral-building financing. Accounts were kept in a money of account, that is, an artificial unit of account, into which all receipts and expenditures in real coin were converted. This money of account did correspond to a fixed quantity of the real coin in which the monetary system was anchored, however. The money of account functioned as a measure of value, the actual coin as a medium of exchange. In the fabric rolls the coin that served as a basis was a small silver coin, the wit (*albus*), and later the stuiver. From 1395 until 1425 accounts were kept in the pound, worth 8 wits, from 1436 until 1463 in the 30-wit arnoldusgulden current, from 1464 until 1544 in the rhinegulden current, worth 240 wits or 20 stuivers, and after 1545 in karolusgulden worth 25 Utrecht stuivers or 20 Holland stuivers.[510]

The wit and the stuiver were subject, like most late medieval silver petty coin, to a constant, if not steady, reduction in value. That depreciation is evident in the exchange rate with the prevailing international gold coin, which saw relatively little decline in purity and weight, as expressed in the silver base coin. For example, during the politically unstable period of the Utrecht Schism (1423-49), the exchange rate of the gold rhinegulden in circulation (not to be confused with the rhinegulden current used as the money of account) rose from 66 wit to 198 wit.[511] In the Sticht, as elsewhere in Europe, there were therefore two types of coin in circulation: the inflationary small silver coin and its derivatives, and the inflation-proof gold or sometimes large silver coin. Broadly speaking, the first was used in small day-to-day monetary transactions such as wage payments, whilst the second was used in international and interregional commerce and in fixed multi-year financial contracts, such as lease agreements and hereditary or life annuity contracts.[512] There is no need in the present context to delve into explanations for the depreciation – punctuated by the occasional value appreciation – of the basic coin of the Utrecht region.[513] However, the question does arise as to whether and to what extent the cathedral fabric suffered financial setbacks as a result of these variable monetary developments, or conversely even profited from them. The fabric did experience small losses now and then, where cash balances had decreased in value.[514] Over the long term, however, monetary factors in no way negatively impacted fabric finances. Things might have been different had it contracted multi-year agreements for important revenues in the money of account or in its depreciating base coin whilst booking allied payments under expenditures in the inflation-proof gold or silver coin. Such is not the case, however.

The most vital revenues, and especially those established by contract or custom for a succession of years, had to be paid in the prevailing international gold coin, or its equivalent value in another currency.[515] This rule applied in particular to the quest monies, at least until 1526, after which quest revenues began to tumble. As we have seen, quests could be farmed out for as long as 20 years, with the fee fixed in gold coin – after 1442 always the gold rhinegulden. Chapter contributions for the *vinalia* were protected against depreciation, as were the trifling revenues issuing from the redemption of the *pannus*.[516]

The relationship between returns and the currency of payment was more complicated where proceeds from the *reportationes* were concerned. As far as we can tell, rents from the *reportationes* were calculated in stuivers[517] in some parishes and in a gold coin in others, mainly the larger ones.[518] But in almost all cases the *reportationes* were eventually fixed at a certain quantity in the money of account.[519] Contributions from the *reportationes* in Zwolle, for example, were expressed in oude schilden, a money of account set at one and a half times the value of the gold rhinegulden in 1418.[520] After 1464, however, the value of the oude schild was recalculated for the Zwolle contribution at one and a half times the rhinegulden current. By contrast, the value of the oude schild as calculated for *reportationes* from the Oude Kerk (Old Church) in Amsterdam remained pegged to the gold rhinegulden.[521] Where income from rents and distributions on immoveable property was concerned, only a few minor associated duties were fixed in the money of account; the rents themselves were almost always in gold coin.[522] Overall, therefore, income sources which the cathedral fabric contracted for multiple years were protected against depreciation of the silver base currency and the money of account that was based upon it.

The same question arises as regards expenditures: Did monetary factors have an impact on their magnitude? Some expense categories were contracted in gold coin, others were not. Wages and purchases of small quantities of building material were usually paid for in small coin of silver or baser metal. Price development in these categories did not keep pace with the value appreciation of the gold coin: for example, the salary of an unskilled labourer, as expressed in the money of account, rose nearly 60 percent between 1442 and 1525, while the value of the gold rhinegulden, as expressed in stuivers, rose by more than 100 percent in the same period. Purchases of large quantities of stone, by contrast, were almost always contracted in gold coin, in which they were – presumably – also paid; the same was true of the cargo price. Not only is this logical given the international context of these types of transactions, but it was probably also stipulated by stone merchants, who wanted to be paid in a coin that remained relatively stable in value rather than in silver money that was sometimes devaluated several times in the space of a single year.[523] As regards the other expenditures, small annual payouts contracted in the money of account often saw virtually no change for years. Obligations arising from credit transactions were almost always negotiated in gold coin.

On the whole, therefore, we may conclude that though the fabric's receipts and expenditures did not profit from monetary factors, neither did they suffer any detrimental effect.[524]

A representation of the cathedral fabric's expenditures in graph form, in rhinegulden current, between the years 1395 and 1580 presents much the same picture as that of its revenues (graph 2). Deficits or surpluses spanning many years are nowhere in evidence. However, not all expenditures were made for construction, furnishing or upkeep. In the period between 1395/96 and 1524/25, the latter being the last year in which the building lodge operated at full steam, those expenses accounted for an average 65 percent of the budget.[525] After that last year the average fell to around 30 percent. Naturally, this begs the question of what the remaining funds were used for. We find them distributed across various expenditure categories in the fabric rolls: the '*exposita in pensionibus fabrice*' (expenditures for the annual payments charged to the fabric), the '*exposita in pensionibus prebende defunctorum*' (expenditures for the annual payments charged to the prebends of the deceased), the '*exposita pro candelis*' (expenditures for the candles) and the collective heading '*exposita extraordinaria*' (special expenditures).[526] The range of expenses at issue here, not connected with construction and furnishing, can be classified into a few simple categories.

To begin with there were the costs of fabric management and administration, which also included costs of litigation to defend its interests, travel costs and, in general, all outlays related to upholding the fabric's rights and safeguarding its sources of income. Second are expenditures for ecclesiastical services in the cathedral church, such as annual remunerations to Church officials and servants and payments for recurrent activities. Amongst the latter were the fee for the organist (with compensation for his tabard and the rent on his house)[527] and remuneration for the singers (choristers), as well as the costs of decorating the church with greenery on certain feast days. Also reckoned in this category were costs '*pro candelis*', these being precisely defined payments for the lighting of candles or torches on certain occasions and/or specific locations.[528] It may be that these entries represent payments that the fabric was obliged to shoulder in connection with its disposal over endowments for certain foundations. After all, properly speaking, it was the treasurer who was tasked with providing lights in the building, with the principal part of his expenses comprising outlays for wax and oil.[529]

Alongside the above categories came costs attending promotion of the general interests of the cathedral chapter and, by extension, of the States of the Nedersticht, which the cathedral chapter administered.[530] These expenditures were chargeable to the fabric treasury, given that the *prebenda defunctorum* fund incorporated within it could be utilized for '*expense, quas capitulum sibi injunxerat*' (expenditures imposed on it by the chapter).[531] Included in this category were wages for messengers, travel expenses, official expenses, gifts and costs of hospitality, on occasion also taxes, and most especially costs for litigation to defend the chapter's interests. Legal proceedings could drag on for decades and could ultimately be a major drain on the fabric fund, particularly when cases were appealed up through the highest authority.[532]

An entirely different category of expenditures were those issuing from credit transactions, and specifically the annual remunerations in conjunction with endowments or profit-bearing assets assigned to the fabric, on the one hand, and incidental payments made to redeem such remunerations or to make profit-bearing investments, on the other. Items that recurred each year included outlays for individual foundations for candles or lights, the annual remuneration paid to the chamberlain of the *Camera Minor* for arranging obit celebrations[533] and the distribution of hereditary and life annuities. In the sixteenth century this last category so grew in number that from 1526/27 they were given their own new category of '*exposita de redditibus redimibilibus*' (expenditures in connection with [payment of] redeemable annual payments) within the special expenditures.[534]

Finally, there are the expenditures already characterized as internal payments, including subsidies given to other chambers for reasons that are not clear in every case. Between 1460 and 1463 the fabric provided a sum of nearly 2400 gulden worth 30 wit – more than a third of the average building expenses in that period – to help pay off a debit balance on the *Camera Minor*'s accounts from the years 1458-1461.[535] In other years – for reasons not clear to us – the master of the fabric was instructed to transfer credit balances not to his successor but to the chapter or else deposit them '*in archivis*' (in the archive). Between 1488 and 1491, 2070 rhinegulden current disappeared *in archivis*,[536] and between 1491 and 1495 the fabric put 1600 rhinegulden current *ad manus capituli* (at the chapter's disposal).[537] Sometimes the fabric accounts were burdened with costs for capitular building activities unrelated to the cathedral building works[538] or for the purchase of estates.[539] These costs could rise as high as the average annual expenses of the cathedral building lodge.[540]

Taken altogether, these expense categories could cut deeply into the funds available for the building works. In the 1518/19 accounting year, for example, which had the highest total expenditures of the entire period between 1395 and 1580, no more than 30 percent of the budget was spent on construction and furnishings. The fabric borrowed 1125 rhinegulden, 875 of which was earmarked for the purchase of wine, participated in lawsuits for a sum of 250 rhinegulden, bought land for the same amount and spent 194 rhinegulden repairing dykes – all on behalf of the chapter.[541] It also paid off sums it had contracted worth more than 1800 rhinegulden.[542] In 1511/12 the aforementioned loan of 2200 rhinegulden needed to fund the war against the lord of IJsselstein ate up so large a share of the resources that only 19 percent remained to spend on building operations. These years of financial prosperity found the chapter all the more inclined to exploit the fabric for interests unrelated to building and outfitting the cathedral church.

Everything changed after around 1525. In the meagre years that followed, the situation reversed, with other chambers coming to the fabric's aid with temporary or permanent support. This period also saw the chapter taking steps to transfer the burden for fixed expense categories previously always charged to the fabric to other chambers.

Around 1550 the *Bona Divisa* fund was charged with paying the – much reduced – official expenses and costs of legal proceedings.[543] And as late as 1576 the chapter made arrangements to ensure '*ut fabrice in quantum possibile est ab omnibus inutilibus expensis exoneretur atque liberetur*' (that the fabric is discharged and freed, insofar as possible, from all unnecessary expenditures).[544]

Despite the continuous depletion of resources caused by expenditures that were only partly or even wholly unrelated to the cathedral fabric's objectives, up until about 1525 the major share of its budget – the stated average 65 percent – could still be spent on building, maintaining and furnishing the cathedral church. What, then, was the actual scale of the building lodge established at Utrecht Cathedral, and at what pace was it capable of working? In answering this question, our most logical and important source of information is the fabric rolls. Before we turn to consult these data, however, it is essential to briefly sketch the influence that certain aspects of the building operations had on the level of costs.

The construction of the main church of the diocese was a lavish undertaking. The chapter opted to have the structure raised chiefly in stone, which was of course not native to the Northern Netherlands. It goes without saying that the cost of using stone could diverge considerably depending on whether a cathedral was being built near a quarry or a long distance away. The difference in price had to do not only with the additional expense of transport and tolls, but also – and quite crucially – with the manner in which the quarry was exploited. Where a cathedral enjoyed a favourable geographic situation, the chapter could itself exploit a quarry that it leased or owned. Such was the case at the cathedrals of Regensburg[545] and Cologne,[546] where the masons who worked the quarry were in the employ of the cathedral fabric. The fabric of Utrecht Cathedral was rather less well-favoured in this respect. Its stone came chiefly from Bentheim and Westphalia, and to a lesser extent from the Rhineland, particularly from the Siebengebirge (Drachenfels) and the Eiffel. Stone from Brabant and Wallonia were never enough to displace supplies from the east.[547] The chapter had to purchase stone on site at the quarry or else place an order with a stone merchant or buy from his stock. The costs of shipment and tolls were high. Calculations made for the church of Xanten have shown that it would have cost not half as much had it been built closer to the Siebengebirge (where the most important quarries were located).[548] Such calculations are more difficult to make in the case of Utrecht as the cathedral chapter usually obtained stone from fixed suppliers, moulded to match wood templates sent to the merchants for that purpose.[549] On those exceptional occasions when the cathedral canons made an expedition to buy stone on site, such as in 1506/07, the net costs of transport and tolls needed to convey a shipment of stone and slates bought in Koblenz and Cologne to the wharf in Utrecht turn out to be not less than 47 percent of the purchase price.[550]

Factors associated with the purchase of stone applied equally to the purchase of other non-native building materials, including metals such as lead and also timber. How much less money might the cathedral chapter have needed to build the cathedral had it opted for an edifice of brick instead of stone? That is a question to which we have no answer.

Our estimates of the varying scale of cathedral-building operations in Utrecht below will be based solely on sums spent on construction, upkeep and furnishings. Construction costs are split into two categories, namely, wages and materials. Costs of furnishing the church have been totalled without making this two-fold distinction.

Wages for bricklayers, stone masons, unskilled labourers, carpenters and slaters who worked *in loedsa* comprise the first expense category in the fabric rolls, and take up the largest part of the *cedula* that the architect submitted to the master of the fabric each month. These twelve *cedulae* aside, builders' wages are also found listed under the '*exposita in pensionibus fabrice*' (expenditures for the annual payments charged to the fabric) and occasionally under the '*exposita extraordinaria*' (special expenditures).

The second category of costs consisted of expenditures for building materials of all kinds. Leading this category were expenditures for stone, recorded for the most part under the heading '*recepta lapidum per totum annum*' (bills for stone over the financial year). The costs of brick and other building materials and their shipment were usually paid by the architect and itemized in his monthly bills. Sums for materials purchases crop up again in the special expenditures. These expenses are also all tallied together.

The third category, expenditures for furnishing the interior, forms a clear group of its own. Here we have outlays for large items of church furniture such as organs, choir stalls, the high altar and its appurtenances, the rood loft, sacrament house and bells, and in addition for paraments and books and reliquaries needed for the liturgy. Division into cost categories is not possible in this rubric as furniture was very often commissioned by contract or bought ready-made. Most expenditures for furnishings are collected under the heading '*exposita extraordinaria*', and a few in the architect's monthly cost schedules.

Graph 5 paints a striking picture of spending levels and by extension of building intensity over the span of nearly two centuries. All amounts have been translated into the annual wages of a building lodge assistant. Here we can draw a number of conclusions. Firstly, it is clear that the Dom building lodge was a continuous enterprise, and the structure of the fabric's finances reflect this permanency from the time of the 1288 *mendicatorium* onwards. In fact, up until around 1350, the cathedral-building lodge was the only ecclesiastical building enterprise in the diocese that had a permanent setup and architect.[551]

The scale of building operations carried out within this permanent framework varied enormously, even sliding or spiking by several dozen percentages from one year to the next. Wage payments remained relatively constant, but expenditures for building materials and, even more so, for furnishings were adjusted to reflect the means available at any given time. A few sharp declines can be attributed to political crises. In 1426 the Utrecht Schism resulted in a long hiatus in construction,[552] whilst the war against Bishop David in 1482 and 1483 paralysed economic activity in the city and countryside,[553] as did the siege laid on Utrecht by the lord of IJsselstein in 1511.[554] Political unrest in 1527 and 1528 had similar effects, except that this time there was no recovery.[555]

Over the long term, however – and such temporary fluctuations aside – we can trace a clear trend. After a fairly energetic period around

1400, the scale of building operations took a significant step back over the course of several decades. The Utrecht Schism (1423-1449) certainly bears part of the blame, given that, as we have seen, cathedral-building funds came to be withheld as a result. Not until 1469 did activity return to a level near that of the booming early years of the century. In the period that followed – lasting up until around 1525 and roughly corresponding with the erection of the former nave – the building lodge thrived. The period between approximately 1490 and 1520 saw an almost unique influx of sufficient funds to purchase precious inventory for the cathedral, including paraments, the high altar with its own candelabra, reliquaries and, most importantly, the thirteen bells that tolled from the cathedral tower – a marvel virtually without equal in Europe.[556] The ultimate peak in construction spending, reached in the year 1505 with a sum equivalent to more than 210 annual wages, came with that last purchase, when over 40 percent of the budget went towards funding the bells. Around the same time, large quantities were also spent on two further projects that, for myriad reasons, never actually got off the ground: the installation of new choir stalls and of a copper fence to set off the indulgence altar in the north transept.[557]

After 1525 building activity withered to its lowest point ever within the space of a few short years.[558] Regular shipments of stone ceased in 1528. The building lodge, or *loedsa*, continued to exist but employed only a few workers. In 1527 the canons reduced the architect's *pensio* (annual payment) by half, and on 1 December 1551, after the architect Claes Martensz.'s death, decided to cease this distribution as well.[559] Five years later the *loedsa* was actually being leased out as a residence. Available funds were barely enough to keep the building in a decent state of repair, and new building activities were slim to none. The largest construction expenditures in these years were in 1543 for extensive restoration of the glazing donated by Bishop David in 1485/86 and the construction of the new St Martin's bridge across the Oude Gracht in 1555.[560] The fabric's financial situation had so deteriorated that during a December 1554 meeting, the cathedral canons decided to refuse a generous offer by Emperor Charles V to donate a stained glass window due to the high costs of having it installed: 'because they did not want to have to bear the costs of installing and removing those windowpanes; they preferred to leave the old glass rather than incur new expenses, given that the cathedral was already heavily burdened with other daily expenditures'.[561]

The manifest prestige that had long surrounded the Dom remained unblemished in these years. In 1540 it served as the grand and impressive backdrop for the royal welcome organized in honour of Charles V, and again in 1549 for Philip II.[562] In January 1546 the twenty-first chapter meeting of the Order of the Golden Fleece, chaired by Charles V, convened in the cathedral chancel.[563] Increasing numbers of tourists came to climb to the top of the tower, especially once the large bells were hung in place.[564]

Not until the final decades of the Reformation do we find any hint of a modest reversal. After 1560 there is enough money to restore the stock of paraments and even buy a few new ones. And, for the first time in many years, we find the chapter once again willing to venture into two projects requiring a relatively large pool of funds. On 15 November 1558 the canons decided to purchase wood for new choir stalls, which were completed in 1562.[565] In 1568 Peter Jansz. Swart began work on an organ, for which he received his final payment in 1573.[566] But the tide had not definitely changed for the better. Several years later, in 1578, the church treasure was melted down, impelled by external pressures as discussed above. All the outward signs of long-forgotten devotions were now erased forever.

On 18 June 1580 a definitive ban on Catholic worship was issued for the city of Utrecht, coupled with the closure of its collegiate churches. This action followed in the wake of a *beeldenstormerije* (iconoclasm) that had swept Utrecht's churches a few months previous, on 7 March.[567] On 19 July the cathedral chapter was itself forced to effect the 'purging' of the cathedral church by dismantling its altars and taking down its images.[568]

Upon the death of Archbishop Frederik Schenck van Toutenburg on 25 August 1580, the city's chapters had to make a unified appeal to the civic administration '*om te bestellen dat die eertsbisschop eerliken nae behoiren begraven wordt ende voorts tgeene dat totten uutfaert is van noode uit te richten*'.[569] The requiem mass held for the repose of his soul was the last Catholic service to be held in the cathedral until the year 1672.

It has been suggested by some that the tornado which wiped out nearly the entire nave on 4 August 1674 owed its devastating effect to the fact that the cathedral church remained unfinished. This is a supposition that can never be proven. But it is certainly true that the cathedral was never fully built. The outermost string of chapels never materialized, nor did the stone vault planned for the nave and transept or the system of nave abutments.[570] That construction had actually reached the state it had was doubtless thanks in large part to the remarkably fast pace of building in the decades just preceding the abrupt abatement of the quest monies around 1525.

CATHEDRAL VERSUS PARISH CHURCH FINANCING: THE DOM AND THE BUURKERK IN UTRECHT

We can shed clearer light on the typical hallmarks of a cathedral fabric by making a comparison between the sources of income utilized by a cathedral fabric and those available to a parish church. In Utrecht, such a comparison logically presents itself with the Buurkerk, which was dedicated to the Virgin Mary and was the oldest and also the largest of the city's four parish churches and – crucially – where the requisite documentation has been preserved.

The final chapter in the construction history of the Buurkerk as we see it today (a church was probably already established here as early as the tenth or eleventh century) opens directly after the city fire in 1279. Various fourteenth-century additions were made to the thirteenth-century building, including the tower around 1370 and a new choir somewhat later on.[571] The churchwarden's accounts, which are preserved from 1435 without any significant lacunae, list only a handful

78

View of the towers of the Dom and the Buurkerk from the immunity of the collegiate church of St Mary
Pen and watercolour,
349 x 501 mm
By Pieter Jansz Saenredam (1597-1665), signed and dated 18 September 1636
Haarlem, Teylers Museum

The church of St Mary, which was one five collegiate churches in Utrecht, was demolished in the nineteenth century.

LITERATURE
Wilmer 2005, p. 284.

of renovations, albeit major ones.[572] Of these, the most important was the campaign between 1430 and 1456 to widen and lengthen the thirteenth-century basilican plan and so create a hall church with aisles. There were no further building campaigns until after 1500, and then several in the period until 1541; these focused largely on expanding the choir and adding new side aisles on both the north and south flanks. The campaign begun in 1430 overshadowed all these other renovations, however. In the years following both building periods, the churchwardens spent large sums on costly inventory such as statues to decorate the nave piers (1456-63), organs (1468-73, 1500, 1543-49), a rood loft (1493-99), a sacrament house (1420, 1522-25), paraments (1466, 1533, 1542-43) and bells (1534, 1542, 1545).

Contrasts with the Dom are already manifest in the way the fabric of the Buurkerk was administered. As was the case in most medieval cities, day-to-day management of the parish church and its fabric lay with the churchwardens, who were appointed by the civic authorities. In Utrecht, two mayors served as *overste kerckmeysters* and as representatives of the parishioners. They in turn appointed two churchwardens, who carried out the actual work and rendered account to the mayors. When the time came for the annual audit of the accounts, parishioners were called to the church by the sounding of the bell;[573] also in attendance were the parish priests, though not as participants, given that they bore no responsibility for the administration of either the building or its inventory.[574] There were countless links binding the Buurkerk with the fabric of urban life. Most of the craft guilds, and certainly the preeminent ones, had their own altar inside the church,[575] as did the plethora confraternities.[576] Two areas of the church building were even reserved for the city's particular use. The council's chapel (*Raadskapel*), situated north of the tower, was where the council exercised its devotions before the altar of St Martin; this was also the site for sessions of the *buurspraken* – that is, where the council's decisions were promulgated.[577] The city subsidized construction of the council chapel, in part by the allocation of *steenboeten*, these being fines reckoned in the provision of a certain number of bricks.[578] The Buurkerk's tower served not only the church itself but was also an instrument of civic security and civic authority.[579] Indeed, not the soaring Dom tower, but the tower of the Buurkerk was that from which Utrecht was guarded, except in times of crisis.[580] Aside from the church bells, the tower also contained the unconsecrated city bells, comprising the council bell and the tocsin (*banklok*).[581] The latter bell, which was by far the heaviest, stood as a symbol of the city's jurisdiction and was sounded when the council wished to call citizens together; rulings and inspections were *ter clocken ghecondicht* (heralded by the bell)[582] It was only natural, then, that the city bells were paid for with civic funds.[583]

The fundamental interconnectedness of civic and Church domains, so entirely absent from the Dom,[584] together with the city magistrate's exclusive control over the governance of the Buurkerk's fabric, in no way detracts from the fact that the fabric's property and income were strictly ecclesiastical, and moreover oftentimes donated under onerous contract. This prevented any intermingling of city and parish finances and spared the Buurkerk from being burdened with expenditures that had no bearing on its real tasks. The churchwardens simply had no power to shuffle revenues, property components and financial obligations back and forth between different reserves as the cathedral canons did. Differences between the fabric of the Buurkerk and that of the cathedral are thrown into even sharper relief when we compare the makeup of their respective revenues.

The fabric of the Buurkerk had its economic basis in its property assets, which comprised various types of annuities, estates held in hereditary or fixed-term tenure, houses held in lease or given *te erve* (in bequest). However, the yield on these holdings was not allocated directly to church-building or maintenance, but to the so-called *Heilige-Geesttafel* (Table of the Holy Spirit), which was incorporated within the fabric of the Buurkerk.[585] This arrangement explains the substantial annual distributions of not only money, but also wool and linen cloth, shoes and bread with which the churchwardens – as administrators of the *Heilige-Geesttafel* – were charged in the terms of the foundation. But many bequests specified that '*wes daer overloept, dat sel der kercken bliven tot horer tymmeringhe*',[586] thus also allowing the building itself to profit from this ever-expanding pool of capital. Im-

79

View across the nave of the Buurkerk in Utrecht from north to south
Black and white chalk, pen in brown ink on blue paper, 269 x 418 mm
By Pieter Jansz. Saenredam (1597-1665), signed and dated 16 August 1636
The Utrecht Archives

LITERATURE
Wilmer 2005, no.299

mediately before the outbreak of the Iconoclasm in 1566, the fabric's income from property totalled 1080 karolusgulden, set off against requisite distributions of no more than 645 karolusgulden.[587]

A second source of income, again bearing no relation to building activity, were the compensations and payments in which the fabric partook in return for services rendered in connection with its parish tasks; most important were the *funeralia* – proceeds from the sale and opening of graves and from the cloth draped on the bier during the funeral service.[588] These generated never more, and usually less than, 10 percent of the total income.

Gifts donated by parishioners of their own free will formed a wholly separate category of income. Though we find such gifts listed in every account, their number and nature varied a great deal depending on whether or not the building lodge was active. Testamentary bequests were one form of voluntary gift.[589] Such bequests as were left in kind usually consisted of a precious – perhaps even the most precious – garment owned by the deceased, which age-old and widespread custom dictated be given to the fabric, or sometimes the parish priest, as a *mortuarium* (mortuary gift).[590] The profit on such items could be considerable. In 1444 '*Jonfrou Proeijs wijf Lichtenberg*' bequeathed a '*bonten tabbert mit open bonten mouwen*' and a '*tabbert mit witten voeder*',[591] which together made up one-fifth of the year's income. Besides tabards, we find countless belts, rosaries, rings and other pieces of jewellery. Some legacies were not cashed in because they were of direct use to the building works: '*item Aernt Tolsz. Gaf onser kerck op zijn dootbedde 6000 leynegel*' (1442).[592] But the majority of bequests were lump sums of money. There was considerable variation in value, ranging from the equivalent of several years' pay for a building labourer to – as was more often the case – a few days' or weeks' worth.[593] The number of bequests received also differed from one year to another, with a clear link between them and the fabric's level of building activity. Though there were usually no more than a handful of legacies to record, we find 58 in 1440, 64 in 1457 and even more than 100 in 1450. There is a logical explanation for these spikes. Whenever a building campaign was underway, churchwardens exhorted parish clergy to urge bequests on their parishioners whenever they were called to administer the last sacrament and draw up wills.[594] For the first time in 1444, the rolls list the name of the parish priest or chaplain who had procured (*geprocureert*) the bequest.[595] Their efforts were rewarded with some token or a meal with the churchwardens.[596] Ten years later, as the building period wound down, the clerics' direct involvement in securing legacies was no longer needed. But the launch of works in the choir after 1503 once again saw the churchwardens adding the heading '*testament bij den pastoren ende capellanen*'.[597]

On occasion, the church fabric was named an heir, even if only as a result of the terms of a contract. It always inherited the estates of residents of the four *godscameren*, which the churchwardens had commissioned using fabric monies in 1457 and were built close to the cathedral. The tenants, usually women living alone, resided there free of charge but were bound to leave their possessions to the fabric.[598] As legatees, the churchwardens settled the deceased's remaining debts, if any, distributed a few bequests and assumed responsibility for the funeral. The yield on the sale of the household goods, combined with cash money and other possessions, could be substantial.[599]

A second category of voluntary gifts can be classified as devotional gifts. On 6 August 1434 Bishop Rudolf van Diepholt granted the customary pardon of 40 days to everyone who made a gift for the building works.[600] Viewed in this light, we might call every gift indulgence money; indulgence monies in the strict sense of the word, however, were of secondary value.[601]

The focus of devotional life in the Buurkerk was, without a doubt, the image of the *Pietà* (*Maria ter Nood Gods*) in the northern transept.[602] It was reputed to have effected miracles, but we find no reflection of this in the account rolls, nor has any 'book of miracles' been preserved. There was, however, a confraternity, established in the fourteenth century, which commissioned masses to be read every Saturday and Marian feast day; this brotherhood had also secured a number of episcopal indulgences.[603] Devotional gifts, both in money and in kind, flooded in. Under the heading '*opboeren dat voer onser liever vrouwen gecomen is*', the accounts list sometimes lengthy series of '*kleinodieën*' (small items), which were liquidated on fixed dates or, where appropriate, used to ornament the statue itself. Offerings even included livestock (a horse), foodstuffs (half an ox, a basket of cherries, grain), flax and wool.[604] The grain was weighed on scales placed before the statue of the Virgin, on which the ailing or, alternatively, healed donor was weighed first so that they could give their weight in grain as a votive offering to Mary. This so-called *ponderatio*, already recorded in the time of Gregory of Tours (d. 594),[605] was a popular custom throughout the Netherlands.[606] In most cases parents had their children weighed, but in 1444 those present could have seen how *'die abdisse van Sinte Servaes gewegen wert onse vrou tot Buerkerc'*.[607] In most cases the measure of wheat was bought for a fixed price.

By far the most important gifts for the building works were those that parishioners gave outside any specific devotional framework. Gains from the offering boxes were never very great, even during building campaigns, and contributed at most five percent of the income. The collection dish – the tin *nap* – generated a good deal more.[608] The churchwardens passed it around the church on Sundays and feast days, and also during Holy Week, when the yield was greatest.[609] There is a manifest connection between the size of these proceeds and building activity. Beginning in 1435 the gains swelled from around 75 rhinegulden current (of 240 wit) to 191 rhinegulden current in 1444, undergoing a slow decline thereafter to finally settle at the fairly constant level of approximately 100 to 75 rhinegulden current after 1465. The construction of both choirs prompted receipts to rise again to 160 rhinegulden current in 1507, and then fall to around 85 rhinegulden current after 1525.

In the period in which the Buurkerk was converted into a hall church, from 1430 to 1455 (fig. 79), the churchwardens took to the roads, accompanied by clerics and designated parishioners, to collect money within – and only within – the boundaries of the parish. Such *ommegangen* were a popular usage in parishes everywhere.[610] In 1435 an *omganc van den coster* (sacristan's collection) was held on 23 successive Saturdays, with fairly slim returns that were recorded as *weeckegelde* (week receipts) with each donor's name.[611] Two years later three members and former members of the church administration and two priests set out *totten husen* (to the houses), amassing 150 gifts along the way from named donors to yield a total of 60 rhinegulden current, or 13 percent of the income.[612] In 1444 and 1446 there were *omgangen totten wagescot* and *totten leyen* (local collection for the wainscot and for the slates). Parishioners themselves conducted collections in each of the eight neighbourhoods into which the parish was divided; the first year's collection on the Thursday before the neighbourhood fair (*buurkerkmis*) saw the delegation of '*vele goede lude omme, elc in sijn achtendeel*'. The results were promising, generating a total of more than 180 rhinegulden current, plus over 100 individual gifts worth 300 rhinegulden current, or 28 percent of the fabric income all told.[613] On New Year's Eve of 1446, the sum of the profits '*so men al Buerkerckers-pel omghinc doen men dat cruuswerc sou vulven*' came to 340 rhinegulden current, or again 28 percent of the income. The parish priests, chaplains and sacristan were all compensated for their work.[614]

Last but not least, each account roll contains a heading for individual gifts, sometimes donated expressly for the building works. Rolls from the years 1435-1443 each contain a list with several dozen entries for '*persoenen die totter tymmeringhe dagelix ende wekelix hoer aelmoesen ende goetduncken gegeven hebben*';[615] later these receipts were grouped together under the heading '*opboeren van allen gemenen ende onsekere dinghen*', sometimes also noting a designation, for example for a component of a large item of inventory such as the organ, rood loft, bells, sacrament house or paraments.[616] Also listed here are goods of uncertain provenance and contested and unlawful goods - which by rights accrued to the cathedral fabric but were probably included in the settlement sum it received for the *reportationes* - to whit: found money, weregild, '*quaden gelde*', '*een rekeninge dair sy om scielden*' and suchlike.[617] Most of these gifts did not exceed the value of a few weeks' income of a building labourer.[618]

The category '*opboeren van onsekeren dinghen*' (receipts from uncertain things) was also where the churchwardens recorded the scant contributions made by the city. The magistrate bore the cost of the city bells and a portion of that for repair of the tower, and allocated fines in stone for construction of the council chapel. Where the actual church works was concerned, he only designated the occasional receipt from a fine,[619] which is exceptionally little compared with other cities, where civic administrations would support church-building by allocating an excise duty over a period of years or donating a large lump sum.[620] Based on the foregoing, we can establish that the extensive rebuilding works that took place at the Buurkerk had to be financed with receipts from parishioners' voluntary gifts in money and in kind, which included bequests, devotional offerings, proceeds from the offering boxes and collecting dish inside and outside the church, and gifts given on an individual basis. In the years between 1430 and 1461, voluntary contributions were enough to cover 93 percent of the costs of building and furnishings (which averaged 60 percent of total expenditures in the same period). Regular fixed income, annuities and rents, parish revenues and a portion of the voluntary contributions were used for distributions to the poor, expenses and salaries associated with religious services in the church, life annuity distributions and other capital expenditures. In years in which no construction works took place, the aggregate of these various payments could consume upwards of 90 percent of expenditures, with the remaining 10 percent spent on standard building maintenance.

The means by which the fabric of the Dom and that of the Buurkerk amassed the resources needed to facilitate church building and maintenance activities are characteristic of all cathedral churches and parish churches, respectively. That said, it is important to keep in mind that the two fabrics did not share a corresponding status within their respective hierarchies. Utrecht Cathedral was the main church of a large and important diocese. The Buurkerk's position within that diocese, by contrast, was never that of an important parish church. Though Utrecht was certainly the largest city in the diocese, with some 20,000 inhabitants around 1500, the four constituent parishes into which it had been divided in the city's glory days were so vast as to make the realization of an imposing church building in any one of them an impossibility. Added to this is the fact that the extant accounts span a period in which the masters of the cathedral fabric were running a permanent building enterprise, whereas the churchwardens of the Buurkerk could only really claim to have been building patrons over a few decades. Even at its most active between 1430 and 1456, the scale of the building lodge at the Buurkerk could not compare with that at the cathedral between 1395 and 1526, being only around one-fifth the size of the latter. The graph showing the Buurkerk's expenditures for construction, upkeep and furnishings, as expressed in the annual wage of a cathedral building lodge assistant, illustrates the striking contrast (graph 6).

From time to time, Utrecht therefore had two church building lodges operating simultaneously a short distance apart, each of which was supported by entirely different forms of financing. Relations between the two churches were very limited but not lacking in warmth. Occasionally, the Dom or the Buurkerk gave the other its surplus building material.[621] When the tocsin broke in 1406, the cathedral chapter offered the temporary use of the Dom tower's Lady Bell that '*slaen ende luden sal als die raet te doen heeft ende des noot is*'.[622] Both churches sometimes relied on the services of the same architects and artists.[623] However, none of this alters the fact that the differences between the two were enormous. The Buurkerk was a civic church, situated in the economic and political heart of the city and charged with civic duties of all kinds. Its fabric was controlled by the civic magistrate. As a parish church, it was by definition a church of and for those of the faithful who lived within the parish boundaries and who accordingly depended on that church for the cure of their souls. As parish church, too, it formed the base of the hierarchical pyramid. The impetus for building started with the churchwardens, who were members of the same urban elite to which the *Heilige-Geesttafel* owed its ever-growing pool of capital and which founded anniversary obits for the families belonging to its class. Voluntary gifts, by contrast, encompassed a broader circle of parish donors who took an interest in the welfare of their church.

Contrast this with the Dom, the star church of the diocese, at the top of the ecclesiastical hierarchy but almost wholly unencumbered by tasks of spiritual care and thus without a flock of faithful dependents. It was the first church of the bishopric, and yet in fact a church without a bishop. But not without a cathedral chapter, placing it first amongst the episcopal city's five aristocratic and purely clerical collegiate churches. It was also a centre of political events, thanks to the cathedral chapter's late medieval political position as the most powerful member of the first estate in the States of the Nedersticht.[624] Where contributions for the building works were concerned, however, the chapter's share was very limited; the lion's share came, albeit indirectly and in stages, from offerings from the faithful across the entire bishopric, facilitated by the cathedral's rank as mother church of all parishes in the diocese. It is fitting here to cite the apt remark that cathedral-building stands for the triumph of the power of Church institutions.[625]

Utrecht Cathedral, like the other collegiate churches, was both topographically and – more to the point – spiritually isolated.[626] We will not be surprised to learn, then, that on Sunday 25 August 1566 it was the Buurkerk that was the first of Utrecht's churches to be targeted by the Iconoclasts, followed by the other parishes and various monastic churches. The Dom and its fellow collegiate churches were left virtually unscathed.

CHAPTER FOUR

A SURVEY OF CONSTRUCTION FINANCING AT SEVERAL CATHEDRALS

INTRODUCTION

The income sources on which the Utrecht Cathedral fabric relied are characteristic of cathedral fabrics in general. Notwithstanding these strong similarities with other cathedrals, there are also some key differences, both positive and negative in nature.

The absence of contributions from the civic government fits the normal picture: scarcely any cathedral fabric north of the Alps could count on funds from this source. Contributions from the pope were equally uncommon. That the lords of diocesan territories over which the bishop exercised only spiritual jurisdiction, such as the counts of Holland and dukes of Guelders, were unwilling to make donations for the building works is wholly understandable; after all, the cathedral church stood in the city of which the bishop – their frequent political opponent – was the lord. For the bishops' part, only a single donation of any note is known to us, namely, John of Arkel's allocation of the episcopal tithes from May 1343 until May 1344.[1] This seems remarkably little when we consider what is known of the contributions made by some French and English bishops to their cathedrals. But it is less unusual when compared with other bishops in the German Empire, who manoeuvred within political relationships analogous to those in the bishopric of Utrecht. At the same time, it is interesting to note that the absence of large donations from overlord or bishop meant the fabric of Utrecht Cathedral was never in a position, as other cathedrals were, to invest a sudden influx of funds in a rapid acceleration of its building works.

It is a curious fact that the fabric never profited from the allocation of annates. On the one occasion that the Utrecht annates were levied for anything other than papal ends, they were used to settle a bishop's debts.[2] Another feature distinguishing the fabric of Utrecht Cathedral is its lack of any significant endowment. Funds contributed by the chapter never strayed from the strictly conventional.

In Utrecht, as in many other dioceses, the basis for the inflow of building funds was laid by the bishops' *mendicatoria*. Parish contributions in the form of the *reportationes*, organized by deanery, are likewise found in other dioceses. But unlike many other cathedrals, the Utrecht Dom boasted no collection of relics – that major draw for the faithful. However, the chapter was able to more than compensate for this lack through the organization of its own diocesan collection and the extremely consistent application – in contrast with most other dioceses – of an admission fee for the limited number of outside collections that it permitted inside its borders. Revenues from the Dom's own collection and, especially, those admitted from outside were exceptionally high.[3] This may have been due to the high population density in the Utrecht region, its wealth of cities and the relative prosperity that the diocese enjoyed in the late medieval period. When looking at receipts from leased quests, which were recorded in the fabric rolls as aggregates, we would do well to remember that the figures conceal a multitude of small, anonymous devotional gifts from faithful parishioners throughout the diocese, and moreover that these gifts were not given to support cathedral-building but as an expression of veneration for saints, most of whom had their locus of worship far beyond the boundaries of the bishopric of Utrecht. It was the sum total of all these revenues that facilitated the continuous operation of a large, permanent building lodge for over two centuries.

This chapter will first explore how the building works or individual building campaigns were financed at eight other cathedrals and at the mother of all churches, St Peter's in Rome. Financial records spanning varying numbers of years from the late thirteenth into the sixteenth centuries have been preserved at an estimated 80 cathedral fabrics.[4] None of these sets of records can compete with the Utrecht cycle in terms of either completeness or coherence, and moreover these data have been published for only a handful of cathedrals. We must therefore limit our survey to a few typical examples of cathedral fabrics in France, Spain, England, Germany and Italy over a period that runs from the beginning of the fourteenth century up to and including the sixteenth. What is relevant for our purposes is not the nature of their income (which has been the subject of extensive analysis in the preceding chapters) but, rather, their constellation and scale. As stated, this section will conclude with a brief consideration of the building fabric of the main church of all Christendom: St Peter's in Rome.

The final section of this chapter will take a broad look at the scale of medieval cathedral and church building enterprises, addressing questions about the amount of time and quantity of resources typically needed to build a cathedral, the maximum scale achieved during this period and, finally, whether building patrons had any real conception of the scope of the task they were taking on when they launched a building project.

ONE THE FINANCING OF BUILDING LODGES AT SEVERAL CATHEDRALS AND ST PETER'S, ROME

THE CATHEDRAL FABRIC OF EXETER, 1300-1514

The cathedral of Exeter was the head church of a diocese of modest proportions, which was subdivided into four archdeaconries. The chapter, which was secular, numbered only 24 prebendary canons, making it one of the smallest and also least-endowed chapters in England. In 1377 the city had more than 3000 inhabitants, of whom an estimated 155 were ecclesiastics.[5] Its sixteen parish churches were extremely small, and not one of them had burial rights. The cathedral dominated the small city completely.

Of exceptional wealth, by contrast, is the capitular archive, and more especially that of the fabric – not only in terms of its comprehensiveness but also in view of the early date at which the cycle of accounts begins. The oldest of these rolls, covering the years 1279 until 1287, is a financial memorandum rather than an annual account in the proper sense; the series of true financial statements begins with the year 1299/1300. This series is more or less complete up through 1352/53. A new cycle begins after 1371 and continues without major lacunae until 1467; between 1479/80 and 1513/14 only five accounts remain.[6] Overall, its records of expenditures have been more fully preserved than those of receipts, and provide a clear picture of the scope of building operations. Graph 7 traces the history of building expenditures, as expressed in the annual wages of an unskilled *operarius* (labourer), over a period in excess of two centuries, albeit with a few large lacunae.

80
The cathedral of Exeter, as seen from the northeast

There is considerable disparity in the pace of building in the first four decades of the fourteenth century and that in the subsequent long period until into the sixteenth century. Construction of a new cathedral to replace the Norman building may have begun a few years before the oldest account of 1279 with the erection of the Lady Chapel, and was largely finished around 1370, though the cathedral building works were also active after this time.

The organizational structure of the fabric was no different from that in place elsewhere. We find the first mention of a *custos operis* as early as 1204, the year in which the bishop also assigned the fabric its first fixed source of income, namely, the prebendary fruits of the parish church in Erth.[7] As in Utrecht, the launch of the new building campaign prompted a division of finances between those to be used for the maintenance of the old cathedral, the *vetus fabrica*, and those for the new building, the *opus novum*. This distinction would be eliminated by the chapter in 1310,[8] when a single *custos operis* was charged with administering all the fabric's accounts.

The pattern of the cathedral fabric's revenues in the period up until 1353 presents a one-sided picture. Aside from its aforementioned profits from the parish of Erth (averaging 10 to 16 annual wages), the fabric disposed over the usual sources of income, namely, proceeds from a number of offering boxes and the Pentecostal oblations (*oblationes pentecostales*) in the cathedral. Having no famous relics or devotions, this category yielded the cathedral very little. There were also the usual bequests and gifts, generating anywhere between 3 d. (two days' wages) and £10 (more than six years' wages) in the first half of the fourteenth century.[9]

Diocesan collections, procured by archdeaconry, also generated very little. When Exeter lost its large episcopal subsidies, the chapter endeavoured to boost income by means of massive propaganda, copying out 1200 letters of indulgence to support the collections[10] and thereby pushing earnings up from £10-15 in the 1330s and 1340s to £24 and £25 (15 annual wages) in 1351 and 1352, respectively.

In periods of heightened building activity, the fabric's finances were driven by large subsidies from the bishops, supplemented by contributions from the chapter. Bishop Thomas Bitton (1292-1307) donated £124 18 s. 4 d. (80 annual wages of a labourer) to rebuild the cathedral in 1303/04, and possibly also in the preceding and following years, and left the fabric a further enormous sum of £1345 5 s. 11 d. in his will.[11] A deed of 1310 has his successor Walter Stapeldon thanking him for his large private contributions, '*pro immensis susidiis fabrice ecclesie* [...] *ad felicem ipsius progressum*' (for his immense subsidies to support the favourable progress of the building works). Stapeldon continued his predecessor's accustomed annual series of gifts until the year 1325. In addition, he seems to have made an agreement with the chapter – including the four dignitaries, dean, precentor, treasurer and chancellor – under which their joint contributions would match exactly half that of the bishop, thus £62 9 s. 4 d. (40 annual wages). In 1310 the bishop levied a three-year tax on the diocesan clergy to support cathedral construction, on the grounds that daughter churches were bound to support their mother church.[12] At his death Stapeldon also left a large sum of 1000 marks, of which £285 13 s. 4 d. (over 180 annual wages) is accounted for in the rolls for 1325/26.[13] Stapeldon, *vir magni meriti*, was buried in his cathedral in a place of honour to the north of the high altar, a spot traditionally reserved for the church founder. His debt-ridden successor John de Grandisson (1327-1369) made only sporadic donations to the fabric during his lengthy term as bishop, but work on the nave could nevertheless continue almost without interruption.[14]

The large sums of money contributed by both the bishops and chapter of Exeter can perhaps be explained by the fact that the chapter was made up in large part of clerics with local roots. Bishops were always elected by the chapter and, like the canons, resided in their episcopal city on a regular basis. Indeed, clerics of the cathedral of this isolated and not particularly wealthy diocese seem to have felt a remarkably strong bond with their church.[15]

THE CATHEDRAL FABRIC OF MILAN: THE FIRST PHASE OF CONSTRUCTION, 1387-1391

81
The cathedral of Milan, view of the apse from the southwest

The campaign to build a new cathedral in Milan is one of the largest, most complex and also best-documented ecclesiastical building projects in Europe.[16] Milan had long been home to a double cathedral – that is, to two cathedral buildings, Santa Tecla and Santa Maria Maggiore, each with its own *baptisterium* – where liturgical services alternated between the summer and winter months, and each with its own chapter. Over time, the Santa Maria Maggiore gained the status of *ecclesia matrix* and religious and political centre of civic life. The decision to demolish the old basilica, which had suffered severe damage when the campanile collapsed in 1353, and build a new cathedral was probably taken in 1385 or 1386.[17] It must have been clear from the beginning that the project would entail a complete redistribution of the ecclesiastical precinct. The basilica dedicated to Mary and its baptistery would have to be torn down, as would a number of canons' residences, the archbishop's palace and local shops. Eventually the ancient Santa Tecla and its baptistery, situated just west of the current façade, were also forced to make way, though it would not be until 1548 – following interminable debate – that the last remnants of the building were removed.[18] Two years later the fabric, or *superstantia*, of Santa Tecla was incorporated within that of the *duomo*.[19]

We have already discussed a few facets of the initial phase of the cathedral's construction: the intricate management structure of the fabric after 1387, the political significance of the lord of Milan, Gian Galeazzo Visconti, at the campaign's start in 1386, followed by his relinquishment of all ambitions for the cathedral building project shortly thereafter, and finally the trivial role of the archbishop.[20]

By far the most vital financial contribution to the *Opera* came in the form of a mass almsgiving movement for the building works that started in 1386.[21] Where precisely this wave of magnanimity came from is not clear – spontaneous when it started, but carefully orchestrated in later stages. Curiously, it was not the promise of indulgences or the translation of relics that supplied the spark but, it seems, the bare fact of the building plans. There appears to have been a tradition of guilds convening in the cathedral on the feast of the Nativity of the Virgin (8 September) to make solemn offerings, as we learn from a decree issued by Gian Galeazzo Visconti on 7 February 1387, in which he assigns the *oblationes* from the feast of the prior September and, provisionally, of all those to come, to the cathedral fabric.[22] In March 1387 residents of each of the city's six districts began organizing collections in aid of the building works, and it became customary to bring the proceeds to the cathedral every Sunday.[23] Eventually the fabric administration assumed charge of this essentially spontaneous initiative, thus giving it the stamp of an official institution. In a letter addressed to Gian Galeazzo Visconti on 6 August 1387, the fabric urged that he and his people join the '*milites, advocati et medici et alii nobiles dictae vestrae civitatis*' (soldiers, counsellors and physicians and other notables of your aforementioned city) on 15 August, the feast of the Ascension of the Virgin, in the solemn almsgiving procession.[24] Invitations were sent out on this same day to high-ranking clerics of the city, including abbots of the preeminent abbeys, to present their offerings on Sunday, 18 August.[25] One after another, the cathedral received all the various leagues and ranks of citizens – members of the guilds, residents of the six districts and clerics, as well as a range of *comitiae* formed specially for the occasion, such as the '*nobiles et notabiles iuvenes Mediolani*' (noble and notable youths of Milan)[26] and the *po-*

destà with his *curia* – as they came to give alms at the high altar on Sundays and '*laborare pro nihilo*' (work for free).[27]

Private individuals, too, provided their services free of charge and made offerings for the building works, no doubt motivated by the prospect of the remission of sins and the need to do penance. In the fabric rolls for 1387 we come across the item '*oblatio per donolam dictam Raffaldam meretricem 3 s. 4 d.*' (offered by a woman by the name of Raffalda, prostitute, 3 s. 4 d.).[28] In a few instances such individual gifts were exceedingly large. An entry for 21 October 1387 reads '*pro oblatione facta per quendam qui noluit nominari nec notitiam aliquam dare, sed dixit quod erat quaedam persona quae venit ad veram poenitentiam 3200 lire*' (presented as an offering by someone who wished not to be named or recognized, but saying that he had come to do genuine penance 3200 lire), which is above 20 percent of the income for that year and equal to some 84 annual wages of a labourer.[29] Many of the faithful offered gifts in kind. Farmers from the surrounding region brought grain and thousands of litres of wine, whilst the citizens of Milan – men and women alike – gave their best garments and most opulent treasures. To receive these various gifts, the fabric stationed two laymen at the former main altar, where a fabric-appointed officer guarded them day and night.[30] This became the backdrop for stirring scenes: in the autumn of 1387, a poor woman donated her cloak for the building works without a thought for the cold, whereupon a gentleman intervened to buy it back and return the garment to her, '*pauperrimae, quae ipsa valde indigebat*' (oh poor woman, to her who also had such need of it herself).[31] On certain fixed dates the fabric had these goods offered for public sale in various locations in the city, whilst another portion was cashed in the fabric's own shop. Proceeds from all these gifts in money and kind were substantial and without question made up the largest share of the extremely high overall income realized during these years.[32] But by 1390 we already see the first clear signs of decline, as revenues dropped from just under 44,000 lire in 1389 to just under 30,000 in 1390.[33]

The fabric now had to go out in search of other prospects. On 11 April 1390 Gian Galeazzo Visconti was already turning to the pope to request a special indulgence for the building works,[34] and it was thanks to his intervention that the cathedral fabric subsequently acquired the *instar jubilei* (as for a Jubilee) indulgence for all of Lombardy from Pope Boniface IX[35] on 1 October 1390[36], still in time to profit from the Jubilee year. The terms under which this indulgence was issued and the resulting financial yield are known to us from detailed accounts. The cathedral fabric had had to pay Rome 1500 gold florins to obtain the bull itself.[37] Anyone who wished to earn the indulgence had to visit five churches in Milan, including the cathedral, and deposit an amount equal to one-third of the costs of a trip to Rome.[38] The bull of indulgence arrived in Milan on 1 February 1391, but did not enter into effect until 15 February. Forty-seven copies were drawn up for circulation throughout the whole of Lombardy.[39] It was a long time before any major influx got underway, with the first major sums '*pro oblationibus jubilei*' not appearing in the fabric rolls until June. Possibly this delay was behind the fabric's massive exertions to get the pope to grant an extension of the initial term, which in itself had been unusually long to start with, running until the Nativity of the Virgin (8 September) 1391.[40] With a great deal of effort, the fabric's agent succeeded in achieving this aim during a personal audience with the pope, who agreed to allow the indulgence to be proclaimed until Easter (14 April) of 1392.[41] It was unheard of and unprecedented for a Jubilee indulgence to be offered within the walls of any single city aside from Rome for more than one year; indeed, usually the time of grace did not extend beyond fourteen or fifteen days.[42] The financial gains must have exceeded all expectations: in 1391 alone at least 34,700 lire imp. (910 annual wages of a building assistant) flowed into the fabric fund,[43] such that income from indulgences made up more than 60 percent of the total. The year of the Jubilee indulgence marked a new and, at the same time, last peak of energetic building activity after 1387. Subsequent papal pardons issued from 1398 onwards met with little financial success.[44]

The nature of cathedral-building ambitions in Milan are manifest not only in the scale on which the works were established from the very start, but also in the conscious decision, made in the spring of 1387, to raise the building not in brick but in the more prestigious marble. The price of marble was exponentially higher, in part because its transportation required an intricate system of waterways to be dug to and from the quarries.[45] To the extremely high overall expenses for building materials, marble contributed a 2.8 percent share in 1387, rising thereafter to 54 percent in 1388, 42 percent in 1389, 79 percent in 1390 and 67 percent in 1391.[46]

Analysis of *Fabbrica* receipts and expenditures between 1387 and 1391 permits a number of conclusions. The *Fabbrica* could not dispose over such revenues as were typically allotted a cathedral fabric: it had no income from annuities or rents, received no contributions from the chapter or canons, utterly trivial sums from the archbishop and never more than paltry gifts from the lord of Milan, and was not apportioned any tax revenues by the civic government.[47] All this points up a financial organization cast in a different mould, entirely borne up during these years of popular enthusiasm by the inhabitants of the city. The nature of their contributions has been set out above. Most were anonymous gifts presented within a scripted devotional framework or gathered in *capse*, *bussule* or *zepi* set up inside or brought to the churches of the city and diocese or picked up at one of the six *porte* encircling the city.[48] Supplementing them were personal gifts, often also anonymously given, a few of which were exceptionally large. Entirely without parallel is the legacy bequeathed by the merchant Marco Carelli, who willed 35,000 ducats in 1393 – worth 1275 annual wages – in return for which the fabric honoured him with a marble sarcophagus bearing an inscription that describes the legacy at length (fig. 82).

In 1387 the fabric reaped a total income of 17,170 lire (550 annual wages of a *manovale*),[49] in 1389 of 26,930 lire (860 annual wages) and in 1391, the year of the indulgence, 57,290 lire (1830 annual wages).[50] In that last year only 30,630 lire (980 annual wages) were spent on cathedral-building, but in the other years building expenditures hardly diverged from the receipts.

The rapid pace of construction set by the *Fabbrica* of Milan Cathedral during the initial years is absolutely without parallel. But 1391 also marked its final high point, after which all ardour quickly deflated. By 1394 the fabric was already suffering a severe lack of monetary resources and was compelled to take out loans in order to pay the labourers.[51] The death of Gian Galeazzo Visconti in 1402 even brought

82
Marble sarcophagus of Marco Carelli (c. 1325-1394), merchant and banker and benefactor of the cathedral of Milan, 1408
Inscription: *Hac admiranda Marcus requiescit archa / Qui de Carellus cognomine dictus erat. / Hic tibi devotus sanctissima virgo Maria / Pro fabrica ecclesie maxima dona dedit. / Milia nam plusquam triginta quinque ducatum / Contulit. Ergo anime tu miserere sue. / Qui dominus Marcus obiit die XVIIII septembris MCCCLXXXXIIII*
After a design by Filippino degli Organi, 1408; sculpture attributed to Jacopino da Tradate and Jacobello delle Masegne
Milan Cathedral

Carved in the stone placed above the gisant is the inscription: 'This glorious shrine is the resting place of Marco, a Carelli by his surname, who in his dedication to you, holy Virgin Mary, made the cathedral fabric a rich gift. For he contributed more than thirty-five thousand ducats. Therefore take pity on his soul. The said lord Marco died on the 18th day of September 1394'.
Marco Carelli was originally interred in the Campo Santo; later the cathedral fabric paid for the transfer of his tomb to the south nave aisle wall.

LITERATURE
Boucheron 1998, pp. 187-188.

building activity to a complete standstill for some time.[52] Building subsequently progressed at a variable but, on the whole, fairly slow pace, and it would take until into the eighteenth century for the vast cathedral church to finally be finished, with the completion of its famous façade in 1888.[53]

THE CATHEDRAL FABRIC OF OSNABRÜCK, 1477-1543

83
The cathedral of Osnabrück, as seen from the northwest

The diocese of Osnabrück, founded around 800, was amongst the smaller dioceses, its pre-Reformation borders encompassing 165 parishes spread across fourteen archdeaconries. The chapter, too, was modest in size, seating 24 canons. At the close of the fifteenth century, the city numbered approximately 8000 inhabitants, distributed across its four parish churches.[54]

The construction, furnishing and upkeep of the city's cathedral of St Peter was entrusted to the *structuarius*, as the master of the fabric was known, to which office the chapter named a chantry priest. A total of 44 financial accounts have been preserved over a time span of 67 years between 1477 and 1544.[55] They cover a period in which the only entries, aside from various reconstruction works and minor building projects, are for a couple of large inventory purchases (paraments in 1477/78 and four bells in 1484/85 and 1485/86), the extensive renovation of the southwest tower (between 1510 and 1525, finished between 1540 and 1544) and the construction of the west portal (1530/31). The cathedral of St Peter is a majestic architectural structure that has in fact seen but few changes or additions since it was built in the eleventh and twelfth centuries.[56]

At the very end of the late Middle Ages, the fabric of Osnabrück Cathedral had an unusually modest budget at its disposal, with yearly expenditures for building and maintenance never rising above an average of 13 annual wages over the entirety of this period. The expense entries for the four church bells, cast by the famed bell founder Gerrit van Wou from Kampen in 1484/85 and 1485/86 at a price equivalent to 57 and 23 annual wages of an unskilled labourer, respectively, are exceptional;[57] the same goes for the funds laid out for paraments in 1477/78 (20 annual wages). The combined costs of building the tower in two phases and the west façade portal amounted to the equivalent of no more than an average of 17 annual wages a year over a period of fifteen years. The overall picture of expenditures for construction, upkeep and furnishings is one of changeability, as is typical for a cathedral fabric that had only intermittent access to a slow trickle of funds (graph 8). Similarly, in terms of the fabric's total expenditures, it is worth noting that the share attributable to construction and furnishing costs ranged from as much as 80 to as little as 5 percent. The fact that expenditures and receipts could only ever diverge in the short term, resulting in annual surpluses or deficits, makes it interesting to analyse the fabric's income. Over the entire period at issue, its net income averaged 24 annual wages, peaking in 1484/85 (for the church bells, 69 annual wages) (graph 9).

The pattern on which the fabric's income was built up reveals a relatively stable share of revenues issuing from leases and annuities. However, most of them also carried financial obligations, chiefly for obits. As such, they contributed little or nothing to the fabric's core task: the care of the building. The fabric's holdings of land and houses or annuities attached to them did allow it the option of redeeming annuities or selling a house to finance spending, however. In 1484/85 the fabric sold seven life annuities for a sum of nearly 20 annual wages. By effecting financial transactions of this kind, the *structuarius* was able to raise the fabric's cash balance and thereby fund comparatively high costs.

Revenues dedicated in their entirety to the building and its interior were the same as everywhere. That the bishop furnished no financial support whatsoever for the cathedral fabric was to be expected; other suffragan bishops of Cologne did no differently. From the beginning of the fifteenth century, the see would moreover unite various Westphalian dioceses, and the bishop was only rarely in residence.

The chapter put in place a series of now-familiar statutory provisions to benefit the cathedral fabric, including admission dues, years of grace, absence dues (from 1538), proceeds from vacant prebends and, sometimes, of incorporated vicariates, which generated varying

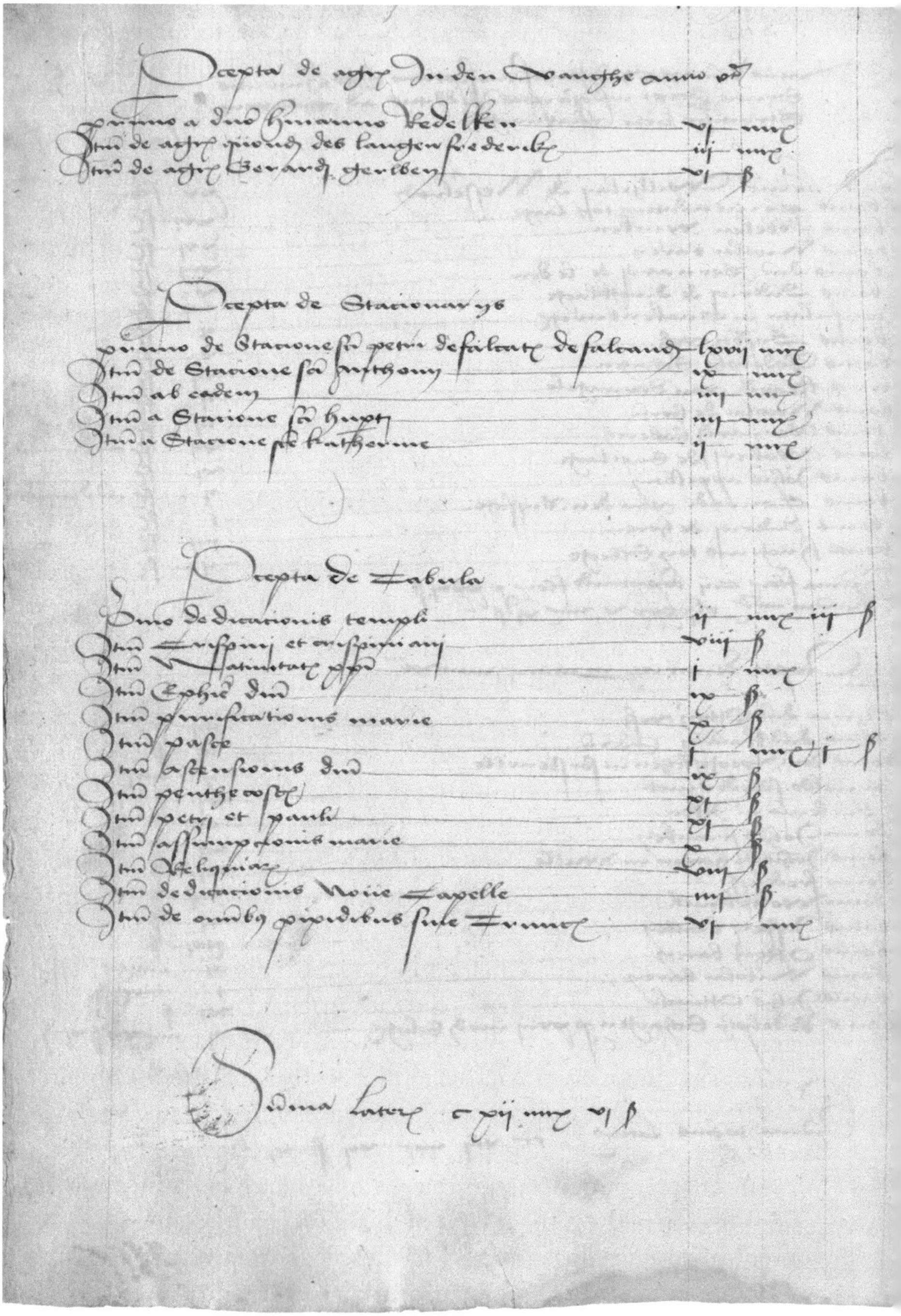

84
Osnabrück Cathedral
Fabric roll with receipts for the year 1507/08, f. 88 v.
Osnabrück, Bistumsarchiv

Page listing income from rents (*de agris*), pardoners (*de stacionariis*), collections held in the cathedral on Church feast days (*de tabula*) and the offertory boxes (*de omnibus pixidibus sive truncis*). The receipts from pardoners concern the quests for St Peter (67 marks), St Anthony (113 marks), St Hubert (4 marks) and St Catherine (2 marks), totalling 86 marks. The fabric had a total income of almost 638 marks in this year.

LITERATURE
Guntermann 2003, pp. 71-75, 134.

amounts of income nearly every year, depending on the circumstances.[58] Additionally, like their counterparts elsewhere, the canons were more inclined than lay people to name the cathedral in their testaments.

Of minor financial import are contributions received from the faithful in the sixteenth century. The cathedral of Osnabrück was no pilgrimage church. Here the faithful brought their offerings for the fabric on eleven set feast days, to be collected in dishes, *tabula*, and during the rest of the year deposited them in the collection boxes. In some years there was a special indulgence on offer.[59] There was also a diocesan fabric confraternity dedicated to the patron saint, '*Sankt Peter*'. It would seem that only inhabitants of the city enrolled as members; they are listed in the registers with surnames and Christian names, but number no more than slightly over 60 between 1477 and 1524/25.

Revenues garnered from the diocesan faithful were utterly insignificant. The chapter never took any trouble whatsoever to develop this source of funds, in sharp contrast to the neighbouring diocese of Utrecht. Only three quests not affiliated with the cathedral were active in the bishopric: one run by the Antonines, one from the abbey of St Hubert in the Ardennes and a certain quest for St Catherine, presumably conducted by the Osnabrück church dedicated to this saint (fig. 84). The admission fee remained fixed at the same rate for nearly the whole of the period between 1477 and 1525, at a combined 19 marks, or the value of approximately one year's wage. The share contributed by the cathedral's own quest for St Peter (comparable with the quest for St Martin in Utrecht) was variable, but sometimes as large as 60 marks.

The decline of revenues from the confraternity and quests was even more abrupt here than in Utrecht. After 1528/29, the already meagre returns dwindled to nought.[60] In reality, the brotherhood had already ceased to exist in 1525/26, '*quia nemo ingressus est*' (because no one joined). Alms deposited in the offering dish and offering box by the faithful likewise diminished to next to nothing. The rising popularity of Luther's teachings in Osnabrück were doubtless at the root of this downward spiral. At the time of the civic uprising in 1525, city residents demanded that '*men schall henforder keine terminarii oder stationern binnen Ossnabrugh tho lathen*' (henceforth no pardoners nor collectors shall be admited inside Osnabrück). Many ecclesiastics, the rector of the cathedral's main altar amongst them, held Lutheran convictions. In 1543, the year of the last extant fabric roll, Prince-Bishop Franz von Waldeck made an attempt to introduce the Lutheran order in his diocese, motivated in part by political considerations of state and in spite of opposition from the chapter. Five years later he was forced to retract his decision, but it was not until 1623 that Osnabrück would once again see its episcopal seat occupied by bishops devoted to the Counter Reformation.[61] Having become isolated from both city and diocese, the completion of the west tower and erection of the west portal had to be realized without any assistance from the faithful.

THE CATHEDRAL FABRIC OF SENS: CONSTRUCTION OF THE TRANSEPT, 1490-1517

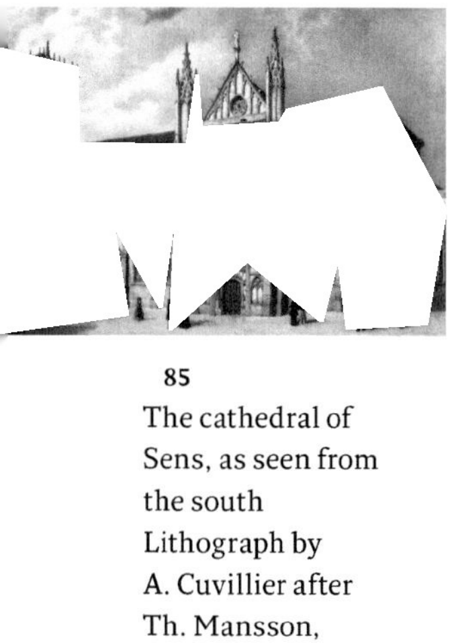

85
The cathedral of Sens, as seen from the south
Lithograph by A. Cuvillier after Th. Mansson, c.1840

Though high up in the ecclesiastical hierarchy, the archbishopric of Sens was only moderate in size, comprising five archdeaconries with twelve deaneries and around 700 parishes in all. There were a total of 50 canons attached to the cathedral.

Built between roughly the years 1140 and 1175, with its large west façade completed early in the thirteenth century, the cathedral of St Etienne belongs to the first generation of Gothic cathedrals. Apart from substantial reconstruction and renovation in the two or three decades after the collapse of the west tower in 1268 and modification of the clerestory and addition of chapels in the fourteenth century, the cathedral has largely preserved its twelfth-century appearance.[62]

Calls for a transept began in the fourteenth century, but troubled times – the Hundred Years' War – put building plans on hold until the end of the fifteenth century.[63] The chapter, which like other chapters commissioned the construction work, had already taken the decision to add a transept in 1465, a full quarter-century before actual building began. From that year on the chapter set money aside from its own income and opened a collection box *pour la croisée*, which yielded a modest total of around 1500 l.t. (over 50 annual wages of a *manoeuvre*).[64] The exceptionally well-preserved archive makes it possible to trace the progression of work on both arms of the transept and their portals in detail. The cycle of fabric rolls – a combined 66 accounts from the thirteenth century and the period between 1319 and 1490 – are amongst the best preserved in France, whilst the years documenting the transept campaign between 1490 and 1517 have come to us almost fully intact.[65]

The cost of building the transept has been calculated at 19,625 l.t. When we add the costs of glazing the south transept (1125 l.t.) and tapestries to screen off the choir (975 l.t.), the total expenditures for building and furnishing the cathedral during these years come to 21,725 l.t. This figure corresponds to upwards of 33 annual wages, spread out over a period of 22 documented years – a markedly modest pace of building compared with the cathedral of Utrecht. These expenses were financed using the fabric's income, made up of shares of a mere 5 percent from the archbishop, more than 25 percent from the canons, over 15 percent from the king and nearly 55 percent from the diocesan faithful.[66]

Archbishop Tristand de Salazar (1475-1519) made a modest contribution to the fabric's overall costs with donations of between 792 and 1192 l.t.[67] over a number of years after 1492. At the same time, he financed the works with loans and paid 3000 l.t. in successive instalments for an altar founded in his name and further donated 300 l.t. for a tapestry for the choir and left 1200 l.t. in his will for the completion of the tower. He also had a direct interest in the construction of the south transept as it provided entry into the bishop's palace, prompting the chapter to have his coat of arms set prominently in the south portal and south transept window, though perhaps more in deference to the bishop's right of access to his cathedral than in gratitude for his gifts.[68] In fact, the true contribution of the archbishop – being a prelate with countless diplomatic and political connections and a benefactor in many guises – lay perhaps more in his initiating role[69] and his successful efforts to solicit donations from the king.

These royal donations, making up 15 percent of the total, were vital and consisted of the allocation of two taxes that were the king's due: the salt tax (*gabelle*) in the diocese of Sens and the civic collection (*aide*) proceeds of 400 l.t. over six years.[70] To these the chapter added a series of customary revenues: the *prebenda defunctorum*, mortuary gifts, admission dues, certain fines and a tax (*tail*) on prebends. Like their counterparts elsewhere, some canons also left a bequest.

More than half of the fabric's income derived from the faithful. The five collection boxes inside the cathedral generated 13 percent of the fabric's income. Proceeds from two of these boxes were shared with the Parisian Hôpital des Quinze Vingts Aveugles and the Hôtel-Dieu, which had been granted permission to install them.

One of the collection boxes, *le grand tronc*, was linked with the thirteenth-century fabric confraternity dedicated to St Stephen (St Etienne). Though it maintained an altar in the cathedral and had its seat there, it was a diocesan organization, as in other places, and each parish church kept its own list of member confraters and consorors. Confraternity dues formed one of the fabric's diocesan income sources. The *quête générale* established by the archbishop in 1440 was affiliated with the confraternity, but receipts from these collections, held in perhaps all 700 parishes and delivered by parish priests via the archdeacons or deans or at the annual *senne* (diocesan synod), were recorded separately. New indulgences and religious privileges such as the suspension of the ban on eating butter and milk during Lent, as offered from 1499 onwards, augmented these receipts. Proceeds from the diocese's one foreign quest, from the priory of St Loup, dried up during the years of the building campaign as a result of conflicts. All told, receipts from diocesan bequests, the *quête générale* and confraternity dues supplied 38 percent of the fabric's income (graph 10).

Construction of the transept was financed using the sources described above. Whilst offerings from the faithful were of paramount importance, both the archbishop and king also played key roles in making the relatively modest building project possible.[71]

THE CATHEDRAL FABRIC OF TROYES, 1294-1550

The cathedral of Sts Peter and Paul in Troyes was the main church in a diocese of some 300 parishes, distributed across nine deaneries. Its chapter numbered 40 prebendary canons. A city fire in 1188 formed the incentive for building a new Gothic cathedral, with work commencing around 1200 and by and large finished - though with successive decades-long interruptions - upon the completion of the west front between 1502 and 1550. The northern St Peter's tower was not fully raised until the seventeenth century, whilst its counterpart, the tower of St Paul, was never realized.

86
The cathedral of Troyes, as seen from the north Lithograph by C. Fichot, nineteenth century

The remarkably early set of fabric rolls, preserved without major gaps, runs from the end of the thirteenth century into the sixteenth and provides insight into the scale of the building lodge and its funding mechanisms.[72] Like Utrecht Cathedral, Troyes had a building lodge in permanent operation, the size of which varied substantially depending on the nature of the campaign. Unlike the cathedral fabric at Utrecht, however, that at Troyes tapped new income sources for special building projects, which brought in large sums for just a few decades.

The cycle of accounts can be split into several groups. In the seven years between 1294/95 and 1300/01, net revenues were an estimated annual 1814 l.t., corresponding to about 18 years' wages for a carpenter.[73] The pattern of the income is dominated by contributions from the faithful, totalling 85 percent, of which 40 percent came from the diocesan collection, procured by the deans, 30 percent from monies offered before the relics or elsewhere in the cathedral and 15 percent from quests from outside the diocese. The remaining receipts derived from legacies and annuities. Neither the bishops nor the chapter made any contributions to the fabric.[74] During a second seven-year period, between 1333/34 and 1339/40, net revenues came to 2146 l.t. a year, representing over 12 annual mason's wages or 24 for an unskilled *operarius*.[75] Though receipts are classified differently in this second period, we can deduce that 60 percent issued from diocesan collections, including at least six different foreign quests.[76]

Only ten annual accounts remain to give a picture of income patterns over the period between 1366 and 1500.[77] During this near century and a half, receipts varied in value from 66 (1390/91) to 16 (1449/50) annual wages of an *ouvrier*, with an average of 37. Building activity was frequent, but fluctuated greatly in scale. This last fact is reflected in the fabric's income infrastructure. Contributions from the diocesan faithful remained relatively constant throughout this whole period, excepting only in times of war, and yielded the equivalent of around 10 to 15 annual wages.[78] Leading this category were receipts from the diocesan collection campaign, which were handed over during the synods. Admission fees (*placet*) charged to foreign quests – sometimes numbering more than ten – generally provided no more than a quarter or a third as much as the cathedral's campaign; the chapter in Troyes, unlike that in Utrecht, made hardly any effort to use its admission jurisdiction to benefit the cathedral building works. There were also proceeds from offering boxes in the churches of the city of Troyes and in the cathedral itself, as well as modest legacies and small sums from confraternities.[79] Contributions from the chapter were made up solely of very small admission dues, never exceeding three years' wages in worth. One special category was the contributions made by the faithful from the diocese of Troyes itself as well as its surrounding dioceses in connection with the papal plenary indulgence of 1451, already discussed above, which yielded generous sums for 20 years after the resumption of the nave building campaign – at times even exceeding half the annual income.[80]

In certain years the fabric's financial clout was determined by lump sum or short-term financial contributions from the bishop, chapter, sovereign, city or citizens of Troyes. Usually there was some specific incentive for such donations or contributions, for example, when the nave collapsed on Christmas day of 1389 after one of the clerestory windows had fallen out.[81] The 1389/90 account lists the following contributions: 300 l.t. from the chapter, 40 l.t. from the bishop and 100 l.t. from the duke of Burgundy; in the following year 200 l.t. from the king, 50 l.t. from the pope and 386 l.t. from the population of the city of Troyes. Almost never did the cathedral fabric receive any sustained form of funding from the bishops. The only exceptions are Louis and Jacques de Raguier, uncle and nephew, who donated sums totalling around 2000 l.t., or some 80 annual wages, in the decade after 1479/80, as mentioned above,[82] '*pour faire la nef neufve*'.

Aside from his 1390 donation, the king also granted a sum of 128 l.t. in 1366, comprising one-fifth of the income in that year. Not until after 1500 did the fabric receive any enduring funding from this source, which was put towards the construction of the west façade.

Aid from the city attests to the good relations between the chapter and civic authorities. This found expression in the large donation made by the *bourgeois, habitans et clers* of Troyes in 1389/90, followed by five annual contributions of 40 l.t. each between 1390 and 1411. As in other dioceses, the construction of the tower – a point of reference for the entire city – was an enterprise uniquely suited to civic support, and it was with precisely such support that the tower above the transept was raised.[83] The chapter furthermore engaged citizens in building operations and in the administration of funds, as it had also done in 1381 during deliberations concerning the choir screen that was to separate the canons' choir from the nave.[84]

The launch of works at the west façade in 1502 heralded a new phase in the cathedral's construction history and was accompanied by a phenomenal increase in the budget.[85] Initially, in 1501/02, this was due to an accumulation of credit balances, which supplied half the funds available in that year, whereas actual revenues supplied only around 45 annual wages of a *manoeuvre*. Net revenues rose rapidly to 60 annual wages in 1506/07 and 145 in 1536/37. Total spending for the lower portion of the west façade between 1506 and 1532 can be estimated at 70,000 l.t., or around 2700 annual wages spread out over a period of more than 25 years. Here the chapter bolstered the fabric's financial capacity in two ways. Firstly, it secured a set share of the *gabelle* revenues from the king in 1506 for a term of six years (with successive renewals until 1536 thanks to the bishop's intervention). This royal tax on salt furnished 40 percent of the fabric's income between 1516 and 1532, placing Troyes amongst the many French cathedrals to profit from this source of funds (graph 12).[86]

Secondly, the chapter was able to significantly boost existing revenues from diocesan contributions, as opposed to alms brought to the cathedral itself, which saw hardly any growth at all.[87] Proceeds did increase from the wooden almsboxes, or *boettes*, which were customary in every parish and delivered to the diocesan synods by parish priests in the usual way; these comprised all monies collected for the cathedral, with Lenten receipts recorded separately – doubtless in view of the lucrative dispensation from the ban on consuming milk and butter in that time. In characteristic fashion, we also see the chapter changing its admission policy for quests from outside the diocese. In 1506/07 it was still willing to admit eleven *quêtes*, which yielded a modest profit of 150 l.t. (six annual wages). Most of these paid no more than a small *placet des questains* (admission fee), except the Quinze Vingt Aveugles from Paris, which was permitted to collect during Eastertide and paid 70 l.t., making up almost half the total.[88] In 1520 the chapter put an abrupt end to this liberal admission scheme: thenceforth, no more foreign quests would be admitted, '*denegantur littere de placet questoribus*' (the pardoners will be refused admission letters).[89] Profits from outside quests thus dried up – and those from the cathedral's own collection soared apace.[90] The canons placed a logical focus on the traditional collections and other profits drawn from the diocese's parishes, utilizing the religious privileges they had secured in aid of the cathedral building works. No longer were the faithful confronted with multitudes of foreign pardoners who came to seek alms for entirely alien ends. The chapter took as its motto: *karitas incipit a semet ipso* (charity starts with you).[91] Wielding this combination of measures, the chapter managed to raise receipts from the diocesan collection to roughly the same level as those from the *gabelle*. Together, they laid the basis for the remarkable multiplication of funds available for building the façade. Further income sources – capitular contributions, legacies, lease fees and rents – did almost nothing to tip the scales (graph 13).

THE CATHEDRAL FABRIC OF BOURGES: CONSTRUCTION OF THE NORTH TOWER, 1508-1537

The cathedral of St Etienne that still stands today was raised at a rapid pace over the course of two building campaigns lasting from the end of the twelfth century through to around 1250. In the fourteenth century this large archbishopric encompassed some 800 parishes, distributed across 20 deaneries.[92] The chapter had 40 prebends, and more than 20 canons of varying status resided in the city.[93]

On New Year's Eve day of 1506, the cathedral's ruinous north tower, the consolidation of which had been planned from 1503, collapsed, destroying a significant portion of the nave as well. The rebuilding campaign got to an energetic start in 1508. A special pool of funds was diverted from the fabric and administered as a separate account, the *oeuvre de la tour*.[94] Between that year and 1537 a total of 81,001 l.t. was spent on building – fully four times the amount spent at Sens over a similar time span for the construction of its transept. The total cost of the project, taking account of payments from other sources for general expenses, is estimated at 100,000 l.t.,[95] an amount roughly equivalent to an average 90 annual wages of a building labourer over 30 years. A further distinction from Sens was the fluctuation in expenditures and, as such, in the size and composition of the Bourges fabric's income patterns. The peak spending year in the 1508-1537 building period came in 1517, with expenditures of 6485 l.t., and the low point in 1530 with 1641 l.t.

87
The cathedral of Bourges, with a view of the north tower and westwork

The most valuable contribution came from the archbishops, who donated a sum total of 34,630 l.t., or more than one-third of the building costs. But it was with antipathy and reluctance that some of them took up their duty of restoring the damaged cathedral to its former glory. Michel de Bucy (1505-1512), who like the majority of archbishops had been appointed at the king's behest, was ordered by Louis XII (his natural father, no less!) to contribute 3000 l.t. each year until the tower was rebuilt, this being the difference between his generous income from the diocese and the basic archiepiscopal expenses. Ultimately, it took a Paris parliamentary arrest in 1510 to compel him to pay.[96] His successor, who showed himself more willing to cooperate with the chapter, succeeded in reducing this amount to 1500 l.t. in his first two years, and to 2000 l.t. a year thereafter. And yet the actual payments came late or not at all, making it extremely difficult for the chapter to pay the building labourers on time. Amongst his successors were some who were better at fulfilling their obligations, for which the chapter rewarded them by displaying their coats of arms on a portal or the tower.

De Bucy demanded that the chapter itself make a contribution proportionate to his own. In fact, the chapter would contribute a total of 8156 l.t., or around a quarter of the amount contributed by the archbishops. The provenance of these funds is not entirely clear, but seems to be from such standard revenues as admission dues as well as an additional levy raised on prebends.

A revenue of particular significance – one also enjoyed by various other cathedrals and churches – was the share in the salt tax (*gabelle*) profits raised in Normandy and Languedoc, allocated by King Francis I in 1515. Between 1515 and 1537 the *oeuvre de la tour* received 19,132 l.t. from this source, representing around one-fifth of the total building costs.

Second in importance after the archbishops' contributions were those from the faithful, who funded more than 26,000 l.t., or approximately one-quarter, of the overall building costs.[97] A very limited portion of these monies derived from gifts and legacies, and the major part from contributions from the fabric confraternity and from the offering boxes, *quêtes* and papal pardons.

The fabric confraternity, which had the customary dedication to the cathedral's patron saint, St Stephan, traced its origins to 1493, but had developed since then – armed with papal pardons – into the *confrérie de la tour.* Its contributions were transferred via the synodal system.

Only two external quests were admitted, being impossible to deny: that of the Hôtel Dieu and that of Les Quinze-Vingts Aveugles in Paris. Both charitable institutions had papal licences to collect across the length and breadth of the kingdom. We have indications that the chapter of Bourges managed to reserve a sizable portion of the large sums gathered by these quests for its own tower building works. We also know that the archbishop was willing to deploy the printing press as a means to promote the collection of the Hôtel Dieu, its indulgences and religious benefits, as is evidenced by a fine printed broadside.[98]

The rebuilding of Bourges Cathedral's north tower is a prime example of a comparatively brief campaign supported by a tailored set of income sources (graph 11). The king's observation in 1512 that the tower's '*ruyne et decadence* [...] *ne seroit estre reparé pour cinquante mille livres tournois* [50,000 l.t.] *ou plus*' is revealing in this respect, though his estimate falls somewhat shy of the actual cost.[99]

THE CATHEDRAL FABRIC OF TOLEDO, 1418-1438

The cathedral of Toledo was amongst the most imposing and richly endowed in Europe, both as a building and, to an even greater extent, as an institution.[100] Captured from the Moors in 1085, the city's archiepiscopate was soon hailed as the primate of the whole of the Iberian peninsula.

Construction of the Gothic cathedral – built, as in many Spanish cities, on the foundations of the *mesquita* – commenced in 1224 and was largely finished in 1493 with the completion of the last vaults at the west end. The cathedral numbered 90 clerics in 1236: 40 canons, 30 *racioneros* entitled to a partial canon's prebend, and 20 chaplains. By the sixteenth century this figure had swelled to a combined 250 clerics. Added to these were hundreds of lay officials and servants, bringing the total number of people attached to the cathedral during this period of prosperity to an estimated 700.[101]

88
The cathedral of Toledo

The cathedral building lodge was administered by the prestigious *Obra y Fabrica*. The office of *Obrero Mayor* was always filled by a canon, who was appointed by the archbishop with the chapter's approval and might remain in office for decades.[102] He had a permanent staff of many dozens of people, some charged with overseeing the building and its facilities over the course of the ecclesiastical year, others with performing duties in association with the *Obra y Fabrica*, and still others with carrying out administrative tasks.[103]

The financial records of the *Obra y Fabrica* provide a clear picture of the nature and size of its receipts and expenditures, which have been analysed in respect of ten accounts from the years 1418-1438.[104] What strikes us here is the sheer size of the receipts, averaging more than 3.5 million maravedís annually for these ten years, or an average 170 annual wages of a *peón* (unskilled labourer) each year, with actual amounts fluctuating between 225 and 131 annual wages.[105]

An unprecedentedly large share of the income, some 90 percent, was garnered from the *excusados*, the second most important tithe of the entire archdiocese. The proceeds were farmed out, thereby avoiding major fluctuations and eliminating the hassles of collection. The remaining ten percent of receipts derived from rents on houses and estates. Alms offered in the cathedral generated at most one percent. Slightly more profitable were the fruits of the *mandas* (bequests and donations), a category that also included a quarter of the revenues collected by diocesan monasteries and churches.[106]

A portion of the fabric's expenditures were designated for the high staff expenses and upkeep of the cathedral; the largest part was spent on building operations and to pay for church inventory, including the organs, liturgical books, paraments, liturgical vessels and the like. The sums entailed could be considerable: the imposing polychrome wooden retable commissioned by Archbishop Cardinal Cisneros in conjunction with the *Obrero Mayor* for the high altar, and constructed between 1497 and 1504, cost at least 2.5 million maravedís, or 333 annual wages.[107]

As the sixteenth century progressed, the *Obra y Fabrica* came to assume the status of a highly bureaucratized organization of impressive proportions. In 1587, 116 people were permanently engaged by the fabric;[108] it drew an income of 15.5 million maravedís, set off against expenditures exceeding 17.5 million maravedís, or 920 annual wages of a *peón*.[109] Its pattern of revenues in this year show no real divergence from that of a century and a half earlier: more than 80 percent was supplied by the *excusados*, which also included the *terzuelos* from territories controlled by the military orders,[110] whilst tenancy and ground rents yielded five percent. The remaining receipts, including alms offered in the cathedral, were utterly insignificant, with the sole exception of a special diocesan collection that furnished more than ten percent of the income on the single occasion it was held.

Expenditures consisted of salaries for the numerous staff members (including the choristers) as well as myriad payments associated with structural maintenance of the vast building and for liturgical requisites like wax and oil, repairs to old paraments, and the purchase of new paraments and liturgical vessels. One unusual entry, representing approximately 10 percent of the total outlays, concerns the ceremonial return of St Leocadia, patroness of Toledo, to the cathedral: after a centuries-long sojourn in an abbey in Hainaut, the saint's relics were rescued by stealth from that newly heretical region.[111]

Expenditures swelled to immense proportions never before equalled by any cathedral fabric in centuries past. They issued not from a large building lodge, but merely from the maintenance of the ecclesiastical building complex and the high materials cost of maintaining ongoing ecclesiastical and liturgical activities in one of the wealthiest and most illustrious cathedrals in Counter Reformation Europe. These expenses were not defrayed to any extent by voluntary contributions from the faithful.[112]

THE CATHEDRAL FABRIC OF SEGOVIA, 1525-1650

The campaign to build a new cathedral in Segovia at a location different from that occupied by its predecessor got off to a dramatic start. The old thirteenth-century cathedral stood on a small piece of land alongside the Alcazar, a site that was unfavourable in many respects: too cramped for a cathedral worthy of the city and too close to the centre of political and military power. The latter half of the sixteenth century saw a busy programme of building activities in spite of this, including the construction of the cloister under the auspices of both the king and bishop in the 1460s.[113] The cathedral enjoyed a flourishing existence; much money was spent on building and decorating its chapels and on furniture such as the organ and choir stalls. On 21 November 1461 a miracle occurred: the bishop, aided by masons in the cathedral's employ, was led to discover the relics of the city and diocese's seventh-century patron saint, San Frutos, and his companions buried in the ground behind one of the altars. A series of additional wonders followed.[114]

89
The cathedral of Segovia

Plans to relocate the cathedral to another part of the city – an unusual and irregular measure[115] – were already being framed by this time.[116] In fact, King Henry IV (1454-1474) had promised the enormous sum of 16 million maravedís, or roughly 1600 annual mason's wages, if the move went ahead. In 1510 the bishop gained renewed approval from the king to relocate the cathedral, together with its chapter and lower clergy – 189 people in all – to the area formerly occupied by the convent of St Clare, a spot situated at an ample distance from the Alcazar and available for the substantial price of 600,000 maravedís.[117]

The situation came to a head when various cities in Castile rose in fierce rebellion primarily against tax measures introduced by the new king, Charles v. On 30 May 1520 a civic representative with royalist sympathies was murdered by wool industry tradesmen. A revolutionary committee of *comuneros* replaced the royalist civic administration. These events set the stage for a full-blown revolt against the authority and power of the throne. Brandishing the motto '*la iglesia es la ciudad*'(the church is the city), a mob of city residents – Segovia had a population of some 12,000 – forced its way into the cathedral and turned it into a base for attacking the royal troops entrenched in the Alcazar. The cathedral became a war zone, with a terrible toll on the building and its contents; the relics of St Frutos only narrowly made it to safety inside the walls of the Alcazar. It was not until a year later that the city made a definitive return to peace, with the offenders granted a general amnesty by Charles v.[118] Heavy fines were imposed, as well as large sums to compensate for damage.[119] The city agreed to pay an initial compensation of 7 million maravedís, later reduced to 3 million, to be taken off its tax profits over a period of ten years.[120]

The relocation of the cathedral could be put off no longer. On 18 August 1523, following the chapter's request and bishop's endorsement, the emperor granted his consent for the move (fig. 91). Before work on the new cathedral could begin, however, some hundred houses still occupying the grounds of the former convent of St Clare would first have to be cleared; a committee was convened to assess the purchase price.[121] The convent church itself would be used by the chapter until the new cathedral was ready. For its cloister walk, the chapter decided to have that from the old cathedral dismantled and carried to the new site stone by stone, where it was rebuilt for 1.5 million maravedís between 1524 and 1530.[122]

On 8 June 1525 the bishop laid the first stone of the new cathedral, a symbolic act of reconciliation between Segovia and the emperor and between the city's lay and clerical populations, and a silver plaque bearing the arms of the emperor and bishop was set behind the first stone to commemorate the event.[123] Work would continue for the better part of 240 years, with the dedication taking place in 1768, though divine services were already being held in the nave of the new cathedral by 15 August 1558.[124] The tower, chapter room and library had also been completed by that date.

The extant fabric rolls provide a detailed window onto the intricate financial provisions made for the building works and the scale of operations for building this last Gothic-style cathedral (fig. 13, 90). Here we can rely on an existing excellent analysis of the records spanning the years 1526-1653.[125]

The fabric's income can be divided into three main categories. There were the traditional fabric revenues also in place before 1525, which yielded 43 percent of the income over this entire period. Alms and other offerings supplied a similar percentage. Special revenues rounded off the earnings with another 14 percent.[126] But within this lengthy time span of almost 130 years, the actual volumes of income and proportional divisions amongst the three categories fluctuated greatly.[127]

The traditional revenues were the same as everywhere in Spain: a quarter of all diocesan collection proceeds, in Segovia from around 375 parishes in all, burial rights and, most importantly, the annates and annuities.[128] The chapter managed to enlarge some of these revenues, for example by reconceiving the *tercias annatas* as the *medias annatas* in 1527 and thereby doubling the proceeds.

The second category, comprising alms and offerings, typically included six different types of contributions. First were those made by the kings. Considered over the entire period (1526-1653), they are remarkably insignificant, providing a share of just over four percent. Only during the very first decades did the emperor make substantial allocations from various of his religious holdings, though the actual receipts fell far short of what was promised.[129] Contributions from the bishops, some contracted and some voluntary, came on a very irregular basis and moreover totalled not more than three and a half percent of the combined alms and offerings. The cathedral chapter and clergy, and occasionally other clerics of the city (the city had 23 parishes),

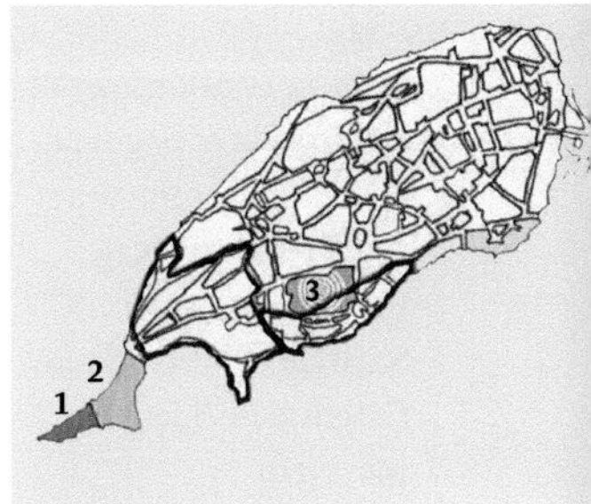

90
Segovia, map showing the location of the old and new cathedrals

1 Alcazar (royal fortress)
2 Site of the old cathedral
3 New cathedral

LITERATURE
Carrero & Rico 2004, p. 232.

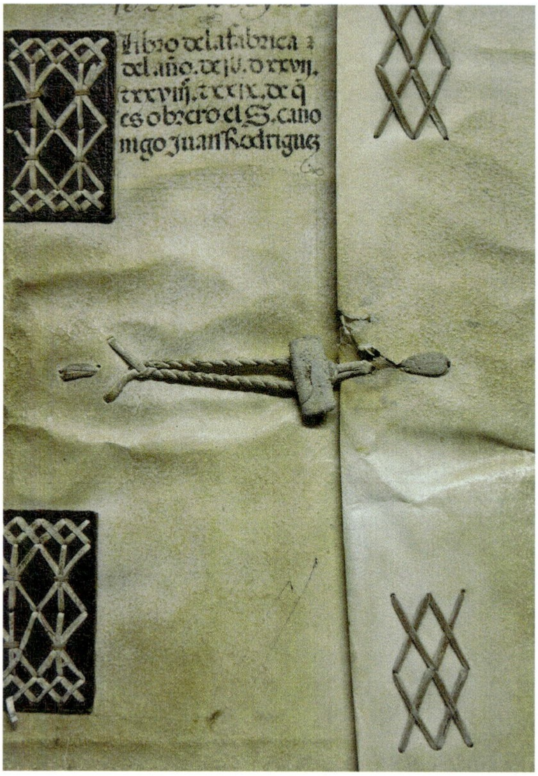

91
Volume containing the fabric rolls of Segovia Cathedral for the years 1527, 1528 and 1529
Parchment
Segovia, Archivo de la Catedral de Segovia, inv. C 219

The volume also states the name of the first master of the fabric (obrero) after the launch of the new building campaign in 1524, the canon Juan Rodriguez.

LITERATURE
Cillanueva de Santos 2009, pp. 278, 288, 322.

generated more than 17 percent of the total. The city itself made a range of different kinds of contributions. Initially it paid the aforementioned 3 million maravedís in damages, and later also the proceeds from an excise duty on olive oil and ham, raised with imperial consent. In fact, the city felt itself to be responsible for the cathedral and ultimately contributed over 27 percent of all the alms and offerings. From time to time we glimpse a measure of rivalry between the city and chapter, such as when the city demanded a stake in the alms administration in the form of one of the keys to the *arca* (strongbox).[130] Yet there was no question of civic control of the fabric as found throughout Italy. A further trivial share was contributed by the *Junta de Nobles Linajes*, a council of aristocratic families who diverted a small portion of the ground rents on their estates to the cathedral building works, generating slightly over five percent of the total offerings.[131]

The lion's share of the offerings, more than 40 percent of the total, came from the trade guilds. This amount also included small sums from the almsboxes, the *çepos en cada yglesiaI*, installed in every diocesan parish.[132] Within the city itself a movement got underway to gather funds, goods and building materials to support the building works – an enterprise trained along a ritualized devotional framework that bore remarkable similarities to Milan's fourteenth-century almsgiving movement.[133] Over the course of 22 Christian feast days, a continually varying assortment of groups of guild and confraternity representatives set out from their parish churches and processed to the ever-waxing cathedral to present their gifts. Devotional processions of this kind continued until far into the seventeenth century and were known as *echar piedra*, or 'giving of stones', suggesting that the ritual may have had its roots in the transfer of stones from the old cloister walk to the site of the new cathedral around 1525.[134] On these occasions we see all the various social and economic echelons of the civic community emerging from the woodwork. The largest share of the resulting receipts always came from the guilds associated with the cloth industry, which formed the backbone of the civic economy.[135] In the words of the chapter, the cathedral was built with the '*sudor y sustancia*' (the sweat and fortune) of the city.[136]

The special revenues making up the third category consisted of receipts from a number of special collections (including one in 1525), several large bequests, the sale of chapels and so on; these receipts were incidental in nature and added little weight to the balance.[137]

The erection of the new cathedral generated a large influx of revenues within a brief span of time. During the initial years after 1526, the fabric's income tripled relative to the years 1515-1517. But this boom period of construction was not destined to last very long. Tracing the entire period from 1526 until 1653, we see that the level of resources available for building could change from year to year. If we deflate the amounts in maravedís by wage indexes and subsequently render the result in the annual wages of an unskilled building labourer,[138] we find that works at the new cathedral were at their most energetic in the years before 1550, especially given the fact that a full 80 percent of the funds were spent on building in those years, as opposed to only 30 percent between 1604 and 1653. As would be expected, expenditures booked for the building lodge during this latter period present a far less rosy picture (graph 14).[139]

The cathedral of Segovia shares a claim with that of Salamanca[140] to being the last to be raised entirely in the Gothic architectural tradition. The funds amassed over the course of more than a century for its construction have rightfully been characterized as the fruits of a mixed patronage. Of these, contributions from the civic community, *el pueblo de Segovia*, expressing the populace's collective pride in its cathedral, were of the most vital significance.[141]

THE *FABBRICA DI SAN PIETRO* OF ROME, 1506-1626

The bishop's seat in Rome was not in St Peter's but in St John Lateran, and it was therefore this church that ranked as the official first church in the hierarchy of churches, the mother church of Christendom, the *cunctarum mater caput ecclesiarum*. It was also this church that housed the papal residence. Even so, the church of St Peter, built by the Emperor Constantine over the grave of St Peter, had long been the most important pilgrimage church in the Christian world, barring only the church of the Holy Sepulchre in Jerusalem. Not until the papacy returned from Avignon in 1377 did the papal court move to the Vatican. That relocation officially sealed the status of St Peter's,[142] with Pope Nicholas v (1447-1455) referring to it in so many words as the first church of the city and of the world.[143] Driven by a vision of transforming the architectural face of Rome, Nicholas was the first pope to take the initiative to rebuild the dilapidated fourth-century basilica, though only certain sections of it and with respect for the old building, replacing the old transepts and apse with models on a much larger scale. But the works were shut down upon his death and remained so for a long time, with only a brief revival under Paul II in 1470.[144]

It was not until the papacy of Julius II (1503-1513) that building activities resumed. On 18 April 1506 he laid the first stone of the new St Peter's, thus opening the architectural history of the largest church in Christendom. It is an architectural history that is exceptionally complex. To begin with, the question would remain right up until the beginning of the seventeenth century of whether the existing, venerable basilica built under Constantine could and should be preserved at least in part '*Ut simul et vetustas serbaretur et venustas adderetur*' (to both preserve its antiquity and increase its beauty).[145] Over the course of the relatively brief building campaign of slightly over 120 years,[146] a succession of architects,[147] brilliant and stubborn by turns, brought with them a changing progression of ideas and concepts about the nature and form of the church. They prompted similarly varying levels of ambition, resulting in the repeated demolition of freshly completed sections of the building[148] and the need to put up expensive temporary facilities, such as the enormous partition wall, the *muro divisorio*, which at once both shielded those parts of the old St Peter's still in use and connected them with the new building via a passageway. [149] Unlike an ordinary cathedral, moreover, the basilica and papal palace existed as a single unit, not only in terms of their geographic situation but also in their administration.[150] The personal interests of the pope – and particularly the plans framed by Julius II to give his tomb chapel a central place in the new church building – added a new component to the construction process and required additional, albeit incalculable, sources of income.[151]

The methods used to amass building funds can only be reconstructed in a general way. The difficultly here lies not only in the fragmentary state of the archives, but also in the manner in which the building was administered. Initially, building works at St Peter's were managed directly by the administration of the papal court, the *Camera Apostolica*,[152] and it was not until later, and then in successive phases, that a separate management body, the *Fabbrica*, was established. The first step was taken in 1510, when Julius II appointed a committee of prelates to collect and administer the offerings.[153] Leo X (1513-1521) subsequently entrusted the issue of indulgences and collection of indulgence monies to a cardinal, placing the financial and executive management of the building lodge itself in the hands of lay persons.[154] It was Clement VII (1523-1534) who finally established an administrative body that would endure unchanged until around 1605. On 12 December 1524 he published the bull *Admonet Nos* and laid the basis for

the *Collegium* LX *Virorum*: a college of 60 prelates from every Christian nation appointed to manage the *Fabbrica di San Pietro*, with the authority to act autonomously and in certain matters even independently of the pope, operating under its own jurisdiction and with a private court of law to settle disputes.[155] It was a form of management that reflected the old notion of St Peter's as the mother church of all churches – the church of universal preeminence.[156] This idea served to legitimize not only the lofty ambitions of the enterprise and the show of *magnificentia* – harking back to the Roman emperors[157] – but also the procurement of construction monies from throughout the whole of Europe. Just as a cathedral fabric could call upon the faithful of the entire diocese, so the construction of St Peter's should be certain of the support of all Christians.[158]

In 1589 Pope Sixtus v curtailed the far-reaching autonomy of the *Collegium LX Virorum* by appointing a single cardinal to direct the college. In 1605 the entire body was replaced with the *Congregazione della Fabbrica*, now under the direction of three cardinals, which introduced a distinction between administrative activities (including the collection of funds), led by the *economo*, and actual building operations as led by the architect.[159]

We have scarcely any quantitative data relating to how the building works were financed during the first critical period before the *Sacco di Roma* in 1527, when the city was devastated by the plundering troops of Charles v. Indeed, there is almost no surviving documentation at all. It is only from 1529 on that the *Fabbrica* archives, and specifically the accounts listing the *'entrata e uscita'* (receipts and expenditures), have been preserved.[160]

The unique significance of the succession of bulls of indulgence promulgated in aid of the construction of St Peter's from 1507 onwards[161] is due in particular to the unusually complicated way in which they were proclaimed and propagandized across the length and breadth of the Christian world, as well as to the contest over how the proceeds were to be divided.[162] These indulgences were no different in nature from the usual plenary pardons. In larger territories north and south of the Alps, the pope assigned the collection to the diverse provinces of the Franciscan Observant Order, with an indulgence commissary appointed to direct affairs and see to the campaign's actual organization. Foremost amongst the his tasks was to negotiate terms with administrators of the cathedrals and churches where the indulgence was to be offered. Here churches always demanded a large share of the local proceeds. In areas with a strongly centralized government, by contrast, such as England, Brittany and Savoy, campaigns were organized along existing secular boundaries, with the division of the proceeds a constant point of negotiation. Secular lords were keen to dictate the terms under which the pardon for St Peter's would be permitted in their lands. As an example, we have the kings of Hungary and Poland, who managed to obtain two-thirds of the indulgence monies to fund their wars against the pagans.[163]

The opposite strategy was also employed. On 2 December 1514 Pope

92
The church of St Peter in Rome, as seen from the east during the construction of the façade, 1610-1611
Pen drawing, 245 x 315 mm
Wolfenbüttel, Herzog August Bibliothek

LITERATURE
Exh. cat. *Barock im Vatikan, Kunst und Kultur im Rom der Päpste II 1572-1676*, Bonn 2005-2006, no. 28.

Leo x proclaimed the pardon for St Peter's for several large territories that included the Low Countries. In the following year, on 7 September 1515, Charles v secured from the pope exclusive rights for another indulgence to fund repairs to the dykes, which would replace the former for a term of three years, though on the condition that one-third of the fruits would go to the works at St Peter's. The dyke indulgence was effectively privileged above that for the church of St Peter, and in so doing the emperor managed to keep the reins well in hand.[164]

Pope Leo x's *Liquet nos* (1513) and *Sacrosanctis Salvatoris* (1515) bulls of indulgence have gone down in history as firing the starting shot for the Reformation. It was against the second of these that Luther posted his 95 Theses in Wittenberg in 1517. This plenary indulgence was issued at the request of Margrave Albert of Brandenburg, who was archbishop of both Mainz and Magdeburg as well as bishop of Halberstadt. During the eight years that followed, all other indulgences issued for any church or cause whatsoever throughout this expansive territory would be suspended. Half the proceeds benefitted Albert (allowing him to pay the Roman Curia the extremely high taxes attached to his agglomeration of ecclesiastical titles), the other half the church of St Peter. The Fugger banking family took charge of the financial arrangements.[165]

Luther aimed his criticism not only at the indulgence in and of itself, but also at the allocation given the indulgence receipts. Why did the pope not build his church of St Peter using his own funds? Ostensibly, because St Peter's belonged to all Christians, but the Germans scoffed at this argument: a church was meant to be the place where the faithful came to hear the word of God and receive the sacraments; yet how many Germans would ever actually visit the church of St Peter? Money earmarked for building and maintenance at parish churches was now diverted to an insatiable, expensive project. For the faithful, large churches served no purpose at all: '*Sanct Peters Münster zu Rom, Coloniae et Ulm templa sunt amplissima et inopportuna*'.[166] And besides, no one could say for certain whether the monies that in theory accrued to the building works at St Peter's ever really made it there. Doubt and rumour were rife as to whether the funds were not in truth being used to meet the pope's personal expenses.[167]

In regions where the Reformation prevailed, the collection of indulgence monies quickly devolved into a fiasco – with major consequences. Only in those areas that remained Catholic were indulgences still promulgated with success. The year 1562 saw the pope repeal the indulgence for St Peter's throughout all of Christendom. In Spain, where the king had regarded the indulgence for St Peter's as direct competition for his immensely successful crusade indulgence to support the war against the Muslims, introduced in 1482, the *Cruzada* was now instituted as the sole permissible indulgence. But even here the Holy See continued to demand a portion of the proceeds, and after difficult negotiations the Spanish crown was made to cede initially half, and later a fixed sum, for the construction and upkeep of St Peter's. Ultimately, the *Cruzada* would evolve into a state tax, a small portion of which continued to go to St Peter's until far into the nineteenth century.[168] During the period of construction between 1529 and 1620, however, an average of 65 percent of St Peter's building income derived from *Cruzada* contributions from Spain and the Spanish territories. To put it succinctly, without the *Cruzada* receipts, St Peter's could never have been completed.[169]

Sufficient data remain from the year in which the first stone was laid in 1506 until the basilica's consecration in 1626, notwithstanding a few lost decades, to allow us to quantify the volume of the *Fabbrica*'s income in broad terms and thereby make a quantitative estimation of the immensely variable scale of building operations.[170] Within that 120-year period, war (the Battle of Lepanto in 1571) and political scheming disrupted the works for an interval of slightly under half a century; here we see that relations between the pope and the Spanish crown were decisive in determining how faithfully the *Cruzada* monies were delivered to Rome. The actual duration of the building campaign can be approximated at between 70 and 80 years.[171] In the first seven years between 1506 and 1512, a sum of at least 70,000 ducats was spent on the building works, thus more than 10,000 a year, equal to around 330 annual wages of a *manovale*.[172] After the Sack of Rome in 1527, building activity all but ceased for seven years. From 1529 we have accounts that span until 1620, making it possible to calculate the income in annual wages of a *manovale*.[173]

Table 2
Average annual expenditures of the *Fabbrica di San Pietro*, as expressed in the annual wage of a *manovale* 1529-1585

1529-42:	**139**	**annual wages**
1543-49:	**547**	**annual wages**
1549-61:	**324**	**annual wages**
1561-70:	**291**	**annual wages**
1572-79:	**244**	**annual wages**
1580-85:	**661**	**annual wages**

Building activity reached a climax with the completion of the dome between 1587 and 1590, when narrative sources estimate the number of labourers involved at 600 or even 800. For 433 working days between July 1588 and May 1590, there may even have been as many as 1000 building labourers simultaneously engaged on the dome's completion.[174] Yet a new peak in building activities came with the start of nave and façade construction in 1608 and 1609, with expenditures topping 140,000 scudi over two years, thus an annual value of approximately 1865 annual wages.[175] In the campaign's final phase under the pontificate of Paul v, between 1605 and 1620, expenditures reached the immense sum of 1,510,406 ducats, or over 1300 annual wages a year and more than what had been spent in all the preceding hundred years (fig. 92).[176]

The lists recording figures and range of other published data relating to the building lodge at St Peter's together yield a fairly consistent picture of its average scale. Considered over the lengthy building period, which saw great fluctuation in the volume of activity, the *Fabbrica di San Pietro* emerges as one of the largest of the ecclesiastical building operations, although only in its concluding phase did it ever manage to surpass the scale of operations at the very largest cathedrals such as Milan and Toledo. The speed with which Bernini's vast colonnade encircling St Peter's Square was built between 1657 and 1667 was equally unprecedented. An estimate of the costs involved reveals that average annual expenditures in this decade came to the equivalent of over 1280 annual wages of a *manovale*,[177] a sum that completely overshadows even the largest of the medieval ecclesiastical building lodges.

TWO DURATION AND PACE OF CONSTRUCTION

The previous section already anticipated questions concerning the scale of ecclesiastical building lodges, and specifically of how many building labourers were employed at any one time, what quantities of building materials were needed, and how much money was spent on the often expensive inventory of bells, organs, altars, stained glass, liturgical vessels, paraments and the like. Given the dearth of relevant sources, it has never been possible to come up with a satisfactory answer to these questions, despite the fact that we have detailed knowledge about the duration of building campaigns at most cathedrals and churches. The remarkable differences in these durations makes the question of scale all the more acute. Utrecht Cathedral was built and furnished in about 275 years – a fairly standard pace of construction for the late medieval period.[178] And yet the time it took to build several of the large Ottonian cathedral churches has been reckoned at no more than a few decades,[179] whilst most of the large twelfth- and thirteenth-century French cathedrals were raised within a time frame of less than a century.[180]

All the same, scholars have attempted to quantify the scale of these building enterprises using other, non-financial data. One such study was prompted in part by the provocative hypothesis offered by Robert S. Lopez in 1952, framed as the question *Economie et architecture médiévale: cela aurait-il tué ceci?*[181] Lopez had observed that medieval Italian cities were in the vanguard of economic growth but lagged behind in terms of the size and wealth of their religious edifices, just like the affluent cities of modern-day America. At the same time, he noted that certain French cities – Beauvais, for instance – that are famed for their awesome cathedrals never achieved any true measure of economic prosperity, though not for lack of trying. Might it be that the construction of cathedrals in Beauvais and elsewhere stunted the economic development of these cities by diverting scarce production resources away from such sectors as trade and industry and putting them towards non-profitable projects instead? Lopez's hypothesis elicited many responses, both positive and negative.[182] One scholar, H.

Thomas Johnson, set about testing his theory against the facts.[183] Based on a single example – the construction of Westminster Abbey in London between 1246 and 1259, for which the financial and budgetary data are known – he endeavoured to calculate the quantity of labour required to build a single specific physical unit: a cubic yard. By extrapolating the resulting data to cathedrals and other large church buildings constructed in England between 1100 and 1400 he was able to compute the number of man-years needed to build them. His conclusion was that only a small share of England's labour pool was actually used to build large churches. Johnson thus comes down on the side of the opponents of Lopez's theory, and quite rightly, as will become clear below. At the same time, however, the essentially accurate tenor of his conclusion does not conceal the fact that his methodology was far too general to produce any kind of reliable result.[184]

An entirely different approach was taken by the Australian architect John James, who calculated the scale of the building lodge at Chartres Cathedral during the most important phase of its building history, between 1194 and 1223. His estimates are the by-product of a minute architectural analysis of the building, on the basis of which he claims to have established that the immense structure was raised and completed layer by layer in a number of annual building campaigns over the course of the stated period, with marked variation in the scale of operations and in the pool of labourers employed there. He approached the problem of quantifying the fluctuating scale of these campaigns by computing the cost price of each year's worth of work as though the cathedral were being built today, that is to say according to current prices and using modern technical apparatus. This approach allowed him to make comparisons between each of the annual building campaigns and to render the distribution of architectural effort invested over these 30 years in the form of a bar graph. The result of this inevitably speculative calculation coincides with everything other sources tell us about the early building history of Chartres Cathedral. It fully captures, for instance, the major acceleration in building operations that followed on the loss of the bishop's and chapter's modest contributions and subsequent succession of miracles and attendant flood of offerings from the faithful. It also manages to provide a historically founded explanation for the 1209 collapse that caused building operations to revert to the low level of the campaign's early years: the crusade against the Albigensians, in which the bishop of Chartres took part.[185]

The changeable pace of building at Chartres is remarkably similar to that characterizing operations at the Dom in Utrecht several centuries later, as well as of a number of other churches where financial records have been preserved. Only where ecclesiastical building expenditures are documented in monetary amounts is it actually possible to paint a reliable picture of the scale of building operations. Though such data have in fact been preserved in a fairly large number of cases, it diverges widely in both place and time. A number of these cases are brought together below, representing not only cathedrals but also other kinds of church buildings such as abbeys, collegiate churches and parish churches. Wherever possible, expenditures for the building lodge and for inventory have been translated into the annual wages of an unskilled labourer. In a few instances we only know the fabric's gross expenditures, in other words including all general costs, which could be considerable. In order to discover the size of the various ecclesiastical building lodges and the rate at which they consumed resources, we must therefore also possess a basic understanding of such general costs. As it turns out, the scale of building operations and of fabric expenditures had an upper limit that was rarely exceeded. A general median value can also be identified. The lower limit is of little interest, as it would have been determined by the basic costs of maintaining the building. Utrecht found itself down at this level in the years after 1525. The first 20 accounts after 1527 reveal an average construction cost corresponding to eleven years' wages of a building lodge assistant; the absolute low points came in 1527, with six annual wages, and 1542, with seven and a half.

Such low-level building expenditures were by no means unusual. Indeed, the majority of cathedral fabrics that were not or only minimally engaged in building would have had to make do with similarly small budgets;[186] the Hundred Years' War (1337-1453) saw a great many French cathedrals even operating under this level.[187] Work was no more intensive at the collegiate church of St Victor in Xanten between 1356 and 1491.[188] In Utrecht, the lowest point of the entire cathedral building campaign came during a period of war, in 1483, when building expenditures dipped to 13 annual wages – still a reasonable level of activity, and moreover one that many cathedrals in France and elsewhere would never or only scarcely match during the fourteenth and fifteenth centuries, even in campaigns that stretched out over many years. In Limoges, heavy repairs to the bell tower between 1388 and 1391 were on a par with the building pace in Utrecht in 1483.[189] Building activity was hardly more energetic in Troyes during the second half of the fourteenth and beginning of the fifteenth centuries, as we have seen.[190] Even the expenses booked by the Buurkerk in Utrecht during the building lodge's most active years between 1430 and 1456, when renovations for the hall church were underway, never topped the equivalent of 17 annual wages.[191]

Cathedral fabrics that financed a permanent or semi-permanent building lodge typically disposed over an annual budget of between 20 and 100 annual wages of an unskilled labourer.[192] At an average of 81 annual wages in the long period between 1395 and 1527, the pace of cathedral-building in Utrecht was exceptionally high. In terms of size, its building lodge was comparable with that of York Minister between 1399 and 1543 and of Exeter Cathedral in the campaign's first decades between 1299 and 1342. Even comparatively extensive, late medieval building programmes were borne to a successful conclusion on a smaller pool of funds; the construction of the transept Sens Cathedral between 1490 and 1516, for example, consumed a yearly average of under 40 annual wages.

It was fairly rare for a church fabric to have long-term access to a building budget of anything over 100 annual wages. The building lodge at the immense church of Our Lady in Antwerp, which was both collegiate and parish church in one of the most affluent cities of northwestern Europe, disposed over an annual budget averaging 112 annual wages for a period lasting more than a century, from 1431 until 1540. The rapid pace of building at Hereford in 1290-1291 no doubt represents a moment in that cathedral's building history that its fortunes were up.[193] The cathedral of Prague, begun in 1344, was still in an early stage of development when it reached its construction peak between

1372 and 1378,[194] with the volume of works declining apace towards the end of the fourteenth century and ceasing almost entirely for the space of nearly a hundred years during the Hussite Wars (1419), until 1509. Building climaxed in 1372 and again in 1377, when expenditures totalled 235 annual wages, just a fraction higher than the maximum total building cost of 212 annual wages booked in Utrecht in 1505. The rate of construction achieved in Milan during the initial campaign years between 1387 and 1391 is utterly unparalleled, at seven to eight times that of the Utrecht Dom. But here, too, the intensity of operations saw a sharp decline even before the century was out.[195]

The largest ecclesiastical building lodge known to us from documentary sources concerns not a cathedral but the royal abbey church of Westminster in London. Over a period of nearly 25 years, from 1246 until 1272, construction spending averaged a sum equal to 710 annual wages, and in one year, 1252, even reached 1185 annual wages. Nearly the entire enterprise was financed by the king, and it was he who determined the pace of building.[196] In March 1251, *in adventu regis* (at the king's arrival), there were to be six to eight hundred labourers at work.[197] Two years later the king demanded that additional workers be hired – 1000 if it came to that – in order to have a particular section of the building finished before Easter.[198] The building lodge at Westminster Abbey resembles that of such large royal castles and fortresses as Beaumaris, Caernarvon and Conway. There the pace of building was even higher: at times there were more than 1600 people labouring on these military structures.[199] Incidentally, the building works at Charles v's Vredenburg Castle in Utrecht also employed 1000 labourers after 1528, who finished the job in ten months.[200]

Church building operations probably never attained this level of intensity, even at large twelfth- and thirteenth-century French cathedrals like Chartres, which were completed within a few decades.[201] One of the very few extant eyewitness accounts describing the size of a building lodge in this period relates to the cathedral of Santiago de Compostela. According to the pilgrim's guide, the campaign years around 1100 saw some 40 to 50 stonemasons working alongside the architect on a daily basis.[202]

Cathedrals and other churches had neither the financial means nor the clout to attract a labour force in the way that some sovereigns could.[203] There was a definite ceiling to the scale of ecclesiastical, and in particular cathedral, building works. As such, it is hardly likely that, as Lopez claims, cathedral-building deterred the economic growth of various episcopal cities.

Observed over the long term, the general pattern of cathedral fabric expenditures paints a picture of instability. This can be explained in part by the fact that certain sources of income might only be available for a circumscribed period, or perhaps just once. Examples include not only pledges from kings and bishops, but also papal pardons issued for a limited term. As a result, the height of expenditures could show powerful growth for one or several years and then revert to former levels. Another factor was crises, whether sustained in character, as in the case of war, or incidental, such as the fire that struck the city of Oviedo. There, two canons were assigned the difficult task of giving notice to the master builder and his staff *con dulçes palabras* (with sweet words), but kept the masons at work in the quarry in order to ensure building materials would be ready when the building campaign could be resumed.[204] In Utrecht, it was the abrupt decline of the quest monies that tore a permanent hole in the fabric's primary source of revenues. At the cathedral of Cologne, the master of the fabric saw himself compelled to fire all the workers in 1530 and shut down the *officina fabrice*, presumably for the same reason.[205]

We may well wonder to what extent bishops and chapters embarking on new building projects sought to form any conception of the financial burdens they were laying on their own shoulders and on those of their successors. In fact, as soon as the floor plan was established, the scale of the works was more or less fixed. The situation was even more set in stone when successive or even simultaneous phases of the campaign were conducted on entirely different sections of the building. In both Utrecht and Cologne, the towers were raised long before anyone had given thought to linking the transepts; indeed, that at Cologne Cathedral would not be anywhere near completed in the Middle Ages. In many cases the cathedrals as conjured in the minds of ecclesiastical building patrons could not actually be realized by their successors. Countless cathedrals were abandoned as torsos, some eventually completed in the nineteenth century, such as Cologne, Beauvais, Clermont-Ferrand, Limoges, Regensburg and Prague. We also encounter a reverse situation: churches conceived on a plan that was too cramped for later, unforeseen requirements. All sorts of tricks were then deployed to equip a building begun too small for heavier demands. A case in point is the church of Our Lady in Antwerp, a collegiate church and, crucially, the sole parish church of a city whose rapid growth from around 1450 onwards and multiplication of confraternities and trade guilds, all needing chapels and altars, far exceeded the capability of its fourteenth-century cathedral to house them.[206] The thirteenth-century Buurkerk, too, required modifications to meet changing demands. It is symptomatic of the diminishing importance of cathedrals in relation to parish churches in the later medieval period that a severe shortage of space was far less of a problem amongst the former.

The layout of medieval cities furnishes an apt comparison. There, too, civic administrations faced the difficulty of treading the fine line between an overly ambitious urban plan that ultimately brought large tracts of undeveloped land inside the walled precincts, where building and maintenance were expensive, and an excessively conservative expansion plan that later demanded constant, costly modification.[207]

In the campaign to build Utrecht Cathedral, there was a definite measure of financial planning, over both the short and long term. Where the short term was concerned, the chapter was highly adept at securing the monetary resources needed to finance unanticipated large expenditures.[208] Where the longer term was concerned, it repeatedly took steps to tap new sources of income and to guarantee their continued profitability. In the strict sense of the word, however – that is, in the sense of drawing up a budget – planning was an unfamiliar concept.[209] Not until the later Middle Ages do we encounter any capacity to estimate the costs entailed in an extensive building project or the length of time needed to complete it.[210] In 1506 the chapter of Palencia concluded an agreement with its master stonemason Joan de Ruesga under which the cathedral was to be finished within a period of five years for a sum of 3.6 million maravedís, or roughly 500 man-

93
Fragment of a design sketch for the west façade of the cathedral of Clermont-Ferrand, 1496
Parchment, 1392 x 676 mm
Clermont-Ferrand, Archives départementales Puy-de-Dôme 3 G arm. 18, sac B, cote 29

The drawing belongs with the itemized cost estimate which the cathedral chapter of Clermont-Ferrand commissioned four architects and the building labourers to have drawn up before a notary on 18 November 1496. It describes building activities associated with necessary repairs to the cathedral and the building's completion. The erection of a new west façade with three portals and two towers would account for half the projected costs, namely, 55,000 l.t. (around 1650 annual wages). The drawing relates to this part of the specification. The prominently placed coats of arms of the king and bishop suggest that years.[211] On 18 November 1496, at the chapter of Clermont-Ferrand's request, four architects drew up an itemized cost estimate for the completion of that cathedral. Included in the plan was the construction of three bays of the nave and side aisles and the west façade with three portals and double towers, as well as minor repairs to the roof, to the two small towers on the south portal and to another tower on the north portal of the Virgin Mary. Appended to the estimate was a surviving presentation drawing on parchment: '*le patron et portraict des portaux et ce qu'il reste a parachever à l'eglise de Clermon*', possibly intended to help solicit funds from the king and bishop (fig. 93).[212] The architects reckoned the total cost of building and repairs at 100,300 l.t. – an extremely large sum, equal to 3240 annual wages of an unskilled labourer, or a period of 40 years of labour at the pace sustained by the Utrecht Cathedral fabric for the whole of the fifteenth and beginning of the sixteenth centuries. It was patently clear to the canons that they were not in any position to complete the task as set. Unlike its counterpart in Utrecht, the fabric of Clermont-Ferrand was not equipped to make such a huge capacity investment. It would not be until Viollet-le-Duc that the original plan could be realized, though adapted as he deemed fit, between 1848 and 1864. The canons of Utrecht Cathedral could count themselves more fortunate. After two and three-quarter centuries, precisely before the definitive turn of the previously favourable tide, they were able – if only barely – to complete their cathedral.

the chapter may have intended to use the drawing to solicit funds from them. The façade as shown here was never built; the current façade was designed by Viollet-le-Duc.

LITERATURE

Davis 1983, pp. 67-83; Recht 1989, pp. 419-420.

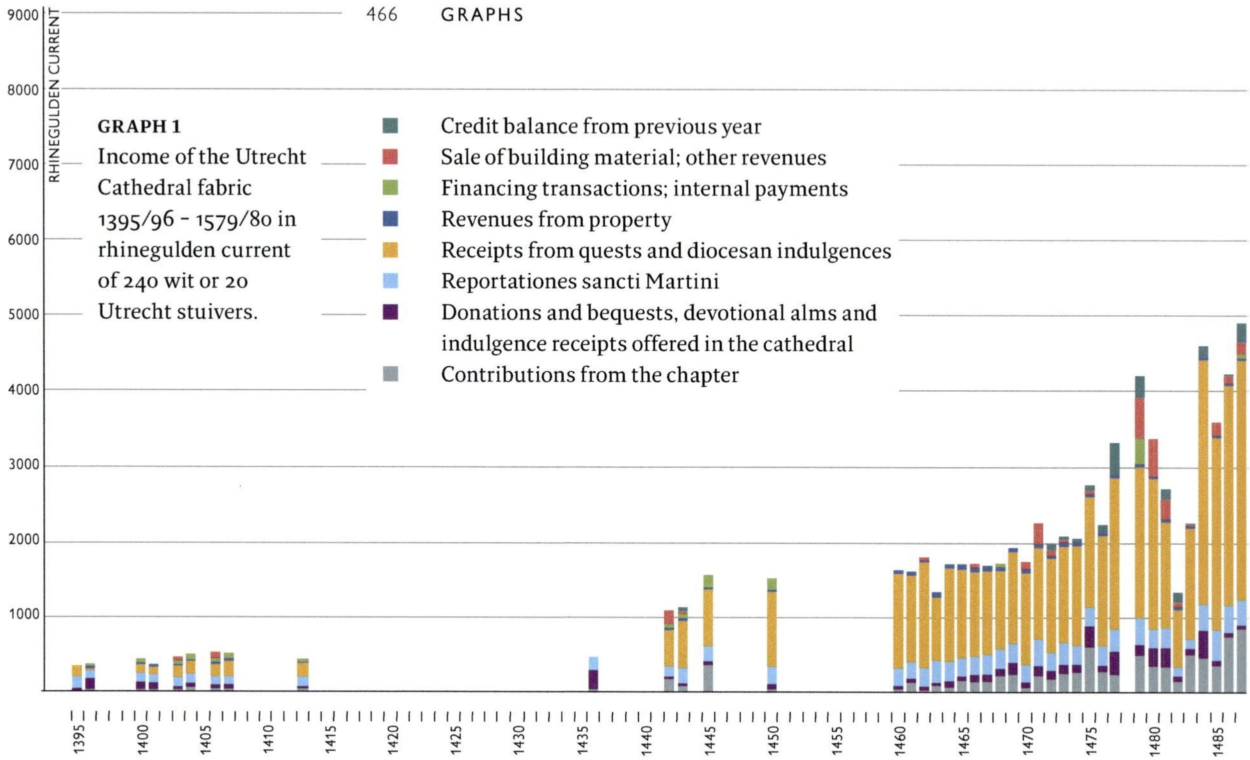
9000
8000
7000
6000
5000
4000
3000
2000
1000
RHINEGULDEN CURRENT
GRAPH 1
Income of the Utrecht Cathedral fabric 1395/96 - 1579/80 in rhinegulden current of 240 wit or 20 Utrecht stuivers.
Credit balance from previous year
Sale of building material; other revenues
Financing transactions; internal payments
Revenues from property
Receipts from quests and diocesan indulgences
Reportationes sancti Martini
Donations and bequests, devotional alms and indulgence receipts offered in the cathedral
Contributions from the chapter
1395
1400
1405
1410
1415
1420
1425
1430
1435
1440
1445
1450
1455
1460
1465
1470
1475
1480
1485

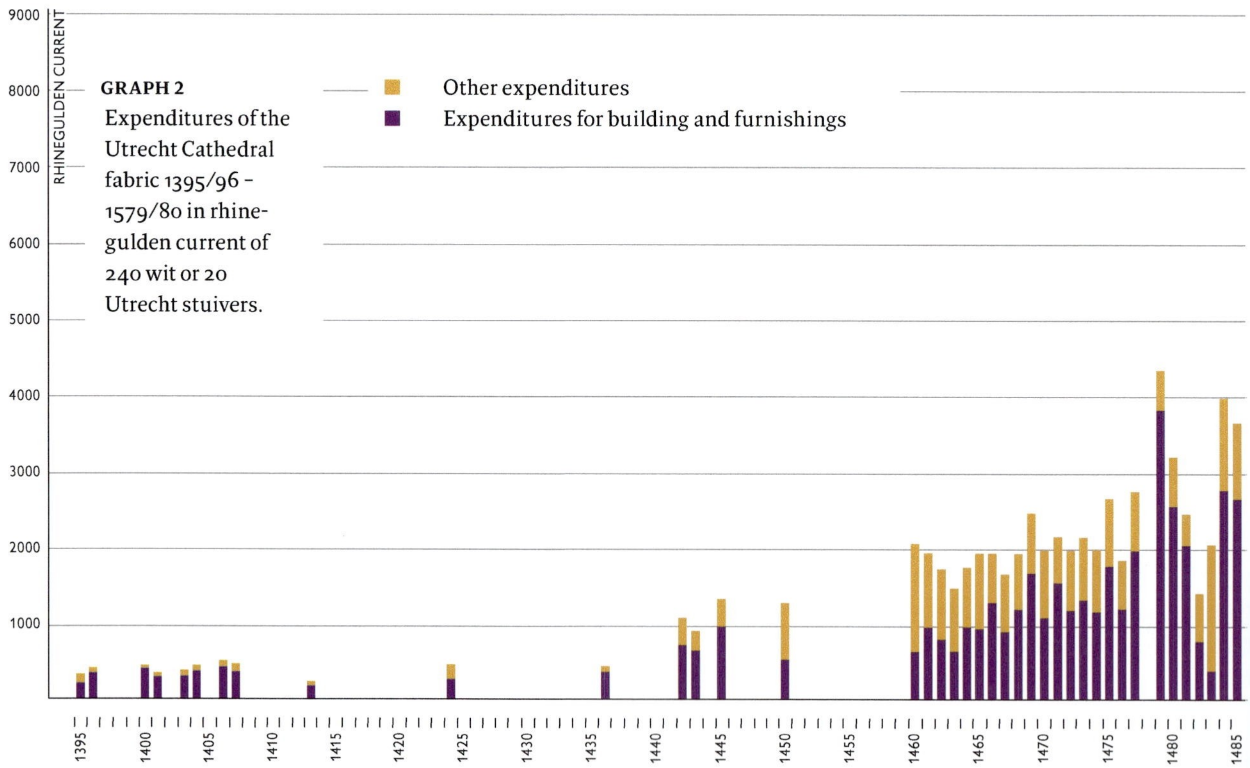
9000
8000
7000
6000
5000
4000
3000
2000
1000
RHINEGULDEN CURRENT
GRAPH 2
Expenditures of the Utrecht Cathedral fabric 1395/96 - 1579/80 in rhinegulden current of 240 wit or 20 Utrecht stuivers.
Other expenditures
Expenditures for building and furnishings
1395
1400
1405
1410
1415
1420
1425
1430
1435
1440
1445
1450
1455
1460
1465
1470
1475
1480
1485

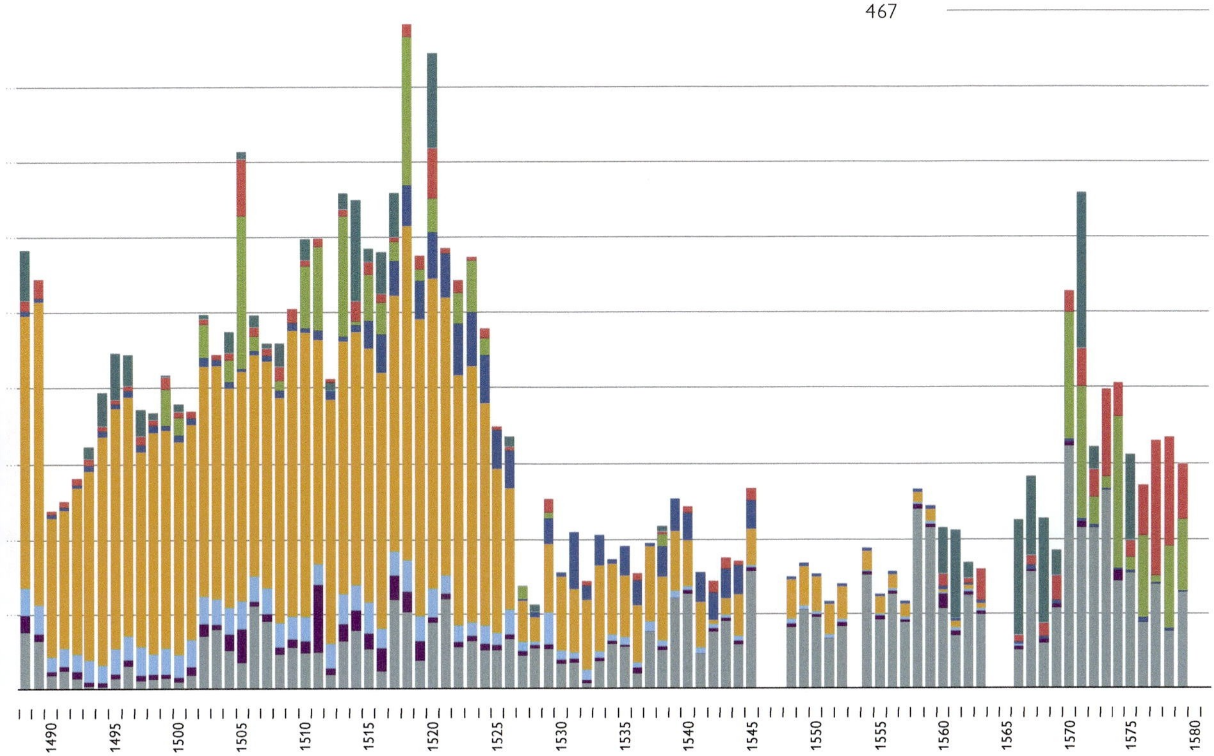
1490
1495
1500
1505
1510
1515
1520
1525
1530
1535
1540
1545
1550
1555
1560
1565
1570
1575
1580

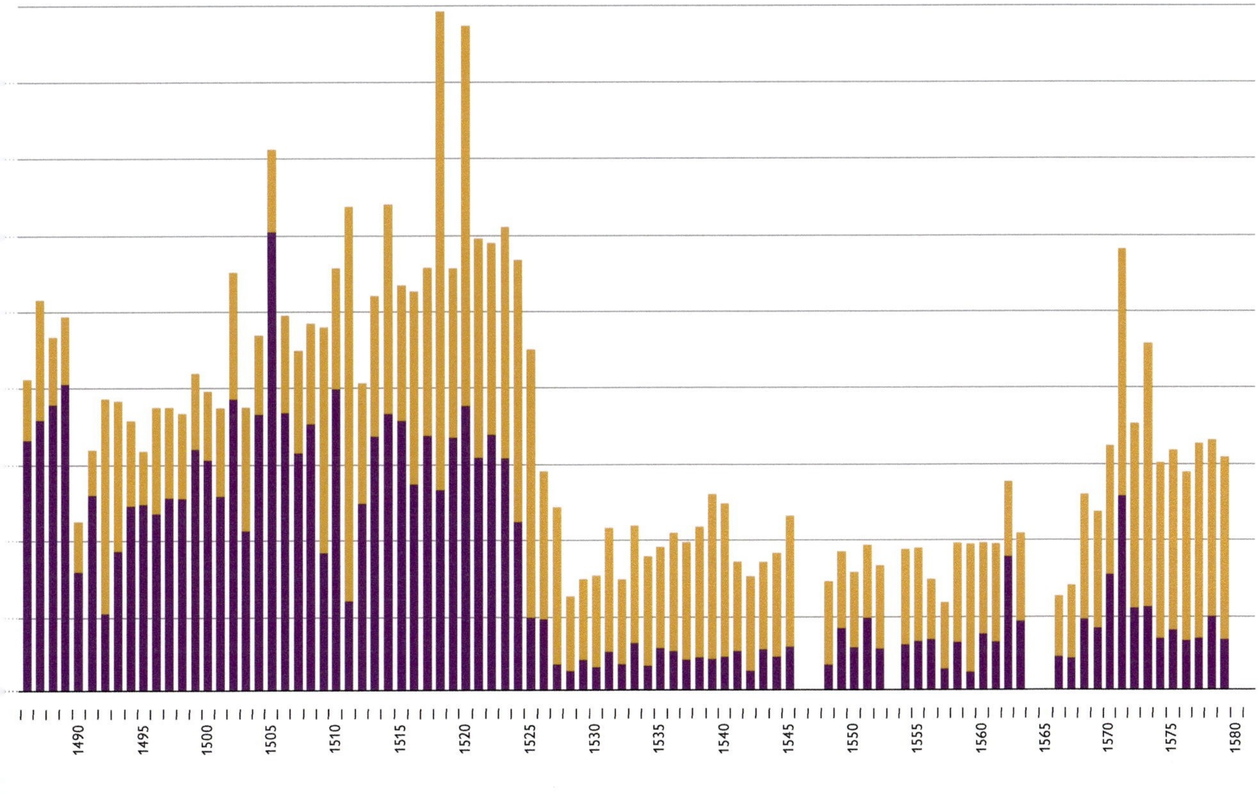
1490
1495
1500
1505
1510
1515
1520
1525
1530
1535
1540
1545
1550
1555
1560
1565
1570
1575
1580

GRAPH 3

Restancie (items in arrears) of the Utrecht Cathedral fabric 1395/96 - 1579/80 in rhinegulden current of 240 wit or 20 Utrecht stuivers.

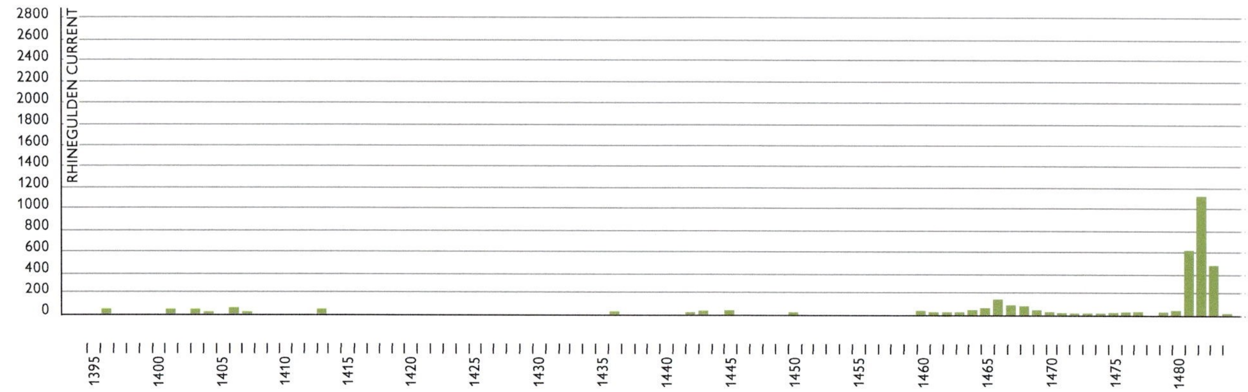

GRAPH 4

Credit and debit balances of the Utrecht Cathedral fabric 1395/96 - 1579/80 in rhinegulden current of 240 wit or 20 Utrecht stuivers

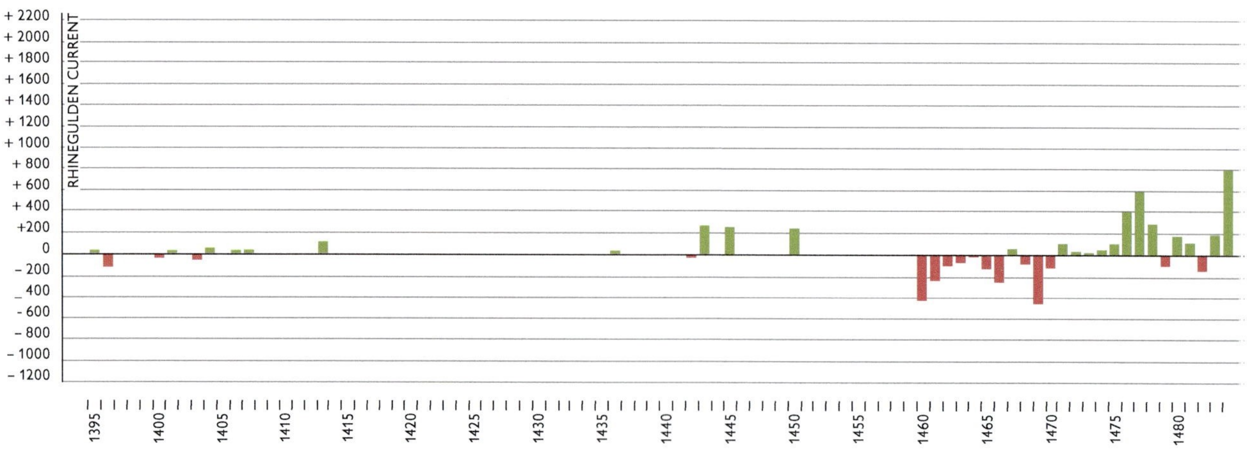

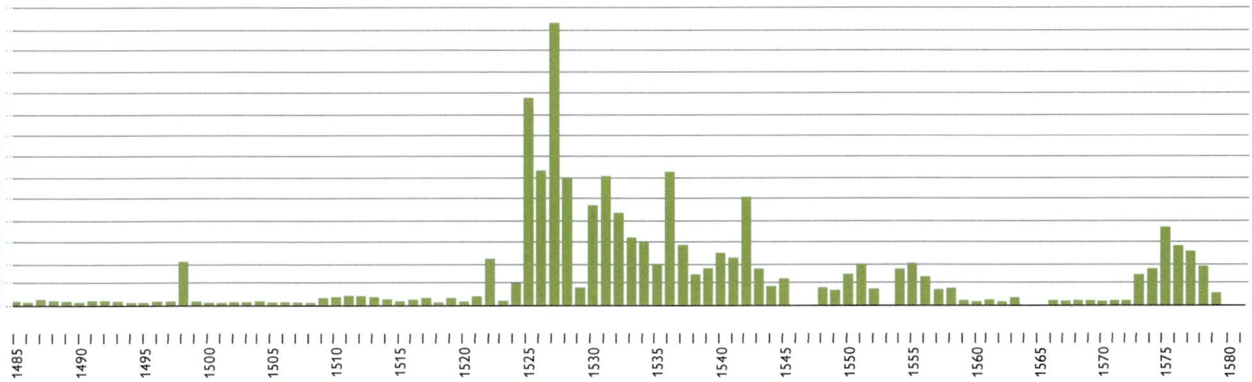
1485
1490
1495
1500
1505
1510
1515
1520
1525
1530
1535
1540
1545
1550
1555
1560
1565
1570
1575
1580

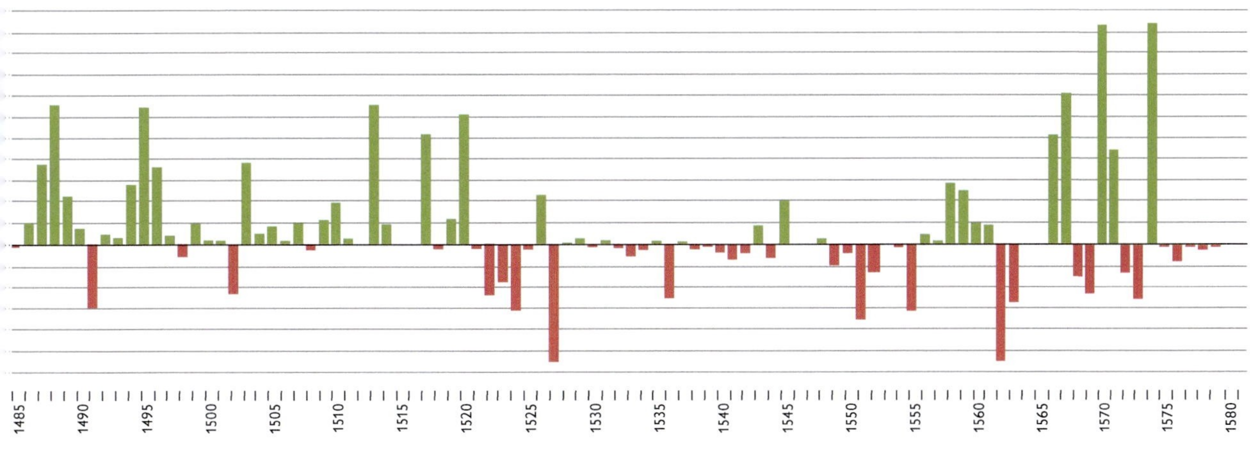
1485
1490
1495
1500
1505
1510
1515
1520
1525
1530
1535
1540
1545
1550
1555
1560
1565
1570
1575
1580

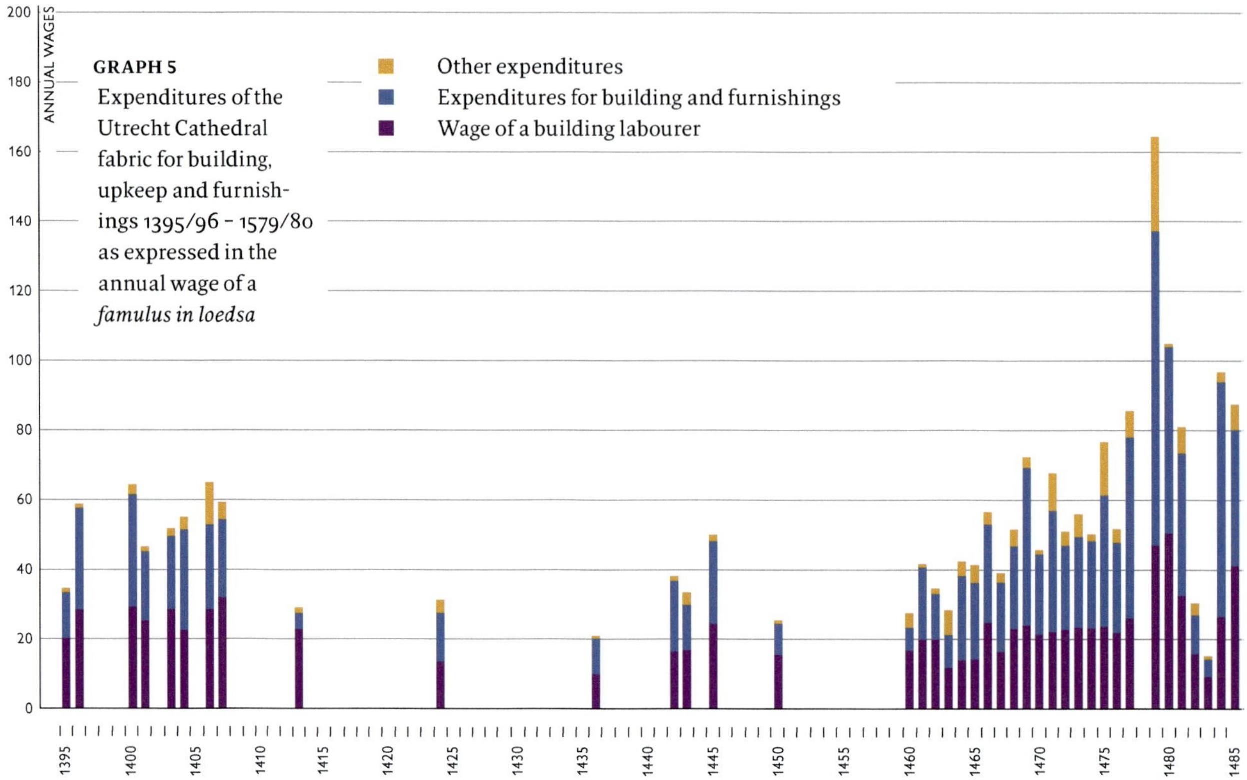

GRAPH 5
Expenditures of the Utrecht Cathedral fabric for building, upkeep and furnishings 1395/96 – 1579/80 as expressed in the annual wage of a *famulus in loedsa*

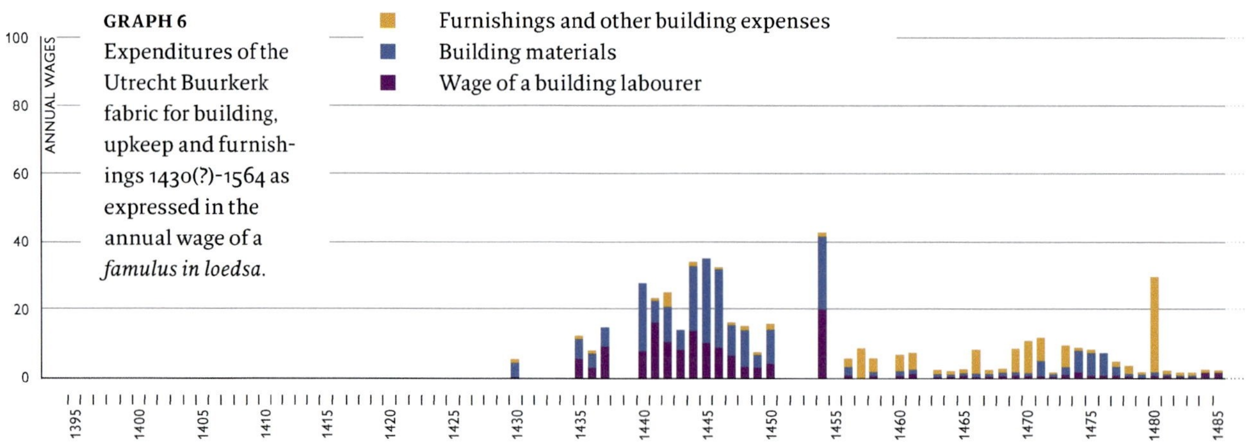

GRAPH 6
Expenditures of the Utrecht Buurkerk fabric for building, upkeep and furnishings 1430(?)-1564 as expressed in the annual wage of a *famulus in loedsa*.

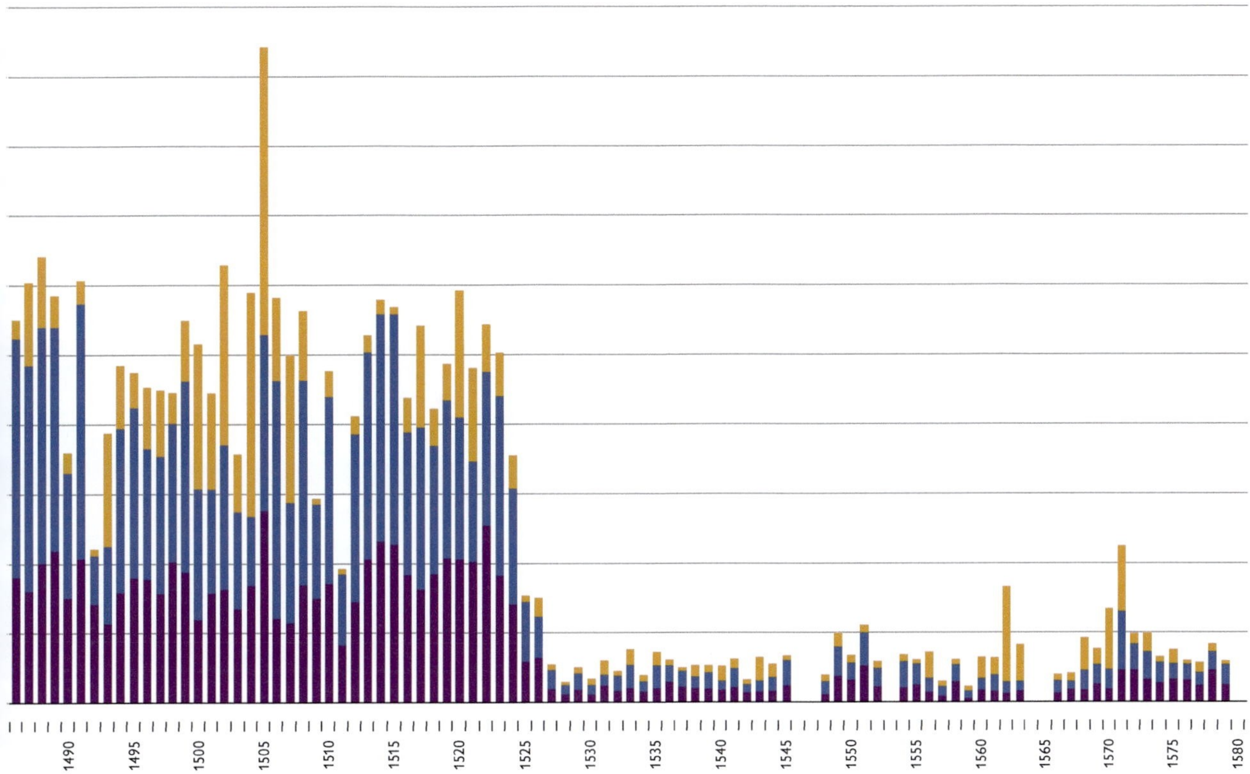
1490
1495
1500
1505
1510
1515
1520
1525
1530
1535
1540
1545
1550
1555
1560
1565
1570
1575
1580

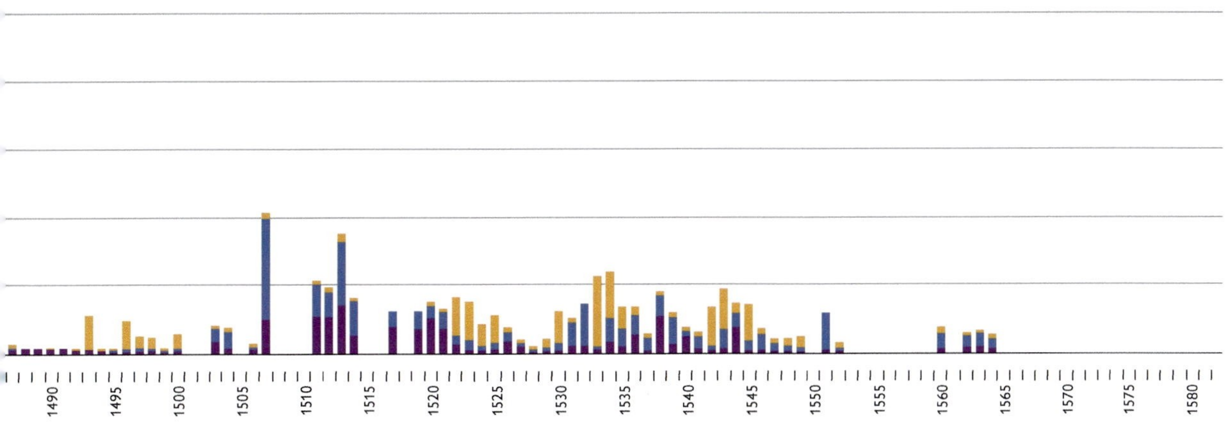
1490
1495
1500
1505
1510
1515
1520
1525
1530
1535
1540
1545
1550
1555
1560
1565
1570
1575
1580

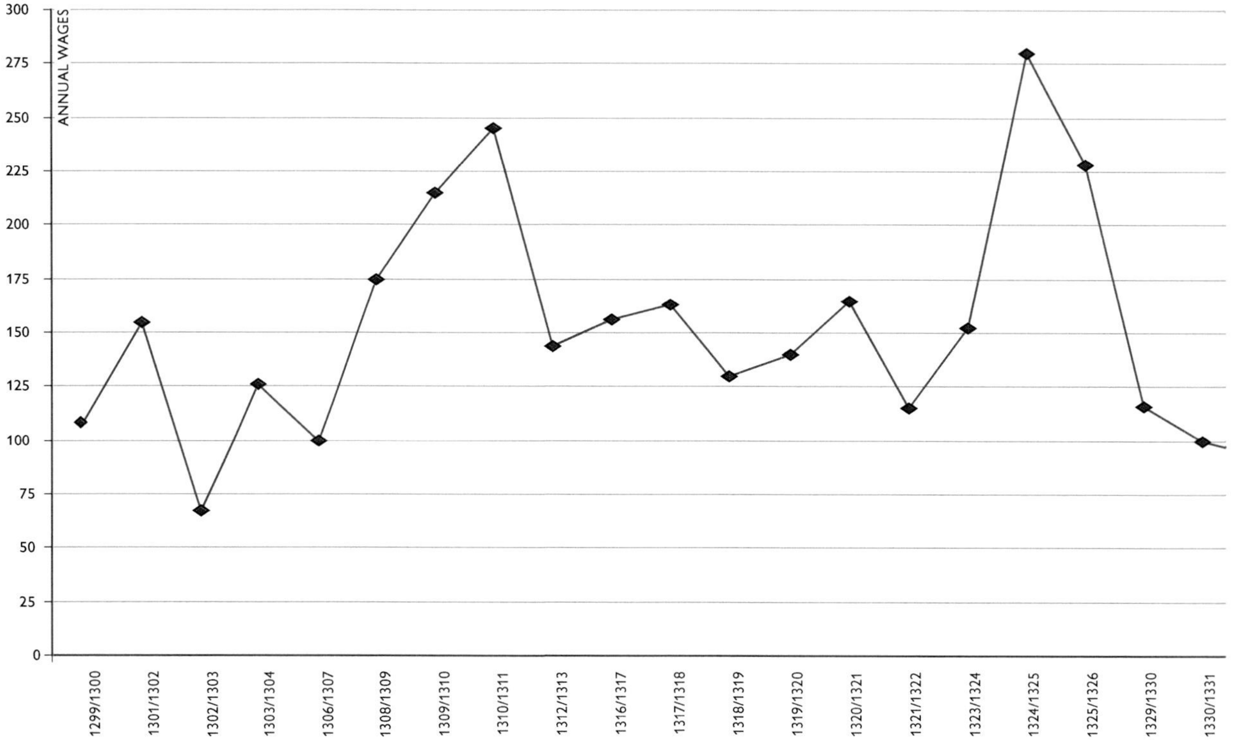
ANNUAL WAGES
300
275
250
225
200
175
150
125
100
75
50
25
0
1299/1300
1301/1302
1302/1303
1303/1304
1306/1307
1308/1309
1309/1310
1310/1311
1312/1313
1316/1317
1317/1318
1318/1319
1319/1320
1320/1321
1321/1322
1323/1324
1324/1325
1325/1326
1329/1330
1330/1331

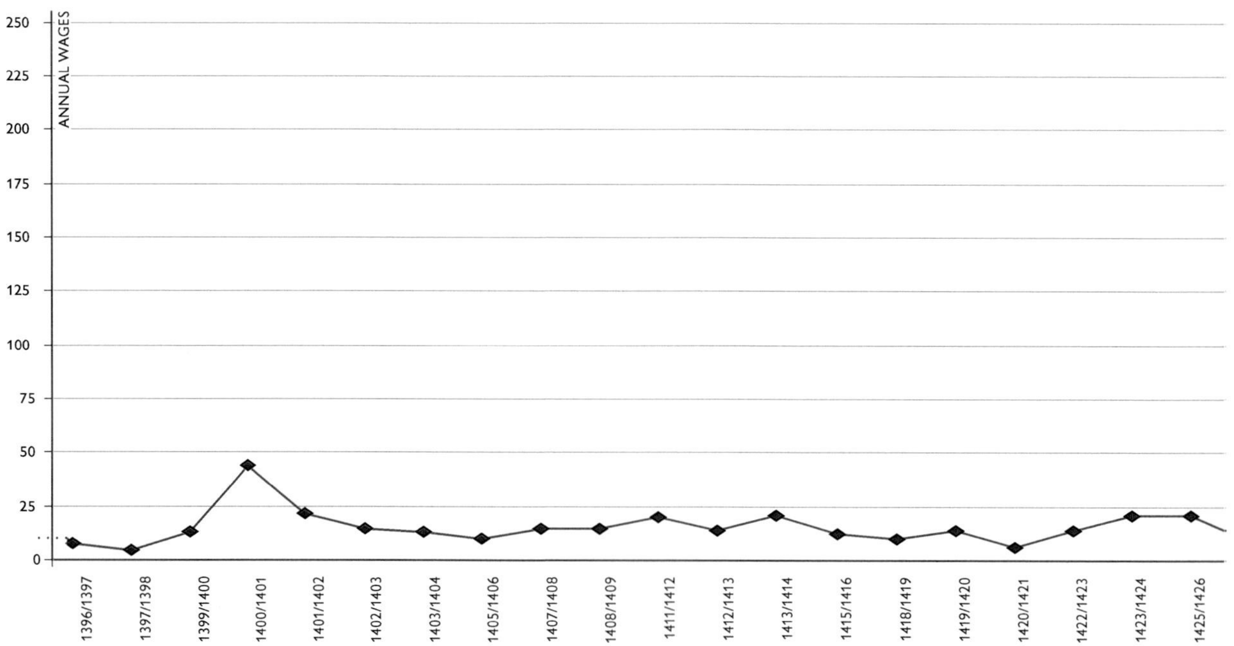
ANNUAL WAGES
250
225
200
175
150
125
100
75
50
25
0
1396/1397
1397/1398
1399/1400
1400/1401
1401/1402
1402/1403
1403/1404
1405/1406
1407/1408
1408/1409
1411/1412
1412/1413
1413/1414
1415/1416
1418/1419
1419/1420
1420/1421
1422/1423
1423/1424
1425/1426

GRAPH 7
Expenditures of the Exeter Cathedral fabric 1299/1300 - 1505/06 as expressed in the 250-day annual wage of an unskilled building labourer: 1300-1350: 2 d. per day; 1351-1372: 2½ d. per day; 1371-1400: 3 d. per day; 1401-1411: 3½ d. per day; 1412- 1505: 4 d. per day.

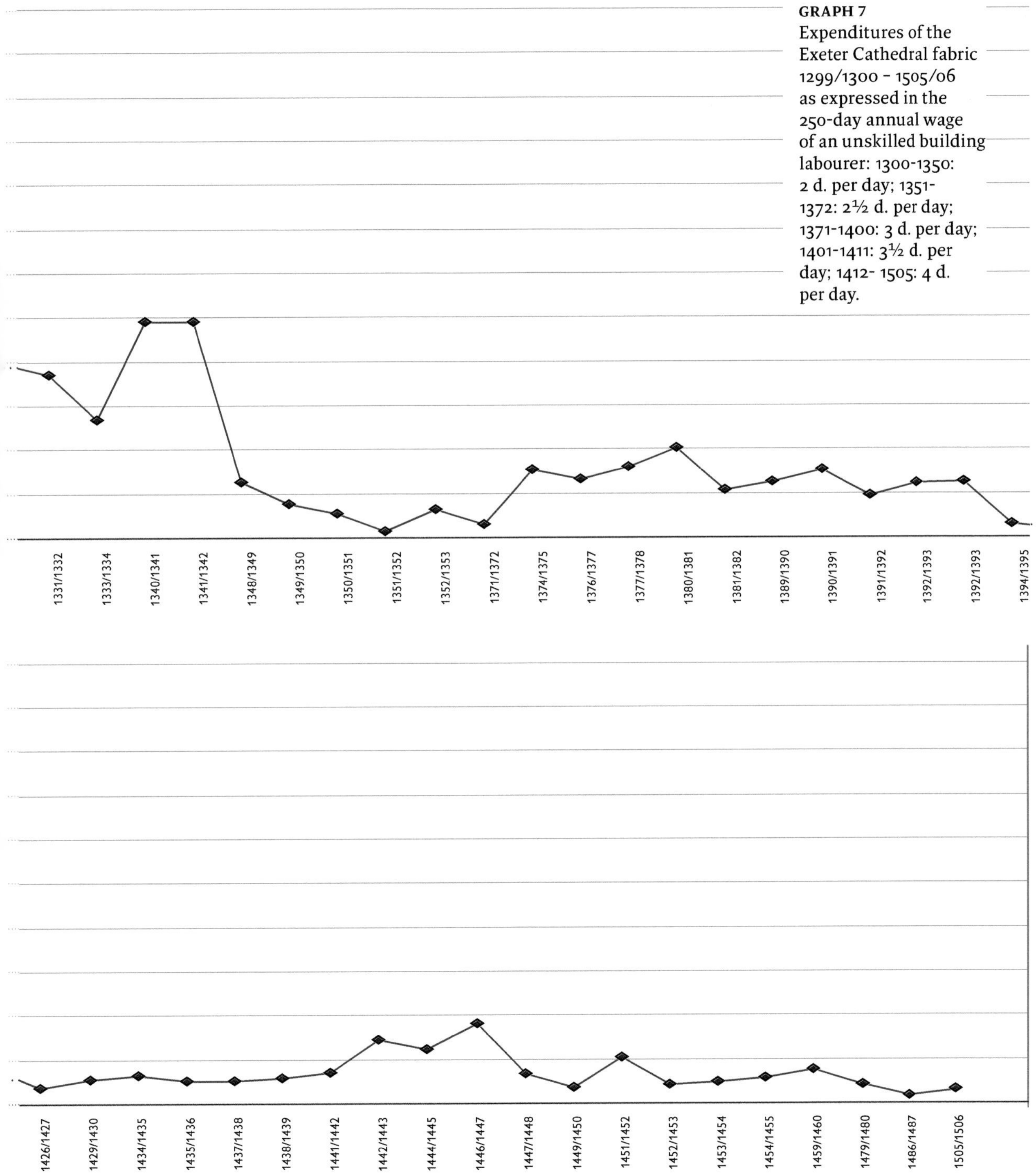

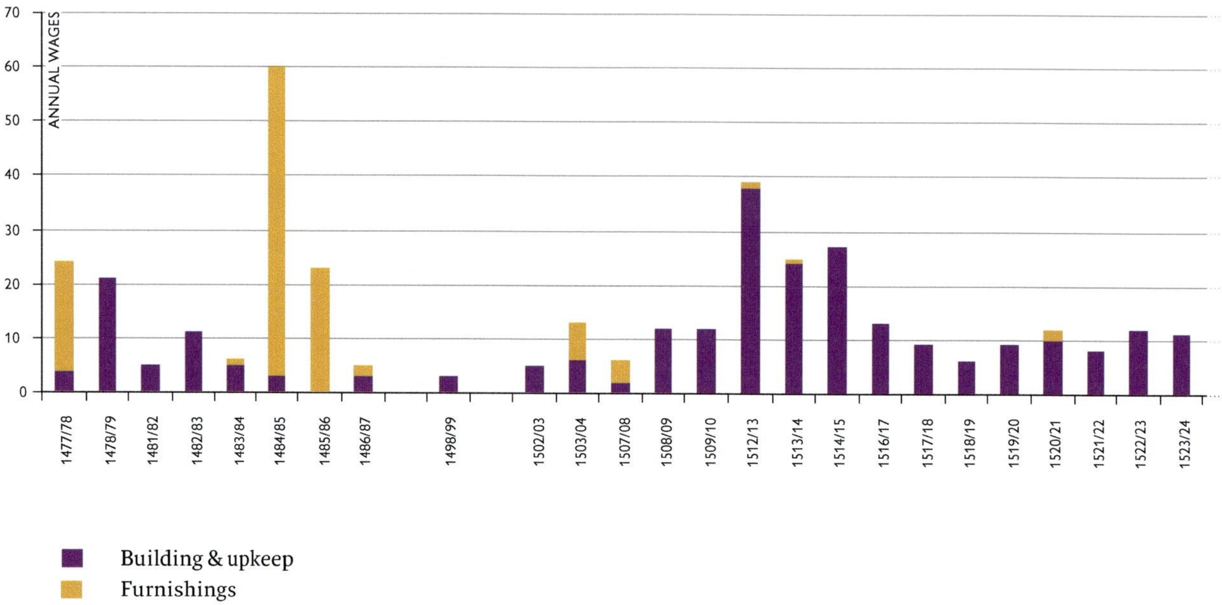
ANNUAL WAGES
70
60
50
40
30
20
10
0
1477/78
1478/79
1481/82
1482/83
1483/84
1484/85
1485/86
1486/87
1498/99
1502/03
1503/04
1507/08
1508/09
1509/10
1512/13
1513/14
1514/15
1516/17
1517/18
1518/19
1519/20
1520/21
1521/22
1522/23
1523/24
Building & upkeep
Furnishings

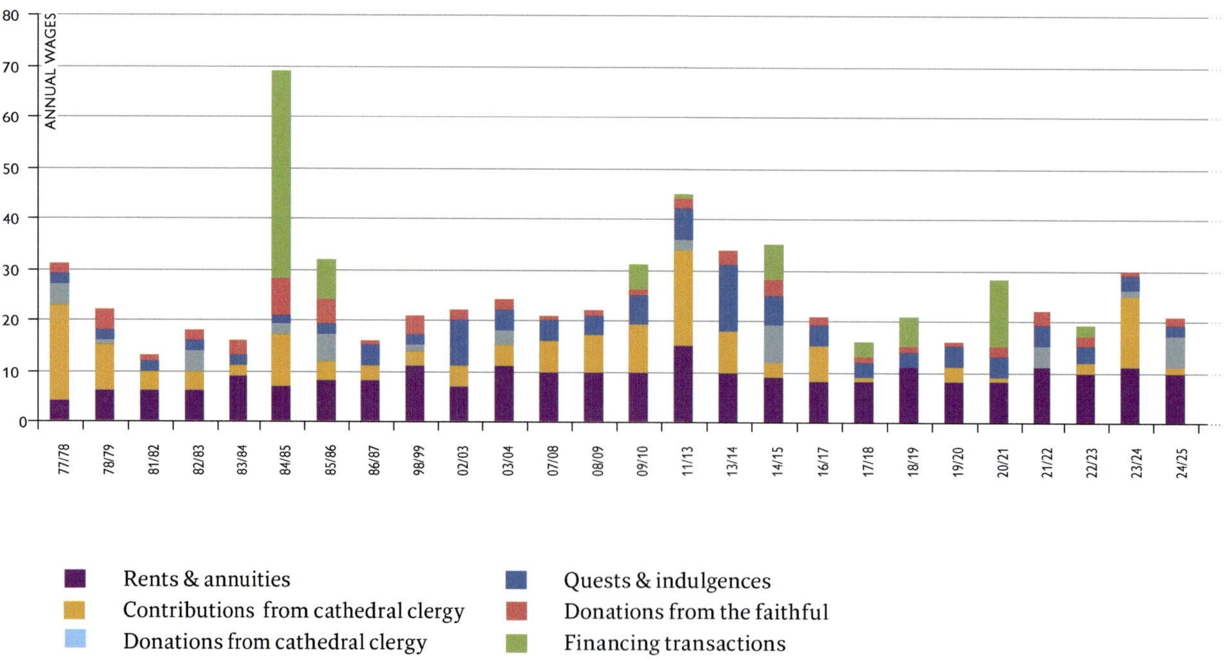
ANNUAL WAGES
80
70
60
50
40
30
20
10
0
77/78
78/79
81/82
82/83
83/84
84/85
85/86
86/87
98/99
02/03
03/04
07/08
08/09
09/10
11/13
13/14
14/15
16/17
17/18
18/19
19/20
20/21
21/22
22/23
23/24
24/25
Rents & annuities
Contributions from cathedral clergy
Donations from cathedral clergy
Quests & indulgences
Donations from the faithful
Financing transactions

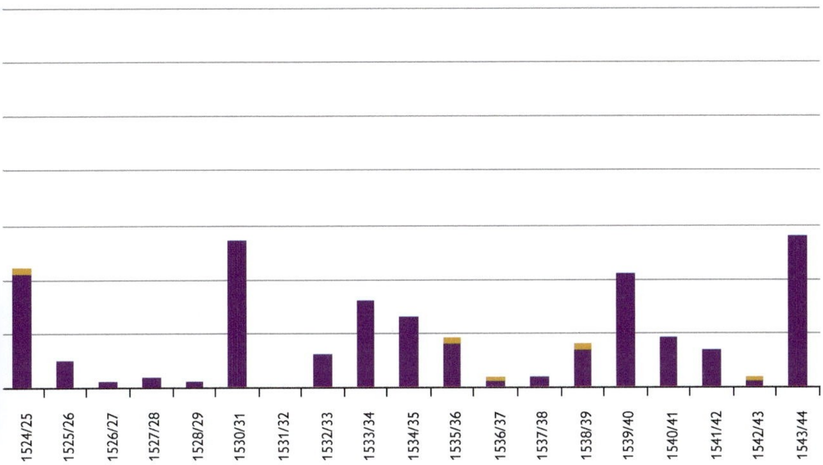

GRAPH 8
Expenditures of the Osnabrück Cathedral fabric for building, upkeep and furnishings 1477-1543 as expressed in the 250-day annual wage of an unskilled building labourer: 1477-79: 8 d.; 1481-84: 10 d.; 1484-1514: 12 d.; 1516-1532: 14 d.; 1533-1537: 15 d.; 1538: 16 d.; 1539: 18 d.; 1540-43: 20 d.

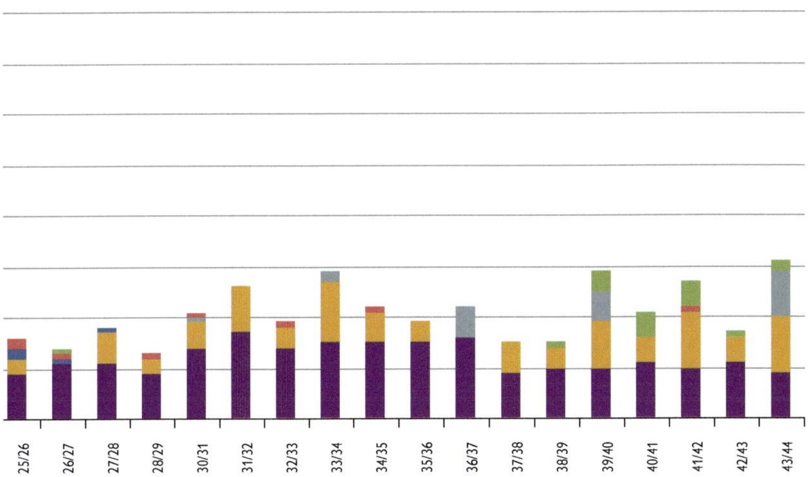

GRAPH 9
Net income of the Osnabrück Cathedral fabric 1477-1543 as expressed in the 250-day annual wage of an unskilled building labourer. Credit balances from previous years are not included.

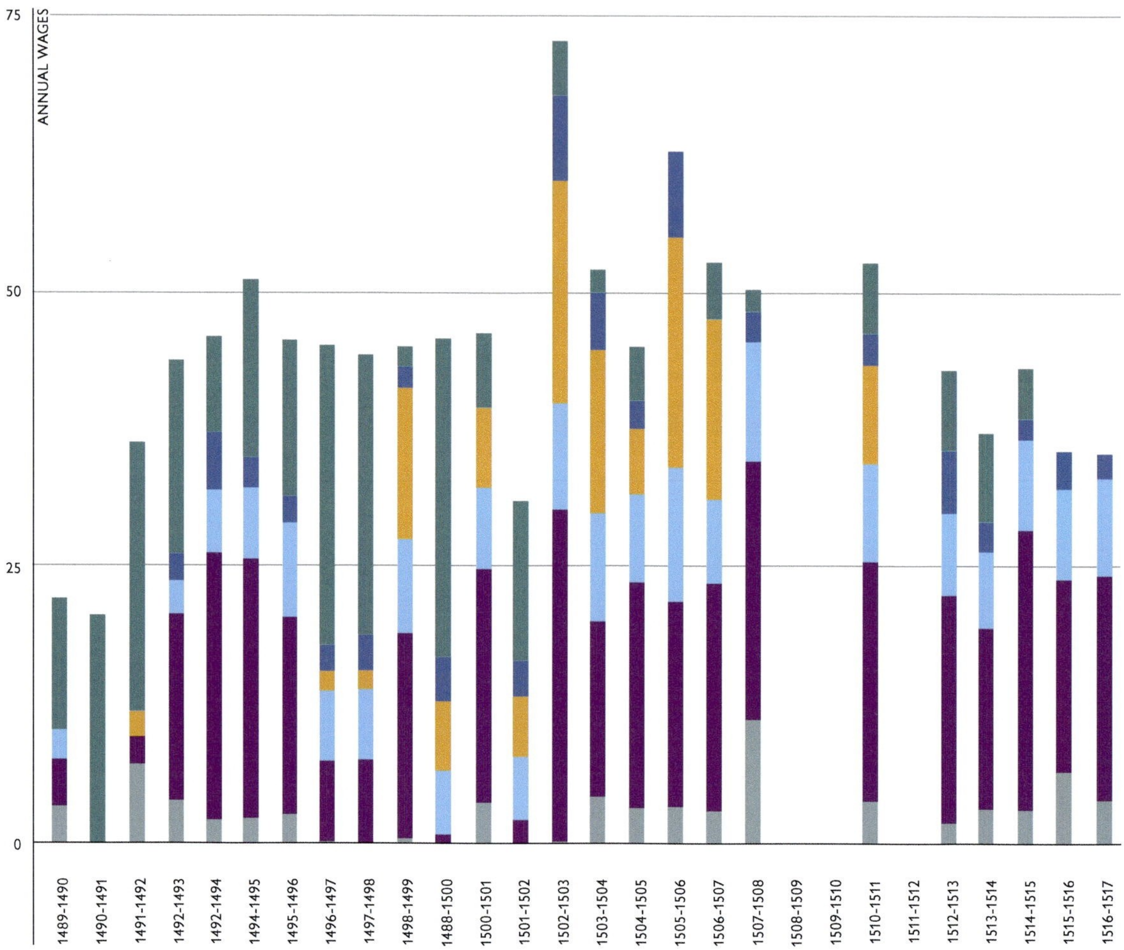

GRAPH 10
Income of the Sens Cathedral fabric 1489/90 - 1516/17 during transept construction as expressed in the annual wage of a manoeuvre (30 l.t. per year).

- Credit balance previous year
- Contributions from the faithful: quests, confraternity, collection boxes, etc.
- Annuities and rents, sale of building material
- Contributions from canons
- Bequests, contributions from the king
- Other revenues: archiepiscopal donations, the *gabelle*, loans

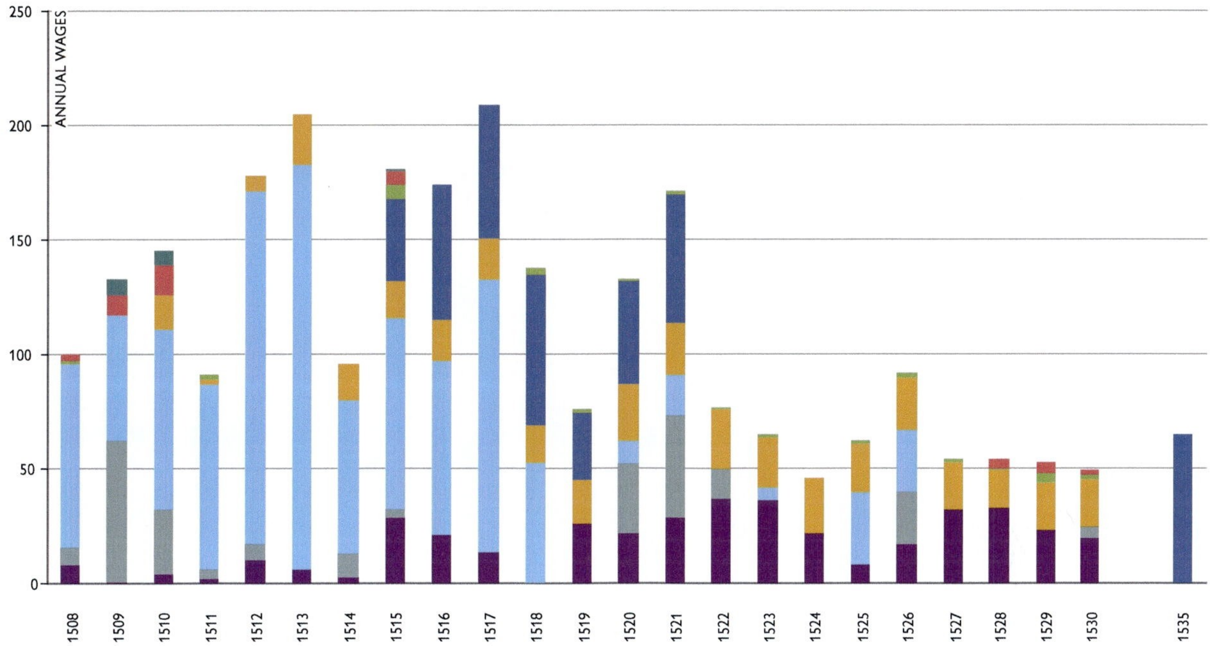

GRAPH 11
Income of the Bourges Cathedral fabric 1508-1535 as expressed in the 250-day annual wage of a manoeuvre (2.s. 6 d. per day).

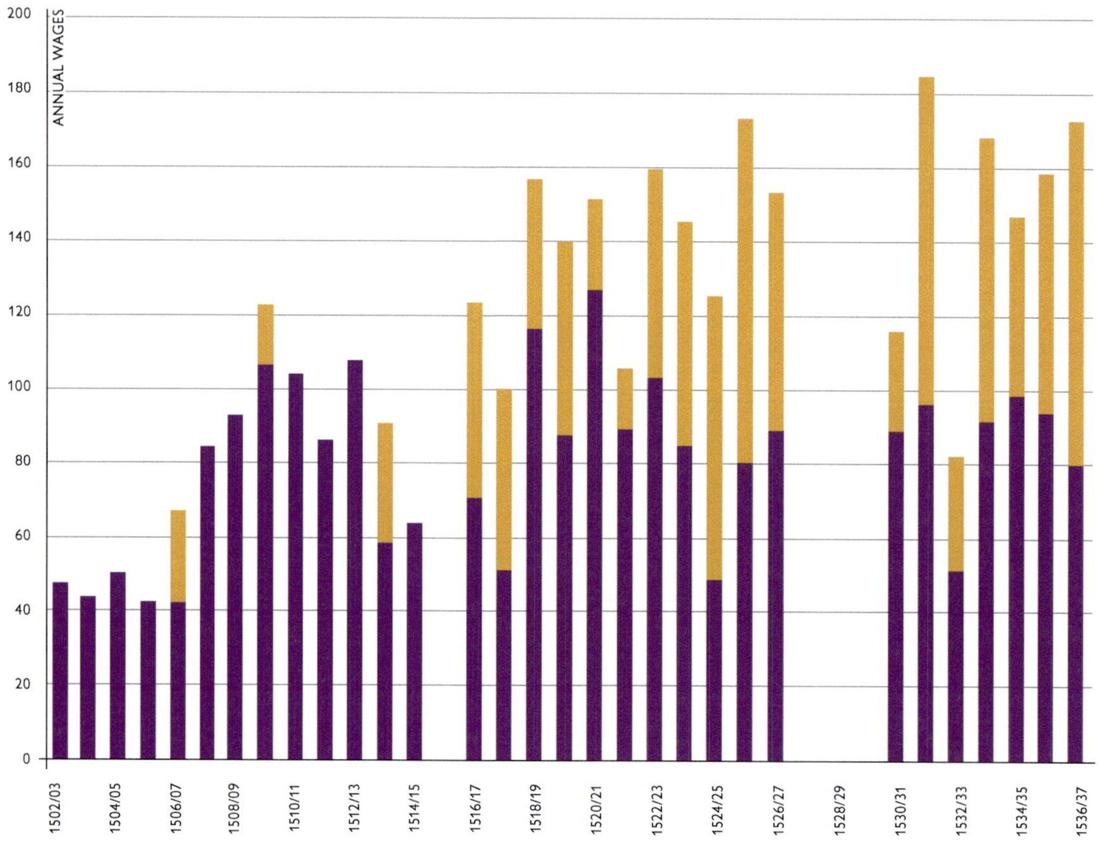

GRAPH 12
Income of the Troyes Cathedral fabric, including the share supplied by the gabelle, 1502/03–1536/37 as expressed in the 250-day annual wage of a manoeuvre (2 s. 1 d. per day). Source: Meunier, forthcoming

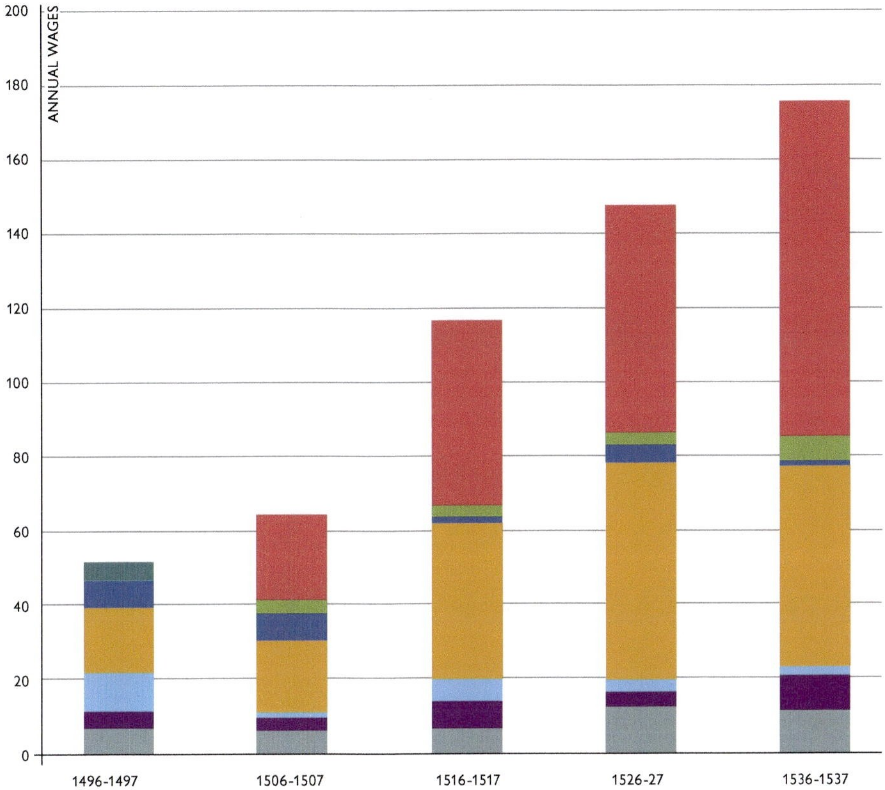

GRAPH 13
Income of the Troyes Cathedral fabric in the years 1496/97, 1506/07, 1516-17, 1526/27 and 1536/37 as expressed in the 250-day annual wage of a manoeuvre (2s.1 d. per day). Source: Meunier , forthcoming

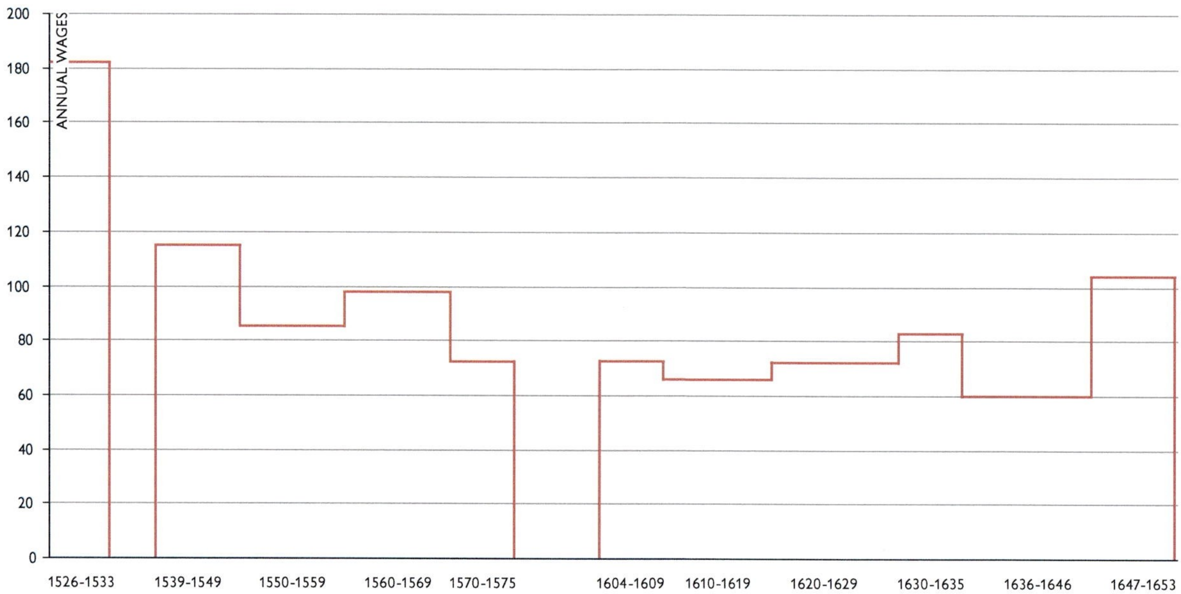

GRAPH 14
Receipts of the fabric of Segovia Cathedral fabric as expressed in the annual wages of an unskilled building labourer, calculated as an annual average for each period.

MONEY AND COINS

NOTES

APPENDICES

ARCHIVES

BIBLIOGRAPHY

INDEX OF PLACE NAMES

MONEY AND COINS

A wide range of different coins and monetary systems are mentioned in this book. There is a very real difference between actual coins made of gold, silver and billion, which were used to make payments and functioned as a medium of exchange and store of wealth, on the one hand, and money of account on the other. The latter did not exist – or at any rate no longer exists – as a real coin, but instead served as a measure of value, and it was in this money of account that financial accounts were kept starting from the twelfth and thirteenth centuries. As a method of accounting and reckoning, this represented the only way to gather the huge array of existing coins under the umbrella of a single system of account. Each money of account was itself anchored in an actual coin, the so-called link or basic coin, and in fact any given coin could in principle serve as the basis for a money of account system. Since the sums cited in this book nearly all derive from financial accounts and other financial documentation, we refer exclusively to such monies of account.

Foremost amongst these was the pound (pfund, pond, libra, livre, lira; abbreviated as pf., lb. or l., etc.), having its origins as a unit of weight measurement. It was divided into 20 solidi (sou, shilling, sueldo; abbreviated as sol. or s., etc.), which in turn was subdivided into 12 denarii (deniers, dinero, denaro, penny, pfennig, penning; abbreviated as den. or d., etc.). The pound was used in various monetary systems, oftentimes together with the designation of the city or region in which it was recognized, such as the l. barc. used in Barcelona, the lb. reg. in Regensburg, the l.rod. in Rodez, and the l.vienn. in Vienne. Large parts of France used the l.par. (*parisis*, Paris) and the l.t. (*tournois*, Tours) to keep financial accounts, with 5 l.par. being equal to 4 l.t. around the year 1350. Most common in the Low Countries were the lb.vls. (*vlaams*, Flanders) and the lb.brab. (*brabants*, Brabant); from around 1430 the value of 3 lb.brab. was equal to 2 lb.vls., with 1 lb. comprising 40 groten or 20 stuivers worth 12 deniers each. In

England accounts were kept in the £ sterling (so-called after a silver penny minted in the twelfth century). Areas of the German Empire used the pfund or talent, bearing a value of 8 schillings worth 30 pfennig or 48 miten each.

The gulden (or florin, originally a gold coin minted in FLORENCE in 1252) could also serve as a unit of account. The rhinegulden was employed as a money of account in the Rhineland region. In the Low Countries around the year 1450, 1 rhinegulden-current (to be distinguished from the gold rhinegulden in circulation) represented 2 stuivers (patards) or 40 groten (grossus denarius, gros, grosso, groschen, etc.) or 144 deniers, and as such was quantified in the same way as the lb.vls. After around 1528 this unit was replaced by the karolusgulden, worth 1¼ rhinegulden current.

The mark, which likewise had its origins as a unit of weight measurement, was used as a money of account in certain regions of the German Empire. Its value was variously reckoned at 60 groschen, 12 Cologne schilling or 16 Lübeck schilling. In England 1 mark equalled ⅔ £.

Castile had the maravedís or morabetino (originally a silver coin minted in the twelfth century), which was subdivided into 10 dineros, with the maravedís being a commonly used money of account.

For the purposes of this book, and specifically to allow comparisons across time and place, these various monies of account are here rendered, where possible, in the wages of an unskilled labourer. See pp. 84-86.

Literature: Spufford 1998, pp. 291-293 and 397-414; Spufford 1986, pp. XX-XXVI, with maps on pp. XXII, XXV and passim.

NOTEN

EPISCOPAL CITIES IN SMALL CAPS FONT

INTRODUCTION

1 De Lange 1991, pp. 70, 73-74: *'Hier op is gebouwt de kerck nostre Dame, een stuck werx sijnde, dat niet schoon, maer wter maete groot is ende veel gecost moest hebben'*. Hooft goes on to write, *'doch soude aansienlijcker sijn ende meer geacht werden, soo ment wel onderhiel'* (but would be more distinguished and esteemed if it were better maintained). P.C. Hooft's (1581-1647) Grand Tour began in La Rochelle; from there he continued to PARIS, travelling on to Italy and returning to the Netherlands by way of Germany.

2 The poet Racine (1639-1699) wrote after visiting CHARTRES: *'la cathédrale de Chartres est grande, mais un peu barbare'*; Michel 1906, p. 11. See also Frankl 1960, p. 237 ff. Marcel Proust famously noted that *'les cathédrales exerçaient un prestige bien moins grand sur un dévot du XVIIe siècle que sur un athée du XXe'*; Prungnaud 2008, p. 247. For a recent, nuanced survey of perspectives on the Gothic architectural style in France, see Rousteau-Chambon 2003, pp. 223-59, 132, 140, 225.

3 Frankl 1960, pp. 440, 481 ff. For the cathedral as a theme in poetry and prose, see Peeters 1986, Emery 2001 and Prungnaud 2008.

4 Duby 1976.

5 See e.g. Knoop & Jones 1949, Booz 1956, Gimpel 1958, Aubert 1960-1961, Salzman 1952, Du Colombier 1973.

6 Frankl 1960, pp. 111-112.

7 See Appendix one.

8 Particularly in Italy, see Haines & Riccetti 1996; *La Fabbrica Eterna*; *Finanziare cattedrali*; Cavaciocchi 2004. The collected papers of the 2003 conference in Vincennes, *Le financement de la construction aux XIIIe-XVIe siècles en France*, have not yet been published; they will contain surveys on, amongst others, LIMOGES (Soulard), SENS (Cailleaux), ROUEN (Foucher-Lefebvre) and TROYES (Meunier).

9 EXETER: Erskine 1981 and 1983. FREISING: Ramisch *et al.* 1998. OSNABRÜCK: Guntermann 2003 [cd].

10 *Spain:* OVIEDO: De Caso Fernández 1981; TOLEDO: Izquierdo Benito 1982; MALAGA: Pérez del Campo 1985; MURCIA: Gutiérrez-Cortinas Corral 1987a; SEGOVIA: Cortón de las Heras 1990; MALLORCA: Sastre Moll 1993 and 1994; Domenge i Mesquida 1997. *France:* TROYES: Murray 1987; ROUEN: Lefebvre 1994; LIMOGES: Soulard 1995; SENS: Cailleaux 1999; BOURGES: Hamon 2001.

11 Bordeaux 1969, p. 2.

12 See the overview of extant fabric accounts in Appendix one.

CHAPTER ONE

Managing the cathedral church: the cathedral fabric

1 Eubel 1898-1901, vol. 1, p. 540 ff., vol. 2, p. 281 ff. This number does not include dioceses that fell under the eastern patriarchates. Le Bras 1959/1964 puts this at 800 dioceses. The frequent changes make it difficult to give a precise number. Today the Roman Catholic church encompasses approximately 2500 dioceses and approximately 260,000 parishes (*Osservatore romano*, 29-10-1984). For a recent overview of the c. 75 dioceses of the Holy Roman Empire, see Gatz *et al.* 2003. For France: the series entitled *Fasti Ecclesiae Gallicanae*, of

which only nine volumes were issued.

2 Brooke 1999, p. 92. Here we make no distinction between dioceses and archdioceses.

3 *Atlas zur Kirchengeschichte*, maps 32 and 71. For France: Dubois 1965; for Germany: Gatz *et al.* 2003.

4 According to an alternative count: 285 dioceses; Edwards 1967, p. 244 n. 2.

5 At any rate in the thirteenth century; Lemarignier *et al.* 1962, p. 160. See also the social geographic study by Chevalier 1997, pp. 12, 13, 31-64.

6 Mansilla Reoyo 1994.

7 Hauck 1898-1920, vol. 3, p. 978 ff., vol. 4, p. 910 ff., vol. 5 (2), p. 1137 ff.

8 Hamilton Thompson 1947, p. 40; Swanson 1989, chapter 1: '*Ecclesia Anglicana*'.

9 Helle 2003, p. 437.

10 For France: *Fasti Ecclesiae Gallicanae*. For Spain the distribution in size has been calculated for the year 1630: of the 36 dioceses, seven had more than 1000 parishes (BURGOS as many as 1693) and ten less than 100 parishes (CADIX had only 14); *Diccionario eclesiastica de España*, p. 1897.

11 Dubois 1965, p. 682.

12 Lemarignier *et al.* 1962, p. 160 (early fourteenth century).

13 *Cartulaire Chartres*, vol. 1, pp. LXIII, XLVI (thirteenth century).

14 Schlicht 2005, p. 15 (c. 1300); *Fasti Ecclesiae Gallicanae*, vol. 2, Rouen, p. 3.

15 KONSTANZ: Krebs 1939-1954, p. 2; LIÈGE: Gatz *et al.* 2003, p. 376. See also *Dictionnaire* [...] *ecclésiastiques*, in voce the various episcopal cities.

16 Gaudemet 1958, p. 322 ff. In the fifth century there were 200 dioceses in central and southern Italy and only 50 in northern Italy; Gaul had 116 dioceses. This distribution lasted until Pope Gregory the Great (590-614).

17 Nottarp 1920, passim.

18 For the northern Netherlands, see Blok 1968, pp. 50-52.

19 Herrmann 2007, p. 9.

20 For instance, the ecclesiastical reorganization in England after 1066 and the Ottonian dioceses in Germany.

21 Concerning the establishment of the southern French dioceses, particularly in connection with Church reform, see Fournié *et al.* 2003.

22 GRANADA, GUADIX, MÁLAGA and ALMERÍA; Riesco Terrero 1987, pp. 89-110.

23 The noun *cathédrale* is first used in France in 1666; Jounel 1988, p. 31. The Second Vatican Council (1962-1965) defines a cathedral as '*ea est, in qua episcopi cathedra sita est*'; exh. cat. RHEIMS 2001, p. 19.

24 '*Omnes de diocesi sunt parrochiani ecclesie cathedralis*'; Gilles 1995, p. 242 n. 45; also *Regesten Köln*, vol. 6, no. 509 (1354).

25 *L'Église et le peuple chrétien*, p. 69.

26 *Archiwa-biblioteki i muzea koscielne* 56 (1988), pp. 198, 248.

27 Charter, bishop of KULM, 22 July 1251; *Urkundenbuch Culm*, no. 29. The four dioceses of the territory of the Teutonic Order later encompassed 719 very small parishes in all, only ten percent of them in cities; Herrmann 2007, p. 150.

28 Gaudemet 1958, p. 308.

29 Stutz 1895, p. 38; Ruffini 1896, col. 161; Schwickerath 1942, p. 59 n. 282. For Spain: Villanueva Estengo 1902-1906, vol. 3, p. 86 ff. and *Diccionario eclesiastica de España*, pp. 1888-1889. A detailed overview of this issue is presented in Schöller 1989, pp. 5-59. In its broader context also in Puza 1989, pp. 335-342.

30 This process had run its course by around 800; Plöchl 1960-1962, vol. 1,

p. 427; Pöschl 1908-1912, vol. 1, p. 32; Liermann 1963, p. 67 ff.

31 Stutz 1895, p. 29; Edwards 1967, chapter 2; Marchal 1999-2000, vol. 94, pp. 783-786.

32 Stutz 1895, p. 320 ff., especially n. 82; Thomassinus 1725, pars 3, liber 2, caput 36, no. 5, contends that quadripartition remained in practice longer at cathedrals than at parish churches.

33 Friedberg 1879/1882, vol. 1, pp. 696, 697.

34 Thomassinus 1725, pars 3, liber 2, caput 23 and 36; also Zindel 1791, p. 83 and Jedin 1979, passim.

35 Exceptions are Spain and Sweden, where in the thirteenth century the fabric share designated for churches was occasionally used – with papal permission – for other causes; see p. 117 ff. Schöller 1989, pp. 60-61, also denies the practical significance of the canonical division.

36 Post 1967, p. 58; Hofman 2003, p. 798. For RHEIMS, compare Durand 1901-1903, vol. 1, p. 108 n. 5.

37 Ruffini 1896, col. 126, 160; Boehmer 1723, par. 57.

38 Thomassinus 1725, pars 3, liber 2, caput 23, no. 11, with more examples; as late as 1771 Pope Clement XIV issued a bull prescribing quadripartition for parish churches; Ruffini 1896, col. 160. See also Herrmann-Mascard 1975, pp. 295-296.

39 See p. 71 ff. on compulsory episcopal contributions.

40 See Lesne 1910 and Pöschl 1908-1912, especially vol. 2, pp. 63 ff. and 153. Private donations, usually granted under onerous terms, oftentimes preceded official division. These and later donations, and not property ceded by bishops, supplied the most important share of new capitular endowments; Pöschl 1908-1912, vol. 2, p. 87. Duby 1973, p. 72 ff., notes differences between central and western Europe and southern Europe as regards this development, in that there was a continuing consciousness – albeit of only theoretical significance – of the original unity of Church property. Cf. Wstinc: '*non est diversitas nisi in amministracione*' (UTRECHT, c. 1345); Muller 1895, pp. 232, 233. Also Schieffer 1976, pp. 262-269, 274, 282, Crosby 1994, and Marchal 1999-2000, vol. 94, pp. 788 ff.

41 Schwickerath 1942, p. 69.

42 *Cartulaire Paris*, no. 35; Lesne 1910, pp. 61, 109; Pöschl 1908-1912, vol. 2, p. 93 n. 2 and p. 70 n. 4; Lesne 1936/1943, vol. 6, p. 270 and n. 2; also *Dictionnaire* [...] *ecclésiastiques*, in voce '*Bénéfices*', col. 1258. In 811, before the property division, the count and countess of Paris had already granted the cathedral an endowment under the express condition that two-thirds of the fruits would accrue to the canons' stipends and one-third '*ad luminaria sive ad restaurandam ipsam ecclesiam*'; the bishop's 829 charter confirms this donation; *Cartulaire Paris*, no. 29; Pöschl 1908-1912, vol. 2, p. 90 n. 4. Schöller 1989, p. 117, supposes this was intended to refer only to the chapter buildings.

43 Hubert 1964, pp. 18, 22, 25. Concerning so-called double cathedrals, see below p. 235 (UTRECHT).

44 See n. 40; also Pöschl 1908-1912, vol. 2, p. 90 n. 4, and p. 99; Schwickerath 1942, pp. 69, 70; Hofmeister 1931, pp. 132, 133.

45 Concerning the so-called *Güntarsche Güterteilung*, see *Regesten Köln*, vol. 1, no. 213; Pöschl 1908-1912, vol. 2, pp. 71, 74; Neuss & Oediger 1964, pp. 257, 420, 421. Pöschl 1908-1912, vol. 1, p. 4 and vol. 2, p. 153, takes the general position, though providing little evidence to support it, that the chapter

buildings and cathedral itself formed part of the divided capitular property. See also Fournier 1942, pp. 146, 160 and Groten 1980, pp. 172, 201-210, 260.

46 Ruffini 1896, col. 161, 164; Hofmeister 1931, p. 131. Cf. the Council of Dioclea 1199; Mansi 1759-1793, vol. 22, col. 70 ff., and the Council of Braga 563; idem, vol. 9, col. 778; Nolet & Boeren 1951, p. 196.

47 Le Bras 1959/1964, p. 378; Hamilton Thompson 1947, p. 5; especially Edwards 1967, chapter 2. For the legal aspects, see Gaudemet 1979.

48 Crosby 1994, p. 389 n. 118; also p. 392.

49 *Serment épiscopal*; see e.g. Amiet 1922, p. 215.

50 Amiet 1923, p. 217; *compositio* of 1328, idem, p. 251 ff.

51 *Inventaire-sommaire Pyrénées-Orientales* G 110. This document is also included in the oath book used by bishops on ascending their see.

52 *Cartulaire Notre-Dame de Paris*, vol. 2, pp. 483-489. Additionally: Lot 1865, pp. 149, 160; Timbal & Metman 1964, p. 55 ff.; Gimpel 1960, pp. 47, 92; Vidrier 1913/1914, vol. 40, pp. 147, 392; Fournier 1942, p. 175; *Bulletin Monumental* 67 (1903), pp. 55-57, and 68 (1904), p. 373. Friction persisted until into the fifteenth century. Similar problems are seen in AMIENS; *Cartulaire Amiens*, vol. 2, p. 99 (19 March 1377). Also, Gaudemet 2001, pp. 269-270: the jurisdictional problems also concerned the precinctal immunity (*parvis*).

53 Timbal & Metman 1964, p. 47 n. 4; also Amiet 1923, p. 27 ff. Concerning the bishop's position at the cathedral of AMIENS, see Durand 1901-1903, vol. 2, p. 155; in RODEZ: Desachy 2005, p. 579 (around 1450 the bishop expressed his wish to determine the '*ordinatio chori et divini cultus celebratio edt ordinatio festivitatum*'; here he was a member of the chapter). Concerning MEISSEN: Rogge 1996, pp. 186-192. Sometimes an unwilling guest: in 1415 the citizenry of STRASBOURG imprisoned Bishop-elect Willem van Diest in the cathedral's chapel of St John; Rapp 1974, p. 124.

54 Luczak 1931, pp. 122, 208, 231. For UTRECHT: Muller 1895, p. 55 ff. For COLOGNE: Janssen 1995, pp. 92-93.

55 For example in TOUL: see Clanché 1926-1927, p. 124 n. 1. For a similar case in COLOGNE, see Ennen 1863/1869, vol. 3, pp. 149-150.

56 Concerning this conflict, see Villard 1968, pp. 358-360. The same happened in LAUSANNE in 1193; Raymond 1907, pp. 98-108.

57 Edwards 1967, pp. 105, 324.

58 Luczak 1931, p. 198.

59 Brühl 1975, pp. 245-250, studied the topography of 21 Gallo-Frankish *civitates*. Crépin-Leblond 1987, vol. 1, p. 4, cites UTRECHT and TOURNAI as examples where passageways spanned a street.

60 In COLOGNE the bishop's palace degenerated into something of a secretariat; Vogts 1930, p. 22. In PADERBORN the palace devolved into a *Absteige-quartier*, later ending up in the hands of the chapter; Hoppe 1975, pp. 43, 60, 190. For Germany, see Hofmann 1914, p. 79, and for England, Hamilton Thompson 1947, pp. 5, 45.

61 Dauch 1913, passim, researched episcopal residences in 33 dioceses in the German Empire; more recently: Press 1992, p. 19. For England: Hamilton Thompson 1947, p. 42 n. 2, and pp. 45, 46. For France: Luchaire 1909, p. 148.

62 '*Sciat dominus quod quicumque est Remensis archiepiscopus duos habet principales adversarios, videlicet capitulum remense et cives*'; Desportes 1979,

p. 173 n. 111, and Gaudemet 2008, p. 416.

63 Luczak 1931, p. 251 ff.

64 Ferraris 1852-1857, vol. 3, in voce *'ecclesia'*, art. 3, no. 13. Southern 1970, pp. 174, 175, cites Carolingian *capitularia*: *'ut ecclesia tectum et luminaria habeat et episcopus provideat'* (813).

65 The mystical marital bond was first and foremost with his diocese; Hofmeister 1931, p. 129; also Crosby 1994, p. 365 n. 15: engagement, marital consent and nuptials are paralleled in the bishop's choice, the *confirmatio* and the consecration. Also Gaudemet 2008, p. 379.

66 Bishops claimed express responsibility for the organization of the liturgy and the choral service, for instance in RODEZ c. 1450: *'ordinatio chori et divini cultus celebratio et ordinatio festivitatum principaliter pertinent ad epicopums quia est caput ecclesie et preordinator in cunctis et hoc est jus officium principale'*; Desachy 1998, n. 62. For TOUL, see Clanché 1926-1927, p. 124 n. 7.

67 See the *Cartularium* of the fabric of UTRECHT Cathedral; *Inventaris Archief kapittel ten Dom*, no. 405. BASEL kept a *Fabriksbuch*, begun in 1496; La Roche 1888, p. 81. STRASBOURG had the *Donationsbuch*, into which these episcopal charters were also copied; *Urkundenbuch Strassburg*, vol. 2, nos 40, 41, 43, etc.

68 See the *Wahlkapitulationen* of MERSEBURG, c. 1265; Range 1910, p. 144, of HALBERSTADT, 28 July 1390; *Urkundenbuch Halberstadt*, vol. 4, no. 3040, and of AUGSBURG, 1463; Leuze 1908, p. 100. Cf. *Urkundenbuch Bremen*, vol. 4, p. 234 n. 8.

69 For example: Barbosa 1656-1665, vol. 2, p. 432, vol. 5, p. 220, vol. 9 (2), p. 53. Modern authors (Enlart 1902, p. 73; Du Colombier 1973, p. 10; Mortet 1898, p. 404; Aubert 1960-1961, vol. 118, p. 245; Pernoud 1966, p. 163) all refer to this canonical provision, but seem to take the position that the rule was applied. Seymour 1968, n. 132, rightly rejects this.

70 Weilandt 1992, p. 20 ff.; also Giese 1982, passim. The two studies complement each other. Also Hirschmann 1998, pp. 492-505; he rightly notes the role that chapters were already playing in the eleventh century, though separate fabric endowments had not yet formed.

71 Coué 1992, pp. 347-415; also Giese 1982, concerning the period from the tenth through the twelfth century, passim, and Weilandt 1992, p. 21 ff. Not all tenth- to twelfth-century bishops were actively involved in cathedral construction: seven of the fourteen bishops of MAGDEBURG, six of the twelve of HAMBURG; Giese 1982, pp. 417, 423.

72 Fernie 1993, p. 159 n. 7: he also made a solemn vow to travel no farther than ten kilometres from his ravaged cathedral until it was fully repaired.

73 Mortet 1911, p. 66: '[...] *quippe timens ne, aut morte preventus, aut qualibet alia causa coactus, opus imperfectum relinquat'*.

74 Giese 1982, p. 410.

75 *Gallia Christiana*, vol. 11, instr. p. 219 ff.; Le Patourel 1944, p. 135 ff.; Musset 1966, p. 310 (*parochia* is diocese); Musset 1987, p. 126. Characteristic of the absolute power that bishops asserted over their cathedrals is the case of Bishop Yves III of SÉES, who in 1048/49 drove his opponents from the city and did not scruple to set his cathedral on fire. This earned him a stern reprimand from the pope and an order to restore his cathedral; *Fasti Ecclesiae Gallicanae*, vol. 9, SÉES, p. 7.

76 Mortet 1911, pp. XXXIX, 62 n. 1, 71 ff., 88, 91, 162 ff. Weilandt 1992, pp. 36-70, 154.

77 Concerning this issue, which is not explored here, see Weilandt 1992, pp. 44, 163, 253-294, also Coué 1992, pp. 269-270. The distinction between the construction of cathedrals and large abbeys is likewise beyond the scope of this study; Weilandt 1992, pp. 158-159.

78 Barlow 1939, pp. XLIX, XLIII, 209, 210; LISIEUX applied a statutory three-part division.

79 Migne 1844-1891, vol. 225, col. 219, see also col. 267.

80 '*Decorem domus Dei cum sancto David sic dilexit, sic desideravit, ut ecclesiam s. Petri renovare fratres hortaretur*'. Reconstruction would not start until 1248; Ennen 1863/1869, vol. 3, p. 961; Clemen 1937, pp. 34, 43, 50.

81 The personal bond a bishop felt with his cathedral may also have depended on the strength of his local loyalty. In the twelfth and thirteenth centuries most French bishops died in the diocese to which they had first been appointed. Starting in the fourteenth century it was common for bishops - now no longer elected by the chapter, but appointed by the pope - to be transferred, and a bishopric was seen simply as one step in a career; Gaudemet 2008, pp. 378-400.

82 *Gallia Christiana*, vol. 10, instr. pp. 264-265; Branner 1962b, n. 16; Murray 1989, pp. 35, 154-155.

83 *Gallia Christiana*, vol. 1, p. 20: '*ac die immediate sequenti ad pacem et unitatem reducens canonicos, qui dudum inter se fuerant plurimum dissidentes, cum eisdem ordinavit concorditer ante etiam quam cibum sumerent, quod nova deberet major ecclesia fabricari*'; also Laran 1931, p. 11. The bishop later came into serious conflict with the chapter and *boni homines* of ALBI, resulting in a famous case lodged against him with the papal court. In 1307 he was transferred to LE PUY; Théry 2004, pp. 192-197. For further examples of episcopal initiatives in dioceses in southern France, see Biget 1982, pp. 22, 57 n. 14. Also in dioceses elsewhere: AUXERRE: *Congrès Archéologique de France* 116 (1958), p. 45; Mortet & Deschamps 1929, p. 203; RHEIMS: Branner 1961, p. 25; BOURGES: Branner 1962a, p. 22 ('*on pourrait comparer leur rôle à celui de modernes présidents de société*'); BORDEAUX: Gardelles 1963, p. 201; NARBONNE: Mortet 1898, p. 404; Freigang 1992, p. 206.

84 *Gallia Christiana*, vol. 11, instr. p. 266E, agreement between the bishop and chapter: '[...] *episcopus* [...] *fabricam er bona fabricae prout consuevit, custodiat; si tamen grande opus immineat in dicta ecclesia faciendum, episcopus illud faciat seu fieri faciat, requisito consilio capituli vel majoris partis praesentium in ecclesia supradicta*'. Also Grant 2005, p. 22; he rightly notes that in building affairs, too, 'the balance of power between bishop and chapter varied according to the personalities involved'.

85 Bouvier 1911, vol. 2, p. 261 ff. The fabric probably acquired its independent administrative status in 1226 under an agreement between the treasurer and chapter on the maintenance of the cathedral; Cailleaux 1999, p. 161.

86 Soulard 1993, p. 229.

87 Enlart 1902, p. 73 n. 2.

88 Vasseur 1882, p. 451; the fabric proper may not have been established until slightly later, around 1385. In 1367 the chapter gave the bishop leave to install a collection box for the building works in the cathedral, to which his servants would keep the keys. Apparently, the bishop

still had control of the fabric at this time; idem, p. 448; also Grant 2005, p. 21.

89 Bion de Marlavagne 1875, pp. 106, 279 (1293/94 account); in RODEZ, the bishop was also a party to all contacts concluded in connection with the building works. Not until the seventeenth century did the chapter make attempts to deprive the bishop of his stake in the fabric's administration.

90 Neuwirth 1890, pp. 367, 389 ff. Construction of the cathedral, which began in 1344, is included amongst the *onera* of the archbishop of PRAGUE; see also Neuwirth 1893, pp. 68-70, 302.

91 Heading of the 1451/52 fabric account; Basin 1859, p. 199 n. 1.

92 Paris, Archives Nationales LL 464, dossier 61 (1360-1522).

93 In 1301 the account was audited *'in aula domini episcopi'* in the presence of the official and a canon representing the bishop and of two canons representing the chapter; Paris, Bibliothèque Nationale, lat. 9111, f. 222; additionally see *Inventaire-sommaire Aube* G 1559; Assier 1855, p. 11 (1419-1420); Murray 1987, p. 233 n. 13.

94 *Monumenta Boica*, vol. 34 (2): *Wahlkapitulation* 1463 (p. 34); capitular statute of 1485 (p. 191 ff.); with papal confirmation in 1486 (p. 206). GNIEZNO also had joint management by the archbishop and chapter; Binder 1912, p. 100 ff., and LEÓN still in 1534; Villacorta Rodriguez 1974, p. 389.

95 Hofmeister 1931, p. 134.

96 *Urkundenbuch Niederrhein*, vol. 3, no. 659 (25 July 1365), vol. 4, no. 276 (17 May 1446); Lacomblet 1868, nos 72, 78, 79, 86, 88, 89, 94; Ennen 1880, pp. 83-84; Ennen 1863/1869, vol. 3, pp. 986-988; Clemen 1937, pp. 60, 63; Wiek 1959b, p. 100 ff.; *Regesten Köln*, vol. 5, nos 1455 (22 December 1347) and 1498 (6 September 1348). Also Berglar & Engels 1986, pp. 224-225.

97 Concerning MAINZ from the beginning of the thirteenth century, see Veit 1912, pp. 150-151.

98 He did this by 'donating' all the cathedral's altars to the chapter; Le Grand 1931, p. 154. Ownership of altars probably entailed an obligation to build or maintain that part of the church. Fournier 1942, p. 173, notes a charter of 1029, which has two canons of the cathedral of NEVERS donating two altars to the chapter, which in turn assumed responsibility to rebuild *'totum membrum basilicae'*. For the building history of LANGRES: *Congrès Archéologique de France* 91 (1928), p. 486.

99 *Registrum Baldock et al.*, pp. 74-75, 91-93 (1308); Edwards 1967, p. 231. Bishops lost their voice in cathedral building affairs at monastic cathedrals, too. A chronicle of DURHAM written around 1150 relates that Bishop William (1081-1093) had established the rule that the bishop would build the church using his own income and the monks the monastic building from theirs. However, the rule died with him as they neglected their own buildings to concentrate their energies on the construction of the church; Salzman 1952, p. 364; Lehmann-Brockhaus 1955-1960, no. 1375; Mortet 1911, p. 286. In the thirteenth century the care of the church building lay with the monastery; the east transept was begun by the prior in 1242; Pevsner 1953, p. 88.

100 *Cartulaire Arras*, no. 176. Papal confirmation in *Registres Innocent IV*, no. 708: '[...] *episcopi ex nunc perpetuo sunt et erunt liberi et immunes ab omnimoda refectione er retentione omnium predictorum et*

omnium aliarum rerum sacrarum vel non sacrarum, ac universorum edificiorum ecclesie, sive sunt intra ecclesiam, sive extra adherentia ecclesie, in qualibet sui parte [...]'. At LIMOGES the bishops provided the driving force for the cathedral building campaign until around 1300, after which control devolved to the chapter. The first reference to an *opus fabrice* occurs in 1308; canons' gifts and foundations grew more numerous from the end of the thirteenth century; Soulard 1993, p. 229 ff.

101 *Diplomatarium Danicum*, vol. 1: 5, no. 65. The bishop refers to '*iuri nostro in hac parte, si quid tamen iuri habuerimus*'.

102 Some examples from France after the Hundred Years' War: VIVIERS after the arrival of the new bishop in 1498; *Congrès Archéologique de France* 150 (1992), p. 327; LAVAUR around 1484 under Bishop Jean Vigier (1469-1497); idem 140 (1982), pp. 336-337; CAHORS after 1493, idem 147 (1989), pp. 55 and 14. For Archbishop Georges d'Amboise (1460-1510) of ROUEN's direct involvement in the construction of his cathedral, see Hamon in Joubert 2006, pp. 329-348.

103 Rodríguez Estévez 1998, p. 56. The famous utterance by a canon in 1401, '*hagamos una iglesia tal, que los que la viesen labrada nos tengan por locos*', has been handed down to us in Ortiz de Zuñiga, *Anales de Sevilla* uit 1677, and is therefore in doubt; Montoto 1952, pp. 31, 123; *La catedral gótica de Sevilla*, p. 42; Falcón Márquez 1980, p. 15.

104 Guenée 1987, p. 214.

105 *Bulletin Monumental* 70 (1906) p. 291 ff.; see also below p. 72.

106 SALZBURG: Leisching 1964, p. 264. CHARTRES: Amiet 1923, p. 218 ff. PARIS: Timbal & Metman 1964, p. 62. The Council of Trent determined that cathedral fabrics had to render their accounts before their bishop; Thomassinus 1725, pars 3, liber 2, caput 36, no. 8.

107 *Dictionnaire* [...] *ecclésiastiques*, vol. 12, p. 369; Le Bras 1959/1964, p. 380; Lemarignier *et al.* 1962, p. 34; Edwards 1967, p. 5. For the German Empire, see in particular Schieffer 1976, pp. 261-287, and Marchal 1999-2000, vol. 94, p. 787 and passim.

108 It was at these meetings that decisions for new building were taken. See e.g. the 1312 minutes of the GERONA chapter: '[...] *Capitulum Gerundense* [...] *more solito congregatum, statuit, voluit et ordinavit, quod caput ipsius ecclesiae de novo construetur et edificaretur et circumcirca ipsum novem capellae fierent*'; *España Sagrada*, vol. 45, p. 3 and Street 1914, vol. 2, p. 92 n. 4.

109 This process was played out particularly in the thirteenth century; Nolet & Boeren 1951, p. 186. For Germany: Hauck 1898-1920, vol. 5 (1), p. 191; Schneider 1885, p. 69. For England: Edwards 1967, p. 33. For France: Browne 1895. As an example: the largest chapter was that of LAON, with 83 members; Gaudemet 2001, p. 274.

110 Plöchl 1960-1962, vol. 1, p. 429, vol. 2, p. 393 ff.; Lemarignier *et al.* 1962, p. 34; Pöschl 1908-1912, vol. 2, p. 90 ff.; Duby 1973, p. 80.

111 Pöschl 1908-1912, vol. 2, pp. 90, 96; Nolet & Boeren 1951, pp. 269, 315.

112 *Dictionnaire de droit canonique*, in voce '*custode*', refers to the major variation in local regulations and authorities. See e.g. Zindel 1791, p. 59 and Mansi, vol. 22, pp. 660-661 (LICHFIELD treasurer, 1195); also Decr. Greg. IX lib. I tit. XXVII, in Friedberg 1879/1882, vol. 2, p. 155. Sometimes the *camerarius* was charged

with overseeing the church building; Nolet & Boeren 1951, p. 196; Mortet 1888, p. 53 (PARIS); *Gallia Christiana*, vol. 11, p. 220 (COUTANCES).

113 Schneider 1885, p. 98; Edwards 1967, pp. 136, 220; Hinschius 1869-1897, vol. 2, p. 103 ff.

114 Feine 1954, p. 341; Plöchl 1960-1962, vol. 2, p. 410; Schneider 1885, p. 98; Edwards 1967, p. 225; Hinschius 1869-1897, vol. 2, p. 110. Local regulations: Range 1910, p. 64 (MERSEBURG); Kaluza-Baumruker 1987, pp. 63-67 (SCHWERIN and northern German dioceses); Quantin 1869, p. 214 (SENS).

115 In SANTIAGO DE COMPOSTELA the treasurer was the *maestro de la Obra* in 1131; López Ferreiro 1898-1911, vol. 4, pp. 158, 160, vol. 5, p. 169. For other examples suggesting that the treasurer was charged with overseeing the cathedral: Hofmeister 1931, p. 31 ff.; for ANGERS, see Joubert 2001, p. 46. In twelfth- and thirteenth-century LAON the treasurer was the most powerful dignitary in the chapter where property management was concerned. He was responsible for the cathedral building itself and had jurisdiction within it. There was also a *fabrica*; Saint-Denis 1994, pp. 353, 472, 476, 526; Clark & King 1983, pp. 19, 21-22. In FREISING the *custos* alternated with the bishop; the fabric was still referred to as the *Dom-custodei* in the fifteenth century; Mitterwieser, pp. 2, 81. In 1337 SALZBURG's *custos* was still *collector fructuum fabricae*; *Regesten Salzburg*, vol. 3, p. 1069. In BASEL the fabric was also run by the *custos*, incidentally as an independent financial body; Hieronimus 1938, p. 13. In 1343 FRAUENBURG fabric was still controlled by the cathedral *custos*, who bore the title *magister fabrice*; Herrmann 2007, p. 123. Regarding the complicated situation in VIENNA, see Flieder 1968, pp. 73, 92, 101, 159, 261.

116 To illustrate: Bishop Walkelin (1070-1098) of WINCHESTER allocated estates belonging to the monastery's *mensa* for the duration of the cathedral building campaign, which had an annual yield of £300; *Chartulary of Winchester Cathedral*, no. 1.

117 *Gallia Christiana*, vol. 11, p. 220; see also Nolet & Boeren 1951, p. 196.

118 Concerning fabrics and canon law, see Gilles 1995, p. 234.

119 In Classical Antiquity the term *Fabrica* was used to designate, amongst other things, a forge or arms manufactory, and in Late Antiquity also a public building; *fabrica ecclesiae* means a church building. See Niermeyer 1954-1976, in voce *'fabrica'*; *Dictionnaire de droit canonique*, in voce *'fabrique'*; Schröcker 1934, p. 72 ff. and Branner 1976.

120 Schröcker 1934, p. 35. In BORDEAUX a *fabrica* is already mentioned in 1195; Gardelles 1963, p. 15. For the fabric in AMIENS, see Durand 1901-1903, vol. 1, pp. 103-124. In PARIS there is no mention of a *fabrica* until the beginning of the fourteenth century; Mortet 1888, p. 53. The first reference to a fabric at Scandinavian cathedrals is in 1275 (UPPSALA); Nylander 1953, p. 198 n. 3 and *La Fabbrica Eterna*, p. 307. The term *opus* is used much earlier, though without any clear indication of what type of organization this was. *Custodes operis* are already being mentioned around 1000 in ORLÉANS; Mortet 1911, p. 4 n. 1. An *opus* is recorded in RHEIMS in 1176; Branner 1961, p. 30 n. 33. In 1196 the archbishop of ARLES allocated certain goods to the *operarius*, one of whose predecessors is known; Mortet & Des-

champs 1929, pp. 171-172; also Esquieu 1992, p. 73. In RODEZ the first mention of a canon as a master of the fabric occurs in 1215, *Fasti Ecclesiae Gallicanae*, vol. 6, RODEZ, p. 8; in ANGERS in 1209, there jointly established by the bishop and dean; idem, vol. 7, ANGERS, pp. 11, 75. 154. The term *labor* is also used, for example in ASTORGA in 1117; *España Sagrada*, vol. 16, p. 474. In PALERMO the fabric was known by the Arabic word *maramma*; Bresc-Bautier 1976, pp. 109, 112.

121 Spieckermann 1935, p. 6. According to the *Rechtsboek* compiled by Wstinc (c. 1345), the UTRECHT Cathedral treasurer was responsible for the bells; Muller 1895, pp. 114-115.

122 *Cartulaire Liège*, vol. 6, no. 480 and pp. 326-328: '*super refectione seu restauratione et detentione nostre ecclesie, ad quas custos, secundum consuetudinem ab antiquo servatam, hactenus teneri dicebatur*'.

123 Hamilton Thompson 1920, p. 14.

124 *Monumenta Boica*, vol. 34 (2), doc. 73 (9 November 1485) and doc. 78 (11 May 1486); Leuze 1908, pp. 62, 63; Hofmeister 1931, p. 134.

125 In CUENCA in Spain the tasks of the treasurer and *obrero* were defined in 1282; Palomo 2002, vol. 1, p. 157, vol. 2, p. 301 (doc. no. 15). In MENDE a statute of 1308 designated two *ouvriers*, who took over some of the competences of the *sacrista*; *Fasti Ecclesiae Gallicanae*, vol. 8, *Mende*, p. 8. As late as 1419 a regulation was instituted in VANNES reducing the *trésorie* to an honorary title; Martinière 1923, p. 114.

126 In some cases the partitioning of the provostal property did not actually take place until long after the fabric was established: in COLOGNE in 1373, in MÜNSTER in 1370, in MINDEN in 1380; Neuss & Oediger 1964, p. 417; Schröer 1966, p. 485. See also Barrow 1990, p. 18; Marchal 1999-2000, vol. 95, pp. 19-20.

127 De Farcy 1901-1926, vol. 4, p. 142 ff.; also vol. 3, pp. 1 and 295, and vol. 1, p. 26; Avril 1984, pp. 743-744 and pp. 428, 633; *Fasti Ecclesiae Gallicanae*, vol. 7, ANGERS, pp. 75, 154. In ROUEN it was because the *thesaurarius* failed to carry out his duties that his tasks and the associated stipends were reassigned to the fabric, by a charter of 3 March 1469. He was compensated with an annuity and was further allowed to attend the opening of the collection boxes and auditing of the accounts; Pommeraye 1686, pp. 346-347, 352, 421-422; Lefebvre in *Notre-Dame de Rouen*, p. 89.

128 Hofmeister 1931, p. 133.

129 In addition to the examples cited below, see also Decr. Greg. IX lib. I tit. XXVI, c. 2, in Friedberg 1879/1882, vol. 2, p. 155.

130 Branner 1961, p. 30 n. 33 and Varin 1838-1848, vol. 1, pp. 497, 498: '[...] *quod ecclesia Remensis libere et integre percipiet omnes oblationes et elemosinas que in ecclesia fient et ubicumque in ea offerentur et capetagia que solent in eadem ecclesia afferri et tam denarios quam obolos quos presbiteri parochiales solent reddere et affere pro cera; et propter hoc faciet eadem ecclesia omnes sumptus necessarios, quales hucusque alii fecerunt thesaurarii, ad luminare, et eadem que circa ornatum er reparationem ecclesie solent expendi, et alia que per manum subthesaurarii solent dari et procurari; excepto* [...]' (here follow a series a obligations which the treasurer continues to fulfil) '*et hec predicta reddendo, liber erit thesaurarius ab omnibus sumptibus et expensis, qui* [!] *pro omnibus quocumque modo ad ecclesiam remensem pertinentibus, solent en*

debent fieri a subthesaurario remensi'. See also *Inventaire-sommaire Marne* G II, 1, p. 140 ff. A similar conflict, the roots of which are not known to me, arose in NOYON in 1288: the sub- treasurer and chapter settled an accord under which he would cede to the chapter all revenues accruing to his office, in return for which he was released from all of his obligations; in 1463 the *sous-trésorie* was incorporated within the fabric, possibly with a view to the great expense of repairs; *Inventaire-sommaire Oise* G I, no. 1390; Seymour 1968, p. 75. Similar kinds of disputes are found not only in cathedral chapters, but also in collegiate ones, such as of the basilica of St Andrew in COLOGNE; Wuerdtwein 1781-1792, vol. 2, p. 176.

131 Pycke 1983-1984, pp. 71-89.

132 *Cartulaire Lausanne*, no. 378 (18 July 1226), no. 743 (4 and 7 August 1226), no. 744 (15 August 1226); Grandjean 1963, pp. 265, 274.

133 Sandron 1998, pp. 38-41. Bishop Nivelon donated 100 l. for the building works as well as a tract of land on which the south transept was to be built.

134 UTRECHT: see below p. 247. LONDON: Edwards 1967, p. 236; Knoop & Jones 1949, p. 45. PRAGUE: Neuwirth 1890, p. 154. Presumably also in AMIENS (the first reference to the fabric is in 1234); Durand 1901-1903, vol. 1, p. 104 ff.

135 Lacomblet 1868, no. 11; Ennen & Eckertz 1860-1879, vol. 2, no. 255; Ennen 1863/1869, vol. 3, p. 962. Also *Ad Summum 1248*, A 7 and G 1, 2 and 3. For the dates of the building campaign, see Wolff 1968.

136 Ennen & Eckertz 1860-1879, vol. 2, p. 277; Wiek 1959b, p. 99 n. 270. A charter of 24 November 1246 records that the treasurer was responsible for, amongst other things, the windows, guarding the altar of St Peter and the lighting; *Regesten Köln*, vol. 3, no. 1296; *Urkundenbuch Coblenz und Trier*, no. 885.

137 Lacomblet 1868, no. 64; *Regesten Köln*, vol. 4, no. 1548; Lacomblet 1857, p. 120 n. 48 (concerning difficulties in the sixteenth century). It is possible that a similar sort of lease was arranged in AUXERRE as shortly before construction commenced in 1220, the *sacrista* ceded certain *oblationes* for the building works, for as long as they took, against a yearly payment of 40 s. from the *confratria operis*; *Inventaire-sommaire Yonne* G 1824. Other cases of disagreement between treasurer and fabric are found in LINCOLN in 1284 (maintenance of windows); *Statutes of Lincoln Cathedral*, vol. 1, pp. 286-287; and in SALISBURY in 1440; *Statutes of Salisbury Cathedral*, pp. 310-319.

138 See e.g. the following monographs on individual chapters. AUGSBURG: Leuze 1908, pp. 62, 63. BREMEN: Müller 1908, p. 67. CHARTRES: Amiet 1922, pp. 135, 138, 150; Jusselin 1915-1922, passim. EXETER: Erskine 1962, passim. HALBERSTADT: Brackmann 1898, p. 107. HAMBURG: Apel 1934, pp. 97, 98. HILDESHEIM: Hoffmann 1911, pp. 3, 76 and n. 5. LANGRES: Le Grand 1931, p. 92. MAGDEBURG: Weber 1912, p. 70. MEISSEN: Kunz von Brunn 1902, p. 109. MERSEBURG: Range 1910, p. 104. MINDEN: Dammeyer 1957, p. 83. MÜNSTER: Nottarp 1909, pp. 8, 9, 36 n. 5; Spieckermann 1935, p. 6. OSNABRÜCK: Hagemann 1901, pp. 99, 100. PADERBORN: Ohlberger 1911, pp. 74, 82 ff.; Bückmann 1912, p. 41. ENGLAND: Edwards 1967, pp. 233-238; Hamilton Thompson 1925, pp. 132-134. Uniformity is of course by no means the rule. In the diocese of AGDE

(southern France) a canon was appointed *operarius* for life in 1229, to which office certain revenues were attached. It is possible that this position should be identified with that of the treasurer in the period before the fabric had been established; *Cartulaire Agde*, nos 311, 312; see also Branner 1976, passim. Concerning the bishop's and chapter's authority to make appointments in NARBONNE after 1267 and elsewhere, see the detailed survey in Freigang 1992, pp. 55-61, 363-370; summary by Freigang in Cassanelli 2005, pp. 171-173. For TOLEDO, see Cardinal-Archbishop Pedro de Mendoza's important and detailed constitution of 24 December 1490, published in Lop Otín 2006, pp. 917-923.

139 Nylander 1953, p. 103 (UPPSALA 1316).

140 As in FREISING in the fifteenth century: '*praesente rev. domino nostro episcopo*', Ramisch *et al.* 1998, passim.

141 Hinschius 1869-1897, vol. 2, p. 109 n. 17; Heintschel 1956, pp. 4, 5; Schneider 1885, p. 84.

142 As in CHARTRES: Jusselin 1915-1922, p. 258: '[...] *et est eisdem provisoribus inhibitum ne ipsi aliquid de novo construant in ecclesia quod sit notabiliter sumptuosum inconsulto capitulo, nisi eciam de conscientia et licencia capituli petita super hiis et obtenta*' (1341). For a sample oath, see Mone 1836, col. 241, doc. 12 (SPEYER). See also *Registrum Sancti Pauli Londinensis*, p. 100 (LONDON, 1332), and *Statutes of Lincoln Cathedral*, vol. 2, p. 356 (LINCOLN, 1440). If they overreached their authorities, they were called to account during the chapter meeting and sometimes fined. Such was the case with a canon of WELLS who in 1501 had ordered the large bell re-cast without consulting the chapter; Reynolds 1881, p. 203.

143 For example, a 1507 epigram relates that Canon Johann von Hattstein (1455-1518), who was *magister et procurator fabricae* of MAINZ Cathedral from 1488 until his death, '[...] *Nec tibi consulto desint res materiae/ lignum, calx, plumbum, clavis, harena, lapis* [...]'; Gottron 1951, p. 59. His Renaissance epitaph by Peter Schro in the ambulatory - a Michelangelesque pietà with Sts John and Mary Magdalene - lauds his erudition and shrewdness (fig. 7); Arens 1982, pp. 83, 156-167.

144 Recio Mir 1999, p. 74.

145 UTRECHT, 1415; *Bronnen bouwgeschiedenis*, vol. 2 (1), p. XXXVII; AUGSBURG, 1485 (no more than 15 rhinegulden); *Monumenta Boica*, vol. 34 (2), p. 192; TOLEDO 1490: no expenditures above 10,000 maravedís; Lop Otín 2006, pp. 520, 920.

146 It is curious that many of the monographs cited in n. 138 make only passing reference to a fabric. For a general overview of the building lodge, see Binding 1993, pp. 31-71.

147 CHARTRES: Jusselin 1915-1922, passim; Amiet 1922, pp. 138, 156, 183. STRASBOURG: Woltmann 1876, pp. 263, 264. ROUEN; Lefebvre in *Notre-Dame de Rouen*, pp. 88-93. BASEL: La Roche 1888, p. 90; Hieronimus 1938, p. 516. MILAN (robes of office, as in COLOGNE): Boito 1889, p. 179; *Annali*, vol. 1, p. 7. SPEYER (official garments for '*des stifts ambts und wercklut*'); Krebs 1968, 24 March 1501 and 18 March 1507. In CAMBRAI a *sagittarius* was charged with shooting down pigeons; Houdoy 1880, p. 181.

148 BASEL: La Roche 1888, p. 109. RODEZ, recorded in 1244: Desachy 2005, p. 145. PALMA: Domenge i Mesquida 1997, p. 78. ANGERS: *Fasti Ecclesiae*

Gallicanae, vol. 7, pp. 102, 106 (no. 112).

149 ROUEN: Lefebvre 1994, vol. 1, p. 58 and vol. 4, doc. 4: the inventory also contains a summary of the books in the procurator's room; there was also a statue of Mary. STRASBOURG: Fuchs 1990b and Fuchs 2000, p. 143 n. 11. We also have good descriptions dating to 1429 and 1436 of the chamber of the *operaio* of the *duomo* of SIENA; Riedl & Seidel 1995, p. 30. The fabric of RODEZ had its own house as from around 1250, alongside the residence of the *ouvrier*, which also housed the fabric archive; Désachy 2005, pp. 146, 169, 542.

150 Edwards 1967, p. 229.

151 Exceptions are the fabrics of the nine so-called monastic cathedrals in England; Edwards 1967, pp. 9-11; Dobson 1991, passim, Lehmberg 1988, pp. 38-42. These cathedrals had no secular chapter, but instead a community of Benedictine monks led by a prior; the *custos operis* was one of the *obedientaries* officers, charged with tending certain organizational aspects of monastic life. The *opus* was set up differently from one place to another. In CANTERBURY the monastic system of management evolved towards a centralized organization; care of the church was entrusted to the *sacrist*, whose income was actually paid by the treasurer, who himself had had charge of centrally controlled finances since around 1150; Smith 1940, passim; Woodruff 1936, p. 79 ff. In ELY, by contrast, the office of the *sacrist* was independent of the common fund; Salzman 1948/1953, vol. 2, p. 205.

152 The duties entrusted to the fabric were furthermore subject to modification. In PADERBORN the care of vestments and liturgical books did not come under the fabric's competences until late in the medieval period; Ohlberger 1911, pp. 83-84.

153 As in UTRECHT; *Bronnen bouwgeschiedenis*, vol. 2 (1), pp. XXI, XLVI; see below p. 253.

154 YORK: Hamilton Thompson 1925, p. 135; Knowles 1936, p. 31. ELY: Chapman 1907, passim. SITTEN: Holderegger 1926, passim. STRASBOURG: see below p. 53 ff.

155 METZ (1445) (chapter ordered the *magister fabrice* to borrow 24 l.t. '*pro negociis ecclesie supportandis*'); Pelt 1930, p. 97. CHARTRES (fourteenth century); Jusselin 1915-1922, p. 261. EXETER; Erskine 1962, pp. 259, 266. COLOGNE (sixteenth century); Schultz 1877, pp. 56, 57. LINCOLN (1439); *Statutes of Lincoln Cathedral*, vol. 2, p. 432 ff. SALISBURY (1440); *Statutes of Salisbury Cathedral*, pp. 310-319. RHEIMS (1325); Varin 1838-1848, vol. 2, p. 411.

156 See Barbosa 1656-1665, vol. 2, p. 432.

157 Concerning this theory, see Wiek 1959b, p. 53; Schröcker 1934, pp. 71, 90.

158 Varin 1838-1848, vol. 2, p. 411.

159 *Statutes of Lincoln Cathedral*, vol. 2, p. 432 ff.

160 *Statutes of Salisbury Cathedral*, pp. 316-319.

161 Jan Kuys cites church fabrics in southwest Flanders after 1180; De Smet *et al.* 2006, p. 84; the oldest fabric rolls date from the latter half of the fourteenth century; idem, p. 96.

162 See Schröcker 1934, passim; Drew 1954, passim; Wiek 1959b, p. 53 ff.; Clément 1895, passim. Recent overview in three articles by Jan Kuys in De Smet *et al.* 2006, pp. 83-91, 93-107, 109-133.

163 Schröcker 1934, p. 148 ff.

164 In the case of cathedrals, too, cities occasionally objected to the bishop's (and chapter's) right to dispose over the *oblationes*, such as in AVILA in the latter half of

the twelfth century; *Dictionnaire* [...] *ecclésiastiques*, in voce 'Avila'.

165 Examples in Schröcker 1934, p. 152 n. 1.

166 Maurer 2002, pp. 250, 252: in dioceses in southern Germany, between 200 and 500 clerics. Maurer gives further illustrations of cathedrals' significance as the main diocesan church in the late Middle Ages, such as the public penances practised in the cathedral of KONSTANZ during Easter week, when sometimes in excess of 1200 sinners from throughout the diocese whose sins could not be absolved by their parish priests would gather in the cathedral. A diocesan synod is a mandatory periodic meeting of ecclesiastics around their bishop in order to be informed and receive instructions; broad overview in Gaudemet 2008, pp. 421-442.

167 Wiek 1959b, pp. 41, 112, describes the cathedral as '*Kult- und Repräsentationsbau einer stadtfremden Macht*' and its '*stadtfremde Zweckbestimmung*'. See also Crosby 1994, p. 13: the cathedral's designation as *ecclesia* had no bearing on the faithful, but rather on the bishop and/or chapter.

168 For France, see Picard 1994, pp. 61-70. In England only eight percent of the high nobility opted to be buried in a cathedral; Rosenthal 1972, pp. 82, 84, 85, 90, 119.

169 Le Bras 1954, pp. 188, 190; see also Lesne 1936/1943, vol. 6, p. 18 ff.

170 The size of the immunity varied from less than ten hectares (AUXERRE 6 ha, UTRECHT 2 ha) to more than 100 (COLOGNE 120 ha). For a general discussion see: Erlande-Brandenburg 1989, pp. 205-234 and Hirschmann 1998, pp. 433-436 (overview of 24 cathedral cities west of the Rhine). ENGLAND: Hamilton Thompson 1925, p. 156 ff.; Lepine 1995, p. 114; Edwards 1939, passim; Hill 1965, pp. 115-130; Gilchrist 2005, p. 27 (NORWICH). FRANCE AND BELGIUM: Lesne 1936/1943, vol. 6, p. 18; Moreau 1940-1948, vol. 2, p. 121 ff.; Brühl 1975, passim, and more recently Esquieu 1992 (with maps), Esquieu 1998 (with maps), Picard 1994, passim; also Freigang 1992, pp. 239-248. GERMANY: Hofmann 1914, Leudemann 1980. ITALY: Braunfels 1953, p. 171.

171 Some examples: LAON, fourteenth century: c. 350 people (Picard 1994, p. 246), LYON: c. 300 people (idem, p. 278); LICHFIELD, a much smaller cathedral: c. 100 people (Barron & Harper-Bill 1985); NORWICH, a monastic cathedral, thirteenth and fourteenth centuries: c. 270 people (Gilchrist 2005, p. 15).

172 Gilles 1995, p. 232.

173 Schieffer 1976, pp. 116-117, 153 ff.

174 Kroesen 2003, p. 180.

175 Freigang 1992, pp. 11, 47, 357.

176 This important issue falls beyond the scope of this study; see Esquieu 1998; also Kurmann 1987, p. 21 n. 24 (e.g. RHEIMS, AMIENS, CHÂLONS-EN-CHAMPAGNE); Erlande-Brandenburg 1977, p. 258 (AMIENS).

177 Hofmann 1914, p. 6 ff. In England such fortification took place from around 1250 until the end of the fourteenth century; Edwards 1939, p. 62 ff.; Hill 1965, p. 115 ff.; Lepine 1995, p. 114. Concerning the relationship between the city and cathedral within the precinctal boundaries in LONDON: Barron 2003, pp. 126-149. Concerning NARBONNE and other cathedrals in southern France, see Freigang 1992, pp. 244-252.

178 Concerning the immunity as a place of commerce: Hofmann 1914, pp. 106-116; Le Bras 1954, pp. 191-192. Houses and shops around the cathedral, in some cases rented out to fund the

fabric, such as in ELY (Atkinson 1933, p. 142); YORK (Raine 1859, p. 68); LAUSANNE, early thirteenth-century '*estaisuns*' (Laufer 1996, pp. 34-44); COLOGNE (Ennen 1880, pp. 19, 40, 58, 72; Ennen 1863/1869, vol. 1, p. 735 n. 1, vol. 3, p. 983; Vogts 1930, p. 22; Gechter 1983, pp. 226-234, 400-403; Lacomblet 1868, no. 102); MAINZ, thirteenth century (Demandt 1977, p. 88 ff.; Gottron 1951, pp. 43-45); STRASBOURG (Winckelmann 1907, p. 255); CHARTRES (Jusselin 1915-1922, p. 268; Lecocq 1876, p. 194 ff.; Merlet 1858, passim; Von Simson 1956, p. 167; Chédeville 1973, pp. 425, 458); BORDEAUX (Le Bras 1954, p. 191; Larcher de Lavernade 1845, p. 90); MILAN (Boito 1889, p. 210; Carotti 1889, p. 280); LIÈGE (*Cartulaire Liège*, vol. 2, no. 480); ROUEN (De Beaurepaire 1909, passim; Lefebvre 1997); METZ (Pelt 1930, nos 16, 33, 36, 39, 43, 48, 59, 74); CAHORS, 1308 (Bénéjeam-Lère 1993, pp. 15,16); AMIENS (Durand 1901-1903, vol. 1 p. 122); QUIMPER (Le Men 1877, pp. 223, 252); TROYES, end of the fifteenth century, '*logettes*' (Murray 1987, p. 63; also Gadan 1851, pp. XL and 10; d'Arbois de Jubainville 1862, p. 223); MEAUX: king orders demolition, 1412 (Stein 1934, pp. 95-107); TOURNAI, fourteenth century (Pycke 1983-1984, n. 43). Concerning the incorporation of the main square and civic market, La Plaza Mayor, into the cathedral precinct in SIGÜENZA around 1500, see La Porte-Fernández Alfaro 1992, pp. 403-415.

179 Feine 1954, p. 178; Schröcker 1934, p. 90; Frölich 1933, p. 262. PARIS (the Notre-Dame was the parish church of the Île de la Cité until 1183, that is for 20 years after building works began): Friedmann 1959, p. 118 ff.; Friedmann 1964, p. 28; instead Bishop Maurice de Sully transformed twelve chapels on the Île de la Cité into small parishes; Lorentz & Sandron 2006, pp. 127-128; Gaudemet 2001, p. 264. COLOGNE: Gescher 1930, passim. MÜNSTER: Schröer 1966, p. 516. SALZBURG: Leisching 1964, p. 260. Additional examples in Erlande-Brandenburg 1977, pp. 309-313. Concerning the conflict of interest between parish and chapter in ROUEN, see Tabbagh 1997, pp. 218-220. Concerning similar conflicts, also in relation to the division of alms, in HEREFORD, see Swanson & Lepine 2000, pp. 70, 79. Their parish rights were not always complete; for example, UTRECHT Cathedral had no baptismal font of its own; De Groot & Van Tongerloo 1997, pp. 209-232. In LIMOGES the cathedral had no parish duties at all, except vis-à-vis the cathedral community.

180 ELY before 1360: Atkinson 1933, p. 7; Salzman 1948/1953, vol. 4, p. 83; Chapman 1907, vol. 1, pp. 30, 101, 103, vol. 2, p. 192. LINCOLN: Cook 1957, p. 27. For England, see the definitive article by Lepine 2006: at least four of the nine secular cathedrals accommodated a parish church, usually in the nave. TOULOUSE: Van der Meer 1967, p. 86.

181 Namely, the parish church established in the chapel of San Pedro from the beginning of the fifteenth century. There was furthermore a separate entrance that could also be used when the cathedral itself was closed; the chapel was administered by the chapel as an independent entity; Lop Otín 2006, pp. 637-643; *Las catedrales españolas*, p. 111. In ROUEN the coexistence of parish and cathedral under one roof gave rise to myriad disputes over competence.

In 1497 the parish was removed to a new chapel near the *Tour de Beurre*. The parish had its own fabric, run by laymen, and was responsible for the costs of services and furniture. A few accounts postdating 1503 are preserved: Lucien-René Delsalle in *Notre-Dame de Rouen*, pp. 124-138.

182 NORWICH: three parishes with burial rights within the monastic precinct; Gilchrist 2005, p. 31, cites additional examples. CHICHESTER: Hamilton Thompson 1925, p. 104. CONDOM after 1531 at the civic consuls' request; the city maintained this building: *Congrès Archéologique de France* 128 (1970), p. 149. Concerning cathedrals' parishional role in Southern France, and the various solutions applied, see Ryckebusch 1995. In the diocese of LAVAUR, established in 1318, the bishop and chapter had use of the apse and two bays, the parish of the remaining three bays. Following renovations begun in 1484, the bishop compensated the parishioners with a new bay and a portal; *Congrès Archéologique de France* 140 (1982), pp. 334, 337. Concerning the Sainte-Croix altar in the cathedral of CLERMONT-FERRAND and its unusual use by the chapter as an instrument with which to increase its civic influence vis-à-vis the bishop and other parishes, see Chagny-Sève 1985.

183 Hubert 1962, p. 114; *Reallexikon zur deutschen Kunstgeschichte*, in voce *'Altar'*, col. 413; Braun 1924, vol. 1, pp. 402-406; Hofmeister 1931, pp. 119, 120. MÜNSTER: Schröer 1966, p. 516. RODEZ: Bion de Marlavagne 1875, p. 105. ROCHESTER: Cook 1957, p. 26. VIENNA: Flieder 1968, pp. 186 n. 313, 189. In late medieval PADERBORN and MAINZ the west choir served as parish church: *Westfälische Zeitschrift* 3 (1961) p. 154 n. 26 (personal communication from Dr C.J.A.C. Peeters). In MAINZ the altar of the Holy Cross that stood before the rood loft still served as the parish altar in 1332; *Willigis und sein Dom*, p. 219 ff. SALISBURY's parish altar, located near the pulpit in the nave, was likewise dedicated to the Holy Cross (1468); Lepine 2006, p. 33.

184 Bion de Marlavagne 1875, pp. 105, 226-228. RODEZ had two parishes, that of the *bourg* and that of the *cité*, i.e. the cathedral; detailed survey in Désachy 1996, pp. 92-98. The consuls, who administered the parish altar, had their own bench in the lower part of the choir by at least 1355. In the seventeenth century the bishop rescinded this right despite protest; idem, pp. 25, 29.

185 Matamoros 1932, pp. 104- 105; Almuni i Balada 1991, pp. 49-50; Almuni i Balada 2007, p. 142 and doc. 101 (26 March 1439).

186 Concerning the involvement of the laity in ecclesiastical decisions, see Avril 1991, p. 253.

187 Mortet & Deschamps 1929, p. 260 (31 March 1236); *Fasti Ecclesiae Gallicanae*, vol. 1, AMIENS, p. 5; Murray 1996, pp. 49-51, 135-137; also Murray 1990, pp. 114, 130-131.

188 'and the clerics, burghers and inhabitants of TROYES who were present always agreed as one to build the said tower'. 'master of the fabric [...] who was charged with informing the residents and reporting to them [...] how the monies and contributions which all of them had pledged would be spent'; account for 1412/13; *Inventaire-sommaire Aube* G 1561; Pigeotte 1877, p. 160; Murray 1987, pp. 59, 141, 175 and 233. In ARLES, the influx of offerings at the

grave of Archbishop Louis Aleman (d. 1450) and ensuing plans for rebuilding the choir prompted the new archbishop to establish a college of four fabric masters, two of whom were appointed by the city; *Congrès Archéologique de France* 134 (1976), p. 365. For additional examples (BOURGES, CHARTRES, DAX, APT), see Schöller 1989, pp. 201-202.

189 For instance in PALMA in 1390; Domenge i Mesquida 1997, pp. 67, 71, 98. HUESCA: Durán Gudiol 1991, p. 73.

190 Schöller 1989, pp. 200-215.

191 Edwards 1967, p. 235; Hill 1965, p. 113; Owen 1994, pp. 121-122: the fabric fund dates from around 1160, and its management was initially charged to a layman and a canon, later to two ecclesiastics who answered to the chapter.

192 Suhr 1938, p. 83 ff.; Wiek 1959b, p. 95; *Urkundenbuch Lübeck*, no. 57.

193 Apel 1934, pp. 97-98; *Urkundenbuch Hamburg*, vol. 1, p. 613 (1269), vol. 2 (4), p. 811 (1336). It should be noted that by the Middle Ages, HAMBURG claimed a cathedral in name only, as the city fell in the diocese of BREMEN. See also Mathieu 1973, pp. 34-36.

194 Wiek 1959a, passim.

195 Donath 2000, pp. 25-27, 39-44: the *fabrica* is first recorded in 1271; not only cathedral canons, but also laymen served as *magistri fabrice*.

196 Especially Wiek 1959b; also the articles by Blumstein 1902; Erler 1954; Hanauer 1900-1901, 1901-1902; Pfleger 1937, passim; Reinhardt 1960; Winckelmann 1907, Fuchs 1974, Binding 1993, pp. 71-75; especially Schock-Werner 1996.

197 Those cathedral fabrics where citizens' involvement was limited to the auditing of accounts, as in NANTES, are not considered here; Le Mené 1961, p. 376; Bordeaux 1969, p. 249 n. 37.

198 Suhr 1938, p. 85 ff.; Schröcker 1934, pp. 59 ff., 85 ff. He speaks of '*das Recht an den Oblationen*', which he defines as all unstructured and freely given offerings made by the faithful, earmarked for pious causes.

199 See the HAMBURG Cathedral statutes of 24 July 1336 (*Urkundenbuch Hamburg*, vol. 2 (4), p. 811): '*qui quidem consul deputabitur et elegitur a capitulo et non a consulibus, et nihil aliud faciet, nisi quod sit conscius, ut nullum dampnum fiat civitati per structuram ecclesie et quod redditus fabrice in usus debitos convertantur*'. This rule was enacted on 8 November 1269; Mathieu 1973, p. 35. In the fourteenth century the consuls appointed the lay *rector structure*. In 1339-1341 the chapter and council went to court in a dispute over the misuse of proceeds from the collection boxes; Salomon & Reetz 1968-1980, vol. 1, pp. 38-41, vol. 2, pp. 246-247, 339, vol. 3, p. 38.

200 Provision issued by the Lateran Council in 1123; Mortet 1911, p. 364.

201 *Urkundenbuch Lübeck*, no. 4066; see also no. 513.

202 *Urkundenbuch Bremen*, vol. 2, no. 108; Wiek 1959a, p. 130.

203 Klink 1988, p. 88. The *buwmeister* was alternatively known as the *procurator fabrice*.

204 *Urkundenbuch Regensburg*, nos 126, 230b, 232; Hubel 1989, pp. 165-167; Hubel & Schuller 1995, pp. 12, 90.

205 Schock-Werner 1983, p. 14.

206 Wiek 1959b, passim; Hanauer 1901-1902, vol. 21, p. 246; texts in Reinhardt 1960. Civic management continued to be a point of contention between the bishop and city even as late as 1393 and 1395; *Urkunden-buch Strassburg*, vol. 6, pp. 408-409, 590-591; Fuchs

1974, p. 23. The high chapter retained a right of inspection over the fabric in the fourteenth century.

207 Pfleger 1937, p. 4; Pfleger 1941, p. 64; Fuchs 1974, p. 23. Day-to-day management of the *Oeuvre Notre Dame* was charged to the *Schaffner* – in most cases an ecclesiastic, at least until the end of the fifteenth century – who was supervised by three *Pfleger* – always laymen from the upper echelons of the community – who in turn were accountable to the civic administrators; see the three fourteenth- and fifteenth-century statues and descriptions of the duties of both types of officers in Fuchs 2000, pp. 139-146.

208 Schock-Werner 1995, p. 225; Signori 1995, p. 257; also Heckert 1993, p. 153.

209 Wiek 1959b, p. 69; also Marie-José Nohlen in Doré 2007, pp. 31-40.

210 The city's official expenses were charged in part to the fabric; in times of famine the *Frauenwerk* sometimes supplied aid; Pfleger 1941, p. 68.

211 Hanauer 1900-1901, vol. 20, p. 16 (1501).

212 Hanauer 1901-1902, vol. 21, p. 49 ff.; Wiek 1959b, p. 84.

213 It is not clear whether what was at issue in 1422 was a renewal of a right fallen into disuse or the institution of a new right. It might be that the chaplain of the *altare civitatis* was replaced by a canon at this time; Fuchs 1974, p. 25.

214 Another example: in the seventeenth and eighteenth centuries the city of ELNE appealed against the appropriation and later liquidation of the cathedral treasure by the chapter, which had relocated with the bishop to PERPIGNAN (1602); the city's plea met with refusal; *Inventaire-sommaire Pyrénées-Orientales* G 110 (1721).

215 Ennen 1880, pp. 83-84; Wiek 1959b, pp. 97-102. It is unknown whether the city succeeded in its endeavour. A charter of 10 June 1315 (Lacomblet 1857, p. 152) appoints a '*cives Coloniensis*' as *rector operis fabrice*, but it is doubtful that he actually functioned as an administrator of the cathedral fabric.

216 This complex issue can only be touched upon briefly here as the financing of the construction of Italian *duomi* falls largely outside the scope of this study. There is a large body of recent literature on this subject. General: Fonseca 1984; Haines & Riccetti 1996; Boucheron 2000; Crouzet-Pavan 2003. BOLOGNA: Fanti 1980 and 1989, pp. 698-742. FLORENCE: Zervas 1987, pp. 3-53; Haines, in Verdon 1994, pp. 71-83; Haines & Riccetti 1996, pp. 267-295; Haines, in *Finanziare cattedrali*, pp. 137-167. GENUA: Polonio, in Haines & Riccetti 1996, pp. 1-71. LUCCA: Concioni 1994-1995, p. 201. MILAN: Rondinini 1984; Welch 1995, pp. 49-114; Boucheron 1998, pp. 127-157; Rondinini in *Finanziare cattedrali*, pp. 107-121, good summary in *Ad Summum 1248*, pp. 185-202; concerning the summer cathedral of Santa Tecla: Chellini 1997. ORVIETO: Riccetti, in Crouzet-Pavan 2003, pp. 245-373 and in *Finanziare cattedrali*, pp. 167-229. PERUGIA: Nicolini 1992, pp. 211-225; Silvestrelli, in Haines & Riccetti 1996, pp. 137-157. PIACENZA: Klein 1995. PISA: Ronzani, in Haines & Riccetti 1996, pp. 1-71. SIENA: Riedl & Seidel 1995, and especially Giorgi & Moscadellli 2005.

217 Orvieto 1138, FLORENCE 1173: Schmid 1957, p. 91 ff.; Kurze 1966, p. 203.

218 Concerning the position of the bishop in thirteenth-century northern Italy, see Southern 1970, pp. 202-213.

219 Crouzet-Pavan 2003, p. 159;

Schmid 1957, p. 106; especially Fonseca 1984, passim.

220 Nicolini 1992, pp. 214, 217-220; Silvestrelli in Haines & Riccetti 1996, pp. 137-156.

221 Haines & Riccetti 1996, p. 386 and index sub nomine '*fra* Melano' and '*fra* Bevignate'.

222 '[...] *esset remotio devotionis civium*'; Haines & Riccetti 1996, p. 259 n. 301.

223 Concerning the complex relationship in a third city – PISA – see Hunnikin 1972-1973, pp. 44-49: the cathedral and baptistery were managed separately.

224 In MILAN the situation was complicated by the fact that there were two cathedrals built in direct proximity to each other: the cathedral dedicated to Mary was the winter cathedral, that of Santa Tecla the summer cathedral. The fabric, or *superstantia*, of Santa Tecla was initially jointly managed by canons of this church and laymen, and after 1417 by the canons alone. Not until 1550, after endless legal wrangling, was the cathedral of Santa Tecla finally demolished; Chellini 1997.

225 Mezzanotte 1955, pp. 871-872; Boito 1889, pp. 34 ff., 179; Bishop 1918, pp. 415-416; *Annali*, vol. 1, passim; Gatti Perer 1969, vol. 1, pp. 53-60; Brivio 1977, especially pp. 1-50.

226 *Annali*, Appendix vol. 1, p. 38; *Annali*, vol. 1, pp. 3-12: '*regolamento generale di amministrazione*'; also in Brivio 1977, pp. 131-142. Gatti Perer 1969, vol. 1, p. 54: the master of the fabric was fired, and replaced on 11 August 1387.

227 The record-highest number of representatives of the six *porte* was 300 in 1395; this number declined to six or twelve after 1468. Brivio characterizes the *fabbrica* as an '*istituzione religiosa e civile insieme*', which was able, by conducting a '*politica dell'equidistanza*' between the archbishop, chapter, city and duke, to carve out a large measure of autonomy and room for independent action; Brivio 1977, pp. 10-25, 37 ff. Incidentally, in MILAN, as in STRASBOURG, monies belonging to the *fabbrica* were also spent for other ends. During the famine of 1402, the *fabbrica* functioned as the *Comune*'s fund for food purchases; during the period of the republic (1447-1450), the *fabbrica* supplied stones for projectiles, financed bridge-building and so on; Mezzanotte 1955, pp. 898, 906, 907.

228 See Grote n.d., passim, and more recently Verdon 1994 and Haines in Haines & Riccetti 1996.

229 Braunfels 1953, pp. 149-150; Davidsohn 1896-1927, vol. 1, pp. 333-334.

230 Grote n.d., p. 33. Here, too, lay influence in the fabric's management did not come without a struggle; Schröcker 1934, pp. 148-149.

231 Grote n.d., pp. 43, 44, 68, 109; Haines & Riccetti 1996, p. 271. Concerning the term *Opera*, see Schmid 1957, p. 105 n. 84.

232 On only one occasion do we find mention of intervention by the bishop, in this case not without cause, in 1341; Grote n.d., p. 57.

233 Grote n.d., p. 31; Schröcker 1934, p. 119. In SIENA the *consilium campanae et populi* voted 219 to twelve on 20 October 1290 to cover the fabric's budget shortfall with civic funds; Norton 1880, pp. 140, 304.

234 Cf. the *Comune*'s deliberation on 7 August 1318 about granting subsidies '*quod nisi per Comune Florentie ad opus ipsum porrigatur pecuniarum subsidium, opus predictum prosecutio et consumatio carebit*'; Grote n.d., p. 31.

235 Grote n.d., pp. 39, 43, 68; Davidsohn 1896-1927, vol. 4 (2), p. 170.

236 Grote n.d., p. 44.

CHAPTER TWO

Sources of income for the building works

Introduction

1 Concerning this issue, see Iogna-Prat 2006. His central question is: '*Pourquoi en Occident Dieu est devenu "de pierre"?*'; see pp. 309, 312, 317, 443, 459, 608 and passim.

2 '*Porro ipsa domus idcirco vocabulum habet ecclesiae, quia continet Ecclesiam, id est populum convocatum ab eo qui facit unanimes habitare in domo*', cited in Platelle 1991, p. 628, also p. 627 n. 6.

3 Pycke 2005, p. 683.

4 An example: letter from the bishop of AVIGNON, 1216: '[...] *attendentes quod inter cetera opera pietatis et misericordie sit templa et monasteria Dei ornare* [...]'; Mortet & Deschamps 1929, p. 222.

5 Psalm 26 (25) : 8; see e.g. Mortet 1911, pp. 69 n. 1, 94, 339.

6 Timmers 1947, no. 1392; Thomassinus 1725, pars 3, liber 2, caput 36, no. 4; also e.g. Mansi 1759-1793, vol. 25, p. 794 (1326), and Quicherat 1886, p. 217. See also the church dedication mass in the *Missale Romanum*; Hull Stookey 1969, passim.

7 For example: LONDON synodal consititution, 1215, 1222; Wooley 1915, p. 301: '*cum fuerit in veteri testamento magnus honor exhibitus templo, ad quod convenire consueverant Hebrei manu non vacua, et hoc tempore gracie succedunt ecclesie cathedrales* [...]'. Extensive discussion by Suger (c. 1081-1151); Panofsky 1946, pp. 64, 65, 185.

8 Faupel-Drevs 2000, p. 213: she paraphrases the *Rationale divinorum officiorum* by Durandus of MENDE (1230/31-1296).

9 Thomas Aquinas 1952, *Summa Theologiae*, II, II, q. 117a.3 ad 1; q. 128a.1c., q. 134 passim. Both *liberalitas* and *magnificentia* were virtues with a bearing on '*circa pecuniam*'. *Liberalitas* fell under the cardinal virtue of *iustitia*, whilst *magnificentia* under that of *fortitudo*: '[*liberalitas* ...] *respicit communiter usum pecuniae*, [*magnificentia* ...] *respicit magnum in pecuniae usu*'; q. 134 a.3 ad 1.

10 Barlow 1939, p. XXIV and 181. Concerning Arnulf as episcopal building patron, see Grant 2005, pp. 21, 28, 85-87, 232.

11 From the outset, arguments for and against monumental church-building were very consistent; even the Church fathers were ambivalent about the splendour of the church building, such as Clement of Alexandria (c. 150-215) (personal communication from Dr C.J.A.C. Peeters).

12 Since the time of Ambrose, much has been written concerning the use of gold and precious materials in divine services and the moral obligation in times of crisis to liquidate them in order to ransom prisoners or aid the poor; see Aston 1987; Sternberg 1996; Bernard of Clairvaux in Rudolph 1990, pp. 80-103.

13 For example in Petrus Cantor (d. 1197); Baldwin 1970, vol. 1, pp. 66, 109 and n. 18 and 31.

14 Bernard of Clairvaux in Rudolph 1990, pp. 11, 280-283, 327-328: '*fulget ecclesia in parietibus et in pauperibus eget*'. Bernard's ideas trace back to the Church fathers Jerome and John Chrysostom; also Fracheboud 1953, passim.

15 For example, Thomassinus 1725, pars 3, liber 3, caput 32 and 33, no. 5.

16 Mortet 1913, especially pp. 113, 114 n. 4, 116.

17 Coulton 1928, pp. 322-337.

18 Post 1967, pp. 24, 25; Hofman 2003, p. 780.

19 Thomassinus 1725, pars 3, liber 3, caput 26 ff.; Bordenave 1643, pp. 625-641.

20 Friedberg 1879/1882, vol. 1, p. 696.

21 Thomas Aquinas 1952, *Summa Theologiae*, II, II, q. 185a.7c.

22 Decr. sec. pars art. XII quest. 11c.7 (Friedberg 1879/1882, vol. 1, p. 710): cited from Jerome: '*non parietes ornare templi sed pauperibus providere gloria episcopi est*'.

23 From *De gemma animae*, c. 1130; Mortet & Deschamps 1929, p. 18. Some synodal statutes, such as those from TOURNAI in the thirteenth century and CAMBRAI in 1260, ruled that no collections would be permitted before those for the poor and needy had taken place; *Statuts synodaux Reims*, p. 335 (sub 7).

24 See Appendix one.

25 The earliest reliable sources date from the twelfth century; Van Caenegem & Ganshof 1962, p. 104; Quicherat 1886, p. 183.

26 Only in a few cases is it possible to render a cathedral fabric's fluctuating budget during a period of key building activity in visual form; Du Colombier 1973, p. 14; Héliot 1965, p. 243. See also Vroom 1981, Appendix 10 and graph 7. Concerning TROYES, see Murray 1975, p. 128, fig. 13.

27 STRASBOURG's cathedral fabric, the *Frauenwerk*, is an example of one that was extremely wealthy; Hanauer 1901-1902, vol. 21, pp. 165, 166. Also Marie-José Nohlen in Doré 2007, pp. 36-37: this wealth was largely amassed in the years after the Black Death, c. 1350.

28 Ferraris 1852-1857, in voce '*ecclesia*', art. 3, no. 68; Zindel 1791, p. 83 (par. 43); Barbosa 1656-1665, vol. 5, p. 220, vol. 9 (1), p. 52; Frances de Urrutigoyti 1665, cap. 12 and 13, to which the description below is primarily indebted. Frances de Urrutigoyti (1600-1670) was professor of canon law in his natal city of ZARAGOZA; *Diccionario eclesiastica de España*, p. 955.

29 Frances de Urrutigoyti 1665, cap. 12, no. 12, cap. 13, nos 4, 5, 99.

30 Idem, cap. 13, nos 96, 97.

31 Idem, cap. 13, no. 13.

32 Idem, cap. 12, no. 8.

33 Idem, cap. 13, no. 9.

34 One exceptional example concerns the cathedral of ABØ in Finland. According to a deed of 1335, the priest of the parish of Sagu, whether on the advice or even the command of the bishop and chapter, put certain goods at the cathedral's disposal until such time as it was finished, because it was unseemly that the rural parishes should prosper even as the cathedral - the mother church of diocese - fell into disrepair: '[...] *indecens esse* [..] *quod ecclesiis ruralibus per dyocesis Finlandem competenter exstructis et decenter ornatis, ecclesia Aboensis aliarum mater eiusdem dyocesis ecclesiarum et domina deserta quasi appareat oculis intuencium et plurimum ruinosa*'; *Diplomatarium suecanum*, no. 3105, 19 January 1335.

35 Frances de Urrutigoyti 1665, cap. 13, no. 67.

36 Idem, cap. 13, nos 120, 130.

37 Idem, cap. 13, no. 100.

38 Idem, cap. 13, no. 105.

39 Cf. definition formulated by E.H. Gombrich, *Meditations on a hobby horse*, London 1963, p. 86: 'social history of art [...] an account of the changing material conditions under which art was commissioned and created in the past'.

40 Sometimes also for worldly objectives, such as the indulgences issued for bridge-building; Paulus 1922-1923, vol. 2, p. 247, vol. 3, p. 439; Boyer 1964, passim; Boyer 1976, pp. 31-60 ('the bridge as a pious work'), especially pp. 49, 92, 112 ff.

41 Compare the classification of income sources at the *Stiftskirche* of Sankt Viktor in Xanten; *Stiftskirche*

Xanten, vol. 3 (2), pp. XVIII-XXV, vol. 4 (2), pp. XVII-XXI.

42 A case in point is the cathedral building campaign at HUESCA, which commenced in 1497 and ended in 1515, and which was not accounted for in the regular fabric rolls; Archivo de la Catedral, cuentas de fábrica.

43 Such as in TROYES; *Inventaire-sommaire Aube* G 1571, 1574, etc., and in SENS 1490; Quantin 1842, p. 22.

44 See chapter 1, n. 177. Revenues accruing to the fabric from such buildings in MILAN and ROUEN, and elsewhere. Not all fabrics enjoyed these revenues, however. In YORK it was a subordinate chapter official - the janitor or the porter - who had the right to establish shops within the immunity; Edwards 1967, p. 228. In COLOGNE a canon commissioned the erection of eight small houses inside the church precinct in 1251, paid for from his own pocket, intending to use the proceeds to fund his obit. Rents from other stalls accrued to the *custos* in the thirteenth and fourteenth centuries. Not until the latter half of the sixteenth century did the cathedral fabric profit from the proceeds of shops built to abut new pillars inside the cathedral; *Urkundenbuch Niederrhein*, vol. 2, no. 378; Ennen 1880, pp. 19, 40, 58; Lacomblet 1868, p. 175. In 1241 the archbishop of MAINZ granted the chapter half the income from shops in the cathedral immunity to enlarge its prebends. In the second half of the thirteenth century, the chapter acquired the titles to these shops but did not allocate the income to the fabric; Demandt 1977, pp. 88-91. For QUIMPER see Le Men 1877, pp. 233, 252.

45 See also Crosby 1994, p. 42.

46 As burial place for bishops from the twelfth century on; Brühl 1975, p. 247.

47 Freigang 2002, in connection with the Notre Dame in PARIS; concerning the chapels and chaplaincies of the Notre Dame also Eldin 1994, pp. 73, 74.

48 Bango Torviso 1992, pp. 126-128. For BURGOS, see Karge 1995, p. 61: not until after 1450, countless chapels, which were always built with the chapter's permission. The enormous *Capilla de Condestables*, erected between 1482 and 1492, was built and furnished entirely at the expense of its commissioners Don Pedro de Velasco and his wife Mencia de Mendoza, with the chapter's consent; Pereda Llarena & De Ceballos 1999, p. 31 n. 3, 6, 7 and 11. Concerning the *capillas reales* in Spanish cathedrals, see Ruiz Sousa 2006; Nogales Rincón 2005. There is scarcely any documentation concerning the financing of the construction of these chapels, which sometimes served as burial places for the kings.

49 Israëls 2006, p. 89. This study traces the evolution of the cathedral of SIENA from the vantage point of a single chapel, which, together with its altarpiece, was founded as one of the cathedral's first private chapels by the deceased *operaio* (master of the fabric) Turino de Matteo between 1423 and 1430; its foundation required no or only little architectural intervention, however.

50 An exception is the famous royal chapel in the cathedral of KRAKOW (1519), founded by King Sigismund I as a burial chapel and site of elaborate obit celebrations and fully funded by him via the allocation of certain fixed revenues; its construction and furnishing were organized without any involvement on the part of the cathedral fabric; Franaszek & Przybyszewski 1991 (including building expenditures for Italian

craftsmen, 1521-1526). Concerning the construction, supply of building material and financing of the San Blas chapel north of the cloister of TOLEDO Cathedral (1397), see Sánchez-Palencia Mancebo 1985. This chapel, founded by Archbishop Pedro Tenorio in 1397 and intended as his burial chapel was fully autonomous up until 1837; also *Las catedrales españolas*, pp. 114-115.

51 Durán Gudiol 1991, p. 72; exact wages for this period are unknown.

52 Almuni i Balada 2007, doc. 30 and 31, pp. 695-700. Permission might also be gained with a large gift to the fabric, such as in 1487, when a benefactor gained '*licentia fabricandi altare Sti Crucifixi* [...] *post altere majus ex eo quod dedit magnam cuantitatem ad prosecuendam fabricam*'; Matamoros 1932, p. 119 n. 1.

53 Almuni i Balada 2007: concrete examples: doc. 48 (1364) and 100 (1438).

54 Based on TORTOSA; Almuni i Balada 2007, p. 696.

55 Concerning the chapels and their respective retables in the cathedral and three parish churches of BARCELONA, see Borau Morell 2003. The contribution was sometimes 130 lliuvres barc.; idem, Appendices 8-11 (1379). Contributions for the building works were in lump sums (albeit sometimes paid in instalments). A benefice or *anniversarium* required a pool of capital from which the annual costs could be paid. A retable cost between 445 and 110 lliuvres barc.; idem, p. 280; also pp. 485-487, 298-370.

56 RODEZ 1299, '*Lego operi in subsidium constructionis unius capellae* [...]'; Desachy 2005, p. 39.

57 See the analysis relating to MURCIA Cathedral by Gutiérrez-Cortines Corral 1987a, pp. 24-26; also Rodríguez Llopis & García Díaz 1994, pp. 82- 87: there were a variety of options available within any single cathedral and period.

58 López de Silanes & Sáinz Ripa 1991, doc. 251; the founder was furthermore free to choose the altar's patron saint.

59 In BOURGES the chapter minutes reveal that canons and other founders themselves managed the commission of their own chapels during their lifetimes. A few canons were put in charge of overall supervision. Each founder was obliged to leave a certain sum in his will to guarantee the chapel's completion.; De Girardot & Durand 1849, pp. 73-117. For PARIS: Aubert 1920, p. 142 and n. 7 (1288). For CAMBRAI: deed of 1418; Houdoy 1880, p. 259. For AMIENS: *Cartulaire Amiens*, vol. 2, p. 99 (fourteenth century). See also Bechle 1954, pp. 68-71. In 1426 Queen Elisabeth founded a chapel and altar in the cathedral of KRAKOW, '*erexit. aedificavit. construxit, dotavit*'; *Zbiór dokumentow katedry diecezji Krakowskiej*, Lublin1973, vol. 2, no. 270.

60 Raine 1859, p. XXI and doc. XXIII, pp. 168-170.

61 As examples of well-documented cathedral furniture and interior in general unconnected with any chapel: CHOIR STALLS: ZARAGOSSA 1445, managed by the *obra del coro*; *La Seo de Zaragoza*, p. 158. ROUEN, 1457-1471; Lardin in Block & Billiet 2003, pp. 33-71; *Fasti Ecclesiae Gallicanae*, vol. 2, pp. 24 ff.: the archbishop paid the 712 l.t., or 23 annual wages, for his own seat himself, whilst the seats of the 88 canons, which cost at least 6485 l.t or over 200 annual wages, were paid for from the fabric fund over a period of eleven accounting years. LEÓN, 1468 et seq., managed by the *obra de la sillería*;

Teijeira Pablos 1993, doc. 23, 24. AMIENS between 1508 and 1519; *Fasti Ecclesiae Gallicanae*, vol. 1, pp. 17-20: 120 seats, costing 9,488 l.t. or more than 300 annual wages, were funded not by the fabric but by the *L'Office des marances* (= fines for absence during choral prayers), with another 10 or more percent funded by contributions from individual canons. RETABLES: PALENCIA 1504-1526; San Martín Payo 1953. HUESCA 1520-1534; Durán Gudiol 1991, pp. 159-161. For Spain: Kroesen 2003, pp. 323-329. CHOIR TAPESTRIES 1402-1532: exh. cat. RHEIMS 2001, pp. 243-252 (Weigert) and Weigert 2004, app. 1 (at 40 churches, half of them cathedrals, these were gifts from the bishop, individual canons or the chapter). BOOKS FOR THE LITURGY: PALENCIA, 7 *cantorales*; San Martín Payo 1985. LITURGICAL VESSELS: CÓRDOBA, *custodia procesional* 1513-1518; Martín Ribes 1983. STAINED GLASS: documentary records only exist from the fifteenth century on; Caviness 1996, p. 73. For a discussion of commissions for stained glass windows in general, see Kurmann & Kurmann-Schwarz 1997 and also, with reference to CHARTRES Cathedral: Kurmann & Kurmann-Schwarz 1995 and Kurmann-Schwarz 1996. Additionally: LEÓN 1423/24: *Documentación medieval León*, nos 109, 129, 137, 142; Yarza *et al.* 2004, p. 296. PALENCIA 1503: twelve windows in the crossing; San Martín 1985. Regarding the UTRECHT Dom, see Appendix five.

62 Pycke 2005, p. 684: '[...] *sed solam per eam* [*ecclesiam*] *et in ea pompose incedentes dilatant fimbrias suas*'.

63 This also applied where the donor's identity was indicated by means of an inscription or family coat of arms. The inclusion of a coat of arms can therefore be seen as a mark of gratitude for a gift, and does not in itself signify that the individual actually supplied all the financing; Meunier 2003. Concerning the chapter's measure of control in the commission of stained glass windows, see Kurmann & Kurmann-Schwarz 1997 and Kurmann-Schwarz 1996; also Lefebvre 1997, p. 422, concerning the donation of statues by citizens of ROUEN. See also n. 137.

64 Cloulas 1993, pp. 139-140; *Carta Mendoza*.

65 Clark 2007, p. 99, draws the same conclusion regarding agricultural labour capacity in England between 1250 and 1600.

66 Research conducted by Phelps Brown & Hopkins 1955-1961 furthermore shows that whilst building wages - here expressed in a unit of consumer goods - did in fact fluctuate greatly in the Middle Ages, this fluctuation was very consistent throughout Europe.

67 The first to apply this measure was Tenhaeff, publisher of the UTRECHT cathedral fabric accounts; Tenhaeff 1949, p. 191; Zervas 1987, p. 53, also uses this measure for her analysis of the *Opera* in FLORENCE. Recent studies: Dirlmeier 1978, pp. 130-135, 141-157; Dirlmeier 1983, pp. 35 ff.; Kimpel & Suckale 1985, p. 447 and n. 51 (period between 1250 and 1300 in France); Jütte 1985, pp. 83-101 and Gechter 1983, p. 267 (COLOGNE); Lardin 1997, pp. 367-370 (ROUEN); Victor 1996, pp. 379-80 (GERONA); Costantini 2003, p. 109 (Chaise-Dieu); and for Italy: *Finanziare cattedrali*, pp. 25, 80, and Giorgi & Moscadelli 2005, pp. 120, 273 (SIENA)

68 It is not always possible to obtain wage information from the source itself, that is from the cathedral fabric

rolls. In such cases it is necessary to rely on comparable published wage records. Nor are both the summer and the winter wages known in every case. Where necessary, wages in England are taken from Phelps Brown & Hopkins 1955-1961, Phelps Brown & Hopkins 1981, and Clark 2007, pp. 130-134; wages in France from d'Avenel 1894-1912. In England, real wages in the building industry developed along more or less the same lines as those in agriculture; Clark 2007, p. 109.

ONE The bishop's contributions

69 *Charters Salisbury*, pp. 229, 230.

70 Peckius 1620, p. 66; Van Espen 1700, pars 2, tit. 16, cap. 2 (= vol. 1, pp. 729-741, cap. 5).

71 The canonists were fully aware of this fact, hence the addition '*seclusa consuetudine*'.

72 *Cartulaire Sens*, p. 93.

73 Clanché 1926-1927, p. 124 n. 1.

74 '*Preceptum cooperture ecclesie b. Marie: [...] trabes autem et tigni, immo omnia alia ecclesie necessaria ab episcopo ecclesie ministrentur*'; Mortet 1911, pp. 350, 351 and *Cartulaire Notre-Dame de Paris*, vol. 1, p. 266; see also Mortet 1888, pp. 24, 25. Concerning the contradiction with the provisions of 829: Lesne 1936/1943, vol. 6, p. 270. See also Erlande-Brandenburg 1997, pp. 23, 24 and Lombard-Jourdan 1997, p. 523 n. 151: the other sections of the roof were funded from the fruits of the vacant episcopal see, which accrued to the king.

75 The arbitral ruling of 8 February 1283: *Cartulaire Notre-Dame de Paris*, vol. 2, p. 483 ff., and Vidrier 1913/1914, vol. 40, pp. 388-398 (no. 9). Also Paris, Archives Nationales LL 270, f. 158 (1392); Lot 1865, passim. Concerning BOURGES: De Girardot & Durand 1849, pp. 30-31. POITIER's bishop was also charged with responsibility for the bells starting from the beginning of the thirteenth century; *Fasti Ecclesiae Gallicanae*, vol. 10, POITIERS, p. 9.

76 Because the division of the bishop's and monastic community's respective endowments (ELY being a so-called monastic cathedral) had taken place in 1109 and the care of the church was entrusted to the monks, it seems likely that the bishop's decision to support the repair of the church in this way was a voluntary one; Salzman 1948/1953, vol. 4, p. 65; Atkinson 1933, pp. 3, 6 ff. One of the rolls refers to *cementarii sacriste* in addition to *cementarii episcopi*; Chapman 1907, vol. 1, p. 47. Nine of England's cathedrals had a Benedictine monastery instead of a secular chapter; Edwards 1967, p. 10.

77 *Cartulaire Arras*, no. 176; *Registres Innocent IV*, no. 7098; Héliot 1953, pp. 14, 15.

78 Weltsch 1968, pp. 37-38; *eclesia* can also refer to the Church as institution.

79 Wardens of monastic churches and abbeys, too, sometimes had to be compelled by the *parlement* to put a portion of their income towards church repairs; Gazzaniga 1973, pp. 99-101, cites two rulings issued by the *parlement* of TOULOUSE in 1454 and 1461, respectively. The fact that from the fourteenth century onwards chapters increasingly sought recourse in not the pope but the French *parlements* points up growing Gallican tendencies: Gaudemet 2001, p. 282.

80 A November 1512 decree of the *parlement* of PARIS ordered the bishop and chapter to each put up a sum of 800 l.t. for the building of the transept, begun in 1510; Leblond 1933,

p. 24. In that year the chapter had complained before the *parlement 'qu'il* [i.e. the chapter] *a employé de grandes sommes et que monsieur l'évesque depuis certaines années y a contribué très peu quoique souvent requis*'. The contribution remained compulsory until 1790; Bonnet-Laborderie 1978, pp. 65, 81. The *parlement*'s ruling is published in Meunier 2003.

81 Cailleaux 2001, p. 71 (1504/05).

82 The obligation on the archbishop to share in the building expenses is recorded as early as 1389. After the start of cathedral reconstruction works in 1510, the chapter found itself forced to launch various legal suits against the archbishop, for example with the *parlement* of BORDEAUX; Gardelles 1963, pp. 23, 25, 28 ff. and *Inventaire-sommaire Gironde* G 330 (1504; the archbishop had to contribute a quarter of his income), G 505, G 508.

83 *Bulletin Monumental* 72 (1908), p. 435 (1526 et seq.).

84 *Congrès Archéologique de France* 90 (1927), p. 273 (1530); Lavergne 1920, passim (1546): here in respect of an obligation in relation to building works begun in 1505 by his predecessor.

85 *Congrès Archéologique de France* 92 (1929), p. 175 (1487); Bagnéris 1986, p. 45; this sum continued to be paid until 1611.

86 *Congrès Archéologique de France* 141 (1983), pp. 302-304; Le Mené 1882, pp. 23-27; *Inventaire-sommaire Morbihan* G, p. 297 (ruling of the *parlement* of RENNES on 23 October 1516: 200 l.t. annually for construction of the transept; the contribution was imposed until into the seventeenth century).

87 Annual contribution of 600 l.t., worth approximately 20 annual wages (ruling of the *parlement* of BORDEAUX in 1492). A contribution was imposed on the chapter too, namely, the fruits of one prebend; Arbellot 1852, pp. 36, 37; Soulard 1993, pp. 216, 217.

88 *Inventaire-sommaire Hautes-Alpes* G 1181.

89 In 1497 the *parlement* of TOULOUSE ordered the new bishop to complete the as yet unfinished work on *'des clouchiers et voultes'*; the priory of LAVAUR became a cathedral in 1318; *Congrès Archéologique de France* 140 (1982), p. 334.

90 *Fasti Ecclesiae Gallicanae*, vol. 5, Agen, p. 12: by the *parlement* of BORDEAUX in 1487 and 1509.

91 Narbonne 1901, p. 36; Mortet 1898, pp. 412, 413; *Bulletin Monumental* 70 (1906), p. 291 (1512 et seq.). Other examples, which relate to small southern French dioceses, in Lemarignier *et al.* 1962, p. 373. Additionally: LECTOURE, 25 May 1487; *Congrès Archéologique de France* 128 (1970), p. 198.

92 Brutails 1899-1901, vol. 12, pp. 390, 408, vol. 13, pp. 188, 437, 440. In VANNES the annual contribution of 200 l.t. carried a value of six to seven years' wages. In LIMOGES the annual contribution of 600 l.t. equalled 82 years' wages; d'Avenel 1894-1912, vol. 3, p. 577.

93 Hamon 2001, pp. 124-126.

94 *Diplomatarium Danicum*, vol. 3: 2, no. 219. On rare occasions the bishop impeded the building works: around 1420 the chapter of SION accused the bishop-administrator André de Gualdo - who was set on reforming the chapter - of not having contributed anything for the cathedral's reconstruction and of actually having imprisoned the canons in charge of the building works; Dubuis 1979, p. 156, n. 51.

95 In LIMOGES the bishop's position as overlord entitled him to offerings made at the

altar of the church in St Léonard, which he allocated to the cathedral fabric in 1388; Arbellot 1852, p. 72.

96 In AMIENS the *Liber Ordinarius* (late thirteenth century) prescribed that the bishop advance the cause of the cathedral fabric (alongside that of several other churches and the Hotel Dieu) during his synodal sermon; Durand 1901-1903, vol. 1, p. 121 n. 2.

97 Dispensation is the remission of or exemption from a Church dictate or obligation. Commutation is the conversion of a dictate or obligation into a different obligation, such as the substitution of a monetary gift for a pilgrimage.

98 In 1512 the bishop of BEAUVAIS described his annual grants of many indulgences, which yielded hundreds of livres (tournois) each year, as being in essence his episcopal contribution for the building works; Meunier 2003, p. 55 (sub 13).

99 The bishop of GENEVA suspended indulgences for the building works in 1232 following a conflict with the chapter concerning the appointment of a collector of the *'eleemosyne'*; the pope ordered him to annul the suspension; *Registres Grégoire IX*, vol. 1, p. 925. See also Baud 1985, pp. 43-49.

100 Caillet 2007, p. 302: the north portal of BOURGES Cathedral is dedicated to St Guillaume (d. 1209); the reliquary shrine of St Etienne (St Stephan) standing before him may refer to his allocation of the devotional offerings to the building works. Caillet discusses bishops' representations in BOURGES, TROYES, RHEIMS, Paris and AMIENS; CHARTRES and LAON have no such representations whatsoever.

101 Bishops' lack of willingness sometimes extended to the point that they demanded payment for lands they ceded for new building works; CLERMONT-FERRAND, deeds of 23 and 30 May 1273: 300 l.t.; Gobillot 1912, p. 18 n. 2; Archives départementales Puy-de-Dôme 3 G arm. 18, sac B, cote 22 and 23.

102 With particular reference to Normandy: Grant 2005, p. 21.

103 A colourful summary of the great variation in the ranks and roles of French bishops in Gaudemet 2008, pp. 403-411.

104 For example De Farcy 1901-1926, vol. 3, p. 26 ff.; *Cartulaire Amiens*, vol. 1, p. 102; *Gallia Christiana*, vol. 8, instr. p. 362, vol. 10, instr. p. 69; De Formeville 1866, p. 487.

105 Weilandt 1992, pp. 71-97, in particular p. 81, distinguishes between *Bischofsmittel* and *Bistumsmittel*: *'ex propriis impensis'* – from private property – on the one hand, and *'ex pontificalibus stipendiis'* or *'de epsicopalibus redditibus'* on the other.

106 *'Quippe circiter septingentas libras de proprio primo anno, preter oblationes fidelium et preter jurisdictionis sue proventus, quos ad hoc ab initio deputavit, in sumptus ejusdem operis erogavit; ceteris vero annis quandoque per hebdomadam decem libras, quandoque centum solidos ad minus, preter premissa et preter questas diocesis sue sive diocesium vicinarum'*; Mortet & Deschamps 1929, pp. 203, 204; *Congrès Archéologique de France* 116 (1958), p. 45; Branner 1961, p. 25. Jurisdictional dues also accrued to the fabric at BOURGES as from 1195 to pay for repairs to the old nave; Branner 1962a, pp. 58-59.

107 Lehmann-Brockhaus 1938, no. 1032; also *Westfälische Forschungen* 19 (1966), p. 156.

108 Lehmann-Brockhaus 1938, no. 115.

109 Idem, nos 656, 962, 1002, 1467, 1479, 1480, etc.

Additionally, CHARTRES, Bishop Fulbert after 1020; Mortet 1911, p. 62. LISIEUX, Bishop Arnulf in a letter to the pope in which he defends himself against the chapter's accusations of embezzlement: *'ipsamque ecclesiam episcopalem ex magna parte sumptibus meis et acquisitionibus innovatam'*; Barlow 1939, p. 209; Hardy 1917, pp. 109-111; Grant 2005, p. 87. PARIS, Bishop Maurice de Sully: *'propriis magis sumptibus quam alienis'*; Mortet & Deschamps 1929, p. 111; Mortet 1888, p. 49; Mortet 1889, pp. 206, 221. A combination of official and private revenues from the bishop of VERDUN in 1144: *'omnibus peregrinorum oblationibus ibi attitulatis et de suo etiam multis addictis*, [...]'; *Congrès Archéologique de France* 96 (1933), p. 394. See also Stalley 1971, pp. 62, 71 and 81 on the builder-bishop Roger of SALISBURY (1102-1139) and the rebuilding of the choir of the cathedral at Sarum.

110 Bouxin 1902, p. 25 n. 1.

111 Kraus 1979, pp. 141-142; Raine 1859, pp. XIV ff., XXII: he estimates the total episcopal contribution between 1361 and 1373 at more than £2500 and 140 marks. Wage figures in Knoop & Jones 1949, p. 236. Also Hughes 1988, pp. 142-143.

112 Archbishop Simon of Sudbury (1375-1381) donated 3000 marks (£ 2250, 720 annual wages) to the *opus* in his own lifetime and left a further 130 marks in his will. His successor William Courtenay (1381-1397) gave 1000 marks for the building works; Woodruff & Danks 1912, p. 163; Woodruff 1932, p. 26 and Woodruff 1936, p. 80.

113 Ramm 1978, pp. 155-163 and n. 457: '[...] *pastor bonus ne domus sua ecclesie sue preciosor videretur et ne quis ipsum magis ad secularia quam spiritualia* [...] *inclinatum diiudicaret* [...]'.

114 Overview of the episcopate (114 bishops and archbishops) in France in 1438: Tabbagh 2006, pp. 87-186; concerning their building activities as connected with their cathedrals, pp. 143-145.

115 Though the financial documentation is lost, there can be no question that the campaign to build the choir of VIVIERS Cathedral between 1516 and 1521 was initiated and financed by the exceptionally wealthy Bishop Claude de Tournon. He commissioned not only the cathedral, but also the bishop's palace and three *chateaux*; Costantini in Bos *et al.* 2006, pp. 289-295.

116 *Inventaire-sommaire Aube* G 1567 and 1568; Murray 1987, p. 63. In the accounts for 1520/21 and 1522/23 (G 1588 and 1589), also episcopal gifts of 400 l.t. and 200 l.t., respectively. See also d'Arbois de Jubainville 1862, p. 404; Assier 1855, pp. 22, 58.

117 Quantin 1842, pp. 23, 29, 35; *Inventaire-sommaire Yonne* G 1141 ff.; Bouvier 1911, vol. 2, p. 421, vol. 3, pp. 179-180. The total cost incurred for both arms of the transept with their portals over a period of 25 years was roughly 22,000 l.t. Also: Carrière 1936, p. 113 and Cailleaux 1999, p. 451 ff. Concerning the inclusion in OVIEDO of the coat of arms of Bishop Angulo (1506-1516) in anticipation - or possibly acknowledgement - of financial support, see Gutiérrez-Cortines Corral 1987a, p. 21: *'las armas de su señoría re. se ponrán en todos lugares de la torre y de las otras obras* [...] *y hazemos saber a vuestra merced que es la mejor y mas sumptuosa que ay en todos reynos de España* [...]'.

118 For England, see Lehmann-Brockhaus 1955-1960, amongst others nos 1040, 1044, 2397, 2398, 2966.

119 Branner 1962b, p. 80.

120 Sandron 1998, pp. 38-41.

121 *Bulletin Monumental* 45 (1879), p. 63; not 1000 l.t. but 100 l.t.; Ledru 1900, p. 336.

122 Bishop William de Greenfield (1306-1315); Raine 1859, p. XI.

123 Bordeaux 1969, p. 235.

124 For example, the will of Bishop Grandisson of Exeter, 1369; *Register John de Grandisson*, pp. 1512, 1550.

125 No systematic research has been conducted on bishops' wills; this conclusion is based on a handful of published wills; *Gallia Christiana*, especially vol. 8, instr. p. 88. Statistical study of English wills between 1480 and 1660 shows that whilst higher clergy, including bishops, left their churches next to nothing, they did leave legacies for social and charitable causes; Jordan 1959, p. 346.

126 Necrology of the Notre Dame: *Cartulaire Notre-Dame de Paris*, vol. 4, pp. 145-146; Mortet 1889, p. 274; Mortet & Deschamps 1929, p. 114; see also Baldwin 2006, p. 36: '*sans doute sa création personelle*'. Concerning the episcopal requirement in respect of the cathedral roof, see n. 74 above. Another example is the 1285 testament of Bertrand de l'Isle, bishop of TOULOUSE and initiator of the campaign to build a new cathedral. He donated 1000 l.t. to the chapter, 1000 l.t. to the fabric (approximately 80 annual wages of a mason), 1000 l.t. for the radiating chapel at the east end, 600 l.t. for the foundation of two banquets and his obit celebration, and 100 l.t. for ornamenting the church; *Congrès Archéologique de France* 154 (1996), pp. 215, 227.

127 *Register Henry Chichele*, pp. 298-301 and XLIV: by far the largest bequest to a fabric of any will published here. Bubwith also left the cathedral a valuable set of paraments. Another example concerns Bishop Bertrand de L'Isle-Jourdain of TOULOUSE (1272-1286), who took the initiative to build the cathedral choir and left 1000 l.t. (80 annual wages of a mason) for the building works in a will encompassing 120,000 l.t. in bequests; Kraus 1979, p. 79 and n. 95.

128 Hill 1965, p. 112.

129 The gift comprised less than two percent of total receipts in 1390; Boito 1889, pp. 64, 65, 77; *Annali*, Appendix vol. 1, p. 108 (11 May). Boito 1889, p. 27, reports an archiepiscopal gift of 2000 lire imp. It is not clear whether this concerns a single gift or an aggregate over multiple years; this sum, too, is modest in comparison with the tens of thousands of lires imp. that the fabric collected each year.

130 Quantin 1869, p. 222 ff.; *Inventaire-sommaire Yonne* G 1124, 1125.

131 Even where it did there could still be discrepancy between the pledge of a bequest and its actual payment. For LIMOGES, see the large bequest left by Bishop Aimeric in 1272, which bore the condition that construction would have to begin within one year. Not until more than ten years after his death, and a tough legal battle, could the sum finally be collected; Soulard 1993, pp. 168-174.

132 Moberley 1893, p. 271; Goodman 1934, passim: contract dated 16 August 1404. The monastery – comparable to chapters at secular cathedrals in England and elsewhere – thus held ultimate decision-making authority over the old building; it had a stake in the administration via a monk who was delegated as *contra rotulator*.

133 Lowth 1777, app. XXXIV and XXXV; Moberley 1893, pp. 344-348 and 99-100 (palace); Hamilton Thompson 1920, pp. 22, 24; Cook 1957, pp. 267, 300; Hayter 1970, passim.

134 Cabié 1892, passim; *Dictionnaire* [...] *ecclésiastiques*, vol. 2, p. 1075. This calculation capitalizes the 100 l.t. for the commemorative mass on 4000 l.t. A sum of 2000 l.t. is equivalent to 64 annual wages of an unskilled labourer.
135 Cf. Duby 1976, p. 237.
136 *Register Henry Chichele*, p. 299.
137 The inclusion of a coat of arms on a given section of the building usually signifies that it was co-financed someone from that family; Enlart 1902, p. 76 n. 1; Gombrich 1960, p. 285; Branner 1965, p. 46 n. 27; Cook 1957, p. 235. But this was by no means always the case. The escutcheons set against the vault of Westminster Abbey in LONDON commemorate not benefactors, but families with whom the king was related by marriage; Colvin 1963, vol. 1, p. 146. There are innumerable documented instances of the representation of the arms of the bishop (or of other benefactors): BEAUVAIS: coats of arms as a tribute and acknowledgement of gifts; Meunier 2003. PALMA DE MALLORCA, fourteenth century; Domenge i Mesquida 1997, pp. 93-96. PALENCIA 1516: large gift for the cloister conditional on the addition of armorial bearings; San Martín Payo 1983, no. 9. AUCH: from the fourteenth century onwards each bishop had his arms set on newly completed sections of the building; 170 escutcheons were removed during the French Revolution; Bagnéris 1986, p. 45. TOLEDO, 1490 constitution of Cardinal Petro de Mendoza for the administration of the *Obra*: the archbishop's coat of arms was to be set on each new section of the building built with his permission; Lop Otín 2006, p. 920. See also n. 63.
138 Martínez y Sanz 1866, pp. 20, 21. It may be for this reason that the chapter archives contain no trace of documentation on its construction.
139 Villers 1901, p. 16 ff. The newly cast bell required as much as 800 l.t. in 1483 alone.
140 Archives départementales Aveyron 3 G 249; Bion de Marlavagne 1875, pp. 85-87, 110. From the witness testimonies we can deduce that the building works were administered without the fabric's involvement; the fabric rolls for these years are missing. Concerning ALBI: testament of Bishop Louis d'Amboise dated 28 January 1485, in which he bequeaths 2000 l.t (around 65 annual wages) each year until completion, plus 500 écus (25 annual wages) at the project's launch; Biget 1982, p. 33 and n. 50. According to the chronicle of Schadaeus (1614), the bishop of STRASBOURG also donated large sums for the tower's construction; Hanauer 1900-1901, vol. 19, p. 760.
141 *Tour de Beurre* (1485-1507); in 1500 Archbishop Georges I d'Amboise gave 2500 marks to fund a large bell for the still unfinished tower, dubbed *La Georges d'Amboise*. In 1503 he took charge of its completion; Fallue 1848, pp. 216-219; Janin 1997, p. 124. His testament in *Inventaire-sommaire Seine-Inférieure* G 3417. For the crossing tower (after 1514-1544) Archbishop Georges II d'Amboise donated a massive lead-clad timber spire, on which work began in 1542. On 29 April 1544 he pledged a sum of at least 18,000 l.t., or roughly 600 annual wages of an unskilled labourer, from his private means as security; Pommeraye 1686, pp. 29-30.
142 De Caso Fernández 1981, p. 374; *Colección documental Oviedo*, no. 202: *'por lo qual le besavan las manos'*. A sum worth around 40

annual wages.

143 Wolf 2006, pp. 422, 442-450.

144 The biographies of many dozens of French bishops from the period 1200-1500, published in what are currently ten volumes of the *Fasti Ecclesiae Gallicanae*, furnish a good insight into the nature of this category of artistic patronage and its significance for the cathedral. Some examples: Gobillot 1912, pp. 32-34 (on patronage by the bishops of CLERMONT-FERRAND between 1415 and 1517); Aubert 1910, p. 17; Janin 1997 (on patronage by Archbishop Georges d'Amboise of ROUEN, 1490-1510).

145 Colchester & Harvey 1974, p. 211. Also Aylmer & Cant 1977, p. 100.

146 Concerning the social and familial factors that went into shaping the French episcopate between 1150 and 1350, as based on 617 bishops in 48 dioceses, see Gaudemet 1965, passim. A similar study relating to England between 1354 and 1485 for 79 bishops from 17 dioceses: Rosenthal 1970, passim. There are virtually no data pertaining to the budgets bishops had at their disposal; see Lemarignier *et al.* 1962, p. 369 ff.

147 Biget 1974, passim, especially pp. 140 ff. and 150 ff.; also Freigang 1992, pp. 166-176 (RODEZ).

148 Deserving of particular mention are revenues that accrued to the fabric on those rare occasions when an episcopal see was occupied by a minor. In 1501 Pope Alexander VI determined that the bishop of METZ would be succeeded on his death by Jean, son of the duke of Lorraine (1497-1550), though the latter would not actually take up these duties before his twentieth birthday and would not be raised to the episcopal dignity until another seven years later. If the see were to fall vacant before these conditions were met, all income belonging to the bishop's *mensa* would be divided into three shares, of which one was allocated for completion of the choir. The bishop died in 1505, meaning the fabric was able to profit from this income for nearly 20 years; Pelt 1930, no. 138. On 16 March 1507 King Louis XII assigned similar revenues to the fabric of BOURGES for rebuilding the tower, which had collapsed in December 1506. His illegitimate son Michel de Bucy was appointed archbishop whilst still a minor. Given that it was reasonable for the archbishop to give financial support for the rebuilding works, the king reserved an annual 3000 l.t. for this purpose for the duration of the rebuilding campaign. These funds provided half the fabric's annual income; De Girardot & Durand 1849, pp. 136, 137.

TWO The chapter's contributions

149 See pp. 64, 71.

150 Concerning the chapter's canonical entitlement to represent all the faithful of the diocese, see Brundage 1995, p. 107.

151 Cf. Decr. Greg. IX lib. III tit. XLVIII c. I, in Friedberg 1879/1882, vol. 2, p. 652.

152 Ferraris 1852-1857, vol. 5, col. 1411-1424 and Decr. Greg. IX lib. V tit. XL c. XXIX, in Friedberg 1879/1882, vol. 2, p. 925.

153 Bordenave 1643, p. 598; Lesne 1936/1943, vol. 3, p. 145 ff.; Fliche & Martin 1934, vol. 7, p. 256.

154 Thomas Aquinas 1952, *Summa Theologiae*, II, II, q. 86a.2c.

155 Lehmann-Brockhaus 1955-1960, no. 831; Foreville 1958, p. 7; Cheney 1968, pp. 30, 31; also in Thomassinus 1725, pars 3, liber 2, caput 23, no. 11. On 25 June 1219 Pope Honorius III authorized the archbishop

to spend one-quarter on the renovation of the choir for as long as work remained to be done; Foreville 1958, pp. 7, 105.

156 The shrine of St Thomas was run as an independent *officium* – as a separate organization with its own financial administration: Druffner 1993, p. 266 and n. 77; Woodruff & Danks 1912, p. 246; Smith 1940, pp. 353, 356; Smith 1943, p. 12; Woodruff 1932, pp. 19, 26. The monastery also covered most of the costs needed to maintain pilgrims. In 1220 the sums of money required to receive pilgrims were so large that the costs could not be covered by the proceeds; Woodruff & Danks 1912, p. 74. In the Jubilee year 1420 a reported 100,000 pilgrims visited the shrine. Proceeds from offerings made that year had a net worth of £644, of which £200 (48 annual wages of an unskilled labourer) were spent on the building works.

157 Nilson 1998, pp. 122-167, specifically pp. 139 and 187.

158 *Regesten Köln*, vol. 2, no. 805.

159 *Urkundenbuch Niederrhein*, vol. 1, no. 519; *Regesten Köln*, vol. 3, no. 1335; cited in Thomassinus 1725, pars 3, liber 2, caput 23. The shrine would later be administered as a separate entity by two canons, the *custodes regum*, on the chapter's behalf, whose duties included attending to the liturgical celebrations, supervision of pilgrims and transcribing pilgrims' testimonies; *Urkundenbuch Niederrhein*, vol. 3, p. 310 (1337); *Achthundert Jahre*, p. 51; Groten 1980, pp. 211-214, 221; Amberg 1989, pp. 20-39. In the fourteenth and fifteenth centuries the city attempted to exercise a claim to the relics; *Achthundert Jahre*, pp. 66, 74 ff.; Ennen 1863/1869, vol. 3, p. 149 ff. The oldest fabric accounts of 1513/14 contain no trace at all of receipts from the shrine of the Three Magi; *Ad summum 1248*, p. 58. Nor is it likely that the fabric profited from the French king Louis XI's exceptionally large gift made in honour of the Three Magi in 1482 in the form of an annuity worth 50 annual mason's wages; idem, pp. 179-180. Similarly, proceeds from the *Heiltumszeigung* in WÜRZBURG have left no trace in the 1529/30 rolls; Von Güldenstubbe 1988.

160 *Statutes of Salisbury Cathedral*, p. 202 (1319).

161 *Statutes of Lincoln Cathedral*, vol. 1, pp. 335-337 (1322).

162 According to a capitular decision of 1248, the '*denarii ciste peregrinorum*' of QUIMPER Cathedral likewise rightfully accrued to the chapter, but as from 1278 actually went to the treasurer; *Cartulaire Quimper*, nos 84, 124. In LAUSANNE, the offerings were brought before the statue of *Notre Dame*, the cathedral's patroness, and divided between the respective *mensae* of the bishop and chapter; Gatz *et al.* 2003, p. 341.

163 Swanson 1993, p. 97. Also Nilson 1998, pp. 137-140, 159-161,182-190.

164 Thomassinus 1725, pars 3, liber 2, caput 36, no. 1.

165 *Gallia Christiana*, vol. 11, instr. p. 218; Mortet 1911, p. 71.

166 Mortet & Deschamps 1929, pp. 199-201; Sandron 1998, pp. 38-41, mentions arrangements made between the treasurer and the – probably newly formed – fabric for the partition of the offerings in 1205 and later; see above p.

167 *Congrès Archéologique de France* 48 (1881), p. 199; Le Mené 1882, p. 13: concerns offerings made by the 'countless numbers of people'; see also De la Martinière 1923, pp. 117-124; Leguay 1975, pp. 113-114 and *Congrès Archéologique de*

France 141 (1983), p. 297. The fabric's share was administered by the bishop, at whose initiative the relics of St Vincent had come to the cathedral. Presumably he took charge of the construction works; De la Martiniére 1923, p. 115.

168 Capitular statute of 19 March 1425: collection box for the recently begun west tower of QUIMPER Cathedral; *Cartulaire Quimper*, no. 499.

169 Capitular statute issued by the chapter of St Paul's in LONDON in 1300: '*quod omnimode oblaciones ad crucem* [...] *in subsidium nove fabrice eiusdem ecclesie convertantur donec perficiatur*'; Lehmann-Brockhaus 1955-1960, no. 2963.

170 Bordenave 1643, p. 601 (no. 41), except for mass oblations. These also occasionally accrued in part to the fabric. As from 23 August 1385 the chaplains of the cathedral of METZ also had to cede to the fabric half the offerings made at the altar, or else forfeit both halves; Pelt 1930, p. 49.

171 *Cartulaire Arras*, no. 202; also Schöller 1989, p. 65 n. 29. In SALISBURY the bishop and chapter agreed to put the *oblationes altarium* towards the building works for a period of seven years (later extended) from 1225, and possibly even from 1218; Lehmann-Brockhaus 1955-1960, nos 4098, 4144; *Charters Salisbury*, pp. 229, 230.

172 Recent research reveals SANTIAGO's importance as a pilgrimage site to have been seriously overrated: relics of St James were scattered everywhere throughout Europe, and all of these locales attracted pilgrims to venerate this extremely popular saint. The huge influx of pilgrims to the distant Santiago did not get underway until the seventeenth and eighteenth centuries; Péricard-Méa 2001, pp. 90-95, with a map locating relics of St James in France.

173 Sigal 1990, passim.

174 This partition is described in the *Liber Sancti Jacobi* (c. 1140); Vielliard 1950, p. 120; also López Ferreiro 1898-1911, vol. 3, pp. 254-255 and vol. 5, p. 179.

175 López Ferreiro 1898-1911, vol. 3, p. 25 and app. 43.

176 Idem, vol. 5, pp. 177-180. The *Obra* in SANTIAGO was not identical to the *fabrica* at other cathedrals; in the thirteenth century it formed a separate corporation made up of 30 families, all with technical or administrative ties to the cathedral; idem, vol. 3, p. 25; vol. 4, p. 159 and app. 6; vol. 5, p. 155; vol. 6, app. 44, p. 172: '*maestre et arquero* [treasurer] *et pedreros* [masons] *et oficiales de la Obra*'. Possibly comparable to the '*maîtrise de l'œuvre*' in CHARTRES; Jusselin 1915-1922, p. 252 ff.

177 The oldest known statutes date to 1228; at this time offerings were also brought to the church treasury; López Ferreiro 1898-1911, vol. 5, pp. 127-128 and app. 13, pp. 40, 41. Concerning the rivalry surrounding gifts left at the *altar mayor* and the fabric's *arca*, see also Pérez Rodríguez 1996, p. 147.

178 López Ferreiro 1898-1911, vol. 5, app. 25; Sumption 1975, p. 160, with a not entirely accurate portrayal of how affairs were arranged.

179 López Ferreiro 1898-1911, vol. 5, p. 183; Santiago Alfeo is St James the Less; see fig. 4.

180 Idem, vol. 6, pp. 255-258 and app. 44. My thanks to H. Brouwer, hispanist in Amsterdam, for his assistance in translating this text.

181 Archives départementales du Morbihan (VANNES), cathedral fabric rolls, e.g. 74 G 6, 1486/87 account, f. 41: '[...] *pour les poblacions et offrandes* [..] *quelles*

appartiennent audit chapitre et que tient ledit procureur a ferme [...]'. The canons also farmed out the right to take the cathedral's relics of St Patern to the parish church dedicated to him in VANNES during the annual pilgrimage past seven Breton churches (*le Tro-Breiz*) and on other feast days to the highest-bidding ecclesiastic, who then took in the offerings; Marsille 1982, p. 80; *Inventaire-sommaire Morbihan* 58G1 pp. 159-171, especially pp. 164-168 (lawsuit 1398-1407) with a spirited account of the course of affairs.

182 Edwards 1967, p. 234 ff.

183 Idem, p. 39.

184 The difficulties surrounding the *prebendae defunctorum* were part of those relating to the fruits of vacant benefices, or *annualia*, which as we shall see were sometimes also assigned to the building works; see p. 112 ff.

185 Von Brünneck 1905, p. 1 ff. One of the earliest examples concerns the collegiate chapter of Brussels in 1047. In AUGSBURG the regulation has its roots in an episcopal measure of 1029; Leuze 1908, p. 33.

186 Schneider 1885, pp. 137-138.

187 Idem, p. 138 n. 3 (LÜBECK); *Urkundenbuch Halberstadt*, vol. 2, no. 1587 (HALBERSTADT); Leuze 1908, p. 33 (AUGSBURG); Spieckermann 1935, p. 19 (MÜNSTER).

188 *Urkundenbuch Bremen*, vol. 2, no. 635 (BREMEN, fourteenth century). Other causes were also supported. In 1130 the chapter at NOYON decided to cede one year's proceeds from all vacant prebends to the Templars until at least 1181 in order to allow them to build their quarters, despite the fact that the new cathedral was also under construction from around 1145; *Cartulaire l'ordre du Temple*, p. XXXI; Seymour 1968, p. 45.

189 *Cartularius Baiocensis*, vol. 1, pp. 104, 105; Vallery-Radot n.d., pp. 10, 11. The regulation was still in force in 1440.

190 *Cartularius Baiocensis*, vol. 1, pp. 217, 218. But compare the view taken by Geert Groote: 'They [*doctores*] denounce the spacious, grand and too-large and beautiful building of churches, equally when funded from the clergy's own property, reasoning that this deprives the poor'; Post 1967, pp. 54, 55.

191 Requests for papal confirmation of such regulations are particularly numerous from the thirteenth century onwards; later, it seems confirmation was deemed unnecessary. See e.g. *Registres Urbain IV*, no. 1630 (TOUL, 1264, for a period of ten years); *Registres Innocent IV*, no. 1190; *Gallia Christiana*, vol. 14, instr. p. 167 (RENNES, 1245); *Congrès Archéologique de France* 83 (1920), p. 7 (METZ 1257). For other causes: *Registres Innocent IV*, nos 1188, 1192, 3481, etc.; *Registres Alexandre IV*, no. 300, etc. COLOGNE in any case already had a grace year in 1179; Groten 1980, p. 218.

192 ANGERS, after 1209: De Farcy 1901-1926, vol. 1, p. 26 n. 4. Speyer, 1220: Mone 1836, pp. 92, 93; *Urkundenbuch Speyer*, vol. 1, nos 1444 and 244. YORK, 1221: Lehmann-Brockhaus 1955-1960, no. 5021.

193 Though the reason for this is not known to this author, it may have to do with the fact that German chapters have been subject to much more thorough and systematic investigation than those in France and England. To name a few: LIÈGE: Görres 1907, p. 60. MÜNSTER: Spieckermann 1935, p. 19; Nottarp 1909, pp. 8, 34 n. 8, 36 n. 5; Dürr 1777, p. 252. PADERBORN: Ohlberger 1911, pp. 32, 83. MEISSEN: Kunz von Brunn 1902, p. 41. HALBERSTADT:

Urkundenbuch Halberstadt, vol. 2, no. 1587 (1292). PRAGUE: Neuwirth 1890, p. 376. VERDEN: Bückmann 1912, p. 34. OSNABRÜCK: Hagemann 1901, p. 34; Rhotert 1916, p. 303; Kirchhoff 1910, p. 70. HILDESHEIM: Hoffmann 1911, p. 67. KONSTANZ: Mone 1852, pp. 41, 50. GNESEN: Binder 1912, pp. 25 n. 2, 37, 100. BRANDENBURG: Dürr 1777, p. 253. WÜRZBURG: idem, p. 250. TRENT: idem, p. 254. TRIER: idem, p. 251.

194 Overview in Dürr 1777, pp. 249-253.

195 Friedberg 1879/1882, vol. 2, pp. 1205, 1206. The decretal is mentioned in every handbook: see e.g. Hinschius 1869-1897, vol. 2, p. 72; also Von Brünneck 1905, p. 8; Kirsch 1903, pp. X, XII; Haller 1903, p. 50; Baix 1942, p. CDVIII; Göller 1910, p. 81 n. 1. Dürr 1777, p. 249, reports that though the decretal was not integrated into the local laws of many German chapters, it was applied nevertheless.

196 For example in MEISSEN; Kunz von Brunn 1902, pp. 41, 42.

197 *Urkundenbuch Halberstadt*, vol. 2, no. 1587 (HALBERSTADT, 1292).

198 PRAGUE: Neuwirth 1890, pp. 376-377.

199 Also sometimes donations of wine; Edwards 1967, pp. 63, 64; cf. the customary term in UTRECHT: *vinalia*.

200 Aubert 1960/1961, vol. 118, p. 246. In CHARTRES from as early as the eleventh century: *Cartulaire Chartres*, vol. 1, p. CXLV.

201 Edwards 1967, p. 66.

202 Lehmann-Brockhaus 1955-1960, no. 1043; Edwards 1967, p. 64.

203 See e.g. in VERDEN: Bückmann 1912, p. 30 n. 6.

204 ARLES furnishes an early example, where with the chapter's permission the bishop allocated to the *operarius* a '*decimam partem oblationum cannonicorum noviter intrantium, mobilium tantum* [...]' (1196); Mortet & Deschamps 1929, p. 171 and n. 3.

205 PRAGUE: Neuwirth 1890, p. 376; TROYES: Murray 1987, p. 233 n. 24.

206 PADERBORN: after 1480; Ohlberger 1911, p. 82.

207 *Inventaire-sommaire Yonne*, G 1131 ff. *Kappegeld* or admission dues to benefit the fabric also in LONDON, WELLS, SALISBURY, YORK, LICHFIELD; Edwards 1967, p. 63 ff. BORDEAUX: Gardelles 1963, p. 27. OSNABRÜCK: Kirchhoff 1910, p. 70. MAGDEBURG: Weber 1912, p. 70. MÜNSTER: Spieckermann 1935, p. 26. HILDESHEIM: Hoffmann 1911, p. 67. PADERBORN: Ohlberger 1911, pp. 35, 83. MEISSEN: Kunz von Brunn 1902, pp. 30, 36. CHARTRES: *Cartulaire Chartres*, vol. 1, p. 283. ANGERS after 1289: De Farcy 1901-1926, vol. 3, p. 2 n. 3. BRESLAU: Sabisch 1965, p. 166. LANGRES: Le Grand 1931, p. 18. QUIMPER: *Cartulaire Quimper*, no. 332. LE MANS: *Cartulaire Le Mans*, no. 1064. AMIENS: *Cartulaire Amiens*, vol. 2, no. 539. NARBONNE: Narbonne 1901, p. 364. KONSTANZ: Mone 1852, p. 41. TROYES: Quicherat 1886, p. 194. PARIS (from the fourteenth until the sixteenth century): Paris, Archives Nationales LL 270, f. 1-52, 65 ff. REGENSBURG: Schuegraf 1855, p. 70. FRAUENBURG: 10 marks, or two annual wages of a mason's assistant; Herrmann 2007, pp. 147, 153. UTRECHT: see below p. 265.

208 Absence from the choir naturally only concerned canons bound by residence.

209 In 1537 a vicar in LÜBECK had berated a colleague as a *schelm et bossewicht*, thrown beer in his face and hit him with the empty mug; the resulting fine was designated for the fabric; Prange 1990/1993, vol. 11, no. 1317.

210 Bird & Baildon 1907/1914, vol. 1, p. 134, vol. 2, p. 122. Additionally: PARIS, as from

1209: Mortet 1888, p. 49. COLOGNE, after 1248: Ennen 1863/1869, vol. 3, pp. 962, 975. PRAGUE, after 1350: Neuwirth 1890, p. 380. OSNABRÜCK: Hagemann 1901, p. 39. AUGSBURG: Leuze 1908, p. 97. TRENT *'de penis inobediencium'*: Santifaller 1948, p. 173. TROYES: Gadan 1851, p. 5. SALISBURY: *Statutes of Salisbury Cathedral*, pp. 252, 258. Concerning monetary fines imposed on ecclesiastics in general, see Hinschius 1869-1897, vol. 5, p. 80 n. 9; 624 n. g; 627 n. 1; Coulton 1928, pp. 363, 364.

211 *Diplomatarium Danicum*, vol. 4: 1, no. 391 (1388).

212 Concerning the problem of residence, see Edwards 1967, pp. 39, 50 ff.

213 De Farcy 1901-1926, vol. 1, p. 26 n. 4.

214 In 1297 it was determined that canons who were absent without permission would forfeit their prebends. Half of the resulting monies were shared out amongst those canons who were in attendance, the other half went into the fabric fund; Bückmann 1912, p. 25. A similar rule applied to vicars; idem, p. 33.

215 From 1401 on the fabric received a portion of the prebends of those absent without leave: *portiones absentium*; Ohlberger 1911, p. 84.

216 Mone 1836, p. 94; *Urkundenbuch Speyer*, vol. 1, no. 421; see also Janner 1876, p. 179; Ferraris 1852-1857, vol. 2, col. 163, 164 (no. 19).

217 In GERONA in 1369/70 and 1370/71, 13 and 15 percent, respectively; Archivo de la catedral, Obra de la Seu VI, 2 and 3.

218 *Lexikon für Theologie und Kirche*, in voce *'mortuarium'*; Lemarignier *et al.* 1962, p. 211; Lentze 1950, p. 343; Coulton 1936, p. 47.

219 For England, see Heath 1964, p. 20 ff.

220 Account item *'de palefrido'*, listing the name of a deceased canon and a specific sum; Raine 1859, pp. XXXV, 31, 36, 49, 184.

221 Sometimes the textile was used to make a chasuble; Piponnier 1997, pp. 4-7. In TROYES this could be bought off for 10 l.t. in the fifteenth century; Gadan 1851, p. 6; Assier 1855, p. 18. In NARBONNE canons handed over a fixed sum of 12 l.t.; Narbonne 1901, p. 364.

222 See AMIENS statute of 16 April 1392: canons and chaplains rendered their best garment, *'suivant la louable coustume'*, which was sold, preferably to the testator's family; Durand 1901-1903, vol. 2, pp. 119-120.

223 Temporary incorporation was also possible; Ferraris 1852-1857, vol. 7, col. 1290.

224 Concerning the incorporation of other benefices into the fabric, see p. 110.

225 This notwithstanding, in 1350 the provincial council of PADUA recommended outright that one or two canon's prebends be incorporated in the event of insufficient regular income; Mansi 1759-1793, vol. 26, p. 232; Hofmeister 1931, p. 87.

226 Hinschius 1869-1897, vol. 2, p. 418; Ferraris 1852-1857, vol. 7, col. 1287, 1293 (in voce *'unio'*).

227 Deed of 2 December 1220: Pelt 1930, no. 1; also *Congrès Archéologique de France* 149 (1991), p. 473 n. 12.

228 Aubert 1931, p. 21, nos 175, 176 (capitular statute of 10 April 1435).

229 *Urkundenbuch Bremen*, vol. 2, no. 635: '[...] *structuarius omni anno percepit prebenda* [...]'. It is possible that this concerns a new prebend as the capitular statute notes that this prebend comes at the expense of the incomes of the other canons.

230 Gardelles 1963, p. 21: '[...] *adeo fructus et proventus et redditus mensae capitularis et fabrice ipsius ecclesie sunt modernis temporibus diminuti, quod vix ad ipsorum capituli et aliorum personarum et servitorum*

ipsius ecclesiae statum decentem ac victum solitum congruentes sunt'. See also *Inventaire-sommaire Gironde* G 503 (1427 account). Incorporation for a very specific purpose is seen elsewhere too, such as at the cathedral of SPEYER, where a chantry was incorporated into the fabric in order to pay for the organ; Krebs 1968, nos 1010, 1024, 1028.

231 *Pouillés Sens*, p. 472.

232 A prebend was incorporated into the treasury under Bishop Simon de Bossy (1362-1404), and not until later - in the sixteenth century (?) - into the fabric, at which time the treasurer was released from certain of his obligations; *Pouillés Reims*, pp. 99, 100.

233 Schuegraf 1847/1848, vol. 12, p. 194.

234 See p. 268.

235 Collegiate churches may have been compelled to seek recourse in incorporation more often than cathedrals because they did not have access to the typical cathedral revenues. For example: the church of St John in UTRECHT in 1518 for a period of 30 years for the construction of the choir, begun in 1508; *Inventaris archief kapittel St.-Jan*, chapter minutes inv. 1, vol. 1, f. 117, 117v. Additionally, Fritzlar in 1231 with the pope's permission: *Registres Grégoire IX*, vol. 1, pp. 646, 647; Wilburg (diocese of TRIER) in 1318 for 30 years: Wuerdtwein 1781-1792, vol. 4, p. 178-179. Also Coulton 1928, p. 576.

236 Examples where the architect received his own prebend: SEO DE URGEL (1175): Mortet & Deschamps 1929, p. 129. AUXERRE, COUTANCES, STRASBOURG (church of St Thomas): *Bulletin Monumental* 83 (1924), p. 89; De Mély 1920/1921, no. 11, p. 294. Xanten (church of St Victor): Wilkes 1946/1947, p. 242; Beissel 1889, vol. 1, p. 97. In Xanten, emoluments from the *prebenda lapicidae* lapsed to the fabric after 1374. In UTRECHT the fabric collected proceeds resulting from the *officium tectoris*, possibly dissolved in the fourteenth century. In CHARTRES the chapter bought off the hereditary office of *magister operis ecclesiae*, which had degenerated into a kind of bookkeeper's post, in the beginning of the fourteenth century. The records reveal nothing about the party to which these proceeds subsequently accrued; Jusselin 1915-1922, p. 235 ff., p. 256 ff.; Von Simson 1956, p. 224 n. 100; *Cartulaire Chartres*, vol. 2, p. 279. The prebend of the *operarius* of MARSEILLE was incorporated into the chapter's *mensa* in 1442; *Gallia Christiana Novissima*, vol. 2, no. 1493. Concerning a goldsmith's prebend in ELY, see Chapman 1907, vol. 2, app. C, pp. 151-166.

237 Naturally, this summary is incomplete; all sorts of revenues could be permanently allocated to the fabric such as, in MERSEBURG, the document sealing fees in 1345; *Urkundenbuch Merseburg*, no. 989.

238 For example, the collegiate church of St Walburgis (diocese of TRIER) in 1318 for a period of 30 years: a) prebend of a non-residentiary canon, b) *prebendae defunctorum*, c) attendance dues for absent canons, and d) *oblationes* on certain feast days; Wuerdtwein 1781-1792, vol. 4, pp. 178-179.

239 Leuze 1908, pp. 96, 97. This *Kammer* was in fact a large strongbox, meant to hold at least 2000 gulden. The revenues moreover issued from the usufruct of absent prebendaries, voluntary gifts and so forth.

240 Lehmann-Brockhaus 1955-1960, no. 1034: *'ut per quinquennium de proventibus et redditibus dignitatum et prebendarum ecclesie nostre vicesima secundum estima-*

cionem in capitulo nostro provisam transeat in usus fabrice eiusdem ecclesie, que multiplici reparatione indigere dinoscitur'.

241 *Charters Hereford*, pp. 80, 81.

242 In 1296 the chapter of YORK levied a two-sevenths tax on its prebends for a period of three years. In 1298 attempts were made to force non-residentiary members of the chapter to pay a contribution as well, with the subcantor setting of for ROME to this end; Raine 1859, p. XI. Nave construction started in 1290.

243 Erskine 1962, p. 265; Hamilton Thompson 1925, p. 171: half of the small prebends worth 6 marks (£4 16 s.) each; the lion's share of the canon's stipends consisted of their attendance dues.

244 Raine 1859, p. 173 (1360).

245 Edwards 1967, p. 92 (1387, a one-seventh portion of the prebends).

246 Archives départementales Nord 4 G 4569: 1360/61 fabric account, tax on non-residentiary canons of 100 s. and on residentiary canons of 40 s. ('*ad succurendum presenci officio*'). Yield: 173 l.par., almost ten percent of the income and equivalent to five annual wages of an unskilled labourer. It is not clear whether these contributions apply to this year alone.

247 *Bulletin Monumental* 45 (1879), p. 63 ff.

248 Porée 1926, p. 18.

249 *Congrès Archéologique de France* 130 (1972), p. 526.

250 Quicherat 1886, p. 185; Mortet & Deschamps 1929, p. 320. The l.vien. was roughly 25 percent weaker than the l.t.; d'Avenel 1894-1912, vol. 1, pp. 44, 488.

251 *Inventaire-sommaire Aube* G 1561.

252 Quantin 1842, p. 23.

253 Cook 1957, p. 124, also p. 246: in 1337 the residentiary canons supplied £1000; the non-residentiary canons £200 once more.

254 'receipts from canons for the tax that was ordained by the chapter'; *Inventaire-sommaire Aube* G 1130; 1383/84 fabric receipts: 326 l.t.; 1394/95: 259 l.t.; 1395/96: 295 l.t. It is possible that this one-time levy continued in the form of an admission due after 1400. As has been noted, it is not always clear whether contributions made to the chapter were assigned on a one-off basis or for multiple years.

255 As in CHARTRES in the fourteenth century: Jusselin 1915-1922, pp. 258, 259.

256 As in AUXERRE in 1535, with the sale of a forest; Porée 1926, p. 19.

257 See regarding UTRECHT p. 323; concerning the reverse situation (fabric resources used to fund capitular interests), see p. 48.

258 This even applied in respect of dioceses in the Teutonic territories: there the bishop had no choice but to initiate building projects quite simply because chapters did not yet exist. From the beginning of the fourteenth century onwards, however, chapters established at the cathedral churches of KULMSEE (CHEŁMŻA), MARIENWERDER (KWIDZYN), FRAUENBURG (FROMBORK) and KÖNIGSBERG came to assume positions fully in line with customary practice elsewhere; Herrmann 2007, pp. 123, 250.

259 For instance the church of St Victor in Xanten; *Stiftskirche Xanten*, passim; Beissel 1889, vol. 2, p. 1 ff.

260 Coyecque 1889/1891, vol. 2; Leblond 1933, p. 20; the pledge drive was also open to the laity.

261 'every person promises to give his offering according to his means for the construction of this sacred tabernacle; the dean promises to donate 100 florins [...] over six years, the cantor sixty francs in

the same term'; Aubert 1931, n. 114; the bishop also pledged money.

262 Evans 1948, p. 109. Financing for the *Capsa beati Peati* in CHARTRES was arranged in the same way; Jusselin 1915-1922, p. 319; Merlet 1906, Appendix 2. In ROUEN canons were given a choice between donating a statue for the large west portal, on which work began in 1509, or a fixed sum of 22 ½ l.t.; De Beaurepaire 1897, p. 219 ff.; 'without the images, which the canons will have made as they desire and at their own cost and account'; *Inventaire-sommaire Seine-Inférieure* G 2524.

263 Some local examples: CAMBRAI (1418): Houdoy 1880, p. 259; VANNES (1537): *Congrès Archéologique de France* 48 (1881), p. 221.

264 Examples are legion. For CAMBRAI, '*registres et dossiers des executions testamentaires*' of cathedral clerics between 1376 and 1582: though the fabric received nothing for construction, it did receive contributions for myriad furnishings; Houdoy 1880, pp. 11, 257-287. For CHARTRES: Jusselin 1915-1922, pp. 319, 323; Lefèvre-Pontalis 1905, pp. 99-107. For PRAGUE: Neuwirth 1893, pp. 83-87. Of the ten predominantly thirteenth-century testaments of LYON canons taken up in the *Cartulaire Lyonnais* (vol. 1, pp. 401, 489, 569; vol. 2, pp. 107, 224, 357) six include a gift to the fabric. The nine canons' testaments in the cartulary of AUTUN (*Cartulaire Autun*, pp. 157, 179, 181, 192, 216, 229, 236, 272, 382) all include a small or larger bequest for the fabric; by contrast, the three bishops' testaments do not. For the large bequest left by COLOGNE Cathedral canon Hermann von Jülich (1315), see Lacomblet 1857, p. 151. In his extensive and elaborate testament of 18 November 1433 the canon-*mayordomo* of the cathedral of SEVILLE, Juan Martínez de Vittoria - one of the founders of the cathedral's *Nueva Fabrica* - named the fabric as his heir; Álvarez Marquez 1990, p. 24 and passim.

THREE Joint contributions from the bishop and chapter

265 Von Simson 1956, p. 176; the reorganization took place between 1171 and 1193; Chédeville 1973, p. 514.

266 '*Episcopus igitur et canonici* [...] *partem reddituum suorum non modicam per triennium conferendam ad reparationem ejus ecclesie absque ulla contradictione concesserunt*'; Thomas 1881, p. 509; Von Simson 1956, p. 162 and n. 14. '*Verum ad tanti structuram operis laicorum munera vel auxilia nequaquam sufficerent, nisi (ut) episcopus et canonici tantam, ut supra dictum est, ex propriis redditibus tribus annis pecuniam contulissent; quod siquidem transaucto eodem triennio, omnibus manifestum apparuit, cum omnis subito pecunia defecisset, ita ut qui preerant operi quod daretur operariis non haberent, aut quid dari posset de cetero non viderent*'; Thomas 1881, p. 511; Mortet & Deschamps 1929, p. 169. French version: '*quand ces trois ans furent passez / Ne porent pas paier assez / Li mestre de l'œvre aus ouvriers / Car ia falloient les deniers*'; Du Colombier 1973, p. 10; Kunstmann 1973, p. 77.

267 Construction at RHEIMS began in 1210; Branner 1961, p. 29.

268 *Regesten Köln*, vol. 3, no. 543; Ennen 1863/1869, vol. 3, p. 961; Clemen 1937, p. 50.

269 Migne 1844-1891, vol. 225, col. 219.

270 *Gallia Christiana*, vol. 10, instr. pp. 264-265.

271 '*Ad quod* [i.e. the building works] *deputavit vicesimam suorum redituum et canonici de suis pariter per temporis*

spatium vicennalis'; *Gallia Christiana*, vol. 1, instr. p. 21; Laran 1931, p. 11; Luchaire 1909, p. 177; Biget 1974, p. 14; Biget 1982, pp. 22-25, 57 n. 14. He also allocated other revenues to the building works, such as the fruits of vacant churches; see below p. 112 ff.

272 *Charters Salisbury*, pp. 229, 230; *Vetus Registrum*, vol. 2, pp. 8, 41, 65. The chapter's contribution, which applied from 1219, was initially set at seven years, but was successively renewed. There is no indication that the bishop was also already contributing at this time. The chapter ceded a portion of its prebendal revenues; Lehmann-Brockhaus 1955-1960, nos 4069, 4072; Le Bras 1954, p. 391.

273 De Farcy 1901-1926, vol. 1, p. 26 n. 3 and 4; the south transept was finished before 1236. Concerning the collaboration between the bishop and chapter of ANGERS, see also Caillet 2007, p. 307. Similar measures were sometimes taken at Spanish cathedrals, for example in LEÓN on 12 April 1240, where both parties pledged equal amounts for a period of five years; Yarza *et al.* 2004, p. 155; Ruiz Asencio & Martín Fuertes 1994, no. 2662. In HUESCA the capitular contribution set for a ten-year term in 1294 was considerably higher than that of the bishop; 552 versus 300 sueldos. This contribution was replaced by an alternate arrangement in 1300; Durán Gudiol 1991, pp. 71, 72.

274 Narbonne 1901, p. 25; Mortet 1898, p. 404 and Biget 1974, p. 140; no term is mentioned. The annates were also allocated to the building works, concerning which see below p. 112. The sum of 300 l.t. corresponded to approximately 15 annual wages of a skilled professional in the building trade; d'Avenel 1894-1912, vol. 3, p. 570. The bishop and chapter of HUESCA also allocated monies to the fabric on 6 September 1294, to whit an annuity of 300 sueldos for a period of ten years; Del Arco 1924, pp. 25-26.

275 Erskine 1983, pp. IX-X.

276 Almuni i Balada 2007, doc. 60, 63 and also 104; also p. 101. In the chapter's case this concerned only the *dignitates*. The contribution was reduced one year later, with the bishop now ceding half the tithes and the prior a sum of 1935 sol.barc., or three years' wages.

277 *Congrès Archéologique de France* 68 (1901), p. 326; 128 (1970), pp. 147-148.

278 The building campaign is exceptionally well documented; Criado Mainar 2000, especially pp. 385-394. Also *La Seo de Zaragoza*, pp. 265-273.

FOUR Papal contributions

279 See Costantini 2003, p. 35 n. 9. Support from the pope/former bishop could not be expected as a matter of course; see Freigang 1992, pp. 254-257 concerning Clement IV and NARBONNE.

280 Concerning COMMINGES: *Regestum Clementis papae V*, no. 9909; De Carsalade du Pont 1892, passim; Van der Meer 1967, p. 141; Boeren 1962, pp. 112, 147; Biget 1974, p. 140. The first stone was laid in 1304; on 15 January 1309 the pope himself came to lift his holy predecessor, Bishop Bertrand (1083-1123), to the sainthood. See also *Dictionnaire [...] ecclésiastiques*, in voce 'Comminges'.

281 Concerning quarantines, see Paulus 1922-1923, vol. 2, p. 80 ff. They suggest a dispensation from the fasting that usually went hand in hand with public penance.

282 Paulus 1922-1923, vol. 2, p. 19; Gardelles 1963, p. 17.

283 The pope had initially pledged a sum of 20,000 fl. '*pro opere dicte ecclesie*'; this

was also to serve as the site of his grave. Immediately before his death, however, he opted for the collegiate church of Uzeste instead and reduced the amount to 10,000 fl. This sum represents a mere one percent of his bequests to ecclesiastical bodies and family members; after his death a case was lodged against the latter legatees; Jansen 2001, pp. 55-58. Daily wage of 9 d.: d'Avenel 1894-1912, vol. 3, p. 573.

284 *Lettres communes Urbain v*, no. 24584: the cathedral '*ad manum suum tenet*'; also '*habet sinceritatem dilectionis*', idem, no. 24577.

285 Idem, no. 23975; also no. 22071, 22 October 1368, five days after the see fell vacant because of the bishop's transfer to the diocese of AVIGNON.

286 Idem, no. 24577; *Fasti Ecclesiae Gallicanae*, vol. 8, MENDE, p. 109.

287 *Inventaire-sommaire Lozère* G 694, 701, 702, 1145, 1148; *Lettres communes Urbain v*, nos 24533, 27248, 27249; *Fasti Ecclesiae Gallicanae*, vol. 8, MENDE, pp. 20, 22.

288 *Lettres communes Urbain v*, no. 24539; *Inventaire-sommaire Lozére* G 1148, 1149; *Fasti Ecclesiae Gallicanae*, vol. 8, MENDE, p. 119: resistance against one canon's plan to offer relics and precious items for sale in order to support the bishop's building campaign in 1393.

289 Bégule 1880, pp. 9, 43; *Cartulaire Lyonnais*, vol. 1, pp. 510, 518, 530, 591, 618, vol. 2, pp. 27-30; Beyssac 1912-1913, pp. 192-197; cf. Boeren 1962, p. 139. Papal letters of this type were not unusual. Innocent IV addressed a similar letter to the faithful of the Church province of COLOGNE on 13 November 1254 with an appeal to support the cathedral of OSNABRÜCK, which had burnt down; *Monumenta Germaniae Historica*, Ep. Saec. XIII Pont., no. 340. On 9 September 1262 Urban IV confirmed a similar letter issued by Innocent IV and Alexander IV on behalf of the cathedral of CLERMONT-FERRAND; Manry *et al.* 1959, p. 167; Gobillot 1912, pp. 14-15.

290 Paulus 1922-1923, vol. 2, p. 218 ff., vol. 3, p. 150 ff., especially pp. 160, 166, 226, 313.

291 See p. 111. Numerous examples in the *Lettres communes Jean XXII* (more than 280 cases); *Regestum Clementis papae v* (82 cases), etc. The earliest papal legislation dates from the twelfth century; Hinschius 1869-1897, vol. 2, pp. 441 ff., 454.

292 Best summary in *Dictionnaire de droit canonique*, in voce '*annates*' (G. Mollat), and in *Dictionnaire* [...] *ecclésiastiques*, in voce '*annates*' (J.P. Kirsch).

293 One single case was incorporated into the collection of decretals and thus also into general canon law: Decr. Greg. IX lib. v tit. XL c. XXXII (Friedberg 1879/1882, vol. 2, p. 926). This case concerned the bishop of TOUL, whom Pope Honorius III (1216-1227) accorded the right to collect proceeds from vacated benefices in his diocese for a period of two years; Kirsch 1903, p. XIII; Haller 1903, p. 50; Thomassinus 1725, pars 3, liber 2, caput 37, no. 3; Feine 1954, pp. 307-309, 428.

294 Baix 1942, p. CDVII n. 2; Kirsch 1903, p. XIII.

295 See p. 112 ff.

296 The pope demanded for his own use half the first-year's fruits of any vacated benefice. For an in-depth description of the *annata* in conceptual terms, see Baix 1942, p. CDVI ff.; Göller 1910, p. 80*; Kirsch 1903, p. IX ff.

297 The Council of FLORENCE (1437-1439) even instituted a tax on the annates not recognized by the pope; Plöchl 1960-1962, vol. 2, p. 381.

298 *Collectories pontificales*, pp. 511, 636, 637; possibly a consequence of the privilege granted by the pope for five years in 1304; *Registres Benoît XI*, p. 575.

FIVE Contributions from the ruler: emperor, king and lord

299 Guéry 1984, p. 1245; *liberalitas* is related to *charitas* and can engender *prodigalitas*.
300 Schwickerath 1942, p. 65.
301 Construction typically spanned no more than a few decades. Weilandt 1992, pp. 162-163.
302 Benz 1975, p. 126; he took a similar interest in the cathedral of BASEL, begun in 1010; idem, pp. 159-166.
303 The city of SPEYER is estimated to have had a population of 2000-3000; Heidrich 1991b, p. 12.
304 Concerning the cathedral of SPEYER, see especially Weinfurter 1991, Heidrich 1991a and 1991b, Engels 1995. SPEYER was the first church in the German Empire to serve as a dynastic final resting place; the gravestones extended across a third of the nave. Concerning the relationship between graves and commemoration in SPEYER, see Schmid & Wollasch 1984, pp. 681-706.
305 'SPEYER is made famous by offerings from King Henry'; in a miniature in the *Codex Aureus*; Weinfurter 1991, p. 74 n. 80.
306 In 1097 the emperor appointed his chaplain, Otto, later bishop of BAMBERG (1102-1033), as administrator of the cathedral building works at SPEYER in order to put affairs in order there: Lehmann-Brockhaus 1938, no. 1366 (*Herbordi vita Ottonis*). For SPEYER: Haas 1966, passim; Binding 1974, pp. 94-96.
307 Especially Heidrich 1991a, pp. 192-199; at the cathedral of SPEYER the partition of goods between the bishop and chapter had already taken place under Henry III; there is no quantitative data.
308 Mone 1836, passim; the earliest document published there dates from 1220. In later centuries imperial initiative and patronage - which continued to make a meaningful contribution up until the thirteenth century - were fairly negligible. Compare the agreement between the Otto of Brunswick (1198-1214), King of the Romans, and the archbishop of MAGDEBURG following the 1207 fire in the Ottonian cathedral, in which the former promised, amongst other things, '*Juvabimus ecclesiam Magdeburgensem ad edificationem suam secundum consilium archiepiscopi*'; *Regesta Magdeburg*, vol. 2, no. 329; Hamann & Rosenfeld 1910, p. 155, no. 39. However, the columns from Ravenna donated by Otto I were conscientiously reused in tribute to the first building. Also Schöller 1995, pp. 217-218, 221, who asserts that the gallery of kings at cathedrals like CHARTRES, PARIS, AMIENS and RHEIMS was symbolic of this '*garde*'.
309 Lemarignier *et al.* 1962, p. 170 ff., 243-246; additionally, Von Simson 1956, p. 173; Seymour 1968, pp. 14-18; also Schöller 1995, p. 217 ('*gardia specialis*'). The common term was '*évêchés royales*'.
310 Some examples: Louis VII (1137-1180) bequeathed 200 l.par. to the Notre Dame of PARIS; Molinier 1902, p. 179; Wolf 1956, p. 38; Aubert 1920, p. 30 n. 6; Kraus 1979, p. 215 n. 28; and a sum of money to the cathedral of SENLIS in 1168; Aubert 1912, p. 20. Philip Augustus (1180-1223) donated 200 l.par. for the construction of CHARTRES; Von Simson 1956, p. 177 and n. 67; Chédeville 1973, pp. 518, 524. Philip the Fair donated a quarry to the cathedral of

NOYON in 1293 for the salvation of his soul; Champollion-Figeac 1868, p. 79; Seymour 1968, pp. 72, 104. Louis IX (1226-1270) did the same for the cathedral of TOURS in 1241 and 1243; Boissonnot 1920, p. 400, doc. 2. In the time before the spectacular growth of the French kingship, cathedral-building also received assistance from the major seigneurial lords. In 1202, as duke of Normandy, the English king John Lackland donated 2000 l. ang. to the cathedral of ROUEN, which had been devastated by a fire in 1200; moreover, he twice granted permits to collect for the building works. Up until 1204 ROUEN Cathedral served as the coronation church and mausoleum of the dukes of Normandy; *Congrès Archéologique de France* 89 (1926), p. 15; Lot 1865, p. 19 ff.; Kraus 1979, p. 179; Grant 2005, pp. 124, 134, 138. See also Mortet & Deschamps 1929, p. 201 and n. 4.

311 Avril 1984, vol. 1, pp. 563, 747.

312 Already during the war, in January 1393, Charles VI (1380-1422) donated 10,000 francs for the completion of the transept of the cathedral of LE MANS; a few months later saw the receipt of the first 1000 francs for the '*ouvrage du Roy*'; Ledru 1900, pp. 331-336.

313 Carrière 1936, p. 109; Dupont-Ferrier 1930-1933, vol. 1, p. 138, vol. 2, pp. 20, 97-129, 211, 235, 320. Other types of building enterprises also profited from this tax, such as the works at the castle of Amboise between 1492 and 1498, where the proceeds yielded 7323 l.t. in 1495/96, or one-sixth of the overall income; *Congrès Archéologique de France* 77 (1910), vol. 2, p. 284. Concerning the importance of indirect taxes, for example on wine, for the erection of city walls from the fourteenth century onwards, see Rigaudière 1985, pp. 45-56, 71.

314 Blanquart 1918, passim; Bonnenfant 1939, p. 18. The first privilege dates from 27 August 1465; renewed in 1469, 1475, 1481 and, with a brief hiatus, in 1485. Also *Congrès Archéologique de France* 138 (1980), p. 302 and n. 20: summary of the sections to be built; the king asks the faithful to remember him in their prayers in view of his massive contribution of personal funds. Glazing for the radiating chapel was also financed with these receipts; Joubert 2001, p. 210.

315 Cailleaux 1999, pp. 192-205; see also *Inventaire-sommaire Yonne* G 711, 1142 ff.

316 Aubert 1912, p. 25; after the 1504 fire; in 1507 initially for six years, later extended: one d.t. of every *minot* of salt sold anywhere in the kingdom; the tax yielded approximately 1200 l.t. a year. This indirect tax, which was levied until 1789, assumed the existence of storehouses or sheds in which salt could be kept in storage.

317 *Inventaire-sommaire Seine-Inférieure* G 4421, 4450; *Congrès Archéologique de France* 89 (1926), p. 21. After the fire of 4 October 1514, Louis XII (1498-1515) pledged 12,000 l.t. (around 400 annual wages of an unskilled labourer) over a period of ten years, to be levied in part from the tax on salt; only 2000 l.t. was ever received. Francis I (1515-1547) promised to pay the remainder in exchange for prayers and two memorial services.

318 Hamon 2001, pp. 128-130, 133; also De Girardot & Durand 1849, p. 36: for reconstruction of the north tower which had collapsed in 1505, proceeds between 1515 and 1521: 9144 l.t., or 27 percent of the total income, and equal to the annual wage of around 160 unskilled building labourers.

319 Desjardins 1865, p. 43; Leblond 1933, pp. 21, 24: from 1514 onwards, interrupted by the imprisonment of Francis I in 1525-1526 after the battle of Pavia; the chapter sold items from the cathedral inventory to help pay the king's ransom; renewed in 1536 for a period of ten years. Transept construction was already well underway by this time. The yield in 1532 was 4086 l.t., against total fabric expenditures of 4955 l.t.

320 *Inventaire-sommaire Aube* G 1574, 2594, 2595 (after 1484).

321 See references in notes 324-331 below.

322 Warnke 1976, pp. 235, 279.

323 See also p. 435, 441 on SENS and BOURGES.

324 *Inventaire-sommaire Aube* G 1559. The 1401/02 account (LONDON, British Museum Add. ms. 15083, f. 112v.) records a royal donation of 100 l.t., representing around 20 percent of the clear income in that year.

325 *Inventaire-sommaire Aube* G 1568.

326 Idem G 1564, 2594, 2595

327 Idem G 1580, 1577.

328 Idem G 1584.

329 Idem G 1585-1591. No figures are recorded for the years 1518/19, 1519/20 and 1524/25. Clear income is gross income less the credit balance carried forward from previous years.

330 Idem G 1589.

331 Idem G 1593, 1595, 4151. The yield in 1530 was 1700 l.t., in 1531 2300 l.t. and in 1532 500 l.t.

332 SANTIAGO 1131; López Ferreiro 1898-1911, vol. 4, app. 6. SALAMANCA 1152; Martín Martín 1975, p. 80. LEÓN, starting in 1277, possibly already after 1266, up into the fifteenth century; *Colección documental León*, nos 2378, 2449, 2543, 2755, 2775, 2891, 3061, 3175, 3337, 3467; Teijeira Pablos 1993, doc. 14 (1462/63: *'estos son les excusados'*, 52 names). BURGOS 1292, 1299; Pereda Llarena 1984, nos 267, 335. CIUDAD RODRIGO 1319 (*'siete excusados'*); Bernal Estévez 1982, pp. 34-36, 140; Azofra 2006, pp. 119, 173. ASTORGA 1374 (the king determines that the city must grant this exemption to the *'Excusados de la obra'*); *Colección documental Astorga*, vol. III, no. 1807. OVIEDO 1388, 1420, 1449; De Caso Fernández 1981, pp. 165 n. 66; *Colección documental Oviedo*, nos 5-8, 11, 12 (*'diez excusados'*); De Caso Fernández *et al.* 1999, vol. 1, pp. 88, 96, 102.

333 Evans 1948, p. 112.

334 CHARTRES: Von Simson 1956, pp. 180, 181; Chédeville 1973, pp. 453-454, 517. COLOGNE: Ennen 1863/1869, vol. 3, p. 1026. YORK: Knowles 1936, p. 42; concerning the history of these windows: Knowles 1936, p. 30 ff. For TROYES and SENS around 1500: Minois 2005, pp. 219-231. Financial data relating to the donation of windows in Damen 2005, pp. 148-150: the sums for fifteen glazed windows donated by Burgundian and Hapsburg rulers to various churches in the Low Countries between 1459 and 1516 ranged from 150 lb.vls. (26 annual wages of an unskilled labourer) to 420 lb.vls. (73 annual wages); Verlinden 1959/1965/1972, vol. 2, pp. 95, 426.

335 Ravaux 1989, pp. 87 and 88, *'vacance royale au moment du don royal'*: CHÂLONS-EN-CHAMPAGNE, also SOISSONS and CHARTRES by Philip Augustus and Louis IX. The French kings, and also the English kings, collected the episcopal mensal revenues attached to vacant sees; see also Crosby 1994, p. 362.

336 For UTRECHT Cathedral, see p. 285 ff.

337 Colvin 1963, passim.

338 Cook 1957, p. 191.

339 *Charters Salisbury*, nos 158 (1227), 210, 211, 302.

340 *'Ad quod opus promovendum non tantum episcopus, immo*

rex et cum eo multi magnates manum porrexerunt adiutricem. Unde quidam ait: rex largitur opes, fert praesul opem, lapicidae dant operam; tribus hic est opus ut stet opus': Lehmann-Brockhaus 1955-1960, no. 4067.

341 Testament in Wolf 1956, p. 38; Branner 1965, pp. 31, 32. Concerning Louis IX's personal involvement in the building works, see Mortet & Deschamps 1929, p. 241.

342 Colvin 1963, vol. 1, pp. 248-257. Edward I's engagement in ecclesiastical building projects was nothing compared with his expenditures for castle-building, totalling £80,000; the same applies to Edward III; idem, pp. 161, 162, 1029.

343 For England, see Colvin 1963, vol. 1, pp. 48-50, 87-93, 157-159.

344 Monget 1898-1901, vol. 1, p. 429 ff. Over a period of 25 years (1377-1403) the average pace of building lay at around a quarter of this peak year.

345 Mezzanotte 1955, pp. 860, 895, 897; Romanini 1964, pp. 351, 426; Boito 1889, pp. 164, 165; Brivio 1977, p. 41. This author contends that the use of marble as the building material and of German Gothic as the architectural style was determined by Gian Galeazzo at the start of the building campaign and imposed on the fabric.

346 Gian Galeazzo granted the fabric a number of tax exemptions. Boito and Mezzanotte estimate his monetary contributions from the *Camera del Principe* to have been more than 12,000 lire imp. up until 1399; receipts over the first five years (1387-1391) alone came to 145,000 lire imp.; Boito 1889, pp. 25, 26, 28; Mezzanotte 1955, pp. 866, 896.

347 Colvin 1963, vol. 1, pp. 147, 151, 155, 157; however, he put around £5000 of this money towards the shrine of his predecessor St Edward (1042-1066), who had been canonized in 1161. During his reign the king spent in excess of £113,000 on castles; idem, p. 109. See also Binski 1995, pp. 1-7, 50, 90, 175, 205.

348 Led by their abbot, the monks resumed the building campaign in 1368; only a quarter of the monies derived from the king. Over the more than 150 years (1376-1552) that it took to erect the nave, total expenditures came to £20,000, as against £50,000 between 1245 and 1272; Rackham 1909-1910, passim; Colvin 1963, vol. 1, pp. 151, 155-157; Knoop & Jones 1949, p. 135.

349 French and English kings almost never choose cathedrals for their interment, whilst the Salian emperors used the cathedral of SPEYER as their mausoleum; Hallam 1982, pp. 367-367. Concerning Norman cathedrals' function as mausoleums for the dukes up until 1204, see Grant 2005, pp. 34, 37. ROUEN was both mausoleum and coronation church; concerning the contribution made by John Lackland, see Grant 2005, pp. 121-122, 124, 134.

350 The cathedral was a pantheon of the Navarran monarchy from 1134 on; *La catedral de Pamplona*, vol. 1, p. 87.

351 Leroy 1985 and Goñi Gaztambide 1996, p. 109; Martínez de Aguirre 1987, pp. 263, 273-274 (*capilla San Esteban*, destroyed with the cathedral's collapse in 1390). In 1351/52 the chapter spent 601 l., or roughly 38 annual wages of an assistant and five percent of the kingdom of Navarre's total expenditures; see also *Diccionario eclesiastica de España*, in voce '*Capilla Real*'.

352 Martínez de Aguirre 1987, p. 259.

353 *La catedral de Pamplona*, vol. 1, pp. 84-88; Goñi Gaztambide 1996, p. 111.

354 Goñi Gaztambide 1955, p. 18

ff. Receipts and expenditures between the years 1398 and 1407, as summarized on p. 20, do not include royal gifts. In his testament of 11 July 1403, the king designated the cathedral as his final resting place, just as his father Charles II had done. He personally commissioned his tomb monument in 1413. After Charles III's death, royal interest in the cathedral waned; idem, p. 30.

355 Ramírez Vaquero 1996, pp. 197-234.

356 Idem, p. 234; *La catedral de Pamplona*, vol. 1, pp. 230-231.

357 Concerning the financing of the building works at the cathedral of PALMA, see Sastre Moll 1993; Sastre Moll in Pascual 1995, pp. 37-41; Sastre Moll 1994; Domenge i Mesquida 1997, pp. 67-123; Domenge i Mesquida in Freigang & Stiglmayr 1999, pp. 159-187.

358 O'Callaghan 2004, p. 204.

359 Domenge i Mesquida 1997, pp. 130-140 and figs 13 and 14; Pascual 1995, pp. 210-215.

360 Sastre Moll 2001, p. 60 ff.: work on the palace, 1309-1314.

361 Other cathedrals also served as temporary or permanent dynastic burial places: LEÓN, TOLEDO (Capilla de Reyes Viejos, 1289), SANTIAGO (after 1535), GRANADA (burial chapel, 1505-1517) and SEVILLE (Capilla Real, early sixteenth century); *Las catedrales españolas*, pp. 274-278, 280.

362 Concerning Castile-León: Nieto Soria 1986a and 1986b; also Rodríguez Estévez 1998, p. 37 n. 7.

363 Concerning BURGOS: Karge 1995, p. 31; concerning CIUDAD RODRIGO: Azofra 2006, pp. 116-120; also Erlande-Brandenburg 1989, p. 252. The failure of the plan, framed after 1280, to build a Gothic choir at the cathedral of SANTIAGO has been blamed on the absence of royal support; SANTIAGO qualifies as the only Gothic cathedral to have been raised without any royal support; Puente Míguiz 1985 and Puente Míguiz in Freigang & Stiglmayr 1999, p. 51. The largest gift of 10,000 maravedís booked by the cathedral of LEÓN came not from the king, but from Infante Alfonso de Valencia (1282-1316), *mayordomo* to the king; he was accorded a privileged site for his grave - '*ad sanctos*', near the relics; Yarza *et al.* 2004, pp. 343-345.

364 Rodríguez Estévez 1998, pp. 55-56; *La Catedral de Sevilla*, pp. 134-137.

365 We know, from what can be gleaned from the scarce sources, that French kings never donated large sums for the building or repair of their coronation church of RHEIMS; Reinhardt 1963, pp. 7-8. The high costs of the coronation itself were regarded as issuing from the king's right of *gistum* and were therefore borne by the archbishop. The latter first managed to avert these costs in 1223 by shifting them onto citizens subject to his bannum; Brühl 1950, p. 65 and passim.

366 It is for this reason that the Scandinavian lands and their national royal saints - St Erik (Sweden), St Knut (Denmark) and St Olaf (Norway) - are left out of the discussion here; see Hoffmann 1975.

367 Cf. Flieder 1968, p. 105.

368 Concerning the veneration of Wenceslas and Adalbert, their graves and relics (incl. illustration), see *The story of Prague Castle*, pp. 89-101.

369 Haussherr 1971, pp. 21-26, 40. My thanks to Prof. Haussherr for sending a copy of the deed, published in *Regesta Bohemiae et Moraviae*, vol. 4, no. 1029; see also Tadra 1880, p. 392, and *The story of Prague Castle*, pp. 166-170 (incl. illustration). Neuwirth 1890,

pp. 373, 380, 386, cites other royal donations.

370 The crown, which had been commissioned by Charles IV (first mentioned in 1346) and given by him in keeping to the chapter, was to be housed at the grave of Wenceslas and was never to leave the cathedral; *The story of Prague Castle*, pp. 172-179, 481-487.

371 See the inscription under his bust in the triphorium: '[...] *fundavit Pragensem ecclesiam de sumptuoso opere* [...] *ac sumptibus propriis laboravit* [...]'; Beneškovská & Hlobil p. 154; *Die Kathedrale von St. Veit*, p. 10. He commissioned the mosaic of the Last Judgement over the south portal, called the *porta aurea*. Likewise, the construction and rich furnishings of the Wenceslas Chapel – which as locus of the grave and relics of St Wenceslas and repository for the coronation insignia and state archives was the religious nexus of dynastic power – were without question also financed by him; *The story of Prague Castle*, p. 181; *Die Kathedrale von St. Veit*, p. 21; Beneškovská & Hlobil 1999, pp. 44-58.

372 Barbara Schock-Werner in Cassanelli 2005, p. 279; also Gatz *et al.* 2003, p. 577.

373 Kovács 1992, pp. 95-99; Grass 1983, pp. 252-276; Dmitrieva & Lambrecht 2000, p. 22: mausoleum after 1365 (not as sole church); the *Kaisergruft* in the Capuchin church not until after 1617.

374 The diocese encompassed only 20 parishes within its narrow borders; the emperor got the right to nominate the bishop; Gatz *et al.* 2003, p. 810.

375 On this subject, see the monograph by Viktor Flieder. He shows that already in the twelfth century St Stephan's was being built as the prospective cathedral; Flieder 1968, especially pp. 27, 45, 57, 102-105, 137, 159, 162, 192-194, 214-224.

376 Though there is no record of King Casimir III the Great making any financial contribution for the construction of KRAKOW Cathedral, he is likely to have done so: the campaign to raise the new choir commenced in 1320, which was also the year of the first coronation; Crossley 1985, pp. 15, 27-51; also the review of this survey in *Zeitschrift für Kunstgeschichte* 1987, pp. 552-560. Crossley (p. 45) says – quite rightly – that the building of the new cathedral cannot be deemed a royal foundation; the king's gifts related to decorative elements and not to the structure itself. Concerning the links between PRAGUE, KRAKOW and VIENNA, see Crossley 1985, pp. 51, 256; Dmitrieva & Lambrecht 2000, pp. 13-24, 103-115. The sovereign's castle and the cathedral also lay close together in NANTES, where the duke of Brittany made contributions for the construction of the cathedral's portals (by allocating a tax on wine, after 1425) and took part in the auditing of the fabric accounts via a delegated ducal officer (*procontrarotulator ducis*, 1457), indicating that the duke had a financial stake; Guillouët 2003, pp. 147-153, 169,183.

377 Weltsch 1968, pp. 59, 64, 108.

SIX Contributions from the civic administration and urban institutions

378 Signori 1995, p. 200 and n. 156.

379 Saint-Denis 2008, pp. 27, 82, 133; also Saint-Denis 1994, pp. 101-103, 194, 603-609. Even before this the king's chancellor had been murdered whilst at prayer in the cathedral. The damage to the cathedral choir was not serious. For an overview of clashes

between bishops and populace in France, see Gaudemet 2008, pp. 417-419.

380 Falque Rey 1988, pp. 201 (1116) and 508-511 (1136): '*proiecerunt in eum* [= archbishop] *lapides et usque ad altaris beati Jacobi introitum insecuti sunt* [...] *cum densitate lapidum et multitudine saxorum*'; Abou-el-Haj 1997, p. 169. Concerning the 1112 revolt of the Commune in LAON, the bishop's murder and fire damage to the Romanesque cathedral, see Clark & King 1983, p. 15; Saint-Denis 1994, p. 104; Saint-Denis 2008, pp. 81-82; publication of all sources in Kaiser 2003, pp. 147-157. Summary in Saint-Denis *et al.* 2002, pp. 71-77. See also Soria Audebert 2005 regarding all forms of violence against bishops in French dioceses, pp. 17, 44, 136, 150, 153,158-159, 213-216,287. She cites 62 cases between 1012 and 1218, thirteen of which ended in fatality. Such violent incidents rarely extended to the cathedral church: besides LAON in 1112, also THÉROUANNE in 1083 (destruction of reliquaries and ornaments).

381 *Registres Grégoire IX*, vol. 2, no. 281 (11 October 1235); Branner 1961, p. 33 ff.; Reinhardt 1963, p. 231; *Inventaire-sommaire Marne G*, vol. 2 (1), p. 248; *Fasti Ecclesiae Gallicanae*, vol. 3, RHEIMS, pp. 161-162. Kurmann 1987, p. 21, voices doubt as to whether the building lodge shut down entirely in these years. In CHARTRES a comparable riot broke out during the building campaign, on October 1210, hinting at major tensions between the chapter and urban population; here a heavy wagon used in the building works was rammed into the dean's house; Chédeville 1973, pp. 499, 524 and n. 105; Williams 1993, pp. 25-26. In AMIENS a handful of civic officials started a fire in the cathedral and opened the chest containing the chapter's privileges in 1258; Murray 1996, pp. 62, 73, 76, 141.

382 Fernie & Whittingham 1972, pp. 27-31: concerning the settlement of the fine imposed on the city. The fine was for 3000 marks or £2000, representing a value of 1475 annual wages, to be paid over six years; it is not clear if these sums were in fact collected. Also Fernie 1993, pp. 163-165, 211-212; Atherton *et al.* 1996, pp. 250, 259-262. Gilchrist 2005, pp. 29-30, also cites conflicts in NORWICH in 1443 and in EXETER in 1283. There were renewed disturbances in 1443.

383 There are countless examples of comparable conflicts, some of which persisted for centuries and could suddenly boil over dangerously. Usually the cathedral did not become a target, unlike the canons' residences situated inside the immunity. For France, see Müller 1998, pp. 67-90: in 1192 the citizens of ROUEN tore down the precinct wall and refused to restore it. Canons' houses were destroyed and shops burnt down, and there were also fatalities. Not until 1256 was the wall rebuilt. See also Mussat 1982 and Grant 2005, p. 123. For England see the fine discussion by Rosser in Slater & Rosser 1998, pp. 20-43: siege of the immunity in HEREFORD in 1262, as well as in EXETER, YORK and, as noted, in NORWICH. Rosser cites the ritual function of processions to resolve such conflicts, whether permanently or temporarily. For Germany, see Radtke 2004, pp. 165-184: in LÜBECK a protracted conflict broke out in June 1299, when 1000 people converged on the immunity, ravaging and looting the canons' houses, drinking the wine and

threatening to despoil the cathedral - which the city council managed to prevent. The interdict was not lifted until 1317. The settlement concluded with the city in 1308 would hold firm for centuries.

384 Freigang 1992, pp. 46-49. The conflict seems to have been resolved in 1361 as the consuls got a passage between the city wall and the choir. Serious disagreement between the citizens and chapter of ROUEN concerning the erection of a wall that hampered tradesmen: Mortet & Deschamps 1929, pp. 165, 166 (1192-1195). In ZAMORA permission for the tower's completion was granted in 1496 under the condition that it would not result in any damage to the city fortifications; De Lera Maíllo 1999, no. 2012.

385 Kroesen 2003, p. 198; concerning the civic administration and the cathedral in BARCELONA, p. 220, in LEÓN, p. 232.

386 Ortí Belmonte 1954; Nieto Cumplido 1998, pp. 499-507; Kroesen 2003, p. 184. Construction was officially launched on 17 September 1523, but in fact large quantities of building material had already been purchased before then.

387 Fournié 1995, pp. 258-262. LAVAUR was home to a cathedral as from 1317. Inscribed at the entrance to the crypt, where the relics were kept, in the basilica of Saint-Sernin in TOULOUSE were the words: *'His sunt vigiles qui custodiunt civitatem'*.

388 Seibrich 1995, pp. 63, 69, 106-107 and n. 444. Under pressure from the archbishop, the city withdrew its demand for access in 1546.

389 Bion de Marlavagne 1875, p. 67.

390 Quantin 1842, p. 19; Bouvier 1911, vol. 2, p. 421. On 13 April 1505 the city administrators and high-standing residents of SENS declared themselves in wholehearted support of the transept's construction, yet failed to pledge any contribution; Cailleaux 1999, p. 56.

391 For instance the accounts for 1402/03 and 1409/10; London, British Museum Add. ms. 15083, f. 133, 169, 183, accounts for 1412 ff.; *Inventaire-sommaire Aube* G 1561, account for 1491/92: G 1569.

392 *Inventaire-sommaire Aube* G 1570, 1571.

393 Almuni i Balada 2007, doc. 101, pp. 814-816 and 141-142.

394 MEAUX 1393: 240 l.t., 1394: 200 l.t., 1495: 240 l.t., 1505: 100 l.t., 1510: 170 l.t.; all small sums worth some ten annual wages; Kurmann 1971, pp. 103, 118, 143-144.

395 Durán Gudiol 1991, p. 137.

396 *Inventaire-sommaire Yonne* G 1128.

397 Chartraire n.d., p. 28; Quantin 1842, p. 35. Relations between the city and fabric were so friendly that in 1480 the latter provided a two-year loan of 100 écus d'or to the former; *Inventaire-sommaire Yonne* G 1139, 1140.

398 *Inventaire-sommaire Seine-Inférieure* G 2503. Also CHÂLONS-EN-CHAMPAGNE: in 1462 100 l.t for new bells, for roof repairs and for the new organ; Ravaux 1977, p. 365.

399 Dubuis 1995, pp. 37-42.

400 Krebs 1952-1959, nos 8103, 8114, 8397, 8407, 8884, 8891, 8896, also 5985, 6010. For the city's rights, see *Regesten Münster Konstanz*, nos 86 (1256) and 367 (1511).

401 Text of a lost deed from the initial phase of building; Braunfels 1953, p. 146 and n. 505.

402 Grote n.d., p. 111, and above p. 57.

403 From the deed of 7 August 1318, in which the city allocates money for cathedral-building for the first time since 1301; Guasti 1887, p. 23; Grote n.d., p. 39.

404 Grote n.d., p. 44.

405 Grote n.d., pp. 21, 35: late thirteenth century. The monastic churches of

Santa Maria Novella and Santa Croce also benefitted from such funds.

406 Grote n.d., pp. 32-34 and n. 85 and 95. There was a similar tax in ORVIETO; Du Colombier 1973, pp. 10, 11.

407 Income from the so-called *directura*; Grote n.d., p. 32.

408 Idem, p. 40 and n. 120.

409 See Lorenzo Fabbri in Crouzet-Pavan 2003, pp. 195-244. The numeric data date from the period after 1446, when the works had already passed their peak; graphs and tables for the years 1446-1494 on pp. 204-208. Also Haines & Riccetti 1996, pp. 267-294; Verdon 1994, and Haines in *Finanziare cattedrali*, pp. 137-166 ('*La grande impresa civica di Santa Maria del Fiore*').

410 Grote n.d., p. 112.

411 In 1352 and between 1360 and 1370; Grote n.d., pp. 62, 102 (1352); Haines, in *Finanziare Cattedrali*, p. 152.

412 Grote n.d., pp. 33, 35.

413 Zervas 1987, p. 12. She publishes tables listing the *Opera*'s receipts and expenditures over the years 1339-1359, as expressed in the wages of an unskilled labourer (*manovale*); the available funds varied, ranging from 285 annual wages in 1339 to 55 annual wages in 1348 and 1349. It is not clear which share derived from the *Comune*. Further analysis of these key cycles of quantitative data fall outside the scope of this study.

414 For SIENA, see Giorgi & Moscadelli 2005, pp. 116-122; 140-189, 388 (graph); Giorgi & Moscadelli in *Finanziare cattedrali*, pp. 112-106; Haines in *Finanziare cattedrali*, p. 141 n. 13, cites the greater efficiency of FLORENCE when compared with SIENA. For ORVIETO, see Haines & Riccetti 1996, pp. 167-229; Riccetti 1988, pp. 139-215; Riccetti in Barlozzetti 1995, pp. 274-334; Riccetti in *Finanziare cattedrali*, pp. 167-228. For PERUGIA, see Nicolini 1992.

SEVEN Contributions from ecclesiastical property and fiscal sources in the bishopric

415 Hinschius 1869-1897, vol. 4, p. 307; Leisching 1964, p. 260. This is the formulation used in the deed of 16 April 1264; *Urkundenbuch Niederrhein*, vol. 2, no. 541.

416 Duby 1976, p. 117; Biget 1974, p. 156, also pp. 137-140.

417 Nolet & Boeren 1951, p. 358 ff; Lindner 1950, p. 207.

418 Vanrie 1965, p. 54.

419 Such large-scale restitution did not take place everywhere; Post 1957, vol. 1, p. 211.

420 Raine 1859, pp. 142-145; p. 29 (account VII); Aylmer & Cant 1977, p. 122; especially Swanson 1999, pp. 105-121. Also Norton 2007, p. 169.

421 Niermeyer 1954-1976, in voce '*beneficium*' sub 24.

422 Especially from the thirteenth century onwards; Lindner 1950, p. 226.

423 Lindner 1950, p. 308; for England, see the Council of LONDON in 1268; Powicke & Cheney 1964, p. 770. In England it was usually the chapter's common fund that profited from an incorporation; Lepine 2006, pp. 48-50.

424 Lindner 1950, p. 310.

425 Idem, pp. 296-306.

426 Since the Council of VIENNE; idem, p. 297.

427 Ruffini 1896, col. 169; Hofmeister 1931, p. 124.

428 *Regestum Clementis papae V*, index p. 120.

429 *Lettres communes Jean XXII*, index, p. 210, in voce '*unio beneficiorum*'.

430 See also Hayez 1985, p. 138, on incorporations of parishes under Urban V (1362-1370), with only one example of incorporation in a cathedral fabric – at ST ANDREW's in Scotland – of a parish that had originally belonged to the

bishop's *mensa* - thus a gift from the bishop.

431 Other beneficiaries, apart from the bishop's *mensa*, could include the chapter endowment or a monastery, universities, hospitals, church fabrics, etc.; Feine 1954, pp. 363, 354 n. 8; Denifle 1897-1899, vol. 1, p. 983. See also Schöller 1989, pp. 267-270.

432 EXETER: Erskine 1962, p. 265, Erskine 1983, p. xx (documented in 1204). CANTERBURY: *Acta Stephani Langton*, p. 144 (1228). HEREFORD: Yates 1973, p. 82 (1270). AGDE: *Cartulaire Agde*, p. 311. RODEZ: Bion de Marlavagne 1875, pp. 26, 109 (1281; presumably a donation by the bishop of two churches already incorporated into his *mensa*). NARBONNE: Champollion-Figeac 1868, p. 312 (1256, two churches). QUIMPER: *Cartulaire Quimper*, no. 190 (as evidenced by a deed of 1299). BÉZIERS: *Regesta Honorii papae III*, vol. 1, p. 40 (26 September 1216). LIMOGES: Biget 1974, p. 139 (1295).

433 HEREFORD: *Registrum Orleton*, p. 158 (1320) (incorporation of a parish in the diocese of Salisbury over which the bishop of HEREFORD held the right of patronage; papal confirmation: *Charters Hereford*, pp. XXXIII, 207, 208). WÜRZBURG: *Monumenta Boica*, vol. 46, pp. 172-174 (1353). WELLS: Bird & Baildon 1907/1914, vol. 1, pp. 204, 540, 547 (deeds of 1306 and 1338: officially the church was incorporated into the chapter, with the fruits assigned to the fabric; upon visitation, however, the chapter proved to be reneging). SALISBURY: the city's parish of St Thomas in 1363, in the face of the tower's imminent collapse; Brown 1995, p. 58. MÜNSTER: Spieckermann 1935, p. 26 (1385). CAMBRAI: Dehaisnes 1886, vol. 1, p. 436; Archives départementales Nord 4 G 4 (1371). SPEYER: Mone 1836, p. 96 (1361, two churches). ANGERS: *Inventaire-sommaire Maine-et-Loire* G, p. 57. Also compare the donations of several villages to the cathedral fabric (administered by the *custos*) by the bishops and chapters of MARIENWERDER (KWIDZYN) and FRAUENBURG (FROMBORK) (areas controlled by the Teutonic Order in eastern Prussia) in 1342 and 1343, respectively, including not only the right of patronage over the churches but also all manorial revenues from hunting, fishing and so on; Pottel 1911, pp. 39, 76; Herrmann 2007, pp. 122, 595; 147, 419.

434 CANTERBURY: Smith 1940, p. 359; Woodruff & Danks 1912, p. 168 (donation by Archbishop Arundel 1396-1414). MAGDEBURG: *Urkundenbuch Magdeburg*, no. 55 (1409). RODEZ: Denifle 1897-1899, vol. 1, no. 669; Bion de Marlavagne 1875, pp. 46, 108 (1427, due to war). UZÉS: Denifle 1897-1899, vol. 1, no. 564 (1444, yielding not more than 10 l.t.). VANNES: *Inventaire-sommaire Morbihan* G, p. 300 ff. (fabric accounts from 1475 on). NEVERS: Denifle 1897-1899, vol. 1, no. 151.

435 METZ: Pelt 1930, no. 201 (1504 and 1511).

436 Archives départementales Aveyron 3 G 249. Worth 20 and 18 annual wages of a *manoeuvre*, respectively.

437 See above n. 184, 271, 274.

438 See also Lunt 1965, p. 94 and Kuys 2004, pp. 194-195.

439 Baix 1942, p. CDXXXV.

440 Niermeyer 1954-1976, in voce *'annata'*; *Dictionnaire de droit canonique*, in voce *'annates'* sub 11, and *Dictionnaire* [...] *ecclésiastiques*, in voce 'annates' sub 1.

441 Powicke & Cheney 1964, p. 44; Colchester & Harvey 1974, p. 201: the decree must date from between

roughly 1176 and 1186.

442 Hefele & Leclercq 1907-1938, vol. 7, p. 496.

443 See Appendix two.

444 Ferraris 1852-1857, vol. 3, col. 398; Barbosa 1656-1665, vol. 5, p. 220, vol. 9 (1), p. 53. They refer to '*fructus beneficiorum vacantium pro fabrica ecclesiae cathedralis*', perhaps intending *intercalares* (?).

445 See for example the various *Registres des Papes*, index, in voce '*annatae*' or '*beneficia*'; other fabrics too were sometimes assigned annates.

446 *Lettres communes Urbain v*, no. 19680 (22 February 1367): '*redditus et facultates fabrice adeo sunt tenues et exiles quod reparationi ipsius fabrice centuplicati nequaquam sufficere possent*'.

447 See p. 96.

448 Gardelles 1963, p. 17; Bion de Marlavagne 1875, pp. 26 n. 1, 39, 52, 109. After 1461 only a quarter of the fruits of vacant benefices in the bishop's and chapter's collation were spent on the building works.

449 Paid until 1664, after which this was converted into a fixed sum of 600 l.t.; Narbonne 1901, p. 37.

450 Freigang 1992, p. 47, refers to a '*Annatensegen*' for the building works; Cassanelli 2005, p. 171.

451 Decr. Greg. IX lib. V tit. XL, c. XXXII, in Friedberg 1879/1882, vol. 2, p. 926. Additionally, see e.g. Baix 1942, p. CDVII n. 2; Kirsch 1903, p. XIII; Haller 1903, p. 50; Thomassinus 1725, pars 3, liber 2, caput 58, no. 2.

452 Appendix two; Desjardins 1865, pp. 5, 6 (incorrectly states 1226); Bonnet-Laborderie 1978, p. 47 (confirmation by the papal legate).

453 Friedberg 1879/1882, vol. 2, p. 1206; additionally, Von Brünneck 1905, pp. 8, 23; Göller 1910, p. 81, n. 1; Baix 1942, p. CDVIII; Dürr 1777, p. 249; Haller 1903, p. 50; Kirsch 1903, pp. X, XII.

454 See Appendix two.

455 Bion de Marlavagne 1875, p. 279; Mortet & Deschamps 1929, p. 311 ff. The rolls were kept in two different pounds of account, making precise quantification impossible.

456 Archives départementales Aveyron 3 G 249; cf. Bion de Marlavagne 1875, p. 312 ff.

457 Archivo de la catedral de GERONA, Obra de la Seu VI, pp. 2, 3 and 4.

458 Archives départementales Pyrénées-Orientales G 111.

459 Quicherat 1886, pp. 185, 186; Mortet & Deschamps 1929, p. 320. Of the *annualia* granted to the cathedral fabric of SENS for five years in 1279, a subsequent item yielded another 116 l.t., or one-third of the receipts; Quantin 1869, p. 222; *Inventaire-sommaire Yonne* G 1174.

460 Domenge i Mesquida 1997, pp. 120, 121, 235.

461 Schmidt 1889, pp. 7, 8.

462 Hillgarth & Silano 1984, no. 126.

463 Excerpt from the account of their journey published by Durán Gudiol 1956, pp. 367-372.

464 As in PARIS, 1347, see Appendix two.

465 Fabrics profited from the tithe proceeds indirectly, through the allocation of revenues from the bishop's and chapter's *mensae*; Biget 1972, pp. 248, 272-273; Biget 1982, p. 23. (ALBI, late thirteenth century); also Erlande-Brandenburg 1989, pp. 261-262.

466 Summary that takes account of new insights into this complex issue in *Diccionario eclesiastica de España*, in voce '*patrimonio eclesiastico*', '*diezmo*' and '*tercias reales*'; *Vocabulario básico*, in voce '*Diezmos*'.

467 Hermann 1988, pp. 33, 34: '*la fiscalité ecclesiastique espagnole se fonde sur la mystique de la croisade*'; also p. 314.

468 We can no more than touch upon this theme here; see e.g. Ladero Quesada 1982, pp. 190-212; Nieto Soria 1986a, pp. 220-221; idem

1986b, pp. 383-403; idem 1988, pp. 118-123; idem 1993, pp. 311-322; Hermann 1988, pp. 16-39, 314. The tithes played a major role in the ecclesiastical and economic life of Spain, and the tax was not conclusively abolished until 1841. There is currently no comprehensive survey of the issues surrounding the tithes.

469 The *Siete Partidas*, the statutory code compiled under King Alfonso X in the second half of the thirteenth century; cited in Hermann 1988, p. 44.

470 Palomo Fernández 2002, vol. 1, p. 142, vol. 2, p. 310 (doc. 324).

471 Clément 1895, p. 390; Karge 1995, p. 168; Linehan 1971, p. 125 and n. 5. Concerning the primate of Toledo: *Enciclopedia de historia de España*, p. 974. Tithes belonging to the fabric's share were also diverted to other ends: in 1220 the pope granted the bishop of PALENCIA permission to spend a portion of these funds on the university; Abajo Martín 1986, nos 146 and 161 (five years, renewed).

472 *Diccionario eclesiastica de España*, p. 2552; *Vocabulario básico*, p. 141.

473 Here we must leave aside the intricate formulae used to divide the tithes into percentages for the bishop, clergy, fabrics and king, not least because they were subject to constant compensatory adjustment and moreover were of chiefly theoretical significance. For TOLEDO, see Sánchez Herrero 1976, pp. 139-140.

474 *Diccionario eclesiastica de España*, p. 2552, in voce '*tercias reales*'; also *Enciclopedia de historia de España*, p. 1144. Additionally: *Registres Innocent IV*, nos 2538, 6214, 6316, 6439, 6497; *Registres Alexandre VI*, no. 1642. Also Thomassinus 1725, pars 3, liber 2, caput 36, no. 9. Concerning the *tercias reales* and the complicated allocation of the resulting revenues, see e.g. Nieto Soria 1988, pp. 118-123; Nieto Soria 1986, pp. 391-396; Nieto Soria 1994, pp. 312-324. The *tercias reales* were repealed along with the tithes in 1837.

475 Karge 1995, pp. 54-57; Rodríguez Molina 1986, p. 217; Azofra 2006, p. 118.

476 *Colección documental León*, no. 2140; *La Catedral de León*, pp. 62-64, 68; Yarza *et al.* 2004, pp. 121-125, 156. In 1258 the king granted the *tercias reales* to the bishop in order to clear the diocese's debts; Fernández Flórez 1985, p. 293. Also *Registres Alexandre IV*, nos 1642 and 1643: with additional confirmation of the allocation of the annates.

477 'the state of the fabric is good, thanks be to God'; *Colección documental León*, no. 2732; *La Catedral de León*, p. 71.

478 *Registres Innocent IV*, no. 6316.

479 Del Arco 1924, p. 23 and n. 1, pp. 24-28, 33; Latorre Ciria 1992, p. 126; Durán Gudiol 1991, p. 69: deed of 1273.

480 Goñi Gaztambide 1955, pp. 21, 55-58. In some Spanish dioceses it was customary to designate the tithes wholly to the day-to-day maintenance of the clergy, and the first fruits of the harvest, the *primicias*, to the maintenance of the parish church instead.

481 The *primitiae* or *primicias* were the first fruits of the harvest, which were collected by the parish clergy, who were required to bring them to the bishop. He then decided on their final designation; *Vocabulario básico*, p. 154 and *Enciclopedia de historia de España*, p. 975. The *primitiae* had a value of one-quarter of that of the *diezmos*.

482 Archivo de la Catedral de

HUESCA, cuentas de fabrica; also Durán Gudiol 1991, p. 99.

483 *Colección documental León. Actas capitulares*, no. 330 (1379); *Documentación medieval León*, nos 13 and 14 (1419). Also elsewhere: MURCIA 1416; Rodríguez Llopis & García Díaz 1994, pp. 131, 148-149.

484 Account of the journey from 18 September 1412 until 1 April 1413 in Domingo Pérez & Gutiérrez Iglesias 1999, pp. 413-451. Cathedrals in not only Castile and León, but also in Aragon profited from various tithe revenues.

485 Concession in 1416, complaint from the city of Orihuela in 1433; Rodríguez Llopis & García Díaz 1994, pp. 131, 149.

486 For example LEÓN; *Colección documental León*, nos 2853, 2952 (1327).

487 Cal Pardo 1992, no. 4501 (25 May 1566); my thanks to Msgr Cal Pardo for his interpretation of the number 366; letter of 3 April 2001.

488 *'Excusado'* – exempted in the sense of not being required to render them to the collectors of the other tithes; not to be confused with those exempted from taxes. Beginning in 1567 the king laid claim to the *excusados* to fund fighting in the Low Countries: *Vocabulario básico*, p. 152; *Diccionario eclesiastica de España*, p. 889.

489 BAEZA-JAEN: Rodríguez Molina 1986, pp. 84, 216 (1368). TOLEDO, the *excusado* is not yet listed in the 1383 account, but is in that from 1418; Torroja Menéndez & Sánchez Palencia 1977, p. 17. LEÓN from the latter half of the fifteenth century; *Colección documental León*, nos 4046, 4057, 4338, 4346, 4784. MALAGA, bishopric as from 1486, granted by the primate of Spain, the archbishop of Toledo, in 1488; Riesco Terrero 1987, pp. 81, 99, 101, 107, 108; Hermann 1988, p. 191.

490 Ten accounts dating from this period have been analysed; see p. xxx.

491 Rodríguez Estévez 1998, pp. 55, 311 (wages); Ladero Quesada 1982, p. 203 (three years: 1491, 1494, 1503).

492 Gutiérrez-Cortines Corral 1987a, p. 106 (the years are mistakenly reversed in the graph).

493 See the interesting but not fully elaborated hypothesis of Gutiérrez-Cortines Corral 1987a, p. 118.

494 OVIEDO 1382, contributions varying in scale from all parishes at the launch of the building works; later converted into a fixed monetary sum of 10 maravedís; De Caso Fernández 1981, p. 162; *Colección documental Oviedo*, no. 4. In ZAMORA likewise a tax levied per parish in 1479; De Lera Maíllo 1999, no. 1681.

495 Concerning the *Voto de Santiago*: *Diccionario eclesiastica de España*, pp. 2783-84; *Enciclopedia de historia de España*, p. 1223; *Vocabulario básico*, p. 456; López Ferreiro 1898-1911, vol. 2, pp. 73-146, especially pp. 132-137, vol. 7, pp. 341 and app. 43; Herbers 1994, pp. 233-239; Pérez Rodríguez 1994, pp. 186-201; González Vázquez 1996, pp. 245-252; Rey Castelao 1987, especially pp. 245-252 and 463-464.

496 Rey Castelao 1987, p. 458 n. 1; Pérez Rodríguez 1994, pp. 187-198: the geography of the *Voto*.

497 González Vázquez 1996, pp. 246. At the time of the definitive formation of the capitular *mensa* in 1228, receipts from the *Voto* were divided between the archbishop and chapter; the fabric's share is not specified; López Ferreiro 1898-1911, vol. 5, p. 126 and app. 13, p. 39.

498 Barreiro Somoza 1987, p. 326.

499 *L'Église et le peuple chrétien*, pp. 73-74; Nylander 1953,

pp. 208, 220.

500 *Kulturhistorisk Leksikon*, in voce *'fabrica'*, pp. 120, 128 and *'tiend'*, passim. Given the absence of quantitative data on cathedral fabrics throughout Scandinavia, only the main points are covered here. For procedural practices at the cathedral of UPPSALA, which disposed over a portion of the rural church tithe from the beginning of the thirteenth century, and later (and following much debate) also over the poor tithe, see Nylander 1953, pp. 230-244. For Finland, see *Diplomatarium suecanum*, no. 3105 (19 January 1335): the rural churches are in good repair, whereas the cathedral of ABØ is *'ruinosa'* and must therefore be aided by its daughter churches.

501 Concerning tithes in the diocese of LINKÖPING, see Nylander 1953, pp. 218-228.

502 *Diplomatarium suecanum*, no. 327; on the same day the cathedral of UPPSALA received a mere 40-day indulgence; no. 326. Also no. 352, 20 December 1245; Nylander 1953, p. 224; *Kulturhistorisk Leksikon*, in voce *'tiend'*, p. 297.

503 *Diplomatarium suecanum*, no. 957 (12 February 1288); Cnattingius *et al.* 1987, pp. 282-286.

504 *Diplomatarium suecanum*, no. 2655 (23 February 1328).

505 Cnattingius *et al.* 1987, p. 286; Nylander 1953, p. 225. There may be a link between the usurpation of the parish church tithes and the fourteenth-century transfer of the relics of local saints to the cathedrals of LINKÖPING and LUND; Fröjmark 1992, p. 198.

506 For example, UPPSALA; *Diplomatarium suecanum*, pp. 238, 242.

507 Cnattingius *et al.* 1987, p. 292: the *capella omnium (fidelium) animarum*, which was later administered by the cathedral fabric, received a third of the share for the poor, or a two-ninths portion.

508 Cnattingius *et al.* 1987, p. 296.

509 *Kulturhistorisk Leksikon*, in voce *'Olafsskatt'* and *'Kyrkans finanser'*, p. 664; *L'Église et le peuple chrétien*, p. 78.

510 Sweden: *Registres Innocent IV*, no. 1088 (20 February 1245): valid for three years in the diocese of LUND.

EIGHT Voluntary contributions from the faithful

511 Lacomblet 1857, p. 172.

512 Mortet & Deschamps 1929, pp. 95-96.

513 Lehmann-Brockhaus 1955-1960, no. 1375; Julier 1970.

514 Passages such as those cited above bear the stamp of commonplaces. Concerning the abbey of Morigni (built 1109-1921) we are told: '[...] *aedificia omnia haec quae cernis ex pauperum eleemosinis construxerunt*'; Mortet 1911, p. 341. The monastery of St Gilduinus was raised at great speed around 1165 *'de minutis fidelium solis eleemosynis'*; Mortet & Deschamps 1929, p. 88. And concerning the abbot of the Andres monastery near Boulognes a source from the latter half of the twelfth century records that *'numquam a principibus et potentibus subsidium mendicavit* [...]'; Fagniez 1898/1900, no. 126; Mortet 1911, p. 391.

515 Thomas 1881, pp. 513, 514. Concerning the different forms of Marian worship practised at CHARTRES and its history in relation to pilgrimage, see J. Bugslag in Blick & Tekippe 2005, pp. 135-183. Such situations were not uncommon; in PAMPLONA the king had to reprieve the building works three years after their launch; Goñi Gaztambide 1955, pp. 18-19.

516 The *Sancta Camisia* worn by the Virgin Mary, which was the cathedral's most important relic is traditionally held to have been a gift from Charles the Bald in

876. Concerning this and other relics at CHARTRES, see Lautier 2003, pp. 23-29. Concerning the role of the pilgrimage, see J. Bugslag in Blick & Tekippe 2005, pp. 135-183, especially p. 153.

517 The revival of the building lodge at CHARTRES made possible with the offerings of the faithful has been rendered in a graph by John James. Having made a minute analysis of the building campaigns between 1194 and 1223, he calculated the cost price of each against 1972 price levels - thus as if the cathedral had been built using modern techniques, as it were. Building activity peaked in 1210; James 1972, pp. 58 (cash-flow chart) and 60; republished in James 2007, pp. 503-519.

518 Mortet 1911, p. 368; Rudolph 1990, pp. 11, 280-281, 322-323. Concerning pilgrims' expectations for a costly shrine, see Sumption 1975, pp. 153, 154.

519 Post 1967, pp. 24-26; Hofman 2003, p. 781.

520 Aubert 1960/1961, vol. 119, p. 112; Kletzl 1939, pp. 11, 12; Roosegaarde Bisschop 1956, pp. 177, 193 ff., 210.

521 '[...] *ingentem molem grandemque machinam tanti edificii eminenciamque turrium antiquorum* [...] *ventorum impulsu ac frequentibus et urentibus magis ac magis quassata et corrosa est ymbribus*'; *Urkundenbuch Lübeck*, no. 1652.

522 *Urkundenbuch Strassburg*, vol. 2, p. 40; Paulus 1922-1923, vol. 2, p. 237. Reinhardt 1960, p. 20. See also the passage from the bishop of CAMBRAI's formal encyclical letter in support of the cathedral building works (fifteenth century): '*columpnarum et testudinum pulcritudine decorata et sculpturarum ad dei laudes artificiocis subtilitatibus adornata*'; Archives départementales Nord 4 G 1082.

523 *Registrum Baldock et al.*, p. 217; Harvey 1972, p. 41.

524 Post 1967, pp. 40, 41; Hofman 2003, p. 788.

525 Cf. Lopez 1952, p. 438.

526 Paulus 1922-1923, vol. 1, pp. 13, 28, 29. '*Sicut aqua extinguit ignem ita elemosina extinguit peccatum*'; *Urkundenbuch Bremen*, vol. 4, no. 264 (1400). Also PALENCIA 1432: '*así como el agua mata el fuego así la limosna mata el pecado*'; García Cuesta 1954, p. 93.

527 The issue of the giving of gifts is a separate area of historical and anthropological study that cannot be broached here; for a recent overview, see Bijsterveld 2007.

528 Concerning the history of the relics and veneration of relics, see Herrmann-Mascard 1975; Heinzelmann 1979; Crook 1999/2000, pp. 6-39. Concise overview of the veneration of saints and their relics in Miedema 2003, pp. 346-377. Research into the significance of relics and the cult of relics, which has seen explosive growth in recent years (see overview in *Kunstchronik* 2007, pp. 271-282), falls outside the scope of this study.

529 Given that every altar held one or more relics, each church had relics of its own; Braun 1924, vol. 1, p. 526.

530 Exh. cat. RHEIMS 2001, pp. 171-172.

531 See Chapter 7 in Crook 1999/2000; Heinzelmann 1979, p. 30; also concerning the concepts of *inventio, elevatio, depositio, translatio, adventus, ingressus* and *ostentatio ad conspectum populi*: pp. 43, 52, 66, 77, 80-82.

532 Mortet 1911, p. 322; Mortet & Deschamps 1929, pp. 67-69, 257-259. Additional examples in Branner 1961, p. 29 and Seymour 1968, p. 47 ff.

533 Southern 1953, p. 286; also Herrmann-Mascard 1975, p. 403.

534 On the distinction between *elevatio* and *translatio*, see

Herrmann-Mascard 1975, p. 82 and n. 40.

535 Herrmann-Mascard 1975, p. 186.

536 Concerning the relationship between the cult of relics and the expectation of miracles up through the thirteenth century, see the extensive survey by Signori 1995.

537 An investigation into 3000 miracles attributed to intercession by a saint after death and recorded as such between 1066 and 1300, primarily in England, has shown that roughly half these miracles occurred at a reliquary shrine in a church, whilst the remaining half took place before the pilgrim set out to give thanks. Ninety percent of miracles concern the healing of physical or mental ailments; the remaining ten percent other incidents such as rescue from a storm at sea; Finucane 1977, pp. 69, 88, 111.

538 Van Cauwenbergh 1922, passim; Boeren 1962, p. 34, Van Herwaarden 1978, passim.

539 Also expressed in portal and window iconography. For CHARTRES, see Lautier 2003; she has established that relics of 64 percent of the 186 saints portrayed in the windows were present in the cathedral before or during the building period.

540 Two examples: Concerning the possession of the true relics of St Eligius, see the legal conflict between the cathedral of NOYON and the abbey of St Eloi that began in 1252. This conflict was settled in the cathedral's favour in a ruling of the Paris *parlement* in 1462; in 1256 the abbey accused the canons that they were diverting *vota et oblationes* away from the abbey and to the cathedral; Guyotjeannin 1990. Concerning rivalry over the *oblationes* arising from the Marian pilgrimage between the cathedral of St Etienne in CHÂLONS-EN-CHAMPAGNE and the collegiate church of Notre-Dame-en-Vaux, resulting in a papal arbitral ruling in 1180, see Villes 2001, p. 225.

541 Mortet & Deschamps 1929, pp. 199-201; see also Cheney 1973, p. 28 and Von Simson 1956, p. 170 ff.

542 The absence of important relics in places like NORWICH explains the lack of any large-scale building plans; Fernie 1993, p. 157; see also Brooke 1999, pp. 183-185, on Norman cathedrals.

543 Heinzelmann 1979, p. 99.

544 In all of the 25 translations performed between 1010 and 1185 throughout the entire territory from the Loire to the Rhine, only one case involved a cathedral (MENDE), whilst the vast majority concerned abbeys; Sigal 1990, p. 214.

545 Coulton 1936, p. 98.

546 Herrmann-Mascard 1975, pp. 409, 412.

547 Deckers 1870, pp. 215-216. The small city of Lier just south of Antwerp saw many miracles take place thanks to the intercession of the parish church's patron, St Gummarus, from 1475 on; the book of wonders records 232; Vroom 1983, pp. 51-53 and 120. Van Drakenborch was appointed master of the cathedral fabric many times between 1462 and 1493; see Chapter 3, n. 164.

548 Ferraris 1852-1857, vol. 4, col. 423 ff. The seminal work on indulgences continues to be Paulus 1922-1923. See also Piekarek 1973 and Moeller 1989, pp. 540-546: the term *indulgentia* dates from the thirteenth century. Good overview in Miedema 2003, pp. 377-397. Also Swanson 2007, p. 8.

549 Paulus 1922-1923, vol. 1, pp. 193, 259 ff., vol. 2, pp. 80 ff., 213, vol. 3, p. 415 ff.

550 Idem, vol. 2, p. 224.

551 Cited in Foreville 1958, p. 50; Paulus 1922-1923, vol. 2, p. 226.

552 STRASBOURG 1275: Maurer 2002, p. 241.
553 Paulus 1922-1923, vol. 2, p. 226 ff., vol. 3, p. 429 ff.
554 Idem, vol. 1, p. 193, vol. 3, p. 516 ff.
555 Idem, vol. 3, p. 450 ff.
556 Idem, vol. 1, p. 132 ff.
557 One of the earliest indulgences was that for the cathedral of MAGUELONE near Aigues-Mortes and dates from between 1030 and 1060; Mortet 1911, pp. 88, 89; Paulus 1922-1923, vol. 1, pp. 143, 144 n. 1. The cathedral lay so isolated in its marshland surroundings that in 1035 the pope granted an indulgence to all who would be conveyed there by boat or via the rickety bridge to be buried; Bonde 1994, pp.180-181; Lemaitre 1995, p. 85.
558 Also '*manum caritativam porrigere*'; Paulus 1922-1923, vol. 3, p. 429.
559 Neuhausen 1994, pp. 219-274. Chiefly in relation to Germany. For Westphalia, see Prinz 1971, pp. 151 ff.: 44 indulgences issued between 1282 and 1302, including one for the cathedral of PADERBORN; between 1312 and 1362 71 so-called collective indulgences were issued, including one for the cathedral of MINDEN and another for that of PADERBORN; of the indulgences issued between 1415 and 1505, not a single one was designated for a cathedral. Also Chiffoleau 1984, p. 258. Of the seven major papal indulgence campaigns between 1505 and 1517, one was designated for the tower of KONSTANZ Cathedral and one for the cathedral of TRIER; Moeller 1989.

NINE Donations made for the fabric in the cathedral

560 See above p. 82. Cheney 1973, pp. 30, 31. Detailed canon law overview in Bordenave 1643, pp. 598-603.
561 Concerning collection boxes and the rituals surrounding the making of offerings in money or in kind, see Kroos 1985, and for the northern Netherlands: Meindersma 1973, both with illustrations of offertory boxes. For Scandinavia: *Kulturhistorisk Leksikon*, in voce '*kiste*'. Detailed description of a richly ornamented and particularly grand '*vasculum tripes pro conservandis oblatis*' dating from 1578 in the chapel of St Sigismund in KRAKOW Cathedral in Franaszek & Przybyszewski 1991, p. 51.
562 Bion de Marlavagne 1875, p. 109 (RODEZ).
563 Mortet & Deschamps 1929, p. 321 (AUTUN).
564 'from the box, which stands in the choir of the said church'; Assier 1855, p. 14 (TROYES).
565 In BASEL the fabric had three collection boxes set up inside the cathedral: at the base of the rood loft (the '*locus petitionis*', fig. 5), at the main entrance and at the crossing; La Roche 1888, p. 91; Hieronimus 1938, p. 590.
566 *Regestum Clementis papae v*, no. 4771. Concerning the indulgence, see Paulus 1922-1923, vol. 2, p. 40.
567 Concerning the highly regimented ritual surrounding the veneration of Thomas Becket at four spots, the *loca sacra*, each linked with his martyrium, see Hearn 1994, pp. 44-47 ('the itinerary of the cult'); Woodman 1981, fig. 136; Nilson 1998, pp. 211-215.
568 'this is the offertory box of the fabric of St James; this is the fabric of the church'. 'To you, sir, from Lombardy, this is the offertory box of the fabric of St James. Go here to give your money'; López Ferreiro 1898-1911, vol. 5, p. 183 and app. 25, pp. 64-65. Exhaustive discussion of this ritual in Vázquez de Parga 1993, vol. 1, pp. 147-150, vol. 3, doc. 80 (1263-1272?). There was a separate ritual for Germans: exh. cat. Munich

1984, p. 257. Also Kroesen 2003, pp. 168-169, and Pérez Rodriguez 1996, pp. 144-154; he points out that not a single medieval documentary record of the proceeds has been preserved. For the practice of loudly promoting the relics, also elsewhere, such as in England, see Nilson 1998, p. 97. In PAMPLONA the *pedidor del obrero* was allowed to grant indulgences from a specific spot, but not - except on three feast days - to go around surpliced with a *bacin*; Goñi Gaztambide 1996, p. 104.

569 On this, see Herrmann-Mascard 1975, pp. 209, 213.

570 Idem, p. 276. Additionally Cheney 1973, p. 30. On arrangements at English cathedrals: Nilson 1998, pp.128-134 (*custos feretri, feretrarius, tumbarius*, etc.); Quicherat 1886, p. 195 (TROYES). Satirical description in Rabelais (1932, pp. 27-31): Panurge hears the pardoner's words '*centuplum accipies*' (thou shalt receive a hundredfold, to whit in Heaven) as '*centuplum accipe*' (take a hundredfold) and devises a trick that he subsequently applies at several different *bassains des pardons*, secretly switching a small coin for a gold one worth a hundred times as much.

571 Brutails 1899-1901, vol. 12, pp. 405, 406 n. 10 (BORDEAUX).

572 Gadan 1851, p. 1; Quicherat 1886, vol. 2, p. 195; Coulton 1928, p. 575; Herrmann-Mascard 1975, p. 289 (TROYES).

573 Assier 1855, p. 14; Quicherat 1886, vol. 2, p. 195. TROYES additionally had a '*rec. du rapport des reliques*' that was registered on a monthly basis.

574 Hieronimus 1938, p. 562, glossary, in voce '*petitio*' as designation of place in the *Münster*; La Roche 1888, p. 91. See also the record of various collection boxes, e.g. in the BASEL fabric accounts for 1481/82 f 47 (BASEL, Stadtarchiv): '*pixis super altare peticionis matricis*', '*nova pixis quam posui ante ymaginem b. Virginis in ambitu*', '*truncus magnus ante peticionem matricis*'. Also exh. cat. BASEL 2001, pp. 330-331.

575 For example in RODEZ: '*pro questa bassini operis que fit in ecclesia*'; Archives départementales de l'Aveyron 3 G 249; BASEL: La Roche 1888, p. 93; In REGENSBURG several times a year: 1459 account; Schuegraf 1855, p. 76. '*Bassin*', '*bashin*' and in Spanish '*bacin*' means collection plate; see for ROUEN *Notre-Dame de Rouen*, p. 128 and below n. 1077.

576 Paulus 1922-1923, vol. 1, p. 132 ff.; vol. 2, pp. 1 ff., 236 ff.; vol. 3, pp. 150, 433 ff. For England, see Swanson 2007, p. 51 ff.

577 Idem, vol. 2, pp. 61-72.

578 See Denifle 1897-1899, vol. 1, passim; vol. 2, pp. 150 ff., 160, 166.

579 Paulus 1922-1923, vol. 2, p. 5. He also issued large indulgences for the cathedral of LYON, where he had resided six years; Bégule 1880, pp. 43, 44.

580 Paulus 1922-1923, vol. 2, p. 19; Gardelles 1963, p. 17. Plus seven years and seven quarantines during the 20 days before and after this feast day and 40 days once daily.

581 Paulus 1922-1923, vol. 3, p. 177.

582 Idem, pp. 153, 450 ff. From the time of Pope John XXII (1316-1334), these fees varied depending on the importance of the bull, ranging from 20 to 100 ducats; Bordeaux 1969, p. 117.

583 In the fourteenth century cardinals received the right to grant indulgences of not more than 100 days; Paulus 1922-1923, vol. 2, p. 218 ff.

584 Delehaye 1926-1928, passim, has compiled all collective indulgence bulls known to him, comprising around 1300 bulls over the

period 1287-1541. Most contain the clause '*manus adiutrices porrigere*'. Also Paulus 1922-1923, vol. 2, p. 61 ff. and Prinz 1971, p. 125 ff.

585 Schuegraf 1847/1848, vol. 11, p. 82; Janner 1876, p. 180.

586 *España Sagrada*, vol. 34, p. 213. Might this and the previous case in fact concern many separate letters, and thus not collective letters in the proper sense? See Prinz 1971, p. 125 ff. A handful of collective letters was embellished with historiated initials; these sumptuous leaves were intended for display in the cathedral church. The oldest painted leaf dates from 1326; none are known from the period between 1364 and 1454. Of the 83 letters issued for Germany, only one was for a cathedral (MINDEN, 1341, no. 36); Delehaye 1926-1928, vol. 46, p. 227; Radocsay 1971, pp. 58-59; Erben 1923, pp. 172, 180 ff.; Prinz 1971, p. 128 ff. See also Fournier 1923, pp. 116, 122-131.

587 Collective indulgence bulls could be valid for ten years; Delehaye 1926-1928, vol. 46, p. 332. The term set for papal indulgences is a complicated matter as the issuing pope or one of his successors could also revoke indulgences; Paulus 1922-1923, vol. 3, p. 159; see below p. 157.

588 Overview of the indulgences and other privileges granted by the archbishops of COLOGNE between 1248 and 1322 in Stehkämper 1979/1980, p. 26.

589 For example, the bishop of STRASBOURG's letter of 28 January 1275; *Urkundenbuch Strassburg*, vol. 2, no. 40.

590 Contemporaries were already voicing theological objections against this practice; see for example the treatise on indulgences attributed to Hugo de Novo Castro (c. 1300); Hauréau 1896, p. 233. See also Angenendt *et al.* 1995 on *gezählte Frömmigkeit* and *Heilsarithmetik*; in French: *comptabilité de l'au-delà*.

591 *Summaria* or *sommaires*; Boeren 1962, p. 90; Fournier 1923, pp. 118, 121.

592 In 1492 a booklet was published in COLOGNE specifying which indulgences were available to earn on which days in which of the city's churches – totalling 27 years and 6230 days, together with the spiritual benefits of 7000 masses – followed by a systematic listing of the relics preserved in each of COLOGNE's churches; Falk 1879, pp. 68, 69; *Ad Summum 1248*, K 4. See fig. 29.

593 Fabric account for 1349/50: 8 s. paid to a scribe to copy out 800 indulgence letters; Erskine 1983, p. 283; Cook 1957, p. 300.

594 The earliest recorded example dates from 1455 (Erfurt); Eisermann in Swanson 2006, p. 311. He describes the issue of printed indulgence letters as a 'media event'; idem, pp. 309-330. For Germany: COLOGNE: Neuhausen 1994, pp. 129-130; also Angenendt *et al.* 1995, p. 55 (on the faithful touching the displayed indulgence letters and seals). Cathedrals had always been a very small minority amongst the institutions issued with indulgences, also before the fifteenth century: of the 142 indulgences allocated to the Westphalian dioceses of MÜNSTER, MINDEN and PADERBORN between 1282 and 1505, only three were for their cathedrals; Prinz 1971, passim. Of the 47 known English printed indulgence letters from between 1498 and around 1525, only one relates to a cathedral (HEREFORD). For Spain: the chapter of ZARAGOZA ordered 5000 indulgence letters in 1501; *La Seo de Zaragoza*, p. 193. In HUESCA the fabric had 6000 letters printed in 1499 and 7000 in 1500, which were

circulated and sold throughout the diocese from on horseback or mule-back. Returns over two years came to 13,263 s., or 25 annual wages; Durán Gudiol 1991, pp. 131, 135. The book printing trade was also deployed to combat false indulgences, as attested by the 1487 fabric account from PAMPLONA for the printing of 2300 '*bulas para los simoniadores que han simoniado las indulgencias de la obra y confratia de la catedral*'; *Tecnología y sociedad*, p. 208.

595 *Reallexikon zur deutschen Kunstgeschichte*, in voce '*Ablass*', c. 82. See also Ramisch *et al.* 1998, no. 10369, 1492 *custos* rolls from FREISING Cathedral, item: '*ain grosse Tafel abgeschriben dar an Indulgenz altaris Sancti Sigismundi sein geschriben*'.

596 'Donate to the construction of Our Lady and earn the great indulgence and great pardon that is granted by holy popes, councils, cardinals, archbishops and bishops, which God in his mercy has made large'; La Roche 1888, p. 93; Mone 1834, p. 323. Different version in Hieronimus 1938, pp. 226, 521 (*ceremoniale Basiliensis episcopatus*, 1517). The cathedral of STRASBOURG followed a similar practice, paying an annual stipend of 3 s. for '*item dem do rûffet "stürent zu dem wercke"*'; Fuchs 1974, p. 31, n. 21.

597 Paulus 1922-1923, vol. 2, p. 106, vol. 3, p. 150; Norman Housley in Swanson 2006, passim and p. 283, overview of indulgences issued for the crusades against the Hussites in Bohemia, the Turks in the Balkan and the Moors in Spain between 1417 and 1517.

598 Nolet & Boeren 1951, p. 290.

599 In 1438 the chapter of OVIEDO managed to secure a Jubilee indulgence valid for sixteen days before and after the feast of the Exaltation of the Holy Cross (14 September), which it sought in connection with the presence of an importance relic of the True Cross in the *Arca de las reliquias*. The indulgence was renewed in 1480 upon payment of a substantial 65,730 maravedís (around ten annual wages) to the curia. A unique aspect of this plenary indulgence was that it was not suspended whilst the crusade indulgence was in effect, as was the case in other dioceses in Spain. The receipts cannot have been large as the fabric, '*estava en grand nesesydad*', had to borrow the sum from the canons. Sanz Fuentes 1998, pp. 783-793; *Colección documental Oviedo*, no. 48.

600 Sachet 1914, pp. 1-5, 145, 187-218; also Hoffman 1984, p. 25.

601 Sachet 1914, pp. 219-248, 281 ff.

602 Idem, pp. 301 ff., 502.

603 Idem, pp. 324-342; 499-528: 43 receipts over 200 years. Also the fabric rolls in the Archives départementales Rhône 10 G 1608 ff. An analogous indulgence was issued in 1395 by Boniface IX for BREMEN for a period of nine years; Klink 1988, pp.124-138, with a detailed description of the procession and displays of relics in the cathedral and four main churches, which together symbolized the five wounds of Christ.

604 Chapman 1907, vol. 1, pp. 111, 116, 119; Atkinson 1933, pp. XXII, 12, 31; Salzman 1948/1953, vol. 4, p. 70 ff.

605 Cook 1957, p. 32 with additional examples; Herrmann-Mascard 1975, p. 170. Especially Nilson 1998, pp. 216-218.

606 For example, the shrine of St Thomas Becket in CANTERBURY; Woodruff & Danks 1912, pp. 78-79; Woodman 1981, pp. 221-222. Also the shrine of St Cuthbert in DURHAM on the saint's and other feast days: evocative description from 1593 in *Rites Durham*, pp. 3-6: underneath the shrine were four places to kneel 'in time of theire devout offeringes and fervent prayers'. CANTERBURY and DURHAM used a hoist to display the shrine. Also Lehmberg 1988, pp. 50-51.

607 See the exhaustive study by Kühne 2000 on the *ostensio reliquiarum* in Germany; see graphs on pp. 581 and 583. Relic displays were organized in many churches, with those in cathedrals being amongst the most important; idem, pp. 645-646. Also Boeren 1962, section 23, 29; Beissel 1890, p. 124; Herrmann-Mascard 1975, pp. 195-203; Braun 1924, vol. 2, p. 545. The relics were announced in loud voice by an *Ausrufer, vocalissimus* or *praecursor.*

608 See Nilson 1998, pp. 144-167, 211-228, with data on the cathedrals of CANTERBURY, ELY, NORWICH, HEREFORD, LINCOLN, DURHAM and also YORK and WORCESTER. Of the 19 cathedrals, 14 had a 'major saint'; Nilson 1998, p. 6. Also Swanson 1989, pp. 225-228; Lehmberg 1988, p. 31 (sharp decline in receipts after c. 1520); p. 69 ff. (dismantling of many shrines under Henry VIII between 1537 and 1540).

609 Boeren 1962, section 30. Ely: Salzman 1948/1953, vol. 4, p. 50. CHARTRES: Von Simson 1956, p. 166. NOYON: Seymour 1968, p. 25.

610 Boeren 1962, p. 5; Kühne 2000, passim. The oldest known indulgence for the veneration of relics dates from 1119. For the veneration of images of saints from 1208 on, see Paulus 1922-1923, vol. 2, p. 234; *Lexikon für Theologie und Kirche*, in voce *'Reliquienverehrung'*.

611 'the sum of items of relics is 7118 items; the sum of the indulgences is 49826 years'; citation from the now untraceable *Heiltumsbuch*; Falk 1879, p. 70; Paulus 1922-1923, vol. 3, p. 290. See also Boeren 1962, p. 85 ff.; Guth 1970, p. 148; Beissel 1892, p. 31. Cf. the list of relics at Reading Abbey around 1190, numbering 242 items; Sumption 1975, p. 116.

612 *Heiltumsbücher* are known to have been printed for the cathedrals of COLOGNE (1492), BAMBERG (1493), WÜRZBURG (1493), VIENNA (1502 and 1514) and TRIER (1513); Boeren 1962, p. 87 ff.; Falk 1879, pp. 59-79; Paulus 1922-1923, vol. 3, p. 287 ff.; Kühne 2000, pp. 34-50. See figs 11 and 12. Large (c. 600 x 750 mm) broadsheets were also occasionally printed. Lists of church treasuries of relics were also copied out by hand, such as in MAGDEBURG - possibly as a template for a printer - and especially the sumptuous codex from BAMBERG of 1509/10, with drawings of all the reliquaries; see the facsimile edition of the *Bamberger Heiltum*. For TRIER after the discovery of the *Sancta Tunica* in 1512, see Scheckmann 1996 and Seibrich 1995, pp. 91-96.

613 Called *'miracula, de quibus facti sunt libelli'* by Augustine (354-430) in his *De Civitate Dei*; Gregory of Tours (538-594) also notes the existence of books of miracles; Beissel 1913, p. 69; Beissel 1890, p. 115; Sumption 1975, p. 151 ff.; Nilson 1998, in voce *'miracula'*. See also the instructions in the *Ordinarius van Sion* (c. 1275) concerning what to do *'si fiant aliqua miracula in aliqua ecclesia'*, which includes having the beneficiary of the miracle swear an oath; Huot 1973, pp. 541, 618. Concerning the procedure for dealing with miracles in early thirteenth-century LINCOLN, see Sigal 1990, p. 208.

614 Delisle 1848, p. 342 n. 3.

615 Concerning books of

miracles, i.e. collected narratives of miracles, see Beissel 1890, p. 115; Beissel 1913, p. 69; Boeren 1962, p. 74 ff.; Schreiber 1938, pp. 135-139; Signori 1995, passim and Karte I and II.

616 The earliest chronicled miracles relate to abbeys; all five Norman miracle compilations from between 1047 and 1100 derive from abbeys. Of the eight miracle compilations dating from between 1106 and 1189, only one relates to a cathedral (COUTANCES); Richard 1975, pp. 185-189.

617 Schreiber 1938, pp. 35, 93 n. 14, 94 n. 21; Mortet 1911, p. 320. DURHAM (St Cuthbert): Aird 1993, pp.19-21. COUTANCES: Pigeon 1876, p. 377 ff.; Signori 1995, pp. 77-99. LAUSANNE: *Cartulaire Lausanne*, no. 804 ff. STRASBOURG: *Monumenta Germaniae Historica* S.S., vol. 17, pp. 114-117 (1280-1290); Signori 1990 and Signori 1995, pp. 247-269 and Karte XI on the geographical distribution. CANTERBURY: *History of Thomas Becket*, vol. 1, pp. 137-545, vol. 2, pp. 21-258; Finucane 1977, p. 121; public readings of the miracle stories were organized in the chapter room ('*publice recitatis*'); Druffner 1993, p. 265 n. 66. NORWICH AND WORCESTER: Finucane 1977, pp. 118, 130. With the exception of CANTERBURY, all of these cases concern regional pilgrimage sites and a travel radius of two to three days, or between 60 and 90 km. The major pilgrimage churches in and en route to ROME and SANTIAGO and that of CANTERBURY all had a range of 500 to 700 km or more: Sigal 1990, p. 199. In the late Middle Ages a great many miracles were further recorded to a set protocol, a case in point being KRAKOW, which produced five compilations, comprising 1446 miracles, between 1430 and 1520, most of them linked with the cathedral; Witkowska 1981, p. 221.

618 Thomas 1881, pp. 514, 515, 517, 520, 521, 522, 539. Concerning the CHARTRES book of miracles, see also Chédeville 1973, pp. 95 n. 92, 511, and Kunstmann 1973, passim; detailed analysis in Signori 1995, pp.174-202.

619 See the proceeds registered in the 1464-1500 *custos* rolls from the cathedral of BAMBERG. The year 1493 was an exception, which saw the issue of the *Heiltumsbuch* in four editions and a corresponding sixfold rise in the offerings – 300 pounds as opposed to 50; Kühne 2000, p. 284.

620 Nilson 1998 p. 139: 'In none of the surviving series of shrine accounts is there a regular entry for transferring offerings in the fabric fund'.

621 Concerning the earliest preserved book of Marian miracles, from COUTANCES (1128-1135), see Signori 1995, pp. 77-98 and 320 (map), p. 92 (regarding Vitalis); she notes the key significance of the cathedral building. Also Le Patourel 1944, p. 138 n. 5; Pigeon 1876, pp. 370-372; Delisle 1848, pp. 345, 346; Mortet 1911, p. 145: '*confitens b. Mariae et ipsius ecclesiae servum emptitium fore* [...] *eidem ecclesiae capitagium proprii capitis annuatim reddere*'.

622 Archives départementales Seine-Inférieure G 2481-2518. This proportion shifts in the sixteenth century: G 2522 ff.

623 Chapman 1907, vol. 1, pp. 17, 74, 119; the figures are added up under a, e and f. See also Atkinson 1933, pp. XXII, XXIII. Additional figures in Nilson 1998, pp. 154-156: the proceeds registered in the sacrist rolls peaked around 1400 at £100 (32 annual wages).

624 Paris, Bibliothèque Nationale, lat. 9111, f. 206 ff. Cf. *Congrès Archéologique*

de France 130 (1972), p. 526.

625 Accounts for 1373/74, 1375/76: Paris, Bibliothèque Nationale, lat. 9113, f. 1 ff.; accounts for 1401/02, 1402/03, 1409/10: LONDON, British Museum Add. ms. 15083, f. 106 ff.

626 *Inventaire-sommaire Aube* G 1585; approximately 20 annual wages of an unskilled labourer; d'Avenel 1894-1912, vol. 3, p. 579.

627 *Inventaire-sommaire Yonne* G 1124 ff. Used for modification of the clerestory and the construction of chapels; Chartraire n.d., p. 15.

628 Ramisch *et al.* 1998, passim; see vol. 2, p. 223, in voce '*Opferstock, cippus, Stock*'.

629 The proceeds ranged from 319 l.t. to 143 l.t. between 1495 and 1502.

630 '*De arche, de bassinis*': 54 l.t. of the 373 l.t. (net); Archives départementales Puy-de-Dôme 3 G arm. 18, sac B, cote 25.

631 Arbellot 1852, pp. 69, 70.

632 '*De tabella et pixidibus ecclesie*': 54 l.t.; '*de tronco*': 18 s. of total receipts of 356 l.t.; *Inventaire-sommaire Somme* G 1157.

633 Collection box (not counting offerings at the grave of Bishop Lescrope): £57 of total receipts of £519; Raine 1859, pp. 30-32.

634 In 1382, 220 l., or seven percent, of the total receipt of 519 lb. (also including gifts in kind), or 20 percent; Hanauer 1901-1902, vol. 21, pp. 162, 166.

635 Schuegraf 1855, p. 75.

636 Archives départementales Aveyron 3 G 249.

637 Here we will not consider conditional donations and bequests, generally comprising property assets (estates, houses, annuities, etc.) burdened with financial obligations, though they were of undeniable significance in determining the structure of fabric finances – for instance in STRASBOURG; Hanauer 1901-1902, vol. 21, p. 162 ff., and Doré 2007, p. 37.

638 Account for 1415; Raine 1859, pp. 28-36: heading '*elemosyna et legata*'.

639 Schuegraf 1855, pp. 73-75.

640 La Roche 1888, p. 102, identifies as the largest gifts: 150 gros, 40 gros and 30 gros.

641 Account for 1419/20: '*rec. de laiz d'argent*', with donor lists; Assier 1855, p. 19; cf. the item: '*de la femme Jacquinot, bourrelier, malade, et lui fut porté le pied de St. Marguerite et fut delivrée* [...]'.

642 Bion de Marlavagne 1875, p. 110.

643 Arbellot 1852, p. 71.

644 Neuwirth 1893, pp. 123-147, discusses artistic patronage amongst the aristocracy and citizens of PRAGUE, with little mention of the cathedral.

645 Such as in CHARTRES after 1194; Thomas 1881, p. 509.

646 The solemn ritual almsgiving movements known as *le feste delle offerte* conducted in the Italian *duomi* are not considered here, since there the building works were run not by the chapter but – usually – by the city or a civic institution. Concerning the almsgiving movement in MILAN between 1387 and 1390, see Vroom 1981, pp. 146-148; in the fifteenth century: Boucheron 1998, pp. 548-552; also Rondinini in *Finanziare cattedrali*, pp. 107-120; Cattaneo 1985, pp. 80-85. Concerning the obligatory '*offerta dei ceri*' (wax and wax candles) in SIENA in the thirteenth and fourteenth centuries, forming by far the largest source of income, see Georgi & Moscadelli in *Finanziare cattedrali*, pp. 11-106 ('*quod omnes ceri ad Opus deveniant*'), graph 3, p. 81. Also in Orvieto: Riccetti in *Finanziare cattedrali*, pp. 214.

647 Enlart 1902, p. 86, cites a passage from Gregory of Tours (538-594). See also Niermeyer 1954-1976, in voce '*matricularius*'.

648 Booz 1956, pp. 25, 92; see also Frances de Urrutigoyti 1665, caput 13, nos 120, 130.

649 David 1965, passim; Van Werveke 1904, p. 343; Du Colombier 1973, p. 18; Lesne 1936/1943, vol. 6, pp. 270-276; Salzman 1952, p. 3; Jones 1952, p. 502; Niermeyer 1954-1976, in voce '*angaria*'. An example of the exploitation of serfs by the bishops of EICHSTÄTT in the first half of the eleventh century in Lehmann-Brockhaus 1938, no. 337; see also Evans 1948, p. 55.

650 David 1965, p. 1122.

651 Lesne 1936/1943, vol. 6, p. 276. Corvee duty was also exacted for the construction of city walls, for example in NANTES in the late fourteenth century (1500 people, also called in from surrounding villages), in ANGERS in 1477 and in NARBONNE in 1355; Rigaudière 1985, pp. 35-36.

652 Enlart 1902, p. 186 n. 3; Aubert 1960/1961, vol. 118, p. 249 ff.; Mortet & Deschamps 1929, pp. 280, 281 and n. 2 (latter half of the thirteenth century in the diocese of RODEZ).

653 Du Colombier 1973, p. 18. Also Iogna-Prat 2006, p. 495. Cf. the abbey of St Rémi in RHEIMS active cooperation in the building works in the first half of the eleventh century '*pro facinorum suorum abolitione* [...]'; Mortet 1911, p. 41.

654 Bishop Hugh of LINCOLN (1135-1200) lent a direct hand in the building works at his cathedral, where miracles occurred; Lehmann-Brockhaus 1955-1960, no. 2364; Harvey 1972, p. 236. This is expressly stated in the canonization proceedings; Vauchez 1988a, p. 345; Owen 1994, p. 121.

655 Louis IX (St Louis; 1226-1270) took part in the works at the abbey of Royaumont: '[...] *et pour ce que il vouloit avoir le pardon* [...] *il portoit a la foiz pour ce pierres ou aueunes choses semblables*'; Mortet & Deschamps 1929, p. 243.

656 Paulus 1922-1923, vol. 1, p. 38; the indulgence for personal participation developed independent of and later than those for almsgiving and churchgoing, and existed alongside them up through the end of the Middle Ages.

657 Paulus 1922-1923, vol. 3, p. 434; Rémy 1928, p. 119 ff.; Fredericq 1922, pp. 39-62.

658 Pfleger 1941, p. 66; Hasak 1927, p. 70. Also at the Cathedral of SION, where in 1312 the bishop offered an indulgence for any labour or carts, stones, mortar, sand and other building materials supplied for the portal's structural foundation; Dubuis 1979, précis 3.

659 Norton 1880, p. 299; Corsepius 1997, p. 40. Of particular interest is a practice recorded in the twelfth century whereby all pilgrims to SANTIAGO were asked to aid the works by carrying a block of stone with them from a certain place to the lime kilns, situated at some distance from the cathedral; López Ferreiro 1898-1911, vol. 3, p. 27.

660 See Corsepius 1997, pp. 35-46, with an excellent overview of the *Karrenkult*; Signori 1995, pp. 152-173, *Wagenprozessionen*; Iogna-Prat 2006, pp. 495-498.

661 St Rémi in RHEIMS (1039): Mortet 1911, p. 41. St-Trond (1055-82): idem, pp. 157-158; Lehmann-Brockhaus 1938, no. 1982; Fagniez 1898/1900, no. 128. Monte Cassino (1058-1087): Lehmann-Brockhaus 1938, no. 2277. St-Pierre-sur-Dive (1145): Mortet & Deschamps 1929, p. 63 ff. Andres (1164 and 1197): Verplaetse 1965, p. 35; Mortet 1911, pp. 390, 394. St Denis (before 1140): Panofsky 1946, pp. 92, 93.

662 Mortet & Deschamps 1929, p. 65 ff.; translation in Branner 1969, p. 93. Chédeville 1973, p. 521,

relates that the quarry of Berchères-les-Pierres was 10 km from the cathedral.

663 Thomas 1881, pp. 510, 513-514.

664 Mortet & Deschamps 1929, p. 205.

665 Idem, p. 257.

666 Cf. text relating to CHÂLONS-EN-CHAMPAGNE: '*Ecce genere nobiles, potentes opibus, honore pollentes, clationis mundane fastu desposito, cervices cordis et corporis sub iugo pietatis humiliant* [...]. *Plaustris igitur ad urbem (deductis), videres milites generosos, matronas potentes, juvenes et virgines, senes cum junioribus, nudo pede, curso festino, jocundo corde, per vicos et plateas in occursum certatim convolare*'; Mortet & Deschamps 1929, p. 110; Demaison 1899, p. 106; David 1965, p. 1116; Van Werveke 1904, p. 344. Also Hirschmann 1998, p. 512: on nobles' sense of shame at performing such ignominious, servile labour.

667 Corsepius 1997, p. 38.

668 '[...] *confessionem* [...] *cum poenitentia, et concordiam de omni malevolentia, et humilitatem veniendi cum obedientia requirimus ab eis cum ad nos veniunt, eosque pie recipimus et absolvimus et benedicimus, si tria illa deférunt*'; Mortet & Deschamps 1929, p. 67; translation in Branner 1969, p. 94.

669 Sigal 1990, pp. 205-207; Signori 1995, pp. 41, 156: there was an entire series of rituals that accompanied the veneration of relics. Gregory of Tours mentions the *incubatio*: whilst sleeping underneath or near the reliquary shrine, the saint would appear and effect a cure (this practice did not die out until the fifteenth century); the *excubiae*: night vigil; the *potatio*: drinking the water used to wash the relics; and the *lavatio*: the washing of ailing limbs.

670 Thomas 1881, pp. 513, 514: '[...] *pernoctabat autem quam plurimis noctibus foris in claustro – non enim omnes infra ambitum ecclesie poterant contineri – peregrinorum maxima multitudo, ita quod clerici qui ad matutinos surrexerant claustrum ingredi pre multitudine populi non valebant. Videres preterea sacerdotes cum suis plebibus adventantes noctis ibidem vigilias observare er una cum clericis pariter advenientibus psalmos, hymnos et cetera cantica spiritualia in honorem et laudem gloriose Virginis altis vocibus decantare* [...]'. See also Kunstmann 1973, p. 86 and Sigal 1990, pp. 205-207. Concerning the pilgrims' conduct inside the cathedral and consequences for the building itself, see Hayes 1999, passim.

671 Work on this section lasted from the day before Easter until the Monday after the octave of Easter, when the translation took place. The source records that '*Qui brevi tempore sponte fecerunt, quod multi conducticii* [paid labourers] *per longa tempore non fecissent*'; Mortet & Deschamps 1929, pp. 258-259.

672 '[...] *multi ad eundem locum e diversis partibus confluxerunt, plaustris siquidem et aliis vehiculorum generibus frumentum, vinum, ferrum et multa hujusmodi ad ecclesie fabricam utilia vel necessaria attrahentes, nichilominus tamen calices, cifos argenteos et alia preciosa donaria deferentes pariter et offerentes*'; Thomas 1881, p. 513; Kunstmann 1973, p. 85. See also Chédeville 1973, p. 515.

673 Mortet & Deschamps 1929, p. 67; translation in Branner 1969, p. 94. '*Disciplina*' here means penance; Niermeyer 1954-1976, in voce '*disciplina*'.

674 The case of CHARTRES Cathedral is particularly famous: of its 140 windows, 44 were donated by guilds and tradesmen, 40 by

members of royalty and the aristocracy, and 16 by ecclesiastics; Von Simson 1956, p. 180; Chédeville 1973, pp. 453, 454, 478, 517.

675 Mortet & Deschamps 1929, p. 529.

676 Early examples relate chiefly to abbeys. Concerning the abbey of St-Trond, one source from the first half of the twelfth century relates: '[...] *inspiravit Deus cuidam matronae* [...], *quae suis sumptibus unum pylarium prima coepit edificare* [...]. *Haec imitatur quidam Libertus, de hac majori curte nostra villicus, aliud iuxta eam incepit et consummavit. Post istos oppidani nostri de suis fraternitatibus quattuor inceperunt pylaria et duo reliqua sunt imperfecta*'; Lehmann-Brockhaus 1938, no. 2004. Additional examples in Verplaetse 1965, p. 36; Van Werveke 1904, p. 345; Rolland 1924, p. 178 and n. 1; Enlart 1902, pp. 76 n. 1, 88 n. 3. Examples from the late medieval period include a nobleman's donation of a pillar to the cathedral of RODEZ in 1470; Bion de Marlavagne 1875, p. 68; and the donation of the large sum of 200 lb.reg. d. for the main portal of the cathedral of REGENSBURG at the end of the fourteenth century by city councillor Gamerad der Sarchingen zu Sarching; Schuegraf 1847/1848, vol. 11, p. 154; Schuegraf 1858, p. 154.

677 One of the earliest references to donor-name inscriptions concerns the cathedral of COUTANCES in the period 1024-1045: '[...] *cooperantibus quoque baronibus et parochianis fidelibus: quod usque hodie contestantur aliquot ipsorum nomina insculpta lapidibus in ecclesie arcubus*'; *Gallia Christiana*, vol. 11, instr. p. 218. Later examples are legion. Inventory of all escutcheons affixed to a cathedral in Boissonnot 1920, p. 421 ff. See *Reallexikon zur deutschen Kunstgeschichte*, in voce '*Bauinschrift*'.

678 Thomas 1881, pp. 539-541, Kunstmann 1973, p. 189.

679 Pigeon 1876, pp. 370-372.

680 Woodruff 1932, p. 22; Woodruff & Danks 1912, pp. 158, 163.

681 'they abided for barely a year'; the source is a later chronicle; Hamann & Rosenfeld 1910, p. 139 and n. 38. Construction of the choir began in 1209. Example of a similar pledge list: *Tour de Beurre*, ROUEN Cathedral after 1485; Fallue 1848, p. 211.

682 See for example Cox 1913, p. 80 ff.; Brutails 1899-1901, vol. 12, p. 409 (BORDEAUX); Van Dalen 1927, p. 234 (Dordrecht).

683 After the Fourth Lateran Council (1215) plenary indulgences could only be issued by the pope; Nolet & Boeren 1951, p. 290; also Paulus 1922-1923, vol. 1, p. 196; Boeren 1962, pp. 93-94.

684 Paulus 1922-1923, vol. 2, pp. 221-222.

685 Idem, p. 106 n. 4; also Sumption 1975, p. 229.

686 Nolet & Boeren 1951, pp. 292, 293; Paulus 1922-1923, vol. 2, p. 117, vol. 3, p. 379 ff. The first mention of indulgences for the deceased occurs in 1457. Concerning the notion of *suffragium*, see *Dictionnaire de Théologie catholique*, in voce '*suffrage*', col. 2738.

687 Alongside *semel in vita*, or *semel in vita et semel in articulo mortis*; Nolet & Boeren 1951, pp. 287-288.

688 Confessional letters emerged between 1250 and 1350, but did not become popular until the late Middle Ages; Paulus 1922-1923, vol. 2, p. 124 ff., vol. 3, p. 303 ff.; Wolfs 1963, p. XV.

689 Large numbers of printed confessional letters were distributed especially from around 1475 on; see *Einblattdrucke des XV. Jahrhunderts*, in voce '*Ablassbriefe*'. These always

left a blank space in which the name of the person receiving this privilege was to be filled in. The incunable literature sometimes refers to indulgence letters where confessional letters is meant. See fig. 13. Also Eisermann in Swanson 2006, pp. 309-330.

690 Paulus 1922-1923, vol. 3, p. 540 ff. Detailed description of how such solemn occasions were orchestrated in BASEL: Hieronimus 1938, pp. 269-272; in BREMEN (May 1503) and in other northern German cities: Röpcke 1992, pp. 70-78.

691 Called the '*Türkenkasten*'; Ennen 1863/1869, vol. 3, p. 305; Paulus 1922-1923, vol. 3, pp. 203, 204.

692 Concerning Peraudi, see especially Paulus 1922-1923, vol. 3, pp. 178-188, 325-332; also Housley in Swanson 2006, pp. 286-307; Röpcke 1992, pp. 43-80; Neuhausen 1994, pp. 133-138; Moeller 1989, pp. 547-557.

693 Crusade indulgences were issued for fighting against the Muslims (in Spain and the Balkans) and against heretics (the Hussites in Bohemia); Housley in Swanson 2006, pp. 277-307; Paulus 1922-1923, passim. The indulgence for St Peter's, proclaimed by Julius II in 1507, also falls into this category; Paulus 1922-1923, vol. 3, pp. 140-147; Hashagen 1931, pp. 167, 168.

694 Paulus 1922-1923, vol. 2, p. 101, vol. 3, p. 357; Boeren 1962, p. 46.

695 Nolet & Boeren 1951, p. 290.

696 Rémy 1928, p. 37; Paulus 1922-1923, vol. 3, p. 181 ff.

697 Specifically in Lombardy, Bavaria, Bohemia, Saxony, Poland, the Scandinavian countries, England, the Low Countries; Paulus 1922-1923, vol. 3, p. 181; Fredericq 1922, nos 27-31; Rémy 1928, p. 35 ff.

698 *Ad instar* indulgences were issued along the same lines as those previously extended to other churches. Best known is the indulgence issued to the Portiuncula Chapel near ASSISI; Paulus 1922-1923, vol. 3, p. 150 ff. The majority date from after the mid-fourteenth century. The earliest known example was granted to the population of MALLORCA in 1352; Sumption 1975, p. 241. Concerning '*städtischen Stellvertreterstätten*' - the possibility of earning Roman indulgences in one's home city - see Miedema 2003, pp. 432-462. Here cathedral cities form a minority amongst instances in Germany and the Low Countries cited from after 1450.

699 See Esch 2004, pp. 110-134, on the journey made by a collector of indulgence monies through Germany, the Low Countries (also stopping at UTRECHT Cathedral) and Austria between 1470 and 1472; Röpcke 1992, on Peraudi's trip through northern Germany in 1505; Moeller 1989, pp. 546-567, on the last large-scale indulgence campaigns.

700 For the Netherlands: Post 1957, vol. 2, p. 42 ff.

701 Paulus 1922-1923, vol. 3, p. 455.

702 Boeren 1962, p. 10 ff., 101, 109 ff.

703 Woodruff 1932, p. 191; Woodman 1981, table on p. 121; Nilson 1998, pp.147-154; Diana Webb in Swanson 2006, p. 267.

704 Boeren 1962, p. 140, with an incorrect date for the first celebration in 1451; Sachet 1886, pp. 90, 186 ff., 431-445.

705 Schulte1904, vol. 1, p. 257 ff.

706 Paulus 1922-1923, vol. 3, p. 182; Rocco Negri 1975, pp. 191-200; Boito 1889, pp. 25-31; *Annali*, vol. 1, p. XII, 33 and Appendix vol. 1, account for 1391. Only very rarely did the time of grace extend to a full year; Paulus 1922-1923, vol. 3, pp. 540-541; Boeren 1962, pp. 93-94.

707 *Inventaire-sommaire Aube* G 2593; also Murray 1987,

pp. 62, 145.

708 Listed under the receipts are also profits from the sale of pilgrim badges: '*pour la vendue des enseignes d'argent dorées et blanches, comme d'aultres d'estain, en sain Pierres et clefz, et aultres achettées de Belin, miraclier, et de la vefve feu Domey, vendue par plusieurs et diverses personnes, la somme de 24 l.t.*'; d'Arbois de Jubainville 1862, p. 393. Concerning the right to sell these mass-produced souvenirs, from which the fabric almost never benefited, see *Achthundert Jahre*, p. 209 (COLOGNE); López Ferreiro 1898-1911, vol. 5, app. 5, 17, 33; González Vázquez 1996, pp. 238-239 (SANTIAGO, *concheiros* 1200 until the fifteenth century); Jusserand 1950, p. 210; Beissel 1913, pp. 247-253, and especially Cohen 1976, passim. Also Houdoy 1880, p. 73 (CAMBRAI 1481: sale by the fabric); Ruiz de la Peña Solar 1990, pp. 258-259 and 59, 63 (contract of 6 July 1481 in which the chapter of OVIEDO commissions the production of 25,000 pilgrim badges intended for sale during the Jubilee).

709 An *operarius* earned a daily minimum wage of 1 s. 8 d.; Murray 1987, p. 206; d'Arbois de Jubainville 1862, p. 395 and doc. XXIX; *Inventaire-sommaire Aube* G 1565. Examples of returns on similar pardons at other cathedrals include: in SENS 746 l.t. at the beginning of transept construction in 1490, with total receipts of 1146 l.t.; *Inventaire-sommaire Yonne* G 1141; in LISIEUX after the collapse of the tower in 1553: 219 l.t. in 1156, 173 l.t. in 1157, 58 l.t. in 1558 and 2 l.t. in 1559; Vasseur 1882, p. 478. For VALENCIA, see Villanueva Estengo 1902-1906, vol. 2, pp. 230-242, 253-256 (1458, 1461, 1469 and 1470).

710 Paulus 1922-1923, vol. 3, p. 200.

711 Le Mené 1882, pp. 13-15. A plenary indulgence was later also available to earn on 1, 2 and 3 May 1514; proceeds came to 400 l.t., against costs of 54 l.t., with a net value equal to eleven annual wages of an unskilled labourer; idem, p. 23; *Congrès Archéologique de France* 48 (1881), p. 251 ff.

712 The miracle is related as follows. A small boy happened on a soldier taking his sweetheart into a lusty embrace. The girl was so afraid that the child would reveal what he had seen to her strict father that, to allay her fears, the soldier stole the boy away and cut out his tongue so he would be unable to speak. Reduced to beggary, the boy - still carrying his tongue with him - came to visit the cathedral of CHARTRES where, on the third day after Easter, his power of speech was miraculously restored to him before the altar of the Virgin Mary; Thomas 1881, p. 511 ff.; Kunstmann 1973, p. 79.

713 '*Audita igitur tanti novitate miraculi, tota civitas commota est et gaudio et exaltatione repleta, sed cum, universis illuc undique concurrentibus, predictus puer multitudinem populi ferre non posset, tandem in eminenti loco super gradum ligneum ad capsam beati Leobini, juxta truncum oblationum, quasi ad spectaculum, immo ad miraculum positus est, ubi recta et aperta pronuntiatione ad opus ecclesie genetricis Dei cunctos invitans multa et a multis oblationum beneficia impetrare promeruit*'; Thomas 1881, p. 512; Kunstmann 1973, pp. 82, 83; Corsepius 1997, p. 44 n. 217.

714 Von Simson 1956, p. 183.

715 Merlet 1906, p. 225 ff. The chapel was under construction from 1324 until 1358; Lautier 2003, p. 41. Saint Piat was the first bishop of TOURNAI, whose remains were later transferred to CHARTRES.

716 Herrmann-Mascard 1975, pp. 183-184.

717 Branner 1961, p. 29. In AUXERRE the bishop's translation of the head of St Amâtre in 1309 rang in the beginning of a new period of building; Porée 1926, p. 14. Seymour 1968, pp. 47, 48, connects the date of the second phase of construction at NOYON Cathedral with the elevation of the relics of St Eligius in 1157. He cites parallel examples from the cathedrals of SENLIS (1177) and AMIENS.

718 On the political backgrounds of many of these devotions, see Jusserand 1950, p. 192 ff.; Cook 1957, pp. 32 ff., 126-133; Coulton 1928, p. 16 ff.; Sumption 1975, pp. 280-282. The politically motivated assassination of Bishop Thomas Becket was the only such to ever inspire an important pilgrimage; Soria Audebert 2005, p. 283.

719 Concerning shrines in England, see Nilson 1998, passim; Lehmberg 1988, pp. 30-49; general: Crook 1999/2000, pp. 242-281. The cathedrals at issue are DURHAM (St Cuthbert), CANTERBURY (St Thomas and Archbishop Winchesley), LONDON (St Erkenwald), YORK (St William), LINCOLN (St Hugh), CHICHESTER (St Richard), LICHFIELD (St Chad), HEREFORD (St Thomas Cantilupe), ELY (St Etheldreda), NORWICH (St William and Bishop Walter), SALISBURY (St Osmund). A few abbeys also possessed a saint's shrine.

720 Woodruff & Danks 1912, pp. 77, 122 ff. See also Petersohn 1989, pp. 35-38, on the connection between the translation of relics and Jubilee years; he points out that there was not yet any question of a plenary indulgence in 1220; also Webb in Swanson 2006, pp. 259-262.

721 Cited in *Registrum Trillek*, p. 147. In HEREFORD too the arrival of the relics of St Thomas Cantilupe was regarded as the catalyst for better harvests, larger catches of fish and fertile livestock; Vauchez 1988a, p. 543.

722 Branner 1960, p. 112; especially Geary 1977, passim.

723 Cf. '*Historia inventionis et miraculorum s. Gilduini*' in relation to the building of the abbey of Saint-Père in CHARTRES; the *inventio* took place in 1165; Mortet & Deschamps 1929, pp. 88-90.

724 'Because of this translation, almost all of the population and devout people of FLORENCE, men and women, small and great, came with great devotion and offerings'; Grote n.d., p. 42; St Zenobius (d. 424) was the bishop of Florence. A similar ceremonial translation was organized for St Eulalia in the cathedral of BARCELONA on 30 June 1339; Puig i Puig 1979, p. 245 ff., doc. CIX and CXI.

725 Cook 1957, p. 32.

726 This category in the rolls bears the heading: '*recepta oblacionum ad sepulturam Magistri Ricardi Lescrope pro stipendiis VIII cementariorum per annum £73 8s*'. The wording of the items that follow also points up the fact that only part of the alms were being spent on building works: '*de £ 62 8s. de oblationibus ad sepulturam magistri Ricardi* [...]'; Raine 1859, p. 32. In 1409 the chapter did however decide to use the offerings for the reconstruction of the fourth pillar of the crossing tower that had collapsed in 1408; Norton 2007, p. 175. Concerning the eminent significance of Richard Scrope for the cathedral of YORK and his cult there: Norton 2007, pp. 138-213.

727 Yates 1973, p. 79.

728 Concerning HEREFORD: *Charters Hereford*, pp. 163-165; Bannister 1902-1904, passim; Yates 1973, p. 79 ff.; Finucane

1977, pp. 135-137, 173-188; Swanson 1993, pp. 93-102; Nilson 1998, pp. 138, 221, 239; Barrow 1999, passim. Nilson 1998, pp. 211-228 and 234-241, has published quantitative data and graphs on the cathedrals of CANTERBURY (1198-1474), ELY (1291-1536), NORWICH (1272- 1535), HEREFORD (1478-1522), LINCOLN (1334-1531) and DURHAM (1376-1537). In view of the fact that it is not clear whether some part - and, if so, which - accrued to the fabric, these figures are by and large left out here. The building works likewise enjoyed only a portion of the offerings in HEREFORD; Swanson 1993, pp. 94, 97. Nilson 1998, p. 241, publishes a schematic graph of all offerings made at English shrines, revealing that they hit their peak in the latter half of the fourteenth century and then quickly tumbled after around 1510.

TEN Money collected in and outside the diocese

729 See recent research into the geographic reach of devotional cults as based on documented miracles: CHARTRES, Chédeville 1973, pp. 510-512 and HEREFORD, Finucane 1977, p. 173 ff. Both of these cults were distinctly local in scope.

730 Rémy 1928, pp. 119-120; Fredericq 1922, nos 48-67: regarding the first well-documented indulgence in the Low Countries.

731 Concerning this indulgence - the best documented of all those in Germany - see Schulte 1904, vol. 1, pp. 79-85, 155-160, vol. 2, pp. 23-62, 70, 127, 129; Krebs 1952-1959, nos 4244-4917, passim; *Regesten Münster Konstanz*, no. 370 ff.; Baier 1911, passim. Moeller 1989, p. 557, sums up the seven large indulgence campaigns conducted between Peraudi's death in 1505 and the beginning of Luther's attack on indulgences in 1517. Of these seven campaigns, two were for cathedrals (TRIER and KONSTANZ), one for the church of St Peter in ROME, one for the Dominican church of AUGSBURG, one the so-called dyke indulgence in the Low Countries, and two for crusades conducted by the Teutonic Order. Concerning the papal indulgence in TRIER, which was preached throughout the entire Church province, see Seibrich 1995, pp. 99-106: 43.6 percent, or 2740 ducats, of the alms accrued to the cathedral and were spent primarily on the casting of two bells.

732 *Regesten Münster Konstanz*, no. 381 ff.

733 Schulte 1904, vol. 2, no. 35, p. 39.

734 Those who wished to gain further spiritual benefits, such as a confessional letter, had to meet additional financial conditions: Schulte 1904, vol. 2, pp. 46-47.

735 '*Ob modernus papa hieran etwas nachlassen wurde*'; Krebs 1952-1959, no. 4595.

736 Perhaps aimed at the Church provinces of MAINZ and MAGDEBURG; Krebs 1952-1959, no. 4872.

737 Schulte 1904, vol. 2, p. 34; Krebs 1952-1959, no. 4882.

738 Krebs 1952-1959, nos 4269, 4672, 4762.

739 Wage derives from the 1499 account.

740 'because they are coins [...] it is difficult to convey them by horse'; Krebs 1952-1959, no. 4718; Schulte 1904, vol. 2, p. 31, vol. 1, p. 156. The settlement statements tendered by indulgence campaign collectors occasionally contain details illustrating the characteristic problems involved in procuring monies in the most diverse currencies and denominations across extensive territories, along with the risks of transport; Esch 2004, p. 126. Concerning the indulgence for the crusade against the king of

Bohemia in 1470-1472, see Finke 1932-1933, e.g. pp. 226 (number of horses), 234 (expenditures '*pro una bursa longa de corio cervino ad portandum pecunias*'), and Esch 2004, pp. 116, 117, 119 ('*moneta minuta quia noluerunt numerare*' are weighed '*propter fastidium* [aversion] *numerandi*').

741 This term was introduced by Voisin 1869, p. 477.

742 See Appendix three.

743 MEISSEN 1413: '*ecclesia* [...] *per improvisam et repentinam aeris intemperiem ac pluviarum ac intollerabilium ventorum tyrannidem* [...] *perpessa;* [...] *quae prae ceteris basilicis nostrae diocesis ut lucerna ardens super mensam domini posita tamqum sidus irradiat matutinam*'; Donath 2000, p. 28.

744 SANTO DOMINGO DE LA CALZADA 1465: '[...] *para se fazeer la obra magnificameente e en tiempo razzonable* [...]'; López de Silanes & Sáinz Ripa 1992, no. 287 (p. 60).

745 Appendix three: *mendicatoria* for UTRECHT of 1288, and STRASBOURG of 1275; Héliot & Chastang 1964/1965, p. 9.

746 Appendix three: *mendicatorium* for BESANÇON; Zink 1973, doc. 71.

747 In STRASBOURG, 1190: '*latores presentium cum testimonio sigilli nostri*'; in COLOGNE, 1264, a *nuntius* is documented by name: '[...] *Gerardo sacerdoti provisori fabrice nostre Coloniensis, presentium exhibitori*'; in UTRECHT they were designated as '*nuncii Sancti Martini, exhibitores presencium*'.

748 See Appendix three: with relics in the *mendicatoria* for TRIER, BREMEN, TOURNAI and TOUL.

749 Appendix three: *mendicatorium* for YORK of 1304.

750 Idem, *mendicatorium* for STRASBOURG of 1275.

751 Idem, *mendicatorium* for BREMEN.

752 Idem, *mendicatoria* for WÜRZBURG, STRASBOURG of 1275, and UTRECHT of 1288.

753 See Appendix three: *mendicatoria* for STRASBOURG of 1275, HALBERSTADT and TOUL (where the parish priest furthermore had to recite the miracles of St Gérard from the pulpit every Sunday; Clanché 1926-1927, p. 159). In the fifteenth-century diocese of BASEL, the *petitio* had to be held four times a year, always in cycles of six successive Sundays plus on the feast days in between; La Roche 1888, p. 99. In the diocese of REGENSBURG, parish priests had to proclaim the indulgences and spiritual benefits on offer from the pulpit starting from the first Sunday of Lent through the octave of Easter; the collection may also have been held at this time; Schuegraf 1847/1848, vol. 11, p. 194 and doc. 11. In the diocese of STRASBOURG, the collection was repeatedly held from 25 July until 2 November and during Lent; Pfleger 1937, p. 7.

754 Appendix three: *mendicatoria* for HALBERSTADT, COLOGNE, STRASBOURG of 1275, UTRECHT, PRAGUE, BREMEN, GERONA, TOUL.

755 Idem, *mendicatoria* for CHÂLONS-EN-CHAMPAGNE, HALBERSTADT, COLOGNE, STRASBOURG of 1275, MAINZ of 1293, YORK of 1304 and 1312, PRAGUE and BREMEN. This period is specified in TOUL as running from the Sunday after St Mansuetus (3 September) until Laetare Sunday in Lent; Clanché 1926-1927, p. 162. CAMBRAI had a similar arrangement for the various archdeaconries making up the diocese; Archives départementales Nord 4 G 101 and 1082. In SANTO DOMINGO DE LA CALZADA (1448 and 1453) the bishop determined that, on pain of excommunication, '*que en ninguna de nuestras iglesias non ande*

ningund vaçin antes que aqueste'.

756 Appendix three: *mendicatoria* for HALBERSTADT, WÜRZBURG, STRASBOURG of 1275, UTRECHT, PRAGUE and TOUL. Already from early on we find synodal statutes from England stipulating that laymen be appointed as co-custodians of offerings made by the faithful for the *petitores*, as in CANTERBURY in 1213-14 and in later statutes; Powicke & Cheney 1964, pp. 33, 34, 85, 194, 623.

757 Appendix three: *mendicatorium* for CLERMONT-FERRAND of 1311; Archives départementales Puy-de-Dôme 3 G arm. 18, sac B, cote 24; Gobillot 1912, pp. 23-24.

758 Appendix three: *mendicatoria* for HALBERSTADT, WÜRZBURG, STRASBOURG of 1275, UTRECHT, PRAGUE, TOURNAI, TOUL. On the *locus reportationes*, see the COLOGNE synodal statutes of 1319; Lepper 1979, p. 354.

759 In the *mendicatoria* for Trier, PRAGUE, TOURNAI, BREMEN and TOUL, amongst others, with the additional provision that where the church is too small, the mass is to be read at a portable altar in the open air; see also Héliot & Chastang 1964/1965, p. 12; Paulus 1922-1923, vol. 2, p. 271 ff. Jongkees 1942, p. 165, incorrectly suggests that parish clergy brought pressure to bear on the faithful of their own volition. Some synodal statutes in effect prohibited this: *'diligenter inducat ad elemosinas erogandas, pietatis intuitu, non animo extorquendi'*; *Statuts synodaux Paris*, vol. 1, pp. 164-165 (ANGERS, first half of the thirteenth century). A document connected with a 1535 lawsuit between the bishop of ANGERS and the Hotel Dieu in PARIS (which held similar privileges) reveals that great significance was attached to celebrating the collection day as a Sunday: '[...] *à tels jours non feriez le peuple ne s'assemble pas et n'est pas en telle devotion que aux jours de feste et ne vouldroit laisser ses oeuvres manuelles pour aller gaigner les pardons*'; Coyecque 1889/1891, vol. 1, p. 140 n. 2.

760 Neuwirth 1890, p. 382 ff., idem 1893, pp. 278-282. We get a very clear picture of how affairs were arranged from a letter that the archbishop of YORK addressed to his clergy in 1352: '[...] *collectam ipsam ad usum fabricae predictae (dumtaxat concessam seu concedendam) personaliter facietis* (de pastoors) *in albis sub pena predicta, cum dicti nostri procuratores et nuncii personaliter non poterint interesse. Er quicquid collectum fuerit in hac partel tam per vos quam per dictos procuratores seu nuncios, latores presencium, sine dilacione vel dimunicione aliqua integraliter liberetis*'; Raine 1859, doc. XXII, pp. 167, 168.

761 Appendix three: *mendicatorium* for MAINZ of 1293.

762 Concerning the messengers we read, *'quod singuli cum singulis famulis vadant per squadras ordinatas in terra vel loco'*. After having read the mass and the sermon, they were to order the '*presbyteris* [i.e. the local clergy], *duobus consulibus et duobus aliis hominibus illius loci vel terrae, quod subsequenter discurrant domos et familias universas, requirendo et colligendo subsidium et oblationes*'. The local collectors were charged with cashing offerings made in kind and presenting these monies plus the other contributions during the office of the Holy Virgin on 1 November, presumably to their parish priests, who then – according to a 1387 document – had to render these results in MILAN on the feast of St Martin (12 November). It was the overlord Gian

Galeazzo Visconti who issued this elaboration of the provisions of the 12 May 1386 *mendicatorium* in a document dated 12 October 1386; *Annali*, Appendix vol. 1, sub 1386 and 1387; Brivio 1977, doc. 2, p. 129.

763 Appendix three: *mendicatoria* for WÜRZBURG, UTRECHT, STRASBOURG of 1275 and TOUL.

764 Idem, *mendicatoria* for HALBERSTADT, UTRECHT, STRASBOURG of 1275, PRAGUE and BREMEN.

765 *Idem, mendicatoria* for WÜRZBURG, HALBERSTADT, COLOGNE, UTRECHT, STRASBOURG of 1275, PRAGUE, BREMEN, TOURNAI, TOUL.

766 *Idem, mendicatoria* for COLOGNE, STRASBOURG of 1275, UTRECHT, TOURNAI, BREMEN and TOUL. A WÜRZBURG charter of 1 September 1237 mentions a confraternity; *Monumenta Boica*, vol. 37, no. 254. For BREMEN, see also *Urkundenbuch Bremen*, vol. 5, no. 70 (1415).

767 Appendix three: *mendicatorium* for STRASBOURG of 1275: '[...] *et ad elemosinas singulis annis reddendas se obligaverunt*'. Similar provisions in TOURNAI and TOUL, where defaulting on payments resulted in excommunication; Clanché 1926-1927, pp. 151, 167.

768 In TOURNAI 6 d., in TOUL 1 gros over a period of 20 years, in BAYEUX five years, in VICH ten years.

769 See Appendix three, *mendicatoria* for, amongst others, HALBERSTADT, UTRECHT and PRAGUE; cf. for YORK: Raine 1859, p. 160.

770 Appendix three: *mendicatoria* for WÜRZBURG and PRAGUE.

771 Idem, *mendicatoria* for PRAGUE and TOUL.

772 Idem, *mendicatoria* for WÜRZBURG, STRASBOURG of 1275, YORK of 1304, PRAGUE, BREMEN and TOUL.

773 Idem, *mendicatorium* for TOUL: Clanché 1926-1927, p. 165.

774 Appendix three: *mendicatoria* for WÜRZBURG, STRASBOURG of 1275, HALBERSTADT, COLOGNE, UTRECHT, PRAGUE, BREMEN and TOURNAI.

775 Concerning *casus reservati*, see Hinschius 1869-1897, vol. 4, pp. 102, 106 ff. They were often summarized in synodal statutes: Mansi 1759-1793, vol. 24, p. 503, vol. 25, pp. 55, 76, etc. Also Van Herwaarden 1978, pp. 45-47.

776 '[...] *vota fracta, si ad ea redierunt*'; Paulus 1922-1923, vol. 2, pp. 90-92.

777 '[...] *offensae parentum sine manuum iniectione violentia*'; idem, pp. 92-93.

778 '[...] *periuria, transgressiones fidei et iuramenti*'; idem, pp. 93-96. Other privileges relate to the sins '*mendacia ex levitate, loco vel pietate dicta*', '*vaniloquia superflua et inutilia*', '*peccata oblita*', '*poenitentiae oblitae et male factae*', '*decimac per ignorentiam detentae*'; see idem, pp. 79, 88 ff.

779 BARCELONA 1343, in Catalan; Puig i Puig 1979, no. CXIII: '*aquests son los pardons qui son atorgats a quiscun dels benfaytors de la obra* [...]''.

780 Appendix three: *mendicatoria* for WÜRZBURG, TRIER, COLOGNE, STRASBOURG of 1275, UTRECHT, TOURNAI, METZ and BREMEN. See Paulus 1922-1923, vol. 2, p. 99, vol. 3, pp. 514-515.

781 Idem, *mendicatoria* for STRASBOURG of 1190 and 1275, PRAGUE and TOUL. See Paulus 1922-1923, vol. 3, p. 512 ff.

782 Idem, *mendicatoria* for WÜRZBURG, COLOGNE, STRASBOURG of 1275, UTRECHT and TOUL.

783 Deed of 14 November 1279; *Urkundenbuch Strassburg*, vol. 2, no. 71.

784 Villanueva Estengo 1902-1906, vol. 7, pp. 264-265. The *mendicatorium* for REGENSBURG from 1525 states 7254 masses; Schuegraf 1847/1848, vol. 11, p. 266.

785 Schuegraf 1847, p. 265: '*summa verum missarum in sepedicta ecclesia Raspon. fundatarum et quot annis perficiendarum sunt septem millia cum ducentis et quinquaginta quatuor*' [=7254].

786 This privilege only applied so long as the interdict or excommunication did not bear on one of the confraternity members personally; Appendix three: *mendicatoria* for STRASBOURG of 1275, UTRECHT and TOURNAI.

787 Clanché 1926-1927, pp. 150, 166.

788 Boniface (674-754) in particular propagated this idea; Le Bras 1940-1941, passim; Paulus 1922-1923, vol. 3, p. 512; Deschamps 1958, passim.

789 Those who became members often received a confraternity letter as proof; Paulus 1922-1923, vol. 3, p. 513; Coulton 1928, p. 358; Cook 1957, p. 300; Swanson 2007, pp. 98-102 and index in voce 'confessional/confraternity letters'. Wolfs 1963 publishes similar *litterae de beneficiis* dating from between 1243 and 1524, though none relate to a cathedral fabric confraternity. With the invention of printing, large numbers of such confraternity letters were issued in printed form; only a very few of those that have been preserved originate from cathedrals. See figs 18 and 19; also Swanson 2007, pp. 165-173, 377.

790 On this see *Synodalbündniss*: *Realencyklopädie*, in voce '*Bruderschaft*'.

791 Confraternities with no connection to the fabric could also be found at cathedrals, for example the *confrérie* Saint-Nicolas de QUIMPER, established with the bishop's consent around 1400; one roll has been preserved for the years 1482-1484 (196 members); Prigent 1991, pp. 276-311.

792 Concerning parish fabric confraternities, see Mortet 1911, p. 200, n. 4; Schröcker 1934, p. 58 and n. 2; Westlake 1919, pp. 138-238; Drew 1954, p. 21 ff.

793 Noordeloos 1959, p. 61; Cheney 1973, pp. 33, 34. Concerning fabric confraternities at abbeys, see Mortet 1911, pp. 341, 374. For England, see Swanson 2007, pp. 65-70.

794 From the eleventh century on, confraternities of this kind were also set up in support of bridge-building; see Boyer 1964; Paulus 1922-1923, vol. 2, p. 252 ff.; *Lexikon für Theologie und Kirche*, in voce '*Brückenbau*'; Kraus 1979, pp. 105-106 (LYON); Boyer 1976, pp. 39-47.

795 *Bulletin Monumental* 55 (1889), p. 55.

796 Puig i Cadafalch & Pujol Tubau 1918, pp. 29-30; Paulus 1922-1923, vol. 1, p. 177 n. 7.

797 Barlow 1939, p. 114. It still existed around 1350; *Pouillés Rouen*, p. 246.

798 *Pouillés Rouen*, p. 246.

799 Graham 1945-1947, passim.

800 *Cartularius Baiocensis*, vol. 1, no. 47.

801 *Urkundenbuch Strassburg*, vol. 1, no. 143; Hasak 1927, p. 21 ff.

802 Initially, there seem to have been quite large differences between cathedral fabric confraternities. Around the mid-twelfth century we find local confraternities forming to make pilgrimages to CHARTRES and other cathedrals and to bring their offerings and join in building activities there. The groups had an ad hoc nature, disbanding and turning homeward after the work was done; on this see p. 45; also Demaison 1899, p. 95.

803 Barlow 1939, p. 88; also Grant 2005, p. 85.

804 Grant 2005, pp. 87, 89; concerning Arnulf himself and his building ambitions also: p. 21.

805 Graham 1945-1947, pp. 74, 75.

806 Almost every cathedral had its own diocesan fabric

confraternity. Schöller 1989, pp. 331-333, cites (in addition to those named) the following: LE MANS (1100), also *Cartulaire Le Mans*, vol. 1, no. 892 (1460), RHEIMS (c. 1223), GENEVA (1234), TOULON (1268), EVREUX (1288), MAINZ (1293), AUTUN (before 1295), SENS (1296), LYON (later thirteenth century), RODEZ (before 1316), also Freigang 1992, p. 174 n. 66, MIREPOIX (1326/27) and TOUL (1336). To these we can add the following: in England: HEREFORD, LICHFIELD, COVENTRY, EXETER, YORK and WELLS; Swanson & Lepine 2000, pp. 77-78; Swanson 2007, p. 67, SALISBURY (1223); Edwards 1967, p. 325, also Brown 1995, pp. 51-52, 59, 64 (late fourteenth century, a confraternity with a distinctly aristocratic character). In France: TOURS (fourteenth-sixteenth centuries); Boissonnot 1920, p. 240 n. 2, LISIEUX (documented in 1350); Vincent 1988, p. 271 n. 24, p. 308, TROYES (established in 1354, again in 1488); *Inventaire-sommaire Aube* G 3868, 1569; d'Arbois de Jubainville 1862, p. 413; Assier 1858, p. 27, SÉES (documented in 1452); Marais & Beaudoin 1876, pp. 114-116, ORLÉANS (re-established in 1487); Denifle 1897-1899, vol. 1, no. 953, LIMOGES (established on 8 April 1501); Arbellot 1852, pp. 37, 79-80, BOURGES (established in 1506); De Girardot & Durand 1849, p. 133, SENLIS (established in 1507); Aubert 1910, pp. 27, 197, CHARTRES (documented in 1516, for tower works); *Inventaire-sommaire Eure-et-Loir* G 1, p. 67; Couturier 1989, p. 898. In Germany: NAUMBURG (1249, religious society with members including both living and deceased donors); Küas 1937, pp. 173-174, OSNABRÜCK (religious confraternity 1254) *Urkundenbuch Osnabrück*, vol. 2, no. 96, HALBERSTADT (documented in 1257); *Urkundenbuch Halberstadt*, vol. 2, no. 937, vol. 4, no. 3146, BREMEN (established by the archbishop in 1415 as a new confraternity to coexist alongside the old, with a sermon for the messengers of the confraternity of St Peter); *Urkundenbuch Bremen*, vol. 5, p. 70; Klink 1988, passim, MÜNSTER (documented in the sixteenth century); Schröer 1966, pp. 522, 523 n. 49. In Switzerland: SION (documented in 1481, pardoners go round to gather contributions); Dubuis 1979, reg. 43 and 47, BASEL (documented in the *Fabrikbuch* in 1496, with vernacular text), La Roche 1888, p. 105. In the Low Countries: CAMBRAI (documented in synodal statutes in 1287/88), Boeren 1953-1954, vol. 4, p. 151; *Lettres Communes Jean XXII*, no. 50537 (1333). In Spain: PALENCIA (1321/22, 1352, 12 May 1432: letter from the bishop); García Cuesta 1954, pp. 93-94, SANTO DOMINGO DE LA CALZADA (documents dating from between 1440 and 1493; the admission due for someone living was 20 maravedís, for someone dead 10 maravedís; contains a detailed summary of how many indulgences were available to earn on which days, with a total value of 28,451 years and 294 days); López de Silanes & Sáinz Ripa 1991, nos 238, 240, pp. 182-188, 242, 287, 314, 315, 336. For the kingdom of LEÓN: nearly every diocese had a building confraternity (*confradias constructoras*), e.g. ASTORGA (1310), ZAMORA, LEÓN (1267), SALAMANCA (1363); Sánchez Herrero 1978, pp. 137-142, 386, 442, 470, 475.

807 The *Petersbruderschaft* may already have been active in 1264, and certainly was in 1319; Lacomblet 1868,

no. 75; Lacomblet 1857, pp. 173-177; Ennen 1880, pp. 59, 100; Fahne 1864, p. 135 ff.; *Ad Summum 1248*, p. 45; Militzer 1997-2000, vol. 2, pp. 1007-1019. For UTRECHT, see below p. 296.

808 As in WINCHESTER (1202): Lehmann-Brockhaus 1955-1960, no. 4779; CANTERBURY, set up in 1186: Cheney 1973, p. 33; WORCESTER, set up by the bishop in 1224, renewed in 1302: Graham 1945-1947, p. 75; VICH (1326), for a period of ten years: Villanueva Estengo 1902-1906, vol. 7, p. 264.

809 'an annual memorial service, vigil and mass at the high altar for all the benefactors of the fabric and the large bells will be sounded'; Pelt 1930, no. 21. The confraternity was formed in March 1330; Aubert 1931, pp. 12, 13.

810 Mortet & Deschamps 1929, p. 205.

811 La Roche 1888, p. 104; Hieronimus 1938, pp. 224, 400 ff., 483, 506.

812 Pfleger 1937, p. 9; Pfleger 1941, p. 65.

813 *Statutes of Lincoln Cathedral*, vol. 2, pp. 357-358; Hill 1965, p. 113 and plate 3; Edwards 1967, pp. 299, 318; Cook 1947, p. 34; Hamilton Thompson 1925, p. 136; Binnall 1962, p. 77; Owen 1994, pp. 121, 144, 149.

814 It is not clear whether this mass was read at a dedicated fabric altar; Assier 1858, p. 46; Assier 1855, p. 24.

815 Haslinghuis & Peeters 1965, p. 271. In the cathedral of SANTIAGO, the *Arca de la Obra* was installed near the altar of the Holy Cross - the traditional altar of the parishioners, and of the faithful in general - in the thirteenth century; López Ferreiro 1898-1911, vol. 5, app. 13, p. 40.

816 *Diplomatarium Danicum*, vol. 4: 2, no. 517.

817 Héliot & Chastang 1964/1965, p. 808.

818 La Roche 1888, pp. 97, 105; Hieronimus 1938, p. 243. Thirty-five processions were organized inside BASEL Cathedral each year; idem, pp. 568-569.

819 BASEL; La Roche 1888, p. 104. From the cathedral of COLOGNE we still have a '*registrum fraternitatis sancti Petri in Pasculo Coloniensis, 1488*' and a '*registrum defunctorum*', 1488-1550; Fahne 1864, p. 134; Lacomblet 1857, p. 178; *Ad Summum 1248*, D 8. In SPEYER the pardoners were also charged with compiling and updating a register of confraternity members; Mone 1836, p. 241 ff.

820 Pycke 2005, publication of this *liber fabricae*, pp. 682-696: '*hec ecclesia est domus dei et porta celi et consolatio omnium recurrencium ad eam. Namque conveniunt singuli et recreantur in ea universi, sicque in ea spiritualibus bonis reficiuntur quicumue fideles devoti*'; also exh. cat. Tournai, no. 19 and Pycke 2005, pp. 133, 190, 198 and nos 183 and 210. The fabric altar was located in the south transept on level with the rood screen and *jubé*.

821 Woltmann 1876, pp. 259-265; Pfleger 1935, p. 101 ff. As a rule, donors were members of the *confraternitas beate Marie Virginis*. Aside from lists of deceased donors, the codex also contains copies of indulgences and other papal and episcopal benefits extended to the fabric.

822 Goods given in kind were cashed to benefit the fabric. These concern mostly garments, jewellery, weapons, artworks, books and sometimes '*omnia bona sua*'; Woltmann 1876, p. 263.

823 The fabric also accepted property components given under onerous conditions, usually consisting of reading masses for the repose of the deceased. The fabric also assumed the burden of so-called

proveniers – people living alone who transferred all their goods and chattels, in this case to the fabric, which in exchange saw to their needs in life and arranged for commemorative obit celebrations after their deaths. The fabric at STRASBOURG was able to take on such obligations thanks to the kitchen, bakery and wine cellar that it operated for the building labourers boarding there; Pfleger 1935, p. 102; Doré 2007, p. 56; Fuchs 1990b, p. 54.

824 'Dear children, help me to pray faithfully with God's aid for all those people, living and dead, who have given their alms and permanent contributions to the fabric of Our Lady and have participated in all the good things taking place here, by singing and by reading; their names are written below and fall within this week; firstly we commemorate by the will of God the honourable man [...]'; text on the first unnumbered folio of the *Liber Donationum*; Woltmann 1876, p. 381; Pfleger 1937, p. 9.

825 'item, died master Johans Schultheis Zorn of blessed memory, a pious, prized knight, an exceptional devotee of Our Lady and her fabric, who in life gifted the fabric with many stallions and horses and now after his death with his harness and a horse: pray for him'; this item dates from around 1410; Woltmann 1876, p. 391; Pfleger 1935, p. 103.

826 Wittmer 1967, passim; illustration of the *liber donationum*: Doré 2007, p. 60; Nolet & Boeren 1951, p. 395; Van Caenegem & Ganshof 1962, p. 101 ff. Concerning the cathedral of DURHAM's *liber vitae*, see Bishop 1918, p. 349 ff.

827 Extensive overview of the period from 1112 (LAON) until 1533/34 (SENS), with particular focus on relic tours, by Léon Pressouyre in exh. cat. RHEIMS 2001, pp. 174-179.

828 Lucas 1986, pp. 13-17.

829 Amongst others, abbeys in Lobbes, ROUEN and MEAUX; Héliot & Chastang 1964/1965, p. 800. Initially, it was mostly abbeys and monasteries that made these circuits; see also Demouy 2005, pp. 201-222. In general: Héliot & Chastang1964/1965, passim; Héliot 1963, passim; Sigal 1976, passim; Kaiser 1995, passim; Signori 1995, pp. 99-125, 229-246; see also Beissel 1892, pp. 1-18. An overview of travelling alms collection campaigns in the period between 1060 and 1350 in Schöller 1989, pp. 298-305: amongst the 109 ecclesiastical institutions, abbeys, etc. are 40 cathedrals (with LAON as the first in 1112). An early and noteworthy example of a cathedral collection concerns that for the cathedral of SEBASTE (SAMARIA) in the Latin kingdom of Jerusalem. Soon after 1170 Bishop Radulph called on all Christians to contribute to the construction of the cathedral. Several canons were despatched – armed with indulgences and other spiritual privileges – with the relics of St John the Baptist, discovered in 1145. The collection is presumed to have been held in French dioceses as SEBASTE itself was a Frankish bishopric; Kedar 1994, passim.

830 Croyland Abbey near LINCOLN; Lehmann-Brockhaus 1955-1960, no. 1183; Paulus 1922-1923, vol. 2, p. 266; Coulton 1928, p. 355.

831 Kaiser 1995, n. 28 and 32.

832 Paulus 1922-1923, vol. 2, pp. 266, 267.

833 Lehmann-Brockhaus 1938, no. 1128: abbey of Petershausen near KONSTANZ, after 1127.

834 Recent edition of the *Miracula sancte Marie Laudunensis* by Saint-Denis 2008.

835 The revolt of the commune, murder of the bishop and fire in the cathedral took place on 24 April; the journey began on 6 June, possibly preceded by a short circuit of LAON and its environs in May; Saint-Denis 2008, pp. 87-92, 145-159. See also n. 380.

836 Héliot & Chastang 1964/1965, p. 797; Mortet 1911, pp. 319, 320; Bouxin 1902, p. 10.
The 1112 trip lasted from 4 June until 21 September and covered a distance of 1000 km, whilst that made in 1113 lasted from 28 March until 6 September and covered 2000 km; Sigal 1976, pp. 80, 81, maps of the routes on pp. 101, 102; also Signori 1995, pp. 99-125 and Karte IV a and b; also Karte IX (journey with the LAUSANNE Cathedral relics in the diocese of GENEVA in 1235). Also Saint-Denis 1994, pp. 96-104, 109-115, and Saint-Denis 2008, pp. 145-195. Clark & King 1983, p. 22. Construction of the present-day cathedral began around 1150.

837 Migne 1844-1891, vol. 156, col. 961-987: 32 chronicled miracles, c. 1145; a version from some 20 years earlier by Guibert de Nogent contains only seven *miracula*. Detailed analysis of both versions in Signori 1995, pp. 105-124.

838 Héliot & Chastang 1964/1965, p. 810: in 1364 the famous shrine of Nicholas of Verdun was carried through the fields of the diocese of TOURNAI; also Pycke 2003, p. 233 and p. 80, no. 112 '*nota de scrinio beate Virginis exportando vel referendo*'. In SENS repairs were made to a shrine in 1457 '*que l'on portait par les champs en faisant la quête*'; Quantin 1842, p. 16. For AMIENS and the precious items borne along there (1347 inventory of the treasurer), see Durand 1901-1903, vol. 1, p. 115.

839 Migne 1844-1891, vol. 156, col. 975; Saint-Denis 2008, pp. 162-165.

840 Borrowed from Verplaetse 1965, p. 36. It is possible that soliciting money was initially not even amongst the chief objectives of the relic tours. Héliot & Chastang 1964/1965, p. 800, also cite factors such as the desire to avert evil, provide defence and secure the borders of the abbey's secular power. Concerning the practice of demarcating jurisdictional or property boundaries by treading along them with the relics, see also Boeren 1962, p. 39; Herrmann-Mascard 1975, p. 221 ff.

841 Typifying the lack of general diocesan acceptance for these collections is the course of events in AMIENS in 1137, where the relics of the civic patron, the martyr and bishop St Firmin, miraculously 'refused' to leave the city gates; the city's inhabitants were themselves opposed to the relics journeying outside the city; Murray 1996, p. 26. Concerning the compilation of the miracles of St Firmin and the relationship between the saint and commune, see Ott 2000, pp. 63-64.

842 *Vetus Registrum*, vol. 2, pp. 11-12.

843 Paulus 1922-1923, vol. 2, p. 266, vol. 3, pp. 230-273.

844 Detailed description in the statutes of the 1261 provincial council of MAINZ; Mansi 1759-1793, vol. 23, p. 1102.

845 In his *De pignoribus sanctorum*; Lefranc 1896, p. 295; Guth 1970, p. 72 ff.; Platelle 1999 p. 118.

846 Mansi 1759-1793, vol. 20, p. 1124; Héliot & Chastang 1964/1965, p. 14, no. 2.

847 Mansi 1759-1793, vol. 22, p. 681; Artonne *et al.* 1963, p. 352.

848 Foreville 1965, pp. 376-380; Friedberg 1879/1882, vol. 2, p. 888.

849 On this see Paulus 1922-1923, vol. 2, p. 268 ff.; Héliot & Chastang

1964/1965, p. 5 ff. Pardoners were forbidden from performing their office by the Council of Trent on 16 July 1562; Mansi 1759-1793, vol. 33, p. 194; Paulus 1922-1923, vol. 3, p. 497.

850 Deed of 2 September 1391 drawn up by the provost and dean of the cathedral of BREMEN and several other high-ranking clerics: *Urkundenbuch Bremen*, vol. 4, no. 134. Concerning false pardoners in England, who went around without papal or episcopal authorization, see Swanson 2007, p. 183 and index, in voce 'questorial licenses'.

851 Already at the provincial council of TRIER in 1227; later also at the provincial council of MAINZ in 1261, and elsewhere; Paulus 1922-1923, vol. 2, p. 269.

852 'that the business of the fabric of our mother church [...] shall in all matters enjoy a special prerogative'; *Regesten Mainz*, vol. 2, 1, no. 569, 15 March 1356; the archbishop revoked all *negotia questuum* except that for the cathedral.

853 *Monumenta Boica*, vol. 37, nos 249-256.

854 *Urkundenbuch Osnabrück*, vol. 2, nos 96-99, pp. 121, 124, 131.

855 *Geschiedenis van de Oude kerk te Delft*, ms. D.P. Oosterbaan (Delft Municipal Archive), pp. 62-64.

856 *Fabrikbuch* BASEL: La Roche 1888, p. 91; PARIS, fourteenth and fifteenth centuries: Aubert 1920, p. 148 and n. 3; UTRECHT: Dodt van Flensburg 1838-1848, vol. 7, p. 232.

857 'Each Sunday the parish priests must recommend the fabric of the church of St Peter in TROYES to their parishioners in the following manner: "I have been charged by the bishop to recommend to you each Sunday the fabric of the church of St Peter, which is the cathedral of this bishopric and is the mother of all other churches, where the holy chrism is obtained with which you were anointed in the holy sacrament of baptism. And for this, one and all must feel special devotion and do good according to their means"'; Assier 1858, p. 57; Artonne *et al.* 1963, p. 464.

858 Blick & Tekipppe 2004, pp. 716-724, also n. 102; In German: *Pflichtprozession*. The custom may have had its roots in northern France and the Southern Netherlands, reaching England via Norman bishops to be introduced there in virtually every diocese; Swanson 1989, pp. 224-225 ('smoke farthing'); Brooke 1995, p. 186; Blair 1988, pp. 56-66, 84.

859 The so-called '*visitatio religiosa*'; also the bishop's recognition as '*primus parochus*'; Kyll 1962, p. 60; Berlière 1922, p. 428.

860 Berlière 1922, p. 425; Boeren 1962, pp. 58, 59.

861 Pigeon 1876, p. 370; Delisle 1848, pp. 345-347; Le Patourel 1944, p. 131 n. 4.

862 Du Cange, *Glossarium ad scriptores mediae et infimae latinitatis*, Paris 1678, in voce '*pentecostalia*' and '*nummi pentecostales*'; Berlière 1922, p. 423; Kyll 1962, p. 114.

863 In TOURNAI, Whitsunday and the fifteen days thereafter were '*quando homines consueverunt oblationes suas offerre ad ecclesiam cathedralem*'; Voisin 1869, p. 475 n. 1. In LINCOLN until into the fifteenth century; Lepine 1995, p. 13; in EXETER until into the sixteenth century; Lehmberg 1988, p. 30; also Erskine 1981, p. 330. Also in DURHAM, as attested by the *feretrarius* (of the relics of St Cuthbert) rolls, from after 1376 until into the sixteenth century, with offerings made '*cum vexiliis ecclesiarum diocesis Dunelmi*' (1376); '*de oblacionibus curatorum tocius diocesis Dunelmi in processionibus infra ebdomadam pentecoste*' (1428/29); absent parish priests were fined; receipts

were minimal and never above 20 days' wages; personal communication from Dr John McKinnell, Durham. See also Lepine 2006, pp. 43-44. In TRIER the *Pflichtwallfahrt* was still conducted back to the cathedral on Whitsunday on into the sixteenth century; Seibrich 1995, p. 102 n. 385 and p. 54 n. 53.

864 Examples in Thomassinus 1725, pars 2, liber 3, caput 42, no. 2. Additionally in e.g. CAMBRAI, 1260, 1287/88 and early fourteenth century: Boeren 1953-1954, vol. 3, p. 378, vol. 4, p. 136; Martène & Durand 1724-1733, vol. 7, p. 1297; Artonne *et al.* 1963, p. 161. EXETER, 1205/07: *Register John de Grandisson*, pp. 785, 786; 1287: Powicke & Cheney 1964, p. 1056. SOISSONS, 1403: Martène & Durand 1724-1733, vol. 8, p. 1549b; Artonne *et al.* 1963, p. 423. NANTES, 1320: Martène & Durand 1724-1733, vol. 4, p. 955d; Artonne *et al.* 1963, p. 317. MEAUX, around 1346: Martène & Durand 1724-1733, vol. 4, p. 902d; Artonne *et al.* 1963, p. 304. TRÉGUIER, 1338, imposed on all clerics charged with cure of souls, and recommended to parishioners: Martène & Durand 1724-1733, vol. 4, p. 1114e; Artonne *et al.* 1963, p. 455. PARIS, first half of the thirteenth century, *Statuts Synodaux Paris*, vol. 1, pp. 88-89. Also Caspers 2006, pp. 93-94.

865 Kyll 1962, p. 23 ff.

866 This in any case is the interpretation given by Berlière 1922, pp. 419, 432. Later writers paint a more nuanced and in some respects diverging picture; see Kyll 1962, pp. 107, 113; Vanrie 1963, passim. Concerning mother and daughter churches in the diocese of UTRECHT, see Kuys 2004, pp. 42-46.

867 Boeren 1962, p. 59; Berlière 1922, p. 440. The abrogation in NORWICH of the *consuetudo paschalis* - contributions from all diocesan churches collected at both synods - once church and cloister construction were concluded in the twelfth century may represent customary practice; Atherton *et al.* 1996, p. 43.

868 For example HEREFORD 1353, ½ d. each for those who were married and 1 farthing for those who were not; *Registrum Trillek*, sub 17 June 1353; LIMOGES, synodal statutes 1519, 1 d. ('*denarius christianitatis*') from each communicant: Arbellot 1852, p. 80. See also SALISBURY, 1251: *Statutes of Salisbury Cathedral*, p. 207 n. 4; SOUTHWELL: Beaumont 1956, p. 14; Livett 1883, p. 11; UPPSALA, 1257: Nylander 1953, p. 295. For France: Vauchez 1988b, pp. 60-64.

869 See for example the constitutions of the bishop of LONDON, 1245-1249; Powicke & Cheney 1964, p. 652; Woolley 1915, p. 301 (with incorrect date). The *registrum ecclesie Londinensis* (late thirteenth century) says: '*quiquis hoc* [i.e. pilgrimage] *devotus impleverit, fraternitatem maioris ecclesie* [...] *accipit*'; Woolley 1915, p. 287. See also Berlière 1922 p. 440; Vanrie 1963, p. 17.

870 For example CHICHESTER, 1247-'48; Powicke & Cheney 1964, p. 416.

871 Berlière 1922, p. 440.

872 For example SALISBURY, synodal statutes of 1238-44: '[...] *oblationes pentecostales* [...] *ecclesie Sar. sicut aliis cathedralibus ecclesiis a fidelibus parochianis de iure communi nomine subiectionis debitas per parochiales presbiteros colligi et nuntiis nostri capituli, ad locas ubi processiones pentecostales convenient sibi occurrentibus, sine omni diminutione et subtractione persolvi precipimus*'; there is also mention of '*nuntios ad dictam collectam deputatos*'; Powicke & Cheney 1964,

pp. 383, 384. See also the WINCHESTER statutes of 1247?; idem, p. 409, and of NORWICH of 1240-66. Both here and in WINCHESTER the collection was conducted by rural deanery: '*ut collecte in quolibet decanatu per duos viros fidedignos, quos sacrista eiusdem ecclesie adhuc ducit deputandos predicto sacriste absque diminutione qualibet fideliter et integre persolvatur*'; idem, p. 363. Also the ELY statutes; idem, p. 520.

873 *Registrum Lincoln*, no. 307. From a letter written by St Hugh of LINCOLN (1186-1200) we learn that parish priests were to record the names of those of the faithful who had and had not come and made payment and to render account of this to the deans and the bishop's clerical delegate; Woolley 1915, p. 288, also Owen 1994, pp. 131-132. This last also in EXETER (1205-1207): *Register John de Grandisson*, pp. 785-786; Powicke & Cheney 1964, p. 3.

874 *Cartulaire Amiens*, vol. 2, p. 102 (1377).

875 On a very few occasions it turns out that a relic tour organized by the cathedral fabric was a commutation of a Whitsuntide procession or at any rate of an annual pilgrimage. In the diocese of TOURNAI, interest in the annual mid-September procession lapsed in the second half of the fourteenth century in the face of war; the dean and chapter therefore decided to send the shrine on a circuit of the diocese: '*decanus et capitulum* [...] *considerantes, quod populus Flandrensis quam plurimum est devotus, concordaverunt, quod feretrum beate Marie in dicta patria et in episcopatu undique portaretur ad promovendum dicta corda ad devotionem* [...] *perpendentes* [...] *quia propter guerras processio Tornacensis non erat visitata*'; Toussaert 1963, pp. 250, 251.

876 For example the bishop of LONDON, early twelfth century; Graham 1945-1947, p. 73.

877 In Lobbes and Tongeren two-thirds accrued to the canons' *mensae*; Vanrie 1963, pp. 18, 26.

878 In CHARTRES one-third accrued to the *chévecier*; *Cartulaire Chartres*, vol. 1, p. LXXXVI. In QUIMPER half went to the *trésorier*; *Cartulaire Quimper*, no. 124 (1278). In TOURS the *trésorier* likewise received half (1290); *Pouillés Tours*, vol. 5, pp. 5-9.

879 As in Lobbes and Tongeren; Vanrie 1963, pp. 18, 26.

880 Graham 1945-1947, p. 73; cf. Thomassinus 1725, pars 3, liber 2, caput 23, no. 2.

881 Powicke & Cheney 1964, p. 819 n. 1.

882 Rolls for 1278-1287, 1310/11, 1312/13, 1324/25 (for '*Venia beati. Petri*'), 1340/41, 1341/42; Erskine 1962, pp. 258, 262, 265; Erskine 1981 and 1983, index pp. 329, 330; also Swanson 2007, p. 151 n. 208. In ROUEN half these monies accrued to the treasurer and half to the fabric from the thirteenth century on, and to the fabric in full as from 1470; Tabbagh 1997, p. 216. In ANGERS the treasurer lost the *pentecostalia* to the fabric in 1294; Avril 1984, p. 749.

883 Printed copy in broadside: Exeter, cathedral library D and C 3498/93. Dr Audrey Erskine, archivist at the Exeter Cathedral Archives, brought this document to my attention.

884 Cf. '*in signum debite subiectionis*'; see Berlière 1922, p. 440.

885 Loth 1879, pp. 117, 573 ff.; Huard 1925, p. 101; cf. *Inventaire-sommaire Seine-Inférieure* G 4420.

886 *Inventaire-sommaire Seine-Inferieure* G 2514 ff.; 1400 l.t. equals 45 annual wages of an unskilled labourer. In PARIS, too, the parish *obuli christianitatis* accured to the fabric; Paris,

Archives Nationales LL 270, f. 90 (1392).

887 Papal collections were held starting with the Second Crusade (1145-1149). These receipts represented just one of the income sources used for the Crusades; most crusaders used private funds to finance their journey to the Holy Land; Phillips 2007, p. 106. Concerning the financing of the Crusades in the twelfth century, see Constable 1982, pp. 64-88.

888 Paulus 1922-1923 vol. 1, p. 138, vol. 2, pp. 206-207 n. 5; Lunt 1939, p. 423; also Riley-Smith 1995, p. 56.

889 Papal mandate of 27 December 1199: translation published in Lunt 1965, vol. 2, pp. 82-86. These collection boxes were fitted with three locks – the bishop's, the parish priest's and one entrusted to a devout layman. Also Lunt 1939 p. 423 and Lloyd 1988, pp. 18, 46-48; this prescript was applied chiefly in England. For France: Clément 1895, p. 405; Bos 1998, p. 54. As early as 1188 a begging expedition was organized in Wales to collect alms for the Crusades; Lloyd 1988, p. 60. Illustration of a chest preserved in Climping (Sussex): Riley-Smith 1995, p. 58, (see fig. 28).

890 Paulus 1922-1923, vol. 2, chapter XXV, especially pp. 271, 273, 277; Héliot & Chastang 1964/1965, p. 12.

891 The documentary sources draw a very clear distinction between crusade preachers and pardoners commissioned by monasteries and churches; Paulus 1922-1923, vol. 2, p. 361 n. 6.

892 '*Populum [...] communem et pauperes, quorum est vivere de labore, diebus etiam non feriatis, suis omissis operibus et dietis, per dictas litteras compellentes ad ecclesias conveniri pro suis praedicationibus audiendis*'; Hauréau 1896, p. 235.

893 Paulus 1922-1923, vol. 2, p. 273.

894 'so that the good people are not for this occasion withheld from their business'; Martène & Durand 1717, vol. 4, p. 1183a; Artonne *et al.* 1963, p. 454.

895 Herrmann & Knies 1976, p. 33. The anonymous author of this address to the MAINZ chapter remarks how the messengers pressed the faithful: '*lucrum sudoris laborum suorum ab ipsis nituntur extorquere*'.

896 The bull *Quam amabilis Deo*; *Cartulaire S. Jean de Jérusalem*, p. 130; Hiestand 1972, no. 57; also Prutz 1908, p. 155. An earlier bull dated 20 February 1131 is a fake; Migne 1844-1891, vol. 174, col. 77, and *Cartulaire S. Jean de Jérusalem*, no. 91.

897 The bull *Milites Christi*, is preserved only as a précis; Hiestand 1972, no. 2.

898 Hiestand 1972, no. 8; *Cartulaire l'ordre du Temple*, no. VIII; Tangl 1894, formula no. XXXIX.

899 *Cartulaire S. Jean de Jérusalem*, no. 356, confirmed many times; Hiestand 1972, no. 95; Tangl 1894, formula no. XXXII. See also Prutz 1908, p. 154. Bishops made similar complaints about those who impeded cathedral works collections; see the letter *Querelam gravem* in Eekhof 1909, Appendix no. 2 (1 October 1327). The assertion of Paulus 1922-1923, vol. 2, p. 289, that this formulation stems from around 1250 is incorrect.

900 Tangl 1894, formulae LVI, LIX, CI; also Barbiche 1975, nos 136, 137, 537, 539, 771, 812, 829, etc. Cf. Paulus 1922-1923, vol. 2, p. 249 ff., vol. 3, p. 238. The Teutonic Order acquired the right to collect on 20 January 1221; Prutz 1908, p. 115.

901 Mortet 1911, p. 374. In 1204 the Order's general chapter banned all pardoners' activities; Mortet & Deschamps 1929, p. 37. Another early example of a

non-cathedral *mendicatorium* is that issued by the archbishop of LYON for the abbey of St Pierre on 4 August 1173; *Cartulaire Lyonnais*, vol. 1, p. 68. See also Paulus 1922-1923, vol. 2, p. 266. The Templars' papal letters were already being confirmed by bishops early on; see the Bishop of ANGERS's letter of between 1128 and 1149; *Cartulaire l'ordre du Temple*, no. XXI.

902 Prutz 1908, p. 167.

903 Idem, pp. 115, 154-155, 206, 227-228, 403. Concerning this competition, see below p. 214 ff.

904 Powicke & Cheney 1964, pp. 417, 1056.

905 Eekhof 1909, p. 90.

906 *Cartularius Baiocensis*, vol. 1, pp. 58, 59. In the 1185 episcopal *mendicatorium* in behalf of the collegiate church of Notre-Dame-du-Port in CLERMONT-FERRAND the stipulated contribution was 3 d. a year; Manry *et al.*1959, p. 66, no. 38.

907 Denifle 1897-1899, vol. 1, no. 953.

908 Arbellot 1852, pp. 37, 79, 80.

909 Aubert 1910, p. 27, The confraternity of HUESCA asked members to contribute 2 s. a year; Del Arco 1924, pp. 37-39.

910 See n. 767.

911 *Regesten Köln*, vol. 5, no. 630; also Militzer 1997-2000, vol. 2, p. 1016.

912 Appendix three: *mendicatoria* for BAYEUX and TOUL.

913 Álamo Berzosa 1968, p. 36.

914 Such as in SENS; *Inventaire-sommaire Aube* G 1134 ff.; Bouvier 1911, vol. 2, p. 446, vol. 3, p. 18; Quantin 1869, p. 225; Quantin 1842, p. 23 ff.

915 Schmidt 1889, pp. 7, 8; Guntermann 2003, pp. 72-75; their number ranged from one to six each year; the admission due for a married couple was around 75 days' wages. There are no new members after 1528, '*nihil, quia nemo ingressus est*' (f 245v).

916 Though an incidental figure from a twelfth-century chronicle does actually hint at stable receipts. Regarding St Hugh, bishop of LINCOLN (1186-1200), sources relate that '*quandam vero fraternitatem in episcopatu suo instituit, ex qua mille marcae singulis annis ad illud opus construendum colligebantur*'; Lehmann-Brockhaus 1955-1960, no. 2369.

917 '[...]*fraternitatem quondam in ecclesia nostra laudabiliter institutam, sed aliquanto tempore* [...] *sopitam innovamus*'; *Cartularius Baiocensis*, vol.1, p. 58.

918 Clanché 1926-1927, passim; Héliot & Chastang 1964/1965, p. 808. Additional examples: in SÉES the bishop reinstituted the old confraternity in 1452 after the cathedral had been ravaged by the English in 1450; Gobillot 1937, p. 22.

919 The maximum annual contribution was 815 l.t., or more than 26 annual wages of an unskilled labourer.

920 De Girardot & Durand 1849, pp. 133, 137.

921 *Charters Hereford*, p. 163.

922 Assier 1855, p. 27; Quicherat 1886, vol. 2, p. 196; 'from all the confraters and consorors from every village in the diocese'; *Inventaire-sommaire Aube* G 1569 ff. Concerning the building dates: *Congrès Archéologique de France* 113 (1955), pp. 10-13. Concerning wages: d'Avenel 1894-1912, vol. 3, p. 578. SÉES experienced similar fluctuation, with 470 l.t. in 1519, 33 l.t. in 1520, 74 l.t. in 1521 and 170 l.t. in 1522; Marais & Beaudoin 1876, pp. 114-116.

923 La Roche 1888, p. 105; Fouquet 1999, p. 201.

924 Couturier 1989, p. 898; Paris wages: Baulant 1971, p. 482.

925 '*Testamenta laicorum non fient sine praesentia sacerdotis parochialis*'; Mansi 1759-1793, vol. 23, p. 416, vol. 24, p. 444, etc.; Adam 1964, pp. 91-95; Bechle 1954, p. 203 and n. 2. Already in 1176 the bishop of VIBORG was

admonishing his priests not to filch the '*elemosinam de mundo transmigrancium*' intended for the cathedral; *Diplomatarium Danicum*, vol. 1: 3, no. 53.

926 '*Praecipitur sacerdotibus, quod diligentes et solliciti sint in monendo parochianos suos de eleemosynis et legatis ad fabricam ecclesiae b. Marie faciendis et legata fideliter quaerant et reservent; scribant etiam nomina eorum, qui legaverint et ad episcopum ad synodum offerant; et sic eis appareat qui fuerint in hoc diligentes et negligentes*'; Mansi 1759-1793, vol. 22, pp. 766-768; Artonne *et al.* 1963, p. 353.

927 Lehmann-Brockhaus 1955-1960, no. 4094; Powicke & Cheney 1964, p. 191.

928 Mansi 1759-1793, vol. 24, p. 938; Schoolmeesters 1908, p. 92: 1278 statutes.

929 '*Praecipimus eciam presbyteris ut solliciti et diligentes sint in monendis parrochianis suis, quod elemosinas et legata faciant ad fabricam ecclesie b. Marie Cameracensis et sub testimonio bonorum per nuntios fideles procuratori fabrice mittant et nomina eorum, qui fabrice legaverint vel confratrias b. Marie solverint ad synodum deferant, ut pro eis in synodo fiat communis oracio et in singulis parrochiis dominicis diebus et festivis fiat specialis oracio et expresse pro benefactoribus ecclesie b. Marie Cameracensis*' (1278/88); Boeren 1953-1954, vol. 3, pp. 154, 155 (before 1238); see also idem, vol. 4, p. 147, and Reusens 1903, p. 32 (1307).

930 Mansi 1759-1793, vol. 25, p. 22; cited in Thomassinus 1725, pars 3, liber 2, caput 26, no. 3: 1300 statutes.

931 Joosting & Muller 1906-1924, vol. 5, pp. 137, 162: 1342-1362 and 1533.

932 Norton 1880, pp. 314, 315 (doc. x): 28 March 1388. In 1296 the civic administration in FLORENCE further ordered that all testaments had to include a gift for the cathedral works; an obligatory bequest for the third enclosure wall was added to this in 1298. Here the monies were collected in each parish by the parish priests, aided by two laymen; Grote n.d., pp. 33, 34; Davidsohn 1896-1927, vol. 4 (1), p. 369. In ORVIETO all notaries were required to advance the cause of the cathedral works; *Finanziare cattedrali*, p. 195 and n. 71.

933 Schuegraf 1847/1848, vol. 11, p. 94.

934 La Roche 1888, p. 102; also in AMIENS: Denifle 1897-1899, vol. 1, no. 14 (1435).

935 Skillington 1966-1967, passim; wage: Salzman 1952, p. 77; Dobson 1983, p. 38: usually ½ mark; also in DURHAM and CARLISLE.

936 Lepine 2006, pp. 45-46.

937 Bijsterveld 1996, p. 460; Bijsterveld 2007, pp. 26, 27, 197.

938 Atherton *et al.* 1996, p. 278.

939 *Ad Summum 1248*, pp. 135-136 and H7; also Ennen 1880, p. 58; Clemen 1937, p. 53.

940 Antwerp, St James' Church Archives, fabric rolls 1535/36, f. 5 (and others). The transaction was not always so profitable; in 1534/35 receipts from bequests for the cathedral yielded only 1 lb. 2 s. 9 d. brab.

941 *Catálogo documental Burgos*, no. 1918 (1408); the rent was 3000 maravedís.

942 GENOA had a stipulation – the earliest instance dates from 1179 – that one-tenth of monies given in connection with the cure of souls be spent on cathedral-building ('*decenum operi Sancti Laurencii*'); Epstein 1984, pp. 140-143, 171-173, 235-237; *Finanziare cattedrali*, p. 197 n. 84, with examples such as MODENA and BOLOGNA.

943 One ducato oro was equal to 1 lire 7 s. 8 d.imp.; personal communication from Dr E. Brivio, MILAN. The annual wage of a *manovale* averaged around 38 lire imp.

944 Mezzanotte 1955, pp. 867, 900; Gatti Perer 1969, vol. 2, pp. 175, 183, 184; especially Ciceri & Rocco Negri 1971, passim; also Brivio 1977, p. 26 n. 3, and Rocco Negri 1975, p. 187 n. 2.

945 La Roche 1888, pp. 102, 103.

946 Boito 1889, pp. 24, 25.

947 Concerning the *votum simplex*, see Ferraris 1852-1857, in voce '*votum*', art. 1, no. 12.

948 See Appendix three, e.g. the *mendicatoria* for STRASBOURG of 1275, BREMEN and HALBERSTADT. Concerning the commutation of vows, see Paulus 1922-1923, vol. 3, p. 506 ff.

949 Hauréau 1896, p. 234.

950 At least according to later canonists like Barbosa: Iuris Eccl. Univ., liber 1, caput 11, nos 21 and 203; only the pope could commutate *perigrationes maiores* to JERUSALEM, ROME and SANTIAGO. Boeren posits that commutation was an authority reserved for the pope, who could in turn delegate this right to his bishops; *Tijdschrift voor Geschiedenis* 80 (1967), pp. 399-400. See for example *Lettres communes Benoît XII*, no. 2498.

951 Paulus 1922-1923, vol. 1, p. 208, vol. 2, p. 32 ff., vol. 3, p. 506; Lunt 1965, vol. 1, p. 117; pilgrimages to Jerusalem could be converted into payment in gold even as early as 1089.

952 Otherwise the commutation leaned towards dispensation, which was subject to other laws; Ferraris 1852-1857, in voce '*votum*', art. 3, no. 119.

953 Eekhof 1909, p. IX.

954 *Bronnen bouwgeschiedenis*, vol. 2 (1), p. 52 and n. 2.

955 Paulus 1922-1923, vol. 3, p. 511 ff.

956 Klink 1988, pp. 122-123.

957 Schuegraf 1858, pp. 170, 184, 196.

958 Brutails 1899-1901, vol. 12, p. 406.

959 Van Havre 1897, under this year.

960 *Inventaire-sommaire Marne* G IV, p. 114. Additional examples in Coulton 1928, p. 363. Also in FREISING, 1492-1497, '*ex esu lacticiniorum*'; Mitterwieser 1918, p. 80 ff.; Ramisch *et al.* 1998, nos 9772, 10138, 11301 (receipts worth 50 rhinegulden).

961 '2 thousand and a half letters made for the butter [dispensation] sent to the rural deans and the parish priests to recommend the fabric'. 'the money which has come from [the dispensation for] butter and milk'; Archives départementales Seine-Inférieure G 2512. For an estimate of the building costs between 1485 and 1507, see Loth 1879, p. 133 ff. The north tower of BOURGES Cathedral (1580-1624) is also called the *Tour de Beurre*; Leblond 1933, p. 20; De Girardot & Durand 1849, p. 21 n. 1.

962 *Dictionnaire de Théologie catholique*, vol. 13, especially col. 2490 (in voce '*restitutio*'). Quoted from the *sermon d'Amiens* (c. 1276); Crampon 1876 p. 587.

963 This episode is related by Caesar of Heisterbach (around 1180-1240) and must have taken place between 1180 and 1196; Baldwin 1970, vol. 1, pp. 307-309; cited in Aubert 1920, p. 28 n. 3, and in Coulton 1928, p. 348 n. 1. An analogous incident is recorded in the LAON book of miracles; Migne 1844-1891, vol. 156, col. 979.

964 Nelson 1947, p. 110.

965 Cf. the adage '*meretrix non peccat quia accipit, sed quia meretrix*'; cited in Baldwin 1970, vol. 1, p. 104; also Baldwin 2006, p. 92.

966 Baldwin 1970, vol. 1, pp. 134-136; Caviness 1996, p. 59 n. 9.

967 Cf. the donation made by a *meretrice* to MILAN Cathedral, p. 147 above.

968 Baldwin 1970, vol. 1,

pp. 244-248.

969 In later UTRECHT *mendicatoria*, e.g. 1398; Eekhof 1909, Appendix no. 40; *Bronnen bouwgeschiedenis*, vol. 2 (1), p. 72 n. 4. We also find mention of '*bona minus justa quesita*'; Eekhof 1909, Appendix no. 4 (1344). Concerning UTRECHT, see below p. 296.

970 'if anyone has unlawfully acquired goods, whether they be found goods, stolen goods or usurious goods, and does not know the legal heir and gives them to the building of Our Lady, he shall be free from guilt'; La Roche 1888, p. 98; a different version in Hieronimus 1938, p. 266 (from the *ceremoniale Basiliensis Episcopatus*, 1517).

971 'all goods that were lost and are given to St Bavo'; Haarlem, Noord-Hollands Archief, St Bavo church archives, no. 147, 1502 account, f. 20.

972 Haarlem, Noord-Hollands Archief, St Bavo church archives, 1492 account, f. 12; also 1486 account, f. IV; 1497 account, f. 24v. (lost ox); 1505, f. 29 (lost sheep).

973 Noonan 1957, p. 30; Nelson 1947, p. 110. See also Thomas Aquinas 1952, *Summa Theologiae*, II, II, q. 32a.7.

974 Hauréau 1896, pp. 233, 234.

975 Post 1967, passim. See the important review by P.C. Boeren in *Tijdschrift voor Geschiedenis* 80 (1967), pp. 399-400. For the date of this treatise, possibly read out during the synod of 1371, see Hofman 2003, p. 761.

976 For example in CAMBRAI, 1238: '*quod si non inveniantur haeredes, fabricae ecclesiae b. Marie Cameracensis restituenda applicentur*'; Boeren 1953-1954, vol. 3, p. 136.

977 Schoolmeesters 1908, p. 10. Amongst these were the aforementioned military orders such as the Teutonic Order, which obtained this privilege in 1257; Prutz 1908, p. 115.

978 Including in: *Monumenta Germaniae Historica*, Ep. Saec. XIII Pont., p. 422 (METZ, 1257); *Gallia Christiana*, vol. 13, instr. 395 (TARENTAISE, 1259); *Registres Urbain IV*, no. 2229 (hospital of Santo Spirito, ROME, 1263); *Registres Honorius IV*, no. 2981 (monastery in FLORENCE, 1286); *Registre Benoît XI*, nos 98, 220, 428, 530, 558, 601, 836, 970 (especially to the Dominicans, 1303-1304); *Regestum Clementis papae V*, nos 768, 4048, 4051, 8459, 8460. Additionally Paulus 1922-1923, vol. 3, p. 501 ff.

979 Allan 1874-1888, vol. 3, p. 77.

980 Prims 1927-1947, vol. 15, p. 142, vol. 18, p. 156. The church fabric paid ROME quite high sums for this privilege, which was valid for a limited period – usually fifteen years. See Vroom 1983, p. 56.

981 Paulus 1922-1923, vol. 3, p. 503; *Dictionnaire de droit canonique*, in voce '*componende*', especially col. 1255. *Compositio* was a right reserved for the pope.

982 Joosting & Muller 1906-1924, vol. 5, pp. 111, 116; Post 1967, p. 68 at line 723; cf. Clem. lib. V tit. VII c. 1, in Friedberg 1879/1882, vol. 2, pp. 1186, 1187; also Hofman 2003 at line 652. Later synodal statutes: Mansi 1759-1793, vol. 25, pp. 498, 756, 757, 1094; also Thomassinus 1725, pars 3, liber 2, caput 10, no. 5.

983 Edler-de Roover 1957, p. 773 ff.; Nelson 1947, p. 110. Popes sometimes recommended this, for instance Pope Eugene IV (1431-1447) to Cosimo de Medici; Gombrich 1960, p. 282; Urban IV in 1264 to a Florentine merchant; Hermesdorf 1963, p. 16. Sometimes popes also advised donating this money to the poor, for instance Clement VI (1342-1352) to the French king; Paulus 1922-1923, vol. 3, p. 510.

984 Fraser Jenkins 1970, p. 163.

985 See for example the 1476 document issued by the archbishop-elect of MAINZ, in which he grants the Franciscans certain pastoral authorities, such as the right to take confessions, but at the same time expressly reserves any incoming *bona vaga* for the cathedral fabric; Wuerdtwein 1781-1792, vol. 9, pp. XXIX-XXX.

986 In 1358 the bishop of BAMBERG allocated local *bona injusta* to the construction of the parish church of St Sebaldus in Nuremberg; Reicke 1926, p. 106.

987 Synodal statutes of 1354-1356; Beissel 1889, vol. 2, p. 19.

988 'item, the forenamed testator gives and bequeaths to the fabric of Our Lady of CAMBRAI his unlawful goods, whom [the owner] he knows not 13 s.'; Antwerp, Archive of the O.-L.-Vrouwekathedraal: testament of A. de Moor, 29 July 1500.

989 See the *Miracula* in Migne 1844-1891, vol. 156, col. 968.

990 Clanché 1926-1927, p. 157; Villes 1983, pp. 46, 49, 142, 176-181. In YORK the *mendicatorium* of 1304 stipulates that the collection will be held until countermanded; Raine 1859, p. 155.

991 Héliot & Chastang 1964/1965, p. 8.

992 *Inventaire-sommaire Yonne* G 1124-1163.

993 *Inventaire-sommaire Seine-Inférieure* G 11, G 347-418.

994 Raine 1859, pp. 196-198.

995 Schuegraf 1847/1848, vol. 11, pp. 55, 209.

996 Ennen 1880, p. 42; Lacomblet 1868, no. 97; *Ad Summum 1248*, p. 48.

997 See p. 321.

998 Goñi Gaztambide 1955, pp. 3, 47.

999 See p. 30. Some additional figures: a 1328 count documents the number of parishes in various French dioceses as follows. SENLIS: 86, NOYON: 295-300, Soissons: 405, LAON: 343, AMIENS: 774, RHEIMS: 774, LIMOGES: 900, SAINTES: 700, AIRE-SUR-L'ADOUR: 230, CLERMONT-FERRAND before 1317: 800; Van der Meer 1967, pp. 10, 41, 60, 153, 184. During the same period the archbishopric of COLOGNE encompassed some 798 parishes; Neuss & Oediger 1964, p. 272. The diocese of BASEL numbered 154 parishes, and LAUSANNE 301; Pfister, p. 195 ff.; Hauck 1898-1920, vol. 4, p. 220 ff.; late fourteenth-century STRASBOURG had 423 parishes; Rapp 1974, p. 22.

1000 'to have renewed the three documents in which all the parish priests of the archbishopric of ROUEN are registered on behalf of the fabric'; *Inventaire-sommaire Seine-Inférieure* G 2484.

1001 Ramisch *et al.* 1998, vol. 2, p. 237, in voce *'Sammlung, [...] collectura'*.

1002 Schuegraf 1855, in voce *'de collecturis ecclesiarum'*, pp. 31-57; also Hubel & Schuller 1995, p. 102, concerning extremely severe sanctions for stubborn parish priests (1405). For the number of parishes, see Gatz *et al.* 2003, p. 603.

1003 *Bronnen bouwgeschiedenis*, vol. 2 (1), pp. 8-29 and below p. 290.

1004 Cf. the difficulties confronting canons in England: Bouxin 1902, p. 12; Héliot & Chastang 1964/1965, p. 17.

1005 *Registres Urbain IV*, no. 2925. On 19 December 1265 his successor Clement IV (1265-1268) granted indulgences to those of the faithful in the Church provinces of BOURGES, NARBONNE and BORDEAUX who donated to the cathedral building works; Du Ranquet 1928, p. 13; Gobillot 1912, pp. 14-16; Manry *et al.*1959, p. 167 (no. 94) (translation); see also Biget 1974, pp. 132-133.

1006 *Registres Innocent IV*, no. 2569. The archbishop of

MAGDEBURG also managed to secure a papal recommendation letter for the whole Church province in 1215; Hamann & Rosenfeld 1910, n. 42.

1007 See Appendix three.

1008 Ennen 1880, p. 42.

1009 *Regesten Köln*, vol. 3, no. 1779.

1010 Fallue 1848, p. 211.

1011 Lehmann-Brockhaus 1955-1960, no. 4095. Elsewhere, the *nuntii* are called '*praedicatores immo magis elemosinarum petitores*'; idem, no. 4072.

1012 Martène & Durand 1717, vol. 1, p. 918; Boissonnot 1920, p. 67; *Congrès Archéologique de France* 155 (1997) p. 291.

1013 Deed of 25 June 1291, valid until 25 May (Whitsunday) 292; *Regesten Köln*, vol. 3, no. 3339.

1014 *Urkundenbuch Strassburg*, vol. 1, p. 564.

1015 Paulus 1922-1923, vol. 2, p. 272. In some cases we do not know the legal grounds on which *nuntii* went round the diocese. On 25 June 1291 the archbishop and cathedral chapter of COLOGNE informed the archbishop and clergy of MAINZ that they had appointed two '*procuratores in negocio fabrice*' for the archdiocese, who were vested with wide-ranging authorities; *Regesten Köln*, vol. 3, no. 3339. *Questores* from BOURGES were active in the diocese of POITIERS; Branner 1962a, p. 25. In the beginning of the thirteenth century, the chapter of CHARTRES despatched '*nuntios per quasdam provincias*'; Thomas 1881, p. 528; see also Héliot & Chastang 1964/1965, pp. 809, 810. In the early fourteenth century collectors working on behalf of SAINT-BERTRAND-DE-COMMINGES, St Sernin in TOULOUSE and NARBONNE Cathedral were making rounds in the diocese of ELNE; Durliat 1960, p. 169 ff.

1016 Later canonists made a point of noting that permission from secular powers was not sufficient; Ferraris 1852-1857, in voce '*quaestuare*', art. 2.

1017 Signori 1995, p. 191; source: the *Miracula*.

1018 Ennen & Eckertz 1860-1879, vol. 2, no. 375; Lacomblet 1868, no. 30; Ennen 1880, p. 42; *Ad Summum 1248*, p. 43.

1019 *Inventaire-sommaire Marne* G IV, 454 (1403).

1020 *Inventaire-sommaire Oise* G 1, 1338 (1477); De la Fons Mélicocq 1848, pp. 31-36.

1021 *Inventaire-sommaire Yonne* G 125; Bouvier 1911, vol. 2, p. 420.

1022 *Congrès Archéologique de France* 112 (1954), p. 55 (1442, 1444). In 1330 it was the king of MALLORCA, James II, who gave permission for the *obrers* of PERPIGNAN to collect in all parishes in the kingdom. The pardoners were to wear a bell and carry a book with them in which to register new confraternity members; Ponsich 1953 p. 141. Additional examples in Héliot & Chastang 1964/1965, vol. 59, pp. 809, 810; vol. 60, p. 6 ff. An early example is SENLIS, letter from Louis VII around 1155; *Gallia Christiana*, vol. 10, instr. p. 1401; *Congrès Archéologique de France* 44 (1877), p. 252; Mortet & Deschamps 1929, pp. 95, 96.

1023 Aubert 1910, pp. 14, 190-191.

1024 Cf. *Regesta Honorii papae III*, no. 4389; also Clark & King 1983, p. 60 n. 24.

1025 The archbishop was summoned before the pope on 6 September 1245; *Registres Innocent IV*, no. 1625.

1026 Decretal '*Romana ecclesia*': Sexti decr. 1. v tit. x de poen. c. 1; Friedberg 1879/1882, vol. 2, p. 1093. Cf. Ferraris 1852-1857, in voce '*archi-episcopus*', art. 2, no. 71. On this conflict, see Varin 1838-1848, vol. 1, pp. 670-687; Paulus 1922-1923, vol. 2, p. 271; Branner 1961, p. 30 and n. 37; Reinhardt 1963, p. 232

n. 3; Héliot & Chastang 1964/1965, p. 10 ff.

1027 CAHORS synod of 1318; Martène & Durand 1717, vol. 4, pp. 688, 689; Artonne *et al.* 1963, pp. 154-155. CAMBRAI: Boeren 1953-1954, vol. 3, p. 27 n. 41, p. 387 n. 10.

1028 Varin 1838-1848, vol. 1, p. 725; Reinhardt 1963, pp. 74, 232 n. 5.

1029 'the rents of the quests contracted [...] in six dioceses of the Church province of ROUEN'; Archives départementales Seine-Inférieure G 2383 ff. (1383 ff.). The six dioceses are SÉES, Evreux, AVRANCHES, LISIEUX, BAYEUX and COUTANCES.

1030 *Inventaire-sommaire Seine-Infèrieure* G 2513, G 2520 ff.

1031 For instance in LINCOLN, 1321; *Statutes of Lincoln Cathedral*, vol. 1 *(liber niger)*, pp. 332-334; cf. REGENSBURG synodal statutes of 1377, caput 35; *Monumenta Boica*, vol. 15, pp. 618-620. For UTRECHT, see below p. 291.

1032 Concerning diocesan synods, see Feine 1954, p. 330; Hinschius 1869-1897, vol. 3, p. 582 ff.; Cheney 1968, p. 5; Foreville 1965, p. 314. Concise overview in Gaudemet 2008, pp. 421-442.

1033 Here just one example of many: 1288 synodal statutes of the bishop of LIÈGE, with provisions concerning the designation of *res aliene*, p. 106; chapter on *de questuariis*, pp. 137-138; encouragement to leave bequests to the fabric, p. 140; Avril 1996.

1034 The *cathedraticum* was also called *synodaticum*.

1035 Paris, Bibliothèque Nationale, lat. 5529b, f. 4v., 5; Mortet & Deschamps 1929, p. 320; Quicherat 1886, vol. 2, p. 185. See endpapers.

1036 Archives départementales Yonne, G 1126 ff.; Bouvier 1911, vol. 2, p. 446.

1037 Paris, Bibliothèque Nationale, lat. 9111, f. 206 (1294/95 account); lat. 9113 (1373/74 account); London, British Museum Add. ms. 15083 (1400/02, 1402/03, 1409/10 accounts); Assier 1855, p. 14.

1038 *Bronnen bouwgeschiedenis*, vol. 2 (1), p. XXXI, and below p. 296 ff.

1039 Account for 1334/35; Archives départementales Puy-de-Dôme 3 G arm. 18, sac. B, cote 25.

1040 Account for 1416/17 ff.; Archives départementales Rhône 10 G 1608 ff.

1041 Diestelkamp 1929, pp. 235, 258-259. A similar measure was taken in MAGDEBURG in 1491.

1042 For actual practice in the diocese of STRASBOURG, see Rapp 1974, pp. 64, 331. For UTRECHT, see Post 1957, vol. 1, p. 253.

1043 On rural synods: *Dictionnaire de droit canonique*, in voce *'archidiacre'* c. 975; in voce *'archiprètre'* c. 1011-1014; Hinschius 1869-1897, vol. 2, p. 269 ff.; Lambrecht 1984; Nolet & Boeren 1951, p. 299 ff.; Kuys 2004, pp. 137-141; Hamilton Thompson 1943, p. 185 ff.; Scammel 1971, p. 7 ff. For practices in the case of STRASBOURG, see Rapp 1974, pp. 63-65, 88, 89, 196, 197, 221-225; Burcklé 1935, especially pp. 92-94.

1044 Mansi 1759-1793, vol. 22, pp. 1234-1235.

1045 Different procurement methods were combined in the diocese of CAMBRAI, too. Recorded together under one item were receipts both *'a commissis ad causam indulgentiarum et privilegiorum concessorum confratribus ecclesie'*, probably to be identified as the *nuntii* of the *mendicatorium*, and *'a decanis christianitatum'*, the rural deans; Archives départementales Nord 4 G 4669 (1461 ff.).

1046 *Inventaire-sommaire Seine-Inférieure* G 2524 (1511/12 account) ff.; Lefebvre 1994, vol. 4, pp. 115-116. The guidelines and set schedule for this expedition in both winter and summer, plus instructions for the distribution of *breves* about the confraternity in each rural deanery, are published in Lefebvre 1994, vol. 4, pp. 19-27: *'Cy apres ensuit ce que le procureur de l'euvre de Nostre Dame de Rouen doibt faire pour la fabrique quant est a aler querre la confrarie par les doyennnés de l'archeveschié'*; my thanks to Ms Lefebvre for making this rare document available to me. WELLS also sent two chapter representatives on horseback to make a several-week circuit of the diocese, stopping in each rural deanery to pick up the monies; WELLS Cathedral Archives, fabric accounts.

1047 *Inventaire-sommaire Seine-Inférieure* G 2490, G 2491 (1431/32, 1432/33 accounts): *'pro vino dato dominis curatis, qui fuerunt in kalendis, in quibus ego procurator antedictus non audebam ire, obstantibus guerris, et pluribus sacculis seu saquetis de pulvere datis decanis ruralibus, qui dictam fabricam curatis recommandaverunt in dictis kalendis 20 s.'* The *kalendes* or *calendes* were the meetings convoked by rural deanery or archpresbytery; they were also known as *concilia, capitula, synode* or *congregatio*; their frequency varied from one diocese to another, decreasing over the course of time from at first monthly to, in the later Middle Ages, a few times or even only once yearly; failure to attend resulted in a fine; Avril 2003, pp. 11-26.

1048 *Inventaris Archief kapittel ten Dom*, no. 405, f. 18.

1049 Mone 1834, pp. 324; La Roche 1888, p. 99; cf. Pfister 1964, pp. 195.

1050 Burcklé 1935, pp. 117-121.

1051 *'Pour grossoyer douze lettres missives pour envoyer au douze doyens pour faire recommander la croysée à leurs curés'*; *Inventaire-sommaire Yonne* G 1142; Bouvier 1911, vol. 2, p. 411; Quantin 1842, p. 16.

1052 *Breviculi*, the purpose of which is not entirely clear but may have been equivalent to confraternity letters, were distributed amongst rural deaneries in the dioceses of ROUEN, CAMBRAI, WELLS and possibly others. In CAMBRAI such *breviculi*, *'recepta queste breviculorum in denariis in toto episcopatu'* are already documented in the fourteenth century; however, as from 1383 the *breviculi*, which the parish priest read from the pulpit, were replaced by *nuntii* sent round to promote the cathedral fabric; Archives départementales Nord 4 G 4560 (1332/33 ff.); Houdoy 1880, p. 134. A *'collectio fraternitatis per brevia'* is documented in WELLS, where these *'brevetts'* - 480 copies in 1457/58 - were distributed to the rural deans; WELLS Cathedral Archives, fabric accounts. See also fig. 15.

1053 Lefebvre 1994, vol. 4, pp. 23, 26. Concerning the diocesan division into 1400 parishes, 28 rural deaneries and six archdeaconries, see *Fasti Ecclesiae Gallicanae*, vol. 2, ROUEN, pp. 3-4. Many hundreds of *'brevetz* [...] *escrip en parchemin distribuez aux doyennés'* are documented annually. From 1489/90 on they were printed, and the number of copies distributed each year rose from 2000 to 5000; *Inventaire-sommaire Seine-Inférieure* G 2491 ff.

1054 For instance in the diocese of COUTANCES, as attested by the 1372 synodal statutes; Pigeon 1876, pp. 258-259, and in CAMBRAI; Houdoy 1880, pp. 33-34.

1055 See Appendix three, also in CLERMONT-FERRAND (1314); Archives départernentales Puy-de-Dôme 3 G arm. 18, sac. B, cote 24.

1056 Eekhof 1909, p. x.

1057 Hauréau 1896, p. 234. Hugh of Newcastle uses the term *convocatio*, which was also used to designate parochial synods in the region of the northern Netherlands; Post 1954, p. 24.

1058 The bishop of PRAGUE allowed parish priests a share; *mendicatorium* for PRAGUE (see Appendix three), p. 355. Synodal statutes also sometimes stipulate integral delivery: '*et quod datur petentibus elemosynas integre restituatur*'; LE MANS 1247 and ROUEN 1231-1235; Mansi 1759-1793, vol. 23, pp. 758, 379; Artonne *et al.* 1963, pp. 247, 378.

1059 De Lacger 1927, p. 463; Artonne *et al.* 1963, p. 29.

1060 AVIGNON synodal statutes of 1344; Martène & Durand 1717, vol. 4, pp. 568-569; Artonne *et al.* 1963, p. 97.

1061 Paulus 1922-1923, vol. 1, p. 202 and n. 6.

1062 Idem, p. 207 n. 5. In 1212 the distribution of these boxes was entrusted to *predicatores* who – again in reference to England – '*cum privilegiis multis per se et coadiutores suos multos signaverunt ad honorem crucis, multa colligentes et truncos per singulas ecclesias statuentes*'; *Annales prioratus de Dunstaplis*; Lehmann-Brockhaus 1955-1960, no. 6724. Also in the case of collections run by the Hospitallers: *Registrum Baldock et al.*, pp. 109-110 (1309).

1063 Martène & Durand 1717, vol. 4, p. 1123; Artonne *et al.* 1963, p. 456.

1064 Mone 1836, p. 243; Schultz 1877, p. 56.

1065 La Roche 1888, p. 91; Mone 1834, p. 323; Janner 1876, pp. 177-178 (fifteenth century).

1066 *Inventaire-sommaire Yonne* G 1137 and subsequent numbers; Bouvier 1911, vol. 2, p. 446.

1067 Quicherat 1886, vol. 2, p. 195; Assier 1858, p. 43 ff., Gadan 1851, pp. 1-5.

1068 Hanauer 1901-1902, vol. 21, p. 162 (fourteenth and fifteenth centuries). Cf. 1437/38 account: '*Dis ist ingenummen uss den buhssen alse man das werck unser lieben frowen in den kirchspeln an den sunnentagen verkundet 157 lb.*'; Archives de l'œuvre Notre-Dame, no. 43 (Archives de la ville de Strasbourg). See also the 1475/78 account: '[...] *innome usser den buhssen als man jn den kyrchspelen sü vmbtreytt jnn der Statt vnd jm lande*' (our receipts from the boxes taken around the parish churches in the city and in the countryside) [to be distinguished from '*inname vsser den stocken jnwendig des münsters*' (receipts from the collection bag inside the *Münster*)]; Fuchs & Holderbach 2008, p. 189; also 1492/93 account, Fuchs 2006, p. 71; the receipts were very small – only 106 lb. in this year, or around ten annual wages of an unskilled workman.

1069 After 1387 '*bussoli, ceppi e casse*' in the cathedral and in all the churches of the city and diocese; Boito 1889, p. 16. *Cippi*, *cassette* and *tronchi* for other Italian *duomi* were also installed in the parish churches. In the case of ORVIETO lists of parishes were maintained in a *Liber cipporum Sancte Marie* (fourteenth century); labourers from the cathedral escorted the delegates from the *Opera* during their annual trip; Riccetti 1988, pp. 147-148 (with a map showing distribution) and p. 171; *Finanziare cattedrali*, pp. 188, 197.

1070 '*De pixidibus episcopatu*'; *Inventaire-sommaire Seine-Inférieure* G 1157 (1357/58 account); Durand 1901-1903, vol. 1, p. 116.

1071 Boissonnot 1920, pp. 238, 239 (early fifteenth century).

1072 *Congrès Archéologique de France* 119 (1961), p. 56 and n. 1 (after 1393).

1073 *Congrès Archéologique de France* 78 (1911), p. 449 (episcopal mandate of 17 April 1403).

1074 Account for 1401/02; London, British Museum Add. ms. 15083, f. 107v.

1075 'receipts from the boxes in each parish in the diocese of TROYES, which contain the collections for the said fabric from the parishes and which are opened by the said masters of the fabric'; Gadan 1851, pp. 1, 2.

1076 Paris, Bibliothèque Nationale, lat. 9111, f. 213.

1077 The following are examples of offerings made for the cathedral fabrics gathered by collection dish (*bacín*) in each parish, in alphabetical order by diocese; how this was organized is not clear in every case. ASTORGA: episcopal dictate of 1444 that each parish was to install a '*bacín para la obra y fábrica*' to benefit the cathedral; *Colección documental Astorga*, vol. III, no. 2047. BURGO DE OSMA, fifteenth century: '*limosna de la Bacineta*' in all diocesan churches on all Sundays and feast days; Hevia Ballina 1993, p. 93. JAÉN: the *obrero* was authorized (in 1386 and later) to install a *vacín* in every parish except BAEZA, home to the former cathedral church; Rodríguez Molina 1986, pp. 70 and 252. MONDOÑEDO: the '*bacines, mandas, limosnas y tabaquez*' (wicker basket) of each diocesan parish, with the exception of the cathedral and those in the city, are leased by the cathedral fabric to the highest bidder (usually a canon) for life or for a certain term. This relates only to monetary offerings, and not those in kind such as precious items, retables and so forth, nor to estates and immoveable property. The parish fabrics were allowed to keep half; Cal Pardo 1992, nos 88 (1498), 92, 94, 138, 153, 1643, 2885, 4506 and 2885 (1593). MURCIA: '*bacín del obispado*', with very meagre receipts in the sixteenth century: Gutiérrez-Cortines Corral 1987a, p. 107. PALMA DE MALLORCA: the cathedral fabric confraternity of *Nostra Dona Santa Maria* organized collections with the cathedral *bacins* (*de la seu*, a cathedral-run collection in the city during Lent), in the city's five parishes (*de Ciutat*) and on the islands of Mallorca, Minorca and Eivissa (*de l'illa*), which in each case were picked up by parochial *baciners*. Gifts in kind (cheese, oil, grain, eggs, figs) were picked up by horse-drawn cart and sold in Palma. Confraternity contributions generated more than half the fabric's receipts in the second half of the fourteenth century; Domenge i Mesquida 1997, pp. 55, 82, 100-108,112-115,120-121, 302-308; Pascual 1995, pp. 38. PAMPLONA: canons were granted (i.e. leased) the right to collect that which had been gathered by the *bacineros* in a certain area, and were further authorized to take action against false '*cuestores y pedidores*', 11 April 1472; Goñi Gaztambide 1996, p. 116 and doc. 19. TORTOSA: *acaptes* (collections) using *bacins* were organized in all diocesan parishes immediately after the first stone had been laid in 1347; '*l'baci d'aquest acapte*' are specifically given priority over other collections; Matamoros 1932, p. 99 n. 2; Almuni i Balada 2007, pp. 81, 100 and doc. 28, 52 and 53. SANTO DOMINGO DE LA CALZADA: the bishop orders a *baçin* for the cathedral and hospital to be passed around during mass on every Sunday and feast day; parish priests are allowed to keep a one-fifth share (1465); López de Silanes & Sáinz Ripa 1992, no. 287. SEGORBE AND ALBARRACÍN (both with cathedral rights; the bishop refers to '*sponsas suas*'): the bishop orders that '*bacinum et questor pro opere et luminaria sedis* [...]' be admitted into all parishes (1357); Blasco Aquilar 1973, p. 293 n. 73. VALENCIA: fabric rolls over the period from 1380 (the earliest) until the mid-sixteenth century record *bacins* or *buzones* in every parish, with a distinction between diocesan parishes' *bacins dla Seu* or *bacins del bispat*, registered monthly with the name of the collector, sometimes together with the *bacins* of the twelve city parishes, and the cathedral's *bacins dels portals*; Archivo catedralicio de Valencia, no. 1473, passim, and Sanchis y Sivera 1909, pp. 9-10.

1078 *Inventaire-sommaire Seine-Inférieure* G 2525 (1512/13 account); G 2539 (accounts for 1540 ff.). Other dioceses also handed out small gifts of this kind to the *collectores*, for example tokens including 2500 small knives in STRASBOURG in 1382 and 1395; Fuchs 1990a, pp. 43, 50, 52.

1079 '[...] *quaestumque sibi fieri praecipiunt* [i.e. pardoners] *et collectam, quandoque tertia vel media dicti quaestus presbyteris portione concessa, ut eos* [i.e. parish priests] *sibi magis alliciant in favorem ad suam fallaciam prosequendam*'; Hauréau 1896, p. 234.

1080 Heath 1964, pp. 28, 30, 35, 36, 42, 43: always as '*de questore s. Wilfridi de Rypon*', etc. Concerning non-cathedral building works collections, see below p. 214.

1081 Post 1967, pp. 44, 45; Hofman 2003, p. 790.

1082 Mone 1834, p. 323; La Roche 1888, pp. 91, 99; Janner 1876, pp. 177-178.

1083 *Bronnen bouwgeschiedenis*, vol. 1 (1), p. XXXI; incorrect reading of the relevant text.

1084 The fabric of the church of St Stephan in VIENNA received one-third of the proceeds collected for the cathedral works at PASSAU; see for example the 1407 account: '*die Samnung gen Passau in der Vasten ist gevallen der drittail der chirchen 10 tl. 7 d.*'; Uhlirz 1902, p. 260. See also Paulus 1922-1923, vol. 3, p. 464. For examples from the diocese of UTRECHT, see below p. 287.

1085 See p. 294.

1086 Krebs 1952-1959, no. 155 (1490).

1087 Idem, no. 5167, also 1837, 3103, 5233, 5791: complaint by the masters of the fabric in 1525 concerning the additional time needed for counting.

1088 LAON: *Hermanni monachi de miraculis s. Mariae Laudunensis*, in: Migne 1844-1891, vol. 156, col. 968; new edition by Saint-Denis 2008; Héliot & Chastang 1964/1965, pp. 810, 814 with varied examples. Also SALISBURY in 1219: *Vetus Registrum*, vol. 2, pp. 11-12.

1089 Barlow 1939, p. 88.

1090 For example at the provincial council of RHEIMS in 1231; Paulus 1922-1923, vol. 2, pp. 266, 269. Cf. the in some indulgence letters customary clause '*quas litteras mitti per questuarios districtius inhibemus*'; idem, vol. 2, pp. 24, 288 and n. 5. In 1486 the abbey of Ste-Colombes near SENS donated one of the saint's ribs to a parish church under her patrocinium under the condition that it would not be circuited abroad; Coulton 1936, p. 124.

1091 A model sermon of c. 1440 drawn up by the Antonines; Mischlewski 1992, pp. 487-488, and one from the abbey of St Hubert in the Ardennes; Eekhof 1909, pp. 79-80. Concerning these two collections and their relevance for the cathedral works, see below p. 363-378.

1092 The sermon was published by Crampon 1876, pp. 553-601, in a fragment of somewhat over 10,000 words in length. Concerning this sermon, see Zink 1976, no. 55 (p. 486); analysis on pp. 240-241; additionally, pp. 42-46, 127, 205-209, 276, 357-358, 369, 424-425, 450. My thanks to Bernard Verhille of AMIENS, who supplied me with a copy of the ms. Picardie 158, f. 131-138, from the Bibliothèque Nationale in Paris. Jacques Ribard is preparing a new edition of the sermon. The *sermon d'Amiens* is a rare example of a sermon possibly transcribed literally as read in the vernacular for an uneducated audience; Zink 1976, p. 276. Murray 1996, pp. 116-117 and 207-208, unjustifiably assumes that the sermon was held in the cathedral.

1093 Crampon 1876, pp. 585 and 553.

1094 'to be forgiven [...] good, gentle folk [...] forgiveness and absolution for all of those men and women who send their alms to the church of Our Lady in AMIENS [...], which is our mother church'; Idem, p. 596.

1095 Spearing 1965, p. 55, see also pp. 75-76, 92-93. Concerning Chaucer's fictional Pardoner and various interpretations of him, see Minnis 2003, pp. 322-334. John Bale's play *The three laws* (c. 1538) contains a similar speech by an Antonine pardoner: 'Good christen people, I come hither verelye / As a true proctour of the howse of Saynt Antonye / [...] Come paye your moneye, and ye shall have letters of me'; Swanson 2007, p. 188.

1096 Bredero 1986, pp. 305-306; also in synodal statutes from NOYON and elsewhere since as early as the late thirteenth century; *Statuts synodaux Reims*, p. 264, no. 28.

1097 Bredero 1986, pp. 305-06. The line '[...] *literas per predicatores questionarios defferri districtius prohibemus sed per singulos nuncios concedimus eas defferri*' recurs in many deeds, for example *Monumenta Boica*, vol. 49, no. 104 (24 Sept. 1279); see also n. 1090.

1098 Héliot & Chastang 1964/1965, p. 796 and n. 7, pp. 810, 813 ff. It is not clear whether this collection was held to benefit the building works.

1099 Mone 1836, p. 242. The *iuramentum petitoris* set the wage at 30 gulden together with reimbursement of expenses.

1100 Hanauer 1901-1902, vol. 21, p. 164 (fourteenth and fifteenth centuries).

1101 RODEZ: Bion de Marlavagne 1875, pp. 110, 111. TOUL in 1347, 1383, 1403 and 1455; this one-third portion then applied '*pour leur paine et pour leur despens*' or '*pour pourchaicier la besoigne de la queste de l'œuvre de l'église de Toul*'; Clanché 1926-1927, pp. 168-175; Héliot & Chastang 1964/1965, p. 816.

1102 Late thirteenth-century synodal statutes in TOURNAI and NOYON expressly prohibited rural deans and parish priests from making deals with pardoners to receive a share from them; *Statuts synodaux Reims*, p. 264, no. 27.

1103 Héliot & Chastang 1964/1965, p. 813.

1104 A similar contract in *Inventaire-sommaire Oise* G 1, 1358 (NOYON, 1463). There were also other variants: on 24 June 1367 the dean and chapter of WELLS leased a lifetime right to collect offerings and bequests of less than 6s. 8d to an officer of the *procurator fabrice*, for which he paid the fabric an annual £20; Bird & Baildon 1907/1914, vol. 2, no. 375.

1105 '*Nec praedicatio alicuius provinciae eis vel quibusdam aliis commitatur ad firmam*'; Paulus 1922-1923, vol. 2, p. 268; also vol. 3, p. 491 ff.

1106 *Inventaire-sommaire Yonne* G 1124, 1125, 1136; Quantin 1869, p. 223; Bouvier 1911, vol. 2, p. 310.

1107 Du Ranquet 1928, p. 16.

1108 Gadan 1851, p. VII; Quicherat 1886, vol. 2, pp. 95, 196.

1109 Eekhof 1909, p. 96 ff.

1110 *Inventaire-sommaire*

Seine-Inférieure G 2513; Imbart de la Tour 1909, p. 262 ff. Valid only for the *quêtes* in suffragan dioceses.

1111 '*Decani et presbyteri non emant a quaestuariis futuros proventus seu questus ficiendos*'; LIÈGE synodal statutes of 1287, cited in Paulus 1922-1923, vol. 2, p. 280 n. 7. Also CAMBRAI synodal statutes of 1307; Reusens 1903, pp. 54, 55.

1112 'from Nicolas Bouclier, resident of Plancy, pardoner of the fabric, leased to him for one year only, to attend the synod of 1383: paying at Christmas and at Easter in halves, here for 16 livres'; Gadan 1851, p. 2 and n. 5; Assier 1858, p. 45.

1113 Swanson 2007, pp. 136-137.

1114 See p. 288.

1115 These do not include diocesan receipts of an obviously different derivation such as the *débite* (Pentecostal oblations) and *quête* in ROUEN, or the Pentecostals offered alongside the *venia s. Petri* in EXETER (Erskine 1962, p. 266), nor collections for other churches, monasteries and institutions, which are considered below.

1116 Paris, Bibliothèque Nationale, lat. 9111, f. 206v ff. In 1373/74 (Bibliothèque Nationale, lat. 9113, f. 2) a distinction is made between receipts from, on the one hand, the city and diocese, '*recepta bustiarum dicte fabrice in quibus erant queste facte pro dicta fabrica in ecelesiis parochialibus Trecensis diocesis et in sancto synode apertis*' and, on the other, '*recepta de bustis parochialium ecclesiarum civitatis Trecensis*'.

1117 Paris, Bibliothèque Nationale, lat. 9111, f. 211v, with the addition: '*deductis expensis factis pro questoribus et eorum servientibus*'. The quest was therefore not farmed out; see f. 206v and f. 209: '*recepta questarum decanatuum Trecensis dyocesis*'. See also Gadan 1851, p. 1; Assier 1858, pp. 44, 45; Assier 1855, p. 17.

1118 'from all the confraters and consorors from all villages in the diocese, brought by the parish priests and the rectors, both during the synods and throughout the year'; *Inventaire-sommaire Aube* G 1569; Assier 1855, p. 27. By 1516 the *bustii* had in any case disappeared; idem G 1585.

1119 *Inventaire-sommaire Yonne* G 1124 and G 1125 (the 1295/96 and 1319/20 accounts both show the quest to be leased); G 1126 (1341/42); Cf. G 1137.

1120 'the general quest of the confraternity of St Stephen as received from throughout the diocese, called the small quest'; *Inventaire-sommaire Yonne* G 1134.

1121 *Inventaire-sommaire Yonne* G 1141 ff.

1122 'From the collection'; 'from the offertory boxes in the bishopric'; *Inventaire-sommaire Somme* G 1157. In the diocese of Autun, collections were held under the auspices of various patron saints, although the procedures always seem the same. Cf. 1295/96 account: '*recepta pro indulgentia benefactoribus ecclesie b. Lazari* [i.e. the cathedral's patron] *concessa*' and '*recepta queste et confratrie b. Nazarii in synodo Penthecoste*', both itemized according to the proceeds from each of the diocese's 24 archpresbyteries and deaneries; Paris, Bibliothèque Nationale, lat. 5529b, f. 4, f. 5; Mortet & Deschamps 1929, p. 320; Quicherat 1886, vol. 2, p. 185.

1123 The south transept portal is dedicated to St Honoré, with one scene in the tympanum depicting a procession with his reliquary shrine; Murray 1996, pp. 118-119, 138-139.

1124 *Cartulaire Lausanne*, no. 891 (November 1236). Concerning miracles during this collection, see nos 807-811 (1235-42); on the fire of 18 August 1235, see no. 805. Detailed discussion in

Signori 1995, pp. 229-246 and Karte IX (journey with the relics).

1125 For example in the diocese of KONSTANZ; see Krebs 1939-1954, in voce 'BASEL', 'Berghausen', 'Rufach', etc.; Barth 1954, pp. 108, 129-131.

1126 In 1254 the archbishop of COLOGNE blocked a collection run by an Augustinian monastery in the diocese of LIÈGE, and in 1318 that of a Benedictine chapel in Dortmund; *Regesten Köln*, vol. 3, no. 1779, vol. 4, no. 1038.

1127 The total number of parish church and chapel *quêtes* authorized by the archbishop of ROUEN are known precisely: only 16 parishes between 1460 and 1491; Vénard 1987, p. 13.

1128 The Antonine collection dates from shortly after 1200, and the first instances of papal involvement from the incumbencies of Gregory IX (1227-1241) and Innocent IV (1243-1254), after which the Antonines continually worked to strengthen ties with the pope; Mischlewski 1976, pp. 35 ff., 45, 46, 50; also Paulus 1922-1923, vol. 2, pp. 289-290. Concerning efforts organized within the commandries and preceptories throughout dozens of bishoprics, see Frieß 1994, pp. 60-64, 66, 97-106, 230-231; Mischlewski 1995, maps of Europe, pp. IX and X.

1129 Vroom 1993, p. 573.

1130 Coyecque 1889/1891, vol. 1, pp. 140-153, with an overview of all extant printed bulls. Also Vénard 1994, pp. 276, on the role of the Hotel Dieu.

1131 From ROME: the hospital of Santo Spirito. From France: the brothers of St Anthony from VIENNE and collections from ARLES, LIMOGES and AMIENS; Pueyo Colomina 2000a, pp. 685-686.

1132 Hugh of Newcastle may be alluding to this when he accuses the *praelati* '[...] *forte donis aut precibus circumventi nugis talibus* [of the pardoners] *acquiescunt per suas litteras dantes eis super his in suis diocesibus licentiam et favorem* [...]'; Hauréau 1896, p. 234.

1133 Voisin 1869, pp. 475, 476, 480-484.

1134 In some cases the cathedral chapter itself profited from the admission fees; in ROUEN these generated 2000 l.t. in 1510, or a quarter of chapter's total receipts; Imbart de la Tour 1909, p. 264.

1135 *Regesten Köln*, vol. 3, no. 3787 (26 January 1301), vol. 4, no. 462 (20 June 1309); Paulus 1922-1923, vol. 2, pp. 290, 291. Also *Ad summum 1248*, C 6. The sum of 30 marks may be a fixed sum; in HALBERSTADT the 1321 rent amount remained unchanged in later years: Diestelkamp 1929, p. 229 n. 34.

1136 *Cartulaire Liège*, vol. 3, no. 1274, 30 June 1342. The admission fees also accrued to the cathedral fabric before 1342; see the Archives de L'évêché de LIÈGE, cathédrale Saint Lambert B I 8, *De materia questarum et de questoribus*, with an overview of statutes bearing on the questing establishment between the end of the thirteenth and fifteenth centuries and documents relating to the admission of the Antonines; *Cartulaire Liège*, vol. 2, nos 823, 824, 825, 827. In TROYES the fabric received the admission fees from 1294-1297, after which the new bishop claimed the monies, at least for a time; Paris, Bibliothèque Nationale, lat. 9111, f. 213v. In the diocese of HALBERSTADT, as also in COLOGNE, the Antonines paid an admission fee of 30 marks of pure silver. In 1321 the bishop allocated this sum to the fabric, but later claimed it for himself. Not until 1369 did he acknowledge the fabric's claims; Schmidt 1889, pp. 5, 6. At the beginning of the fourteenth century, profits from the admission of the Antonines in EXETER also accrued at least in part to the fabric; Swanson 2007, p. 128.

1137 'that no one may promulgate indulgences or any other benefits in the diocese of UTRECHT, and these must first be evaluated and admitted by the aforementioned dean and canons of the cathedral chapter'; Dodt van Flensburg 1838-1848, vol. 7, p. 232; Eekhof 1909, Appendix no. 48.

1138 '[...] so too we shall and intend each year give to our fabric at the wonted times our wonted sealed letters, in their official forms, regarding the business with our lords St Stephan and St Anthony. And what this may yield, and all other monies and accruals which this same fabric has and shall have, we intend to proceed unhindered to benefit the building of the cathedral [...]'. *Urkundenbuch Halberstadt*, vol. 4, no. 3040; Schmidt 1889, p. 6.

1139 '*Volumus* [...], *ut nullos questuarios ad colligendas et petendas elemosinas, de quorum admissione nostra interest, nos vel nostri successores per ambitum nostrarum civitatis et diocesis de cetero admittemus tacite vel expresse, nisi iidem questuarii cum provisore fabrice* [...] *super portione fabrice debita ita prius convenerit cum effectu, quod dictorum* [...] *decani et capituli ac ipsius provisoris accedat expressum ad hoc beneplacitum et voluntas*'; *Urkundenbuch Westfalen*, vol. 8, p. 321 (25 June 1314).

1140 *Statutes of Salisbury Cathedral*, pp. 200, 201.

1141 See Noordeloos 1959, p. 31, in respect of UTRECHT. In the archdiocese of HAMBURG, admission policy was the responsibility of the provost, but he never acted without first consulting the masters of the fabric and obtaining their consent; cf. capitular statutes of 24 July 1336 under '*de officio prepositi*': '[...] *item non admittet questuarios vel literas quaslibet eis dabit pro ellemosinis colligendis sine structurariorum ecclesie consilio et assensu*'; *Urkundenbuch Hamburg*, vol. 2 (4), p. 795. This provision stems from an agreement made between the chapter and provost on 8 July 1320; idem, vol. 2 (3), p. 373. The bishoprics of UTRECHT and TRENT placed official admission policymaking power in the hands of the vicar-general, who was the bishop's principal assistant in the execution of his religious duties; Post 1957, vol. 2, p. 30; Santifaller 1948, p. 290.

1142 Concerning these collections: Paulus 1922-1923, vol. 3, pp. 238-252.

1143 Paris, Bibliothèque Nationale, lat. 9111, f. 206 ff.; 9113, f. 1 ff.; LONDON, British Museum Add. ms. 15083, f. 106 ff.; Gadan 1851, pp. 2, 3: rubric: '*receptes des questains, qui questent au diocese de Troies*'. These were chiefly the major international quests: those of the Antonine Order, the hospital of Santo Spirito, the hospice of St Bernard, the Hospitallers in Jerusalem and St James of Altopascio; cf. Assier 1858, p. 45.

1144 Assier 1855, p. 15.

1145 Barth 1954, p. 128: the hospital order of Santo Spirito, the Antonines, the hospice of St Bernard, the quest for St Valentine and several local collections; in 1331 only the first three of these (p. 112), but 19 around 1550 (pp. 127-128).

1146 Goñi Gaztambide 1955, p. 34.

1147 Mone 1836, p. 100: the hospital order of Santo Spirito, the Antonines, the hospice of St Bernard and the quest for St Valentine.

1148 Boeren 1953-1954, vol. 3, p. 384; Artonne *et al.* 1963, p. 158.

1149 Wuerdtwein 1772-1780, vol. 5, pp. 142, 143. The bishop of BRIXEN (BRESSA-

NONE) issued 36 *litterae quaestus* between 1473 and around 1500 for eight churches and institutions, including the Antonines and the hospital of Santo Spirito in ROME; Frieß 1994, p. 102.

1150 See p. 305 ff.

1151 *Urkundenbuch Bremen*, vol. 4, no. 276, charter issued between 11 February 1397 and 14 March 1401. The chapter later changed this arrangement to have the pardoner pay 50 gulden; Müller 1908, p. 68; Wiek 1959a, p. 125; Klink 1988, p. 77. In AUTUN the fabric also received a third of the proceeds from foreign quests; cf. 1294/95 account: '*item pro tercia parte indulgenciarum concessarum benefactoribus ecclesiarum et hospitalium beate Marie Claromontensis, Podiensis* [LE PUY], *Sancti Justi* [St Just, LYON] *et pontis Rodani Lugdunensis 12 l.vien.*'; Mortet & Deschamps 1929, p. 321.

1152 Including in the dioceses of CALAHORRA, CALZADA, LEÓN and TOLEDO; Goñi Gaztambide 1970, pp. 453, 454 (1418); Torroja Menendez & Sanchez Palencia 1977, p. 18. Also in OVIEDO: *Colección documental Oviedo*, nos 26, 34 (1462 and 1471); De Caso Fernández 1981, p. 226. On SANTO DOMINGO DE LA CALZADA also: López de Silanes & Sáinz Ripa 1991 and 1992, concerning the period between 1409 and 1496: nos 172, 187, 193, 258, 334; also no. 339 concerning the division between the bishopric's two cathedrals (CALAHORRA and SANTO DOMINGO DE LA CALZADA). Elsewhere the bishop granted half the quest proceeds to the cathedral building works, such as in LAUSANNE in 1267; Grandjean 1963, p. 272.

1153 Vénard 1994, p. 276.

1154 According to a 1336 letter from the bishop's official; Crosnier 1854, pp. 412, 413.

1155 UTRECHT: Noordeloos 1959, p. 35; LIÈGE: *Cartulaire Liège*, vol. 2, no. 825.

1156 Goñi Gaztambide 1955, p. 34.

1157 Paulus 1922-1923, vol. 3, p. 491.

1158 Cf. deed dated 26 January 1293, issued for the Antonines by the court official of LIÈGE; *Cartulaire Liège*, vol. 2, no. 823; similar document from 1397 issued by the archbishop of BREMEN for the messengers of the Antonines; *Urkundenbuch Bremen*, vol. 4, no. 199.

1159 Summary of the spiritual benefits offered by the Antonines in Noordeloos 1959, p. 49 ff.

1160 Confraternity of St Anthony: Noordeloos 1959, p. 60 ff.; confraternity of St Hubert: *Inventaris Archief kapittel ten Dom*, no. 405 (cathedral fabric cartulary), f. 99, 100.

1161 *Mendicatorium Assche*, p. 222; additional examples in Laenen 1924, pp. 151, 187 (Zoutleeuw, Mechelen). See also Krebs 1939-1954, in voce 'Berghausen', 'Rufach', etc.

1162 Between 1294/95 and 1300/01 revenues from foreign quests amounted to between 45 l.t. and 42 l.t. (except in 1297/98, when the bishop received a portion); after 1373/74 always 28 l.t. or 27 l.t., which in the final quarter of the fourteenth century was equal to only one annual wage of an unskilled labourer; Gadan 1851, p. XVIII.

1163 Paris, Bibliothèque Nationale, lat. 5529b, f. 5, 5v; Mortet & Deschamps 1929, p. 320; Quicherat 1886, vol. 2, p. 183 ff.

1164 *Inventaire-sommaire Yonne* G 1124, 1125, 1126.

1165 Goñi Gaztambide 1955, p. 34.

1166 The restored cathedral was dedicated on 6 September 1114; Saint-Denis 2008, pp. 158, 198-201.

1167 Ennen 1880, p. 44.

1168 *Inventaire-sommaire Yonne* G 1133.

1169 Archives départementales Yonne G 1124 ff.

1170 Schuegraf 1855, p. 57 and Schuegraf 1858, pp. 161, 183, 193.

1171 Archives départementales Puy-de-Dôme 3 G arm. 18, sac. B, cote 25.

1172 WELLS Cathedral Archives, fabric accounts; my thanks to L.S. Colchester in WELLS, who allowed me to consult his transcriptions of the accounts.

1173 Archives départementales Rhône 10 G 1607 ff.

1174 Paris, Bibliothèque Nationale, lat. 9111, 9113; LONDON, British Museum Add. ms. 15083. In ROUEN we find a reverse process at work. A few random samples show that the percentage rose from 14 percent in 1432 to 26 percent in 1457 and 45 percent in 1508; Archives départementales Seine-Inférieure G 2491,G 2492, G 2523.

1175 Bion de Marlavagne 1875, pp. 279-283, 311; Mortet & Deschamps 1929, p. 310 ff.; Héliot & Chastang 1964/1965, p. 24; Archives départementales Aveyron 3 G 249.

1176 *Inventaire-sommaire Somme* G 1157.

1177 Archivo de la catedral de GERONA: Obra de la Seu Inv. VI, f. 1 ff.; recorded as '*summe acapitorum*'; '*acaptiri*', that is to collect money. Cf. in BORDEAUX: '*Acaptadores*', that is *amassadores* or *queteurs*; Brutails 1899-1901, vol. 12, pp. 404, 405.

1178 Hanauer 1901-1902, vol. 21, pp. 162-163. As attested by a random sampling from the accounts (Archives de la ville de Strasbourg), this percentage fluctuated between ten and four percent of the net receipts up until the Reformation (1529).

1179 For the calculation method, see p. 84-86.

1180 *Inventaire-sommaire Seine-Inférieure* G 2534 ff.; Archives départementales Seine-Inférieure G 2491; wages in Baulant 1971, pp. 482, 483.

1181 Schuegraf 1855, p. 57 and Schuegraf 1858, pp. 161, 183, 193.

1182 Ramisch *et al.* 1998, vol. 2, p. 237, in voce '*Sammlung,* [...] *collectura* '.

1183 WELLS Cathedral Archives, fabric accounts; see Appendix one under WELLS.

1184 La Roche 1888, p. 105; Mone 1834, 'BASEL', sub v. Similar amounts in PAMPLONA in 1487; Goñi Gaztambide 1955, pp. 33-34.

1185 Fabric rolls 1373/74, 1401/02, 1402/03, 1409/10; see Appendix one under TROYES.

1186 Fabric rolls 1367/68, 1369/70, 1370/71, 1375/76, 1376/77; see Appendix one under GERONA.

1187 *Inventaire-sommaire Somme* G 1157.

1188 Archives départementales Yonne G 1141.

CHAPTER THREE
The financing of the building works at UTRECHT Cathedral: a case study

INTRODUCTION

1 See Appendix one.

2 *Inventaris Archief kapittel ten Dom*, nos 651 and 659; *Bronnen bouwgeschiedenis*, vol. 2 (1, 2 and 3): fabric rolls, 1395/96-1528/29.

3 *Inventaris Archief kapittel ten Dom*, nos 1 and 2.

4 Published by S. Muller Fzn.; see Muller 1895 and Muller 1903.

5 *Inventaris Archief kapittel ten Dom*, no. 405; we were grateful to have at our disposal the précis compiled by Tenhaeff, preserved at Utrecht University's Institute for Medieval History (Instituut voor Middeleeuwse Geschiedenis). The cartulary was formed at the chapter's behest in 1415, and would have been in the fabric master's care; *Inventaris Archief kapittel ten Dom*, no. 67, f. 4 vo.

6 *Inventaris Archief kapittel ten Dom*, especially nos 403-515.

THE CATHEDRAL CHURCH

7 Post 1957, vol. 1, p. 47; after 1039 also the diocese of CAMBRAI.

8 Mulders 1943, pp. 34-36, including map.

9 Peeters 1966, passim; also his contribution in Haslinghuis & Peeters 1965, pp. 145-167; Van Moorsel 1968, passim; also Fritze 1971, passim.

10 Most recent summary in *De oudste kerken van Utrecht*; Van Vliet 2002, pp. 71-89. Hirschmann 1998, pp. 65-80, examines developments in the diocese of UTRECHT within a broad context.

11 Van Vliet 2002, pp. 242, 275, 286.

12 Concerning the UTRECHT immunities, see De Bruijn 1994. On this 'cross' of churches, see recent discussion in Van Vliet 2002, p. 293 ff.; also Herzog 1964, p. 241.

13 De Bruijn 1994, pp. 82-83 and loose map. The medieval fortress extended 25 to 50 metres beyond the walls of the Roman *castellum* on all sides; De Bruijn 1994, p. 99.

14 De Bruijn 1994, pp. 143, 411; De Groot 1994, pp. 41-42; De Groot 2006, Chapter 10.

15 Struick 1968, p. 57.

16 For the building history and all related literature, see Haslinghuis & Peeters 1965, p. 167 ff., especially pp. 336-344, and Haakma Wagenaar 1975, pp. 16-24.

17 Heeringa 1927.

18 Concerning the twelve chantries founded in *novo opere* at the master of the fabric's instigation between 1295 and 1303, see Rikhof 2006, pp. 55-61, 78.

19 It is possible that the collapse of the Romanesque St Martin's tower, now dated at 1308, was one of the incentives for building a new tower; Haakma Wagenaar 1975, pp. 22, 93.

20 A lengthy polemic on the building, location and function of the Dom tower has developed between Aart Mekking, Martin de Bruijn and Arie de Groot, amongst others, but is of only ancillary interest in the present context. The most recent summary can be found in De Groot 1998, pp. 20-29.

21 The outer bounds of the Dom's and Oldminster's respective immunities were established in 1320 when construction of the tower began; De Bruijn 1994, pp. 113, 160.

22 The situation remained obscure after the tower's completion as well. A new arrangement was put in place between 1399 and 1418. In 1399 the cathedral chapter obtained a parcel of land northwest of the tower via an exchange, which it promised to leave undeveloped and use to enlarge the churchyard; *Bronnen bouwgeschiedenis*, vol. 2 (1), p. 43 n. 3, p. 74 n. 6; *Inventaris archief kapittel Oudmunster*, no. 448. The city was also involved in this exchange; *Regesten bisschoppen Utrecht*, pp. 527, 528.

23 *Bronnen bouwgeschiedenis*, vol. 2 (2), pp. 132, 238, 334; also still in 1518/19: idem, vol. 2 (3), p. 422.

24 Idem, vol. 2 (2), p. 156.

25 See graph 5.

26 Concerning the cathedral's annexes, see De Groot 2006, Chapter 9.

27 This date derives from De Groot 2006, Chapter 9, pp. 1-22.

28 Haakma Wagenaar 1934; Haakma Wagenaar 1975, pp. 50 ff., 84 ff.

THE CATHEDRAL FABRIC AND IT'S SOURCES OF INCOME

29 *Bronnen bouwgeschiedenis*, vol. 2 (1), p. XXI.

30 Idem, pp. XXI, 271 n. 1; Muller 1895, pp. 194-195.

31 *Oorkondenboek Utrecht*, nos 558, 812, 715, also 1164. St Mary's already had a year of grace in the twelfth century; Van den Hoven van Genderen 1997, p. 71.

32 *Inventaris Archief kapittel ten Dom*, no. 659, all

published in *Bronnen bouwgeschiedenis*, vol. 2 (1), pp. 271-343, 363-366; the *prebenda defunctorum* rolls 1487-1492 have not been published; *Inventaris Archief kapittel ten Dom*, no. 659. See also *Bronnen bouwgeschiedenis*, vol. 2 (2), p. XIII-XIV. Such fusion also occurred elsewhere. From 1375 CAMBRAI had an '*officium fabrice et ornamentorum*'; Archives départementales Nord 4 G 4594.

33 *Bronnen bouwgeschiedenis*, vol. 2 (1), p. XVIII.

34 However, there was only ever one procurator or *magister fabrice* in charge; see also Muller 1895, p. 114.

35 Ibidem.

36 *Inventaris Archief kapittel ten Dom*, no. 67, f. 3v, 4r, 4v; *Bronnen bouwgeschiedenis*, vol. 2 (1), p. XVIII.

37 *Bullarium Trajectense*, no. 1632 (5 November 1359); Rutgers 1970, p. 179.

38 *Bronnen bouwgeschiedenis*, vol. 2 (1), p. 95 n. 1; vol. 2 (2), p. 113 (listing the names and '*episcopus*').

39 *Bronnen bouwgeschiedenis*, vol. 2 (2), pp. 705, 768.

40 He was a member of the cathedral chapter in UTRECHT, but had no prebend; *Inventaris Archief kapittel ten Dom*, p. V.

41 *Bullarium Trajectense*, no. 1632.

42 *Bronnen bouwgeschiedenis*, vol. 2 (2), p. 113.

43 Van Asch van Wijck 1846-1848, vol. 2, p. 72 (6 March 1466); '*item nuncius missus fuit ad dominum rev. in facto electionis magistri fabrice*'; *Bronnen bouwgeschiedenis*, vol. 2 (2), p. 667. Additionally *Regesten bisschoppen Utrecht*, nos 5452 (7 January 1519), 5505 (21 January 1521), 5535 (12 March 1524); *Inventaris Archief kapittel ten Dom*, no. 406 (1533); no. 1, vol. 19, f. 46 (14 March 1569), also f. 193v, 261; vol. 20, sub 5 March 1575. The introduction to the *Inventaris Archief kapittel ten Dom* (p. XVII, n. 2) states that certain aspects have already been recorded in Wstinc's *Rechtsboek*.

44 Concerning the bishop's alternating right of appointment up to as late as 1562 '*iuxta antiquam laudabilemque* [...] *consuetudinem*'; De Groot 2006, Chapter 2, n. 12.

45 Esch 2004, p. 116; Fink 1932-1933, pp. 211-242, collector's rolls sub 19 July 1472: '*item magistro fabrice pro fabrica ecclesie quia sic voluit dominus episcopus Trajectensis 10 fl*'; also *Bronnen bouwgeschiedenis*, vol. 2 (1), p. 464. The rolls list only one entry of this kind.

46 *Bronnen bouwgeschiedenis*, vol. 2 (2), p. 237.

47 Van Asch van Wijck 1850-1853, vol. 1, p. 155, letter 219; Haslinghuis & Peeters 1965, p. 359.

48 Vroom 1964.

49 Van Vliet 2002, p. 241.

50 Séjourné 1921; Post 1957, vol. 1, p. 210; Nolet & Boeren 1951, p. 184; Muller 1914, p. 34 ff. Concerning the endowment of the chapter of St John's in UTRECHT, see Palmboom 1995, especially pp. 64-66. This process occurred all over Europe: Lemarignier *et al.* 1962, p. 190.

51 Muller 1903, p. 23; publication of the *Liber Camerae*, idem, pp. 23-57.

52 Van den Hoven van Genderen 1997, p. 53; Palmboom 1995, pp. 27-28.

53 Muller 1890, p. 8 ff.; this was in fact permitted under the rule of Chrodegang.

54 Muller 1903, p. 51.

55 *Inventaris Archief kapittel ten Dom*, no. 2670; Muller 1903, p. 7.

56 Edwards 1967, pp. 5 n. 2, 39, 40.

57 *Inventaris Archief kapittel ten Dom*, no. 599 and introduction, p. XVI; *Bronnen bouwgeschiedenis*, vol. 2 (1), p. 273 n. 5; Muller 1903, pp. 20, 169, 174.

58 Muller 1895, passim.

59 Both Van der Donck's and Brock's *Talmuds* and a report concerning the

management after 1585/86 are published in Muller 1903, p. 75 ff. Overview of the sixteenth-century accounts in Moore 1988, Appendices 2-6.

60 Muller 1895, p. 106 ff. The chambers already existed before this; *Inventaris Archief kapittel ten Dom*, nos 597-624.

61 Muller 1903, p. 20; *Inventaris Archief kapittel ten Dom*, p. XVL.

62 *Inventaris Archief kapittel ten Dom*, pp. XVIII, XIX.

63 Idem, pp. XIV and 286; Muller 1903, pp. 181-182.

64 Muller 1895, p. 113; *Inventaris Archief kapittel ten Dom*, no. 1474.

65 *Inventaris Archief kapittel ten Dom*, pp. XVI, XVII.

66 Muller 1895, pp. 171, 226. There were 41 stipendiaries; from 1118 onwards the dean also held that belonging to the bishop. Concerning the remaining three stipendiaries, see *Inventaris Archief kapittel ten Dom*, p. V.

67 Muller 1903, p. 20.

68 Muller 1895, p. 114, also pp. 105 and 115.

69 Idem, p. 112. The *Camera Major* was also encumbered with '*expensas incumbentes capitulo, quas sibi capitulum committit*, [...] *exponere et facere*'; idem, p. 107.

70 *Bronnen bouwgeschiedenis*, vol. 2 (1), pp. XXI, XLI.

71 See p. 48.

72 *Inventaris Archief kapittel ten Dom*, no. 2541 (1554/55, 1562/63, 1565/66 accounts).

73 Muller 1895, p. 90 ff.; *Inventaris Archief kapittel ten Dom*, no. 2505 ff. Also De Groot 1994, p. 80.

74 *Inventaris Archief kapittel ten Dom*, no. 575 (accounts for the construction of the Borchtbrug, 1406); no. 562 (account for the digging of a canal, 1412); no. 531 (account for choir stalls, 1568). Cf. no. 2508 (memorial service connected with reliquary shrine for St Pontian, 1460 and 1502); Brom 1900, pp. 238-251: though the goldsmith received gold and silver not accounted for in the fabric rolls. On deliveries of stone, see Alberts 1954, pp. 8, 18.

75 *Inventaris Archief kapittel ten Dom*, nos 2506, 2507; *Bronnen bouwgeschiedenis*, vol. 2 (1), pp. 283, 285, 286, 287, 289. Tenhaeff did not consult these sources, leading him to misinterpret several items in the fabric rolls. The *capsa* fund served primarily to finance the creation of the *Capsa S.-Agnetis*, a gold shrine into which the relics of St Agnes were to be translated in 1419 (Calkoen 1897-1898, vol. 1, f. 31). The fund was administered within the fabric, despite possessing its own revenues. Foremost amongst them were receipts from the quest for Nostra Domina, which do not appear in the fabric rolls until 1424/25, and which presumably were reserved for this purpose until the shrine's completion. The *capsa* fund also received a few small donations in money and in unvalued gold statuettes that were affixed to the shrine; these are not mentioned anywhere in the fabric rolls. The *capsa* fund also financed the purchase of a set of paraments. Diversions and intermediate loans aside, paraments were also funded from revenues that usually accrued to the fabric (such as a compensation paid by the city of UTRECHT for the demolition of two houses near St Martin's bridge). However, expenditures relating to the above projects were also booked in the *prebenda defunctorum* rolls; some amounts correspond with those in the *capsa* rolls, but a handful of items remain enigmatic. The 1413/14 rolls (*Bronnen bouwgeschiedenis*, vol. 2 (2), p. 155) list, under the heading *immolaciones*: '*nihil, quia magister Wysso recepit ad usum crucis fiende*'. In 1513/14 the notary financed the commission of the reliquary for the head of

St Adrian; *Bronnen bouwgeschiedenis*, vol. 2 (3), pp. 210 and 237.

76 De Groot 1994, p. 45.

77 Rikhof 2006: between 1243 and 1484: 54 chantry foundations, after 1451 solely mass foundations.

78 Muller 1895, pp. 261, 262; lay assistants, which also included the cathedral building labourers, are described in so many words as entitled to a gravesite within the immunity.

79 Haslinghuis & Peeters 1965, pp. 362-403.

80 Idem, pp. 477-478.

81 Muller 1895, p. 261.

82 Slothouwer & De Jonge 1919; Haslinghuis & Peeters 1965, p. 354 ff.

83 Calkoen 1897-1898, vol. 1, f. 30, 50, vol. 2, f. 46, vol. 3, f. 12 ff.; *Inventaris Archief kapittel ten Dom*, pp. 333-368; Heeringa 1927, p. 66 ff.; Muller 1895 pp. 26-34. In addition to the 29 endowed altars, there were also several, including the high altar and the indulgence altar, which had no dotation; maintenance of these altars therefore also fell within the competence of the fabric. The figure of 40 altars derives from De Groot 2006, Chapters 4 and 5, and the map of altars (*altaren*).

84 De Groot 2006, Chapter 5, p. 27 and n. 82. The terms *vicaris/vicarie* (chantry/chantry priest) and *kapelaan/kapelanie* (chaplaincy/chaplain) are treated as synonymous.

85 *Inventaris Archief kapittel ten Dom*, no. 2678; also Rikhof 2006, p. 70.

86 Such as the Lokhorst Triptych by Jan van Scorel; Haslinghuis & Peeters 1965, p. 403. Amongst other things the sources list: a memorial tablet for the provost Naturelli, a statue of St Sebastian at the grave of the canon Fred. de Coninc, a statue of St Adrian at the grave of Canon Adriaan Ram, a *tabula lapidea* on the altar of Sts Peter and Paul commissioned by Canon G. Strijt (1563); see Calkoen 1915, f. 19, 31, 33; Muller 1906, p. 16a; *Inventaris Archief kapittel ten Dom*, no. 1, vol. 18, f. 31.

87 Chapels of Guy of Avesnes, Frederik II van Sierck, John of Arkel.

88 Chapels of Zweder van Uterlo (d. 1378), Simon van der Sluys (d. before 1506). Concerning the former chapel, see Rikhof 2006, pp. 63-64.

89 Cathedral Dean Ludolf van den Veen (d. 1508), Cathedral Dean Johan van der Vecht (d. 1572), Treasurer Henric Raescop (d. 1455), Treasurer Gerard Soudenbalch (d. 1524), Canon Abraham van Leeuwenberch (d. 1523), Canon Anthonie Taets van Amerongen (d. 1555).

90 *Burggraaf* (Viscount) Jan van Montfoort (d. 1521), Cornelis de Wael (d. 1505), architect, to be identified with the Taets Chapel; Muller 1906, p. 7a and n. 2.

91 This applies in the case of the cathedral canons Van der Vecht and Taets.

92 Haslinghuis & Peeters 1965, pp. 258-265, 289-291; *Bronnen bouwgeschiedenis*, vol. 2 (2), pp. 490, 491, 497, 588.

93 For example in RODEZ, where the executors of a 1299 will had to pay 25 l.t. directly to the building labourers every Saturday; Bion de Marlavagne 1875, p. 28 and n. 1.

94 *Inventaris Archief kapittel ten Dom*, nos 2873 and 652; (1456, receipt belonging to Van der Borch), p. 82; Muller 1916, passim; Bouvy 1947, pp. 70-71.

95 'to help make the chapel to good account'; De Groot 2006, Chapter 8, n. 41: aside from the receipt of 20 January 1456, he also cites the 19 January 1456 building contract between the dean and chapter with Jacob van der Borch for a sum of 650 rhinegulden, or around 26 annual wages, to be paid in

two instalments.

96 'to help found his memorial service, chapel and tomb'; 'for the creation and adornment of Bishop Roelof's chapel and tomb'; Van Asch van Wijck 1846-1848, vol. 2, p. 82 (letter of 2 September 1473); concerns a claustral house: Calkoen n.d., vol. 1, claustral house Bc.

97 Muller 1916, p. 4.

98 And yet it can be no coincidence that one of the will's executors, Dirk Uterweer, charged with supervising the chapter's completion in a capitular resolution of 7 July 1473, was also the master of the cathedral fabric in that year; Muller 1916, p. 4; *Bronnen bouwgeschiedenis*, vol. 2 (1), p. 474.

99 There is even less information regarding the construction and furnishing of the chapel of the cathedral dean Ludolf van den Veen (d. 1508). The chapter minutes of 1511 refer to a disagreement between the cathedral canons and the executors of Van den Veen's complicated will. The canons stipulated that the will's executors *'die capell doen stofferen ende cyren ter somme toe van 200 gouden rijnsguldens'*, as the will prescribed. The adornments would then seem to have been contracted without the fabric's involvement; the fabric rolls contain no related entries. Nothing is known about how its actual construction was financed. The only thing we know for certain is that an opening was hewn and then resealed in the wall separating the respective immunities of the Dom and Oldminster so that Van den Veen's sarcophagus could be carried in, the costs of which were charged to the deceased. See Calkoen n.d., vol. 2, f. 149, and *Inventaris Archief kapittel ten Dom*, no. 1, vol. 12, f. 75, no. 2, vol. 1, f. 75-95. Also De Groot 2006, Chapter 8, p. 20 and n. 102.

100 See Appendix five.

101 *Inventaris Archief kapittel ten Dom*, no. 2505: inventories from the years 1498, 1504, c. 1530, 1543 and 1571. The 1504 inventory is published in Brom 1900.

102 Buchelius 1906, p. 182; Muller 1906, p. 10 ff.; Calkoen 1897-1898, vol. 1, f. 23, 24; also De Groot 2006, Chapter 7, pp. 7-14. Additionally: *Bronnen bouwgeschiedenis*, vol. 2 (1) in voce *'ecclesia'* and *'vitra'*. Installation costs were charged to the fabric; the cathedral fabric paid for the glazing of the nave clerestory; idem, vol. 2 (2), p. 156.

103 Muller 1906, p. 16 ff. Especially De Groot 1994, pp. 51 and 79 ff. and De Groot 2006, Chapter 8, pp. 38-44 and Appendix. He distinguishes between the statues of the Apostles in the choir, which were donated by canons and members of the nobility in the circle of Bishop John of Arkel (1343-1364) and the approximately 20 statues in the transept and choir that were donated privately by canons, usually in connection with their own graves or altars.

104 *'Soe bin ic* [Canon Joh. Foyt] *gecomen tot hem* [the master of the fabric], *soe als ic te syn hadde twee heyligen te setten in den doem, als daer nu staen; nae gewoonten der kercken soe pleech men de fabrycmeisters te kennen te geven als men wat nyes maect* [...]', *Inventaris Archief Kapittel ten Dom*, no. 282 (1495); *'item ontfangen van heer Geerloff van der Donck van steyn ende calck*: 15 *st.*'; *Bronnen bouwgeschiedenis*, vol. 2 (2), p. 459. Additional examples in De Groot 1994, pp. 77-80; also De Groot 2006, Chapter 8, p. 39.

105 De Groot 2006, pp. 103-104.

106 De Groot 2006 rightly points this out.

107 *Inventaris Archief kapittel ten Dom*, no. 2507, f. 3: summary of *'ymagines capse

sancte Agnetis' together with their donors, mostly canons.

108 Idem, no. 2508; Brom 1900, pp. 249-251.

109 *Inventaris Archief kapittel ten Dom*, no. 2513; see Appendix five. Also: *Bronnen bouwgeschiedenis*, vol. 2 (1), pp. 439, 463, 464, 475, 505, 539, 552; Haslinghuis & Peeters 1965, p. 360.

110 Van Vliet 2002, pp. 172-174.

ONE Contributions from the chapter

111 Van den Hoven van Genderen 1997, p. 56. See also Moore 1988, p. 149, for a comparison with other cathedrals.

112 Muller 1895, p. 194; *Inventaris Archief kapittel ten Dom*, no. 157; good summary in *Bronnen bouwgeschiedenis*, vol. 2 (1), p. 271 n. 1, and pp. XXI, XXXIV.

113 An older regulation of 1234 determined that any canon who entered a monastery kept his right to a year of grace, unlike cathedral canons who relinquished (*resignatio*) or exchanged (*permutacio*) their prebends for some other reason. In such cases the *prebenda defunctorum* fund may already have been collecting the full fruits of the three years of the expectative grace even then; Muller 1895, pp. 42, 43.

114 Muller 1903, pp. 48, 17; Muller 1895, p. 195; *Inventaris Archief kapittel ten Dom*, nos 158, 159.

115 Muller 1895, pp. 106, 110-112: a 1312 statute reprises that of 1257; Muller 1895, p. 197; *Inventaris Archief kapittel ten Dom*, no. 160; see also Rutgers 1970, pp. 178, 209.

116 See p. 87 ff., also Muller 1895, pp. XXIII and 177, and Van den Hoven van Genderen 1997, p. 172 n. 23.

117 There was a further stipulation that the *prebenda defunctorum* fund would also benefit from the fruits of all years of the expectative if the deceased had for whatever reason had no claim to the years of grace, for example in the event that he had not yet fully come into his prebend; Muller 1903, p. 116. Summary of those entitled to a year of grace in Muller 1895, p. 47.

118 Muller 1903, pp. 61, 62, 75; *Bronnen bouwgeschiedenis*, vol. 2 (1), p. 515: confirmation from Rome for a fourth year for expectatives. Elsewhere in the *Talmud*: Muller 1903, pp. 86, 87, 93, 94, 95.

119 Muller 1903, pp. 75-83; also pp. 117, 118, 146 ff. Muller and Tenhaeff give an erroneous description of these terms in my view: Muller 1903, p. 74 and *Bronnen bouwgeschiedenis*, vol. 2 (1), p. 272 n. 3.

120 Actual practice was far more complex, because the *prebenda defunctorum* partook in neither the daily commons nor in the credit balances on particular accounts; see *Inventaris Archief kapittel ten Dom*, no. 737.

121 *Bronnen bouwgeschiedenis*, vol. 2 (1), p. 310.

122 Rubriek '*exposita in pensionibus prebende defunctorum*'; see below p. 354.

123 *Bronnen bouwgeschiedenis*, vol. 2 (1), pp. XXXIII and 49 n. 2; in 1450 the payment in beer was replaced with payment in oats.

124 Muller 1895, p. 234; *Inventaris Archief kapittel ten Dom*, p. XII.

125 Muller 1903, pp. 77, 121; *Bronnen bouwgeschiedenis*, vol. 2 (1), pp. 185.

126 *Bronnen bouwgeschiedenis*, vol. 2 (1), pp. XXXIII, 484 (1473/74 account).

127 Idem, p. 506 n. 5.

128 Van de Graft 1924, p. 81 ff.; *Bronnen bouwgeschiedenis*, vol. 2 (1), index in voce '*festi et ludi*'; *Bronnen bouwgeschiedenis*, vol. 2 (2), p. 672. Also De Groot 1994, p. 82

129 See p. 337 ff.

130 Muller 1903, p. 150 n. 2. Canons may not all have

had their own signets.

131 Muller 1895, p. 261; *Bronnen bouwgeschiedenis*, vol. 2 (1), pp. 272-343 passim, only until 1443. On the Oldminster, see Van den Hoven van Genderen 1997, p. 598.

132 Muller 1903, p. 150 and n. 4; prelates paid double this amount. See *Bronnen bouwgeschiedenis*, vol. 2 (1), p. 523 and *Inventaris Archief kapittel ten Dom*, no. 651: accounts for 1502/03, 1511/12, 1518/19, 1574/75.

133 Muller 1895, p. 112; *Bronnen bouwgeschiedenis*, vol. 2 (1), p. XXI.

134 Conflict with the provost: *Inventaris Archief kapittel ten Dom*, no. 1, vol. 14, f. 199v (1543), and with the dean: vol. 16, f. 131r, 131v, 268r (1550-1553).

135 Muller 1903, p. 124; the sums booked in the accounts do not always correspond with the stipulated 100 oude schilden.

136 Muller 1903, p. 124; *Inventaris Archief kapittel ten Dom*, no. 1, vol. 17, f. 359v.

137 *Inventaris Archief kapittel ten Dom*, no. 1, vol. 18, f. 175v (29 April 1567).

138 Idem, no. 1, vol. 17, f. 302v-305.

139 Fabric rolls 1529/30, f. 4v: '*item superfuerunt ex pulsationibus mortuorum deductis consuetis laboris oneribus 44 rijnsgulden 10 st. 9 d.*'

140 Rates varied from 12 karolusgulden (the St Salvator for canons from elsewhere) to 2 karolusgulden.

141 Fabric rolls 1562/63: 11 December 1562; the painter died on 6 December.

142 *Inventaris Archief kapittel ten Dom*, no. 1, vol. 18, f. 133 (8 March 1566), f. 144 (10 May), f. 147 (31 May); no. 2799. Concerning this chantry, see Rutgers 1970, p. 181 and Rikhof 2006, n. 94. Other chantries incorporated by the chapter: *Inventaris* o.c., nos 365, 378.

143 *Ex Injuncto* bull: Dierickx 1960-1962, vol. 1, p. 14, vol. 2, p. 414 n. 1.

144 Idem, vol. 2, nos 668, 669.

145 Idem, vol. 2, no. 381; also nos 380, 382, 389.

146 Receipts over 1570-1579: 5647 karolusgulden; paid in 1568-1579: 5006 karolusgulden. In 1571/72 the archbishop remitted one instalment. *Inventaris Archief kapittel ten Dom*, no. 1, vol. 19, f. 101v, 102v ('*prebenda fabrice ratione prebende archiepiscopalis*').

147 '[it] being a jewel and an ornament for the entire city'; *Inventaris Archief kapittel ten Dom*, no. 2499, pp. 311, 312.

148 Idem, p. 378; Muller 1903, p. 80.

149 Muller 1903, p. 80, n. 6, pp. 84, 153-154; *Inventaris Archief kapittel ten Dom*, no. 1, vol. 10, sub 9 June 1506.

150 *Inventaris Archief kapittel ten Dom*, nos 2499, pp. 311-312.

151 The system of compensation was moreover subject to all sorts of modification; see *Inventaris Archief kapittel ten Dom*, no. 649, vol. 3, 1518 account: annotation to the credit balance '*ad usum fabrice*'. This year also marks the first time in which we find annotated in the margins for the respective chantries: '*prima* [...], *secunda vicaria pro fabrica*', and so on. Up until 1525, the fabric received roughly the same amounts as it had to compensate in deficits. In addition, the fabric subsidized the choral fund on a regular basis; see *Bronnen bouwgeschiedenis*, vol. 2 (1), pp. 276, 279, 283, 293, 285, vol. 2 (2), pp. 169, 396, vol. 2 (3), pp. 431, 471, and fabric rolls 1529/30, f. 26. Between 1526 and 1533 the fabric was unable to shoulder the debit balances on this account group as it had shortages of its own.

152 Between 1534 and 1554 the fabric dipped into its surpluses on only seven occasions, to an amount of

around 725 rhinegulden, but after 1554 nearly every year until 1579/80, to a total of 5660 karolusgulden.

153 *Inventaris Archief kapittel ten Dom*, no. 1, vol. 19, f. 257v, also f. 261 (20 July 1574).

154 Years in which debit balances were not or not wholly transferred to expenditures in the succeeding account: *prebenda defunctorum* rolls 1422/23; fabric rolls 1442/43, 1460/61, 1469/70, 1498/99, 1522/23, 1523/24, 1525/26, 1527/28, 1532/33, 1533/34, 1534/35, 1536/37, 1540/41, 1542/43, 1544/45, 1548/49 until 1552/53, 1555/56, 1562/63, 1568/69, 1569/70, 1572/73, 1573/74. Years in which the master of the fabric provided credit balances not to his successor but to some other chapter officer: 1484/85, 1488/89, 1489/90, 1490/91, 1495/96, 1496/97, 1503/04, 1526/27, 1529/30, 1535/36, 1543/44, 1571/72. For actual figures see graph 4.

155 Between 1540 and 1543 approximately 300 rhinegulden were paid from the so-called '*rekening van de 10863 g 2 st. 3 wit*', probably related to the States treasury; *Inventaris Archief kapittel ten Dom*, no. 1, vol. 14, f. 4.

156 See for example *Inventaris Archief kapittel ten Dom*, no. 639, vol. 6, f. 37v (1552).

157 Idem, no. 1, vol. 16, f. 306, 307 (1554), vol. 18, f. 122 (1571) and 193v (1573). In 1572 and 1573 the dean and chapter had to shoulder the salary owed to the lawyer.

158 A capitular statute of 22 June 1579 and 30 October 1579 gave the fabric access to collected debts by drawing of lots; *Inventaris Archief kapittel ten Dom*, no. 1, vol. 20 under these dates; no. 745.

159 See Appendix five.

160 'a labyrinth, a maze, in which one can find neither beginning nor end [...] and must ultimately be likened to a haystack'; Muller 1903, p. 168. 'To be able to see at a glance [*in een oogopslag*] in a single account, in a single itemization, in a single balance, all our poverty and wealth, all our expenses, all our debts remaining and paid, revenues and arrears on any single day'; Muller 1903, p. 218.

161 An exception to some degree was the choir building campaign begun at the church of St John in 1508 – a modest project that was not to be completed until 1539. Even the fortuitous discovery of the relics of St Bernulf, the celebration of this discovery with the subsequent issue of a 40-day indulgence by the bishop (18 June 1514) and, more especially, another by the pope (23 February 1519) – acquired through the intermediation of the provost of St John's, Johan Ingenwinckel, who also worked for the papal court – were unable to effect devotions of any significance. At 80 rhinegulden or less a year, revenues from indulgence receipts were never large. The chapter financed the building works by selling life and redeemable annuities. No record of the choir building campaign remains. However, see *Inventaris archief kapittel St.-Jan*, nos 104 (indulgences), 105 (register of annuities sold), 162 (fabric rolls without expenditures for choir-building) and no. 1 (capitular resolutions), vol. 1, especially sub 13 October 1518 (f. 117r, 117v), 18 May 1520 (f. 137v). Also Calkoen 1902, p. 85 ff.

TWO Gifts and bequests

162 *Bronnen bouwgeschiedenis*, vol. 2 (2), p. 671; *Inventaris Archief kapittel ten Dom*, no. 2196. On De Wael as architect, see Haslinghuis & Peeters 1965, p. 344. Moreover, he paid 250 rhinegulden current into the fabric treasury to fund perpetual annual remunerations of 9 rhinegulden current to the choristers and 1 rhinegulden current to workers in the building lodge, bought a life annuity of 781½ rhinegulden current for his natural daughter and her son, and founded a burial chapel; *Bronnen bouwgeschiedenis*, vol. 2 (2), p. 694 and successive years; Muller 1906, p. 11a; also De Groot 2006, Chapter 5, p. 25 and n. 116.

163 *Bronnen bouwgeschiedenis*, vol. 2 (1), p. 522.

164 Here follow only those bequests worth five annual wages of an unskilled building labourer or more. See also Moore 1988, p. 413, n. 118. In 1508 CATHEDRAL DEAN LUDOLF VAN DEN VEEN left 400 gold rhinegulden, equalling almost 25 annual wages of a building labourer; *Bronnen bouwgeschiedenis*, vol. 2 (3), p. 146 (1511/12 account); *Inventaris Archief kapittel ten Dom*, no. 1, vol. 12, f. 71 ff. Van den Veen also made further large bequests and endowments. In 1503 GERLACUS VAN DER DONCK, compiler of one of the cathedral capitularies (*rechtsboek*) and former master of the fabric, bequeathed half the net revenues of his canon's residence (Calkoen n.d., vol. 1, claustral house Eb), a sum of 262½ rhinegulden current and the fruits of his year of grace, to whit 278 rhinegulden current, *'ad structuram et reparationem ornamentorum'*: totalling 540½ rhinegulden current, or more than 19 annual wages of a building labourer. Though the preserved codicil reveals that the bequest for the Dom was by far the single largest, it was overshadowed by the aggregate of some 60 mostly small bequests worth a combined 1222 rhinegulden current; *Bronnen bouwgeschiedenis*, vol. 2 (2), pp. 641, 650, 672; *Inventaris Archief kapittel ten Dom*, no. 264; Muller 1903, p. 67 ff. CANON JOH. VAN DRAKENBORCH, whose former offices included master of the fabric, bequeathed the net profits of his house in 1498, yielding more than 457½ rhinegulden current, or 16½ annual wages of a building labourer; *Bronnen bouwgeschiedenis*, vol. 2 (2), pp. 506, 514, 541; Calkoen n.d., vol. 1, claustral house Ad; *Inventaris Archief kapittel ten Dom*, no. 1, vol. 10, sub 19 March 1499. CANON NICOLAAS DE LAVENNIS, also a former master of the cathedral fabric, bequeathed the fruits of both his years of grace, totalling nearly 381 rhinegulden current, or 14 annual wages of a building labourer, *'ten nutte van de paramenten'* in 1517; *Bronnen bouwgeschiedenis*, vol. 2 (3), pp. 394, 436; *Inventaris Archief kapittel ten Dom*, no. 2, vol. 1, f. 123 (27 June 1517). The fabric assumed the obligation to pay out 5 s.bon. to the choristers each month, totalling a negligible 1½ rhinegulden current annually. CANON WILLEM VAN BROECKHUYSEN, who died in 1511, bequeathed 162½ rhinegulden current *'voor nieuwe paramenten'* and furthermore donated the profits of his canon's residence of more than 201 rhinegulden current. However, this house was subject to an annual payment (*pensio*) of 7 rhinegulden current, for which the commutation can be established at 175 rhinegulden current. The net value of his bequest can therefore be estimated at 188½ rhinegulden current, or seven years' wages of a building labourer; *Bronnen bouwgeschiedenis*, vol. 2 (3), pp. 146, 173, 210; *Inventaris Archief kapittel ten Dom*, no. 1, vol. 12, f. 10v, 11v; no. 2, vol. 1, f. 100 ff.; Calkoen n.d., vol. 1, claustral house Ca 1. For the annual payment, see

Inventaris Archief kapittel ten Dom, no. 651, loose leaf belonging to the account for 1515/16. The following bequests – likewise all from canons – were worth between two and five annual wages of a building labourer. GOESWINUS GROLL: 100 rhinegulden current, or almost four and a quarter years' wages; *Bronnen bouwgeschiedenis*, vol. 2 (1), p. 447 (1469/70). JOH. FOYT: donation (?) of 100 rhinegulden, or three and a half years' wages, for choir tapestries; *Bronnen bouwgeschiedenis*, vol. 2 (2), p. 252 (1488/89). ERNEST VAN STEENRE: 50 rhinegulden current, or more than two annual wages; *Bronnen bouwgeschiedenis*, vol. 2 (2), p. 522 (1475/76).

165 *Bronnen bouwgeschiedenis*, vol. 2 (2), pp. 199, 240, 242, 399, 514, 540; *Inventaris Archief kapittel ten Dom*, no. 1, vol. 10, 21 February 1500; Van der Monde 1844, vol. 2, p. 168.

166 See p. 255.

167 De Groot 1994, passim; especially De Groot 2006 passim; with the 1571 sacristy inventory as an appendix.

168 *Inventaris Archief kapittel ten Dom*, no. 2505. The 1504 inventory is published in Brom 1900; that of 1571 in De Groot 2006, Appendix 3, pp. 237-256.

169 De Groot 2006, Chapter 2, p. 34, and Chapter 8, pp. 45-51.

170 Bishops Burchard (1100-1112), Guy van Avesnes (1303-1317), bishops-elect Nicolo van Caputio (1341), John of Arkel (1314-1367), David of Burgundy (1457-1496), Frederick IV of Baden (1496-1517), George van Egmond (1534-1551) and Frederik Schenk van Toutenburg (1560-1580). Some donated more than one item. Muller 1906, p. 12, mentions the donation by Bishop Frederick IV of Baden of a sword (of precious metal) for the statue of St Martin above the indulgence altar, probably around 1510; De Groot 2006, p. 92.

171 Muller 1906, p. 16; Haslinghuis & Peeters 1965, p. 347. The statue of St Martin was donated by Count William III of Holland.

172 De Groot 2006, pp. 38-44; see also n. 104.

173 See De Groot 1994, passim, and especially De Groot 2006. Additionally, *Bronnen bouwgeschiedenis*, vol. 2 (1), in voce '*ecclesia, vitra*'; the window installation costs were for the cathedral fabric's account. Donors sometimes purchased stone for the statues from the fabric.

174 Concerning Philip the Good's window in 1449: Damen 2005, pp. 154 n. 55, 165; on the adjacent window of Frank van Borselen in 1456/57: Arkenbout 1967, pp. 124-125; also De Groot 2006, pp. 111, 266, 339 (nos 65 and 66).

175 De Groot 2006, Chapter 7, pp. 7-13; also n. 49 and 50.

176 Including some who also left a monetary bequest, such as Ernest van Steenre and Joh. van Drakenburch; Muller 1906, p. 9. Concerning the donations and bequests of Evert van Zoudenbalch (d. 1503), see Suir 1977, p. 46.

THREE Devotional and indulgence monies offered in UTRECHT Cathedral

177 Muller 1895, p. 114.

178 For example: *Inventaris Archief kapittel ten Dom*, no. 1, vol. 9, f. 63 (22 February 1489), no. 651, fabric rolls 1529/30, f. 26.

179 Muller 1895, pp. 263, 264.

180 *Bronnen bouwgeschiedenis*, vol. 2 (1), p. 8 n. 3; this chantry priest would later also be given the title of *indulgentiarius*; fabric rolls 1557/58, f. 300; also De Groot 2006, Chapter 11, p. 23.

181 Muller 1906, pp. 11-12. See *Bronnen bouwgeschiedenis*, vol. 2 (3), p. 123 ('*dat offlaet daer sint Merten op staet*'),

p. 155 (*'in den back onder die orgelen dair die reliquien van den oflaet in staen'*), p. 341 (*'outaer voor 'toflaet van sinte Merten'*). In COLOGNE Cathedral the altar dedicated to its patron, St Peter, was likewise the locus of gifts for the church; at the same time, however, this altar was also the main altar and parish altar of the *Edelfreien* of the diocese; Stehkämper 1979/1980, p. 27. In ROUEN an alabaster statue of Mary was a centre of devotion. It was the only statue in the church that fell under the fabric's administrative authority and stood on the altar of St Mary in the nave against the rood loft; this is also where masses for benefactors of the fabric were read; Foucher-Lefebvre in Bos *et al.* 2006, pp. 144-149.

182 *Inventaris Archief kapittel ten Dom*, no. 405, f. 1 ff. Concerning medieval indulgences and devotional life in the Netherlands, see the relevant chapter in Herwaarden 2003, pp. 86-122.

183 *Bronnen bouwgeschiedenis*, vol. 2 (1), p. 559; Fredericq 1922, no. 258; Dodt van Flensburg 1838-1848, vol. 7, p. 232.

184 *Oorkondenboek Utrecht*, no. 1660.

185 Idem, no. 2496.

186 Idem, no. 2760.

187 Eekhof 1909, Appendix no. 35; dates from Tenhaeff.

188 *Inventaris Archief kapittel ten Dom*, no. 415. Curiously, the indulgence of one year and 40 days that Bishop John of Arkel requested from and – according to the petition (*supplicatorium*) – was granted by the pope in 1359 is missing; Rutgers 1970, p. 178; was it ever actually proclaimed?

189 *Oorkondenboek Utrecht*, no. 1722.

190 Idem, nos 2364, 2397.

191 'item from cardinals, legates, archbishops and bishops, indulgences worth 7 years, 1380 days, and 12 quarantines'; Dodt van Flensburg 1838-1848, vol. 7, pp. 232, 253; *Inventaris Archief kapittel ten Dom*, no. 419.

192 Recent overview of relics owned by the Dom and their veneration by Frans Rikhof in Margry & Caspers 1997, pp. 737-747.

193 Peeters 1966, p. 90; Haslinghuis & Peeters 1965, p. 160; Van den Hoven van Genderen 1997, p. 35; Van Vliet 2002, pp. 172-174; Beissel 1890, p. 88.

194 Obtained from the monastery of Marienweerd near Culemborg; Matthaeus 1703, p. 7 (c. VII).

195 Eekhof 1909, p. 53 and Appendix nos 96, 97. The fabric had to pay a substantial 175 rhinegulden current to send a canon to the monastery; a remuneration was also paid to a canon in Antwerp, Heda; the abbot of Cognac received the gift of a *bracchium argentium* worth 96 rhinegulden current; *Bronnen bouwgeschiedenis*, vol. 2 (3), pp. 469, 470, 510.

196 Brom 1900, p. 270; exh. cat. UTRECHT 1972, no. 36.

197 The Oldminster had already owned a relic of St Willibrord since 1301; from a deed of 1 July 1520 (erroneously listed as no. 436x in the *Inventaris Archief kapittel ten Dom*) we learn that the Oldminster hoped to exchange its relics of Bishop Frederick (820-835) for relics of Sts Willibrord and Boniface; Visser 1934, p. 168 ff.; Eekhof 1909, p. 14 (incorrect); Van den Hoven van Genderen 1997, p. 621.

198 The relics were *'presentate'* to the chapter on 26 September 1519; *Inventaris Archief kapittel ten Dom*, no. 2, vol. 2 sub dato. But on 22 October 1520 the city of UTRECHT approached the archbishop of TRIER to act as the Dom's intermediary with the abbot of Echternach; Van Asch van Wijck 1838, pp. 68-70; Van Asch van Wijck 1850-1853 vol. 2,

1852, pp. 268-269. Later relic inventories sometimes do list a set of relics of St Willibrord, but not the head or body the request referred to; Van Asch van Wijck 1838, pp. 63-68. There is also mention of a book, the *de vita et miraculis S. Willibrordi*, which apparently was obtained; Van Asch van Wijck 1850-1853, vol. 2, 1852, p. 251 (3 November 1519); *Bronnen bouwgeschiedenis*, vol. 2 (3), pp. 465-470, 505; also Calkoen 1915, p. 39.

199 Appears for the first time in the 1413/14 fabric rolls, and from 1466/67 every seven years; *Bronnen bouwgeschiedenis*, vol. 2 (1), p. 161, vol. 2 (2), pp. 237, 239. For the protocol: Eekhof 1909, p. 16 and *Inventaris Archief kapittel ten Dom*, no. 419. Pilgrims were granted safe-conduct; Matthaeus 1703, p. 8, c. VIII (1522). Also Boeren 1962, p. 156, Van den Hoven van Genderen 1987, p. 37, and De Groot 1994, p. 81.

200 Van Asch van Wijck 1838, pp. 163-166; *Inventaris Archief kapittel ten Dom*, no. 419. All the reliquaries and shrines have been lost. However, recent research has uncovered various relics from the Dom, including the charred remains of St Agnes and St Pontian and the thumb and skull of St Martin, in the Old Catholic cathedral of St Gertrude in UTRECHT; De Kruijf 2009, pp. 53-58.

201 Episcopal indulgence dated 13 August 1418 for those present at the translation to the new shrine; *Inventaris Archief kapittel ten Dom*, no. 418; see above, p. 254.

202 See Appendix five.

203 Van Asch van Wijck 1838, p. 166; Rutgers 1970, p. 183.

204 *Inventaris Archief kapittel ten Dom*, no. 419.

205 The cathedral of UTRECHT was one to which judges only rarely imposed a pilgrimage as penalty. Of the 3170 penal pilgrimages imposed in Antwerp between 1383 and 1513 (of which, incidentally, only 1826 were actually carried out, whilst the rest were bought off), only twelve stipulated UTRECHT, as opposed to 293 imposed for COLOGNE Cathedral; this places COLOGNE at the top of the list, and UTRECHT thirty-eighth. The penalty books (*correctieboeken*) of Leiden document 840 imposed pilgrimages between 1434 and 1557, of which 233 to ROME, 116 to Einsiedeln, 75 to COLOGNE and only two to UTRECHT. The UTRECHT Dom is also named as a destination – albeit only sporadically – in Lier, LIÈGE, Maastricht and Lille; Van Herwaarden 1978, pp. 181, 186, 701, 705, 709, 730; Van Cauwenbergh 1922, p. 139.

206 The relics were set up in a wooden case in the cathedral. *Bronnen bouwgeschiedenis*, vol. 2 (3), pp. 411, 449 (1518/19 and 1519/20 accounts).

207 See Appendix five under 1517, including literature.

208 *Inventaris Archief kapittel ten Dom*, no. 651, fabric rolls 1557/58, f. 300.

209 Fredericq 1922, pp. 323, 396.

210 The two sums were entered in different categories; see for example *Bronnen bouwgeschiedenis*, vol. 2 (2), pp. 115, 116.

211 Idem, vol. 2 (2), pp. 41-42: payment for *pixides* and for three tablets to which the indulgence bulls were affixed.

212 'shall be available to earn in the cathedral of St Martin on Friday, Saturday and Sunday next, to which end confessors will be engaged for three days before and three days afterwards'; Dodt van Flensburg 1843, p. 63 *buurspraakboek*; the profit for the cathedral fabric was minimal, only 11 rhinegulden current; *Bronnen bouwgeschiedenis*, vol. 2 (2), p. 252.

213 Rémy 1928, p. 110 ff. Part

of the proceeds were designated for a crusade against the Turks. *Inventaris Archief kapittel ten Dom*, no. 1, vol. 10, sub 9 October 1502; *Bronnen bouwgeschiedenis*, vol. 2 (2), pp. 591, 615, 616.

FOUR Episcopal mendicatoria and synodal statutes

214 The Portiuncula indulgence (less costs) yielded at least 6000 lb. of 8 wit (around 40 annual wages) in 1396, 1400/01 and 1402/03; the data are incomplete; *Bronnen bouwgeschiedenis*, vol. 2 (1), pp. 62, 68, 80. In 1477 and 1502 the Jubilee indulgence yielded 125 rhinegulden (4 percent, four and a half annual wages) and 60 rhinegulden (1.5 percent, two annual wages), respectively, the 1481 Crusade indulgence more than 130 rhinegulden (5 percent, four and a half annual wages), the 1484 SAINTES indulgence more than 100 rhinegulden (2 percent, three and a half annual wages), the indulgence for the crusade against the Turks in 1514 more than 150 rhinegulden (3 percent, five annual wages), the indulgence for the hospital of the Santo Spirito in ROME in the same year nearly 100 rhinegulden (2 percent, three annual wages) and the indulgence for the construction of St Peter's in ROME '*in commodum et utilitatem immensi operis Basilice principis apostolorum de Urbe*' almost 400 rhinegulden (3.5 percent, thirteen annual wages) between 1516 and 1518; Fredericq 1922, nos 190, 223 ff., 280 ff., 332 ff., 364 ff.; *Inventaris Archief kapittel ten Dom*, no. 494.

215 See Appendix three.

216 *Oorkondenboek Utrecht*, no. 2249. Another quest predating 1288 is that of the Carmelite monastery in Haarlem, 1284; Eekhof 1909, p. 22.

217 *Oorkondenboek Utrecht*, no. 1722.

218 Joosting & Muller 1906-1924, vol. 5, pp. 54-60, 60-68, 69-72; the statutes of 1310; idem, pp. 96-97. LIÈGE: Post 1957, vol. 1, p. 187.

219 Translation in Appendix four.

220 The synodal statutes date from 31 March 1318; Joosting & Muller 1906-1924, vol. 5, p. 100. Following Bishop John of Arkel, synods were held on the Tuesday following the fourth Sunday after Easter (Cantate Sunday) and on 20 October; Post 1957, vol. 1, p. 251; see also Van Vliet 2002, p. 332.

221 Tangl 1894, p. 267; *Cartulaire S. Jean de Jérusalem*, p. 246 (no. 346).

222 Post 1933, p. 96.

223 *Inventaris Archief kapittel ten Dom*, no. 405, f. 20.

224 Joosting & Muller 1906-1924, vol. 5, pp. 96, 97.

225 Noordeloos 1959, p. 30.

226 Eekhof 1909, pp. X-XI (passage from '*ceterum vobis*' up to '*inobedientes vero sacerdotes*').

227 '*In capitulis vestris generalibus aut in diebus et locis reportacionum vestrarum solitis et ad hoc deputatis*'; ibidem.

228 Deeds of 26 November 1339 and 18 March 1340 (Eekhof 1909, Appendix 3) reveal that Bishop Jan III van Diest had '*certis et racionabilibus ex causis*' revoked privileges relating to the *bona injusta* and commutations, which he overturned in this deed.

229 Rutgers 1970, p. 176.

230 '*Igitur quartam partem omnium decimarum ad nos ordinario iure pertinencium* [...] *ad consummacionem dicti operis deputamus*'; *Inventaris Archief kapittel ten Dom*, no. 405, f. 75v.

231 Rutgers 1970, pp. 24 ff., 166 ff.

232 Joosting & Muller 1906-1924, vol. 5, pp. 111, 116; Rutgers 1970, pp. 176, 177; Nolet & Boeren 1951, p. 154.

233 Rutgers 1970, pp. 20, 21.

234 Post 1967, p. 16; Hofman

2003, pp. 777, 778; see above, p. 195.

235 De Blécourt 1950, p. 145.

236 Post 1967, p. 38; Hofman 2003, p. 788

237 Joosting & Muller 1906-1924, vol. 5, pp. 110-111 (1345 sub F, J, K, L, M); pp. 115-116, 118, 119, 120 (1347); pp. 125, 126 (1350); p. 130 (1351); p. 132 (1352); p. 133 (1353); pp. 136-137 (n.d.); pp. 137-138 (n.d.); also Rutgers 1970, pp. 176-177.

238 Rutgers 1970, p. 173.

239 Joosting & Muller 1906-1924, vol. 5, pp. 137-138. Tenhaeff (*Bronnen bouwgeschiedenis*, vol. 2 (1), p. XXXI), Post 1967, p. 8, and Rutgers 1970, p. 173, incorrectly interpret this passage as giving the cathedral fabric a claim to a quarter of all local offerings.

240 The *mendicatorium* of Frederick of Blankenheim is only partly legible.

241 The bishop's proclamation of the *mendicatorium* on 31 March was amongst his first official acts after being appointed on 18 March 1517; Sterk 1980, p. 33. Bishop Philip's incumbency is the first since that of John of Arkel from which synodal statutes have been preserved, namely, from 2 October 1517; Joosting & Muller 1906-1924, vol. 5, pp. 148-156; concerning the fabric: pp. 150, 153.

FIVE The reportationes sancti Martini

242 Joosting & Muller 1906-1924, vol. 1, pp. 40-160, vol. 2, pp. 11-22.

243 Idem, vol. 2, p. 51 ff., 68 ff., map in Mulders 1943. See also *Bronnen bouwgeschiedenis*, vol. 2 (1), pp. 8-29.

244 Mol 2004, n. 2.

245 Eekhof 1909, Appendix 7.

246 Incidentally, Friesland managed to shirk all Church taxes and levies; Van Buijtenen in Rutgers 1978, p. 4. On the ecclesiastical situation in Friesland in particular, see also Mol 2004.

247 *Bronnen bouwgeschiedenis*, vol. 2 (1), p. 8 n. 5, p. 110, p. 225 n. 2: Zeelandic Flanders as from 1406, Drenthe from 1436, West Friesland from 1460.

248 In 1530: 190 parishes, in 1540: 100, in 1550: 84, in 1555: 22.

249 Alberts 1966, p. 211 n. 34 (second edition 1978, p. 222 n. 40).

250 The cities of Leiden, Delft, Noordwijk, Schoonhoven, Emmerich, Haarlem, Amsterdam, Gouda, Deventer, Kampen, Zwolle and Dordrecht.

251 *Bronnen bouwgeschiedenis*, vol. 2 (1), p. 203 n. 5, p. 254 n. 2; cf. *Inventaris Archief kapittel ten Dom*, no. 430.

252 In ordinary years receipts came to 220 rhinegulden current, in 1528 only 44 rhinegulden current. Concerning these years, see Van Kalveen 1972, passim. By contrast, the war led by David of Burgundy (1482-84) resulted in only a temporary downturn, followed by recovery; *Bronnen bouwgeschiedenis*, vol. 2 (2), p. 771.

253 The bookkeeping system allowed for payment defaulting on a large scale; see waste books in *Bronnen bouwgeschiedenis*, vol. 2 (1), p. 173 and n. 4, pp. 418 and 507.

254 See p. 287. This was customary in the case of other diocesan collections also, where the rural deans who gathered the *cathedraticum* were allowed to keep a third of the proceeds.

255 'to demand and to receive on behalf of our fabric the conveyance for Saint Martin, here called the *reporatationes b.Martini*'; *Inventaris Archief kapittel ten Dom*, no. 1, vol. 1, f. 69v, 71v: contracts with Zwolle, Polsbroek, Oostzanen, Middelburg, Delft and other parishes. The earliest capitular resolutions date from 1402. Additionally *Inventaris* o.c., no. 429: Ingen (1456, ten years); Delft, church of St Hippolytus (Oude Kerk) (1460, ten years); Arkel (1473, ten years); Lekkerkerk (1477,

twelve years); Oudewater (1486, ten years).

256 Both these factors played a part in the *reportationes* in the parish of Zwolle. Its contribution fell from 10 oude schilden in around 1400 to 4 oude schilden in 1464; moreover, whereas the oude schild had initially equalled 1½ gold rhinegulden, it was worth only 1½ rhinegulden current after 1464; *Bronnen bouwgeschiedenis*, vol. 2 (1), pp. LXXVIII, 125, 422, vol. 2 (2), p. 27.

257 Receipts did increase in some parishes, such as Haarlem.

258 *Inventaris Archief kapittel ten Dom*, no. 419; Dodt van Flensburg 1838-1848, vol. 7, pp. 232-233. Also Oosterbaan 1958, pp. 62-64.

259 *Bronnen bouwgeschiedenis*, vol. 2 (3), pp. 65, 66.

260 Oosterbaan 1973, pp. 484-485; Haarlem, Noord-Hollands Archief, St Bavo church archives, no. 147, 1248 account, f. I *'item opten pinxterdach van de bede mit sunte Martijns'*; also in other years; UTRECHT, Buurkerk: Van Rappard 1880, p. 70.

261 'and for this the church has granted a great many indulgences for the conveyance for St Martin on major feast days'; Regionaal Archief Alkmaar, archives of the church of St Lawrence, no. 1824, f. 79.

262 The churchwardens of Haarlem always entered receipts from their collection together with the *'Sinte Martijnsgeld'* (money for St Martin); see n. 260.

263 'the commander advised us not to go'; Overvoorde 1906, pp. 87, 88, 118.

264 Regionaal Archief Leiden, churchwardens' rolls, church of St Peter, 1428, f. 36v (not in Overvoorde); *'Item so was sinte Martinsbede gepacht 10 jair lanc ende die jaren waren nu ommegecomen. Doe hebben die kercmeesters weder in pacht 10 jair lanc om 8 wilhelmus scilde tsiaers'*; see also Overvoorde 1906, p. 123.

265 'conveyance for St Martin in excess of the 8 [oude] schilden handed over in this year'; Overvoorde 1906, pp. 124 and 88.

266 Verhoeven 1992, pp. 172-177, with graphs showing the receipts.

267 'under the condition that the aforementioned churchwardens shall nonetheless bring with them and deliver there any bequests reserved for our cathedral church and any unlawful goods or spoils that have come into their hands'; *Inventaris Archief kapittel ten Dom*, no. 429; also *Bronnen bouwgeschiedenis*, vol. 2 (3), pp. 163 and 160: this entry makes clear the difference between *reportationes*, on the one hand, and bequests, wills, *bona injusta* and so on, on the other.

268 Conscience monies in e.g. *Bronnen bouwgeschiedenis*, vol. 2 (1), p. 6 n. 4, pp. 52, 66, 108, 171, 172, 219, etc., vol. 2 (2), p. 713. This category also contains the somewhat mysterious *'recepta de casibus episcopalibus et homicidiis'*, which are found only in the first seven accounts and which receipts were thenceforth spent on books for the choral service; *Bronnen bouwgeschiedenis*, vol. 2 (1), p. XXIX, p. 50 n. 7, pp. 66, 78, 88, 97, 108, 145.

269 *Bronnen bouwgeschiedenis*, vol. 2 (1), p. 88, 97, etc., vol. 2 (2), pp. 5, 54, etc., vol. 2 (3), pp. 2, 36, etc. We cannot rule out that testamentary bequests formed a much more important income source during the period over which no fabric rolls have been preserved than they did later on. The 1358 will of Elisabeth Huge Nagels of Haarlem designated its largest bequest of 2 lb. for the UTRECHT Dom, twice the amount she left to the church of St Bavo in Haarlem; Henderikx 1977, p. 130 and n. 54.

270 *Bronnen bouwgeschiedenis*, vol. 2 (1), p. 52 and n. 2.

271 Idem, vol. 2 (2), p. 339. The masters of the fabric attempted to revive the confraternity. On 31 July 1504 Cardinal Raymund Peraudi granted the confraters and consorers an indulgence worth 100 days and confirmed all former privileges; *Inventaris Archief kapittel ten Dom*, no. 435. The institution was never to flourish, despite having its own seal and a registry of members (*rotulus de confraternitate scti Martini*), and had already disappeared from the *mendicatoria* in 1364; Fredericq 1922, no. 242; *Inventaris Archief kapittel ten Dom*, no. 483: both documents concern Friesland.

272 Van Rappard 1880, p. 74 (1440-41). Also Oosterbaan 1973, pp. 488; Inventory of the diocese of Haarlem, précis 252.

273 Van der Horst 1866, p. 175.

274 Another reason, though one that did not generally weigh heavily, is that the pope had granted some parish churches the privilege of accepting *bona injusta*. This papal privilege was at odds with the cathedral fabric's claim. St Bavo's in Haarlem received this privilege in 1309 (renewed in 1397); Allan 1874-1888, vol. 3, pp. 76, 78.

275 'was sent to UTRECHT on Cantate [Sunday], that is the third Sunday before Whitsunday'; Regionaal Archief Alkmaar, archives of the church of St Lawrence, no. 1824, f. 79.

276 *Inventaris Archief kapittel ten Dom*, no. 67, f. 3v-4; at both the spring and autumn synods.

277 *Bronnen bouwgeschiedenis*, vol. 2 (1), pp. 419 ff., 507 ff.

278 Account for 1395-1424; *Bronnen bouwgeschiedenis*, vol. 2 (1), passim; also later; idem, p. 549. There was also an even simpler form of collection: at the church of St Nicholas in UTRECHT, the churchwardens gave their contribution directly to the cathedral's *magister fabrice*; *Catalogussen archief stad Utrecht, tweede afdeeling*, no. 706, church of St Nicholas, churchwardens' rolls 1505, f. 3 and other years.

279 *Bronnen bouwgeschiedenis*, vol. 2 (1), p. 204 n. 2, pp. 418, 603; *Inventaris Archief kapittel ten Dom*, no. 2, vol. 1, f. 170 (1510).

280 Especially in Delfland: *Bronnen bouwgeschiedenis*, vol. 2 (2), pp. 54, 115, 200, 213, 244, 274, 315, 376, 401, 426, 670; concerning the provisor: Nolet & Boeren 1951, p. 227.

281 *Bronnen bouwgeschiedenis*, vol. 2 (1), p. 514, vol. 2 (3), p. 384.

282 Idem, vol. 2 (2), p. 627, n. 1, p. 665; also vol. 2 (3), pp. 312, 384. More commissioners are recorded later on, who were charged with accepting monies and goods for the fabric; idem, vol. 2 (3), p. 163; also cathedral fabric rolls 1529/30, f. 25v, 1537/38, f. 161v.

283 *Bronnen bouwgeschiedenis*, vol. 2 (3), p. 714.

284 Concerning the bookkeeping system, see idem, vol. 2 (1), p. 418 n. 4. Debtor lists were also drawn up; see for example cathedral fabric rolls 1529/30, f. 36v.

285 Idem, vol. 2 (3), p. 66.

286 *Inventaris Archief kapittel ten Dom*, no. 431 (1463, 9 May); *Bronnen bouwgeschiedenis*, vol. 2 (2), p. 393 (parish priest of Hulst in 1494).

287 *Bronnen bouwgeschiedenis*, vol. 2 (2), p. 170 (1485/86).

288 Idem, vol. 2 (2), p. 334 (1491/92). Other examples of legal action: idem, vol. 2 (1), pp. 371, 471, 500, vol. 2 (2), p. 245: *monitorium* from the bishop's official directed against the fabric masters of nine churches '*de non solutione reportationes b. Martini*' (1487/88).

289 In the fifteenth century – pursuant to the West Frisian schism – West Frisian priests refused to

yield up these monies; *Bronnen bouwgeschiedenis*, vol. 2 (1), pp. 464, 471, 475.

290 Idem, vol. 2 (3), p. 711.

291 Verhoeven 1992, pp. 174, 176.

292 Fabric rolls 1529/30, f. 25v: '*Item diversis commissariis per dyocesim pro restantiis multiplicibus reportationibus b. Martini habendis et recipiendis pro eorum magna diligencia precipue hoc tempore lutheriano solutionem negantes et solvere in multis locis nolentes, necnon pro expensis per eosdem iuridice procedendo, itinerando et nuncios de loco ad locum mittendo per dyocesim factis, solet fabrica istis dare tertium denarium de receptis, iam tantum dedit per composicionem de 180 fl. quintum denarium facit 36 rijnsgulden*'. First reference to Luther in the fabric rolls: 1522/23; *Bronnen bouwgeschiedenis*, vol. 2 (3), p. 582. His writings were already being printed in the Low Countries in 1520; Visser 1909, p. 29 ff.; Fredericq 1922, p. 595. Receipts from diocesan collections witnessed a decline elsewhere in Europe, too: in 1524 the canons of KONSTANZ complained that the '*petitio matricis, die vor jaren ain namhafftige summ geltz ertragen hab, in grossen mercklichen abfal komen*'; Krebs 1952-1959, no. 7934. Thanks in part to the position taken by King Henry VIII, Luther's influence was barely felt in England; on the contrary, indulgence receipts rose over the first three decades of the sixteenth century, possibly boosted by efficient propaganda via the printing presses. Not until after the break with Rome were indulgences discredited once and for all; Swanson 2007, pp. 360-361, 475.

293 For example: deanery of the Veluwe in 1515/16; Zwolle in 1528/29; *Inventaris Archief kapittel ten Dom*, no. 1, vol. 13, f. 27v.

294 *Inventaris Archief kapittel ten Dom*, no. 1, vol. 17, f. 30v (9 December 1554); a *patronus* or design was used here.

295 Idem, no. 434.

296 Idem, no. 1, vol. 16, f. 192v, 202; idem, no. 651, fabric rolls 1552/53, f. 182v, 184, 187v. The legal grounds for these imperial letters is not known to me. The *reportationes* appear to have enjoyed the overlords protection from an early date; cf. Bishop Philip of Burgundy's 1454 order to pay the *reportationes*, preserved in the cathedral fabric cartulary, idem no. 405, f. 67. Other legal actions against defaulters also continued as normal: cathedral fabric rolls 1537/38, f. 161v, 1545/46, sub Walcheren, 1550/51, f. 104v, 1552/53, f. 183, 1562/63, f. 29.

297 *Inventaris Archief kapittel ten Dom*, no. 408.

298 In 1567 the receipts came to 5 stuivers, nothing in 1568, 11 stuivers in 1569, and nothing in 1570 and the years following, excepting one solitary back payment of 2½ stuivers in 1578.

299 The '*collecturae ecclesiariam*' amounted to 37 percent of the receipts in 1459, 65 percent in 1487, 70 percent in 1488 and 76 percent in 1489; see p. 221.

SIX The quest monies

300 Paulus 1922-1923, vol. 2, p. 492; Post 1957, vol. 2, p. 47; also Caspers in Swanson 2006, pp. 68-71.

301 Noordeloos 1959, p. 30.

302 Eekhof 1909, p. XV; successively renewed, e.g. p. XXXII; Joosting & Muller 1906-1924, vol. 5, p. 153 n. 2 (12 October 1393); Noordeloos 1959, p. 30 n. 5.

303 Eekhof 1909, p. XXXII; Heeringa 1932, vol. 2, pp. 55, 56, 71, 94, 116, 129, 145, 170, 197, 211, 246; vol. 3, p. LXI. On one occasion, in the war year of 1482/83, the vicar-general collected '*propter guerras*' more than half the quest receipts;

Bronnen bouwgeschiedenis, vol. 2 (2), pp. XII, 94.

304 *Inventaris Archief kapittel ten Dom*, no. 405, f. 40v; confirmed by Bishop Rudolf van Diepholt in 1451; Matthaeus 1703, p. 9.

305 On 19 December 1396, at the request – as the pope explicitly states – of the dean and chapter, Boniface IX gave his permission for pardoners from the cathedral to visit churches within the diocese, notwithstanding the constitutions of diocesan or provincial synods; this represented a relatively harmless confirmation of an existing situation; Eekhof 1909, Appendix no. 37; *Inventaris Archief kapittel ten Dom*, nos 428 and 405, f. 2v. On 5 September he confirmed the bishop's letter concerning '*bona injusta et vaga*'; *Inventaris* o.c., no. 405, f. 25-27, f. 41-44, nos 420, 421; Eekhof 1909, Appendix no. 40.

306 *Inventaris Archief kapittel ten Dom*, no. 405 f. 6-7.

307 With reference to the letter of 11 October 1393; Eekhof 1909, Appendix no. 36.

308 *Inventaris Archief kapittel ten Dom*, nos 423, 405, f. 35v-38v; Eekhof 1909, Appendix no. 48. Confirmations by Sixtus IV: *Inventaris* o.c., no. 405, f. 159v, f. 169-171, no. 439. Confirmations by Alexander VI: no. 426; Eekhof 1909, Appendix no. 103; cf. *Inventaris* o.c., no. 425.

309 Post 1957, vol. 2, pp. 2-18.

310 *Bronnen bouwgeschiedenis*, vol. 2 (1), p. 203 n. 5, p. 254 n. 2.

311 The following documents relate to this matter: *Inventaris Archief kapittel ten Dom*, nos 505 (i.e. no. 4051 f. 5-6), 506 (i.e. no. 405, f. 8r, 8v), 507 (i.e. no. 405, f. 30v-34), 508 (i.e. no. 405, f. 34v), 509 (i.e. no. 405, f. 8v), all from 1434. Similar sorts of difficulties had already been encountered in 1427, no. 504 (i.e. no. 405, f. 27-30v).

312 Noordeloos 1959, p. 30.

313 Eekhof 1909, passim.

314 See p. 288.

315 Eekhof 1909, p. 73 and Appendix no. 9; *Bronnen bouwgeschiedenis*, vol. 2 (1), p. XXVIII; *Inventaris Archief kapittel ten Dom*, no. 441; Van Kalveen 1968, p. 31; Bloemen 1961, pp. 96, 105. A miracle involving the host took place at the beginning of the thirteenth century; the fire of 1465, in which the host was spared, gave renewed impetus both to veneration and the church building works. The collection campaign certainly also toured the diocese of LIÈGE after 1472; Habets 1888, pp. 80, 126-127, Caspers in Swanson 2006, p. 71, Margry & Caspers 2008 pp. 297-298.

316 Kühn 1994, pp. 96, 102. This collection also operated in the dioceses of TOURNAI, ARRAS and THÉROUANNE; Zender 1959, pp. 148-150.

317 Eekhof 1909, p. 66; *Bronnen bouwgeschiedenis*, vol. 2 (1), p. 50 n. 6; Paulus 1922-1923, vol. 3, pp. 252, 290; *Inventaris Archief kapittel ten Dom*, no. 442; Zender 1959, pp. 144-177.

318 In 1350 the abbot determined that quest receipts would henceforth be spent on building the abbey; one monk was appointed to supervise; Vroom 1993, p. 579 n. 13.

319 Eekhof 1909, p. 44 ff. and Appendix no. 11; *Bronnen bouwgeschiedenis*, vol. 2 (1), p. 50 n. 6; Paulus 1922-1923, vol. 3, p. 252 (pardoners documented as early as 1330). Hubert was not only the patron saint of hunters, but also, especially in the fifteenth century, a protector against rabies; Dierkens 1999, pp. 244, 250.

320 Eekhof 1909, p. 70 and Appendix no. 12; *Bronnen bouwgeschiedenis*, vol. 2 (1), pp. XXXVIII, 108 n. 2; *Inventaris Archief kapittel ten Dom*, no. 459; Heeringa 1932, vol. 2, p. 145. Verbal communication by Louise van Tongerloo.

321 Eekhof 1909, p. 72; *Inventaris Archief kapittel ten Dom*, no. 458; *Catalogussen archief stad Utrecht, tweede afdeeling*, p. 106 ff.; Weiler & Geirnaert 1980, pp. 427-452.

322 Eekhof 1909, Appendix no. 14; *Inventaris Archief kapittel ten Dom*, no. 460.

323 Eekhof 1909, Appendix nos 17 and 20; *Inventaris Archief kapittel ten Dom*, no. 461; Van Kalveen 1968, passim.

324 Eekhof 1909, p. 55 ff.; especially Noordeloos 1959, p. 27 ff. Earliest record in the UTRECHT sources: 1387; *Inventaris Archief kapittel ten Dom*, no. 405, f. 68. It was already operating in COLOGNE long before this, in 1301; *Regesten Köln*, vol. 3, no. 3787, vol. 4, no. 462 (1309).

325 The succession of papal benefits and privileges began under Innocent IV (1243-1254) and his successors; Mischlewski 1976, pp. 44, 45, 50, and other publications by him.

326 Eekhof 1909, pp. 69-70; *Inventaris Archief kapittel ten Dom*, nos 487 (i.e. Eekhof 1909, Appendix no. 68) and 488. Connection with Neuss: *Bronnen bouwgeschiedenis*, vol. 2 (2), pp. 308-310; *Kronijk Historisch Genootschap* 4 (1848), p. 141; Paulus 1922-1923, vol. 3, p. 252. Concerning veneration for St Quirinus: Köster 1960, passim.

327 *Lexikon für Theologie und Kirche*, in voce *'Marschälle'*, who were venerated in the Church province of COLOGNE in particular, see Hüffer 1938. Zender 1959, p. 153, provides a map showing veneration of the Four Holy Marshals; he emphasizes the ethnological factors; see also p. 177. Similar associations are also found elsewhere. The diocese of STRASBOURG also had Four Marshals: St Anthony, St Quirinus, St Hubert and St Valentine; Barth 1954, p. 103. In the bishopric of KONSTANZ the quests of St Anthony, St Valentine, St Bernard and the Santo Spirito had special rights; Barth 1954, p. 108.

328 Adriaanse 1932, p. 80; Voisin 1869, pp. 481-482.

329 Eekhof 1909, Appendix nos 98, 100, 101, 102; *Inventaris Archief kapittel ten Dom*, no. 496; see Nolet & Boeren 1951, p. 463. Similar conditions were applied to the collection run by the Bridgettines from Dendermonde in 1535; *Inventaris Archief kapittel ten Dom*, no. 1, vol. 14, f. 38.

330 Beissel 1889, vol. 2, pp. 27-28; Rotthoff 1973, pp. 14-15; *Stiftskirche Xanten*, vol. 4 (2), p. XXI. The papal indulgence was granted on the occasion of the so-called *Viktortracht*, a procession held on a regular basis. In Holland receipts came to 354 marks (equalling eleven annual wages of a building labourer), which was around a quarter of the total - very high - income that flowed into the fabric in Xanten that year. Concerning the *Viktortracht* in 1288, 1376, 1400, 1421, 1464 and 1487, see Hawicks 2004, pp. 53, 57, 65.

331 The question of how many of these sporadic collections operated in the diocese without the cathedral fabric's official sanction remains unanswered; see Jongkees 1942, p. 163. Habets 1979, p. 78, cites six begging letters from the Heilige Geest Gasthuis in Groningen dating from 1448, 1506, 1519, 1528, 1541 and 1543, and lists begging letters from other religious houses there. My thanks to the late Dr F.J. Bakker of Groningen, who sent me transcriptions of several of these letters.

332 On 2 March 1421 Bishop Frederick of Blankenheim granted the Cistercian convent in Assen a diocesan collection; UTRECHT, UTRECHTS Archief, episcopal archives, no. 9, f.

79v; my thanks to Dr F. Bakker for the transcription and translation.

333 Jongkees 1942, p. 163.

334 *Inventaris Archief kapittel ten Dom*, no. 4116. Van Lokhorst was also accused of concealing the strongbox (*cista*) with its contents, which had been handed over to him in Rotterdam.

335 Eekhof 1909, Appendix no. 52; incorporated in the fabric cartulary, (*Inventaris Archief kapittel ten Dom*, no. 405) f. 195 ff.; Paulus 1922-1923, vol. 3, p. 256.

336 *Bronnen bouwgeschiedenis*, vol. 2 (1), p. 348 and n. 6: 1460/61 account, admission fee of 840 gulden (of 30 wit); in this particular instance the bishop asked for a quarter of the receipts.

337 Jongkees 1942, p. 164.

338 *Inventaris Archief kapittel ten Dom*, no. 405, f. 199r and v: vidimus dated 6 June 1486; bull of 14 April 1485; later bulls on 14 July and 12 October 1486; idem, f. 201v, 202r.

339 *Bronnen bouwgeschiedenis*, vol. 2 (1), pp. 206 and 204 (1486/87 account).

340 Eekhof 1909, Appendix nos 71, 72, 73 (agreement of 17 May 1494). On 1 May 1495 the bishop granted an indulgence to benefactors of the Trinitarians; Fredericq 1922, no. 259; also on 30 January 1497, Eekhof 1909, Appendix no. 74.

341 *Inventaris Archief kapittel ten Dom*, no. 478 (20 June 1490). The Trinitarians had already illicitly begun their begging campaign in 1490; *Inventaris* o.c., no. 659, *prebenda defunctorum* rolls 1490, f. 9; possibly also *Bronnen bouwgeschiedenis*, vol. 2 (2), p. 309.

342 *Bronnen bouwgeschiedenis*, vol. 2 (2), pp. 376, 401, 777, 779. In 1494 a 'recognition fee' (*recognitiegeld*) of 13 gold rhinegulden was divided out amongst the canons '*pro admissione questus sancte Trinitatis ad tres annos*'; Muller 1903, p. 133.

343 *Bronnen bouwgeschiedenis*, vol. 2 (1), p. 539 n. 2, p. 540 n. 9 and vol. 2 (3), p. 555 (1522/23); Fredericq 1922, no. 370; *Inventaris Archief kapittel ten Dom*, no. 405, f. 239-240 and 242; nos 489, 490. Also Paulus 1922-1923, vol. 3, p. 238 ff. and Barth 1954, pp. 114-115.

344 *Bronnen bouwgeschiedenis*, vol. 2 (3), pp. 74, 108 (1509/10 and 1510/11). Probably identical with the papal indulgence for the crusade against the schismatical Russians, known as the crusade against the Tartars; Eekhof 1909, Appendix no. 81; Fredericq 1922, p. 449 ff.; Rémy 1928, p. 206. The indulgence offered by the hospital of the Holy Spirit in BESANÇON also yielded a small profit of 94 rhinegulden in 1515/16; Fredericq 1922, no. 331; *Bronnen bouwgeschiedenis*, vol. 2 (3), pp. 230, 232, 233, 235, 275, 280, 314.

345 Concerning receipts in the cathedral, see p. 279 ff.

346 Rémy 1928, p. 131 ff.; Paulus 1922-1923, vol. 3, pp. 212 ff. and 541 ff.; Fredericq 1922, no. 223. *Bronnen bouwgeschiedenis*, vol. 2 (2), pp. 98, 115, 179, 205 (incorrectly held for Xanten, see index) and *Inventaris Archief kapittel ten Dom*, no. 659, *prebenda defunctorum* rolls 1487, f. 4 (fine for exceeding the collection term). On this indulgence, see also Corsten 1975, p. 62 ff.

347 Rémy 1928, p. 151; Fredericq 1922, p. 498 ff.; *Inventaris Archief kapittel ten Dom*, nos 491-494. See also *Bronnen bouwgeschiedenis*, vol. 2 (3), p. 515 (1521/22).

348 Hofman 1894, pp. 10-11; *Kronijk Historisch Genootschap* 2 (1846), pp. 106-107; *Bronnen bouwgeschiedenis*, vol. 2 (2), p. 420 ('*hollandie*' to be read as '*Hallensis*'), p. 445.

349 *Bronnen bouwgeschiedenis*, vol. 2 (2), p. 303. Another example: the quest for St Bernardus in 1507, 1514 and 1520: Fredericq 1922,

no. 316; *Kronijk Historisch Genootschap* 3 (1847), p. 174; Van Asch van Wijck 1850-1853, vol. 2, p. 264.

350 Fredericq 1922, no. 255 ff.

351 Some examples: indulgences without permission from the chapters of Hoevelaken and Arnhem (1483/84); *Bronnen bouwgeschiedenis*, vol. 2 (2), p. 110. In Kampen pardoners operated illegally (?) with papal letters of indulgence (1506/07); idem, vol. 2 (2), p. 762. The parish priests of Biervliet and Putten admitted unknown pardoners; *Inventaris Archief kapittel ten Dom*, no. 1, vol. 10, f. 18, 23r, 23v (1495). In SAINTES, indulgence collectors were fined because they had gone on collecting longer than agreed (1486/87); *Bronnen bouwgeschiedenis*, vol. 2 (2), pp. 180, 205, 206. Action taken against the unsanctioned *'de Barbaris'* indulgence (1507/08); idem, vol. 2 (3), p. 25. Action taken against the unsanctioned false quest for Mount Sinai: idem, vol. 2 (3), p. 814, in voce *'Synay'* (between 1510/11 and 1520/21); Fredericq 1922, no. 327; Eekhof 1909, pp. 24, 25 and Appendix no. 85. Imprisonment of a pardoner who had proclaimed indulgences with the bishop's, but without the chapter's, permission; idem, vol. 2 (3), p. 505. Two *questores extranei* were apprehended in West Friesland and brought to UTRECHT; idem, vol. 2 (3), pp. 539, 540, 541; cf. Fredericq 1922, no. 242. Imprisonment of a pardoner bearing certain indulgences of the Premonstratensian order, followed by consultation with the bishop (1520/21); *Bronnen bouwgeschiedenis*, vol. 2 (3), pp. 496, 500.

352 In relation to the Mount Sinai quest, see n. 351.

353 Fabric rolls 1510/11, *Bronnen bouwgeschiedenis*, vol. 2 (3), p. 141.

354 *'Item dedi Henrico Backer quia abstraxit litteras indulgentiae s. Brigitte singulis portis et valvis ecclesiarum trajectensis'*; *Bronnen bouwgeschiedenis*, vol. 2 (2), p. 420. Concerning this indulgence, see Dodt van Flensburg 1843, 'St.-Birgitte'; Paulus 1922-1923, vol. 3, p. 270.

355 Jongkees 1942, p. 79; Eekhof 1909, p. 25 ff. and Appendix nos 57-60, 62, 83, 84, 91, 92, 104; Matthaeus 1703, pp. 9-11; *Inventaris Archief kapittel ten Dom*, nos 439, 498-502, 405, f. 104-106 and 175.

356 SENLIS, Louis VII in 1155; Mortet & Deschamps 1929, pp. 95-96 n. 1.

357 Hashagen 1931, pp. 168-170.

358 Thus, the 1493 conflict between the prince-elector and the bishop of MEISSEN, in which the chapter was also involved, hinged on the admission of the quest for St Valentine. The bishop got the better end of the deal as the quest disposed over papal and even imperial privileges; Rogge 1996, pp. 202-203.

359 Eekhof 1909, p. CV.

360 Jongkees 1942, p. 160 ff., Appendix 18. There was opposition in, for instance, the cities of Delfland and around Leiden, where proceedings were launched against the *rectores*: *Bronnen bouwgeschiedenis*, vol. 2 (1), pp. 372, 374, 401 and n. 4, 402. Complaints concerning indulgences and quests are the tenth item on the list of objections that the cities laid before the lords in 1462.

361 *Bronnen bouwgeschiedenis*, vol. 2 (3), pp. 133, 136, 137, 140 (1510/11); 310, 313 (1515/16); 351 (1516/17); 419, 420, 421 (1518/19). Also: Eekhof 1909, p. 31; Post 1954, p. 477; Fredericq 1922, no. 339. Open conflicts were rare. One example is the imprisonment of pardoners from Zeelandic Flanders in Ghent (*Bronnen bouwgeschiedenis*, vol. 2 (3), pp. 233, 239 (1513/14), because all collections were barred in this area, including the

cathedral's for the dyke indulgence; Eekhof 1909, pp. 29, 30. For other instances in which the account rolls refer to letters of approval from the overlord: *Bronnen bouwgeschiedenis*, vol. 2 (1), pp. 372, 455, 491, vol. 2 (2), pp. 134, 136. *Inventaris Archief kapittel ten Dom*, no. 651, fabric rolls 1529/30, f. 24, 1535/36, f. 71, 1543/44, f. 407, 408. The duke of Guelders also occasionally intervened with quests in his domain: *Kronijk Historisch Genootschap* 2 (1846), p. 113 (1496), and Van Asch van Wijck 1846-1848, vol. 4, p. 157 (1516). Also the count of Berg; *Bronnen bouwgeschiedenis*, vol. 2 (3), pp. 679, 682, 683, 708, 711.

362 Noordeloos 1959, p. 31.

363 Fredericq 1922, no. 338 (10 June 1515). '*Et super illis litteris revocacionis expedivit* [Canon Deel] *mandamentum penale publicandum ad omnia oppida et dominia principis; et misit diversos ianitores ad publicandum*'; *Bronnen bouwgeschiedenis*, vol. 2 (3), p. 314.

364 Letters of recommendation for the 1500 Jubilee indulgence and others; Van Asch van Wijck 1850-1853, vol. 1, nos 148, 157, 176-179; cf. *Bronnen bouwgeschiedenis*, vol. 2 (2), p. 555; Van Kalveen 1974, p. 115; see above, n. 348

365 Eekhof 1909, p. 61 ff. and Noordeloos 1959, passim, especially pp. 27 and 39.

366 Noordeloos 1959, p. 75; Rauch 1950, p. 163.

367 In HALBERSTADT 30 marks, in AUGSBURG 30 pfund heller, in MAINZ 40 gulden, in KONSTANZ 1 gulden in letter-sealing duties; Mischlewski 1958, p. 63 n. 287; Rauch 1950, p. 164. In OSNABRÜCK the Antonines paid the fabric 13 marks and the bishop's official 3 marks; Beming 1940, p. 164. In STRASBOURG the Antonines paid the bishop and his diocesan chancery 23 florins, which was slightly more than the other quests; Barth 1954, p. 127. In COLOGNE the Antonines were made to pay a sub- stantially larger sum; 200 rhinegulden in 1534; Rauch 1950, pp. 164, 173. Also Mischlewski 1976, p. 282.

368 *Inventaris Archief kapittel ten Dom*, no. 405, f. 44v.

369 Idem, f. 44v-52v; Noordeloos 1959, pp. 33-34.

370 Letter of 19 October 1424 in Van Mieris 1756, pp. 738-739; Jongkees 1942, p. 79. However, cf. letter of 18 January 1425 admitting the Antonines on the basis of their papal letters; Matthaeus 1703, pp. 12-13.

371 *Inventaris Archief kapittel ten Dom*, no. 464 (not mentioned in Noordeloos 1959). The volume of presumed damages is a shot in the dark; idem, f. 5, note *in margine*: '*primo videtur probandum dampnum quod sit fabrice per questum et utrum hoc sit satis in articulis specificatum*'.

372 Noordeloos 1959, p. 35. See *Inventaris Archief kapittel ten Dom*, nos 466, 467 (Eekhof 1909, Appendix nos 69 and 70), 468, 469 (Eekhof 1909, Appendix no. 79), 470 (Eekhof 1909, Appendix no. 93), 471 and 472 (Eekhof 1909, Appendix no. 106).

373 Eekhof 1909, p. 63 and Appendix no. 111; Noordeloos 1959, p. 33; *Bronnen bouwgeschiedenis*, vol. 2 (3), pp. 382, 427.

374 Previously, the Antonines had been granted reductions, for example in 1450; *Inventaris Archief kapittel ten Dom*, nos 465 and 405, f. 52-54.

375 See also the document dated 20 February 1533 in the second waste book (*memoriaal*) of the provincial court of UTRECHT in N. van der Monde, *Tijdschrift* 9 (1843), p. 103; Eekhof 1909, p. 64.

376 See *Inventaris Archief kapittel ten Dom*, no. 55 (cathedral chapter cartulary) f. 349-351: on 14 February 1420 the provisor of the

cathedral fabric at COLOGNE farmed out the quest on behalf of the abbot of St Hubert to the cathedral chapter for a period of ten years (my thanks to Kees Smit, who brought this deed to my attention), also no. 445; Eekhof 1909, Appendix no. 49; *Bronnen bouwgeschiedenis*, vol. 2 (1), p. 170 n. 7. Concerning the relationship with COLOGNE, see *Ad Summum 1248*, pp. 48-49.

377 Vroom 1993, p. 73: LIÈGE, TRIER, STRASBOURG, SENS, LANGRES, AUTUN, MÂCON, NEVERS, TOUL, CHÂLON-SUR-SAÔNE, CAMBRAI, TOURNAI and THÉROUANNE. Also for a description of various forms of cooperation.

378 *Inventaris Archief kapittel ten Dom*, nos 447, 448, 451 (1444-1512); Eekhof 1909, Appendix nos 50, 56, 64, 67, 76, 77, 78, 80, 82, 86, 88; *Bronnen bouwgeschiedenis*, vol. 2 (1), pp. 355, 356, 362, 372, 385, etc.

379 Eekhof 1909, Appendix nos 54 and 55. Concerning the role of Evert van Zoudenbalch, see Suir 1977, pp. 37-38.

380 For a discussion of what is meant by 'net proceeds', see below p. 317.

381 To compare: in the far smaller diocese of OSNABRÜCK (163 parishes), the St Hubert quest yielded 24 gold rhinegulden in 1522, of which 15 gold rhinegulden were designated for the abbey; Beming 1940, p. 264.

382 The following documents relate to this dispute: 25 MARCH 1510: Hofman 1894, pp. 56-58; 11 MAY 1510: idem, pp. 58-60; 30 MAY 1510: idem, pp. 60-61; 18 JUNE 1510: idem, pp. 61-62; 21 JUNE 1510: *Inventaris Archief kapittel ten Dom*, no. 454; 15 JUNE 1510: Hofman 1894, pp. 63-64; 2 SEPTEMBER 1510: *Inventaris* o.c., no. 454; 10 SEPTEMBER 1510: Hofman 1894, pp. 64-65; 24 NOVEMBER 1510: *Inventaris* o.c., no. 454; 28 NOVEMBER 1510: ibidem; 9 SEPTEMBER 1512: Eekhof 1909, p. 47; 24 NOVEMBER 1512: idem, Appendix no. 87; 7 DECEMBER 1512: *Inventaris* o.c., no. 405, f. 129; 10 DECEMBER 1512: Eekhof 1909, Appendix no. 88; 20 DECEMBER 1512: idem, Appendix no. 89; 3 JANUARY 1513: idem, Appendix no. 90; 7 JANUARY 1513: *Inventaris* o.c., no. 405, f. 125-126. Also *Bronnen bouwgeschiedenis*, vol. 2 (3), pp. 130, 133, 136, 137, 139, 140 (1510/11), 202, 204 (1512/13).

383 Hofman 1894, pp. 56-58.

384 Through Margaret of Austria, regent of the Low Countries, the emperor declared categorically that no one was permitted to conduct quests or proclaim indulgences in his domains without his authorization; Laurent 1893, p. 229.

385 Letter dated 21 June 1510 (see note 382): '*obventiones non tam ratione reliquarum quam - autoritatis diocesane - obveniant in certis dispensationibus et indulgentiis, qui nuntiis questuum committuntur*'. The other canon was Willem Heda, who resided in Antwerp.

386 *Inventaris Archief kapittel ten Dom*, no. 405, f. 125v (7 January 1513).

387 See lists in Brom 1900, passim.

388 Exh. cat. COLOGNE 1989, p. 14 (Angenendt); *Eglise de Saint-Hubert*, pp. 11, 12, 173, 176.

389 *Bronnen bouwgeschiedenis*, vol. 2 (3), pp. 128, 129, 139, 161, 163, 164.

390 Hofman 1894, pp. 75-79 (29 June 1521); Eekhof 1909, p. 67. The chapter appears to have been against admitting the quest; On 28 April 1521 Charles v appealed to the chapter to do so; Van Asch van Wijck 1846-1848, vol. 3, no. 216. See also *Bronnen bouwgeschiedenis*, vol. 2 (3), pp. 624, 625, 730.

391 Hofman 1894, p. 78. The abbot appears to have gotten farther than his

confrere of St Hubert, regularly taking one (additional?) seventh of the proceeds in receipt; *Bronnen bouwgeschiedenis*, vol. 2 (3), pp. 624, 625; fabric rolls 1529/30, f. 24, 1534/35, f. 47, 1536/37, f. 131, 1537/38, f. 161.

392 See the case of the bishopric of OSNABRÜCK cited in n. 381.

393 Eekhof 1909, pp. 63, 96; Noordeloos 1959, p. 32 ff. The Antonine commandries organized their quests in one of two ways: they either ran their *viagium* or *cursus* themselves, or farmed out the collection to a fellow Antonine, cleric or even layman. The second form was used in UTRECHT; Mischlewski 1958, p. 62 ff.; Rauch 1950, p. 163 (with a good description of the *viagia*); Mischlewski 1976, p. 273 ff.

394 Eekhof 1909, pp. 96-100 gives a good overview; see also the tables in *Bronnen bouwgeschiedenis*, vol. 2 (1, 2 and 3).

395 *Inventaris Archief kapittel ten Dom*, no. 1: capitular resolutions, passim.

396 Idem, no. 440: register of leases 1449-1517; Eekhof 1909, Appendix no. 68.

397 *Inventaris Archief kapittel ten Dom*, no. 1, vol. 2, f. 33v, sub 1414: the canons entrusted two pardoners with '*duo monstrancias, unam argenteam ad modum crucis factam et desuper imaginem b. Martini in equo deauratam, ponderantem 45 loet argenti; item aliam monstranciam cupream deauratam ad utendum cum questu b. Martini*'. See also the summary of parapher-nalia in idem, no. 1, vol. 6, f. 51 and no. 651, fabric rolls 1529/30, f. 26, 1563/64, f. 64. Concerning the book with route descriptions, see Noordeloos 1959, p. 39; Rauch 1950, p. 163; Mischlewski 1976, p. 280. Regarding the eight major collection expeditions undertaken by the St Hubert quest in the archdiocese of COLOGNE, see *Ad Summum 1248*, pp. 48-49.

398 COLOGNE Cathedral had acquired a large collection of reliquaries, chains, crosses and bells associated with the quest for St Hubert, which the master of the fabric handed over to the cathedral treasury in 1557; today, only a reliquary for St Hubert remains; *Ad Summum 1248*, p. 52, c 12 and c 9 and fig. 7.

399 Occasionally, the debts of deceased pardoners led to problems; see the action taken against the daughter of a pardoner for St Martin; fabric rolls 1530/31, f. 18v. In this case the pardoner was obviously a layman. Amongst the pardoners were also renowned and accomplished canons, such as Evert van Zoudenbalch; Suir 1977, p. 37; see fig. 28.

400 *Inventaris Archief kapittel ten Dom*, no. 1, vol. 10, sub 7 May 1499.

401 *Bronnen bouwgeschiedenis*, vol. 2 (1), pp. 362, 395, 402, vol. 2 (2), pp. 92, 94-95 (in Gouda due to the war), 392, vol. 2 (3), pp. 163, 238; cf. *Inventaris Archief kapittel ten Dom*, no. 513.

402 Assistants were officially sanctioned and enjoyed the same protection; Eekhof 1909, Appendix no. 23.

403 *Catalogussen archief stad Utrecht, tweede afdeeling*, no. 1 (Buurkerk cartulary, UTRECHT), f. 91: '*daer en zellen die kerkmeysters geen tortisen toe lenen mede te halen noch laten beyaarden ten si dat si der kerken also vele ghelts gheven als een take wijns wardich is of de kercmeysters ghemoede te hebben, uutghenomen sunte Martinsbede*' (for which the churchwardens shall not provide torches to fetch them nor sound the bell unless they give the church as much money as the value of a *take* of wine, or what the churchwardens will accept, with the exception of the *reportationes* for St Martin). All the fabric rolls

record a small sum in receipts in each of the seven *cassen*. See also the church of St James, Utrecht: Riemsdijk 1888, p. 43; Hulst: Caland 1883, p. 447; Gouda: Noordeloos 1959, p. 43; Hoorn: Municipal Archives, civic rolls 1494 ff.

404 Noordeloos 1959, p. 43.

405 Zierikzee: *Bronnen bouwgeschiedenis*, vol. 2 (3), p. 133 (1510/11). Amsterdam: idem, p. 167 (1511/12) and Van Asch van Wijck 1846-1848, vol. 2, p. 185 (1503). Leiden: *Kronijk Historisch Genootschap* 2 (1846), p. 82; also Matthaeus 1703, pp. 8-9.

406 Jongkees 1942, p. 167. Not just cities, but local lords too could make things difficult for pardoners; *Bronnen bouwgeschiedenis*, vol. 2 (2) (Guelders), p. 451, vol. 2 (3), pp. 679, 682, 683, 708, 711 (count of Berg); also *Inventaris Archief kapittel ten Dom*, no. 513.

407 Post 1954, p. 473.

408 *Inventaris Archief kapittel ten Dom*, no. 1, vol. 5, f. 193 (1460) against the quest for St Quirinus; *Bronnen bouwgeschiedenis*, vol. 2 (1), pp. 362, 455, vol. 2 (3), pp. 129, 540 (Ouderkerk aan de IJssel *'super diffamationibus per fratrem minorem factis in ambone contra questores nostros'*), 580, 650 (Deventer, a chantry priest *'valde inhoneste predicavit contra questores nostros et nos etiam diffamavit'*), 651.

409 Fredericq 1922, no. 241 (8 August 1488); Paulus 1922-1923, vol. 3, pp. 529-530.

410 'certain miraculous signs contradicting Luther's doctrine'; *Bronnen bouwgeschiedenis*, vol. 2 (3), p. 582.

411 *Inventaris Archief kapittel ten Dom*, no. 2, vol. 2, f. 28v (31 March 1522).

412 *Bronnen bouwgeschiedenis*, vol. 2 (1), p. 601: Rents for the quest for St Martin fell from 1580 to 627 gulden, and for the quest for Our Lady from 1035 to 143 gulden (1 gulden = 30 wit). Was resistance from the cities of Holland to blame for this decline? Cf. Jongkees 1942, p. 164.

413 Something similar happened in the case of the quest for St Quirinus in 1488, when the rent jumped from 90 to 225 rhinegulden (until 1519).

414 See tables a-3 and c-3 in *Bronnen bouwgeschiedenis*, vol. 2 (1) and table c in idem, vol. 2 (2 and 3).

415 A single example: in 1487 PAMPLONA Cathedral's share in the nine foreign quests amounted to just ten percent of the total receipts of its own quest; Goñi Gaztambide 1955, p. 34.

416 Rauch 1950, p. 163 ff., describes how a trip of this kind was organized by Antonines from the monastery of Höchst, whence a major expedition set out with two clerics and five servants, all on horseback.

417 Between 1482 and 1483 an exchange rate reduction of more than 30 percent was granted *'ex gratia speciali propter guerras et inconvenientia temporis'*; *Bronnen bouwgeschiedenis*, vol. 2 (2), pp. 78, 98. From 1503 until 1512 (expect 1509) and from 1521 until 1525 all pardoners - with the exception of the Antonines - enjoyed a small reduction in the exchange rate; idem, pp. 623, 649, 670, 713 and fabric rolls passim; the reduction was between 6 and 15 percent.

418 The karolusgulden comprised 20 st. hollands; the gold rhinegulden 28 st. hollands. On the value of the karolusgulden vis-à-vis the rhinegulden current, see p. 338.

419 See p. 337 ff.

420 Regarding the bookkeeping method, see Tenhaeff 1949, vol. 1, p. 194.

421 There are also instances in which the masters of the fabric granted pardoners a reduction in view of exceptional circumstances, which they effected in the form of an exchange rate

reduction (see note 417) or a temporary reduction in the rent, as for example in 1485/86 and 1488/89 due to turmoil in Flanders; *Bronnen bouwgeschiedenis*, vol. 2 (2), pp. 140, 251. Between 1491 and 1495 three quests: for St Quirinus, St Hubert and Our Lady; idem, pp. 335, 354, 373, 397. The reduction was between 10 and 20 percent.

422 *Bronnen bouwgeschiedenis*, vol. 2 (1), pp. 96, 106, 144.

423 Jongkees 1942, p. 164; *Bronnen bouwgeschiedenis*, vol. 2 (1), pp. 401, 403 (*caristia*), 438.

424 *Bronnen bouwgeschiedenis*, vol. 2 (2), pp. 14, 177, 214, 252.

425 Idem, vol. 2 (3), p. 657.

426 *Inventaris Archief kapittel ten Dom*, no. 2, vol. 2, f. 28v.

427 It is possible that the political situation in Guelders played a role; *Inventaris Archief kapittel ten Dom*, no. 651, fabric rolls 1543/44, f. 374: '*casu quo dicti questus in patria de Gelria exercere non potuerunt*'.

428 *Inventaris Archief kapittel ten Dom*, no. 1, vol. 14, f. 8v (1536); no. 2, vol. 6, f. 54v (1543). Also no. 471: agreement with the Antonines dated 17 February 1542, in which the chapter promised the pardoners '*van der tijdt der heresien ende ketterien mit alle billicheyt, discretie ende redenen [te] tracteren*' (to treat them with due fairness, consideration and reasonableness in such times of heresies and apostacies).

429 Eekhof 1909, p. 105; Paulus 1922-1923, vol. 3, p. 497.

430 *Inventaris Archief kapittel ten Dom*, no. 1, vol. 18, f. 176 (29 April 1567); cf. Muller 1903, p. 111.

431 For similar developments in the dioceses of COLOGNE and TRIER, see Vroom 1993, pp. 576-579 and n. 15. A letter of 21 July 1533 documents how the master of the fabric in COLOGNE was obliged to fire the labourers and '*officinam claudere et obserare donec uberiora tempora receperimus*'; cathedral construction was still underway in 1528; *Ad Summum 1248*, p. 36, B 5 and pp. 53-54.

432 Letter to Thomas Wolsey dated 7 August 1520; cited in Van Herwaarden 2003, p. 109 n. 79.

433 See Goudriaan 1994, pp. 66-74, for further interpretation of these numbers.

SEVEN Income from property: rents and annuities

434 *Bronnen bouwgeschiedenis*, vol. 2 (3), p. 35.

435 Only four items 50 years later; *Bronnen bouwgeschiedenis*, vol. 2 (1), pp. 218, 242 and n. 4; concerns items 75, 76, 77, 91.

436 Tenhaeff 1949, vol. 1, p. 194.

437 Idem, p. 189 ff. Tenhaeff paints a somewhat overly dark picture, having failed to consider that the so-called *antique restantie* from all the chambers were collected by a separate *receptor*; the fabric had such old *restantie* in 1470, 1476, 1491/93, 1496, 1500, 1512, 1516, 1519/21 and 1524 were shared out amongst the canons, *Inventaris Archief kapittel ten Dom*, no. 668, vols 1 and 2: 1442-1529.

438 Tenhaeff 1949, vol. 1, p. 198, nos 5, 11, 17, 29 (houses); p. 198, no. 3 and p. 201, no. 10 (estates). Tenhaeff wrongly neglects to take this aspect into account.

439 Especially in the years 1481-83, 1527-28 and 1541-43.

440 This happened to the oude schild (*scutum antiquum*) in the case of some house rents; Tenhaeff 1949, vol. 1, p. 176.

441 For example the four *jugera* in Lopik, who make their first appearance in the fabric rolls in 1460/61, and were charged with paying an allowance of an eighth share of the receipts to the

chamberlain of the *Camera Minor*; *Bronnen bouwgeschiedenis*, vol. 2 (1), pp. 347 n. 6, 353 n. 2, 266 n. 2; also *Inventaris Archief kapittel ten Dom*, no. 1189 and no. 405, f. 38v, 39v.

442 For example the relationship between the Jutfaas tithes, recorded in the accounts from 1507/08 onwards, and the allowance paid to Splinter Jacobsz.; see Vroom 1981, p. 515.

443 See idem, p. 515.

444 See idem, pp. 517-518.

445 See idem, pp. 516-517.

446 '*De memoriis translatis ex fabrica ad minorem cameram*'; *Inventaris Archief kapittel ten Dom*, no. 2, vol. 2, f. 59 (8 November 1525); *Bronnen bouwgeschiedenis*, vol. 2 (3), pp. 689, 701-703: this concerns an annual contribution of approximately 150 rhinegulden. A similar exchange was presumably made in 1487; *Bronnen bouwgeschiedenis*, vol. 2 (1), p. 299 n. 3, vol. 2 (2), p. XXVI; cf. *Inventaris Archief kapittel ten Dom*, no. 659, vol. 2, *prebenda defunctorum* rolls 1488: from this date almost all payments of 60 rhinegulden to the *Camera Minor* for memorial services cease; perhaps the fabric's commitments had been paid off; see also the 1500/01 account; *Bronnen bouwgeschiedenis*, vol. 2 (2), pp. 550, 551.

447 Calkoen n.d., vol. 1, claustral house Ea 1; bought by the cathedral fabric in 1480/81 and 1481/82; the old lodge was torn down in 1488/89. *Bronnen bouwgeschiedenis*, vol. 2 (2), pp. 50, 51, 72, 255.

EIGHT Financing transactions: the cathedral fabric as lender and borrower

448 De Blécourt 1950, pp. 196-202; Kernkamp 1954, p. 10.

449 De Blécourt 1950, pp. 198, 200 ff.

450 Not considered here are instances in which the cathedral fabric received or provided credit for brief periods, in which case the rules of *mutuum* applied, meaning no annual distribution was paid. Examples in *Bronnen bouwgeschiedenis*, vol. 2 (2), pp. 641, 671, vol. 2 (3), pp. 432, 475.

451 The dean of the Dom was chairman, the chapter secretary was also secretary of the States. Meetings were held in the cathedral's small chapterhouse. The administration of the States was regarded as an extension of the activities of the cathedral chapter; Van Kalveen 1974, p. 29.

452 Van Kalveen 1974, pp. 431, 434, 438.

453 '*Ex cista communi trium statuum*'; cf. Van Kalveen 1974, pp. 26, 66. Additionally: *Bronnen bouwgeschiedenis*, vol. 2 (2), pp. 353, 358 and index in voce '*Rotel*'.

454 *Bronnen bouwgeschiedenis*, vol. 2 (2), p. 650.

455 Van Kalveen 1974, p. 171.

456 Idem, pp. 177, 180.

457 This amount was the equivalent of an annual wage for 114 unskilled labourers. See *Bronnen bouwgeschiedenis*, vol. 2 (3), p. 166; Van Kalveen 1974, pp. 170-180.

458 *Bronnen bouwgeschiedenis*, vol. 2 (3), p. 228 and n. 4. Some of these annuities were redeemed from the fabric's 'sixteenth penny' fund; idem, pp. 228 and 340.

459 Idem, pp. 279, 317 n. 1.

460 The fabric rolls covering the period 1546/47 and 1547/48 are missing. See chapter minutes, *Inventaris Archief kapittel ten Dom*, no. 1, vol. 15, f. 87 sub 10 June 1547; idem, no. 2, vol. 1, f. 67 ff.

461 *Bronnen bouwgeschiedenis*, vol. 2 (2), p. 694 (first partial payment of the remuneration), vol. 2 (3), p. 3 (first tithe receipts), vol. 2 (3), pp. 275, 418 (redemption of the annuity).

462 *Bronnen bouwgeschiedenis*, vol. 2 (1), p. 266, vol. 2 (3),

pp. 228, 346, 509.

463 For the church of Our Lady in Antwerp, see Vroom 1983, pp. 91-94.

464 One of the few examples: life annuities purchased in 1505 by the testamentary executors of the architect Cornelis de Wael in behalf of his natural daughter Cornelia and her child for the sum of 30 gold philippi at the 16th penny. The life annuity was paid until 1559/60; *Inventaris Archief kapittel ten Dom*, no. 651, fabric rolls 1559/60, f. 348v, 349.

465 Muller 1903, p. 48; Muller 1895, p. 199 (statute of 1257); Muller 1903, pp. 150-152. In the earlier accounts the endowment was 20 times the payment.

466 *Bronnen bouwgeschiedenis*, vol. 2 (1), p. 285 n. 1; *Inventaris Archief kapittel ten Dom*, no. 2506.

467 *Bronnen bouwgeschiedenis*, vol. 2 (1), p. 290 n. 5. Another example: the testamentary executors of the canon Dirk van Amsterdam sold an annuity from a claustral house and invested the capital in the *prebenda defunctorum* fund, on the condition that the master of the fabric would thenceforth pay out five percent, or 3 oude schilden, annually to the *Camera Minor*; *Inventaris Archief kapittel ten Dom*, no. 2188; *Bronnen bouwgeschiedenis*, vol. 2 (1), p. 228 and n. 2, pp. 332, 517. Another option was a combined form of life annuity and obit foundation, in which case the fabric received the endowment and bound itself to pay the founder a life annuity until his death and the same amount thereafter to the *Camera Minor* to fund his commemoration; for example, the foundation established by Canon Leeuwenberg: *Bronnen bouwgeschiedenis*, vol. 2 (3), p. 209 and *Inventaris Archief kapittel ten Dom*, no. 1, vol. 12, f. 88.

468 *Bronnen bouwgeschiedenis*, vol. 2 (1), pp. 296, 300, 538.

469 *Bronnen bouwgeschiedenis*, vol. 2 (2), p. 671.

470 Foundation of Canon Boeckelaer; *Bronnen bouwgeschiedenis*, vol. 2 (3), p. 318; *Inventaris Archief kapittel ten Dom*, no. 2, vol. 1, f. 178. See also the foundations established by the architect Cornelis de Wael for the choristers and building labourers of the *loedsa*; *Bronnen bouwgeschiedenis*, vol. 2 (2), p. 671.

471 See *Bronnen bouwgeschiedenis*, vol. 2 (2), index, p. 908, sub Jansveld.

472 The *quattor tempores* are around Ash Wednesday, Whitsunday, the Exaltation of the Holy Cross and St Lucy's Day. See also *Bronnen bouwgeschiedenis*, vol. 2 (2), p. 592.

473 De Bruijn 1994, pp. 126-143.

474 Idem, pp. 238-245.

475 Muller 1890, pp. 34-35.

476 See p. 272 ff.

477 Concerns Calkoen n.d., vol. 1, claustral house Dc. See *Inventaris Archief kapittel ten Dom*, no. 592 and *Bronnen bouwgeschiedenis*, vol. 2 (2), p. 715, vol. 2 (3), p. 37, additionally pp. 100, 128, 160, 196, 224, 227, 260, 263, 300, 304, etc. Also Muller 1890, p. 139.

478 *Inventaris Archief kapittel ten Dom*, no. 592 (deed of 17 December 1512); Muller 1890, pp. 34, 128.

479 *Bronnen bouwgeschiedenis*, vol. 2 (3), p. 555. The fabric was still paying an outstanding annual fee from this house in 1531/32, fabric rolls f. 19v. See also Muller 1890, pp. 46-47.

480 See Vroom 1981, pp. 506-520 (Appendix four), under column 7; in 1406/07 the chapter conducted its transactions without involving the fabric fund.

481 For example: *Bronnen bouwgeschiedenis*, vol. 2 (3), p. 469: investment of 200 rhinegulden current, against 6.25% (the sixteenth penny).

482 Some examples: 820 rhinegulden current in 1511,

or 13 percent of the fabric's income, from Cathedral Dean Ludolf van den Veen, *Bronnen bouwgeschiedenis*, vol. 2 (3), p. 46. In 1515/16, 631 rhinegulden current, or 11 percent of the fabric's income, from Canon Tulman; idem, vol. 2 (3), pp. 279-280; this edition does not include the separate folio of commentary on these items appended to the rolls. Concerning Tulman, see also Vlam & Vente 1965, pp. 248 ff., 273. In 1518/19 Bishop Frederick of Baden's testamentary executors deposited 28 times the annual payment - a sum of 1575 rhinegulden current, or 18 percent of the fabric's income - for a series of memorial services; *Bronnen bouwgeschiedenis*, vol. 2 (3), p. 395.

483 See Vroom 1981, Appendix four, column 7.

484 The most important expenses for investments and redemptions are: 1492/93: purchase of *redditus a Rotel*, 312 rhinegulden current. 1511/12: purchase of revenues from the Hinderdam and the wine duty, 3213 rhinegulden current. 1513/14: redemption of an 'eleventh penny' annuity, 269 rhinegulden current. 1514/15: redemption of a commitment connected with the tithes in Jutfaas, 1115 rhinegulden current. 1516/17: redemption of a 'sixteenth penny' annuity, 106 rhinegulden current. 1518/19: redemption of a commitment connected with the tithes in Jutfaas, 1813 rhinegulden current. 1519/20: purchase of periodic revenues, 275 rhinegulden current. 1520/21: redemption of a redeemable 'sixteenth penny' annuity, 225 rhinegulden current, and investment of the principal for an obit endowment, 275 rhinegulden current; see also *Inventaris Archief kapittel ten Dom*, no. 1, vol. 12, f. 80. 1523/24: redemption of *een redditus redimibilis*, 164 rhinegulden current; *Bronnen bouwgeschiedenis*, vol. 2 (2), p. 353, vol. 2 (3), pp. 166, 167, 228, 275, 340, 418, 469, 496, 506, 627.

485 *Bronnen bouwgeschiedenis*, vol. 2 (2), pp. 671-672.

486 Idem, vol. 2 (3), p. 768.

487 *Inventaris Archief kapittel ten Dom*, no. 651, fabric rolls 1532/33, f. 15v.

488 Idem, no. 1, vol. 19, f. 101v and 102v (February 1571) and no. 651, fabric rolls 1570/71, annotations at '*pensiones fabrice*'.

NINE The sale of building materials and church treasure

489 *Bronnen bouwgeschiedenis*, vol. 2 (1), p. XXXII, vol. 2 (2), p. XIII; from 1527/28 this disappears as a separate category in the accounts; idem, vol. 2 (3), p. 718.

490 Relatively large sums were still recorded in 1542/43, 1545/46 and 1563/64. See *Inventaris Archief kapittel ten Dom*, no. 651, under the relevant years.

491 In 1423 the canons of Xanten sold a reliquary shrine with the archbishop of COLOGNE's consent for 548 marks, or 65 percent of that year's income, '*pro utilitate eclessie et ad usum fabrice*'; *Stiftskirche Xanten*, vol. 3 (2), pp. 310, 312, 314; Beissel 1889, vol. 2, p. 21. In 1393/94 the canons of MENDE Cathedral sold jewels given by Pope Urban V, with the pope's approval but against opposition from the bishop, city and diocesan clergy, in order to finance new building works; *Inventaire-sommaire Lozère* G 702, G 1149. In 1284, after the collapse of the choir vaults at BEAUVAIS, the canons sold the crosier of Bishop Milon de Nanteuil - who had himself established income sources for the new building works in 1225 - in order to fund

repairs. When the tower collapsed in 1573, cathedral repairs were similarly funded by the sale of chalices and other precious items; Desjardins 1865, pp. 17, 101.

492 Van Werveke 1927, p. 344; also Lehmann-Brockhaus 1938, no. 2747 (c. 1100).

493 'observing that the urgent need for money and the great necessity of the fabric [...] demands this'; Struick 1968, pp. 169, 170.

494 *Inventaris Archief kapittel ten Dom*, no. 1, vol. 20, sub 18 and 30 June 1577; also complaint sub 15 March 1576; additionally, p. xx n. 1.

495 *Inventaris Archief kapittel ten Dom*, no. 1, vol. 20, sub 18 and 19 February 1578; Willem van Lamsweerde's account reports the date as 17 February; Dodt van Flensburg 1838-1848, vol. 1, p. 257 (i.e. *Inventaris Archief kapittel ten Dom*, no. 2148).

496 'having assisted overtime on various days and [at various] hours, and most of these at night, and indeed whole nights through'; *Inventaris Archief kapittel ten Dom*, no. 2148 (not in Dodt van Flensburg).

497 'to pay the knights and servants'; Dodt van Flensburg 1838-1848, vol. 1, p. 218.

498 Muller 1897, pp. 293-296.

499 Idem, pp. 309 ff. and 286; Dodt van Flensburg 1838-1848, vol. 1, p. 258 ff. The liquidation had taken place on 19, 21 and 27 February.

500 Muller 1897, pp. 310-312; Dodt van Flensburg 1838-1848, vol. 1, pp. 260-262; *Inventaris Archief kapittel ten Dom*, no. 1, vol. 20, sub 8 April 1578.

501 'was so far in arrears, not even knowing what to do to keep its church intact and provide for necessary repairs'; Dodt van Flensburg 1838-1848, vol. 1, pp. 261-262.

502 *Inventaris Archief kapittel ten Dom*, no. 651, fabric rolls 1577/78, f. 30v, 1578/79, f. 57v, 1579/80, f. 91v and idem, no. 2148 (payment of 1200 karolusgulden, not in Dodt van Flensburg). Also idem, no. 1, vol. 20, sub 20 April 1579 and 22 and 23 June 1579. The figures entered in the fabric rolls do not entirely match up with those in the settlement statement.

503 See Appendix five. In 1511 Floris van Egmont wrote the regent that the cathedral chapter had melted the shrines of Sts Pontian and Agnes down into coin; Sterk 1980, p. 24. However, this was never actually done.

504 UTRECHT's other collegiate churches managed to save a few precious items from their treasuries, most of which are now preserved in the Rijksmuseum Amsterdam. To my knowledge the only item preserved from the Dom is the hammer of St Martin, now in the Rijksmuseum Het Catharijne Convent, Utrecht; Haslinghuis & Peeters 1965, p. 403; Exh. cat. Utrecht 1972, no. 36.

THE FINANCING OF BUILDING AND FURNISHING UTRECHT CATHEDRAL

505 For tables listing actual figures for the Dom's receipts and expenditures, and also those of the Buurkerk, together with detailed commentary on various items, refer to my doctoral dissertation: Vroom 1981, pp. 506- 530, 542-552.

506 Tenhaeff 1949, vol. 1, p. 64; elsewhere he was known as the *Hüttenknecht* or *valet de la fabrique*; Lardin 1997 for ROUEN. For the purposes of this book, a standard year equals 250 working days (170 summer days and 80 winter days).

507 There is no definitive break; from 1499/1500 onwards income from credit transactions begins to play a significant role.

508 Tenhaeff 1949, vol. 1, pp. 194-195.

509 See previous discussion of the *vinalia*; the *reportationes*; the quests and land ownership.
510 Posthumus & Ketner 1964, p. 19; *Bronnen bouwgeschiedenis*, vol. 2 (1), p. 166 n. 1 for the date of 1425. The best explanation of how the medieval monetary system worked is Cipolla 1956, especially pp. 38-51. On the monetary system in UTRECHT, see De Meyer, pp. XLIII-LVI and Van Gelder 1971-1972, p. 12 ff. See additionally Posthumus & Ketner 1964, pp. XLI-XLIX and 12-30, and the important review of this work in Morineau 1968, especially pp. 178-186. On monies of account, see also Spufford 1988, pp. 411-414.
511 Posthumus & Ketner 1964, p. 17. Spufford 1986, p. 256.
512 Cipolla 1956, p. 34.
513 On the diverging development of prices in Utrecht as opposed to Holland, see Morineau 1968, pp. 184-186, 201 (fig. 3). A revaluation took effect on 1 February 1490, aimed at stopping the strong devaluation of the stuiver: the exchange rate of the gold rhinegulden was brought down from 48 to 19 stuivers, following a similar measure by Philip the Handsome on 14 December 1489; Van Gelder 1951, passim; Pusch 1932, p. 15 ff.; Van der Chijs 1859, pp. 361, 363, 369. Spufford 1986, pp. 256-257.
514 See *Bronnen bouwgeschiedenis*, vol. 2 (1), p. 686 (in voce '*perdicio monete*') and p. 541 n. 2, vol. 2 (2), p. 291.
515 It is impossible to tell from the account rolls which coins were actually used for payments as they only list the coin in which they were calculated and how much that coin was worth in the money of account.
516 See p. 266.
517 *Inventaris Archief kapittel ten Dom*, no. 429; Oudewater (20 stuivers, 1486 contract for ten years), Lekkerkerk (17 stuivers, 1477 contract for twelve years).
518 *Inventaris Archief kapittel ten Dom*, no. 429: Ingen (1 arnoldusgulden, 1456 contract for ten years); Delft, Oude Kerk (4 Bavarian gulden, 1460 contract for ten years); Arkel (1 Bavarian gulden, 1443 contract for ten years).
519 We recorded yields from the *reportationes* from 1395 until 1535 (in which year only one of all the parishes still paid) in the parishes of Rotterdam, Leiden, Delft, Alkmaar, Haarlem, Hoorn, Amsterdam, Gouda, Deventer, Kampen, Elst, Groningen and Zwolle, where the volume of contributions was remarkably high.
520 *Bronnen bouwgeschiedenis*, vol. 2 (1), pp. LXX and 294, n. 2.
521 Example from the fabric rolls for 1480/81: (*Bronnen bouwgeschiedenis*, vol. 2 (2), pp. 25, 27): 2 oude schilden was 3 rhinegulden current, 18 stuivers in Amsterdam; 4 oude schilden was 6 rhinegulden current in Zwolle.
522 See p. 325.
523 Concerning the role of gold in international monetary transactions, see Cipolla 1956, pp. 33-35.
524 Tenhaeff's observations in this connection in *Bronnen bouwgeschiedenis*, vol. 2 (1), p. LXXVIII, are incorrect.
525 See Vroom 1981, Appendix five; the sums spent on building ranged anywhere between 19 and 97 percent.
526 Division amongst these categories was customary as from 1463/64; *Bronnen bouwgeschiedenis*, vol. 2 (1), p. 377 ff.
527 Tenhaeff 1949, vol. 1, p. 83 ff.
528 *Bronnen bouwgeschiedenis*, vol. 2 (2), p. XX ff. In 1436 these expenditures were booked under different categories; idem, vol. 2 (1), p. 263, n. 6.
529 *Inventaris Archief kapittel ten Dom*, nos 2514 ff.
530 Van Kalveen 1974, p. 29.

531 *Bronnen bouwgeschiedenis*, vol. 2 (1), p. XLI, vol. 2 (2), p. XXI-XXII.

532 The proceedings against Otto de Jonghe 1445-1448 cost around 2000 gulden of 30 wit; *Bronnen bouwgeschiedenis*, vol. 2 (1), p. 340 n. 11. In 1445/46 proceedings in Rome cost around 1250 gulden of 30 wit; idem, p. 250. Proceedings connected with the provostry in West Friesland cost roughly 1500 rhinegulden; idem, p. 471. The case against the lord of Brederode (1512-1527) regarding goods bequeathed by the canon Willem van Weerdenborch, cost at least 1500 rhinegulden. Proceedings against the treasurer Albert Pigghe cost approximately 250 rhinegulden between 1540 and 1542.

533 *Bronnen bouwgeschiedenis*, vol. 2 (1), p. 290 n. 5, p. 365 n. 8, p. 383 n. 1; vol. 2 (2), pp. XXVI, 233, 390 n. 1. These payments stopped in 1488; *Inventaris Archief kapittel ten Dom*, no. 659, 1488 account, f. 4.

534 *Bronnen bouwgeschiedenis*, vol. 2 (3), p. 707.

535 Idem, vol. 2 (1), pp. 357, 374; the amounts match the debit balances of the *Camera Minor*; *Inventaris Archief kapittel ten Dom*, no. 633, vol. 6; cf. *Bronnen bouwgeschiedenis*, vol. 2 (2), p. 371.

536 *Bronnen bouwgeschiedenis*, vol. 2 (2), pp. 271, 292, 312, and *prebenda defunctorum* rolls 1488, *Inventaris Archief kapittel ten Dom*, no. 659, vol. 2. However, *ex archivis* at least 348 rhinegulden current was paid to a supplier of cloth for paraments, cf. *Bronnen bouwgeschiedenis*, vol. 2 (2), p. 310. On the archive's location above the east portal, see idem, vol. 1 (1), p. 361 n. 4.

537 Idem, vol. 2 (2), pp. 423, 427, 455. Similar agreement in 1519, although there is no record of it in the account rolls; *Inventaris Archief kapittel ten Dom*, no. 2, vol. 2, f. 10v.

538 Water mill at Raven (1461-1463), 1000 gulden of 30 wit, *Bronnen bouwgeschiedenis*, vol. 2 (1), p. 361, 374. New house in the seigneury (*heerlijkheid*) of Egdam near Amersfoort (1487), 250 rhinegulden current, idem, vol. 2 (2), p. 246. The house *'in Veno'* (1501-1503), approximately 800 rhinegulden current, idem, vol. 2 (2), p. 603 and in voce *''t Veen'*. Hospital in the Vuilsteeg (1524/25), contribution of 400 rhinegulden current, idem, vol. 2 (3), p. 656 and *Inventaris Archief kapittel ten Dom*, no. 1, vol. 13, f. 9.

539 Acquisition of the estate of Egdam, 1484 contribution *'de mandato capituli'* of 622 rhinegulden current, *Bronnen bouwgeschiedenis*, vol. 2 (2), p. 138: the amount was settled with the credit balance; *Inventaris Archief kapittel ten Dom*, nos 1914-1917 *'Emptio dominii et bonorum'* in Hagestein, 2800 rhinegulden current (1509/10-1511/12), *Bronnen bouwgeschiedenis*, vol. 2 (3), pp. 104, 138; for dykes there (1517-1519), 500 rhinegulden current, idem, pp. 389, 424, 432.

540 For example the estate of Hagestein.

541 *Bronnen bouwgeschiedenis*, vol. 2 (3), pp. 431, 432.

542 Idem, p. 418; *Inventaris Archief kapittel ten Dom*, no. 886: concerns a commitment resting on certain tithes from which the cathedral fabric drew the profit.

543 *Inventaris Archief kapittel ten Dom*, no. 639, vols 4, 5 and 6 (*Bona Divisa* rolls). We find the first traces of this development back in the separate account drawn up for the sale of life annuities in 1532, which records a number of expenditures related to quests. On 16 February 1571 the decision was taken to split the official expenses: the *Bona Divisa* would pay the deputations, the fabric the

hospitality costs; *Inventaris* o.c., no. 1, vol. 19, f. 102v. Incidentally, the cathedral chapter's waning political role is clearly mirrored in its diminishing official and legal expenses.

544 *Inventaris Archief kapittel ten Dom*, no. 1, vol. 20, sub 15 March 1576.

545 Schuegraf 1855, p. 83 ff.

546 Alberts 1954, p. 36; Du Colombier 1973, p. 19; see also Salzman 1952, p. 219 ff.

547 Stone merchants like Lieven Boegel from Brussels and later the Keldermans family, who exploited quarries in Brabant and Wallonia, did not enter the picture until later; they are first mentioned in the fabric rolls in 1484/85; *Bronnen bouwgeschiedenis*, vol. 2 (2), p. 126. On the provenance of the stone, idem, p. XV-XVIII and Haslinghuis & Peeters 1965, p. 193.

548 Beissel 1889, vol. 2, pp. 29-45.

549 *Bronnen bouwgeschiedenis*, vol. 2 (1), p. 370 n. 2, p. 378 n. 3.

550 Alberts 1954, p. 34 and passim. The cathedral chapter managed to get various reductions in toll payments from the authorities by sending a canon to personally escort the shipment; stone price/cost price ratios were different for other types of stone from quarries elsewhere.

551 Meischke 1964, p. 123.

552 *Bronnen bouwgeschiedenis*, vol. 2 (1), p. 314 n. 2, p. 310 n. 4; only the *prebenda defunctorum* rolls are preserved for this year.

553 *Bronnen bouwgeschiedenis*, vol. 2 (2), p. 102 ff.; Tenhaeff 1949, vol. 1, p. 95 ff.

554 *Bronnen bouwgeschiedenis*, vol. 2 (1), p. 314 n. 2; Van Kalveen 1974, pp. 182, 199.

555 Hazewinkel 1928, passim.

556 Fehrmann 1967, p. 87.

557 Coster 1909, passim; Vroom 1964; Appendix five and the literature cited there.

558 Such a sudden reduction in the size of a building lodge was not unusual. In KONSTANZ the cathedral chapter determined on 24 November 1524 that *'den angefangten buw nitt vollenden moge* [...]'; on 5 May 1525 it decided to shut down the *Bauhütte* and fire the masons; Krebs 1952-1959, nos 8246, 8391, 8398. More than a year later, in September 1526, the reformed city council assumed control of the fabric; *Regesten Münster Konstanz*, no. 474. The immediate cause was - as in UTRECHT - an abrupt decline in diocesan revenues (*petitio matricis*) as from 1524; Krebs 1952-1959, nos 7934, 8114.

559 *Inventaris Archief kapittel ten Dom*, no. 1, vol. 16, f. 186v, 187.

560 Idem, no. 1, vol. 17, f. 103, sub 11 March 1555, and no. 651, fabric rolls 1555, f. 241v; Haslinghuis & Peeters 1965, first document, p. 58; De Groot 1994, p. 66.

561 *'verum se nullas velle subire ratione positionis et depositionis eiusdem vitree fenestre expensas, potius malle tenere veterem fenestram quam expensas facere, attento quod ecclesia multum est onerata aliis quotidianis expensis'*. *Inventaris Archief kapittel ten Dom*, no. 1, vol. 17, f. 30v.

562 Van Asch van Wijck 1838, p. 14 and Van Asch van Wijck 1846, pp. 28, 41.

563 Haslinghuis & Peeters 1965, p. 352.

564 In 1524 the *campanarius* had to promise to admit no one who was not a chapter member to the tower, except with the treasurer and fabric master's permission; Matthaeus 1703, p. 25. Nevertheless, by 1570 trips to the top of the tower had proved such a lucrative source of additional income for the *custos* that he had to be indemnified when events connected with the war made it necessary to close the tower; *Inventaris Archief kapittel ten Dom*, fabric rolls 1570/71 f. 206.

565 *Inventaris Archief kapittel ten Dom*, no. 1, vol. 17, f. 136v, sub 15 November 1558; a large portion of the costs was registered in the 1556/57 accounts, which were not yet closed; see also no. 1, vol. 17, f. 210 and vol. 18, f. 26.
566 See Appendix five.
567 Muller 1903, p. 161; *Inventaris Archief kapittel ten Dom*, no. 1, vol. 20, sub 10 March 1580.
568 De Groot 1994, pp. 39 and 85, with an overview of events up until 1595.
569 Struick 1968, p. 188; 'to effectuate that the archbishop will be buried honourably and befittingly and additionally to do that which is necessary for the funeral'; *Inventaris Archief kapittel ten Dom*, no. 1, vol. 20, sub 26 August 1580. The first reformed sermon given in the Dom was on 15 January 1581.
570 Haslinghuis & Peeters 1965, p. 333.

CATHEDRAL VERSUS PARISH CHURCH FINANCING: THE DOM AND THE BUURKERK IN UTRECHT

571 Haakma Wagenaar 1935, pp. 78-126 (thirteenth century), 126-167 (fourteenth century); Haslinghuis 1926, pp. 140-142.
572 *Catalogussen archief stad Utrecht, tweede afdeeling*, nos 47, 43, 44, 45; excerpt published in Van Rappard 1880, pp. 25-225 and Kist 1847, p. 307 ff. The archives of the Buurkerk are without a doubt the richest parish church archives of the former diocese of UTRECHT. Fabric rolls from the end of the fourteenth, the fifteenth and the sixteenth centuries are preserved from St Peter's in Leiden: Overvoorde 1906, pp. 61-144; Hulst: Adriaanse 1930, p. 66 n. 16, 1932, p. 83; St Bavo's in Haarlem, waste books: *Inventaris archieven kerken Haarlem*, no. 147; the former church of St John in Culemborg: Van de Ven 1938, no. 656, and from three other parish churches in UTRECHT, namely, those of St James, St Nicholas and St Gertrude; *Catalogussen* o.c., nos 423, 706, 797.
573 Van Rappard 1880, p. 197; Muller 1900, pp. 202-204.
574 Post 1954, pp. 428, 430.
575 Bogaers 1999, p. 111: there are extant data concerning eight confraternities at the Buurkerk; it is presumed there were 18. Concerning the religious and social position and significance of the Buurkerk in medieval UTRECHT, see also Bogaers 2003 and Bogaers 2008, pp. 371-493.
576 Overvoorde & Joosting 1896-1897, vol. 1, pp. 145-153.
577 Muller 1900, p. 215; Muller 1883-1885, Introduction, p. 48. Concerning the council chapel, see Heckert 1993, p. 141 and passim.
578 Haakma Wagenaar 1935, p. 174. Concerning the *steenboeten* – a very common form of civic fine, usually for the city walls – see Hollestelle 1961, pp. 135-137. For UTRECHT: Muller 1883-1885, Introduction, pp. 70, 76, 162, 237, and Van der Monde 1842.
579 Concerning the church tower's civic function, see Nolet & Boeren 1951, p. 102 n. 2. In France: Evans 1948, p. 242. In England: Cook 1954, pp. 55, 59. In Flanders: Toussaert 1963, pp. 325, 751. Several individual cities: Louvain: Van Uytven 1961, pp. 137, 172; Arnhem: Rosenberg 1962, p. 292; Breda: Scherft 1956, passim; Nijmegen: Van Schevichaven 1900, p. 192 ff.; Frankfurt am Main: Schoenberger 1927, p. 152; Wolff 1892, pp. 39-50; Fribourg (Switzerland): Isele 1955, p. 79; Blavignac 1858, p. XLIII; Vroom 1983, p. 41.
580 Van der Monde 1844, vol. 1, pp. 187-189.
581 Haakma Wagenaar 1935, in voce '*klokken*', and Appendix 9: the third unconsecrated bell, the *Uurklok*,

hung in the small crossing tower.

582 Haakma Wagenaar 1935, pp. 313, 315-318; Muller 1885; Muller 1883-1885, Introduction, pp. 240-241.

583 Haakma Wagenaar 1935, pp. 309, 318, n. 1, 321; Buurkerk churchwardens' rolls 1477 f. 16v; 1481B, f. 10v. (see note 572). We have no data concerning the financing of the tower's construction; it would appear that the costs of upkeep and renovation were usually borne by the church or, when they related to the city bells (bell cage and the like), by the city alone or the city and church jointly.

584 For other evidence of the ties between the parish church and city, see Muller 1883-1885, Introduction, p. 343, vol. 2, p. 230; *Catalogus Archief Gemeente Utrecht*, p. 103 (church as repository for the city archives); Hollestelle 1961, p. 83 (the city's standard brick size hung in the church).

585 Muller 1900, p. 239 ff.; Van der Graft 1926, p. 85.

586 'what remains in excess of this the church shall retain for its building works'; *Catalogussen archief stad Utrecht, tweede afdeeling*, no. 1 (*registerboeck*), f. 54; also fabric rolls 1463, f. 5 ('*één vierde ter tymmeringhe*').

587 To compare: income from property (*de bonis*) yielded roughly 35 karolusgulden during this period.

588 The differentiated rate was fixed by the civic authorities; *Catalogussen archief stad Utrecht, tweede afdeeling*, no. 1, f. 31, 32, 33; no. 3, f. 25. Also Muller 1883-1885, vol. 1, pp. 23, 24 and Muller 1900, pp. 245, 246. Another income source was the sale of seats, which yielded sporadic receipts: Buurkerk churchwardens' rolls, 1513 f. 17, and *Catalogussen* o.c., no. 1, f. 31, 43, 44. Similar income sources are also found at cathedrals that simultaneously fulfilled parish functions: see VANNES Cathedral rolls; *Inventaire-sommaire Morbihan*, p. 300 ff.

589 Bequests comprised of financial assets are not considered here; these were almost always meant to fund distributions to the poor: see n. 585.

590 *Lexikon für Theologie und Kirche*, in voce '*mortuarium*'; Lemarignier *et al.* 1962, p. 211.

591 'fur tabard with open sleeves of fur'; 'tabard with a white lining'; Van Rappard 1880, p. 101.

592 'item Aernt Tolsz. gave our church 6000 slate nails on his deathbed'; Idem, p. 86.

593 A few large bequests, not counting those naming the fabric as heir under onerous terms: Van Rappard 1880, p. 130 (1447), 47 rhinegulden of 240 wit, or approximately two years' wages of a building labourer; p. 151 (1454), 150 rhinegulden, or nearly seven years' wages; pp. 139, 140 (1449), 73 rhinegulden and 37½ rhinegulden, or roughly 3½ and 1½ years' wages.

594 Muller 1883-1885, Introduction, p. 97 n. 1; cf. '*item Lysbeth Witten die stierf in de Donkerstraat ende Her Myl gaf hoor dat sacrament ende sy gaf 3 gouden arnouds gulden*'; Van Rappard 1880, p. 129 (1446).

595 Van Rappard 1880, p. 119; Muller 1900, p. 255.

596 Van Rappard 1880, p. 127: '*item doe wij onse papen ten eten hadden*'.

597 'wills, via the parish priests and chaplains'; Buurkerk churchwardens' rolls, 1507 f. 7v; registered thus up through 1525.

598 De Blécourt 1950, p. 354; Van Iterson 1960, p. 240. Concerning the Ambachtstraat: Van der Monde 1844, vol. 1, p. 238.

599 Van Rappard 1880, pp. 122, 205. Buurkerk churchwardens' rolls, 1498 f. 9v, 1503 f. 11, 1504 f. 7v, 1511 f. 12v, 1514 f. 17, 1532 f. 15, 21, 1535 f. 13v, 20v, 1536 f. 15v, 1541

f. 13v, 1548 f. 15, 1552 f. 15.

600 Haakma Wagenaar 1935, pp. 178, 179.

601 Muller 1900, p. 252. The church did have an indulgence chest; proceeds *'voer die aflaatskist'* were booked together with those from the collection dish, such that these receipts cannot be distinguished from each other. Other indulgences may have been 'guests' in the Buurkerk; Buurkerk churchwardens' rolls, 1469 f. 9v, 1489 f. 8v, 1494 f. 9, 1498 f. 13, 1500 f. 13, 1537 f. 14v, 22; Van Rappard 1880, pp. 213, 214.

602 Muller 1900, pp. 252-254; Kronenburg 1904-1931, vol. 4, p. 126, vol. 6, p. 221. Other devotions need not concern us here, since they yielded the fabric little. An exception to this was the veneration of the Holy Cross, which generated only a third of receipts in 1484; Buurkerk churchwardens' rolls, 1484 f. 18v; Van Rappard 1880, p. 191. See also Muller 1900, p. 258.

603 *Catalogussen archief stad Utrecht, eerste afdeeling*, p. 30: indulgences in 1380, 1381, 1394; the city directed futile appeals to ROME in 1387 and 1510.

604 'fruits rendered for Our Lady'; Van Rappard 1880, pp. 45, 63, 65, 175, 187, 214; Kist 1847, p. 307.

605 MEISSEN 1936, n. 57; Beissel 1892, pp. 15 n. 7, 131, 185; Kronenburg 1904-1931, vol. 4, p. 246. Weights were taken in grain, wax, flax and even gold and silver.

606 's-Hertogenbosch: Mosmans 1931, pp. 409, 410 n. 5. Hulst: Adriaanse 1932, p. 81. Breda: Van Keppel n.d., p. 79. Alkmaar: Lampen 1929, p. 137. Delft: Oosterbaan 1958, pp. 152, 159, 171 ff. The Hague: Wildeman 1897, pp. 80, 81, 126. Arnhem: Alberts 1962, p. 1 ff. See also Zender 1959, p. 157.

607 'the abbess of St Servatius's was weighed [before] Our Lady at the Buurkerk'; Van Rappard 1880, p. 101; Kist 1847, p. 308.

608 Van Rappard 1880, p. 200.

609 In some years the proceeds were specified by period, see for example Buurkerk churchwardens' rolls, 1470 f. 13.

610 Nijmegen, 1559, for bells, by six councillors and four churchwardens; Schevichaven 1900, p. 210. Dordrecht, 1461, for bells; Van Dalen 1927, p. 165, no. 12. Gouda, 1552 and 1553 after the fire, Walvis 1713, pp. 55, 60. Delft, 1560, for the north transept of the Oude Kerk; Oosterbaan 1973, p. 473. Arnhem, 1431, for the tower, by mayors and churchwardens; Rosenberg 1962, p. 194. Antwerp, after the fires of 1434 and 1533, for bells in 1431 and 1507; see Vroom 1983. TROYES, for the rood loft of Ste Madeleine, 1511/12 and 1512/13; Assier 1854, pp. 37, 44, 46. TROYES, St Jean, 1526 and 1528; Prévost 1936, p. 84. VIENNA, for St Stephan's in 1455 by two clerics and two distinguished citizens in four districts; Flieder 1968, p. 106.

611 Van Rappard 1880, pp. 47-52.

612 Buurkerk churchwardens' rolls, 1437 f. 12-17.

613 'many good folk [went] round, each in his local eighth'; Van Rappard 1880, pp. 102, 122, 124; Buurkerk churchwardens' rolls, 1444 f. 13-17v; 1446 f. 12, 12v, 18. The 17 gulden in profits booked in 1445 would appear to be a subsequent payment; Van Rappard 1880, p. 113.

614 'such as was collected around the parish of the Buurkerk to complete the crossing'; Van Rappard 1880, pp. 151, 152.

615 'persons who have daily and weekly given their alms and prayers for the building works'; Idem, p. 40.

616 'fruits from all suspect and uncertain things'; see Appendix six.

617 'ill-gotten monies', 'a bill on which they disagreed'; Van

Rappard 1880, pp. 69, 74, 82, 87, 88, 92, 94, 95, 96, 113; Buurkerk churchwardens' rolls, 1454 f. 13; 1512 account f. 12v; Muller 1900, p. 251.

618 A sum of 96 rhinegulden current of 240 wit received from Jan Knoop in 1444, representing more than four annual wages of a building labourer, may have been obtained via a collection; Van Rappard 1880, p. 103; cf. Buurkerk churchwardens' rolls, 1444 f. 21.

619 Amongst others, Van Rappard 1880, pp. 68 (1438), 75 (1440), 103 (1444), 111 (1445); Buurkerk churchwardens' rolls, 1448 f. 10v.

620 Bergen op Zoom: Juten 1923-1924, vol. 30, p. 302, vol. 31, p. 44 ff.; also Vroom 1983 on the church of Our Lady in Antwerp.

621 *Bronnen bouwgeschiedenis*, vol. 2 (1), pp. 221, 235, 247, vol. 2 (2), pp. 487, 541; Haslinghuis 1926, p. 144; Van Rappard 1880, p. 111; Buurkerk churchwardens' rolls, 1513 f. 28v.

622 'will strike and sound when the council meets and in emergencies'; Haakma Wagenaar 1935, p. 315; Van den Hoven van Genderen 1987, p. 37.

623 Jacob van der Borch: Van Rappard 1880, p. 154 n. 1; Willem van Boelre: *Bronnen bouwgeschiedenis*, vol. 2 (1), p. 213 n. 1; Adriaan van Wesel: Van Rappard 1880, p. 198 (1487); *Bronnen bouwgeschiedenis*, vol. 2 (2), pp. 281, 291.

624 Van Kalveen 1974, p. 28 ff., 190 (conclusion of peace treaty on 7 September 1511). The Dom was the scene of struggles and schemes in times of war and political conflict, too; Zilverberg 1951, pp. 77, 82.

625 Le Bras 1954.

626 Cf. De Jong 1964, p. 10.

CHAPTER FOUR
A survey of construction financing at several cathedrals

INTRODUCTION

1 See p. 286.

2 *Registres Nicolas IV*, nos 5840, 5841 (year 1291); Mulders 1943, pp. 104-105, 132; the allocation was valid for three years.

3 See p. 314, compare with the neighbouring diocese of OSNABRÜCK; Berning 1940, pp. 29, 164, 261 ff.

4 See Appendix one and p. 62.

ONE The financing of building lodges at several cathedrals and St Peter's, Rome

5 Kowaleski 1995, pp. 371-377.

6 See Appendix one.

7 Erskine 1981 p. XI.

8 Erskine 1991, p. 7.

9 Buck 1983, p. 51 n. 106. The bequest of £20 by a canon in 1312/13 was exceptional; Erskine 1981 p. 62.

10 Erskine 1981, p. 288 (1351/52 account). Another 800 letters were written in 1325/26; Erskine 1981, p. 172.

11 Buck 1983, p. 50; this amount appears nowhere in the rolls; also Erskine 1983, p. IX.

12 Erskine 1981, p. 61; Buck 1983, p. 51.

13 Erskine 1981, p. 164; Buck 1983, p. 52 n. 111.

14 Grandisson donated £60 in 1330/31, £20 in 1341/42 and £10 in 1347; Erskine 1983, pp. 233, 266, 275.

15 Buck 1983, pp. 47-55.

16 Brooke 1999, p. 92.

17 Concerning the six possible dates, see Braunstein 1985, p. 88; Welch 1995, p. 55; Boucheron 1998, p. 160.

18 Boucheron 1998, p. 157 and fig. 17; Welch 1995, p. 40.

19 Concerning the church of Santa Tecla, its fabric and the administration thereof by the chapter – not by laymen, as at the cathedral – see Chellini 1997. The archbishop's remark made in 1349 is typical in this respect: '*honestius sit et tutuis quod ea quae ecclesiastica sunt potius per clericos quam per laicocs gubernantur*'; idem, p. 406.

20 The oldest documents

relating to the new cathedral are an indulgence issued by the archbishop, dated 12 May 1386, and Gian Galeazzo Visconti's admission of the pardoners in his lands, dated 12 October 1386; Boucheron 1998, p. 156 n. 78; Cattaneo 1985, docs 1 and 2.

21 The oldest document relating to the construction of the cathedral is a bull of indulgence dating to 12 May 1386. The day on which the first stone was laid, possibly without much ceremony, might have been 18 June 1386; *Annali*, Appendix vol. 1, sub 1386; Boito 1889, pp. 15, 61; Mezzanotte 1995, p. 864; Bishop 1918, p. 413; Brivio 1977, p. 6.

22 Gian Galeazzo determined that '[...] *quod denarii soluti per paratica dictae nostrae civitatis, tam pro oblatione festae S.Mariae mensis septembris lapsi, quam solvendi in futurum die dictae festae usque ad beneplacitum nostrum, in opus dictae fabricae convertantur*'; *Annali*, vol. 1, XI and under 1387; Mezzanotte 1995, p. 866. Starting from 1388 the cathedral fabric administration moved the '*solemnis oblatio ad majorem Ecclesiam Virginis*' to 7 September, the eve of the feast of the Birth of the Virgin, in gratitude for the birth of Gian Galeazzo's eldest son on this day in 1388; Gatti Perer 1969, vol. 2, p. 64. SIENA instituted a similar annual almsgiving ritual, perhaps in emulation of MILAN, on Easter of 1389 in the presence of all the assembled guilds in order to support the completion of the building; Norton 1880, pp. 315-318.

23 The six *porte* each had their respective turns on 7, 14, 21 and 28 July and 11 August; Bishop 1918, p. 413.

24 In their invitation letter the *presidentes fabrice* write (amongst other things) '[...] *quod oblatio* [...] *iam facta est cum magna devotione per homines tam divites quam pauperes, intrinsicos et extrinsicos, quincumque portarum civitatis eiusdem, qui satis copiose et liberaliter eidem fabricae manus porrexerunt adiutrices*'; *Annali*, vol. 1, p. 2; Mezzanotte 1995, p. 866.

25 *Annali*, vol. 1, p. 2; *Annali*, Appendix vol. 1, p. 31 under 18 August: '*pro oblatione facta per clerum Mediolani 299 lire. 4 s. 3 d.*'; Bishop 1918, p. 415.

26 *Annali*, Appendix vol. 1, 1387 account; Boito 1889, p. 16 ff.; Bishop 1918, p. 418.

27 Account entry for 23 September 1387: '*oblationes per servitores, qui venerunt pro volendo laborare pro nihilo, sed plovit sic quod non potuerunt 14 lire 3 s. 5 d.*'; *Annali*, Appendix vol. 1, sub 1387 B.

28 Boito 1889, p. 20. Though it was not compulsory for earnings from fornication to be spent *ad pias causas*, the scholastics did advise this; Thomas Aquinas 1952, *Summa Theologiae*, II, II, q. 32 a. 7; Noonan 1957, p. 30; Baldwin 1970, vol. 1, p. 134 ff.

29 *Annali*, Appendix vol. 1, sub 1387 C, 21 October. Boito 1889, p. 27, suggests the likelihood that this gift came from Gian Galeazzo Visconti. Another gift, registered as '*pro oblatione super majus altare nomine cujusdam illustris et excelsae dominae, quae noluit nominari 320 lire*', would have been donated by his wife. Another anonymous '*devotus beatae Virgini Mariae*' donated 160 lire over a period of eleven months in 1390 (i.e. 1760 lire); *Annali*, Appendix vol. 1, pp. 108-119.

30 Boito 1889, p. 20 ff.

31 Boito 1889, p. 21; Bishop 1918, p. 419 (4 November 1387).

32 The exact size is impossible to calculate on the basis of the accounts; the proceeds were registered in a separate account; Gatti

Perer 1969, vol. 1, p. 57.
33 Boito 1889, p. 77.
34 *Annali*, vol. 1, p. 33.
35 Concerning the excessively high and numerous indulgences that this pope issued, only to revoke most of them again at a later date, see Paulus 1922-1923, vol. 3, p. 152 ff.; Foreville 1958, pp. 61, 62.
36 Gian Galeazzo's letter to the pope was dated 11 April 1390; *Annali*, vol. 1, pp. XII, 33; Gatti Perer 1969, vol. 1, p. 58; Rocco Negri 1975, passim; Brivio 1977, p. 25 ff.
37 Paulus 1922-1923, vol. 3, p. 453; Rocco Negri 1975, p. 191.
38 Boito 1889, p. 30; Paulus 1922-1923, vol. 3, p. 182.
39 *Annali*, Appendix vol. 1, 1391 account, expenditures sub February.
40 Paulus 1922-1923, vol. 3, p. 182 n. 1.
41 *Annali*, Appendix vol. 1, p. 191; Boito 1889, p. 31; Rocco Negri 1975, p. 200: '*de alia gratia jubilei aliquo die nullo modo voluit* [= the pope] *voluit facere; nam dicit et verum dicit quod numquam alicui ecclesiae mundi hoc fuit concessum*' (report of an audience with the pope on 21 August 1391). Gian Galeazzo was no longer involved by the time of the bull's renewal.
42 In only a few churches did the time of grace last a full year; Boeren 1962; pp. 93, 94; also Paulus 1922-1923, vol. 3, pp. 540, 541. Concerning the Jubilee indulgence in UTRECHT Cathedral after 1475 and 1500, see p. 279.
43 A *manovale* earned a wage of c. 38 lire imp. a year; Boito 1889, pp. 64, 65. Total receipts over 1391 came to 57,287 lire imp.; *Annali*, Appendix vol. 1, p. 9; Boito 1889, p. 78.
44 Paulus 1922-1923, vol. 3, p. 152 and n. 10, p. 435. The indulgence had a term of fifteen years. Renewal of the 1398 indulgence in 1404 by Pope Boniface IX's successor, Innocent VII; Paulus 1922-1923, vol. 3, p. 154. 1403 indulgence: Mezzanotte 1995, p. 898. Jubilee indulgence of 1452: Paulus 1922-1923, vol. 3, p. 544; Brivio 1977, pp. 32-36.
45 Welch 1995, pp. 71, 76, was the first to point this out. For the waterways see also Braunstein 1985, figs 2 and 3.
46 Braunstein 1985, p. 92. The *fabbrica* in its turn supplied marble for ecclesiastical and other building projects; Boucheron 1998, pp. 473-482.
47 Rondinini 1984, p. 105.
48 See the map of MILAN in Boucheron 1998, p. 107; Welch 1995, p. 35.
49 A *manovale* earned at least 3 s. a day; Braunstein 1985, pp. 96, 128, 130.
50 *Annali*, Appendix vol. 1, pp. 20-155. There is absolutely no data concerning the receipts for 1388. The occasional transferred monthly credit balances are not included in this number; the debit balances added onto the receipts in 1390 are a mystery; these are small amounts.
51 Boito 1889, p. 32.
52 Cattaneo 1985, p. 31 ff.
53 Boito 1889, p. 236; Mezzanotte 1955, pp. 902, 906, 915, 986.
54 Gatz *et al.* 2003, pp. 529-533; Guntermann 2003, p. 80. To compare: the neighbouring diocese of UTRECHT bounded 1100 parishes; its chapter numbered 40 canons. The city of UTRECHT also had four parishes, but a population of some 20,000 people around the year 1500.
55 There is an excellent analysis of the accounts, also transcribed on CD-ROM, in Guntermann 2003. The first entry in which a *structuarius* is referred to by name dates from 1366.
56 The cathedral's reconstruction after the fire of 1254 (finished in 1272), along with a number of renovations in the fourteenth and

fifteenth centuries, need not concern us here; the same goes for building activities that were never registered in the fabric rolls such as those relating to the chapel of the Holy Cross; see Guntermann 2003, p. 91.

57 Concerning the two large and two small church bells, see also Fehrmann 1967, pp. 56-60, 255-256.

58 For a detailed description, see Guntermann 2003, pp. 78-88.

59 For example in 1486/87, 1503 and 1509/10; Guntermann 2003, pp. 68-69, 76-77.

60 Guntermann 2003, p. 69. In that same year the fabric booked the first payments for two men to carry the processional cross during Lent and on Whitsunday '*quia nemo gratis portare voluit*', fabric accounts f 249v; Guntermann 2003, p. 61 n. 152.

61 Gatz *et al.* 2003, p. 533; Guntermann 2003, p. 110.

62 *Bulletin Monumental* 140 (1982), pp. 98-102 (Jacques Henriet).

63 Cailleaux 1999, pp. 11, 110.

64 Idem, p. 111.

65 Idem, pp. 49-58; three years are missing: 1508/09, 1509/10 and 1511/12. See Appendix one.

66 The following is fully indebted to Cailleaux 1999, Cailleaux 2002 and Cailleaux (forthcoming).

67 Cailleaux 1999, p. 142.

68 Cailleaux 2001, p. 81. De Salazar's coat of arms was added again to the façade of the north transept, but now alongside that of the chapter; Cailleaux 1999, pp. 39-40.

69 The building campaign for the south tower, begun in 1517, was called to an immediate halt on the archbishop's death in 1519; Cailleaux 1999, p. 146.

70 Idem, pp. 191-210.

71 A broad analysis of the budget available from the end of the thirteenth century until the end of the fifteenth, as based on a scattered body of data, provided in several graphs in Cailleaux (forthcoming), ; this does not take price and wage inflation into account.

72 Fabric rolls covering approximately 170 years have been preserved over the period between 1294 and 1550.

73 d'Avenel 1894-1912, vol. 3, p. 586: at a day's wage of 14 d.

74 Murray 1987, pp. 23, 212; not including transferred credit balances.

75 Wages: Murray 1987, p. 203.

76 Idem, pp. 24, 25, 213.

77 Idem, pp. 209-214 (with bar graphs for each year). It is regrettable that the author did not analyse all the relevant accounts in this way.

78 For example in 1422/23; Murray 1987, p. 48.

79 Not including contributions from the newly formed fabric confraternity from 1491/92 on.

80 See p. 157.

81 Murray 1987, pp. 35, 42.

82 See p. 92.

83 Murray 1987, pp. 46, 47, 59 and 237 n. 8.

84 See p. 51.

85 Murray 1987, pp. 87-109; Meunier 2001 and Meunier (forthcoming). My thanks to Florian Meunier for sharing his information.

86 See p. 124

87 The cathedral fabric confraternity founded in 1488 generated next to no income, as was also true of the cathedral's other confraternities.

88 Personal communication from Meunier. The abbey of St Hubert paid 12 l.t.; two other organizations paid 10. l.t. apiece. Twelve quests were admitted in 1496/97.

89 Chapter minutes of 15 February 1520; Meunier 2003, n. 30.

90 Four quests were admitted in 1536/37, amongst them that of the Hôtel Dieu in Paris and the abbey of St Hubert.

91 Meunier 2003, n. 24 and 26.

The issue of the admission of extra-diocesan quests had already been broached by the bishop in 1510.

92 Devailly 1973, p. 75.

93 Sibille 1991, pp. 206, 209.

94 This fund was subsumed back into that of the fabric in the early 1530s; Hamon 2001, p. 131.

95 Hamon 2001, p. 132.

96 Meunier 2003, p. 37; a remarkably large sum – three times that contributed by the bishop of BEAUVAIS in 1512.

97 All figures cited in the foregoing are borrowed from the table in Hamon 2001, p.133. The categories designating miscellaneous sums and loans are of practically no significance and are therefore not included in the total.

98 Jenny 1977, pp. 1-21, with illustration on p. 19.

99 'ruinous and decayed state [...] can only be repaired with 50,000 l.t. or more'; Hamon 2001, p. 131.

100 Records of the bishops' income from the period after 1565 reveal TOLEDO to be far and away the wealthiest of any Spanish archdiocese or diocese, being roughly three times as rich as the runner-up, the diocese of SEVILLE; Hermann 1988, p. 155.

101 Fernández Collado 1999, pp. 13, 15, 28.

102 Idem, p. 44. Between 1458 and 1584 there were only ten *Obreros Mayor.*

103 Idem, pp. 107-121, provides a listing of the staff employed in the sixteenth century. Also Santolaya Heredero 1979, pp. 98-102.

104 Izquierdo Benito 1982; also Torroja Menendez & Sanchez Palencia 1977, pp. 16-20 and nos 761-770. The oldest account, dating to 1383, is incomplete.

105 Izquierdo Benito 1985, p. 484. Wage of a *peón*: 9 maravedís per day in the summer, 7 maravedís per day in the winter; Izquierdo Benito 1982, p. 156.

106 Izquierdo Benito 1982, p. 474, lists 16; see also Torroja Menendez & Sanchez Palencia 1977, p. 18. The minimal gains indicate that these profits were bought off.

107 Fernández Collado 1999, pp. 219-228. It is likely that the archbishop shouldered a large share of the costs; he signed a number of subcontracts worth c. 1.6 million maravedís.

108 Santolaya Heredero 1979, p. 42. In the latter half of the sixteenth century the diocese encompassed 854 parishes, the city 20; the population was between 45,000 and 62,000; Marías 1983, pp. 109, 116.

109 Santolaya Heredero 1979, pp. 97, 117. Wage of a *labourer*: 76½ maravedís per day; Hamilton 1970, p. 399.

110 *Excusados* and *terzuelos*: Santolaya Heredero 1979, pp. 60-86.

111 Santolaya Heredero 1979, pp. 111, 141; Vroom 1992, pp. 11-14.

112 See also Rodríguez G. de Ceballos 1989, pp. 79-85.

113 Sanz y Sanz 1967, p. 188.

114 Contreras Jiménez 1989, pp. 508-531, based on an examination of the fabric rolls for 1458-1472. Also Sanz y Sanz 1967, pp. 161-190.

115 The only other example known to this author is the relocation of the cathedral from Old Sarum to Salisbury in 1218.

116 Recent overview by María Soto Cano in Carrero & Rico 2004, pp. 215-241.

117 Villalpando 1962, p. 392; Sanz y Sanz 1967, pp. 185-190; wage p. 189, number of clerics p. 195.

118 Haliczer 1981, pp. 1-6; Álvarez de Frutos 1988, pp. 41-50; De Colmenarez [1637] 1969-1974, vol. 2, pp. 196-205.

119 Álvarez de Frutos 1988, p. 71.

120 Villalpando 1962, p. 394; Sanz y Sanz 1967, p. 199; García Sanz 1999, pp. 18,19, 29.

121 De Colmenares 1969-1974,

vol. 2, p. 210; Villalpando 1962, p. 394.

122 Villalpando 1962, p. 399.

123 De Colmenares 1969-1974, vol. 2, p. 212.

124 Villalpando 1962, p. 406; Sanz y Sanz 1967, p. 204; Cortón de las Heras 1990, pp. 797, 807.

125 García Sanz deals with the period 1525-1650 (taken up in Cortón de las Heras 1990, vol. 1, pp. 707-766). Also Casaseca Casaseca 1988, pp. 85-95. Rodríguez G. de Ceballos 1989, p. 80, compares sixteenth-century Spanish cathedral fabrics, including SEGOVIA. More recently, Cillanueva de Santos 2009, in particular pp. 35-195; the results of his study have been incorporated in this book; the numbers published by García Sanz have served as a basis, with the exception of those relating to the building lodge, Cillanueva Santos, p. 180 and graph on p. 165.

126 García Sanz 1999, tables 5 and 9.

127 Fabric accounts are missing for the years 1533-1539 and 1575-1604.

128 García Sanz 1999, pp. 13, 14 and table 6, with a detailed breakdown: annates and annuities generated 80 percent of this category over the entire period, with these profits directly reflecting trends in the agrarian market.

129 Soto Cano in Carrero & Rico 2004, p. 229.

130 García Sanz 1999, pp. 19, 22-23.

131 Idem, p. 24.

132 Cortón de las Heras 1990, doc. 63 (1534?).

133 See p. 425.

134 De Colmenares 1969-1974, vol. 2, pp. 312-215; Villalpando 1962, pp. 398-400; Sanz y Sanz 1967, pp. 200-202; García Sanz 1999, pp. 20-22; Rodríguez G. de Ceballos 1989, p. 80.

135 García Sanz 1999, tables 2 and 8: in 1561 the largest part of the population of Segovia, some 60 percent, was employed in the cloth industry.

136 As related in the *Actas capitulares* in the seventeenth century; García Sanz 1999, p. 15.

137 García Sanz 1999, pp. 24-25; tables 5 and 9; also Cillanueva de Santos 2009, pp. 97-101, with graphs providing a breakdown of the revenues in percentages between 1529 and 1699.

138 See García Sanz 1999, table 4. The indices, with the decade of 1520-1529 as base years, are borrowed from Hamilton 1970, pp. 267-268; the wages are also taken from Hamilton 1970, p. 395: the average daily wages of a labourer or a mason's helper over the period 1520-1529 can be estimated at 34 maravedís, yielding an annual wage of 8500 maravedís.

139 García Sanz 1999, p. 27. The proportion of the total expenditures spent on construction during the period from 1524 until 1699 was an average of 46 percent, peaking at 83 percent in 1524-1530; Cillanueva de Santos 2009, p. 164.

140 Construction began in 1513; in 1560 the cathedral had been built up to the crossing, after which a second campaign got underway in 1589. The cathedral was not actually finished until the eighteenth century. The collegiate church of Valladolid, begun in 1527, was designated as the cathedral in 1595.

141 García Sanz 1999, p. 36; also Cillanueva de Santos 2009, p. 193. There have been a number of recent studies dealing with the financing of cathedral-building in Spain, mostly concentrating on the post-medieval period. Gutiérrez-Cortinas Corral 1987a has published graphs setting out receipts and expenditures at the cathedral of MURCIA between 1521 and 1572. Total outlays for construc-

tion of the tower for a period of seven years between 1519 and 1525 came to 3.4 million maravedís, which at a day's wage of 30 maravedís comes to around 65 annual wages per year. Also Gutiérrez-Cortinas Corral 1987b, pp. 110-117. The *diezmos* were by far the most valuable source of income. Latorre Ciria 1992, pp. 120-134, analyses receipts and expenditures at the fabric of HUESCA Cathedral between 1510 and 1700. Perez del Campo 1985 analyses how construction of the nave and façade of MALAGA were financed between 1719 and 1782. The leading income source was the combined excise duties levied with the king's consent. The building lodge operated on a minimal scale: slightly over 1 million reales de vellón were spent on construction and furnishings over a period of 64 years, thus a yearly rate of 16 annual wages of a *peón*; Pérez del Campo 1985, pp. 133,155, 212.

142 Westfall 1974, pp. 4, 5; Magnuson 1958, pp. 163-166; Bredekamp 2000, p. 21.

143 Westfall 1974, p. 19.

144 Magnuson 1958, pp. 163-214; also Günther 1997, pp. 71-75, Bredekamp 2000, p. 24 and Roser 2005, pp. 16, 69-74, 117-118, 251-252; we have records of various expenditures over a number of years for this building plan. The building plans of Nicholas V and Paul II were known as far north as Germany; p. 117 n. 376.

145 '*Ut simul et vetustas serbaretur et venustas adderetur*', as per Alfonso Chacón (1540-1599), in Varangoli 2008, p. 239. See also Francia 1989, p. 110.

146 Piola Caselli 1996, p. 56. Leaving aside the years of war and other political upsets, actual construction took up 70-80 years.

147 Bramante, Raphael, Sangallo, Michelangelo, Maderno and Bernini; Bredekamp 2000, passim. Complete list: Basso 1987-1988, vol. 1, p. 98; Bosman 2004, pp. 152-153.

148 Bredekamp 2000, calls this '*das Prinzip der produktiven Zerstörung*' in his book title.

149 From 1538 until 1615 the *muro divisorio* was also in use '*ad ventos arcendos*'; see also Rice 2007, p. 17. Bosman 2004, pp. 92-99, questions the wall's temporary character, positing that it was built to connect the old St Peter's with the new. There was a strict administrative division between the old St Peter's (managed by the chapter) and the new building (managed by the *Fabbrica)*. Even before this, in 1513/14, the *tegurium* designed by Bramante was built, forming a temple-like structure above the high altar and papal throne that must have provided protection from the wind and rain during the time that the roof was being raised, in 1526; by 1592 it had already been torn down; Bredekamp 2000, pp. 52-53 and Bosman 2004, pp. 105-113. There were around 100 ecclesiastics attached to the chapter: 30 canons, 36 *beneficiati* and 26 *chierici*; Rice 2007, p. 13.

150 Westfall 1974, pp. 120, 147.

151 Bredekamp 2000, p. 24; Kempers 1996, p. 227.

152 Frommel 1991, p. 175; Ait & Vaquero Piñeiro 2000, p. 154; Jones 2002, pp. 399-406; Frommel 1976, pp. 74-81.

153 *Liquet omnibus* bull; *Bullarum diplomatum*, vol. 5, pp. 481-488; Jones 2002, p. 399.

154 Ait & Vaquero Piñeiro 2000, p. 157: two Florentine merchants served as treasurers; the building lodge's financial administration lay in the hands of the Roman merchant Giuliano Leni. It is possible that Leo X, a Medici, was inspired by the way in

which affairs were run in the *Opera* of FLORENCE Cathedral and by that city's banking system; Basso 1987-1988, vol. 1, p. 412.

155 *Bullarum diplomatum*, vol. 6, pp. 448-54; Basso 1987-1988, vol. 1, pp. 41-42; 119-141 (concerning the *tribunale*); Ait & Vaquero Piñeiro 2000, pp. 170-172; Jones 2002, p. 399.

156 Frommel 1976, p. 77 n. 44; Günther 1997, p. 99 and n. 187.

157 Thoenes 1998, passim.

158 See also Thoenes 2008, p. 14.

159 Rice 2007, pp. 9-11.

160 Basso 1987-1988, vol. 1, p. 35. The archival annotations from the first period are a later reconstruction by Francesco Magalotti, administrator of the *Fabbrica*. Also Francia 1977, p. 55.

161 Frommel 1976, pp. 102 (bull of 4 November 1507), 103, 106, 109, 115.

162 The intricate arrangements are described in Schulte 1904, vol. 1, p. 243, index sub '*Rom*'; and in Paulus 1922-1923, vol. 3, pp. 147-151.

163 Frommel 1976, nos 173-175; Günther 1997, p. 77.

164 Fredericq 1922, nos 332 and 343; Schulte 1904, vol. 1, p. 171; Caspers in Swanson 2006, pp. 83-86.

165 Concerning this indulgence and the role of the Fuggers banking house, see Schulte 1904, vol. 1, pp. 93-150.

166 'The churches of St Peter's in ROME, of COLOGNE and of Ulm are too large and unsuitable'; Günther 1997, pp. 99-101 and n. 199.

167 Schulte 1904, vol. 1, pp. 174, 178; Günther 1997, p. 99.

168 Goñi Gaztambide 1949, pp. 10-28, 33; Goñi Gaztambide 1958, pp. 462-509 and doc. 20 (bull issued by Paul III, 25 November 1538); *Diccionario eclesiastica de España*, in voce '*Bula de la Cruzada*'; Piola Caselli 1996, p. 61; Rietbergen 1983, pp. 122, 137-140. The last payment was made in 1851; 1966 marked the official end of the *Cruzada*.

169 See the recent definitive article by Dandelet 2008, especially pp. 43-47; he is the first to make an analysis, albeit broad, of the '*entrata e uscita*' account books of the *Fabbrica*. See also Basso 1987-1988, vol. 1, pp. 107-110: '*redditi delle crociate: Spagna, Portogallo, Sicilia, Napoli, Sardegna*'; Portugal fell under the Spanish empire from 1580 until 1640.

170 These estimates do not include financing for individual chapels; on this, see Rice 2007 pp. 162-164: in the early seventeenth century a large altar cost 800-1000 scudi, a small one 300-400 scudi; the annual wage of a *manovale* was around 78 scudi.

171 Piola Caselli 1996, p. 56.

172 Frommel 1976, p. 62; Francia 1977, p. 20: there is some slight variation in the figures. Wages: Vaquero Piñeiro 1996, p. 144. The ducato di camera was a gold coin, as was the scudo; 80 bolognini = 1 scudo; 100 ducats (24 carats) = 109 scudi (22 carats); Piola Caselli 1996, p. 57; the wage is in silver bolognini. Concerning the relationship between the various coins, see Francia 1977, pp. 7, 62 n. 9; Francia 1989, p. 16; Basso 1987-1988, vol. 1, p. 104.

173 We have no precise figures for before 1529; see Francia 1977, p. 86 n. 18. Figures in the table are borrowed from Dandelet 2008.

174 Francia 1977, p. 115; Francia 1989, pp. 21-23, 40. Piola Caselli 1996, p. 55; Bredekamp 2000, p. 92; Thoenes 1978, pp. 479-480, deems these numbers to be exaggerated, though there seems to be no cause to think so. Nothing has been published concerning the years leading up to the church's dedication in 1626.

175 Francia 1989, p. 128, also

pp. 135-138.

176 Dandelet 2008, p. 47; Bredekamp 2000, p. 110.

177 Concerning the construction of the colonnade, see Rietbergen 1983, passim; concerning in particular the financing and scale of the building lodge, pp. 148-154. Bernini was the architect of St Peter's from 1629 until 1680.

TWO Duration and pace of construction

178 Scott 2003, pp. 38-42, 136, estimates the average period of building at 250-300 years, based on data from English cathedrals.

179 Weilandt 1992, pp. 160-163.

180 See overview in Kimpel & Suckale 1985, pp. 503-547.

181 'Economy and medieval architecture: was the one the undoing of the other?'; Lopez 1952, pp. 433-439. See also Ricetti in *Finanziare Cattedrali*, pp. 167-175.

182 In support of Lopez's hypothesis: Bordeaux 1969, p. 255, and Dieter Kimpel in *Bulletin Monumental* 135 (1977), p. 217. Against Lopez's hypothesis: Biget 1974, pp.157-158; Chédeville 1973, p. 519, and Duby 1976, pp. 115 ff., 137. See also Schöller in Cavaciocchi 2004, pp. 219-228.

183 Johnson 1967a and 1967b.

184 Alford & Smith 1969 and Johnson 1969.

185 James 1972, passim and p. 58 (graph); also James 2007, pp. 503-519; James 1977/1979, pp. 9-18, 120 n. 45 (revised graph). An alternate calculation of the scale of the building lodge, based on the actual construction volume completed within a given time span, in Wolff 1968, pp. 113-114, who posits that between 69 and 100 building labourers were employed at COLOGNE Cathedral during the construction of its string of radiating chapels (completed in 1261).

186 For example OSNABRÜCK, 1415, see also Vroom 1981, Appendix 10.

187 LYON 1401/02: 8½ years' wages; 1417/18: 4½ years' wages; SENS 1433-1444: 2 years' wages, the smallest budget in the period 1319-1490, from which 66 accounts are preserved.

188 *Stiftskirche Xanten*, vols 3 (2) and 4 (2); Beissel 1889, vol. 1, pp. 100-140, vol. 2, p. 2.

189 Arbellot 1852, pp. 72-79.

190 See Vroom 1981, Appendix 10; building continued until the dedication in 1429.

191 Minimum: six annual wages in 1449 and 1456; maximum: 41 annual wages in 1454.

192 Knoop & Jones 1949, p. 45, distinguish between a semi-permanent versus an ad hoc building lodge.

193 Pevsner 1963, p. 148.

194 Neuwirth 1893, p. 76. Possibly this figure is inflated on account of the notably low wage of the unskilled *famulus* in PRAGUE; translated into wages of a skilled building labourer, the PRAGUE building lodge expended an equivalent of 68 annual wages, that in UTRECHT 51.

195 Mezzanotte 1955, p. 896 ff.

196 This is also true of the building of the Chartreuse van Champol in Dijon by the dukes of Burgundy. Here the building lodge reached its upper limit in 1386-1387, when building expenditures totalled 520 annual wages; see Vroom 1981, Appendix 10.

197 Colvin 1971, pp. 192, 193; cf. Johnson 1967a, p. 198 ff.

198 Salzman 1952, p. 36.

199 Du Colombier 1973, p. 8; Knoop & Jones 1949, p. 3; Colvin 1963, vol. 1, p. 1029.

200 Struick 1968, p. 131. Similar numbers are recorded for the construction of the Teutonic Order's fortresses in Prussia, which sometimes required a pool of 1200 labourers; Dewischeit 1899, p. 168.

201 Salzman 1952, p. 36; Aubert 1960-1961, vol. 118, p. 256. James estimates there to

have been a total of some 300 building labourers working at the cathedral and in the stone quarry during active years; James 1977/1979, p. 12 n. 9.

202 Vielliard 1950, pp. 116-118; Du Colombier 1973, p. 8.

203 Concerning the king's mustering of manpower in England, see Salzman 1952, p. 37; Also Dewischeit 1899, p. 168.

204 *Colección documental Oviedo*, nos 196, 197; De Caso Fernández 1981, pp. 371-374: gifts from the bishop and king made it possible to resume building in 1526.

205 Vroom 1993, p. 179.

206 See Vroom 1983, pp. 16-21.

207 Mols 1954-1956, vol. 2, pp. 61-65.

208 A method in use elsewhere was to create a building fund from aggregate credit balances over a succession of decades, which could then be used to meet certain large expenses. In TROYES 2198 l.t. was amassed in 1506/07 to fund construction of the façade; *Inventaire-sommaire Aube* G 1577. See also Beissel 1889, vol. 2, p. 6.

209 See the polemic concerning the question of whether 'there was no programming or estimate of cost and/or time' in the major twelfth- and thirteenth-century church building enterprises, between Branner on the one hand and Von Simson on the other, in *The Art Bulletin* 1955, pp. 235-237, provoked by Branner's review of Du Colombier 1973. Du Colombier and Von Simson deny this, rightly so in my view.

210 In 1451 the papal bull of indulgence for the cathedral of VANNES judged the number of years needed to complete the cathedral at a minimum of 20; the nave could be dedicated in 1476; Rosenzweig 1936-1938, no. 722. The completion of the megalomaniacal expansion of the cathedral of SIENA, begun in 1339, was estimated in 1356 - when the project was aborted - to require 100 years, as based on the income of the *Opera*; Van der Ploeg 1993, p. 116.

211 García Cuesta 1954, no. 7 (pp. 119-130); the contract of 27 April 1506 replaced that of 9 May 1504, no. 6 (idem, pp. 109-119): the activities are described at great length and also included the supply of building materials. Concerning the contracts preserved in the cathedral archive, see San Martín Payo 1983, pp. 34-36.

212 'the pattern and drawing of the portals and of what remains to be finished of the church of Clermont'; Davis 1983, passim; *Congrès Archéologique de France* 158 (2000), p. 142. Also: Bibliothèque de la ville, Clermont-Ferrand, ms. 634 (copy Michel Cohendy). The construction of the façade of NANTES Cathedral was estimated at 75,000 l.t. in 1438, of which 15,000 l.t. had already been spent; Guillouët 2003, p. 163.

APPENDIX ONE

MEDIEVAL CATHEDRAL FABRIC ACCOUNTS

The following overview is arranged alphabetically by country and therein by date. Accounts postdating 1550 are for the most part not included.
Literature: Schöller 1989, pp. 361-379; Cailleaux 1999, p. 157.

ENGLAND

EXETER
1279-1353 (36 accounts); published in excerpts in Erskine 1981 and Erskine 1983; and 1371-1467 (67 accounts) and 1479-1514 (only a few accounts); typed transcriptions in Findlay 1939; cited in Erskine 1962, p. 257; Erskine 1981, p. VIII; Erskine 1991, pp. 1-9; excerpts in Oliver 1861, pp. 379-408.

HEREFORD
1290/91, 1384, 1387,1447; *Charters Hereford*, pp. 163-165; Lehmann-Brockhaus 1855-1960, no. 2084; Yates 1973, pp. 79-86; Nilson 1998, p. 160 n. 52.

ELY
1291-1517 (45 accounts); the years 1291-1360 published by Chapman 1907; cited in Brooke *et al.* 1976, p. 175.

NORWICH
1297-1430 (obedientary rolls, after 1313/14 communar rolls, around half of the accounts are preserved); analysed and partially published in Fernie & Whittingham 1972; cited in Atherton *et al.* 1996, pp. 165-174.

YORK
1360-1639 (64 accounts, of which 30 accounts from between 1415 and 1515); excerpts in Raine 1859; cited in Aylmer & Cant 1977, p. 185; Nilson 1998, p. 163.

WELLS
1390, 1457, 1480/81, 1492/93, 1500/01,1505/06, 1549/50; excerpts in Bird & Baildon 1907/1914, vol. 2, passim; typed transcription by L.S. Colchester, Wells.

CANTERBURY
1492, 1494-97 (expenditures); analysed in Woodman 1981, pp. 203-205.

LINCOLN
1504-1517, 1525, 1528/29; cited in Owen 1994, p. 168.

FRANCE

Archives of cathedral fabrics make up part of cathedral chapter archives. They are preserved in the various Archives départementales of the French departmental capitals, under series G. The *Inventaires-sommaires*, which appeared in print around 1860, contain excerpts from the account rolls; the *Répertoires numériques* contain only brief references. For construction accounts, see Locatelli & Vergnolle 1995; for later accounts see Rousteau-Chambon 2003, pp. 62-64.

SENS
1283/84, 1295/96, 1319/20, 1341/42, 1360/61, 1377/78, 1393-1396, 1396-1401, 1401-1406, 1407-1417, 1427-1437, nearly complete from 1439 until 1770; *Inventaire-sommaire Yonne* G 1123-1199; cited in Schöller 1989, pp. 371-372; Cailleaux 1999, pp. 49-53, 463-618; Cailleaux (forthcoming).

RODEZ
1288/89, 1293/94, 1459 (expenditures), 1507/08, 1509/10; Archives départementales Aveyron 3 G 249; published in Mortet & Deschamps 1929 (1293), p. 310; Bion de Marlavagne 1875, pp. 279-283; cited in Desachy 2005, p. 169, pp. 296-300 (expenditures 1459/60); pp. 311-315 (1507/08, 1509/10, extracts).

AUTUN
1294/95; Paris, Bibliothèque

Nationale, lat. 5529B; published by Mortet & Deschamps 1929, p. 320; analysed in Quicherat 1886, pp. 183-191; Gimpel 1960, pp. 63-66; cited in Schöller 1989, p. 362.

TROYES
1294-1301,1327/28, 1333/34, 1339/40, 1366-1574, with a few lacunae; Paris, Bibliothèque Nationale, lat. 9111, 9112, 9113; Troyes, *Inventaire-sommaire Aube* G. II, pp. XVIII- XXI and G 1559 ff.; Dublin, Trinity College and Cheltenham, Bibl. Phil; published by Gadan 1851, Assier 1855b, Assier 1858 and d'Arbois de Jubainville 1862; analysed in Murray 1987, pp. 113-115, 199-216; cited in Roserot de Melin 1966 and Schöller 1989, pp. 373-375.

EMBRUN
1298, Archives départementales Hautes-Alpes E 521; cited in Schöller 1989, p. 365.

CAMBRAI
1310, 1318 and 1329 (fragments), also 1332-1786 (454 accounts, 53 missing); *Répertoire numérique Nord* 4 G 813 and 4560-4765; excerpts in Houdoy 1880, pp. 4 and 157- 221 (1310-1598); cited in Schöller 1989, p. 363.

NOYON
1333/34 (expenditures), 1462/63, early sixteenth century; *Inventaire-sommaire Oise* G 1380; Mathon 1864, pp. 587-600; cited in Seymour 1968, p. 181.

PARIS
1333-1340, 1378-1380, 1386/87, 1392-1394; excerpts from Canon Sarasin (1744-1766), Paris, Archives Nationales LL 270; cited in Vidrier 1913/1914, vol. 40, pp. 177-205; Schöller 1989, p. 368; Davis 1998, pp. 60-61.

CLERMONT-FERRAND
1334/35, Archives départementales Puy-de-Dôme 3 G arm. 18, sac B, cote 25; cited in Davis 1983, n. 19, 20; Schöller 1989, p. 364.

STRASBOURG
1329, 1338, 1382/83, 1389, 1398 (year-end accounts only), 1414-1436 (incomplete series of half-year accounts), 1437-1513 (25 accounts), a few accounts after 1532; Archives de la ville de Strasbourg, série II, 45a-46 and Archives de l'Oeuvre Notre-Dame, no. 43; published in Fuchs 1990 (1382/83 and 1385); cited in Forté 1978, pp. 55, 69-70, 78-79; Schock-Werner 1983, pp. 248-249; Marie-José Nohlen in Doré 2007, pp. 38, 36 (fig.).

AMIENS
1357/58; *Inventaire-sommaire Somme* G 1157; cited in Durand 1901-1903, vol. 1, p. 124; Schöller 1989, p. 362.

ANGERS
1378 and after 1416/17 with lacunae; cited in De Farcy 1901-1926, vol.1, pp. 24, 70, 106, 173, vol. 2, p. 70, vol. 3, p. 296 ff., vol. 4, p. 144.

ROUEN
1383-1387, 1406/07, 1414/15, 1419-1421, 1426/27, 1430-1433, 1457/58 until 1788; *Inventaire-sommaire Seine-Inférieure (Maritime)* G 2481-2627; cited in Beaurepaire 1897, p. 204; Lefebvre 1994, vol. 1, p. 113; Schöller 1989, p. 370; Foucher-Lefebvre (forthcoming), annexe 1; Lardin in *Notre-Dame de Rouen*, pp. 96-121 (accounts spanning 1383-1387).

LIMOGES
1388-1391, 1404-1408, 1412/13, 1415/16, 1443/44, 1459/60, 1468, 1501, 1503, 1508 and later accounts; *Répertoire numérique Haute Vienne* G 669-679; cited in Arbellot 1852, p. 68 ff.; Leroux 1910, p. 427; Soulard 1993, pp. 254-265.

ARRAS
1384 and 1391; cited in Schöller 1989, p. 362; De Mély 1920/1921, no. 11, p. 336.

LYON
1401/02, 1414-1419, 1429/30, 1457-1469, 1481/82, 1488/89, 1493/94, 1498-1501, 1524-1529; Archives départementales Rhône 10 G 1607-1612; cited in Sachet 1914, p. 331 n. 2.

QUIMPER
1409/10, 1458/59, 1468/69, 1477-1480, 1514, 1524; *Répertoire numérique Finistère* 12G 70-79; cited in Le Men 1877, p. 260 ff.

AIX-EN-PROVENCE
1410-1427; cited in Altet 1986, p. 24.

ELNE
1415-1417,1441/42, 1448/49; *Inventaire-sommaire Pyrenées-Orientales* G 111-114.

CHARTRES
1415/16, 1586-1595; *Inventaire-sommaire Eure-et-Loir* G I, p. 69 ff. 1415 account published in Merlet 1889, pp. 35-94.

LISIEUX
1424-1426, 1451/52, 1462/63 and a few later accounts; Basin 1859, pp. 199-207; cited in Vasseur 1882, p. 454 ff.

TOURS
1431-1433 (fragment); Gasnault 1962; also Boissonnot 1920, p. 239 n. 2.

BOURGES
1460, 1507-1537; De Girardot & Durand 1849, passim; analysed by Hamon 2001, passim.

VANNES
1474/75, 1485-1489, 1491-1494, 1496-1498, 1502/03, 1504/05, 1516-1519, 1533/34, 1545/46; *Inventaire-sommaire Morbihan* 74 G 2 ff.; cited in Mussat 1983, p. 299 ff.

BAYEUX
1484-1486; cited in Villers 1901.

BEAUVAIS
1499 (fragment); published in Coyecque 1891.

SENLIS
1503/04- 1505/06; cited in Aubert 1910, pp. v, 25; also Meunier 2002, p. 4 n. 6.

BORDEAUX
1508, 1510-1512, 1515-1529; *Inventaire-sommaire Gironde* G 504-509.

BOURGES
1508-1530; Hamon 2001, p. 133.

GERMAN EMPIRE

HALBERSTADT
1367; Staatsarchiv Magdeburg; published by Schmidt 1889; several accounts from the sixteenth century, idem, p. 2 n. 4; Schöller 1989, p. 366.

PRAGUE
1372-1378; published by Neuwirth 1890; also *The story of Prague Castle*, pp. 188-189 and *Die Kathedrale von St. Veit*, pp. 50, 51 (fig.).

TRIER
1381, 1387, 1388; cited in Schöller 1989, p. 373.
Magdeburg
1417/18, 1424/25,1445/46, 1446/47, 1455/56; cited in Wentz & Schwineköper 1972, p. 73.

FREISING
1447-1500; Custos-Rechnungen; published by Ramisch *et al.* 1998; cited in Mitterweiser 1918, pp. 2, 84.

REGENSBURG
1459, 1487-1489; published by Schuegraf 1855 and 1858; and 1517, 1530, 1538, 1557 ff.; cited in Schuegraf 1855, p. 12.

OSNABRÜCK
1415/16 (now lost), 1477/78, 1478/79, 1481/82-1486/87, 1498/99, 1502/03,1503/04, 1507/09-1509/10, 1512/13-1514/15, 1516/17-1528/29, 1530/31-1543/44; Guntermann 2003, pp. 112-203, published on accompanying CD-ROM; Rhotert 1916.

COLOGNE
1513/14, 1559/60, 1568/69; described, analysed and charted by Manfred Huiskes in *Ad Summum 1248*, pp. 43-55, 58-61.

WÜRZBURG
1529/30; published by Von Güldenstubbe 1988.

ITALY

In view of the diverging form of cathedral building works administration in Italy, only a few exceptionally significant series of fabric accounts are listed here.

SIENA
1320-1825 ('*entrata e uscita*'); Riedl & Seidel 1995, p. 142 ff.

ORVIETO
1321-1450 and later years;

Riccetti 1988, p. xv n. 20 and pp. 138-215; Kosegarten 1996, p. 29.

MILAN
1386-1605 with a few lacunae; 1387-1391 accounts published in *Annali*, Appendix vol. 1, pp. 20-211; cited in Verga 1908, p. 79.

BRIXEN/BRESSANONE
1460-1504; cited in Tavernier 1996, p. 183; Egg 1987, p. 332 n. 25.

LOW COUNTRIES

UTRECHT
1395-1595; *Inventaris Archief kapittel ten Dom*, no. 651; the accounts for 1395-1528 are published in *Bronnen bouwgeschiedenis*.

TOURNAI
1455 (fragment), 1566, 1571; 1455 account published in Duvosquel 1973.

LIÈGE
1454-1506 (with a few lacunae) and 1517-1532; Archives de l'Évêché de Liège; cited in Poncelet 1934, p. 8 ff.

SPAIN

The majority of fabric accounts are preserved in the Archivos Catedralicios of the various cathedrals; see *Archivos Iglesia and España*, vol. 1

BARCELONA
1325-1327, 1357-1359, 1361-1367, 1369-1373, 1377-83, 1389-1393, 1397 with lacunae up until 1804; Vallés i Botey 1987, pp. 32-34; Sanabre 1948, pp. 32, 99, 339; cited in Fábrega Grau & Baucells Reig 1969, p. 15; Borau Morell 2003, pp. 58-59. The majority of *llibres de l'obra* relate only to expenditures; the oldest only to receipts.

PALMA DE MALLORCA
1327-1345, 1368-1371 (ten accounts), 1389-1790 (with a few lacunae); cited in Miralles Sbert 1941-1943, nos 1701-1971; Sastre Moll 1993; Sastre Moll 1994; Domenge i Mesquida 1997, pp. 49-63, 120-121, 283-323; fig.: Pascual 1995, pp. 7, 36, 123, 128.

SEO DE URGELL
1334, 1452, 1485; *Llibre de l'obra de la Seu d'Urgell*; cited in Puig i Cadafalch & Pujol Tubau 1918, p. 61 n. 1.

TORTOSA
1345-1463 (41 accounts, accounts over the period 1350-1375 are missing); Almuni i Balada 1991, pp. 41, 273-282; Almuni i Balada 2007, pp. 29, 31, 869-870.

ZARAGOZA
1346-1347, 1376-1401, 1400-1402, 1409-1410, 1412-1413, 1413, 1415-1425, 1471-after 1548 (with lacunae), 1346 account published by Lacarra Ducay & Monterde Albiac 1989; cited in Buesa Conde 1987, p. 353 (some inaccuracies); illustration in *La Seo de Zaragoza*, pp. 131 and 405. Most of these accounts relate solely to expenditures.

GERONA/GIRONA
1367-1498 (with lacunae); Archivo Catedralicio, Obra de la Seu inv VI, nos 1. ff.; cited in Victor 1996, p. 367 n. 12.

VALENCIA
1380, 1389-1822 (with a few lacunae); Chabás Llorens 1997, no. 1540; Olmos Canalda 1950, nos 1388-1505; cited in Sanchis y Sivera 1909, pp. XII, 442.

LERIDA/ LLEIDA
1356-1707; exh. cat. Lleida 1991, cat. 19 and p. 78; cited in *Censo*, p. 598.

TOLEDO
1383 (expenditures), 1418, 1424-1429, 1431/32, 1448, 1450, 1453/54, 1458, 1459, 1461, 1463, 1465-1470, 1478, 1483/1484, 1494-1503, 1505-1600; cited in Torroja Menendez & Sanchez Palencia 1977, no. 760 ff.; Izquierdo Benito 1982; Santolaya Heredero 1979.

CUENCA
1396-1398, 1400-1408 (incomplete accounts), 1434-1459, 1470-1480, 1547 ff.; Chacón Gómez-Monedero & Palomo Fernández 2002, pp. 33-36; Palomo

Fernández 2002, vol. 2, pp. 294-296, 409-475 (extracts) and p. 168 n. 133.

PAMPLONA

1398-1407, 1439, 1440-1474, 1480/81; Goñi Gaztambide 1965, nos 1616, 1617, 1626, 1767, 1917, 2004; analysed in Goñi Gaztambide 1955, p. 20 and doc. 20; *Tecnología y sociedad*, p. 200; Martínez de Aguirre 1987, p. 267.

HUESCA

1421-1457, 1498-1522, 1523-1540, 1581-1631, 1631-1718; cited in *Censo*, p. 587; Latorre Ciria 1992, p. 318.

SEVILLE

1424-1740 (with lacunae, e.g. 1467-1487); Rubio Merino 1987/1988, vol. 1, pp. 121 ff. and 309, vol. 2, pp. 26, 185 ff.; see also *La Catedral de Sevilla*, pp. 767-770, and *La catedral gótica de Sevilla*, pp. 48-113.

SEGORBE

1438, 1446, 1449, 1457, 1583 ff.; cited in Llorens y Raga 1970, nos 361-365.

LEÓN

1440, 1450, 1458/59, 1530-1553, 1555 ff.; cited in García Villada 1919, nos 9391- 1908, see also 5790-5793; excerpts in Merino Rubio 1974, pp. 343-379.

SEGOVIA

1458-1472, 1475, 1477, 1479, 1483, 1514-1517, 1524-1575 (with only a few lacunae), 1603-1653; Contreras Jiménez 1989, pp. 507-531; Casaseca Casaseca 1988, pp. 86-95; Cortón de las Heras 1990, pp. 717-762; García Sanz 1999, n. 2; Cillanueva de Santos 2009, pp. 211-212 (complete summary) and p. 327 n. 102.

SANTO DOMINGO DE LA CALZADA

1483-1486, 1489-1514, 1524, 1527, 1531-1562 (with lacunae); excerpts in Moya Valgañón 1986, doc. 11, 22, 27 , 36, 44, 50, 53, 56, 65, 72, 75, 82, 85, 87, 94, 98, 100, 104-105, 111, 123, 125, 134; cited in López de Silanes & Sainz Ripa 1992, no. 317.

SIGÜENZA

1498-1556; Pérez-Villamil 1899, p. 416 and passim; cited in *Censo*, p. 562.

SALAMANCA

1499-1841; cited in Marcos Rodríguez 1962, p. 216; Chueca 1951, p. 25.

CORIA

1500 ff.; cited in *Censo*, p. 366; García Mogollón 1999, p. 127.

MURCIA

1521, 1522,1523, 1525, 1534-1573; Gutiérrez-Cortines 1987a, pp. 171 n. 1, 101-119; Gutiérrez-Cortines 1987b, p. 192 n. 67.

OURENSE

1505-1565; cited in *Censo*, p. 711.

OVIEDO

1511, 1516-1521, 1526-1529; *Colección documental Oviedo*, nos 161, 166, 168, 172, 184, 190, 209, 215, 222, 227; De Caso Fernández 1981, pp. 362-368, 503.

BURGOS

From 1514 on; cited in Sanz, p. 19 n.1; Mansilla Reoyo 1956, p. 96.

ÁVILA

1520, 1522, 1524, 1529, 1530, 1536-1559; cited in Ajo González 1962, nos 583-843; account for 1546 published in López-Arevalo 1966, pp. 203-212.

GRANADA

1514-1951, with lacunae; *Archivos Iglesia and España*, pp. 256, 259; Marín López 1998, p. 465; excerpts for the years 1514, 1521-1532, 1544-1546, 1560-1564, 1569, 1576-1588, 1592-1593 in Rosenthal 1961, pp. 173-210.

SWITZERLAND

SION

1333-1342; published in Holderegger 1926; cited in Schöller 1989, p. 372.

FRIBOURG

1376 ff., 1470-1490; published in Blavignac 1858; cited in Schöller 1989, p. 365.

BASEL

1399-1487 (41 accounts); Staatsarchiv Basel; cited in *Baugeschichte des Basler Münsters*, p. 168; La Roche 1888, p. 79 ff.; Schöller 1989, p. 362.

APPENDIX TWO

LAUSANNE
1445-1449; 1505/06, 1530/31; cited in Rück 1975, p. 161.

GENEVA
1469-1471, 1520/21; Archives d'État KAa 54 and 56.

KONSTANZ
1499, 1505/07, 1513/14, 1528 and subsequent years; Landes Archiv Karlsruhe; excerpts in Mone 1852, p. 38; cited in *Regesten Münster Konstanz*, pp. vii, xv and passim; Degler-Spengler 1996, p. 789.

ANNATES

The following is a partial overview of annates/*annualia* granted to cathedral fabrics, presented in chronological order. See also Schöller 1989, pp. 270-279, which contains a summary.

1225 BEAUVAIS; granted by the bishop and chapter for a period of ten years. *Gallia Christiana*, vol. 10, instr. pp. 284-285.

1239 QUIMPER; granted by the bishop; annual fruits of all the churches in his collation; for the cathedral fabric and hospital. *Cartulaire Quimper*, no. 50; extended (?), see no. 136 (1285) and no. 244 (1335).

1245, 30 March GENEVA; papal confirmation of a decree issued by the bishop and chapter; first-year's fruits of benefices in their collation, except for benefices belonging to the bishop's *mensa*; allocated in part to the cathedral fabric. *Registres Innocent IV*, no. 1180.

1253 and 1289 CLERMONT-FERRAND; granted by the pope; benefices in the bishop's and chapter's collation. *Registres Nicolas IV*, nos 1066, 1067, 1626; Du Ranquet 1928, p. 11; Gardelles 1963, p. 17.

1263, 20 March LANGRES; granted by the pope after a fire; first-year's fruits of all benefices that fell vacant within a period of two years. *Registres Urbain IV*, c. 257.

1264, 21 May LIMOGES; granted by the bishop for three years, extended in 1290 until 1327, thereafter from 1344; half-year's fruits of all vacant parishes. Arbellot 1852, pp. 24-28, 66; *Congrès Archéologique de France* 84 (1921), p. 4; Evans 1948, p. 94 n. 2; Soulard 1993, pp. 179-180.

1267, 4 July NARBONNE; decree issued by the archbishop and chapter: full-year's fruits of vacant benefices; at the order of Pope Clement IV reduced in this year to a half-year's fruits. Renewed by Pope Nicholas IV on 23 May 1291 for the full-year's fruits of vacant benefices for a period of five years, except those in the collation of exempt ecclesiastical institutions; thereafter extended in perpetuity; levied until 1664. Narbonne 1901, pp. 25, 26, 37; Mortet 1898, p. 405 ff.; *Registres Nicolas IV*, nos 5183, 5184; Freigang 1992, p. 51.

1268 MEAUX; granted by the bishop and chapter; full-year's fruits of vacant parish churches for a period of ten years, though renewed in 1282. Kurmann 1971, n. 240, 242, 297.

Between 1269 and 1293 SEO DE URGELL; granted by the bishop Pere de Urg (1269-1293) for a period of four years; full-year's fruits of all benefices vacated due to death, except for those of the cathedral; successively extended. Puig i Cadafalch & Pujol Tubau 1918, pp. 76 n. 2, 77.

1277 RODEZ; granted by the pope and bishop; the fruits of benefices in the bishop's and chapter's collation; successively extended until into the sixteenth century, but for only a quarter of these fruits as from 1461. *Registres Nicolas IV*, no. 1426 (1289); Denifle 1897-1899, vol. 1, no. 669 (1433); Bion, pp. 26 n. 1, 39, 52, 109.

1277 ALBI; granted by the bishop for a period of 20 years; first-year's fruits of all churches (in the bishop's and chapter's collation?). *Gallia Christiana*, vol. 1, p. 21; Laran 1931, p. 11; see also Biget 1974, p. 148 and Biget 1982 p. 23.

1278-1296 REGENSBURG; granted by the bishop; concerns only one parish. Schuegraf 1847/1848, vol. 11, p. 93.

1279 SENS; granted by the pope for a period of five years; extended in 1285. Bouvier 1911, vol. 2, p. 261; *Registres Honorius IV*, p. 59; *Inventaire-sommaire Yonne* G 11, p. 39.

Between 1279 and 1295 TOUL, granted by the bishop and chapter for a period of three years; fruits of all vacant parishes on the condition that the priest got a sufficient income, designated to fund the erection of the vaults above the choir and side aisles. *Congrès Archéologique de France* 164 (2006), p. 221 and n. 56.

1280 BOURGES; granted by the pope for a period of three years. Branner 1962a, p. 68 n. 3.

1284 PASSAU; granted by the bishop; benefices in the bishop's collation. Dürr 1777, p. 210; Kirsch 1903, p. XIII; Baix 1942, p. CDVII n. 2.

1285, 15 December CHÂLONS-EN-CHAMPAGNE; granted by the pope for a period of five years; benefices in the bishop's and chapter's collation; renewed in 1289 and 1303. *Registres Honorius IV*, no. 308; *Registres Nicolas IV*, no. 1066; *Registres Benoît XI*, no. 85; *Congrès Archéologique de France* 135 (1977), p. 365.

1285 CAHORS; granted by the bishop and chapter; half the first-year's fruits of all churches in the diocese; extended in 1308 under the restriction that the designation was fixed until at least the end of the fifteenth century. *Bulletin Monumental* 137 (1979), p. 288; *Congrès Archéologique de France* 147 (1993), p. 12.

1289 YORK; granted by the pope for a period of three years. *Registres Nicolas IV*, pp. 767-768; cf. *Registres Honorius IV*, p. 280 and Raine 1859, p. 121.

1289 AUTUN; granted by the pope; successively extended for a period of ten years, e.g. in 1347. *Registres Nicolas IV*, nos 1635, 1636. *Cartulaire Autun*, pp. 256-259; *Registres Urbain IV*, pp. 257, 258; Mortet & Deschamps 1929, p. 320.

1298, 7 May BARCELONA; granted by the bishop and chapter for a period of ten years at the start of construction; full-year's fruits of all churches in the bishop's and chapter's collation; the first stone was laid on 1 May 1299. Puig i Puig 1929, Appendix CII.

13th century VANNES; as evidenced in fabric accounts from after 1475 until the end of the eighteenth century. *Inventaire-sommaire Morbihan*, p. 300 ff.; Le Mené

1900, pp. 213, 226.
1300, 1 January HUESCA; granted by the bishop and chapter more than 25 years after the start of construction for a period of ten years; full-year's fruits of the canonries and dignities of the diocese as well as the half-year's fruits of lower benefices in the bishop's collation. Extended many times in somewhat modified form until into the sixteenth century. Del Arco 1924, pp. 26, 32, 39, 41; Durán Gudiol 1956, p. 367.
1304, 8 March THÉROUANNE; granted by the pope for a period of five years. *Registres Benoît XI*, no. 575.
1307 BORDEAUX; granted by the pope for a period of 20 years. Gardelles 1963, p. 17.
1309, 15 May, 31 December AGEN; granted by the pope for a period of ten years. *Regestum Clementis papae V*, nos 5281, 4276; Gardelles 1963, p. 17; Haller 1903, pp. 50, 51.
1309, 25 February TOULOUSE; granted by the pope for a period of five years; half-year's fruits. *Regestum Clementis papae V*, no. 4240.
Early 14th century BAZAS; granted by the bishop and chapter for a period of five years. Gardelles 1963, p. 17.
Early 14th century (before 1317) ZARAGOZA; renewed by the bishop in 1328: first-year's fruits of benefices in the city and diocese. *La Seo de Zaragoza*, pp. 127, 128.
1310 CHALON-SUR-SAÔNE; granted by the bishop and chapter for a period of ten years; extended in e.g. 1329. *Congrès Archéologique de France* 91 (1928), p. 427.
1311 ELNE; granted by the bishop; full-year's fruits of all benefices and half-year's fruits of all dignities in his collation during his lifetime; later statute of 1380 granted papal approval on 13 October 1400 and remained valid until the cathedral's completion; these proceeds still recorded in fifteenth-century fabric accounts. Archives départementales Pyrénées-Orientales G 110, 111.
After 1313 HALBERSTADT; granted by Pope Boniface IX. *Urkundenbuch Halberstadt*, vol. 4, no. 3164 (1401); Dürr 1777, p. 210; Schmidt 1889, pp. 7, 8.
1315, 1 May SION; granted by the bishop for a period of five years; all vacant benefices in the diocese. Dubuis 1979, p. 152, reg. 4.
1320-1330 SALZBURG, granted by the archbishop after a fire, remaining valid until repealed; half-year's fruits of parish churches in his collation. *Regesten Salzburg*, vol. 3, pp. 195, 969, 1069, 1121.
1323 LYON; granted by the archbishop for a period of three years to fund tower construction. Bégule 1880, p. 9.
1339, 21 December TORTOSA; granted by the bishop for a period of 20 years, extended by 50 years in 1375, and also thereafter; full-year's fruits of all benefices in the city and diocese. Almuni i Balada 1991, p. 50; Almuni i Balada 2007, doc. 13, pp. 660-662; also doc. 14 and 15, pp. 662-666 and doc. 51, pp. 738-742; doc. 98 (1436) p. 810.
1342 SENLIS; granted by the bishop; a quarter or a sixth of the fruits. Aubert 1910, p. 20.
1347 PARIS; granted by the bishop and chapter for a period of two years for urgent repairs; a third of the year's fruits of benefices in their collation. Paris, Archives Nationales LL 537, no. 2 bis.
1351, 31 July PALMA DE MALLORCA; granted by the bishop (possibly also by his predecessor). Domenge i Mesquida 1997, pp. 98-100 and 120-121 (table with proceeds in 1393/94 and 1397/98).
1357 SEGORBE; granted by the bishop; half the first-year's fruits of all benefices in the city and diocese. Blasco Aguilar 1973, p. 293 n. 71.

1361, 23 December TARAZONA; granted by the bishop and chapter pursuant to the king of Castile's destruction of the cathedral; all benefices including and not including cure of souls. *España Sagrada*, vol. 49, p. 463; Harvey 1957, p. 187.

1365, 22 June SARLAT; papal permission issued to the bishop and chapter for a period of four years; fruits of vacant benefices where the first fruits were not reserved for the pope. Denifle 1897-1899, vol. 2, p. 648 n. 3.

1367, 22 February TOURNAI; papal permission issued to the bishop and chapter for a period of two years; the *fructus primi anni* of prebends in their collation, except where the Camera Apostolica was entitled thereto, and with allocation of the *congrua portio* to the observers. *Lettres communes Urbain V*, no. 19680.

1369 KRAKOW; decree issued by the provincial council; half the year's fruits. Mansi 1759-1793, vol. 26, p. 557.

1369 FF. GERONA; as attested by the fabric accounts. Archivo de la Catedral, Obra de la Seu VI, p. 2 ff.

1372, 23 November ARRAS; granted by the pope for a period of six years to repair the nave. Héliot 1953, p. 15; Denifle 1897-1899, vol. 2, p. 225.

1457, 19 February ZAMORA; granted by the pope; extended in 1505. De Lera Maíllo 1999, nos 1589 and 2197.

1459 LIMOGES; permission requested from the pope. Soulard 1993, pp. 216-217.

1471, 2 May OVIEDO; permission issued by the bishop for a period of ten years; half the fruits of benefices in the diocese, as also determined by previous bishops. *Colección documental Oviedo*, no. 33.

1476, 18 September ASTORGA; papal permission issued to the bishop and dean for a period of one year; the fruits of all vacant benefices. *Colección documental Astorga*, vol. II, no. 2187.

1486, 1 December PALENCIA; granted by the pope for a period of 35 years for the cathedral's completion. San Martín Payo 1954, p. 161, nos 6, 6 bis.

1529 CORDOBA; *Medias annnates* of all benefices in the diocese. Nieto Cumplido 1998, p. 509.

1522, 6 May MONDOÑEDO; repetition of a synodal decree; allocation of a quarter share of the fruits of vacant benefices in perpetuity. Cal Pardo 1992, nos 3349, 3368, 3370, 4460.

1591 SALAMANCA; request by the chapter from the bishop; half-year's fruits in perpetuity. Chueca 1951, p. 185.

16th century AVILA; half the year's fruits for an indefinite period; as evidenced in the fabric's administrative records. López-Arevalo 1966, p. 208.

APPENDIX THREE

LIST OF *MENDICATORIA*

- BAYEUX, Bishop Henri II, between 1165 and 1205; in *Cartularius Baiocensis*, vol. 1, no. 47.

- STRASBOURG, Bishop Konrad, between 1190 and 1202; in *Urkundenbuch Strassburg*, vol. 1, no. 143; Hasak 1927, p. 21 ff.; also 28 January 1275 in *Urkundenbuch Strassburg*, vol. 2, no. 240; Hasak 1927, p. 33 ff.

- BESANÇON, Archbishop Amadeus, between 1203 and 1220; in Zink 1973, doc. 71, 76 and 78.

- CAMBRAI, bishop, c. 1212; Archives départementales Nord 4 G 99 (fiche 1382); renewed March 1236 (fiche 1384).

- WÜRZBURG, bishop, 1 January 1240; in *Monumenta Boica*, vol. 37, no. CCLIX.

- TRIER, Church of Our Lady, letter from the archbishop of Cologne, 3 June 1243; in *Urkundenbuch Coblenz und Trier*, vol. 3, no. 770.

- CHÂLONS-EN-CHAMPAGNE, bishop's official on behalf of the bishop, 2 April 1255; in Bibliothèque Georges Pompidou, Châlons-en-Champagne, mss 250, p. 764 (Jean-Pierre Ravaux, personal communication).

- HALBERSTADT, bishop of Metz, 29 August 1258; in *Urkundenbuch Halberstadt*, vol. 2, no. 972; for later mandates: idem, vol. 4, nos 2928 and 2960; also Diestelkamp 1929, Appendix 2.

- COLOGNE, archbishop, 26 April 1264; in *Urkundenbuch Niederrhein*, vol. 2, no. 541; also *Regesten Köln*, vol. 6, nos 778, 935, 957, 959 (1356 and 1357), 1124 (1358), vol. 7, no. 364a (1365).

- OLOMOUC, bishop, 6 December 1265; in *Codex regni Bohemiae*, no. 462.

- PRAGUE, bishop, 18 October 1266, for the cathedral of Olomouc; in *Codex regni Bohemiae*, no. 481.

- FREISING, bishop, 1274, for the cathedral of Bamberg for a period of five years; cited in Von Winterfeld 1979, p. 35.

- BAZAS, bishop, c. 1280, for the cathedral of Pamplona; in Goñi Gaztambide 1996, p. 106 and Appendix 3.

- UTRECHT, Bishop-elect John I of Nassau, 8 September 1288; in *Oorkondenboek Utrecht*, vol. 4, no. 2349; Rutgers 1978, pp. 149-153. For the other Utrecht *mendicatoria*, see below.

- MAINZ, archbishop, 7 January 1293; *Regesten Mainz*, vol. 1, no. 303.

- BARCELONA, bishop, 4 March 1302; in Puig i Puig 1929, pp. 458-460, Appendix CIII; also 1343, Appendix CXIII, in Catalan.

- YORK, archbishop, 3 June 1304; in Raine 1859, p. 154.

- YORK, bishop of Durham, 30 September 1312; in Raine 1859, p. 156.

- SALISBURY, bishop, 1319; in *Statutes of Salisbury Cathedral*, pp. 194-201.

- CALAHORRA, bishop, 10 June 1322; cited in Sáinz Ripa 1995, pp. 156-157.

- GERONA, bishop, 13 March 1325; in *España Sagrada*, vol. 44, p. 320 ff.

- VICH, bishop, 17 February 1326; in Villanueva Estengo 1902-1906, vol. 7, pp. 261-270.
- METZ, bishop, 18 February 1326; in Pelt 1930, no. 5; cf. *Congrès Archéologique de France* 83 (1920), pp. 7, 8.
- ELNE, bishop, 1336; in *Inventaire-sommaire Pyrénées-Orientales* G 110.
- NEVERS, bishop, 1336; in Crosnier 1854, p. 412 ff.
- PRAGUE, Archbishop Ernst, shortly after 1355, for the cathedral and bridge; in Tadra 1880, p. 395 ff.; Neuwirth 1890, pp. 382-386.
- HUESCA, bishop, 7 August 1346; in Durán Gudiol 1991, p. 74; also 1500 in Del Arco 1924, pp. 37-39.
- TORTOSA, bishop, 1346-1348; in Almuni i Balada 2007, doc. 28, pp. 690-693; also doc. 52 and 53 (1375).
- MILAN, archbishop, 12 May 1386; in *Annali*, Appendix vol. 1, sub 1386 and 1387; cf. Boito 1889, p. 15 ff.
- BREMEN, archbishop, 21 February 1396; in *Urkundenbuch Bremen*, vol. 4, no. 177.
- CAMBRAI, bishop, 1373; in Houdoy 1880, p. 34.
- TOURNAI, bishop, 22 October 1364; in Voisin 1869, p. 477 ff.
- MEISSEN, bishop, 16 October 1413; cited in Donath 2000, pp. 26, 48.
- SANTO DOMINGO DE LA CALZADA, bishop, 15 July 1448, for the cathedral and hospital; in Moya Valgañon 1986, no. 254; also nos 271, 274, 287.
- REGENSBURG, bishop, 9 January 1525; in Schuegraf 1847/1848, pp. 262-266.
- TOUL, bishop, 19 October 1525; in Clanché 1926-1927, p. 153 ff.

The majority of *mendicatoria* are letters issued by a bishop for his own cathedral [exceptions are Bazas, Freising, Halberstadt, Prague, Trier and York (1312)]. Only the oldest *mendicatorium* from each respective cathedral is listed here. The content of these letters was transcribed into official form books; see Rockinger 1863/1961, p. 458: *'forma litere indulgentialis, quam deferant elemosinarum petitores'* (Zürich, after 1250) and p. 547: *'forma litterarum pro recolligendis elemosinis ad opus hospitalium et piorum locorum'* (c. 1280). Occasionally the existence of a *mendicatorium* can be deduced from other deeds, such as in the case of a 20-day papal indulgence for the cathedral of Bremen, dated 18 March 1224 (*'cum eorum nuncius ad vos accesserit'*), *Urkundenbuch Bremen*, vol. 1, no. 129).

MENDICATORIA RELATING TO UTRECHT CATHEDRAL

- 1288, 8 September, Bishop-elect John I of Nassau (1267-1290); *Inventaris Archief kapittel ten Dom*, no. 405 (i.e. the cartulary of the cathedral fabric), f. 9v. Published in Eekhof 1909, Appendix no. 1; *Oorkondenboek Utrecht*, no. 2349, translation follows in Appendix 4 of this book.
- 1307, 2 March, Bishop Guy van Avesnes (1301-1317); *Inventaris* o.c., no. 405, f. 70r, 70v, no. 408a.
- 1318, 30 March, Bishop Frederik II van Sierck (1317-1322); *Inventaris* o.c., no. 405, f. 68v ff., no. 408a.

- 1322, 18 December, Bishop-elect Jan van Bronkhorst (1322-1323); *Inventaris* o.c., no. 405, f. 18-20. Cited in Noordeloos 1959, p. 30 n. 3.

- 1327, 11 October, Bishop Jan van Diest (1322-1340); *Inventaris* o.c., no. 405, f. 12v ff., no. 400, no. 409. Published in Eekhof 1909, Appendix 2.

- 1340, 11 May, Bishop Jan van Diest (1322-1340); *Inventaris* o.c., no. 405, f. 703 et seq.

- 1343, 12 May, Bishop John of Arkel (1342-1364); *Inventaris* o.c., no. 405, f. 75v ff. Cited in Rutgers 1970, p. 176.

- 1344, 3 May, Bishop John of Arkel (1342-1364); *Inventaris* o.c., no. 405, f. 77 ff., no. 409. Published in Eekhof 1909, Appendix no. 4; cited in Rutgers 1970, p. 176.

- 1358, 25 March, Bishop John of Arkel (1342-1364); *Inventaris* o.c., no. 405, f. 79 ff., no. 409. Published in Eekhof 1909, Appendix no. 5 (précis).

- 1364, 22 November, Bishop Jan van Virneburg (1364-1371); *Inventaris* o.c., no. 405, f. 82 ff.

- 1364, 22 November, Bishop Jan van Virneburg (1364-1371); *Inventaris* o.c., no. 405, f. 16v. Published in Matthaeus 1703, pp. 17-19; Eekhof 1909, Appendix 6 (précis).

- Undated, Bishop Jan van Virneburg (1364-1371); *Inventaris* o.c., no. 405, f. 20v ff. and no. 418.

- 1371, 12 October, Bishop Arnold van Horn (1371-1379); *Inventaris* o.c., no. 405, f. 85v.

- 1371, 12 October, Bishop Arnold van Horn (1371-1379); *Inventaris* o.c., no. 405, f. 87-90.

- 1371, 12 October, Bishop Arnold van Horn (1371-1379); *Inventaris* o.c., no. 409. Published in Eekhof 1909, Appendix no. 8.

- 1379, 23 October, Bishop Floris van Wevelinkhoven (1379-1393); *Inventaris* o.c., no. 405, f. 90v, no. 409. Published in Eekhof 1909, Appendix no. 19 (précis).

- 1379, 23 October, Bishop Floris van Wevelinkhoven (1379-1393); *Inventaris* o.c., no. 405, f. 22, no. 420.

- 1394, 20 March, Bishop Frederick of Blankenheim (1393-1423); *Inventaris* o.c., no. 409.

- 1463, 10 May, Bishop David of Burgundy (1457-1496); *Inventaris* o.c., no. 405, f. 116v ff., no. 409.

- 1518, 31 March, Bishop Philip of Burgundy (1517-1524); *Inventaris* o.c., no. 418; Published in Eekhof 1909, Appendix no. 94 (précis).

Additional *mendicatoria* lay down provisions for collecting in a given area or for a certain aspect of the collection; Eekhof 1909, including Appendix nos 7, 23, 25, 36, 40, 43, 47.

APPENDIX FOUR

Mendicatorium of Bishop-elect John of Nassau (1267-1290) for the construction of Utrecht Cathedral, 8 September 1288.

John, by the grace of God Bishop-elect of Utrecht, to all those abbots, priors, provosts, deans, canons, parish priests and vicars of churches, or priests serving in chapels in the city and the diocese of Utrecht, dearly beloved in Christ, who shall see this letter: eternal blessings in the Lord.

Whereas concerning our venerable mother church of Utrecht, first of all churches in the city and diocese of Utrecht, being especially dear to us before all other churches of which we by the grace of God are called founder, it is fitting that, in order to honour the most glorious Virgin Mary and our most pious patron the blessed confessor Martin, and in view of her great old age, she be entirely and honourably restored from the foundations up. Because her own means are insufficient for her construction, unless she is favoured with the pious alms of the faithful, we most diligently appeal for her and with her to you, beloved in Christ, who have seen fit to place divine authority under the rule of our crosier, and we appeal also for Him who prayed on the cross to the Father that He would liberate us from the curse of eternal death, and we exhort and command you for the forgiveness of your sins to render pious alms and charitable offerings for this purpose, wherefore you shall earn treasures in Heaven. For we who are born naked into this world can take nothing with us when we die except our alms and good works, as is read in Revelations: 'and their works do follow them' [Rev. 14:13]. Therefore, brothers, let no one, rich or poor, at a time of such great necessity shrink before the almighty God and blessed Virgin Mary and our pious patron saint from offering his due service, but let each and every one from his possessions make in such measure as the Lord has given him a gift of alms to render for the construction of this great work, so that on the Day of Judgement he may be granted eternal life, and that you who are amongst those standing on the right-hand side shall deserve to hear: 'Come, ye blessed of my Father' who have joyfully and piously built a house on this earth for Me and for my Mother, the Virgin Mary, and for the blessed Martin, 'inherit the kingdom prepared for you from the foundation of the world'. [Mat. 25:34]

Moreover we desire that your loyalty to us and our church, your mother church, which we believe you have until now had and will continue to have, shall be the more clearly manifested in the faithful advancement of this cause. We therefore order you and by virtue of the sacred obedience prescribe on pain of suspension that you receive the messengers of our aforementioned church, when they come to you, into your churches and homes with courtesy and charity and that you diligently urge the people of God who are entrusted to you to give generously of the goods that God has bestowed upon them for this so pious work.

Moreover we prescribe on pain of suspension that you appoint two upright and trustworthy men from amongst your subordinates as collectors of the alms to be obtained, who shall faithfully gather, discerningly receive and assiduously preserve these until a specific day and place that the bearer of these documents, the special messenger of our aforementioned church, shall make known to you and them. They shall then, together with you and without making any subtraction, deliver them there and render them without any wicked postponement or opposition.

However, if after the time established by the messenger any of your parishioners should fail to render or defiantly reserve these alms, you must by our authority compel such men, using ecclesiastical penalties and having given sufficient advance warning, to make due payment, and if they should persevere in their defiance, you must take harsher action until appropriate satisfaction has been made.

We furthermore desire that you make particular mention of the matter of the aforementioned church with your parishioners when they approach death and make up their wills, in order that all who die in the Lord give according to their means.

However, if anyone should prove disobedient or rebellious against this order, then he will be made to appear before us or before the procurator of the aforementioned church, the provost of Tiel, in Utrecht on a day to be specified by the messenger to receive a fitting punishment for his disobedience.

These messengers and their task we place under the protection and safe-conduct of the blessed Martin, our illustrious patron saint, and of ourselves, and we shall excommunicate anyone, whether clergyman or layman, who would presume to disturb them during their business or attempt by rede and deed, by word and works to impede this business.

And should it repeatedly happen when the children of God appear in the sight of the Lord that a gainsaying Satan stands with them and offers obstinate resistance, then we wish and by virtue of the sacred obedience prescribe that, when that son of perdition is revealed by his opposition amidst the assembled flock of the faithful, he be summoned before us or our aforementioned procurator at the direction of the bearer of these documents for his offence of disobedience and be made to appear on the appropriate day before the procurators and the messengers of the aforementioned church. We admonish you altogether, beloved by us in Christ, and in the Lord we exhort you, should any see this fault in themselves they admit this to God, who sees into the conscience, and to their confessors, with penance and reverence so that they shall not subsequently do such things again.

Let those who on the contrary know themselves free of such obstinacy, persevere with devotion and sacred obedience and offer continuous and faithful resistance to those obstructers, by rigorously publicizing the sentence of excommunication that we have imposed on those people, certain in the knowledge that, aside from the heavenly merits, we shall reward them on fitting occasions. In this manner shall those who are a burden and not an honour to us and ours deserve the force of ecclesiastical judgement in such measure that God and the Church shall have from them a worthy and payable penance, or else they must die in their iniquities.

We also wish and command you on pain of the aforementioned penalty that, where there are those who value the favour of men more highly than that of God, and who scorn the Apostolic indulgences and those of the venerable fathers, the lords archbishops and bishops, and also dishonour the keys of the one universal Church, outside of which, as the true and Apostolic faith proclaims, there is no salvation, and who defame the indulgences granted to the church or the delegated persons, you declare them excommunicated the moment they raise this business in your churches, and order all of the faithful to avoid them.

To amplify and encourage the devotion of the faithful in the Lord, we verily grant to all the faithful who render their alms for the building works of the oft-named church, according to the means available to them, or to those who out of ardent faith and piety join the confraternity to be founded for them, an indulgence of one year and forty days and one quarantine [fasting period], and we release them from the sins they have forgotten to confess, from broken vows if they have repented, from offences to fathers and mothers if no violence was committed, from forgotten and poorly performed penances, from oaths sworn rashly and without restraint, from lies and false talk, whether spoken in jest or in goodness, and also from tithes that have been withheld in ignorance, this on the authority of the almighty God, of his glorious Mother Mary and the pious and blessed confessor Martin, our patron saint; and we wish you parish fathers to bear witness of this with us.

Moreover we decree that any who have kept in their possession any form of unlawfully acquired goods, whether from plunder, theft or usury, and are now desirous to make recompense to God insofar as they are able, but perhaps do not know to whom they should make restitution of these goods, wherefore with pious intentions they transfer them to the fabric of our mother church, shall on the aforementioned authority be fully and completely absolved in these matters; and we order you, priests, to induce your subordinates all the more to do this, admonishing them to make to themselves friends with the said mammon of unrighteousness in order that they may be received after death into everlasting habitations [after Luke 16:9].

We furthermore wish and diligently urge you in the Lord, on account of the pressing need, to commute periods of fasting and pilgrimages, excepting those to Jerusalem, which you have imposed or shall impose on your subordinates, and also vows, by whomsoever they be made, concerning which you are called to give counsel, into a redemption of commensurate size in support of the said church fabric.

For these things we verily grant, by virtue of the authority vested in us by God, to all who come on Maundy Thursday and on the day of the dedication of this same church, that is the feast of Mary Magdalene, until the octave of both feast days, to the oft-mentioned mother church on account of their piety and who give their alms at these times, for each one of the said feasts an indulgence of one year and forty days and one quarantine, together with all the indulgences and benefits that have been granted by the venerable cardinals, legates, archbishops and bishops who were present at the dedication of this church.

Moreover we confirm all other indulgences that anyone whomsoever has conferred on this church or that shall be dispensed in our diocese, as described in letters patent to be shown to you, in order that they may bring all those who are settled in our diocese everlasting happiness; and if certain churches have been placed under interdict by us or by our subordinates, then they may upon the joyous arrival of these great benefits, except where such interdict is by name, be opened and rejoice in the divine services, as often as the said work shall be promoted there.

We have also decreed that every priest in our diocese, both regular and secular, shall celebrate two masses each month, one for all the living and one for all the deceased brothers and sisters who have been benefactors to our church and who have joined the confraternity out of ardent faith, whom we wish also to be rewarded in this world in such manner, that if the churches to which they belong have been placed under interdict on our authority or on that of our subordinates and if they should die during that time, except where such interdict is by name they shall be granted an official church burial and the people thereabouts shall be called on to pray for them with humility and devotion.

To you rural deans of the congregations of Christians, we prescribe on pain of the aforementioned penalty that within your deaneries you order all these of our established decrees to be steadfastly observed by your subordinates, on pain of excommunication.

Additionally, for the priests and clerics who labour faithfully in this matter, to any who have out of weakness or negligence or forgetfulness been remiss in performing their ecclesiastical duties during the mass or the canonical hours, provided that they have made repentant confession, we have in fatherly compassion deemed it fitting to grant merciful pardon.

We also earnestly ask and prescribe that you render every comfort and every manner of hospitality in your homes and monasteries to the messengers of Saint Martin, bearers of these documents, out of reverence for the blessed Martin and on account of the obedience due us, lest by chance whilst staying in the homes of laypersons or in inns these messengers and their business should be brought into disrepute.

Do thusly in these things, in order that we may praise your devotion in the Lord as befits its merits.

Additionally, to fortify your munificence in respect of the said church, and wishing to add grace to grace and virtue to virtue, we shall give you to share in every good thing that passes in our diocese.

Done at Utrecht in the year of our Lord's Incarnation the twelve hundred eighty-eighth on the day of the Nativity of the blessed Virgin.

APPENDIX FIVE

CHURCH INVENTORY ITEMS FUNDED BY THE FABRIC OF UTRECHT CATHEDRAL, 1400-1576

The following list is mainly restricted to inventory items that were fully or partially funded by the cathedral fabric treasury and which laid a relatively heavy burden on the fabric's budget. For a complete overview, see De Groot 2006. All amounts are rounded off and converted into annual wages of the building lodge assistant.

1400/01
CAMPANA CRUCIS, RE-CAST HOLY CROSS BELL, WEIGHING 1397 POUNDS
Source Fabric accounts; *Bronnen bouwgeschiedenis*, vol. 2 (1), p. 74.
Literature Van der Hegge Zijnen 1925, p. 29; Van der Elst 1929, p. 18; Van den Hul 1982, pp. 18, 25.
Cost 457 lb. worth 8 wit (c. 2 ½ annual wages).

1406-1408
NOVA ORNAMENTA RUBEA: SIX COPES, ONE CHASUBLE, TWO TUNICS, THREE ALBS AND ACCOMPANYING STOLES AND MANIPLES
Source Prebenda defunctorum accounts; *Bronnen bouwgeschiedenis*, vol. 2 (1), pp. 283-287; also *Inventaris Archief kapittel ten Dom*, mss 2506 and 2507.
Maker Jacobus Botterman, supplies embroidered borders.
Cost 1788 gulden worth 30 wit (c. 37 ½ annual wages).

1405-1409
CAPSA S. *AGNETIS*, GILDED SILVER RELIQUARY SHRINE, FITTED WITH EIGHTEEN STATUETTES OF GILDED SILVER, DONATED BY THE BISHOP AND MEMBERS OF THE CHAPTER
Source Inventaris Archief kapittel ten Dom, no. 2507 (*capsa* administration account), no. 418 (indulgence of 13 August 1418); Heeringa 1932, p. 33 (1408-1409); Dodt van Flensburg 1838-1848, vol. 1, p. 259; Buchelius 1906, p. 177.
Literature Van den Bergh-Hoogterp 1990, pp. 216-217, 389, 697-699; De Groot 1994, p. 54; De Groot 2006, p. 52.
Cost Unknown.
Note On 2 September 1418 the bones of St Agnes were transferred from a wooden case to the gilded shrine, and the indulgence is linked with this event ; see Calkoen 1897-1898, vol. 1, f. 31. The shrine was melted down on 27 February 1578, at which time it was valued at 2210 karolusgulden.

1424/25
YMAGO SIVE PICTURA, IN QUA CONTINETUR CAPUT S. ELISII (painted reliquary containing the head of St Elysius)
Source Waste book of the fabric accounts; *Bronnen bouwgeschiedenis*, vol. 2 (1), p. 198; De Groot 2006, p. 53.
Cost 140 lb. worth 8 wit (c. ½ annual wage).

1424(?)-1434
ORGAN
Source Fabric accounts (payment in one term); *Bronnen bouwgeschiedenis*, vol. 2 (1), p. 197; *Inventaris Archief kapittel ten Dom*, no. 1, vol. 3, f. 24 and no. 533 (bill of receipt).
Literature Vente 1942, pp. 11, 54, 163; Vlam & Vente 1965, p. 247.
Maker Anthonius van Elen, cantor of the basilica of St Servatius in Maastricht.
Cost 534 rhinegulden (c. 7900 lb. worth 8 wit, 1430 exchange rate, c. 25 annual wages), paid in multiple terms.

1424/25-1450(?)
SACRAMENT HOUSE, BEGUN BY THE CATHEDRAL FABRIC; CANON BEERNT UTEN ENGE DONATES THIRTEEN STATUES AND FIVE IRON LATTICES
Source Fabric accounts 1424/25, 1443/44, 1450/51; *Bronnen bouwgeschiedenis*, vol. 2 (1), pp. 194, 236, 257, 259; *Inventaris Archief kapittel ten Dom*, no. 2513 (contract of 1442).
Literature *Obreen's Archief voor Nederlandsche Kunstgeschiedenis*, vol. 5, p. 9; Haslinghuis & Peeters 1965, p. 360; De Groot 1994, p. 48; De Groot 2006, pp. 50-51.
Makers Master Heynric van Boutsvoort, architect; Jan Bude, sculptor; Willem Koernken, locksmith.
Cost Canon Uten Enge finances statues at a sum of 744 gulden worth 30 wit and lattices at 320 gulden worth 30 wit; the cathedral fabric pays 94 gulden for lattices and 19 gulden worth 30 wit for statues (6 ½ annual wages altogether). The production costs are not booked separately in the fabric accounts.

1453-1455
LARGE '*HOIRCLOCK*' (STRIKING CLOCK), WEIGHING 6255 POUNDS
Source *Inventaris Archief kapittel ten Dom*, no. 540 (bill of receipt), no. 605 (cathedral fabric cartulary), f. 58v.
Literature Van der Hegge Zijnen 1925, p. 28; Van der Elst 1929, p. 20 ff.; De Waard *et al.* 1963, pp. 248, 249, 241; Haslinghuis & Peeters 1965, pp. 449-451; Van den Hul 1982, p. 36.
Makers Peter Boyden and Steven Butendiic, bellfounders.
Cost 656 rhinegulden (= 4375 gulden worth 30 wit) (c. 24 annual wages).

1459-1502
FERETRUM S. PONCIANI (reliquary shrine of gilded silver for St Pontian)
Source Fabric accounts 1466/67, *Bronnen bouwgeschiedenis*, vol. 2 (1), p. 410; 1468/69, pp. 439, 445; 1469/70, p. 454; 1473/74, p. 489; 1475/76, pp. 521-531; 1476/77, p. 538; 1477/78, p. 548; 1489/90, *Bronnen bouwgeschiedenis*, vol. 2 (2), p. 290; 1490/91, p. 311; 1494/95, p. 395 ff.; 1495/96, p. 421; 1496/97, p. 453; 1497/98, pp. 480, 482; 1498/99, p. 506; 1499/1500, p. 534; 1502/03, p. 620; 1504/05, p. 663. See also *Bronnen bouwgeschiedenis*, vol. 2 (1), pp. 463, 475, 505-572, vol. 2 (2), p. 213; Brom 1900, pp. 238 ff., 249 ff. (sacristy inventory); Dodt van Flensburg 1838-1848, vol. 1, p. 259; Buchelius 1906, p. 177: '*Pontiani loculum, vix quattor ferebant viri, ex puro argento*'.
Literature Van den Bergh-Hoogterp 1990, pp. 212, 218-239, 700; De Groot 1994, p. 54; De Groot 2006, p. 52.
Makers Tideman IJsbrantsz. and Abel van der Vechte, goldsmiths.
Cost 2181 rhinegulden current, not counting gifts in gold and silver from the canons (c. 70 annual wages).
Note The shrine was melted down on 23 February 1578, yielding 4344 karolusgulden.

c. 1460/61
HOROLOGIUM (clock)
Source Fabric accounts; *Bronnen bouwgeschiedenis*, vol. 2 (1), p. 355.
Literature Haslinghuis & Peeters 1965, p. 451.
Maker Gerard Alardsz.
Cost Unknown, the last payment was for 391 gulden worth 30 wit (c. 2 annual wages).

1463/64
CANDLEHOLDERS IN FRONT OF THE HIGH ALTAR
Source Fabric accounts; *Bronnen bouwgeschiedenis*, vol. 2 (1), pp. 384, 489.
Literature De Groot 2006, p. 70.
Maker Unnamed '*gheelghieter*' (pewter-melter).

Cost 885 gulden worth 30 wit (c. 4 ½ annual wages).

1471-1476
FIVE *NOVAE CAPPAE LASURINI/BLAVII COLORIS* (new blue copes)
Source Fabric accounts 1471/72, 1472/73, 1475/76; *Bronnen bouwgeschiedenis*, vol. 2 (1), pp. 472, 481, 531, 532; *Inventaris Archief kapittel ten Dom*, no. 2507.
Cost 342 rhinegulden current (c. 14 annual wages).

1479/80
NOVAE CAMPANAE, SCILICET HOROLOGII IN TURRI NOSTRA (new bells, to whit the chimes in our tower)
Source Fabric accounts; *Bronnen bouwgeschiedenis*, vol. 2 (1), p. 562.
Literature Haslinghuis & Peeters 1965, p. 451; Fehrmann 1967, pp. 41, 86, 250; Van den Hul 1982, p. 27.
Maker Gerard van Wou, bellfounder in Kampen.
Cost 350 rhinegulden current (c. 12 ½ annual wages).

1487-1494
ONE CHASUBLE, TWO TUNICS, SIX COPES OF SILK VELVET
Source Fabric accounts 1487/88, 1488/89, 1490/91, 1493/94; *Bronnen bouwgeschiedenis*, vol. 2 (2), pp. 237, 238, 240, 270, 310, 372; *Inventaris Archief kapittel ten Dom*, no. 659 (*prebenda defunctorum* accounts) 1487, f. 8, 1488, f. 5v, f. 6, 1489, f. 4; no. 1 (chapter minutes), vol. 9, f. 112 (16 November 1491); Brom 1900, p. 254 (sacristy inventory).
Supplier Nicolaas Basijn of Antwerp, 101½ ell silk.
Makers Damass de Setten de Dordraco, Gerardus Arnoldi de Buscumducis, Petrus Theodorici, Theodorus Roberti, embroiderers.
Cost c. 1445 rhinegulden current, of which 348 rhinegulden current drawn from the chapter treasury (c. 45 annual wages).

1487-1491
TAPESTRY CYCLE WITH THE HISTORY OF ST MARTIN, IN THE CHOIR
Source Fabric accounts 1487/88, 1488/89, 1490/91; *Bronnen bouwgeschiedenis*, vol. 2 (2), pp. 244, 269, 308.
Literature De Groot 2006, p. 67.
Makers Magister Jodocus die Vos and Petrus Pijll, tapestry makers in Brussels.
Cost 160 rhinegulden current (c. 6 annual wages).

1489-1498
HIGH ALTAR: WOODEN PREDELLA AND PAINTED ALTARPIECE
Source Fabric accounts 1489/90, 1496/97, 1497/98; *Bronnen bouwgeschiedenis*, vol. 2 (2), pp. 281, 291, 453, 477.
Literature Muller 1906, p. 17b; Haslinghuis & Peeters 1965, p. 360; De Groot 1994, p. 48; De Groot 2006, pp. 46-47.
Makers Adriaen van Weesel, sculptor; Jan Aertsz, cabinetmaker; Ernest van Schayck, painter.
Cost Predella: 95 rhinegulden current; altarpiece: 196 rhinegulden current (c. 9 annual wages).
Note The fact that the churchwardens of the Nieuwe Kerk in Delft referred to the high altar of Utrecht Cathedral in their contract with the painter Jan van Scorel (1550) suggests that the whole of this altarpiece, excepting the predella, was also painted.

1499-1501
TWO CANDLEHOLDERS FOR THE HIGH ALTAR, GILDED SILVER
Source Fabric accounts 1499/1500, 1500/01; *Bronnen bouwgeschiedenis*, vol. 2 (1), pp. 557, 558.
Literature Van den Bergh-Hoogterp 1990, pp. 244-245; De Groot 2006, p. 70.
Maker Abel van der Vechte, goldsmith.
Cost 417 rhinegulden current (c. 13 annual wages).
Note Cf. Brom 1900, p. 267 (sacristy inventory), '*septem*

candelabra argentea in parte deaurata facta expensis ecclesie anno 1501 [...] simul 954 floreni aurei'; the fabric accounts do not record all expenditures related to this purchase.

1500-1511

NOVA ORNAMENTA IN HONOREM NOSTRE DOMINE, PARAMENTS COMMISSIONED ON THE CHAPTER'S ORDERS, WHITE DAMASK

Source Fabric accounts 1500/01 (482 rhinegulden current, white damask), 1501/02 (c. 200 rhinegulden current, also for borders), 1502/03 (716 rhinegulden current, primarily for borders), 1503/04 (264 rhinegulden current, also for *nolae* and curtains), 1510/11 (damask embroidery); *Bronnen bouwgeschiedenis*, vol. 2 (2), pp. 561, 582, 620, 639, 640, vol. 2 (3), pp. 136, 141.
Literature De Bodt 1991, pp. 9,12, 28.
Maker Jacob van Malboirch, embroiderer.
Cost c. 1803 rhinegulden current (c. 58 annual wages).

1500/01

THREE STOLES, THREE MANIPLES, ALBS AND AMICES, TO ACCOMPANY THE RED COPES (see 1487-1494)

Source Fabric accounts; *Bronnen bouwgeschiedenis*, vol. 2 (2), p. 555 ff.; Brom 1900, p. 254 (sacristy inventory).
Literature De Bodt 1991, p. 28.
Makers Petrus Theodrici, Jacob van Malboirch, embroiderers; Anthonius de Corcellis supplies the fabric.
Cost c. 260 rhinegulden current (c. 8 annual wages).

1500-1522

CHOIR STALLS, NEVER MADE

Source Fabric accounts 1500/01, 1501/02, 1505/06, 1508/09, 1509/10, 1517/18, 1520/21, 1521/22; *Bronnen bouwgeschiedenis*, vol. 2 (2), pp. 561, 580, 680 ff., 698; vol. 2 (3), pp. 60, 87, 88, 38S, 386, 501, 505, 508, 510, 537.
Literature Vroom 1964, passim; Sterk 1980, p. 131.
Maker Jan Gossaert van Mabuse, painter and draughtsman.
Cost c. 875 rhinegulden current (c. 28 annual wages).

1500-1502

CURTAINS FOR LENT, IN THE CHOIR

Source Fabric accounts 1500/01 ('*tafftaff*', silk), 1501/02, 1502/03 ('*pannus lineus cum floribus*'); *Bronnen bouwgeschiedenis*, vol. 2 (2), pp. 561, 583, 614; Brom 1900, p. 258 (sacristy inventory), '*4 cortinee linee nove satis presiose ad modum damasti, facte pro quadragesima pro summo altari*'.
Literature De Groot 2006, n. 337.
Supplier Flemish nuns in Antwerp.
Cost 454 rhinegulden current (c. 15 annual wages).

1501/02

TWO *BACULI S. CRUCIS, UTENDI CIRCA FESTA PASCHALIA* (poles to carry the processional crosses used at Eastertide)

Source Fabric accounts; *Bronnen bouwgeschiedenis*, vol. 2 (2), p. 582. Brom 1900, p. 264 (sacristy inventory), '*5 baculi cum argento vestiti, quorum duo noviter facti sunt*'.
Literature Van den Bergh-Hoogterp 1990, p. 245.
Maker Abel van der Vechte, goldsmith.
Cost 188 rhinegulden current (c. 6 annual wages).

1501-1503

FERETRUM IN DEPORTATIONE VENERABILIS SACRAMENTI (gilded wooden litter for the Blessed Sacrament)

Source Fabric accounts 1501/02, 1502/03; *Bronnen bouwgeschiedenis*, vol. 2 (2), pp. 573, 618.
Makers Henrick Bontmaker and Jacop van Ghenderen, woodcarvers; Th. Schaey, painter.
Cost 94 rhinegulden current (3 annual wages).

1502/03
PICTURA ET DEAURATIO YMAGINIS S. JOANNIS BAPTISTE, IN NAVI ECCLESIE AD PILERNUM STANS
(polychroming of the statue of St John the Baptist, at a pier in the nave)
Source Fabric accounts; *Bronnen bouwgeschiedenis*, vol. 2 (2), p. 618.
Maker Th. Schaey, painter.
Cost 60 rhinegulden current (c. 2 annual wages).

1502-1504
TAPESTRIES WITH THE LAST JUDGEMENT AND '*CUM YMAGINE S. MARTINI*', BOTH IN THE SMALL CHAPTER ROOM
Source Fabric accounts 1502/03, 1503/04; *Bronnen bouwgeschiedenis*, vol. 2 (2), pp. 596, 612, 639.
Maker Henricus de Rossem, tapestry maker.
Cost 120 rhinegulden current (c. 4 annual wages).

1502-1509
COPPER GATE FOR THE HOLY SEPULCHRE
Source Fabric accounts 1502/03 (31 rhinegulden current), 1506/07 (242 rhinegulden current), 1508/09 (44 rhinegulden current); *Bronnen bouwgeschiedenis*, vol. 2 (2), pp. 602, 751, 764, 766, vol. 2 (3), p. 69.
Literature Haverkorn van Rijsewijk 1900-1901, passim; De Groot 1994, p. 59; De Groot 2006, p. 95.
Makers Claes Egberts, sculptor (design, '*patroen*'); Master Willem Looman of Ordingen near Krefeld, blacksmith.
Cost c. 320 rhinegulden current (c. 10 annual wages).
Note The Holy Sepulchre itself was made in 1500/01 and 1502/03; the sculptor Gerrit Splinters was employed for a daily wage of 6 stuivers. In 1506/07 Master Arnoldus, *lapicida*, produced statues and appurtenances for 43 rhinegulden current. It is possible that canons donated a few individual statues.

1504-1514
THIRTEEN BELLS, OF WEIGHTS VARYING FROM 296 KG TO 8222 ½ KG, TOTALLING WITH THE TONGUES 32,045 KG
Source Fabric accounts 1504/05 (1348 rhinegulden current), 1505/06 (2544 rhinegulden current), 1506/07 (183 rhinegulden current), 1507/08 (781 rhinegulden current), 1508/09 (466 rhinegulden current), 1510/11 and 1511/12 (207 rhinegulden current for installing the bells), 1513/14 (420 rhinegulden current for installing the bells and the clock); *Bronnen bouwgeschiedenis*, vol. 2 (2), pp. 664, 667, 689 ff., 757, 765, vol. 2(3), pp. 32, 63, 138, 166, 218, 238.
Literature Van der Hegge Zijnen 1925, p. 33; Van der Elst 1929, p. 33 ff.; Van Asch van Wijck 1850-1853, vol. 1, pp. 155, 159, 212, 215; Fehrmann 1967, pp. 86 ff., 275 ff.; Haslinghuis & Peeters 1965, p. 447 ff; Van den Hul 1982, pp. 27-34.
Maker Gerrit van Wou, bellfounder from Kampen.
Cost c. 5950 rhinegulden current (c. 190 annual wages).

1504-1509
EMBROIDERED BORDERS, ON VARIOUS PARAMENTS
Source Fabric accounts 1504/05 (84 rhinegulden current), 1506/07 (74 rhinegulden current, *cum legenda et vita b. Marie Magdalene*), 1507/08 (165 rhinegulden current, borders on red tunics), 1508/09 (54 rhinegulden current, 6 borders on 3 albs); *Bronnen bouwgeschiedenis*, vol. 2 (2), pp. 663, 667, 767, vol. 2 (3), pp. 33, 67.
Literature De Bodt 1991, p. 28.
Maker Jacob van Malboirch, embroiderer.
Cost 337 rhinegulden current (c. 11 annual wages).

1504-1506
BLACK PARAMENTS, EMBELLISHED WITH GOLD THREAD

Source Fabric accounts 1504/05 and 1505/06; *Bronnen bouwgeschiedenis*, vol. 2 (2), pp. 664, 704.
Cost 251 rhinegulden current, possibly plus 136 rhinegulden current for gold thread (c. 12 annual wages).
Note These paraments were financed from the bequest of Canon Gerlacus van der Donck.

1504-1507
ANTEPENDIUM, WHITE DAMASK WITH AND WITHOUT GOLD FLOWERS
Source Fabric accounts 1504/05 (98 rhinegulden current), 1506/07 (34 rhinegulden current, borders on white damask and other deliveries); *Bronnen bouwgeschiedenis*, vol. 2 (2), pp. 664, 764.
Maker Jacob *'die wapenstick-er'* (the embroiderer of escutcheons) (that is Van Malboirch).
Cost c. 132 rhinegulden current (c. 4 annual wages).

1507/08
CAPUT S. ADRIANI (silver reliquary for the head of St Adrian)
Source Fabric accounts 1507/08 (478 rhinegulden current); *Bronnen bouwgeschiedenis*, vol. 2 (3), p. 33, also pp. 210, 237; *Inventaris Archief kapittel ten Dom*, no. 2509 (commissioning contract 16 August 1504, labour: between 80 and 125 gold rhinegulden (between 140 and 218 ½ rhinegulden current)); Dodt van Flensburg 1838-1848, vol. 1, pp. 259-260.
Literature Van den Bergh-Hoogterp 1990, pp. 211, 222; De Groot 2006, p. 53.
Maker Abel van der Vechte, goldsmith.
Cost At least 478 rhinegulden current, possibly partially paid in kind (c. 15 annual wages).
Note The reliquary was melted down in April 1578, yielding 1360 karolusgulden.

1512/13
RELIQUARY, ST BLAISE
Source Fabric accounts; *Bronnen bouwgeschiedenis*, vol. 2 (3), p. 203; see also 1514/15 (payment of 56 rhinegulden current), idem, p. 273.
Literature Van den Bergh-Hoogterp 1990, p. 246.
Maker Abel van der Vechte, goldsmith.
Cost 92 rhinegulden current, possibly plus 56 rhinegulden current (c. 5 annual wages altogether).

1515-1517
ANTIPHONARY, SUMMER PART
Source Fabric accounts 1515/16 and 1516/17; *Bronnen bouwgeschiedenis*, vol. 2 (3), pp. 312, 349.
Maker Henricus de Roy *'pro pergameno, scriptura, floratura et ligatura'*.
Cost 87 rhinegulden current (c. 2½ annual wages).

1516-1518
GOLD BORDERS, ON COPES
Source Fabric accounts 1516/17 and 1517/18; *Bronnen bouwgeschiedenis*, vol. 2 (3), pp. 350, 424.
Literature De Bodt 1991, p. 29.
Maker Jacob van Malboirch, embroiderer.
Cost 247 rhinegulden current (c. 8 annual wages).

1517/18
LATTICES FOR THE HOUSE OF ST PONTIAN
Source Fabric accounts; *Bronnen bouwgeschiedenis*, vol. 2 (3), pp. 360, 371.
Literature De Groot 2006, p. 52.
Maker Henric van Bemmel, spurrier.
Cost 163 rhinegulden current (c. 5 annual wages).
Note The house of St Pontian – a stone reliquary shrine inside the cathedral – was financed from the fabric treasury without itemization of the costs; the first stone was laid in 1516/17; *Bronnen bouwgeschiedenis*, vol. 2 (3), p. 326.

1517-1523
COPPER GATE FOR THE INDULGENCE ALTAR, NEVER MADE
Source Fabric accounts 1517/18, 1518/19, 1519/20, 1520/21, 1521/22, 1522/23; *Bronnen bouwgeschiedenis*, vol. 2 (3), pp. 369, 371, 385, 410, 411, 430, 431, 549 (not in Coster), 463, 464, 465, 467, 507, 538, 547, 581, 582.
Literature Coster 1909, pp. 215-217; Van Rappard 1881-1882, passim; Sterk 1980, pp. 46-47, 131-132, 290 n. 10; De Groot 2006, pp. 92-93.
Makers Jan van Eynde, Gregorius Wellemans and others.
Cost 890 rhinegulden current (c. 28 annual wages).

1517-1519
THREE METAL UNICORNS, USED AS CANDLEHOLDERS
Source Fabric accounts 1517/18, 1518/19; *Bronnen bouwgeschiedenis*, vol. 2 (3), pp. 366, 372, 421.
Literature Van den Bergh-Hoogterp 1990, p. 247; De Groot 2006, p. 71.
Makers The 'meyster van Mechelen', that is Jan van Eynde, copper founder; Abel van der Vechte, goldsmith.
Cost 567 rhinegulden current (c. 8 annual wages).

1519-1526
BISHOPS' PORTRAITS, IN THE CHOIR
Source Fabric accounts 1519/20 (4 or 8 portraits?), 1520/21 ('2 *parcken van der memorien der bisscoppen Willems van Mechelen myt syn gesellen*'), 1524/25 ('*twee biscopen als Baden ende Philips van Bourgongen*'), 1525/26; *Bronnen bouwgeschiedenis*, vol. 2 (3), pp. 446, 447, 449, 453, 454, 486, 642, 664, 667, 668; see also fabric accounts 1533/34, f. 15 and 1567/68, under October expenditures.
Literature Muller 1906, p. 13; Sterk 1980, p. 89; De Groot 2006, pp. 121-123.
Makers Splinter van Nyewenroede; Goyert '*die scilder*' (the painter).
Cost c. 105 rhinegulden current (c. 3 ½ annual wages).
Note No entries have been found in the fabric accounts for the other bishops' portraits.

1521/22-1524/25
HEAD OF ST BLAISE: SILVER RELIQUARY
Source Fabric accounts; *Bronnen bouwgeschiedenis*, vol. 2 (3), pp. 544, 550, 551, 653; Dodt van Flensburg 1838-1848, vol. 1, p. 258.
Literature Van den Bergh-Hoogterp 1990, p. 247; De Groot 2006, p. 53.
Maker Abel van der Vechte, goldsmith.
Cost 279 rhinegulden current (c. 9 annual wages).
Note This reliquary was melted down in February 1578, yielding 479 karolusgulden.

1521/22
BENCHES IN THE LARGE CHAPTERHOUSE
Source Fabric accounts; *Bronnen bouwgeschiedenis*, vol. 2 (3), pp. 531, 548, 649.
Literature Haslinghuis & Peeters 1965, p. 481.
Makers Claes van Esbroeck, sculptor; Godefridus de Greeff, painter; Jan van Oey, boxmaker.
Cost 144 rhinegulden current (c. 4 ½ annual wages).

1524/25
BORDERS ON PARAMENTS
Source Fabric accounts; *Bronnen bouwgeschiedenis*, vol. 2 (3), pp. 650, 651.
Literature De Bodt 1991, p. 29.
Maker Jacob van Malboirch, embroiderer.
Cost 143 rhinegulden current (c. 4 ½ annual wages).

1535/36
TWO COPES
Source Fabric accounts, f. 72.
Cost 60 rhinegulden current, the velvet only (c. 1½ annual wages).

1538/39
CANCELLI FERREI ANTE RELIQUIAS S. PONTIANI (iron lattices for the relics of St Pontian)
Source Fabric accounts, f. 193, 197, 198.
Literature De Groot 2006, p. 52.
Makers Henrick van Bemmel, spurrier; Cornelis Gerardi, *pictor*.
Cost 77 rhinegulden current (c. 2 annual wages).

1544/45
EIGHT STONE STATUES ON THE EAST PORTAL
Source Fabric accounts, under monthly schedules for July and f. 453v.
Literature Swillens, *Jaarboekje van Oud-Utrecht*, 1950, pp. 72-73.
Makers Rijck van Beest, sculptor (18½ karolusgulden); Johannes Block, *pictor* (32½ karolusgulden).
Cost 51 karolusgulden (64 rhinegulden current) (c. 1½ annual wages).

1556-1563
WOODEN CHOIR STALLS
Source Fabric accounts 1556/57, f. 278v (240 karolusgulden), 1558/59, f. 328 (53 karolusgulden), 1559/60, f. 349 (14 karolusgulden), 1562/63, f. 50 ff. (905 karolusgulden); *Inventaris Archief kapittel ten Dom*, no. 1, vol. 18. Separate document, bill of receipt drawn up by Anthonisz. Peters on 1 March 1564 for the receipt of 800 karolusgulden; idem, no. 513.
Literature Haslinghuis & Peeters 1965, pp. 351-352; De Groot 2006, pp. 57-60.
Maker Thonis. Petersz, cabinetmaker.
Cost 1212 karolusgulden (1515 rhinegulden current) (c. 39 annual wages).

1560/61
PARAMENTS OF BLACK SILK, INCLUDING THREE CHASUBLES, TWO DALMATICS, TWO COPES
Source Fabric accounts, f. 375; *Inventaris Archief kapittel ten Dom*, no. 1, vol. 17, f. 136v.
Supplier Fabric purchased in Antwerp, partially exchanged.
Cost 190 karolusgulden (238 rhinegulden current) (c. 6 annual wages).

1563/64
PARAMENTS FOR THE MASS OF THE BLESSED SACRAMENT, RED SILK CHASUBLE AND DALMATICS
Source Fabric accounts, f. 81.
Supplier Textile purchased in Antwerp.
Cost 239 karolusgulden (299 rhinegulden current) (c. 7½ annual wages).

1568-1574
ORGAN, TWENTY-FIVE STOPS, SIX BELLOWS
Source Fabric accounts 1568/69 (230 karolusgulden), 1569/70 (170 karolusgulden), 1570/71 (768 karolusgulden), 1571/72 (1055 karolusgulden), 1573/74 (100 karolusgulden); Buchelius 1906, p. 177.
Literature Vente 1942, pp. 26, 36, 80, 164; Vlam & Vente 1965, p. 258 ff.; Haslinghuis & Peeters 1965, pp. 272, 354; De Groot 1994, p. 63; De Groot 2006, pp. 96-97.
Makers Peter Jansz. de Swart, organ maker; the Van Schayck brothers, painters; and others.
Cost c. 2333 karolusgulden (2916 rhinegulden current) (c. 75 annual wages).
Note Buchelius cites: '*organicum […] summis sumptubus aere archipresbiteri Cornelii Miropii perfectum*'; contributions from the provost Myerop appear nowhere in the accounts.

1575/76
IRONWORK ON THE SMALL BELLS OF THE CHIMES
Source Fabric accounts, under February expenditures.
Cost 106 karolusgulden (133 rhinegulden current) (c. 3½ annual wages).

APPENDIX SIX

CHURCH INVENTORY ITEMS FUNDED BY THE FABRIC OF THE BUURKERK, 1420-1566

The following list is restricted to inventory items that laid a relatively heavy burden on the budget of the fabric. See also Bogaers 2008, pp. 827-832 (Appendix five) and pp. 390-392. Objects made of precious metal, such as the statue of the Virgin Mary (1529), are not included here as the silver, gold and precious stones that went into making them were donated; Van den Bergh-Hoogterp 1990, pp. 353-365, 721-726. All amounts are rounded off and converted into annual wages of the Utrecht Cathedral building lodge assistant. For the churchwardens' accounts, see *Catalogussen archief stad Utrecht, tweede afdeeling*, no. 47.

1420
STONE SACRAMENT HOUSE
Source Churchwardens' accounts; Van Rappard 1880, pp. 28-30.
Cost 37 rhinegulden current (c. 4 annual wages).

1456-1463
SEVENTEEN POLYCHROME STONE STATUES ON THE NAVE PIERS
Source Churchwardens' accounts; Van Rappard 1880, pp. 156, 160-163.
Literature Haakma Wagenaar 1935, pp. 42 n. 1, 72 n. 1; Bouvy 1947, pp. 72, 74.
Makers Jacob van der Borch, architect and sculptor; Willam Tonsz. and Hilbrant *'die maelre'*, polychromers.
Cost c. 350 rhinegulden current (c. 14 annual wages).

1466
CHASUBLE, TUNIC AND DALMATIC
Source Churchwardens' accounts; Van Rappard 1880, pp. 165, 166.
Maker Claes Pagant van Brug, supplies borders.
Cost 157 rhinegulden current (c. 6 annual wages).

1468-1473
ORGAN
Source Churchwardens' accounts; Van Rappard 1880, pp. 169, 172, 174, 177, 179.
Literature Muller 1900, p. 213; Vente 1942, pp. 78, 166.
Maker Master Peter, organ maker.
Cost c. 530 rhinegulden current (c. 21 annual wages).

1493, 1496, 1497, 1499
ROOD LOFT, 34 COPPER COLUMNS ON WOODEN BASES WITH CRUCIFIXION GROUP
Source Churchwardens' accounts; Van Rappard 1880, pp. 205-212, 223.
Literature Muller 1900, pp. 206-208; Haakma Wagenaar 1935, p. 248.
Makers Henrick Bontmaker, woodcarver; Gijsbert van Laer, copper founder; and others.
Cost c. 520 rhinegulden current (c. 16½ annual wages).

1522-1525
SACRAMENT HOUSE, REFURBISHMENT
Source Churchwardens' accounts 1522, f. 25v, 26; 1523, f. 24v; 1524, f. 22; 1525, f. 23v.
Maker Claes van Esbroeck, stonecutter.
Cost c. 1124 rhinegulden current (c. 36 annual wages).

1533
CRIMSON RED PARAMENTS, CHASUBLE, TWO DALMATICS, THREE COPES AND AN ANTEPENDIUM
Source Churchwardens' accounts 1533, f. 25, also 1530, f. 25v; *Catalogussen archief stad Utrecht, tweede afdeeling*, no. 49.

Literature Van den Berg-Hoogterp 1990, p. 145.
Maker Cornelis van der Goude supplies borders; fabric purchased in Antwerp; also payments to several goldsmiths.
Cost c. 1125 rhinegulden current (in total) (c. 29 annual wages).
Note Approximately half the costs were paid from the fabric treasury, the remaining half by donors whose coats of arms were applied on the items; recorded in separate accounts.

1534-1542
ST MICHAEL BELL AND LADY BELL
Source Churchwardens' accounts 1534, f. 23 ff.; 1542, f. 21.
Literature Haakma Wagenaar 1935, pp. 161, 320, 333, 342, 370-371; De Waard *et al.* 1963, pp. 266-267; Van den Hul 1982, pp. 52-54.
Maker Master Jan Tolhuys *'die clockgieter'* (the bellfounder).
Cost c. 600 rhinegulden current (c. 15 annual wages).
Note The St Michael bell had to be re-cast in 1542.

1542-1543
PARAMENTS OF WHITE DAMASK, CHASUBLE, TWO DALMATICS, THREE COPES AND AN ANTEPENDIUM
Source Churchwardens' accounts 1542, f. 21v; 1543, f. 21 (?).
Maker Reyer, embroiderer; damask purchased in Antwerp.
Cost Probably c. 410 rhinegulden current (c. 10½ annual wages).

1543-1549
ORGAN
Source Churchwardens' accounts 1543, f. 21 ff.; 1544, f. 26v; 1545, f. 22v ff.; 1546, f. 23v; 1547, f. 23v; 1548, f. 23v; 1549, f. 23v ff.
Literature Haakma Wagenaar 1935, p. 335; Vente 1942, pp. 79-167.
Maker Master Cornelis Gerritz., organ maker.
Cost c. 930 rhinegulden current (c. 24 annual wages).

1545
ST SALVATOR BELL
Source Churchwardens' accounts, f. 23v.
Literature Van den Hul 1982, p. 53.
Cost c. 180 rhinegulden current (c. 4½ annual wages).
Note The bell was purchased.

No large sums were spent on furnishing the Buurkerk between 1549 and 1566, the latter being the year of the Iconoclasm.

ARCHIVES

The locations of the archives consulted for this book are provided in the notes. The bibliography lists those archive inventories that have been published.

BELGIUM

Antwerp, Stadsarchief: archives of the collegiate church of Our Lady
Antwerp, archives of the church of St James
Liège, Archives de l'Évèché

GERMANY

Karlsruhe, Badisches Generallandesarchiv: Konstanz Cathedral

ENGLAND

Exeter, Cathedral Archives
London, British Museum, Add. mss 15083: Troyes Cathedral
Wells, Cathedral Archives

FRANCE

Auxerre, Archives départementales de l'Yonne, série G: Sens Cathedral
Clermont-Ferrand, Bibliothèque municipale et universitaire, ms. 634
Clermont-Ferrand, Archives départementales du Puy-de-Dóme, série G
Lille, Archives départementales du Nord, série G: Cambrai Cathedral
Lyon, Archives départementales du Rhóne, série G
Paris, Archives Nationales, LL. 270: Notre Dame
Paris, Bibliothèque Nationale, ms. lat. 5529 B: Autun Cathedral and ms. lat. 9111 and 9113: Troyes Cathedral
Perpignan, Archives départementales des Pyrénées-Orientales, série G: Elne Cathedral
Rodez, Archives Départementales de l'Aveyron, série G
Rouen, Archives départementales de la Seine-Maritimc (previously Seine-Inférieure), série G
Strasbourg, Archives de la ville de Strasbourg: Strasbourg Cathedral
Vannes, Archives départementales du Morbihan, série G

THE NETHERLANDS

Alkmaar, Regionaal Archief Alkmaar: church of St Lawrence
Haarlem, Noord-Hollands Archief: church of St Bavo
Hoorn, Westfries Archief: civic accounts
Leiden, Regionaal Archief Leiden: church of St Peter
Utrecht, Het Utrechts Archief: archives of the cathedral chapter and the Buurkerk

SPAIN

Gerona, Archivo catedralicio
Huesca, Archivo de la Catedral
Valencia, Archivo capitular de la catedral de Valencia

SWITZERLAND

Basel, Staatsarchiv: Domstift

BIBLIOGRAPHY

A

ABAJO MARTÍN 1986 Abajo Martín, T., *Documentación de la catedral de Palencia (1035-1247)*, Palencia 1986.

ABOU-EL-HAJ 1988 Abou-El-Haj, B., 'The urban setting for late medieval church building : Reims and its cathedral between 1210 and 1240', *Art History* 11 (1988), no. 1, 17-41.

ABOU-EL-HAJ 1997 Abou-El-Haj, B., 'Santiago de Compostela in the Time of Diego Gelmírez', *Gesta* 36 (1997), no. 2, 165-179.

Achthundert Jahre Verehrung der heiligen drei Könige in Köln 1164-1964, *Kölner Domblatt* 23-24 (1964).

Acta Stephani Langton, Cantuariensis archiepiscopi A.D. 1207-1228, Oxford 1950.

ADAM 1964 Adam, P., *La vie paroissiale en France au XIVe siècle*, Paris 1964.

ADRIAANSE 1930/1932 Adriaanse, J., 'Het Hulstersche kerkgebouw, zijn bediening en zijn bedienaars in den loop der eeuwen', *Jaarboek van de Oudheidkundige Kring De Vier Ambachten*, 1930, 61-83, 1932, 65-95.

Ad Summum 1248, Der gotische Dom im Mittelalter. Ausstellung des Historischen Archivs der Stadt Köln aus Anlaß der Grundsteinlegung des Kölner Doms vor 750 Jahren, Cologne 1998.

AIRD 1993 Aird, W.M., 'The making of a medieval miracle collection : The Liber de Translationibus et Miraculis Sancti Cuthberti', *Northern History* 29 (1993), 1-24.

AIT & VAQUERO PIÑEIRO 2000 Ait, I. & M. Vaquero Piñeiro, *Dai casali alla fabbrica di San Pietro : I Leni : uomini d'affari del Rinascimento*, Rome 2000.

AJO GONZÁLEZ 1962 Ajo González, C., *Historia de la Iglesia en la hispanidad: Avila*, vol. 1, *Fuentes y archivos*, Madrid 1962.

ÁLAMO BERZOSA 1968 Álamo Berzosa, G., *Iglesia catedral de Jaen, historia e imagen*, Jaen 1968.

ALBERTS 1954 Alberts, W. Jappe, 'Leveranties van steen uit het Rijnland voor de dombouw te Utrecht en tolheffing op de Rijn, in W. Jappe Alberts & F. Ketner, *Nederrijnse studiën* XIIIe-XVe *eeuw*, Groningen 1954, 1-48.

ALBERTS 1962 Alberts, W. Jappe, 'De verering van Sint Eusebius', *Archief voor de geschiedenis van de Katholieke Kerk in Nederland* 4 (1962), 1-10.

ALBERTS 1966 Alberts, W. Jappe, *Geschiedenis van Gelderland van de vroegste tijden tot het einde der middeleeuwen*, The Hague 1966.

ALFORD & SMITH 1969 Alford, B.W.E. & M.O. Smith, 'The economic effects of cathedral and church building in medieval England: a reply, *Explorations in entrepreneurial history* 6 (1969), 158-169.

ALLAN 1874-1888 Allan, F., *Geschiedenis en beschrijving van Haarlem*, 4 vols, Haarlem 1874-1888.

ALMUNI I BALADA 1991 Almuni i Balada, V., *L'obra de la Seu de Tortosa (1345-1441)*, Tortosa 1991.

ALMUNI I BALADA 2007 Almuni i Balada, V., *La catedral de Tortosa als segles del gòtic*, vols 1 & 2, Barcelona 2007.

ALTET 1986 Altet, X.B.I. (ed.), *Artistes, artisans et production artistique au Moyen-Âge*, vol. 1, Paris 1986.

ÁLVAREZ DE FRUTOS 1988 Álvarez de Frutos, P., *La revolución comunera en tierras de Segovia*, Segovia 1988.

ÁLVAREZ MÁRQUEZ 1990 Álvarez Márquez, C., 'Notas para la historia de la

Catedral de Sevilla en el primer tercio des siglo XV', *Laboratorio de Arte* 3 (1990), 11-32.

AMBERG 1982 Amberg, G., *Ceremoniale Coloniense : Die Feier des Gottesdienstes durch das Stiftskapitel an der Hohen Domkirche zu Köln bis zum Ende der Reichsstädtischen Zeit*, Siegburg 1982.

AMBERG 1989 Amberg, G., 'Eine Läuteordnung des Domes und Aufzeichnungen über die Beleuchtung im Dom zu den einzelnen Gottesdiensten aus dem Jahre 1580', *Kölner Domblatt* 54 (1989), 73-88.

AMIET 1922 Amiet, L., *Essai sur l'organisation du chapitre cathédral de Chartres du XIe au XVIIIe siècle*, Chartres 1922.

AMIET 1923 Amiet, L., 'La juridiction privilegiée spirituelle du chapitre cathédral de Chartres', *Revue historique de droit français et étranger* 2 (1923), 210-272.

ANGENENDT *et al.* 1995 Angenendt, A. *et al.*, 'Gezählte Frömmigkeit', *Frühmittelalterliche Studien : Jahrbuch des Instituts für Frühmittelalterforschung der Universität Münster*, 1995, 1-73.

Annali della fabbrica del Duomo di Milano dall'origine fino al presente; pubblicati a cura della sua Amministrazione, Milan, vol. 1, 1877; appendix vol. 1, 1883.

APEL 1934 Apel, G., *Die Güterverhältnisse des hamburgischen Domkapitels*, Hamburg 1934.

ARBELLOT 1852 Arbellot, F., *Cathédrale de Limoges, histoire et description*, Paris/ Limoges 1852.

D'ARBOIS DE JUBAINVILLE 1862 Arbois de Jubainville, M.H. d', 'Documents relatifs aux travaux de construction faits à la cathédrale de Troyes pendant les XIIIe, XIVe et XVe siècles', *Bibliothèque de l'École des chartes* 23 (1862), 214-248, 393-423.

Archivos Iglesia en España Guía de los archivos y las bibliotecas de la Iglesia en España, vol. 1: *Archivos*, León 1985.

DEL ARCO 1924 Arco, R. del, *La Catedral de Huesca*, Huesca 1924.

ARENS 1982, Arens, F., *Der Dom zu Mainz*, Darmstadt 1982.

ARKENBOUT 1967 Arkenbout, A.A., 'De Heren van Voorne als opdrachtgevers van de 15de eeuwse glasschilderkunst', *Rotterdams Jaarboekje*, 1967, 121-138.

ARTONNE *et al.* 1963 Artonne, A., L. Guizard & O. Pontal, *Répertoire des statuts synodaux des diocèses de l'ancienne France du XIIIe à la fin du XVIIIe siècle*, Paris 1963.

VAN ASCH VAN WIJCK 1838 Asch van Wijck, A.M.C. van, *Plegtige intrede van Keizer Karel den Vijfden in Utrecht in den jare 1540*, Utrecht 1838.

VAN ASCH VAN WIJCK 1846 Asch van Wijck, A.M.C. van, *Plegtige intrede van Philips II binnen de stad Utrecht in den jare 1549*, Utrecht 1846.

VAN ASCH VAN WIJCK 1846-1848 Asch van Wijck, A.M.C. van, 'Inventaris der brieven uit het archief der 5 kapittelen 1380-1517', *Kronijk van het Historisch Gezelschap te Utrecht*, vols 2-4, 1846-1848.

VAN ASCH VAN WIJCK 1850-1853 Asch van Wijck, A.M.C. van, *Archief voor kerkelijke en wereldlijke geschiedenis van Nederland, meer bepaaldelijk van Utrecht*, 3 vols, Utrecht 1850-1853.

ASSIER 1854 Assier, A., *Comptes de la fabrique de l'église Sainte-Madeleine de Troyes, suivis de l'histoire de la construction du jubé et de plusieurs pièces curieuses conservées aux archives de l'Aube*, Troyes 1854.

ASSIER 1855 Assier, A., *Comptes de l'œuvre de l'église de Troyes avec notes et éclaircissements ou nouvelles recherches sur la construction des églises et sur les usages du moyen-âge*, Troyes 1855.

ASSIER 1858 Assier, A., *Construction d'une Notre-Dame au XIIIe siècle suivie des comptes de l'œuvre de l'église de Troyes au XIVe siècle*, Paris 1858.

ASTON 1987 Aston, M., 'Gold and Images', in W.J. Sheils & D. Wood (eds), *The church and wealth*, Oxford 1987, 189-207.

ATHERTON *et al.* 1996 Atherton, I., E. Fernie, C. Harper-Bill & S. Hassell (eds), *Norwich Cathedral : Church, City and Diocese, 1096-1996*, London/Rio Grande 1996.

ATKINSON 1933 Atkinson, Th.D., *An architectural history of the Benedictine monastery of Saint Etheldreda at Ely*, 2 vols, Cambridge 1933.

Atlas zur Kirchengeschichte, Die christlichen Kirchen in Geschichte und Gegenwart, Freiburg im Breisgau 1970.

AUBERT 1910 Aubert, M., *Monographie de la cathédrale de Senlis*, Senlis 1910.

AUBERT 1912 Aubert, M., *Senlis*, Paris [1912].

AUBERT 1920 Aubert, M., *Notre-Dame de Paris : La place dans l'histoire de l'architecture du XIIe au XIVe siècle*, (diss.), Paris 1920.

AUBERT 1931 Aubert, M. (ed.), *La cathédrale de Metz*, Paris 1931.

AUBERT 1960-1961 Aubert, M., 'La construction au moyen-âge', *Bulletin Monumental* 118 (1960), 241-260; 119 (1961), 7-43, 81-121, 181-209, 297-325.

D'AVENEL 1894-1912 Avenel, G. d', *Histoire économique de la propriété, des salaires, des denrées et de tous les prix en général depuis l'an 1200 jusqu'en l'an 1800*, 6 vols, Paris 1894-1912.

AVRIL 1984 Avril, J., *Le gouvernement des évêques et la vie religieuse dans le diocèse d'Angers (1148-1240)*, 2 vols, Lille 1984.

AVRIL 1991 Avril, J., 'La participation du clergé diocésain aux décisions épiscopales', in *Á propos des actes d'évêques : Hommage à Lucie Fossier*, Nancy 1991, 251-263.

AVRIL 1996 AVril, J., *Les statuts synodaux de Jean de Flandre, évêque de Liège (1288): Édition critique précédée d'une étude de leurs sources et de leur contenu*, vol. 61, Liège 1996.

AVRIL 2003 Avril, J., 'Les réunions de prêtres (calendes, chapitres) au Moyen Age', in M. Ascheri *et al.* (eds), *'Ins Wasser geworfen und Ozeane durchquert', Festschrift für Knut Wolfgang Nörr*, Cologne/Weimar/Vienna 2003, 11-26.

AYLMER & CANT 1977 Aylmer, G.E. & R. Cant (eds), *A history of York Minster*, Oxford 1977.

AZOFRA 2006 Azofra, E. (ed.), *La catedral de Ciudad Rodrigo a través de los siglos : Visiones y revisiones*, Salamanca 2006.

B

BAGNÉRIS 1986 Bagnéris, F., *La cathédrale d'Auch et son quartier de chanoines*, Paris 1986.

BAIER 1911 Baier, H., 'Neue Nachrichten über den Konstanzer Ablass von 1513 und 1514', *Zeitschrift für die Geschichte des Oberrheins* 65 (1911), 193-203.

BAIX 1942 Baix, F., *La chambre apostolique et les 'Libri Annatarum' de Martin V (1417-1431)* Brussels/Rome 1942.

BALDWIN 1970 Baldwin, J.W., *Masters, princes and merchants; the social views of Peter the Chanter and his circle*, 2 vols, Princeton 1970.

BALDWIN 2006 Baldwin, J.W., *Paris, 1200*, Aubier 2006.

Bamberger Heiltum Baumgärtel-Fleischman, R. (ed.), *Das Bamberger Heiltum von 1508/1509 in der British Library London* (Add ms 15689), facsimile, Bamberg 1998.

BANGO TORVISO 1992 Bango Torviso, I.G., 'El espacio para enterramientos privilegiados en la arquitectura medieval española', *Annuario del departamento de historia y teoría del arte* 4 (1992), 93-131.

BANNISTER 1902-1904 Bannister, A.T., 'The Hereford miracles', *Transactions of the Woolhope Club*, 1902-1904, 377-383.

BARBICHE 1975 Barbiche, B., *Les Actes Pontificaux Originaux des Archives Nationales de Paris*, vol. 1, Vatican City 1975.

BARBOSA 1656-1665 Barbosa, Aug. [1590-1649], *Opera omnia*, 10 vols, Lyon 1656-1665.

BARLOW 1939 Barlow, F. (ed.), *The letters of Arnulf of Lisieux*, London 1939.

BARLOZZETTI 1995 Barlozzetti, G. (ed.), *Il Duomo di Orvieto e le grandi cattedrali del Duecento (Atti del Convegno Internazionale di Studi, Orvieto, 12-14 novembre 1990)*, Turin 1995.

BARON 1999 Baron, F., 'Effigies sculptées à Notre-Dame de Paris aux XIVe et XVe siècles', in F. Joubert & D. Sandron (eds), *Pierre, lumière, couleur : Études d'histoire de l'art du Moyen Âge en l'honneur d'Anne Prache*, Paris 1999, 327-340.

BARREIRO SOMOZA 1987 Barreiro Somoza, J., *El Señorío de la Iglesia de Santiago de Compostela (Siglos IX-XIII)*, La Coruña 1987.

BARRON 2003 Barron, C.M., 'London and St Paul's Cathedral in the Later Middle Ages', in J. Backhouse (ed.), *The medieval English cathedral, papers in honour of Pamela Tudor-Craig, proceedings of the 1998 Harlaxton Symposium*, Donington 2003, 126-149.

BARRON & HARPER-BILL 1985 Barron, C.M. & Chr. Harper-Bill, *The Church in pre-Reformation society: essays in honour of F.R.H. Du Boulay*, Woodbridge/Suffolk 1985.

BARROW 1990 Barrow, J., 'German cathedrals and the monetary economy in the twelfth century', *Journal of Medieval History* 16 (1990), 13-38.

BARROW 1999 Barrow, J., 'The canons and citizens of Hereford c.1160-c.1240', *Midland History* 24 (1999), 1-23.

BARTH 1954 Barth, M., 'Heiltumführer und Almosensammler des Mittelalters : Die Mandate des Strassburger Bischofs Wilhelm von Honstein (1506-1541)', *Freiburger Diözesanarchiv*, 3rd Series, 6 (1954), 100-131.

BASIN 1859 Basin, T., *Histoire des règnes de Charles VII et de Louis XI*, vol. 4, Paris 1859.

BASSO 1987-1988 Basso, M., *I privilegi e le consuetudini della Rev.da Fabbrica di San Pietro in Vaticano (sec. XVI-XX)*, 2 vols, Rome 1987-1988.

BAUD 1985 Baud, H. (ed.), Le diocèse de Genève-Annecy, Histoire des diocèses de France, vol. 19, Paris 1985.

Baugeschichte des Basler Münsters, Herausgegeben vom Basler Münsterbauverein, Basel 1895.

BAULANT 1971 Baulant, M., 'Le salaire des ouvriers du bâtiment à Paris 1400-1726', *Annales, économies, sociétés, civilisations* 26 (1971), 463-483.

BEAUMONT 1956 Beaumont, R.M., *The chapter of Southwell Minster*, Southwell 1956.

DE BEAUREPAIRE 1897 Beaurepaire, Ch. de, 'Notice sur le grand portail de la cathédrale', in *Mélanges historiques et archéologiques concernant le département de la Seine-Inférieure et plus spécialement la ville de Rouen*, Rouen 1897, 203-224.

DE BEAUREPAIRE 1909 Beaurepaire, Ch. de, 'Boutiques du portail des libraires', in *Derniers mélanges historiques et archéologiques concernant le département de la Seine-Inférieure et plus spécialement la ville de Rouen*, Rouen 1909, 161-177.

BECHLE 1954 Bechle, E., *Das Begräbnisrecht im Schwaben bis zur Reformation*, (inaug. diss. Tübingen), Wablingen 1954 (typescript).

BÉGULE 1880 Bégule, L., *Monographie de la cathédrale de Lyon, précédée d'une notice historique par M.C. Guigue*, Lyon 1880.

BEISSEL 1889 Beissel, S., *Die Bauführung des Mittelalters : Studie über die Kirche des hl. Victor zu Xanten*, 3 vols, Freiburg im Breisgau 18892 (reprint Osnabrück 1966).

BEISSEL 1890 Beissel, S., *Die Verehrung der Heiligen und ihrer Reliquien in Deutschland bis zum Beginne des 13. Jahrhunderts*, Freiburg im Breisgau 1890.

BEISSEL 1892 Beissel, S., *Die Verehrung der Heiligen und ihrer Reliquien in Deutschland während der zweiten Hälfte des Mittelalters*, Freiburg im Breisgau 1892.

BEISSEL 1913 Beissel, S., *Wallfahrten zur unseren Lieben Frau in Legende und Geschichte*, Freiburg im Breisgau 1913.

BÉNÉJEAM-LÈRE 1993 Bénéjeam-Lère, M., 'La Cathédrale Saint-Étienne de Cahors', *Congrès Archéologique de France* 147 (1993), 9-89.

BENEŠKOVSKÁ & HLOBIL 1999 Beneškovská, K. & I. Hlobil, *Peter Parler & St Vitus's Cathedral 1356-1399*, Prague 1999.

BENZ 1975 Benz, K.J., *Untersuchungen zur politischen Bedeutung der Kirchweihe unter Teilnahme der deutschen Herrscher im hohen Mittelalter : Ein Beitrag zum Studium des Verhältnisses zwischen weltlicher Macht und kirchlicher Wirklichkeit unter Otto III. und Heinrich II*, Kallmünz 1975.

VAN DEN BERGH-HOOGTERP 1987 Bergh-Hoogterp, L. van den, 'Een vorstelijke geschenk van David van Bourgondië aan de Domkerk te Utrecht', *Antiek* 21 (1987), no. 9, 510-515.

VAN DEN BERGH-HOOGTERP 1990 Bergh-Hoogterp, L. van den, *Goud- en zilversmeden te Utrecht in de late middeleeuwen*, The Hague/ Maarssen 1990.

BERGLAR & ENGELS 1986 Berglar, P. & O. Engels (eds), *Der Bischof in seiner Zeit : Bischofstypus und Bischofsideal im Spiegel der Kölner Kirche*, Cologne 1986.

BERLIÈRE 1922 Berlière, U., 'Les processions des croix banales', *Académie royale de Belgique : Bulletin de la classe des lettres et des sciences morales et politiques*, 5th Series, 8 (1922), 419-446.

BERNAL ESTÉVEZ 1982 Bernal Estévez, A., *Ciudad Rodrigo en la Edad Media*, Salamanca 1982.

BERNING 1940 Behring, W., *Das Bistum Osnabrück vor Einführung der Reformation (1543)*, Osnabrück 1940.

VAN BEUNINGEN & KOLDEWEIJ 1993 Van Beuningen, H.J.E & A.M. Koldeweij, *Heilig en profaan : 1000 laatmiddeleeuwse insignes uit de collectie H.J.E. van Beuningen*, Rotterdam papers no. 8, Cothen 1993.

VAN BEUNINGEN, KOLDEWEIJ & KICKEN 2001 Van Beuningen, H.J.E & A.M. Koldeweij, D. Kicken, *en profaan 2 : 1200 laatmiddeleeuwse insignes uit openbare en particuliere collecties*, Rotterdam papers no. 12, Cothen 2001.

BEYSSAC 1912-1913 Beyssac, J., 'Les Papes ayant appartenu au chapitre de Lyon', *Bulletin de la Société littéraire, historique et archéologique de Lyon* 5 (1912-1913), 191-218.

BIGET 1972 Biget, J.-L., 'La restitution des dîmes par les laïcs dans le diocèse d'Albi à la fin du XIIIe siècle : contribution à l'étude des revenus de l'évêché et du chapitre de la cathédrale', in *Les évêques, les clercs et le roi (1250-1300)*, Cahiers de Fanjeaux, vol. 7, Toulouse 1972, 211-283.

BIGET 1974 Biget, J.-L., 'Recherches sur le financement des cathédrales du Midi au XIIIe siècle', in *La naissance et l'essor du gothique méridional au XIIIe siècle*, Cahiers de Fanjeaux, vol. 9, Toulouse 1974, 127-164.

BIGET 1982 Biget, J.-L., 'La cathédrale Sainte-Cécile d'Albi : L'architecture', *Congrès Archéologique de France* 140 (1982), 20-62.

BIJSTERVELD 1996 Bijsterveld, A.-J.A., 'Middeleeuwse vrome schenkingen als instrument van sociale integratie en politieke machtsvorming. Een historiografisch overzicht', *Tijdschrift voor Geschiedenis* 109 (1996), 443-464.

BIJSTERVELD 2007 Bijsterveld, A.-J.A., *Do ut des : Gift giving, memoria, and conflict management in the Medieval Low Countries*, Hilversum 2007.

BINDER 1912 Binder, B., *Das Domkapitel zu Gnesen, seine Entwicklung bis zur Mitte des 15. Jahrhundert*, (diss.), Greifswald 1912.

BINDING 1974 Binding, G., *Beiträge über Bauführung und Baufinanzierung im Mittelalter*, Cologne 1974.

BINDING 1993 Binding, G., *Baubetrieb im Mittelalter*, Darmstadt 1993.

BINNALL 1962 Binnall, P.B.G., 'Notes on the medieval altars and chapels in Lincoln cathedral', *The Antiquaries Journal* 42 (1962), 68-80.

BINSKI 1995 Binski, P., *Westminster Abbey and the Plantagenets : Kingship and the Representation of Power 1200-1400*, New Haven/ London 1995.

BION DE MARLAVAGNE 1875 Bion de Marlavagne, L., *Histoire de la cathédrale de Rodez* [...], Rodez/Paris 1875 (reprint Nîmes 2007).

BIRD & BAILDON 1907/1914 Bird, W.H.B. & W.P. Baildon (eds), *Calendar of the manuscripts of the dean and chapter of Wells*, 2 vols, London 1907 & 1914.

BISHOP 1918 Bishop, E., *Liturgica historica : papers on the liturgy and the religious life of the western church*, Oxford 1918.

BLAIR 1988 Blair, J. (ed.), *Minsters and parish churches*, Oxford 1988.

BLANQUART 1918 Blanquart, F., *Quelques dons royaux en faveur de travaux de reédification à la cathédrale d'Evreux pendant les* XVe, XVIe *et* XVIIe *siècles. Documents publiés par -*, s.l. 1918.

BLASCO AGUILAR 1973 Blasco Aguilar, J., *Historia y derecho en la catedral de Segorbe : Antecedentes histórico-jurídicos y derecho privilegiado*, Valencia 1973.

BLAVIGNAC 1858 Blavignac, J.D., *Comptes de dépenses de la construction du clocher de Saint-Nicolas à Fribourg en Suisse de 1470 à 1490*, Paris 1858.

DE BLÉCOURT 1950 Blécourt, A.S. de, *Kort begrip van het Oud-Vaderlands Burgerlijk Recht*, edited by H.F.W.D. Fischer, Groningen 1950[6].

BLICK & TEKIPPE 2005 Blick, S. & R. Tekippe (eds), *Art and architecture of late medieval pilgrimage in northern Europe and the British Isles*, Leiden 2005.

BLOCK & BILLIET 2003 Block, E.C. & F. Billiet (eds), *Les stalles de la Cathédrale de Rouen : Histoire et iconographie*, Rouen 2003.

BLOEMEN 1961 Bloemen, C., *De basiliek van Meerssen, pronkstuk van de Maasgothiek*, s.l. 1961.

BLOK 1968 Blok, D.P., *De Franken : Hun optreden in het licht der historie*, Bussum 1968.

BLUMSTEIN 1902 Blumstein, F., 'L'Oeuvre Notre-Dame et sa légende', *Revue catholique d'Alsace*, New Series, 21 (1902), 519-531, 588-595, 701-708, 780-786, 821-832.

DE BODT 1991 Bodt, S. de, 'Borduurwerkers aan het werk voor de Utrechtse kapittel- en parochiekerken 1500-1580', *Oud-Holland* 105 (1991), no. 1, 1-31.

BOEHMER 1723 Boehmer, J.H., *Ius ecclesiasticum protestantium, liber 3*, Halle 1723.

BOEREN 1953-1954 Boeren, P.C., 'Les plus anciens statuts du diocèse de Cambrai', *Revue de droit canonique* 3 (1953), 1-32, 131-172, 377-415; 4 (1954), 131-158.

BOEREN 1962 Boeren, P.C., *Heiligdomsvaart Maastricht : Schets van de geschiedenis der heiligdomsvaarten en andere jubelvaarten*, Maastricht 1962.

BOGAERS 1999 Bogaers, L.C.J.J., 'Broederschappen in laatmiddeleeuws Utrecht op het snijpunt van religie, werk, vriendschap en politiek', *Trajecta, tijdschrift voor de geschiedenis van het katholiek leven in de Nederlanden* 8 (1999), 97-119.

BOGAERS 2003 Bogaers, L.C.J.J., '"God wouts". De financiering van de Buurkerk (1435-1569) als spiegel van groepsvorming en belangentegenstellingen binnen de parochie', *Jaarboek Oud-Utrecht*, 2003, 67-123.

BOGAERS 2008 Bogaers, L.C.J.J., *Aards, betrokken en zelfbewust : De verwevenheid van cultuur en religie in katholiek Utrecht, 1300-1600*, Utrecht 2008.

BOISSONNOT 1920 Boissonnot, H., *Histoire et description de la cathédrale de Tours*, Paris 1920.

BOITO 1889 Boito, C., *Il Duomo di Milano e i disegni per la sua facciata*, Milan 1889.

BONDE 1994 Bonde, S., *Fortress-Churches of Languedoc : Architecture, religion and conflict in the High Middle Ages*, Cambridge (USA) 1994.

BONNENFANT 1939 Bonnenfant, G., *La cathédrale d'Evreux*, Paris 1939.

BONNET-LABORDERIE 1978 Bonnet-Laborderie, Ph., *Cathédrale Saint-Pierre, Beauvais : Histoire et architecture*, Beauvais 1978.

BOOZ 1956 Booz, P., *Der Baumeister der Gotik*, Munich/Berlin 1956.

BORAU MORELL 2003 Borau Morell, C., *Els promotors de capelles I retaules a la Barcelona del segle XIX*, Barcelona 2003.

BORDEAUX 1969 Bordeaux, M., *Le patrimoine ecclésiastique à la fin du moyen-âge : Évolution économique des diocèses et abbayes de France aux XIVe et XVe siècles*, (diss.), Bordeaux/Paris 1969.

BORDENAVE 1643 Bordenave, J. de, *L'estat des églises cathédrales et collégiales*, Paris 1643.

BOS 1998 Bos, A., 'Les archives des fabriques parisiennes à la fin du Moyen Âge et à l'époque moderne', *Bibliothèque de l'École des chartes* 156 (1998), 369-405.

BOS *et al.* 2006 Bos, A. *et al.*, *Materiam superabat opus : hommage à Alain Erlande-Brandenburg*, Paris 2006.

BOSMAN 2004 Bosman, L., *The power of tradition : Spolia in the architecture of St. Peter's in the Vatican*, Hilversum 2004.

BOUCHERON 1998 Boucheron, P., *Le pouvoir de bâtir : Urbanisme et politique édilitaire à Milan (XIVe-XVe siècles)*, Rome 1998.

BOUCHERON 2000 Boucheron, P., 'À qui appartient la cathédrale? La fabrique et la cité dans l'Italie médiévale', in *Religion et société urbaine au Moyen Âge : Études offertes à Jean-Louis Biget par ses anciens élevès*, Sorbonne 2000, 95-117.

BOUVIER 1911 Bouvier, H., *Histoire de l'église et de l'ancien archidiocèse de Sens*, vol. 2 (1122-1519), vol. 3 (1519-1789), Amiens 1911.

BOUVY 1947 Bouvy, D.P.R.A., *Middeleeuwsche beeldhouwkunst in de Noordelijke Nederlanden*, Amsterdam 1947.

BOUXIN 1902 Bouxin, A., *La cathédrale Notre-Dame de Laon; historique et description*, Laon 1902.

BOYER 1964 Boyer, M.N., 'The bridgebuilding brotherhood', *Speculum* 39 (1964), 635-650.

BOYER 1976 Boyer, M.N., *Medieval French bridges : A*

history, Cambridge (USA) 1976.

BRACKMANN 1898 Brackmann, A., *Urkundliche Geschichte des Halberstadter Domkapitels im Mittelalter*, (diss.), Wernigerode 1898.

BRANNER 1960 Branner, R., 'Les débuts de la cathédrale de Troyes', *Bulletin Monumental* 118 (1960), 111-121.

BRANNER 1961 Branner, R., 'Historical aspects of the reconstruction of Reims cathedral 1210-1241', *Speculum* 36 (1961), 23-37.

BRANNER 1962A Branner, R., *La cathédrale de Bourges et sa place dans l'architecture gothique*, Paris/Bourges 1962.

BRANNER 1962B Branner, R., 'Le maître de la cathédrale de Beauvais', *Art de France* 2 (1962), 77 ff.

BRANNER 1965 Branner, R., *St. Louis and the court style in gothic architecture*, London 1965.

BRANNER 1969 Branner, R., (ed.), *Chartres cathedral: illustrations, introductory essay, documents, analysis, criticism*, New York 1969.

BRANNER 1976 Branner, R., '"Fabrica, opus" and the dating of medieval monuments', *Gesta* 15 (1976), 27-30.

BRAUN 1924 Braun, J., *Der christliche Altar in seiner geschichtlichen Entwicklung*, 2 vols, Munich 1924.

BRAUNFELS 1953 Braunfels, W., *Mittelalterliche Stadtbaukunst in der Toskana*, Berlin 1953.

BRAUNSTEIN 1985 Braunstein, P., 'Les débuts d'un chantier: Le Dôme de Milan sort de terre 1387', in O. Chapelot & P. Benoit (eds), *Pierre et métal dans le bâtiment au Moyen Âge*, Paris 1985, 81-102.

BREDEKAMP 2000 Bredekamp, H., *Sankt Peter in Rom und das Prinzip der produktiven Zerstörung : Bau und Abbau von Bramante bis Bernini*, Berlin 2000.

BREDERO 1986 Bredero, A.H., *Christenheid en christendom in de Middeleeuwen : Over de verhouding van godsdienst, kerk en samenleving*, Kampen 1986.

BRESC-BAUTIER 1976 Bresc-Bautier, G., 'La "maramma" de la cathédrale de Palerme aux XIVe e XVe siècles', *Commentari : Rivista di critica e storia dell'arte* 27 (1976), 109-120.

BRIVIO 1977 Brivio, E., 'La fabbrica del Duomo; storia e fisionomia', *Archivio Ambrosiano* 32 (1977), 5-145.

BROM 1900 Brom, G., 'Middeleeuwsche kerksieraden', *Archief voor de geschiedenis van het aartsbisdom Utrecht* 26 (1900), 233-324.

Bronnen bouwgeschiedenis Tenhaeff, N.B. & W. Jappe Alberts (eds), *Bronnen tot de bouwgeschiedenis van den Dom te Utrecht*, Rijks Geschiedkundige Publicatiën grote serie, The Hague 1948-1976, vol. 2 (1): *Eerste stuk: Rekeningen 1395-1480* (no. 88): vol. 2 (2) *Tweede stuk: Rekeningen 1480/81-1506/07* (no. 129): vol. 2 (3): *Derde stuk: Rekeningen 1507/08-1528/29* (no. 155).

BROOKE 1995 Brooke, C.N.L., 'English Episcopal *Acta* of the Twelfth and Thirteenth Centuries', in M.J. Franklin & C. Harper-Bill (eds), *Medieval ecclesiastical studies in honour of Dorothy M. Owen*, Woodbridge 1995, 41-45.

BROOKE 1999 Brooke, C.N.L., *Churches and Churchmen in Medieval Europe*, London/Rio Grande 1999.

BROWN 1995 Brown, A.D., *Popular piety in late medieval England : the Diocese of Salisbury 1250-1550*, Oxford 1995.

BROWNE 1895 Browne, G.F., 'On the constitution of French chapters', *Transactions of the St. Pauls' Ecclesiological Society* 3 (1895), 225-240.

BRÜHL 1950 Brühl, C., *Reims als Krönungsstadt des französischen Königs bis zum Ausgang des 14. Jahrhun-*

derts, Frankfurt am Main 1950.

BRÜHL 1975 Brühl, C., *Palatium und Civitas*, vol. 1: *Gallien*, Cologne 1975.

DE BRUIJN 1994 Bruijn, M.W.J. de, *Husinghe ende Hofstede : Een institutioneel-geografische studie van de rechtspraak over onroerend goed in de stad Utrecht in de middeleeuwen*, (diss.), Utrecht 1994.

BRUNDAGE 1995 Brundage, J.A., *Medieval canon law*, London/New York 1995.

VON BRÜNNECK 1905 Brünneck, W. von, *Zur Geschichte und Dogmatik der Gnadenzeit*, Stuttgart 1905.

BRUTAILS 1899-1901 Brutails, J.-A., 'Deux chantiers bordelais', *Le Moyen-Age* 12 (1899), 385-412; 13 (1900), 169-192, 437-452; 14 (1901), 1-30.

BUCHELIUS 1906 Buchelius, A., 'Trajecti Batavorum Descriptio', *Bijdragen en mededelingen van het Historisch Genootschap* 27 (1906), 131-269.

BUCK 1983 Buck, M., *Politics, finance and the church in the reign of Edward II*, vol. 19, Cambridge 1983.

BÜCKMANN 1912 Bückmann, R., *Das Domkapittel zu Verden im Mittelalter*, (diss.), Münster 1912.

BUESA CONDE 1987 Buesa Conde, D.J. (ed.), *Las catedrales de Aragon*, Zaragoza 1987.

Bullarum diplomatum et privilegiorum sanctorum romanorum pontificum Taurinensis editio [...], vols 5 & 6, Turin 1860.

Bullarium Trajectense Brom, G. (ed.), *Bullarium Trajectense*, 2 vols, The Hague, 1891-1896.

Bulletin Monumental, vol. 1 (1835) - vol. 166 (2008).

BURCKLÉ 1935 Burcklé, J., *Les chapitres ruraux des anciens évêchés de Strasbourg et de Bâle*, Colmar 1935.

C

CABIÉ 1892 Cabié, E., 'Testament de Louis Ier d'Amboise, évêque d'Albi, 1485', *Revue du Tarn* 9 (1892), 4-20.

VAN CAENEGEM & GANSHOF 1962 Caenegem, R.C. van & F.L. Ganshof, *Encyclopedie van de geschiedenis der middeleeuwen; inleiding tot de geschreven bronnen van de geschiedenis der Westerse middeleeuwen*, Ghent 1962.

CAILLEAUX 1999 Cailleaux, D., *La Cathédrale en chantier : La construction du transept de Saint-Étienne des Sens d'après les comptes de la fabrique, 1490-1517*, Paris 1999.

CAILLEAUX 2001 Cailleaux, D., 'Chanoines et archevêques : recherches sur les commanditaires des travaux de la cathédrale de Sens à la fin du XVe et au début du XVIe siècle', in O. Chapelot (ed.), *Du projet au chantier : Maîtres d'ouvrage et maîtres d'œuvre aux XIVe-XVIe siècles*, Paris 2001, 69-86.

CAILLEAUX 2002 Cailleaux, D., 'Les comptes de construction des cathédrales médiévales', in *Cahiers de la sauvegarde de l'art français* 15 (2002), 20-33.

CAILLEAUX (FORTHCOMING) Cailleaux, D., 'Les ressources de la fabrique de la cathédrale de Sens au Moyen Age', in *Le financement de la construction aux XIIIe-XVIe siècles en France*, Paris (forthcoming).

CAILLET 2007 Caillet, J.-P., 'La figure de l'évêque dans les programmes des cathédrales françaises des XIIe-XIIIe siècles : Un programma assez contrasté', in A.C. Quintavalle (ed.), *Medioevo: l'Europa delle cattedrali (Atti del convegno internazionale di studi Parma 19-23 settembre 2006)*, Parma/Milan 2007, 301-309.

CALAND 1883 Caland, F., 'Oudste rekening der kerk van Hulst 1 October 1409 tot 30 September 1410', *Archief, vroegere en latere mededeelingen voornamelijk in betrekking tot Zeeland*, vol. 5, 1883, 409-475.

CALKOEN N.D. Calkoen, G.G., *De burch van Utrecht en haar*

naaste omgeving, manuscript, 3 vols, n.d., Het Utrechts Archief.

CALKOEN 1897-1898 Calkoen, G.G., *Beschrijving van de Dom of St.-Maartenskerk*, manuscript, 3 vols, 1897-1898, Het Utrechts Archief.

CALKOEN 1902 Calkoen, G.G., *Het Sint Janskerkhof en de St. Janskerk*, manuscript, 1902, Het Utrechts Archief.

CALKOEN 1915 Calkoen, G.G., *Aanteekeningen omtrent den Dom van Utrecht, hoofdzakelijk uit de 16e eeuw*, manuscript, 1915, Het Utrechts Archief.

CAL PARDO 1992 Cal Pardo, E., *Mondoñedo - Catedral, Ciudad, Obispado en el siglo XVI. Catálogo de la documentación del del archivo catedralicio*, Mondoñedo 1992.

CAROTTI 1889 Carotti, G., 'Vicende dei Duomo di Milano e della sua facciata', *Archivio storico dell'arte* 2 (1889), 113-126, 279-292.

CARRERO & RICO 2004 Carrero, E. & D. Rico (eds), *Catedral y ciudad medieval en la Península Ibérica*, Murcia 2004.

CARRIÈRE 1936 Carrière, V., *Introduction aux études d'histoire ecclésiastique locale*, vol. 3, Paris 1936.

DE CARSALADE DU PONT 1892 Carsalade du Pont, J. de, 'Clément V et l'église de Comminges', *Revue de Comminges* 7 (1892), 197-203.

Carta Mendoza 'Carta del Gran Cardenal Mendoza al Cabildo de Toledo sobre su sepultura', *Boletin de la Sociedad Española de Excursiones : Arte - Arqueologia - Historia* (1915), 161-162.

Cartulaire Agde Terrin, O. (ed.), *Cartulaire du chapitre d'Agde*, Nîmes 1969.

Cartulaire Amiens Roux, J. & E. Soyez (eds), *Cartulaire du chapitre de la cathédrale d'Amiens*, 2 vols, Amiens 1905, 1912.

Cartulaire Arras Guesnon, A. (ed.), *Cartulaire de l'évêché d'Arras* [...], Arras 1902.

Cartulaire Autun Charmasse, A. de (ed.), *Cartulaire de l'église d'Autun*, 2 vols, Paris/Autun 1865, 1900.

Cartulaire Chartres Lépinois, E. de & L. Merlet (eds), *Cartulaire de Notre-Dame de Chartres*, 3 vols, Chartres 1862-1864.

Cartulaire Lausanne Roth, Ch. (ed.), *Cartulaire du chapitre de Notre-Dame de Lausanne*, vol. 1, Lausanne 1948.

Cartulaire Le Mans Broussillon, B. de (ed.), *Cartulaire de l'évêché du Mans (965-1786)*, Le Mans 1908.

Cartulaire Liège Bormans, S., E. Schoolmeesters & E. Poncelet (eds), *Cartulaire de l'église Saint-Lambert de Liège*, Brussels, vol. 2, 1895; vol. 3, 1898; vol. 6, 1933.

Cartulaire Lyonnais Guigue, M.-C. (ed.), *Cartulaire Lyonnais* [...], 2 vols, Lyon 1885, 1893.

Cartulaire Notre-Dame de Paris Guérard, B.E.C. (ed.), *Cartulaire de l'église Notre-Dame de Paris*, 4 vols, Paris 1850.

Cartulaire l'ordre du Temple Albon, Marquis d' (ed.), *Cartulaire général de l'ordre du Temple (1119?-1150)*, 2 vols, Paris 1913, 1922.

Cartulaire Paris Lasteyrie, R. de (ed.), *Cartulaire général de Paris* [...], vol. 1: *528-1180*, Paris 1887.

Cartulaire Quimper Abbé Peyron (ed.), *Cartulaire de l'église de Quimper*, Quimper 1909.

Cartulaire S. Jean de Jérusalem Delaville le Roulx, J. (ed.), *Cartulaire général de l'ordre des hospitaliers de S. Jean de Jérusalem*, vol. 1: *1100-1200*, Paris 1894.

Cartulaire Sens Chartraire, E. (ed.), *Cartulaire du chapitre de Sens*, Sens 1904.

Cartularius Baiocensis Bourrienne, V. (ed.), *Antiquus Cartularius Ecclesiae Baiocensis*, 2 vols, Rouen 1902-1903.

CASADO ALONSO 1985 Casado Alonso, H., 'La construction à Burgos à la fin du Moyen Age, prix et salaires', *Cahiers de la Méditerranée* 31

(1985), 125-149.
CASASECA CASASECA 1988 Casaseca Casaseca, A., *Rodrigo Gil de Hontañón (Rascafría, 1500 - Segovia, 1577)*, Salamanca 1988.
CASPERS 2006 Caspers, Ch., 'Indulgences in the Low Countries, c. 1300 - c. 1520', in R.N. Swanson (ed.), *Promissory notes on the treasury of merits : Indulgences in late Medieval Europe*, Leiden/Boston 2006, 65-101.
CASSANELLI 2005 Cassanelli, R. (ed.), *Die Baukunst im Mittelalter*, Düsseldorf 2005.
Catálogo documental Burgos Mansilla Reoyo, D., *Catálogo documental del archivo catedral de Burgos (804-1416)*, Madrid/Barcelona 1971.
Catalogus Archief Gemeente Utrecht Muller Fzn., S. & C.L. de Leur, *Catalogus van het Archief; supplement, bijvoegselen en indices : Openbare verzamelingen der Gemeente Utrecht*, Utrecht 1914.
Catalogussen archief stad Utrecht Muller Fzn., S., W.C. Schuylenburg & J.G.C. Joosting, *Catalogussen van de bij het stadsarchief bewaarde archieven. Eerste afdeeling: De aan de stad Utrecht behoorende archieven. Tweede afdeeling: De aan de stad Utrecht in bewaring gegeven archieven*, Utrecht 1911, 1912.
La catedral gótica de Sevilla, Fundación y fábrica de la obra nueva, Seville 2006.
La Catedral de León, Mil años de historia, León 2002.
La catedral de Pamplona, 2 vols, Pamplona 1994.
La Catedral de Sevilla, Seville 1985.
Las catedrales españolas, fuente de cultura, historia y documentación, Lope de Barientos, seminario de cultura no. 1, Cuenca 2008.
CATTANEO 1985 Cattaneo, E., *Il Duomo nella vita civile e religiosa di Milano (terza edizione ampliata)*, Milan 1985.
VAN CAUWENBERGH 1922 Cauwenbergh, E. van, *Les pèlerinages expiatoires et judiciaires dans le droit communal de la Belgique au moyen-âge*, Louvain 1922.
CAVACIOCCHI 2004 Cavaciocchi, S. (ed.), *L'edilizia prima della rivoluzione industriale secc XIII-XVIII : Atti della 'Trentaseiesima settimana di studi'*, 26-30 April 2004, Prato 2004.
CAVINESS 1996 Caviness, M.H., *Stained glass windows*, Turnhout 1996.
Censo-Guia de archivos españoles, 2 vols, Madrid 1972.
CHABÁS LLORENS 1997 Chabás Llorens, R., *Índice del archivo de la Catedral de Valencia*, Arxius Valencians, vol. 16, Valencia 1997.
CHACÓN GÓMEZ-MONEDERO & PALOMO FERNÁNDEZ 2002 Chacón Gómez-Monedero, F.A. & G. Palomo Fernández, *Inventario de la sección Fabrica del Archivo de la Catedral de Cuenca*, Cuenca 2002.
CHAGNY-SÈVE 1985 Chagny-Sève, A.-M., 'La Paroisse Sainte-Croix de Clermont du XIIIe au XVIe siècle', in *L'encadrement religieux des fidèles au Moyen-Âge et jusqu'au Concile de Trento*, Paris 1985, 257-279.
CHAMPOLLION-FIGEAC 1868 Champollion-Figeac, A., *Documents paléographiques relatifs à l'histoire des beaux-arts et des belles-lettres pendant le moyen-âge*, Paris 1868.
CHAPMAN 1907 Chapman, F.R., *Sacrist rolls of Ely*, 2 vols, Cambridge 1907.
Charters Hereford Capes, W.W. (ed.), *Charters and records of Hereford Cathedral*, Hereford 1908.
Charters Salisbury Jones, W.R. & W. Dunn Macray (eds), *Charters and documents illustrating the history of the cathedral, city and diocese of Salisbury in the twelfth and thirteenth centuries*, London 1891.
CHARTRAIRE N.D. Chartraire, E., *La cathédrale de Sens*, Paris n.d.
Chartulary of Winchester

cathedral Goodman, A.W. (ed.), *Chartulary of Winchester Cathedral*, Winchester 1927.

CHÉDEVILLE 1973 Chédeville, A., *Chartres et ses campagnes (XIe-XIIIe s.)*, Paris 1973.

CHELLINI 1997 Chellini, I., 'Superstantia e superstantes: alcuni aspetti della fabbrica di Santa Tecla di Milano', *Nuova revista storica* 81 (1997), 401-424.

CHENEY 1968 Cheney, C.R., *English synodalia of the thirteenth century*, Oxford 1968[2].

CHENEY 1973 Cheney, C.R., 'Church building in the middle ages', in *Medieval texts and studies*, Oxford 1973, 346-363.

CHEVALIER 1997 Chevalier, M., *La France des cathédrales du IVe au XXe siècle*, Rennes 1997.

CHIFFOLEAU 1984 Chiffoleau, J., 'Pour une économie de l'institution ecclésiale à la fin du Moyen Âge', *Mélanges de l'Ecole française de Rome : Moyen Âge, temps modernes* 96 (1984), 247-279.

VAN DER CHIJS 1859 Chijs, P.O. van der, *De munten der bisschoppen van de heerlijkheid en de stad Utrecht, van de vroegste tijden tot aan de Pacificatie van Gent*, Haarlem 1859.

CHUECA 1951 Chueca, F., *La catedral nueva de Salamanca : Historia documental de su construcción*, Salamanca 1951.

CICERI & ROCCO NEGRI 1971 Ciceri, A. & V. Rocco Negri, 'Marco Carelli, benefattore del Duomo di Milano (sec. XIV)', *Archivio Ambrosiano* 21 (1971), 365-385.

CILLANUEVA DE SANTOS 2009 Cillanueva de Santos, M.A., *La construcción de la catedral de Segovia a través de sus cuentas : Estudio patrimonial, financiero y contable de la edificación de la Dama de las Catedrales*, Segovia 2009.

CIPOLLA 1956 Cipolla, C.M., *Money, prices and civilisation in the Mediterranean world*, Princeton 1956.

CLANCHÉ 1926-1927 Clanché, G., 'Quêtes et confrérie de Saint Gérard pour l'achèvement de la cathédrale de Toul, d'après la charte inédite de l'évêque Hector d'Ailly, 1525', *Mémoires de la Société d'archéologie lorraine et du Musée historique lorrain* 67, 1926-1927, 124-190.

CLARK 2007 Clark, G., 'The long march of history: farm wages, population, and economic growth, England 1209-1869', *The economic history review* 60 (2007), 97-135.

CLARK & KING 1983 Clark, W.W. & R. King, *Laon Cathedral : Architecture (1)*, London 1983.

CLEMEN 1937 Clemen, P., *Der Dom zu Köln*, Düsseldorf 1937.

CLÉMENT 1895 Clément, M., 'Recherches sur les paroisses et les fabriques au commencement du XIIIe siècle d'après les registres des papes', *Mélanges d'archéologie et d'histoire* 15 (1895), 387-418.

CLOULAS 1993 Cloulas, A., 'La sculpture funéraire dans l'Espagne de la Renaissance : Les commandes ecclésiastiques', *Gazette des Beaux-Arts* 135 (1993) 140-163.

CNATTINGIUS *et al.* 1987 Cnattingius, B., R. Edenheim, S. Ljungstedt & M. Ullén, *Linköpings domkyrka*, vol. 1: *Kyrkobyggnaden*, Stockholm 1987.

Codex regni Bohemiae Codex diplomaticus et epistolaris regni Bohemiae, vol. 5, fasc. 1, Prague 1974.

COHEN 1976 Cohen, E., 'In haec signa: pilgrim-badge trade in southern France', *Journal of Medieval History* 2 (1976), 193-214.

COLCHESTER & HARVEY 1974 Colchester, L.S. & J.H. Harvey, 'Wells Cathedral', *The Archeological Journal* 131 (1974), 200-215.

Colección documental Astorga Cavero Domínguez, G. & E. Martín López, *Colección documental de la Catedral de Astorga II (1126-1299), III*

(1300-1499), León 2000.

Colección documental León Ruiz Asencio, J.M. *et al.* (eds), *Colección documental del archivo de la Catedral de León*, vols VIII (1230-1269) - XIIII (1474-1534), León 1993-1999.

Colección documental León. Actas Capitulares Álvarez Palenzuela, V.A., *Colección documental del archivo de la Catedral de León. Actas Capitulares I (1376-1399)*, León 1999.

Colección documental Oviedo De Caso Fernández, F., *Colección documental sobre la catedral de Oviedo*, vol. 1 (1300-1520), vol. 2 (1520-1599), Gijón 1982-1983.

Collectories pontificales Berlière, U. (ed.), *Les collectories pontificales dans les anciens diotèses de Cambrai, Thérouanne et Tournai au XIVe siècle*, Rome 1929.

DE COLMENARES 1969-1974 Colmenares, D. de, *Historia de la insigne ciudad de Segovia y compendio de las historias de Castilla, nueva edición anotada*, 3 vols, Segovia [1637] 1969-1974.

DU COLOMBIER 1973 Colombier, P. du, *Les chantiers des cathédrales*, Paris 1973².

COLVIN 1963 Colvin, H.M. (ed.), *The History of the Kings' Works*, vols 1-2: *The middle ages*, London 1963.

COLVIN 1971 Colvin, H.M. (ed.), *Building accounts of King Henry III*, Oxford 1971.

CONCIONI 1994-1995 Concioni, G., *San Martino di Lucca : La cattedrale medioevale*, special issue of *Rivista di Archeologia Storia Custome* (1994-1995), nos 1-4.

Congrès Archéologique de France, session I (1839) - session 164 (2006), Paris 2008.

CONSTABLE 1982 Constable, G., 'The financing of the crusades in the twelfth century', in B.Z. Kedar *et al.*, *Outremer, studies in the history of the crusading Kingdom of Jerusalem, presented to Josua Prawer*, Jerusalem 1982, 64-88.

CONTRERAS JIMÉNEZ 1989 Contreras Jiménez, M.E., 'Noticias sobre la antigua Catedral de Segovia', *Anuario de estudios medievales : Consejo superior de investigaciones científicas*, 1989, 507-531.

COOK 1947 Cook, G.H., *Medieval chantries and chantry chapels*, London 1947.

COOK 1954 Cook, G.H., *The English medieval parish church*, London 1954.

COOK 1957 Cook, G.H., *The English cathedral through the centuries*, London 1957.

CORSEPIUS 1997 Corsepius, K., *Notre-Dame-en-Vaux : Studien zur Baugeschichte des 12. Jahrhunderts in Chalons-sur-Marne*, Stuttgart 1997.

CORSTEN 1975 Corsten, S., 'Der Ablass zugunsten der Kathedrale von Saintes; seine Verkündigung am Niederrhein im Spiegel der Wiegendrucke', *Annalen des historischen Vereins für den Niederrhein* 177 (1975), 62-76.

CORTÓN DE LAS HERAS 1990 Cortón de las Heras, M.T., *La construccion de la Catedral de Segovia (1525-1607)* (diss.), Madrid 1990.

COSTANTINI 2003 Costantini, F.-A., *L'abbatiale Saint-Robert de la Chaise-Dieu: Un chantier de la papauté d'Avignon (1344-1352)*, Paris 2003.

COSTER 1909 Coster, H.P., 'Het koperen hek voor het altaar van St. Maarten in den Dom te Utrecht', *Bulletin van den Nederlandschen Oudheidkundigen Bond*, 2nd Series, 2 (1909), 196-218.

COUÉ 1992 Coué, S., 'Acht Bischofsviten aus der Salierzeit - neu interpretiert', in S. Weinfurter (ed.), *Die Salier und das Reich*, vol. 3, Sigmaringen 1992, 347-415.

COULTON 1928 Coulton, G.G., *Art and the Reformation*, Oxford 1928.

COULTON 1936 Coulton, G.G.,

Five centuries of religion, vol. 3: *Getting and spending*, Cambridge 1936.

COUTURIER 1989 Couturier, M., 'Les investissements culturels des institutions religieuses à Chartres (1480-1600)', in *Investimenti e civiltà urbana secoli XIII-XVIII: Atti della 'Nona settimana di studi', 22-28 aprile 1977*, Prato 1989, 883-910.

COX 1913 Cox, J.Ch., *Churchwardens' accounts from the fourteenth century to the close of the seventeenth century*, London 1913.

COYECQUE 1889/1891 Coyecque, E., *L'Hôtel-Dieu de Paris au Moyen Age : Histoire et documents*, 2 vols, Paris 1889, 1891.

COYECQUE 1891 Coyecque, E., 'Le transept de la cathédrale de Beauvais 1499-1500', *Nouvelles Archives de l'art français*, 3rd Series, 7 (1891), 101-103.

CRAMPON 1876 Crampon, A., 'Un sermon prêché dans la cathédrale d'Amiens vers l'an 1270', in *Mémoires de la Société des Antiquaires de Picardie* (1876), 57-61, 551-601.

CRÉPIN-LEBLOND 1987 Crépin-Leblond, Th., *Recherches sur les palais épiscopaux en France au Moyen Age (XIIe-XIIIe siècles); d'après divers exemples des provinces ecclésiastiques de Reims et de Sens*, 4 vols, (unpublished diss. École des chartes), Paris 1987.

CRIADO MAINAR 2000 Criado Mainar, J., 'La administración de la fábrica de la Seo de Zaragoza en la ampliación del arzobispo Hernando de Aragón (1546-1550)', *Memoria Ecclesiae* 17 (2000), 377-398.

CROOK 1999/2000 Crook, J., *The Architectural Setting of the Cult of Saints in the Early Christian West c. 300-1200*, Oxford 1999/2000.

CROSBY 1994 Crosby, E.U., *Bishop and chapter in twelfth-century England : A study of the mensa episcopalis*, Cambridge 1994.

CROSNIER 1854 Crosnier, A.J., *Monographie de la cathédrale de Nevers*, Nevers 1854.

CROSSLEY 1985 Crossley, P., *Gothic Architecture in the Reign of Kasimir the Great : Church architecture in lesser Poland 1320-1380*, Kraków 1985.

CROUZET-PAVAN 2003 Crouzet-Pavan, E. (ed.), *Pouvoir et édilité : Les grands chantiers dans l'Italie communale et seigneuriale*, École française de Rome 2003.

D

VAN DALEN 1927 Dalen, J.L. van, *De Groote Kerk te Dordrecht*, Dordrecht 1927.

DAMEN 2005 Damen, M.J.M., 'Vorstelijke vensters : Glasraamschenkingen als instrument van devotie, memorie en representatie (1419-1519)', *Jaarboek voor Middeleeuwse Geschiedenis*, 2005, 140-200.

DAMMEYER 1957 Dammeyer, W., 'Der Grundbesitz des Mindener Domkapitels: Ein Beitrag zur Güter- und Wirtschaftsgeschichte der deutschen Domkapitel', *Mindener Jahrbuch*, 1957.

DANDELET 2008 Dandelet, Th.J., 'Financing New Saint Peter's 1506-1700', in G. Satzinger & S. Schütze (eds), *Sankt Peter in Rom 1506-2006 : Beiträge der internationalen Tagung vom 22.-25. Februar 2006 in Bonn*, Munich 2008, 41-49.

DAUCH 1913 Dauch, B., *Die Bischofsstadt als Residenz der geistlichen Fürsten*, Berlin 1913.

DAVID 1965 David, M., 'La fabrique et les manœuvres sur les chantiers des cathédrales en France jusqu'au XIVe siècle', in *Etudes d'histoire du droit canonique dédiées à Gabriel Le Bras*, vol. 2: *1113-1130*, Paris 1965.

DAVIDSOHN 1896-1927 Davidsohn, R., *Geschichte von Florenz*, 4 vols, Berlin 1896-1927.

DAVIS 1983 Davis, M.T.,

'"Troys portaulx et deux grosses tours" : The flamboyant façade project for the cathedral of Clermont', *Gesta* 22 (1983), no. 1, 67-83.

DAVIS 1998 Davis, M.T., 'Splendor and peril: The cathedral of Paris, 1290-1350', *The Art Bulletin* 80 (1998), no. 1, 34-66.

DE CASO FERNÁNDEZ 1981 De Caso Fernández, F., *La construccíon de la catedral de Oviedo (1293-1587)*, Oviedo 1981.

DE CASO FERNANDEZ *et al.* 1999 De Caso Fernández, F. *et al.* (eds), *La Catedral de Oviedo*, vol. 1: *Historia y restauración*; vol. 2: *Catálogo y bienes muebles*, Oviedo 1999.

DECKERS 1870 Deckers, P.G.L., *Leven en eerdienst van den heiligen Ridder Gummarus, beschermheilige der stad Lier [...]*, Lier 1870.

DEGLER-SPENGLER 1996 Degler-Spengler, B. (ed.), *Das Bistum Konstanz. Das Erzbistum Mainz. Das Bistum St. Gallen*, Helvetia Sacra, Section 1, vol. 2, Basel 1996.

DEHAISNES 1886 Dehaisnes, Chr., *Documents et extraits divers concernant l'histoire de l'art dans la Flandre, l'Artois et le Hainaut avant le* XV*e siècle*, 3 vols, Lille 1886.

DELEHAYE 1926-1928 Delehaye, H., 'Les lettres d'indulgences collectives', *Analecta Bollandiana* 44 (1926), 342 ff.; 45 (1927), 97 ff., 323 ff.; 46 (1928), 149 ff., 287 ff.

DELISLE 1848 Delisle, L.V., 'Notice sur un traité inédit du douzième siècle, intitulé "Miracula ecclesiae Constantiensis"', *Bibliothèque de l'École des chartes* 9 (1848), 339-352.

DEMAISON 1899 Demaison, L., 'Les chevets des églises Notre-Dame de Châlons et Saint-Rémi de Reims', *Bulletin archéologique du Comité des travaux historiques et scientifiques* (1899), 84-108.

DEMANDT 1977 Demandt, D., *Stadtherrschaft und Stadtfreiheit im Spannungsfeld von Geistlichkeit und Bürgerschaft in Mainz (11.-15. Jahrhundert)*, Wiesbaden 1977.

DENIFLE 1897-1899 Denifle, H., *La désolation des églises, monastères et hôpitaux en France pendant la guerre de cent ans*, vol. 1: *Documents relatifs au* XV*e siècle*, Paris 1897, vol. 2: *La guerre de cent ans jusqu'à la mort de Charles* V, Paris 1899.

DE OLAGUER-FELIU ALONSO 1980 De Olaguer-Feliu Alonso, F., *Las rejas de la Catedral de Toledo*, Toledo 1980.

DESACHY 1996 Desachy, M., *Le Chapitre Cathédral de Rodez (v. 1350-v. 1450)*, Paris 1996.

DESACHY 1998 Desachy, M., 'Querelles et conflicts autour de la cathédrale de Rodez (1300-1500)', in N. Coulet & O. Guyotjeannin (eds), *La ville au Moyen Âge : Actes du 120e congrès national des sociétés historiques et scientifiques, 1995, Aix-en-Province, section histoire médiévale et philologie*, Paris 1998, 133-144.

DESACHY 2005 Desachy, M., *Cité des hommes : Le chapitre cathédral de Rodez (1213-1562)*, Rodez 2005.

DESCHAMPS 1958 Deschamps, J., *Les confréries au moyen-âge*, Bordeaux 1958.

DESJARDINS 1865 Desjardins, G., *Histoire de la cathédrale de Beauvais*, Beauvais 1865.

DESPORTES 1979 Desportes, P., *Reims et les Rémois aux* XIII*e et* XIV *siècles*, Paris 1979.

DEVAILLY 1973 Devailly, G., *Le diocèse de Bourges*, Paris 1973.

DEWISCHEIT 1899 Dewischeit, C., 'Der deutsche Orden in Preussen als Bauherr', *Altpreussische Monatschrift*, New Series, 36 (1899), 145-223.

Diccionario eclesiastica de España Aldea Vaquero, Q., T. Marin Martínez & J. Vives Gatell (eds), *Diccionario de historia eclesiastica de*

España, 4 vols, Madrid 1972-1975.

Dictionnaire de droit canonique, Paris 1935-...

Dictionnaire ecclésiastiques Baudrillart, A. (ed.), *Dictionnaire d'histoire et de géographie ecclésiastiques*, Paris 1912-...

Dictionnaire de Théologie catholique, Paris 1923-1950.

DIERICKX 1960-1962 Dierickx, M., *Documents inédits sur l'érection des nouveaux diocèses aux Pays Bas*, 3 vols, Brussels 1960-1962.

DIERKENS 1999 Dierkens, A., 'Du bon (et du mauvais) usage des reliquaires au Moyen Âge', in E. Bozóky & A.-M. Helvétius (eds), *Les reliques : Objets, cultes, symboles: Actes du colloque international de l'Université du Littoral-Côte d'Opale (Boulogne-sur-Mer), 4-6 septembre 1997*, vol. 1, Turnhout 1999, 239-252.

DIESTELKAMP 1929 Diestelkamp, A., 'Geschichte der Dombaubrüderschaft St. Stephani in Halberstadt : Ein Beitrag zur Geschichte des mittelalterlichen Brüderschaftswesens', in R. Holtzmann & W. Möllenberg (eds), *Sachsen und Anhalt : Jahrbuch der Historischen Kommission für die Provinz Sachsen und für Anhalt*, 1929, 220-265.

Diplomatarium danicum, 28 vols, Copenhagen 1938-2000.

Diplomatarium suecanum, 10 vols, Stockholm 1829-1982.

DIRLMEIER 1978 Dirlmeier, U., *Untersuchungen zu Einkommensverhältnissen und Lebenshaltungskosten in oberdeutschen Städten des Spätmittelalters (Mitte 14. bis Anfang 16. Jahrhundert)*, Abhandlungen der Heidelberger Akademie der Wissenschaften, Philosophische-Historische Klasse, vol. 1, Heidelberg 1978.

DIRLMEIER 1983 Dirlmeier, U., 'Zu Arbeitsbedingungnen und Löhnen von Bauhandwerkern in Spätmittelalter', in R.S. Elkar, *Deutsches Handwerk in Spätmittelalter und früher Neuzeit*, Göttingen 1983, 35-54.

DMITRIEVA & LAMBRECHT 2000 Dmitrieva, M. & K. Lambrecht, *Krakau, Prag und Wien : Funktionen von Metropolen im frühmodernen Staat*, Stuttgart 2000.

DOBSON 1983 Dobson, R.B., 'Cathedral chapters and cathedral cities: York, Durham and Carlisle in the fifteenth century', *Northern History* 19 (1983), 15-44.

DOBSON 1991 Dobson, R.B., 'The English monastic cathedrals in the fifteenth century', *Transactions of the Royal Historical Society* (1991), 151-172.

Documentación medieval León Bautista Bautista, M., M.T. García García & M.I.N. Crispín, *Documentación medieval de la iglesia catedral de León (1419-1426)*, Salamanca 1990.

DODT VAN FLENSBURG 1838-1848 Dodt van Flensburg, J.J., *Archief voor kerkelijke en wereldsche geschiedenissen, inzonderheid van Utrecht*, vols 1-7, Utrecht 1838-1848.

DODT VAN FLENSBURG 1843 Dodt van Flensburg, J.J., 'S. Brigitte en hare aflaten te Utrecht', *Tijdschrift voor Geschiedenis, Oudheden en Statistiek van Utrecht* 9 (1843), 60-65.

DOMENGE I MESQUIDA 1997 Domenge i Mesquida, J., *L'Obra de la Seu : El procés de construcció de la catedral de Mallorca en el tres-cents*, Palma 1997.

DOMINGO PÉREZ & GUTIÉRREZ IGLESIAS 1999 Domingo Pérez, T. & M.R. Gutiérrez Iglesias, 'La gracia del quinto diezmero concedida en el año 1409 a la Fábrica de la Seo por Benedicto XIII y su primera ejecución en 1412', in *Aragón en la Edad Media* (1999), nos 14-15, 413-450.

DONATH 2000 Donath, M., *Die Baugesichte des Doms zu Meißen 1250-1400*, Leipzig 2000.

DORÉ 2007 Doré, Mgr J. (ed.),

Strasbourg, la grâce d'une cathédrale, Strasbourg 2007.

DREW 1954 Drew, Ch., *Early parochial organisation in England : The origins of the office of churchwarden*, London 1954.

DRUFFNER 1993 Druffner, F., 'Hagiographie und Sakraltopographie in Canterbury', in G. Kerscher (ed.), *Hagiographie und Kunst : Der Heiligenkult in Schrift, Bild und Architektur*, Berlin 1993, 255-272.

DUBOIS 1965 Dubois, J., 'La carte des diocèses de France avant la révolution', *Annales, économies, sociétés, civilisations* 20 (1965), 680-691.

DUBUIS 1979 Dubuis, P., 'Documents relatifs à la cathédrale de Sion au moyen âge', *Vallesia* 34 (1979), 149-173.

DUBUIS 1995 Dubuis, P., 'Les premieres horloges de Lausanne (1400-1430)', *Mémoire Vive* (1995), 34-42.

DUBY 1973 Duby, G., 'Les chanoines réguliers et la vie économique des XV en XII siècles', in *Hommes et structures du moyen-âge*, Paris/The Hague 1973, 203-212.

DUBY 1976 Duby, G., *Le temps des cathédrales : L'art et la société 980-1420*, Paris 1976 (first edition 1962).

DUPONT-FERRIER 1930-1933 Dupont-Ferrier, G., *Etudes sur les institutions financières de la France à la fin du moyen-âge*, 3 vols, Paris 1930-1933.

DURAND 1901-1903 Durand, G., *Monographie de l'église Notre-Dame cathédrale d'Amiens*, vol. 1: *Histoire et description de l'édifice*, vol. 2: *Mobilier et accessoires* Amiens/Paris 1901-1903.

DURÁN GUDIOL 1956 Durán Gudiol, A., 'Un viaje por la diócesis de Huesca en el año 1338', *Argensola* 7 (1956), 367-372.

DURÁN GUDIOL 1991 Durán Gudiol, A., *Historia de la Catedral de Huesca*, Huesca 1991.

DURLIAT 1960 Durliat, M., 'Contribution roussillonnaise à la construction de la cathédrale de Saint-Bertrand-de-Comminges', *Revue de Comminges* 73 (1960), 169-174.

DÜRR 1777 Dürr, A., 'Dissertatio de annis carentiae canonicorum ecclesiarum cathedralium et collegiatarum in Germania' [1772], in A. Schmidt, *Thesaurus iuris ecclesiastici potissimum Germanici* [...], vol. 6, Heidelberg 1777, 204-270.

DUVOSQUEL 1973 Duvosquel, J.-M., 'Fragments d'un compte de la fabrique de la cathédrale de Tournai (1455) à la Bibliothèque Vaticane', *Bulletin de l'institut historique Belge de Rome* 43 (1973), 377-399.

E

EDLER-DE ROOVER 1957 Edler-de Roover, F.M., 'Restitution in Renaissance Florence', in *Studi in onore di Armando Sapori*, vol. 2, Milan 1957, 773-790.

EDWARDS 1939 Edwards, K., 'The houses of Salisbury Close in the fourteenth century', *The Journal of the British Archeological Association*, 3rd Series, 4 (1939), 55-117.

EDWARDS 1967 Edwards, K., *The English secular cathedrals in the middle ages: A constitutional study with special reference to the fourteenth century*, Manchester 1967[2].

EEKHOF 1909 Eekhof, A., *De questierders van den aflaat in de Noordelijke Nederlanden*, The Hague 1909.

EGG 1987 Egg, E., 'Die Bauhütte von Brixen', in J. Nössing & H. Stampfer (eds), *Kunst und Kirche in Tirol : Festschrift zum 70. Geburtstag von Karl Wolfsgruber*, Bozen 1987, 301-334.

L'Église et le peuple chrétien dans les pays de l'Europe du centre-est et du nord (XIVe-XVe siècles), Rome 1990.

Eglise de Saint-Hubert L'ancienne église abbatiale de

Saint-Hubert, Etudes et Documents, Monuments et Sites, vol. 7, Namur 1999.

Einblattdrucke des XV. *Jahrhunderts, Ein bibliographisches Verzeichnis herausgegeben von der Kommission fur den Gesamtkatalog der Wiegendrucke*, Halle am Saal 1914.

EISERMANN, F., *Verzeichnis der typographischen Einblattdrucke des 15. Jahrhunderts im Heiligen Römischen Reich Deutscher Nation*, 3 vols, Wiesbaden 2004.

ELDIN 1994, Eldin, G., 'Les chapellenies à Notre-Dame de Paris (XIIe-XVIe siècle) : Recherches historiques et archéologiques', *Positions des thèses soutenues à l'École des chartes*, Paris 1994, 69-75.

VAN DER ELST 1929 Elst, W. van der, *De klokken van den Domtoren te Utrecht*, Amsterdam 1929.

EMERY 2001 Emery, E., *Romancing the cathedral, gothic architecture in fin-de-siècle French culture*, New York 2001.

Enciclopedia de historia de España, vol. 5: *Diccionario temático*, Madrid 1991

ENGELS 1995 Engels, O., 'Die kaiserliche Grablege im Speyerer Dom und die Staufer', in J. Dahlhaus & A. Kohnle (eds), *Papstgeschichte und Landesgeschichte : Festschrift für Hermann Jakobs zum 65. Geburtstag*, Cologne 1995, 227-254.

ENLART 1902 Enlart, C., *Manuel d'archéologie française*, vol. 1: *Architecture religieuse*, Paris 1902.

ENNEN 1863/1869 Ennen, L., *Geschichte der Stadt Köln*, Cologne vol. 1, 1863, vol. 3, 1869.

ENNEN 1880 Ennen, L., *Der Dom zu Köln von seinem Beginne bis zu seiner Vollendung*, Cologne 1880.

ENNEN & ECKERTZ 1860-1879, Ennen, L. & G. Eckertz, *Quellen zur Geschichte der Stadt Köln*, 6 vols, Cologne 1860-1879.

EPSTEIN 1984 Epstein, S., *Wills and Wealth in Medieval Genua, 1150-1250*, Cambridge (USA)/London 1984.

ERBEN 1923 Erben, W., 'Bemalte Bittschriften und Ablassurkunden', *Archiv für Urkundenforschung* 8 (1923), 160-188.

ERLANDE-BRANDENBURG 1977 Erlande-Brandenburg, A., 'La façade de la cathédrale d'Amiens', *Bulletin Monumental* 135 (1977), 253-293.

ERLANDE-BRANDENBURG 1989 Erlande-Brandenburg, A., *La Cathédrale*, Paris 1989.

ERLANDE-BRANDENBURG 1997 Erlande-Brandenburg, A., *Notre-Dame de Paris*, New York 1997.

ERLER 1954 Erler, A., *Das Strassburger Münster im Rechtsleben des Mittelalters*, Frankfurt 1954.

ERSKINE 1962 Erskine, A.M., 'The medieval financial records of the cathedral church of Exeter', *Journal of the Society of Archivists* 2 (1962), 254-266.

ERSKINE 1981 Erskine, A.M., *The accounts of the fabric of Exeter Cathedral, 1279-1353. Part 1: 1279-1326*, Devon & Cornwall Record Society, New Series, vol. 24, Torquay 1981.

ERSKINE 1983 Erskine, A.M., *The accounts of the fabric of Exeter Cathedral, 1279-1353. Part 2: 1328-1353*, Devon & Cornwall Record Society, New Series, vol. 26, Torquay 1983.

ERSKINE 1991 Erskine, A.M., 'The Documentation of Exeter Cathedral: The Archives and their Application', in F. Kelly (ed.), *Medieval art and architecture at Exeter Cathedral, The British Archaeological Assosciation, conference transactions for the year 1985*, vol. 11, London 1991, 1-9.

ESCH 2004 Esch, A., 'Aus dem Alltag eines Ablasskollektors : Eine Reise durch Deutschland, die Niederlande und Österreich anhand der Buchführung 1470-1472', in *Päpste, Pilger,*

Pönitentiarie : Festschrift für Ludwig Schmugge zum 65. Geburtstag, Tübingen 2004, 109-131.

España Sagrada, theatro geographico-historico de la Iglesia de España, 52 vols, Madrid 1754-1918.

VAN ESPEN 1700 Espen, Z.B. van, *Ius ecclesiasticum universum*, 2 vols, Louvain/ Brussels 1700.

ESQUIEU 1992 Esquieu, Y., *Autour de nos cathédrales : Quartiers canoniaux du sillon rhodanien et du littoral méditerranéen*, Paris 1992.

ESQUIEU 1998 Esquieu, Y., *Quartier cathédral : Une cité dans la ville*, Paris 1998.

EUBEL 1898-1901 Eubel, C., *Hierarchia catholica medii aevi*, 2 vols, Münster in Westfalen 1898-1901.

EVANS 1948 Evans, J., *Art in medieval France : A study in patronage*, Oxford 1948.

EXH. CAT. BASEL 2001 *Der Basler Münsterschatz*, Basel (Historisches Museum) 2001.

EXH. CAT. COLOGNE 1989 *Reliquien, Verehrung und Verklärung*, Cologne (Schnütgen-Museum) 1989

EXH. CAT. LLEIDA 1991, *La Seu Vella de Lleida : La catedral, els promotors, els artistes s. XIII a S. XV*, Barcelona 1991

EXH. CAT. MUNICH 1984 *Wallfahrt kennt keine Grenzen*, Munich (Bayerischen Nationalmuseum) 1984.

EXH. CAT. RHEIMS 2001 *20 siècles en cathédrales*, Rheims (Palais du Tau) 2001.

EXH. CAT. TOURNAI 1971 *Trésors Sacrés : Cathédrale Notre-Dame de Tournai*, Tournai (Musée d'histoire et d'archéologie) 1971.

EXH. CAT. UTRECHT 1972 *Van Willibrord tot Wereldraad*, Utrecht (Aartsbisschoppelijk Museum) 1972.

F

La Fabbrica Eterna, Cultura, logica strutturale, conservazione delle cattedrali gotische, Vigevano 1993.

FÁBREGA GRAU & BAUCELLS REIG 1969 Fábrega Grau, A. & J. Baucells Reig, *Catálogo del archivo capitular de la S.I. Catedral Basílica de Barcelona : Indice general de las series documentales*, Barcelona 1969.

FAGNIEZ 1898/1900 Fagniez, G., *Documents relatifs à l'histoire de l'industrie et du commerce en France*, 2 vols, Paris 1898, 1900.

FAHNE 1864 Fahne, A., 'Urkundliches aus dem Mittelalter über das Aufbringen der Kosten für den Cölner Dombau', *Forschungen auf dem Gebiete der Rheinischen und Westphälischen Geschichte* 1 (1864), no. 1, 133-140.

FALCÓN MÁRQUEZ 1980 Falcón Márquez, T., *La catedral de Sevilla, estudio arquitectónico*, Seville 1980.

FALCON PEREZ *et al.* 1986 Falcon Perez, M.I., M.L. Ledesma, C. Orcastegui & E. Sarasa, 'La construction à Saragosse à la fin du Moyen Âge : Conditions de travail, matériaux, prix et salaires', *Cahiers de la Méditerranée* 31 (1986), 73-93.

FALK 1879 Falk, F., *Die Druckkunst im Dienste der Kirche zunächst in Deutschland bis zum Jahre 1520*, Cologne 1879.

FALLUE 1848 Fallue, M., 'Construction de la tour de la cathédrale de Rouen dite Tour de Beurre', *Académie de Rouen, classe des Belles-Lettres, séance 2 juin 1848*, 209-220.

FALQUE REY 1988 Falque Rey, E., *Historia Compostellana*, Corpus Christianorum : Continuatio Mediaeualis, vol. 70, Turnholt 1988, 218-227.

FANTI 1980 Fanti, M., *La fabbrica di San Petronio in Bologna dal XIV al XX secolo: Storia di una instituzione*, Italia Sacra : Studi e documenti di storia ecclesiastica, vol. 32, Rome 1980.

FANTI 1989 Fanti, M., 'La fabbrica della Basilica di San Petronio in Bologna tra il XIV e il XV secolo', in *Investimenti e civiltà urbana secoli XIII-XVIII: Atti della*

'Nona settimana di studi', 22-28 aprile 1977, Prato 1989, 699-742.

DE FARCY 1901-1926 Farcy, L. de, *Monographie de la cathédrale d'Angers*, 4 vols, Angers 1901-1926.

Fasti Ecclesiae Gallicanae, répertoire prosopographique des évêques, dignitaires et chanoines de France de 1200 à 1500, 9 vols, Turnhout 1996-2005.

FAUPEL-DREVS 2000 Faupel-Drevs, K., *Vom rechten Gebrauch der Bilder im liturgischen Raum : Mittelalterliche Funktionsbestimmungen bildender Kunst im Rationale divinorum officiorum des Durandus von Mende (1230/1-1296)*, Leiden 2000.

FEHRMANN 1967 Fehrmann, C.N., *De Kamper klokgieters, hun naaste verwanten en leerlingen*, Kampen 1967.

FEINE 1954 Feine, H.E., *Kirchliche Rechtsgeschichte*, vol. 1: *Die katholische Kirche*, Weimar 1954[2].

FERNÁNDEZ COLLADO 1999 Fernández Collado, Á., *La Catedral de Toledo en el siglo XVI: Vida, arte y personas*, Toledo 1999.

FERNÁNDEZ FLÓREZ 1985 Fernández Flórez, J.A., *El patrimonio del Cabildo Catedralicio de León en la segunda mitad del siglo XV*, Valladolid 1985.

FERNIE 1993 Fernie, E., *An Architectural History of Norwich Cathedral*, Oxford 1993.

FERNIE & WHITTINGHAM 1972 Fernie, E. & A.B. Whittingham, *The early communar and pitancer rolls of Norwich cathedral priory with an account of the building of the cloister*, Norwich 1972.

FERRARIS 1852-1857 Ferraris, L., *Prompta Bibliotheca canonica, juridica, moralis, theologica* [...]. *Editio novissima*, 8 vols, Amboise 1852-1857.

Finanziare cattedrali e grandi opere pubbliche nel medioevo nord e media Italia (secoli XII-XV), Biblioteca della 'Nuova Rivista Storica', no. 39, Rome 2003.

FINDLAY 1939 Findlay, D.F., 'The fabric rolls of Exeter Cathedral 1374-1514, 3 vols, typescript, 1939, Exeter cathedral library.

FINK 1932-1933 Fink, K.A., 'Die Kreuzablass gegen Georg Podiebrad in Süd- und Westdeutschland', *Quellen und Forschungen aus italienischen Archiven und Bibliotheken* 24 (1932-1933), 207-235.

FINUCANE 1977 Finucane, R.C., *Miracles and pilgrims : Popular beliefs in medieval England*, London 1977.

FLICHE & MARTIN 1934 Fliche, A. & V. Martin (eds), *Histoire de l'église depuis des origines jusqu'à nos jours*, 24 vols, Paris 1934-...

FLIEDER 1968 Flieder, V., *Stephansdom und Wiener Bistumgründung : Eine diözesan- und rechtsgeschichtliche Untersuchung*, Vienna 1968.

FONSECA 1984 Fonseca, C.D., '"Ecclesia matrix" e "Conventus civium" : l'ideologia della Cattedrale nell'età comunale', in *La pace di Costanza 1183 : un difficile equilibrio di poteri fra società italiana ed impero. Milan-Piacenza, 27-30 aprile 1983*, Bologna 1984, 135-149.

DE LA FONS MÉLICOCQ 1848 Fons Mélicocq, A. de la, *Les artistes et les ouvriers du Nord de la France (Picardie, Artois, Flandre) et du Midi de la Belgique aux XIVe, XVe et XVIe siècles*, Béthune 1848.

FOREVILLE 1958 Foreville, R., *Le Jubilé de Saint Thomas Becket du XIIIe au XVIe siècle (1220-1479) : Etude et documents*, Paris 1958.

FOREVILLE 1965 Foreville, R., *Latran I, II, III et Latran IV*, Paris 1965.

DE FORMEVILLE 1866 Formeville, H. de, 'Notice sur les chanoines de l'ancienne cathédrale de Lisieux', *Mémoires lus à la Sorbonne 1865*, Paris 1866, 477-499.

FORTÉ 1978 Forté, M.-J., *L'œuvre Notre-Dame : fabrique de la cathédrale de*

Strasbourg, typescript 1978.

FOUCHER-LEFEBVRE (FORTHCOMING) Foucher-Lefebvre, E., 'La comptabilité de la fabrique de la cathédrale Notre-Dame de Rouen (fin XIV-début XVIe s.)', in *Le financement de la construction aux XIIIe-XVIe siècles en France*, Paris (forthcoming).

FOUQUET 1999 Fouquet, G., *Bauen für die Stadt : Finanzen, Organisation und Arbeit in kommunalen Baubetrieben des spätmittelalters. Eine vergleichende Studie vornehmlich zwischen den Städten Basel und Marburg*, Cologne/Weimar/Vienna 1999.

FOURNIÉ 1995 Fournié, M., 'Confréries, bassins et fabriques dans le sud-ouest de la France : Des œvres municipales', in A. Vauchez (ed.), *La religion civique à l'époque médiévale et moderne (Chrétienté et Islam)*, Nanterre 1995, 245-263.

FOURNIÉ *et al.* 2003 Fournié, M., R. Ryckebusch & A. Dubreil-Arcin, 'Jean XXII et le remodelage de la carte ecclésiastique du midi de la France: une réforme discrète', *Revue d'histoire ecclésiastique* 98 (2003), 29-60.

FOURNIER 1923 Fournier, P.-F., 'Affiches d'indulgences manuscrites et imprimées des XIVe, XVe et XVIe siècles', *Bibliothèque de l'École des chartes* 84 (1923), 116-160.

FOURNIER 1942 Fournier, E., *Nouvelles recherches sur les curés, chapitres et universités de l'ancienne église de France*, Paris 1942.

FRACHEBOUD 1953 Fracheboud, M.A., 'Saint-Bernard est-il seul dans son attitude face aux œuvres d'art?', *Collectanea ordinis cisterciensium reformatorum* 15 (1953), 113-130.

FRANASZEK & PRZYBYSZEWSKI 1991 Franaszek, A. & B. Przybyszewski, *Kaplica Zygmuntowska : Materialy zródlowe 1517-1977*, Kraków 1991.

FRANCES DE URRUTIGOYTI 1665 Frances de Urrutigoyti, M.A., *De ecclesiis cathedralibus earumque privilegiis et praerogativis tractatus*, Lyon 1665.

FRANCIA 1977 Francia, E., *1506-1606 : Storia della costruzione del nuovo San Pietro*, Rome 1977.

FRANCIA 1989 Francia, E., *Storia della costruzione del nuovo San Pietro da Michelangelo a Bernini*, Rome 1989.

FRANKL 1960 Frankl, P., *The Gothic : Literary sources and interpretations through eigth centuries*, Princeton 1960.

FRASER JENKINS 1970 Fraser Jenkins, A.D., 'Cosimo de Medici's patronage of architecture and the theory of magnificence', *Journal of the Warburg and Courtauld Institutes* 33 (1970), 162-170.

FREDERICQ 1922 Fredericq, P., *Codex documentorum sacratissimarum indulgentiarum neerlandicarum*, Rijks Geschiedkundige Publicatiën, kleine serie, vol. 21, The Hague 1922.

FREIGANG 1992 Freigang, C., *Imitare ecclesias nobiles : Die Kathedralen von Narbonne, Toulouse und Rodez und die nordfranzösische Rayonnantgotik im Languedoc*, Worms 1992.

FREIGANG 2002 Freigang, C. 'Chapelles latérales privées: Origines, fonctions, financement : le cas de Notre-Dame de Paris', in *Art, cérémonial et liturgie au Moyen Age : Actes du colloque de 3e cycle Romand de lettres, Lausanne/Fribourg 2000*, Rome 2002.

FREIGANG & STIGLMAYR 1999 Freigang, C. & C.M. Stiglmayr, *Gotische Architektur in Spanien/La arquitectura gótica en España : Akten des Kolloquiums der Carl Justi-Vereinigung und des kunstgeschichtlichen Seminars der Universität Göttingen, 4-6 Februar 1994*, Frankfurt am Main/Madrid 1999.

FRENCH 1999 French, T., *York Minster : The St William*

window, Oxford 1999.

FRIEDBERG 1879/1882 Friedberg, Ae. (ed.), *Corpus Iuris Canonici*, 2 vols, Leipzig 1879, 1882.

FRIEDMANN 1959 Friedmann, A., *Paris: ses rues, ses paroisses du moyen-âge à la révolution : Origine et évolution des circonscriptions paroissiales*, Paris 1959.

FRIEDMANN 1964 Friedmann, A., 'Notre-Dame et les paroisses de Paris au XIIIe siècle', *Revue d'histoire de l'Eglise de France* 50 (1964), 27-34.

FRIESS 1994 Frieß, P. (ed.), *Auf den Spuren des heiligen Antonius : Festschrift für Adalbert Mischlewski zum 75. Geburtstag*, Memmingen 1994.

FRITZE 1971 Fritze, W.H., 'Zur Entstehungsgeschichte des Bistums Utrecht: Franken und Friesen 690-734', *Rheinische Vierteljahrsblätter* 35 (1971), 107-151.

FRÖJMARK 1992 Fröjmark, A., *Mirakler och helgonkult : Linköpings biskopsdöme under senmedeltiden*, Studia Historica Upsaliensia, vol. 171, Uppsala 1992.

FROMMEL 1976 Frommel, Ch.L., 'Die Peterskirche unter Papst Julius II im Licht neuer Dokumente', *Römisches Jahrbuch für Kunstgeschichte*, 1976, 57-137.

FROMMEL 1991 Frommel, C.L., 'Il cantiere di S. Pietro prima di Michelangelo', in *Les chantiers de la Renaissance : Actes des colloques tenues à Tours en 1983-1984*, Paris 1991, 175-190.

FRÜLICH 1933 Frülich, K., 'Kirche und stadtisches Verfassungsleben im Mittelalter', *Zeitschrift der Savigny-Stiftung für Rechtsgeschichte, Kanonistische Abteilung* 22 (1933), 188-288.

FUCHS 1974 Fuchs, J., 'L'Oeuvre Notre-Dame et la cathédrale de Strasbourg à travers les archives', *Bulletin de la société des amis de la cathédrale de Strasbourg* 11 (1974), 21-34.

FUCHS 1990A Fuchs, F.J., 'Les comptes de l'oeuvre Notre-Dame des années 1382-83 et 1385, *Bulletin de la Société des Amis de la Cathédrale de Strasbourg* 19 (1990), 41-52.

FUCHS 1990B Fuchs, F.J., 'Un inventaire inédit du mobilier de l'œuvre Notre-Dame de la fin du XIVième siècle', *Bulletin de la Société des Amis de la Cathédrale de Strasbourg* 19 (1990), 53-60.

FUCHS 1998 Fuchs, F.J., 'Comptes de la Fondation de l'œuvre Notre-Dame-Année 1414, *Bulletin de la Société des Amis de la Cathédrale de Strasbourg* 23 (1998), 33-71.

FUCHS 2000 Fuchs, F.J., 'Les administrateurs et les régisseurs de l'œuvre Notre-Dame de Strasbourg : trois réglements inédits des XIVième et XVième siècles', *Bulletin de la Société des Amis de la Cathédrale de Strasbourg* 24 (2000), 139-148.

FUCHS 2004 Fuchs, F.J., 'Comptes de la Fondation de l'œuvre Notre-Dame - Année 1419', *Bulletin de la Société des Amis de la Cathédrale de Strasbourg* 26 (2004), 9-52.

FUCHS 2006 Fuchs, F.J., 'Les comptes de l'œuvre Notre-Dame de 1492-93', *Bulletin de la Société des Amis de la Cathédrale de Strasbourg* 27 (2006), 55-112.

FUCHS & HOLDERBACH 2008 Fuchs, F.J. & J.M. Holderbach, 'Les comptes de lOeuvre Notre-Dame de 1475-76', *Bulletin de la Société des Amis de la Cathédrale de Strasbourg* 28 (2008), 133-168.

G

GADAN 1851 Gadan, J.F., *Comptes de l'église de Troyes 1375-'85*, Troyes 1851.

Gallia Christiana, in provincias ecclesiasticas distributa, Paris, 16 vols, 1715-1874.

GARCÍA CUESTA 1954 García Cuesta, T., 'La catedral de Palencia según los protocolos : La obra de cantería', *Boletín del*

Seminario de Estudios de Arte y Arqueología 20 (1954), 91-142.

GARCÍA MOGOLLÓN 1999 García Mogollón, F.-J., *La catedral de Coria : Arcón de Historia y Fe*, Edilesa 1999.

GARCÍA SANZ 1999 García Sanz, A., 'Un mecenazgo de reyes, estamentos y corporaciones de menestrales en Castilla: la catedral de Segovia (1525-1650)', in *Gli aspetti economici del mecenatismo in Europa (secoli XIV-XVIII) : Atti della 'Diciassettesima settimana di studi', 19-24 aprile 1985*, Prato 1999 [CD-ROM].

GARCÍA VILLADA 1919 García Villada, Z., *Catálogo de los códices y documentos de la catedral de León*, Madrid 1919.

GARDELLES 1963 Gardelles, J., *La cathédrale Saint-André de Bordeaux : Sa place dans l'évolution de l'architecture et de la sculpture*, Bordeaux 1963.

GASNAULT 1962 Gasnault, P., 'Un fragment d'un compte de l'œuvre de la cathédrale de Tours du XVe siècle', *Bulletin de la Société Nationale des Antiquaires de France* (1962), 94-110.

GATTI PERER 1969 Gatti Perer, M.L (ed.), *Il Duomo di Milano : Congresso Internazionale, Milano, Museo Nazionale della Scienza e della Tecnica, 8-12 settembre 1968*, 2 vols, Milan 1969.

GATZ *et al.* 2003 Gatz, E., C. Brodkorb & H. Flachenecker, *Die Bistümer des Heiligen Römischen Reiches von ihren Anfängen bis zur Säkularisation*, Freiburg im Breisgau 2003.

GAUDEMET 1958 Gaudemet, J., *L'église dans l'empire romain (IV-V siècles)*, Paris 1958.

GAUDEMET 1965 Gaudemet, J., 'Recherches sur l'épiscopat médiéval en France', in *Proceedings of the second international congress of medieval canon law*, Rome 1965, 139-155.

GAUDEMET 1979 Gaudemet, J., 'Evêques et chapitres (Législation et doctrine à l'âge classique)', in *Mélanges offerts à Jean Dauvillier*, Toulouse 1979, 317-328.

GAUDEMET 2001 Gaudemet, J., 'Le chapitre cathédral de Paris aux XIIe et XIIIe siècles', *L'année canonique* 43 (2001), 259-282.

GAUDEMET 2008 Gaudemet, J., *Formation du droit canonique et gouvernement de l'église de l'antiquité à l'âge classique*, Strasbourg 2008.

GAZZANIGA 1973 Gazzaniga, J.-L., *L'église du midi à la fin du règne de Charles VII (1444-1461) d'après la jurisprudence du Parlement de Toulouse*, (diss.), Toulouse 1973.

GEARY 1977 Geary, P.J., 'Saint Helen of Athyra and the cathedral of Troyes in the thirteenth century', *The Journal of Medieval and Renaissance Studies* 7 (1977), 149-168.

GECHTER 1983 Gechter, M., *Kirche und Klerus in der stadtkölnischen Wirtschaft im Spätmittelalter*, Wiesbaden 1983.

VAN GELDER 1951 Gelder, H.E. van, 'De muntpolitiek van Philips de Schone 1482-1496', *Jaarboek van het Koninklijk Nederlands Genootschap voor Munt- en Penningkunde*, 1951, 42-55.

VAN GELDER 1971-1972 Gelder, H.E. van, 'De Utrechtse munten ten tijde van bisschop David van Bourgondië', *Jaarboek van het Koninklijk Nederlands Genootschap voor Munt- en Penningkunde*, 1971-1972 (issued 1975), 10-50.

GESCHER 1930 Gescher, F., 'Der Kölner Dom des Mittelalters als Pfarr- und Sendkirche des hohen Adels', in *Der Dom zu Köln : Festschrift zur Feier der 50. Wiederkehr des Tages seiner Vollendung am 15. Oktober 1880*, Cologne 1930, 215-230.

GIESE 1982 Giese, W., 'Zur Bautätigkeit von Bischöfen und Äbten des 10. bis 12. Jahrhunderts', *Deutsches Archiv für Erforschung des Mittelalters* 38 (1982), 388-438.

GILCHRIST 2005 Gilchrist, R., *Norwich cathedral close : The evolution of the English cathedral landscape*, Woodbridge 2005.

GILLES 1995 Gilles, H., 'La cathédrale dans les textes canoniques méridionaux', in *La cathédrale (XIIe-XIVe siècle)*, Cahiers de Fanjeaux, vol. 30, Toulouse 1995, 231-243.

GIMPEL 1958 Gimpel, J., *Les batisseurs de cathédrales*, Paris 1958.

GIORGI & MOSCADELLI 2005 Giorgi, A. & S. Moscadelli, *Costruire una cattedrale : L'Opera di Santa Maria die Siena tra XII e XIV secolo*, Munich 2005.

DE GIRARDOT & DURAND 1849 Girardot, A. de & H. Durand, *La cathédrale de Bourges, description historique et archéologique*, Moulins 1849.

GOBILLOT 1912 Gobillot, Ph., *La cathédrale de Clermont*, Clermont-Ferrand 1912.

GOBILLOT 1937 Gobillot, R., *La cathédrale de Sées*, Paris 1937.

GÖLLER 1910 Göller, E., *Die Einnahmen der apostolischen Kammer unter Johann XXII*, Paderborn 1910.

GOMBRICH 1960 Gombrich, E.H., 'The early Medici as patrons of art : A survey of primary sources', in E.F. Jacob (ed.), *Italian Renaissance Studies : A tribute to the late Cecilia M. Ady*, London 1960, 279-312.

GOÑI GAZTAMBIDE 1949 Goñi Gaztambide, J., 'Los cuestores en España y la regalia de indulgencias : Los cuestores en los siglos XIV y XV', *Hispania Sacra revista de historia eclesiastica* 2 (1949), 1-43.

GOÑI GAZTAMBIDE 1955 Goñi Gaztambide, J.G., 'Nuevos documentos sobre la catedral de Pamplona', *Principe de Viana* 16 (1955), 133-200 (offprint paginated 3-70).

GOÑI GAZTAMBIDE 1965 Goñi Gaztambide, J., *Catálogo del Archiva Catedral de Pamplona*, vol. 1: *829-1500*, Pamplona 1965.

GOÑI GAZTAMBIDE 1970 Goñi Gaztambide, J., 'Santo Domingo de la Calzada: El santo, el puente y la catedral (1418-1362)', *Hispania Sacra* 23 (1970), 451-458.

GOÑI GAZTAMBIDE 1996 Goñi Gaztambide, J.G., 'Nuevos documentos sobre la Catedral de Pamplona', *Príncipe de Viana* 57 (1996), no. 207, 101-142.

GONZÁLEZ VÁZQUEZ 1996 González Vázquez, M., *El arzobispo de Santiago : Una instancia de poder en la edad media (1150-1400)*, Coruña 1996.

GOODMAN 1934 Goodman, A.W., 'The transformation of the nave: prior Nevyle and William of Wykeham', *Winchester Cathedral Record* (1934), no. 3, 12-14.

GÖRRES 1907 Görres, J., *Das lütticher Domkapitel bis zum 14. Jahrhundert*, (diss.), Berlin 1907.

GOTTRON 1951 Gottron, A.B., 'Johann von Hattstein, ein Mainzer Domherr im Zeitalter des Humanismus', in F. Knöpp (ed.), *Archiv für hessische Geschichte und Altertumskunde*, Darmstadt 1951, 37-62.

GOUDRIAAN 1994 Goudriaan, K., 'Het einde van de Middeleeuwen ontdekt?', *Madoc, tijdschrift over de Middeleeuwen* 8 (1994), 66-75.

VAN DE GRAFT 1924 Graft, C.C. van de, 'Over het spel van Herodes in den Dom te Utrecht', *Jaarboekje van Oud-Utrecht*, 1924, 71-103.

VAN DE GRAFT 1926 Graft, C.C. van de, 'De armenpotten van de St. Nicolaas- en de St. Geertruidakerk te Utrecht', *Jaarboekje van Oud-Utrecht*, 1926, 84-114.

GRAHAM 1945-1947 Graham, R., 'An appeal about 1175 for the building fund of St. Pauls' cathedral church', *The Journal of the British Archaeological Association*, 3rd Series, 10 (1945-1947), 73-76.

LE GRAND 1931 Grand, M. le, *Le chapitre cathédral de*

Langres de la fin du XIe siècle au concordat de 1516, Paris 1931.

GRANDJEAN 1963 Grandjean, M., 'A propos de la construction de la cathédrale de Lausanne (XII-XIIIe siècle) : Notes sur la chronologie et les maitres d'œuvre', *Genava* 11 (1963), 261-287.

GRANT 2005 Grant, L., *Architecture and society in Normandy 1120-1270*, New Haven 2005.

GRASS 1983 Grass, N., *Königskirche und Staatsymbolik : Ausgewählte Aufsätze zur Rechtsgeschichte und Sakralkultur der abendländischen Capella regia*, Innsbruck 1983.

DE GROOT 1994 Groot, A. de, 'Beelden in de Dom van Utrecht in de zestiende eeuw', *Nederlands Kunsthistorisch Jaarboek*, 1994, 38-99.

DE GROOT 1998 Groot, A. de, 'Een droom van een Dom : De Dom van Adelbold II, bisschop van Utrecht : Kanttekeningen (geen reconstructie)', *Jaarboek Oud-Utrecht*, 1998, 6-44.

DE GROOT 2006 Groot, A. de, *De Dom van Utrecht in de zestiende eeuw: inrichting, decoratie en gebruik van de katholieke kathedraal*, (unpublished diss. VU University Amsterdam), Amsterdam 2006.

DE GROOT & VAN TONGERLOO 1997 Groot, A. de & L. van Tongerloo, 'Kinderzegening en doop in Dom en Oudmunster, een zeldzaam liturgisch gebruik in het kathedraalcomplex van Utrecht', *Trajecta, tijdschrift voor de geschiedenis van het katholiek leven in de Nederlanden* 6 (1997), 209-232.

GROTE N.D. Grote, A., *Das Dombauamt in Florenz 1285-1370 : Studien zur Geschichte der Opera di Santa Reparata zu Florenz im vierzehnten Jahrhundert*, Munich n.d. (c. 1960).

GROTEN 1980 Groten, M., *Priorenkolleg und Domkapitel von Köln im Hohen Mittelalter*, Bonn 1980.

GUASTI 1887 Guasti, C., *Santa Maria del Fiore : La costruzione della chiesa e del campanile*, FLORENCE 1887.

GUENÉE 1987 Guenée, B., *Entre l'église et l'état : Quatre vies de prélats Français à la fin du moyen âge (XIIIe-XVe siècle)*, Paris 1987.

GUÉRY 1984 Guéry, A., 'Le Roi Dépensier : Le don, la contrainte, et l'origine du système financier de la monarchie française d'Ancien Régime', *Annales, économies, sociétés, civilisations* 39 (1984), 1241-1269.

GUILLOUËT 2003 Guillouët, J.-M., *Les portails de la cathédrale de Nantes: Un grand programme sculpté du XVe siècle et son public*, Rennes 2003.

VON GÜLDENSTUBBE 1988 Güldenstubbe, E.S. von, 'Die Würzburger Dombauamtsrechnung des Rechnungsjahres 1529/30', in *Würzburger Diözesan-Geschichtblätter*, vol. 50 (1988), 659-686.

GUNTERMANN 2003 Guntermann, R.-M., *Turmbau und Totengedenken: Die Domfabrik zu Osnabrück im späten Mittelalter*, Osnabrück 2003 [with CD].

GÜNTHER 1997 Günther, H., '"Als wäre die Peterskirche mutwillig in Flammen gesetzt", zeitgenössische Kommentare zum Neubau der Peterskirche und ihre Massstäbe', *Münchener Jahrbuch der bildenden Kunst*, 1997, 67-112.

GUTH 1970 Guth, K., *Guibert von Nogent und die hochmittelalterliche Kritik an der Reliquienverehrung*, Ottobeuren 1970.

GUTIÉRREZ-CORTINES CORRAL 1987A Gutiérrez-Cortines Corral, C., *Arquitectura, Economía e Iglesia en el siglo XVI (Murcia y su entorno)*, Murcia 1987.

GUTIÉRREZ-CORTINES CORRAL 1987B Gutiérrez-Cortines Corral, C.,

Renacimiento y arquitectura religiosa en la antigu diócesis de Cartagena (Reyno de Murcia, Gobernación de Orihuela y Sierra del Segura), Murcia 1987.

GUYOTJEANNIN 1990 Guyotjeannin, O., 'Les reliques de Saint Éloi a Noyon : Procès et enquêtes du milieu du XIIIe siècle', *Revue Mabillon : Revue internationale d'histoire et de littérature religieuses* 62 (1990), 57-110.

H

HAAKMA WAGENAAR 1934 Haakma Wagenaar, Th., 'De eerste omloop van den Domtoren in de XIVe en XVe eeuw', *Jaarboekje van Oud-Urecht*, 1934, 58-84.

HAAKMA WAGENAAR 1935 Haakma Wagenaar, Th., *De bouwgeschiedenis van de Buurkerk te Utrecht; proeve eener historische voorbereiding van de restauratie van een middeleeuwsch monument*, Utrecht 1935.

HAAKMA WAGENAAR 1975 Haakma Wagenaar, Th., *Memorandum Domtoren*, vol. 1: *Architectuur en bouwgeschiedenis*, vol. 2: *De restauratie van 1901-1931*, vol. 3: *Tekeningen en foto's*, Utrecht 1975.

HAAS 1966 Haas, W., 'Die Erbauer des Domes zu Speyer : Bauherren-Architekten-Handwerker', *Zeitschrift für Kunstgeschichte* 29 (1966), 223-241.

HABETS 1888 Habets, J., *Beknopte geschiedenis der proostdij van Meerssen*, Moordrecht 1888.

HABETS 1979 Habets, J., 'Bedelbrieven uit het archief van het Heilige Geest Gasthuis in Groningen', in *Excursiones Mediaevales : Opstellen aangeboden aan Prof. Dr. A.G. Jongkees door zijn leerlingen*, Groningen 1979, 77-93.

HAGEMANN 1901 Hagemann, H., *Das Osnabrücker Domkapitel in seiner Entwicklung bis im 14. Jahrhundert*, (diss.), Greifswald 1901.

HAINES & RICCETTI 1996 Haines, M. & L. Riccetti (eds), *Opera : Carattere e ruolo delle fabbriche cittadine fino all'inizio dell'Età Moderna. Atti della Tavola Rotonda, Villa i Tatti, Firenze, 3 aprile 1991*, Florence 1996.

HALICZER 1981 Haliczer, S., *The Comuneros of Castile : The Forging of a Revolution, 1475-1521*, Wisconsin 1981.

HALLAM 1982 Hallam, E.M., 'Royal burial and the cult of kingship in France and England', *Journal of Medieval History* 8 (1982), 359-380.

HALLER 1903 Haller, J., *Papsttum und Kirchenreform: Vier Kapitel zur Geschichte des ausgehenden Mittelalters*, vol. 1, Berlin 1903.

HAMANN & ROSENFELD Hamann, R. & F. Rosenfeld, *Der Magdeburger Dom*, Berlin 1910.

HAMILTON 1970 Hamilton, E.J., *American treasure and the price revolution in Spain, 1501-1650*, [first edition 1934], New York 1970.

HAMILTON THOMPSON 1920 Hamilton Thompson, A., 'Medieval building documents and what we learn from them', *Proceedings of the Somersetshire Archaeological and Natural History Society* 66 (1920), 1-25.

HAMILTON THOMPSON 1925 Hamilton Thompson, A., *The cathedral churches of England*, London 1925.

HAMILTON THOMPSON 1943 Hamilton Thompson, A., 'Diocesan organization in the middle ages; archdeacons and rural deans', *Proceedings of the British Academy* 29 (1943), 153-194.

HAMILTON THOMPSON 1947 Hamilton Thompson, A., *The English clergy and their organization in the later middle ages*, Oxford 1947.

HAMON 2001 Hamon, É., 'Le financement du chantier de la tour nord de la cathédrale de Bourges au début du XVIe siècle', in O. Chapelot (ed.), *Du projet au chantier : Maîtres d'ouvrage et maîtres d'œuvre aux XIVe-XVIe siècles*, Paris 2001, 117-139.

HANAUER 1900-1901 Hanauer, A., 'L'œuvre Notre-Dame de Strasbourg', *Revue catholique d'Alsace*, New Series, 19 (1900), 752-766, 801-818; 20 (1901), 7-32.

HANAUER 1901-1902 Hanauer, A., 'Nouvelles notes sur l'œuvre Notre-Dame', *Revue catholique d'Alsace*, New Series, 20 (1901), 807-817, 906-913; 21 (1902), 49-57, 81-97, 161-178, 241-254.

HARDY 1917 Hardy, V., *La cathédrale St.-Pierre de Lisieux*, Paris 1917.

HARVEY 1957 Harvey, J., *The cathedrals of Spain*, London 1957.

HARVEY 1972 Harvey, J., *The mediaeval architect*, London 1972.

HASAK 1927 Hasak, M., *Das Münster unserer Lieben Frau zu Strassburg im Elsass*, Berlin 1927.

HASHAGEN 1931 Hashagen, J., *Staat und Kirche vor der Reformation; eine Untersuchung der vorreformatorischen Bedeutung des Laieneinflusses in der Kirche*, Essen 1931.

HASLINGHUIS 1926 Haslinghuis, E.J, 'De Buurkerk te Utrecht en hare bouwgeschiedenis', *Oudheidkundig Jaarboek*, 1926, 122-148.

HASLINGHUIS & PEETERS 1965 Haslinghuis, E.J. & C.J.A.C. Peeters, *De Dom van Utrecht*, The Hague 1965.

HAUCK 1898-1920 Hauck, A., *Kirchengeschichte Deutschlands*, 5 vols, Leipzig 1898[2]-1920.

HAURÉAU 1896 Hauréau, M.B., 'Notice sur le numéro 16089 des manuscrits latins de la Bibliothèque Nationale', *Notices et extraits des manuscrits de la Bibliothèque Nationale et autres bibliothèques* 35 (1896), 208-239.

HAUSSHERR 1971 Haussherr, R., 'Zu Auftrag, Programm und Büstenzyklus des Prager Domchores', *Zeitschrift für Kunstgeschichte* 34 (1971), 21-46.

HAVERKORN VAN RIJSEWIJK 1900-1901 Haverkorn van Rijsewijk, P., 'Het heilig Graf in de Domkerk te Utrecht', *Bulletin van den Nederlandschen Oudheidkundigen Bond* 2 (1900-1901), 39-43.

VAN HAVRE 1879 Havre, G. van (ed.), *Chronijck der Stadt Antwerpen, toegeschreven aan den notaris Geeraard Bertijn*, Antwerp 1879.

HAWICKS 2004 Hawicks, H., 'Zur wirtschaflichen Bedeutung der Heiligenverehrung für die Errichtung gotischer Sakralbauten am Niederrhein : Das Beispiel von Viktortracht un Viktordom in Xanten im Kontext des Prozessions- und Kirchbauwesens', in D. Geuenich (ed.), *Heiligenverehrung und Wallfahrten am Niederrhein*, Essen 2004, 50-70.

HAYES 1999 Hayes, D.M., 'Mundane uses of sacred places in the central and later Middle Ages, with a focus on Chartres cathedral', *Comitatus: A journal of Medieval and Renaissance Studies* 30 (1999), 11-36.

HAYEZ 1985 Hayez, A.-M., 'Problèmes paroissiaux vus de la cour d'Avignon sous le pontificat d'Urbain V (1362-1370)', in *L'encadrement religieux des fidèles au Moyen-Âge et jusqu'au Concile de Trento*, Paris 1985, 135-169.

HAYTER 1970 Hayter, W., *William of Wykeham, patron of the arts*, London 1970.

HAZEWINKEL 1928 Hazewinkel, H.C., 'Voor 400 jaar', *Jaarboekje van Oud-Utrecht*, 1928, 47-88.

HEARN 1994 Hearn, M.F., 'Canterbury Cathedral and the Cult of Becket', *The Art Bulletin* 76 (1994), no. 1, 19-52.

HEATH 1964 Heath, P., *Medieval clerical accounts*, York 1964.

HECKERT 1993 Heckert, U., 'Die Ratskapelle als Zentrum bürgerlicher Herrschaft und Frömmigkeit : Struktur, Ikonographie und Funktion', *Blätter für deutsche Landesgeschichte : Neue Folge des Korrespondenz-*

blattes 129 (1993), 139-164.

HEERINGA 1927 Heeringa, K., 'Het zesde altaar in het nieuwe werk van den Dom', *Jaarboekje van Oud-Utrecht*, 1927, 61-71.

HEERINGA 1932 Heeringa, K., *Rekeningen van het Bisdom Utrecht 1378-1573*, vol. 2: *Rekeningen over het geestelijk gezag van den bisschop*, vol. 3: *Inleiding en indices*, Utrecht 1932.

HEFELE & LECLERCQ 1907-1938 Hefele, J. & H. Leclercq, *Histoire des conciles d'après les documents originaux*, 19 vols, Paris 1907-1938.

VAN DER HEGGE ZIJNEN 1925 Hegge Zijnen, B.A.J. van der, 'De klokken van den Utrechtschen Dom', *Jaarboekje van Oud-Utrecht*, 1925, 25 ff.

HEIDRICH 1991A Heidrich, I., 'Bischöfe und Bischofskirche von Speyer', in *Die Salier und das Reich*, vol. 2: *Die Reichskirche in der Salierzeit*, Sigmaringen 1991, 187-224.

HEIDRICH 1991B Heidrich, I., 'Die Bischöfe von Speyer in der Salierzeit und der Dombau', *Rheinische Vierteljahrsblätter* 55 (1991), 1-20.

HEINTSCHEL 1956 Heintschel, D.E., *The medieval concept of an ecclesiastical office (1140-1300)*, Washington 1956.

HEINZELMANN 1979 Heinzelmann, M., *Translationsberichte und andere Quellen des Reliquienkultes*, Typologie des sources du Moyen Âge occidental, vol. 33, Turnhout 1979.

HÉLIOT 1953 Héliot, P., 'Les anciennes cathédrales d'Arras', *Bulletin van de koninklijke commissie voor monumenten en landschappen* 4 (1953), 11-109.

HÉLIOT 1963 Héliot, P., 'Voyages de reliques au profit des églises françaises du moyen-âge', *Académie des Inscriptions et Belles Lettres; comptes rendus des séances de l'année 1963*, 90-96.

HÉLIOT 1965 Héliot, P., 'L'étude de l'architecture française au moyen-âge: bilan, perspectives et programme', *Gazette des Beaux-Arts* 107 (1965), 240-246.

HÉLIOT & CHASTANG 1964/1965 Héliot, P. & M.-L. Chastang, 'Quêtes et voyages de reliques au profit des églises françaises du moyen-âge', *Revue d'histoire ecclésiastique* 59 (1964), 789-822; 60 (1965), 5-32.

HELLE 2003 Helle, K. (ed.), *The Cambridge history of Scandinavia*, vol.1: *Prehistory to 1520*, Cambridge 2003.

HENDERIKX 1977 Henderikx, P.A., *De oudste bedelordekloosters in het graafschap Holland en Zeeland*, Dordrecht 1977.

HERBERS 1994 Herbers, K., 'Politik und Heiligenverehrung auf der Iberischen Halbinsel : Die Entwicklung des "politischen Jakobus"', in J. Petersohn (ed.), *Politik und Heiligenverehrung im Hochmittelalter*, Sigmaringen 1994, 177-275.

HERMANN 1988 Hermann, Ch., *L'Église d'Espagne sous le patronage royal (1476-1834)*, Madrid 1988.

HERMESDORF 1963 Hermesdorf, B.H.D., 'Thomas van Aquino als raadsman van Toskaanse kooplieden', *Mededelingen der Koninklijke Nederlandse Akademie van Wetenschappen afd. Letterkunde*, New Series, 26 (1963), no. 1.

HERRMANN 2007 Herrmann, Chr., *Mittelalterliche Architektur im Preussenland: Untersuchungen zur Frage der Kunstlandschaft und -Geographie*, Petersberg 2007.

HERRMANN & KNIES 1976 Herrmann, F. & H. Knies, *Die Protokolle des Mainzer Domkapitels*, vol. 1: *Die Protokolle aus der Zeit* 1450-1484, Darmstadt 1976.

HERRMANN-MASCARD 1975 Herrmann-Mascard, N., *Les reliques des saints, formation coutumière d'un droit*, Paris 1975.

VAN HERWAARDEN 1978 Herwaarden, J. van,

Opgelegde bedevaarten : Een studie over de praktijk van opleggen van bedevaarten (met name in de stedelijke rechtspraak) in de Nederlanden gedurende de late middeleeuwen (ca. 1300-ca. 1500), Assen/Amsterdam 1978.

VAN HERWAARDEN 2003 Herwaarden, J. van, *Between Saint James and Erasmus : Studies in late-medieval religious life: devotion and pilgrimage in the Netherlands*, Leiden/Boston 2003.

HERZOG 1964 Herzog, E., *Die ottonische Stadt : Die Anfänge der mittelalterlichen Stadtbaukunst in Deutschland*, Berlin 1964.

HEVIA BALLINA 1993 Hevia Ballina, A.H. (ed.), *Memoria Ecclesiae IV : La Catedral y la Diócesis en los Archivos de la Iglesia. Santoral hispano-mozárabe en España*, Oviedo 1993.

HIERONIMUS 1938 Hieronimus, K.W., *Das Hochstift Basel im ausgehenden Mittelalter : Quellen und Forschungen*, Basel 1938.

HIESTAND 1972 Hiestand, R., *Papsturkunden für Templer und Johanniter: Archivberichte und Texte*, Abhandlungen der Akademie der Wissenschaften in Göttingen, Philosophische-Historische Klasse, 3rd Series, no. 77, Gottingen 1972.

HILL 1965 Hill, F., *Medieval Lincoln*, Cambridge 1965[2].

HILLGARTH & SILANO 1984 Hillgarth, J.N. & G.Silano, 'A compilation of the Diocesan synods', *Mediaeval Studies* 46 (1984), 78-157.

HINSCHIUS 1869-1897 Hinschius, P., *System des katholischen Kirchenrechts, mit besonderer Rücksicht auf Deutschland*, 6 vols, Berlin 1869-1897.

HIRSCHMANN 1998 Hirschmann, F.G., *Stadtplanung, Bauprojekte und Grossbaustellen im 10. und 11. Jahrhundert : Vergleichende Studien zu den Kathedralstädten westliches des Rheins*, Stuttgart 1998.

History of Thomas Becket Materials for the history of Thomas Becket, archbishop of Canterbury, 2 vols, London 1875-1876 (reprint 1965).

HODGES 2005 Hodges, L.F., *Chaucer and clothing, clerical and academic costume in the General Prologue to the Canterbury Tales*, Cambridge 2005.

HOFFMAN 1984 Hoffman, P.T., *Church and community in the Diocese of Lyon, 1500-1789*, New Haven 1984.

HOFFMANN 1975 Hoffmann, E., *Die heilige Könige bei den Angelsachsen und den skandinavischen Völkern : Königsheiliger und Königshaus*, Neumünster 1975.

HOFFMANN 1911 Hoffmann, R., *Die wirtschaftliche Verfassung und Verwaltung des Hildesheimer Domkapitels bis zum Beginn der Neuzeit*, (diss.), Münster 1911.

HOFMAN 1894 Hofman, J.H., 'Kerkelijke stukken uit de 15e en 16e eeuw', *Archief voor de Geschiedenis van het aartsbisdom Utrecht* 21 (1894), 1-80.

HOFMAN 2003 Hofman, R. (ed.), 'Gerardi Magni Contra Turrim Trajectensem', in *Gerardi Magni Opera Omnia*, vol. I, Turnhout 2003, 745- 805.

HOFMANN 1914 Hofmann, K., *Die engere Immunität in deutschen Bischofsstädten im Mittelalter*, Paderborn 1914.

HOFMEISTER 1931 Hofmeister, Ph., *Bischof und Domkapitel nach altem und nach neuem Recht*, (diss.), Tübingen 1931.

HOLDEREGGER 1926 Holderegger, H., 'Eine Domfabrikrechnung aus dem 14. Jahrhundert', *Zeitschrift für Schweizerische Geschichte* 6 (1926), 234-279.

HOLLESTELLE 1961 Hollestelle, J., *De steenbakkerij in de Nederlanden tot omstreeks 1560*, Assen 1961.

HOPPE 1975 Hoppe, U., *Die Paderborner Domfreiheit : Untersuchungen zu Topographie, Besitzgeschichte und Funktionen*, Munich 1975.

VAN DER HORST 1866 Horst,

J.J. van der, 'Kerkelijk Veere, proeve eener bronnenstudie', *De Katholiek: godsdienstig, geschied- en letterkundig maandschrift* 48 (1866), 160-183.

HOUDOY 1880 Houdoy, J., *Histoire artistique de la cathédrale de Cambrai, ancienne église métropolitaine : Notre-Dame, comptes, inventaires et documents inédits*, Lille 1880 (reprint Geneva 1972).

VAN DEN HOVEN VAN GENDEREN 1987 Hoven van Genderen, B. van den, *Het kapittel-generaal en de staten van het Nedersticht in de 15e eeuw*, Zutphen 1987.

VAN DEN HOVEN VAN GENDEREN 1997 Hoven van Genderen, B. van den, *De Heren van de Kerk : De kanunniken van Oudmunster te Utrecht in de late middeleeuwen*, Zutphen 1997.

HUARD 1925 Huard, G., 'La paroisse et l'église Saint-Pierre de Caen des origines au milieu du XVIe siècle', *Mémoires de la Société des Antiquaires de Normandie* 35 (1925), 1-300.

HUBEL 1989 Hubel, A., 'La fabrique de Ratisbonne', in R. Recht (ed.), *Les batisseurs des cathédrales gothiques*, Strasbourg 1989, 165-177.

HUBEL & SCHULLER 1995 Hubel, A. & M. Schuller, *Der Dom zu Regensburg : Vom Bauen und Gestalten einer gotischen Kathedrale*, Regensburg 1995.

HUBERT 1962 Hubert, J., 'La vie commune des clercs et l'archéologie', in *La vita commune del clero nei secoli XI e XII: Atti della settimana di studio, Mendola settembre 1959*, Milan 1962, vol. 1, 90-116.

HUBERT 1964 Hubert, J., 'Les origines de Notre-Dame de Paris', *Revue d'histoire de l'Eglise de France* 50 (1964), 5-26.

HÜFFER 1938 Hüffer, M., 'Iets over de HH. Vier Maarschalken', *Studiën, tijdschrift voor godsdienst, wetenschap en letteren* 130 (1938), 439-447, 498-505.

HUGHES 1988 Hughes, J., *Pastors and visionaries : Religion and secular life in late medieval Yorkshire*, Woodbridge/Suffolk 1988.

VAN DEN HUL 1982 Hul, D. van den, *Klokkenkunst te Utrecht tot 1700*, Zutphen 1982.

HULL STOOKEY 1969 Hull Stookey, L., 'The Gothic cathedral as the heavenly Jerusalem: liturgical and theological sources', *Gesta* 8 (1969), 35-41.

HUNNIKIN 1972-1973 Hunnikin, C., 'A note on the administration of the projects of the Piazza del Duomo in Pisa', *Marsyas* 16 (1972-1973), 43-59.

HUOT 1973 Huot, F., *L'Ordinaire de Sion : Etude sur la transmission manuscrite, son cadre historique et sa liturgie*, Fribourg 1973.

I

IMBART DE LA TOUR 1909 Imbart de la Tour, P., *Les origines de la Réforme*, vol. 2, Paris 1909.

Inventaire-sommaire des archives départementales antérieures à 1790: archives ecclésiastiques série G, clergé séculier [with the name of the département], 1862-...

Inventaris Archief kapittel ten Dom Heeringa, K., *Inventaris van het Archief van het kapittel ten Dom*, Utrecht 1929; Hinsbergen, Ph.J.G.G. van, *Index van persoons- en plaatsnamen*, The Hague 1951.

Inventaris archief kapittel Oudmunster Jonge van Ellemeet, B.M. de, *Inventaris van het archief van het kapittel van Oudmunster*, typescript, n.d., Rijksarchief Utrecht.

Inventaris archief kapittel St.-Jan Jonge van Ellemeet, B.M. de, *Inventaris van het archief van het kapittel van St.-Jan*, typescript, 1934, Rijksarchief Utrecht.

Inventaris archief kapittel St.-Marie Jonge van Ellemeet, B.M. de, *Inventaris van het archief van het kapittel van*

St.-Marie, typescript, 1937, Rijksarchief Utrecht.
Inventaris archieven kerken Haarlem Verhoofstad, P.M., *Inventaris der archieven van kerken, kloosters en staties, berustend in het archiefdepot van het bisdom van Haarlem*, Haarlem 1959.
IOGNA-PRAT 2006 Iogna-Prat, D., La Maison Dieu: Une histoire monumentale de l'Église au Moyen Âge, Paris 2006.
ISELE 1955 Isele, E., *Das Freiburger Münster St. Nikolaus und seine Baulast: Rechtsgeschichte einer Kirche*, Freiburg 1955.
ISRAËLS 2006 Israëls, M., *Sassetta's Madonna della Neve : An image of patronage*, (diss. UvA), Leiden 2006.
VAN ITERSON 1960 Iterson, W. van, *De stad Rhenen: De resultaten van een rechtshistorisch onderzoek*, Assen 1960.
IZQUIERDO BENITO 1982 Izquierdo Benito, R., 'Bienes, ingresos y gastos de la Obra de la catedral de Toledo durante la primera mitad del siglo XV', *En la España medieval* 2 (1982), 476-484.
IZQUIERDO BENITO 1985 Izquierdo Benito, R., 'Datos sobre la construcción en Toledo en el s. XV: materiales, herramientas y ordenanzas', *Cahiers de la Méditerranée* 31 (1985), 151-164.

J

JAMES 1972 James, J., 'What price the cathedrals?', *Transactions of the Ancient Monuments Society*, New Series, 19 (1972), 47-65.
JAMES 1977/1979 James, J., *Chartres, Les constructeurs*, vols 1 & 2, Chartres 1977, 1979.
JAMES 2007 James, J., *In search of the unknown in medieval architecture*, London 2007.
JANCEY 1982 Jancey, M., *St Thomas Cantilupe Bishop of Hereford : Essays in his honour*, Hereford 1982.
JANIN 1997 Janin, F., 'Georges d'Amboise, archevêque de Rouen, et son chapitre (1493-1510)', in S. Lemagnen *et al.* (eds), *Chapitres et cathédrales en Normandie*, vol. 2, Caen 1997, 123-137.
JANNER 1876 Janner, F., *Die Bauhütten des deutschen Mittelalters*, Leipzig 1876.
JANSEN 2001 Jansen, Ph., 'Un nouveau chantier dans la ville : Construction du choeur de la cathédrale à la fin du XIIIe et au début du XIVe siècle', in M. Agostino (ed.), *La cathédrale Saint-André, reflet de neuf siècles d'histoire et de vie bordelaise*, Bordeaux 2001, 47-61.
JANSSEN 1995 Janssen, W., *Das Erzbistum Köln im späten Mittelalter 1191-1515*, Cologne 1995.
JEDIN 1979 Jedin, H., 'Bona ecclesiae - Bona pauperum : Zur Vierteilung des Kircheneinkommens vor und auf dem Tridentium', in E. Gatz (ed.), *Römische Kurie. Kirchliche Finanzen. Vatikanisches Archiv : Studien zu Ehren von Hermann Hoberg*, vol. 1, Rome 1979, 405-413.
JENNY 1977 Jenny, J., 'Sur une lettre d'indulgence de l'archevêque de Bourges en faveur de l'Hôtel-Dieu de Paris (1er quart du XVIe siècle)', *Cahiers d'archéologie et d'histoire du Berry* 49 (1977), 1-21.
JOHNSON 1967A Johnson, H. Th., 'Cathedral building and the medieval economy', *Explorations in entrepreneurial history* 4 (1967), 191-209.
JOHNSON 1967B Johnson, H. Th., 'Note: relation of building volume and construction inputs', *Explorations in entrepreneurial history* 5 (1967), 108-110.
JOHNSON 1969 Johnson, H. Th.,'The economic effects of cathedral and church building in medieval England : A rejoinder', *Explorations in entrepreneurial history* 6 (1969), 170-174.
JONES 1952 Jones, G.P., 'Building in stone in medieval Western Europe', in *The Cambridge Economic History of Europe*, vol. 2., Cambridge 1952, 493-519.
JONES 2002 Jones, I.,

'L'archivio della Fabbrica di San Pietro', in A. Pinelli (ed.), *La Basilica di San Pietro in Vaticano*, Rome 2002, 399-407.

DE JONG 1964 Jong, O.J. de, *Beeldenstormen in de Nederlanden*, Groningen 1964.

JONGKEES 1942 Jongkees, A.G., *Staat en Kerk in Holland en Zeeland onder de Bourgondische hertogen 1425-1744*, Groningen 1942.

JOOSTING & MULLER 1906-1924 Joosting, J.G.C. & S. Muller Fnz., *Bronnen voor de geschiedenis der kerkelijke rechtspraak in het bisdom Utrecht in de middeleeuwen*, 7 vols, The Hague 1906-1924.

JORDAN 1959 Jordan, W.K., *Philanthropy in England 1480-1660 : A study of the changing pattern of English social aspirations*, London 1959.

JOUBERT 2001 Joubert, F. (ed.), *L'artiste et le commanditaire aux derniers siècles du Moyen Âge, XIIIe-XVI siècles*, Paris 2001.

JOUBERT 2006 Joubert, F. (ed.), *L'Artiste et le Clerc : La commande artistique des grands ecclésiastiques à la fin du Moyen Âge (XIVe-XVIe siècle)*, Paris 2006.

JOUNEL 1988 Jounel, P., 'La cathédrale, maison de Dieu et du peuple de Dieu', in *La cathédrale demeure de Dieu, demeure des hommes (Actes du Colloque de Pont-à-Mousson, 26-28 juin 1987)*, Paris 1988, 29-49.

JULIER 1970 Julier, J., 'Modo intentius modo remissius agebatur; zur Baufinancierung im Mittelalter', *Der Heidelberger Portländer* 1 (1970), 7-11.

JUSSELIN 1915-1922 Jusselin, M., 'La maîtrise de l'œuvre à Notre-Dame de Chartres : La fabrique, les ouvriers et les travaux du XIVe siècle', *Mémoires de la Société Archéologique d'Eure-et-Loir* 15 (1915-1922), 233-348.

JUSSERAND 1950 Jusserand, J.J., *English wayfaring life in the middle ages*, London 1950[4].

JUTEN 1923-1924 Juten, G.C.A., 'De St.-Geertruikerk te Bergen op Zoom', *Taxandria* 30 (1923), 297-306; 31 (1924), 25-29, 43-48, 73-76, 115-91.

JÜTTE 1985 Jütte, R., 'Feier- und Arbeitstage im alten Köln: Ein Beitrag zur Bestimmung des Einkommens aus Tagelöhnen im Spätmittelalter und der Frühen Neuzeit', *Jahrbuch des Kölner Geschichtsvereins*, 1985, 83-102.

K

KAISER 1995 Kaiser, R., 'Quêtes itinérantes avec des reliques pour financer la construction des églises (XIe-XIIe siècles)', *Le Moyen Age : Revue trimestrelle d'histoire et de philologie* 91 (1995), 205-225.

KAISER 2003 Kaiser, R., 'Guibert de Nogent und der Bischofsmord in Laon (1122): Augenzeuge, Akteur, Dramaturg', in N. Fryde & D. Reitz (eds), *Bischofsmord im Mittelalter*, Göttingen 2003, 121-157.

KALUZA-BAUMRUKER 1987 Kaluza-Baumruker, M., *Das Schweriner Domkapitel (1171-1400)*, Cologne/Vienna 1987.

VAN KALVEEN 1968 Kalveen, C.A. van, 'Oorkonden betreffende de Sacramentsverering te Amersfoort 1340-ca. 1440', *Jaarboekje van Oud-Utrecht*, 1968, 27-40.

VAN KALVEEN 1972 Kalveen, C.A. van, 'De gildenbeweging van april 1525 en haar voorgeschiedenis', *Jaarboekje van Oud-Utrecht*, 1972, 113-114.

VAN KALVEEN 1974 Kalveen, C.A. van, *Het bestuur van bisschop en Staten in het Nedersticht, Oversticht en Drenthe, 1483-1520*, Groningen 1974.

KARGE 1995 Karge, H., *La catedral de Burgos y la Arquitectura del siglo XIII en Francia y España*, León 1995.

Die Kathedrale von St. Veit, vol. 1: *Der Dombau*, Prague 1994.

KEDAR 1994 Kedar, B.Z.,

'Raising funds for a Frankish cathedral: The appeal of bishop Radulph of Sebaste', in P. Klep *et al.* (eds), *Entrepreneurship and the transformation of the economy (10th-20th centuries)*, Louvain 1994, 443-453.

KEMPERS 1996 Kempers, B., 'Diverging perspectives - New Saint Peter's : Artistic ambitions, liturgical requirements, financial limitations and historical interpretations', *Mededelingen van het Nederlands Instituut te Rome* 55 (1996), 213-251.

VAN KEPPEL N.D. Keppel, J.R. van, *Eenige wetenswaardigheden betreffende de Groote- of Lieve Vrouwenkerk te Breda in de XVIde eeuw uit oude rekeningen medegedeeld*, Breda n.d.

KERNKAMP 1954 Kernkamp, J.H., *Vijf jaar praktijk in dienst van het economisch- en sociaalhistorisch hoger onderwijs : Met illustratieve beschouwingen over stedelijke rentebrieven en een keukenboek van 1596*, The Hague 1954.

KIMPEL & SUCKALE 1985 Kimpel, D. & R. Suckale, *Die gotische Architektur in Frankreich 1130-1270*, Munich 1985.

KIRCHHOFF 1910 Kirchhoff, J., *Die Organisation des Osnabrücker Kirchenvermögens in der Zeit vom 12.-14. Jahrhundert*, Osnabrück 1910.

KIRSCH 1903 Kirsch, J., (ed.), *Die päpstlichen Annaten in Deutschland während des XIV. Jahrhunderts*, vol. 1, Paderborn 1903.

KIST 1847 Kist, N.C., 'De rekeningen der parochiekerken te Utrecht, dienstbaar gemaakt aan de geschiedenis', in J.J. Dodt van Flensburg, *Archief voor kerkelijke en wereldsche geschiedenissen, inzonderheid van Utrecht*, vol. 6, Utrecht 1847, 307 ff.

KLEIN 1995 Klein, B., *Die Kathedrale von Piacenza : Architektur und Skulptur der Romanik*, Worms 1995.

KLETZL 1939 Kletzl, O., *Plan-Fragmente aus der deutschen Dombauhütte von Prag in Stuttgart und Ulm*, Stuttgart 1939.

KLINK 1988 Klink, L., *Johann Hemelings 'Diplomatarium fabricae ecclesia Bremensis' von 1415/20*, Hildesheim 1988.

KNOOP & JONES 1949 Knoop, D. & G.P. Jones, *The mediaeval mason : An economic history of English stone building in the later middle ages and early modern times*, Manchester 1949[2].

KNOWLES 1936 Knowles, J.A., *Essays in the history of the York school of glass-painting*, London 1936.

KOSEGARTEN 1996 Kosegarten, A.M., *Die Domfassade in Orvieto : Studien zur Architektur und Skulptur 1290-1330*, Munich/ Berlin 1996.

KÖSTER 1960 Köster, K., 'St. Quirinus-Wallfahrten und ihre Pilgerandenken', *Neusser Jahrbuch*, 1960, 8-27.

KOVÁCS 1992 Kovács, E., 'Die Heiligen und heiligen Könige der frühen Habsburger (1273-1519)', in K. Schreiner & E. Müller-Luckner (eds), *Laienfrömmigkeit im späten Mittelalter : Formen, Funktionen, politisch-soziale Zusammenhänge*, Munich 1992, 93-105.

KOWALESKI 1995 Kowaleski, M., *Local markets and regional trade in medieval Exeter*, Cambridge 1995.

KRAUS 1979 Kraus, H., *Gold was the mortar : The economics of cathedral building*, London 1979.

KREBS 1939-1954 Krebs, M., 'Die Investiturprotokolle der Diözese Konstanz aus dem 15. Jahrhundert', *Beilage zum Freiburger Diözesan-Archiv* 66-74 (1939-1954).

KREBS 1952-1959 Krebs, M. (ed.), 'Die Protokolle des Konstanzer Domkapitels 1487-1526, No. 1-No. 9024', *Zeitschrift für die Geschichte des Oberrheins* 100 (1952), 128-257; 101 (1953), 74-136; 102 (1954), 274-318; 103 (1955), Beiheft; 104 (1956),

Beiheft; 106 (1958), Beiheft; 107 (1959), Beiheft.

KREBS 1968 Krebs, M. (ed.), *Die Protokolle des Speyerer Domkapitels*, vol. 1, 1500-1517, Stuttgart 1968.

KROESEN 2003 Kroesen, J.E.A., *Het middeleeuws altaarretabel op het Iberisch schiereiland : Vorm, plaats, boodschap*, Groningen/Tilburg 2003.

KRONENBURG 1904-1931 Kronenburg, J.A.F., *Maria's heerlijkheid in Nederland. Geschiedkundige schets van de vereering der H. Maagd in ons Vaderland van de eerste tijden tot op onze dagen*, 9 vols, Amsterdam 1904-1931.

KROOS 1985 Kroos, R., 'Opfer, Spende und Geld im mittelalterlichen Gottesdienst', *Frühmittelalterliche Studien : Jahrbuch des Instituts für Frühmittelalterforschung der Universität Münster*, 1985, 502-519.

DE KRUIJF 2009 Kruijf, A. de, 'Terug van weggeweest, de thuiskomst van Utrechtse relieken na de reformatie', *Jaarboek Oud-Utrecht*, 2009, 38-66.

KÜAS 1937 Küas, H., *Die Naumburger Werkstatt*, Berlin 1937.

KÜHN 1994 Kühn, N., 'Die Reichsabtei Kornelimünster', in J. Mötsch & M. Schoebel (eds), *Eiflia Sacra : Studien zu einer Klosterlandschaft*, vol. 30, Mainz 1994, 89-114.

KÜHNE 2000 Kühne, H., *Ostensio Reliquiarum : Untersuchungen über Entstehung, Ausbreitung, Gestalt und Funktion der Heiltumsweisungen im römisch-deutschen Regnum*, Berlin 2000.

Kulturhistorisk Leksikon for Nordisk Middelalder, 22 vols, Roskilde 1956-1982.

KUNSTMANN 1973 Kunstmann, P. (ed.), *Jean le Marchant : Miracles de Notre-Dame de Chartres*, Ottawa/Chartres 1973.

KUNZ VON BRUNN 1902 Kunz von Brunn genannt von Kauffungen, *Das Kapitel von Meissen im Mittelalter; ein Beitrag zur Verfassungs- und Verwaltungsgeschichte der deutschen Domkapitel*, (diss.), Leipzig 1902.

KURMANN 1971 Kurmann, P., *La cathédrale Saint-Etienne de Meaux : Etude architecturale*, Paris 1971.

KURMANN 1987 Kurmann, P., *La façade de la cathédrale de Reims : Architecture et sculpture des portails, étude archéologique et stylistique*, Lausanne 1987.

KURMANN & KURMANN-SCHWARZ 1995 Kurmann, P. & B. Kurmann-Schwarz, 'Chartres Cathedral as a Work of Artistic Integration: Methodological Reflections', in V.C. Raguin *et al.* (eds), *Artistic Integration in Gothic Buildings* :Toronto/Buffalo/London 1995, 131-152.

KURMANN & KURMANN-SCHWARZ 1997 Kurmann, P. & B. Kurmann-Schwarz, 'Französische Bischöfe als Auftraggeber und Stifter von Glasmalereien. Das Kunstwerk als Geschichtsquelle, *Zeitschrift für Kunstgeschichte* 60 (1997), no. 4, 429-450.

KURMANN-SCHWARZ 1996 Kurmann-Schwarz, B., 'Récits, programme, commanditaires, concepteurs, donateurs : Publications récentes sur l'iconographie des vitraux de la cathédrale de Chartres', *Bulletin monumental* 154 (1996), 55-71.

KURMANN-SCHWARZ & KURMANN 2001 Kurmann-Schwarz, B. & P. Kurmann, *Chartres : Die Kathedrale*, Regensburg 2001.

KURZE 1966 Kurze, O., *Pfarrerwahlen im Mittelalter, ein Beitrag zur Geschichte der Gemeinde und des Niederkirchenwesens*, Cologne/Graz 1966.

KUYS 2004 Kuys, J., *Kerkelijke organisatie in het middeleeuwse bisdom Utrecht*, Nijmegen 2004.

KYLL 1962 Kyll, N., *Pflichtprozessionen und Bannfahrten im westlichen Teil des alten Erzbistums Trier*, Bonn 1962.

L

LACARRA DUCAY & MONTERDE ALBIAC 1989 Lacarra Ducay, M.C. & C. Monterde Albiac, 'Un libro de fábrica de la Seo de Zaragoza del año 1346', *Aragón en la Edad Media* (1989), no. 8, 363-381.

DE LACGER 1927 Lacger, L. de, 'Statuts synodaux inédits du diocèse d'Albi au 13ème siècle', *Revue historique du droit français et étranger* 6 (1927), 463 ff.

LACOMBLET 1857 Lacomblet, Th.J., 'Der Dom zu Cöln ist 1248 nicht abgebrannt', *Archiv für die Geschichte des Niederrheins* 2 (1857), 103-180.

LACOMBLET 1868 Lacomblet, Th.J., 'Urkunden und Regesten zur Geschichte des Cölner Dombaues, aus Lacomblet's Nachlasse, mit Einleitung und Erganzungen vom Herausgeber', *Archiv für die Geschichte des Niederrheins* 6 (1868), 9-62.

LADERO QUESADA 1982 Ladero Quesada, M.A., *El siglo XV en Castilla : Fuentes de renta y politica fiscal*, Barcelona 1982.

LAENEN 1924 Laenen, J., *Introduction à l'histoire paroissiale du diocèse de Malines : Les institutions*, Brussels 1924.

LAMBRECHT 1984 Lambrecht, D., *De parochiale synode in het oude bisdom Doornik gesitueerd in de Europese ontwikkeling, 11de eeuw - 1559*, Brussels 1984.

LAMPEN 1929 Lampen, W., *Alcmaria eucharistica : Ter gelegenheid van het vijfde eeuwfeest van het eucharistisch wonder te Alkmaar*, Alkmaar 1929.

DE LANGE 1991 Lange, J. de, *P.C. Hoofts Reis-heuchenis, naar de autograaf uitgegeven, ingeleid en toegelicht*, Amsterdam 1991.

LA PORTE FERNÁNDEZ-ALFARO 1992 La Porte Fernández-Alfaro, P., 'La Plaza Mayor de Sigüenza', *Archivo Español de Arte* (1992), no. 259/260, 403-415.

LARAN 1931 Laran, J., *La cathédrale d'Albi*, Paris 1931.

LARCHER DE LAVERNADE 1845 Larcher de Lavernade, M.Ch., *Histoire de la ville de Sens*, Sens 1845.

LARDIN 1997 Lardin, P., 'Un manœuvre privilégié le valet de la fabrique de la cathédrale de Rouen à la fin du Moyen Âge', in S. Lemagnen *et al.* (eds), *Chapitres et cathédrales en Normandie*, vol. 2, Caen 1997, 361-373.

LA ROCHE 1888 La Roche, E., 'Bauhütte und Bauverwaltung des Basler Münsters', *Beiträge zur vaterländischen Geschichte. Herausgegeben von der historischen und antiquarischen Gesellschaft zu Basel* 12 (1888), 77-113.

LATORRE CIRIA 1992 Latorre Ciria, J.M., *Economía y Religión : Las rentas de la Catedral de Huesca y su distribución social (siglos XVI-XVII)*, Zaragoza/Huesca 1992.

LAUFER 1996 Laufer, A., 'Au pied de la cathédrale: échoppes, ateliers autour de 1220', *Mémoire Vive* (1996), no. 5, 34-44.

LAUTIER 2003 Lautier, C., 'Les vitraux de la cathédrale de Chartres: Reliques et images', *Bulletin Monumental* 161 (2003), 3-97.

LAVERGNE 1920 Lavergne, G., 'Travaux à la cathédrale de Sarlat au XVIe siècle', *Bulletin de la Société historique et archéologique du Périgord* 47 (1920), 155-161.

LEBLOND 1933 Leblond, V., *La cathédrale de Beauvais*, Paris 1933.

LE BRAS 1940-1941 Le Bras, G., 'Les confréries chrétiennes : Problèmes et propositions', *Revue historique de droit français et étranger*, 4th Series, 19-20 (1940-1941), 310-364.

LE BRAS 1954 Le Bras, G., 'L'invasion de l'église dans la cité : Programme de recherche historique sur les rapports de l'urbanisme et du droit canon', in *Urbanisme et architecture; études écrites et publiées en l'honneur de Pierre Lavedan*, Paris 1954.

LE BRAS 1959/1964 Le Bras, G., *Institutions ecclésiastiques de la chrétienté médiévale*, in A. Fliche & V. Martin (eds), *Histoire de l'église depuis les origines jusqu'à nos jours*, vol. 12, 1 & 2, Paris 1959, 1964.

LECOCQ 1876 Lecocq, A., 'Recherches sur les enseignes de pélerinages et les chemisettes de Notre-Dame de Chartres', *Mémoires de la Société Archéologique d'Eure-et-Loir* 6 (1876), 194-243.

LEDRU 1900 Ledru, A., *La cathédrale Saint-Julien Du Mans, ses évêques, son architecture, son mobilier*, Mamers 1900.

LEFEBVRE 1994 Lefebvre, E., *La fabrique de la cathédrale de Rouen : Présentation et Édition des Comptes (1406-1458)*, (unpublished diss. École des chartes), Paris 1994.

LEFEBVRE 1997 Lefebvre, E., 'La cour des libraires de la cathédrale Notre-Dame de Rouen', in S. Lemagnen *et al.* (eds), *Chapitres et cathédrales en Normandie*, vol. 2, Caen 1997, 417-424.

LEFÈVRE-PONTALIS 1905 Lefèvre-Pontalis, E., 'Les architectes et la construction des cathédrales de Chartres', *Mémoires de la Société nationale des antiquaires de France* 64 (1905), 69 ff.

LEFRANC 1896 Lefranc, A., 'Le traité des reliques de Guibert de Nogent et les commencements de la critique historique au moyen-âge', in *Etudes d'histoire du moyen-âge, dédiées à Gabriel Monod*, Paris 1896, 285-306.

LEGUAY 1975 Leguay, J.P., 'Vannes au XV siècle : Aspects institutionels, économiques et sociaux, *Bulletin mensuel de la Société Polymatique du Morbihan* 103 (1975), 45-120.

LEHMANN-BROCKHAUS 1938 Lehmann-Brockhaus, O., *Schriftquellen zur Kunstgeschichte des 11. und 12. Jahrhunderts für Deutschland, Lothringen und Italien*, 2 vols, Berlin 1938.

LEHMANN-BROCKHAUS 1955-1960 Lehmann-Brockhaus, O., *Lateinische Schriftquellen zur Kunst in England, Wales und Schottland vom Jahre 901 bis zum Jahre 1307*, 5 vols, Munich 1955-1960.

LEHMBERG 1988 Lehmberg, S.E., *The Reformation of Cathedrals : Cathedrals in English society, 1485-1603*, New Jersey 1988.

LEISCHING 1964 Leisching, P., 'Die Rechtsverhältnisse des Salzburger Domes', *Österreichisches Archiv für Kirchenrecht* 15 (1964), 259-276.

LEMAITRE 1995 Lemaitre, J.-L., 'Une cathédrale en son île : MAGUELONE', in *La cathédrale (XIIe-XIVe siècle)*, Cahiers de Fanjeaux, vol. 30, Toulouse 1995, 79-95.

LEMARIGNIER *et al.* 1962 Lemarignier, J.-F., J. Gaudemet & G. Mollat, *Histoire des institutions françaises au moyen-âge*, vol. 3: *Institutions ecclésiastiques*, Paris 1962.

LE MEN 1877 Le Men, R.F., *Monographie de la cathédrale de Quimper* (XIIIe-XVe *siècle)*, Quimper 1877.

LE MENÉ 1882 Le Mené, J.M., *Histoire de l'église cathédrale de Vannes*, Vannes 1882 (extract from *Bulletin de la Société polymathématique du Morbihan*).

LE MENÉ 1900 Le Mené, M.l., 'Le chapitre de la cathédrale de Vannes', *Bulletin de la Société Polymatique du Morbihan* (1900), 149-261.

LE MENÉ 1961 Le Mené, M., 'La construction à Nantes au XVe siècle', *Annales de Bretagne* 68 (1961), 361-402.

LENTZE 1950 Lentze, H., 'Begrabnis und Jahrtag im mittelalterlichen Wien', *Zeitschrift der Savigny-Stiftung für Rechtsgeschichte, Kanonistische Abteilung* 36 (1950), 328-364.

LEPINE 1995 Lepine, D., *Brotherhood of Canons*

Serving God : English Secular Cathedrals in the Later Middle Ages, Woodbridge 1995.

LEPINE 2006 Lepine, D., '"And alle oure paresshens" : Secular cathedrals and parish churches in late medieval England', in C. Burgess & D. Eamon (eds), *The Parish in late medieval England, proceedings of the 2002 Harlaxton Symposium*, Donington 2006, 29-53.

LEPPER 1979 Lepper, H., 'Unbekannte Synodalstatuten der Kölner Erzbischöfe Heinrich von Virneburg (1306-1332) und Wilhelm von Gennep (1349-1362)', *Annuarium Historiae Conciliorum* 11 (1979), 339-355.

DE LERA MAÍLLO 1999 Lera Maíllo, J.C. de, *Catálogo de los documentos medievales de la catedral de Zamora*, Zamora 1999.

LEROUX 1910 Leroux, A., 'De l'introduction du français en Limousin du XIVe au XVIe siècle', *Bulletin historique et philosophique du Comité des travaux historiques et scientifiques* (1910), 427-435.

LEROY 1985 Leroy, B., 'Les grands chantiers publics en Navarre, sous la dynastie d'Evreux (1328-1430)', *Cahiers de la Méditerranée* 31 (1986), 55-71.

LESNE 1910 Lesne, E., *L'origine des menses dans le temporel des églises et des monastères de France au IXe siècle*, Paris 1910.

LESNE 1936/1943 Lesne, E., *Histoire de la propriété ecclésiastique en France*, Lille, vol. 3, 1936; vol. 6, 1943.

Lettres communes Benoît XII Vidal, J.-M. (ed.), *Benoît XII (1334-1342), lettres communes, Analysées d'après les registres dits d'Avignon et du Vatican*, Paris 1903-1911.

Lettres communes Jean XXII Mollat, G. (ed.), *Lettres communes de Jean XXII (1316-1334)*, Paris 1904-1947.

Lettres communes Urbain V Hayez, M. & A.M. (eds), *Urbain V (1362-1370), Lettres communes, analysées d'après les registres dits d'Avignon et du Vatican*, 12 vols, Rome 1954-1989.

LEUDEMANN 1980 Leudemann, N., *Deutsche Bischofstädte im Mittelalter : Zur topographischen Entwicklung der deutschen Bischofsstadt im Heiligen Römischen Reich*, Munich 1980.

LEUZE 1908 Leuze, O., *Das Augsburger Domkapitel im Mittelalter, (*diss.), Tübingen 1908.

Lexikon für Theologie und Kirche, Freiburg im Breisgau 1957-1966[2].

LIERMAN 1963 Lierman, H., *Handbuch des Stiftungsrecht*, vol. 1, *Geschichte des Stiftungsrecht*, Tübingen 1963.

LINDNER 1950 Lindner, O., 'Die Inkorporation im Bistum Regensburg wahrend des Mittelalters', *Zeitschrift der Savigny-Stiftung fiir Rechtsgeschichte, Kanonistische Abteilung* 36 (1950), 205-328.

LIVETT 1883 Livett, G.M., *Guide to Southwell Minster*, Southwell 1883.

LLORENS Y RAGA 1970 Llorens y Raga, P.-L., *Inventario de los fondos del archivo histórico de la catedral de Segorbe*, Castellón 1970.

LLOYD 1988 Lloyd, S., *English society and the crusade 1216-1307*, Oxford 1988.

LOCATELLI & VERGNOLLE 1995 Locatelli, R. & E. Vergnolle (eds), 'Les comptes de construction médiévaux et l'histoire de l'architecture', *Revue de l'art* 110 (1995), 42-67.

LOMBARD-JOURDAN 1997 Lombard-Jourdan, A., 'L'invention du "Roi Fondateur" à Paris au XIIe siècle : De l'obligation morale au thème sculptural', *Bibliothèque de l'École des chartes* 155 (1997), 485-542.

LOPEZ 1952 Lopez, R.S., 'Economie et architecture médiévale: cela aurait-il tué ceci?', *Annales, économies, sociétés, civilisations* 7 (1952), 433-439.

LÓPEZ-ARÉVALO 1966 López-Arévalo, J.R., *Un cabildo catedral de la vieja Castilla. Avila: su estructura juridica, s. XIII-XX*, Madrid 1966.

LÓPEZ FERREIRO 1898-1911 López Ferreiro, L.P.A., *Historia de la Santa A.M. Iglesia de Santiago*, 11 vols, Santiago de Compostela 1898-1911.

LÓPEZ DE SILANES & SÁINZ RIPA 1991 López de Silanes, C. & E. Sáinz Ripa, *Colección diplomática calceatense. Archivo Catedral (1400-1450)*, Logroño 1991.

LÓPEZ DE SILANES & SÁINZ RIPA 1992 López de Silanes, C. & E. Sáinz Ripa, *Colección diplomática calceatense. Archivo catedral (1451-1499) y Archivo del Hospital (1431-1497)*, Logroño 1992.

LOP OTÍN 2006 Lop Otín, M.J., *El cabildo catedralicio de Toledo en el siglo XV : Aspectos institucionales y sociológicos*, (diss.), Madrid 2006 [CD].

LORENTZ & SANDRON 2006 Lorentz, Ph. & D. Sandron, *Atlas de Paris au Moyen Âge : Espace urbain, habitat, société, religion, lieux de pouvoir*, Paris 2006.

LOT 1865 Lot, H., 'Une querelle de l'évêque de Paris et du chapitre de Notre-Dame au XIIIe et XVe siècle', *Bibliothèque de l'École des chartes* 26 (1865), 149-162.

LOTH 1879 Loth, J., *La cathédrale de Rouen, son histoire, sa description depuis les origines jusqu'il nos jours*, Rouen 1879.

LOWTH 1777 Lowth, R., *The life of William of Wykeham, bishop of Winchester*, Oxford 1777.

LUCAS 1986 Lucas, A.T., 'The social role of relics and reliquaries in ancient Ireland', *Journal of the Royal Society of Antiquaries in Ireland* 116 (1986), 5-37.

LUCHAIRE 1909 Luchaire, A., *La société française au temps de Philippe-Auguste*, Paris 1909[2].

LUCZAK 1931 Luczak, J., *La résidence des évêques dans la législation canonique avant le concile de Trento*, Paris 1931.

LUNT 1939 Lunt, W.E., *Financial relations of the papacy with England to 1327*, Cambridge (USA) 1939.

LUNT 1962 Lunt, W.E., *Financial relations of the papacy with England 1327-1534*, Cambridge (USA) 1962.

LUNT 1965 Lunt, W.E., *Papal revenues in the middle ages*, vols 1 & 2, New York 1965 (first edition 1934).

M

MAGNUSON 1958 Magnuson, T., *Studies in Roman Quattrocento Architecture*, Stockholm 1958.

MANHES-DEREMBLE 1993 Manhes-Deremble, C., *Les vitraux narratifs de la cathédrale de Chartres : Étude Iconographique*, Paris 1993.

MANRY *et al.* 1959 Manry, A.G., R. Sève & M. Chaulanges, *L'Histoire vue de l'Auvergne : Choix de documents*, Clermont-Ferrand 1959.

MANSI 1759-1793 Mansi, J.O., *Sacrorum conciliorum nova et amplissima collectio*, 51 vols, Florence 1759-1793.

MANSILLA REOYO 1956 Mansilla Reoyo, D., *El archivo capitular de la catedral de Burgos : Breve guía y sumaria descripción de sus fondos*, Burgos 1956.

MANSILLA REOYO 1994 Mansilla Reoyo, D., *Geografía Eclesiástica de España : Estudio histórico-geográfico de las Diócesis*, vols 1 & 2, Rome 1994.

MARAIS & BEAUDOIN 1876 Marais, H. & H. Beaudoin, *Essai historique sur la cathédrale et le chapitre de Séez*, Alençon 1876.

MARCHAL 1999-2000 Marchal, G.P., 'Was war das weltliche Kanonikersinstitut im Mittelalter? Dom- und Kollegiatstifte : Eine Einführung und eine neue Perspektive', *Revue d'histoire ecclésiastique* 94 (1999), 761-807; 95 (2000), 7-53.

MARCOS RODRÍGUEZ 1962 Marcos Rodríguez, F.,

Catálogo de documentos del archivo catedralicio de Salamanca (siglos XII-XV), Salamanca 1962.

MARGRY & CASPERS 1997 Margry, P.J. & Ch. Caspers, *Bedevaartplaatsen in Nederland*, vol. 1: *Noord- en Midden-Nederland*, Amsterdam/Hilversum 1997.

MARGRY & CASPERS 2008 Margry P.J. & Ch. Caspers, *101 bedevaartplaatsen in Nederland*, Amsterdam 2008.

MARÍAS 1983 Marías, F., *La Arquitectura del Renacimiento en Toledo (1541-1631)*, vol. 1, Toledo 1983.

MARÍN LÓPEZ 1998 Marín López, R., *El cabildo de la catedral de Granada en el siglo XVI*, Granada 1998.

MARSILLE 1982 Marsille, H., 'La petite guerre des chanoines', *Bulletin de la Société Polymatique du Morbihan* 109 (1982), 79-86.

MARTÈNE & DURAND 1717 Martène, E. & U. Durand, *Thesaurus Novus Anecdotorum*, 4 vols, Paris 1717.

MARTÈNE & DURAND 1724-1733 Martène, E. & U. Durand, *Veterum scriptorum et monumentorum historicorum, dogmaticorum, moralium amplissima collectio*, 9 vols, Paris 1724-1733.

MARTÍN MARTÍN 1975 Martín Martín, J.L., *El Cabildo de la Catedral de Salamanca (siglos XII-XIII)*, vol. 26, Salamanca 1975.

MARTÍN RIBES 1983 Martín Ribes, J., *Custodia procesional de Arfe*, Córdoba 1983.

MARTÍNEZ DE AGUIRRE 1987 Martínez de Aguirre, J., *Arte y monarquía en Navarra, 1328-1425*, Pamplona 1987.

MARTINEZ Y SANZ 1866 Martínez y Sanz, D., *Historia del templo catedral de Burgos, escrita con arreglo a documentos de su archivo*, Burgos 1866.

DE LA MARTINIÈRE 1923 Martinière, J. de la, 'Vannes dans l'ancien temps : Comment Maître Vincent enrichit l'Église de Vannes', *Bulletin de la Société Polymatique du Morbihan* (1923), 108-124.

MATAMOROS 1932 Matamoros, J., *La catedral de Tortosa*, Tortosa 1932.

MATHIEU 1973 Mathieu, K., *Der Hamburger Dom : Untersuchungen für Baugeschichte im 13. und 14. Jahrhundert (1245-1329) und eine Dokumentation zum Abbruch in den Jahren 1804-1807*, Hamburg 1973.

MATHON 1864 Mathon, M., 'Documents concernant l'œuvre de la cathédrale de Noyon', *Revue des sociétés savantes des départements* (1864), 587-600.

MATTHAEUS 1703 Matthaeus, A., *Fundationes et fata ecclesiarum quae et Ultrajecti et in ejusdem suburbiis et passim alibi in diocesi*, Leiden 1703.

MAURER 2002 Maurer, H., 'Zur Bedeutung der Kathedrale für die Diozöse des späten Mittelalters : Beobachtungen an Bischofskirchen der Alemania', *Römische Quartalschrift für christliche Altertumskunde und Kirchengeschichte* 92 (2002), 238-256.

VAN DER MEER 1940 Meer, F.G.L. van der, *Geschiedenis eener kathedraal*, Utrecht 1940.

VAN DER MEER 1967 Meer, F.G.L. van der, *Onbekende kathedralen in Frankrijk*, Amsterdam/Brussels 1967.

MEINDERSMA 1973 Meindersma, K. T., 'Offerblokken in Nederland', *Bulletin van de Koninklijke Nederlandse Oudheidkundige Bond* 72 (1973), 23-44.

MEISCHKE 1964 Meischke, R., 'Drie kerken van Rutger van Kampen', in *Opus Musivum : Een bundel studies aangeboden aan Prof. Dr. M.D. Ozinga ter gelegenheid van zijn zestigste verjaardag op 10 november 1962*, Assen 1964, 115-161.

MEISEN 1936 Meisen, K., 'Ein Mirakelbüchlein des 15. Jahrhunderts aus der Wallfahrtskirche Marienthal bei Hamm an der Sieg',

Annalen des historischen Vereins für den Niederrhein 129 (1936), 88-115.

DE MÉLY 1920/1921 Mély, F. de, 'Nos vieilles cathédrales et leurs maîtres d'œuvre', *Revue archéologique*, 5th Series, 11 (1920), 290-362; 13 (1921), 77-108.

Mendicatorium Assche 'Mendicatorium ou lettre de recommandation donnée par l'évéque de Cambrai à ceux qui quêtaient pour la reconstruction de l'église d'Assche', *Analectes pour servir à l'histoire ecclésiastique de la Belgique* 1 (1864), 222-226.

MERINO RUBIO 1974 Merino Rubio, W., *Arquitectura hispano flamenca en León*, León 1974.

MERLET 1858 Merlet, L., 'Boutiques au cloître Notre-Dame (Chartres)', *Mémoires de la Société Archéologique d'Eure-et-Loir* 1 (1858), 79-89.

MERLET 1889 Merlet, L., 'Compte de l'œuvre de la cathédrale de Chartres en 1415-'16', *Bulletin archéologique du Comité des travaux historiques et scientifiques* (1889), 35-94.

MERLET 1906 Merlet, R., 'Les architectes de la cathédrale de Chartres et la construction de la chapelle Saint-Piat au XIVe siècle', *Bulletin Monumental* 70 (1906), 218-234.

MEUNIER 2002 Meunier, F., 'Les Chambiges à Senlis : L'art flamboyant sous François Ier', in *Comptes rendus et mémoires de la Société et d'archéologie de Senlis années 2000 et 2001*, Senlis 2002, 1-22.

MEUNIER 2003 Meunier, F., 'Les travaux de la cathédrale de Beauvais dans un arrêt du Parlement de Paris (1512)', *Bibliothèque de l'École des chartes* 161 (2003), 33-57.

MEUNIER (FORTHCOMING) Meunier, F., 'Le financement de la cathédrale de Troyes dans le premier tiers du XVIe siècle', in *Le financement de la construction aux XIIIe-XVIe siècles en France*, Paris (forthcoming).

MEZZANOTTE 1955 Mezzanotte, P., 'Il Duomo', in *Storia di Milano*, vol. 6 (1392-1450), Milan 1955, 857-931.

MICHEL 1906 Michel, A., *Histoire de l'art*, vol. 2 (1), Paris 1906.

VAN MIERIS 1756 Mieris, F. van, *Groot charterboek der graven van Holland, van Zeeland en Heeren van Vriesland*, vol. 4, Leiden 1756.

MIGNE 1844-1891 Migne, J.P., *Patrologiae cursus completus [...] series latina*, 235 vols, Paris 1844-1891.

MILITZER 1997-2000 Militzer, K. (ed.), *zur Geschichte der Kölner Laienbruderschaften vom 12. Jahrhundert bis 1562/63*, 4 vols, Düsseldorf 1997-2000.

MINNIS 2003 Minnis, A., 'Reclaiming the pardoners', *Journal of medieval and early modern studies* 33 (2003), 311-334.

MINOIS 2005 Minois, D., *Le vitrail à Troyes: les chantiers et les hommes (1480-1560)*, Paris 2005.

MIRALLES SBERT 1941-1943 Miralles Sbert, J., *Catálogo del archivo capitular de Mallorca*, 3 vols, Palma de Mallorca 1941-1943.

MISCHLEWSKI 1958 Mischlewski, A., 'Der Antoniterorden in Deutschland', *Archiv für mittelrheinische Kirchengeschichte* 10 (1958), 39-66.

MISCHLEWSKI 1976 Mischlewski, A., *Grundzüge der Geschichte des Antoniterordens bis zum Ausgang des 15. Jahrhunderts*, Cologne/Vienna 1976.

MISCHLEWSKI 1992 Mischlewski, A., 'Eine deutsche Antoniterpredigt aus dem 15. Jahrhundert', in H. Mordek (ed.), *Aus Archiven und Bibliotheken, Festschrift für Raymund Kottje zum 65. Geburtstag*, Frankfurt am Main/Bern/New York/Paris 1992, 477-488.

MISCHLEWSKI 1995 Mischlewski, A., *Un ordre hospitalier au Moyen Age :*

Les chanoines regulier de Saint-Antoine-en-Viennois, Grenoble 1995.

MITTERWIESER 1918 Mitterwieser, A., 'Der Dom zu Freising und sein Zubehör zu Ausgang des Mittelalters', *Sammelblatt des historischen Vereins Freising* 11 (1918) 1-98.

MOBERLY 1893 Moberly, G.H., *Life of William of Wykeham*, Winchester/London 1893.

MOELLER 1989 Moeller, B., 'Die letzten Ablaßkampagnen : Der Widerspruch Luthers gegen den Ablaß in seinem geschichtlichen Zusammenhang', in H. Boockmann *et al.* (eds), *Lebensleren und Weltentwürfe im Übergang vom Mittelalter zur Neuzeit : Bericht über Kolloquien der Kommission zur Erforschung der Kultur des Spätmittelalters 1983 bis 1987*, Göttingen 1989, 539-567.

MOL 2004 Mol, J.A., *Friezen en de zeggenschap over hun kerken in de Middeleeuwen*, (inaugural address), Leiden 2004.

MOLINIER 1902 Molinier, A. (ed.), *Obituaires de la Province de Sens*, vol. 1, Paris 1902.

MOLS 1954-1956 Mols, R., *Introduction à la démographie historique des villes d'Europe du XIVe au XVIIIe siècle*, 3 vols, Louvain 1954-1956.

VAN DER MONDE 1842 Monde, N. van der, 'Over de steenboeten te Utrecht', *Tijdschrift voor Geschiedenis, Oudheden en Statistiek van Utrecht* 8 (1842), 325-338.

VAN DER MONDE 1844 Monde, N. van der, *Geschied- en oudheidkundige beschrijving van de pleinen, straten, stegen, waterleidingen, wedden, putten en pompen der stad Utrecht*, 3 vols, Utrecht 1844.

MONE 1834 Mone, F.J., 'Die Münsterfabrik zu Basel', *Anzeiger für Kunde des deutschen Mittelalters* 3 (1834), 205-208, 319-329.

MONE 1836 Mone, F.J., 'Über die Domfabrik zu Speyer', *Anzeiger für Kunde der deutschen Vorzeit* 4 (1836), 92-103, 241-252.

MONE 1852 Mone, F.J., 'Beitrage zur Kunstgeschichte vom 10. bis 16. Jahrhundert in Konstanz, Reichenau, Basel, Freiburg, Landau und Neustadt', *Zeitschrift fur die Geschichte des Oberrheins* 3 (1852), 17-57.

MONGET 1898-1901 Monget, C., *La Chartreuse de Dijon d'après les documents des archives de Bourgogne*, 2 vols, Montreuil-sur-Mer 1898-1901.

MONTOTO 1952 Montoto, S., *La catedral y el alcázar de Sevilla*, Madrid 19522.

Monumenta Boica, Munich 1763-...

Monumenta Germaniae Historica, Hannover 1826-...

MOORE 1988 Moore, S.F.C., *The Cathedral Chapter of St. Maarten at Utrecht before the Revolt*, (unpublished diss. University of Southhampton) 1988.

MOORSEL 1968 Moorsel, P.P.V. van, *Willibrord en Bonifatius*, Bussum 1968.

MOREAU 1940-1948 Moreau, E. de, *Histoire de l'église en Belgique*, vols 1-4, Brussels 1940-1948.

MORINEAU 1968 Morineau, M., 'D'Amsterdam à Seville: de quelle réalité l'histoire des prix est-elle le miroir ?', *Annales, économies, sociétés, civilisations* 23 (1968), 178-206.

MORTET 1888 Mortet, V., *Etude historique et archéologique sur la cathédrale et le palais épiscopal de Paris du VIe au XIIIe siècles*, Paris 1888.

MORTET 1889 Mortet, V., 'Maurice de Sully, évêque de Paris (1160-1196) : Etude sur l'administration épiscopale pendant la seconde moitié du xiie siècle', *Mémoires de la Société de l'histoire de Paris et de l'Ile de France* 16 (1889), 105-280.

MORTET 1898 Mortet, V., 'Notes sur la cathédrale, le cloître et le palais archiépiscopal de Narbonne (XIIIe-XVIe siècles)', *Annales du Midi*, 1898, 401-414.

MORTET 1911 Mortet, V., *Recueil de textes relatifs à l'histoire de l'architecture et à la condition des architectes en France au moyen-âge XIe-XIIe siècles*, Paris 1911.

MORTET 1913 Mortet, V., 'Hugue de Fouilloi, Pierre le Chantre, Alexandre Neckam et les critiques au douzième siècle contre le luxe des constructions', in *Mélanges d'histoire offerts à M. Charles Bémont*, Paris 1913, 105-137.

MORTET & DESCHAMPS 1929 Mortet, V. & P. Deschamps, *Recueil de textes relatifs à l'histoire de l'architecture et à la condition des architectes en France, au moyen-âge XIIe-XIIIe siècles*, Paris 1929.

MOSMANS 1931 Mosmans, J., *De St.-Janskerk te 's-Hertogenbosch*, Den Bosch 1931.

MOYA VALGAÑÓN 1986 Moya Valgañón, J.G., *Documentos para la historia del arte del archivo catedral de Santo Domingo de la Calzada (1443-1563)*, Logroño 1986.

MULDERS 1943 Mulders, H.J.B., *Der Archidiakonat im Bistum Utrecht bis zum Ausgang des 14. Jahrhundert: Eine rechtshistorische Studie zur kirchlichen Verfassungsrecht*, Utrecht/Nijmegen 1943.

MÜLLER 1908 Müller, A., *Das Bremische Domkapitel im Mittelalter*, (diss.), Greifswald 1908.

MULLER 1883-1885 Muller Fzn., S. (ed.), *De middeleeuwsche rechtsbronnen der stad Utrecht*, 4 vols, The Hague 1883-1885.

MULLER 1885 Muller Fzn., S., 'De Banklok van Utrecht', in *Etudes archéologiques, linguistiques et historiques dédiées à M. le dr. C. Leemans*, Leiden 1885, 298-302.

MULLER 1890 Muller Fzn., S., *Over claustraliteit*, Verhandelingen der Koninklijke Akademie van Wetenschappen, afd. Letterkunde, vol. 29, 1890.

MULLER 1895 Muller Fzn., S. (ed.), *Het Rechtsboek van den Dom van Utrecht door Mr. Hugo Wstinc*, The Hague 1895.

MULLER 1897 Muller Fzn., S., 'Inventaris van het goud- en zilverwerk der Utrechtsche geestelijke gestichten in 1578', *Archief voor de geschiedenis van het aartsbisdom Utrecht* 7 (1897), 284-324.

MULLER 1900 Muller Fzn., S., *Schetsen uit de middeleeuwen*, Amsterdam 1900.

MULLER 1903 Muller Fzn., S. (ed.), *Rechtsbronnen van den Dom te Utrecht*, The Hague 1903.

MULLER 1906 Muller Fzn., S., *De Dom van Utrecht*, Utrecht 1906.

MULLER 1914 Muller Fzn., S., *Schetsen uit de middeleeuwen: Nieuwe bundel*, Amsterdam 1914.

MULLER 1916 Muller Fzn., S., 'De beelden der graftombe van bisschop Rudolf van Diepholt', *De Nederlandsche Musea* 1 (1916), 1-8.

MÜLLER 1998 Müller, H., 'Rouen contra Rouen: Der Konflikt zwischen Bürgern und Kathedralkapitel am Ende des 12. Jahrhunderts im Spiegel der Papsturkunden', in L. Kéry, D. Lohrmann & H. Müller (eds), *Licet preter solitum : Ludwig Falkenstein zum 65. Geburtstag*, Aachen 1998, 67-90.

MURRAY 1975 Murray, S., 'The completion of the nave of Troyes cathedral', *Journal of the society of architectural historians* 34 (1975), 121-139.

MURRAY 1987 Murray, S., *Building Troyes Cathedral : The Late Gothic Campaigns*, Bloomington/Indianapolis 1987.

MURRAY 1989 Murray, S., *Beauvais Cathedral, architecture of transcendence*, Princeton 1989.

MURRAY 1990 Murray, S., 'Looking for Robert de Luzarches: The Early Work at Amiens Cathedral', *Gesta* 29 (1990), no. 1, 111-131.

MURRAY 1996 Murray, S., *Notre-Dame, Cathedral of Amiens : the Power of Change in Gothic*, Cambridge

(USA) 1996.

MUSSAT 1982 Mussat, A., 'Les cathédrales dans leurs cités', *Revue de l'Art* 55 (1982), 9-22.

MUSSAT 1983 Mussat, A., 'La Cathédrale Saint-Pierre de Vannes', *Congrès Archéologique de France* 141 (1983), 294-312.

MUSSET 1966 Musset, L., 'Les conditions financières d'une réussite architecturale : Les grandes églises romanes de Normandie', in *Mélanges offerts à René Crozet*, Poitiers 1966, 308-314.

MUSSET 1987 Musset, L., 'Le mécénat des princes normands au XIe siècle', in X.B.I. Altet (ed.), *Artistes, artisans et production artistique au Moyen Âge*, vol. 2, Paris 1987, 121-134.

N

NARBONNE 1901 Narbonne, L., *La cathédrale Saint-Just de Narbonne : Guide historique, archéologique et descriptif*, Narbonne 1901.

NELSON 1947 Nelson, B., 'The usurer and the merchant prince : Italian businessmen and the ecclesiastical law of restitution', *The Journal of Economic History*, Supplement 7 (1947), 104-122.

NEUHAUSEN 1994 Neuhausen, C., *Das Ablaßwesen in der Stadt Köln vom 13. bis zum 16. Jahrhundert*, Cologne 1994.

NEUSS & OEDIGER 1964 Neuss, W. & F.W. Oediger, *Geschichte des Erzbistums Köln*, vol. 1: *Das Bistum Köln von den Anfängen bis zum Ende des 12. Jahrhunderts*, Cologne 1964.

NEUWIRTH 1890 Neuwirth, J., *Die Wochenrechnungen und der Betrieb des Prager Dombaues in den Jahren 1372-'78*, Prague 1890.

NEUWIRTH 1893 Neuwirth, J., *Geschichte der bildenden Kunst in Böhmen, vom Tode Wenzels III bis zu den Husitenkriegen*, vol. 1: *Allgemeine Verhältnisse, Baubetrieb und Baudenkmale*, Prague 1893.

NICKEL 2001 Nickel, H.L., *Das Hallesche Heiltumbuch von 1520 : Nachdruck zum 450. Gründungsjubiläum der Marienbibliothek zu Halle*, Halle an der Saale 2001.

NICOLINI 1992 Nicolini, U., 'Una cattedrale per un popolo', in M.L.C. Pierotto (ed.), *Una città e la sue cattedrale : il duomo di Perugia*, Perugia 1992, 211-225.

NIERMEYER 1954-1976 Niermeyer, J.F., *Mediae latinitatis lexicon minus*, Leiden 1954-1976.

NIETO CUMPLIDO 1998 Nieto Cumplido, M., *La catedral de Córdoba*, Córdoba 1998.

NIETO SORIA 1986A Nieto Soria, J.M., 'Las realidades cotidianas de las relaciones Monarquía-Episcopado en Castilla, siglos XIII-XIV', in *Etat et Eglise dans la genèse de l'état moderne: Actes du colloque organisé par le Centre National de la Recherche scientifique et la Casa de Velásquez*, Madrid 1986, 217- 225.

NIETO SORIA 1986B Nieto Soria, J.M., 'Le pouvoir royal de l'épiscopat en Castille XIIIE-XIVE siècles', *Le Moyen Age: Revue trimestrelle d'histoire et de philologie* 92 (1986), 383-403.

NIETO SORIA 1988 Nieto Soria, J.M., *Iglesia y poder real en Castilla : El episcopado 1250-1350*, Madrid 1988.

NIETO SORIA 1993 Nieto Soria, J.M., *Iglesia y genesis del estado moderno en Castilla (1369-1480)*, Madrid 1993.

NILSON 1998 Nilson, B., *Cathedral Shrines of Medieval England*, Woodbridge 1998.

NOGALES RINCÓN 2005 Nogales Rincón, D., 'Las capillas y capellanías reales Castellano-Leonesas en la Baja Edad Media (siglos XIII-XV): algunas precisiones institucionales', *Anuario de estudios medievales* 35 (2005), 737-766.

NOLET & BOEREN 1951 Nolet, W. & P.C. Boeren, *Kerkelijke instellingen in de middeleeuwen*, Amsterdam 1951.

NOONAN 1957 Noonan jr., J.T., *The scholastic analysis of usury*, Cambridge (USA) 1957.

NOORDELOOS 1959 Noordeloos, P., 'Antoniana', *Archief voor de geschiedenis van de katholieke kerk in Nederland* 1 (1959), 27-107.

NORTON 1880 Norton, C.E., *Historical studies of church-building in the middle ages; Venice, Siena, Florence*, London 1880.

NORTON 2007 Norton, Ch., 'Richard Scrope and York Minster', in P.J.P. Goldberg (ed.), *Richard Scrope: archbishop, rebel, martyr*, Donington 2007, 138-214.

Notre Dame de Rouen, XVIE *centenaire de la cathédrale Notre Dame de Rouen 396-1996 : Colloque international 5, 6 et 7 décembre 1996*, Rouen 2005.

NOTTARP 1909 Nottarp, H., 'Die Vermögensverwaltung des Münsterischen Domkapitels im Mittelalter', *Zeitschrift für Vaterländische Geschichte und Altertumskunde* 67 (1909), 1-49.

NOTTARP 1920 Nottarp, H., *Die Bistumserrichtung in Deutschland im achten Jahrhundert*, Stuttgart 1920.

NYLANDER 1953 Nylander, I., *Das kirchliche Benefizialwesen Schwedens während des Mittelalters : Die Periode der Landschaftsrechte*, Stockholm 1953.

O

O'CALLAGHAN 2004 O'Callaghan, J.F., *Reconquest and crusade in medieval Spain*, Philadelphia 2004.

OHLBERGER 1911 Ohlberger, J., *Geschichte des Paderborner Domkapitels im Mittelalter*, (diss.), Münster 1911.

OLIVER 1861 Oliver, G., *Lives of the bishops of Exeter and a history of the cathedral*, Exeter 1861.

OLMOS CANALDA 1950 Olmos Canalda, E., *Guía del archivo de la catedral de Valencia*, Madrid 1950.

Oorkondenboek Utrecht Muller Fnz., S. *et al.* (eds), *Oorkondenboek van het Sticht Utrecht*, 5 vols, Utrecht 1920-1959.

OOSTERBAAN 1958 Oosterbaan, D.P., 'Kroniek van de Nieuwe Kerk te Delft', *Bijdragen voor de geschiedenis van het bisdom Haarlem* 65 (1958), 2-336.

OOSTERBAAN 1973 Oosterbaan, D.P., *De Oude Kerk te Delft gedurende de middeleeuwen*, The Hague 1973.

ORTÍ BELMONTE 1954 Ortí Belmonte, M.A., 'Oposición del Cabildo municipal de Córdoba a la construcción del crucero de la Mezquita', *Boletin de la Real Academia de Córdoba de Ciencias, Bellas Letras y Nobles Artes* 25 (1954), no. 71, 271-277.

OTT 2000 Ott, J.S., 'Urban Space, Memory, and Episcopal Authority: The Bishops of Amiens in Peace and Conflict, 1073-1164', *Viator, medieval and renaissance studies* 31 (2000), 43-77.

De oudste kerken van Utrecht Special issue of the *Bulletin van de Koninklijke Nederlandse Oudheidkundige Bond* 93 (1994), no. 4/5.

OVERVOORDE 1906 Overvoorde, J.C., 'Rekeningen uit de bouwperiode van de St. Pieterskerk te Leiden', *Bijdragen voor de geschiedenis van het bisdom Haarlem* 30 (1906), 61-144.

OVERVOORDE & JOOSTING 1896-1897 Overvoorde, J.C. & J.G.C. Joosting, *De gilden van Utrecht tot 1528*, 2 vols, The Hague 1896-1897.

OWEN 1994 Owen, D., *A History of Lincoln Minster*, Cambridge 1994.

P

PALMBOOM 1995 Palmboom, E.N., *Het kapittel van Sint Jan te Utrecht : Een onderzoek naar verwerving, beheer en administratie van het oudste goederenbezit (elfde-veertiende eeuw)*, Hilversum 1995.

PALOMO FERNÁNDEZ 2002 Palomo Fernández, G., *La catedral de Cuenca en el contexto de las grandes canterías catedralicias castellanes en la Baja Edad*

Media, 2 vols, Cuenca 2002.

PANOFSKY 1946 Panofsky, E. (ed.), *Abbot Suger on the abbey church or St.-Denis and its art treasures*, Princeton 1946.

PASCUAL 1995 Pascual, A. (ed.), *La catedral de Mallorca*, Palma de Mallorca 1995.

LE PATOUREL 1944 Patourel, J. le, 'Geoffrey of Montbray, bishop of Coutances 1049-1093', *The English Historical Review* 59 (1944), 129-161.

PAULUS 1922-1923 Paulus, N., *Geschichte des Ablasses im Mittelalter*, 3 vols, Paderborn 1922-1923.

PECKIUS 1620 Peckius, P., *Tractatus de sacrosanctis et catholicis Christi ecclesiis reparandis ac reficiendis*, Münster 1620 (first edition 1573).

PEETERS 1966 Peeters, C.J.A.C., 'De oudste bisschopskerken van Utrecht', in *Feestbundel F. van der Meer*, Amsterdam/ Brussels 1966, 73-127.

PEETERS 1986 Peeters, K., 'Dichterlijke visies op de gotische kathedraal : van Verlaine tot Marsman', in F. Kuyvenhoven & B. Treffers (eds), *Nader beschouwd : Een serie kunsthistorische opstellen aangeboden aan Pieter Singelenberg*, Nijmegen 1986, 87-106.

PELT 1930 Pelt, J.B., *Etudes sur la cathédrale de Metz : Textes extraits principalement des registres capitulaires (1210-1790)*, Metz 1930.

PEREDA LLARENA 1984 Pereda Llarena, F.J., *Documentación de la Catedral de Burgos*, vol. 1:*1254-1293*, vol. 2: *1294-1316*, Burgos 1984.

PEREDA LLARENA & DE CEBALLOS 1999 Pereda Llarena, F.J. & A.R.G. de Ceballos, '"Coeli enarrant gloriam Dei": Arquitectura, iconografia y liturgia en la capilla de los Condestables de la Catedral de Burgos', *Annali di architettura: rivista del Centro Internazionale di studi di architettura Andrea Palladio* 9 (1999), 17-34.

PÉREZ DEL CAMPO 1985 Pérez del Campo, L., *Arte y economía : La construcción de la Catedral de Málaga*, MÁLAGA 1985.

PÉREZ RODRÍGUEZ 1994 Pérez Rodríguez, F.J., *El dominio del Cabildo Catedral de Santiago de Compostela en la Edad media (siglos XII-XIV)*, Santiago 1994.

PÉREZ RODRÍGUEZ 1996 Pérez Rodríguez, F.J., *La Iglesia de Santiago de Compostela en la Edad Media: el Cabilco Catedralicio (1100-1400)*, Santiago 1996.

PÉREZ-VILLAMIL 1899 Pérez-Villamil, M., *La catedral de Sigüenza*, Madrid 1899.

PÉRICARD-MÉA 2001 Péricard-Méa, D., 'Le pèlerinage de Compostelle a-t-il existé?', *L'Histoire* (2001), no. 258, 90-95.

PERNOUD 1966 Pernoud, R., 'Comment on construisait une église', in *Histoire générale des églises de France, Belgique, Luxembourg, Suisse*, vol. 1, Paris 1966, 137-166.

PETERSOHN 1989 Petersohn, J., 'Jubiläumsfrömmigkeit vor dem Jubelablaß : Jubeljahr, Reliquientranslation und "remissio" in Bamberg (1189) und Canterbury (1220)', *Deutsches Archiv für Erforschung des Mittelalters* 45 (1989), 31-53.

PEVSNER 1953 Pevsner, N., *The buildings of England : Country Durham*, Harmondsworth 1953.

PEVSNER 1963 Pevsner, N., *The buildings of England : Country Herefordshire*, Harmondsworth 1963.

PFISTER 1964 Pfister, R., *Kirchengeschichte der Schweiz*, vol. 1, Zürich 1964.

PFLEGER 1935 Pfleger, L., 'Das Schenkungsbuch des Strassburger Münsters', *Elsass Land* 15 (1935), 101 ff.

PFLEGER 1937 Pfleger, L., 'Die Stadt- und Ratsgottesdienst im Strassburger Münster', *Archiv für Elsässische Kirchengeschichte* 12 (1937), 1-56.

PFLEGER 1941 Pfleger, L.,

Kirchengeschichte der Stadt Strassburg im Mittelalter, Colmar 1941.

PHELPS BROWN & HOPKINS 1955-1961 Phelps Brown, E.H. & S.V. Hopkins, 'Seven centuries of building wages', *Economica*, New Series, 22 (1955), 195-207; 23 (1956), 296-314; 24 (1957), 289-306; 26 (1959), 18-38 and 28 (1961), 30-36.

PHELPS BROWN & HOPKINS 1981 Phelps Brown, H. & S. Hopkins, *A perspective of wages and prices*, London/ New York 1981.

PHILLIPS 2007 Phillips, J.,*The second crusade, extending the frontiers of christendom*, New Haven/London 2007.

PICARD 1994 Picard, J.-C. (ed.), *Les chanoines dans la ville : Recherches sur la topographie des quartiers canoniaux en France*, Paris 1994.

PIEKAREK 1973 Piekarek, R., 'Die Braunschweiger Ablaßbriefe : Eine quellenkundliche Untersuchung über die Finanzierung der mittelalterlichen Kirchenbauten im Hinblick auf die damalige Bußpraxis', *Braunschweigisches Jahrbuch*, 1973, 74-137.

PIGEON 1876 Pigeon, E.A., *Histoire de la cathédrale de Coutances*, Coutances 1876.

PIGEOTTE 1877 Pigeotte, L., 'Le grand clocher de la cathédrale de Troyes', *Mèmoires de la société académique d'agriculture, des sciences, arts et belles-lettres du département de l'Aube* 41 (1877), 149-210.

PIOLA CASELLI 1996 Piola Caselli, F., 'Public finances and the arts in Rome: the Fabbrica of St Peter's in the 17th century', in M. North (ed.), *Economic history and the arts*, Cologne 1996, 53-66.

PIPONNIER 1997 Piponnier, F., 'Purchases, gifts and legacies of liturgical vestments from written sources, in the fourteenth and fifteenth centuries', *The Journal of the Costume Society* 31 (1997), 1-7.

PLATELLE 1991 Platelle, H., 'La cathédrale et le diocèse : Un aspect religieux du rapport ville-campagne : L'exemple de Cambrai', in J.M. Duvosquel & A. Dierkens, *Villes et campagnes au moyen âge : Mélanges Georges Despy*, Liège 1991, 625-637.

PLATELLE 1999 Platelle, H., 'Guibert de Nogent et le "De pignoribus sanctorum": Richesses et limites d'une critique médiévale des reliques', in E. Bozóky & A.-M. Helvétius (eds), *Les reliques : Objets, cultes, symboles: Actes du colloque international de l'Université du Littoral-Côte d'Opale (Boulogne-sur-Mer) 4-6 septembre 1997*, vol. 1, Turnhout 1999, 109-121.

PLÖCHL 1960-1962 Plöchl, W.M., *Geschichte des Kirchenrechts*, 2 vols, Vienna 1960-1962².

VAN DER PLOEG 1993 Ploeg, K. van der, *Art, architecture and liturgy : Siena cathedral in the Middle Ages*, Groningen 1993.

POMMERAYE 1686 Pommeraye, J.-F., *Histoire de l'église cathédrale de Rouen, metropolitaine et primatiale de Normandie*, Rouen 1686.

PONCELET 1934 Poncelet, E., 'Les artistes de la cathédrale Saint-Lambert de Liège', in *Chronique archéologique du pays de Liège* 25 (1934), 5-38.

PONSICH 1953 Ponsich, P., 'La cathédrale de Saint-Jean de Perpignan', *Etudes Rousillonnaises* 3 (1953), 137-215.

PORÉE 1926 Porée, C. *La cathédrale d'Auxerre*, Paris 1926.

PORTELA SILVA *et al.* 1985 Portela Silva, E. *et al.*, 'La bâtiment à Saint-Jacques de Compostelle (1075-1575) : Demande, financement, travail et techniques', *Cahiers de la Méditerranée* 31 (1985), 3-34.

PÖSCHL 1908-1912 Pöschl, A., *Bischofsgut und Mensa episcopalis : Ein Beitrag zur Geschichte des kirchlichen Vermögensrechtes*, 3 vols,

Bonn 1908-1912.

POST 1928 Post, R.R., *Eigenkerken en bisschoppelijk gezag in het diocees Utrecht tot de XIIIe eeuw*, Utrecht 1928.

POST 1933 Post, R.R., *Geschiedenis der Utrechtsche bisschopsverkiezingen tot 1535*, Utrecht 1933.

POST 1954 Post, R.R., *Kerkelijke verhoudingen in Nederland vóór de Reformatie van ± 1500 tot ± 1580*, Utrecht 1954.

POST 1957 Post, R.R., *Kerkgeschiedenis van Nederland in de middeleeuwen*, 2 vols, Utrecht 1957.

POST 1967 Post, R.R. (ed.), *Geert Grootes tractaat Contra turrim Traiectensem teruggevonden*, The Hague 1967.

POSTHUMUS & KETNER 1964 Posthumus, N.W. & F. Ketner, *Nederlandse Prijsgeschiedenis*, vol. 2, Leiden 1964.

POTTEL 1911 Pottel, B., *Das Domkapitel von Ermland im Mittelalter : Ein Beitrag zur Verfassungs- und Verwaltungsgeschichte der deutschen Domkapitel, insbesondere der des deutschen Ordensstaates in Preussen*, Leipzig 1911.

Pouillés Reims Longnon, A. (ed.), *Pouillés de la Province de Reims*, Paris 1908.

Pouillés Rouen Longnon, A. (ed.), *Pouillés de la Province de Rouen*, Paris 1903

Pouillés Sens Longnon, A. (ed.), *Pouillés de la Province de Sens*, Paris 1904

Pouillés Tours Longnon, A. (ed.), *Pouillés de la Province de Tours*, Paris 1903

POWICKE & CHENEY 1964 Powicke, F.M. & C.R. Cheney (eds), *Councils and synods with other documents relating to the English Church*, vol. 2 (1205-1313), Oxford 1964.

PRANGE 1990/1993 Prange, W. (ed.), *Die Protokolle des Lübecker Domkapitels*, vol. 11: *1535-1540*, vol. 12: *1522-1530*, Schleswig-Holsteinische Regesten und Urkunden, Neumünster 1990/1993.

PRESS 1992 Press, V., *Südwestdeutsche Bischofsresidenzen außerhalb der Kathedralstädte*, Stuttgart 1992.

PRÉVOST 1936 Prévost, A., *Histoire de Saint Jean, quartier el paroisse de Troyes*, Troyes 1936.

PRIGENT 1991 Prigent, C., 'Le compte de la confrérie Saint-Nicolas de Quimper (1482-1484)', *Bulletin de la Société nationale des antiquaires de France* (1991), 277-311.

PRIMS 1927-1947 Prims, F., *Geschiedenis van Antwerpen*, 24 vols, Antwerp 1927-1947.

PRINZ 1971 Prinz, J., 'Vom mittelalterlichen Ablasswesen in Westfalen : Ein Beitrag zur Geschichte der Volksfrömmigkeit', *Westfälische Forschungen* 23 (1971), 107-171.

PRUNGNAUD 2008 Prungnaud, J., *Figures littéraires de la cathédrale 1880-1918*, Villeneuve-d'Ascq 2008.

PRUTZ 1908 Prutz, H., *Die geistlichen Ritterorden : Ihre Stellung zur kirchlichen, politischen, gesellschaftlichen und wirtschaftlichen Entwicklung des Mittelalters*, Berlin 1908.

PUENTE MÍGUIZ 1985 Puente Míguiz, J.A., 'La catedral gótica de Santiago de Compostela : Un proyecto frustrado de D. Juan Arias (1238-1266)', *Compostellanum : Sección des estudios Jacobeos* 30 (1985), 245-275.

PUEYO COLOMINA 2000 Pueyo Colomina, P., 'Licencias para pedir limosnas, con y sin indulgencias, otorgadas por los arzobispos de la diócesis de Zaragoza en la segunda mitad des siglo XIV', *Aragón en la Edad Media* (2000), no. 16, 683-707.

PUIG I CADAFALCH & PUJOL TUBAU 1918 Puig i Cadafalch, J. & P. Pujol Tubau, *Santa Maria de la Seu d'Urgell*, Barcelona 1918.

PUIG I PUIG 1929 Puig i Puig, S., *Episcopologio de la Seda Barcinonense : Apuntes para la historia de la iglesia de Barcelona y de sus prelados*, vol. 1, Barcelona 1929.

PUSCH 1932 Pusch, G., *Staatliche Münz- und Geldpolitik in den Niederlanden unter den burgundischen und habsburgischen Herrschern, besonders unter Kaiser Karl V*, (diss.), Munich 1932.

PUZA 1989 Puza, R., 'Die Finanzierung der katholischen Kirche im historischen Rückblick', in L.C. Morsak & M. Escher (eds), *Festschrift für Louis Carlen zum 60. Geburtstag*, Zurich 1989, 335-351.

PYCKE 1983-1984 Pycke, J., 'Le chanoine trésorier et la fabrique de la cathédrale de Tournai dans la première moitié du XIIIe siècle d'après des documents inédits', *Mémoires de la Société Royale d'Histoire et d'Archéologie de Tournai* 4 (1983-1984), 71-90.

PYCKE 2003 Pycke, J., *Sons, couleurs, odeurs dans la cathédrale de Tournai au 15e siécle*, vol. 1: *Edition du cérémomial et des ordinaires suivie du commentaire (1) : Les acteurs, les lieux et le mobilier liturgique*, Tournai/ Louvain-la-Neuve 2003.

PYCKE 2005 Pycke, J., 'Un témoignage inédit sur le culte de la Croix, de Notre-Dame et des reliques á la cathédrale de Tournai au XVe s.: Le 'Liber confraternitatis fabricae ecclesiae Tornacensis', in *'Scribere sanctorum gesta', receuil d'études d'hagiographie médiévale, offert à Guy Philippart*, Turnhout 2005, 673-696.

Q

QUANTIN 1842 Quantin, M., *Notice historique sur la construction de la cathédrale de Sens*, Auxerre 1842.

QUANTIN 1869 Quantin, M., 'Mémoire sur l'organisation et le régime économique et financier de l'ancien chapitre cathédrale de Sens', in *Mémoires lus à la Sorbonne en 1868*, 1869, 197-235.

QUICHERAT 1886 Quicherat, J, *Mélanges d'archéologie et d'histoire*, vol. 2, Paris 1886.

R

RABELAIS 1932, Rabelais, F., *Oeuvres de François Rabelais: Gargantua & Pantagruel*, vol. 2, Paris 1932.

RACKHAM 1909-1910 Rackham, R.B., 'The Nave of Westminster', *Proceedings of the British Academy* 4 (1909-1910), 33-97.

RADOCSAY 1971 Radocsay, D., 'Über einige illuminierte Urkunden', *Acta Historiae Artium* 17 (1971), 31-61.

RADTKE 2004 Radtke, Ch., 'Si non facietis voluntatem nostram ... Zum Lübecker Kirchenkampf im 13 Jahrhundert', in *Bischof und Bürger: Herrschaftsbeziehungen in den Kathedralstädten des Hoch- und Spätmittelalters*, Göttingen 2004, 165-184.

RAINE 1859 Raine, J. (ed.), *The fabric rolls of York Minster*, Durham 1859.

RAMÍREZ VAQUERO 1996 Ramírez Vaquero, E., 'La fábrica de la catedral de Pamplona : ¿Una obra pública?', in *Tecnología y sociedad: las grandes obras públicas en la Europa medieval : XXII Semana de Estudios Medievales, Estella, 17 a 21 de julio de 1995*, Pamplona 1996, 197-234.

RAMISCH *et al.* 1998 Ramisch, H., C.A. Harrer & A. Heß (eds), *Die Freisinger Dom – Custos – Rechnungen von 1447-1500*, 2 vols, Munich 1998.

RAMM 1978 Ramm, P., *Der Merseburger Dom : Seine Baugeschichte nach den Quellen*, Weimar 1978.

RANGE 1910 Range, F., *Die Entwicklung des Merseburger Domkapitels von dem Anfange bis zum Ausgang des 14. Jahrhunderts*, Hildesheim 1910.

DU RANQUET 1928 Ranquet, H. du, *La cathédrale de Clermont-Ferrand*, Paris 1928.

RAPP 1974 Rapp, F., *Réformes et réformation à Strasbourg;*

église et société dans le diocèse de Strasbourg (1450-1525), Paris 1974.

VAN RAPPARD 1880 Rappard, F.A.L. van (ed.), 'De rekeningen van de kerkmeesters der Buurkerk te Utrecht in de 15e eeuw', *Bydragen en mededeelingen van het historisch genootschap* 3 (1880), 25-225.

VAN RAPPARD 1881-1882 Rappard, F.A.L. van, 'Verzameling van bescheiden betreffende het maken van een koperen hek voor een altaar in den Dom te Utrecht (1519)', *Archief voor Nederlandschen Kunstgeschiedenis* 4 (1881-1882), 246-264.

RAUCH 1950 Rauch, J., 'Die Almosenfahrten der Höchster Antoniter am Ausgang des Mittel-alters', *Archiv für mittelrheinische Kirchengeschichte* 2 (1950), 163-174.

RAVAUX 1977 Ravaux, J.-P., 'La Cathédrale de Châlons-sur-Marne', *Congrès Archéologique de France* 135 (1977), 360-399.

RAVAUX 1989 Ravaux, J.-P., 'Les vitraux de l'abside de la cathédrale de Châlons-sur-Marne donnés par saint Louis', *Mémoires de la Société d'agriculture, commerce, sciences et arts de la Marne* 104 (1989), 73-89.

Realencyklopädie für protestantische Theologie und Kirche, Leipzig 1896-1908.

Reallexikon zur deutschen Kunstgeschichte, Stuttgart 1937-...

RECHT 1989 Recht, R. (ed.), *Les batisseurs des cathédrales gothiques*, Strasbourg 1989.

RECIO MIR 1999 Recio Mir, Á., *'Sacrum Senatum' : Las estancias capitulares de la Catedral de Sevilla*, Seville 1999.

Regesta Bohemiae et Moraviae Emler, J. (ed.), *Regesta diplomatica nec non epistolaria Bohemiae et Moraviae*, pars 4 (6 vols), Prague 1885-1892.

Regesta Honorii papae III Pressuti, P. (ed.), *Regesta Honorii papae III [1216-'27]*, 2 vols, Rome 1888-1895.

Regesta Magdeburg Mülverstedt, G.A. von (ed.), *Regesta archiepiscopatus Magdeburgensis*, 4 vols, Magdeburg 1876-1899.

Regesten bisschoppen Utrecht Muller Fzn., S. (ed.), *Regesten van het archief der bisschoppen van Utrecht (722-1528)*, 3 vols, Utrecht 1917-1922.

Regesten Köln Die Regesten der Erzbischöfe von Köln im Mittelalter, 12 vols, Cologne 1901-2001.

Regesten Mainz Regesten der Erzbischöfe von Mainz von 1289-1396, Leipzig 1913.

Regesten Münster Konstanz Reiners-Ernst, E., *Regesten zur Bau- und Kunstgeschichte des Münsters zu Konstanz*, Konstanz 1956.

Regesten Salzburg Die Regesten der Erzbischöfe und des Domkapitels von Salzburg 1247-1343, 3 vols, Salzburg 1928-1934.

Regestum Clementis papae V [1305-1314], ex Vaticanis archetypis [...] editum cura et studio monachorum ordinis s. Benedicti, 8 vols, *Tables des registres de Clément V*, Rome 1884-1888, Paris 1948-1957.

Register Henry Chichele The register of Henry Chichele archbishop of Canterbury 1414-1443, vol. 2: Jacob, E.F. (ed.), *Wills proved before the archbishop or his commissaries*, Oxford 1937.

Register John de Grandisson Hingeston-Randolph, F.C. (ed.), *The register of John de Grandisson, bishop of Exeter (1327-1369)*, 3 vols, London/Exeter 1894-1899.

Registre Benoît XI Grandjean, Ch. (ed.), *Le registre de Benoît XI [1303-1304], recueil des bulles de ce pape*, Paris 1905.

Registres Alexandre IV Bourel de la Roncière, C. *et al.* (ed.), *Les registres d'Alexandre IV [1254-1261], recueil des bulles de ce pape*, 3 vols, Paris 1859-1960.

Registres Grégoire IX Auvray, L. (ed.), *Les registres de Grégoire IX* [1227-1241], *recueil des bulles de ce pape*, 4 vols, Paris 1896-1955.

Registres Honorius IV M. Prou, M. (ed.), *Les registres d'Honorius IV [1285-1286]*, Paris 1888.

Registres Innocent IV Berger, E. (ed.), *Les registres d'Innocent IV [1243-1254]*, 4 vols, Paris 1884-1921.

Registres Nicolas IV Langlois, E. (ed.), *Les registres de Nicolas IV [1288-1292], recueil des bulles de ce pape*, 2 vols, Paris 1887-1893.

Registres Urbain IV Guiraud, J. (ed.), *Les registres d'Urbain IV [1261-1264], recueil des bulles de ce pape*, 4 vols, Paris 1899-1958.

Registrum Baldock et al. Fowler, R.C. (ed.), *Registrum Radulphi Baldock, Gilberti Segrave, Ricardi Newport & Stephani Gravesend, episcoporum Londoniensium [1304-1338]*, London 1911.

Registrum Lincoln Foster, C.W. (ed.), *The Registrum Antiquissimum of the Cathedral Church of Lincoln*, vol. 1, Hereford 1931.

Registrum Orleton Bannister, A.T. (ed.), *Registrum A. de Orleton episcopi Herefordensis [1317-1327]*, London 1908.

Registrum Sancti Pauli Londinensis Sparrow Simpson, W. (ed.), *Registrum statutorum et consuetudinum ecclesie cathedralis Sancti Pauli Londinensis*, London 1873.

Registrum Trillek Parry, J.H. (ed.), *Registrum Johannis de Trillek episcopi Herefordensis [1344-1361]*, London 1912.

REICKE 1926 Reicke, S., 'Stadtgemeinde und Stadtpfarrkirche der Reichsstadt Nürnberg im 14. Jahrhundert : Eine rechtsgeschichtliche Untersuchung'. *Mitteilungen des Vereins für Geschichte der Stadt Nürnberg* 26 (1926), 1-110.

REINHARDT 1960 Reinhardt, H., 'Les textes relatifs à l'histoire de la cathédrale de Strasbourg depuis les origines jusqu'à l'année 1522', *Bulletin de la Société des amis de la cathédrale de Strasbourg*, 2nd Series, 7 (1960), 11-30.

REINHARDT 1963 Reinhardt, H., *La Cathédrale de Reims: Son histoire, son architecture, sa sculpture, ses vitraux*, Paris 1963.

RÉMY 1928 Rémy, F., *Les grandes indulgences pontificales aux Pays-Bas à la fin du moyen-âge (1300-1531)*, Louvain 1928.

REUSENS 1903 Reusens, E.H.J. (ed.), 'Statuta antiquissima dioecesis Cameracensis', *Analectes pour servir à l'histoire ecclésiastique de la Belgique*, 1903, 1-116.

REY CASTELAO 1987 Rey Castelao, O., 'La protección jurídica de las rentas ecclesiasticas en España: El ejemplo del Voto de Santiago', *Hispania Sacra* 39 (1987), 457-503.

REYNOLDS 1881 Reynolds, H.E., *Wells Cathedral : Its foundation, Constitutional History and Statutes*, Wells 1881.

RHOTERT 1916 Rhotert, J., 'Die älteste erhaltene Strukturrechnung des Domes vom Jahre 1415', *Mitteilungen des Vereins für Geschichte und Landeskunde von Osnabrück* 39 (1916), 303-316.

RICCETTI 1988 Riccetti, L. (ed.), *Il duomo di Orvieto*, Rome/Bari 1988.

RICE 2007 Rice, L., *The altars and altarpieces of new St. Peter's: Outfitting the Basilica 1621-1666*, Cambridge 2007.

RICHARD 1975 Richard, J.C., '"Les miracula" composés en Normandie aux XIe et XIIe siècles', *Positions des thèses soutenues à l'École des chartes*, Paris 1975, 183-189.

RIEDL & SEIDEL 1995 Riedl, P.A. & M. Seidel (eds), *L'Archivio dell'Opera della Metropolitana di Siena : Inventario a cura di Stefano Moscadelli*, vol. 1, Munich 1995.

RIEMSDIJK 1888 Riemsdijk, Th.H.F., *Bijdragen tot de geschiedenis van de kerspelkerk van St. Jacob te Utrecht*, Leiden 1888.

RIESCO TERERO 1987 Riesco Terero, A., *Erección canónica de las cuatro catedrales del reino de Granada*, Málaga 1987.

RIETBERGEN 1983 Rietbergen, P.A.N., 'A vision come true : Pope Alexander VII, Gianlorenzo Bernini and the colonades of St. Peter's, 1655-1667', *Mededelingen van het Nederlands Instituut te Rome* 44-45 (1983), 111-163.

RIGAUDIÈRE 1985 Rigaudière, A., 'Le financement des fortifications urbaines en France du milieu du XIVe siècle à la fin du XVe siècle', *Revue historique* 273 (1985), 19-95.

RIKHOF 2006 Rikhof, F., 'Kapelaniën in de middeleeuwse Utrechtse Dom', *Jaarboek Oud-Utrecht*, 2006, 43-83.

RILEY-SMITH 1995 Riley-Smith, J. (ed.), *The Oxford Illustrated History of the Crusades*, Oxford/New York 1995.

Rites Durham Rites and monuments of the Cathedral Church of Durham, 'A description or breife declaration of all the ancient monuments, rites, and customes belonginge or beinge within the monasticl church of Durham before the supression. Written in 1593' (facsimile reprint of the Surteees Society edition of 1842), Felinfach 1998.

ROCCO NEGRI 1975 Rocco Negri, V., 'Storia e cronologia del primo giubileo Milanese (1390-1392) nei documenti inediti dell' archivio della Ven. Fabbrica del Duomo', *Archivio Ambrosiano* 28 (1975), 186-209.

ROCKINGER 1863/1961 Rockinger, L., *Briefsteller und Formelbücher des elften bis vierzehnten Jahrhundert*, Munich 1863, New York 1961.

RODRÍGUEZ ESTÉVEZ 1998 Rodríguez Estévez, J.C., *Los canteros de la Catedral de Sevilla : Del Gótico al Renacimiento*, Seville 1998.

RODRÍGUEZ G. DE CEBALLOS 1989 Rodríguez G. de Ceballos, A., 'Aspectos económicos y administrativos en las fábricas de las catedrales españolas durante el siglo XVI', *Anuario del Departemento de Historia y Teoría del Arte*, 1989, 79-86.

RODRÍGUEZ LLOPIS & GARCÍA DÍAZ 1994 Rodríguez Llopis, M. & I. García Díaz, *Iglesia y sociedad feudal : El Cabildo de la Catedral de Murcia en la baja edad media*, Murcia 1994.

RODRÍGUEZ MOLINA 1986 Rodríguez Molina, J., *El Obispado de Baeza-Jaén : Organización y Economía Diocesanas (Siglos XIII - XVI)*, Jaén 1986.

ROGGE 1996 Rogge, J., 'Zum Verhältnis von Bischof und Domkapitel des Hochstifts Meißen im 14. und 15. Jahrhundert', *Römische Quartalschrift für christliche Altertumskunde und Kirchengeschichte* 91 (1996), 182-206.

ROLLAND 1924 Rolland, P., 'L'expansion tournaisienne aux 11e et 12e siècles; art et commerce de la pierre', *Annales de l'académie royal d'archéologie de Belgique* 72 (1924), 175-219.

ROMANINI 1964 Romanini, A.M., *L'architettura gotica in Lombardia*, vol. 1, Milan 1964.

RONDININI 1984 Rondinini, G.S., 'La fabbrica del duomo come espressione dello spirito religioso e civile della società Milanese (fine sec. XIV- sec. XV)', in *Religion et culture dans la cité Italienne de l'Antiquité à nos jours (Actes du Colloque du Centre Interdisciplinaire de Recherches sur l'Italie des 8-9-10 novembre 1979)*, Strasbourg 1984, 101-115.

ROOSEGAARDE BISSCHOP 1956 Roosegaarde Bisschop, G., 'De geschilderde maquette in Nederland', *Nederlands Kunsthistorisch Jaarboek*, 1956, 167-217.

RÖPCKE 1992 Röpcke, A., 'Geld und Gewissen : Raimund Peraudi und die Ablaßverkündung in Norddeutschland am Ausgang des Mittelalters',

Bremisches Jahrbuch, 1992, 43-80.

ROSENBERG 1962 Rosenberg, H.P.R., 'De Sint Eusebiuskerk te Arnhem', *Bulletin van de Koninklijke Nederlandsche Oudheidkundige Bond*, 6th Series, 15 (1962), kol. 189-211.

ROSENTHAL 1961 Rosenthal, E. E., *The cathedral of Granada : A study in the Spanish Renaissance*, Princeton 1961.

ROSENTHAL 1970 Rosenthal, J.T., 'The training of an elite group : English bishops in the fifteenth century', *Translations of the American Philosophical Society*, New Series, 60 (1970), 1-54.

ROSENTHAL 1972 Rosenthal, J.T., *The purchase of paradise : Gift giving and the aristocracy* 1307-1485, London 1972.

ROSENZWEIG 1936-1938 Rosenzweig, L., 'Cartulaire général du Morbihan', *Bulletin de la Société Polymatique du Morbihan* (1936-1938).

ROSER 2005 Roser, H., *St. Peter in Rom im 15. Jahrhundert : Studien zu Architektur und skulpturaler Ausstattung*, Munich 2005.

ROSEROT DE MELIN 1966 Roserot de Melin, J., *Bibliographie commentée des sources d'une histoire de la Cathédrale de Troyes*, vol. 1: *Construction*, Troyes 1966.

ROTTHOFF 1973 Rotthoff, G., *Organisation und Finanzierung des Xantener Dombaues im 15. Jahrhundert*, Krefeld 1973.

ROUSTEAU-CHAMBON 2003 Rousteau-Chambon, H., *Le gothique des Temps modernes: Architecture religieuse en milieu urbain*, Paris 2003.

RUBIO MERINO 1987/1998 Rubio Merino, P., *Archivo de la Santa Metropolitana y Patriarcal Iglesia Catedral de Sevilla*, 2 vols, Madrid 1987, 1998.

RÜCK 1975 Rück, P., 'Les registres de l'administration capitulaire de Lausanne (XIIIe-XVIe siècle)', *Revue historique Vaudoise* (1975), 135-186.

RUDOLPH 1990 Rudolph, C. (ed.), *'The things of greater importance' : Bernard of Clairvaux's Apologia and the medieval attitude toward art*, Philadelphia 1990.

RUFFINI 1896 Ruffini, F., 'La rappresentanza giuridica delle parrocchie', *Giurisprudenza italiana, raccolta generale, periodica e critical* [...], 48 (4) (1896), kol. 113-kol. 273.

RUIZ DE LA PEÑA SOLAR 1990 Ruiz de la Peña Solar, J.I. *et al.*, *Las peregrinaciones a San Salvador de Oviedo en la Edad Media*, Oviedo 1990.

RUIZ SOUSA 2006 Ruiz Sousa, J.C., 'Capillas Reales funerarias catedralicias de Castilla y León : Nuevas hipótesis interpretativas de las catedrales de Sevilla, Córdoba y Toledo', *Anuario del Departamento de Historia y Teoria del Arte* 18 (2006), 9-29.

RUTGERS 1970 Rutgers, C.A., *Jan van Arkel, bisschop van Utrecht*, Groningen 1970.

RUTGERS 1978 Rutgers, C.A. (ed.), *De Utrechtse bisschop in de middeleeuwen*, The Hague 1978.

RYCKEBUSCH 1995 Ryckebusch, F., 'La fonction paroissiale des cathédrales du Midi à la fin du Moyen Âge', in *La cathédrale (XIIe-XIVe siècle)*, Cahiers de Fanjeaux, vol. 30, Toulouse 1995, 295-336.

S

SABISCH 1965 Sabisch, A., 'Breslauer Domherren des 16. Jahrhunderts', in *Reformata reformanda, Festgabe für Hubert Jedin*, vol. 2, Münster 1965, 144-176.

SACHET 1886 Sachet, A., *Le Grand Jubilé séculaire de Saint-Jean de Lyon: 1451, 1546, 1666, 1734*, Lyon 1886.

SACHET 1914 Sachet, A., *Le pardon annuel de la Saint-Jean et de la Saint-Pierre à Saint-Jean de Lyon, 1392-1790*, vol. 1 (*1392-1562*), Lyon 1914.

SAINT-DENIS 1994 Saint-Denis, A., *Apogée d'une cité*

Laon et le Laonnois aux xiie et xiiie siècles, Nancy 1994.

SAINT-DENIS 2008 Saint-Denis, A. (ed.), *Hériman de Tournai : Les miracles de Sainte Marie de Laon*, Paris 2008.

SAINT-DENIS *et al.* 2002 Saint-Denis, A., M. Plouvier & C. Souchon, *Laon, la cathédrale*, Paris 2002.

SÁINZ RIPA 1995 Sáinz Ripa, E., *Sedes episcopales de la Rioja, siglos xiiv-xv*, Logroño 1995.

SALOMON & REETZ 1968-1980 Salomon, R. & J. Reetz, *Rat und Domkapitel von Hamburg um die Mitte des 14. Jahrhunderts*, vols 1-3, Hamburg 1968-1980.

SALZMAN 1948/1953 Salzman, L.F. (ed.), *The Victorian history of the county of Cambridge and the isle of Ely*, London vol. 2, 1948, vol. 4, 1953.

SALZMAN 1952 Salzman, L.F., *Building in England down to 1540 : A documentary history*, Oxford 1952.

SANABRE 1948 Sanabre, J., *El archivo de la Catedral de Barcelona*, Barcelona 1948.

SÁNCHEZ HERRERO 1976 Sánchez Herrero, J., *Concilios provinciales y Sínodos toledanos de los siglos XIV y XV : La religiosidad cristiana del clero y pueblo*, La Laguna 1976.

SÁNCHEZ HERRERO 1978 Sánchez Herrero, J., *Las diócesis del reino de León : siglos xiv y xv*, León 1978.

SÁNCHEZ-PALENCIA MANCEBO 1985 Sánchez-Palencia Mancebo, A., *Fundaciones del Arzobispo Tenorio : La capilla de San Blas, en la Catedral de Toledo*, Toledo 1985.

SANCHIS Y SIVERA 1909 Sanchis y Sivera, J., *La Catedral de Valencia : Guía histórica y artística*, Valencia 1909.

SANDRON 1998 Sandron, D., *La cathédrale de Soissons : Architecture du pouvoir*, Paris 1998.

SAN MARTÍN PAYO 1953 San Martín Payo, J., *El Retablo Mayor de la Catedral de Palencia : Nuevos datos*, Palencia 1953.

SAN MARTÍN PAYO 1954 San Martín Payo, J., 'Catalogo del Archivo de la Catedral de Palencia : Fabrica de la Santa Iglesia Catedral', *Publicaciones de la Institución Tello Téllez de Meneses* (1954), no. 2, 143-178.

SAN MARTÍN PAYO 1983 San Martín Payo, J., *Catalogo del Archivo de la Catedral de Palencia*, vol. 50, Palencia 1983.

SAN MARTÍN PAYO 1985 San Martín Payo, J., 'Contratos sobre siete cantorales y las vidrieras del crucero de la catedral', *Publicaciones de la Institucíon Tello Téllez de Meneses* 52 (1985), 175-193.

SANTIFALLER 1948 Santifaller, L., *Urkunden und Forschungen zur Geschichte des Trientner Domkapitels im Mittelalter*, vol. 1, Vienna 1948.

SANTOLAYA HEREDERO 1979 Santolaya Heredero, L., *La obra y fábrica de la catedral de Toledo a fines del siglo xvi*, Toledo 1979.

SANZ FUENTES 1998 Sanz Fuentes, M.J., 'Documentos pontificios medievales referentes al jubileo ovetense de la Santa Cruz', in K. Borchardt & E. Bünz (eds), *Forschungen zur Reichs-, Papst- und Landesgeschichte : Peter Herde zum 65. Geburtstag von Freunden, Schülern und Kollegen dargebracht*, Stuttgart 1998, 783-793.

SANZ Y SANZ 1967 Sanz y Sanz, H., 'Bosquejo histórico de dos Catedrales', *Estudios Segovianos* (1967), no. 19, 161-204.

SASTRE MOLL 1993 Sastre Moll, J., 'La financiación de las obras de la Catedral de Mallorca siglo XIV', in *Homenatge a Antoni Mut Calafell, arxiver*, Palma 1993, 277-294.

SASTRE MOLL 1994 Sastre Moll, J., *El primer llibre de fàbrica i sagristia de la Seu de Mallorca (1327-1345)*, Mallorca 1994.

SASTRE MOLL 2001 Sastre

Moll, J., *Els llibres d'obra del palau reial de l'Almudaina*, Palma 2001.

SCAMMEL 1971 Scammel, J., 'The rural chapter in England from the eleventh to the fourteenth century', *The English Historical Review* 86 (1971), 1-21.

SCHECKMANN 1996 Scheckmann, J., *Der Heilige Rock von Trier, ausgestellt im Jahre 1513, Faksimile-Nachdruck der Postinkunabel*, Briedel 1996.

SCHERFT 1956 Scherft, P., 'Het H. Sacrament van Mirakel van de Niervaart en de bouw van de Bredase toren', *Jaarboek van de Geschied- en Oudheidkundige Kring van stad en land van Breda 'De Oranje boom'*, 1956, 59-65.

VAN SCHEVICHAVEN 1900 Schevichaven, H.D.J. van, *De St. Stephenskerk te Nijmegen*, Nijmegen 1900.

SCHIEFFER 1976 Schieffer, R., *Die Entstehung von Domkapiteln in Deutschland*, Bonn 1976.

SCHLICHT 2005 Schlicht, M., *Un chantier majeur de la fin du Moyen Âge : La cathédrale de Rouen vers 1300 : Portail des libraires, portail de la Calende, chapelle de la Vierge*, Caen 2005.

SCHMID 1957 Schmid, H.F., 'Das Weiterleben und die Wiederbelebung antiker Institutionen im mittelalterlichen Stadtewesen', *Annali di storia del diritto* 1 (1957), 85-135.

SCHMID & WOLLASCH 1984 Schmid, K. & J. Wollasch (eds), *Der geschichtliche Zeugniswert des liturgischen Gedenkens im Mittelalter*, Munich 1984.

SCHMIDT 1889 Schmidt, G., 'Baurechnung des Halberstädter Doms von 1367', in *Programm des Königlichen Dom-Gymnasiums zu Halberstadt*, 1889, 1-19.

SCHNEIDER 1885 Schneider, Ph., *Die bischöfliche Domkapitel : Ihre Entwicklung und rechtliche Stellung im Organismus der Kirche*, Mainz 1885.

SCHOCK-WERNER 1983 Schock-Werner, B., *Das Strassburger Münster im 15. Jahrhundert : Stilistiche Entwicklung und Hüttenorganisation eines Bürger-Doms*, Cologne 1983.

SCHOCK-WERNER 1996 Schock-Werner, B., 'Le chantier de la cathédrale de Strasbourg : L'Oevre Notre-Dame', in *Chantiers médiévaux*, Paris 1996, 221-249.

SCHOENBERGER 1927 Schoenberger, G., *Beiträge zur Baugeschichte des Frankfurter Doms*, Frankfurt am Main 1927.

SCHÖLLER 1989 Schöller, W., *Die rechtliche Organisation des Kirchenbaues im Mittelalter vornehmlich des Kathedralbaues: Baulast – Bauherrenschaft – Baufinanzierung*, Cologne/Vienna 1989.

SCHÖLLER 1995 Schöller, W., 'Die französische Königskathedrale : Revision eines Topos', in H-R. Meier *et al.* (eds), *Für irdischen Ruhm und himmlischen Lohn : Stifter und Auftraggeber in der mittelalterlichen Kunst*, Berlin 1995, 213-226.

SCHOOLMEESTERS 1908 Schoolmeesters, E. (ed.), *Les status synodaux de Jean de Flandre, évêque de Liège, 16 février 1288*, Liège 1908.

SCHREIBER 1938 Schreiber, G., *Deutsche Mirakelbücher : Zur Quellenkunde und Sinngebung*, Düsseldorf 1938.

SCHRÖCKER 1934 Schröcker, S., *Die Kirchenpflegschaft : Die Verwaltung des Niederkirchenvermögens durch Laien seit dem ausgehenden Mittelalter*, Paderborn 1934.

SCHRÖER 1966 Schröer, A. (ed.), *Monasterium, Festschrift zum siebenhundertjährigen Weihegedächtnis des Paulus-Domes zu Münster*, Münster 1966.

SCHUEGRAF 1847/1848 Schuegraf, J.R., 'Geschichte des Domes von Regensburg und der dazu gehörigen Gebäude', *Verhandlungen des historischen Vereins von*

Oberpfalz und Regensburg 11 (1847), 1-267; 12 (1848), 1-223.

SCHUEGRAF 1855 Schuegraf, J.R., 'Nachtrage zur Geschichte des Domes von Regensburg: Regensburger Dombaurechnung von dem Jahre 1459', *Verhändlungen des historischen Vereins von Oberpfalz und Regensburg* 16 (1855), 1-223.

SCHUEGRAF 1858 Schuegraf, J.R., 'Drei Rechnungen über den Regensburger Dombau aus den Jahren 1487, 1488 und 1489', *Verhändlungen des historischen Vereins von Oberpfalz und Regensburg* 18 (1858), 135-205.

SCHULTE 1904 Schulte, A., *Die Fugger in Rom 1495-1523, mit Studien zur Geschichte des kirchlichen Finanzwesens jener Zeit*, 2 vols, Leipzig 1904.

SCHULTZ 1877 Schultz, A., 'Die deutschen Dombaumeister', in R. Dohme (ed.), *Kunst und Künstler Deutschlands und der Niederlände*, vol. 1, 1877, 49-72.

SCHWICKERATH 1942 Schwickerath, W., *Die Finanzwirtschaft der deutschen Bistümer*, Breslau 1942.

SCOTT 2003 Scott, R.A., *The gothic enterprice; a guide to understanding the Medieval Cathedral*, Berkeley 2003.

SEIBRICH 1995 Seibrich, W., 'Die Trierer Heiltumsfahrt im Spätmittelalter', *Archiv für mittelrheinische Kirchengeschichte* 47 (1995), 45-125.

SÉJOURNÉ 1921 Séjourné, P., 'Oorkondenhoek van het Sticht Utrecht tot 1301', *De Katholiek* 159 (1921), 195-200.

La Seo de Zaragoza, Gobierno de Aragón 1998.

SEYMOUR 1968 Seymour, Ch., *Notre-Dame of Noyon in the twelfth century : A study in the early development of gothic architecture*, New York 1968[2].

SIBILLE 1991 Sibille, C., 'Les archevêques de Bourges et le chapitre cathédrale de 1482 à 1525', *Positions des thèses soustenues à l'École des chartes*, Paris 1991, 204-212.

SIGAL 1976 Sigal, P.A., 'Les voyages de reliques aux onzième et douzième siècles', *Sénéfiance* 2 (1976), 73-104.

SIGAL 1990 Sigal, P.A., 'Reliques, pèlerinage et miracles dans l'église médiévale (XIe-XIIIe siècles)', *Revue d'histoire de l'Eglise de France* 76 (1990), 193-211.

SIGNORI 1990 Signori, G., 'Hagiographie, Architektur und Pilgerwesen im Spannungsfeld Städtischen Legitimations- und Integrationsstrebens', *Zeitschrift für Historische Forschung* 17 (1990), 279-297.

SIGNORI 1995 Signori, G., *Maria zwischen Kathedrale, Kloster und Welt : Hagiographische und historiographische Annäherungen an eine hochmittelalterliche Wunderpredigt*, Sigmaringen 1995.

VON SIMSON 1956 Simson, O. von, *The gothic cathedral : The origin of gothic architecture and the medieval concept of order*, London 1956.

SKILLINGTON 1966-1967 Skillington, F.E., 'Enclosed in clay: a study in Leicester wills', *Leicestershire archaeological and historical society* 42 (1966-1967), 35-53.

SLATER & ROSSER 1998 Slater, T.R. & G. Rosser (eds), *The Church in the Medieval Town*, Aldershot 1998.

SLOTHOUWER & DE JONGE 1919 Slothouwer, D.F. & C.H. de Jonge, 'Enige vondsten in de Utrechtsche Domkerk', *Bulletin van den Nederlandschen Oudheidkundigen Bond*, 2nd Series, 12 (1919), 219-227.

DE SMET *et al.* 2006 Smet, M. de, J. Kuys & P. Trio, *Processions and church fabrics in the Low Countries during the late Middle Ages : An inquiry into secular influence on ecclesiastical and religious matters on a local urban level*, Louvain/ Kortrijk 2006.

SMITH 1940 Smith, R.A.L., 'The central financial system of Christ Church Canterbury 1186-1512', *The English Historical Review* 55, (1940), 353-370.

SMITH 1943 Smith, R.A.L., *Canterbury cathedral priory : A study in monastic administration*, Cambridge 1943.

SORIA AUDEBERT 2005 Soria Audebert, M., *La crosse brisée: des êveques agressés dans une église en conflit, royaume de France fin Xe début XIIIe siècle*, Turnhout 2005.

SOULARD 1993 Soulard, T., *La cité episcopale de Limoges au moyen age, enquête autour d'une cathédrale*, (diss.), Paris 1993.

SOULARD 1995 Soulard, T., 'Le financement du chœur gothique de la cathédrale de Limoges', *Bulletin de la Société nationale des antiquaires de France* (1995), 76-92.

SOULARD (FORTHCOMING) Soulard, T., 'Le financement de la cathédrale de Limoges aux XIIIe et XIVe siècles', in *Le financement de la construction aux XIIIe-XVIe siècles en France*, Paris (forthcoming).

SOUTHERN 1953 Southern, R.W., *The making of the Middle Ages*, London 1953.

SOUTHERN 1970 Southern, R.W., *Western society and the church in the middle ages*, Harmondsworth 1970.

SPEARING 1965 Spearing, A.C. (ed.), *The Pardoner's prologue and tale from the Canterbury tales by Geoffrey Chaucer*, Cambridge 1965.

SPIECKERMANN 1935 Spieckermann, H., *Beiträge zur Geschichte des Domkapitels zu Münster im Mittelalter*, (diss.), Münster 1935.

SPUFFORD 1986 Spufford, P., *Handbook of medieval exchange*, London 1986.

SPUFFORD 1988 Spufford, P., *Money and its use in medieval Europe*, Cambridge 1988.

STALLEY 1971 Stalley, R.A., 'A twelfth-century patron of architecture : A study of the buildings erected by Roger, bishop of Salisbury 1102-39', *Journal of the British Archeological Association* 1971, 62-83.

Statutes of Lincoln Cathedral Bradshaw, H. & Chr. Wordsworth (eds), *Statutes of Lincoln Cathedral*, 3 vols, Cambridge 1892-1897.

Statutes of Salisbury Cathedral Wordsworth, Chr. & D. Macleane (eds), *Statutes and customs of the cathedral church of the blessed Virgin Mary of Salisbury*, London 1915.

Statuts synodaux Paris Les statuts synodaux français du XIIIe siècle, vol. 1: Pontal, O. (ed.), *Les statuts de Paris et le synodal de l'ouest (XIIIe siècle)*, Paris 1971.

Statuts synodaux Reims Les statuts synodaux français du XIIIe siècle, vol. 4: Avril, J. (ed.), *Les statuts synodaux de l'ancienne province de Reims (Cambrai, Arras, Noyon, Soissons et Tournai)*, Paris 1995.

STEHKÄMPER 1979/1980 Stehkämper, H., 'Die Kölner Erzbischöfe und das Domkapitel zwischen Grundsteinlegung und Chorweihe des gotischen Domes (1248-1322)', *Kölner Domblatt* 44 & 45 (1979/1980), 11-34.

STEIN 1934 Stein, H.M., 'Nouveaux Documents relatifs à la cathédrale de Meaux', *Mémoires de la Société Nationale des Antiquaires de France* 8 (1934), 86-107.

STERK 1980 Sterk, J.J.B.M.M., *Philips van Bourgondië (1456-1524) bisschop van Utrecht als protagonist van de Renaissance, zijn leven en maecenaat*, Zutphen 1980.

STERNBERG 1996 Sternberg, T., 'Aurum utile', *Jahrbuch für Antike und Christentum*, 1996, 128-148.

Stiftskirche Xanten Die Stiftskirche des Hl. Viktor zu Xanten, vol. 3 (2): C. Wilkes & G. Rotthoff (eds), *Die Baurechnungen der Jahre 1356 bis 1437*, Berlin 1957, vol. 4 (2): G. Rotthoff (ed.), *Die Baurechnungen der Jahre 1438/39 bis 1491/92*, Kevelaer 1975.

The story of Prague Castle, Prague 2003.

STREET 1914 Street, G.E., *Some account of Gothic architecture in Spain*, 2 vols, London/New York 1914[2].

STRUICK 1968, Struick J.E.A.L., *Utrecht door de eeuwen heen*, Utrecht 1968.

STUTZ 1895 Stutz, U., *Geschichte des kirchlichen Benefizialwesens von seinen Anfängen bis auf Alexander III*, vol. 1, Berlin 1895.

SUHR 1938 Suhr, W., *Die Lübecker Kirche im Mittelalter : Ihre Verfassung und ihr Verhältnis zur Stadt*, Lübeck 1938.

SUIR 1977 Suir, E.T., 'Evert Zoudenbalch, domkanunnik te Utrecht in de tweede helft van de 15de eeuw', *Jaarboek van Oud-Utrecht*, 1977, 7-55.

SUMPTION 1975 Sumption, J., *Pilgrimage, an image of medieval religion*, London 1975.

SWANSON 1989 Swanson, R.N., *Church and society in late medieval England*, Oxford 1989.

SWANSON 1993 Swanson, R.N., 'Devotional offerings at Hereford cathedral in the later middle ages', *Analecta Bollandiana* 111 (1993), 93-102.

SWANSON 1999 Swanson, R.N., 'An appropriate anomaly: Topcliffe parish and the fabric fund of York Minster in the later middle ages', in D. Wood (ed.), *Life and thought in the Northern church c.1100-c.1700 : Essays in Honour of Claire Cross*, York 1999, 105-121.

SWANSON 2006 Swanson, R.N. (ed.), *Promissory notes on the treasury of merits : Indulgences in late medieval Europe*, Leiden/Boston 2006.

SWANSON 2007 Swanson, R.N., *Indulgences in late medieval England : Passports to Paradise?*, Cambridge 2007.

SWANSON & LEPINE 2000 Swanson, R.N. & D. Lepine, 'The Later Middle Ages, 1268-1535', in G. Aylmer & J. Tiller (eds), *Hereford Cathedral*, London/Rio Grande 2000, 48-86.

T

TABBAGH 1997 Tabbagh, V., 'Une cathédrale et ses fidèles : Notre-Dame de Rouen à la fin du Moyen Âge', in S. Lemagnen *et al.* (eds), *Chapitres et cathédrales en Normandie*, vol. 2, Caen 1997, 215-230.

TABBAGH 2006 Tabbagh, V., 'Les évêques de royaume de France en 1438', in *Gens d'Église, gens de pouvoir (France, XIIIe-XVE siècle)*, Dijon 2006, 87-187.

TADRA 1880 Tadra, F. (ed.), 'Cancellaria Arnesti : Formelbuch des ersten Prager Erzbischofs Arnest von Pardutic', *Archiv für Osterreichische Geschichte* 61 (1880), 267-568.

TANGL 1894 Tangl, M. (ed.), *Die päpstlichen Kanzleiordnungen von 1200-1500*, Innsbruck 1894.

TAVERNIER 1996 Tavernier, L., *Der Dombezirk von Brixen im Mittelalter : Bauhistorische Studien zur Gestalt, Funktion und Bedeutung*, vol. 294, Innsbruck 1996.

Tecnología y sociedad, Las grandes obras públicas en la Europa medieval (Actas de la XXII Semana de Estudios Medievales de Estilla. 17 al 21 de julio de 1995), Pamplona 1996.

TEIJEIRA PABLOS 1993 Teijeira Pablos, M.D., *La influencia del modelo gótico flamenco en Léon : La sillería de coro catedralicia*, León 1993.

TENHAEFF 1949 Romein, J. (ed.), *Tenhaeff's, N.B., Verspreide Geschriften*, vol. 1, Groningen/Jakarta 1949.

THÉRY 2004 Théry, J., 'Fama, enormia. L'enquête sur les crimes de l'évêque d'Albi Bernard de Castanet (1307-1308) : Gouvernement et contestation au temps de la théocratie pontificale et l'hérésie des bons hommes', *Heresis* 40 (2004), 192-197.

THOENES 1978 Thoenes, Ch., 'Ennio Francia 1505-1606,

Storia della costruzione del nuovo San Pietro', (review), *Kunstchronik* 31 (1978), 474-489.

THOENES 1998 Thoenes, Ch., '"Il primo tempio del mondo" : Raffaello, S. Pietro e il denaro', *Casabella continuitá, rivista internazionale di architettura* 62 (1998), no. 654, 56-65.

THOENES 2008 Thoenes, Ch., 'Über die Grösse der Peterskirche', in G. Satzinger & S. Schütze (eds), *Sankt Peter in Rom 1506-2006: Beiträge der internationalen Tagung vom 22.-25. Februar 2006 in Bonn*, Munich 2008, 9-28.

THOMAS 1881 Thomas, A. (ed.), 'Les miracles de Notre-Dame de Chartres, texte latin inédit', *Bibliothèque de l'École des chartes* 42 (1881), 505-550.

THOMAS AQUINAS 1952 Thomas Aquinas, *Sancti Thomae Aquinatis Summa Theologiae, Secunda Secundae*, Madrid 1952.

THOMASSINUS 1725 Thomassinus, L. [1619-1695], *Ancienne et nouvelle discipline de l'église touchant les bénéfices et les bénéficiers*, vol. 3, Paris 1725 (first edition 1678-1679).

TIMBAL & METMAN 1964 Timbal, P.-C. & J. Metman, 'Évêque de Paris et chapitre de Notre-Dame : La juridiction dans la cathédrale au moyen-âge', *Revue d'histoire de l'Eglise de France* 50 (1964), 47-73.

TIMMERS 1947 Timmers, J.J.M., *Symboliek en iconographie der Christelijke kunst*, Roermond 1947.

TORROJA MENÉNDEZ & SÁNCHEZ PALENCIA 1977 Torroja Menéndez, C. & A. Sánchez Palencia, *Catálogo del archivo de obra y fabrica de la catedral de Toledo*, vol. 1: *Serie de libros, Siglos XIV-XVI*, Toledo 1977.

TOUSSAERT 1963 Toussaert, J., *Le sentiment religieux en Flandre à la fin du moyen-âge*, Paris 1963.

U

UHLIRZ 1902 Uhlirz, K., *Die Rechnungen des Kirchenmeisteramtes von St. Stephan zu Wien*, Vienna 1902.

Urkunden Eichstätt Steinberger, L. & J. Sturm (eds), *Urkunden des Hochstifts Eichstätt, Urkunden von 1306-1365*, Monumenta Boica, vol. 50, Munich 1932.

Urkundenbuch Bremen Ehmck, D.R. & W. von Bippen (eds), *Bremisches Urkundenbuch*, 5 vols, Bremen 1873-1902.

Urkundenbuch Coblenz und Trier Eltester, L. & A. Goerz (eds), *Urkundenbuch zur Geschichte der jetzt die preussischen Regierungsbezirke Coblenz und Trier bildenden mittelrheinischen Territorien*, vol. 3 (1212-1260), Koblenz 1874.

Urkundenbuch Culm Woelky, C.P. (ed.), *Urkundenbuch des Bisthums Culm*, Danzig 1884.

Urkundenbuch Halberstadt Schmidt, G. (ed.), *Urkundenbuch des Hochstifts Halberstadt und seiner Bischöfe*, vols 2-4, Leipzig 1884-1887.

Urkundenbuch Hamburg Lappenberg, J.M. *et al.* (eds), *Hamburgisches Urkundenbuch*, 3 vols, Hamburg 1907-1953.

Urkundenbuch Lübeck Leverkus, W. & W. Prange (eds), *Urkundenbuch des Bistums Lübeck*, vol. 1, vol. 2 (*1220-1439*), vol. 3 (*1439-1509*), Oldenburg 1865 / Neumünster 1994-1995.

Urkundenbuch Magdeburg Hertel, G. (ed.), *Urkundenbuch der Stadt Magdeburg*, vol. 2 (1403-1464), Halle 1894.

Urkundenbuch Merseburg Kehr, P. (ed.), *Urkundenbuch des Hochstifts Merseburg*, vol. 1, Halle 1899.

Urkundenbuch Niederrhein Lacomblet, Th.J. (ed.), *Urkundenbuch zur die Geschichte des Niederrheins*, 4 vols, Düsseldorf 1840-1853.

Urkundenbuch Osnabrück Philippi, F. (ed.), *Osnabrücker Urkundenbuch*, vols 2, 3 & 4, Osnabrück 1896-1969.

Urkundenbuch Regensburg

Widemann, J. (ed.), *Regensburger Urkundenbuch*, Monumenta Boica, vol. 53, Munich 1912.

Urkundenbuch Speyer Remling, F.X., *Urkundenbuch zur Geschichte der Bischöfe zu Speyer*, vols 1 & 2, Mainz 1852-1853 (reprint Aelen 1970).

Urkundenbuch Strassburg Wiegand, W. (ed.), *Urkundenbuch der Stadt Strassburg*, 6 vols, Strasbourg 1879-1899.

Urkundenbuch Westfalen *Wesfälisches Urkundenbuch*, 9 vols, Münster 1847-1982.

VAN UYTVEN 1961 Uytven, R. van, *Stadsfinanciën en stadsekonomie te Leuven van de XIIIe tot het einde der XVIIe eeuw*, Brussels 1961.

V

VALLERY-RADOT N.D. Vallery-Radot, J., *La cathédrale de Bayeux*, Paris n.d.

VALLÉS I BOTEY 1987 Vallés i Botey, A., *La construcció de la catedral de Barcelona segons els llibres de l'obra 1325-1383*, (diss.), Barcelona 1987.

VANRIE 1963 Vanrie, A., 'Les croix banales aux abbayes en Belgique au moyen-âge', *Contributions à l'histoire économique et sociale* 2 (1963), 6-26.

VANRIE 1965 Vanrie, A., 'L'Incorporation des églises paroissiales au moyen-âge', in *Hommage au professeur Paul Bonenfànt*, Brussels 1965, 47-54.

VANWIJNSBERGHE 2002 Vanwijnsberghe, D., 'Réalité et fiction chez le Maître du Livre d'Heures de Dresde : Le frontispice du Cartulaire de l'hôpital Saint-Jacques de Tournai (Tournai, Bibliothèque de la ville, Ms. 27), in B. Cardon *et al.* (eds), *Als ich can : Liber amicorum in memory of Professor Dr. Maurits Smeyers*, Paris/ Louvain/Dudley (MA) 2002, 1509-1546.

VAQUERO PIÑEIRO 1996 Vaquero Piñeiro, M., 'Ricerche sui salari nell'edilizia romana (1500-1650)', *Rivista Storica del Lazio* 5 (1996), 131-158.

VARANGOLI 2008 Varangoli, C., 'La conservación de San Pedro del Vaticano', in *La Europa de las catedrales : Conservación y gestión : Actas simposio internacional*, Valladolid 2008, 233-271.

VARIN 1838-1848 Varin, P. (ed.), *Archives administratives de la ville de Reims*, 3 vols, Paris 1838-1848.

VASSEUR 1882 Vasseur, Ch., 'Etudes historiques et archéologiques sur la cathédrale de Lisieux', *Bulletin de la Société des antiquaires de Normandie* 10 (1882), 419-501.

VAUCHEZ 1988A Vauchez, A., *La sainteté en occident aux derniers siècles du Moyen Age : D'après les procès de canonisation et les documents hagiographiques*, Rome 1988.

VAUCHEZ 1988B Vauchez, A., 'Les cathédrales : approches historiques', in *La cathédrale demeure de Dieu demeure des hommes (Actes du Colloque de Pont-à-Mousson, 26-28 juin 1987)*, Paris 1988, 51-69.

VÁZQUEZ DE PARGA *et al.* 1993 Vázquez de Parga, L., J.M. Lacarra & J. Uría Riu, *Las peregrinaciones a Santiago de Compostela*, vols 1-3, Navarra 1993.

VEIT 1912 Veit, A.L. 'Archivalische Nachrichten über den Dom zu Mainz bis zum 16. Jahrhundert', in D.F. Hermann (ed.), *Archiv für hessische Geschichte und Altertumskunde*, Darmstadt 1912, 147-171.

VAN DE VEN 1938 Ven, A.J. van de, *Het oud-archief van de gemeente Culemborg*, Utrecht 1938.

VÉNARD 1987 Vénard, M., 'La construction des églises paroissiales, du XVe au XVIIIe siècle', *Revue d'histoire de l'Église de France* 73 (1987), 7-33.

VÉNARD 1994 Vénard, M., 'Les ventes d'indulgences au temps de Luther', in M. Aubrun *et al.* (eds), *Entre idéal et réalité : Actes du colloque international d'histoire finances et religion,*

Le Poiré-sur-Vie (Vendée) 1994, 275-285.

VENTE 1942 Vente, M.A., *Bouwstoffen tot de geschiedenis van het Nederlandse orgel in de 16e eeuw*, Amsterdam 1942.

VERDON 1994 Verdon, T., *Alla riscoperta di Piazza del Duomo in Firenze*, vol. 3: *Il Campanile di Giotto*, Florence 1994.

VERGA 1908 Verga, E., *L'archivio della fabbrica del Duomo di Milano*, Milan 1908.

VERHOEVEN 1992 Verhoeven, G., *Devotie en negotie : Delft als bedevaartplaats in de late middeleeuwen*, Amsterdam 1992.

VERLINDEN 1959/1965/1972 Verlinden, C. (ed.), *Dokumenten voor de geschiedenis van prijzen en lonen in Vlaanderen en Brabant*, vol. 1 (*xve-xviiie eeuw*); vol. 2 (*xive-xixe eeuw*), vol. 3 (*xvie-xixe eeuw*); Bruges 1959, 1965, 1972.

VERPLAETSE 1965 Verplaetse, A., 'L'Architecture en Flandre entre 900 et 1200 d'après les sources narratives contemporaines', *Cahiers de civilisation médiévale x-xiiie siècles* 8 (1965), 25-42.

Vetus Registrum Rich Jones, W.H. (ed.), *Vetus Registrum Sarisberiense alias dictum Registrum s. Osmundi episcopi*, 2 vols, London 1883-1884.

VICTOR 1996 Victor, S., 'Les salaires des ouvriers du bâtiment à Gérone au XVème siecle', *Anuario de Estudios Medievales* 26 (1996), 365-390.

VIDRIER 1913/1914 Vidrier, A., 'Les marguilliers laïcs de Notre-Dame de Paris 1204-1790', *Mémoires de la Société de l'histoire de Paris et de l'Ile-de-France* 40 (1913), 117-402; 41 (1914), 131-346.

VIELLIARD 1950 Vielliard, J., (ed.), *Le guide du pèlerin de Saint-Jacques de Compostelle*, Mâçon 1950[2].

VILLACORTA RODRIGUEZ 1974 Villacorta Rodriguez, T., *El cabildo catedral de León : Estudio historico-juridico: siglos xii-xix*, León 1974.

VILLALPANDO 1962 Villalpando, M., 'Origenes y construccion de la Catedral de Segovia', *Estudios Segovianos* (1962), 391-408.

VILLANUEVA ESTENGO 1902-1906 Villanueva Estengo, J.L., *Viage literario a las iglesias de España*, Madrid vol. 2, 19022; vol. 3, 19022; vol. 7, 1906.

VILLARD 1968 Villard, F., 'Le conflit entre l'évêque Pierre d'Amboise et le chapitre cathédrale pour la juridiction ecclésiastique', *Bulletin de la Société nationale des antiquaires de l'Ouest et des Musées de Poitiers*, 4th Series, 9 (1968), 341-360.

VILLERS 1901 Villers, G., 'La Tour du Patriarche', *Société des Sciences, Arts et Belles-Lettres de Bayeux* 6 (1901), 11-39.

VILLES 1983 Villes, A., *La cathédrale de Toul : Histoire et architecture*, Toul/Metz 1983.

VILLES 2001 Villes, A., 'L'ancienne grande flèche de la cathédral Saint-Étienne de Châlons-en-Champagne', *Umeni* 49 (2001), 220-234.

VINCENT 1988 Vincent, C., *Des charités bien ordonnées : Les confréries normandes de la fin du xiiie siècle au début du xvie siècle*, Paris 1988.

VISSER 1909 Visser, C.Ch.G., *Luther's geschriften in de Nederlanden tot 1546*, Assen 1909.

VISSER 1934 Visser, W.J.A., 'Reliquieën van de H.H. Willibrordus en Bonifacius naar de Oudmunster te Utrecht in 1520 overgebracht', *Archief voor de geschiedenis van het Aartsbisdom Utrecht* 58 (1934), 167-172.

VLAM & VENTE 1965 Vlam, C.C. & M.A. Vente (eds), *Bouwstenen voor een geschiedenis der toonkunst in de Nederlanden*, Utrecht 1965.

VAN VLIET 2002 Vliet, K. van, *In kringen van kanunniken : Munsters en kapittels in het bisdom Utrecht 695-1227*, Zutphen 2002.

Vocabulario básico Teruel Gregorio de Tejada, M., *Vocabulario básico de la Historia de la Iglesia*, Barcelona 1993.

VOGTS 1930 Vogts, H., 'Der Kölner Dom im Stadtplan und Stadtbild im Laufe eines Jahrtausends', in *Der Dom zu Köln : Festschrift zur Feier der 50. Wiederkehr des Tages seiner Vollendung am 15. Oktober 1880*, Cologne 1930, 1 ff.

VOISIN 1869 Voisin, C.J., 'Mendicatorium accordé par l'évêque de Tournai, Philippe d'Arhois, pour la restauration et l'entretien de la cathédrale de Tournai', *Analectes pour servir à l'histoire ecclésiastique de Belgique* 6 (1869), 474-480.

VROOM 1964 Vroom, W.H., 'Jan Gossaert van Mabuse als ontwerper van koorbanken in de Dom van Utrecht', *Oud-Holland* 79 (1964), 172-175.

VROOM 1981 Vroom, W.H., *De financiering van de kathedraalbouw in de middeleeuwen, in het bijzonder van de dom van Utrecht*, Maarssen 1981.

VROOM 1983 Vroom, W.H., *De Onze-Lieve-Vrouwekerk te Antwerpen : De financiering van de bouw tot de beeldenstorm*, Antwerp/Amsterdam 1983.

VROOM 1989 Vroom, W.H., 'La construction des cathédrales au Moyen Âge : Une performance économique', in R. Recht (ed.), *Les batisseurs des cathédrales gothiques*, Strasbourg 1989, 81-90.

VROOM 1992 Vroom, W.H., *'In tumultu gosico', over relieken en geuzen in woelige tijden*, Nijmegen 1992.

VROOM 1993 Vroom, W.H., 'Het jachtgebied van Sint-Hubertus', in *Bouwkunst : Studies in vriendschap voor Kees Peeters*, Amsterdam 1993, 571-580.

VROOM 1996 Vroom, W.H., 'The Financing of the Construction of the Gothic Cathedral in Utrecht', in E. De Bièvre (ed.), *Utrecht: Britain and the continent. Archaeology, Art and Architecture*, Leeds 1996, 183-188.

VROOM (FORTHCOMING) Vroom, W.H., 'Les mendicatoria de la cathédrale d'Utrecht (1288-1518) : Les contributions des fidèles du diocèse pour la constructions de la cathédrale', in *Le financement de la construction aux XIIIe-XVIe siècles en France*, Paris (forthcoming).

W

DE WAARD *et al.* 1963 Waard, R. de *et al.*, *Klokken en klokkengieters, bijdragen tot de campanologie door de historische commissie van de Nederlandse klokkenspelvereniging*, Culemborg 1963.

WALVIS 1713 W[alvis], J., *Beschrijving der stad Gouda*, Gouda/Leiden [1713].

WARNKE 1976 Warnke, M., *Bau und Überbau : Soziologie der mittelalterlichen Architektur nach den Schriftquellen*, Frankfurt 1976; reviews: J. Wollasch in *Kunstchronik* 1977, 269-273; D. Kimpel & R. Suckale in *Kritische Berichte* 5 (1977), 62-70.

WEBER 1912 weber, E., *Das Domkapitel von Magdeburg bis zum Jahre 1567 : Ein Beitrag zur Verfassungs- und Verwaltungsgeschichte der deutschen Domkapitel*, (diss.), Halle 1912.

VAN DER WEE 1956 Wee, H. van der, *Bijdragen tot de prijzengeschiedenis*, Louvain 1956.

WEIGERT 2004 Weigert, L., *Weaving sacred stories : French choir tapestries and the perfomance of clerical identity'*, Ithaca/London 2004.

WEILANDT 1992 Weilandt, G., *Geistliche und Kunst : Ein Beitrag zur Kultur der ottonisch-salischen Reichskirche und zur Veränderung künstlerischer Traditionen im späten 11. Jahrhundert*, Cologne/Weimar/Vienna 1992.

WEILER & GEIRNAERT 1980

Weiler, A.G. & N. Geirnaert (eds), *Monasticon Windeshemense*, vol. 3: *Die Niederlande*, Brussels 1980.

WEINFURTER 1991 Weinfurter, S., 'Herrschaftslegitimation und Königsautorität im Wandel : Die Salier und ihr Dom zu Speyer', in S. Weinfurter (ed.), *Die Salier und das Reich*, vol. 1, Sigmaringen 1991, 55-95.

WELCH 1995 Welch, E.S., *Art and authority in Renaissance Milan*, New Haven/London 1995.

WELTSCH 1968 Weltsch, R.E., *Archbishop John of Jenstein (1348-1400) : Papalism, Humanism and Reform in Pre-Hussite Prague*, The Hague/Paris 1968.

WENTZ & SCHWINEKÖPER 1972 Wentz, G. & B. Schwineköper (eds), *Das Erzbistum Magdeburg*, Band 1, Teil 1, Berlin/New York 1972.

VAN WERVEKE 1904 Werveke, A. van, 'Het verhuren van reliquieën in de XVe en in de XVIe eeuw', *Volkskunde* 16 (1904), 33-76.

VAN WERVEKE 1927 Werveke, H. van, 'Over kerkbouw vóór de 13de eeuw', in *Album opgedragen aan Prof. Dr. J. Vercoullie*, Brussels 1927, 343-349.

WESTFALL 1974 Westfall, C.W., *In this most perfect paradise: Alberti, Nicolas v, and the invention of conscious urban planning in Rome, 1447-55*, London 1974.

WESTLAKE 1919 Westlake, H.F., *The parish guilds of medieval England*, London 1919.

WIEK 1959A Wiek, P., 'Die bürgerliche Verwaltung der Bremer Domfabrik im Mittelalter', *Bremisches Jahrbuch*, 1959, 121-134.

WIEK 1959B Wiek, P, 'Das Strassburger Münster : Untersuchungen über die Mitwirkung des Stadtbürgertums am Bau bischöflicher Kathedralkirchen im Spätmittelalter', *Zeitschrift für die Geschichte des Oberrheins* 107 (1959), 40-114.

WILDEMAN 1897 Wildeman, M.G., *Aanteekeningen uit de rentmeestersrekeningen der Groote of St. Jacobskerk te 's-Gravenhage 1557-1567*, The Hague 1897.

WILKES 1946/1947 Wilkes, C., 'Die Xantener Dombauhütte', *Annalen des historischen Vereins für den Niederrhein* 144/145 (1946/1947), 240-248.

WILLIAMS 1993 Williams, J.W., *Bread, wine & money : The windows of the trades at Chartres Cathedral*, Chicago 1993.

Willigis und sein Dom Brück, A.Ph. (ed.), *Willigis und sein Dom : Festschrift zur Jahrtausendfeier des Mainzer Domes 975-1975*, Mainz 1975.

WILMER 2005 Wilmer, C.C.S., *De getekende stad : Utrecht in oude tekeningen, 1550-1900*, Utrecht 2005.

WINCKELMANN 1907 Winckelmann, O., 'Zur Kulturgeschichte des Strassburger Münsters im 15. Jahrhundert', *Zeitschrift für die Geschichte des Oberrheins*, New Series, 22 (1907), 247-290.

VAN WINTER 1972 Winter, J.M. van, 'Utrecht am Rhein : Mittelalterlicher Rheinlauf und Entstehungsgeschichte der Stadt Utrecht', in *Die Stadt in der europäischen Geschichte : Festschrift Edith Ennen*, Bonn 1972, 138-153.

VON WINTERFELD 1979 Winterfeld, D. von, *Der Dom in Bamberg, vol. 1: Die Baugeschichte bis zur Vollendung im 13. Jahrhundert*, Berlin 1979.

WITKOWSKA 1981 Witkowska, A., 'Functions of Votive Practices and Revitalization Rites in Folk Religiousness of the Late Middle Ages', in J. Kloczowski (ed.), *The Christian Community of Medieval Poland : Anthologies*, Wroclaw 1981, 217-243.

WITTMER 1967 Wittmer, Ch., 'L'Obituaire de la cathédrale de Strasbourg et les sciences auxiliaires de l'histoire 1263-1520', in *Hommage à Hans Haug*,

Strasbourg 1967, 357-363.
WOLF 1956 Wolf, G. (ed.), *Florilegium testamentorum*, Heidelberg 1956.
WOLF 2006 Wolf, S., 'Le portrait d'un archevêque: Pey Berland : Vie et carriére d'un clerc bordelais', *Zeitschrift der Savigny-Stiftung für Rechtsgeschichte, Kanonistische Abteilung* 92, 123 (2006), 410-452.
WOLFF 1968 Wolff, A., 'Chronologie der ersten Bauzeit des Kölner Doms 1248-1277', *Kölner Domblatt* 28-29 (1968), 68 ff.
WOLFF 1892 Wolff, C., *Der Kaiserdom in Frankfürt am Main : Eine baugeschichtliche Darstellung*, Frankfurt am Main 1892.
WOLFS 1963 Wolfs, S.P., *Litterae de beneficiis O.P. (1243-1524)*, Groningen 1963.
WOLTMANN 1876 Woltmann, A., 'Das Wohlthäterbuch des Frauenwerkes zu Strassburg', *Repertorium für Kunstwissenschaft* 1 (1876), 259-265, 375-393.
WOODMAN 1981 Woodman, F., *The Architectural History of Canterbury Cathedral*, London/Boston/Henley 1981.
WOODRUFF 1932 Woodruff, C.E., 'The financial aspect of the cult of St. Thomas of Canterbury as revealed by a study of the monastic records', *Archaeologia Cantiana* 44 (1932), 13-32.
WOODRUFF 1936 Woodruff, C.E., 'The Sacrists' rolls of Christ Church, Canterbury', *Archaeologia Cantiana* 48 (1936), 38-80.
WOODRUFF & DANKS 1912 Woodruff, C.E. & W. Danks, *Memorials of the cathedral and priory of Christ in Canterbury*, London 1912.
WOOLLEY 1915 Woolley, R.M., 'Constitutions of the diocese of London c. 1215-1222', *The English Historical Review* 30 (1915), 285-302.
WUERDTWEIN 1772-1780 Wuerdtwein, S.A., *Subsidia diplomatica ad selecta juris ecclesiastici germaniae et historiarum capita elucidanda*, 13 vols, Heidelberg 1772-1780.
WUERDTWEIN 1781-1792 Wuerdtwein, S.A., *Nova subsidia diplomatica ad selecta juris ecclesiastici germaniae et historiarum capita elucidanda* [...], 14 vols, Heidelberg 1781-1792.

Y

YARZA *et al.* 2004 Yarza, J., M.V. Herráez, & G. Boto (eds), *Congreso Internacional : La Catedral de León en la Edad media: Actas*, León 2004.
YATES 1973 Yates, W.N., 'The fabric rolls of Hereford cathedral 1290/1 and 1386/7', *The National Library of Wales Journal* 18 (1973), 79-86.

Z

ZENDER 1959 Zender, M., *Räume und Schichte mittelaltlicher Heiligenverehrung in Ihrer Bedeutung für die Volkskunde*, Düsseldorf 1959.
ZERVAS 1987 Zervas, D.F., 'Un nuovo documento per la storia del duomo e del Campanile di Firenze (1333-1359)', *Rivista d'arte : Studi documentari per la storia delle arti in Toscana* 39 (1987), 3-53.
ZILVERBERG 1951 Zilverberg, S.B.J., *David van Bourgondië, bisschop van Terwaan en van Utrecht (± 1427-1496)*, Groningen 1951.
ZINDEL 1791 Zindel, J.Ch., 'De ecclesia cathedralibus dissertatio canonico iuridica', in A. Mayer, *Thesaurus Novus iuris ecclesiastici potissimum Germaniae* [...], vol. I, Ratisbonne 1791, 33-84.
ZINK 1973 Zink, J., *Die mittelalterliche Kathedrale von Besançon bis zum 13. Jahrhundert*, (diss.), Freiburg im Breisgau 1973.
ZINK 1976 Zink, M., *La prédication en langue romane avant 1300*, Paris 1976.

INDEX OF PLACE-NAMES

EPISCOPAL CITIES IN SMALL CAPS FONT

KEY

A Austria
B Belgium
CH Switzerland
CZ Czech Republic
DK Denmark
F France;
G Germany;
GB Great Britain;
I Israël;
IT Italy
L Luxembourg;
N Norway
NL Netherlands;
P Poland;
R Russia;
SE Sweden
SP Spain
T Turkey

ILLUSTRATION CREDITS

p. 15. Archive of the Cathedral of Mallorca.

p. 26-27. Map: UvA-Kaartenmakers, Amsterdam.

p. 32, 76, 77, 328, 329, 340, 343, 410, 411. Het Utrechts Archief.

p. 36. Universiteitsbibliotheek Utrecht, Ms. 400, fol. 63v
p. 40. © Rudolf Wakonigg.

p. 45. © Chanoine Gabriel Normand, Metz.

p. 55. Bischöfliches Dom- und Diözesanmuseum Mainz.

p. 61. Musée de l'Oeuvre Notre Dame de Strasbourg, photo: E. Bacher.

p. 64. Musée de l'Oeuvre Notre Dame de Strasbourg, photo: M. Bertola.

p. 71. Archive of the Cathedral of Mallorca © Cabildo Catedral Mallorca.

p. 74. Prague Castle Archive, Metropolitan Chapter Archives, sign. Cod.XI/1, f.28v

p. 74. Prague Castle Archive, Metropolitan Chapter Archives, sign. Cod.XI/1, front cover.

p. 103 Bibliothèque de la Ville de Tournai.

p. 112. © Courtesy of M. Hubert Colin, Toul.

p. 126. © Courtesy of G. Bussery, Lyon.

p. 133. Cathedral of S Vitus at the Prague Castle, © The Prague Castle Administration, photo: Jan Gloc.

p. 157. © The British Library Board, Add MS 15689.

p. 171. Staatsarchiv Basel-Stadt, Bild 6, 1654.

p. 174. Photo Rachel Moriarty; with the permission of the Dean and Chapter, Chichester Cathedral, and the Rector and Churchwardens of the Parish of Climping, Sussex.

p. 178. © Photo: Janos Stekovics.

p. 182-183 and cover. Cathedral of León.

p. 184. ÖNB, Bildarchiv, Ink. 25.G.22, fol. 1r

p. 184. ÖNB, Bildarchiv, Ink. 25.G.22. fol. 3r

p. 186. © Photo: B. Verhille.

p. 187. La Nuée Bleue, Strasbourg, cliché E. List; Fabrique de la Cathédrale de Strasbourg.

p. 190. Collectie familie van Beuningen, inv.nr.2130.

p. 198. Städtisches Museum, Braunschweig, Museumsfoto.

p. 202. Reims, BM, Inc. 195.

p. 206. © The Dean and Chapter of Hereford Cathedral.

p. 210. Courtesy of Geert-Jan Koot, Rijksmuseumbibliotheek Amsterdam.

p. 222, 223. Courtesy of Canon Nicholas Bennett, Lincoln Cathedral Libary.

p. 242. Bibliothèque Nationale de France.

p. 247. Cathedral of Reims.

p. 251. Cl. E. Berry, Musées de Sens.

p. 266. Reproduced by kind permission of the Syndics of Cambridge University Library. The 'Pardoner' from The Canterbury Tales by Geoffrey Chaucer (1343 ?-1400), Parchment, Cambridge, University Library, MS. Gg. IV. 27, f. 306r

p. 286, 289. Rijksmuseum Amsterdam.

p. 303. Image & copyright Centraal Museum, Utrecht/Ernst Moritz.

p. 311. © The Trustees of the British Museum.

p. 356. Collectie familie van Beuningen, inv.nr.0895.

p. 356. Pelgrimsinsigne Sint Maarten, Cultuurhistorie Gemeente Utrecht, photo: Hans Lägers.

p. 356. Collectie familie van Beuningen, inv.nr.2054.

p. 357. Pelgrimsinsigne Theobaldus, Bureau Monumenten en Archeologie, Amsterdam.

p. 357. Pelgrimsinsigne Cornelius, Archeologische Dienst Zwolle.

p. 357. Collectie familie van Beuningen, inv.nr.2284.

p. 357. Collectie familie van Beuningen, inv.nr.1693.

p. 380, 381,382. Rijksprentenkabinet Amsterdam.

p. 406, 407. Teylers Museum Haarlem, Nederland.

p. 424. Archivio Duomo Milano.

p. 429. Archivio Duomo Milano.

p. 432. Bistumsarchiv Osnabrück, BAOS Ma 24 fol. 88r and 88v

p. 441. Photo © Etienne Hamon.

p. 464. Archives Départementales de Clermont-Ferrand.